Business Law

**Wm. C. Brown
Company
Publishers**
*Dubuque,
Iowa*

Joseph L. Frascona
University of Colorado

Business Law
Text and Cases

Contributing Authors

Edward J. Conry
Utah State University

Gerald R. Ferrera
Bently College

Terry L. Lantry
Colorado State University

Bill M. Shaw
University of Texas at Austin

George J. Siedel III
The University of Michigan

George W. Spiro
University of Massachusetts at Boston

Arthur D. Wolfe
Michigan State University

wcb

Wm. C. Brown
Chairman of the Board

Book Team

G.W. Cox
Editor
Rus Caughron
Production Editor
Barbara J. Grantham
Designer

Wm. C. Brown Company Publishers College Division

Lawrence E. Cremer
President
Raymond C. Deveaux
Vice President/Product Development
David Wm. Smith
Assistant Vice President/National Sales Manager
Matthew T. Coghlan
National Marketing Manager
David A. Corona
Director of Production Development and Design
William A. Moss
Production Editorial Manager
Marilyn A. Phelps
Manager of Design
Mary M. Heller
Visual Research Manager

to Students

The Authors

Joseph L. Frascona, J.D.
Professor of Business Law at the University of Colorado, a member of the faculty of the C.P.A. Institute at Denver University, and the director of the Colorado School of Banking. He is a member of the New York, Colorado, and Federal Bars; a past president of the American Business Law Association; a member of the Rocky Mountain Business Law Association; and is on the Commercial Arbitration Panel of the American Arbitration Association. Professor Frascona was formerly an Associate Attorney in the office of the Attorney General of the United States and General Counsel to the Office of the Foreign Liquidation Commission, U.S. Department of State, in England. He is the author of numerous books and articles on business law and serves as a consultant to business and industry and the accounting profession. He earned his B.S. from City College, City University of New York and his J.D. from Harvard University.

Edward J. Conry, J.D.
Assistant Professor of Business Law, Utah State University. He has both worked in and served as a consultant to businesses, and he has written extensively on consumerism and real estate topics. Professor Conry is a past president of the Rocky Mountain Business Law Association, is a member of the governing body of the American Business Law Association, and serves as a reviewer for the *American Business Law Journal.* He has a B.A. from California State University at Fullerton and an M.B.A. and J.D. from the University of California.

Gerald R. Ferrera, J.D.
Professor of Business Law and Chairman of the Law Department, Bentley College. He is president of the North Atlantic Regional Business Law Association and Editor-in-Chief of the *North Atlantic Regional Business Law Review.* Under a grant from the National Endowment for the Humanities, Professor Ferrera developed an interdisciplinary course on "Law and Philosophy." He is a legal consultant to professional and business associations and is a member of the Massachusetts and Federal Bars. Professor Ferrera earned his B.S. from Boston College and J.D. from the New England School of Law.

Terry L. Lantry, J.D.
Professor of Accounting and Business Law at Colorado State University. He is a member of the Colorado and Indiana State Societies of Certified Public Accountants and of the Colorado, Indiana, and Federal Bars. He is a past president of the American Business Law Association. Professor Lantry is the author or co-author of numerous articles, monographs, and textbooks. He has a B.A. and J.D. from Valparaiso University and an M.B.A. from Indiana University.

Bill M. Shaw, J.D., LL.M.
Associate Professor of Business Law at the University of Texas at Austin. He is particularly interested in environmental law and technology assessment and has written extensively on these topics. Professor Shaw is a staff editor of the *American Business Law Journal,* an officer of the Southern Business Law Association, and on the Arbitration Panel of the American Arbitration Association, among other professional associations. He is a member of the Texas and Louisiana Bars. He earned a B.S. and M.B.A. at Louisiana Tech University, a J.D. at Tulane University, and an LL.M. at the University of Texas at Austin.

George J. Siedel III, J.D., D.C.L.S.
Associate Professor of Business Law at The University of Michigan. The subjects of his several books have ranged from hospital health care administration to environmental law to real estate law, and his articles have covered an even wider field. Professor Siedel has been an officer of the Tri-State Regional Business Law Association, is presently Chief Editor of the *Michigan Real Property Review,* and is a Council member of the State Bar of Michigan Real Property Law Section. Professor Siedel has a B.A. from the College of Wooster, a J.D. from The University of Michigan, and a Dipl. Comp. Legal Studies from Cambridge University.

George W. Spiro, J.D.
Associate Professor of Law and Management at the University of Massachusetts at Boston. He specializes in labor relations and labor studies and has written primarily on the interfaces of law, management theory, jurisprudence, and labor studies. Professor Spiro has a B.S. in Personnel and Industrial Relations and a J.D. from Syracuse University and an M.S. in Labor Studies from the University of Massachusetts at Amherst.

Arthur D. Wolfe, J.D.
Associate Professor of Business Law at Michigan State University. He is a past president of the Tri-State Regional Business Law Association and currently a Senior Staff Editor of the *American Business Law Journal.* He is a member of the Indiana and Ohio Bars. His articles and books cover such topics as "Analysis of Human Service Agencies" and "Undergraduate Legal Instruction and the Development of Cognitive Behaviors." Professor Wolfe earned a B.A. in history and a J.D. from Ohio State University and an M.A. in economics from the University of Illinois.

Contents

ix

Illustrations

Preface

To the Student

Congratulations *to you* as a student for wishing to learn about the law of business! You and other students have motivated us authors to write this book for you to enjoy, find interesting and stimulating, and serve you well both in and outside the classroom.

This book is not designed to make you a lawyer but, rather, to help you recognize and understand the legal significance of the business transactions occurring around you and in which you will participate, and to know when to call a lawyer. It is so written as to cause you to *want* to read it and to hold your attention and interest as you proceed through the book, building on what you have read as you go along.

This text has not been "leveled down," but has been authoritatively written to "lift up" the subject in a very innovative, current, and useful manner. The book is continually addressed to you, involving you in the text discussion. It will challenge you, as well as the instructor, by its smooth and deceptively easy style. Everything has been done to be helpful to you, as a student. Easily understandable language is used throughout the text, which is thoroughly up to date.

Each of the book's ten parts begins with a very brief overview statement of the chapters in that part and a summary paragraph covering the whole part. Each chapter begins with a list of the learning objectives for that chapter. Then comes an introduction leading you into the subject of that chapter. The text reads easily and logically as the subject is developed progressively. Many legal forms and diagrams are used at points in the book where they will be helpful. As you read through the text, guides and definitions of important legal terms appear in the margins highlighting topics discussed in the text.

Important legal terms are clearly defined and printed in bold type *as soon as they appear* in the text so that you can quickly understand their meaning and how they are used. They are included in the Glossary at the end of the book. Many factual examples appear in the text as you read along, illustrating how the legal principles apply.

A great many condensed court cases occur throughout the text showing how the courts use these principles in live situations. There is an introductory sentence leading into each case indicating the point of that case and tying the case into the text. First the "Facts" are presented, then the "Decision," and finally the

"Reasoning" of the court for its decision. These cases are carefully selected so as to be interesting to you and are *not* a lot of legal verbiage. Most of them are recent cases.

At the end of each chapter is a Summary Statement, briefly pointing up some of the high points that you should have learned from the chapter. This is helpful in your review of what you have read. Following the summary is a carefully selected *long* interesting case that will give you the "feel" of a court's thinking as the court analyzes the facts and moves toward its decision. The case illustrates the application of an important legal principle that you have learned as you read through the chapter. Like the first famous long case in the book, all these long cases should be very interesting to you. Many of these are *the* outstanding cases on the subject, guiding the courts and followed by the courts as new cases are later considered.

At the back of the book are three appendices to provide you ready access to source material. Appendix A is "An Explanation of the Civil Trial Process." This explains in detail, with illustrative forms of a Summons and a simple Complaint, how a civil case proceeds and how the judgment is appealed. Appendix B is the "Uniform Partnership Act (1914)." Appendix C is the "Uniform Commercial Code (1978 Text)." Throughout the book many footnote references are made to the Code, which is here in its complete up-to-date form.

The Code is followed by a "Table of Cases" listing the cases (with page references) that have occurred throughout the book. Next is an extensive "Glossary of Legal Terms and Definitions," followed finally by an Index to the book.

After the table of Contents there is a list of the many helpful Illustrations that occur in the book (by figure number, title, and page reference).

A Note on Sexism
Particular efforts have been made in the preparation of this volume to avoid derogatory references to feminine and masculine genders. In modern society, sexist references to either are insulting to both and certainly have no place in a textbook geared to men and women students.

At the same time, the English language offers no generic singular for "they" or "them." The sole option is to use combinations of singulars such as "she and he," "his or her," and so forth. Unfortunately, such combinations become unwieldy, especially when repeated frequently, and interrupt reading flow. In some cases the problem can be corrected by simply restructuring the sentence; where that has been workable, it has been done. In cases where revision does not effect a solution, the singular pronoun "he" or "his" has been employed. It has been employed *only* in its traditional function of serving as the singular of "they" or "them" and *not* as the *masculine* singular as such.

To the Instructor
Part 1 is "The Foundations of Legal Systems." This subject is discussed in four chapters: 1, "The Nature of Legal Systems and Law"; 2, "Organization of the United States Legal System"; 3, "Criminal Law"; and 4, "The Law of Torts." This part is unique in two respects. First, it attempts to show how the concept

of law has evolved over time. Rather than treating each view of law as *independent* of other points of view, the authors attempt to *integrate* all the views and material. Second, the areas of criminal law, torts, and procedural law are *related directly* to the world of business, rather than being treated as separate unrelated areas.

Part 2 is "Contracts." This subject is the basis of all business transactions, its principles of law permeating all other areas of the law. Accordingly, the text treatment is very extensive in its nine chapters, 5 through 13. This part is thoroughly up-to-date and is in conformity with Restatement (Second) of Contracts, recently approved after many years of deliberation and research.

Part 2 is innovative in that it rearranges the material in a very natural flow pattern causing the subject to seem neither structured, stilted, nor of an inflexible mold. It all "fits" easily, based on *the freedom to contract* and its social limitations. It reflects the *thinking* of society and why this freedom and its social limitations exist. It shows the *trend* of society's thinking and WHY the law is as it is. Accepted principles of contract law are being changed by society and the courts, and this part shows this by the text and the *startling* new cases indicating this development. This treatment of the subject is unique. The continuing theme throughout, tying all the chapters together, is *freedom to contract*. This approach allows the student to constantly return to a central focal point and allows the instructor to build upon prior material as new contractual concepts unfold. Many of the cases used were deliberately chosen to emphasize the role that contract law plays in the general development of the perceived needs of society.

One further comment about part 2. Most instructors of business law are used to a book that concludes "Contracts" with a chapter on remedies. In this text, remedies are considered to be among the various *rights* that parties acquire *as a part of their contract*. Accordingly, remedies as a topic is introduced in the chapter on *rights* preceding the concluding chapter on duties.

Part 3 is "Agency and Employment." The subject is discussed in chapters 14 through 18. This is probably the most risk-laden area of the law. Often it is considered to be one of the most difficult areas of the law because, since business transactions usually occur through agents, the law of agency integrates, and must be consistent with, all the areas of the law. Accordingly, this portion on agency is especially carefully explained in understandable terms with frequent use of examples. The subject is carefully tied into the Restatement (Second) of Agency, which is referred to continually in the text. The last chapter, "Employment," is short for two reasons. First, it is an extension of the law of agency. Second, the very extensive, separate chapter 34 covers the labor and collective bargaining aspects of employment in part 7, "Government Regulation of Business."

Part 4 is "Personal Property and Bailments." This subject is discussed in three chapters: 19, "Personal Property"; 20, "Bailments"; and 21, "Carriers, Documents of Title, and Innkeepers." Private ownership of personal property is widespread and is an integral part of the American concept of the right to own property. The concept of personal property is carefully explained and such property is distinguished from other kinds of property, as are the various forms of ownership of such property. The different kinds of bailment are discussed with unusually well-selected examples and cases to make the subject both very interesting and personal to students. Since personal property is warehoused and transported by carrier, with the consequent issuance of warehouse receipts and bills of lading, these two areas of the law come under Article 7 of the Uniform Commercial Code and are discussed and integrated into the law of business. The complex and vitally important portion on the transfer and negotiation of these documents of title is very carefully discussed so as to be clear and meaningful to students. The front of two forms, a negotiable bill of lading and a non-negotiable warehouse receipt, are reproduced in the text. The subject of innkeepers is included in the text discussion.

Part 5 is "Sales." The five chapters, 22 through 26, are very extensive in coverage. The treatment of the text material in this part is unique in several ways. First, the subject is introduced by a discussion of the *thinking* and philosophical *realism* of Article 2 of the Code, which is the law of the sales of *goods*. In this way students begin to see WHY the Code is as it is and its objectives. Second, the text uses the central image of two large corporate merchants doing business by the exchange of their various business forms to explain most of the Article 2 sections. Here we have the "battle of the forms" very carefully analyzed, explained, and illustrated by examples and cases. This helps students grasp what the Code is attempting to do in some of its more complicated sections. The portion of the law that concerns the individual consumer, such as the creation and breach of warranties, is included in chapter 26, "Consumer Law." Third, while the material does not attempt to cover every section of the Code, certain sections of the Code being more important than others, the latter sections are very carefully selected and analyzed thoroughly. For example, the subjects of the Statute of Frauds, the Parol Evidence Rule, Additional Terms in Acceptance, Unconscionability, and Remedies are emphasized. Fourth, through the use of longer appellate cases at the end of each chapter, students can see how legal issues intertwine, as is always the case in reality. Often one finds statute of frauds problems intertwined with the application of the parol evidence rule, waiver of warranties, etc. These key features of the text material on Article 2 make it easier for students to understand and apply the legal principles of sales law.

Part 6 is "Commercial Paper." This part has five chapters, 27 through 31. This subject with all of its complexities and extensive detailed coverage can be one of the most difficult areas of the law for students to grasp. This text carefully discusses the subject of *commercial paper* under Articles 3 and 4 of the Code. It is unique in its step-by-step coverage in its manner of presentation, in easily understood terminology, and with a profusion of excellent examples and cases so as to be meaningful and understandable to students. The subject matter begins by linking up the material with the fundamentals of the law of contracts generally. It compares "assignments" with "negotiation" and stresses, from the very outset, the importance of complying with the stringent formal requirements of section 3–104 of the Code. Practical applications of the Code are emphasized, and student interest will be enhanced with case summaries and hypotheticals, as well as explanatory text material, that establish a reasonable pace through: transfer and negotiation; the holder, holder in due course, and defenses; bank collections; deadlines and discharge. Each chapter's objective is to communicate the fundamentals in a straight-forward manner so that the instructor can utilize classroom time more efficiently.

Part 7 is "Government Regulation of Business." This part has four chapters: 32, "Antitrust Law"; 33, "Administrative Law"; 34, "Labor Law"; and 35, "Environmental Law." It attempts to show how important government regulation of the private sector of business has become in recent years. By highlighting and stressing recent developments in the law these chapters come alive. Students will see the importance of understanding government regulation. A unique portion of this part is chapter 35, "Environmental Law." The subject is of ever-growing importance to all of society, and the text in this book is, in our opinion, the most extensive and authoritative treatment of the subject in any business law book in the United States. It is so written that students can easily understand this lengthy subject. For example, it is not usually understood that the National Environmental Policy Act (NEPA), the kingpin of all United States environmental laws, firmly commands a rigorous decision-making process for *all* agencies of the federal government. *All* federal laws, policies, and regulations of the United States must be interpreted and administered in accordance with NEPA.

Part 8 is "Business Organizations" with two subdivisions: "A. Partnerships and Special Ventures," with four chapters; and "B. Corporations," with five chapters. Partnerships and corporations are common forms of business organization. It is necessary that students acquire a clear introduction into their formation, operation, rights, duties, ownership of interests in the partnership and corporation, management, dissolution, and termination of their legal entities.

The text on partnerships is based on the Uniform Partnership Act to which reference is made continually. Special Ventures, such as the limited partnership, joint ventures, and others, are also explained with reference made to the Uniform Limited Partnership Act. The text points out some of the changes made in the new Uniform Limited Partnership Act of 1976, which the various states have not had a real opportunity to consider for adoption. A short form of partnership agreement is reproduced.

The five chapters on corporations are built around the Model Business Corporation Act. A form of a certificate of stock is reproduced. Article 8 of the Code on Investment Securities, as recently amended, is discussed.

Part 9, "Real Property," consists of three chapters: 45, "Real Property and Its Ownership"; 46, "Transferring Ownership of Realty"; and 47, "Renting Realty." Many diagrams are used. The chapters provide a broad overview of the field of real property in a somewhat unusual manner. Thus, the chapter "Renting Realty" discusses the landlord-tenant relationship extensively and, whenever possible, the material is discussed from the perspective of the student tenant. Similarly, the chapter on transfer of ownership is structured in a way that parallels the procedures involved in the typical residential sale.

Part 10 is "Secured Transactions, Insurance, and Bankruptcy," consisting of five chapters. Under *secured transactions,* the lengthy and complex Article 9 of the Code is carefully integrated into the text in a manner that makes for an easy, graduated learning process in studying the most important parts of this difficult subject. The short but very important subject of *suretyship* is carefully considered. *Insurance* is important to most Americans from cradle to grave. The approach begins with an examination of the general principles of insurance law, followed by a review of the three common types of insurance—life, fire, and automobile. The last chapter on *bankruptcy* includes a succinct up-to-date examination of the new 1978 Bankruptcy Reform Act. Important aspects of the new law are highlighted. Students should find the text of more than general interest because every person who borrows money or extends credit will be exposed to the potential application of the new law.

In order for the instructor to have ready access to source material there are three appendices. First is Appendix A, "An Explanation of the Civil Trial Process," which explains in detail, with illustrative forms of a Summons and a simple Complaint, how a civil case proceeds and how the judgment is appealed. Next is Appendix B, "Uniform Partnership Act (1914)," followed by Appendix C, "Uniform Commercial Code (1978 Text)." Since many footnote references in the text refer to the Code, it is felt that instructors would like to have the Code in its complete up-to-date form.

Also included at the end of the book is a convenient table of the cases (with page references) discussed in the text and included in the case problems, followed by the "Glossary of Legal Terms and Definitions" and an Index.

There are many helpful illustrations in the book. They are listed by figure number, title, and page reference on the Illustrations page after the table of Contents.

Lastly, an innovative and helpful Instructor's Manual and a comprehensive Student Study Guide are available to accompany this text.

Acknowledgments

As in all research and writing, there are always those persons—silent and unsung—whose efforts, patience, and sacrifices are quietly intertwined into the final product. The authors are deeply grateful for such help afforded to them by their families in this process. Also, the authors wish to acknowledge with thanks the excellent assistance of Professor Oscar J. Miller, librarian of the School of Law, University of Colorado.

Further, the authors wish to acknowledge with appreciation the permissions to reprint the following material: the 1978 text of the Uniform Commercial Code and Official Comments to various sections therein copyrighted 1978 by and reprinted herein with the permission of both The American Law Institute and the National Conference of Commissioners on Uniform State Laws; the Restatement (Second) of Torts, section 402A, copyrighted 1965, and various sections from the Restatement (Second) of Agency, copyrighted 1958 by and reprinted herein with the permission of The American Law Institute; the text of the Uniform Partnership Act, copyrighted 1914 by and reprinted herein with the permission of the National Conference of Commissioners on Uniform State Laws; and two forms, General Partnership Agreement (Short Form) and Limited Partnership Certificate (Short Form), reprinted with permission from Edmund O. Belsheim's "Modern Legal Forms," copyrighted 1971 by West Publishing Company.

Without the excellent, constructive, patient reviews of the manuscript for this text by the following faculty, this book could not have achieved its present excellence. Thank you, very much: Kurt Engbritson, Sacramento City College; Christopher L. Hamilton, Golden West College; Beverly Hunt, The Thomas M. Cooley Law School; J. Roland Kelley, Tarrant County Junior College, Northeast Campus; George N. Plavac, Cuyahoga Community College; Gary R. Schwartz, Harrisburg Area Community College; William S. Vanderpool, John A. Walker College of Business, Appalachian State University; Gola E. Waters, Southern Illinois University at Carbondale; and Murray Woodrow, Westchester Community College.

Joseph L. Frascona

Business Law

Part 1

The Foundations of Legal Systems

1. **The Nature of Legal Systems and Law**
   The concept of jurisprudence and its relationship to the role of law in society.

2. **Organization of the United States Legal System**
   Why the United States system of jurisprudence exists and how it operates.

3. **Criminal Law**
   The role of criminal law in society and legal rights and duties as they appear in a relationship between an individual and society.

4. **The Law of Torts**
   The role of tort law in society and legal rights and duties as they involve individual relationships.

Summary

Part 1 of this text introduces you to the subject matter of law and the nature and functions of law in our nation. You will learn as you progress through this text how law is used to improve our society.

Part 1 opens with an attempt to provide a workable definition of law. Next we move to an outline of the workings of the United States legal system. Finally we turn to two subject areas which are of increasing importance to managers—criminal law and the law of torts.

1 The Nature of Legal Systems and Law

After you have read this chapter, you should be able to:

1. Define "legal system."
2. Define "norm."
3. Distinguish between positive and negative sanctions.
4. Identify St. Thomas Aquinas's concept of law.
5. Identify Aristotle's concept of law.
6. Identify Friedrich Karl von Savigny's concept of law.
7. Explain why contemporary social scientists study our legal system.
8. Distinguish between formal and informal norms.
9. Explain the historical school of jurisprudence.
10. Explain natural law.
11. Explain social engineering.
12. Define "law."

Introduction

You are about to embark on a study of the subject of law. You may be surprised to discover that the search for an accurate, all-encompassing definition of law has gone on for thousands of years and will not end as long as people continue to think about the subject. Today researchers are studying legal systems throughout the world to make them work better for all of us. While you may not have an exact definition of law in mind as you pick up this textbook, you certainly are affected by law each and every day. Think about the incident described below.

In Dubuque, Iowa a farmer closes a deal to sell a portion of his land to some investors from Boston, Massachusetts. The investors plan to build condominiums to house the town's growing population. The farmer thinks about all the other dwellings in town and wonders what the difference is between an apartment and a condominium. His daughter, a legal secretary, says that a condominium is an individually-*owned* apartment in a multiunit facility, whereas a typical apartment is merely a *rented* unit.

In this case and in thousands like it each day, individuals or groups of people try to understand or work with a little piece of something we call "law." Every nation in the world has a legal system, and law touches each of us as we go about the business of participating in society. If we are to be effective citizens and participate fully in society, it becomes important for each of us to have a knowledge about and a concern for law.

Importance of Law

Legal systems have always been an important part of every society. In the cases mentioned above and in thousands of instances each day, the **legal system** helps us resolve conflicts, punish individuals who violate societal norms, and solve some of our most pressing problems. Indeed, as our society becomes more complex, we tend to rely more heavily on law to guide our conduct.

legal system
a set of laws adopted by a society or group of people

Just as individuals look to the law as a guide in their personal affairs, so do business people look to the law in their business activities. In the United States today there are over 1,733,000 corporations doing business. Many of these corporations are so large that what they do has an impact on the entire world. Examples of firms with a worldwide reach are Ford Motor Company and American Telephone and Telegraph Company. As large as these firms are, they look to the law to help structure their operations. Even though there may be significant differences in the laws of the countries in which these firms do business, the firms' managers expect certain rules imposed by society to be followed in doing business. Without some shared expectations about how people will behave—as spelled out by a society's legal system—how could a business person expect to run an organization, even for a day?

For example, assume that General Electric agrees to deliver 3,000 citizens band radios to Ajax, Inc. in Newark, New Jersey and another 3,000 radios to LeFleur, Inc. in Paris, France. The sales manager at GE needs to be able to rely on the laws of contracts and sales in both nations so he can properly manufacture and deliver the radios and make a profit. He needs to know that if Ajax or LeFleur decides not to make payments when they are due, the court in Newark or Paris will make them perform as agreed or make some other fair adjustment. The following case illustrates the need of the medical profession for guidance by law in the area of abortions.

Facts

Two Missouri-licensed physicians—one performs abortions at hospitals and the other supervises abortions at Planned Parenthood, a not-for-profit organization—brought this action challenging the constitutionality of the Missouri abortion statute. They believed that certain of its provisions deprived them and their patients of various constitutional rights: the right to privacy in the physician-patient relationship; the physician's right to practise medicine; the female's right to determine whether to bear children; the patient's right to life due to the inherent risk involved in childbirth.

Decision

The court held that portions of the Missouri law were constitutional and portions were not.

Reasoning

The portions of the Missouri law requiring a woman's consent before abortion were constitutional, as were the portions of the law defining viability of the fetus and certain record-keeping requirements. However, the portion which spoke to the issue of the technique of producing an abortion by the physician was unconstitutional because it was an arbitrary regulation designed to prevent the vast majority of abortions from taking place.

Planned Parenthood of Central Missouri et al. v. Danforth, 96 S.Ct. 2831 (1976).

Thus, law is an important element of society, both in our private lives and in the world of work. As vital as law is to our lives, however, many students are not given an opportunity to study it in any formal way before they attend college. In fact, many people are not exposed to law even during their years as undergraduates. To many, law remains a mystery understood only by a select number of craftsmen known as lawyers or judges.

We hope to take some of the mystery out of law through the pages of this text. We plan to do this by giving you a look at law as a major institution in our society. You will learn how law affects our society and how we can make social changes by using law. Our focus will be on those portions of law which are of most immediate value to someone in business. We start by familiarizing you with some basic notions about law and legal systems. These concepts provide a foundation upon which you can build.

What Is Law?

Anthropologists, philosophers, historians, sociologists, and political scientists are only a few of the kinds of scholars who have tried to give an accurate definition of the term "law."[1] A practising lawyer would probably give yet another definition. Your own idea of law might include legal craftsmen, such as judges, police, bailiffs, and lawyers; the places where these craftsmen work, such as courts and jails; and the endless stream of books they refer to, such as *Black's Law Dictionary,* the criminal codes, and the *Uniform Commercial Code.* Indeed, each of these is a part of the legal system in the United States. But this is not the whole picture. The historical background of law plays a large part in our understanding.

Aristotle (384–322 B.C.)

If you could turn back the calendar to the years between 384 and 322 B.C., you might have the opportunity to meet Aristotle. Locating him would probably not be too difficult, because he spent much of his time at a school near Athens called the Lyceum, which he founded. The Lyceum was a beautiful place to visit, with elaborate gardens and imposing statues of the Greek gods. In these gardens Aristotle taught students about his concept of law.

Aristotle built upon the Greek notion that the world was ordered by cosmic law, or, to use his term, **natural law**. He simply meant that there is a law higher than that which is made by mortals—a kind of ideal law. Aristotle tried to connect moral principles and legal principles.

natural law
an ideal or cosmic law

St. Thomas Aquinas (1225–1274)

In order to become a Dominican friar, Thomas Aquinas attended the University of Paris and obtained a doctorate in theology. Soon afterward he became a leader in the Roman Catholic Church, an advisor to Pope Urban IV, and a prolific writer. We can learn about his theory of law by reading his *Summa Theologica,* in which he suggests that law is given to us by God and then interpreted by man's "natural reason." Man's law may err, God's law cannot err.

As part of their philosophies of law, Aristotle and St. Thomas Aquinas shared a belief in a transcendent law given to man. Both men saw a relationship between moral justice and law. Others also have worked with the concept of natural law. To pursue this perspective on the law somewhat further, you might examine the works of Emmanuel Kant or John Locke. But if this perspective is unsatisfactory, your thoughts may be closer to those of Friedrich Karl von Savigny.

---

[1] For a more complete picture of the various perspectives on law, see the original works by any of these philosophers or one of the many fine texts on jurisprudence, such as J. Feinberg and H. Gross, *Law in Philosophical Perspective* (Encino, California: Dickenson Publishing Co., 1977); or C. Morris, *The Great Legal Philosophers* (Philadelphia: University of Pennsylvania, 1959).

Friedrich Karl von Savigny (1779–1861)

Savigny was an orphan of German origin and received his education by moving about from university to university. While still in his twenties, he took a teaching position at Marburg, and there he produced a highly renowned legal treatise. Savigny continued his writing at a number of educational institutions in Prussia, Berlin, and Paris.

Savigny was instrumental in developing the **historical school of jurisprudence.** This school of thought suggests that law evolves as a result of a particular nation's entire history; that lawyers or judges simply interpret the historical direction of the nation. Even legislators, Savigny would suggest, merely put into words that which is embedded in the larger web of a given nation's history. The name that Savigny gave this expression of the spirit of the people is *Volksgeist.* Critics of the historical school of jurisprudence in general and of Savigny in particular ask whether law simply reflects the common consciousness of the nation, as he suggests, or helps to mold the future.

The most important feature of Savigny's work for our purposes is that it marked a move away from traditional generalizations about law toward a more careful pattern of study of society. Indeed, contemporary social scientists are indebted to Savigny for his work. Students interested in learning more about the historical school of jurisprudence might look into the writings of Sir Henry Maine, another legal philosopher of similar persuasion.

Why Is Law Investigated?

It should be clear by now that there are a number of different ways of viewing law, each of which has a particular strength or weakness. Yet contemporary legal scholars are always searching for new and workable models of law which would be useful in organizing and analyzing the information that they are continually uncovering. Why are social scientists dissatisfied with the traditional models?

Social scientists.

Today's rapidly changing world presents us with issues which were rare or unheard of only a short while ago. This is particularly true in the world of work. In our society, people are calling upon business to have a heightened sense of social responsibility, and law is ever more frequently the vehicle used to move business people in the desired direction. Product liability[2] cases reflect this trend.

We have all been disappointed by products at some time in our lives. Some people have found unusual substances in soft drink bottles, and others have been hurt by machines that contained defective parts. For many years consumers had little recourse against companies that put defective or harmful products on the market. For example, in the case of *MacPherson v. Buick Motor Co.,*[3] a person was injured when a wheel on an automobile collapsed because of a defect and thus caused an accident. In order to recover damages caused by such an incident,

---

[2] Product liability is discussed below, pp. 65–66, 455–56, 468–80.

[3] 111 N.E. 1050 (N.Y. 1916).

The Foundations of Legal Systems

the court said, the driver had to prove that the company failed to use reasonable care in assembling the car or, to use the legal terms, that the company was **negligent** in manufacturing the car. The driver also had to defend against the company's assertion that he was **contributorily negligent**—that he failed to exercise reasonable care as a driver and so could not blame the motor company for his misfortune.

Needless to say, it was difficult to establish that the company did not use reasonable care in assembling the car. The problem of defending against the company's assertion of contributory negligence merely complicated the situation. In recent years, the buying public has demanded that this burden be lifted in instances where a particular product is unreasonably dangerous to the customer, so people have turned to law to resolve this difficulty. The legal system has responded to this social pressure by increasing business responsibility. In more than 60 percent of our states, those who sell products that will reach the consumer virtually unchanged are responsible for injury if the product is defective, even if due care was used in putting together the item.

You can expect to see changes in this and almost every other area of law discussed in this text. Clearly, law is not a set of unchanging rules; rather, it changes to reflect movements in our society and, at times, even leads the way for change. The following case illustrates a change in law awarding damages for emotional trauma and upset from witnessing an automobile accident.

negligence (conduct) failure to use the degree of care demanded by the circumstances

contributory negligence plaintiff's conduct which falls below the standard to which he should conform for his own protection and which is a legally contributing cause with the defendant's negligence causing the plaintiff's harm

Facts
Defendant drove his automobile in a southerly direction on Bluegrass Road, and at that time plaintiff mother's infant daughter, Erin, lawfully crossed Bluegrass Road. Defendant's negligent operation of his vehicle caused the death of Erin. Erin's sister, also a plaintiff, and the mother both witnessed the accident from different distances. The surviving mother and daughter join in an action for damages for their emotional trauma.

Decision
Judgment for the plaintiffs.

Reasoning
Damages may be had for emotional trauma and physical injury resulting from plaintiff's witnessing of an accident in which a closely related person is injured or killed if an ordinary person should have foreseen injury to the plaintiff. The possibility that the witnesses may feign trauma to collect damages does not justify a different result. The court recognizes that it is creating a *new* concept of duty by including a right to recovery for injury experienced within an *emotional* impact zone, where before one could only recover for injury experienced within a *physical* impact zone.

Dillon v. Legg, 441 P.2d 912 (Cal. 1968).

Because the range of disputes which are considered amenable to solution through legal systems continues to grow, and because the complexity of the issues within the range increases all the time, we need to study our legal machinery constantly to make sure that it is functioning at its best. Social scientists who study the legal system perform that task. They seek new models of law because the older models do not enable them to study how law and legal systems really function.

How Is Law Perceived?

As was suggested several times above, there are a number of different ways of understanding what is meant by the term "law." In this section we present a view shared by a significant number of contemporary writers about the subject. We begin by learning certain fundamental concepts.

Norm

norm
a group's standard of behavior

A **norm** is a standard shared by members of a group about how they should behave. We all adhere to standards of behavior which we learned as members of a family, a town, and our society as a whole. Many of us have learned these standards so well that we do not even consciously think about them unless we deviate from the norm.

Several years ago a music group called the Beatles created quite a stir when they violated a norm. Until then most men had worn their hair rather short. The Beatles violated the norm by growing their hair so that it covered their ears. Many people considered their action outrageous and looked upon these young men with scorn. Other simple examples of norms are that people should have three meals a day, that dogs in fire stations should be dalmations, and that nurses should wear white uniforms while working in hospitals.

The kind of norms just mentioned are largely "informal." That means that although they define how a person should behave, they are really casual in that enforcement is not usually strict and punishment for deviation is minor. The norm which dictates that forks be placed on the left side of a plate is another informal norm. Although you might raise some eyebrows or be chastised for failing to follow the correct procedure, you probably would not receive any more than a serious reprimand.

Norms may be very "formal," and deviation may be punished severely. Any number of standards for performance fit into this category. Society as a whole does not approve of one person taking another's life, nor do we approve of embezzlement, forgery, arson, etc. In each case we have defined the norm in legal words, in something we call the "criminal code." Violations of the code bring punishments ranging from fines to loss of one's own life.

Norms and Freedom of Choice

sanction
a group's technique for controlling its members

The term **sanction** may be used to describe the techniques for maintaining social control over the members of a group. As was suggested above, a violation of a society's criminal code can bring a sanction ranging from a fine to loss of one's own life. In the following case the court upheld a state's statutory sanction of capital punishment for the crime of murder.

Facts

Gregg was accused of killing and robbing two men and was charged with armed robbery and murder. Following his conviction, Gregg challenged the imposition of the death penalty as "cruel and unusual" punishment under the Eighth and Fourteenth Amendments of the United States Constitution.

Decision

The punishment of death for the crime of murder does not, under all circumstances, violate the Eighth and Fourteenth Amendments.

Reasoning

Capital punishment for the crime of murder can not be viewed as invariably disproportionate to the severity of that crime. What is required is a carefully drafted statute that ensures that the sentencing authority is given adequate information and guidance. The Georgia statutory system under which Gregg was sentenced to death is a constitutional one.

Gregg v. State of Georgia, 428 U.S. 153 (1976).

This kind of sanction is called a **negative sanction** because failure to adhere to the norm brings punishment to the individual. Negative sanctions are the kind most often used by our legal systems. We punish our wrongdoers.

Psychologists tell us that there are also **positive sanctions.** When a person does something particularly good, he or she is rewarded. A child knows that if he or she washes the dishes, he or she will be rewarded by mother or father. A sales employee knows that if he or she achieves a certain level of sales in a month, he or she will receive a bonus, which is a positive sanction. An employee who works hard all year long may expect a positive sanction in the form of a raise in pay or a promotion.

Basically, people are free to choose how they behave. Whether you wear a sport jacket and tie to school or a sweat shirt and blue jeans is a matter of your own choice. Not all people choose to follow the norms prescribed by their peer group or by the larger society. A course in psychology would probably help you begin to understand the reasons for that kind of decision. Here it is important to note that all of us have a range of choices from which we may choose our behavior. If we choose within the norms, we are rewarded; a choice outside the norms results in a negative sanction.

negative sanction
punishment for deviating from the norms of a group

positive sanction
reward for an action approved by a group

Conflict Between Norms

Difficult choices arise when the norms of one group of people come into conflict with society's formal norms. In certain groups—particularly among young people—individuals are pressured to conform to norms that advocate drinking or the use of drugs. The larger society has norms which severely punish such behavior; hence, there is a potential for conflict. In the following case the norm of society for appropriate operation of a school was upheld by the court as superior to the norm of a group of students who were interfering with society's norm.

Facts

Certain students enrolled at Tarrant County Junior College were extremely upset by the possibility that one of their associates was scheduled for a disciplinary hearing at the school which could result in dismissal, and they threatened violence if their friend was dismissed. Following the dismissal they did in fact commit acts of violence. Do the First and Fourteenth Amendments of the United States Constitution guarantee the students' rights, in violation of a state statute, to threaten, curse, and abuse their deans and to generally make trouble at the college?

Decision

No, they may be enjoined from such actions.

Reasoning

The rights of free speech and assembly, while fundamental in our society, still do not mean that everyone with opinions or beliefs to express may address a group at any public place at any time. There is an implied guaranty of order in our society. In the case at bar there was "more than a mere desire on the part of the deans to avoid the discomfort that always accompanies an unpopular view." There was conduct which would materially interfere with the appropriate operation of the school.

Hughes v. Board of Trustees, Tarrant County Jr. College, 480 S.W.2d 289 (Tex. 1972).

The strains can be great in business as well. A company may be able to maximize profits by polluting the atmosphere instead of purchasing expensive pollution control equipment, and many firms have a norm which dictates that managers should try to maximize the company's profits. Even so, in the United States today, many norms have developed which apply powerful sanctions to firms that destroy the environment. The manager may find himself or herself in a terrible bind, torn between competing norms.

Law as a Form of Norm

Some social scientists could argue persuasively that law can exist in any number of situations. For example, in a family, parents "make laws" that children must obey; in a company, the personnel director makes rules that employees must obey. In fact, whenever a group gets together, law may appear. These laws, which are not supported by the official sanctions of the government, are called "private laws" and are generated in "private legal systems."

This text, however, takes the position that law is one type of norm or, more specifically, that *norms established by the official leaders of society may be characterized as law.* We will limit our discussion to the study of the United States legal system—those norms established by any part of our government— and we will not discuss private legal systems, except to note that they are actively studied by people interested in the sociology of law.

law
norms established by the official leaders of society; also those desires recognized and secured by society

The Foundations of Legal Systems

Legal Systems

Once you understand the concept of law, you can imagine a number of different *ways* of putting together the laws of a particular society. Lawmakers can put together laws to create a very democratic or a very autocratic society. For example, the American system of government allows individual citizens to participate extensively in creating laws. On the other hand, for decades Spain's legal system was dominated by the whims of its dictator, General Franco. In fact, there are an enormous number of different ways to construct a legal system.

The late Karl Llewellyn, an American legal scholar, developed what he called the **law-government continuum** to illustrate the point that legal systems can be constructed in an infinite number of ways. He suggested that, in a legal system at the government end of the continuum, decisions would be made according to the arbitrary whim of a leader. Laws would exist or disappear depending on the leader's mood. Llewellyn called this extreme situation the *government pole.* The other end of the continuum is the *law pole.* At the law pole, the rules of law would be so complete that there would be no need for human judgment. Whim would play no role in such a system.

Both ends of the continuum are extreme systems, and it is difficult to imagine any modern legal system at either extreme. It is possible, however, to place nations closer to one pole than the other.[4] For example, countries controlled by a dictator are closer to the government pole than to the law pole. The United States and Great Britain are closer to the law pole, as diagrammed in figure 1.1.

Our text will focus on the legal system of the United States. However, students should remember that the laws of other nations may vary significantly from ours. For students interested in legal history, some legal systems predate the United States' legal system—for example, the Code of Hammurabi (2000 B.C.) and the Mosaic Code (1200 B.C.). The laws of other nations are very important for future business managers. Many firms in the United States actively do business all over the world. The laws governing business transactions vary

law-government continuum
a method of showing the numerous ways of constructing legal systems

Figure 1.1   The Law-Government Continuum

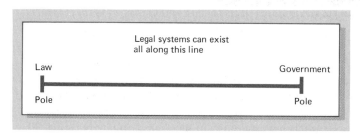

---

[4] For more complete explanation, see H. Richard Hartzler, *Justice, Legal Systems and Social Structure* (Port Washington, N.Y.: Kennikat Press, 1977), p. 62.

from nation to nation. Managers should be very careful not to assume that rules of law and interpretation of them are the same worldwide. In the following case, the English court reflected upon the laws of other nations in deciding the law of liability for negligence in England in connection with impure food.

Facts

A woman became ill while drinking some carbonated beverages. She traced the illness to the fact that she had swallowed a bit of decomposed snail which was found in the bottle of soda. She did not see the impurity at first because of the dark color of the bottle. Will she be allowed to recover from the manufacturer?

Decision

Yes, there is a sufficient degree of **privity** between the consumer and the manufacturer.

Reasoning

After looking at the laws of several nations and the laws of Great Britain, the court announced that "a manufacturer of products . . . who sells those products in the form intended for the consumption of the ultimate consumer, and with the knowledge that the absence of reasonable care in the preparation will result in an injury to the consumer's life or property, owes a duty to the consumer to take that reasonable care."

Donoghue v. Stevenson, (1932) L.R., A.C. 562.

privity
a mutuality of relationship between persons or between persons and a particular transaction

social engineering
using the law to bring about social change

Social Engineering

One of the beauties of our legal system is that it is flexible. New laws are continually being created and old laws set aside or amended. This enables us to work within the system in building our nation. Working within the legal system to bring about desired change is quite common. This process of development and control through law was called **social engineering** by Roscoe Pound, a legal scholar. In speaking of legal systems, Pound said:[5]

Today, in my judgment, the most important problem which confronts the jurist is the theory of interests. A legal system attains the ends of the legal order (1) by recognizing certain interests, individual, public and social; (2) by defining the limits within which these interests shall be recognized legally and given effect through legal precepts; and (3) by endeavoring to secure the interests so recognized within defined limits. I should define an interest, for the present purpose, as a demand or desire which human beings either individually or in groups . . . seek to satisfy, of which, therefore, the ordering of human relations must take account.

Thus, under this concept, law could be defined as those desires recognized and secured by society, such recognition and security being established by a legal system.

Social engineering is clearly evident today in the area of minority rights. The United States has citizens from many different ethnic backgrounds; most of us can think of several different examples of ethnic minority groups, such as Spanish

---

[5] Roscoe Pound, *My Legal Philosophy,* edited by Julius Rosenthal Foundation (Boston: Boston Book Company, 1941), p. 247.

The Foundations of Legal Systems

Americans, American Indians, or Black Americans. Difficulties often arise because minority groups are, by definition, a small part of the population and because their habits and characteristics derived from their backgrounds are often different from those of the majority. One problem that these minority groups face is discrimination in employment. That minority groups are "different" from the majority does not mean that they are "bad" or "useless," but some people take this view; the effect of this error can be devastating on an individual. Many victims of discrimination have no way of supporting their families, even if they have valuable skills. Minority groups which have faced this kind of problem have increasingly turned to law craftsmen for help. In the following case the court declared the law prohibiting discrimination on the basis of color.

Facts

Mr. Faraca wanted to be employed by the Georgia Retardation Center. He had several favorable interviews and was told that he was the best-qualified applicant. All that remained was to route his application to Personnel; there was no doubt that his application would be accepted. Faraca was Caucasian. His wife, Ophelia, was black. This fact caused a Dr. Clements, another official at the center, to reject Faraca because of his concern of possible adverse reaction by the public and the legislators of the state. Does this racial discrimination require monetary relief?

Decision

Yes, **monetary relief** is warranted here.

Reasoning

The civil rights laws cover refusal to enter into a contract, and the director was properly held liable for compensatory damages for refusal to employ plaintiff on the grounds that it would not be proper to have a racially mixed couple in the cottage administrator position.

Faraca v. Clements, 506 F.2d 956 (1975).

monetary relief
a court award of money

The earliest form of such help came from the Constitution of the United States, which has been the major vehicle for reducing discrimination. The Fourteenth Amendment, which provides all people with equal protection of the laws, has been a powerful force for assuring the civil rights of all of our citizens. The Constitution is not the only source of aid. Federal legislation, such as the Civil Rights Act of 1964, prohibits discrimination based on race, color, sex, or national origin. Federal agencies have also been called upon to help. The Equal Employment Opportunity Commission provides help to employees who feel that they have been discriminated against on the job because they are members of a minority group.

Most recently, women have been looking to the law to help them obtain rights equal to those of men. The equal rights movement, as it is sometimes called, is trying to obtain passage of a constitutional amendment guaranteeing that equality of rights shall not be abridged because of sex.

Summary Statement

In this chapter we have learned that:

1. It is important for every citizen to have a knowledge of, and a concern for, law.
2. Our society relies upon law as it becomes more complex.
3. An all-encompassing definition of law has not yet been agreed upon.
4. Different theories of jurisprudence exist.
5. Law changes, and it is a fertile field of research for determining why it changes.
6. Norms can have negative or positive sanctions.
7. Law is a form of a norm, and is defined as norms established by the official leaders of society.
8. In our system of government, the individual participates extensively in creating laws.
9. Our legal system is close to the "law pole continuum."
10. Our legal system is involved in social engineering.
11. Our legal system deserves our support.

The point made in this chapter that there is a difference between morals, norms, and law is illustrated in the following famous English case. The idea that what one might consider morally right does not necessarily protect one in a criminal action is shown by this case.

Regina v. Dudley and Stephens
[1884] L.R., Q.B. 61

Lord Coleridge, C.J. The . . . verdict . . . [for the crime of murder] as it is finally settled before us is as follows:

On July 5, 1884, . . . Thomas Dudley and Edward [sic] Stephens, with one Brooks, . . . English seamen, and the deceased also an English boy, between seventeen and eighteen years of age, . . . were cast away in a storm on the high seas 1,600 miles from the Cape of Good Hope, and were compelled to put into an open boat belonging to the said yacht. That in this boat they had no supply of water and no supply of food, except two 1 lb. tins of turnips . . . [and a small turtle which they caught]. That on the twelfth day the remains of the turtle were entirely consumed, and for the next *eight days* they had nothing to eat. That they had no fresh water. . . . That the boat was drifting on the ocean, and was probably more than 1,000 miles away from land. That on the eighteenth day, when they had been seven days without food and five without water, the prisoners spoke to Brooks as to what should be done if no succour came, and suggested that some one be sacrificed to save the rest, but Brooks dissented, and the boy to whom they were understood to refer, was not consulted. That on the 24th of July, the day before the act now in question, the prisoner Dudley proposed to Stephens and Brooks that lots should be cast who should be put to death to save the rest, but Brooks refused to consent, and it was not put to the boy. . . . Dudley proposed that if there was no vessel in sight by the morrow morning the boy should be killed. That next day, the 25th of July, no vessel appearing, . . .

the prisoner Stephens agreed to the act, but Brooks dissented from it. That the boy was then lying at the bottom of the boat quite helpless and extremely weakened by famine and by drinking sea water, and unable to make any resistance, nor did he ever assent to his being killed. . . . That Dudley, with the assent of Stephens, went to the boy, and telling him that his time was come, put a knife into his throat and killed him then and there; that the three men fed upon the body . . . of the boy . . . ; that on the fourth day after the act had been committed the boat was picked up by a passing vessel, and the prisoners rescued. . . . That they were carried to the port of Falmouth, and committed for trial at Exeter. That if the men had not fed upon the body of the boy they would probably not have survived to be so picked up and rescued, but would within the four days have died of famine. . . . That at the time of the act in question there was no sail in sight, nor any reasonable prospect of relief. That under these circumstances there appeared to the prisoners every probability that unless they then fed or very soon fed upon the boy or one of themselves they would die of starvation. That there was no appreciable chance of saving life except by killing some one for the others to eat. . . . [If] upon the whole matter the Court shall be of opinion that the killing of Richard Parker be felony and murder, then the jurors say that Dudley and Stephens were each guilty of felony and murder as alleged in the indictment.

. . . [This case differs from killing done] in the service of . . . [the] Sovereign and in the defense of . . . [the] country. Now it is admitted that the deliberate killing of this unoffending and unresisting boy was clearly murder, unless the killing can be justified by some well-recognized excuse admitted by the law. It is further admitted that there was in this case no such excuse, unless the killing was justified by what has been called "necessity." But the temptation to the act which existed here was not what the law has ever called necessity. Nor is this to be regretted. Though law and morality are not the same, the many things may be immoral which are not necessarily illegal, yet the absolute divorce of law from morality would be of fatal consequence; and such divorce would follow if the temptation to murder in this case were to be held by law an absolute defense of it. It is not so. . . .

It must not be supposed that in refusing to admit temptation to be an excuse for crime it is forgotten how terrible the temptation was; how awful the suffering; how hard in such trials to keep the judgement straight and the conduct pure. We are often compelled to set up standards we cannot reach ourselves. . . . A man has no right to . . . allow compassion for the criminal to change or weaken in any manner the legal definition of the crime. It is therefore our duty to declare that the prisoners' act in this case was willful murder, that the facts as stated in the verdict are no legal justification of the homicide; and to say that in our unanimous opinion the prisoners are upon this special verdict guilty of murder.

Questions and Case Problems

1. Alan Bakke applied to the Medical School at the University of California at Davis under the regular admissions program for one of 100 seats. He was rejected. Under a special admissions procedure, certain minority group members with lesser academic credentials were admitted. Does this represent reverse discrimination? Does this illustrate social engineering? [*Regents of the University of California v. Alan Bakke,* 438 U.S. 265 (1978).]

2. Read the following statute: "When any person shall be convicted of two or more offenses, before sentence shall have been pronounced upon him for either offense, the imprisonment to which he shall be sentenced upon the second or other subsequent conviction shall commence at the termination of the term of imprisonment to which he shall be adjudged upon the prior conviction." It is clear that the purpose of this statute is to ensure that *some* multiple criminal offenders are to be punished more severely than others by having criminal sentences run consecutively rather than concurrently. However, it is also clear that the section does not apply to *all* convicted multiple offenders. It applies if, but only if, a defendant at the same time in one trial is convicted of at least two offenses before he is sentenced for either offense. Is this a reasonable way to punish people? [*State of Missouri v. Baker,* 524 S.W.2d 122 (Mo. 1975).]

3. Esop, a native of Bagdad, is aboard a ship docked in Great Britain. While in port he was indicted for committing an unnatural act which from his background he did not know was wrongful or illegal. Should he be punished? [*Rex v. Esop,* 7 Car. & P 456 (1836).]

4. A passenger runs to catch a train which is leaving a railroad station. In an attempt to help the potential passenger, a trainman pulled the man aboard and dislodged a package from his arms. The package, which contained fireworks, exploded and overturned some distant scales which fell upon plaintiff and injured her. The courts have for years argued the question of to what extent one person should be liable to another where the injury is not clearly foreseeable. What practical norm might you create which would allow you to answer the question posed? Would you hold the Long Island Railroad responsible for the injury to the woman hurt by the scales? [*Palsgraf v. Long Island R. Co.,* 162 N.E. 99 (N.Y. 1928).]

5. "In each of the cases before us, minors of the Negro race, through their legal representatives, seek the aid of the courts in obtaining admission to the public schools of their community on a nonsegregated basis. In each instance, they had been denied admission to the schools attended by white children under laws requiring or permitting segregation according to race. This segregation was alleged to deprive the plaintiffs of equal protection." Does segregation of children on the basis of race, even though physical and other factors may be equal, represent discriminatory and illegal treatment? [*Brown v. Board of Education,* 347 U.S. 483 (1954).]

6. Plaintiff is a physician. One of the people in a relatively small community repeats on at least six occasions: "He is no good, only a butcher. I would not have him for a dog. . . ." Would you stop the person from continuing to use such language? What norm is illustrated? [*Cruikshank v. Gorden,* 23 N.E. 457 (N.Y. 1890).]

7. An actor is seen in a television commercial with a stain on his shirt. He is then immersed up to his chin in water. Soap is poured in the water. When the water recedes, the garment is clean. Is this deceptive if, in fact, the garment had to be cleaned by normal means? What rule would you establish as head of the Federal Trade Commission? [See Trade Regulation Reporter #2, 7533.]

8. A television commercial attempting to illustrate the moisturizing capacity of a shaving cream is demonstrated to be capable of making it possible to shave sandpaper. In fact, sandpaper is not used. Rather, Plexiglass with sand sprinkled on it is used. What rule would you establish as head of the FTC? What norm is illustrated? [*Colgate-Palmolive Co. v. FTC,* 310 F.2d 89 (1962).]

9. On July 20, 1958 an elderly couple were beaten to death by intruders. Petitioner was not brought to trial for more than five years. Petitioner made no objections to continuances until 3½ years after he was arrested. Does the law do itself a disservice by not punishing or freeing individuals rapidly? [*Barker v. Wingo,* 407 U.S. 514 (1972).]

10. The case of *Regina v. Dudley and Stephens,* Queen's Bench Division, 1884 [1881–85] All England Law Reports 61,[6] illustrates a case in which a judge is trying to apply the law without allowing his personal reaction to the facts to enter into his judgment. Is this always appropriate?

---

[6] Above, pp. 16–17.

2

Organization of the United States Legal System

After you have read this chapter, you should be able to:

1. Identify and explain several techniques for resolving disputes.
2. Explain the advantages and disadvantages of arbitration, mediation, and conciliation.
3. Explain the roles of different kinds of law craftsmen: lawyers, judges, paralegals.
4. Identify the different kinds of state and federal courts.
5. Explain the process of beginning a lawsuit.
6. Distinguish between statutory law, common law, administrative law, case law, and constitutional law.

Introduction

In a society as large as our own, people are bound to have conflicting ideas about how things ought to be done. Indeed, even in a relatively small group such as a family or business organization, it is likely that from time to time individuals will disagree. Fortunately, most of the time these disagreements can be settled promptly and with no formal proceeding necessary. But what happens when the problem is complex or difficult to resolve? For example, what happens when a truck owned by Kross Kuntrie Freight, Inc. collides with another truck owned by One Way, Inc. and both drivers deny that they are the cause of the accident?

Suppose that in the situation just mentioned one of the drivers decides that the best way to resolve the dispute is to start a fight with the other driver and the fight results in serious injury to that other driver. Further, what happens if some of the cargo is damaged as a result of the accident? Who should be held responsible—the trucking firm, the individual drivers, the seller, the purchaser? As we will see, these perplexing issues can be resolved in a number of ways.

How the United States legal system resolves such disputes is illustrated in this chapter.

Response of the Law

In the next few pages we will first examine the nonjudicial procedures that people use to resolve grievances among themselves. Then we will look at the legal forums available for resolving disputes. This material is preparation for treatment in later chapters of the substantive rules applied to particular cases. We will focus primarily on a branch of the U.S. legal system known as civil procedure, although we will first look at alternatives to using law, such as compromise, arbitration, or mediation.

Forums.

No time will be spent in this chapter on the U.S. criminal law. But students should bear in mind that the procedures used for resolving criminal cases are markedly different from those described here, as illustrated by the following case, which discusses the burden of proof of the prosecution in a criminal case.

Facts
In June 1966 a jury found respondent Stillman E. Wilbur, Jr. guilty of murder. However, on appeal, Mr. Wilbur's attorney argued that the charge should be reduced to manslaughter. The State of Maine requires a defendant to establish by a preponderance of the evidence that he acted in the heat of passion on sudden provocation in order to have a murder charge reduced to manslaughter. Is this violative of due process?

Decision
Yes, because under this burden of proof a defendant can be given a life sentence when the evidence indicates that he could deserve a lesser sentence.

Reasoning
The due process clause of the United States Constitution requires the *prosecution* to prove beyond a reasonable doubt the absence of heat of passion on sudden provocation when the issue is presented in a homicide case.
Mullaney v. Wilbur, 421 U.S. 684 (1975).

Most of the events mentioned in the introductory statement for this chapter would be handled in the *civil* courts of the United States. *Criminal* courts deal with individuals who have wronged *society* by committing a crime defined by one of the various criminal codes. In our truck driver incident the fight might result in criminal charges of assault and/or battery being filed. All the other disputes would involve interpreting contracts between the parties or ascribing the fault to one of the drivers for causing the accident or deciding who bears the burden for damaged cargo. They would all lie within the purview of a *civil* court of law, and will be resolved by the parties either nonjudicially or by the use of the legal procedures discussed later.[1]

Alternative Mechanisms—Nonjudicial, or Use of the Legal System

Suppose you purchase a stereo system from a reputable store in your community and the system simply does not live up to your expectations. What do you do? It is highly unlikely that your first response would be to sue the department store. Rather, you would probably begin by taking the set back to the store and asking for a refund or a replacement. You have a grievance and you are looking for the simplest, most direct route toward a solution. Most reliable stores would be happy to replace the set or refund your money if the cause of the difficulty could not be traced to something you had done. That is the simple case. But let's make the problem more difficult. Suppose the problem is that you discovered a large scratch on the speaker cabinet. You know you did not cause the problem. But what if the retail dealer thinks that the scratch looks like something you might have done through your carelessness in unpacking the speaker and, thus, the dealer is unwilling to take it back or refund your money? What can you do without resorting to the courts?

Nonjudicial Mechanisms

Compromise
The chances are you would still not run off to your lawyer in preparation for a lawsuit. Even if you did, a responsible attorney would not instantly file a suit. Rather, a more logical step would be to seek a **compromise** solution. A compromise is an agreement resolving a dispute reached through concessions offered by the aggrieved parties. In the case of the stereo, you might start with requesting a refund, or you might indicate that you would be willing to accept the unit at a reduced cost with the defect. Likewise, the retailer might agree to offer you a discount if you kept the damaged speaker. Each of you has moved slightly from your original position to some acceptable middle ground. The dispute is over and each party is satisfied with the result.

compromise
an agreement resolving a dispute outside of court reached through concessions offered by the aggrieved parties

---

[1] See below, pp. 32–36, A1–8.

Why should a business person ever compromise? There are a number of good reasons for settling a dispute through compromise. The first reason has to do with the cost of litigation. Hiring a lawyer to resolve a simple business disagreement is an expensive proposition. A lawyer's fee could easily exceed the value of the item in question. For example, a five dollar discount in the cost of the speaker is far simpler to grant and far less costly than consulting a lawyer on the issue.

A second reason for compromise is the speed of resolution. Litigation takes time. Civil courts in certain parts of the country have extremely heavy workloads, and it is possible that they would be unable to hear a case for months; in some cases years might go by before the issue is heard. A compromise satisfactory to both parties is rapid—indeed, even instantaneous.

Arbitration

Another alternative to litigation is **arbitration.** Arbitration is the process of resolving a dispute by using a third party chosen for his or her neutrality to decide the disputed issue or issues. Arbitration usually implies that the parties agree to be bound by the decision of the intermediary. It is sometimes called "binding arbitration." For example, in the case of the scratched stereo, if the purchaser and retailer could not agree on a precise compromise position, they might have chosen to arbitrate the dispute. That is, they could have called upon a neutral third party to decide what should be done. In the following case the court declared that the common law requirement of unanimous decision by all the arbitrators is no longer applicable today, a majority is sufficient.

arbitration
a method for deciding disputes outside of court by persons called arbitrators, appointed by the disputing parties

Facts
The plaintiffs are tenants of premises leased to them by their landlord, the defendant, and used as a golf course. In 1971 they sought to exercise the option to renew the lease, but the defendant refused. According to their lease, if a dispute arose in the lease it would be settled by a panel of three arbitrators. The arbitrators met and found for the plaintiff, 2 to 1. Must the arbitrators decide cases unanimously?

Decision
No.

Reasoning
It is true that the common law rule was that unanimity is required unless otherwise specified. However, whatever validity the common law rule may originally have had, It Is clear that it has no proper place in current times.

La Stella v. Garcia Estates, Inc. 331 A.2d 1 (N.J. 1975).

Anyone can be an arbitrator of a dispute. All that is required is that the parties to the dispute have trust in the chosen neutral and that the neutral have the intelligence necessary to understand the dimensions of the particular problem presented. The case of the scratched stereo is relatively simple, but not all issues amenable to arbitration are so simple to resolve. For example, labor relations disputes often involve multimillion dollar business operations and complex employee contracts. When such affairs demand the attention of an arbitrator, the individual chosen must have special skills. There are a number of ways of locating individuals with the desired experience. One possibility is to contact a local university and find a professor with the skills you require. Another, somewhat more direct, route is to contact a specialized arbitration organization, such as the American Arbitration Association. They in turn will help you select an appropriate individual for your particular needs.

The practice of arbitration is not so clearly defined as formal legal procedure. An arbitrator may hold an informal hearing with the disputing parties or may be very formal and require that the parties prepare evidence, bring forward witnesses, and the like. Further, an arbitrator may serve one company on a permanent basis, agreeing to handle all complaints presented over a year, or may serve a given firm only once. Arbitration has many of the same advantages that compromise has. *First,* arbitration is a rapid way of dealing with disputes. Once an arbitrator is located, it is merely a matter of scheduling an appropriate hearing time and waiting for a decision to be made. Thus the problem of the overburdened court is eliminated.

Second, although arbitration is more costly than compromise, it still is not so costly as settling a dispute in court. This is because you are not required to have a lawyer present to argue your case in front of an arbitrator, there does not need to be as much preparation, and no papers need to be filed.

Third, arbitration can generate goodwill. If compromise does not lead to a solution, arbitration may be an easy way to settle the dispute without generating a great deal of hostility. For example, a retail department store may want to maintain good customer relations with the residents of the town in which it is located. If the store or the grievant feels that a compromise solution to their problem cannot be found without sacrificing future relations, they might still agree to arbitrate. The arbitrator need not worry about hostility being directed toward him or her, since the relationship is short-term.

Fourth, the parties may call upon experts in particular areas to decide disputes. Judges often are unfamiliar with highly complex, technical areas, and the parties may feel more comfortable having their dispute argued before an expert.

Mediation

Sometimes the disputing parties would like the help of a third individual but would not like to feel bound to follow the solution proposed by arbitration. In that case an alternative mechanism for dispute resolution is **mediation.** Mediation is the process of intervention of a third party between two disputing parties for the purpose of moving them closer to a compromise position.

The most familiar contemporary illustration of mediation is one drawn from international relations. Former presidential advisor Henry Kissinger used the term "shuttle diplomacy" to describe his efforts to mediate the differences of opinion in a Middle East controversy. President Carter did the same in the Egyptian-Israeli dispute in 1979. Some examples of mediation may be as close

mediation
the process of using a third party to bring disputants closer to resolution of their differences

The Foundations of Legal Systems

as the college you are attending. Many schools have people known as "ombuds-men" on campus. These are people who were chosen for their rapport with students, faculty, and administrators and for their ability to act as an interme-diary (or mediator) in disputes which may arise among these three groups. Another example of a mediator might come from the area of labor law. Many firms turn to state-run mediation services when contract negotiations break down.

Just as in the case of arbitration, the profession of mediator is ill-defined. A mediator may be a highly skilled person with a great deal of expertise in a particular subject area, or he or she might just be a person respected for his or her neutrality. Mediation can be a full-time position, as with the state or federal government, or it might be a part-time occupation for such a person as a uni-versity professor or clergyman.

Using The Legal System: Craftsmen

Lawyers

If compromise, arbitration, or mediation should fail to result in a solution, the next step might be to turn to the law. For most people this means turning to a lawyer. In the next few pages we will review the roles that various individuals play in the legal system.

A **lawyer** is an individual trained as an advocate to represent clients in the legal process. The training involved normally amounts to four years of college followed by three years of law school. Even after this rather lengthy period of time, each state requires that potential lawyers pass a bar examination which tests their understanding of basic legal concepts and special understanding of particular states' laws. Although most people imagine that lawyers spend the majority of their time in court, this is not true. In the following case the court indicated that discussion giving legal advice is practising law, which occurs outside the courtroom, but that the activities of the defendants, nonlawyers, were not of that character and did not constitute practising law.

lawyer
a person who is licensed to practise law by advising and representing clients in legal matters

Facts
The defendants maintained an office in Portland and advertised in the Portland papers. One sample ad read as follows: "Divorce. Join the thousands of people who have been successful in securing their own non-contested divorce. Oregon Divorce Council."

The plaintiff, Oregon State Bar, brought suit to enjoin the defendants from practising law through advertising and sale of do-it-yourself divorce kits. None of the defendants is a lawyer. May they be enjoined?

Decision
Some of their activities may continue.

Reasoning
The defendants did not actually practise law by publishing and advertising and selling such kits. But any *discussion* they might have with the parties is a violation of the law.

Oregon State Bar v. Gilchrist, 538 P.2d 913 (Or. 1975).

Lawyers enter into a relationship with their clients based upon the client's trust that the lawyer will help to resolve his concerns in an expeditious manner. This trust is called a "fiduciary" relationship. In the following case the court points out that the conduct of the applicant for admission to the bar would not interfere with his obligation to assist in the administration of justice and should not be a basis for not admitting him as an attorney.

Facts

The petitioner, Terence Hallinan, was faced with a problem when the committee of bar examiners refused to certify him for admission to the bar in the State of California. He had passed the bar examination but they argued that he did not meet their standard of "good moral character." The evidence was his habitual resort to fisticuffs to settle personal differences and his participation in acts of civil disobedience. Are these acts sufficient to prevent him from entering the practice of law in California?

Decision

The committee of bar examiners was in error.

Reasoning

Preliminarily, we note that every intentional violation of the law is not, ipso facto, grounds for excluding an individual from membership in the legal profession. The court found that the committee's investigation should be limited to the assurance that, if admitted, he will not obstruct the administration of justice or otherwise act unscrupulously in his capacity as an officer of the court. This was not shown here.

Hallinan v. Committee of Bar Examiners, 421 P.2d 76 (Cal. 1966).

Many problems simply do not require that a lawyer spend time in court. For example, the procedures involved in many real estate transactions require the talents of an attorney but often do not require his or her appearance before a judge. Similarly, many problems require a great deal of out-of-court time in relation to the time spent in court. For example, many states have uncontested or no-fault divorce statutes. An attorney may spend days working out the dimensions of the separation agreement with the couple and only a few minutes in the actual courtroom appearance.

Further, some lawyers take jobs which require that they use their legal training to perform other kinds of tasks. Some people, for example, use their training in large corporations as managers. Others are employed in government agencies working on administrative law problems. Still others teach law and do extensive research into perplexing contemporary problems. All of the foregoing should not lead you to the conclusion that lawyers rarely use the courts. Rather, you should realize that there are many opportunities for people to use their law-trained minds both inside and outside the courtroom.

judge
the government officer who presides over a court

Judges

There are two systems of courts in the United States, state and federal. This leads us to the fact that there are two systems of **judges,** state and federal. If some of you have had contact with a judge, it is likely that it was a judge working in the state system. Many communities have municipal court judges who handle routine minor cases such as parking and other traffic violations. The municipal judge may also decide simple disorderly conduct or shoplifting cases.

Another kind of state judge that many people are familiar with is the "justice of the peace." J.P.s usually have the power to hear minor violations of the law and often have the power to perform civil marriage ceremonies. J.P. courts have come under increasing criticism in the last few years because the judges are often not trained in law or legal processes and are often merely political appointees.

At the higher levels of court, state judges are often elected for a long term in office. The reason for the long term is to free the judge from being concerned that unpopular (but fair) decisions will potentially cost him or her a job. At these upper levels, judges are usually well trained in law, often having practised or taught law for several years, and have undergone careful scrutiny by the state bar association.

The length of time in office for federal judges is defined by the U.S. Constitution, which states that all federal judges serve in office so long as they maintain good behavior. Thus, federal judges may hold their offices for an unlimited period of time. This makes it important that the individuals be carefully chosen for the job. All federal judges are chosen by the president of the United States and are reviewed by the Senate before they sit on the bench.

One additional kind of judge is an "administrative law judge." Many federal agencies have the power to create rules and regulations which have the force of law. For example, the Federal Communications Commission creates rules to govern citizen band radios. Some of these agencies have established tribunals in which they judge people accused of violating their rules, and those who judge are specialists called administrative law judges. In the following case the Federal Trade Commission rendered an administrative decision ordering a firm to stop unfair competition.

Facts

Sears advertised its sugar. The advertisements implied or stated that: (1) they could sell sugar inexpensively because they purchased such large quantities, (2) the competitors charged more than a fair price, and (3) the merchandise sold by the competition is inferior. In actuality, Sears was able to sell the sugar at less than cost and make a profit only on the condition that the customer simultaneously purchased other merchandise at prices which gave Sears a profit. It did not let the customers know these facts. Is this advertisement enjoinable by the FTC?

Decision

Yes, the commission has authority over unfair methods of competition.

Reasoning

Congress has the right to delegate its legislative and judicial powers to stop unfair methods of competition. That is what happened in this instance. The commission may issue a cease and desist order.

Sears, Roebuck & Co. v. FTC, 258 F. 307 (1919).

Other Law Craftsmen

It would take almost an entire volume to describe in detail all of the different jobs people do in order to make the legal system function. Many of these make interesting and rewarding careers. Inside the courthouse, people hold such law-related positions as clerk, bailiff, court reporter, and some larger courts have law librarians and judicial administration officers as well. Outside the courtroom, law crafts abound. These include positions such as police officer, corrections officials, and legislative research aides.

Paralegals

An emerging occupation for people interested in law but not interested in attending years of law school is that of **paralegal.** Persons in paralegal positions assist lawyers in a number of different ways. They may complete preliminary interviews with clients, thus saving the lawyer a great deal of time. After proper training, paralegals may do legal research, file and prepare papers with the proper court authorities, and generally perform other tasks under the supervision of an attorney. Since the job title "paralegal" is relatively new, the exact tasks that any individual can expect to do will vary with the inclinations of the paralegal's employer. For most employers, paralegal work will be a research-oriented position with a great deal of client contact. Some colleges offer programs leading to certification as a paralegal assistant.

Using the Legal System: The Courts

It was mentioned above that the United States has a dual system of **courts.** What this means is that each state has a court structure and the federal government also has a structure. The courts may be diagrammed as in figures 2.1 and 2.2.

State Courts

State Inferior Courts. **State inferior courts** are the lowest order of state courts and they are sharply limited in **jurisdiction.** Jurisdiction is the power of a court to hear and to decide a case involving a person or subject matter properly brought before the court. Every state decides what configuration of courts it needs to deal with the case load which it faces. Therefore it would be difficult to list every kind of inferior court. However, typically, states have *probate courts* designed to work on the estates of the deceased. They also have *small claims courts,* which can hear cases involving relatively small amounts of money, the amount varying from state to state. *Traffic courts, criminal courts, mayor's courts, municipal courts,* and *county courts* are other relatively common inferior courts. Note that the word "inferior" refers to the fact that these courts are the lowest in the state system, not that they are of lesser quality. These inferior courts are *trial* courts, but they may not hear cases outside their jurisdiction. For example, a traffic court may not hear a case involving the probate (proof) of a will, nor may a small claims court hear controversies which exceed a certain dollar limit.

Figure 2.1   State Court System

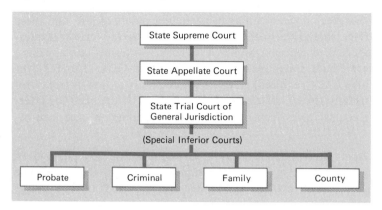

Figure 2.2   Federal Court System

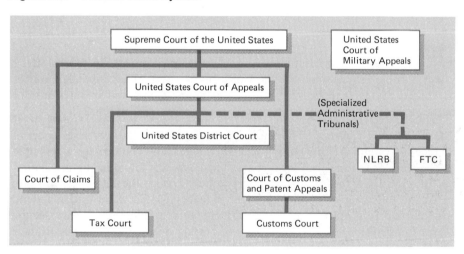

State Courts of General Jurisdiction.   **State courts of general jurisdiction** have many different names, such as *circuit court* or *court of common pleas.* In all states these represent the highest *trial* level court. Since all cases begin in a trial level court, they begin at an inferior court which can hear the case or, if appropriate, a court of general jurisdiction. Also, if a lawyer gets an unsatisfactory result in the inferior court and wishes to further argue a point of law, he or she may appeal to the court of general jurisdiction. These courts are called general jurisdiction courts because they may hear any type of case. However, if there is an inferior court which can hear the case, they will allow it to hear the case first. Technically, its only limitation is territorial. For example, a Texas court of general jurisdiction would not hear a case involving an incident which took place in New York and involved disputants also from New York.

state court of general jurisdiction
the highest order state *trial* court

question of fact
a dispute over what
happened

question of law
a dispute over the
legal effect of what
happened

State Intermediate Appellate Courts. **Questions of fact** (e.g., did he sign the paper?) are settled in trial courts and many can not be appealed. But lawyers and judges often disagree on the meaning of particular points of law, and these **questions of law** (e.g., should the witness have been required to answer a question?) may be appealed to the next higher level court—intermediate appellate courts. Since intermediate appellate courts are not involved in disputes over factual issues, a jury is not required. Lawyers argue points of law in front of a panel of judges (usually three). Just as with inferior courts, the need for intermediate appellate courts varies from state to state depending on case load requirements.

State Supreme Court. If a question of law is particularly troublesome, lawyers may appeal to the highest level court—the supreme court of the state. The supreme court, again, is not involved in disputes over questions of fact and so does not require a jury. Rather, a panel of between five and nine judges listens to the lawyers argue their points of law. If there is no federal issue involved in a case (such as a constitutional question), the determination of law by the supreme court would terminate a case. There then could be no appeal to the federal court system.

Federal Courts

The United States Constitution authorizes the creation of the federal court system. Article III, section 1 of the Constitution says: "The Judicial Power of the United States shall be vested in one Supreme Court and in such inferior courts as the Congress may from time to time ordain and establish."

federal district court
the *trial* level court of
the federal legal
system

Federal District Courts. The **federal district court** is the *trial* level court of the federal system. At this point you may wonder how one decides whether to use the state or federal trial level court. The answer is found in the procedural law. In order for a federal district court to hear a case, the case must fall into one of the following categories. (1) One category is that it may be a federal question (that is, it must be a question arising out of a federal law, treaty, or the federal Constitution). (2) Another way of getting into federal court is to have a question which deals with a federal law which has no dollar requirements, such as civil rights issues or copyrights. (3) A final way of getting into federal court requires that the disputants be from different states or from a state and a foreign nation *and* the amount in controversy must be *over* $10,000. If there are a number of disputants, no plaintiff (the person bringing the case to court) and defendant (the person brought to court) can be from the same state. These requirements are known as subject matter requirements because they literally define which subjects the federal courts will hear and which will be heard by state courts. In addition to subject matter jurisdiction, courts must also have jurisdiction over the person (in personam) or property (in rem) in dispute, and there are additional rules of civil procedure which define these requirements.

In the following case the court held that it did not have jurisdiction over the case because the rules required that all the parties had to be joined in the suit and this had not occurred.

Facts	Reasoning
This is a case involving the question of diversity of citizenship. Almost all of the plaintiffs in the lawsuit were residents of Massachusetts, but not all of them. The defendants were also stated to be citizens of the same state, except Curtiss, who was a citizen of Vermont. Is jurisdiction by the federal court proper?	Jurisdiction can not be supported. The court understood the Congress to mean that each distinct interest should be represented by persons, all of whom are entitled to sue, or may be sued, in the federal courts. That is, where the interest is joint, each of the persons concerned in that interest must be competent to sue, or liable to be sued, in these courts.

Decision

No.

Strawbridge v. Curtiss, 7 U.S. 267 (1806).

U.S. Court of Appeals.   There are eleven courts of appeals in the federal system. Just as with intermediate appellate courts in the state system, the court of appeals does not have "original" jurisdiction over cases. That is, it is not the first court to hear a particular federal case. Rather, the district court or some other federal inferior court holds the trial and the appellate court hears appeals on questions of law. Each of the cases brought before it is heard by a panel of three judges.

U.S. Supreme Court.   Of course, the highest court within the federal system is the Supreme Court of the United States. In rare cases it has original jurisdiction, such as in cases involving ambassadors and in controversies between two or more states or between a state and citizens of another state. But the vast majority of its time is spent on appeals made to it from other courts. The Supreme Court is established by the federal constitution and is composed of nine justices, each of whom has lifetime tenure in the job. These justices hear certain appeals to it and also decide which limited number of cases they will certify for review by it during the upcoming year. The term used to denote a review by the Supreme Court is "certioriari."

Other Federal Courts and Administrative Tribunals.   There are several additional federal courts, each with limited subject matter jurisdiction. The *tax court* is a specialized federal court which deals with questions which arise concerning federal taxation. Before using the tax court, individuals must first exhaust their administrative remedies through the Internal Revenue Service. The *court of claims* hears cases which deal with claims made by individuals against the U.S. government. Many administrative agencies are also administrative tribunals which are also part of this federal system. Examples are the National Labor Relations Board and the Federal Trade Commission. Appeals from these special courts and administrative tribunals are heard first by the U.S. Court of Appeals and later, if further litigation is needed, by the U.S. Supreme Court. The U.S. Court of Military Appeals is worth noting here as a separate federal court. It is important to note that the U.S. Supreme Court can not review decisions of the U.S. Court of Military Appeals.

Using The Legal System: The Lawsuit

Once the proper court is chosen by your attorney, he or she must begin the case by notification of the grievance to the court and the person or group you wish to proceed against. Instituting a lawsuit is a complex branch of a discipline known as civil (or criminal) procedure. In the next few pages we will sketch an outline of a civil cause of action. Later in the book there is a detailed outline of the civil trial process.[2]

Parties to the Suit

In addition to the various law craftsmen described earlier in this chapter, the two primary parties are the **plaintiff** and the **defendant.** The plaintiff is the person who has a grievance and wishes to begin a civil lawsuit. The defendant is the party against whom the lawsuit is brought and who must be notified of the case.

Complaint and Response

The plaintiff must notify both the court and the defendant that he wishes to begin a lawsuit. In order to do this he prepares papers known as a **complaint** or **pleading** (see figure 2.3), which set forth in detail the cause of action that the plaintiff has against the defendant. It states the position of the plaintiff in clear and concise language. The plaintiff's attorney or paralegal assistant then takes the papers to the appropriate court. The plaintiff's attorney usually also prepares a **summons** (see figure 2.4), which is delivered along with a copy of the complaint to the defendant.

The summons sets forth the place for the trial as determined by the court, and the complaint tells the defendant why he or she is being sued. Obviously, care must be taken to assure that the defendant is actually notified, so ideally a court officer or other proper person must personally serve the summons or mail it via registered mail.

Upon receiving the summons and complaint, the defendant then has several alternatives. The simplest thing to do, although probably the least wise, would be to disregard the summons. This would result in a *default* judgment being filed against the defendant when the trial day arrived. A default means that you have automatically lost the case.

A wiser course of action would be for the defendant to choose a lawyer and turn over the summons and complaint to him or her. Lawyers can be located through friends or through the state or local bar associations. If the defendant cannot afford a lawyer, there are a number of organizations which may provide assistance. In criminal cases, the court would appoint a lawyer in order to assure that the defendant receives competent legal assistance in protecting his rights. In civil cases, organizations such as legal aid societies, the American Civil Liberties Union, and special interest groups such as public interest research groups might wish to assist.

---

[2] See below, pp. A1–8.

plaintiff
the party who initiates a civil suit by filing a complaint in the proper court

defendant
the party against whom a civil suit is brought

complaint
the first pleading in a civil action

pleadings
the formal documents filed with a court that usually include the complaint, answer, and motions regarding them

summons
a writ or process served on the defendant in a civil action notifying him of the action and summoning him to appear and plead

The Foundations of Legal Systems

Figure 2.3   Example of a Summons

IN THE...DISTRICT.......COURT

IN AND FOR

...............COUNTY OF....BOULDER...............

·AND STATE OF COLORADO

Civil Action No. .... Div. ....

QUICK COMMERCIAL LOANS, INC.
A Colorado Corporation

Plaintiff.........,

vs.

GERALD K. JONES

Defendant..........

SUMMONS

THE PEOPLE OF THE STATE OF COLORADO
TO THE ABOVE NAMED DEFENDANT........., GREETINGS:

You are hereby summoned and required to file with the clerk an answer to the complaint within 20 days after service of this summons upon you. If you fail so to do, judgment by default will be taken against you for the relief demanded in the complaint.

If service upon you is made outside the State of Colorado, or by publication, or if a copy of the complaint be not served upon you with this summons, you are required to file your answer to the complaint within 30 days after service of this summons upon you.

Warning: If this summons does not contain the docket number of the civil action, then the complaint may not now be on file with the clerk of the court. The complaint must be filed within ten days after the summons is served, or the court will be without jurisdiction to proceed further and the action will be deemed dismissed without prejudice and without further notice. Information from the court concerning this civil action may not be available until ten days after the summons is served.

This is an action* in debt, as set forth more fully in the Complaint.

Dated......June..20.............................., 19..79..........

FISH, FISH and LAKE
Attorneys at Law

....
Clerk of said Court

By...
Deputy Clerk

....
Attorney for Plaintiff
Frank R. Fish, Jr. #2232
1909 Pearl Street, Suite 1300
Boulder, Colorado 80302
Address of Attorney 499-1058

(Seal of Court)

*This summons is issued pursuant to Rule 4, C.R.C.P., as amended. If the summons is published or served without a copy of the complaint, after the word "action" state the relief demanded. If body execution is sought the summons must state, "This is an action founded upon tort."

Figure 2.4 Example of a Complaint

IN THE DISTRICT COURT IN AND FOR THE

COUNTY OF BOULDER AND

STATE OF COLORADO

Civil Action No._____

```
QUICK COMMERCIAL LOANS,      )
INC. A Colorado Corporation,)
                            )
             Plaintiff,     )        COMPLAINT ON
                            )
v.                          )        PROMISSORY NOTE
                            )
GERALD K. JONES,            )
                            )
             Defendant.     )
```

COMES NOW the Plaintiff, by and through its counsel, FISH, FISH, and LAKE, and complains and alleges as follows:

1. That the amount involved herein is in excess of $1,000.00.

2. That venue is proper in this Court because Defendant resided at 621 Pine Street, Boulder, Colorado (Boulder County) as of the commencement of this action.

3. That the Defendant, on or about March 30, 1977 executed and delivered to Plaintiff a Promissory Note, a copy of which is attached hereto and hereby made a part of this Complaint.

4. That the Defendant on or about March 30, 1977 received $5,000.00 as a loan under the terms of the Promissory Note above referenced.

5. That the Defendant has refused to make payments when due and there remains yet due and payable the sum of $3,652.19.

WHEREFORE, Plaintiff demands Judgment against the Defendant in the amount of $3,652.19 together with interest and legal fees as provided in said note, for the costs of suit and collection of the Judgment, interest on the entire amount due at the legal rate from date of Judgment and such other relief as the Court may deem just and proper.

FISH, FISH and LAKE
Attorneys at Law

Plaintiff's Address

828 Arapahoe Street
Boulder, Colorado 80302

By: Frank R. Fish, Jr. #2232
1909 Pearl Street, Suite 1300
Boulder, Colorado 80302
Telephone: (303) 499-1058

The defendant's lawyer would then choose from a number of options. Often the lawyer will file an *answer* to the complaint by agreeing with, or denying, each of the points raised in the plaintiff's pleading. The defendant may add some additional points or may even choose to **counterclaim,** which means a cause of action asserted by the defendant against the plaintiff. The entire process is designed to focus attention on those points about which there is disagreement.

counterclaim
a claim asserted by the defendant against the plaintiff's claim in a civil action

Of course, lawyers should make every effort to resolve cases before they come to trial. It may be clear from the pleadings that a ground for compromise exists, and lawyers often negotiate with each other compromise solutions which are in the best interests of all of the parties to the dispute. Compromise solutions to civil disputes are encouraged by the courts, and it is possible to compromise at any time prior to the trial.

Appearing in Court

If the lawyers can not settle out of court and if the pleadings have been finalized, it is time to prepare for trial. Each of the lawyers marshals as much **evidence** as possible in anticipation of the courtroom appearance. If there are both questions of law (e.g., was the writing a contract?) *and* questions of fact (e.g., was he negligent?) to be decided, then there is a need to have a **jury.** Either party may demand a jury; but if both parties decide not to have a jury, the judge alone will decide the questions of fact. If no dispute exists as to the facts of a case (i.e., what happened), then there is no need for a jury and the case can be tried in front of a judge. Choosing a jury must be done with the utmost care to avoid bias.

evidence
a fact from which an inference can be drawn of another fact

jury
a group of people selected to decide the facts in a trial

Once the jury is chosen the trial may begin. Each side presents its evidence to the judge and jury. Lawyers must be careful that they present their views without violating the rules of evidence for the admission of materials to the court. Lawyers not only present their best evidence, but they try to find flaws in their opponents' evidence. For example, oral evidence which is presented by a witness for the plaintiff may be rebutted through skillful cross-examination by the defendant's lawyer—the process of questioning an opposing witness following his or her original testimony.

When both sides have concluded their presentation, including their summations, the judge makes a statement to the jury explaining what law they must consider in coming to a verdict. This statement to the jury is called the *charge to the jury.*

The jury then retires to a private room in the courthouse to deliberate the **verdict.** When this is done they return to the court and announce their decision. The judge then renders **judgment.**

verdict
a jury's finding of fact

judgment
the final decision of a case by a court

The losing side then has a set period of time within which it must decide whether or not to appeal to a higher court. Again, the appeal must be based upon a disagreement about a point of *law,* either substantive or some procedural violation. There can be no appeal of questions of *fact.* For example, if we go back to the case of the scratched stereo, a question of *fact* would be: Who scratched the speaker cabinet? A question of *law* might be centered around the interpretation of some aspect of contract law, such as determination of the meaning of unconscionable contracts, or whether the conduct of the parties created a contract.

On appeal, the case is heard by a panel of judges. Normally a party has the right to one appeal. Prior to the hearing date, each lawyer submits a written report outlining his or her position on the disputed point of law. This document is called a *brief*. On the day of the hearing, each lawyer argues the points of law before the panel of judges, and the panel at some later time files a written decision. This decision may in certain instances be appealed to the next highest court in the particular system. Sooner or later final resolutions of the dispute occur either because the parties are satisfied or because there are no additional grounds or opportunities for appeal.

The Law Relevant to the Situation

Statutory Law

statutory law
bills passed by a legislature and signed into law by president or governor

The form of law that most people think of when asked to answer the question "What is a law?" is **statutory law.** Federal statutory laws are bills passed by the United States House of Representatives and Senate, signed by the president, and not declared unconstitutional by the court system. Each of the states also has statutory laws, passed through their equivalents of the House and Senate and signed by the governor and allowed to stand by the courts. Further, cities, towns, and other municipalities have the authority to pass *ordinances,* which are forms of statutory law. But statutory law is not the only source of law.

Common Law

In the previous chapter we discussed how norms of a society can become translated into law. When settlers came to America, there obviously were no laws for them to follow but they did have norms for behavior based on the laws of their native lands. Many of these norms, mostly from England, have been incorporated by reference into the laws of the United States, both federal and state. This happens when courts of law refer to these norms and use them in deciding cases. Norms may not be in statutory form but are reflected in the principles of law made by courts in their decisions. Judges often refer to these principles as **common law,** the common concept of justice *not in statutory form.* And the principles are just as binding as statutory law. The early colonies in America had the common law of England, much of which continues as a part of the law in the states today, except for Louisiana, where the civil code or roman law influence continues.

common law
principles of nonstatutory law reflecting the customs and usages of society and found in judicial decisions

Administrative Law

administrative law
rules and regulations created by an administrative agency, thereby becoming law

Chapter 33, on **administrative law,** is devoted to discussion of the administrative rules and regulations that implement constitutional and statutory law. For the time being it is important to realize that both state and federal administrative agencies have the power to make such rules, all of which have the strength of law. There are a number of reasons for granting administrative bodies the power

The Foundations of Legal Systems

to make rules which have the force of law. One of the most important reasons is that administrative agencies have expertise which goes far beyond the expertise of the legislative bodies who would otherwise have to create the rules.

Case Law

Every time a case is heard, a judge is asked to interpret the law in the light of a new set of facts and apply case precedent if it is still applicable—a doctrine called **stare decisis.** When a judge is called upon to interpret the meaning of a word in a statute or administrative rule, or even interpret what a previous judge has said, he is in a position to "make law." All the decisions he writes are filed in court reports by court reporters, and his interpretations become binding on lower courts in the same jurisdiction as they consider future cases on the same point of law. In effect, the legislatures and administrative agencies leave to the judges the task of making more meaningful and clear these pronouncements, which need such attention when they create law. Judges, in doing their job, make law which we call **case law.**

Constitutional Law

Along with the constitutions of each of the states of the union, the U.S. Constitution provides yet another source of law. One of the major purposes of the U.S. Constitution is to provide an organizational framework for the federal government. The federal government has three major branches—legislative, executive, and judicial. The U.S. Constitution explains in broad terms the powers and responsibilities of each of these branches.

A second function of the U.S. Constitution is its declaration of the rights of individuals. Portions of the Constitution, in particular the amendments, spell out freedoms that all of us share by virtue of being citizens of the United States. For example, the due process clauses of the First, Fifth, and Fourteenth Amendments guarantee that, among other things, people shall "not be deprived of life, liberty or property without due process of law."

Summary Statement

In this chapter we have learned:

1. There are alternatives to the legal system for resolving disputes. Not all problems need to be brought to a lawyer. Compromise, arbitration, and mediation are natural alternatives. If the dispute can not be settled in any other way, the legal system presents the forum for grievance resolution.
2. Lawyers and judges are not the only persons who serve and are employed in the United States legal system.
3. The basic design of all state legal systems is the same, and in both the federal and state systems we have courts of general and special jurisdictions and courts of trial and review.
4. The legal process is a series of interrelated actions that are normally taken in an attempt to resolve controversies over the applicability of law in a given situation.

5. Law that can be applied to a dispute varies. The law of any one state consists of the U.S. Constitution, the public Acts of Congress, its own state constitution, the public Acts of its own legislature, case decisions of the Supreme Court of the United States on a constitutional question, case decisions of its own courts, federal and state administrative law, and the private law of individuals within its boundaries.

The following is a classic case which illustrates the purpose of pleadings and the need for a lawyer, and how the United States legal system works.

Dioguardi v. Durning
139 F.2d 774 (1944)

Clark, Circuit Judge. In his complaint, obviously home drawn, plaintiff attempts to assert a series of grievances against the Collector of Customs . . . of New York growing out of his endeavors to import . . . bottles of "tonics." We may pass certain of his claims as either inadequate or inadequately stated and consider only these two: (1) that on the auction day, October 9, 1940, when defendant sold the merchandise at "public custom," "he sold my merchandise to another bidder with my price of $110, and not of his price of $120," and (2) "that three weeks before the sale, two cases, of 19 bottles each case, disappeared." Plaintiff does not make . . . clear how these goods came into the collector's hands . . . but he does say he made a claim for "refund of merchandise which was two-thirds paid in Milano, Italy," and that the collector denied the claim. These and other circumstances alleged indicate . . . that his original dispute was with his consignor. . . . *This complaint was dismissed by the District Court* . . . [because] it "fails to state facts sufficient to *constitute a cause of action.*"

. . . [P]laintiff filed an amended complaint, wherein, with an obviously heightened conviction that he was being unjustly treated, he vigorously reiterates his claims, including those quoted above and now stated as that his "medicinal extracts" were given to the Springdale Distilling Company "with my betting [bidding?] price of $110: and not their price of $120," and "It isn't so easy to do away with two cases with 37 bottles of one quart. Being protected, they can take this chance." . . . [D]efendant . . . explained the loss of the two cases by "saying that they had leaked, which could never be true in the manner they were bottled." *On defendant's motion for dismissal on the same ground as before, the court made a final judgment dismissing* the complaint, and plaintiff now comes to us with increased volubility, if not clarity.

. . . [H]owever, . . . he has stated enough to withstand a mere formal motion, directed only to the face of the complaint, and . . . here is another instance of judicial haste which in the long run makes waste.

We think that . . . the plaintiff has disclosed his claims; as it stands, we do not see how the plaintiff may properly be deprived of his day in court to show what he obviously so firmly believes and what for present purposes defendant must be taken as admitting. . . . The record indicates that he refused further help from a lawyer . . . ,and his brief (which was a recital of facts, rather than an argument of law) shows distrust of a lawyer of standing at this bar. . . . [This] is the plaintiff's privilege . . .; but we fear that he will be indeed ill advised to attempt to meet a motion for summary judgment or other similar presentation of the merits without competent advice and assistance.

Judgment is reversed and the action is remanded for further proceedings not inconsistent with this opinion.

Questions and Case Problems

1. Assume that you own a small retail store in Miami, Florida. You value your customers and wish to maintain their goodwill. Could you recommend two ways of resolving customer complaints other than a lawsuit?

2. Appellant, a twelve-year-old boy, had entered a locker and stolen $112 from a woman's pocketbook. The petition charged appellant with delinquency for the act, which, if performed by an adult, would be larceny. Is proof beyond a reasonable doubt due even to a child? [*In re Winship*, 397 U.S. 358 (1970).]

3. Just before leaving office, John Adams, president of the United States, appointed 42 Federalists. The Senate confirmed these appointments, but the new president told his secretary of state, Madison, not to deliver 17 of these commissions. William Marbury was to have received one of the commissions. Marbury appealed to the Supreme Court of the United States for his appointment under legislation passed by Congress which was contrary to the United States Constitution. Must legislation which is contrary to a constitution give way to the constitution under our system of law? [*Marbury v. Madison*, 1 Cranch 137 (1803).]

4. Johnny Williams was a defendant in a robbery prosecution in Dade County, Florida. As part of the trial, the court impaneled a six-person jury. Is this a violation of his rights? [*Williams v. State of Florida*, 90 S.Ct. 1893 (1970).]

5. Standard Oil Company of New Jersey and thirty-three other corporations, John D. Rockefeller, William Rockefeller, and five other individuals decided to seek a reversal of a decree in a lower court which attempted to dissolve a holding company which was believed to be a violation of a certain federal antitrust law because its actions were in restraint of trade. The statute did not define "in restraint of trade." The court developed a rule of reason which gave meaning to the words "restraint of trade." This rule of reason is an example of what type of law? [*Standard Oil Company of New Jersey v. United States*, 221 U.S. 1 (1910).]

6. Goldfarb tried to find a lawyer who would perform a title examination for less than the fee stated in the minimum bar association fee schedule. Unable to locate a lawyer who would agree, Goldfarb brought a class action suit claiming that fee schedules constituted illegal price fixing. Should Goldfarb prevail? [*Goldfarb v. Virginia State Bar*, 421 U.S. 773 (1975).]

7. Respondents are operators of a California "hot plant" at which asphalt concrete for surfacing highways is manufactured and sold. According to section 2(a) of the federal Robinson-Patman Act, it is forbidden for any person engaged in commerce to discriminate in price where the result has a substantial anticompetitive effect. Since respondents' services were

performed totally within one state, the court had to determine whether or not the respondents were engaged "in commerce." Is the court dealing with a question of fact or law? [*Gulf Oil Corp. v. Copp Paving Company, Inc.* 419 U.S. 186 (1974).]

8. Tompkins, a citizen of Pennsylvania, was injured on a dark night by a passing train of the Erie Railroad. He claimed the accident occurred through the train company's negligence. The action was brought in the Southern District New York Federal Court. The case resulted in a battle over the appropriate law to apply since there was a diversity of citizenship. It was held in the case that the federal court had to apply state law to determine whether Tompkin's complaint contained a cause of action, and it could not create by case decision a federal right for Tompkins. This means there is one type of law which the federal system does not have. What is this law? [*Erie Railroad v. Tompkins,* 304 U.S. 64 (1938).]

9. The complainant is an institution which extensively advertises its chiropractic school. It stated that it had a faculty and a staff, and it claimed incomes for its graduates. An ex-employee of the school who resides in the same state where the school is located is attempting to organize a similar school in the same state. The complainant objects to the ex-employee's efforts. What mechanism might be used by the parties to resolve their dispute? [*American University v. Wood,* 128 N.E. 330 (Ill. 1920).]

10. One of the most basic rights of our legal system is that every individual is entitled to his day in court. It has also been said that a lawyer who represents himself has a fool for a client. Evaluate these statements in the light of *Dioguardi v. Durning,* 139 F.2d 774 (1944).[3] Notice that Mr. Dioguardi was unable to communicate his claim very clearly. Should this make any difference in proceeding with a legal case?

---

[3] Above, pp. 38–39.

Criminal Law 3

After you have read this chapter, you should be able to:

1. Distinguish between criminal law and tort law.
2. Identify the different categories of crime: felony, misdemeanor, treason, violation.
3. Explain the difference between legality and morality.
4. Describe the requisites for crime.
5. Explain several defenses to criminal acts.
6. Explain several different business crimes: arson, forgery, bad checks, embezzlement, burglary.

Introduction

Unfortunately, the number of crimes committed in the United States provides convincing evidence of the necessity for spending some time discussing criminal law. The FBI reported that in 1940 there were approximately 100 crimes committed per 100,000 population; 118 crimes per 100,000 in 1950; 145 in 1960, and 180 in 1965. Subsequent figures available from the FBI indicate that in 1975 over 11 million serious crimes were committed (approximately 5,000 per 100,000 population). The number of crimes continues to rise. White collar crime alone in the United States today is a serious problem. In two recent years more than $500 million in securities were stolen.[1]

Alarming as these figures are, they tell only part of the story. Increasingly, business organizations have had to face the reality that the number of "white-collar" crimes is also increasing. These are offenses such as embezzlement or larceny. In the next few pages we will discuss the nature of criminal law and review some criminal laws.

The substantive law of crime is concerned with defining what duties we owe to society and what rights we have as members of society. Thus, a study of criminal law is important to us so that we may know our legal rights and duties.

Moreover, because crime has a significant impact upon us as individuals and has an impact upon business, it is important for us to have an exposure to this area of law.

Concern of the Law

crime
an act committed or omitted in violation of a public law governing it

tort
a civil (private) noncontractual wrong

The greater part of this text discusses civil law and civil procedure. In this chapter we will examine briefly "the other half of the law" known as criminal law. A **crime** is an act, committed or omitted, in violation of a public law governing it[2] (e.g., robbery, traffic violation). The major difference between a crime and a **tort** is that a crime is an offense against the state (a public wrong) in which the *state prosecutes* the individual, whereas a tort is a civil (private) wrong to a person other than breach of contract and the *injured party must bring the civil lawsuit* himself (e.g., negligence). For example, a negligent car driver is civilly liable to the pedestrian injured by such negligence.

In a criminal offense, the society as a whole takes action against an individual who has violated a formalized norm. Nobody likes murderers, burglars, arsonists, and other such offenders, and all of us, collectively, have delegated the responsibility of dealing with accused criminals to various governmental prosecutors. If an individual is found to be guilty of an offense, he or she is punished by the government. We are saying that society as a whole found the act reprehensible. Some acts are reprehensible to both society as a whole *and* to private individuals who are hurt. Therefore, certain acts are considered both torts and crimes.

---

[1] See FBI statistics, *Uniform Crime Reports,* 1975 (Washington, D.C., U.S. Government Printing Office), as well as *New York Times,* June 10, 1971, p. 22, col. 3, and June 9, 1972, p. 1, col. 2.

[2]*Shick v. United States,* 195 U.S. 65 (1904).

The Foundations of Legal Systems

Categories of Crime

Felony

A **felony** is the most serious category of crime. It is a crime for which, usually, the punishment can be more than one year in prison. Some states have an alternative definition for felony: any crime punishable by death or imprisonment in the state prison. Examples of felonies include murder, robbery, and rape.

felony
a serious crime for which, usually, the punishment can be more than one year in prison

Misdemeanor

Another kind of criminal act is a **misdemeanor.** It is a crime for which the punishment is imprisonment for less than one year, usually in a city or county jail. Once again, an alternative definition adopted by some jurisdictions is that a misdemeanor is any crime not punishable by death or imprisonment in a state prison. Examples of misdemeanors include shoplifting and petty larceny.

misdemeanor
a crime for which the punishment is less than one year in prison

Violation

Some jurisdictions have an additional classification for offenses of lesser importance, such as parking or traffic citations. These are called *violations* and are generally distinguished by the minimal nature of the punishment, such as a fine. Usually they are classified as misdemeanors.

Treason

Treason is a felony which is specifically defined in the U.S. Constitution as "levying war against them [the states], or in adhering to their enemies, giving them aid and comfort."[3]

treason
a felony specifically defined by the U.S. Constitution

Requisites for Crime

Morality Versus Criminality

Just as in the law of torts, certain acts may seem reprehensible to you, but they may be only morally wrong and not criminal in nature. You will not be treated as a criminal if you do not yield your seat in a crowded bus to an elderly individual, or if you fail to remember an engagement (even if it's a promise to witness your best friend's wedding). Similarly, commission of certain infractions generally is insufficient to label someone a moral bankrupt. For example, few would argue that overtime parking at a meter is an indication of immorality.

Act and Intent

Every crime requires either an act or an omission (failure to **act**) when action is required by law. This very simple statement is an extremely important base of criminal law. If people could be punished without having committed an act or for omitting an act required by law, we would be liable to punishment just for our thoughts. In the following case the defendants had not committed a crime because, while they may have intended to commit a criminal act, they did not do so.

act
every crime requires an act or omission

---

[3] U.S. Constitution, Art. III, sec. 3.

Facts

Two men were tried, convicted, and sentenced on an indictment charging them with manufacturing whiskey. There was no evidence of an overt act on their part in the manufacture of whiskey and no circumstantial evidence tending to prove guilt. They appealed the decision.

Decision

The verdict was overturned and the decision reversed. Judgment for defendants.

Reasoning

The court thought that there could be no doubt but that the evidence strongly tends to show an intention on the part of the appellants to engage in the manufacture of liquor; certainly such inference may reasonably be drawn. But intent alone, not coupled with some overt act toward putting the intent into effect, is not cognizable by the court.

State v. Evans, 57 S.E.2d 756 (S.C. 1950).

mens rea
the mental element
required for a crime

This mental element of intent stated by the court in the decision is sometimes given the name **mens rea.** However, students should not confuse *mens rea* with *motive.* You do not have to prove a motive to prove a crime. Different kinds of intent are required for different crimes. Some crimes require *specific intent,* which means they require the proof that the accused intended to commit the particular wrongful act proscribed by law. For example, a general definition of forgery is the false making or materially altering, with intent to defraud, of any writing which, if genuine, might apparently be of legal efficacy. To be guilty of forgery you must have the intent to defraud. If you are merely reproducing an item with the honest belief that you have permission, you will not be held criminally responsible.

Some crimes require only *general intent* but not *specific intent*. This means that you do not have to have the particular intent to commit a certain crime, but only an intent to be doing what you did. An example of a crime usually involving simply general intent is robbery. Robbery often is defined as "taking property from the person or presence of another by use of force or threatening the imminent use of force." Note that no specific intent is spelled out in such statutory language.

Sometimes the mere agreement to commit an offensive act is regarded as violative of the law. For example, if two individuals communicate to each other the desire to commit embezzlement, they have committed a crime. That crime is known as *conspiracy*. Notice that the act of communicating this desire is enough to warrant a criminal charge. Some states require also an overt act.

Defenses.

Ability to Commit Crime—Defenses

Insanity

The classic defense to crime is that the actor was insane *at the time that he committed the offense.* There are a number of definitions of legal insanity. Traditionally, two tests were employed to prove insanity. The first is the *McNaghten test.* Under this older rule, the accused would have to prove that either he did not know the nature of the act, or, if he did know the nature of the act, he did not know that it was wrong. A second traditional test is the *irresistible impulse test.* This requires that the defendant prove that he was suffering from a mental

The Foundations of Legal Systems

disease which caused him to act in the criminal way (irresistible impulse) even though he knew right from wrong.

More recently, two additional tests have been added. According to the *Durham test,* insanity is demonstrated by proof that the actor was suffering from a mental condition and that the act was a result of that condition. The *American Law Institute Model Code test* suggests that a person is not responsible if, as a result of his disease, he lacked substantial capacity "to appreciate the criminality of his conduct or to conform his conduct to the requirements of the law." Additionally, the term "mental disease" does "not include an abnormality manifested only by repeated criminal or otherwise anti-social conduct."[4] In the following case the court held that the trial judge did not instruct the jury that the necessary relationship between the defendant's mental disease and the criminal act must be established beyond a reasonable doubt.

Facts

Defendant was convicted of murder. He was mentally ill at the time that the alleged murder was accomplished. Four doctors testified at the trial as experts. Fifteen witnesses testified concerning Carter's life history, his personality and habits. The jury was instructed to find the defendant not guilty if, at the time of the killing, his insanity caused the act of taking human life. On conviction, the defendant appealed.

Decision

Reversed and remanded for a new trial.

Reasoning

There must be a relationship between the disease and the criminal act; and the relationship must be such as to justify a reasonable inference that the act would not have been committed if the person had not been suffering from the disease.

Carter v. United States, 252 F.2d 608 (1957).

Minors

At common law there existed a sliding scale for determining the responsibility of children (minors) for the commission of a crime. Under seven years old a child is conclusively presumed not to have the ability to commit a crime. Between seven and fourteen the child is presumed incompetent, but the state may rebut the presumption. Finally, between fourteen and adulthood the child is presumed to have the ability, but he or she may rebut that presumption.

Figure 3.1   Scale of Responsibility of Minors for Committing a Crime

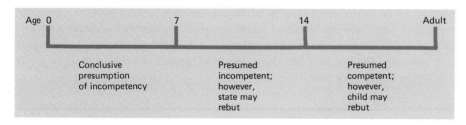

---

[4] American Law Institute Model Penal Code Proposed Official Draft, May 4, 1962, sec. 4.01.

Duress

duress
wrongful inducement to do that which a reasonable person would have been unable to resist

If a defendant commits a wrongful act because he or she was induced to do so by the use of, or threat to use, unlawful force against the defendant or another, which a reasonable person would have been unable to resist, the defendant can assert the defense of **duress.** For example, if someone orders you to rob a bank while holding a gun at you and threatening your life if you do not cooperate, you can later use the defense of duress to charges of robbery leveled at you by the state.

Corporate Responsibility

For years, a perplexing problem facing criminal lawyers was whether to hold corporations liable for criminal acts. The answer today is generally yes. Although corporations obviously can not be imprisoned, they can be fined for offenses. An officer of the corporation will be held criminally liable only if he or she actually committed the wrongful act or directed that the act be done.

Other Defenses

Intoxication is often used as a defense to criminal culpability. However, voluntary drunkenness will not help you avoid liability. *Consent*—that is, voluntary agreement to have a crime committed—may sometimes be a defense. For example, bodily harm which might be criminal in nature is consented to by the participants in a boxing match.

Select Crimes Relevant to Business[5]

For a more complete treatment of any of the following business crimes, see one of the many excellent legal encyclopedias such as *Corpus Juris Secundum* or *American Jurisprudence.*

Arson

arson
the willful and malicious burning of the dwelling house of another (at common law); today, by statute, arson includes one's own insured house and the buildings of another

Arson may be defined as the willful and malicious burning of the dwelling house of another. This is a common law definition, which today has been extended to include one's own insured house and the buildings of another, depending on the particular state statute. Recall that common law consisted of those norms of behavior which became embodied in the case law over time. Each state has its own definition of arson. For example:

West Virginia Code 61–31–1: "Any person who willfully and maliciously sets fire to or burns or causes to be burned or aids, counsels or procures the burning of any dwelling house whether occupied, unoccupied or vacant, or any kitchen, shop, barn, stable or other outhouse that is parcel thereof, or belonging to or adjoining thereto, whether the property of himself or another shall be guilty of arson in the first degree."

---

[5] The definitions that follow are useful *for teaching purposes only.* Students with legal problems are reminded that the best source of advice for their particular problems is an attorney.

Forgery

The false making or altering, with intent to defraud, of any writing which, if genuine, might be of legal efficacy is known as common law **forgery.** In a business setting, forgery might include altering public records, issuing false certificates, or falsifying a doctor's prescription. Altering of checks is also considered forgery and is a particularly common form of forgery.

forgery
the unauthorized act of imitating or altering a writing with the intent to defraud and impose liability

Issuing a Bad Check

As stated in the consolidated laws of New York, a person is guilty of issuing a bad check when: (a) as a drawer or representative drawer, he utters a check knowing that he or his principal, as the case may be, does not then have sufficient funds with the drawee to cover it, and (b) he intends or believes at the time of utterance that payment will be refused by the drawee upon presentation, and (c) payment is refused by the drawee upon presentation.

Embezzlement and Larceny

Larceny and embezzlement are two closely related crimes. **Embezzlement** involves depriving someone of his property through breach of a trust relationship.[6] Note that the property is generally obtained lawfully but later converted to the embezzler's own use. **Larceny** is a common law crime which involves the taking and carrying away of the personal property of another by someone who does not have the right to do so. Notice that there is no relationship of trust between the parties to larceny. In the following case the court held that the same set of facts may result in the commission of two crimes, and it was not improper for the district attorney to prosecute for one rather than the other crime.

embezzlement
depriving someone of his property through breach of a trust relationship

larceny
the taking and carrying away of the personal property of another without the right to do so

Facts
Defendant was convicted of stealing a $5 pair of shoes. He claims that an error was made in convicting him of larceny, that he should have been convicted of shoplifting. Shoplifting (in Tennessee) occurs when "any person . . . shall willfully take possession of any goods . . . not exceeding the value of $100 offered for sale by any store or mercantile establishment."

Decision
Conviction sustained.

Reasoning
Larceny is defined as "felonious taking and carrying away the personal goods of another." The fact that a person may be charged with violation of either a larceny statute or a shoplifting statute at the discretion of the district attorney does not deny equal protection of the law.

Yearwood v. State of Tennessee, 455 S.W.2d 612 (Tenn. 1970).

robbery
the taking of money or goods of value from the person of another or in his presence, against his will, by force or fear

Burglary versus Robbery

Two crimes which are often confused by laymen but which are actually quite different are burglary and robbery. Both are common law crimes. **Robbery** is the taking of money or goods of value from the person of another or in his presence, against his will, by force or fear. In effect, it is an aggravated larceny. **Burglary,**

burglary
the breaking and entering in the night of the home of another with the intent to commit a felony therein

---

[6] 26 AM. JUR.2d *Embezzlement,* secs. 1–7 (1966).

however, is the breaking and entering in the night of the home of another with the intent to commit *any* felony therein. Many states have amended the burglary statute or have alternative laws to deal with burglary-type offenses during the daylight hours.

Commercial Bribing
All states have laws regulating *bribery*. Some have special statutes which regulate bribery in a business setting. For example: New York sec. 180.00 ". . . guilty of commercial bribing when he confers, or offers or agrees to confer, any benefit upon any employee, agent or fiduciary without the consent of the latter's employer or principal, with intent to influence his conduct in relation to his employer's or principal's affairs."

Preparatory Crimes
Sometimes merely preparing to commit a crime results in a criminal offense being committed. *Solicitation* involves inciting someone else to commit a felony. It is a common law crime. Contemporary laws would include inciting to commit misdemeanors as solicitation. **Attempt** is a preparatory crime. Here an actor has the specific intent to commit a crime; makes some act toward accomplishing the crime which goes beyond mere preparation; and has the apparent ability to complete the crime but is stopped by something beyond his control.

attempt
a preparatory crime

Violation of the Antitrust Laws
Violation of the antitrust laws can be a crime. Antitrust laws are discussed in chapter 32.

Summary Statement

1. Crime has a significant impact on society, and an individual will want to know his legal rights and duties as defined by criminal law.
2. There is a difference in rights and duties as defined by the substantive areas of crime, tort, and contract law.
3. Crimes have been categorized according to the seriousness of the end result of the crime—a felony being the most serious, followed by misdemeanor and violation.
4. In criminal law, act plus intent (mens rea) determine whether or not a crime was committed; motive is not a requisite element.
5. There are limits to the rights society has under criminal law inherent in defenses to crimes. Some defenses are insanity, minority, consent, duress.
6. Certain crimes have special significance for business. These include arson, larceny, forgery, embezzlement, and burglary. Statutory definitions of the various crimes differ from state to state.

The following case illustrates the insanity defense to crime. Defenses, as has been noted, limit the right that society has against the individual. This case explores and discusses how and why the rights of society can be limited in criminal law.

Durham v. United States

214 F.2d 862 (1954)

Bazelon, Circuit Judge. Monte Durham was convicted of housebreaking by the District Court. . . . The only defense asserted at the trial was that Durham was of unsound mind at the time of the offense. We are now urged to reverse the conviction. . . .

Durham has a long history of imprisonment and hospitalization. In 1945, at the age of 17, he was discharged from the Navy after a psychiatric examination had shown that he suffered "from a profound personality disorder which renders him unfit for Naval service." In 1947 he pleaded guilty to violating the National Motor Theft Act and was placed on probation for one to three years. He attempted suicide, was taken to Gallinger Hospital for observation, and was transferred to St. Elizabeth's Hospital, from which he was discharged after two months. In January of 1948, as a result of a conviction . . . for passing bad checks, the District Court revoked his probation and he commenced service of his Motor Theft sentence. His conduct . . . in jail led to a lunacy inquiry in the Municipal Court where a jury found him to be of unsound mind. . . . [At] St. Elizabeth's, he was diagnosed as suffering from *"psychosis with psychopathic personality."* . . . [H]e was discharged in July 1949 as "recovered" and was returned to jail to serve the balance of his sentence. In June 1950 he was conditionally released. He violated the conditions by leaving the District. . . . After he was found and returned to the District, the Parole Board referred him to the District Court for a lunacy inquisition, wherein a jury again found him to be of unsound mind. He was readmitted to St. Elizabeth's in February 1951. This time the diagnosis was "without mental disorder, psychopathic personality." He was discharged for the third time in May 1951. The housebreaking which is the subject of the present appeal took place two months later, on July 13, 1951.

. . . [T]he psychiatrist who examined him in September 1951 [said] he suffered from hallucinations immediately after his May 1951 discharge from St. Elizabeth's. Following the present indictment, in October 1951, he was adjudged of unsound mind. . . . He was committed to St. Elizabeth's for the fourth time and given subshock insulin therapy. This commitment lasted 16 months . . . when it was certified . . . that he was "mentally competent to stand trial. . . ."

He was thereupon brought before the court on the charge involved here.

It has been ably argued by counsel for Durham that the existing tests in the District of Columbia for determining criminal responsibility, i.e., *the so-called right-wrong test supplemented by the irresistible impulse test, are not satisfactory criteria for determining a criminal responsibility.* We are urged to adopt a different test to be applied on the retrial of this case. . . .

. . . It is simply that *an accused is not criminally responsible if his unlawful act was the product of mental disease or mental defect.*

We use "disease" in the sense of a condition which is considered capable of either improving or deteriorating. We use "defect" in the sense of a condition which is not considered capable of either improving or deteriorating and which may be either congenital, or the result of injury, or the residual effect of a physical or mental disease.

Whenever there is "some evidence" that the accused suffered from a diseased or defective mental condition at the time the unlawful act was committed, the trial court must provide the jury with guides for determining whether the accused can be held criminally responsible. We . . . could not formulate an instruction which would be either appropriate or binding in all cases. But under the rule now announced, any instruction should in some way convey to the jury the sense and substance of the following: If you the jury believe beyond a reasonable doubt that the accused was not suffering from a diseased or defective mental condition at the time he committed the act charged, you may find him guilty. If you believe he was suffering from a diseased or defective mental condition when *he committed the act, but believe beyond a reasonable doubt that the act was not the product of such mental abnormality, you may find him guilty.* Unless you believe beyond a reasonable doubt either that he was not suffering from a diseased or defective mental condition, or that the act was not the product of such abnormality, you must find the accused not guilty by reason of insanity. . . . He would still be responsible for his unlawful act if there was no causal connection between such mental abnormality and the act. These questions must be determined by you from the facts which you find . . . in this case.

In leaving the determination of the ultimate question of fact to the jury, we permit it to perform its traditional function. . . . Juries will continue to make moral judgments, still operating under the fundamental precept that "Our collective conscience does not allow punishment where it cannot impose blame." But in making such judgments, they will be guided by wider horizons of knowledge concerning mental life. The question will be simply whether the accused acted because of a mental disorder, and not whether he displayed particular symptoms which medical science has long recognized do not necessarily . . . accompany even the most serious mental disorder.

The legal and moral traditions of the western world require that those who, of their own free will and with evil intent (sometimes called mens rea), commit acts which violate the law, shall be criminally responsible for those acts. Our traditions also require that where such acts stem from . . . the product of a mental disease or defect as those terms are used herein, moral blame shall not attach, and hence there will not be criminal responsibility. The rule we state in this opinion is designed to meet these requirements.

Reversed and remanded for a new trial.

Questions and Case Problems

1. Robert Irwin committed a series of murders. Following these crimes he was able to prove that he was mentally ill at the time of the commission of the crimes. Without more data, can you find him an adequate defense to the murder charge? [*People v. Irwin,* 166 Misc. 751 (N.Y. 1938).]

2. Defendant had broken a glass and entered a store. Merchandise including cigarettes had been placed in a bag near a window. Defendant had drunk a quantity of whiskey before breaking into the store. Is he guilty of anything? [*Bradford v. State of Tennessee,* 347 S.W.2d 33 (Tenn. 1961).]

The Foundations of Legal Systems

3. Kalbfeld decides that he no longer likes the way his home looks and burns it to the ground. There is no intent to defraud his insurance company or anyone else. No one is endangered by his act. Is this arson? [*People v. Kalbfeld*, 124 Misc. 200 (N.Y. 1924).]

4. Defendant is an official of a local government. He is approached by an individual who wishes him to vote in a certain way on a pending matter. Defendant offers his vote in exchange for money. Assuming no immunities and assuming that no money is passed, has a crime been committed? [*Rudolph v. State*, 107 N.W. 466 (Wis. 1906).]

5. Jack Jones is in the process of breaking and entering the home of one Frank Franklin. The time is midnight. Jones has the intent to commit a felony, but only puts one finger inside Franklin's home after breaking down the door. Is this a burglary? [*State of Missouri v. Whitaker*, 275 S.W.2d 316 (Mo. 1955).]

6. Lance is a youngster of age seventeen who wished to obtain alcoholic beverages. Since he is under the legal drinking age, he reproduces a driver's license and changes the date of birth. Whereupon he uses the license to procure alcoholic beverages. Has he committed a crime? [*People v. Prata*, 47 Misc.2d 55 (N.Y. 1965).]

7. Defendant issued a check in the amount of $14.50 to plaintiff. This check was submitted to a bank for payment but it was refused because defendant's account was then short. It had been short at the time of issue and defendant knew this when issuing the check. Is this an offense? [*Helman v. Dixon*, 71 Misc.2d 1057 (N.Y. 1972).]

8. Jim Jones hates his professor and one day announces to his roommate, "I wish him dead." Is this the crime of solicitation?

9. Jim Jones offers his professor a cup of coffee which he has laced with a substance he thought was arsenic. In fact, the substance was sugar. Has he committed a crime?

10. In *Durham v. United States*, 214 F.2d 862 (1954),[7] the following quote can be found:

It has been ably argued by counsel for Durham that the existing tests in the District of Columbia for determining criminal responsibility, i.e., the so-called right-wrong tests supplemented by the irresistible impulse test, are not satisfactory criteria for determining a criminal responsibility. We are urged to adopt a different test to be applied on the retrial of this case. This contention has behind it nearly a century of agitation for reform. . . . The rule we now hold must be applied on the retrial of this case and in future cases is not unlike that followed by the New Hampshire court since 1870. It is simply that an accused is not criminally responsible if his unlawful act was a product of mental disease or a mental defect.

The more liberal tests for insanity described in the quotation are fair not only to the individual but for society in general. Evaluate this statement. In order to evaluate this statement, you should think about the difference between legal insanity and medical insanity. Should the standards be the same for each type? Why or why not?

---

[7] Above, pp. 49–50.

4

The Law of Torts

After you have read this chapter, you should be able to:

1. Identify and explain the concept of tort.
2. Distinguish between a tort and a crime.
3. Distinguish between an intentional tort and a negligent tort.
4. Explain assault and battery.
5. Define at least an additional kind of intentional tort.
6. Explain defenses to intentional torts.
7. Define negligent torts.
8. Explain proximate cause as a legal concept.
9. Explain the concept of immunity from tort liability.

Introduction

The word **tort** is not a part of the vocabulary of most people. Yet, torts are committed every day in almost every community in the United States. In fact, the chances of you or a member of your family having committed a tort or being otherwise involved in a tort action at one time or another are reasonably high. The reason is that the number of different kinds of torts is very large. The next few paragraphs will give you a few examples of kinds of problems included within the subject matter of torts.

The most common kind of tort action in the United States is the typical automobile accident. It happens in every large city every single day. Driver X drives his car in a careless manner and dents the fender of driver Y's car. Add passengers to either car or more automobiles or trucks to the accident and you have made the tort more complex—but it is still a tort action.

If the drivers of the cars involved in the accident get out of their cars and exchange more than driver's licenses and ultimately end up in a fight, this too can result in a tort action. If the driver of car X is hurt very badly and is rushed to a hospital, where the doctor in charge carelessly administers the wrong drug or performs the wrong operation, this can result in a tort.

If driver X begins to recuperate in the hospital and is served food with an unwanted foreign object (such as a cigarette butt in his milk) or becomes sick from being carelessly served spoiled food, there is a chance for a tort action. If, in reconstructing the accident, the police discover that the incident was caused by a poorly constructed steering column rather than the driver's carelessness, once again there is a possible tort action.

Torts exist in the business world in the form of trademark infringement, copyright abuse, product liability, and more. Almost any time a person acts below a generally accepted standard of behavior, he or she is risking becoming involved in a tort action.

Response of the Law

All of us are involved in incidents at one time or another for which we are at fault. These incidents may be as simple as accidentally tripping someone in a hallway or as severe as an auto accident involving damages which might exceed a million dollars. In the vast majority of these cases nobody accused you of being a criminal although you may have angered others or even cost them large sums of money.

Assuming that no *contractual* arrangement exists and no *crime* has been committed, a **wrong** is still apparent, and our legal system has developed a body of rules for redressing these wrongs. The late William L. Prosser was the foremost scholar of his time concerning the law of torts. He said that a precise definition of tort was difficult if not impossible to provide but suggested that, "broadly speaking, a tort is a civil wrong, other than breach of contract for which the

tort
a civil (private) noncontractual wrong

wrong
the illegal invasion of another person's interest

court will provide a remedy in the form of an action for **damages**." It is an area that is at once exciting and rapidly changing. We will look at the three major subdivisions of tort law and see how it is evolving. The three major subdivisions are intentional torts, negligent torts, and strict liability torts.

Intentional Torts

While we are free to do as we please in the United States, if we *intentionally* hurt others in the process, we can be held responsible. Certain acts are so repulsive that all members of our society agree to punish the wrongdoer through the vehicle of criminal law. But, for example, assume X strikes you in the nose and society demands that X spend some time in jail for violating the criminal law. The problem of paying your doctor's bills remains even if society is satisfied that X is behind bars. You, as the individual damaged, still are personally unsatisfied even though society as a whole has achieved relief. For this reason there are several *intentional* torts which parallel criminal acts. However, the causes of action are different, and students should not confuse criminal actions with their parallel intentional tort actions.

Battery and Assault

One of the incidents cited in the first part of this chapter was a fist fight between two individuals. This is an example of a battery. A **battery** is committed when an individual acts *intentionally* to cause a harmful or offensive bodily contact with another and a harmful or offensive bodily *contact* directly or indirectly results.[1] The following case illustrates that, without the intent to cause harmful bodily contact, there cannot be a battery.

Facts
Perkins, plaintiff, alleged that the defendant, Stein and Co., was the owner of a large brewery and numerous brewery wagons; that while delivering company beer the defendant's drivers carelessly, negligently, and recklessly ran into, over, and upon the plaintiff. Suit brought for battery.

Decision
This is not a battery. Judgment for defendant.

Reasoning
The intent to do harm is not present. A battery is more than an attempt to do corporal (bodily) hurt to another; but any intentional injury whatsoever, be it ever so small, is a battery.

Perkins v. Stein et al., 22 S.W. 649 (Ky. 1893).

Note that the court is not concerned with the fact that a small injury or a large injury resulted. It is concerned with *intentional* harm and the factual issue of *bodily contact,* which is what differentiates battery from assault. An **assault** is an unprivileged act by a person intentionally causing another to *apprehend* that a harmful or offensive bodily contact will occur. In order for an assault to

---

[1] See, generally, RESTATEMENT (SECOND) OF TORTS sec. 13 (1958).

exist, it is not necessary that the actor have the ability to carry out his threat, as long as he has the *apparent* ability to do so. It is necessary only that the receiver of the threat believes that the actor has the ability to carry out the threat. Battery and assault are separate torts which may occur separately or at the same time. It should be noted that battery and assault can also be separate crimes.

False Imprisonment

False imprisonment, often called *false arrest,* is another intentional tort which may be of concern to business people. False imprisonment may be defined as the unprivileged act of intentionally restraining the movement of another who is aware of such restraint. As with other intentional torts, the actor must have the requisite intent to confine another. Further, the confined party must know he or she is restrained. For example, if you were working with a friend taking inventory of goods in a warehouse and accidently locked your friend in the warehouse, this would not be false imprisonment. You simply do not have the requisite intent. If your friend had continued to work while you left on an errand and had been unaware of having been locked up, this also would not be false imprisonment. But in the following case, grabbing a person was false imprisonment.

false imprisonment
an unprivileged act
intentionally restraining
the movement of
another who is aware
of such restraint

Facts
Plaintiff visited the defendant's store. After she made a small candy purchase, Mr. Vaughn, the store's agent, suddenly grabbed her in the presence of others, accused her of having stolen certain articles, against her will detained her and deprived her of her right of freedom and locomotion, and, finding nothing in her shopping bag except what had been bought and paid for, he released her. Plaintiff sued for false imprisonment.

Decision
This is false imprisonment. Judgment for plaintiff.

Reasoning
Any exercise of force by which, in fact, a person is deprived of his liberty and compelled to remain where he does not wish to remain, or go where he does not wish to go, is an imprisonment.

Great Atlantic & Pacific Tea Co. et al. v. Smith, 136 S.W.2d 759 (Ky. 1939).

Invasion of Privacy

There are a number of additional intentional torts. However, brief mention should be made of one other intentional tort which may occur in a business setting. A tort that has increased in importance in recent years is the *intentional invasion of one's privacy.* Here the cause of action often arises in a business situation when a company unauthorizedly uses an individual's name or likeness for profit,[2] or where very objectionable highly private information about an individual is unauthorizedly made public. The following case illustrates such unwarranted publicity amounting to an invasion of privacy.

---

[2] *Carlisle v. Fawcett Publications, Inc.,* 201 Cal. App.2d 733 (1962).

Facts

The defendant owns a garage in Kentucky, and the plaintiff, Dr. W. Morgan, a veterinarian, was offended when the garage put a sign in its window which read: "*Notice:* Dr. W. R. Morgan owes an account here of $49.67, and if promises would pay an account, this account would have been settled long ago. This account will be advertised as long as it remains unpaid." Plaintiff sued for invasion of privacy.

Decision

There is a right of privacy which has been violated. Judgment for plaintiff.

Reasoning

The court held that there is a right of privacy and that unwarranted invasion of such right may be made the subject of an action in tort to recover damages.

Douglas v. Stokes, 149 S.W. 849 (Ky. 1912).

Some Other Intentional Torts

A few other intentional torts should be mentioned here briefly.

1. *Malicious prosecution* is concerned with a person's initiation or procurement of criminal proceedings against an innocent person, done without probable cause and with malice, the proceedings terminating in favor of the accused person.
2. *Mental and emotional disturbance* is a relatively new and developing tort consisting of outrageous conduct interfering with another person's mental and emotional tranquility.
3. *Deceit* occurs when a person knowingly misrepresents a material fact, intending to mislead another person by inducing him to rely on the misrepresentation and to act in a particular business transaction, causing financial damage to him.
4. *Trespass to chattels* is concerned with a person's wrongful interference with another person's possession of **chattels** (e.g., automobile, furniture) causing damage to the other person's interest in the chattels.
5. *Conversion* is a more serious type of wrongful interference with another person's possession of chattels by wrongfully exercising control and dominion over them.
6. *Trespass to land* is concerned with a person's wrongful interference with another person's possession of land.
7. *Public nuisance and private nuisance* are concerned with a person's unreasonable, substantial interference with either the *public's* use and enjoyment of *public* land (e.g., blocking a public highway), or with a *private* person's use and enjoyment of his *private* land (e.g., excessive and continuous loud noise or offensive odors from a neighbor).
8. Miscellaneous torts concerned with unfair trade practices, such as: *fraudulent marketing* of goods or services (e.g., S markets and sells goods or services to P, misrepresenting that they are made or provided by R when, instead, they are from Z); and wrongful *imitation of physical appearance* of goods.

chattel
a tangible, movable thing

The Foundations of Legal Systems

Defenses to Intentional Torts

Occasionally there exists a legally justifiable *reason* for committing what would otherwise be an intentional tort. Some of these reasons provide enough protection for the actor so that he or she is shielded from what would otherwise be wrongful with resulting liability. These reasons create a *privilege* so to act.

Privilege.   A **privilege** is that which exempts a person from liability for his conduct which, but for the privilege, would subject him to liability for such conduct. A privilege may be in the form of *consent* to such conduct by the person affected or by operation of law.

privilege
that which exempts a person from liability for his conduct which, but for the privilege, would subject him to liability for such conduct

consent
a person's approval of something, made with full capacity, freely and without fraud or mistake, permitting what would otherwise be an intentional tort

1. Consent. A person's **consent** to the illegal invasion of his interest by another person privileges such invasion. The person consenting must have had full capacity to consent and have acted freely, without fraud or mistake, in assenting to the invasion. For example, in all body contact sports the participants consent to body contact by each other, thus precluding the commission of the tort of battery. This is the subject of the following case.

Facts
Plaintiff entered into a boxing match while attending a carnival in the hope of winning some prize money. The match resulted in injury to the plaintiff by the defendant. Plaintiff sued for battery.

Decision
There is no battery. Judgment for defendant.

Reasoning
An assent which satisfied the rules stated prevents an invasion from being tortious and, therefore, is not actionable.

Hudson v. Craft et al., 204 P.2d 1 (Cal. 1949).

It should be clear that consent can not be allowed if it was induced through fraudulent means. For example, if a person assents to eat a tablet which he believes to be an aspirin and which was intentionally misrepresented to be such when in fact it was actually LSD, the victim has not consented to the negative consequences and has a valid cause of action for tort. Finally, consent may be expressly stated or may be implied from the situation.

2. By Operation of Law. There are various privileges given by operation of law and without the consent of the person whose interest is threatened with invasion or has been invaded.

   a. Self-Defense. If there is an *assault,* the person assaulted has the privilege of *self-defense,* which includes the right to self help by him by the use of such physical force as is reasonably required under the circumstances to protect himself from *the threatened battery.* If the threat is danger of substantial bodily harm or danger to life itself, the person assaulted may use force amounting to substantial bodily harm or death to the assaulting party.[3] The following case illustrates reasonable conduct in self-defense when there is reasonable belief of danger of substantial bodily harm.

---

[3] See, generally, RESTATEMENT (SECOND) OF TORTS secs. 63–76 (1958).

Facts

Plaintiff seeks damages for unlawful arrest and personal injuries resulting from being shot by an arresting officer. Plaintiff was denied a drink at a private Christmas party at a Club 21. A disturbance arose when plaintiff refused to leave the club and the bartender called the police. Later, while walking toward the police vehicle, plaintiff began cursing and grabbed for the officer. The officer stepped back and fired one shot into plaintiff's neck.

Decision

This is self-defense on the part of the defendant officer. Judgment for defendant.

Reasoning

The court held that Officer Randolph reasonably believed he was in danger of substantial physical harm and that the force which he used to resist was not unreasonably excessive.

G. Roberts Jr. v. American Employers Insurance Co., Boston, Mass., et al., 221 So.2d 550 (La. 1969).

The privilege of self-defense extends to one person protecting a second person from a third person.

b. Possessory Interests in Property. A person whose *possessory interest in property is superior* to that of a person *threatening to interfere with such property interest* has the privilege to use such physical force as is reasonably required under the circumstances as protection against *such interference,* but the force may not amount to substantial bodily harm or death. An example is a person threatening to commit a trespass to land or chattels of another who has a superior right to possession of such land or chattels. However, if the threatening person also threatens *assault,* then the privilege of *self-defense* becomes available to the person assaulted.

A person with a *superior right to possess* land or chattels *which are in another person's possession* has a privilege of *recapturing* such property. Whether he may use physical force to recapture depends upon whether or not the person in possession *initially* obtained possession rightfully or wrongfully. If the person in possession was *initially rightfully in possession,* then physical force can not be used to recapture. For example, if you defaulted in making an installment payment on your automobile and your creditor, with the right to repossess the automobile on your default, seeks to repossess it, he can not use physical force on you to do so if you refuse to consent to his repossession. You were initially rightfully in possession. However, if the person in possession *initially obtained possession wrongfully,* and the person with a superior right to possession seeking to recapture the property acts *promptly* to repossess after wrongful dispossession has occurred, then reasonable force may be used, but not amounting to substantial bodily harm or death. For example, if you see a thief running off with your tires, you can chase him and use reasonable physical force on him to recapture your tires.

Another illustration of this privilege to recapture chattels is in the area of merchandising. Some states allow shopkeepers the privilege of detaining an individual suspected of shoplifting. Thus, in the previously considered case of *Great Atlantic & Pacific Tea Co. et al. v. Smith* on false imprisonment, if that woman had been detained in a state granting the privilege, she probably would not have succeeded in her cause of action.

Negligent Torts

In this section we turn to the largest subdivision of the law of torts, in terms of the number of cases litigated each year. It is the branch of the law which uses *fault* rather than *intent* for imposing liability. However, not all incidents for which a person is at fault result in legal liability. There are a number of issues to consider before legal liability may be established.

Negligent Torts and Morality

As small children, our parents direct us in our activities. When we make a mistake, we are punished and taught the correct behavior. As we grow older, we discover that the community in which we live has standards of behavior to which we must adhere. However, no one ever can or does tell us the precise behavior deemed acceptable for every conceivable situation. Nonetheless, a certain standard of conduct prevails in all situations, and if we fail to live up to the prevalent standard of conduct, we will be held responsible either morally or legally.

On occasion, certain behavior will fail to meet the community's standard of care but will not be a legal wrong. For example, assume that Franklin Moneypockets is a multimillionaire. Years ago Franklin had his life saved by Ben Pennyless, an extremely poor individual. If Franklin knows of Ben's financial plight, many of us would expect that Franklin would come to Ben's aid. However, there is no legal responsibility to do so. This is because there is *no legal duty* which extends from Franklin to Ben no matter how strong the moral obligation seems to be. The elements involved in suing for the tort of negligence are: a duty of care and its breach; causation, called *proximate cause;* and damage, or loss or harm.

Legal Duty

This leads us to the *first step* of establishing tort liability through *negligence*. There can be an established case of negligence only where there is a *legal duty which extends between the parties*. The question of whether such a legal duty *exists* is strictly a question of law and not a question of fact subject to jury interpretation.

Standard of Care

On the assumption that a legal duty exists, the *next step* would be to establish that the person committing the *tort* of negligence *acted below the prevailing standard of care*. The term we use to describe such *conduct* is **negligence.** Negligence (careless conduct) is the failure to use the degree of care demanded by

negligence (conduct) failure to use the degree of care demanded by the circumstances

the circumstances[4] at the time of the act or failure to act. Another definition for negligence is the failure to use the care which an ordinary, prudent person would use under the same or similar circumstances to avoid causing injury to another or to protect another from injury.[5] Negligence (careless conduct) should be distinguished from the **tort of negligence,** which occurs when (1) a person's negligence (2) proximately causes (3) injury to another person's interest. Until negligence proximately causes such injury, the tort does not exist. In the following case, reasonable care was exercised and, therefore, there being no negligence, no tort of negligence had occurred.

tort of negligence
negligence proximately causing injury to another person's interest

Facts
James Fred Morris suffered personal injuries while attending an automobile mechanics class at Tucson High School. His teacher, defendant, wanted the class to dismantle an automobile and prepare a cut-away view of it. Pieces of the auto were cut off and an attempt was made to bend the top preparatory to placing it on the scrap pile. Jim was trying to lift the piece when another student jumped on it, thus cutting Jim's hand. Plaintiff sued for negligence.

Decision
The teacher was not negligent. Judgment for defendant.

Reasoning
The standard of care for negligence is, of course, the failure to act as a reasonable and prudent person would act in like circumstances. The teacher was acting properly. In this case, the utmost that could be claimed was negligence committed by the students.

J. Morris v. R. Ortiz, 437 P.2d 652 (Ariz. 1968).

A question which must naturally arise is: How do you determine if a person is acting as an ordinary, prudent person would act under the same or similar circumstances? The answer to that question lies within the province of the jury. In each case that comes before it, the jury listens to the fact pattern as explained by the lawyers and decides whether the parties were acting above or below the standard. If the actor was below the standard, he or she is negligent.

Not only is the standard of care a difficult thing to measure for the reason noted above, but the standard varies for other reasons as well. For example, if an individual has certain special skills which he or she is using (usually those licensed), such as a physician or beautician, then he or she must adopt as their standard of conduct the standard of care of the reasonable person within that profession or specialty. The question faced by the jury would be: What would the reasonable and prudent doctor have done under the same or similar circumstances? This is called the "reasonable person test."

Obviously, the standard is not a precise line, and that is one of the major issues of debate in a negligence trial. Lawyers may present *expert witnesses* to testify on the issue of negligence in the particular situation. For example, the lawyer may get a physician to testify before the jury about the standard of conduct among doctors. Lawyers may also be able to put together a fact pattern

---

[4] *Fort Smith Gas Co. v. Cloud,* 75 F.2d 413 (1935).

[5] *Hewlett v. Schadel,* 68 F.2d 502 (1934).

in which the facts speak for themselves, which is called **res ipsa loquitur.** This involves inferring negligence from the fact pattern. For example, a tack in a can of beans bought at a store implies negligence by the manufacturer. Yet another way of building a case of negligence is by illustrating that trade rules were not adhered to, or in select cases that a statute was violated. Once again, it is for the jury to decide if a person was acting as he should. It may well be that the jury will decide that, even if a person followed trade standards or adhered to a statute, the person's conduct was still negligent.

res ipsa loquitur
the thing speaks for itself

Condition and Use of Land. Chapter 45, Real Property and Its Ownership, discusses the duty and standard of care and liability for the condition and use of land.

Proximate Cause of Injury by Negligence

After negligence is proved, the *third step* is to prove that the negligent conduct in question was the **proximate cause** of the injury. Proximate cause refers to the *legal cause* of the injury. The definition of proximate cause most often quoted is "that cause which in natural and continuous sequence, unbroken by an intervening cause, produces the injury, and without which the result would not have occurred." The courts often discuss the issue of the *foreseeability* of the incident when determining proximate cause. However, the terms "proximate cause" and "foreseeability" are not interchangeable. Foreseeability of injury from negligence is an element in proximate cause. The following case makes this distinction.

proximate cause
the cause of an injury without which the injury would not have occurred

Facts

Plaintiff, a longshoreman, employee of the defendant vessel owner, was injured while working aboard ship. The defendant failed to provide adequate flooring to support the weight of a loaded handtruck used by the plaintiff. The flooring collapsed and the plaintiff and the loaded handtruck fell into the hole. The plaintiff, in trying to get the truck and load out of the hole, strained the muscles in his rib cage. He sued for this injury, claiming that the *inadequate flooring* was the proximate cause of his injury. Defendant claimed that he could not reasonably *foresee* that plaintiff would go into the hole and, therefore, he should not be liable because the inadequate flooring was not the proximate cause of plaintiff's injury; his going into the hole was the nonforeseeable proximate cause.

In a suit for negligence against the defendant, the court found that the flooring was insufficient and the proximate cause of plaintiff's injury. Defendant appealed.

Decision

Affirmed for plaintiff. In a case for the tort of negligence, there was no error in finding that the insufficient flooring was the *proximate cause* of plaintiff's injury.

Reasoning

The court concluded that foreseeability was an element of proximate cause. The court held that the failure to furnish adequate flooring prompted the plaintiff, when he fell, to act as he did. Plaintiff's attempt to lift the truck out of the hole was a normal response of a worker under the circumstances and, therefore, foreseeable. It was part of the flooring collapse, which was the proximate cause of plaintiff's injury.

Dewey v. A. R. Klaveness & Co., 379 P.2d 560 (Or. 1963).

The Law of Torts   61

Defenses to the Tort of Negligence

In an accident it is often the case that each party blames the other for the occurrence. Sometimes only one party is at fault, but at other times each party's fault may contribute to the incident. At still other times one party or the other may assume a risk as part of the activity in which they are participating. These points lead us to a discussion of the defenses to the charge of negligence.

Contributory Negligence.   Suppose you were involved in a minor car accident and that you were at fault. Suppose, further, that you knew that the driver of the other car was not driving very carefully either. Would you willingly agree to pay for all the damage done? Probably not! **Contributory negligence** may be the doctrine you use to protect yourself. It is "conduct on the part of the plaintiff which falls below the standard to which he should conform for his own protection, and which is a legally contributing cause cooperating with the negligence of the defendant in bringing about the plaintiff's harm."[6] In the following case the plaintiff's contributory negligence prevented him from obtaining a judgment against the defendant who was negligent.

contributory negligence
plaintiff's conduct which falls below the standard to which he should conform for his own protection and which is a legally contributing cause with the defendant's negligence causing the plaintiff's harm

Facts
Defendant put a pole across the road while making repairs to his home. Plaintiff was riding a horse at top speed and it tripped over the pole. Plaintiff sued for negligence.

Decision
Contributory negligence was present. Judgment for defendant.

Reasoning
A party is not to cast himself upon an obstruction which had been made by the fault of another, and avail himself of it, if he does not himself use common and ordinary caution to be in the right.

Butterfield v. Forester, K.B. 11 E 60 (1809).

Last Clear Chance and Comparative Negligence.   As we have seen, in the simplest of *negligence* cases there is merely one argument:

1. X accuses and proves Y negligent.

In the case of *contributory negligence,* the problem becomes slightly more difficult:

1. X accuses and proves Y negligent, but
2. Y claims X was negligent also (i.e., contributory negligence).

In yet another possible ripple, we can add a *third* stage which would look like this:

1. X accuses and proves Y negligent.
2. Y claims X was negligent also (contributory negligence).
3. X says "I may have been contributorily negligent, but you (Y) had the *last clear chance* to avoid the incident."

---

[6] Restatement (Second) of Torts sec. 464 (1958).

Indeed, *last clear chance* is a well established line of defense to a charge of contributory negligence. Along with each of these charges comes the difficulty of proof. Each claim of negligence, contributory negligence, or last clear chance must be substantiated using the patterns of proof we have been discussing throughout this chapter. This is why even seemingly simple automobile accidents can result in large, elaborate, and costly trials. It is almost an endless cycle with each of the participants claiming the other is at fault.

Some jurisdictions have established a system of *comparative negligence.* Under this system the jury is not required to determine ultimate responsibility, as it must in a system using negligence, contributory negligence, and last clear chance. Rather, comparative negligence merely asks the jury to apportion the percentage of fault among the parties to the case. Thus, driver X may be 30 percent at fault and must pay 30 percent of the cost, while driver Y is 70 percent at fault and pays 70 percent of the cost. In contrast, in many jurisdictions *any* amount of contributory negligence will preclude recovery by the contributorily negligent party.

Assumption of the Risk. One final defense which is frequently used by attorneys is **assumption of the risk.** This involves a situation in which a person *knowing* of the risk of harm agrees to voluntarily assume the risk of harm. The effect of this defense is that the defendant may claim that the plaintiff agreed to subject himself to potential danger and so if he gets injured he may not be successful in collecting damages. In the following case the injured plaintiff did not assume any risk because he was not aware of the specific danger.

assumption of the risk
voluntarily assuming a known risk of harm

Facts
Plaintiff, Vierra, was injured when a piece of *steel* dislodged from a broken tool being used by the defendant and flew several feet striking him in the eye. Plaintiff knew only of the danger from flying particles of *concrete* within a range of seven feet. However, he was standing more than nine feet from the tool. Judgment for the defendant, and plaintiff appealed, claiming error in that the court should not have instructed the jury on the doctrine of assumption of the risk.

Decision
The lower court was not correct in its instructions; reversed.

Reasoning
"The basic question in this case is whether the trial court was justified, under the facts, in instructing on the doctrine of assumption of risk. We have concluded that it was in error . . . and therefore reversible to have instructed on this doctrine. To warrant the application of the doctrine of assumption of the risk, the evidence must show that the victim appreciated the *specific* danger involved. He does not assume any risk he does not know or appreciate."

Vierra v. Fifth Avenue Rental Service, 383 P.2d 777 (Cal. 1963).

immunity
exemption from liability

Immunities.   On occasion, certain categories of persons are granted an **immunity** from tort liability. There must be a very special underlying policy reason for granting such an immunity, and these immunities are greatly limited in number and scope. Historically, both *charitable organizations* and *governmental organizations* were granted such a shield. The policy reason for this was that both these groups were working so much for the public good that they should not be subject to tort liability. Further, governmental liability was based on the common law principle that the "King can do no wrong." Over the years these two immunities have come under severe attack. Charitable organizations are often big businesses and can insure against loss. Thus, the underlying reason for protection is less strong today. Governmental immunity has always been stronger than charitable immunity, but even it has come under attack. Indeed, under the *Federal Tort Claims Act* the federal government can be held liable for *negligent* torts. Even under the Federal Tort Claims Act the government can not be sued for intentional or strict liability torts. Further, most high-ranking government officials are immune provided they do not act with malice.

There is also an *intra family immunity.* In order to promote family harmony, there was a common law immunity between *parent and child.* However, today this immunity is limited to negligent torts. Thus, children can sue their parents for intentional torts.

Finally, there was a *husband/wife* immunity based on the old common law policy that considers husband and wife as one in law. Recently some areas have rejected husband/wife immunities entirely in response to a number of pressures, including pressures from insurance companies which were faced with collusive suits designed to fraudulently collect money.

Liability Without Regard to Negligence or Fault: Strict Liability

In the first part of this chapter we spoke of torts which were intentional in nature. Next we turned to torts which were caused through someone's negligence. In this section we turn to those instances in which courts are not concerned with negligence at all. Rather, they believe that the action was of such a nature that the defendant should accept responsibility without reference to their standard of conduct.

Hazardous Activities

strict liability
absolute liability
irrespective of the
absence of negligence
or fault

The courts state that if you are involved in activity which involves a danger of serious harm to another person or property, which can not be eliminated even using due care and which is not a matter of common usage, you may be held **strictly liable** without reference to your standard of care. This is illustrated in the following famous English case.

Facts

Defendants owned a mill and, in order to supply it with water, constructed a reservoir on some nearby land. Plaintiff owned a nearby coal mine which was inundated by water that escaped from the reservoir. There is proof that the defendant used a great deal of care in building the reservoir.

Decision

Defendant should be held liable.

Reasoning

"We think . . . that the person who for his own purpose brings on his lands . . . anything likely to do mischief if it escapes must keep it at his peril, and if he does not do so, is prima facie answerable for all the damage which is a natural consequence of its escape."

Rylands v. Fletcher, [1868] L.R., 3 H.L. 330.

Animals

Another area in which there is strict liability without reference to negligence is in the keeping of wild animals. Thus, people who want to keep exotic pets such as snakes or tigers are in most cases responsible for their pets' activity even if they use due care in keeping them restrained. This rule does not apply to animals kept in a zoo.

Workmen's Compensation

State Workmen's Compensation laws impose upon an employer strict liability to most employees for personal injury in the course of and arising out of employment, except for self-inflicted injury and intoxication. This subject is discussed in chapter 18, Employment.

Products Liability

This is one of the most rapidly growing fields of tort liability in the United States today. Until recently, people injured while using a product had to demonstrate that the producer was negligent in manufacturing the product. The plaintiff had the difficult task of proving that the manufacturer had fallen below the standard of care required. As you can imagine, this was a difficult task. For example, if you were hurt because of a defect in your car, you would have to collect evidence that the person who put together your particular automobile was negligent at the particular time he was working on your car.

Even if you could accomplish that task, you still had to avoid the defenses to a charge of negligence, such as contributory negligence. You had to prove that you did not contribute to the carelessness of the situation resulting in the accident. These problems are being resolved today through the application of the doctrine of *strict liability* in tort to those who put products on the market. That is, *in certain areas,* the courts will impose liability on the manufacturer without reference to negligence.

At first, the scope of products liability was sharply limited to a select number and kinds of products. The first cases demanded that there had to be direct contact between the manufacturer and purchaser, called *privity*. This meant that, if you purchased a defective product from a middleman or retailer, you could not sue the manufacturer. You lacked privity with the manufacturer. Gradually, the privity doctrine gave way in select cases, such as those involving drugs or poisoned foods.

Soon even this requirement gave way, and you now can sue a manufacturer in some instances without having privity of contract with him. Today the manufacturer of a chattel which he knows or reasonably should believe to be *inherently dangerous* for the use supplied is strictly liable for harm caused by the chattel unless he gives adequate warning of the danger. An example is an explanatory label on a container of poison. Also, a manufacturer is held liable for manufacturing a chattel which, he should realize, *if negligently manufactured,* would create an *unreasonable risk of substantial bodily harm* when used for the purpose for which it was manufactured. In this case, what is important is the risk of harm from the *imperfect manufacture* of the chattel rather than the *inherently dangerous character* of the chattel. For example, a glass coffee urn is not inherently dangerous, but its negligent manufacture could cause it to be an unreasonable risk of substantial bodily harm to a consumer. This trend in the case law has caused concern to many manufacturers since they are increasingly subject to lawsuits brought by injured consumers. In the following famous case the court made new law by extending the duty to manufacture carefully to the remote consumer, thereby hurdling the privity of contract rule.

Facts

The defendant, Buick Motor Company, purchased automobile wheels from a wheel manufacturer. A wheel was defective and the defendant could, by reasonable care, have discovered the defect. However, the defendant did not exercise such care and overlooked the defect. The defendant attached the wheel to one of its automobiles, which was sold to a retailer who, in turn, resold the car to the plaintiff consumer, who was unaware of the defective wheel. The wheel collapsed because of the defect, causing the car to collapse, and the plaintiff was injured. Plaintiff sued the defendant for such injury.

Decision

The defendant manufacturer owed a duty of care to the remote plaintiff consumer. Judgment for plaintiff.

Reasoning

"We hold that when the nature of a thing is such that it is reasonably certain to place life and limb in peril when negligently made, it is then a thing of danger. [If] . . . its nature gives warning of the consequences to be expected [then] . . . the manufacturer is under a duty to make it carefully." The court extended the manufacturer's duty under the facts to the remote consumer, plaintiff, even though there was no privity of contract between the plaintiff and the defendant.

MacPherson v. Buick Motor Company, 111 N.E. 1050 (N.Y. 1916).

Protection of Inventions, Authorship, Identification of Products, Certain Contractual Business Relationships, and Reputation Through Tort Law

At the beginning of this chapter it was suggested that tort law provided a wide range of protection to persons. Before we close this chapter, brief mention should be made of the use of tort law to protect personal and business creations, certain contractual business relationships, and reputation.

Inventions, Authorship, and Identification of Products

A **patent** protects an invention for a nonrenewable period of seventeen years. The tort for using a person's invention without permission is *patent infringement.* Under the new federal copyright law effective 1978, a **copyright** protects original works in a tangible medium of expression, such as literary, musical and dramatic works, television or radio shows.[7] Copyright laws sharply limit a person's ability to reproduce others' work since in doing so you may infringe on the copyright holder's proprietary interests. Finally, a **trademark** or trade name is an identifying designation by which a manufacturer differentiates his or her goods from those of another. It may take the form of a name or symbol. Trademarks are governed by the Lanham Act, also known as the Trademark Act of 1946. *Copyright infringement* and *trademark infringement* are torts.

The original reason for these protections can be traced at least to the United States Constitution, which states in article I, section 8, clause 8, that Congress shall have the power "to promote the progress of science and useful arts, by securing for limited times to authors and inventors the exclusive right to their respective writings and discoveries."

Certain Contractual Business Relationships

People have a right to deal and contract with whom they please, and also to refuse to do so if they please, unless their conduct is wrongful because it breaches a duty to another person or is contrary to law. It is wrongful intentionally to induce other persons to breach their contracts with third persons or to induce other persons to refuse to deal or to continue a business relationship with third persons, thereby causing damage to such third persons. These are the torts of *inducing breach of contract* and *inducing refusal to deal.*

Reputation

Persons have an interest in their reputations and they have a right to freedom from false disparagement of their reputations. It is wrongful intentionally, without privilege, to publish matter which is false and disparages another person's reputation, thereby causing damage to that person's reputation. Published matter

patent
a governmental grant of protection of an invention

copyright
a governmental grant of protection of original works in a tangible medium of expression

trademark
an identifying designation differentiating one's goods from those of another

---

[7] Beginning with 1978, with certain limitations and variations, the period of protection is the author's life plus fifty years after his death; or, if there are two or more authors, then for the life of the last surviving author plus fifty years after his death. There is special provision for works prior to 1978.

is disparaging if it tends to belittle or diminish the esteem in which the defamed person is held by third persons or by the community. *Slander* is an oral disparagement, while *libel* generally is a written disparagement or any other form than oral. The tort is called *defamation.* In the following case the plaintiff could not prove libel by the defendant's *oral* statement.

Facts

Plaintiff was a physician and a candidate for political office. Defendant, his opponent, called out, "Here comes Doctor E. (Plaintiff), the spick and span practitioner. . . . Sufficient be it that we do not look to a quack to set us right in the matter." Plaintiff sued for libel.

Decision

This is not libel. Judgment for defendant.

Reasoning

Without more, this is not libel. "That the court erred in submitting the primary question of respondent's liability to the jury, we regard so clear that we are not justified in saying more."

Elmergreen v. Horn, 91 N.W. 973 (Wis. 1902).

1. Tort law has a significant impact on our society, and an individual will want to know his legal rights and duties as defined by tort law.
2. There is a difference between rights and duties as defined by the legal areas of tort, crime, and contract.
3. There are three major subdivisions of tort liability—namely, intentional torts, negligent torts, and strict liability.
4. Intentional torts include assault and battery, false imprisonment, invasion of privacy, and others.
5. There are defenses to the commission of intentional torts, among which are consent, self-defense, and privilege.
6. Negligent torts involve careless behavior and require that a complainant prove three things: a legal duty of care, a breach of a standard of care, and proximate cause of damage or harm.
7. There are defenses to liability for negligent torts, among which are contributory negligence, last clear chance, comparative negligence, assumption of risk, and immunities.
8. That society has imposed strict liability in certain instances upon suppliers of chattels irrespective of any lack of privity with the injured user.
9. Governmental protection is extended to certain intellectual property (e.g., copyrights) and the rights of persons in their contractual relationships and in their reputations.

The following case illustrates the emerging area of product liability. It shows how a right is created in an individual for the purpose of accomplishing a goal which is to the benefit of society generally.

Greenman v. Yuba Power Products, Inc.

377 P.2d 897 (Cal. 1963)

Traynor, Justice. Plaintiff brought this action for damages against the *retailer* and the *manufacturer* of a Shopsmith, a combination power tool that could be used as a saw, drill, and wood lathe. He saw a Shopsmith demonstrated by the retailer and studied a brochure prepared by the manufacturer. He decided he wanted a Shopsmith . . . and his wife bought and gave him one for Christmas in 1955. . . . After he had worked on . . . [a] piece of wood several times without difficulty, it suddenly flew out of the machine and struck him on the forehead, inflicting serious injuries. About ten and a half months later, he gave the retailer and the manufacturer written notice of claimed breaches of warranties and filed a complaint against them alleging such breaches and negligence.

After a trial before a jury, the court ruled that there was no evidence that the retailer was negligent or had breached any express warranty and that the manufacturer was not liable for the breach of any implied warranty. Accordingly, it submitted to the jury only the cause of action alleging breach of implied warranties against the retailer and the causes of action alleging negligence and breach of express warranties against the manufacturer. The jury returned a verdict for the retailer against plaintiff and for plaintiff against the manufacturer. . . . The manufacturer and plaintiff appeal. . . .

. . . [A] manufacturer is strictly liable in tort when an article he places on the market, knowing that it is to be used without inspection for defects, proves to have a defect that causes injury to a human being.

Although in these cases strict liability has usually been based on the theory of an express or implied warranty running from the manufacturer to the plaintiff, the abandonment of the requirement of a contract between them, the recognition that the liability is not assumed by agreement but imposed by law . . . make clear that the liability is not one governed by the law of contract warranties but by the law of strict liability in tort. Accordingly, rules defining and governing warranties that were developed to meet the needs of commercial transactions cannot properly be invoked to govern the manufacturer's liability to those injured by their defective products unless those rules also serve the purposes for which such liability is imposed.

We need not recanvass the reasons for imposing strict liability on the manufacturer. . . . The purpose of such liability is to insure that the costs of injuries resulting from defective products are borne by the manufacturers that put such products on the market rather than by the injured persons who are powerless to protect themselves. Sales warranties serve this purpose fitfully at best. . . . In the present case, for example, plaintiff was able to plead and prove an express warranty only because he read and relied on the representations of the Shopsmith's ruggedness contained in the manufacturer's brochure. Implicit in the machine's presence on the market, however, was a representation that it would safely do the jobs for which it was built. Under these circumstances, it should not be controlling whether plaintiff selected the machine because of the statements in the brochure, or because of the machine's own appearance of excellence that belied the defect lurking beneath the surface, or because he merely assumed that it would safely do the jobs it was built to do. . . . The remedies of injured consumers ought not to be made to depend upon the intricacies of the law of sales. . . . To establish the manufacturer's liability it was sufficient that plaintiff presumed that he was injured while using the Shopsmith in a way it was intended to be used as a result of a defect in design and manufacture of which plaintiff was not aware that made the Shopsmith unsafe for its intended use. . . .

[Affirmed.]

Questions and Case Problems

1. Plaintiff was a schoolgirl fifteen years of age. She was told by her teacher that if she did not confess to certain statements she would be sent to reform school. To avoid being imprisoned, she confessed. Is this an assault? [*Johnson v. Sampson,* 208 N.W. 814 (Minn. 1926).]

2. Plaintiff was engaged in the practice of healing with clay, herbs, and minerals—as practised, simply quackery. Defendant—Time, Inc.—published in its magazine an article including pictures entitled "Crackdown on Quackery." Assuming that the defendant used a ruse to gain entry to plaintiff's home, may plaintiff sue for invasion of privacy? [*Dietemann v. Time, Inc.,* 449 F.2d 245 (1971).]

3. Plaintiff, an automobile passenger, is involved in an automobile accident and claims that defendant, a liquor merchant, was partially at fault for having sold the driver intoxicating liquors while the driver was inebriated at a time just prior to the accident. Assuming that no laws other than tort law are to be considered, is defendant responsible? [*Mary Ann Waynick v. Chicago's Last Department Store,* 269 F.2d 322 (1959).]

4. Plaintiff is a paying guest at a dance held in a hall owned by defendant. While taking part in a dance she fell and was injured. If the floor is slippery from a perfect waxing, may she sue for negligence? If so, work through what would have to be proven. [*Gough v. Wadhams Mills Grange,* 279 App.Div. 825 (N.Y. 1952).]

5. In the question above, suppose that the dance floor was of the "portable variety" and that a crack existed between sections about which the owner knows. Is there an action for negligence? [*Toftoy v. Ocean Shores Properties, Inc.,* 431 P.2d 212 (Wash. 1967).]

6. An unsupervised youngster gets into his parent's car and begins to play. The car begins to roll when the brake was released by him. In a panic he jumps from the car and is injured. May he sue his mother for leaving the car unlocked leading to his injury? [*Badigian v. Badigian,* 174 N.E.2d 718 (N.Y. 1961).]

7. Defendant operated a hospital which accepted indigent patients. It was a charitable hospital operated as a not-for-profit institution. Plaintiff received an injection, carelessly administered into his left arm, which resulted in paralysis. May he recover damages? [*Rabon v. Rowan Memorial Hospital, Inc.* 152 S.E.2d 485 (N.C. 1967).]

8. A young lady orders baked beans in Boston. "I started to eat [them] and there were two or three dark pieces which I thought were hard beans; that is, baked more than the others, and I put it in my mouth [and bit down and hurt myself]." If there was no evidence of negligence on the part of the dining hall which baked the food, may she recover damages? [*Friend v. Childs Dining Hall, Co.,* 120 N.E. 407 (Mass. 1918).]

9. Joe Smith, a toothpaste manufacturer, knows that Jim Goodheart has a contract with Great Toothpaste Company to deliver fifty boxes of a chemical needed to manufacture Crest. Smith attempts to induce Goodheart to deliver the chemical to him instead of Crest. Is this a violation of the law?

10. In *Greenman v. Yuba Power Products, Inc.,* 377 P.2d 897 (Cal. 1963),[8] the court indicated that product liability could be imposed by law, even in the absence of an agreement (contract), for the purpose of shifting to manufacturers loss caused by defective products which injure consumers. It could be said that tort law is being used as a tool for social change. The case would seem to suggest that the law should place the burden of payment on those who are best able to prevent the loss. Does this standard satisfy you? Assume that you are a member of top management of a major manufacturing firm. Would your answer be the same?

---

[8] See pp. 69–70.

Contracts

Summary

While a contract can be simply stated as "a promise which the law recognizes as creating a legal obligation of performance," *the finding of a contract* requires that a proper contractual purpose be manifested by genuineness of assent, by parties with capacity to contract, who have exchanged consideration. A contract will be *enforced* if its contractual purpose is not in conflict with public policy and, in certain instances, only if the contract is in writing or there is a proper written note or memorandum of the oral contract. A contract is property which, in certain instances, can be transferred to third parties. The property interest in the contract is protected by law. Legal obligations to perform a contract end by performance or by other methods of discharge.

5

Concept of Contractual Agreement

After you have read this chapter, you should be able to:

1. Discuss the concept of "freedom of contract" and its current applications.
2. Understand the distinction between the terms "promise" and "agreement."
3. Understand the full importance and complexity of the definition of a contract.
4. Use those words and phrases which are currently used in the law of contracts.
5. Realize the significance of the fact that legal terms convey the basics of contract law.

Introduction

The Constitution of the United States of America guarantees to each of us the *freedom to contract.*[1] Such a guaranty ensures that you and I may become personally involved in the legal environment in which we all reside. We do this every day by creating *rights and duties* for ourselves and others. This direct participation by us in our legal environment takes place when we buy groceries at the store, rent an apartment, buy a car, enroll in a course at a university, or do many other activities.

Generally, a right is that which one is legally entitled to have, or to do, or to receive from others within limits prescribed by law. Generally, a duty is a legal obligation owing from one person to another.

Without freedom to contract, called "freedom of contract," business in the United States as we know it would cease to exist and our ability to maintain our standard of living would be reduced.

It is important, therefore, that every person understand, use wisely, and preserve such a basic freedom so necessary to our way of life.

The important point you should note in this chapter and throughout Part 2 is that *the concept of freedom to contract has legal limitations.* It is not an absolute freedom.

What Constitutes a Contract

The law specifies what promises can form the basis of a contract. Some promises create only an "agreement," while some create a "contract" in which the promises create legal obligations to perform them. Thus there is a difference between the words "agreement" and "contract." To have a contract, there must be (1) mutual assent with a promise or promises, (2) consideration, (3) capacity to contract, and (4) legality. These will be discussed in separate chapters.

How You Might View It

"We agreed." "We shook hands." "You said you would do it!" "But Mom, Dad said I could have the car tonight." To the casual observer these statements imply the existence of an **agreement.** Each statement suggests that some accord or understanding might exist. In a nonlegal sense we might have an agreement or understanding.

agreement
a manifestation of mutual assent between parties by offer and acceptance

What the Dictionary Says

The dictionary defines an "agreement" as an "arrangement" and notes certain equivalent words—namely, "bargain," "compact," and "contract."[2]

What the Law Says

Two bodies of law are applicable here: the **Uniform Commercial Code** (statutory law) and the common law (the nonstatutory law common to the people and to society). The Code defines an agreement as a "bargain in fact" between parties.

Uniform Commercial Code
a body of statutory law governing commercial transactions concerning personal property (movable things)

---

[1] U.S. Constitution, Art. I, sec. 10: "No State shall . . . pass any . . . law impairing the obligation of contracts. . . ."

[2] *The American College Dictionary* (New York: Random House, 1963), p. 26.

Whether an agreement has *legal consequences* is determined by the Code, when applicable, or by the *common law of contracts*.[3] Whether an agreement will result in a *contract,* which imposes *legal obligations on the parties,* is also determined by the Code and the common law of contracts.[4]

The Uniform Commercial Code.   An application of the Uniform Commercial Code definition of an agreement is found in UCC 2–106. In that article, an agreement must be for the present or future *sale* of **goods** to result in a contract. This Code article limits the subject matter of a sales contract to goods and excludes land and services. Another application is found in UCC 2–204. There the Code requires that an agreement exist before a contract can be formed. Both definitions and applications under the Code lead one to the conclusion that the words "agreement" and "contract" have different meanings under the Code—that agreement is a part of, and necessary to, a contract.

The Common Law.   Under the **common law,** certain arrangements or understandings with regard to social obligations or illegal activities might be recognized as agreements but not as contracts. This is done because the purpose of the understanding is considered to be of minor importance, or it conflicts with what law seeks to prevent others from doing because society has determined such conduct to be undesirable. Thus, under the common law, a contract and an agreement have different meanings—again, agreement being a part of, and necessary to, a contract.

Definition of Contract

A **contract** is *a promise which the law recognizes as creating a legal obligation of performance.* A minimum of two persons, called *parties,* are required in order to have a contract. The definition of contract requires a *promise. Thus, we have the rule that a contract can be formed only if we have at least one promise and two parties.* In the following case the court found that, since the defendant had not made a promise, he had not made a contract.

goods
tangible, movable things

common law
principles of nonstatutory law reflecting the customs and usages of society and found in judicial decisions

contract
a promise which the law recognizes as creating a legal obligation of performance

plaintiff
the party who initiates a civil suit by filing a complaint in the proper court

defendant
the party against whom a civil suit is brought

Facts

Plaintiff, Clark and Enersen, brought an action against Schimmel Hotels, **defendant,** to recover for preliminary architectural and engineering services performed in connection with an addition to a hotel on which construction was never begun. The plaintiff alleges that defendant made representations and led plaintiff to believe that defendant would pay plaintiff fees for architectural services in connection with the project. The plaintiff offered in evidence an AIA (American Institute of Architects) standard form of agreement between the owner and architect prepared for execution by the plaintiff and the defendant. The form was never executed by any of the parties.

---

[3] UCC 1–201(3).

[4] UCC 1–201(11).

Decision

Judgment for defendant.

Reasoning

The plaintiff's contention that the unexecuted form represents a promise or agreement was not sustained by the court. An action in contract inevitably rests upon a promise or set of promises. A promise may be stated in words, either oral or written, or may be inferred wholly or partly from conduct. Quasi contracts, unlike true contracts, are not based on the apparent intention of the parties to undertake the performance in question, nor are they promises. They are obligations created by law for reasons of justice. In this case no express contract was formed. No promise was present upon which an express contract could be formed.

Clark & Enersen, etc. v. Schimmel Hotels, Corp., 235 N.W.2d 870 (Neb. 1975).

Certain promises will not be *enforced* by law as legal obligations. Social obligations, promises which violate a strongly felt public policy, and usually promises to do illegal acts or promises that will produce **unconscionable** results are not enforced by law as contracts. Except for these types of promises, all other promises normally can form the basis for a contract. In the following case the court refused to enforce a contract which was unconscionable and against public policy as determined by the court.

unconscionable
offends the conscience; immoderate, too one-sided

Facts

A motion was made by a divorced husband Garlinger, plaintiff, to eliminate an alimony contract and to sell the marital home which had been awarded to the ex-wife. The grounds were that a married man had moved into the marital home after the divorce had been granted, cohabited and engaged in sexual intercourse with the wife, and moved out only after the filing of the husband's motion.

Decision

The court held for the plaintiff.

Reasoning

Alimony payments were suspended and the marital home ordered sold. The court's reasoning was that it was inconsistent with the purpose of alimony, justice, public policy, and morality for the husband to continue to pay alimony under such circumstances. A court of equity will not enforce specific performance of a contract where, from change of circumstances or otherwise, it would be unconscionable to enforce it or when specific performance would be contrary to public policy.

Garlinger v. Garlinger, 322 A.2d 190 (N.J. 1974).

formal contract
a contract which must be in a certain form

recognizance
an obligation acknowledged by a person in a court to do something—e.g., to appear in court at a later time—i.e., personal bond

check
a draft drawn on a bank payable on demand

Formal and Informal Contracts

A written promise which the law will enforce because it is in a certain required form is called a **formal contract.** Examples of formal contracts would be a contract under seal, a **recognizance,** and various types of negotiable commercial paper such as a **check.**

Figure 5.1 A Check

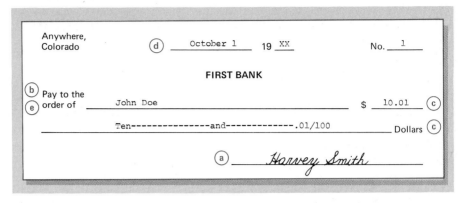

Figure 5.2 A Simple Contract

Sale

Agreement (a) between (c) Barnes and Smith whereby this day Smith has sold and Barnes has bought the (b) entire crop of Niagra grapes, same to be (d) clean and free of mildew and fungi diseases, now growing on the ranch of Smith, situate at Fort Collins, Colorado, consisting of 50 acres, more or less, and the crop estimated as 1,000 tons. Above grapes to be packed and delivered by seller to buyer's packing house at Loveland, Colorado, at such times as may be desired by buyer. Terms (b) $1,000 cash, payment as follows: Net 30.

_____June 1, 19XX_____ Date   Signature _____*Barnes*_____ buyer

                        Signature _____*Smith*_____ seller

Required Form for a Negotiable Instrument. As figure 5.1 illustrates, a negotiable instrument must (a) be in writing and signed by the drawer. It must (b) contain an unconditional order or promise (c) to pay a sum certain in money. It must (d) be payable on demand or at a definite time. It must (e) be payable to order or bearer.

An *informal* or **simple contract** contains a promise which the law does not require to be in any particular form—e.g., a promise to employ a person. It may or may not be in writing. Figure 5.2 is an example of a simple contract, with identification of (a) mutual assent, (b) the consideration, (c) the parties, and (d) legality.

simple contract
a contract which need not be in any particular form

Elements of a Contract

The elements necessary for a *promise* to become a simple contract are: (a) mutual assent, (b) consideration, (c) capacity to contract, and (d) legality. Accordingly, we will first examine the promise which leads to mutual assent and an agreement.

The Promise

The Character of a Promise.   The expression of a **promise** necessary to the formation of a contract looks to the future and is one person's assurance to another or others that something in the future shall happen or not happen. "I'll build the bridge" or "the can will not leak" are examples.

The Number of Promises.   While we must have at least one promise to create a contract, the contract can contain any number of promises. If the promise seeks the performance of an act (e.g., dig a ditch), or a forbearance (refraining from doing something), the contract, if it comes into being, will be called a **unilateral contract** because there is only *one* promise. If the promise seeks a return promise and the contract comes into existence, it will be called a **bilateral contract** because there is *more than one* promise. For example, A promises to pay B $200 for certain services to be rendered by B, and B promises to render such services.

Communication of the Promise.   The promise necessary to the formation of a contract must be *communicated* to another party before it can act as an effective basis for forming a contract. The person who initiates the process for formation of a contract by making the original promise is called the **promisor.** The person to whom a promise has been made is called the **promisee.**

The person who has the duty to carry out the promise is called the **obligor.** The person who has the right to the benefit of the promise is called the **obligee.** (In a contract, A promises to pay B $100. A is the promisor and obligor. B is the promisee and obligee.)

An agreement which manifests by oral or written words the terms of a promise in a unilateral situation, and the return promise in a bilateral situation, is called an *express contract,* provided that the other requirements of a contract are present.

An agreement which can be inferred only from the conduct of persons and which has the other requirements of a contract is called a *contract implied in fact.* For example, J enters D's drugstore, picks up a magazine for sale, waves it in the air to get D's attention, and D nods his head. Upon leaving the store, J will have communicated to D a promise to pay for the magazine and D will have accepted the promise—all by action.

The Implied Promise.   When no promise was intended, yet one is implied in law to prevent **unjust enrichment,** and an agreement is found by law, we have a *contract implied in law, or* **quasi** *contract.* This is illustrated by the following case.

promise
an assurance or undertaking that something shall or shall not happen

unilateral contract
a contract in which the consideration for a promise is an act or a forbearance

bilateral contract
a contract in which the consideration is mutual promises

promisor
the person who makes a promise

promisee
the person to whom a promise is made

obligor
the person who owes a legal obligation

obligee
the person to whom a legal obligation is owed

unjust enrichment
a legal doctrine that prevents persons from profiting or enriching themselves inequitably at the expense of others

quasi
as if

Facts

Plaintiff, Hertz, a former tenant of Ficus, brought this action based on *unjust enrichment* to Ficus, defendant, for expenditures Hertz made in remodeling a restaurant-lounge business owned by Ficus. While the *lease contract* was being negotiated, Hertz remodeled the premises with the knowledge and consent of the owner, Ficus. Because of failure to pay the rent, Hertz was evicted.

Decision

Judgment for Hertz for his expenditures to remodel the restaurant.

Reasoning

The court noted that, under a theory of quasi contract, recovery does not require the existence of a contract. The defendant had received a benefit which it would be inequitable to allow him to retain without compensating Hertz. A contract implied in law is not a contract at all but an obligation imposed by law for the purpose of bringing about justice.

Hertz v. Ficus, 567 P.2d 1 (Ida. 1977).

Joint and Several Promises. We can have any number of parties in a contract. Also we can have any number of promises in a contract. When we relate parties to promises, we have three basic relationships present.

When more than one party appears on either side of a contract, depending upon their intentions, their promises will be considered *joint, several,* or *joint and several.*

If there is only *one promise* and more than one party *together* obligate themselves to perform the *same* promise, the parties' obligation is *joint*; their obligation is to perform together, **jointly.** They are collectively **liable** and can be sued only together.

If the *same* performance is *separately promised* by each party, the obligation is **several,** performable by each of the several parties. They are individually **liable** and can be sued individually.

If the promise is in terms of "I promise" rather than "we promise," and is undertaken by more than one party, the obligation assumed is *joint and several,* so that the parties are liable and can be sued together or individually. This is illustrated in the following case where the court interpreted the word "does" in the contract to mean that each party is jointly and severally liable.

joint liability
occurs when parties together obligate themselves to perform the same promise

several liability
occurs when the same performance is separately promised by each party

confession of judgment
a party's consent to jurisdiction and judgment of a court without a trial in a civil case

Facts

The plaintiff, United States, had obtained a **confession of judgment** award on a debt which had been defaulted by defendant. The loan had been made by a bank, and the loan had been insured by the Small Business Administration. Upon default, the security went to the Small Business Administration of the United States. The defendant brought a motion to vacate the judgment on the ground that the confession of judgment could not be had against only her without joining her husband in the suit on the debt. The defendant's husband was dead. The confession of judgment clause in the debt contract provided that the undersigned "does" authorize such confession, and it had been signed by the defendant wife and her husband.

Decision
Judgment for plaintiff.

Reasoning
The defendant's motion failed because the promise in the confession of judgment was determined to be joint and several. The word "does" is a singular expression. A promise by several persons expressed in the singular binds them jointly and severally. The language is tantamount to stating that each "does," thus authorizing the action against the wife singularly or severally.

United States v. Stuart, 271 F.Supp. 939 (1967).

Objective Test

In express and implied *in fact* contracts, the law looks to the *objective evidence* that parties normally *manifest* in a *bargain* situation in order to determine whether a contract has been formed and then whether it is express or implied in fact.

If I **subjectively** (personally) do not want a contract but my actions or words, oral or written, would lead a reasonable person to understand or presume that I do intend a contract, that presumption will control. A promise communicated in a bargain setting raises a strong presumption that a contractual intent is present. The following case so holds.

subjectively
existing only in one's mind

Facts
Appellant, Mrs. Slade, seeks to set aside a **summary judgment** obtained by appellee, Phelps, preventing her from suing for personal injuries and property damage from a vehicle collision. The summary judgment was rendered by the court on the basis of a voluntarily executed release for valuable consideration which was introduced into evidence. Appellant Slade had signed the release at the hospital without reading the form. She contended that she thought the settlement might not be enough after she read the release which she had signed.

Decision
Affirmed for appellee.

Reasoning
The court held that when the entire testimony of Mrs. Slade was viewed, they thought that it had become rather clear that she knew she was executing the release in question. In addition, the court found in favor of Phelps by applying the rule that there must be a meeting of the minds of the parties to create a contract. However, determination of whether the minds of the parties had met and whether there was an offer and an acceptance must be based on an objective standard— what they said and did—and not on their alleged subjective state of mind.

Slade v. Phelps, 446 S.W.2d 931 (Tex. 1969).

summary judgment
a judgment rendered on a motion by a party in a civil action that, solely on the basis of the pleadings, judgment should be rendered without the necessity of a trial on the facts

Risk

When one makes a promise, one assumes all the risks associated with its performance. Where the promise can not be fulfilled because of **factual impossibility** of carrying it out, one is excused from the consequence of the promise. *Subsequent*

factual impossibility
the facts make performance of the promise impossible

illegality of the contractual obligation contained in the promise (a later event makes performance illegal) and *destruction of the subject matter* of the promise (the building to be painted burns) will in proper cases *excuse* the promisor from the risk consequence involved in making the promise. In the following case the promisor was not excused from performing because he had assumed the risk of unfavorable weather and there was only partial frustration in performing the contract.

Facts
Pete Smith Co., Inc., plaintiff, a contractor, had agreed with the defendant, City of El Dorado, to construct a golf course for a specified price. The plaintiff is seeking relief from his obligation to construct the golf course under the doctrine of commercial frustration after a torrential rainfall caused substantial erosion after clearing and dirt work had been performed. Evidence was introduced that the plaintiff would be required to spend $60,000 to restore the ground for the golf course to its condition prior to the rain. Evidence was also introduced that the contract itself expressed an intent that the contractor bear the risk of unfavorable weather. Evidence was introduced that the destruction of the preliminary work done by the contractor would not make it impossible for the golf course to be constructed.

Decision
Judgment for defendant.

Reasoning
The contract expressed an intent that the contractor bear the risk of unfavorable weather, and there was only partial frustration, which merely increased the cost of performance.

Where the assumed possibility of a desired object or effect to be obtained by either party to the contract forms the basis on which both parties enter into it, and this object or effect is or surely will be frustrated, a promisor who is without fault in causing the frustration, and who is harmed thereby, is discharged from the duty of performing his promise unless a contrary intention appears and unless there is only a partial frustration of purpose, which only increased the cost of performance.

Pete Smith Co., Inc. v. City of El Dorado, 529 S.W.2d 147 (Ark. 1976).

Classification of Agreements

Void Agreement.   A void *agreement* is one which the law will not enforce as a legal obligation, nor does the law recognize its performance as a duty. It is not a contract because the promise or promises do not create a legal obligation of performance.

voidable contract
a contract which can be avoided by one or more of the parties

Voidable Agreement.   A voidable agreement can result in a **voidable contract.** However, it gives one or more of the parties to a contract the alternative of avoiding it or of enforcing it. (A fraudulently induced B to enter into a contract. It is voidable by B.) In the following case a minor, through the minor's mother, could avoid the minor's contract.

Facts

A child actor's mother signed a contract with a manager whereby the manager was to receive 10 percent of the minor's earnings. The mother subsequently avoided the contract on behalf of the minor, defendant. The contention of the plaintiff manager is that a parent by contract may in effect indenture a minor to perform services to or for another, and the contract cannot be avoided.

Decision

Judgment for defendant.

Reasoning

The court allowed the contract to be avoided. The court determined that the contract was a contract of a minor. The court held that, in view of a public policy protecting children from abuse through unreasonable employment and preventing abuses by employment agencies in dealing with minors seeking work, a parent or guardian in law could avoid the contract of a minor for the minor.

Deane v. Rippy, 134 Cal. Reptr. 436, XX (1977), opinion withdrawn from publication by order of the court.

Unenforceable Agreement. An unenforceable agreement is an agreement which can not be successfully sued upon or proved. It can not be enforced in the courts. If it is a contract, it is called an **unenforceable contract.**

Executed Agreement. An **executed contract** is a contract which has been completely performed by all the parties to it.

Executory Agreement. In an **executory contract** something has not been accomplished. The contract can be completely executory—i.e., none of the parties to it has performed their respective duties. A contract can also be partially executory—i.e., one party has performed but the other party has not performed.

Unconscionable Agreement. An **unconscionable contract** for the *sale of goods* under the Uniform Commercial Code is a contract which the court may refuse to enforce or which the court may modify because one of the parties is in too unequal a bargaining position. The crucial test is whether the bargain is so one-sided in its benefit to one party as to strike the conscience of the court.[5]

While freedom of contract is basic to our way of life, we see a number of developments in our law, perhaps best represented by the Uniform Commercial Code, which temper the results of an application of freedom of contract contained in the words "buyer beware." Certainly the concept of the unconscionable contract is designed to soften the harshness of the marketplace.

A total concept of freedom, it could be argued, would allow each state to develop its own law of contracts. The purpose of the statutory Uniform Commercial Code is, because of the needs of commerce and the economy, to bring uniformity in all states to the law of commercial transactions, such as in sales of goods, which is a part of contract law.

Other statutes which have as their purpose the protection of the consumer make inroads on the concept of freedom of contract. Some of them are the Consumer Product Safety Act and the Truth-in-Packaging Act, discussed in

unenforceable contract
a contract which the courts will not enforce

executed contract
a contract which has been performed by all the parties to it

executory contract
a contract which has not been performed by all the parties to it

unconscionable contract
a contract in which one of the parties is in too unequal or one-sided a bargaining position

---

[5] UCC 2–302.

chapter 26; the Federal Trade Commission Act, discussed in chapter 32; the Securities Acts, discussed in chapter 43, and other Acts discussed in the chapters of Part 7, Government Regulation of Business.

The labor relations Acts—i.e., the Wagner Act, the Taft-Hartley Act, and the Landrum-Griffin Act, discussed in Part 3, Agency and Employment—have their impact on the freedom of labor and management to contract.

The conclusions to be drawn from observation of the evolutionary process of contract law are that the concept of *freedom* of contract has been questioned and found wanting, that the concept of **caveat emptor** (let the buyer beware) continues to erode, and is being replaced by the concept of *caveat venditor* (let the seller beware).

caveat emptor
let the buyer beware

Summary Statement

1. The concept of freedom to contract is not unlimited. The understandings we reach with others in our daily lives are not always contracts. The law does not give importance to social obligations.
2. In law, the word "contract" has a very special meaning separate from what we find in the dictionary.
3. In application, the definition of a contract as a promise which creates a legal obligation of performance becomes quite complex.
4. The promise creates a legal obligation and becomes a contract when four things are present: (1) mutual assent, (2) consideration, (3) capacity to contract, and (4) legality.
5. While we require at least one promise and two parties as a minimum for a contract, any number of parties, relationships, and promises can become part of a contract.
6. The importance of the need to communicate the promise by language and/ or action before a contract is formed has been illustrated. The objective analysis of the actions of the parties was developed as a critical concept to determine if there is a manifested meeting of the minds.
7. The importance of terminology as a way of expressing conceptual ideas about contracts has also been illustrated.
8. This chapter has evaluated the concept and evolution of contract law and indicated the path of its future development.

The following case has been chosen for you to read because it represents current thinking on what *freedom of contract* should really mean. The implications of the case are far-reaching, and no doubt you will have a strong feeling for or against the court's decision. The case highlights the importance of contract law both to an individual and to business organizations.

Johnson v. Mobil Oil Corporation

415 F.Supp. 264 (1976)

Plaintiff, Johnson, brought this action against Mobil Oil Corporation to recover for losses suffered when the service station he operated was destroyed by fire. Plaintiff alleges that the fire was caused by events following delivery of gasoline containing water, and seeks to recover for the loss of inventory and other **consequential damages.** Defendant moves for a partial summary judgment dismissing plaintiff's claim for consequential damages. Defendant seeks to limit any recovery to the difference of the value of the gasoline as gasoline and its value as watered gasoline.

Defendant relies on a clause contained in a contract between itself and the plaintiff which reads as follows: *"In no event shall seller be liable for prospective profits or special, indirect or consequential damages."*

Plaintiff opposes the motion on the ground that the clause excluding consequential damages is unconscionable.

The court noted that the law in Michigan was such that unreasonable terms in a contract for goods and services used by a significant segment of the public and obtainable from limited sources would not be enforced as a matter of public policy. In the eyes of the court this *might* represent a departure from the majority view in a direction away from the freedom to contract but was the law in Michigan.

Since gasoline is used by a significant body of consumers and is available from limited sources, the court felt the question of unconscionability was properly before it.

The court noted that unconscionability can be shown in two ways: by proving either *substantive unconscionability* or *procedural unconscionability.*

The court noted that under the Uniform Commercial Code the clause of the contract in question would not be *prima facie* unconscionable in a commercial setting. Thus a finding of substantive unconscionability might not be present.

On the other hand, the court found procedural unconscionability present. The court noted that the plaintiff could not read, except perhaps for certain items in the sports section of the newspaper, and therefore could not understand the significance of the clause in question. Moreover, the court found that neither was the clause brought to plaintiff's attention nor was its legal significance explained to him.

The court found the clause to be unconscionable and not binding on the plaintiff.

In the court's words:

However, before a contracting party with the immense bargaining power of the Mobil Oil Corporation may limit its liability vis-a-vis an uncounseled layman, as it seeks to do in this case, to 'difference money damages,' it has an affirmative duty to obtain the voluntary, knowing assent of the other party. This could easily have been done in this case by explaining to plaintiff in layman's terms the meaning and possible consequences of the disputed clause. Such a requirement does not detract from the freedom to contract, unless that phrase denotes the freedom to impose the onerous terms of one's carefully drawn printed document on an unsuspecting contractual partner. Rather, freedom of contract is enhanced by a requirement that both parties be aware of the burdens they are assuming. The notion of free will has little meaning as applied to one who is ignorant of the consequences of his acts.

Motion of defendant Mobil Oil Corporation denied.

> **consequential (or special) damages** the money judicially awarded for loss which the breaching party reasonably could foresee would be a consequence of his breach

Concept of Contractual Agreement

Questions and Case Problems

1. The plaintiff, Crosby, a construction contractor, is seeking compensation from a company named APL for the use or rental of his equipment. Crosby originally had a contract for the rental of his drag line with Mr. Smith. Mr. Smith had a contract with APL, where he was using Crosby's equipment. APL terminated its contract with Mr. Smith and hired another general contractor to complete certain work.

   APL received a monthly billing from Mr. Crosby for the rental of his drag line. APL promptly responded to this billing by a letter informing Mr. Crosby that the new general contractor was making a survey of its equipment needs and, until it was determined whether the drag line was needed, there would be no responsibility for rental payments. Included in the letter was a statement that, until Mr. Crosby was advised by the new general contractor that the drag line was needed, any rental charges were the obligation of Mr. Smith. Mr. Crosby charged that an implied in-fact contract came into existence because he was not informed until some period of time had passed that his equipment would not be used on the job. What result? [*Crosby v. Paul Hardeman, Inc.,* 414 F.2d 1 (1969).]

2. The defendant, Dynamics, agreed by letter that the following forms and documents had been exchanged with the plaintiff buyer, General Electric Co.: a Dynamics letter of price quotations on a gas purifying machine; a General Electric Co. purchase order for said machine and specifications requiring in part that no impurities should be introduced into affluent nitrogen by the machine; a Dynamics agreement to comply with the terms of the purchase order, including a specified **guaranty** that the equipment would purify a quantity of acid specified to a level required; and a guaranty of a supply of chemicals and a patent **indemnity** agreement. The plaintiff buyer seeks in this action to rescind a contract for sale for the purchase of the machine due to its failure to exclude hydrogen. What forms the basis of the contract? Why can the buyer rescind the contract? [*General Electric Co. v. United States Dynamics, Inc.,* 403 F.2d 933 (1968).]

guaranty
a type of suretyship

indemnity
an absolute obligation to pay for another's loss

3. The plaintiff is a teaching assistant seeking unemployment compensation for periods between school terms. The court found that the teaching assistant had an expectation to be hired each term. Whether he would be hired depended upon the budget for the college and the enrollment in the college. At some time in the beginning of each term for which teaching assistants were hired they received a "statement of appointment" providing "this appointment is for one term; no promise is made for additional terms." The defendant, State Employment Division, contends that the teaching assistants did not have a contract within the meaning of the unemployment compensation law. Thus they were not entitled to unemployment benefits for the periods between school terms. Is the teaching assistant entitled to unemployment compensation? You decide. [*Ashby v. Employment Division,* 534 P.2d 1160 (Or. 1975).]

4. Knack, a cook, and plaintiff in this case, is suing under an Arizona workmen's compensation statute for injuries sustained on a job. The defendant, State Industrial Commission, contends that the plaintiff was hired to perform a series of unilateral contracts to act as cook in various states for an employer who

provided services to railroad track-laying crews. Both parties agree that the terms of the agreement were communicated in Arizona. The defendant contends that the contract was not formed until the acts were performed in the other states. The defendant maintains that the plaintiff is not entitled to the protection of the workmen's compensation statutes of Arizona since the contract was not formed in Arizona. On the other hand, Knack contends that a bilateral contract, in which he promised to act as a cook and his employer promised to pay for his services as a cook, was formed in Arizona, one of the conditions of the contract being that the performance of his services as a cook was to take place in various other states. What result? [*Knack v. Industrial Commission of Arizona,* 503 P.2d 373 (Ariz. 1972).]

5. Sylvestre, plaintiff, a judge, brought an action seeking a declaration of judgment that 1967 and 1968 legislative enactments to a judges' retirement statute were unconstitutional. The amendments to the original retirement statute would cause a diminishment of benefits to Sylvestre. Sylvestre contends that a retirement statute as it exists at the time a person enters into a public office constitutes an offer of a unilateral contract by the government and can not be changed so long as the public official continues to perform according to the terms of the original offer. What result? [*Sylvestre v. State,* 214 N.W.2d 658 (Minn. 1973).]

6. The plaintiff, Mignot, sued to recover money claimed to be due him under an employment contract. The defendant had expressly engaged the services of Mignot and had promised to pay whatever the services were reasonably worth. Mignot brought this action on an express contract to recover money he claimed was due for the work performed in connection with defendant's business. The defendant contends that Mignot could only prove a quasi contract and, therefore, should not be allowed to recover on his claim of an express contract. What result? [*Mignot v. Crater Plywood, Inc.,* 433 P.2d 237 (Or. 1967).]

7. The plaintiff, Clayton, sold his radio station. Suit is being brought against the purchasers upon a promissory note given by a now-bankrupt corporation formed by the purchasers. The contract of sale stipulated that the balance of the purchase price was to be paid by a note of either the buyers or a corporation formed by them. The defendants, purchasers, contend that the contract was executed and that they were discharged when the note was issued to the plaintiff upon formation of the corporation. What result? [*Clayton v. Communications Capital Corporation,* 440 P.2d 330 (Ariz. 1968).]

8. The plaintiff seeks to recover $1,000. The plaintiff contends that a contract had been made whereby, if plaintiff could prove that a daily dose of four glasses of fluoridated water would not cause certain disorders, plaintiff was to receive $1,000 from defendant. The challenge had been made by the defendant to the plaintiff in the heat of an upcoming election. Voters were to decide in a referendum whether or not a community water supply was to be fluoridated. In the eyes of the law, exactly what is this sort of challenge made in the heat of an election? Is it an offer that upon acceptance became a binding contract? Is it a reward, like the sums of money offered for information leading to the arrest and conviction of a perpetrator of a crime? Is it a bet, a wagering of $1,000 against a possibility? You decide. [*Cudahy Junior Chamber of Commerce v. Quirk,* 165 N.W.2d 116 (Wis. 1969).]

9. The plaintiff, Electrical Co., sought to enforce an alleged oral contract against the defendant. Electrical Co. contends that it agreed to submit a higher bid to the defendant's competitors on a certain atomic energy commission project if the defendant would assure the plaintiff that it would get the electrical subcontract on a different project. The effect of this action would be to cause the competitor's bid to be higher than the defendant's bid on the project if the plaintiff's subcontract bid was accepted by the competitor and built into its overall bid for the project. The subcontract on the second project was ultimately given to another electrical company by the defendant. Can the subcontractor successfully sue for breach of contract? [*Premier Electrical Constr. Co. v. Miller-Davis Company*, 291 F.Supp. 295 (1968).]

10. In *Johnson v. Mobil Oil Corporation*, 415 F.Supp. 264 (1976),[6] the court held that a contracting party having immense bargaining power has an affirmative duty to explain in layman's terms the meaning and possible consequences of a contractual obligation to be assumed by another contracting party who is an uncounseled layman. Evaluate this holding by the court.

---

[6] See p. 85.

Contracts

Formation of a Contract

6

After you have read this chapter, you should be able to:

1. Discuss the law of offer and acceptance, recognizing that it acts as a limitation on the freedom to contract.
2. Recognize that the law of offer and acceptance is evolving and moving to facilitate broad social objectives.
3. Appreciate how the promise necessary to the formation of a contract is absorbed into an offer.
4. Understand the complexity of the creation of an offer which places a power in another.
5. Note how the law of offer and acceptance can create rights and duties not previously recognized by law.
6. Note the critical importance of the agency authorized to communicate the acceptance.
7. Realize the critical impact the Uniform Commercial Code has had upon the law of offer and acceptance.

Introduction

The *offer and acceptance* process is critical to the formation of a simple express, or implied-in-fact, contract. One reason is that the offer normally contains the promise required for the formation of a contract. Another reason is that by offer and acceptance there is an apparent meeting of the minds of the parties resulting in an agreement. Before we can have a contract, except for the implied-in-law (quasi) contract, *we need an offer.*

The importance of offer and acceptance to the formation of a contract is apparent from the role the concept is designed to play in the law of contracts. (A *offers* to sell a house to B for $100,000, and B *accepts*. A is *promising* to sell and B is *promising* to buy the house.)

Necessary to the finding of an offer is the satisfaction of *two tests: a quantity test and a quality test.* The law, having given us the *freedom to contract* and the ability to create *rights and duties,* is concerned that we truly *want* to assume certain duties which would not otherwise be imposed upon us by law, and that we truly *want* to gain rights which we would not otherwise be entitled to by law. To satisfy its concerns, the law limits *our freedom to contract* until the two tests necessary for the existence of an offer are satisfied—the quantity and quality tests. These two tests will be examined later.

The important point in this chapter is the concern of the law for determining *from the parties' conduct whether or not the minds of the parties have apparently met in order to have a contract.* The need to determine this factor *objectively* has resulted in the law of offer and acceptance.

The Offer

Terms of an offer must be communicated to an offeree before we place in the offeree the power to accept and to create a contract—to spring a contract into existence.

Once the terms of an offer are communicated to an offeree, the power to spring a contract into existence does not last forever. It ends with the passage of time, or it can end prematurely through acts of the parties to the proposed contract.

The Uniform Commercial Code has brought major changes to the common law of *offer* where the subject matter of the offer is *goods.*

Major changes are made to the common law of *acceptance* by the Uniform Commercial Code where the subject matter of the contract is *goods.* These changes will be discussed later in this chapter under the subsection "Acceptance."

An important point to watch for in this chapter is how the law of offer and acceptance is *evolving* to accomplish social objectives.

Offer Contains a Promise

An **offer** is a promise made in exchange for another's act, forbearance, or return promise. The offer gives the offeree the legal power to accept the offer and to spring a contract into existence. Except for the *inverted unilateral contract* in which we have an act in search of a promise, the offer will contain the promise necessary to the formation of a contract. The promisor, who makes the promise contained in the offer, becomes an **offeror.** The promisee, to whom the promise is made, becomes the **offeree** when he receives the offer. It should be recognized that in the law of contracts the promise is merged into the concept of offer. The following case dealt with an inverted unilateral contract. It involved an idea for a film for which a promise to pay was enforced as a contract.

Facts

Plaintiff, Blaustein, is suing Richard and Elizabeth Burton for breach of contract, unjust enrichment, breach of confidential relationship, services rendered, and benefits conferred on the grounds that the defendants had used plaintiff's idea for filming "The Taming of the Shrew" without compensating plaintiff. Blaustein had come to the Burtons and had explained to them his ideas about making the film.

Decision

Judgment for plaintiff.

Reasoning

The court held the Burtons liable for breach of contract on the basis that they had breached an inverted unilateral contract. The court noted that a contract for the conveyance of, and payment for, an idea may be either express or implied where an idea has been conveyed with the expectation that compensation will be paid by the recipient if the idea is used. The recipient may thereafter gratuitously promise to pay a reasonable compensation for the idea and create a valid obligation. This is what happened in this case when an inverted unilateral contract was created. The conveyance of the idea was the act in search of a promise to compensate.

Blaustein v. Burton, 88 Cal.Rptr 319 (1970).

offer
a promise made in exchange for another's act, forbearance, or return promise

offeror
the promisor making an offer

offeree
the promisee to whom an offer is made

Quantity Test

Before a *proper promise*[1] can result in an offer, it must have *certainty of terms.* A promise can promise *only three things,* and it can ask for only three things: an *act,* a *forbearance* (refraining from doing something), or a *return promise* from the offeree. The **objective manifestation** of the promise must tell the offeree what the offeree is to do (an act) or refrain from doing (a forbearance), and what the offeror will do or not do. (I'll pay you $100 for digging the ditch. The offeror's *promise* is to do an act, *to pay $100,* and the offeree is to do an *act, to dig the ditch.*) If the offer does not satisfy the *quantity test,* it will fail for uncertainty

quantity test
the promise must have certainty of terms in what it promises and what it asks for

objective manifestation
the word, writing, or actions which communicate the offer containing the promise

---

[1] See p. 76. In chapter 5 we noted that social obligations, illegal objectives, and objectives violative of public policy contained in promises would not be enforced as contracts.

Figure 6.1 Quantity Test: Some Situations Which Satisfy the Requirement of Certainty of Terms

Offeror	What I will do	What I will do and not do	What I will not do	The point of the table is that some statement referring to what must be done or not done must exist for both offeror and offeree before we have certainty of terms.
Offeree	What I want you to do	What I want you not to do	What I want you to do or not do	

of terms, and no contract can be formed. There are a number of combinations of statements which satisfy the quantity test. Some of these combinations are illustrated in figure 6.1.

One can understand why advertisements fail as offers. Advertisements normally state what the promisee is required to do but do not normally state what the offeror will do because no limit is placed upon what the promisor will be required to do. Is the promisor willing to sell one item, two hundred, or an infinite quantity? This question is not answered in the typical advertisement; therefore, it fails as an offer. Normally an advertisement is construed as *soliciting or inviting offers.* (A reads an advertisement in her local paper for frying chickens at 49¢ per pound. When A takes a chicken to the checkout counter she is making the offer to the clerk to buy the chicken for 49¢ per pound.)

Similar criticisms can be raised as to catalogs, or with regard to requests for bids to be made by contractors on jobs. These are not offers but *invitations to make offers.*

Under the common law, if the promise contained in the offer includes a formula which will in the future provide the terms of the quantity test, the offer will not fail for uncertainty of terms. An example of a contract which contains a formula that provides certainty of terms would be a **cost-plus contract.**

cost-plus contract
a contract in which the price is the cost of production or performance (whatever it turns out to be) plus an agreed-upon profit

quality test
the promise must cause the offeree reasonably to believe that the promise was intended to be an offer

Quality Test

A **quality test** must also be satisfied for an offer to exist. Is the promise of such quality that it is an offer? Whatever form the *quantity* statement takes, it must be done with the *intent* to make an offer. The quantity statement taken alone is *not* enough to be construed as an offer.

The quality test is *subjective.* From the actions and words of the party making the promise, would a reasonable person presume that *an offer was intended?* The quality test, or *intent to make an offer,* will not result in an offer without the quantity test being satisfied. *Both* quantity test and quality test must be satisfied before an offer will exist. In the following case the court found an expression to be reasonably understood as manifesting an intent to make an offer and not to be a joke.

Facts

Plaintiff, Barnes, sued Treece, vice president of a punch board corporation, who publicly stated that he would pay $100,000 to anyone who could find a crooked punch board. Plaintiff, who read the offer, presented two rigged punch boards to the defendant but was denied payment. Defendant contends that he made the statement in jest and had no serious contractual intent.

Decision

Judgment for plaintiff.

Reasoning

The court found for the plaintiff on the basis that there was sufficient manifestation of mutual assent to form a contract. The court stated that when expressions are intended as a joke and are understood or would be understood by a reasonable person as being so intended, they cannot be construed as an offer and accepted to form a contract. But if the jest is not apparent, and a reasonable hearer would believe that an offer was being made, then the speaker risks formation of a contract which he has not intended. It is the objective manifestations of the offeror which are important and not the secret unexpressed subjective intentions of the offeror.

Barnes v. Treece, 549 P.2d 1152 (Wash. 1976).

The Power Concept

If the quantity and quality tests of an offer are satisfied, and if the offer has been communicated to the offeree, the offeror has given the offeree the power to spring a contract into existence by the offeree's *acceptance* of the offer. In the *unilateral contractual* situation, this is done by the offeree's *acceptance* in performing, or refraining from doing, a *requested act*. In the *bilateral contractual* situation, this is done by the offeree's *acceptance* in giving the *requested promise* to the offeror.

power concept
the offeree has the power to create a contract by making an acceptance knowingly complying with the offer

Communicating the Offer: Express and Implied Terms

In order for the offeree to spring a contract into existence the offeree must have notice of the offer. This requires that the offer be communicated to the offeree in some fashion. The offeror may *communicate* the offer to the offeree directly or through some third party or other *agency*. If the offeree does what the offeror requests without notice of the offer, no contract results because, since the offeree did not rely on any offer, there is no acceptance.

Terms of an offer can be distributed to the general public at large by announcements, such as for rewards, or to particular members of the public by the use of tickets or stubs, such as terms on the back of airline tickets or claim tickets. In the following case the court held that, since there was no **bailment** contract, the terms on a parking lot ticket applicable to a bailment did not apply.

In a **bailment**, goods are *delivered* by a bailor to a bailee, who is liable for damage to the bailed goods caused by his negligence, unless the bailment contract provides otherwise.

Facts

Plaintiff, Shabala, is suing for damage to his car, which was broken into after he had parked it in defendant's parking lot. The plaintiff entered the defendant's parking lot, parked his automobile, locked it, kept the keys, and paid the attendant his fee. Attendant gave the plaintiff a parking ticket which plaintiff did not read. The ticket stated, "Lot closes at 9:30 P.M. Important. Read carefully." Another part of the ticket stated, "Articles left in car at owner's risk."

Decision

Judgment for defendant.

Reasoning

The court held that no bailment contract existed between plaintiff and defendant and, therefore, the defendant was not liable for loss of contents from the automobile. Only a contract for a lease of parking space had been created. The court recognized the trend in law toward not limiting the bailee's liability by a ticket unless the attention of the bailor is called to the ticket and the bailor has knowledge of its contents. In this case, however, the lot was not fenced, the plaintiff retained control over the automobile by taking the keys with him, and limitations were *printed on the ticket*. All of these facts taken together indicated a lease rather than a bailment.

Allright Phoenix Parking, Inc. v. Shabala, 429 P.2d 513 (Ariz. 1967).

Duration of the Offer

In the absence of a time period stated in the offer, an offer *expires* after the passage of a *reasonable time*. The reasonable time period can be short or long, depending upon whether the subject matter of the offer is perishable or fluctuating greatly in value over short periods of time. Also, the offer expires and ceases to exist if the offeror or offeree becomes insane or dies. If *performance* of the contemplated contract to be formed in the future becomes illegal—normally because of enactment of a criminal statute—the offer which looks to the formation of the future contract expires.

The offer can end also by *revocation, rejection and counteroffer,* and *subsequent illegality.* These means of ending an offer are equally applicable to the potential bilateral or unilateral contract.

revocation
the offeror's recalling of the offeree's power to accept as contained in the offer

Revocation of an offer occurs when the offeror recalls the power to accept the offer, which is contained in the offer. Revocation takes place when notice is *received* by the *offeree* that the offer no longer exists. *Actual notice* of the ending of the offer need not be received by the offeree *from the offeror* to cause the offer

---

Figure 6.2 Stated Time Periods Measuring Duration of Offer

Dated Offer	Undated Offer	Delayed Undated Offer
May 1. Stated time period 10 days. Offer ends on May 11.	Received June 6. Stated time period 20 days. Offer ends on June 26.	Received June 9, should have been received June 6. Stated time period 20 days. With notice of delay, offer ends on June 26. Without notice of delay, offer ends June 29.

to end. For example, if the offeree finds out that the subject matter of the offer has been disposed of by the offeror, the offer is revoked. Revocation also occurs when the offeror *delivers* a notice of revocation to the offeree's place of business, personal residence, or **agent** with authority or apparent authority to receive notices for the offeree. The notice of revocation is effective whether or not it is read by the offeree.

However, a public offer, as in reward situations, is revoked when a revocation is distributed using the same means which were used to communicate the offer. In the following case an offeror could revoke its continuing offer in letting a customer have a credit card.

agent
a person authorized to act on behalf of another and subject to the other's control

Facts

A clerk at defendant's store had refused without prior notice to honor credit cards issued by the store to the plaintiff, Mrs. Henderson. One card had been surrendered to the clerk at the store upon his request. At a later time, demand by letter was made upon the plaintiff to return a second card still in possession of the plaintiff, who refused to do so.

Decision

Judgment for defendant.

Reasoning

The court held that the store had a right to request the return of the credit cards. The court reasoned that the issuance of a credit card is but an offer to extend a line of credit. Such an offer is supported by no consideration and may be revoked at any time for any reason or for no reason at all. Acceptance and use of credit cards by customers makes a contract between the store and the customer, but such contract may be terminated by either party at any time. In this case there is a continuing offer which was effectively revoked by the clerk's demand for return of the first card, and by letter demanding the return of the second card.

City Stores Company v. Henderson, 156 S.E.2d 818 (Ga. 1967).

Two kinds of irrevocable offer which are of great importance in business are the option and the firm offer.

Option, Under the Common Law. Under the common law, an *option contract* is a contract to keep an offer stated therein open for a definite time. The offer is irrevocable and is called an **option.** The option offer looks to the formation of a future contract. The effect of an option contract is to prevent the offeror from withdrawing the option offer for a stated period of time or until a specified date, unless the offeror wishes to take the risk of being sued for breach of the option contract. The offeree must pay (give consideration) for the option in order to have an option contract. (I'll sell you this land for $30,000, and I'll keep my offer open for 90 days if you will pay me $1,000—which the offeree then pays.)

option
the irrevocable offer in an option contract

merchant
a person who deals in goods or, by occupation, holds himself out as having knowledge or skill in a transaction concerning goods, or who uses someone who holds himself out as having such knowledge or skill in a transaction concerning goods

Firm Offer, Under the Code. The Uniform Commercial Code[2] has its kind of option. The Code provides that a *written* offer signed by a **merchant** to buy or sell *goods* which gives assurance that it will be held open is not revocable for a stated time or, if no time is stated, for a reasonable time. The maximum amount

---

[2] UCC 2–205.

of time that the offer will not be revocable is three months. Such an offer is called a **firm offer.** (I'll sell you this machine for $900, and I'll keep my offer open for 60 days—which is in writing and signed by the merchant offeror.)

The offeree need not pay (give consideration) for the firm offer to make it binding upon the offeror, as is necessary to the creation of the option contract under the common law. However, the offeror will not be bound to the firm offer if it is contained in a form supplied by the offeree and the offeror has not **signed** *the clause* containing the firm offer provision.

Rejection of an offer occurs by the offeree's act refusing the offer. Rejection takes effect when a rejection or counteroffer to an original offer is *received* by an *offeror*. The same requirements for notice discussed for revocation are applicable to rejection and counteroffer. A rejection is some expression by the offeree which indicates that he is not interested in the offer. A **counteroffer** is an offer made by the offeree which changes the terms of the original offer made to him and, therefore, under the *common law* is a rejection of the original offer.

In the situation where the offer is seeking an act (*unilateral contract*), the offeror can revoke the offer only before the offeree starts to perform. Once the offeree has *substantially performed* the requested act, the offeror is required to allow the passage of a reasonable amount of time before revoking the offer to allow the offeree opportunity to complete performance of the act necessary *to spring the contract into existence.* In the following case the employer could not revoke its offer for a unilateral contract pension plan once the employee had substantially begun to comply with the offer.

Facts
Plaintiff, a retired employee, brings a suit against his employer for breach of contract with regard to an employee pension plan. Plaintiff had been notified by his employer of changes to be made in the existing pension plan. Plaintiff had agreed to enter into the pension plan, allow deductions from his pay, and had worked for some seven months before he received notice of the potential change in benefits. The employer informed the employee that he would not be covered by the pension plan.

Decision
Judgment for plaintiff.

Reasoning
The court held that the signing of the plan and the employee's engaging in work for the employer constituted substantial performance, after which the employer's unilateral contract offer, embodied in the original announcement for enrollment in the pension plan, could not be revoked. The court held that an offer for a unilateral contract may not be revoked after substantial performance has taken place.

Miller v. Dictaphone Corporation, 334 F.Supp. 840 (1971).

Under the Uniform Commercial Code
The Uniform Commercial Code article on sales of goods places a heavy reliance upon the *quality test*—that is, the *intent* of the parties to make an offer.[3] This can be seen in the Code's reliance upon conduct of the parties in determining whether an offer was made[4] and the Code's lack of concern with regard to the

---

[3] UCC 2–204(3).   [4] UCC 2–204(1).

moment when the offer effectively formed the basis for springing a contract into existence.[5]

The Code deemphasizes the *quantity test* of an offer and is willing to rely heavily upon flexible terms like "reasonable" and "seasonable" in the determination of *what the offeror has stated will be done or not done and what the offeree must do or not do.*[6] The Code also relies heavily upon "course of dealing" and "usage of trade" in interpreting terminology used in an offer.[7]

The approach used in the Uniform Commercial Code provides significant differences from the common law of offer. *The changes are limited to offers which have goods as their subject matter.*

Code Offer.   Under the Uniform Commercial Code an offer will not fail for *uncertainty of terms* if price is not stated[8] if the parties intend a contract for sale with price to be established in the future.

Nor will a contract of purchase fail though no quantity is specified if the contract provides for a portion of the seller's "output" or for the buyer's "needs" or "requirements."

In each case the Code establishes and relies upon formulas external to the offer to establish the terms of price and quantity. In the case of price, the market itself establishes the terms. The controlling price will always be a reasonable price for like goods as the goods would have sold for at the time and place of delivery. In the case of quantity, past ability to produce or consume the items in question provides the formula which will determine quantity.[9]

In the following case the court held that a contract to supply coal in sufficient quantity to supply the buyer's needs was interpreted to mean the needs existing at the time the contract was made and not as later increased.

Facts

Plaintiff, a mining company, brought this action against defendant, electrical wholesalers, seeking a declaration of the plaintiff's rights and duties under a contract for sales of coal to the defendant wherein it was promised that the plaintiff was to supply coal requirements for two electrical generating units. Prior to the plaintiff's performance of the contract, the defendant decided to increase the size of its generating units and did not notify the plaintiff coal company of its intended increased needs. It contends that the increased needs must be supplied by the mining company.

Decision

Judgment for plaintiff.

Reasoning

The court held the plaintiff coal company did not need to supply the increased needs of the utility company. A party to a contract may not unilaterally alter the obligations of any parties to that contract. A needs and requirement contract contemplates at the time of contracting the fulfillment of the existing needs of the contracting party. An intentional increase in capacity, thus increasing requirements, will not bind the supplier to the increased quantity.

Utah International, Inc. v. Colorado-Ute Electric Association, Inc., 425 F.Supp. 1093 (1976).

---

[5]UCC 2–204(2).   [6] UCC 1–204.   [7]UCC 1–205.   [8] UCC 2–305.   [9] UCC 2–306.

The end result of this approach is to use reliable formulas to ensure commercial honesty and restrict sharp business practices and yet facilitate the transaction of business.

The Acceptance

The Power Concept

acceptance
the offeree's
expressed assent to
the offer in reliance on
and in compliance with
the offer

An **acceptance** is the offeree's exercise of the power given by an offer to assent to the offer by performing the act or forbearance, or by giving a return promise, in reliance on and in compliance with the offer. By accepting an offer, the offeree has exercised the power given in the offer to spring a contract into existence.

In the *bilateral* contractual situation, the contract comes into existence the moment the return promise requested is *effectively* communicated to the offeror.

In the *unilateral* situation, the contract comes into existence the moment the requested act or forbearance has been performed. If the offer requires notice of performance by the offeree, then such notice must be given. However, on performance of the act or forbearance, there *is an acceptance* and the contract immediately comes into existence irrespective of whether or not notice has been given. While the offer may not *expressly* require notice, it may *impliedly* require notice if the offeree reasonably can believe that the offeror will not learn of his performance within a reasonable time in the ordinary course of affairs. Failure to give such notice causes the offeror to be **discharged** from his contract. It should be noted that, once performance is begun by the offeree, the offer is irrevocable by the offeror and can be accepted only by *full* performance. In the following case full performance of the act did not occur; so, without an acceptance, there was no unilateral contract.

discharged
termination of a
contractual duty to
perform a promise

Facts
Plaintiff, Miyakawa, brings this action against the defendant bowling establishment to recover a prize which he alleges he had won in a bowling competition sponsored by the Bowlerama of Texas, Inc. For five months prior to the competition, house rules had been displayed in the bowling establishment indicating that contestants would be eligible for the prize only if their scores were kept by scorers *selected by a clerk in charge of a control desk*. Plaintiff *kept his own score* and contends he is entitled to the prize because his score was the highest.

Decision
Judgment for defendant.

Reasoning
The court held that, since the plaintiff had kept his own scores and had not complied with the house rule that scores were to be kept by scorers selected by a particular clerk, he could not recover the prize. The court noted that while it is generally held that a party publishing to the world an offer seeking an act and, before the offer is withdrawn, a person acts in reliance on it, the party making the offer will be bound to perform as promised. The rights of a contestant, however, who has performed the act required in a promoter's offer are limited by the terms of the offer, that is, by the conditions and rules of the contest as made public.

Bowlerama of Texas, Inc. v. Miyakawa, 449 S.W.2d 357 (Tex. 1970).

To be effective, the acceptance must be unqualified or unconditional *under the common law* and made by the offeree. An attempt to accept an offer by someone other than the offeree will not cause a contract to come into existence. Only the intended offeree can accept the offer.

The offeree usually has the choice of accepting or rejecting the offer. Inaction on the part of the offeree normally results in the offer *expiring* because of the passage of time. If, however, past course of dealings has made silence an acceptance, active rejection of the offer by the offeree will be necessary to prevent the formation of a contract. *Silence* plus the offeree's *use* of the subject matter of the offer normally results in an implied acceptance of the offer under the common law. However, by statute, unsolicited items received through the mail can be used without creating a contract. In the following case the buyer's silence in not objecting to an arbitration clause continually included in the seller's invoices did not constitute an acceptance of such clause.

Facts

Plaintiff, Tanenbaum Textile Company, Inc., is suing the defendant seeking to enforce an arbitration clause purported to be contained in a contract. On some twenty-seven occasions plaintiff sold and delivered a quantity of textiles to defendant. An invoice was sent on delivery of each order indicating the quantity and price associated with the delivery. Also, on each invoice and stamped in red ink were the words, "All controversies arising from the sale of these goods are to be settled by arbitration."

Decision

Judgment for defendant.

Reasoning

The court hold that the defendant was not subject to having the dispute settled by arbitration. The court noted that it is true that acceptance of a document which plainly purports to be a contract gives rise to an implication of assent to its terms despite ignorance of the contents thereof. In this instance, an invoice is not purported to be a contract. The applicable principle which decides this particular case is that a party can not be held to a contract where there is no assent. Silence operates as an assent and creates an estoppel only when it has the effect to mislead. When a party is under a duty to speak, or when his failure to speak is inconsistent with honest dealings and misleads another, then his silence may be deemed to be acquiescence. Absent this situation, a person is under no obligation to do or say anything concerning a proposition which he does not choose to accept. There must be actual acceptance or there is no contract as in this case.

Tanenbaum Textile Co., Inc. v. Schlanger, 40 N.E.2d 225 (N.Y. 1942).

There are exceptional instances where the offeree can not refuse to accept the offer. These instances arise primarily because of statutory law, the typical example of which would be antidiscrimination laws which prevent an individual who has solicited offers from the public to refuse to accept the tendered offer because of color, religion, sex, race or nationality. This is a further inroad on the freedom to contract but an inroad approved of by legislative bodies for some more important, usually public, purpose.

Communication of the Acceptance

medium
an agency, instrument, means, or channel

Expressly Authorized Medium.   If the offeror stipulates or makes the use of a particular **medium** for communicating the acceptance a *condition* of acceptance, then the use of any other medium will result in a counteroffer. If the offeree uses the expressly authorized medium for accepting the offer, the acceptance becomes *effective* when sent. The contract is formed the moment the message is delivered to the indicated medium. For example, the acceptance would be *effective* the moment the letter was mailed, the telegram handed to the telegraph clerk, or the acceptance spoken into the phone. The acceptance is *effective* though it might never be received by the offeror.

The offeror can stipulate actual receipt of the acceptance as necessary to the formation of a contract. In this circumstance a contract can result only if the acceptance is actually received while the offer continues in existence.

Both the common law and the Uniform Commercial Code are in agreement on the above points.[10] In the following case the company's offer required receipt of acceptance at its home office to be effective as an acceptance, and, since the offeree died before his acceptance was received, there was no acceptance. The offer had expired by the offeree's death.

Facts
Plaintiff, Winney, sought to recover death benefits under a life insurance policy. Said policy contained an offer which allowed the owner to terminate the policy and receive its cash value. The company required that a written request be received at the home office per the policy before a policyholder would be entitled to cash value of the insurance policy. A letter by the owner requesting cash value was not received at the insurance company's office until after the owner-insured's death. The representative of the deceased owner contends that the decedent's estate is entitled to death benefits under the life insurance policy.

Decision
Judgment for plaintiff representative.

Reasoning
The court held for the deceased, reasoning that the acceptance never became effective since the insured died before his letter was received by the insurance company. The court reasoned that an offeror can specify any mode of acceptance he pleases and can require that the acceptance of his offer not be operative until received by him. In this case, this was the impact of the clause requiring written request to be filed at the home office. It was not to be effective until received.

Franklin Life Insurance Company v. Winney, 469 S.W.2d 21 (Tex. 1971).

Impliedly Authorized Medium.   If the offeror does not require actual receipt of the acceptance and does not stipulate the communication medium, the medium used by the offeror to send the offer becomes impliedly authorized as a medium for acceptance. Also, impliedly authorized is any medium customarily used for transactions of that nature at the place where the offer was received.

---

[10] UCC 2–206(1).

The use of the impliedly authorized means by the offeree to communicate the acceptance will cause the acceptance to become *effective* and springs the contract into existence the moment the acceptance is delivered to the medium of communication. Again, the acceptance is *effective* though it might never be received by the offeror.

Unauthorized Medium.   Any medium not expressly nor impliedly authorized is unauthorized. If the offer *requires* the use *exclusively* of a specific medium for acceptance, the offeree's use of an unauthorized medium is not an acceptance but, instead, is a rejection and a counteroffer. If the offer *does not require* such an *exclusive* medium but *suggests* or *invites* a medium, then the offeree's use of an unauthorized medium is not an acceptance *when sent,* but it is effective as an acceptance *when received* by the offeror. Such receipt, however, must be within the time expectations that the offeror had for receipt from the impliedly authorized agency. (A uses the mail asking for an acceptance by mail. It takes three days for the letter to get to B without delay. A's expectation, at the outside, for the receipt of the acceptance by mail is probably six days. If B uses a telegram and the telegraphed acceptance arrives ten days after the offer was sent by A, under the *common law* the letter will be treated as a counteroffer.)

Timeliness.   In order for the acceptance to be *timely* in the expressly and impliedly *authorized* medium situations, it should be *capable of being received* within the stated time required by the offeror; and in the absence of a stated time, then within a reasonable time. If the acceptance is not timely, then the offer expires, and the offeree's late-attempted acceptance is a new offer.

The only difference in the *unauthorized* situation is that the acceptance *must be received* within the stated time required by the offer or, in the absence of a stated time, within a reasonable time.

Under the Uniform Commercial Code

Under UCC 2–206, unless the offeror *clearly requires* otherwise, if the offeree uses a *medium reasonable in the circumstances* to communicate an acceptance, such use will spring a contract into existence immediately when the acceptance is sent even though it is never received by the offeror.

A medium reasonable in the circumstances is one which the offeree calculates will enable the timely receipt of the acceptance by the offeror—e.g., mail, telegram, telephone, depending on the circumstances.

Thus the Code's major impact or change in the common law is that an unauthorized means used to send a timely acceptance can result in a contract when *sent* rather than when *received*.

Another Code change in the common law is that an offer to buy goods to be shipped may be accepted either *by shipment,* creating a *unilateral* contract, or by a *prompt promise to ship,* creating a *bilateral* contract. Under the common law, such a *promise* to ship would have been construed as a counteroffer.

In addition, the seller's shipment of nonconforming goods will be an acceptance and result in a contract unless the seller clearly indicates that such shipment is a counteroffer being made for the accommodation of the buyer. Under the common law such a shipment would always have resulted in a counteroffer.

Confirmation, and Additional Terms in Acceptance. Under UCC 2–207, the offeree's written confirmation of an offer is an acceptance. This is not so under the common law, because a confirmation merely acknowledges receipt of the offer and does not assent to the offer.

Also under the Code, a definite and reasonable expression of acceptance can act as an acceptance though it states terms additional to or different from those offered, unless the offeree clearly indicates that he is making a counteroffer. In such a case, *there is a contract to the extent* that the terms of the offer are accepted, and the additional terms stated by the offeree are a counteroffer by the offeree. Under the common law the result is always a counteroffer in the described situation. (S offers to sell B 1,000 raincoats at $20 each. B replies that he'll take 500 at $20 and 500 at $18 each. Under the common law of contracts, there is no acceptance and no contract. Under the Code, there is an acceptance and a contract for 500 at $20 each and a counteroffer for 500 at $18 each.)

The Code provides formulas to determine what the terms of the contract will be. Between the parties, the changes must be consented to by the offeror before they become part of the contract.

Between merchants, the additional terms automatically become part of the contract unless (a) the offer expressly limits acceptance to the terms of the offer, (b) the changes materially alter the offer, or (c) notification of objection to changes in the terms of the offer has already been given or is given within a reasonable time after notice of them is received. In the above raincoats example, B's counteroffer of $18 materially alters the offer.

If parties by their conduct recognize the existence of a contract, then there is a contract. The terms of the contract will be established by the writings of the parties where agreement exists and also by supplementary terms incorporated under any other provision of the Code such as has been illustrated in this chapter for open quantity and price terms.[11] In the following case the court recognized that a contract existed by the conduct of the parties, the offeree's oral notification constituting an acceptance.

Facts

Maryland Supreme Corporation, a general contractor, filed a counterclaim against the Blake Co., a subcontractor, for his breach of contract to supply concrete at a set price. The general contractor received a letter from the subcontractor which stated a quotation on readimix for a project to be built by the general contractor, asserting that the price will be guaranteed to hold throughout the job period. Upon successfully being awarded the contract, the general contractor orally notified the subcontractor that the subcontractor had the job and that they were to supply the concrete. As the job progressed, the subcontractor began to raise the price. The subcontractor now contends that the general contractor's oral notification was not an acceptance of the subcontractor's original offer and higher prices can now be charged.

Decision

Judgment for Maryland Supreme Corporation.

---

[11] See pp. 97–98.

Reasoning

The court held that, under the Uniform Commercial Code, any reasonable manner of acceptance is intended to be regarded as available to the offeree unless the offeror has made it quite clear that it will not be acceptable. Former technical rules as to acceptance are rejected in favor of a substitute criterion that the acceptance be in any manner and by any medium reasonable under the circumstances. The general contractor's oral acceptance of the subcontractor's written offer was reasonable under the circumstances in this case. (Note: the court applied the Uniform Commercial Code because the contract was for the *sale of goods*.)

Maryland Supreme Corporation v. Blake Co., 369 A.2d 1017 (Md. 1977).

Summary Statement

1. The offer contains the required promise necessary for the formation of a contract.
2. To be effective, an offer must be communicated to the offeree, be intended to be an offer, and in addition must contain certainty of terms (quantity and quality tests).
3. Offers do not last forever. Some expire after the passage of a stated period of time; some end after the passage of a reasonable time; and others end by the death or insanity of the offeror or offeree.
4. Offers can also end by revocation, rejection and counteroffer, and subsequent illegality.
5. The concept of option and firm offer limits the ability of the offeror to revoke the offer without being responsible to the offeree for damages for breach of contract on his acceptance.
6. The Uniform Commercial Code has vastly changed the impact of the common law on offers which have goods as their subject matter. The purpose of these changes is to facilitate commercial transactions and promote commercial honesty.
7. The act of acceptance springs a contract into existence.
8. The acceptance must be unqualified and made with the intent to accept.
9. An authorized means for communicating an acceptance must be used in order for the **deposit rule** to be applicable.
10. The use of an unauthorized means for communicating the acceptance can result in a counteroffer.
11. The Uniform Commercial Code significantly changes the common law of acceptance when the subject matter of the contract is goods.
12. In addition to the Uniform Commercial Code, other statutes have an impact on the law of offer and acceptance in order to accomplish other goals.
13. The law of offer and acceptance conceptually sets a limit on the freedom of contract by the requirements needed to be fulfilled before a contract can come into existence.
14. This area of contract law is still evolving.

deposit rule
an acceptance is effective when sent, though never received, if an authorized medium is timely used by the offeree

The point made in chapter 5 that it may be unlawful *not* to contract is illustrated by the following case. Because of a right guaranteed to one party by statute, another party loses the right *not to contract*. The point being made by this case is that the freedom to contract does not necessarily include the freedom *not* to contract.

Faraca v. Clements
506 F.2d 956 (1975)

Plaintiffs, Andrew Faraca, a Caucasian, and his wife, Ophelia, a black, brought an action against Dr. James D. Clements, the Director of the Georgia Retardation Center, requesting an order **enjoining** the defendant from engaging in discriminatory employment practices and seeking general, special, and punitive damages and attorneys' fees and costs.

enjoining
an order from a court to desist from doing

The Georgia Retardation Center began operations under the direction of Dr. Clements, who is largely responsible for its success. It has about 550 racially integrated residents. Staff also are integrated.

Mr. Faraca filled out an employment application with the center. Mr. Faraca specifically sought employment as a Cottage Program Specialist, while Mrs. Faraca made an "open" application, hopeful that she and her husband could both obtain employment with the center.

Being impressed with Mr. Faraca's credentials, a center employee suggested that he apply for the position of Cottage Program Administrator. This position required that Mr. Faraca and his spouse be present at the center twenty-four hours a day.

Dr. Mills, who was to be Mr. Faraca's supervisor, considered Mr. Faraca the best applicant for the job and wished to hire him. Dr. Clements vetoed the hiring for two reasons: (1) the effects of the racially mixed couple on visitors, and (2) possible adverse reactions from state legislators.

Dr. Clements contends that he should not be held liable for damages because he had proceeded in good faith to protect the program and not out of any personal bias or prejudice.

proscribe
to prohibit

Dr. Clements contends that an existing civil rights statute granting all persons the right to make and enforce contracts was only intended to **proscribe** a breach of contract, not, as in this case, the refusal to enter into a contract.

The court specifically disagreed with this latter position, using the following language:

The statute expressly equalizes the right of all citizens *"to make* and enforce contracts." By specifically protecting the right to make contracts Congress must have meant to protect black citizens from racially biased interference with *prospective contract rights*, otherwise the words italicized would be redundant.

prospective contract rights
contract rights contemplated in the future

The court pointed out that any other interpretation would thwart the purpose of civil rights legislation by the **expedience** *of refusing to contract with blacks.*

As to Dr. Clements' first argument, the court held that public officials can not find sanctuary from the consequences of an act of discrimination in a fear that public reaction will bring unfavorable results.

expedience
means to an end

Judgment for personal damages of $7,188.75 against Dr. Clements affirmed on appeal.

Contracts

Questions and Case Problems

1. Sheehan Company, a plaintiff subcontractor, sued to recover alleged excess charges for plumbing supplies from their supplier. The court found that the defendant supplier had orally quoted prices for copper pipe and tubing from its manufacturer's price sheet with nothing being said by the parties as to quantity, terms of payment, or time of acceptance and delivery. The defendant contends: that its communication was only an invitation to the plaintiff to deal with the defendant; and that since no promise had been contained in the communication, no offer had been made and it was thereby not bound to supply the goods at the price on the price sheet. What result? [*Thos. J. Sheehan Co. v. Crane Company,* 418 F.2d 642 (1969).]

2. Plaintiff, Lefkowitz, is suing the Great Minneapolis Surplus Store, Inc. for refusal to sell to the plaintiff a fur piece which it had offered for sale in a newspaper advertisement that read as follows: "Saturday 9 a.m. sharp, three brand new fur coats worth $139.50, first come, first serve. $1 each." The defendant's contention is that a newspaper advertisement offering items of merchandise for sale at a named price is a unilateral offer which may be withdrawn without notice. Plaintiff was first in line but was refused when he offered $1 for the fur coat advertised. Is the contention of the defendant correct, or can the plaintiff buy the fur coat for $1? [*Lefkowitz v. Great Minneapolis Surplus Store, Inc.,* 86 N.W.2d 689 (Minn. 1957).]

3. The plaintiff, a fabricator of steel and wire products, brought this action against the defendant, a steel broker, and the defendant filed a contractual counterclaim. The plaintiff orally offered the defendant a specified quantity of two different sizes of steel rods at specified prices. The defendant responded that he thought he wanted the rods but he wanted to check with his customers. Some five weeks later the defendant called the plaintiff and agreed to buy one size of rods and then two days later agreed to purchase the other size at the price originally discussed. The defendant contended that the plaintiff replied, "Fine, thank you," to both telephone calls. Was there a timely acceptance of the offer of the plaintiff? You decide. [*Textron, Inc. v. Froelich,* 302 A.2d 426 (Pa. 1973).]

4. Plaintiff, the Union Trust and Savings Bank, brought an action against the State Bank, conservator of an individual who had guaranteed certain notes of a third person which were due and owing to the plaintiff. At the time the guaranty was issued, the plaintiff was aware that the individual had been determined to be a ward of a conservator. It is the contention of the defendant, conservator, that the plaintiff bank's knowledge of the mental disability of the individual caused the individual's offer to act as guarantor to be revoked and of no legal force and effect. You decide. [*Union Trust and Savings Bank v. State Bank,* 188 N.W.2d 300 (Ia. 1971).]

5. Plaintiff general contractor, Gordon Construction Company, brought this action against Coronis Associates for breach of an alleged firm offer contract. The subcontractor, Coronis, had submitted a bid to the general contractor for the sale of structural steel. Such bid was used with other bids by the general contractor for submission to the governmental body. Shortly before notification of acceptance of the subcontract bid, the subcontractor withdrew the offer. The general contractor contends that the subcontractor had no right to withdraw the offer because it was a firm offer. What result? [*E. A. Coronis Assocs. v. M. Gordon Construction Co.*, 216 A.2d 246 (N.J. 1966).]

6. Plaintiff, Standard Oil Company of Indiana, is suing the defendant, Schmieder, for oil equipment per an option contained in a contract with the defendant. The option clause in question provided that the plaintiff could purchase the equipment at a price equal to the defendant's cost minus depreciation as may be mutually agreed upon. The defendant's contention is that the offer contained in the option fails for uncertainty of terms since price is not stated. You decide the issue. [*Schmieder v. Standard Oil Co. of Indiana*, 230 N.W.2d 732 (Wis. 1975).]

7. Plaintiff Roberts, insurance agent, sent defendant a policy which was a renewal of one which defendant's father previously held. Defendant had not ordered or requested issuance of this policy, but he accepted it and paid the premium. At a later date, just prior to the expiration date of the renewed policy a second unsolicited renewal was sent by the plaintiff to the defendant and attached to it was a printed notice stating that, if defendant did not wish to accept it, he must return it or be liable for the premium. Defendant made no response. The plaintiff inquired about the premium by telephone with the defendant. Defendant informed him that he had purchased another policy elsewhere. Plaintiff sues on the second renewal. What result? [*Roberts v. Buske*, 298 N.E.2d 795 (Ill. 1973).]

8. The defendant, Systems Engineering and Manufacturing Company, made a proposal to the plaintiff and required as a condition of acceptance that a signed copy of the proposal and 25 percent down payment be hand delivered to the defendant in order to form the contract. Plaintiff accepted this proposal by telephone, indicating that the proposal had been approved and the defendant could start working on it immediately. The defendant expressed his appreciation and said that they would probably start on it immediately. Subsequently, the defendant found an error in the price it quoted in the proposal and telephoned the plaintiff indicating that it was withdrawing its offer. Had the offer been accepted? You decide. [*Golden Dipt Company, Etc. v. Systems Engineering and Mfg. Co., Etc.*, 465 F.2d 215 (1972).]

9. Plaintiff, CIC, sought to enforce a reorganization plan tendered by defendant, CAC, wherein money loaned by the defendant would be converted into other long-term debts and stock. A proposal for the reorganization was delivered to the plaintiff on September 27. The entire plan of reorganization was by the terms the proposal to be completed by November 1. Contained in this

proposal were the following words: "Will you kindly examine this proposal and let us know your reaction to it at the earliest possible time. We wish to point out that it is not an inflexible proposal, but we also point out that a recapitalization along these lines is imperative." CIC prepared a written acceptance of the offer, dated it October 8, but deliberately withheld mailing the letter until October 19, and it was not received by the offeror defendant until October 21. The offeror contends that the offer expired before it was accepted due to the passage of a reasonable amount of time. What result? You decide. [*Central Invest. Corp. of Denver v. Container Advertising Co.*, 471 P.2d 647 (Colo. 1970).]

10. In *Faraca v. Clements*, 506 F.2d 956 (1975),[12] the court held that one could lose his right not to contract in order to further a legislative purpose contained in a statute. It is quite appropriate to use business law as a tool for social change. Evaluate this statement.

---

[12] See p. 104.

7 Relief from Contractual Obligations

After you have read this chapter, you should be able to:

1. Discuss the law associated with the law of relief from contractual obligation and recognize that it acts as a legal safeguard on the freedom to contract.
2. Recognize that the law of genuineness of assent is a strongly felt force in society.
3. Understand the philosophical importance of the fact that the promise forming the basis of a contract must be fairly and voluntarily given.
4. Realize how the concept of unconscionability has given new importance to the exercise of free will in the contractual setting.
5. Recognize that this area of law is still evolving.

Introduction

In the formative stage of a simple express or implied in-fact contract, the concern of the law is to determine whether or not the parties to the contract *truly intended to create rights and duties not otherwise imposed by law.* The preceding chapter developed an *objective* test to determine the existence of a contract. The law also approaches the parties through a *subjective* test to ascertain *whether they are acting with free will or* **genuineness of assent** in their manifestations of mutual assent, i.e., offer and acceptance.

It is not the intent of the law to protect the fool from folly. The intent of the law is to protect the freedom of voluntary action of the individual.

As it provides *relief from contractual obligations,* the law looks at the parties as individuals and applies a subjective test which considers the traits and characteristics of the individual.

The importance of this chapter to the concept of *freedom to contract* is with regard to what the law means by a promise *voluntarily made* as being basic to the formation of a contract. A proper promise *voluntarily and fairly made* is necessary to the formation of an *enforceable* contract.

> **genuineness of assent**
> reality of consent to an offer or acceptance

Concern of the Law

After it has been determined that the requirements of offer and acceptance have been satisfied, the concern of the law is to see whether or not the **manifestations of mutual assent** to a contract were freely given. In the requirements necessary to satisfy offer and acceptance, parties who choose to contract must pass an *objective* test (quantity and quality tests). (A, evidencing a serious contractual intent, offers to sell his car to B for $2,000. B accepts the offer with the intent to buy the car.)

Genuineness of assent presents parties to a contract with a second test which must be passed before a contract at its formative stage becomes enforceable. Was the offer and/or acceptance an act of free will? The answer to the question necessarily is very *subjective* (personal). Each individual has a different strength of will.

Both the *objective* and *subjective* tests must be satisfied in order to successfully form a contract.

> **manifestation of mutual assent**
> offer and acceptance

Result

If genuineness of assent is not present (the manifestation of mutual assent was not an act of free will), then the party to the contract not exercising free will has the right to avoid, **rescind,** or set aside what objectively appears to be a contract.

The act of *avoidance* must be timely or it is lost. Conduct which is inconsistent with avoidance will reaffirm the contract. This is illustrated by the following case.

> **rescind**
> to cancel

Facts

This is an action by the plaintiff employee against the defendant employer for rescission of an employment contract on the ground that, as a result of duress, threats, and coercion, he was compelled to sign an agreement with respect to his employment. The court found as a matter of fact that the employee who executed an employment contract did not voice any objection to circumstances leading up to the contract nor did he protest to any official of the employer, but the employee recognized the contract in all its terms and provisions and wrote letters to the employer in which he did not question the validity or enforceability of the contract. It was not until thirteen months later that he took the action to rescind or cancel the contract.

Decision

Judgment for defendant.

Reasoning

The court held that because of the inconsistent action of the employee he had ratified the contract as a matter of law. The following reasoning was used. A contract entered into as a result of duress is not void, but merely voidable and is capable of being ratified after duress is removed; ratification results if the party who executed the contract under duress accepts benefits flowing from it or remains silent or acquiesces in the contract for any considerable length of time after opportunity is afforded to annul or avoid it. The conduct of the employee in this case was ratification.

Gallon v. Lloyd-Thomas Co., 264 F.2d 821 (1959).

In the case of fraud (intentional misrepresentation), one can rescind *or* waive his power to avoid the contract and, instead, seek damages for the tort of deceit.[1] (S sold a twelve-year-old tractor to B misrepresenting it to be ten years old. B kept the tractor and sued S for deceit for the difference in value between a ten-year-old tractor and a twelve-year-old tractor.) Under the Code,[2] a party can rescind *and* seek damages. A mistake in drafting a contract will be corrected by **reformation.**

Mistake

In certain situations one can avoid the consequences of the offer or acceptance by proving a **mistake.** A mistake of *law* does not allow *one* to avoid a contract; we are all presumed to know the law. A mistake of *fact* may justify avoidance of a contract. If only one party is mistaken without the other party knowing of the mistake, avoidance of the contract *is not allowed.* (A contracts to sell certain goods to B, forgetting that he had already sold them to C. A can not avoid for his mistake of fact.) If the other party knows a mistake is being made by a party to a contract, avoidance by the mistaken party *is usually allowed.* This is the situation of *unilateral mistake*—one party making the mistake.

In the *mutual* or *bilateral mistake* situation, *both* parties to the contract are mistaken and either party can avoid the contract. It is most commonly said that *the minds of the parties never met.* Most often this occurs in a situation of

---

[1] For the tort of deceit, see above, p. 56.

[2] UCC 2–720, 2–721.

reformation
an action to correct a writing so as to reflect correctly the intentions of the parties which mistakenly were not properly expressed in the writing

mistake
believing a fact to exist when it does not exist, or believing a fact not to exist when it does exist

Contracts

ambiguity. In an ambiguous fact situation the fact is capable of two meanings. Each of the contracting parties associates with a different fact meaning. *Objectively* their minds seem to have met but *subjectively* no meeting of the minds has taken place. Additionally, if both parties assume a fact to be in existence when it is not in existence, or not to be in existence when it is in existence, mutual mistake occurs. This is illustrated in the following case.

Facts

The plaintiff, Dover Pool and Racquet Club, Inc., sought rescission of a land sale contract and return of the money deposit where, unknown to the parties to the contract, a retroactive zoning change would affect the use of the property in question. The court found as a fact that, at the time of the signing of the land sale contract, both parties assumed that zoning bylaws interposed no obstacle to the contemplated use of the premises by the purchaser as a nonprofit tennis and swimming club.

Decision

Judgment for plaintiff.

Reasoning

The court held that, where at the time of signing of a land sale contract *both parties assumed that zoning bylaws* interposed no obstacle to contemplated use of the premises by the purchaser, there was mutual mistake. Although the purchaser's principal purpose could not be said to have been frustrated, a right of vital importance to the purchaser did not exist, and the contract was voidable by the purchaser for *mutual mistake of fact. Both* parties had assumed the zoning laws to be favorable when, in fact, the laws were not favorable to the requirements of the purchaser.

Dover Pool and Racquet Club, Inc. v. Brooking, 322 N.E.2d 168 (Mass. 1975).

The area of mistake reflects the concern of the law that the parties contract knowing the reality of the situation. Without this assurance, the law can not ascertain if the parties to the contract would have entered into it voluntarily. On the other hand, as between two innocent parties, the one causing his own distortion of reality and the other contracting in reality, the court will hold for the latter and against the former. Thus, if one negligently signs a contract misinterpreting its impact or terms or mistakenly assumes he or she is contracting with a named party but is actually contracting with someone else, he or she will be bound to the contract.

Misrepresentation

When one *unintentionally* misrepresents a *material* fact and this induces another to enter into a contract, the misled party can avoid the contract if the party reasonably relied upon the **misrepresentation.** This is so because the law can not assure itself that if the true state of affairs had been known the misled party would have freely entered into the contract. In the following case the plaintiff sought to avoid the contract, alleging that the defendant knew, or should have known, that its representation was false. The court held that the complaint sufficiently stated a cause of action justifying avoidance.

misrepresentation
a representation of
what is not true

Facts

Plaintiff purchased an automobile business from defendant believing the business included the Oldsmobile agency and franchise. Plaintiff alleged that the defendant knew, or should have known, that the franchise was not saleable as part of the business. General Motors refused to transfer the franchise to plaintiff, who then returned the business to defendant and demanded rescission of the purchase contract. Defendant **demurred** to the complaint on the basis that it failed to allege that defendant intentionally made false representations that the plaintiff would receive the franchise.

Decision

Demurrer overruled, for plaintiff.

Reasoning

The court noted that, in an action for deceit, the basis for responsibility is the intent to deceive, proved by the fact that the speaker believes the statement to be false or the representation is made without any belief in its truth. Recovery in damages is also allowed for fraud not amounting to deceit where there was a representation of fact or the speaker is supposed to possess complete knowledge of the facts. In negligence actions, defendant need only fail to exercise ordinary care in making a representation or in ascertaining facts, but, like other cases of negligence, it requires a duty of care or an assumption of a duty. Recovery is allowed even though representations are innocently made, because it would be unjust to allow one making false representations to retain the fruits of a bargain induced by them. A misrepresentation may be innocent, negligent, or known to be false. If innocently made, the contract is still voidable. Since the defendant here was alleged to know or should have known that the franchise was not saleable as part of the business, the order overruling the demurrer was sustained.

Whipp v. Iverson, 168 N.W.2d 201 (Wis. 1969).

Fraud

In **fraud,** a person intentionally misrepresents a present or past fact in an attempt to induce another person to enter into a contract. Opinion is not a statement of fact.

If one reasonably relies upon the false inducement, the contract can be avoided or damages sought under the common law. (A fraudulently induced B to contract with A. B may avoid the contract.)

Concealment

Both in misrepresentation and fraud there is action which distorts reality. In concealment normally there is passive *inaction,* a failure to disclose. Concealment may also occur by *actively* hiding the facts—e.g., an owner of a house covering a wall damaged by termites so that a prospective buyer of the house will not see this. In the following case the court held that, since a particular matter was discussed by the parties, there was, as a matter of fair dealing, a duty to disclose a material fact about the subject discussed.

---

demurrer
a pleading which states that a preceding pleading does not state a cause of action

fraud
(in contracts) a misrepresentation of fact, known to be false, made to induce another person to make or to refrain from making a contract, and relied on by the other person

Facts

This is an action by purchasers for rescission of a land sales contract. During the negotiations for the purchase and sale of a lodge, the sellers and purchasers discussed water rights connected with the property to be sold. The sellers failed to disclose past and pending water disputes of an adjoining landowner. The buyers contend that such failure to disclose entitles them to rescind the contract.

Decision

The court held that the vendors as a matter of law had misrepresented facts concerning the water during negotiations by not disclosing the disputes concerning the water rights.

Reasoning

Even though one is under no obligation to speak as to a matter, if he undertakes to do so, either voluntarily or in response to enquiries, he is bound not only to state truly what he tells but also not to suppress or conceal any facts within his knowledge which will materially qualify those statements. If he speaks at all he must make a full and fair disclosure. The attitude of the courts toward nondisclosure is undergoing a change. The objective of the law is changing so as to impose on the parties to a transaction a duty to speak whenever justice, equity, and fair dealing demand it.

Russ v. Brown, 529 P.2d 765 (Ida. 1974).

A growing body of law is accumulating which requires parties to disclose what reality is so that the law can be assured that the parties are exercising *free will* in the contractual setting.[3] This is especially true under the Uniform Commercial Code, as illustrated by the following case.

Facts

This is a suit by a buyer, Wells, for revocation of his acceptance in regard to his purchase of a new Volvo automobile. The dealer defends on the basis of a **disclaimer** which was contained in a warranty manual. The disclaimer was in slightly different print than other provisions in print in the warranty manual.

Decision

Judgment for buyer.

Reasoning

This disclaimer of warranties was not sufficiently revealed to be binding upon the buyer. The court held that, under the requirements of the Uniform Commercial Code, section 2–316, the disclaimer had been concealed. In order to be an effective disclaimer, it had to be in bold print or in enlarged print such that it would be conspicuous in order to come to the attention of the buyer. (Note: the court applied the Uniform Commercial Code because the contract was for the *sale of goods*.)

Volvo of America Corp. v. Wells, 551 S.W.2d 826 (Ky. 1977).

disclaimer
denial of an obligation or a claim

---

[3] See chapter 26, Consumer Law, for a discussion of the Magnuson-Moss Warranty–Federal Trade Commission Improvements Act.

Duress

duress
wrongful inducement to do that which a reasonable person would have been unable to resist

Duress is wrongful pressure by threat which induces one to enter into a contract, without freedom of choice, because of fear that the threatened, *wrongful* act will be carried out. Its effect is to make a contract *voidable* by the injured party if he *knew* the character of the transaction. If he *did not know* the character of the transaction, there is *no contract*. (X is wrongfully induced to sign a paper evidencing a contract. If X knew the contents of the paper, the contract is voidable by him. If he did not know, there is no contract.) The most crude form of duress which prevents the exercise of *free will* is when one is threatened with criminal or tortious conduct if a contract is not formed. More subtle forms of duress are recognized where free will is controlled by threat to bring criminal action, or by **abuse of civil legal process,** or by threat to withhold goods. The key to understanding duress is to recognize that the law is identifying conduct of one party which is wrongful and calculated to control the will of another in the contractual setting. In the following case the court held that the threat of a civil justifiable suit did not constitute duress nor prevent the other party's free exercise of will.

abuse of civil legal process
to make excessive and improper use of the right to sue in an attempt to exhaust someone into submission

Facts
Plaintiffs brought suit to set aside a contract of sale of realty to the United States for the purpose of a reservoir on the basis that an agent of the United States had expressed duress forcing the plaintiffs to make the contract. The alleged duress was the expression by the agent that, if they did not sell their lands, their lands would be condemned and they would be required to pay lawyers' fees which would eat up amounts awarded them, and that they would not receive temporary leases from the United States on the same basis as those voluntarily selling land to the United States.

Decision
Judgment for defendant.

Reasoning
There was no duress. It is never duress to institute civil suits if there is an honest belief that a good cause of action exists. One is always entitled to say without being guilty of "duress" that if his offer to purchase is not accepted, he will avail himself of his legal rights. Only the threat of a wrongful or unlawful act constitutes "duress," and such a threat will amount to "duress" only if it is sufficient to overpower the will of another party and prevent free exercise of will. Duress did not exist in this case because the plaintiffs were free to fight the condemnation action should it have come forth.

Beatty v. United States, 168 F.Supp. 204 (1958).

Undue Influence

undue influence
unfair persuasion by one who, because of his relationship with another, dominates the other

The law recognizes that, because of closeness of relationship, age, physical or mental condition, the will of a person can be manipulated—called **undue influence.** If, because of the unique relationship, contemplated undue contractual advantage is taken of the manipulated party by *unfair* persuasion, the contract can be avoided. Mere persuasion is proper and does not cause the contract to be voidable. In the following case the court held that there was a **fiduciary** relationship between the parties which was violated by the undue influence of the party with the fiduciary duty to act for the benefit of the other.

fiduciary
a person with a duty to act primarily for the benefit of another

Facts
This is an action by an administrator to have set aside a bill of sale for animals and a warranty deed to a farm which had been executed by decedent. The basis for the case that the transfer to defendant was null and void was (1) exercise of undue influence by defendant over the decedent, (2) lack of mental capacity by the decedent, and (3) lack of consideration for the transfer. The defendant denied all material allegations in the complaint.

It was determined at the trial that a fiduciary relationship existed between the decedent and the defendant by reason of a power of attorney given by the decedent to the defendant while the aged decedent was recovering from an injury. Testimony shows that the defendant knew of the decedent's income and affairs, transacted business for the decedent, and was his constant friend and advisor. Upon his death, she (the defendant) recorded the disputed deed and attempted to gain entrance to the decedent's safe deposit box and she cashed a check made out to him. No consideration was given by the defendant for the half of the farm deeded to her and for the animals covered by the technical bill of sale.

Decision
The court held that the defendant stood in a fiduciary relationship with decedent and had failed to prove that the deed was free from the taint of undue influence. Therefore, the deed

was declared null and void and the property interest reinstated in the administrator.

Reasoning
It is well established that the existence of a fiduciary or confidential relationship between the parties to a transaction creates a presumption of undue influence, which imposes upon the one receiving the benefit the burden of rebutting the presumption by showing that the transaction was **bona fide.** Courts of equity have carefully refrained from identifying particular instances of confidential or fiduciary relationships in such a manner that other, perhaps new, cases might be excluded. It is settled by an overwhelming weight of authority that the principle of undue influence extends to every possible case in which a fiduciary relationship as a fact exists. The term fiduciary or confidential relationship is a very broad one. The rule embraces both technical fiduciary relationships and those informal relationships which exist whenever one man trusts and relies upon another. The defendant failed to establish by clear and convincing evidence that the deed in question was free from the taint of undue influence.

bona fide
in good faith

Earls v. Johnson, 172 So.2d 602 (Fla. 1965).

The Uniform Commercial Code

unconscionable
offends the
conscience,
immoderate, too one-
sided

Under the Uniform Commercial Code,[4] the court is allowed to test the subjective question of the exercise of free will in the commercial setting. The question the court answers is whether or not the contract is **unconscionable.** The test is whether, in light of the general commercial background and the commercial needs of the particular trade or case, the clauses are so *one-sided* as to be unconscionable under the circumstances existing at the time of the making of the contract. If the conclusion is yes, the contract can be avoided. In the area of genuineness of assent, the law's concern is to give relief from contractual obligations not fairly and voluntarily assumed.

Summary Statement

1. Not only must we satisfy the requirements of manifestation of mutual assent before there is an *enforceable* contract, but genuineness of assent must also exist.
2. In the absence of genuineness of assent, a contract can be avoided through rescission, and in some instances damages will be given.
3. The traditional areas wherein problems of exercise of free will may result are mistake, misrepresentation, fraud, concealment, duress, and undue influence.
4. The Uniform Commercial Code in its development of the concept of unconscionability has given renewed importance to problems involving the exercise of free will in a contractual setting.

The most modern form of relief from contractual obligation can be found in the application of avoidance of contractual responsibility found in UCC 2–302. The following case is included in depth to illustrate how the concept of unconscionability is applied in a commercial setting.

Wille v. Southwestern Bell Telephone Company
549 P.2d 903 (Kan. 1976)

The question before the court is whether an advertiser can recover damages for breach of contract from a telephone company for an omission in the yellow pages of its telephone directory when the contract entered into by the parties limits the company's liability for errors and omissions to an amount equal to the cost of advertisement. The trial court granted summary judgment for the telephone company, and the advertiser has appealed.

The facts of the case are that the plaintiff has operated a heating and air conditioning business in Wichita for some thirteen years and has had some listing in the yellow pages of the phone directory for his business over this period of time.

---

[4] UCC 2–302.

In the year involved in this case plaintiff was in the process of expanding his business and sought additional telephone listings. Additional listings were given by the defendant but one of the telephone numbers was inadvertently omitted from the directory. Upon learning of the omission plaintiff began advertising the omitted number on television, incurring expenditures of some $5,000.

The written contract contained a *conspicuous* clause which limited defendant's damages in case of breach of contract:

The applicant agrees that the Telephone Company shall not be liable for errors in / or omissions of the directory advertising beyond the amount paid for the directory advertising omitted, or in which errors occur, for the issue life of the directory involved.

Plaintiff contends the **exculpatory clause** is contrary to public policy and should not be enforced. He asserts unconscionability of contract in two respects: the party's unequal bargaining position, and the form of the contract and the circumstances of its execution.

exculpatory clause
a clause which relieves one from liability

The court noted that the traditional view is that competent adults may make contracts on their own terms, provided they are neither illegal nor contrary to public policy. *Absent fraud, mistake, or duress,* a party who has fairly and voluntarily entered into such a contract is bound thereby, notwithstanding that it is unwise or disadvantageous to him. However, *such a rule is tempered by the principle of unconscionability.*

The UCC neither defines the concept of unconscionability nor provides the elements or perimeters of the doctrine. To define the doctrine is to limit its application, and to limit its application is to defeat its purpose.

Aids to a determination of whether a contract is unconscionable include:

1. Use of printed form or boilerplate contracts drawn skillfully by the party in the strongest economic position, which establish industrywide standards offered on a take-it-or-leave-it basis to the party in the weaker economic position.
2. A significant cost-price disparity or excessive price.
3. A denial of basic rights and remedies to a buyer of consumer goods.
4. Inclusion of penalty clauses.
5. Circumstances surrounding execution of the agreement including its commercial setting, purpose, and effect.
6. Hiding of disadvantageous clauses in a mass of fine print trivia or in places which are inconspicuous.
7. Phrasing clauses in language that is incomprehensible to a layman or that divert his attention from the problems raised by them or the rights given up through them.
8. Overall imbalance in the obligations and rights imposed by the bargain.
9. Exploitation of the underprivileged, unsophisticated, uneducated, and illiterate.
10. Inequality of bargaining or economic power.

The doctrine of unconscionability is used to police the excesses of certain parties who abuse their right to contract freely. It is directed against one-sided, oppressive, unfairly surprising contracts and not against the consequences per se of uneven bargaining power or even a simple old-fashioned bad bargain.

In this case the contract was not unconscionable because the form of the agreement directed the reader's attention to the clause limiting damages. The clause was clearly legible and was phrased in common words and was not one-sided. Moreover, the advertiser was an experienced businessman, and the omission arose from a clerical error which in its commercial setting was reasonably contemplated as falling within the purview of and purpose of the clause.

Judgment for defendant telephone company was affirmed.

Questions and Case Problems

1. The plaintiff, a union local, brought an action for damages resulting from the cancellation of a group life insurance policy by the defendant insurance company. The defendant seeks rescission of the contract because of an arithmetical error made by one of its employees in computing the premium rate. The court noted, and this was important to its decision, that the insurance company itself did not discover the mistake for over a year, and the estimate was within the same range of figures as other bids. Will the policy be rescinded? Why or why not? [*International Union of Operating Engineers Local 953 v. Central Nat. Life Ins. Co.*, 501 F.2d 902, cert. denied 420 U.S. 926 (1974).]

2. Two ships both named Peerless were leaving Bombay, India, one in October and the other in December. An offer was made to sell 125 bales of a commodity to be shipped from Bombay, India, to arrive on the ship Peerless. The buyer accepted the offer and had in mind the ship that sailed in October. The seller, on the other hand, believed that the agreement referred to the ship Peerless which was sailing in December. Each party, seller and buyer, believed in good faith that a different ship was intended in the contract. What result? [*Raffles v. Wichelhaus*, (English) 2 Hurlstone & Coltman 906 (1864).]

3. Plaintiff, Ott, an employee of the defendant, brought an action under the Age Discrimination In Employment Act, asserting fraud and breach of contract. The plaintiff had been discharged at the age of sixty, allegedly because of his age. He filed a complaint with the Department of Labor. He was notified that the defendant would voluntarily comply with the Act and that he would be reinstated in his job. The plaintiff claims that, while he was awaiting a job assignment, the defendant falsely represented to him that, if he would forego his rights under the Act, he would be hired as a consultant at least ten days each month and that he would make more money under the arrangement. The plaintiff accepted early retirement based upon the inducement of the defendant corporation and entered into the consulting agreement, which he now seeks to avoid. Can the agreement be avoided? [*Ott v. Midland-Ross Corp.*, 523 F.2d 1367 (1975).]

4. Plaintiff company, a creditor of the decedent, believed that a farm was jointly owned by the decedent and his wife and that the decedent's estate was insolvent. Defendant, the widow and **executrix,** did not disclose to plaintiff that the farm was owned solely by the decedent before plaintiff signed a release of its claim. Plaintiff now learns of the sole ownership of the decedent and seeks to set aside the release. What result? [*Hartford Accident & Indemnity Company v. Aiello*, 497 F.2d 257 (1974).]

executrix
a woman who is named in and administers a will

5. The defendants, who were convicted of offenses arising out of a jail break, appealed the conviction on the grounds that certain agreements had not been enforced. The first alleged agreement was with the commissioner of corrections, made while the commissioner was a hostage. It was that the inmates would not be punished for crimes arising out of the jail break attempt. The second alleged agreement was an order issued by a federal judge, in the presence of the inmates and their hostage, that no action be taken against the inmates for their participation in the jail break. Can the agreements be avoided? [*United States v. Gorham,* 523 F.2d 1088 (1975).]

6. The plaintiff, wife, discovered her husband, the defendant, in a homosexual act during their marriage. The husband and wife legally separated and a separation agreement was reached. Both parties were represented by counsel in negotiating the agreement. The defendant testified that he was very upset and was under psychiatric care throughout the period, and he executed the agreement only because of his fear of the disclosure of his homosexuality. He testified further that on one or two occasions when his wife was pressing for a resolution of their problems she remarked that he wouldn't want her to tell anyone about the incident but that plaintiff told members of her family, her roommate, and a mutual friend or two of the reason for the breakup of their marriage. Defendant had made all payments required under the agreement until he was hospitalized for a serious illness. After his recovery he decided not to make any further support payments. Can the defendant rescind the agreement based upon mental duress? [*Smith v. Jones,* 76 Misc.2d 656 (N.Y. 1973).]

7. This is an action by Mrs. Clark to set aside and reform a deed which was conveyed through a straw man to Mrs. Clark's sister and brother-in-law, as joint tenants. The plaintiff claimed that she had agreed to have the home constructed on the disputed property with the understanding that she would receive a fee simple title. The defendants contend that they had agreed to give the property to the plaintiff only on the condition that the property be titled in the three names as joint tenants. The court found that Mrs. Clark was sixty years of age, was managing all her affairs successfully, and had made arrangements with the contractor who built the house independent of her brother-in-law. Because of the marriage and blood relationship and the age of Mrs. Clark, can the deed be reformed because of a confidential relationship? [*McCoy v. Clark,* 319 A.2d 314 (Md. 1974).]

8. Plaintiff, wife, brought action for breach of contract based upon terms of a separation and property settlement agreement. Defendant, husband, admitted having executed the agreement approximately one year after institution of a divorce action but denied its validity, alleging undue influence and unfair persuasion exercised by the wife over his free will. Some pertinent facts are that the husband rejected prior offers of settlement attempts. In general, he conducted himself in a manner consistent with furthering his own individual interests. The lower trial court, however, had said that the agreement did not represent a fair and equitable distribution of community property, noting the burdensome requirement of alimony payment upon the husband. Should the contract be set aside on the grounds of undue influence? [*Wick v. Wick,* 489 P.2d 19 (Ariz. 1971).]

9. Plaintiff, a wholesale parts distributor, distributes appliance parts of approximately forty manufacturers to local servicemen and retail dealers. Plaintiff entered into a distribution agreement with Philco. This agreement provided that either party could terminate at any time upon written notice of ninety days. Under the agreement, plaintiff was required to carry an adequate inventory of Philco parts. The agreement further provided that, upon termination of this agreement, the distributor shall cease to be an authorized Philco distributor and will resell and deliver to Philco *upon demand* such Philco products still within the hands of the distributor. This repurchase will be at a mutually agreed price but not in excess of Philco's current distributor price for said products and materials. Upon termination of the agreement, Philco notified the plaintiff that they did not intend to demand repurchase of the parts. Plaintiff was unable to market most of his remaining Philco inventory. Philco refused a later demand to buy back the parts. Plaintiff's complaint alleges that the termination provisions of the contract were unconscionable and sought reimbursement for its damages arising out of the termination. Should plaintiff be allowed to recover? You decide. [*W. L. May Co., Inc. v. Philco-Ford Corporation*, 543 P.2d 283 (Or. 1975).]

10. In *Johnson v. Mobil Oil Corporation*, 415 F.Supp. 264 (1976),[5] the court held that a contracting party having immense bargaining power has an affirmative duty to explain in layman's terms the meaning and possible consequences of a contractual obligation to be assumed by another contracting party who is an uncounseled layman. Because this was not done, a clause limiting liability was declared null and void. In *Wille v. Southwestern Bell Telephone Company*, 549 P.2d 903 (Kan. 1976),[6] a clause limiting liability was deemed valid and binding. Reconcile the two cases. Why in one instance deny the freedom to contract and in the next instance enforce it? Are the cases inconsistent?

---

[5] See p. 85.

[6] See p. 116.

Consideration/Value Given for a Promise

8

After you have read this chapter, you should be able to:

1. Discuss the law of consideration, recognizing that it acts as a limitation on the freedom to contract.
2. Recognize that the law is moving in the direction of not requiring consideration in more and more instances so as to achieve a better sense of fairness to the parties involved and a better understanding of their intentions about assuming legal obligations.
3. Appreciate the differences between the requirements of consideration, manifestation of mutual assent, and genuineness of assent.
4. Note the exceptions to the requirement of consideration in both the common law and the Uniform Commercial Code.
5. Apply the objective tests used to determine whether consideration exists.

Introduction

consideration
the legal price bargained for a promise and inducing a party to enter into a contract

Consideration as *value* and as the *price for a promise* is a basic requirement for a contract. The concept of consideration is: What did the promisor request and receive for his or her promise to which he or she was not already legally entitled? (A promises B $5 for mowing A's lawn. Mowing the lawn is the consideration/ value for A's promise, which, stated legally, says "In consideration of your mowing my lawn, I'll pay you $5.")

However, the law, by case decision and by statute, is reflecting a trend in public policy of making more and more exceptions to this requirement in order to achieve a better sense of fairness to the parties in particular transactions and a better understanding of their intentions about assuming legal obligations.

The fact that the requirement of consideration must be satisfied to have a *simple contract* can be better understood by learning how the concept of consideration developed and how it relates to the *freedom to contract.*

seal
a symbol attached to a writing attesting that it is a legal document

A type of formal contract, a *contract under* **seal,** did not require consideration to prove its validity or enforceability. It was presumed that if one pressed his signet ring into wax on a contractual document, the person had committed himself to the obligation evidenced by the document and truly intended to be bound by his word.

A signet ring bearing some symbol normally was restricted in use to nobles. Merchants wishing to engage in trade and commerce found it necessary to prove to the court that they truly wanted and intended to be bound to a contractual obligation. In most cases merchants were not nobles and therefore could not resort to the use of a seal to satisfy the concerns of the law. Thus, the concept of consideration developed to substitute for the necessity of a seal to show that a common person intended to be bound to a contractual obligation.

Historically, then, it is easily seen why the requirement of consideration is important to the freedom to contract. It is a *further limitation on our ability to create a contract.* By requiring that consideration be present, as well as manifestation of mutual assent and genuineness of assent, the law can be more satisfied that the parties to a contract *want to be bound to the obligation.* Otherwise, consideration as value would not be requested and given for a promise.

By case development and under the Uniform Commercial Code numerous exceptions to the requirement of consideration are being discovered.

Consideration—A Third Test to Determine Intent to Contract

In previous chapters we discussed the concern of the law to determine *whether the parties to a contract truly wanted and intended to be bound to an obligation.* There are three tests to make this determination, all of which are necessary elements in order to have a *contract.* They are: (1) manifestation of mutual assent by offer and acceptance; (2) genuineness of assent; and (3) consideration. We have already discussed the first two, and now we will consider the third, *consideration.*

Unlike the concept of *genuineness of assent,* wherein a *subjective test* was applied to determine whether the parties' manifestation of mutual assent was an act of free will, consideration requires the satisfaction of two *objective* requisites. One is that **detriment** be given for the return obligation by both parties to the contract under the assumption that detriment to one party is normally of benefit to another party. The other requisite is that the detriment be bargained for. (A contracted with B to dig a ditch for B. A's digging is a detriment to A given by A in return for B's obligation to pay A. A's digging is a benefit to B, and B's payment is a benefit to A.)

detriment
the doing, or forbearing from doing, something by a party who had no previous legal obligation so to do or refrain from doing

The detriment by one party is the price, value, or consideration for the promise of the other party justifying enforcement of the promise. The detriment also indicates the intent to contract, as does the promise requesting the detriment.

The Bargain Theory

Under the common law, the basic theory of consideration was the *bargain* theory with two major exceptions, *promissory estoppel* and *moral basis of consideration.* Only the bargain theory demands the satisfaction of the requirements of *detriment bargained for,* next to be explained. When applicable, the two exceptions require something different to show that consideration is present. The concerns of the promissory estoppel and moral basis of consideration are different from that which is traditional to the concept of consideration. The concern is that *equity and justice be done* in the contractual setting rather than the concern about whether the parties intended to commit themselves to a contractual obligation.

The concept of detriment.

Detriment Bargained For

Detriment is legal value. Legal value is *the giving up of a legal right that one has by law to do or not do something (forbearance), or the assumption of a legal duty to do or not do something not otherwise imposed by law.* In the following case the plaintiff mother gave up a legal right which she honestly believed she had, even though its exercise would not have produced a result in her favor. Her forbearance constituted a detriment and consideration for the defendant's promise, making it a contract.

Facts

Plaintiff, mother, brought suit against a claimed putative father to recover for breach of an oral agreement under which he was to pay birth expenses and to support a child upon condition that the plaintiff would refrain from instituting bastardy proceedings. The putative father did not carry out his part of the oral agreement and, in a subsequent bastardy proceeding, upon medical proof in the form of blood tests, it was shown that he could not have fathered the child.

Decision

Judgment for the mother. The court enforced the agreement.

Reasoning

Forbearance to sue for a lawful claim or demand is sufficient consideration where the promise to pay is for a forbearance. The party forbearing must have an honest intention to prosecute litigation which is not frivolous, vexatious, or unlawful and which he or she believes to be well founded. The court found in this case that the mother believed the putative father to actually be the father of the child, and therefore her forbearance to sue was valid, good, and sufficient consideration.

Fiege v. Boehm, 123 A.2d 316 (Md. 1956).

Forms of Detriment

The quantity test[1] illustrates some forms that detriment can take. Consideration is unique in that it requires that the offer and acceptance contain bargained-for legal rights and duties.

Objective Test.   Whether the above requirement of detriment has been met can be objectively determined by ascertaining if legal value has been given by the parties to the contract. Such legal value need not have economic value. In the following case the court held that the detriment may be in the form of a buyer's promise to purchase all its requirements exclusively from a particular supplier, as well as in the form of a supplier's promise to supply all such buyer requirements.

appellee
a party against whom an appeal is taken

appellant
a party who appeals a case decision against him

Facts

Colorado Central Power Co., a wholesaler, had contracted to supply Intermountain Rural Electric Ass'n., a retailer, with all its requirements of electricity for a stated period of time. Intermountain purchased some of its requirements from Colorado but also purchased some of its requirements from others. Colorado sought damages for the lost purchases made from others. The lower court found for Intermountain. Colorado appealed.

Decision

The court of appeals found for the wholesaler, Colorado, reversing the lower court.

Reasoning

The appeals court held that, under Colorado law, a contract which provides that one will purchase requirements for a specified term is *not* unenforceable on the ground that it lacks mutuality of obligation. Consideration is present because one party has promised to supply a reasonable quantity and the other party has promised not to buy its requirements from anyone else.

Intermountain Rural Electric Ass'n. v. Colorado Central Power Co., 322 F.2d 516 (1963).

---

[1] See pp. 91–92.

Bargained For.   Whether or not legal value has been *bargained for* is decided by whether legal value was *mutually requested. This determination will be made objectively by looking at the facts of the contractual setting and deciding as a reasonable person whether the request has been made.* This is illustrated by the following case.

Facts

The plaintiff, executor of the deceased payee, not a **holder in due course,** sued to recover an amount allegedly due on a promissory note. The defendant stated that he was asked by the decedent woman to sign, with her son, as an accommodation co-maker on a promissory note payable to the decedent as payee (the person named in the note to whom it was to be paid). Defendant stated that he told her he was not interested in financing her son, but she said "I will never ask you or call on you for paying this note or any part of this note." Defendant further stated that the decedent had asked him to sign the note as a favor to her so as to give her son as the other co-maker an added sense of responsibility.

Decision

Judgment for the defendant.

Reasoning

The court concluded that there was no consideration for the note. The court pointed out that the plaintiff's argument failed to recognize the fundamental principle that the consideration must be bargained for; it must be the thing which the parties agree shall be given in exchange for the promise. The court recognized that the alleged benefits to the decedent and detriment to the defendant of the note *could* have been consideration for the promise of the defendant *had they been bargained for and intended it as such.* But, since it was *not* bargained for as such, it could *not* act as consideration for the note.

Colorado National Bank of Denver v. Bohm, 286 F.2d 494 (1961).

holder in due course
the innocent holder for value of a negotiable instrument (e.g., check, negotiable promissory note)

Adequacy and Mutuality of Obligation

If only one party to a proposed contract has been requested to give legal value, no binding contractual obligation will be formed, under the general principle that if one party is not bound to a contract (did not give consideration), the other is not bound.

Adequacy of consideration does not deal with a problem of economic value directly. However, where the detriment (legal value) exchanged is economically worthless or *greatly* disproportionate in value, it will not be adequate consideration if it can be shown it was *not intended* to be consideration. *Adequacy questions* for the most part limit themselves to questions of *whether consideration was intended or whether a contract was intended at all.* (For example, perhaps a gift was intended and the object of the gift was not meant to be consideration for any promise.) This is illustrated by the following case where the $1.00 was never paid and was not meant to be consideration for the promise of the defendants to divide sale proceeds according to an agreement.

Facts

This is an action by one brother and by an administrator of a second brother against a sister and a third brother, defendants, for shares in proceeds of the sale of realty as promised by the sister and the third brother under a written contract with the mother. The agreement with the mother was as follows: "In consideration of the sum of $1 to them paid by Julia A. Allen (the mother) the receipt whereof is hereby acknowledged, (they) promised and agreed that, in the event of the sale of the property during their lifetime, they would divide the proceeds equally among themselves. . . ." This they did not do. They introduced oral evidence that they were never paid $1 by the mother.

Decision

Judgment for the sister and the third brother, defendants.

Reasoning

The court found that the written agreement was without consideration and unenforceable. The court reasoned as follows: if, under a written contract, $1 is intended as the consideration and is paid and accepted as such, it is sufficient consideration. If, however, no consideration for a contract was intended and none is given, recital of a consideration in the written contract cannot make the promise enforceable. Therefore, a stated consideration which is a mere pretense and not a reality is not sufficient consideration. The court indicated that the $1 was never paid by the mother and that the defendants signed the agreement to please their mother. Thus, where there was no actual consideration but only a stated consideration in the written agreement, the promise contained in such agreement was without consideration and was unenforceable because it was never intended to act as consideration.

Allen v. Allen, 133 A.2d 116 (D.C. 1957).

Applications

Past Consideration.   Under the bargain theory, "past consideration" is no consideration. Thus, legal value given to support a *prior* contract can not be used or brought forward to support a new contract. (A promises to pay B an additional $1,000 if B will perform the contract previously made by them. B's obligation to perform the previous contract is not legal value for A's new promise. A's promise is not a contract.) Nor can one already under a *legal duty* offer the performance of that duty as consideration for a contract. The right already exists for the other contracting party. Therefore, a promise not to commit a tort or crime, or a promise by a public official to perform a public duty, can not act as consideration for a contract. In the following case a husband's promise to his wife to pay her for performing services which a wife was reasonably expected to perform was not a contract because, by marriage, she was already obligated to render such services.

Facts

At the age of 31, plaintiff married the decedent, 71 years old, and lived with him until his death fifteen years later, with a child born of the marriage. Plaintiff sued the executor of the estate of the decedent seeking performance of his following statement: "I promise to pay to my wife, on condition, the sum of $5,000 providing she stays with me while I live and takes care of things as she always has done; this note not due for six months after my death, and to bear no interest until due. This note to have no lien on my property while I live. Providing that should my wife die before me, this note will become due to her father, Curtis Stanfield. Signed and dated."

Decision

Judgment for the executor.

Reasoning

The court held that the agreement was without consideration. The court held that the agreement to pay the wife for performing services imposed by marital relations was void as against public policy. The services contemplated in the note are reasonably to be performed by a wife under the surrounding circumstances and are implied in the marital contract and furnish no consideration for the obligation. A wife can only contract with her husband for services as are outside of the purely domestic relations implied in the marital contract. The wife here was doing nothing more than she was already legally bound to do.

Frame v. Frame, 36 S.W.2d 152 (Tex. 1931).

Liquidated and Unliquidated Debt. In a *liquidated debt,* the *amount* of the debt has been agreed to by the parties or is ascertainable by a standard. In an *unliquidated debt,* the amount of the debt is unascertained. (Pursuant to the contract, A performed services for B. The contract did not state what amount B was to pay A.) In a *disputed debt* or claim, the person against whom the debt is asserted *honestly and reasonably believes it not to be valid,* but the claimant disagrees. (A performs a service for B and claims $150 as its value, but B honestly and reasonably believes and contends that he never requested the service.)

An attempt to discharge a liquidated debt by doing something *less* than what is required by the contract even though accepted is ineffective, unless a *gift* is made by the creditor of the remaining legal duty not performed. The doing of something *more* than what was initially bargained for will discharge the debt. Thus, when a creditor promises to discharge the debtor if he will pay a *lesser* amount *at an earlier date* is something *more* than he was obligated to do and, therefore, he is discharged from the debt.

A **composition** (agreement) outside of bankruptcy will discharge liquidated debts. The agreement by some or all of the creditors with their insolvent or financially embarrassed debtor, each to take something less than what is owed to him, is sufficient new legal detriment bargained for to bind the creditors to the new agreement which, when performed, will discharge the previous liquidated debts. The mutual promises of the creditors provide the consideration for each other. This reflects public policy.

composition (outside of bankruptcy) an agreement among some or all of the creditors with their insolvent or financially embarrassed debtor, each to take something less than what is owed to him and, on the debtor's performance, the debtor is discharged fully

Consideration/Value Given for a Promise   127

An acceptance of something *less* than what is demanded satisfies and discharges an *unliquidated debt* because each of the parties to the contract has suffered detriment by foregoing the opportunity to have a court determination of what is owed. This type of discharge is a form of compromise which, when performed, is technically called an **accord and satisfaction.**

Promissory Estoppel

The concept of **promissory estoppel** is an exception to the bargain theory of consideration. It requires that certain elements exist: (1) an existing promise (2) made with the expectation that it will be relied upon (3) justifiably relied upon substantially (4) to the injury of the promisee should the promise not be enforced. In the typical situation, no detriment or benefit is given by one of the parties to the contract. Under the *bargain theory of consideration* there would be no contract because of lack of mutuality of obligation. However, *in limited circumstances,* a contract will be found because of the need to promote strongly felt public policy, justice, and equity. In the following case a promise was enforced to avoid injustice even though it did not ask for the legal detriment which was rendered.

Facts
The plaintiff, a low bidder for a public works contract, brought an action against the defendant following the defendant's awarding of the contract to a higher bidder. The plaintiff sought to recover the expense it incurred in its unsuccessful participation in the competitive bidding process, the monies it had expended in a successful prior litigation setting aside the contract awarded to the higher bidder, and lost profits.

Decision
Judgment for the plaintiff. The plaintiff had stated a cause of action for the recovery of monetary damages in promissory estoppel.

Reasoning
In its solicitation for bids, the defendant had clearly promised to award the contract to the lowest responsible bidder and the plaintiff had reasonably relied on that promise to his detriment. The court held that injustice could only be avoided by reaching the conclusion it had. The court concluded that an award of monetary damages would be in the public interest as well as in the plaintiff's interest, since it would deter future misconduct by public entities.

Swinerton & Walberg Co. v. City of Inglewood-Los Angeles County Civic Center Authority, 114 Cal.Rptr. 834 (1974)

Pledge of a Gift
A pledge to an **eleemosynary** institution (e.g., church, United Way) is not enforceable under the bargain theory of consideration because the one making the promise to give a gift has not bargained for anything (detriment) in return. For

---

accord and satisfaction
a new contract (accord) which discharges a party from a previous contractual obligation; the old contract is discharged (satisfied)

promissory estoppel
an equitable principle enforcing a gratuitous promise as a contract, without consideration

eleemosynary
charitable, benevolent

example, A promises to contribute $100 toward the cost of a new organ for a church. However, a promise has been made. It is calculated to be relied upon. It may be justifiably relied upon. If relied on, the institution will suffer loss if it is not carried out, and there is a strongly felt public policy to assist such organizations by promissory estoppel.

In limited situations, promises between closely related parties have been enforced under the concept of promissory estoppel because of the need of justice.

The evidence of the need to do **equity** and fair dealing is causing the courts to apply the concept to the *business* promise in limited circumstances. The following case illustrates the application of promissory estoppel in enforcing a business promise.

equity
principles of justice and fairness which developed when the relief at common law was inadequate

Facts
The decedent purchased a life insurance policy from the plaintiff insurance company on the representation made by its agent that the policy would cover war and aviation risks. The decedent relied on the representation and canceled his existing insurance coverage which covered such risks in order to buy the new insurance. The new policy, however, did not cover war or aviation risks. The decedent was killed in a helicopter crash in Viet Nam while in the Marines. The claim was submitted to the plaintiff's chief claims consultant, who approved the payment of the claim. The plaintiff thereafter sought to recover the money paid.

Decision
The court held that the money need not be returned.

Reasoning
The insurance agent's promise to obtain a policy covering war and aviation risks induced the deceased defendant to drop his other policy in reliance on the promise and, therefore, under the doctrine of promissory estoppel, plaintiff was bound to honor the claim. *This is an example of an application of promissory estoppel to a business promise.*

Prudential Insurance Company of America v. Clark, 456 F.2d 932 (1972).

Moral Obligation

The **moral obligation** of consideration is another exception to the bargain theory of consideration. It bears some relationship to quasi contract. The reader will remember that in quasi contract the court finds that the promise necessary to the formation of a contract exists as a matter of law. Under the moral obligation theory of consideration, the court causes consideration to exist *as a matter of law* when no basis exists under either the bargain theory of consideration or promissory estoppel. Consideration is made to exist because the law recognizes that, morally, in a *limited set of circumstances,* the promise should be enforced. This is illustrated by the following case.

moral obligation
an exception to the bargain theory of consideration

Facts

The father of a minor operating an automobile, which in an accident overturned and injured a minor guest passenger, promised to furnish the guest medical assistance and care to relieve the suffering of the guest. The father had partially executed this promised obligation by making partial payment for medical expenses and then refused to pay the rest of the reasonable value of medical and surgical expenses necessarily incurred for the further treatment of the injuries of the minor guest. The minor guest, plaintiff, sued the father of the minor driver.

Decision

Judgment for the plaintiff, minor guest.

Reasoning

While the court agreed that the obligation was without the normal basis of consideration, it held that the father of the minor driver was obligated to pay the medical expenses on the basis that he had expressed sympathy and anxiety for the care of the plaintiff and was aware of the fact that such care was needed. He was also aware that the plaintiff did not have the financial ability to obtain the needed medical services. Under such circumstances, the court felt there was some moral obligation resting on the defendant. The partial performance of the obligation was believed by the court to evidence a recognition from the start of this moral obligation. It was the opinion of the court that the defendant should be bound to pay the reasonable value of the medical services.

Medberry v. Olcovich, 59 P.2d 551 (Cal. 1936).

Statutes

statute of limitations
a statute limiting the time in which a claim may be asserted in court; expiration bars enforcement of the claim

In situations where contractual obligations have been discharged by the passage of a **statute of limitations** or a proceeding in bankruptcy, a promise to pay a debt due under the discharged contract will reinstate the debt even though this runs counter to the rule that past consideration is no consideration. The new promise is enforceable *in accordance with its terms.* In most cases the new promise must be in writing. There is some justification for this holding when one recognizes that good and adequate consideration was given in the previous contract and that the court is merely requiring a party, by his new promise, to carry out what he was obligated to carry out before he was discharged by an operation of law.

bankruptcy
a federal procedure whereby a debtor's nonexempt assets are gathered together and used to discharge the debtor from most of his debts

The new federal Bankruptcy Reform Act of 1978, sec. 524(c)(d), makes new special provision for a debtor who wishes to reinstate, wholly or partially, his obligation discharged in **bankruptcy,** distinguishing between *any* debtor in (c), and a debtor who is an *individual* in (c) and (d). The subject is discussed in chapter 52, Bankruptcy under the Bankruptcy Reform Act of 1978. Basically, any agreement between the debtor and the creditor for such reinstatement will be enforced only if: the agreement was made before discharge was granted; it was not rescinded within thirty days after it became enforceable; and, if the debtor is an individual and it is a consumer debt not secured by real property, it is in the debtor's best interest and it will not impose undue hardship on the debtor or his dependent. If the debtor is an individual, in addition to this the court shall hold a hearing and inform the debtor in person that such an agreement is not required and the legal effect and consequences of such an agreement.

The Uniform Commercial Code

Under the Uniform Commercial Code, consideration no longer is required in the following instances: to support a "firm offer"[2] (UCC 2–205); to support an agreement which modifies a contract for the sale of goods (UCC 2–209(1)); to discharge a claim arising out of an alleged breach of contract, if the aggrieved party has signed and delivered a written waiver or renunciation (UCC 1–107). In other sections of the Code, consideration has been dispensed with for other purposes.[3]

In the following case under the Code, the court would have enforced a subcontractor's bid as a firm offer, which does not require consideration, except that the bid was not a firm offer.

Facts

A subcontractor, defendant, had bid on a subcontract for a general contractor, plaintiff, who used this bid along with others for his own bid on a job which he was awarded. The subcontractor refused to honor its bid. The subcontractor's bid was contained in a letter which identified it as an estimate and closed with this line "Thank you very much for the opportunity to quote" and the signature of the subcontractor. The general contractor sued for breach of contract.

Decision

For the defendant subcontractor.

Reasoning

The court noted that the firm offer provision in the Code reverses the common law rule that an offer for a period of time which is not supported by *consideration* can be revoked anytime prior to acceptance. The court held that the bid did not meet the requirements of a writing under UCC 2-205, which by its terms gives assurance that it will be held open for a stated or *reasonable time*. The court stated that the concept of promissory estoppel might be applicable to this case.

E. A. Coronis Assocs. v. M. Gordon Constr. Co., 216 A.2d 246 (N.J. 1966).

Summary Statement

1. Consideration is a necessary element to the existence of a contract though numerous exceptions exist.
2. Under the bargain theory of consideration, two objective tests must be satisfied before consideration will be found. These are (a) detriment and (b) bargained for.

---

[2] See pp. 95–96.

[3] See Commercial Paper, UCC 3–605, Letters of Credit, 5–105.

3. Detriment bargained for requires that the giving of legal value be a condition for bringing the contract into existence.
4. Legal value can be recited as a formula: doing or refraining from doing something which one was under no previous legal obligation to do or not do.
5. Mutuality of obligation requires that if one is not bound to a contract, the other party to the contract is not bound.
6. Adequacy of consideration deals with a question of intention.
7. Past consideration is no consideration, with exceptions.
8. An unliquidated debt can be discharged by compromise.
9. Promissory estoppel is applied in situations where the doing of equity is required.
10. The moral basis of consideration, like quasi contract, dispenses with the requirement of consideration as defined in the bargain theory or in promissory estoppel.
11. The Uniform Commercial Code in many instances has dispensed with requiring that consideration be present in order to have a contract.

The following case is included in depth to illustrate why consideration exists in contract law.

Baehr v. Penn-O-Tex Oil Corporation
104 N.W.2d 661 (Minn. 1960)

Plaintiff, Baehr, sued the defendant, Penn-O-Tex Oil Corporation, for rent because of an alleged breach of contract. Baehr leased gasoline filling stations to one Kemp, who was heavily in debt to the defendant. The plaintiff received a letter from Kemp stating that his (Kemp's) assets were all tied up by the defendant and this was why he had not paid the rent due on the leased stations.

A short time after receiving Kemp's letter, Baehr called the agent of the *defendant* and asked about payment of the filling station rents. Defendant told Baehr "that Mr. Kemp's affairs were in a very mixed up form but that he would get them straightened out and mail *Baehr* . . . checks for the rents."

Hearing nothing further, plaintiff wrote a letter to defendant asking what he had to do to get his rent checks and added "or will I have to give it to an attorney to sue?"

Defendant wrote the plaintiff indicating that they were trying to help Kemp "but in no way *were* they operating the business." The letter denied knowledge of or responsibility for any rent due the plaintiff.

After receiving the letter, the plaintiff called the defendant demanding payment of the rent.

The defendant's agent said the defendant would pay the rent. He would take it up with the home office.

The rent was never paid by defendant, and the communications described took place over an eighteen-month period of time.

The court reasoned that if it accepted the plaintiff's version of the statements made by the agent of the defendant as recorded, there was an unequivocal assurance given that the rents would be paid—a promise.

But the court noted "the fact that a promise is given does not necessarily mean a contract was made." Not every promise is legally enforceable. It is not practical nor reasonable to expect full performance of every assurance given whether it be thoughtless, casual, and gratuitous, or deliberately and seriously made.

The test, the court stated, that has been developed by the *common law* for determining the enforceability of promises is the *doctrine of consideration*. Consideration requires that a contractual promise be the product of a bargain. It means a negotiation resulting in the voluntary assumption of an obligation by one party upon condition of an act or forbearance by the other *(legal value)*. *Consideration thus ensures that the promise enforced as a contract is not accidental, casual, or gratuitous but has been uttered intentionally as the result of some deliberation, manifested by reciprocal bargaining or negotiation.* In this view, the requirement of *consideration is no mere technicality, historic anachronism, or arbitrary formality.* It is an attempt to be as reasonable as we can in deciding which promises constitute contracts.

Consideration, as essential evidence of the parties' intent to create a legal obligation, must be something adopted and regarded by the parties as such. In substance, a contractual promise must be of logical form: "If . . . [consideration] is given . . . then I promise . . ."

In this case, though a promise was made by the defendant, a contract was not created. While plaintiff suffered detriment by forbearing to sue Kemp, such detriment was not bargained for by the defendant. Hence the plaintiff did not give consideration for the defendant's promise. The voluntary relinquishment of a legal right is not consideration. Nor did the court find factually that there was evidence that either party took the defendant's assurances seriously or acted upon them in any way. Judgment for defendant.

Questions and Case Problems

1. Under the original contract, the contractor and landowner believed that there would be sufficient dirt available upon the northern half of a unit of a farm to complete the terms of a contract to level and plane farm land. Both parties contemplated that this would be accomplished by moving dirt from high points to low points within the unit. This turned out not to be possible, and the landowner and the contractor subsequently orally agreed to an additional payment for the work to be done by obtaining dirt from the southern half of the unit in order to complete the job. Was there sufficient consideration for the agreement to make it a contract? [*Gannon v. Emtman*, 405 P.2d 254 (Wash. 1965).]

2. An agreement was made between prisoners, plaintiffs, and a director of a department of correction who was a hostage of a prisoner which gave the prisoners absolute immunity from prosecution if they would cease engaging in further violence in a prison uprising. The prisoners subsequently were tried and convicted for the criminal acts, and they then sued the U.S. Government, defendant, for breach of contract. Judgment for plaintiffs and the defendant appealed. What result? [*United States v. Bridgeman*, 523 F.2d 1099 (1975).]

3. The plaintiff, purchaser, sued for specific performance of an option contract for the sale of a trucking company. Defendant, seller, argued that there was no contract for lack of consideration because it provided that, as the company prospered, the purchase price would be reduced. What result? [*Ligon v. Parr,* 471 S.W.2d 1 (Ky. 1971).]

4. The plaintiff, Wells, entered into an agreement with one Lester Riley, the agreement stating that, in the event of a judgment against Lester Riley, the plaintiff would not garnishee his wages or levy on his property except that which could be obtained from insurance coverage. The agreement contained the following clause: "All this will be done in consideration of the sum of *one dollar and other value consideration paid* to him by defendant, Lester Riley." The plaintiff subsequently joined Lester Riley with the other defendants in this action contending that the agreement did not bind the plaintiff because the one dollar was never paid. What result? [*Wells v. Hartford Accident and Indemnity Company,* 459 S.W.2d 253 (Mo. 1970).]

5. The plaintiff, an 83-year-old married woman, contended that she was enticed and induced to leave her apartment and move in with the defendant, a 79-year-old widower, in a house on land which at the time he owned in fee simple. At a later date the defendant deeded to the plaintiff a fee simple interest in the house and land, reserving a life estate to himself. Shortly thereafter relationships became strained and an agreement was entered into. The agreement stated, "It is mutually agreed by and between the parties hereto that during the remainder of their life-times, they shall live together in harmony in the above-described residential premises. Neither shall have the right to dispossess the other from these premises." Shortly after the signing of this agreement, the defendant changed the locks on the doors of the house and refused to allow the plaintiff to reenter. The plaintiff claims that she has a right to reside in the house and brings this suit to enforce the contract. What result? [*Maszewski v. Piskadlo,* 318 So.2d 226 (Fla. 1975).]

6. The plaintiffs sued the representative of the estate of a man with whom they had signed a "contract" with a clause providing that the agreement could be cancelled by either party at any time they desired. What result? [*Cooper v. Jensen,* 448 S.W.2d 308 (Mo. 1969).]

7. Plaintiff, purchaser, brought this action for damages after defendant allegedly breached a contract by failing to convey the real property to the plaintiff in accordance with the terms of a deposit receipt (a form of real estate contract with a real estate agent) which the parties had executed. The contract for the sale of the real estate provided that the agreement was subject to the purchaser obtaining leases satisfactory to the purchaser. The lower court held for the defendant stating that the agreement was illusory and lacking in mutuality. The case has been appealed to the Supreme Court of California. What will the result be? [*Mattei v. Hopper,* 330 P.2d 625 (Cal. 1958).]

8. A retired union officer brought suit to compel a union retirement committee to pay the retired officer an increased pension. A compromise, arising from a disagreement between the retirement committee and the retired officer as to the salary on which the pension was to be based, was reached after the retired officer agreed to accept a pension based on a certain salary, waiving his right to a pension based on a higher salary. Over a period of time the union officer accepted retirement benefits based upon this compromise. Approximately two and a half years later the retired officer argued that his pension should be increased, alleging that it should have been based upon a higher salary. The request was denied. The officer filed a complaint in equity seeking to compel the retirement committee to pay him the requested higher pension. What result? [*Cohen v. Sabin,* 307 A.2d 845 (Pa. 1973).]

9. This is an action by plaintiff, an attorney, against a corporate client for compensation for legal and other services allegedly rendered by him to the corporation over a thirty-year period of time. As a defense to the action, defendant raises the statute of limitations, contending that the period of time required for discharging the obligation had passed previous to the institution of the suit by the plaintiff. Plaintiff had provided the defendant with a statement of charges owed to him shortly before the suit was instituted. The defendant responded to the statement of charges owed by acknowledging the debt and stating that it thought this was all that was due and owing. Without giving new consideration for the promise, can the attorney be successful in this suit? [*Beck v. Dutchman Coalition Mines Co.,* 269 P.2d 867 (Utah 1954).]

10. In *Baehr v. Penn-O-Tex Oil Corporation,* 104 N.W.2d 661 (Minn. 1960),[4] the court said "the requirement of consideration is no mere technicality, historic anachronism, or arbitrary formality. It is an attempt to be as reasonable as we can in deciding which promises constitute contracts." Evaluate this statement.

---

[4] See pp. 132–33.

9 Capacity / Ability to Create a Contract

After you have read this chapter, you should be able to:

1. Discuss the concept of capacity to make a contract and explain what purpose it serves in the law of contracts.
2. Recognize that there are individuals (a) who have no capacity to contract, (b) who have a limited capacity to contract, and (c) who can avoid the consequences of contract.
3. Be aware of the similarities and differences in the way classes of individuals avoid and ratify contracts.
4. Understand that necessaries occupy a unique position with regard to avoidance of contracts.
5. Perceive the current movement of the law to expand contractual capacity.

Introduction

The existence of the necessary *contractual capacity* of the parties is *an element* necessary to the formation of *a contract*. It is important to note that the capacity to create a contract provides yet *another barrier to our freedom* to create, through a contract, rights and duties not otherwise imposed by law.

The law associated with the capacity to create a contract recognizes that there are certain situations in which one should *not* be *allowed* to contract. Moreover, there is a recognition that certain persons should be given a chance to *escape* the consequences of a contract because they need protection. These are the important *value judgments* which have resulted in the law which determines one's capacity to create a contract.

A study of the law relating to the capacity to create a contract is a study of who has no capacity to contract, who has limited capacity to contract, and who can avoid the consequences of a contract.

Protection—Limited or No Capacity

When one is **adjudged** insane, any attempt to contract is **void**. He has no *capacity* to contract. A **trust** will normally give a trustee a *limited power* to contract to further the purpose of the trust. A corporation, which contracts through agents, can enter into contracts that only further the purpose contained in the corporate charter. Convicted felons in some states have a limited capacity to contract. In some states, as a protective public policy, a married woman can not act as a **surety** for her husband's debts. Enemy aliens can not contract or sue on contracts. Infants who are so young that they *can not understand* the significance of a contract have no capacity to contract.

These various situations, which run the full spectrum from no ability to contract to partial inability to contract, exist for various purposes—mainly protection and punishment.

Protection—Right to Avoid

A **voidable** contract is one which is subject to being avoided by a party or the parties and, on avoidance, is discharged. (A fraudulently induces B to contract with A. B has a power of avoidance, so the contract is voidable by B.) It *is* a good contract until it is avoided.

Those persons who are minors or infants under the law (below the age of 18 in most states, below 21 in a few states)[1] can *avoid* (rescind) their contracts. Avoidance of the contractual obligation is possible by those who are induced to enter into a contract because of insane delusions or by those who are so under the influence of drugs or alcoholic beverages that they *do not know* they are

adjudged
the result of a formal legal process

void
of no legal effect

trust
a legal device whereby legal title to property is held by one person (a trustee) for the benefit of a beneficiary

surety
a person who is legally obligated by contract for the performance of another's obligation to a third person

voidable contract
a contract which can be avoided by one or more of the parties

---

[1] The law disregards fractions of a day. Thus, a person born at 1:00 P.M. on November 11, 1960 becomes 18 at the *beginning* of the day of November 10, 1978.

Figure 9.1   Incapacity Table

Category of Person	Incapacity		Reason for Determination of Incapacity
	Total	Limited	
Adjudged insane	Yes		Inability to protect oneself
Trustee		Yes	To ensure that the purpose of a trust is carried out
Corporation		Yes	To ensure that the purpose of a corporation is carried out
Convicted felons		Yes	Punishment
Married women in special situations		Yes	Protection from undue influence
Infants of tender age	Yes		Inability to protect oneself
Infants not of a tender age		Yes	Inability to protect oneself
Enemy alien	Yes		Punishment

entering into a contract. Only the party with the power of avoidance can avoid the contract—e.g., the minor, not the adult; the insane person after becoming sane, but not the other contracting party.

The purpose for giving the right to avoid a contract is the value judgment of the law that these classes of people need protection from what might turn out to be an improvident act. This principle of law is in a state of evolution. In the following case a contract was set aside (avoided) because of a party's limited mental capacity and business competence.

Facts

This is an action to set aside certain business transacted by one deemed to be limited in mental capacity and business competence. The court found that the defendant ingratiated himself into the confidence of the plaintiff and fraudulently took advantage of the plaintiff's mental and physical infirmities and incompetency to induce the business which has been transacted. Both plaintiff and defendant immigrated to the United States from Austria, had known each other for many years, had common tastes and interests, and both spoke the Croatian language. Plaintiff was unable to read or write English, and because of his injuries it was extremely difficult for him to understand matters read or related to him, and he relied upon the defendant for explanations. The eyesight of the plaintiff was also impaired due to an unsuccessful operation on cataracts. He was also quite hard of hearing.

Decision

Judgment for plaintiff.

Reasoning

The court set aside the contract. The court stated that, where it is established that the mind of a party to a transaction has become infirm or his comprehension weakened by age, accident, or illness, the usual presumption of normality and capacity to contract is dissipated. The weakness of mind may not amount to absolute incapacity to transact any business at all, and the mental infirmity need not have been established judicially in order to require the person who has received benefits from dealings with one so afflicted to prove that they were not affected thereby. If one does not have sufficient understanding to protect one's own interests and mental strength to compete in the marketplace, he lacks capacity to transact ordinary business, and dealings with him may be viewed with caution.

Paskvan v. Mesich, 227 F.2d 646 (1955).

Avoidance is the **disaffirming** of a contract. This is done by a party to the contract manifesting that he or she no longer intends to be bound by a contract previously made by him or her. The following case illustrates how conduct was held to manifest an intent to avoid a contract.

Facts

The plaintiff obtained a confession of judgment against defendant on a note, and defendant sought to have the judgment set aside, arguing that he had timely disaffirmed the note. The defendant as a minor had used the proceeds of the note for the purchase of an automobile. He had made two payments on the car and was then drafted by the armed forces. He contacted the bank and told them to pick up the car, which they did and sold it for salvage for $30.

Decision
Judgment for defendant.

Reasoning
The court held that the contract had been disaffirmed. The court reasoned that, as a general rule, a contract of a minor may be avoided by any act showing unequivocally his renunciation of, or a disposition not to abide or be bound by, the contract made during minority. The court noted that disaffirmance or renunciation is a question of intent, and it seemed to the court that when the minor called the bank to pick up the car it was his manifestation of intent to disaffirm the note. There is no requirement for the nth degree of unequivocalness. To impose specificity and formality in the act of disaffirmance is to disregard the basis for the policy of law that protects minors from their improvident actions and which accords to them the right to disaffirm.

Logan County Bank v. Taylor, 295 N.E.2d 743 (Ill. 1973).

Avoidance (Disaffirmance) by Minors

When disaffirming a contract, a minor must return the consideration received by the minor if the minor still has it. Disaffirmance by a minor for contracts concerning **personal property** can occur anytime during minority and within a *reasonable time* after reaching majority. For **real property** contracts, most states

majority
the legal age at which
a minor becomes an
adult

require the minor to wait until reaching **majority** and give to him as a new adult a *reasonable time* thereafter in which to disaffirm. In the following case, forty years was held to be an unreasonable time.

Facts

Plaintiff filed this suit to establish his right to certain land in Macon County forty years after he became an adult. The plaintiff seeks to disaffirm a real property mortgage signed by him during his minority. The father of the plaintiff was the owner of a life estate in the real property, and the plaintiff was the **remainderman.** Both plaintiff and his father signed two notes and a mortgage encumbering the land. The mortgage was foreclosed on the land, and a judicial sale was held and the property was purchased by a third party. The defendant, an assignee of a judgment creditor, redeemed the property at a later date and received a sheriff's deed, which was recorded. The present defendants are children of the individual who redeemed the property. These children contend that they hold a fee simple interest through the sheriff's deed.

Decision

Judgment for defendants.

remainderman
a person who was not
a grantor of an estate
in land but who will
acquire the estate
after a preceding
estate has terminated

Reasoning

The court held that a deed or contract executed by a minor is only voidable, not void. It may be disaffirmed by the minor within a reasonable time after reaching majority. The court noted as a fact that forty years had gone by since plaintiff achieved his majority, that most of that time he knew that the mortgage had been foreclosed. Even though he had received advice from attorneys that his interest would be preserved because he signed the mortgage note when he was a minor, this does not preserve his right to disaffirm. Ignorance of legal rights and erroneous legal advice will not excuse delay in suing. The court held as a matter of law that the forty-year postponement under the circumstances in this case was a clear-cut unreasonable delay. The property remains in the defendants.

Longstreet v. Morey, 364 N.E.2d 602 (Ill. 1977).

The minor is entitled to get back all that was given by the minor as consideration for the contract, unless what was given was tangible personal property which was sold to another for value without notice that the property once belonged to a minor. This result is based upon section 2–403 of the Uniform Commercial Code.

Avoidance by Others

An insane person, alcoholic, or drug addict, if they qualify for the right to avoid a contract, must exercise the right within a *reasonable time* and must give back to the other party the consideration received or its equivalent value if they still have it.

If the other party *knew and took advantage of the disabled party,* the disabled party, like the minor, can avoid the contract and must return only that portion of the consideration he received and still has, and he, in turn, has the right to receive back what he gave as consideration. This is illustrated by the following case involving a mentally incompetent person.

Facts

Plaintiff, an administrator for the decedent, brought suit for the cancellation of a contract resulting in a note and for return of stock certificates securing such note from the defendant bank. The plaintiff alleges that the decedent was mentally incompetent at the time of the loan transaction and that the defendant bank's officers knew or should have known such incompetency, and that decedent received no benefit from the purported transaction. The defendant filed a motion to dismiss.

Decision

Motion denied.

Reasoning

The court stated that the general rule applicable to the issue before the court is that an instrument obtained from an incompetent person by one who is *ignorant* of the incompetency and who acted in good faith and gave a fair consideration will not be set aside unless the parties can be restored to their original positions. The court said this rule is not without its exceptions however. Where an instrument is obtained from an insane person by one having knowledge of his incompetence, the instrument will be set aside without requiring the restoration of the consideration received, this on the principle that anyone dealing with an insane person, knowing him to be insane, deals with him at his own peril and must bear the loss.

McElroy v. Security National Bank of Kansas City, Kansas, 215 F.Supp. 775 (1963).

Necessaries

What is a "necessary" is a question of fact. All authorities agree that those things *actually needed* for survival (food, clothing, shelter, and medical care) are necessaries. Generally, for the *minor* those things needed to maintain a social status equal to the station in life of one's peers are deemed to be necessaries. The flexibility of the concept as it has been applied to minors has resulted in contracts which indirectly provide survival needs (employment agency services, tools, etc.) and tuition fees for an undergraduate college education being considered necessaries. Something is not a necessary for a minor if the parents are willing, able, or have already provided necessaries. A contract for these items by a minor is considered not to be for a necessary. In the following case the court held that it was for the trial court to decide whether retaining an attorney for a minor was a necessary.

Facts

This action was brought by the plaintiff, father of an injured minor child. The minor had been injured in an accident and the father had sought legal advice. The father, on behalf of the child, entered into a contingent fee arrangement which allowed the attorney to recover forty percent of any judgment returned. The following question was certified to the Florida Supreme Court: "Is the contingent fee agreement binding on the minor child or is it the duty of the court to set a reasonable attorney's fee for services rendered to the minor child without regard to the contingency agreement?"

Decision

It depends upon necessity and reasonableness.

Reasoning

The court held as follows. A contingent fee arrangement entered into on behalf of a minor will be binding on the minor if the trial court determines that it was reasonably *necessary* to employ an attorney on behalf of the minor and that the contract by which the attorney was employed was fair and reasonable at the time it was entered into.

Phillips v. Nationwide Mut. Ins. Co., 347 So.2d 465 (Fla. 1977).

While those who have the right to avoid a contract can avoid a contract for *necessaries,* they must *keep* the necessaries, and they remain liable to the other party to pay a *reasonable value* for the items or services provided. Reasonable value will normally be something less than the usual contract price.

Ratification

ratification
(in contracts) a person's waiver of his power of avoidance

Ratification is the opposite of avoidance. It is a party's manifestation of intent to continue to be bound by a contract which he could have avoided. The ratifying party waives his power of avoidance.

Ratification by a minor can occur only within a reasonable time *after the minor reaches the age of majority.* For insane persons or those under the disability of alcohol or drugs, ratification can take place only *after the disability is removed, or* through the action of a **guardian** or other legal representative. Ratification may be made by conduct, as is illustrated by the following case in which a minor's conduct after majority ratified his contract made during minority.

guardian
a person legally entrusted with the custody and/or the property of another

Facts

This suit by a father against a son was based on an alleged contractual agreement of the son to repay college expenses. The father had discussed with the son upon graduation from high school the financing of his education to lead to a degree of doctor of dental surgery. Eight years later, after the son completed graduate school, the father discussed with the son the fact that the cost of the son's education had amounted to some $30,000 and

that he expected repayment in monthly installments of $400. Shortly after this discussion, the son wrote the father contending that only $24,000 was due for his education and that he would repay this at $100 per month. He paid under this letter agreement for some three years before contending that nothing was owed to the father.

Decision

Judgment for plaintiff, father.

Reasoning

Contracts of infants can be ratified upon attaining majority. Ratification does not require new consideration to make it binding. The writing by the infant acknowledging a $24,000 debt and the payments for three years after majority in honoring of that statement could be construed as ratification. Since the jury determined that it was ratification, its finding should stand.

Robertson v. Robertson, 229 So.2d 642 (Fla. 1969).

Minor's Misrepresentation of Age

It has been said that the right of a minor to disaffirm a contract, while shielding the minor, could be used by the minor as a sword against an adult. Thus, if the minor misrepresented his age and induced the adult to enter into a contract thinking the minor was an adult, the minor would have the possibility of avoidance but the adult would be bound to the contract.

In earlier common law, the court did not allow the adult to sue the minor (who generally is responsible for his own crimes and torts) for the damage caused by misrepresentation. The principle was that one could not do indirectly what one could not do directly. Allowing the suit in tort would have the indirect effect of holding the minor to the contract which he was capable of avoiding.

Today in misrepresentation cases a compromise seems to be developed by case law which retains the right of the minor to avoid the contract but requires him to return the *total* consideration given by the adult for the contract. Also, in some cases the minor's misrepresentation causes the contract to be *voidable by the adult party* to the contract. This is illustrated by the following case.

Facts

Plaintiff sued to recover on a loan of $22,000 made to defendant and her husband on a real estate mortgage to build a home. The defendant, who was nineteen and a minor at the time of taking out the loan, recited in an affidavit of title in three places that she was of the age of majority in seeking a loan. After the loan was made, she and her husband built the home, separated, abandoned the property, and defaulted on the mortgage payments. In a subsequent foreclosure suit on the mortgage, the defendant counterclaimed, asserting her infancy, and disaffirmed the mortgage agreement, and she demanded a return from the plaintiff of personal funds used by her in making the mortgage payments and improving the premises.

Decision

Judgment for plaintiff.

Reasoning

The court held for the plaintiff because the defendant misrepresented her age. Infancy is no defense to an action to recover money advanced to an infant on the basis of misrepresentation of majority reasonably relied upon by a lender. While the defendant here tenders her entire interest in the real estate to the plaintiff for the return of her advances, the difficulty is that the plaintiff can not be made whole. It is entitled to be made whole, and the plaintiff is entitled to complete foreclosure free of any claim of the defendant except that she may have an interest in surplus funds.

Manasquan Savings and Loan Ass'n. v. Mayer, 236 A.2d 407 (N.J. 1967).

Special Cases

In some cases a minor can not disaffirm a contract completely or can only partially disaffirm it. Contracts which, by statute, can not be disaffirmed include purchases of corporate investments, insurance policy purchases, contract of marriage, and enlistment in the armed forces. An **emancipated minor** does not lose his power of avoidance.

emancipated minor
a minor whose parents have given up their rights to take care of the minor and to have custody of and to claim the minor's earnings

Contracts that can be only partially disaffirmed would be partnership contracts. While the contract creating the partnership can be avoided, the capital committed by the minor to the partnership must remain available to the creditors of the partnership.

Summary Statement

1. Certain classes of persons have no capacity to contract, others have limited capacity to contract, and still others can escape the consequence of a contract.
2. The right to avoid a contract is in a process of evolving in two directions: one, contract law is becoming more specific about who can avoid a contract; two, it is limiting the right to avoid a contract.
3. Avoidance and ratification require a person's manifestation of an intent within a reasonable time. In avoidance, the intent is that one will no longer be bound to a contract; in ratification, the intent is that one will remain bound to a contract by waiving the power to avoid.
4. Normally a minor or a disadvantaged party with limited capacity to contract need only return what remains of that consideration which he received in order for him to get restitution—get back all consideration which he had given.
5. In cases of a minor's misrepresentation of age, or of contracts by those not known to be incapacitated, *all* consideration must be returned by such persons. For contracts where the subject matter is necessaries, such persons must keep what they have received and pay for their reasonable value.
6. This area of law is still evolving.

The following case is included in depth to illustrate the value judgment that the law needs to protect people in the legal area of capacity. The case also illustrates the current trend in this area of law of making limitations on who and what will be protected and how protection will be afforded.

Gastonia Personnel Corporation v. Rogers
172 S.E.2d 19 (N.C. 1970)

The defendant was graduated from high school when he was seventeen. By the time he was nineteen years old he was emancipated and married. He needed only "one quarter, or 22 hours" for completion of the course requirements at Gaston Tech for an A.S. degree in civil engineering. His wife was employed as a computer programmer at First Federal Savings and Loan. He and she were living in a rented apartment. They were expecting a baby in September. Defendant had to quit school and go to work.

For assistance in obtaining suitable employment, defendant went to the office of the plaintiff, an employment agency. Defendant signed a contract which contained the following: "If I ACCEPT employment offered me by an employer as a result of a lead . . . from you within twelve (12) months of such lead . . . I will be obligated to pay you as per the terms of (this) contract."

After making several phone calls, the employment agency was successful in obtaining an interview for the defendant for a draftsman job. Defendant was interviewed and hired.

The plaintiff has sued for its service charge, and the defense of the defendant was infancy (below twenty-one years of age at that time).

The court held the infant liable for the service charge. The court noted that the early common law recognized that *"an infant may bind himself to pay for his necessary meat, drinks, apparell, necessary physicke, and* such other necessaries, *and likewise for his good teaching or instruction whereby he may profit himself afterwards."* The court continued by recognizing the ancient rule of the common law that an infant's contract, unless for "necessaries" or unless authorized by statute, is voidable by the infant, at his election.

Such other necessaries, the court noted, traditionally meant those articles suitable to the infant's degree and estate. The court also stated that today such other necessaries has become a very flexible concept.

The dominant purpose of the law in permitting infants to disaffirm their contracts is to protect children and those of tender years from their own improvidence, or want of discretion, and from the wiles of designing men.

Society, the court said, has a moral obligation to protect the interest of infants from overreaching adults. But this protection must not become a straight jacket, stifling the economic and social advancement of infants who have the need and maturity to contract. Nor should infants be allowed to turn that protective legal shield into a weapon to wield against fair-dealing adults. It is in the interest of society to have its members contribute actively to the general economic and social welfare, *if this can be accomplished consistently with the protection of those persons unable to protect themselves in the market place.*

The court concluded that the common law rule by judges centuries ago was in need of modification. One of the great virtues of the common law is its dynamic nature that makes it adaptable to the requirements of society at the time of its application in court.

While the court noted that prior decisions were to the effect that the "necessaries" of an infant, his wife and child include only such necessities of life as food, clothing, shelter, medical attention, etc., its view is that the concept of "necessaries" *should be enlarged* to include such articles of property and such services as are reasonably necessary to enable an infant to earn money required to provide the necessities of life for himself and those legally dependent upon him.

Questions and Case Problems

1. The plaintiff sued for money contained in a survivor's account in the defendant bank. The plaintiff contended that a purported agreement under which he and a deceased opened and maintained a survivor account constituted an enforceable contract. The defendant opposed that contention, claiming that the purported agreement was void because it was entered into after the deceased had been adjudged an incompetent under pertinent state statutes. What result? [*O'Brien v. United Bank & Trust Co. of California*, 279 P. 1048 (Cal. 1929).]

2. A provision in a testamentary trust provided that no extension of promissory notes due to the trust fund from a land development corporation would be made after a specified date. It was decided by the trustee to collect the notes as rapidly as possible without insisting on immediate payment in full as they came due. Beneficiary of the trust objected, insisting that this is an extension beyond the power of the trustee. What result? [In re *Estate of Gilliland*, 140 Cal.Rptr. 795 (1977).]

3. Plaintiff stockholder brought this action against the railroad corporation on behalf of himself and all stockholders to enjoin it from continuing to employ unnecessary personnel under "featherbedding" labor union rules and practices, and from paying excessive amounts as compensation to employees under such rules and practices, on the grounds that such a contract was **ultra vires,** or beyond the capacity of the corporation to contract. What result? [*Halpern v. Pennsylvania Railroad Company*, 189 F.Supp. 494 (1960).]

ultra vires
beyond the powers

4. The plaintiff, a prisoner for life, brought this action against the state penal institution seeking an order to allow him to appear in court to sue on several contracts made by him through his attorney while in prison. What result? [*Courtney v. Bishop*, 409 F.2d 1185, cert. denied 396 U.S. 915 (1969).]

5. The plaintiff bank credited a personal bank account of a married woman with a deposit of a portion of a check payable to her husband and indorsed to the order of the wife and indorsed by her for collection. Subsequently, the check was returned to the bank unpaid and the bank charged back the amount of the check against the account, which resulted in an overdraft. The bank sought to recover from the wife the amount of the overdraft, relying on her contractual and statutory liability. Is the wife liable for the obligation of her husband as represented by the check? [*Preston State Bank v. Finberg*, 305 S.W.2d 654 (Tex. 1957).]

6. The plaintiff was refused employment as fruit picker when he could not prove to the owner of a farm that he was an alien *lawfully* in the United States to work as a farm laborer during the harvest season. Is this a violation of a freedom to contract? [*Alonso v. State of California*, 123 Cal.Rptr. 536, cert. denied 425 U.S. 903 (1976).]

7. A contract was signed by a mother of a minor as parent for, and on behalf of, a minor. It provided that, in return for defendant's services as a personal manager of the minor entertainer, the manager would receive ten percent of the minor's earnings received by the mother or minor during the term of the contract. The mother sought to avoid the contract on behalf of the minor. What result? [*Deane v. Rippy,* 134 Cal.Rptr. 436, XX (1977), opinion withdrawn from publication by order of the court.]

8. The defendant, thirteen years of age, was told by her mother that her father had been found dead and that his body was decomposing and in order to pick up the body her signature was needed on a certain document. The defendant signed a document which turned out to be a confession note and an assignment for beneficial interest in an insurance policy on her father's life. The note was for funeral services conducted by the plaintiff in the burial of the minor's father. One year after reaching her majority, defendant filed a motion which is before the court to set aside the confession judgment. What result? [*Terrace Company v. Calhoun,* 347 N.E.2d 315 (Ill. 1976).]

9. This action against a mentally incompetent widow, through her guardian, was based upon a contract which she entered into with plaintiff for the conduct of her deceased husband's funeral services. At the time of the contract, the estate of the husband was insolvent, and the funeral director could not observe any mental impairment on the part of the widow. Are funeral services a necessary? What is the measure of recovery if they are found to be necessaries? [*Charles Melbourne & Sons, Inc. v. Jesset,* 163 N.E.2d 773 (Ohio 1960).]

10. In the case of *Gastonia Personnel Corporation v. Rogers,* 172 S.E.2d 19 (N.C. 1970)[2], the court implied that traditional cases of incapacity should be viewed on individual merits. What implications does this have for the law governing one's ability to make a contract?

---

[2] See pp. 144–45.

10 Public Policy and Contractual Purpose

After you have read this chapter, you should be able to:

1. Ascertain that the subject matter reflects a value judgment that the courts should scrutinize contractual purposes for the good of society.
2. Recognize that there are both traditional and nontraditional contractual purposes that do not further the interests of society.
3. Note how the concept of public policy and contractual purpose limits the freedom of individuals to contract.
4. Discuss the most recent development of importance in the area of contractual purpose and public policy, namely, "unconscionability."
5. Recognize that the law of public policy and contractual purpose is evolving to facilitate a broad social objective—greatest good.

Introduction

In the preceding chapters of this Part we discussed three of the four elements required for a contract: mutual assent, consideration, and capacity to contract. We will now consider the fourth element, legality.

The importance of **public policy** and contractual purpose is evident in that this area of contract law requires that the interests of society or the *community* be *balanced* against the interests of *individuals* in the contractual setting. The end result of this balancing or weighing process directed toward the *greatest good* is that an *agreement* between individuals may be held to be unenforceable *as a contract* because it works against the good of the community.

The study of public policy and contractual purpose reveals a *further restriction upon an individual's freedom to contract*. The rights of a "third party" must be considered—society's rights.

public policy
the concept of law under which the freedom to act is limited for the good of the community

What Is Illegal?

It can be said that if a contractual purpose looks to the doing of something which is **illegal,** then that agreement *violates public policy* and will not be **enforced** *as a contract* by the courts. It is a void *agreement;* there is no contract because there is no legal duty to perform a promise.

What is illegal in the contractual setting is a contractual *purpose* which is directed toward the commission of a tort or a crime.

illegal
contrary to law

enforce
to compel performance

Crime and Tort

The definition of a **crime** can be found in criminal codes. Generally it is a wrong *against society*. A **tort** is normally defined by the common law—by case decision. Generally it is a *civil* (private), noncontractual wrong (*against person or property*). In the following case the court held void as against public policy a *clause* in a contract which, while valid originally, later prohibited a party from disclosing criminal and tortious activity.

crime
an act, committed or omitted, in violation of a public law governing it

tort
a civil (private) noncontractual wrong

Facts
Plaintiff brought an action for breach of contract against the defendant, who had conducted a directional survey of an oil well on plaintiff's land. The contract for the survey prohibited the defendant from giving any information concerning the survey to any third party. The well deviated from the vertical and was actually producing oil from an adjoining tract. In essence, the plaintiff was trespassing. The defendant informed the adjoining owner of the **trespass.**

Decision
Judgment for the defendant.

Reasoning
The court dismissed the plaintiff's suit, holding that the provision for silence in the contract, while valid initially, *became* void when it economically harmed the plaintiff's neighbors. The court noted that such conduct would conceal potential criminal activity and conflicted with a strongly felt stated public policy of encouraging disclosure of criminal and tortious activity. If the defendant had been held to the clause in the contract, he would have committed a tort of fraud.

Lachman v. Sperry-Sun Well Surveying Company, 457 F.2d 850 (1972).

trespass
to wrongfully interfere with another's possession of land or chattels

Illegality by Statute

Something declared by **statute** not to be a proper contractual purpose is deemed to be in violation of public policy and *unenforceable.*

Revenue Versus Regulatory Licenses

If licensing is required by statute *to protect the public,* such as licensing of medical doctors or lawyers to practise a profession or real estate brokers or beauticians to engage in a business, the absence of such a license will cause the objective of the *agreement* to be *violative of public policy,* and the *agreement* will not become a contract. However, if the purpose of the license is *to raise revenue* for the state, the agreement is enforceable as a *contract.*

Sunday Agreements

In certain states, by statute, any attempt *to form a contract* on Sunday is a **nullity.** *Negotiations* of contracts on Sunday are allowed. Exceptions exist in these statutes for contracts directed toward humanitarian purposes, i.e., the sale of a life-saving drug. Normally, the formation on Sunday of those *ordinary* contracts that allow one to earn a living is prohibited.

Usury Law

Most states have declared by statute a *maximum rate* of interest which it is unlawful to exceed in a contract to lend money. Various penalties exist for violation of this statutory provision, ranging from loss of interest to loss of interest and principal. In some states, corporations can borrow money at any rate of interest. If no rate of interest has been stated in a contract, then the *legal rate* of interest will apply. The declared legal rate of interest by statute may be less than the maximum rate.

Discounting loans, service charges, points, requiring insurance, and other charges must all be taken into account to determine whether the maximum rate has been exceeded. In the following case the court held that usury had occurred.

Facts

This was an action on a note due the plaintiff. As proven by a promissory note which he drafted, the plaintiff, an attorney at law, lent a sum of money to the defendants. The note showed that the obligation became due at a certain date and was payable with interest at 7½ percent per annum compounded quarterly. The maximum rate permitted by law was 7½ percent. Plaintiff moved for summary judgment for the plaintiff. Defendants moved for summary judgment for the defendant, asserting the affirmative defense of usury.

Decision

The defendants' motion was granted.

Reasoning

The lending at a maximum rate of simple interest which the law allowed at the time (7½ percent) and then adding in the note that the interest was to be compounded quarterly was usury and in violation of the law. The amount of simple interest at the highest permitted rate, when compounded as required, would exceed the highest permitted rate of interest.

Giventer v. Arnow, 333 N.E.2d 366 (N.Y. 1975).

Exceptions. Credit sales made on the installment basis and lending by certain financial institutions such as small loan companies in some states can be at a rate of interest which would exceed the normal maximum rate.

Discrimination

It is interesting that there are statutes which *require* a contracting party *to contract* with another party on a *nondiscriminatory* basis. The primary impact areas are employment, housing, and the service industry, e.g., businesses providing food, drink, lodging. What is violative of public policy in these areas is not in doing something but in *having not done something*. One is required *not* to discriminate on the basis of color, race, national origin, religion, or sex. The following is an early leading case under the then new 1964 Civil Rights Act holding that peaceful refusal to be discriminated against in an eating establishment on the basis of color did not constitute criminal trespass.

Facts

The defendants, six Negroes, were indicted and convicted under an antitrespass statute. The defendants had been refused service at the Varsity Drive-In of Georgia, Inc. and had been requested to leave the premises by the owner. They had refused and were arrested by the local police. In this action, they appealed their conviction under the Civil Rights Act of 1964.

Decision

For defendants. The conviction was set aside.

Reasoning

The court reasoned that the business place in question was a public eating place offering to serve interstate travelers and that the Civil Rights Act of 1964 forbids discrimination in specified places of public accommodations and removes peaceful attempts to be served on an equal basis from the category of punishable activities. Thus, any conviction for trespass must be vacated and overturned.

Bolton v. State, 140 S.E.2d 866 (Ga. 1965).

"Contracts" of Chance

What is called a "contract of chance" is really an *agreement* creating a risk of loss rather than the legal shifting of an existing risk of loss from a possible future event (e.g., insurance against loss of property by fire). The parties do not have any legal interest in the subject matter at the time the agreement is made.

Gambling or wagering agreements meet the criteria of a contract of chance. Insurance contracts are nothing more than contracts which share *existing* risks. Buying stock, hedging contracts, and transactions in futures are speculative but valid business contracts. In the great majority of states, contracts of chance are against public policy and are *void agreements*. In the following case hedging transactions as explained in the case were not wagering agreements and were lawful.

Facts

Plaintiff creditors of the estate of a deceased person objected to the defendant executor's conduct in having made a compromising agreement for the estate for transactions made by the decedent in the commodities market for future delivery.

Decision

Judgment for defendant.

Reasoning

The court held that the executor was not negligent for proceeding as he had done because the agreement between the decedent and the claimants on the estate was perfectly legal. The court reasoned that an agreement is not illegal as a wagering agreement merely because it provides for the purchase and sale of commodities for future delivery. An agreement is illegal only if parties intend at the time of the agreement that no delivery of the commodity shall be made but that settlement between them is to be effected on the basis of fluctuations in market price. Hedging transactions by those dealing in commodities for future delivery are not necessarily unlawful.

In re *Dana's Estate*, 206 Misc. 1038 (N.Y. 1954).

The Uniform Commercial Code

The broad and general concept of *unconscionability,* as it appears in UCC 2–302, has allowed for a *flexible* determination of what contractual purpose is a violation of public policy. This statutory concept has had its impact upon the common law by making a contract otherwise enforceable under the common law void or unenforceable under the Code. In the following case an **exculpatory clause** in a contract was held to be unconscionable and against public policy and, therefore, void.

exculpatory clause a clause which relieves one from liability

Facts

This was an action on behalf of the plaintiff, Weaver, to set aside an exculpatory clause in a lease. The plaintiff leased a service station from the defendant, American Oil Company. The lease contained a clause relieving the lessor oil company from liability for any and all negligence. The court found it a matter of fact that the clause in question had not been explained to Weaver, who had left high school after 1½ years and had worked in unskilled jobs.

Decision

Judgment for plaintiff.

Reasoning

The court held that the clause in question was violative of public policy and on this basis unenforceable. The court noted that the take-it-or-leave-it basis of the contract and the ignorance of the plaintiff in business matters met the definition of an unconscionable contract.

Weaver v. American Oil Company, 276 N.E.2d 144 (Ind. 1972).

Other Statutes

Under federal legislation, antitrust Acts prohibit contracts which reduce competition, such as contracts in restraint of trade.[1] Various consumer protection legislation, such as labeling requirements promulgated by the Federal Trade Commission, make sales of mislabeled products unlawful.

Illegality by Case Law—Reflection of Community Standards

What is *violative of public policy* has also developed by *case law* (common law). Contractual purposes which violate community standards of morals and ethics is a very *flexible concept.* The court will look to the values of the community, and that community may be the nation or it may be the block you live on. There are some well established concepts of what is a violation of public policy in this area.

Restraint of Trade

A *national value judgment* is presumed to exist which suggests that competition is good and that any contract which has the elimination of competition as its purpose is bad. Thus, any contract whose sole purpose is the elimination of competition violates public policy.

If the agreement not to compete exists to protect some other worthwhile purpose, such as the goodwill in the sale of a business, then it is deemed to be *not in violation of public policy* if it is *reasonable for the benefit of the person to be protected.*

Thus, if a business and its goodwill are being sold, whether or not the restraint provision in the contract for sale is in *reasonable* restraint of trade is tested by what is reasonable in time, geographical area, and subject matter *for the benefit and protection of the buyer.* (S sells his drugstore to B, who would not want S to open (1) another competing drugstore (2) across the street (3) within the next six months. A restraint provision to this effect in the contract for sale would be reasonable in (1) subject matter, (2) geographical area, and (3) time.

If the restraint provision is in an employment contract, it must be reasonable only to the extent of the *protection needed by the person to be benefited.* It must not be unduly harsh and burdensome *on the employee.* In the following case the court held that the restrictive clause in the employment contract was too broad and was excessive for the protection of the employer.

---

[1] See chapter 32, Antitrust law.

Facts

Plaintiff brought suit against a competing car rental company for inducing one of the plaintiff's rental clerks to breach her employment contract and work for the defendant. The employee had worked for the plaintiff at its airport rental desk and was now working for the defendant at its railroad station desk. A restrictive covenant existed in the original contract between the plaintiff and the employee not to work for a local competitor for one year after leaving the employment of plaintiff.

Decision

Judgment for defendant.

Reasoning

The court held that the restrictive covenant was invalid as a matter of law. The court cited a state statute which provided that such an agreement was enforceable only if reasonably necessary to protect the employer. The court noted that the clerk possessed no special skills or customer lists and was not working for the defendant at the airport, which would have competed directly with the plaintiff, but she was in another facility. Thus, the clause in restraint was unreasonable and the contract was void as a matter of law.

Behnke v. Hertz Corp., 235 N.W.2d 690 (Wis. 1975).

Corruption

Agreements which cause a fiduciary to ignore duties that are owed to others and agreements that have a tendency to corrupt a public official are against public policy. This judgment seeks to prevent self-dealing on the part of fiduciaries and partiality in treatment by public officials.

Conflict

substantive law
that part of the law which creates, defines, and regulates rights

Substantive areas of law usually complement each other. If substantive areas of law were in conflict with each other, the logic of the law would be impaired. It follows, therefore, that *contract law should complement the law of crime and tort.*

Contract Against Liability for Illegality

It would be against public policy to allow a contracting party, by the contract, to relieve himself from liability for the consequences of *criminal* action. It is lawful to limit one's liability for *negligent* acts by contract, as illustrated by the following case in which a waiver of liability for negligence was upheld as valid.

Facts

Garretson, an experienced ski jumper, brought this negligence action against the owner of land used for an amateur ski jumping tournament and against the tournament sponsors for injuries he sustained in a ski jump. Garretson had signed an entry blank which contained a waiver of all liability for personal injuries. Defendants moved for summary judgment for the defendants.

Decision

The defendants' motion was granted.

Reasoning

The court reasoned that the plaintiff read and understood the waiver before he signed the entry form. He had signed similar waivers in the past, and *the waiver was reasonable concerning the nature of the activity.* The waiver did not fall greatly below the standard established by law for the protection of others against unreasonable harm.

Garretson v. United States, 456 F.2d 1017 (1972).

Legality of Purpose

The *law* always *presumes* that parties to a contract intend a *lawful result.* If the purpose of the contract can be interpreted either as lawful or unlawful, the lawful result will be preferred. If the contractual purpose is unlawful (illegal or violative of public policy), the general rule is that the court will leave the parties where it finds them. The court will not lend its aid to enforce the agreement.

Divisible Contract.   A contract can consist of more than one promise or more than one act. If the contractual promises and/or acts can be *divided* into lawful contractual purposes and unlawful contractual purposes without destroying the substance of the agreement, the lawful contractual purposes will be enforced. See the previous case of *Lachman v. Sperry-Sun Well Surveying Company,* 457 F.2d 850 (1972).[2]

Exceptions

A party to an *illegal* agreement may enforce it if the person is one of the class of individuals *for whose protection the agreement was made illegal.* For example, a bank can enforce an agreement for an investment made illegal by banking regulation in order to protect depositor's assets. Additionally, a party who *withdraws* from an illegal agreement before its purpose is carried out is entitled to return of the consideration given by him or her for the agreement. A party who was misled or pressured into an illegal agreement may rescind it. In the following case a bank recovered money loaned to a party who had misled the bank to act illegally in making the loan.

Facts
A bank, plaintiff, sued to recover money which it loaned defendant in violation of a statute. The court found that the defendant had intentionally deceived the plaintiff bank's employees for the purpose of inducing the plaintiff to make illegal loans. The court found that the plaintiff had been misled by the defendant's conduct.

Decision
Judgment for plaintiff bank.

Reasoning
The court held that the bank could recover the principal loan but without interest. The court reasoned that the worst that could be said of the bank was that it did not exercise ordinary banking procedures, which would have prevented it from being "taken." The bank was not equally guilty of engaging in an illegal act with the defendant, and the defendant should not be allowed to profit by his wrongful conduct.

Goldman v. Bank of the Commonwealth, 467 F.2d 439 (1972).

---

[2] See p. 149.

Summary Statement

1. The rights of society, as they are impacted by a contract, are given due consideration by the law.
2. There are three aspects of identified contractual purposes that work against the greatest good—namely, torts and crimes, those declared so by statutes, and those deemed unconscionable at common law by case decision.
3. The traditional areas that have been identified as having contractual purposes which violate public policy are licensing, Sunday agreements, usury, contracts of chance, restraint of trade, corruption, and conflict.
4. Nontraditional areas having contractual purposes violative of public policy which are growing in importance are governmental regulation, discrimination, and unconscionability.
5. Exceptions exist to defined areas of public policy violations such as in lending institutions and usury, speculative business contracts, and exculpatory clauses.
6. Exceptions exist to the normal result that the court leaves the parties in "illegal" agreement where it finds them. This occurs when the one who seeks to enforce it was the one to be protected or when one withdraws or when one was "forced" into the agreement.
7. The end of what is necessary to protect society is not yet in sight.

The following case is included in depth as an illustration of how the interests of society, here represented by a child's welfare, can restrict the ability of individuals to contract.

In re Adoption of Brousal
66 Misc.2d 711 (N.Y. 1971)

The husband of the natural mother seeks to adopt her son, James, born out of wedlock. The birth certificate bore the surname of the child's natural father. There is no issue as to paternity.

Despite the fact that neither notice of nor consent to the adoption was required of the father of a child born out of wedlock, the natural father was joined in the action for adoption.

He appeared and filed an answer. He set up a written contract entered into between the natural mother and himself. Under the contract the father has been paying for the support of the child until the commencement of this adoption proceeding. In more pertinent part the contract provides: "The partial relinquishment of the custody by the father to the mother, as in this paragraph provided, shall not be construed to be a consent on the part of the father to the adoption of the child by another person."

In their submission of the issue to the court, the parties treat this provision as an agreement by the mother that the child will not be offered for adoption. On its face, the court said it is nothing of the kind. It is merely a declaration that the agreement shall not be considered as a consent to such an adoption.

No "consent" is required of the father of a child born out of wedlock. The statute is explicit. It states that only the consent of the mother of a child born out of wedlock is required. The natural father simply has no standing before the court to object to the adoption by the husband of the natural mother.

Even if this were, however, a contract not to offer the child for adoption, it would be against public policy.

The welfare of a child simply cannot be the subject of barter. Adoption is a status created by statute. The statutes vest in courts the determination of the child's welfare. The rights of unoffending natural parents must of course be considered and their wishes will rarely be disregarded. However, even natural married parents may not contract between themselves or with others concerning the welfare of the child. A court, and a court alone, must make each and every determination affecting the child's status.

As noted, the statutes give the father of a child born out of wedlock no rights in such determination. This has always been so. It represents a legislative determination that only by marriage to the mother may the father attain status.

The answer to the petition for adoption is stricken. The adoption by the husband of the natural mother of the child is approved.

Questions and Case Problems

1. Plaintiff, Ms. Tyranski, brought this action against the defendant, an administrator of the decedent's estate, claiming that she was entitled to a house held in the decedent's name. The plaintiff contended that, although the decedent was married to another, she and the decedent had been involved in a sexual relationship and had lived together in the house for many years. She alleged that she and the decedent had entered into an oral agreement in which the house was to be conveyed to her. The defendant did not dispute the oral agreement but contended that the illegal relationship itself negated the validity of the agreement. What result? [*Tyranski v. Piggins,* 205 N.W.2d 595 (Mich. 1973).]

2. Thorpe, a real estate broker, sued Carte, his client, for his commission for finding a buyer for Carte's property under an exclusive listing agreement. In an oral and written contract the plaintiff had agreed to share his commission with the finder of a buyer. The finder was not licensed to do this sort of work. What result? [*Thorpe v. Carte,* 250 A.2d 618 (Md. 1969).]

3. A case was brought before the court to determine the timeliness of a lessee's notice to renew a lease. The lease required notice to renew at least thirty days prior to the expiration of the current term, which notice would be considered given at the time of mailing. The thirtieth day prior to the expiration date was a Sunday. On the following Monday, the lessee mailed the notice of election to renew the lease. Was the lease renewed in a timely fashion? [*First National Bank of Oregon v. Mobil Oil Corp.,* 538 P.2d 919 (Or. 1975).]

4. A corporation borrowed money from the plaintiff and agreed to a provision that, in addition to ten percent interest, the principal would be adjusted for inflation on a formula reflecting increases in the consumer price index. Assuming that the maximum rate of interest is ten percent, is the agreement usurious? [*Aztec Properties, Inc. v. Union Planters National Bank of Memphis*, 530 S.W.2d 756 (Tenn. 1975).]

5. This was an action based upon an appeal objecting to a summary judgment which granted the plaintiff's motion for cost of goods sold on an open account in the amount of $1,438.78. The New York State Installment Sales Act is not applicable to a sale of goods by a wholesaler distributor to a retailer for the purpose of resale. Defendant sought and was denied opportunity to raise a defense of usury in the lower court, contending that the supplies of Quasar television sets and parts and the amount stipulated along with a service charge of $155.59 was a usurious transaction. The inventory had been bought by the retailer on credit from the wholesaler. Was usury present in this situation? [*GTP Leisure Products, Inc. v. Cannella*, 397 N.Y.Supp.2d 292 (1977).]

6. Cunningham, a newspaper carrier, brought this action against a newspaper publisher for breach of contract. The defendant, publisher, used an identical contract with all carriers, which contained an agreement that fixed the market price of newspapers. This contract had been signed by plaintiff and other carriers. Can the carrier recover for breach of contract when his route was given to another? [*Cunningham v. A. S. Abell Company*, 288 A.2d 157 (Md. 1972), cert. denied 409 U.S. 865 (1972).]

7. The plaintiffs, directing and managing officers of a corporation, brought this action for an alleged breach of contract by the defendant. The plaintiffs had a contract with the defendant which provided for the exchange of stock in the plaintiffs' corporation for the stock in the defendants' corporation; for the plaintiffs' promise to continue as management; and for a loan by the defendant to the plaintiffs so they could buy out the other shareholders of the plaintiffs' corporation; which acts and promises were not carried out by the defendant. Will the plaintiffs succeed in their suit? [*Childs v. RIC Group, Inc.*, 331 F.Supp. 1078 (1970), aff'd 447 F.2d 1407 (1970).]

8. Burne, as beneficiary under an insurance policy, sued for double indemnity accidental death benefits because of the death of the insured. The insured had been struck by an automobile and was kept alive in a vegetative state for four and a half years before he died. The policy provided that the accidental death benefits would be paid only if death occurred within ninety days of the accident, and that such benefits would not be paid if death occurred during a time when premiums were being waived due to the insured's disability. Will the beneficiary be allowed to recover the insurance? [*Burne v. Franklin Life Ins. Co.*, 301 A.2d 799 (Pa. 1973).]

9. The plaintiff, Schara, brought this action for breach of a contract against the defendant, a tavern owner. The agreement provided that the plaintiff would operate a tavern business as his own for the remainder of the term of the defendant's liquor license, which would be in violation of a licensing statute. It was alleged that the defendant had agreed that, if the plaintiff performed his

duties as manager until a specified date, the plaintiff would be given a one-year lease in the tavern and could thereafter operate the tavern as his own. Plaintiff never carried out the agreement. The plaintiff's contention is that, while parts of the agreement are illegal, the illegal provisions are severable and the agreement to execute a one-year lease is enforceable as a contract. What result? [*Schara v. Thiede,* 206 N.W.2d 129 (Wis. 1973).]

10. Discuss the merits and demerits of the legal system acting as the final judge on what is for the greatest good of society in the contractual setting. Consider the implications of the statement in In re *Adoption of Brousal,* 66 Misc.2d 711 (N.Y. 1971):[3] "However, even natural married parents may not contract between themselves or with others concerning the welfare of the child. *A court, and a court alone, must make each and every determination affecting the child's status.*"

---

[3] See pp. 156–57.

11 Contractual Form—Requirement of a Writing for Enforceability, Statute of Frauds

After you have read this chapter, you should be able to:

1. Recognize that the law tries to assure itself that it is not being misled when it enforces a contract.
2. Understand that the law has developed many exceptions to the rule that certain contracts must be in writing or that there must be a written memorandum of an oral contract in order for the contract to be enforced.
3. Note how the concept of contractual form limits the freedom of individuals to contract.
4. Appreciate the interrelationship between the statute of frauds, the parol evidence rule, and rules of interpretation.
5. Discuss how the evolution of the law associated with the concept of the statute of frauds may be leading to a substantial limitation in its application.

Introduction

Jim claims that he had a contract with Mary, who denies this. Was there a contract, and if so what were its terms? Would this kind of problem be solved if the law required that, for the purpose of proving a contract and its terms, all contracts must be in writing or that there be a written memorandum of an oral contract? Obviously it would be very inconvenient, and all transactions would be much slowed down if such a writing were required for *all* contracts. Also, the opportunity to escape from being bound by a contract is present by showing that there is no writing. Or should only selected kinds of contract be required to be proved by a writing?

The Statute of Frauds

Any statutory provision in the law which requires that a contract be *proved only by a proper writing* is called a **statute of frauds.** Its purpose is to prevent fraud by perjured testimony in proving the existence of a contract. The statute applies only to certain selected kinds of alleged contract which over many years have been the subject of much fraud in proving their existence.

statute of frauds
a statute requiring that certain kinds of contract be proved only by a proper writing

Compliance with the statute's requirement of proof by a writing is necessary for a contract to be *enforced*. Failure to comply with the statute does *not* affect a contract's validity, only its **enforceability.** The courts will not *enforce* the contract if it can not be proved by a proper writing.

enforceable contract
a contract which can be proved and enforced by the courts

Often when a contract does exist but can not be proved because a required writing does not exist, fraud has been perpetrated upon a contracting party and not prevented. Therefore, to be safe, one is well advised to have all contracts in writing, to the extent possible, and not be caught in the pitfall of the statute of frauds requirements.

While there are contracts for which there must be a writing to be proved, numerous exceptions exist which allow many of these *kinds* of contract to be proved orally. Even if the writing does not exist to support these contracts, the party who can not enforce the contract is not always without a remedy.

If the *subject matter* of a contract does *not* fall within the statute of frauds, the contract can be proved orally. Such oral proof of a contract must be sufficiently definite that a court of law can ascertain that the elements necessary for the formation of a contract are present.

An *oral contract* which is written up so that the writing becomes the final expression of the agreement between the parties *normally can not* be modified by oral testimony. In the following case a deposit receipt could not be varied by oral evidence, but note how the court sought to achieve justice by treating the case as one of tort for fraud rather than as a contract case.

Facts

Kett, purchasers of realty, brought this action against the sellers on an alleged collateral oral promise by vendors to a written contract to make certain specific repairs to realty sold. Kett alleged that they were induced to buy a home when the seller agreed to repair a leaky shower, splits in the cement driveway, split bricks in the fireplace, and split kitchen walls. The defendant raised the statute of frauds as a defense and referred to a deposit receipt which stated, "This agreement contains the entire agreement and all representations not herein set forth are deemed waived."

Decision

Judgment for Kett.

Reasoning

The court reasoned that while the writing was the final expression of the oral agreement, and oral evidence could not be introduced to vary its terms, the plaintiff here could proceed on the basis of tort in an action for fraud. The plaintiff was, therefore, not suing on a sales contract, and the statute of frauds did not apply.

Kett v. Graeser, 50 Cal.Rptr. 727 (1966).

executor
a man who is named in and administers a will

administrator
a court-appointed person not named in a will who administers the estate of a decedent

decedent
one who is dead

parol
oral

parol evidence rule
a rule of law which provides that, when there is a written contract, it can not be *contradicted* (added to or varied) by any prior or contemporaneous oral agreement or by a prior written agreement

Contracts Within the Statute

Traditionally, and *under the law of contracts,* the following kinds of contract can not be proved unless there is a proper writing: (1) contracts which will take more than one year to perform; (2) contracts concerning the sale of real property; (3) a promise given in consideration of marriage but not between the parties to be married; (4) a promise to answer for the debt, default, or miscarriage of another; (5) a promise by an **executor** or **administrator** to answer personally for the debt of a **decedent's** estate; and *now, under the Uniform Commercial Code,* (6) a contract for the *sale of goods for $500 or more.*[1]

Effect of the Parol Evidence Rule

Common Law. Under the common law, when there is a written contract, it can not be *contradicted* (added to or varied) by any prior or contemporaneous oral agreement or by a prior written agreement. This is called the **parol evidence rule.** All the terms and conditions should have been included in (integrated into) the writing.

However, there are exceptions when certain *oral evidence* can be introduced in a legal action seeking to enforce a written contract. Under the common law, oral evidence could be introduced to prove the nonexistence of a contract. This is done most often by proving the *absence* of one of the elements necessary to the formation of a contract—namely, *genuineness of assent.*[2] Oral evidence can also be introduced (1) to show that the written contract *violates public policy;*[3] (2) to

---

[1] UCC 2–201. Other Code sections requiring a writing are UCC 8–319, sale of securities; 9–203, security agreement; 9–106, general intangibles; and 1–206, sale of other personal property.

[2] See chapter 7, Relief from Contractual Obligations.

[3] Ibid.

show that a condition which was to occur before the contract was to be enforced failed to happen; (3) to show that the contract is voidable; (4) to show that the contract was discharged by a subsequent oral or written agreement; and (5) to show the meaning of ambiguous language in a contract or to fill in obvious gaps in an *incomplete* written contract.

In the following case the court permitted proof of a condition precedent to show that a written contract never came into existence.

Facts
Plaintiff, Watts, sued to recover a real estate commission. Watts alleged that he obtained a purchaser who was ready, willing, and able to purchase real property in which the defendant, Hogan, had an interest. The defendant contended that a binding contract never existed because of the failure of a condition precedent—the obtaining of the assent and signatures of other parties who were part-owners of the real estate in question. Both plaintiff and defendant have moved for summary judgment. Watts and Hogan had discussed the possibility of selling a parcel of land to Hogan, and a document was signed by Watts and Hogan for its sale.

Decision
The defendant's motion was granted.

Reasoning
The court reasoned that to allow proof of a condition precedent is not in violation of the parol evidence rule since it is not introduced to amend the terms of the contract but to show that the contract never came into existence. The court found as a fact that the contract was never to become effective until all parties who had an interest in the land agreed to its sale and that the signature on the document was only conditional.

Watts v. Hogan, 534 P.2d 741 (Ariz. 1975).

The Uniform Commercial Code. UCC 2–202 broadens the traditional parol evidence rule by permitting the introduction of **course of dealing** and **usage of trade** orally to *explain* terms in a written contract where the subject matter is *goods*. Additional terms can be introduced orally despite the writing when the court is not convinced that the writing was intended to be the *complete* and *exclusive* agreement of the parties to the contract.

course of dealing
conduct of the parties prior to making their contract

usage of trade
commercial usage; regularity of how things are done in a place

The Required Writing

The best writing to prove a contract is *the written contract!* However, if the contract is oral, what kind of a writing or written memorandum of the oral contract will be sufficient to prove the oral contract?

The Common Law of Contracts
A writing which will satisfy the requirements of the statute of frauds can be in *any form* (need not be labeled a contract). It can be pieced together if one document *refers* to another (one letter refers to another letter). To be complete,

however, the memorandum of an *oral contract* must (1) identify the parties to the contract and their relationship (e.g., seller and buyer); (2) describe the subject matter of the contract; and (3) state all the terms and conditions of each promise and to whom made (e.g., price and credit terms). The writing must be signed by the party charged with having made the contract—namely, the party *against whom* the enforcement of the contract is sought. For example, if A orally contracts with B and A wishes to enforce the contract against B, A must prove that a memorandum was signed by B or by his lawfully authorized agent. B is the party charged by A with having made the contract.

In the following case the various writings were *unconnected* and, therefore, they collectively did not constitute a sufficient memorandum to satisfy the statute of frauds requirement.

Facts

Young, buyer, sued McQuerrey, seller, and obtained a judgment directing McQuerrey to convey to Young forty acres of land in California described in an unsigned document. This order was entered in specific performance of an undertaking of the defendant in another signed document which stated the acreage of land to be conveyed and otherwise gave no description of the land. McQuerrey appealed.

Decision

Judgment reversed, for McQuerrey.

Reasoning

The court reasoned that, where there was a memorandum signed by the vendor which did not describe land, and an unsigned deed, neither of which contained express reference to the other, and where there is nothing in the signed memorandum which gave an appearance that it was signed in reference to the unsigned memorandum, these separate writings did not satisfy the statute of frauds requirement for a written memorandum signed by the party to be charged. The documents could not be incorporated by reference. For the writings to have been connected, the connection must appear on their faces and the writings must contain either an express reference to each other or internal evidence of their unity, relation, or connection sufficient to make parol evidence of their relation unnecessary. This could not be done in this case.

Young v. McQuerrey, 508 P.2d 1051 (Hawaii 1973).

The Uniform Commercial Code

Under UCC 2—201, a writing is necessary to prove a contract for the sale of goods for $500 or more. However, such a writing is not required if: (1) *part payment* or *part delivery* for goods has been accepted; (2) the goods are to be specially manufactured for the buyer, are not suitable for sale to others in the ordinary course of the seller's business, and the seller has either substantially begun their manufacture or made commitments to procure them; or (3) the oral contract has been *admitted in court proceedings*.[4] Under (2) and (3) above, the

---

[4] For a more detailed discussion of these exceptions see pp. 357–59.

contract is enforceable without a writing only to the extent of goods for such part payment or goods delivered, and to the extent of such court admission.

All the writing needs are: (1) an overall expression of an intent to contract; (2) the statement of some quantity of goods; and (3) the signature of the party (or his agent) against whom the contract is to be enforced. Any symbol may be used or adopted by a party as a signature if done with the intention of authenticating the writing. However, *as between merchants,* if a *merchant* does not object *seasonably* (within ten days) to a sufficient writing from the other merchant after receipt, he will be deemed to have authenticated it as his own, causing the contract to be proved and enforceable against him. In the following case all three of these items were present, and the court held that the defendant's letter was sufficient to comply with the Code's requirement of a proper writing.

Facts

Plaintiff, Fortune Furn. Mfg. Co., and defendant, Mid-South Plastic Fab. Co., agreed orally, respectively, to purchase and to supply plastic products. The president of Fortune told the sales representative of Mid-South to send him a letter containing the terms of the contract. The following letter was sent: "Mr. Sidney Widcock, President, Fortune Furn. Mfg. Co., Inc., Okolona, Mississippi 38860, Dear Sid: This is to confirm the agreement entered into this date between Phil on behalf of Mid-South Plastic Co., Inc. and you on behalf of Fortune Furn. Mfg. Co., Inc. We agree to maintain expanded and 21-ounce plastic in the warehouse of Mid-South Furniture Suppliers, Inc. in sufficient amounts to supply all the plastics for your plant's use, and if for any reason we do not have the necessary plastic you will be at liberty to purchase the plastic from any other source and we will pay the difference in price between the other source and our current price. We also agree to pay Fortune a 2 percent rebate on the gross sales price of our plastic as an advertisement aid to your company, which rebate to be paid at your request. We assure that all fabrics you need will be in our warehouse at all times and we

appreciate your agreeing to buy all of your plastics from us. Very truly yours, /s/ W. E. Walker, President." The plaintiff's contention to a **counterclaim** by the defendant is that the document does not satisfy the statute of frauds.

Decision

Judgment for the defendant, Mid-South.

Reasoning

The court noted there are only three requirements to make a memorandum sufficient to take the case outside of the statute of frauds provision of the Uniform Commercial Code. Those requirements are (1) the memorandum must evidence a contract for sale of goods, (2) it must be signed by the party against whom enforcement is sought, and (3) it must specify a quantity. The court held that the letter in question satisfied all three requirements.

Fortune Furn. Mfg. Co., Inc. v. Mid-South Plastic Fabric Co., 310 So.2d 725 (Miss. 1975).

counterclaim
a claim asserted by the defendant against the plaintiff's claim in a civil action

Interpretation

In interpreting a written contract, usually ordinary words are given their ordinary meaning and technical words their technical meaning. Each part—i.e., paragraph in the contract—will be interpreted so that it is compatible with the primary purpose of the contract. Special terms will prevail over general terms, and written terms will prevail over printed terms in a form contract. In the following case the added written words prevailed over conflicting printed words in a printed form contract.

Facts

An airplane owned by the plaintiff, Marson Coal Co., collided with a high-tension wire. This action is being brought by the plaintiff to determine whether or not the insurance company is liable under a policy issued on this aircraft. The policy was a standard printed form policy with the following typewritten addition: "When in flight, the aircraft will be piloted only by Harry Marson, provided he is a private or commercial pilot properly certified by the FAA having a minimum of 1900 logged flying hours, including 200 hours on helicopters; or any private or commercial pilot with a helicopter rating properly certified by the FAA having 500 logged helicopter flying hours." The individual flying the plane at the time of the accident did not have the requisite *logged* flying hours. There was an attempt to prove sufficient hours by the introduction of *oral evidence* of additional hours flown.

Decision

Judgment for the defendant insurance company.

Reasoning

Where a printed form contract contains both the form printing and written or typewritten insertions as well, and there appears an irreconcilable conflict between the printed and written portions which requires interpretation, the writing will prevail over the printing to determine the intention of the parties. The written part of the insurance policy required a certain number of *logged* flying hours which was not satisfied by the record book maintained by the pilot. The *log record* indicated that the coverage provision in the policy had not been met. The plaintiff failed to prove the fulfillment of a condition necessary to hold the defendant liable on the policy.

Marson Coal Co. v. Insurance Co. of State of Pennsylvania, 210 S.E.2d 747 (W.Va. 1974).

All writings making up the contract are interpreted together as a whole agreement.

As was stated and explained in chapter 10, Public Policy and Contractual Purpose, a legal rather than an illegal result will be presumed.

Conduct with regard to terminology and circumstances surrounding the creation of the contract will be considered in interpreting words.

Usage of trade, or custom, is used to explain ambiguous terms, and such terminology is construed when needed against the interest of the party who wrote the contract.

One Year Plus

For a *bilateral* contract that will require more than one year to perform from the date of its *formation,* there must be a writing for the contract to be enforceable. When computing time, the day upon which the contract is *formed* is not counted. Thus, a contract made on the first day of the month to start on the third day of the month and to run for one year would require a writing to render it enforceable. The contract runs for one year and one day. The extra day is the second day of the month. A writing will not be required when it is *possible* that the consideration promised can be given within one year. A promise to work for one's life is capable of performance in one year because one might die within a year.

If the contract is *unilateral* and the act *has been performed,* though the promise for the act will take more than one year to perform, no writing will be required to prove its existence. This is illustrated by the following case.

Facts

The plaintiff, Trimmer, seeks to enforce an agreement made orally on December 5, 1965 which contemplated performance to begin on January 1, 1966. This oral agreement required him to perform certain services for the defendant, Short, for the entire year of 1966, which he did, in return for a stated percentage of profits. The court certified the following question: Does the 26-day period which must have elapsed before performance was to begin cause the statute of frauds to be operative because plaintiff could not fully perform within one year from the making of the agreement?

Decision

Yes. Judgment for the plaintiff, Trimmer.

Reasoning

The court held that the statute of frauds is not to be applied where there has been a full and complete performance of the contract by one of the contracting parties which benefits the other and where there is reasonable proof of the oral agreement.

Trimmer v. Short, 492 S.W.2d 179 (Mo. 1973).

Real Property

A writing is needed to prove a contract which concerns itself with the *sale of land* or of an *interest in land.* A lease of land, **easement,** and real property mortgage are illustrations of interests in land. However, by statute, often leases for not more than one year are not included within the statute and are enforceable without a writing.

Contractual purposes which touch or are collateral to an interest in land need not be in writing to be enforced. Thus, a commission agreement with a broker who is to produce a purchaser of real property (absent a statutory requirement for a writing), or a contract to paint or repair a house on land, touch an interest in land but are not concerned with the *sale* of an *interest in land* and, therefore, *need not be in writing to be enforceable.*[5]

easement
a right to the limited use of another's land which can not be revoked by the latter owner

---

[5] For more detail on what is an interest in land, see pp. 812–17.

However, if there is an oral contract for the sale of land and the seller conveys the title to the land to the buyer, who is to pay the purchase price to the seller later, the contract is no longer within the statute of frauds. The reason is that the purpose for protecting the seller against a fraudulent charge that he made a contract is no longer applicable since the seller has conveyed the title to the buyer. Therefore, the seller can enforce the oral contract against the buyer for the purchase price without proof by any writing.

Marriage

The exchange of promises to marry are enforceable and can be proved without a writing. However, a writing is required to prove a promise made by a person *other than* those to be married which induces one to enter into a marriage, such as a promise by the bride's father to the groom to provide some form of **dowry** on the occurrence of the marriage.

dowry
traditionally, property that the wife brings to the marriage

default
a failure to perform a legal duty

Debts and Defaults

A promise to answer for (be responsible for) the debt, **default,** or miscarriage *of another* is unenforceable unless proved by a writing. S orally promises C that, if C will extend credit to D and if D does not pay, then S will pay C. Or X orally promises Y that, if Z does not build the building pursuant to his contract with Y, then X will be liable for Z's default in not performing his contract. In both of these examples the promises of S and X must be proved by a writing for them to be enforceable.

However, for a promise to come within this part of the statute of frauds, *all* of the following three things must occur.

1. The promise must be made to the obligee, the person to whom the obligation is owing. Thus, C and Y are the obligees—C the creditor, and Y the person for whom the building was to be built. If S had made the promise to D, or X had made the promise to Z, their promises would *not* be made to the obligees and would *not* be within the statute and, therefore, would be enforceable without a writing.

2. The promise must not *assume* the obligation of performance but, rather, must be to perform if *another* did not perform. Thus, S and X promised to perform if D and Z did not perform. If S had promised to be liable with D as a co-debtor, or X had promised to build the building with Z, the promises of S and X would *not* be to answer for the debt or default *of another* (D and Z), and their promises would *not* be within the statute. They would have *assumed* the obligations, and their promises would be enforceable without a writing.

3. The promise must be made *primarily* for the *benefit of another,* namely the obligor, and not for the promisor. Thus, if S's promise was made primarily so that D could buy goods from C and supply them to S, or if X's promise was made primarily so that X could lease and occupy the building from Y, the promises of S and X would *not* be *primarily for the benefit of D and Z,* and their promises would *not* be within the statute. They would be enforceable without a writing. This is illustrated by the following case.

Facts

Plaintiffs, two engineering and survey firms, brought this action to recover from defendant, a corporate stockholder, the amounts due for professional services rendered to a corporation which was engaged in developing a tract of land for home building. The plaintiffs contend that the defendant orally agreed to pay for their services to the corporation. The court found as matters of fact that the defendant owned more than 18 percent of the capital stock of the corporation, that he acted as its corporate counsel, and that the corporation owed him $14,000 in legal fees, which could be paid only if the development was financially successful.

Decision

Judgment for the plaintiffs.

Reasoning

The court reasoned that when a promise is given which may be beneficial *both* to the promisor (defendant) and the original debtor (corporation), the factor determinative of whether the statute of frauds applies is whether such consideration was *mainly* desired by the promisor for its benefit or for the benefit of the original debtor. The court held that the oral promise by the defendant stockholder was outside the statute of frauds since the consideration was *mainly* desired for *his* personal benefit.

Howard M. Schoor Associates, Inc. v. Holmdel Heights Constr. Co., 343 A.2d 401 (N.J. 1975).

By "miscarriage" is meant misdoing, a miscarriage of justice. An example is a bonding or insurance company promising to an employer that, if an employee cashier embezzles the employer's money, the company will pay the employer its loss. There must be a writing to prove the company's promise.

Decedent's Estate

A special application of answering for the debt, default, or miscarriage of another is recognized—namely, for the obligations of a deceased person. The process of winding up the affairs of a decedent are normally handled by an executor or an administrator, who pays the decedent's debts out of the money in the decedent's estate. If this personal representative promises to become personally responsible for a debt of the decedent's estate, there must be a writing proving the promise.

Result If No Writing, in General

A *defendant* who raises the defense of the lack of a writing where required by the *statute of frauds* renders the contract *unenforceable* because it can not be proved by a writing. It should not be forgotten that an oral contract *not* within the statute of frauds is enforceable if proved without any writing.

Quasi Contract

In many instances where performance has been rendered under an oral agreement which is not provable, recovery can be obtained for unjust enrichment under the theory of a contract implied in law, namely quasi contract.[6]

---

[6] See p. 79.

Partial Performance

Partial performance, as we have seen in the sale of goods under the Code,[7] can be proved. Under the common law of contracts, when, with the permission of the owner (seller), one (buyer) has taken possession of land under an oral contract and vastly improves the property, the court, if convinced of the existence of an oral contract, will enforce it without a writing.

Full Performance

Full performance of all duties by both parties to the contract prevents the introduction of the plea of the statute of frauds. The defense of the statute of frauds applies only to executory contracts; it does not apply to executed contracts because there is no longer any contract to enforce.

Equity

To promote justice and fairness should the situation demand it, a court can employ equity and thereby waive the requirement of compliance with the statute of frauds. An example is promissory estoppel, discussed previously.[8]

Summary Statement

1. As a practical matter, all contracts should be in writing.
2. Most oral contracts can be proved orally.
3. If the writing is the contract, *previous* oral or written evidence or *contemporaneous* oral evidence should not be heard that would *contradict* its terms.
4. There are the following *six* types of contract (the first five being under the law of contracts), which must be proved by a writing: (a) more than one year to perform; (b) sale of real property; (c) marriage consideration; (d) debt, default, or miscarriage of another; (e) executor's or administrator's promise; and (under the Uniform Commercial Code) (f) sale of goods for $500 or more.
5. Under the common law, oral evidence can be introduced irrespective of the content of a writing in *five* general instances: (a) violation of public policy; (b) failure of conditions; (c) voidable contracts; (d) discharge by subsequent oral or written agreement; and (e) ambiguity and incompleteness.
6. The parol evidence rule under the Code is more liberal than the common law in allowing oral testimony to explain terms in a *written* contract where the subject matter is goods.
7. Under the common law, there are *three* requirements for a writing which will satisfy the requirements of the statute of frauds if the contract is oral. The writing must: (a) identify the parties and their relationship; (b) describe the subject matter; (c) state all the terms and conditions of each promise and to whom made.

---

[7] See pp. 164–65.

[8] See pp. 128–29.

8. There are *three* exceptions under the Code to the necessity for a writing to prove an oral contract for the sale or purchase of goods for $500 or more: (a) part performance; (b) specially manufactured goods; and (c) admitting contract in court proceedings.
9. Under the Code, if the contract for the sale of goods is oral, for a writing to be sufficient there are only *three* requirements: (a) quantity of goods; (b) a writing showing intent to contract; and (c) signature. Between merchants, the writing of one may become that of the other. The signature on a writing must be that of the party sought to be charged with the contract.
10. There are a limited number of rules of interpretation of a writing.
11. There are numerous exceptions which allow enforcement of contracts normally not provable because of the lack of a writing.
12. Equity—through the concept of part performance, quasi contract, and promissory estoppel—has provided remedies when parties can prove contracts at law in the absence of a writing.

The following case illustrates how the court circumvented the requirements of the statute of frauds to prevent fraud.

Harold v. Harold
543 P.2d 1019 (Kan. 1975).

An oral agreement was entered into between Ralph and his wife, Mary, to the effect that if Ralph would execute a will leaving all of his property to Mary, then after his death Mary would convey by deed to Elizabeth a section of Wallace County land previously conveyed to Ralph by Elizabeth. This agreement was made in the presence of witnesses and was reaffirmed on two occasions by Mary. Ralph died and his will was admitted for probate.

Plaintiffs claim they are third-party beneficiaries to the oral agreement as children of Elizabeth. They contend Ralph fully performed all of his obligations under the oral agreement by executing a will leaving all of his real estate to Mary. Mary has refused to deed the property to the children. She denies the existence of the oral agreement and asserts the statute of frauds as a defense. Plaintiffs seek specific performance—i.e., an order directing Mary to execute and deliver a deed to the property in question to the children of Elizabeth.

The pertinent portion of the statute of frauds applicable to this case was quoted by the court:

No action shall be brought whereby to charge a party upon any special promise . . . upon any contract for the sale of lands, tenements, or hereditaments, or any interest in or concerning them; or upon any agreement that is not to be performed within the space of one year from the making thereof, unless the agreement upon which such action shall be brought . . . shall be in writing and signed by the party to be charged. . . .

The court directed the lower court to hear the oral testimony of the oral agreement existing between Ralph and Mary.

The court noted that a statute of frauds was enacted to prevent fraud and injustice, not to foster or encourage it, and a court of equity will not ordinarily permit its use as a shield to protect fraud or enable one to take advantage of his own wrong.

Contractual Form—Requirement of a Writing for Enforceability, Statute of Frauds   171

There is no good reason in equity and good conscience why a defendant . . . should be permitted to hide behind his own wrongdoing upon a defense of the statute of frauds. In such cases one is equitably estopped from relying upon the statute of frauds as a defense.

The more than one year to perform part of the statute of frauds is not applicable to this case because the contract was capable of performance within a year. Ralph had fully performed his part of the bargain within a year from the making of the oral agreement by making the will and dying. Mary could have conveyed the property to Elizabeth's children within the year.

As to the real property section of the statute of frauds, the equitable rule is that a verbal contract affecting or concerning an interest in land may be enforced, notwithstanding the statute of frauds, if it has been so far performed so that to permit the party to repudiate it would of itself be a fraud. Under such circumstances . . . the Statute of Frauds can not be asserted. Ralph's execution of the will was a performance which met the criteria of the rule.

Questions and Case Problems

1. Sunseri brought suit against RKO-Stanley Warner Theatres to rescind a contract for the sale of recreational equipment, the value of which exceeded $500. Sunseri sought to introduce oral evidence that he was induced to enter into the contract because the defendant had represented ownership of the goods. It turned out that the goods belonged to a third party, who had successfully reclaimed the goods from Sunseri. RKO-Stanley Warner Theatres contends that the parol evidence rule will be violated if the oral testimony is admitted. A writing was in existence which was as follows: "RKO-Stanley Warner Theatres Inc. does hereby sell, assign, convey, transfer and deliver to Sunseri *any* right, title and interest the seller may have in the following goods and chattels." What result? [*Sunseri v. RKO-Stanley Warner Theatres, Inc.,* 374 A.2d 1342 (Pa. 1977).]

2. Manning brought the action against the defendant, Metal Stamping Corporation, under a written contract for commissions related to a successful bid for the manufacture of Illinois license plates. The defendant offered to prove orally that part of the agreement with the plaintiff was that the plaintiff was to bribe, and did bribe, the late secretary of state to obtain the contract. The plaintiff objects to the introduction of the oral evidence as a violation of the parol evidence rule. What result? [*Manning v. Metal Stamping Corporation,* 396 F.Supp. 1376, aff'd 530 F.2d 980 (1975).]

3. Plaintiff, a purchaser of land, brought action for specific performance of a contract for the sale of land and introduced the following memorandum dated 4-20-72:

Contract of sale of property known as George Nusbaum tract and Percy Burns property located between old Balto Pike and Route 140. Bounded on the north side by Ethel Williams property and on the south side by old Sam Sulser property for $28,000. Terms $7,000 pd. at time of signing of contract on June 1 and $7,000 to be paid each three months until amt. of sale satisfied. Mr. George Nusbaum to receive no interest for the unpaid balance and he be allowed to live rent free in his house until the money is paid in full. Deposit pd. 4-20-72 in the amount of $500 to bind the agreement. Signed James G. Saffell, George A. Nusbaum. Witness Earl H. Younger.

The court noted the following issue in this case: whether the written memorandum of April 20, 1972 is sufficiently definite and certain to permit specific performance. What conclusion? [*Nusbaum v. Saffell,* 313 A.2d 837 (Md. 1974).]

4. A buyer brought action against a seller for an alleged breach of an oral contract for the sale of a piece of construction equipment. A material fact in issue was whether seller's alleged receipt and retention for thirty days of the buyer's check constituted such an acceptance of payment as to take the alleged oral contract outside the Uniform Commercial Code's statute of frauds provision. What result? [*Kaufman v. Solomon,* 524 F.2d 501 (1975).]

5. Plaintiff, Lambert, sought a court order of specific performance of an oral contract with the defendant, who was to furnish him financing for the construction of an apartment building in the amount of $2,910,000 and for damages for breach of a contract to supply financing. Lambert was to convey an interest in real property as security for the loan. Can Lambert prove the oral contract? [*Lambert v. Home Federal Savings and Loan Association,* 481 S.W.2d 770 (Tenn. 1972).]

6. The plaintiff, a husband, brought a suit for divorce. The wife in her answer prayed that, if he should be granted the divorce, she be awarded custody of their minor child, her husband be required to perform specifically an alleged oral contract made prior to their marriage to adopt her daughter of a previous marriage, and that she be awarded temporary and permanent alimony in support of their minor child. The wife's daughter filed a petition to intervene to require the husband to specifically perform the alleged oral agreement to adopt her as his child. Can the oral agreement be proved? [*Maddox v. Maddox,* 161 S.E.2d 870 (Ga. 1968).]

7. Thomas was awarded a finder's fee of $25,000 to be paid to Thomas for procuring a buyer for the sale of controlling stock of a company. The stock was held by executors in trust for themselves as beneficiaries of the trust for various decedents. Hill, representing the executors, was the one who made the oral promise to Thomas to pay him $25,000 if he could find a desirable buyer. The executors asserted the defense of the statute of frauds when Thomas sued them for the commission. Hill and others are appealing the award to Thomas. What result? [*Hill v. Thomas,* 462 S.W.2d 922 (Ky. 1970).]

8. The plaintiff alleged that the defendants, through an agent, entered into an oral contract for the sale to plaintiff of real property, which is the subject of this litigation and for which the plaintiff seeks specific performance. Plaintiff contended that, in reliance upon the oral contract, it immediately made engineering studies of the property at great cost and made arrangements to obtain $292,830 for the cash down payment which would be required, thereby temporarily interfering with its other financing programs. Plaintiff further contended that it advised its staff to its great detriment to cease efforts to seek other comparable property for its future home building scheduling needs. The contention of the alleged buyer plaintiff was that the defendants can not raise the defense of the statute of frauds because of the part performance of the plaintiff in reliance upon the oral agreement. What result? [*Gene Hancock Constr. Co. v. Kempton & Snedigar Dairy,* 510 P.2d 752 (Ariz. 1973).]

9. The plaintiff, general contractor, brought suit against the supplier of Subaqueous Concrete Pipe, alleging that the defendant breached an oral contract to furnish to plaintiff suitable and acceptable pipe for a marine construction project. The general contractor was to submit a bid on the marine project. He had received another bid from another supplier at a much higher price for pipe. He sought assurances from the defendant that they would stand by their bid for pipe at a lower price, which they said they would. He thereby submitted his bid with the cost of the pipe included and won the contract. The contractor, after receiving notice of his successful bid, informed the defendant that he accepted their price for supplying the needed pipe. At that point the defendant informed the contractor that it could not stand by its original bid. Can the general contractor introduce oral evidence to prove the contract between himself and the supplier? The cost of the pipe is more than $500. [*Janke Constr. Co., Inc. v. Vulcan Materials Co.*, 386 F.Supp. 687 (1974).]

10. It has been said that the statute of frauds probably has perpetrated as much fraud as it has prevented. *Harold v. Harold,* 543 P.2d 1019 (Kan. 1975)[9], is a case example wherein we have an illustration of how the court attempted to prevent fraud. Evaluate the pros and cons of the court's action.

---

[9] See pp. 171–72.

Contractual Rights, Third Parties, and Remedies for Breach of Contract

12

After you have read this chapter, you should be able to:

1. Discuss the law associated with contractual rights, recognizing that the concern of the law in this area is to enhance and protect contract rights gained by exercising the freedom of contract.
2. Appreciate that exercising one's freedom of contract and assuming duties is not viewed lightly by the law.
3. Understand how third parties become associated with a contract.
4. Realize that a remedy is normally a substitute for the right acquired by contract.
5. Note that the Uniform Commercial Code does not differ substantially from the common law in this area of contractual rights.

Introduction

The creation of a simple contract creates property, rights, and duties.

Property usually refers to a *thing*—for example, that house, that bag, that typewriter is my property. It belongs to me; I have an interest in it, a right to it, and other persons have a duty not to interfere with my property. Legally, then, *property* is a thing, and also an interest and a right in a thing, recognized by law.

My *desire* to enjoy a thing exclusively has been recognized as proper by society. An **interest** is a person's *desire* which has been legally recognized as *dominant* over a similar desire of another person. For example, an owner's title to his house is a legal interest in the house recognized by law.

I have the right to *claim* that others will not interfere with my legal interest. So a **right** is a legal claim by the owner of an interest that others shall not interfere with his interest. For example, the owner of a house has the right to claim that others are not to interfere with his enjoyment of the house.

Other persons have a legal obligation to respect my legal interest and not to interfere with it. So a **duty** is a legal obligation not to interfere with another person's legal interest. For example, other persons have a duty not to interfere with my enjoyment of my house.

Thus, the creation of a simple contract gives to each of the immediate parties to the contract: (1) an *interest* in the other party's performance of what he contracted to do; (2) a *right* to have the other party not violate that interest by his failure to perform; and (3) a *duty* to perform the contract and not fail to perform.

These interests, rights, and duties can be transferred to third persons who are not immediate parties to the original contract. Often interests in things are transferred for security. For example, I borrow $100 from you and deliver my ring to you as security, and you now have a security interest in the ring which includes the right to sell it if I don't pay you. A contract right can be transferred or *assigned* and a contract duty can be transferred or *delegated* to a third person. Also, the contract may provide for a benefit to a third person who, as a third-party beneficiary of the contract, thereby obtains a right to enforce the contract to which he is not a party. For example, a husband contracts with an insurance company and obtains a policy of life insurance in which his wife is named as the beneficiary on his death.

The important point in this chapter is the concern of the law with enhancing and protecting the rights which parties gained by exercising the *freedom of contract*.

The Concept of Parties

As was discussed previously,[1] there can be any number of parties to a contract. The obligations of the immediate parties to the contract may be *joint, several,* or *joint and several.*

---

[1] See p. 80.

property
a thing; also an interest or right in a thing

interest
a person's desire which has been legally recognized as dominant over a similar desire of another person

right
a legal claim by the owner of an interest that others shall not interfere with his interest

duty
a legal obligation not to interfere with another person's interest

Unless the contracting parties otherwise agree, if two or more parties *to-gether* are obligated to perform the *same* duty to the *same* person, the obligation is *joint* (collective). They can sue and be sued only together. If each of the several parties *separately* promises to perform the *same* obligation, the obligation is *several* (independent). Each of them can sue and be sued separately. The obligation to perform a duty can be both *joint and several*.

Only the parties to a contract have the *right* to enforce it, called **privity of contract,** with two exceptions to be discussed, namely, *assignments* and *third-party creditor or donee beneficiary contracts*.

privity of contract
two parties have rights or duties relating to each other which were created by a contract

Rights

Rights *under a contract* are normally capable of transfer by the process of **assignment.** The party to a contract who assigns the right under a contract is called an **assignor,** and the person who receives the right is called an **assignee.** For example, B owes S $10, and S assigns to E his right against B for $10. S is the assignor and E is the assignee.

assignment
the transfer of a contract right

assignor
the transferor of a contract right

Figure 12.1   Assignment

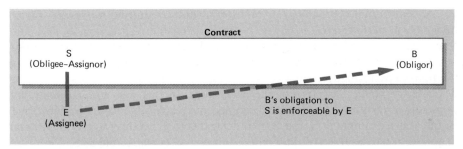

assignee
the person to whom a contract right is transferred

An assignment can take any form as long as the original party to the contract indicates a present intent to transfer a contract right to another. In the following case the assignment took the form of an irrevocable instruction to an escrow agent to pay his **escrow** money to a third person, assignee.

escrow
the conditional delivery of property to a person who is to deal with it on the occurrence of specified conditions

Facts
A debtor of the plaintiff, United States, had, in escrow, proceeds due him from the sale of his house. The debtor gave an irrevocable instruction to the escrow agent to pay the money in the escrow account to the defendant, Hanson. Subsequently, the United States brought an action to garnish (reach) the escrow proceeds. Hanson objected, claiming that the irrevocable instruction to the agent constituted an assignment of the funds of the debtor to the defendant which was superior to the plaintiff's garnishment request. The lower court sustained the defendant's position, and the plaintiff is appealing this judgment in this proceeding.

Decision
Judgment affirmed for the defendant, Hanson.

Reasoning

The court's reasoning was that where the instruction to an escrow agent is irrevocable and designates a specific portion of a fund in an account in existence for disbursement to another, that instruction constitutes an assignment of funds because it evidences a present intent to transfer a right to another. Though the funds have not been disbursed, the right has been effectively vested in another. Whether an agreement constitutes an equitable assignment depends upon the intent of the parties as evidenced by the terms of the agreement in light of all the surrounding circumstances. Here that intent was evident.

United States Fidelity and Guaranty Company v. Hanson, 492 P.2d 754 (Ariz. 1972).

When an effective assignment has been accomplished, the assignee has the assignor's right to enforce the contract against the party who had contracted with the assignor. In the above example of S's assignment to E, E has S's right to enforce the contract against B.

Duties

delegation
the transfer of one's duty to another, the transferor still being responsible for the duty

While contract *rights* are *assignable,* contract *duties* are only **delegable.**

A contractual mechanical or ministerial duty, requiring no special factor necessary to performance, is normally freely delegable. When a party to a contract delegates a contractual duty to another, he, as the original obligor, remains responsible for seeing that the *duty* is performed. The obligee, the one holding the *right* to performance, can hold responsible either the obligor or his consenting delegate for nonperformance of the owed duty. In this way a *third party* not originally a party to "the contract" can become responsible for its performance. In the above example of S and B, if B delegates to C his duty to pay S $10 and C agrees to pay S, B is still liable to S and now C is also liable to S.

Other Third Parties

Third Party Donee and Creditor Beneficiaries—Intended Beneficiaries

beneficiary
a person who is to receive a benefit

There are three types of **beneficiaries** to a contract: donee, creditor, and incidental. The first two are *intended beneficiaries;* that is, *the contract provides* that they are to receive certain contract rights. This is not true of the incidental beneficiary.

donee
the recipient of a gift

A **donee** *beneficiary* of a contract is a third person who has been given the right *under the contract* as a *gift* by a contracting party. For example, the life insurance policy of a husband designates his wife as the beneficiary.

creditor
one to whom money is owed

A **creditor** *beneficiary* is a third person who is given the right *under the contract* to obtain performance by one of the parties of *an obligation owing to him* by the other contracting party in discharge of the latter's *duty* to him. For example, S contracts with B to sell his house to B, who agrees to pay S's mortgage (real property security) debt to C, the mortgagee (secured creditor). C is a third-party creditor beneficiary of the contract between B and S, and B is now liable to C for S's *duty* to pay C on the mortgage debt. S is still liable to C on his mortgage contract with C.

Figure 12.2 Third Party Creditor or Donee Beneficiary Contract

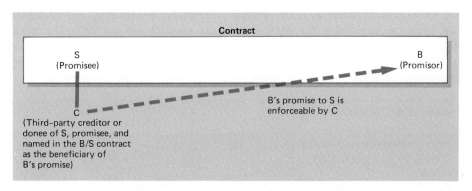

An *incidental beneficiary* has *no* claim to a right under a contract but *anticipates a benefit* if the contract is performed. Beneficiaries can enforce the contracts naming them as beneficiaries and to which they are not parties only *when the contract right is created for their benefit*. The following case illustrates an incidental beneficiary—labor union members.

Facts

The plaintiff, as acting president of a labor union, brings this class action suit on behalf of his union members, who are employees of defendant, a meatpacker. The action was brought as a third party creditor beneficiary under a consent decree agreement between the United States and the defendant which resulted in an agreement to continue normal operations of a particular plant pending a divestiture order of certain packing plants. The argument of the president of the labor union is that the fundamental purpose of the federal Clayton Antitrust Act was to benefit employees in situations such as are covered by this particular case.

Decision

Judgment for the defendant, meatpacker.

Reasoning

The court held that, at most, the members of the labor union were no more than incidental beneficiaries to the agreement between the United States and the packing company. The court reasoned that the fundamental purpose of the Clayton Act was to control monopolies for the direct economic benefit of the entire public, and Congress did not intend employment opportunities to be any more than incidental benefits arising from the enforcement of the Act. Thus, no preexisting duty existed under the Clayton Act to which the plaintiffs could resort as a basis for finding a third party creditor beneficiary relationship to the agreement in question.

Bailey v. Iowa Beef Processors, Inc., 213 N.W.2d 642 (Iowa 1973), cert. denied 419 U.S. 820 (1974).

novation

a new contract with a
new party immediately
discharging the old
contract

Novation

In a **novation** (novo—new), a *new* person becomes a party to a *new* contract with the same general duties as under a prior contract *by substitution.* For example, the bank creditor holds the debtor's land as security for the debt; the bank discharges the debtor's contract; and the bank takes in its place the new contract of the buyer of the land, who contracts with the bank to pay the bank on the new debt, the bank holding the same land as security for the buyer's debt.

Figure 12.3　Novation

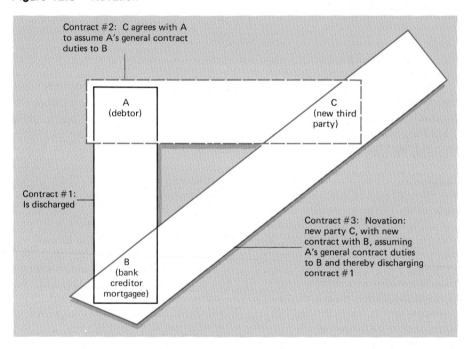

Contract #2: C agrees with A to assume A's general contract duties to B

A (debtor)

C (new third party)

Contract #1: Is discharged

B (bank creditor mortgagee)

Contract #3: Novation: new party C, with new contract with B, assuming A's general contract duties to B and thereby discharging contract #1

The *consideration* given by one of the original parties to the contract (the bank in the example) for the substitution of a *new third party* (the buyer in the example) who assumes the duty to perform the obligations of the original contract is the discharge of the other original contracting party. In the following case the court held that there was a novation by which the defendant, an original party to the contract, was discharged.

Facts

The plaintiff, the United States, sought a deficiency judgment for the unpaid balance of four loans secured by a mortgage obtained from the Small Business Administration. Subsequent to the making of all loans, title to the mortgage property—which then rested in the defendant, Hastings Motor Truck Co.—was conveyed to a third party, and this party also assumed the promissory notes with the knowledge and the consent of the Small Business Administration. This third party defaulted on the loans, and the United States seeks recovery for the debt from Hastings Motor Truck Co.

Decision

Judgment for the defendant.

Reasoning

The court stated that the defendant was no longer liable for the loans. The court reasoned that there was a novation of the loans because the third party signed an agreement to assume the promissory notes, the creditor (the United States) knew of and consented to the change, and the creditor assured the debtor that they were released from further liability. Such is a novation which discharges the original debtor and subjects the third party to duty to the creditor.

United States v. Hastings Motor Truck Co.,
460 F.2d 1159 (1972).

Creation of Third Party Relationships

At the Time the Contract Is Formed

The rights of a *third party beneficiary* in the contract in which the beneficiary is named are created *at the time the contract is formed.* A *donee* beneficiary's rights arise the moment the contracting party who owns the right acknowledges that the right is being held for the beneficiary. If the contracting party reserves the right to change beneficiaries, the beneficiary's right is subject to divestment (termination) should the contracting party change the beneficiary. For example, H takes out a life insurance policy naming W, his wife, as a donee beneficiary, H reserving the right to change the beneficiary. H can inform the insurance company to change the beneficiary. If the contracting party does not reserve this right in a life insurance policy, the interest of the beneficiary is vested (fixed and irrevocable), and change can not be made without the beneficiary's consent.

The interests of *creditor* beneficiaries normally vest in the contract after they have knowledge of it and move in reliance upon the right given. The beneficiary must be a creditor of the party (promisee) to whom the assuming party's (promisor) contract obligation is owed. For example, D takes out a policy of car collision insurance with I company, naming B bank as beneficiary, from whom D had borrowed the money to buy the car. B is a third party creditor beneficiary of the policy, the insurance company is the assuming party promisor, and D is the debtor promisee. In summary, the assuming party's promise is made to the debtor promisee to perform his duty to the creditor third party.

In the following case the sales contract provided that purchase money was to be placed in trust for the seller's creditors, thereby creating a third party creditor beneficiary contract for the benefit of such creditors.

Facts

The United States Internal R...
Service sought fu...
delinquent tax as...
the seller of a bea...
the bounty na... to...
equalling the selling ...
attorney, who in turn p...
trust for the seller's cred...
defendants. The defendan...

Contractual Rights, Third Pa...

Decision

Judgment for the defendants, creditors.

Reasoning

The court reasoned that the seller's creditors were third party creditor beneficiaries of the purchase contract. Thus, the creditors had a direct right against the property. Having previously relied upon the agreement between the buyer and the seller, the creditors have a direct interest in the proceeds of the sale. The only right that the Internal Revenue Service would have would be as to surplus after their claims were satisfied.

Crapper v. Berliner's Inc., 523 P.2d 1025 (Or. 1974).

Since beneficiaries take their rights through a contracting party, they are subject to all the terms of the contract. If the contract provides that only the original parties to the contract may enforce it, then, although the right is created in the beneficiary *at the time of the formation of the contract,* such right can not be directly enforced by the beneficiary.

After the Contract Is Formed

Rights taken under a contract by novation or assignment occur *after* a contract is formed.

A contract may prohibit assignment by the creditor obligee of his *right to payment of money* from the debtor, or the contract may prohibit assignment of one party's *right to performance other than to pay money* by the other party. With respect to the prohibition of assignment of the *right to payment of money,* some courts hold that such a prohibition is contrary to public policy and of *no legal effect* because it limits the *assignor's freedom to contract* with third persons. Other courts hold that the prohibition is *valid.*

With respect to the prohibition of assignment of the *right to performance other than to pay money,* such a provision is valid and will cause the contract to be "personal" in character and nonassignable without the other party's consent.

A contractual promise *to* assign *future* contract rights in an *existing contract* gives only an expectation to an assignee which can be enforced in the future.

Figure 12.4   **Rights of Third Parties**

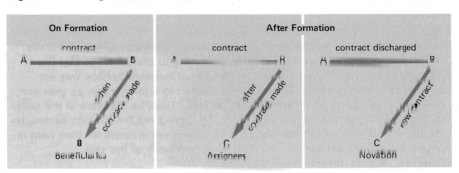

Contracts

Special Rules for Assignment and Delegation

Notice to Obligor of Assignment

Notice of an assignment of right *not for the purpose of security* is normally given by an assignee to the obligor who owes a duty under the contract in order to cut off *defenses* of the obligor which may occur subsequently. Notice is also given to prevent the *discharge* of the obligor by his *innocent* performance of his duty for the benefit of the obligee. For example, D owes money to C, who assigns his right to the money to E. D is unaware of the assignment and he pays C. E has no right against D, but only against C. If E had notified D of the assignment, then D must pay only E. In the following case the defendant's prior interest in property was held to be superior to plaintiff's because the plaintiff had delayed giving notice to defendant of assignment.

Facts

Plaintiff bank brought this action for the recovery of proceeds of a certificate of deposit held by defendant bank. Defendant moved for summary judgment and was granted same. The defendant had retained the deposit as a setoff against the default of a loan. Defendant's right to set off arose prior to notification by the plaintiff bank of its interest in the certificate as a subassignee (an assignee of an assignee).

Decision

Judgment affirmed for the defendant bank.

Reasoning

The court held that plaintiff bank could not have established a firm legal interest in the certificate until it notified defendant that the certificate had been assigned to it as security on a loan. The court found that the plaintiff bank had not exercised ordinary diligence because it failed to so notify defendant bank before its own interest arose in the security.

United States Nat. Bk. of Galveston, Tex. v. Madison Nat. Bk., 355 F.Supp. 165, aff'd 489 F.2d 1273 (1974).

Obligor's Defense Against the Assignee

Since the assignee takes rights under the contract through the assignor, any defenses *arising from the contract itself* are *not* cut off by the assignee giving notice to the obligor of the assignment to him of the contract right. *The assignee gets only what his assignor has.* For example, A fraudulently induced B to contract with him. Later, A assigns to C his right against B for $100 owing by B to A under the contract. B can avoid the contract and assert the fraud as a defense to C's claim against him.

If a defense *separate from the contract* arises between the obligor and the obligee-assignor *after* notice is given by the assignee to the obligor, such defense is cut off. This is not the result if the "separate defense" came into being *before* notice of the assignment was given to the obligor.

Discharge

If the obligor performs the duty owing to the assignor *before he receives notice* from the assignee of the assignment of the right, the assignee has no claim against the obligor. The obligor having performed his contractual obligation innocent of the assignment is discharged of his obligation. The assignee's claim is directed at the *assignor* for breach of his warranty not to defeat or impair the value of the assignment.

Since most assignments are made *for the purpose of security for a debt,* when this occurs the Uniform Commercial Code then *governs* and provides in Article 9 on Secured Transactions that, if the assignee of an account receivable wishes the obligor *to pay directly to the assignee,* the assignee must not only give the obligor notice of the assignment but he must also *demand payment* from the obligor. If this is done, then the obligor *must* pay only the assignee. Notice of assignment alone is not enough to prevent the obligor from paying the assignor and thereby being discharged. In the following case notice was given and demand made by the assignee and the debtor's payment to the assignor did not discharge the debtor's obligation to pay the assignee.

Facts

Plaintiff is an assignee of a construction contract debt bringing suit against the defendant debtor on the assigned debt. Notice of the assignment and demand for payment had been given by the plaintiff to the debtor. Subsequently the debtor disregarded the notice and the demand and paid the assignor instead of the assignee.

Decision

Judgment for the plaintiff assignee.

Reasoning

The court held that the debtor was still liable to the assignee for the assigned debt. The court reasoned that a debtor is liable to pay the assignee of a contractual claim if notice of assignment and demand for payment is received by the obligor before the obligor's payment to the obligee assignor. It does not make a difference to the result that the assignee has the right to bring suit against the assignor for monies wrongfully received. The assignee is not required to make an election of remedies between the assignor and the debtor. A suit against the assignor does not bar a subsequent suit against the debtor.

Van Waters & Rogers, Inc. v. Interchange Resources, 484 P.2d 26 (Ariz. 1971).

Warranty

warranty
an express or implied assurance that certain facts exist

The **warranty** an assignor makes to his assignee is that the contract is valid and that the right exists which the assignor can assign. The assignor warrants there will be no interference with the assignee's perfection of the right. By the assignor accepting performance from the obligor of the duty owed under a contract, the assignor has interfered with the assignee's right. An assignor does not warrant that the obligor is solvent (pays his debts), nor that the obligor will perform the obligation due under the contract.

Priority Among Successive Assignees When the Assignment is Not Made for the Purpose of Security

If an assignor *wrongfully* assigns a right *for value* to several assignees who are *innocent* of a prior assignment, there exist several claimants, only one of which is entitled to performance of the duty owed by the obligor. Under the American rule in the majority of the states and the Restatement (Second) of Contracts, sec. 174, *generally* the first assignee in time has the best claim. Under the English rule, the first assignee to give notice to the obligor of the assignment to him has the best claim to the right. However, irrespective of the rights of several assignees among themselves, performance by the *innocent* obligor to *any* assignee discharges the obligor of his obligation.

Nonassignability

Certain *rights acquired* under a contract are nonassignable. Assignment may be prohibited by law. Also, if the contract expressly or impliedly precludes assignment, it is personal in character, and the contract rights are not assignable by the obligee without the consent of the obligor. It is personal to the *obligor*.

A contract is impliedly personal in character and *nonassignable* when either (1) it involves the personal taste, skill, judgment, character, credit, or fancy of the obligor or (2) assignment would materially change the duties of the obligor or impose additional material risks or burdens upon him or change his duty.

For example, the contracts of lawyers and public accountants with their clients are personal in character and nonassignable because of the skill and judgment of the lawyer and the accountant. The clients *can not assign* their rights to such legal and accounting services without the consent of the lawyer and the accountant.

Basically, *assignment* here is *not* allowed because it violates the *obligor's freedom of contract*.

However, a right as to *what is due* under an *executed nonassignable* contract is enforceable by the assignee. For example, the fire insurance contract on O's house prohibited assignment of the contract. A fire occurred and O assigned to E his right to the insurance proceeds due him under the policy. E can enforce his right to the proceeds. The *contract* had not been assigned, only the *right to the proceeds* had been assigned.

Nondelegability

Certain *duties imposed* by contract can not be delegated. Delegation may be prohibited by law. Also, if the contract expressly or impliedly precludes delegation, it is personal in character, and the contract duties are not delegable by the obligor without the consent of the obligee. It is personal to the *obligee*.

A contract is impliedly personal in character and nondelegable when either (1) it involves the personal taste, skill, judgment, character, credit, or fancy of the obligor or (2) delegation would materially alter the performance due to the obligee.

In the lawyer and accountant example given above, their contracts are impliedly personal and nondelegable for the same reason. The lawyer and the accountant *can not delegate* their duties without the consent of their clients.

Basically, *delegation* here is *not* allowed because it violates the *obligee's freedom to contract*. In the following case the court held that, since the contract was not for personal service, contract duties were delegable.

Facts

A vending machine company and the defendant pizza company had a contract for the installation of vending machines on the defendant's premises and payment to the vending machine company of a percentage of gross sales from these machines as a concession fee or as rent. The vending machine company assigned the contract to the plaintiff, Macke Company. The defendant repudiated the contract on the basis that it was relying upon the personalized service of the owner president of the vending machine company to keep their machines in working order.

Decision

Judgment for plaintiff, Macke Co.

Reasoning

The court held the contract to be assignable. The court reasoned that, in the absence of a contrary provision, rights and duties under an executory bilateral contract may be assigned and delegated, subject to exceptions that duties under a contract to provide personal services may never be delegated nor rights be assigned under a contract where one relies upon the character, credit, or special ability of another. The court held in this particular case that the vending machine contract was not a contract for a personal service and, therefore, could be assigned.

Macke Co. v. Pizza of Gaithersburg, Inc., 270 A.2d 645 (Md. 1970).

Some Code Provisions

Assignment.   We have already seen that the Uniform Commercial Code requires that, when an assignment is made *for the purpose of security,* the assignee is to give *notice* to the obligor of the assignment and to *demand performance directly to the assignee* to assure that the obligor must perform only to the assignee. If the obligor, not knowing of any assignee prior to the demanding assignee, performs to the latter, the obligor is discharged.[2]

Also under the Code,[3] a *right* as to what is due under an *executed* contract is assignable, and *its* assignment can not be prohibited by the contract. In the following case, although the assignee notified the plaintiff debtor of the assignment and was paid by the debtor, since the assignor's claim against the debtor was inferior to the claim of another creditor against the debtor, the assignee had to return the money to the debtor to be made available to the other creditor.

---

[2] See p. 185 for priorities among successive assignees.

[3] UCC 2–210.

Contracts

Facts

Plaintiff, DeLozier, a general contractor, was working on a construction project. He contracted with one named Diviney to install drywall on the project. Before beginning the work, Diviney obtained a personal loan from the Farmers Acceptance Corporation, for which Diviney executed a promissory note. As security for the loan, Diviney assigned to FAC all right to payment with regard to his contract with DeLozier. FAC notified DeLozier of the assignment. DeLozier paid FAC what was due to Diviney under the contract. A supply company that had supplied Diviney with drywall for the project then sued the general contractor for payment. DeLozier sought to recover the payment made to FAC so as to apply it to the material costs.

Decision

Judgment for the plaintiff, DeLozier.

Reasoning

DeLozier is entitled to return of the money paid FAC. The court held that in Colorado a contract *right* can be assigned even though the *contract itself* may not be assigned. This is true even if a contractual term prohibits assignment of the payment. The assignee, FAC, was subject to the terms of the contract and to any defense arising out of the contract. Since the material costs incurred by the subcontractor Diviney exceeded the amount of payment made, and to which the subcontractor thereby was not entitled, neither could FAC, which stood in the shoes of the subcontractor, claim rightfully that it was entitled to payment.

Farmers Acceptance Corporation v. DeLozier, 496 P.2d 1016 (Colo. 1972).

Delegation. The common law of delegation is changed by the Uniform Commercial Code,[4] which provides that, in the absence of anything to the contrary, an assignment *in general terms* is also a delegation of the assignor's duties, *and* the assignee's acceptance is a promise to perform them. When both right and duty are simultaneously assigned and delegated to a third party, the original party to the contract affected thereby may demand additional assurances, such as a bond or deposit, from the *third party* that the contractual duty he assumed will be performed.

Remedies

The Concept of Remedy

We are still considering rights, but these are *new* rights contained *in remedies* for breach of contract. When a right is acquired by contract, the legal system will seek to protect it. If the one who owes the duty wrongfully does not perform, a **breach of contract** exists for which the law provides relief by giving a **remedy.** The various remedies available are money *damages, specific performance* by order or **injunction,** and *restitution.* These will be considered in turn.

breach of contract
wrongful nonperformance of a contractual promise

remedy
the means by which a right is enforced or protected

injunction
a court order requiring a person to do or not to do something

---

[4] Id.

damage
loss or harm

damages
the money judicially awarded for another's wrongful conduct

nominal damages
the money judicially awarded when no damage has occurred from another's wrongful conduct

anticipatory repudiation
a party's manifestation of an intent not to perform his contractual obligation, made before his performance is due

compensatory damages
the money judicially awarded to compensate for damage caused by another's wrongful conduct

consequential (or special) damages
the money judicially awarded for loss which the breaching party reasonably could foresee would be a consequence of his breach

punitive (or exemplary) damages
the money judicially awarded in excess of compensatory damages to punish for malicious, wanton, or intentional wrongful conduct

Since the party enforcing the *remedy* may in all probability not get the *original right* due him under the contract, it should be recognized that the *right* which the remedy affords is a *second* type of *right* with its corresponding duty. For example, S contracts to dig a ditch for B. B has a *right* to have the ditch dug by S. On S's wrongful refusal to dig the ditch, B now has a *remedy* for S's breach of contract and, thus, a *new right* against S for one of the three remedies.

Damages

A breach of contract is a *wrongful* nonperformance of a contractual duty. The word **damage** means loss or harm. **Damages** means the money judicially awarded (by the court) for another's wrongful conduct. If a breach of contract has occurred but the injured party can not show that he actually suffered damage, a symbolic award of **nominal damages** can be obtained. Usually the money award is $1.

Damages are determined as of the time of the breach, except that for an **anticipatory repudiation** and breach, damages are determined as of the time performance was to have occurred. For example, E employs X on Wednesday, X to report for work on the following Monday. On Thursday E tells X not to report for work. E has committed an anticipatory repudiation and breach of the contract. If X sues E on Friday, damages will be fixed as of Monday when X was to have begun work.

When loss due to breach of contract is something other than nominal, one is entitled to recover **compensatory damages,** compensating for damage actually sustained. One measure of compensatory damages is the difference between fair market value (the cost of a substitute performance) and the contract price. Another measure of compensatory damages (for a defective performance rather than no performance) is the difference between the value of a performance as promised or warranted and the actual value received. Compensatory damages could also be lost profits on lost sales or the cost necessary to make a defective performance whole.

Consequential (or special) damages for loss *foreseeable* from a breach of contract are recoverable. For example, if A knows B's plant will be shut down if a promised machine is not delivered by a promised date by A, A can be held liable for B's loss of profit from lost production as a consequence of A's nonperformance and breach of contract. Consequential damages, when applicable, are given in addition to compensatory damages.

Punitive (or exemplary) damages are given in certain *tort* actions, but not for *contract* loss. Punitive damages seek to punish a wrongdoer and they need bear no relationship to *actual damages (compensatory and/or consequential)*. Victims of *intentional torts* can receive punitive damages awards. Under the common law, if one is defrauded into making a contract, one can either: avoid the contract;

or affirm the contract, sue for the tort of **deceit,** and obtain punitive damages. In the following case punitive damages were not awarded, both because the action was for *breach of contract,* and because the defendant had not *intentionally* committed a tort.

deceit
briefly, a tort consisting of contractual fraud causing loss

Facts

Ledingham, plaintiff, brought an action against the defendant, an insurance company, on a health service policy, claiming that the defendant had refused, in bad faith, to pay under the policy. Two days after the policy went into effect, the plaintiff's wife experienced a serious illness which led to a hysterectomy. The insurance company, relying on the statement of the insured's doctor that he could not be certain whether the illness developed before or after the issuance of the policy, refused payment of Ledingham's claim. Justification for refusal was based upon an exemption in the policy for illnesses occurring within 270 days before the effective date of the policy. The jury awarded Ledingham both actual and punitive damages, and the insurance company appealed the punitive damages award.

Decision

Judgment for the defendant insurance company.

Reasoning

The defendant claimed that punitive damages should not have been awarded since punitive damages were not properly awarded in a suit on contract. The appellate court, although agreeing with defendant that punitive damages could not be collected in a contract action, held that Ledingham had also stated a cause of action in tort by alleging that the defendant had breached its duty to act in good faith and deal fairly with Ledingham. The court held, however, that, since the defendant's decision to deny the benefits was made in good faith on the basis of the insured's doctor's statements, Ledingham had failed to show that the defendant had committed a tort, and, therefore, punitive damages were not recoverable.

Ledingham v. Blue Cross Plan for Hospital Care of Hospital Service Corp., 330 N.E.2d 540, rev'd 356 N.E.2d 75 (Ill. 1976).

Liquidated damages is the judicial award of the money agreed upon by the contracting parties as compensatory for a breach of contract *before* the breach is experienced. For example, a contract for the sale of real estate may provide that, if the buyer does not pay the purchase price at the time of the closing of the deal, the buyer's money deposit shall be the liquidated damages. If the liquidated damages provision bears some reasonable relationship to the *actual damage,* it will be awarded for breach of the contract. If the liquidated damages provision is excessive, it will be denied. Such excessive damages agreements are considered penalties which are not enforced by law.

liquidated damages
the money judicially awarded in the amount as agreed to by the parties as reasonable compensation for damage which may be caused by the wrongful conduct of one of the parties in the future

Mitigation. If the party to the contract who is not in breach can lessen the damages caused by a breaching party, he will be required by law to act to so minimize the damages. For example, if an employer wrongfully discharged an employee under a contract with three months remaining, the employee has a duty to seek employment elsewhere for the three months period and thereby reduce his loss of wages under the first contract. In the following case the defendant could not prove that the plaintiff had failed to minimize the damages.

Facts

Ballard, plaintiff, sued the defendant, El Dorado Tire Co., his former employer, seeking damages for alleged wrongful discharge. The trial court awarded damages to Ballard for breach of the employment contract. The defendant appealed, claiming that the trial court erred in failing to reduce the plaintiff's damages by the amount he might have earned in other employment during the unexpired term of the contract. At trial, the defendant had introduced evidence to the effect that there was an extremely low rate of unemployment for professional technicians and managers in the geographical area and that the plaintiff had not taken advantage of this opportunity for employment.

Decision

Judgment affirmed for the plaintiff, Ballard.

Reasoning

The appellate court upheld the trial court's damages award, holding that El Dorado Tire Co. had not met its burden of proving that a similar employment opportunity was available to Ballard. The court reasoned that in order to establish that Ballard had failed to mitigate damages, it was necessary to demonstrate with reasonable certainty that employment was available in the *specific line of work* in which the plaintiff was engaged.

Ballard v. El Dorado Tire Co., 512 F.2d 901 (1975).

Specific Performance

If damages will adequately compensate one for a breach of contract, an order from a court with equity power to specifically perform the contract will not be given. If the subject matter of the contract is *land* or a *unique item of personal property,* an order to specifically perform the contract will be given by a court of equity. Normally, before one is entitled to an equitable remedy, one must show that: (1) *his remedy at law for damages is inadequate;* (2) such equitable relief will *not* work an extreme hardship on the party in breach; (3) there is an enforceable contract; and (4) the court can grant such an *effective remedy.*

In contracts for *personal services,* a mandatory injunction ordering specific performance by a party will not be issued. Such an injunction would be in violation of the U.S. Constitution prohibition of "involuntary servitude" and also would be difficult to enforce. Also, a prohibitory injunction ordering that an act *not* be done will not be issued unless there is a threat of *irreparable harm* to the wronged party. Failure to comply with an injunction invites punishment for contempt of court.

restitution
a legal remedy restoring one to his original position prior to the particular transaction

Restitution

Restitution is a remedy which is an alternative to damages for material breach of contract. One can not have both restitution and damages, nor restitution and specific performance. In restitution, the parties to the breached contract return what they have received, or the value of what was given if what was given can not be returned. The objective is to restore the contracting parties to the positions they occupied before the contract was formed. This is illustrated by the following case.

Facts

Conway, plaintiff, operated a real estate brokerage firm and had orally agreed to furnish Jobin, defendant, with office space and to pay Jobin's expenses in the operating of his insurance business until such time as Jobin could pay his own expenses. In return, Jobin had agreed that when his insurance business produced an income in excess of $10,000 after payment of expenses, Jobin would divide any profits in excess of $10,000 evenly with the plaintiff Conway. After four and a half years had passed, Jobin repudiated the agreement. Plaintiff brought suit for the unpaid divided profits.

Decision

Judgment for the plaintiff, Conway.

Reasoning

The court stated that Conway was entitled to restitution and reimbursement for benefits furnished under the agreement. The court made the point that the recovery of damages would not be the division of the profit but the value of the services and facilities rendered to the defendant. The court reasoned that this would return the contracting parties to the position they occupied before the contract was formed.

Conway v. Jobin, 345 A.2d 903 (N.H. 1975).

Election of Remedies

A party suing for breach of contract will be required to select a remedy. If one seeks damages, one is not entitled to restitution. If one seeks restitution, one is not entitled to specific performance. One can join an action for specific performance with a request for damages.

Under the Uniform Commercial Code

Generally. Special damages under the Uniform Commercial Code are called consequential damages and can be recovered.[5] Under the Code, an action by the seller for the price of goods sold can be maintained when the goods are damaged or destroyed and risk of loss has passed to the buyer.[6]

Specifically. The remedies of an unpaid seller under the Code are: (1) actions directed toward the goods for security for payment of price; (2) mitigation of damages by reselling the goods; (3) suit for price and incidental damages; (4) damages; and (5) cancellation of the contract.

Under the Code, the remedies of a buyer are: (1) damages; (2) specific performance; (3) obtaining a security interest in goods and sale of the goods; and (4) cancellation of the contract.[7]

---

[5] UCC 2–714 and 2–715.

[6] UCC 2–509 and 2–510.

[7] For detailed information on Code remedies in sales of goods, see pp. 422–44.

Summary Statement

1. The creation of a simple contract creates property, rights, and duties.
2. An obligation assumed by contract may be joint, several, or joint and several. Each of the contracting parties has rights and duties.
3. Rights are normally freely assignable unless the contract is personal in character. Duties are normally freely delegable if mechanical or ministerial in nature, but they are not delegable if the contract is personal in character.
4. A contract is personal in character if it expressly or impliedly precludes assignment or delegation.
5. The assignee gets only what the assignor has.
6. There are three types of third party beneficiaries: donee, creditor, and incidental.
7. Rights of a third party beneficiary arise at the moment the contract is created.
8. Rights taken by contract through the process of novation or assignment occur after the contract is formed.
9. When an assignment of a contract right is *not made for the purpose of security,* if the assignee *notifies* the obligor of the assignment, the obligor must pay only to the assignee. If no such notice is given and the obligor innocently pays the obligee assignor, the obligor is discharged.
10. When the assignment is made *for the purpose of security,* under the *Code* the assignee must notify the obligor of the assignment and *demand* payment so that the obligor must pay only the assignee. If no such demand is made, the obligor may pay the obligee assignor and be discharged.
11. Under the Uniform Commercial Code, rights for what is due under an executed contract remain assignable, and the right to payment can not be made nonassignable.
12. The remedies available for breach of a sales contract are numerous and varied under the Uniform Commercial Code. Under the common law of contracts, remedies for breach of contract are damages, specific performance, and restitution.
13. There are five types of damages: nominal, compensatory, consequential, punitive, and liquidated. Restitution is a remedy which is an alternative to damages and to specific performance.
14. One must mitigate damages.
15. The remedy of specific performance is given in limited circumstances.
16. The law associated with contractual rights seeks to enhance and protect rights created by one's exercise of the freedom to contract.

This chapter has made the point that the creation of a contract creates rights which are capable of transfer to third parties and which the law will protect.

The following case is presented to illustrate how personal service contracts not normally considered assignable can, in certain instances, be assigned and how the law protects rights.

Munchak Corporation v. Cunningham

457 F.2d 721 (1972)

This is a suit by owners and operators of a professional basketball club to enjoin one of its players from performing services as a player for any other basketball club.

Cunningham, a basketball player of special, exceptional and unique knowledge, skills and ability, was under contract to play basketball for the Philadelphia 76ers. Cunningham's contract was about to run out with the 76ers, although they had a right under the contract to prevent him from playing basketball with any club for one year if he did not renew his contract with them.

A team called the Cougars entered into contract negotiations by intermediaries with Cunningham whereby they agreed to compensate Cunningham if he sat out a year under the "penalty" clause in the Philadelphia contract and, if he agreed for a stipulated compensation, to play for them for an extended period of time after the one year suspension was over.

Cunningham entered into a contract with the Cougars, then owned by Southern Sports Corporation, on the terms previously indicated, but required in his contract with Southern Sports Corporation that it be prohibited from assigning its contractual right to his services to another "club" without his consent. *This contract contained no prohibition against its assignment to another owner of the same club.*

Subsequent to the contract, Southern Sports Corporation assigned its franchise to the plaintiffs, Munchak Corporation. Cunningham was not asked to consent, nor has he consented to this assignment. *The club "Cougars" still remains the same, only the ownership has changed.*

Cunningham wishes now to remain with the 76ers. His contention is that his contract with the Cougars was not assignable and that, by reason of a purported assignment, he is excused from performance of the previous contract.

The court recognized that, generally, the right to performance of a personal service contract requiring special skills and based upon the personal relationship between parties cannot normally be assigned without the consent of the parties rendering those services. However, the court held that such contracts may be assigned when the character of the performance and the obligation will not be changed. Change of ownership of a franchise does not change the character of the performance or obligation assumed by contract. The right is assignable and will be enforced by granting the injunction.

Questions and Case Problems

1. The plaintiff is a transferee of a certificate for tax or fee exemption granted to a previous corporation. The general law of assignment states that, in the absence of language prohibiting an assignment, claims against a government are freely assignable and should be sustained. In reliance upon this general principle, the plaintiff seeks to enforce the assignment of the exempt taxation status against the government of the Virgin Islands, contending that, since the filing of reports was mechanical and ministerial, the duties assumed with regard to the assignment should not cause the assignment to be null and void. What result? [*Antilles Industries, Inc. v. Government of the Virgin Islands*, 388 F.Supp. 315 (1975), vacated 529 F.2d 605 (1976).]

2. The defendant, City of Winston-Salem, has a contract with a state board of transportation to do work and repairs on streets within the city which are part of the state highway system. Matternes brings this action against the city for wrongful death, personal injuries to a minor, property damage, and medical expenses resulting from an accident in which his deceased wife's car went out of control on a bridge on which there was an accumulation of ice and snow. Plaintiff claims a beneficiary status to the contract and, because it was not enforced by the city, he is suing the city. He asks for summary judgment in his favor. Judgment in the lower court was for the defendant. Plaintiff appeals. What result? [*Matternes v. City of Winston-Salem,* 209 S.E.2d 481 (N.C. 1974).]

3. Plaintiff, an administrator of an estate of a buyer of two certificates of deposit, brings this action against the buyer's daughter, seeking to recover the certificates which were delivered to the daughter after the buyer's death. The certificates of deposit were made out to the buyer or her daughter with the rights of survivorship and not as tenants in common. The daughter was unaware of the existence of the certificates until her mother's death. The certificates had been bought by the mother with her own funds. What type of beneficiary is the daughter, if any? [In re *Estate of Fanning,* 333 N.E.2d 80 (Ind. 1975).]

4. Plaintiff, a bonding company, seeks to recover payments due to a subcontractor from a general contractor. The plaintiff fulfilled its bonding obligation when the subcontractor defaulted by providing the services of a substitute subcontractor. The subcontractor before default but after obtaining the bond opened up a revolving line of credit with a bank, assigning as security the future payments from the general contractor. A dispute has arisen between the plaintiff bonding company and the bank as to who should be preferred on payments owed by the general contractor to the subcontractor in default. Who should receive the payments—the plaintiff bonding company or defendant bank? [*American Fire & Cas. Co. v. First Nat. City Bank of New York,* 411 F.2d 755, 757 (1969), cert. denied 396 U. S. 1007 (1970).]

5. American Air Filter Company, Inc., is suing McNichol, a former employee, for an alleged breach of a restrictive covenant and employment contract not to compete. American Air Filter Company, Inc., claimed that McNichol in his new sales position had been competing with them in violation of the covenant. What is the compensatory measure of damages for a salesman's breach of a covenant not to compete? [*American Air Filter Company, Inc. v. McNichol,* 527 F.2d 1297 (1975).]

6. Walther & Cie, a German corporation, brings this suit against the defendant, an American corporation, for failure to carry out the terms of a settlement agreement. The plaintiff contends that the defendant had failed to provide plaintiff with a negotiable promissory note pursuant to an agreement, and that this failure caused it to sustain loss as a result of a decline in the mark/dollar ratio which occurred between the date that the plaintiff was to receive the note and the date on which it received a check in the amount of the face value of the debt. What is the measure of damages? [*Walther & Cie v. U. S. Fidelity & Guaranty Co.,* 397 F.Supp. 937 (1975).]

7. A real estate broker brought suit pursuant to an exclusive listing agreement wherein the seller provided that, should the property be sold by any other broker during the exclusive period, the plaintiff real estate broker would still receive the amount of the commission. Defendant contends that this provision was unenforceable because it was a penalty. What result? [*Dean Vincent Inc. v. Chef Joe's Inc.*, 541 P.2d 469 (Or. 1975).]

8. Richter decided to purchase a used 1971 Ferrari Daytona Coupe automobile for $17,500 from Tatum, a dealer in foreign cars. Tatum did not have a car in stock but purported to locate one in the hands of another dealer which he described in some detail, giving serial number and other pertinent information on an order form and a bill of sale. These documents were used to support a bank loan for purchase of the car by Richter. Richter placed a deposit of $7,500 for purchase of the car with Tatum. Within a day or two after the cashing of the check, a car was delivered to Tatum which was a European version of a 1971 Ferrari Daytona Coupe intended for racing and not for operation on highways. Tatum took the position that it was not the car which Richter had ordered and refused to deliver the car, saying that he would try to locate another car. Tatum failed to produce another car. Richter brings this action for specific performance of the contract for the sale of the car. What result? [*Tatum v. Richter*, 373 A.2d 923 (Md. 1977).]

9. Plaintiff, Rosenblatt, is suing Credit Discount Company, et al., defendants, to establish who has the best interest in assigned accounts receivable. The owner of the accounts receivable had for value assigned the same accounts receivable to both parties. The defendants were the first assignees in time but did not give notice to the debtors. Plaintiff Rosenblatt was then assigned the receivables and gave notice to the debtors. Who has priority to the receivables—Rosenblatt or Credit Discount Company, et al.—and why? [*Rosenblatt v. Credit Discount Company, et al.*, 98 P.2d 747 (Cal. 1940).]

10. In *Munchak Corporation v. Cunningham*, 457 F.2d 721 (1972),[8] the court perfected the assigned right to personal services by preventing the basketball player from playing basketball for any club but the Cougars. Evaluate the action by the court.

---

[8] See p. 193.

13 Contractual Duties of Performance, Nonperformance, and Discharge

After you have read this chapter, you should be able to:

1. Discuss the law of contractual duties, recognizing that it is directed at ending a contract.
2. Recognize that the law of contractual duties is evolving and is constantly balancing the rights of society and the rights of the immediate parties to the contract.
3. Understand the complexity of determining when one should be allowed to be discharged of a contractual obligation when in breach of contract.
4. Note the role of conditions in contract law.
5. List the methods of discharge.
6. Appreciate the thrust of the Uniform Commercial Code in this area of law.

Introduction

The duties assumed when a contract is created do not last forever. The law, as it has provided for the creation of a contract, also provides for its ending. As it was important for an individual to know how to create a right, it is equally important to know how to *discharge* (end) an obligation assumed under a contract.

Society has a concern that contractual duties be performed. To bring assurance to the community that contractual obligations will be carried out, the law can not lightly discharge an individual from duties assumed by contract.

There is, however, a line of reasonableness between an individual's need to be discharged from a specific contractual obligation and society's interest in seeing that all contractual obligations be enforced. This line constantly shifts as law reflects the collective judgment of the community.

The important point in this chapter is the concern of the law for providing means and ways whereby contractual obligations are terminated.

The Concept of Performance

The expectations of parties when they contract is that they will receive what was promised in a contract. A substitute performance provided by a remedy or something less than complete **performance** was not thought of by the parties when the contract was made. We are, however, human beings and as such not always reliable. The law has taken this into account when it determines what will be required when complete performance of a contractual obligation is not forthcoming.

Performance

Performance means complete performance. If one party to a contract has *completely performed* his obligation under the contract, *he* is **discharged.** He has met the original expectation, and the law will not hold him to any further obligation. As far as he is concerned, *his part* of the contract is **executed** (performed). If all parties to the contract have completely performed, the contract is *executed* and all the parties are discharged.

If the parties have not performed, the **contract is executory;** if only one party has not performed, as to that party's *obligation* the contract is *executory*. Only when the contract is *executory* and there is *wrongful* nonperformance of a promise is there a **breach of contract** by the nonperforming party. In the following case the contract of the debtor on a promissory note was executory and he would be liable only as he failed to pay each installment.

performance
the fulfillment of a contractual obligation

discharge
termination of a contractual duty to perform a promise

executed contract
a contract which has been performed by all the parties to it

executory contract
a contract which has not been performed by all the parties to it

breach of contract
wrongful nonperformance of a contractual promise

Facts

The defendant, Ginsberg, was a maker of a promissory note payable in installments. The note did not contain an acceleration clause (permits the holder to declare the note to be fully payable on default of an installment). The defendant missed only one or two installments. The plaintiff owned the note and brought suit for the face value of the note.

Decision

Judgment for the defendant, Ginsberg.

Reasoning

The court held that the suit for the full value of the note was premature. The plaintiff could sue only for those installments past due. The defendant's duty to pay installments not yet due was executory, and until the date for the payment of the installments passed, no breach of contract would be present and, thus, no basis for plaintiff's suit existed.

L.C. Fulenwider, Inc. v. Ginsberg, 539 P.2d 1320 (Colo. 1975).

Substantial Performance

Performance means *complete* performance. Sometimes the expectations of the parties are not met in that they receive only *substantial* or *partial* performance.

Substantial performance is some performance *slightly less than complete performance. The main purpose of the contract has been performed or not defeated.* The nonperformance is *not material* and there is a *nonmaterial breach* of contract. *When substantial performance has been rendered* but it can not be returned to the performing party and the breach of contract is not intentional, the law will allow both parties to be discharged by giving to the party in breach what he was originally entitled to less what it will cost the nonbreaching party to get complete performance elsewhere. For example, B substantially performs his contract to build a building for C. B painted the front door brown instead of yellow. There is substantial performance and a nonmaterial breach by B. C must pay to B the contract price less what it will cost to repaint the door yellow. This prevents a **forfeiture** and is considered a just result in law. The expectations of the parties have been *approximately* met.

Partial Performance

Partial performance *is only slight performance.* The nonperformance is *material* and there is a *material breach* of contract. The expectations of the nonbreaching party have *not even approximately* been met. *The main purpose of the contract has not been performed or has been defeated.* A material breach normally happens at the *threshold* or beginning stages for *time* of performance under the contract. Since the expectation of future performance is dim and will not be forthcoming, the nonbreaching party can discharge himself from the obligation and seek damages.[1] This is illustrated in the following case of partial performance in which the plaintiff was awarded damages against the defendant who had only partially performed, and the plaintiff was discharged.

---

[1] See pp. 188–90 for damages.

substantial performance
incomplete performance which is sufficient to accomplish, and does not defeat, the main purpose of a contract

forfeiture
to lose a legal right as a penalty

partial performance
incomplete performance which is insufficient to accomplish, or which defeats, the main purpose of a contract

Facts

The defendant failed to fully perform for Golob, the plaintiff, nine types of services, part of an interdependent whole, having the ultimate common purpose of improving the profit level of Golob's business. Golob introduced evidence that the partial performance of the defendant was worthless and that all work would have to be done over by another consulting firm.

Decision

Judgment for plaintiff, Golob.

Reasoning

The court held that the reasonable measure of damages for Golob would be the reasonable cost of obtaining a substitute performance less contract price of the defendant's service. The court said that when part performance is worthless, such performance should not be used to reduce damages for a breach of contract.

Golob v. George S. May International Company, 468 P.2d 707 (Wash. 1970).

Nonperformance

If *no performance* is given as of the date of expected performance under the contract, the nonbreaching party is discharged. He can also **cover** his lost performance, and he can also seek damages.

Threat of No Performance. *A threatened nonperformance* of a *bilateral* contract is an *anticipatory repudiation* resulting in an **anticipatory breach.** However, the party not in breach is not discharged unless he *materially changes his position in reliance* on the anticipatory repudiation. He may immediately bring a suit for damages for such breach. (On September 1, A hires B as a secretary to begin work on September 10. On September 5, A tells B he will not need her. B immediately gets a job with C. A can not withdraw his anticipatory repudiation, which he could have done *before* B obtained employment elsewhere. A is liable to B for his anticipatory breach.) There can not be an anticipatory breach of a proposed *unilateral* contract because, until performance of the act or forbearance occurs, there is no acceptance and no contract.

Failure Midway

If a *failure to perform* happens *midway* through the contract but before substantial performance occurs, the party not in breach is not automatically discharged. For example, if A contracts with B for twenty tons of coal to be delivered by B to A over twenty months at one ton per month, A is not automatically discharged if B misses the eleventh delivery. A must wait until, perhaps, the time for delivery of the twelfth installment before the breach will be material. After the passage of a reasonable time such that a reasonable person would assume that the remainder of performance was not forthcoming, his discharge will then take place.

nonperformance
no performance

cover
to seek a substitute performance

anticipatory breach
a party's material breach of contract made by his repudiation before his performance is due

Figure 13.1   Performance

Type of Performance Rendered	Resulting in Type of Nonperformance	Time of Occurrence Relative to the Contract	Resulting in Type of Breach of Contract
None ▶	Material ▶	At formation ▶	Anticipatory
Partial ▶	Material ▶	Beginning of ▶ performance	Threshold
Substantial ▶	Not material ▶	Midpoint plus ▶	Breach
Complete ▶	None ▶	At end ▶	None

Personal Satisfaction

If one has agreed to perform his obligation to the *personal* satisfaction, judgment, or taste of the other contracting party, he will not have *performed* his obligation nor be discharged from the contract until the other party has acknowledged that the *personal* standard has been met.

If, however, the obligation involves a matter of *mechanical fitness or suitability* for a particular purpose, a *reasonable person* test will be applied to determine whether satisfactory performance had been rendered resulting in discharge of the performing party. The following case is one of personal satisfaction as determined by interpreting the word "happy."

Facts

Defendant Nelson agreed to "trade back in twelve months" Fulcher's Ford car if Fulcher, plaintiff, was not "happy" with a Cadillac he bought from Nelson. Fulcher was not happy with the Cadillac on the day he bought it and, when he sought return of his Ford, Nelson informed him it was sold. Fulcher sued, claiming it was a personal satisfaction contract.

Decision

Judgment for the plaintiff, Fulcher.

Reasoning

The term "happy" meant personally satisfied, according to the court's interpretation. Since plaintiff in good faith was not personally satisfied with the Cadillac, he was entitled to the return of his Ford. Since the Ford could not be returned, the court gave the plaintiff damages which would place him as near as possible to the position he occupied before he entered into a contract with Nelson.

Fulcher v. Nelson, 159 S.E.2d 519 (N.C. 1968).

Time of the Essence

The time for performance of a contract is normally a *reasonable time* under the circumstances *if* no time is stated in the contract.

If time is of the essence because it is *expressly* made so by the contract or because a nontimely performance will be *valueless,* any performance other than on time results in a *material breach* and a *discharge* of the nonbreaching party.

In the following case neither the contract nor the facts indicated that time was of the essence.

Facts

String, the plaintiff, entered into a contract for a house to be built by the defendant contractor within 130 days of the signing of the contract. Some 70 days before the 130-day period was to expire String rescinded the contract, contending that time was of the essence because he needed the home before school started and he did not feel that the construction progress would allow completion of the house within 70 days. The house was substantially completed one month after the 130 days expired. String sues for the return of his deposit and rescission of the contract.

Decision

Judgment for the defendant contractor.

Reasoning

The court reasoned that time was not made of the essence by establishing a completion date for the contract. To make time of the essence the terms of the contract must unambiguously show such intent by the parties, or the facts must be so evident that such intent can be implied. The 130-day period here only established a date for performance.

String v. Steven Development Corp., 307 A.2d 713 (Md. 1973).

Impossibility of Performance

Concept

Impossibility of performance discharges one's obligation assumed by contract. Impossibility means "*it can not factually be done*" as opposed to "it is more difficult or less profitable for me to do it."

impossibility
performance can not factually be done

When Impossible

There are four situations where the law deems that factually something can not be done:

1. where the *personal services of the obligor* are so necessary to the performance of the contract that his *death* or *incapacitation* can make a *personal service obligation* impossible of performance;
2. where the performance of the obligation is deemed, after the formation of the contract but before the date of performance, to violate public policy;
3. where the subject matter essential to the performance of the contract is destroyed; and
4. where **commercial frustration** is experienced and the contract is deemed commercially impracticable.

commercial frustration
an excuse offered by a party to a contract justifying nonperformance of an obligation, usually because performance has been made impossible in fact

The following case illustrates impossibility of performance by supervening later illegality resulting in a discharge of the contract.

Facts

A contractor ceased the building of a home when he found that he could not follow the designer's instructions and specifications to build a home on a lot and give the homeowner a "view." The contractor found he would have to violate later-enacted zoning ordinances and subdivision restrictive covenants if he followed the designer's instructions. The homeowner sued the contractor for breach of contract.

Decision

Judgment for the contractor.

Reasoning

The court allowed the contractor to rescind the contract because it was impossible for him to perform it. When it becomes impossible for one to perform a contract without breaking the law, no contract remains which can be breached.

Quagliana v. Exquisite Home Builders Inc., 538 P.2d 301 (Utah 1975).

The Concept of Conditions

The *duty to perform* arises when the contract is created. The *time for performance* is normally at a later time. If a **condition** must happen *before* one is *required to perform,* the *promise* forming the basis of the contract is deemed *dependent* for its *performance* upon the *occurrence of the condition.* For example, A's promise to pay B for digging a ditch is performable when the condition occurs, namely when B has dug the ditch. A's promise is a **dependent promise,** dependent for its performance on condition of B's digging the ditch. A promise which forms the basis of a contract and renders the promisee *unconditionally* responsible to carry out the obligation contained in the promise is an **independent promise.** A *dependent promise* can be *discharged* by the *happening or nonhappening* of a *condition.* An independent promise is *discharged* by *its performance.* In the above example, if A's promise asked for and received *B's promise* to dig the ditch, B's promise is not dependent upon any condition. B's promise is an *independent promise* and B's duty to perform is discharged when he has dug the ditch. *A's* promise is still a *dependent promise,* performable on the occurrence of the condition of B's performing his promise by digging the ditch. In the following case the defendant was discharged from performing his dependent promise because the condition did not occur.

Facts

Walker, plaintiff, sued the defendant corporation for payment of a bonus under a plan initiated by the defendant while Walker was employed by them. One of the requirements of the plan was that, in order to receive the bonus, the employees be employed by the defendant at the time of the payment of the bonus. The plaintiff had terminated his employment with the defendant before the date of payment of the bonus.

Decision

Judgment for the defendant corporation.

Reasoning

The court determined that the plaintiff was not entitled to the payment of the bonus. An employee's right to compensation can be made expressly conditional upon rendition of a specified performance, and such a provision is not regarded as a penalty.

Continued employment was a condition for the payment of the bonus. Since that condition was not met, the defendant was not required to pay the bonus to Walker.

Walker v. American Optical Corporation, 509 P.2d 439 (Or. 1973).

Kinds of Condition

Conditions are either express, implied in fact, or implied in law and are classified as *precedent, concurrent,* or *subsequent.*

An *express* condition becomes part of a contract by words, written or oral. It is expressly stated. ("I'll repair your watch *if* you deliver it to me." Delivery is an express condition.) *Implied in fact* conditions are part of the contract though not expressed. They are inferred by the promisee because they are necessary for performance of the promisor's promise. (If A wants his watch fixed by B as B promised to do, A has to deliver his watch to B. Delivery is the condition implied in fact. If A can not deliver his watch to B, B has no duty to perform his promise to repair.) *Implied in law* conditions exist to ensure fairness between parties. (A and B enter into a contract and nothing is said about the time for payment of price. Payment upon delivery is implied in law. Delivery is the condition implied in law.) Implied in law conditions need only be substantially performed.

Conditions are normally introduced by words like "if," "when," "after," "as soon as," "provided that," "on condition that."

A **condition precedent** requires something to occur or not to occur *before* the performance of a duty is required (e.g., "dig the ditch and then I'll pay you."). **Concurrent conditions** are mutual conditions which are required to happen theoretically simultaneously (e.g., unpaid seller is to deliver the goods at the same time that payment is made). On the other hand, a duty to perform will be excused upon the occurrence or nonoccurrence of a **condition subsequent.** For example, a contract for transportation of goods provides that, after delivery, any claim for damage to the goods must be made within thirty days. The carrier's promissory duty to pay for any such damage will be excused if the condition subsequent, namely thirty days, expires before any claim is made.

The Concept of Discharge

As we have seen, discharge takes place by performance or by the occurrence or nonoccurrence of a condition. Discharge can also take place *by acts of the parties* or *by operation of law.*

condition precedent
a condition which must occur or not occur before a dependent promise becomes performable

condition concurrent
a condition which must occur at the same time as another condition

condition subsequent
a condition, on the occurrence or nonoccurrence of which, after a promise becomes performable, excuses the duty of performance

Discharge by Acts of the Parties

Novation.   We have previously discussed novation.[2] This is an act by the parties to a contract who mutually discharge their obligations under their contract so that a new contract with a new party can replace it. It is (1) a *new contract* with (2) a *new party* (3) *immediately discharging the old contract.* It is also an *accord and satisfaction.*

Accord, and Accord and Satisfaction.   When a subsequent new contract is made *between the same parties*, it is called an **accord**. The old contract still exists and will be discharged only by performance of the new contract. For example, M defaults on his promissory note held by the bank and he gives the bank his renewal note, the bank keeping both notes. M is still obligated on the original note, as well as on the new note which is an accord with the bank. However, if at the time of its formation the new contract *satisfies* the old contract and thereby causes its discharge, the new contract is called an **accord and satisfaction.** In the above example, if the bank returned the old note to M, the old note is discharged and the renewal note is an accord and satisfaction.

Mutual Rescission, Waiver, and Release.   Some other acts of the parties may cause a discharge. If the parties mutually agree to discharge each other from obligations assumed by a contract, *mutual* **rescission** occurs. If one party knowingly accepts a defective performance, this is a waiver of the nonperformance and is a discharge of the other party's duty to perform. One party can also extinguish a claim to performance by *releasing* the other party from his obligation to perform.

Intentional Material Alteration of a Written Contract.   A written contract which is *intentionally* and *materially altered* by a party to a contract without the consent of the other contracting party *discharges* the other party.

Destruction of a Sealed Contract.   The intentional physical destruction of a contract under seal by the person entitled to its performance discharges the person obligated to perform under the contract.

Discharge by Operation of Law

Statute of Limitations.   By statute in each state, the law gives a specific limited time period for the bringing of a suit for breach of contract. The time varies from three to ten years, depending upon whether the contract was oral or written. These time periods are contained in what is called a *statute of limitations.* The time period starts from the moment of breach of the contract, but it is suspended for periods when the breaching party is not within the jurisdiction of the court. If the *statute of limitations runs*, this acts as a barrier to suit for the nonperformance of a contract which is now *unenforceable* and thus, *in effect, discharges* the party who is in breach of contract.

---

[2] See p. 180.

accord
a new contract which provides that, on its performance, a previous contract as well as the new contract are discharged

accord and satisfaction
a new contract (accord) which discharges a party from a previous contractual obligation; the old contract is discharged (satisfied)

rescission
cancellation

Bankruptcy Discharge. A discharge in *bankruptcy* acts as a barrier to the enforcement of a contract. It terminates the bankrupt debtor's duty to perform and, therefore, is a discharge of such duty.

Judgment. Contracts are also discharged by mergers into **judgments** of claims for performance of a contractual duty. (A sues B for nonperformance and obtains a judgment. The contract is discharged and is merged into the judgment.)

Arbitration Award. Contracts are also discharged by an **arbitration** award by an arbitrator on the existence and violation of a contractual duty which merges the duty into the award and discharges the duty.

judgment
the final decision of a case by a court

arbitration
a method for deciding disputes outside of court by persons called arbitrators, appointed by the disputing parties

The Uniform Commercial Code

Performance Under the Code

The Code does not require performance to one's personal satisfaction but, rather, requires a *good faith performance*[3] in all applicable cases, thus requiring that the *reasonable expectations* of a contracting party be met. This is illustrated by the following case.

Facts

Terry, a gasoline dealer, sued the defendant for breach of contract. Defendant, in a time of gasoline shortage, was required to allocate gasoline supplies among its dealers, including Terry. The defendant found it *impossible* to fully meet its contractual commitments to its dealers due to the energy crisis. The defendant allocated its supplies among its customers on a quota-percentage basis based upon previous year's gallon usage.

Decision

Judgment for the defendant.

Reasoning

The court noted that under the Uniform Commercial Code as it is enacted in California, partial performance will discharge one from his obligation to multiple customers when suppliers *inadvertently* become short, making full performance impossible. What is required is that the party allocating scarce supplies act *in good faith* and proceed in *a fair and reasonable manner.* The court concluded that the quota system met the criteria for discharging the contractual obligation of the defendant.

Terry v. Atlantic Richfield Co., 140 Cal.Rptr. 510 (1977).

Discharge Under the Code

In the case of a *material breach*, the Code provides that the nonbreaching party may *cancel* a contract reserving, however, remedies for nonperformance.[4] In the case of one party's repudiation by anticipatory breach, the Code seeks to encourage performance and, therefore, permits the repudiating party to retract his repudiation before his performance is due if, meanwhile, the party not in breach

---

[3] UCC 1–203.

[4] UCC 2–106(3).

has not *cancelled* the contract or *materially changed his position in reliance* on the repudiation.[5] However, the party not in breach, upon such repudiation, can ask for *additional assurances*—e.g., a bond.[6] If such assurances are not forthcoming, the nonbreaching party can *discharge* himself by *cancellation*.

Termination of a contract occurs *without a breach* but, rather, by one party exercising a power (e.g., exercising a power of avoidance caused by a contract fraudulently induced). Termination acts as a discharge of all parties to a contract, reserving, however, to the party not in breach any remedies for a *prior* breach or defective performance.[7]

The Code provides for a four-year statute of limitations for a sales contract which, in effect, can discharge the contract by its running.[8] Moreover, unlike the common law of contracts, a *written* waiver or renunciation of an obligation owed under a sales contract acts as a discharge even though it is not supported by consideration.[9]

Summary Statement

1. Normally parties to a contract expect complete performance, but the law recognizes other types of performance—namely, substantial and partial. Partial performance when coupled with a damage award will discharge contracts.
2. In special cases, such as anticipatory breach, personal satisfaction, and time of the essence, a party can be discharged from performing his side of the contractual commitment.
3. Four situations exist in law which are deemed factual situations of impossibility which will discharge one's duty assumed by contract.
4. There are conditions precedent, concurrent, subsequent, and also express, implied in fact, and implied in law. The failure of a condition may cause a contract obligation to cease to exist or never to come into existence.
5. Discharge of obligations assumed by contract can happen by acts of the parties through novation, an accord and satisfaction, mutual rescission, waiver, release, intentional material alteration of a written contract, and destruction of a sealed contract.
6. By operation of law, a contract can be discharged by (in effect) the running of the statute of limitations, discharge in bankruptcy, judgment, and arbitration award.
7. The primary interest of the Code is to encourage a good-faith performance of contractual obligations.

The following case illustrates how the interest of society in seeing that contracts are performed is balanced against impossibility of performance.

---

[5] UCC 2–611.   [8] UCC 2–725.

[6] UCC 2–609.   [9] UCC 1–107.

[7] UCC 2–106(4).

Transatlantic Financing Corp. v. United States

363 F.2d 312 (1966)

This case involves an appeal from a judgment entered in favor of the United States. Transatlantic sued the United States for additional cost of carriage pursuant to a contract for the shipment of wheat on the vessel *S.S.Christos* from Texas to Iran.

The carriage cost of $43,972 above and beyond the contract price of $305,842.92 resulted from an extension of a 10,000 mile voyage by about 3,000 miles around the Cape of [Good Hope] Africa after the closing of the Suez Canal by the Egyptian government through obstruction by sunken vessels. This action by the Egyptian government took place on November 2, 1956 shortly after the invasion of Egypt by Israel on October 29, 1956 and the invasion of the canal zone by Britain and France on October 31, 1956. The canal had been nationalized by Egypt on July 26, 1956.

It was on October 2, 1956 that the contract was made by the plaintiff and defendant in an atmosphere of international tension. On October 27, 1956 the *S.S. Christos* sailed from Galveston, Texas for Bandar Shapur, Iran on a course which would have taken her through Gibraltar and the Suez Canal.

On November 7, 1956 a representative of Transatlantic contacted the United States government, requesting instructions concerning the disposition of the cargo and an agreement for payment of additional compensation for a voyage around the Cape of Good Hope. The United States informed Transatlantic that *they were expected to perform their obligation assumed by contract without additional compensation.* The *Christos* changed course following this discussion and delivered the wheat in December at Bandar Shapur, Iran.

Plaintiff seeks additional compensation denied to them by the United States District Court.

This court affirmed the judgment of the district court denying relief to the plaintiff.

The court recognized the plaintiff's argument that implicit in the contract was the contemplation that the *Christos* would use the "usual and customary" route to deliver the wheat (a constructive condition), such route would normally include passage through the Suez Canal, and when that route was closed, the contract was impossible to perform as originally contemplated, and because of the need for altered performance, additional compensation was owed.

The court rejected the plaintiff's argument, holding that *"a thing is impossible in legal contemplation when it is not practicable, and a thing is impracticable when it can only be done at an excessive and unreasonable cost."* The court noted that this approach ultimately represents the ever-shifting line drawn by courts hopefully responsive to commercial practices and mores, at which the community's interest in having contracts enforced according to their terms is outweighed only by the commercial senselessness of requiring performance.

In order to apply the ever-shifting line to excuse one from performance of obligations assumed by contract by applying the doctrine of impossibility the court noted the need to satisfy three reasonably definable steps. First, a contingency, something unexpected, must have occurred. Second, the risk of the unexpected occurrence must not have been allocated either by agreement or custom. Finally, occurrence of the contingency must have rendered performance commercially impracticable.

The court held the timing of the closing of the canal met the first requirement of an unexpected event. The contingency of foreclosure of the route was to a certain extent, in the eyes of the court, somewhat foreseen by Transatlantic (international tension) and since the continued passage of the canal was not made an *express condition* of the contract, it could be argued to have been assumed by them. Thus, requirement two *could* be interpreted adversely against Transatlantic.

The court, however, decided the case based upon the third element, of commercial impracticability. The court pointed out that (any) *increased cost and difficulty of performance never constitutes impracticability.* Justification for relief in this case would require more of a variation between expected cost and the actual cost of performing by the available alternative route.

Questions and Case Problems

1. A contract of sale of a broadcasting corporation provided that a certain purchase price was to be paid by the buyer by executing a personal note *or* by executing a note by a corporation formed by the buyer. The corporation was formed and it issued the note. The corporation was unable to pay the note, and the seller sued the buyer for payment. What result? [*Clayton v. Communications Capital Corp.,* 440 P.2d 330 (Ariz. 1968).]

2. An action was brought by a contractor to foreclose a material-man's lien for some $6,000 on a $25,000 home he contracted to build. The owners counterclaimed for $2,000 for repairs on the new structure. What result? [*Hafer v. Horn,* 515 P.2d 1013 (Ida. 1973).]

3. A maker of a promissory note, some two years before the note is payable, informs the payee that he does not intend to pay the note. Can the payee immediately sue for breach of contract? [*Bertolet v. Burke,* 295 F.Supp. 1176 (1969).]

4. Plaintiff signed a contract for $25,000 worth of dancing lessons from the defendant. A clause in the contract read "NONCANCELLABLE NEGOTIABLE CONTRACT" and "I UNDERSTAND THAT NO REFUNDS WILL BE MADE." Plaintiff had some lessons, and then he was involved in an automobile accident and suffered injuries which prevent him from dancing. Can the defendant enforce the contract? [*Parker v. Arthur Murray, Inc.,* 295 N.E.2d 487 (Ill. 1973).]

5. Seller of a restaurant agreed to a condition being placed into a contract for the sale of the restaurant for the benefit of the purchasers. The sale of the restaurant was conditioned upon the transfer of a liquor license. Taxes were assessed on the sale of the property under a statute passed on Sept. 1. The contract was formed in August and the liquor license was transferred in mid-September. Is the seller or the buyer responsible for payment of the sales tax? [*Kubly v. Wisconsin Dept. of Revenue,* 233 N.W.2d 369 (Wis. 1975).]

6. A shipment of defective lumber was received by a manufacturer. In order to settle the matter, the wholesaler broker supplier agreed to give a credit to the manufacturer on the bill. A letter confirming the allowance of the credit was received by the manufacturer. The wholesaler broker supplier is now suing for the full contract price. What result? [*Ruble Forest Products, Inc. v. Lancer Mobile Homes of Oregon, Inc.,* 524 P.2d 1204 (Or. 1974).]

7. The defendant paid a general contractor and received from the plaintiff subcontractor a promise not to sue on a **mechanic's lien.** When the subcontractor did not receive payment from the general contractor, the subcontractor sued the defendant homeowner, asserting that the homeowner could not set off a breach of contract not to sue under a statute which provided that claims arising out of the same transaction can not be offered as a counterclaim to a mechanic's lien. What result? [*Malin v. Nuss,* 338 A.2d 676 (Pa. 1975).]

8. A supplier sought to foreclose a mechanic's lien on the defendant's property. The general contractor had made a payment to the supplier out of his general fund. The supplier applied these payments to the contractor's bill but *not* for supplies used in the defendant's home. The defendant had paid the general contractor for the supplies. Must the landowner pay twice for the supplies? [*Lumber Supply, Inc. v. Hull,* 158 N.W.2d 667 (Iowa 1968).]

9. The defendant lost several crops valued at $20,000 due to the fact that a defective pump was not adequately repaired by the plaintiff. Plaintiff sued for $550 for repair of the pump. Defendant claims he owes plaintiff nothing. What result? [*Widner Electric & Industrial, Inc. v. Lee,* 537 P.2d 527 (Or. 1975).]

10. In *Transatlantic Financing Corp. v. United States,* 363 F.2d 312 (1966),[10] the court held that the concept of impossibility ultimately represents an ever-shifting line drawn by courts responsive to commercial practices and mores which shows that the community's interest in having contracts enforced according to their terms is outweighed only by commercial senselessness of requiring performance. Discuss the significance of this statement.

mechanic's lien
a statutory lien on real property given to a person who, pursuant to contract, has rendered labor, services, or materials for the improvement of the property and who has not been paid

---

[10] See pp. 207–8.

Agency and Employment

Summary

An agency relationship is created by agreement for the purpose of transacting business affairs by one party with a person acting on behalf of another. The primary objective of the agency is to give authority and power to an agent to create a contract between his principal and a third person. In the process, various rights, duties, and liabilities are created on the part of the principal, agent, and third person.

As with other legal relationships, the law provides for termination of the agency relationship through freedom of individual action and by operation of law.

Any discussion of employment involves not only the agency relationship between employer and employee, covered in chapters 14-17, but also an examination of the regard which society has for employees as reflected in federal and state legislation affecting their employment, protection from injury, compensation for injury, and financial security. Chapter 18 is concerned with such legislation.

14 Nature and Creation

After you have read this chapter, you should be able to:

1. Define the agency relationship.
2. Identify the source of agency law.
3. Describe the relationship of agency law to business transactions.
4. Indicate how an agent's conduct may affect the liabilities of the agent, the principal, and the third person.
5. Explain why it is important to determine whether an agent is a servant.
6. Distinguish an agent from
   a. an independent contractor,
   b. a real estate broker,
   c. a bailee,
   d. a trustee.
7. Distinguish a general power of attorney from a limited power of attorney.
8. Describe the relationship of agency law to business associations.
9. Explain who may be a principal and who may be an agent.
10. Distinguish a general from a special agent.
11. Explain how an agency is created.
12. Define ratification; what are its five elements?
13. Explain who must prove the agency relationship.

Introduction

All around us are **agents,** persons acting on behalf of others. During your business career and private life you will have various dealings with agents. In some manner you will be involved as an agent in the selling of goods or services to the general public. As a consumer you will go to the marketplace for your "daily bread" and there deal with persons representing others. In these transactions the work process is delivered to society through the "hands of agents."

Because the laws of **agency** enter into all forms of business activity, this chapter will explain the nature of the agency relationship within the corporation, partnership, and sole proprietorship.

The rights and duties of the parties involved in agency create a series of potential lawsuits. This chapter will examine and illustrate this liability exposure.

In order for you to recognize an agency problem, it is necessary to distinguish other types of somewhat similar business relationships. This chapter will explain the reasons for the difference based upon agency law.

An important point to watch for in the chapter is how the law applies the value judgment that someone who uses another to create rights and duties should be liable for the consequences of the other's acts.

Nature of the Agency Relationship

Agency Concept
Business associations rely on their employees and other representatives to contract and to act on their behalf in the delivering of goods and services. The relationships formed by this process have legal consequences governed by agency law.

Source of Agency Law
The source of agency law is the common law created through each state's judicial system where the agency agreement was made.[1] Rights and duties conflict in this three-party relationship (the business or individual is referred to as the **principal** in agency law; the representative acting under the authority and on behalf of the principal is called the *agent;* and the person with whom the agent contracts is called the *third party*). The courts, in resolving these disputes, establish a body of law relevant to almost every business transaction. To a much lesser extent, statutes assist in the creation of agency law. Statutory laws have adopted agency principles to provide a legislative remedy to aggrieved parties.

Throughout Part 3, Agency and Employment, reference will be made to the *Restatement of Agency,* which is an authoritative general compilation of the common law of agency throughout the country and constantly referred to in judicial decisions and opinions.

---

[1] RESTATEMENT (SECOND) OF CONFLICT OF LAWS sec. 291 (1969).

agent
a person authorized to act on behalf of another and subject to the other's control

agency
a legal relationship between two persons who agree that one is to act on behalf of the other, subject to the other's control

principal
a person who has authorized an agent to act on his behalf and subject to his control

Business Organizations and Agency Law

Agreements that are commonly made in dealings with business associations frequently involve agency issues. For example, a salesman (agent) who contracts with the customer (third party), on behalf of his company (principal), is acting pursuant to an agency relationship, and a consequent series of rights and duties arises for all parties to the transaction.

The laws governing the *operation* of the corporation, partnership, and the sole proprietorship illustrate the application of agency laws.

Corporations

corporation
a legal entity created by statute authorizing an association of persons to carry on an enterprise

The **corporation** is an artificial person or legal entity created by law.[2] State statutory law has authorized it to deliver goods and services through the "hands of agents" acting on its behalf. Ordinarily, the officers of a corporation and certain other designated employees are those agents through whom the corporation acts.[3] The board of directors is not an agent of the corporation because it is not under the direct control of the stockholders, and the board makes its own managerial decisions.[4]

Partnerships

partnership
an association of two or more persons to carry on as co-owners a business for profit

Partnerships are governed by the Uniform Partnership Act and the owners' partnership agreement.[5] The U.P.A. sec. 9(1) provides: "Every partner is an agent of the partnership for the purpose of its business . . ." and thus establishes the statutory foundation for the application of agency law to partnership transactions.[6]

Sole Proprietorships

A sole proprietor has the legal right and exclusive ownership to his or her business. The agency relationship occurs when the proprietor owner hires employees or other representatives to contract with customers on his behalf. For example, a real estate broker who owns houses (principal) hires a salesman (agent) to sell his houses. The contract that the agent (salesman) makes with the buyer (third person) to sell him a house will bind the proprietor principal (broker).

---

[2] *Black's Law Dictionary,* Rev. 5th ed., 307 (1979); see Part 8B, Business Organizations: Corporations.

[3] *Model Business Corporation Act,* sec. 4(j), General Powers: "Each corporation shall have power to conduct its business, carry on its operations, . . . have offices and exercise the powers granted by this Act . . ."; and *Phoenix Savings and Loan, Inc. v. Aetna Casualty & Surety Co.,* 266 F.Supp. 465 (1966).

[4] RESTATEMENT (SECOND) OF AGENCY sec. 14C. (1958): "Neither the board of directors nor an individual director . . . is an agent of the corporation."

[5] The Act has been adopted in all states except Georgia, Louisiana, and Mississippi.

[6] See Part 8A, Business Organizations: Partnerships and Special Ventures.

Figure 14.1   Relationships Among Principal-Agent-Third Party

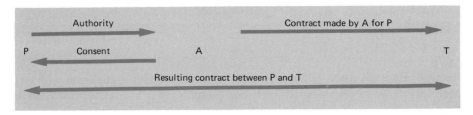

Most business transactions involve one person acting for another person and, therefore, agency law applies. All parties concerned in the agency relationship should understand the legal consequences of their actions. This chapter will help you to identify the agency issues.

Definition of Agency

Agency is a **fiduciary** relationship based upon an express or implied *agreement* whereby one party, the agent, is authorized to act *on behalf* and *under the control* of another, the principal, when the agent consents so to act.[7] Basically, agency is a legal relationship between two persons who agree that one (agent) is to act on behalf of the other (principal), subject to the other's control. Throughout Part 3, Agency and Employment, we will often use the following abbreviations: P (principal), A (agent), T (third party). This relationship may be diagrammed as in figure 14.1.

fiduciary
a person with a duty to act for the benefit of another

Liability Under the Agency Relationship

Although agency may appear to be a simple legal relationship, the following examples illustrate possible grounds for liability through agency.

T v. P

The intended result of creating an agency is to make the *principal* liable and to protect the agent from *personal liability* to third parties. When an agent acts within the scope of his **actual** or **apparent authority** and makes a contract with a third party on behalf of his disclosed or partially disclosed principal, he is not liable on the contract to either the third party or the principal. Only the principal is liable to the third party.

Whether a principal is a disclosed principal, partially disclosed principal, or an undisclosed principal depends upon the knowledge of the third party (T). If T knows or reasonably should know:

1. that A is an agent for a principal and T knows who he is, the latter is a disclosed principal;
2. that A is an agent for a principal but T does not know who he is, the latter is a partially disclosed principal.

authority
an agent's power to act for his principal in accordance with the principal's manifestation of consent to the agent

actual authority
express and implied authority

apparent authority
the power of a person (A) to act as though he were an agent, created by another's (P's) manifestation to a third person (T) that A is P's agent

---

[7] RESTATEMENT (SECOND) OF AGENCY sec. 1 (1958); and *Tonka Corp. v. Commissioner of Taxation*, 169 N.W.2d 589, 593 (Minn. 1969).

If T does not know or reasonably should not know that A is an agent for a principal, the latter is an undisclosed principal. The law of agency applicable to disclosed principals is, generally, equally applicable to partially disclosed principals.

P v. T

The business association (P) may sue on its contract with a customer (T) authorizedly made by its salesman (A). For example, A is a salesman for P shoe store and sells a pair of shoes to T, who is now liable to P for the price.

T v. A

The agent must carefully comply with agency law or he may incur personal liability for making an authorized contract. For example, if the agent does not disclose his principal or his agency status but purports to act on his own behalf, he is a party to the contract with T.

The agent may also be personally liable for committing a tort against the third party. For example, a principal instructs an agent to **slander** a competitor, which the agent does.

slander
a defamatory publication by spoken words, gestures, or other nonpermanent form

A v. T

The agent may sue the third party in contract or in tort in certain circumstances. The third party is liable to the agent in contract if the agent did not disclose to the third party that he was acting for a principal. The third party intended to contract with the agent and, therefore, he is liable to the agent on the contract.

The third party is liable to the agent in tort if he wrongfully injures the agent or his property.

A v. P

The agent normally has an employment contract with the principal and can sue him for its breach. For example, P may wrongfully discharge or not pay A a due commission. It should be carefully noted that, under sec. 441 of the Restatement of Agency: "Unless the relationship of the parties, the triviality of the services, or other circumstances indicate that the parties have agreed otherwise, it is inferred that (P) promises to pay for services which he requests or permits another to perform for him as an agent."

P v. A

When the principal authorizes the agent to act on his behalf, various legal duties come into existence obligating the agent to perform in a certain manner. Violation of these duties will allow the principal to sue the agent. The next chapter will discuss these duties.

Master and Servant Relationship

To the extent that a person has the right of control, or exercises control, over another person, he is liable for the other person's conduct. The principal's control may or may not be over the agent's *physical* conduct. If control is not over

Agency and Employment

physical conduct, then the principal is not liable for the agent's *physical* conduct. (P retains A, a real estate broker, to produce a willing and able buyer of P's house and land. A drives his own car negligently and hits X, a pedestrian. P is not liable to X; only A is liable to X. P did not have the right to control the *physical* conduct of A, a special agent, in driving A's automobile.)

However, if a principal has the right to control, or exercises control, over the *physical* conduct of his agent, he is liable to third persons for *physical* harm caused to them by the agent's wrongful *physical* conduct. Such an agent is called a "servant," or often "employee," and the principal is called a "master." (P's truck driver negligently drives into T while delivering P's goods. Since P has the right to control A's *physical* conduct, A is a servant and P is liable to T for T's *physical* injury caused by A's negligence.) Most agents are servants.

The terms of *master* and *servant* are used in the *employment* relationship only to determine the liability of an employer principal for the *physical harm* caused to third persons by the servant employee's *torts*. This legal relationship exists when the master (principal) controls the *physical conduct* of the servant (agent). The master is held responsible for the negligence of his servant causing physical injury to the third party.[8]

Agency Distinguished from Other Business Relationships

Independent Contractor

For agency to exist, the principal must have the right to exercise *control*, or actually exercise control, over the agent. An **independent contractor** hired to accomplish a physical *result* is not an agent primarily because he is not under the *supervision and control* of the hiring party. He acts independently on his own and makes his own contracts. The following case illustrates how the courts use agency principles in distinguishing the independent contractor and establishing his liability for negligence.

independent contractor
a person who contracts independently for himself to render a result, and who is not acting on behalf of another nor subject to another's control

Facts
Andrew & Dawson, general contractors, agreed with Klein, defendant, to build an addition to a building owned by Klein. Mr. Transmission, Inc. occupied an adjoining building. A wall of the new addition collapsed and fell through the roof of the building occupied by Mr. Transmission, Inc. This is a suit brought by Mr. Transmission, Inc., plaintiff, to hold Klein liable for damage to the adjoining building caused by the general contractor's negligence.

Decision
Judgment for defendant, Klein.

Reasoning
An owner is not liable for property damage to a third person caused by the negligence of an independent contractor. The general contractor was not under the control of the owner and was not an agent.

Klein v. Mr. Transmission, Inc., 318 So.2d 676 (Ala. 1975).

---

[8] *Smalich v. Westfall*, 269 A.2d 476 (Pa. 1970).

An independent contractor may become an agent if he is subject to the *control* of the principal in the performance of service. The degree of control the principal exercises over the hired party is decisive, and the courts will disregard the professional status of the hired party and examine the facts of the situation on the issue of control.

Some independent contractors retain their status as such when retained to act. Examples are doctors, certified public accountants, and engineers. If control should be exercised over their conduct, then they become agents. Examples are hiring a doctor to be an employee in the employer's plant, hiring the C.P.A. as the treasurer or comptroller of a firm, and hiring the engineer as a member of the employer's staff.

Some independent contractors lose this status as such while they are retained to do a job; they become agents. Examples are lawyers, real estate **brokers, auctioneers,** and **factors.** They become "special agents" or "professional agents."

Real Estate Broker.   A real estate broker is licensed by the state to represent sellers in the sale of their real property (land). He is compensated for this service on a commission basis. A real estate broker has very limited authority—generally to state the asking price and identify the owner's property—and in such capacity he is an agent. The broker may be given authority to represent the seller and to contract on his behalf rather than just to negotiate for him.[9]

broker
a person authorized to represent another and to negotiate for him with others

auctioneer
a person licensed by law to sell property of another at a public sale

factor
a person in business for himself with authority to buy goods, or to sell goods in his possession, in his own name for another

bailment
delivery of goods by a bailor to a bailee which are to be returned to the bailor or as he directs in accordance with the bailment agreement

trustee
a person who has title to property in trust for the benefit of someone

Bailee

Bailed property is goods delivered by a bailor to another, the bailee, to be returned to the bailor or as he directs.[10] As business associations continue to rent equipment, the incidents of bailed property become very common. A bailee is not an agent, but he can become an agent if he has possession with authority to buy, sell, or otherwise deal with the bailed goods on behalf of the bailor.

Trustee

A **trustee** is a party to whom the legal title of property has been transferred for the purpose of managing the property for a beneficiary.

Although the trustee acts on behalf of the beneficiary, generally he is not an agent because:

1. he has title to the property held in trust, while an agent normally does not have title;
2. he has no authority to make the beneficiary a party to a contract with anyone, while an agent has the authority to make his disclosed principal a party to the contract;

---

[9] *Knudson v. Weeks,* 394 F.Supp. 963 (Okla. 1975).

[10] See Part 4, Personal Property and Bailments; and *English v. Dhane,* 286 S.W.2d 666 (Tex. 1956).

3. he acts in his own name, while an agent normally acts in the name of his principal; and

4. the trust is not revocable by the trustee, while agency is usually revocable by the agent or the principal.[11]

However, in a grantor/trust the grantor (the transferor of the property) has the right to *control the management* of the property during his life. In this instance and to that extent, the trustee is an agent of the grantor.[12] For a trustee to be an agent, he must, under the terms of the trust, be subject to the control of another.

The following case illustrates the distinction between a "trust" and an "agency." Notice that the court is not concerned with a written document that describes the parties as "escrow agent" or "trustee" but, rather, with the relationship as determined by the facts.

Facts

The Merchants National Bank of Aurora sued Walter Frazier for a court order directing the bank to deliver to Frazier securities and cash, held under a written "escrow agent" agreement for his benefit, and the bank requested to be relieved of responsibility as an agent under the agreement. Frazier, the beneficiary, filed a counterclaim that the bank was a *trustee* and had mismanaged the alleged trust funds with a loss to the trust estate. Was the bank an agent or a trustee?

Reasoning

No particular formality is required in the creation of a trust. From the time the deposit was made in escrow with the bank it became the trustee of Frazier, the beneficiary. Although the bank, as trustee, was not subject to the control of the beneficiary, it was under a duty to manage the trust property for the beneficiary and can be compelled by him to perform its duties.

Merchants National Bank of Aurora v. Frazier, 67 N.E.2d 611 (Ill. 1946).

Decision

A trustee. Judgment for Frazier.

Power of Attorney

A written authorization to act as an agent is called a **power of attorney** (see figure 14.2). There are two types based upon the extent of the authority given to the agent.

power of attorney
written authority by a principal to an agent

Limited Power of Attorney

When the power to act or contract is *restricted* to a certain period of time and to specific transactions, it is a *limited power of attorney*.

---

[11] See Joseph L. Frascona, *C.P.A. Law Review,* 5th ed. (Homewood, Ill.: Richard D. Irwin, 1977), p. 568; *Cassedy v. Connecticut Gen. Life Ins. Co.,* 56 Misc.2d 970 (N.Y. 1968); and RESTATEMENT (SECOND) OF TRUSTS sec. 8 (1957).

[12] See Warren A. Seavey, *Agency* (St. Paul: West Publishing Co., 1964), p. 19.

Figure 14.2 Power of Attorney

Form **2848**
(Rev. July 1976)
Department of the Treasury
Internal Revenue Service

Power of Attorney
(See the separate Instructions for Forms 2848 and 2848–D.)

Name, identifying number, and address including ZIP code of taxpayer(s)

hereby appoints (Name, address including ZIP code, and telephone number of appointee(s)) (See Treasury Department Circular No. 230 as amended (31 C.F.R. Part 10), Regulations Governing the Practice of Attorneys, Certified Public Accountants, and Enrolled Agents before the Internal Revenue Service, for persons recognized to practice before the Internal Revenue Service.)

as attorney(s)-in-fact to represent the taxpayer(s) before any office of the Internal Revenue Service for the following Internal Revenue tax matters (specify the type(s) of tax and year(s) or period(s) (date of death if estate tax)):

The attorney(s)-in-fact (or either of them) are authorized, subject to revocation, to receive confidential information and to perform on behalf of the taxpayer(s) the following acts for the above tax matters:
(Strike through any of the following which are not granted.)

To receive, but not to endorse and collect, checks in payment of any refund of Internal Revenue taxes, penalties, or interest. (See "Refund checks" on page 2 of the separate instructions.)

To execute waivers (including offers of waivers) of restrictions on assessment or collection of deficiencies in tax and waivers of notice of disallowance of a claim for credit or refund.

To execute consents extending the statutory period for assessment or collection of taxes.

To execute closing agreements under section 7121 of the Internal Revenue Code.

To delegate authority or to substitute another representative.

Other acts (specify) ....

Send copies of notices and other written communications addressed to the taxpayer(s) in proceedings involving the above matters to (Name, address including ZIP code, and telephone number):

and

This power of attorney revokes all earlier powers of attorney and tax information authorizations on file with the same Internal Revenue Service office for the same matters and years or periods covered by this form, except the following:

....
(Specify to whom granted, date, and address including ZIP code, or refer to attached copies of earlier powers and authorizations.)

Signature of or for taxpayer(s)
If signed by a corporate officer, partner, or fiduciary on behalf of the taxpayer, I certify that I have the authority to execute this power of attorney on behalf of the taxpayer.

....
(Signature)   (Title, if applicable)   (Date)

....
(Signature)   (Title, if applicable)   (Date)

(The applicable portion of the back page must also be completed.)   Form **2848** (Rev. 7–76)

For example, P authorizes A to withdraw a specified amount of money from his personal checking account while P is in the hospital. The restrictions here are to a certain amount and during hospitalization.

General Power of Attorney

An authorization to do any and all things necessary to carry on with the principal's legal affairs is a *general power of attorney*.

Notice how the court strictly interprets the terms of the power of attorney in the following case.

Facts

The defendant, owner of a plot of land, employed an agent to develop it by drilling for gas and oil, and he executed a power of attorney authorizing the agent "to do and perform each and every act and thing necessary or requisite to be done in the handling, contracting for purchasing or selling any and all property in the name of Florence Oil Company and to execute all necessary decision orders, leases, and assignments, and all other contracts affecting the interest of the Florence Oil Company." The owner claimed that the power of attorney did not give the agent authority to make a loan to the drillers in order that the work might continue.

Decision

Judgment for defendant owner.

Reasoning

Powers of attorney are strictly construed, and the power to sell does not include the power to make a loan.

First National Bank of Troup, Texas v. Blades, 93 F.2d 154 (1937).

Capacity to Be Principal, Agent

Principal

Generally, if a person has the legal capacity to act, he can act through an agent.[13] If the principal has limited capacity, the appointment of an agent is void or voidable in accordance with contract law. For example, P, a minor, authorizes A, an adult, to purchase a television set from a merchant. Both the appointment of the agent and the purchase contract made under it are voidable by the minor. The contract may be ratified after the infant reaches majority.

Agent

Any person may act as an agent, even if he lacks contractual capacity. The contract is between the principal and the third party; the agent is not a party to the contract. Thus, although a minor/agent can avoid his contract with his principal who appointed him an agent, he has the power to bind the principal with a third party. The infant's power of avoidance is personal to the infant and is not available to the principal.

---

[13] See chapter 9, Capacity/Ability to Create a Contract.

Classification of Agents

Agents are classified in accordance with the extent of their authority. There are two classes of agents, "general" and "special," both of whom receive a delegation of authority from the principal to perform on its behalf. If an agent exceeds the scope of his authority, he is personally liable and the principal is not bound.

General Agent

general agent
an agent authorized to conduct a series of transactions involving a continuity of service

A **general agent** has been defined as "an agent authorized to conduct a series of transactions involving a continuity of service." [14] An example of a *general agent* is the manager of a retail hardware store employed to perform all the acts connected with managing the store. Limiting the agent's authority to the hardware store does not make the agency special. The *continuity of services* would involve such acts as personnel responsibility, buying merchandise, and dealing with customer relations on a daily basis. Other examples are sales personnel, truck drivers, secretaries, and clerks on salary.

Special Agent

special agent
an agent authorized to conduct a single transaction or series of transactions not involving continuity of service

"A **special agent** is an agent authorized to conduct a single transaction or a series of transactions not involving continuity of service." [15] A power of attorney given by a stockholder to a broker to sell a stock certificate is an example of a special agency. The single transaction of selling stock will terminate the broker's authority. There is no continuity of service involved in the sale transaction.

A universal agent is a sort of unlimited general agent, and is an agent authorized by the principal to transact all business of every kind. This is usually given in an emergency situation and can be created only by clear and unambiguous language. It is rarely used but, if used, it should be limited to a stated period of time. For example, "to do anything that must be done during my stay in the hospital."

Creating the Agency

Appointment—Consent of the Principal and Agent

The agency relationship is based on an implied or express agreement between the principal and the agent, as found in the facts of each case. For example, P expressly appoints A to act for and on behalf of P, and A consents. An agency relationship may be created in an informal manner without compensation being paid to the agent. Although the agency relationship usually is contractual, it may be a *gratuitous* undertaking by the agent. [16] If the agency is created by a

---

[14] RESTATEMENT (SECOND) OF AGENCY sec. 3 (1958); and *Kelly v. U.S. Steel Corporation and The Thew Shovel Company,* 170 F.Supp. 649 (1959).

[15] RESTATEMENT (SECOND) OF AGENCY sec. 3 (1958).

[16] *Groh v. Shelton,* 428 S.W.2nd 911 (Mo. 1968).

contract between the principal and the agent, the law of contracts applies to its enforcement.[17]

Form

Unless state statutory law requires a writing, the appointment of an agent may be oral or by conduct. For example, if P authorizes A *to sell his land,* the appointment must be in writing.

Ratification

Ratification by one person of an unauthorized act by another person does *not* create agency because there is no *initial* agreement between the two persons that one is to act for the other.

Ratification is the affirmation by a person of a prior act which did not bind him but which was done on his account and is given effect as if originally authorized by him.[18]

But it has the *effect* of agency. Ratification becomes important when an agent exceeds his authority when dealing in the principal's name with a third party, or when a person, not an agent, acts on behalf of another in the latter's name. In both cases, *unless the principal ratifies his actions with the third party,* the principal is not liable but the agent is personally liable on the contract. The doctrine of ratification may be useful when a principal, with knowledge of the unauthorized transaction, accepts the benefit or affirms the "agent's" conduct and thereby becomes bound with the same effect as though the agent had authority so to act. (An unauthorized real estate agent, in P's name, signs a purchase and sale agreement with T to sell P's house above its appraised market value; if P wants the benefit of this contract, his subsequent written ratification will bind himself and T.)

The courts in the following cases applied the doctrine of ratification (a) when the principal knowingly accepted the benefit of an unauthorized loan, and (b) when the city council expressly confirmed the authority of the city manager.

Facts

Serges' managing agent exceeded his authority when he borrowed $3,500 from David, plaintiff, for Serges, defendant, for his use in his business, a retail meat market. Serges paid to David $200 on the alleged loan and stated on several occasions that the full sum would eventually be paid. David sued Serges on the loan.

Decision

Judgment for plaintiff, David.

Reasoning

When an agent purporting to act for a principal exceeds his actual or apparent authority, the act of the agent may still bind the principal if he ratifies it. When Serges, after the unauthorized loan, paid $200 to David and stated the full amount would eventually be paid, he ratified the loan for which he originally was not liable.

David v. Serges, 129 N.W.2d 882 (Mich. 1964).

---

[17] *Automotive Finance Co. v. Kesk, Inc.,* 200 So.2d 136 (La. 1967).

[18] RESTATEMENT (SECOND) OF AGENCY sec. 82 (1958).

Facts

Los Angeles Dredging Co., plaintiff, had a dredging contract with the City of Long Beach, defendant. It was discovered that the dredging operations were polluting the harbor. The city manager, acting for the city, entered into a contract with the dredging company under which the dredging company was to cease work temporarily and carry already dredged materials through longer lines to avoid injury to health. The contract was *later* affirmed by the city council. The dredging company sued the city on the contract. Did the city manager have power to bind the city without authorization by the council?

Decision

Yes. Judgment for plaintiff, Los Angeles Dredging Co.

Reasoning

The city council expressly confirmed the city manager's authority and ratified the contract. Ratification is equivalent to a previous authority: it operates upon the contract in the same manner as though the authority to make the contract had originally existed.

Los Angeles Dredging Co. v. City of Long Beach, 291 P.2d 839 (Cal. 1930).

Elements of Ratification. For ratification, the principal must *intend* to affirm the transaction and the following conditions must be satisfied:

1. The principal must have had *legal capacity* when the act or transaction occurred.
2. The principal must ratify the *entire* contract; he can not accept the benefits and reject the obligations. For example, A, without authorization, sold P's merchandise on credit, payable in installments. P can not ratify the sale and exclude the installment sale provision. P has to ratify the contract in its entirety or not at all. In the following case the court held that the principal's acceptance of benefits was a ratification of the entire contract.

Facts

Martin, a general contractor, was hired to construct a cabin on property owned by the Millers, defendant. Plaintiff, Park Lumber, the materialman, furnished lumber at the request of the general contractor for use in the construction of the Miller home. Prior to anyone being paid, the building collapsed. The Millers claimed that the construction contract had not been performed and that the cabin was negligently erected with resulting damage to them. Park Lumber seeks payment from the Millers, who refused to pay for the lumber used in the construction of the cabin *because it did not enhance the value of their property.* Are the property owners liable to the suppliers of material when the erected cabin collapsed?

Decision

Yes. Judgment for plaintiff, Park Lumber.

Reasoning

The principals (Millers) who have accepted the benefits of a contract made by their agent, the general contractor, may not ratify part and reject the rest. The ratification by the property owners of the general contractor's account with the materialman may not be conditioned upon the principal not suffering a loss.

Lewis v. Martin, 492 P.2d 877 (Colo. 1971).

3. The transaction to be ratified must be *legal*. For example, a loan unauthorizedly obtained by A on P's behalf that violates a usury statute can not be ratified.

4. The agent must disclose to the third person the identity of the principal on whose behalf the agent *purports* to act. It is not necessary that the person who is acting as an agent have any authority at this time. Ratification will not apply in the case of an undisclosed principal. For example, if A never informed T that he was selling a boat on P's behalf, P can not ratify the contract made with T. The reason is that T never intended to contract with P, and it would be unfair to permit P to impose himself upon T by ratification. T intended to contract with *A*.

5. The ratification must occur before the third person withdraws. For example, if T sues A for breach of contract because A never had the authority, P can not then decide to ratify the contract.

Agency by Operation of Law
The courts will infer an agency if it appears from the facts that there was an implied intention to create one.

Marital Relationship. The marital relationship does not, in itself, create authority for one spouse to act for the other. However, if a wife is customarily permitted by her husband to order household supplies, authority or apparent authority to purchase things needed in the household can be inferred.[19] A husband is under a legal duty to financially provide the necessities of life for his family. A wife or child to whom a husband or parent has failed to provide the necessities has the power to contract for the purpose of necessities.[20]

Proving the Agency Relationship

When an agency question is relevant to a case, the burden of proving that the agency relationship existed is on *the party who claims it existed*.[21] As illustrated in the combinations of agency liability, this may be the principal, agent, or third party. The agency relationship is not presumed and must be proved by the evidence. For example, if T sues P, claiming that A acted as P's agent, T has the burden of proving the agency between P and A.

Burden of proof.

---

[19] RESTATEMENT (SECOND) OF AGENCY sec. 22, comment b (1958); and *Melton v. Mire,* 268 So.2d 123 (La. 1972).

[20] RESTATEMENT OF RESTITUTION sec. 113 (1936).

[21] *Reed v. Bunger,* 122 N.W.2d 290 (Iowa 1963).

Summary Statement

1. The source of agency law is the common law.
2. Corporations, partnerships, and sole proprietorships all act through agents.
3. Agency is a fiduciary relationship based on an express or implied agreement whereby one party, the agent, is authorized to act on behalf and under the control of the principal.
4. If a principal has the right to control, or exercises control, over the *physical* conduct of his agent, he is liable to third persons for *physical* harm caused to them by the agent's wrongful *physical* conduct. Such an agent is called a "servant" or "employee," and the principal is called a "master."
5. The terms "master" and "servant" are used in the employment relationship only to determine the liability of an employer principal for the physical harm caused to third persons by the servant employee's torts.
6. An independent contractor is hired to accomplish a physical result and is not under the direct supervision and control of the hiring party.
7. A real estate broker is an independent contractor but, when retained by a client, he becomes a general agent and generally has authority only to state the asking price and identify the owner's property.
8. A power of attorney is a written authorization to act as an agent. A limited power is restrictive, a general power is not.
9. Any person with legal capacity to act can act through an agent.
10. Any person can act as an agent even if he lacks contractual capacity.
11. A "general agent" is authorized to conduct a series of transactions involving a continuity of service.
12. A "special agent" is authorized to conduct a single transaction or a series of transactions not involving continuity of service.
13. The agency relationship is based on an implied or express agreement between the principal and the agent.
14. The relationship of master and servant is a type of agency. One can be a servant even though the service is gratuitously performed.
15. Ratification is the affirmation of an unauthorized act having the effect of binding the ratifying party as though the act had been authorized previously.
16. The agency relationship is not presumed, and the burden of proving it is on the party who claims it exists.

Notice in the following case how the court requires the party that seeks to benefit from the agency relationship to prove its existence.

McLaughlin v. Chicken Delight, Inc.
321 A.2d 456 (Conn. 1973)

Bogdanski, Associate Justice. This is an action where McLaughlin, administrator of decedent's estate, alleged that the motor vehicle which struck and killed the decedent was owned by the defendant, Chicken Delight, Inc., and that the operator of the vehicle was its agent. The superior court held the operator of the vehicle was not the agent of the franchisor, defendant, and rendered its judgment for the defendant. Plaintiff appealed.

The following is a summary of the facts found by the court. The defendant was the **franchisor**, and Food Caterers, Inc. was the franchisee, under the terms of an agreement whereby the defendant granted solely to Food Caterers, Inc. the right to use at its store in East Hartford the name, symbols, methods, and systems of operations of "Chicken Delight." The franchise agreement was designed to control the quality and taste of all "Chicken Delight" products sold to the public. It provided that the defendant should have the privilege of complete inspection of the business and books of the franchisee. Under the agreement, the franchisee was required to deliver promptly and at the time designated by the customer hot and freshly prepared foods from the "Chicken Delight" store. The franchisee agreed to purchase or lease an adequate number of delivery vehicles and to "maintain a free and adequate delivery system." There are seven such franchises in Connecticut and 400 throughout the United States.

The franchisee owned and operated the East Hartford store already mentioned. Above its entrance was a sign with "Chicken Delight" in large letters and "free delivery" in smaller letters. The motor vehicle in question was owned by the franchisee. There were no markings, printing, or signs on it. Inside the vehicle at the time of the accident and next to the operator was a cardboard box imprinted with the words "Chicken Delight." Next to the carton was a heater to keep the food products warm during delivery to customers. At the time of the accident, the heater was in operation and Carfiro was in the process of making a delivery to a customer. Carfiro was hired by Mrs. Joyce Morrison, widow of Robert Morrison, who, prior to his death, managed the business. While Morrison was alive, he instructed operator employees how to make deliveries. After his death Mrs. Morrison took over the task. There was no evidence that Carfiro was hired, paid, or instructed by or known to the defendant.

The packaged foods to be sold were limited and the only name that could be used was "Chicken Delight," the place of business had to be known as "Chicken Delight," and the precise method and manner of cooking was specifically defined. The franchisee had to purchase numerous articles and equipment stated by the franchisor to be essential. This equipment had to be purchased from the franchisor or meet the standards prescribed by it. The franchisee was required to sell its food in a container bearing the trademark "Chicken Delight" and buy its entire requirements for the various packaging kits defined by the franchisor. The business could be conducted only at an approved location, and its construction and remodeling had to meet the franchisor's standards. The preparation and cooking of all foods had to meet specific standards.

The trial court concluded that "although the financial interest of Chicken Delight, Inc. is advanced and the reputation and good will of Chicken Delight, Inc. are enhanced by the delivery of hot Chicken Delight food products, such is not sufficient to establish a basis for the imposition of liability on Chicken Delight, Inc."

It is the plaintiff's contention that the facts found by the trial court show beyond dispute that, at the time of the accident resulting in the death of the decedent, Carfiro in operating the delivery vehicle was acting in furtherance of and for the "benefit" of the business affairs of the defendant, Chicken Delight, Inc.

franchise
a business relationship between a "franchisor" who markets goods or services through a "franchisee" who has the right to use the franchisor's tradename, trademark, and methods of operation

"(1) Agency is the fiduciary relationship which results from manifestation of consent by one person to another that the other shall act on his behalf and subject to his control, and consent by the other so to act. (2) The one for whom action is to be taken is the principal. (3) The one who is to act is the agent." Restatement (Second) 1 Agency, sec. 1. An essential factor in an agency relationship is the right of the principal to direct and control performance of the work by the agent.

The question presented to this court is whether it must be held as a matter of law that the trial court, on consideration of all the evidence in the case, could not reasonably and logically have reached any conclusion other than that Carfiro was the agent of Chicken Delight. The question of the existence or nonexistence of any agency relationship is ordinarily one of fact to be determined by the trier of fact.

It is true that the provisions of a written contract may be relevant to the fact question of whether an agency relationship exists. The plaintiff has totally failed to point to any portion of the contract or to any other evidence in the case which would sustain his burden of establishing that Carfiro was an agent of Chicken Delight. The court concluded that "at the time of the accident, Michael J. Carfiro, Jr., was operating a vehicle owned by Food Caterers, Inc. as an employee of said corporation," and that "at the time of the accident Michael J. Carfiro, Jr., was operating said automobile as the agent of Food Caterers, Inc., acting within the scope of his employment."

The record discloses that the trial court carefully and thoroughly considered all of the evidence claimed by the plaintiff to have a bearing on the finding of an actual agency relationship. The above findings, however, and others found by the court amply support its conclusion that the plaintiff failed to establish the requisite agency relationship claim. This conclusion cannot be disturbed.

Questions and Case Problems

1. Plaintiff owned and operated a business engaged in selling mobile homes and developing mobile home parks. In May 1969 plaintiff employed defendant, a licensed real estate broker in the State of Maine, with the special assignment of acquiring land for development as mobile home parks. Defendant received a weekly salary of $125 for his work. During May and June of 1969 plaintiff requested defendant to negotiate for plaintiff the purchase of a particular tract of land suitable for the company to develop as a mobile home park. When defendant related that the land in question was available, plaintiff requested defendant to purchase the land as a straw man (in defendant's name and not disclosing his agency), in the course of his employment, and then to convey the land to plaintiff.

During the period when the defendant was negotiating for the purchase of the land, he repeatedly told plaintiff that the land would cost $32,400.00 although defendant knew the land could be purchased for $15,474.62. Defendant made these false statements for the purpose of inducing plaintiff to deliver to him the sum of $32,400.00. Relying on defendant's false statements as to the cost of the land, plaintiff delivered $32,400.00 to defendant, it being plaintiff's intention to deliver only the money necessary to make the purchase. On June

23, 1969, using plaintiff's money, defendant paid the owner of the land $14,474.62 to close the sale; defendant took title in his own name and promptly conveyed the land to the plaintiff and plaintiff's wife. After paying out the sum necessary to complete the purchase of the land, defendant retained the balance of the $32,400.00 which plaintiff had given him. Is the defendant real estate broker entitled to his commission of $1,546? Is the plaintiff entitled to sue for deceit? Is the defendant an agent? [*Desfosses v. Notis*, 333 A.2d 83 (Me. 1975).]

2. A fraternal society issued an insurance policy to its members. The bylaws provided that members who had failed to pay dues could be reinstated only if they were in good health; that the officers of local lodges, who were elected by the members, were agents of the local lodge only but were authorized by the "grand lodge" to forward to it money received from dues; and that no agent had authority to waive the rules as to reinstatement. The secretary of the local lodge accepted dues from the decedent, who had failed to pay on time, with knowledge that she had been ill. Did the local secretary of the fraternal society have the authority to "waive" the requirement for reinstatement? [*Bloodgood v. Woman's Ben. Ass'n.*, 13 P.2d 412 (N.M. 1932).]

3. Following an accident, plaintiff was taken to a hospital where he was received by an intern and prepared for an operation which the intern could perform only if authorized by a staff surgeon. The defendant, a staff surgeon, authorized an operation by the intern and was in the operating room during its progress. Following the operation the intern ordered that the plaintiff be given penicillin, to which the plaintiff was allergic, and which caused serious harm. Suit was brought for negligence. Was the intern the servant of the hospital and the staff surgeon? [*Yorston v. Pennell*, 153 A.2d 255 (Pa. 1959).]

4. The driver, Andrew Kowaleski, and the car owner, Antone Kowaleski, are brothers. They operate a service station in Portland. After work Antone planned to go to Andrew's home and have dinner with Andrew and Andrew's wife, the plaintiff. Antone owned a farm at Scappoose, Oregon, a town about 25 miles from Portland. When the plaintiff came over to pick up her husband, Andrew, Antone asked Andrew to drive Antone's car to Scappoose and do the necessary chores at the farm. Andrew agreed and drove away in Antone's car. Antone's car, driven by Andrew, collided with Andrew's car, driven by plaintiff, Andrew's wife, and in which Antone, defendant, was riding as a passenger. Andrew received no compensation for his efforts. Is Antone liable, as a matter of law, for the acts of a friend or relative (Andrew) driving the owner's car in the gratuitous performance of an errand for the owner? [*Kowaleski v. Kowaleski*, 385 P.2d 611 (Or. 1963).]

5. Peters and English were attached to the same organization and quartered in the same barracks at Sheppard Air Force Base at Wichita Falls. During the early part of the evening prior to the collision which occurred about midnight, Peters borrowed English's automobile for his own personal use. Prior to that time English had permitted Peters and other Air Force personnel to use his car for their personal pleasure when he did not have occasion to use it himself. About 8:00 P.M. Peters drove the car to the noncommissioned officers club on the base for the purpose of meeting his date. They danced at the club

until about 10:30. After turning the car over to Peters, English, who was on town patrol duty in Wichita Falls, secured a date for later on that night, after he was to be relieved from duty, and he wanted his car to use on that date. During the time that Peters was at the club, English returned to the base and left a note in the car requesting Peters to call him. After finding the note, Peters drove the car off the base and to a drive-in cafe known as Pioneer No. 3, between the base and the city of Wichita Falls. He had arranged to meet his date again at the Pioneer. About 11:30 or later Peters called English over the telephone from the Pioneer and was told that English wanted him to bring the car to Wichita Falls Police Station between 12:00 and 1:00 and "pick him up." Almost immediately after the telephone conversation, Peters started to make the trip to the police station, meeting his date coming into the cafe with other friends as he went out. It was while Peters was on his way to Wichita Falls in response to English's request that the accident in question occurred. While driving the car from the Pioneer to the Wichita Falls Police Station, was Peters an agent of English? [*English v. Dhane*, 286 S.W.2d 666 (Tex. 1956).]

6. Ulsch & Sons promoted sales of Dempster products and serviced customers' accounts in an assigned geographical area pursuant to an agreement with Dempster Brothers, Inc., plaintiff. Ulsch sold some Dempster equipment to Waste Control of Florida, delivery to be made at Dempster's plant in Tennessee. Ulsch provided an airplane piloted by Ivens, its employee, which took off for Tennessee with two passengers, the president of Waste and one of its employees. The plane crashed, killing the pilot and the two passengers. Their personal representatives brought actions in the Florida courts against Dempster, Ulsch, and the estate of Ivens, claiming that the plane was operated negligently. Dempster was insured by the defendant insurance company, United States Fidelity & Guaranty Company, who refused to defend Dempster in the Florida suits on the ground the complaints in the Florida suits failed to allege that Ulsch was an independent contractor as to Dempster. The insurance policy provided that "the policy does not apply: Under coverages A and C, except with respect to the operations performed by independent contractors. . . ." Fidelity claimed that Ulsch was not an independent contractor and that Dempster's relationship with Ulsch was vendor/vendee. Dempster did not reserve any right of control over Ulsch, who chose its own means of performance. Dempster claimed Ulsch was an independent contractor and brought this suit against Fidelity for the proceeds of the insurance policy. Was Ulsch an independent contractor? [*Dempster Brothers, Inc. v. United States Fidelity & Guaranty Company*, 388 S.W.2d 153 (Tenn. 1964).]

7. Plaintiff, Clarice Paulson, brought this suit against defendants, Madison Newspapers, Inc., Edward Bierer, doing business as Madison Transit Company, and William Crapp, employee of Madison Transit Company, for damages arising out of personal injuries sustained when she fell over a mail sack of newspapers lying on the sidewalk in the city of Lodi. Defendant William Crapp made the Madison newspapers deliveries to Lodi. He could not

recall where he left the sack on the day in question but testified that he usually carried them across the sidewalk and placed them against the post office building, which was in compliance with the instructions of his employer, the defendant. Madison Newspapers obtained authority from the postmaster general to transport mail to certain post offices at its own expense. For many years the defendant, Bierer, under an oral contract with Madison Newspapers, hauled its papers to such post offices upon terms agreed upon with the circulation manager. Bierer testified that Madison Newspapers determined the pick-up and delivery schedules, established the routes, and directed the details of delivery. Madison Newspapers gave him directions as to the equipment he used and its maintenance and made suggestions as to the hiring and firing of drivers, which suggestions Bierer followed. Madison Newspapers maintains that Bierer was an independent contractor and not its agent, and that Bierer was responsible for Crapp's conduct. Was Bierer an independent contractor or an agent of Madison Newspapers? [*Paulson v. Madison Newspapers, Inc.,* 80 N.W.2d 421 (Wis. 1957).]

8. Plaintiff brought suit against the defendants, United States Steel Corporation and The Thew Shovel Company, alleging that a crane manufactured by Thew was of defective construction and while lifting a heavy object the object fell, striking a gas line, causing a fire and explosion which resulted in injuries to the plaintiff. The defendant, The Thew Shovel Company, thereafter filed a motion to dismiss on the grounds that there was insufficient service of process (summons and complaint) upon it. The plaintiff takes the position that the Atlas Equipment Company is the general agent of The Thew Shovel Company and that service upon the Atlas Equipment Company through its president was proper service and was service upon Thew. Defendant, on the other hand, maintains that Atlas is not the general agent of Thew and that they were never authorized to accept any process on behalf of Thew. Atlas is in the business of distributing and marketing constructional and industrial equipment. They distribute products of twelve different manufacturers, including Thew and International Harvester Company. They have an agreement with Thew under which they agree to purchase and Thew agrees to sell to them equipment which Atlas might order at a certain price. It is clear that the equipment becomes the property of Atlas, and Atlas sells their own equipment. They maintain a stock of Thew parts, but Atlas owns these parts. There is absolutely no interlocking directorate, there is no cross-stock ownership, and there are no common officers. Atlas has not been subject to the control of Thew, and certainly Atlas has never been authorized to conduct a series of transactions for Thew, nor were any matters pertaining to Thew's business entrusted to Atlas. Thew's name, however, is listed in the Pittsburgh telephone directory with the Atlas telephone number and at the Atlas address. Is Atlas Equipment Company the general agent of Thew? [*Kelly v. United States Steel Corporation and The Thew Shovel Company,* 170 F.Supp. 649 (1959).]

9. Plaintiff, Menenberg, a certified public accountant and attorney at law, was an accountant for the Felsot Building Company. The Carl R. Sams Company, a partnership consisting of Sams, Merrill, and Threm, was engaged in the real estate brokerage business and was interested in arranging an agreement to sell property for Felsot. Sams proposed to Menenberg that if he would be able to arrange the agreement, the partnership would compensate him for his services. Menenberg was successful in his endeavors, the partnership becoming exclusive selling agent and agreeing to compensate plaintiff $40 for each sale as a "legal fee for services rendered." A short time later the Carl R. Sams Company dissolved and the sales agency was taken over by a new partnership formed by Merrill and Threm. Menenberg no longer received his fee and sued the Merrill-Threm Company, contending that it assumed the obligations of the Sams Company just as it succeeded to the rights, contracts, and benefits of the sales agency agreement. Did the Merrill-Threm Company assume the agency relationship of the Sams Company? [*Menenberg v. Carl R. Sams Realty Co.,* 59 N.W.2d 125 (Mich. 1953).]

10. The case of *McLaughlin v. Chicken Delight, Inc.,* 321 A.2d 456 (Conn. 1973)[22] holds that the person claiming that an agency existed had the burden of proving the agency. It also held that, while a third person may benefit from the agency, nevertheless the third person is not a principal of the person providing the benefit. Discuss the court's holding in light of the fact that, in proving agency, actually two parties are benefiting from services rendered by an agent but only one of the parties benefited is the principal.

------

[22] See pp. 226–28.

Duties of Principal and Agent to Each Other

15

After you have read this chapter, you should be able to:

1. Define the following kinds of authority:
   a. express authority,
   b. implied authority,
      i. incidental authority,
      ii. customary authority,
   c. apparent authority.
2. Know whose duty it is to determine the extent of the agent's authority.
3. Explain the effect of limitations on the agent's authority.
4. Explain the instances when an agent may delegate authority to another.
5. List and explain the five duties an agent owes to a principal.
6. List and explain the four duties a principal owes to an agent.
7. Explain the effect of proper exercise on the agent's authority.
8. Explain the meaning of a fiduciary.

Introduction

It is almost certain that at some time in your life you will find yourself involved in a business agency relationship either as a principal or as an agent.

Such a relationship for both parties creates rights and duties not previously existing, both by the act of creating the agency and in its day-to-day operation.

The concept of authority and power implicit in the agency relationship can lead to the creation of rights, duties, and great potentiality for loss.

Accordingly, it is very important for you to consider carefully your obligations before you enter into an agency relationship. It is, therefore, for your own well-being and future conduct that you, as a student, should understand the perspective in this chapter.

Agent's Authority

Scope of Agent's Authority

An agent may properly contract with a third party *only if authorized by the principal* in words or other conduct. The agent has no power to create his own authority nor extend its scope. The essence of **authority** is a person's (principal) consent to another (agent) to act on the principal's behalf.

The following types of authority will allow you to identify authority and decide whether the agent is acting with the principal's consent.

Express Authority.   If the principal orally or in writing specifies what the agent is to do, the agent has **express authority** to act. For example, if P tells his stockbroker A to sell P's stock at a certain price, A has been given *express authority* to sell the stock at a specified price.

Implied Authority.   The agent's duty is to carry out his express authority *as reasonably understood by the agent*. He must interpret his principal's words of consent in order to understand what they mean. The principal's words *imply* to the agent, and the agent *infers* from those words what the agent reasonably understands he is to do. Thus we have **implied** (or inferred) **authority.** Implied authority can be described as incidental or customary.

1. Incidental Authority. An agent is authorized from the circumstances to perform those acts that are reasonably necessary to carry out the express authority. Suppose an agent is authorized to use a company car on a business trip to effect a sale with a third party. The salesman/agent has implied **incidental authority** to charge the gasoline used to the principal.
2. Customary Authority. The traditional trade or professional practice in which the agent acts creates an implied authorization to conform with the general custom. This is referred to as **customary authority.**

---

authority
an agent's power to act for his principal in accordance with the principal's manifestation of consent to the agent

express authority
an agent's authority specifically expressed in his principal's manifestation to him

implied authority
an agent's authority which the agent reasonably can understand he has from his principal's manifestation to him, but not expressed therein

incidental authority
implied authority to do what is incidental in carrying out the express authority

customary authority
implied authority to do those acts that conform to the general custom or usage

---

By agreement between the principal and the agent, the agent *may not* have incidental and customary authority.

Some common examples of implied authority may be helpful.

1. In *authority "to sell" personal property*, if the agent has *received possession* of the property, then his implied authority is to *contract* in his principal's name and sell and transfer the *title* to the property. If the agent has *not received possession*, his implied authority is solely to *produce a willing and able buyer*. In *authority "to sell" real property*, if the agent's *authority is in writing* (e.g., power of attorney) and there is *nothing* to the contrary, his implied authority is to *contract* in his principal's name and sell and transfer the *title* to the property. If the authority is *oral*, his implied authority is solely to *produce a willing and able buyer*.

2. *Authority to receive payment* implies authority to receive only *cash* for the entire amount or to take a *check as conditional payment*—on condition that it is paid. Authority to receive payment does not authorize the agent to accept credit.

3. *Authority to sign checks and other negotiable instruments in the name of a principal* is not implied easily, in the absence of special circumstances (e.g., emergency).

Apparent Authority.   Agency and authority are created by the principal's expression of consent *to the agent. If P represents to T,* a third person, that A is P's agent, there is no agency nor authority because P never expressed consent *to A* that he was to be P's agent. But as far as T is concerned, A *apparently* is P's agent because P said so *to T.* Therefore, A is an *apparent agent* with **apparent authority** to act for P in accordance with P's representation *to T.* The extent of A's apparent authority will depend upon *T's* reasonable understanding of P's representation to T. If A acts within the scope of his apparent authority, P will be bound to T by A's conduct with the same effect as though A had authority so to act. Under apparent authority, sometimes called "ostensible authority," *the principal's expression of consent is to the third person* rather than to the agent.

A person may be an agent with authority and, at the same time, have apparent authority. For example, P employs A as a salesman in P's store, and P informs T that A is P's salesman. A's authority and apparent authority are to act as a salesman is reasonably expected to act.

An intent to authorize an act may be found from the *principal's conduct.* For example, a store clerk who reasonably appears to a vendor/third party to have authority to purchase supplies from him has apparent authority to do so, and the owner of the store will be liable to the vendor on a sale.

The following case illustrates how the agent's apparent authority must be based upon *conduct of the principal* and not of the agent. The insurance company in this case did not permit its life insurance agent to make loans to new companies and was not responsible for payment made to the agent on the loan.

> **apparent authority**
> the power of a person (A) to act as though he were an agent, created by another's (P's) manifestation to a third person (T) that A is P's agent

Facts

Johnson is the organizer of a consumer finance company which wanted a loan of $400,000. In order to get the loan, it would be necessary to insure Johnson's life, the policy of insurance to be security for the loan. Johnson contacted Thompson, a life insurance agent of Shenandoah Life Insurance Co., to get the loan from Shenandoah, and Johnson gave to Thompson $28,000 earnest money for the loan to show his "good faith" in completing the transaction. Thompson, without express authority from Shenandoah, placed the loan with an outside company and paid to the latter the $28,000 to place the loan. Thompson told Johnson that the outside company was a subsidiary of Shenandoah, which was not true; Thompson was interested in placing the loan only to get the commission on the life insurance policies on Johnson's life necessary to secure the loan. The outside company never granted the loan nor did it return the $28,000 earnest money. This is an action by Johnson against Shenandoah seeking recovery of the earnest money paid to Thompson, its agent. Did Thompson, the life insurance agent of Shenandoah, have apparent authority to bind Shenandoah?

Decision

No. Judgment for Shenandoah.

Reasoning

Representations of the agent can not be the basis for a finding of apparent authority. Apparent authority must be traceable to the principal who holds the agent out to a third party as having authority. Shenandoah never gave to third persons any appearance of authority in their agents to lend money or to promise funds to start a business.

Johnson v. Shenandoah Life Insurance Co., 281 So.2d 636 (Ala. 1973).

Legal Effect of a Contract Properly Executed by an Agent

If an agent acts within the express or implied authority in the name of his principal, there is a contract between the third party and the principal. Accordingly, a salesman is not personally liable for a breach of warranty for goods made to a customer/third party because the sales contract is made *with the principal* through the agent; the agent is not a party to the contract.

Third Party's Duty to Determine the Extent of the Agent's Authority

The third party is under a legal obligation not only to identify the *existence* of the agent's authority but also to determine the *extent* of his authority. If the agent exceeds his authority, the principal will not be bound. Suppose a life insurance agent changes the terms of a life insurance contract without the consent of his company. It is the customer/third party's responsibility to determine whether the agent had the power to change the insurance contract. If he *fails to inquire,* he acts at his peril.

The third party can not rely upon statements made by the agent unless the principal has invited him to do so. For example, a customer is invited by the store owner to rely upon the salesman's statement of the price of goods.

The following case illustrates how a third party can bind a principal for authorized acts, even though he does not inquire into the extent of the agent's authority.

Facts

Plaintiff, Loper Lumber Company, a corporate owner of timber, brings this action to recover payment for timber cut and removed from its land pursuant to an agreement made by the defendant, Windham, through his agent. Windham refused to pay on the grounds that Loper Lumber Company made no inquiry as to the extent of the agent's authority, and they were thereby released from responsibility for the agent's authorized act. If the agent does not exceed his authority, does a third party have an obligation to determine the extent of the authority?

Decision

No. Judgment for plaintiff, Loper.

Reasoning

While a third party dealing with an agent is held to be subject to the burden of ascertaining the extent of the powers of the agent, it seems that where the agent is, in fact, acting within the scope of the authority granted to him, the principal ought to be bound for the acts of the agent, whether the third party made any inquiry as to the extent of the agent's authority or not. The decision as to the principal's liability ought to rest on the actual extent of the authority granted to the agent and not on the fact that the third party dealing with the agent made inquiry to ascertain the agent's authority.

Loper Lumber Co. v. Windham, 282 So.2d 256 (Ala. 1973).

Limitation on the Agent's Authority

As between the principal and the agent, any expressed limitations on the scope of the agent's authority are valid. However, a third party without knowledge of the private and *secret* limitations is not bound by them. The third party has the duty of determining the extent of an agent's authority, and since he can not determine the secret limitations on such authority made by the principal, the limitations are not effective as to the third party. If the agent has *express, implied,* or *apparent authority* to act, he can make a contract with the third party that will bind the principal.

For instance, if it is customary in the used car trade to warrant a used car for thirty days and the principal instructs the salesman/agent to warrant the car for only fourteen days, unless disclosed to the customer/third party, the latter can assume that the agent has authority to give a thirty-day warranty. The agent has such *apparent authority.*

In the following case the court held that, although the agent had limitations on his actual authority, the principal was estopped (precluded) from setting aside the *apparent authority* of the agent.

Facts

Caloin Casteigne, an employee of Foti, purchased from the plaintiff, Dart Distributors, a carpet for his own private use. Casteigne represented at the time of purchase, with the apparent acquiescence of his employer, Foti Enterprises, that he was purchasing in the name of his employer. When the carpet was originally purchased, no indication was given to Dart that it was not being purchased through the account Foti had with them. When Casteigne became employed by Foti as a construction foreman in the building of residential units, he had a number of accounts which were transferred to Foti for credit purposes, and when the subject carpet was purchased, it was advantageous to him to pay through Foti Enterprises to obtain discount advantages. He continued to use the Foti account with the plaintiff after the original purchase. Mrs. Foti, secretary-treasurer of Foti, freely acknowledged that Mr. Casteigne had the authority to purchase carpets from Dart on the account of Foti Enterprises, Inc. When the particular account was not paid, Dart made a demand upon Foti, who responded that they were not personally responsible for this particular item. Dart's position was that they were not advised that the purchase of the carpet by Mr. Casteigne was for his personal use and that Foti was responsible. Was the express limitation to purchase carpets only for business use sufficient to preclude any apparent authority?

Decision

No. Judgment for plaintiff, Dart.

Reasoning

Where the principal clothes an agent with apparent authority to perform certain acts, and a third person (such as plaintiff here) who has no knowledge of or reason to believe that there are limitations on that authority deals with the agent, then the principal is estopped from setting aside the acts of the agent which, although beyond the actual power delegated to him, are within his apparent authority.

Dart Distributors, Inc. v. Foti Enterprises, Inc., 271 So.2d 705 (La. 1972).

delegation
the transfer of one's duty to another, the tranferor still being responsible for the duty

Delegation of Authority by Agent

When a principal selects an agent to contract with others on his behalf, he usually does so on the *personal qualifications* of the agent. The agent generally will exercise *discretion, special skill,* or *judgment* in the performance of his contract and *fiduciary duties.* Hence, it usually is held that an agent does not have implied (or apparent) authority to delegate his authority to another (subagent) without the consent of the principal.

subagent
the person appointed by an agent and as to whom the appointing agent is a principal

If the agent's discretion, special skill, or judgment are not required for the agent's performance, unless the principal has indicated to the contrary, the agent has implied (and apparent) authority to delegate his performance to a **subagent.** On delegation, the subagent is an agent both of the agent appointing him and also of the agent's principal. He has two principals who are both liable for his conduct, the appointing agent being ultimately liable. For example, P insurance company appoints A as its general manager in a particular geographical area, A agreeing to be responsible for personnel hired by him. A employs insurance salesmen working out of A's office. The salesmen sell insurance in P's name to third persons, binding P to them. The salesmen are subagents with A and P as their principals. Both A and P are liable for the salesmen's conduct but, as between A and P, A is ultimately liable.

An agent's *delegation* of his authority to a *subagent* is different from an agent's *appointment* of *another agent*. The appointed agent and the appointing agent have only one principal—namely, the person who created the original agency. For example, P owns a retail store and employs A as general manager. A appoints S as a salesman in the store. P is the principal, and both A and S are his agents. S is not an agent of A, who is not liable for S's conduct. Only P is liable for the conduct of A and S.

An agent may delegate his authority in the following four instances.

1. Ministerial or Mechanical Duties.   In certain cases the act to be performed by the agent does not require anything more than a ministerial (nondiscretionary) or mechanical duty. For example, a general agent parking attendant may delegate the duty to collect parking tickets because it requires no special skill, discretion, or judgment. The following case illustrates how the *showing* of land is a ministerial act and can be delegated to a subagent.

Facts

Heritage Land Sales entered an agreement with Freeport Ridge Estates to act as Freeport's broker for the sale of real estate in the Bahamas. Heritage was to get a commission on each lot sold. Reckner, the plaintiff, was retained by Heritage to fly prospective buyers from the United States to Grand Bahama Island *to view* lots that were for sale. Reckner sued Freeport for services rendered. Was Reckner a subagent of Freeport?

Decision

Yes. Judgment for plaintiff, Reckner.

Reasoning

Heritage, as the agent of Freeport, had the implied authority to delegate its authority to a subagent, Reckner, regarding the ministerial act of *showing* land and flying prospective purchasers to Grand Bahama Island. In his capacity as a subagent, Reckner can look directly to the principal for his compensation.

Freeport Ridge Estates, Ltd. v. Richard G. Reckner, 266 So.2d 129 (Fla. 1972).

The principal may prohibit the delegation of even a ministerial act, providing it is clearly indicated to the agent. It is usually good practice to do so because the principal is responsible to compensate the subagent.

2. Business Custom.   It is implied that the agent has authority to delegate if the trade or profession in which the agency is to be performed has an established custom to employ subagents. The following case was decided on the custom of co-brokerage of real property for sale.

Facts

On April 22, 1963, Rosenthal, plaintiff, telephoned General Dynamics, informing it of the availability of the Art Metal plant in Woodbridge, New Jersey. Rosenthal was not solicited by General Dynamics but called because of his knowledge that a fire had destroyed the General Dynamics plant and that Feist & Feist, a licensed real estate broker and his former employer, was one of the six brokers chosen by Art Metal to procure a purchaser for its Woodbridge property.

Rosenthal spoke with Mr. Kahn of Feist & Feist the same morning, requesting the plans and further information about the Art Metal property. After informing Kahn of the prospective purchaser, he was given a plot plan and a listing sheet. At this time Feist & Feist agreed with Rosenthal to co-broker the property—that is, if Rosenthal effectuated the sale of the Art Metal property, Feist & Feist would divide its commission with him. Rosenthal forwarded the plot plan and other information to General Dynamics the same day.

These were the only acts done by Rosenthal in regard to the sale of the property. At no time did Feist & Feist take any steps to procure General Dynamics as a purchaser of the Art Metal property. Sometime later Art Metal sold its Woodbridge plant to General Dynamics, no commission being paid to Rosenthal or Feist & Feist. Rosenthal brought this suit against Art Metal for his real estate broker's commission. Was the delegation of Feist & Feist's authority to sell Art Metal, Inc. to a co-broker valid?

Decision

Yes. Judgment for plaintiff, Rosenthal.

Reasoning

In real estate trade it is a common custom to co-broker properties, and the power to delegate authority is implied. Thus, if the co-brokerage agreement between Feist & Feist and Rosenthal is valid and Rosenthal was the efficient cause of the sale, then Art Metal is liable to the co-brokers for the commission agreed upon in the listing agreement.

Rosenthal v. Art Metal, Inc., 229 A.2d 676 (N.J. 1967).

For example, if it is customary in the real estate agency business to have subagents show the house and accept counteroffers, the agent would be authorized to do so.

3. Unforeseen Emergency.   If the circumstances surrounding the agent's acts create a sudden emergency, and it is impracticable for the agent to communicate with the principal, he may appoint a subagent to protect the principal's interest and do what he reasonably can believe the principal would want done if he were aware of the circumstances. To illustrate, if the principal delivers perishable food to a carrier/agent with instructions to transport and sell it to a third party, if the carrier/agent can not communicate with the principal that the third party refuses to purchase it and if the food will be worthless unless refrigerated in a warehouse, the carrier/agent has authority to store it and charge the principal's account, the warehouseman being a subagent of the principal to care for the food.

4. Contemplated Conduct of Principal's Business So Requires.   Although not expressed in the agency contract, if it is reasonably inferred from the principal's business that the parties contemplated the appointment of subagents, then the agent may delegate his authority. For example, a general insurance agent ordinarily has the power to appoint subagents to sell insurance for the company. Also, an agent corporation has implied authority to act through its officers and other employees, and an agent partnership through its partners.

Duties and Liabilities Of Principal and Agent

Agent to Principal

A's duties to P.

The basis of liability resulting from an agency relationship is contractual. The agreement, express or implied, between the agent and the principal creates a series of rights and duties. An understanding of this contract is necessary for both parties to properly perform. The following duties are imposed upon the agent in compliance with his contract and the **fiduciary** relationship. They may be expressed in the contract, but frequently are implied. The principal may sue the agent in contract or tort, depending on the nature of the duty violated. In general, the agent has five duties to his principal.

fiduciary
a person with a duty to act primarily for the benefit of another

1. Loyalty.   The agreement between the principal and agent creates a *fiduciary relationship.* An agent acts solely for the benefit of his principal, and he thereby incurs a duty of loyalty which is imposed on all fiduciaries.

A's duty to be loyal to P.

For example, if A has been authorized to negotiate the sales price and sell a house for P, and A sold the house to his friend, T, below the fair market value, A has committed a breach of duty to P.

An agent can not enter into a contract with a third party that would create a *conflict of interest* with the principal. The purpose of his contracts with others is to benefit the principal. Even though this may not be expressed in the agency contract, it is implied by the fiduciary relationship.

For instance, if A is P's agent and he convinces P to sell his product to T, a corporation in which A owns a substantial amount of stock, of which P is unaware, A has violated his duty of loyalty. However, if P knew of A's interest in the corporation, there is no breach. A is liable even if he acts in good faith and believes the transaction is appropriate.

2. Obedience and Performance.   The contractual relationship between the principal and the agent may be an ongoing process creating a variety of *instructions* the agent is obligated to follow. An agent generally is obligated to comply with the principal's reasonable instructions. If A violates the instructions, causing harm to P, even if acting in good faith, he is liable to P. Accordingly, if A, acting in good faith, sells to an unauthorized company in violation of P's instructions, he is liable to P for any resulting injury to P.

A's duty to obey P and to perform his contract with P.

The agent is never obligated to perform illegal or unethical acts. Codes of trade practice and professional responsibility will determine whether the principal's instructions are reasonable. For example, a stockbroker may engage in proper customary trade practice in the sale of stock without objection by the principal/customer.

The following case established liability of an agent under an agreement to purchase and deliver stock where no time was stated for delivery. Where the agent waited three years before delivery, the court held he violated his instructions and fiduciary duty of obedience regardless of the degree of care exercised.

Facts

J. David Chestnut, executor of the estate of John Harvey Chestnut (the principal), sued William H. Cutcliffe (the agent), alleging that on February 10, 1966 the agent entered into an agreement with the principal to purchase for him shares of stock in Monterey Management Company from William H. Murray; that the agent received $25,000 for this service from the principal; that the principal died some six months later on October 1, 1966 and plaintiff qualified as his executor; that the shares of stock were never delivered to the principal during his lifetime and the $25,000 was never returned to the principal, his executor, or anyone on his behalf; and that the agent was therefore indebted to the executor "for the return of said sum of $25,000, for which this action is brought." Did the agent's nonperformance violate his agreement?

Decision

Yes. Judgment for the executor, J. David Chestnut.

Reasoning

Where specific instructions are violated, the agent is responsible in damages for any loss which results from the violation, regardless of the degree of care exercised and irrespective of the intent to benefit the principal. The effect of a failure to obey the principal's instructions will enable the principal to terminate the agency immediately.

Violation or nonperformance of instructions may be considered as a breach of two obligations—the obligation in the contract of agency, and the fiduciary obligation of obedience to the principal's instructions raised by the agency relationship. The agent has shown merely that he tendered the stock on March 28, 1969, some three years after the purchase of property of presumably fluctuating value, and only after demand for return of the purchase price, with no explanation for the delay and for the acts of dominion over the stock. This is a breach of his contract and fiduciary duty of obedience.

William H. Cutcliffe v. J. David Chestnut, Executor, 176 S.E.2d 607 (Ga. 1970).

A's duty to exercise reasonable care.

3. Reasonable Care. An agent is not only subject to the express and implied contract terms with the principal, as well as the fiduciary obligations imposed by the common law, but also the tort law of negligence as it applies to the transaction. He has a duty to exercise proper care in acting as an agent. Under section 379 of the *Restatement (Second) of Agency:* "Unless otherwise agreed, a paid agent is subject to a duty to the principal to act with standard care and skill . . . in the locality for the kind of work which he is employed to perform and . . . to exercise any special skill that he has."

For example, if A, a real estate agent, does not advertise an exclusive listing, he may be liable to P for not complying with the local trade practice.

4. Accounting.   Whatever an agent receives during and as a result of his agency he holds in trust for his principal. He can not secretly keep profits from the agency; they belong to the principal. For example, if T owes P money and T pays P's agent, A, who has authority to receive such payments, A holds the money in trust for P and can not secretly keep it for himself. One of the implied fiduciary duties requires the agent to keep an account of all the property and money belonging to the principal. This is a serious obligation and need not be expressed in the agency contract. Unless otherwise provided in the agency contract, the agent may render an account within a reasonable time after receipt or disbursement of funds. He must present an account upon termination of the agency.

A's duty to account to P.

If the agent is sued by the principal for failure to properly account, the agent has the burden of proving that he paid the principal. For example, if A should deposit corporate funds in his personal checking account, the corporation could claim the funds in A's account.

The agent has a duty to keep a separate account of his principal's funds. The agent will be held personally liable for the loss of any commingled funds.

5. Information.   An agent has a duty to communicate information to the principal even though not instructed to do so under the express terms of the contract.

A's duty to inform P.

Principal to Agent

P's duties to A.

The contract between the principal and agent creates the duties the principal owes to the agent. The implied terms of the contract common to this relationship may create duties of the principal to pay the agent for the performance of services, to reimburse the agent for authorized advances and expenses, and to indemnify the agent against liability to third parties. In general, the principal has four duties to the agent.

1. Duty of Compensation.   An agent is entitled to the agreed compensation or the fair value of his services. If the agent is hired by the principal, the resulting employment contract will determine the *compensation* and duration of the agency. For example, if a stockbroker is hired without an agreed commission rate, he is entitled to the customary trade commission.

P's duty to compensate A.

2. Duty to Comply with the Agency Contract.   The principal has a duty to comply with the terms of the agency contract and to allow the agent to perform under the contract. If a real estate agent is given an "exclusive agency" to list the principal's house for sale for ninety days, the principal can not terminate the agency before that time nor employ another agent for the same purpose. Under an "exclusive sale contract," only the agent may make the sale.

P's duty to perform his contract with A.

3. *Duty of Reimbursement.* The intent of the principal and the agent as *expressed in their contract* determines the right of the agent to recover expenses incurred while *authorizedly* performing the agency contract.

If the principal *requests* the agent to expend the agent's own money in the performance of the agency, the agent has the authority to do so and the principal has a duty to **reimburse** the agent for such expense. The principal's request may be express, or implied from performance pursuant to his authority which required the agent to incur expense. A typical example is a principal's request that the agent is to do something which will require the agent to travel and incur travel expense.

4. *Duty of Indemnity.* **Indemnity** is an obligation to pay for another's loss. A principal has the duty, unless their contract provides otherwise, to indemnify the agent for his *payment of damages to third persons* because of the proper performance of the agency contract or a resulting tort. There is an implied duty a principal owes to an agent to indemnify the agent for the payment of damages the agent was required to make for loss he sustained without his fault while acting pursuant to his authority.

Summary Statement

1. *Express authority* occurs when the principal specifies, either orally or in writing, what the agent is authorized to do.
2. *Implied authority* is customary or incidental, and consent for the agent to perform occurs when the agent reasonably believes that it is necessary to carry out the express authority.
3. *Incidental authority* occurs from the circumstances allowing the agent to perform those acts that are incidental to perform his express authority.
4. *Customary authority* is found when the trade or professional practice in which the agent acts creates an implied authorization to conform with the general custom.
5. *Emergency authority* occurs when the agent is confronted with circumstances that the agent reasonably can believe the principal did not foresee would occur and that require action which the agent reasonably believes is what the principal would do if he were aware of the circumstances.
6. *Apparent authority* occurs when the principal's words or other conduct addressed to a third party reasonably cause him to believe that someone is the principal's agent with authority. Under this theory, it is sometimes said that the principal is "estopped" from denying such agency and authority.
7. The third party is under a duty to determine the extent of the agent's authority.
8. A third party is not bound by secret limitations on the agent's authority. However, as between the principal and the agent, any express limitations on the scope of the agent's authority are valid.

9. Generally, an agent can not delegate to another his authority to act for the principal. However, if the agent's special skill, discretion, or judgment are not involved, he may delegate:
   a. ministerial or mechanical duties,
   b. when there is an established custom to employ subagents,
   c. if an unforeseen emergency arises making it impracticable to communicate with the principal, and
   d. if it is reasonably inferred from the principal's business that the parties contemplated the appointment of subagents.
10. As a result of the fiduciary relationship, an agent owes to the principal the following duties:
   a. loyalty,
   b. obedience and performance,
   c. reasonable care,
   d. to account for agency funds, and
   e. to keep the principal informed.
11. The principal owes to the agent the following duties:
   a. to compensate the agent,
   b. to comply with the agency contract,
   c. to reimburse the agent for expenses authorizedly incurred, and
   d. to indemnify the agent for losses caused to him by the agency relationship through no fault of the agent.
12. The agency relationship creates a fiduciary obligation on the agent toward his principal. A fiduciary is a person with a duty to act primarily for the benefit of another. The law imposes special duties to perform with a high degree of care.

The following case interrelates the master-servant relationship (see chapters 14, Nature and Creation, and 16, Agency and the Law of Contracts and Torts) with the doctrine of apparent authority. Note how liability can be found under either legal theory.

Chevron Oil Company v. Sutton
515 P.2d 1283 (N.M. 1973)

McManus, Chief Justice. Sutton sought damages for death by wrongful act against Chevron Oil Company (Chevron), Lee Sharp (station lessee for Chevron), and Herbert R. Buss (Sharp's employee). Sutton's wife had died from injuries sustained in a car accident when a wheel of a car repaired by Buss came off the vehicle.

The district court granted Chevron's motion for a summary judgment. On appeal to the Court of Appeals, the summary judgment was reversed. The matter is now before this court on certiorari given to the Court of Appeals. . . .

The main issue before this court is whether Chevron asserted enough control over its lessee to constitute a master-servant relationship. If such relationship is present, then Chevron could be found liable under the doctrine of **respondeat superior**. . . .

respondeat superior let the master (superior) be responsible for the torts of his servant committed while acting within the scope of his employment

"Whether a station operator is an employee of an oil company or an independent contractor depends on the facts of each case, the principal consideration being the control, or right to control, of the operation of the station."

The fact in dispute is whether or not Chevron exercised such control over Sharp as to bring the doctrine of respondeat superior into play. * Independent stations of the appellant (Chevron) were required to: (1) diligently promote the sale of Chevron's brand products; (2) remain open for certain hours and days and "meet the operating hours of competitors"; (3) keep the premises, restrooms and equipment in a "clean and orderly condition"; (4) present a "good appearance"; and (5) promote Chevron's image to the motoring public. In addition, Sharp also (6) sold Chevron products and dispensed gasoline and oil provided by the Chevron organization; (7) received the benefit of Chevron advertising; (8) wore uniforms containing the Chevron emblem; (9) used calling cards which billed the station as "Lee Sharp Chevron and Four Wheel Drive Equipment" (apparently with Chevron's consent); and (10) the customers of the Sharp station were permitted to charge purchases of both products and repairs on Chevron credit cards. No one of these factors is controlling, but all are useful in determining whether or not control was present. *By using all of these factors, there is a sufficient factual question as to whether or not there was an actual master-servant relationship.* *

Even if there were not a material issue as to whether or not Chevron asserted enough control as to create an actual master-servant relationship, there still exists a material issue as to whether or not Chevron had clothed the lessee with apparent authority. *

"The apparent authority of an agent is to be determined by the acts of the principal, and not by the acts of the agent; a principal is responsible for the acts of an agent within his apparent authority only where the principal by his acts or conduct has clothed the agent with the appearance of authority. . . . The apparent authority of an agent results from statements, conduct, lack of ordinary care, or other manifestation of the principal's consent, whereby third persons are justified in believing that the agent is acting within his authority. . . . The acquiescence of the principal in an extension of his authority by an agent in the transaction in question may be sufficient to create the appearance of authority in the agent to [do] such act. . . . In such case, the appearance of authority is created because of the fact that the third person is entitled to assume that the principal is cognizant of authority and would forbid it if it were unauthorized. . . ."

Here, Chevron knew of and allowed Sharp to conduct his Four Wheel Drive Fixit Shop and it would be reasonable to assume that, if Chevron did not want Sharp to continue such a business, it should have forbidden such activities or at least have put the public on notice that Sharp did not have the authority to make repairs and that it would not be responsible for such repair activities. Instead of putting the public on notice that Sharp did not have the authority to make such repairs, Chevron advertised in the telephone directory that its stations performed auto repairs, and that its repairmen were skillful.

Sutton relied on such statements, in addition to relying on signs, uniforms and credit card privileges which indicated to the public that Sharp was under the control and was an agent of Chevron. . . . Thus, because Sutton relied on such statements and indicia of authority, there is a material question of fact present as to whether or not Sharp had been clothed with apparent authority by Chevron to act as Chevron's agent. . . .

The cause [case] is reversed and remanded to the District Court of Bernalillo County for action consistent with this opinion.

*[Emphasis added.]

Questions and Case Problems

1. Bromber, the general manager of a hotel, offered a $1,000 reward in a newspaper for information leading to the arrest and conviction of the person who killed the hotel clerk during a hotel robbery. Plaintiff, Jackson, claimed the reward, and the defendant, hotel owner Goodman, denied that Bromber had the authority to make the reward offer. Was there sufficient evidence to present a jury question that Bromber, as the hotel manager, had apparent authority to make the reward offer? The jury returned a finding in favor of Jackson, but the judge set aside the jury's finding and entered judgment for the defendant as a matter of law. Defendant appealed. [*Jackson v. Goodman,* 244 N.W.2d 423 (Mich. 1976).]

2. Glen Wood, an executive vice president of SAR Manufacturing Company, checked into the Holiday Inn facility at Phenix City, Alabama during the late afternoon of February 1, 1972. When Wood checked in, he tendered payment for his room by using his Gulf Oil Company credit card. An imprint was made of his card and it was returned to him, as was the normal practice. Sometime during the early morning of February 2 1972, Jessie Goynes, the "night auditor" of the Phenix City Holiday Inn, called National Data in Atlanta on a toll-free number provided by Gulf in order to confirm the plaintiff's credit card number and receive an authorization to extend credit on the basis of the card. He received a communication from National Data advising him: "Do not honor this sale. Pick up the credit card and send it in for reward." Goynes stated that, after getting the directive from National Data, he telephoned the plaintiff's room at 7:00 A.M. and advised him that he was unable to obtain credit authorization and requested plaintiff to surrender the card. Goynes said that Wood voluntarily complied. Wood then paid in cash and left the motel. Upon returning home, Wood called Gulf and explained that he used the card for business purposes. He complained that his account was current, and his credit was immediately reinstated. Wood sued the Gulf Oil Corporation, Holiday Inns, Inc., Interstate Inns, Inc. (the owner of the Phenix City Holiday Inn), and Jessie Goynes. Interstate and Goynes denied any negligence or wrongful conduct and asserted by way of cross-claim that they were acting under the direction of Gulf and were therefore entitled to indemnification by Gulf.

    (a) Was the Holiday Inn clerk the agent of the Gulf Oil Company? (b) Is Gulf liable for the clerk's tortious conduct? (c) Is Gulf required to indemnify the Holiday Inn for its clerk's negligence? [*Wood v. Holiday Inns, Inc.,* 508 F.2d 167 (Ala. 1975).]

3. Z, a traveling salesman for X Co., had authority to solicit orders for X products. He solicited an order from Y and collected the purchase price for the goods from Y. He put the money in his pocket and never turned it over to X. X shipped the goods to Y and later billed him for the purchase price. Y claimed he had already paid because he paid Z. X claimed he would have to pay again. Must he do so?

4. P, the owner of land, appointed A to be his real estate agent to sell the land. A owned 80 percent of the stock in XYZ, Inc. and served on its board of directors. P was not aware of this. A sold the land to XYZ, Inc. at its appraised fair market value. When P discovered A's interest in XYZ, Inc., he sued XYZ, demanding that it return the land to P. You decide who should prevail.

5. Davis was a salaried outside salesman of defendant, International Playtex Corporation. His duties included selling Playtex products to retail stores. He worked out of his home and was required to own and operate a motor vehicle for business use. He had no set hours of employment and was urged by Playtex's district manager to work evenings and weekends. While traveling to his girlfriend's home to do paperwork for Playtex, Davis was involved in a collision with Barnum, who died from his injuries. Rappaport, the plaintiff, the executor of Barnum's estate, brought this suit against Playtex. Was Davis acting within the scope of his employment at the time of the accident? [*Rappaport v. International Playtex Corporation,* 352 N.Y.Supp.2d 241 (1974).]

6. Mueller Travel Agency was purchased by Fetherston, who became an officer and director. Among the rights transferred to it was a contract to sell tickets for Air Traffic Conference of America (ATC) member carriers. ATC was an agency representing various airplane companies and had negotiated the contract between Mueller Travel Agency and each individual member carrier. This contract provided: (a) that all ticket forms supplied by the carrier to the agent were to be held "in trust" by the agent; (b) that the agent was to report three times per month on tickets sold on the carrier and to submit a check for the amount of business written on that carrier during the previous ten-days sales period; and (c) that all agents were to maintain special deposit accounts for the proceeds of ticket sales. However, some two and a half years before the sale of the agency the requirement of maintaining special deposit accounts was eliminated and replaced with a requirement that the travel agent obtain a surety bond. Mueller deposited the proceeds of its ticket sales for ATC member carriers, together with income from ticket sales for other carriers, into a general commercial checking account in the First National Bank of Madison. Did Mueller Travel Agency hold the funds in trust as trustee or as an agent? [In re *Mueller Travel Agency, Inc.,* 201 N.W.2d 589 (Wis. 1972).]

7. State Automobile and Casualty Underwriters brought this action against Richard J. Salisbury and Diversified Insurance Agency, agent of State Auto, to recoup $19,758.54 plaintiff had paid out under a policy which it claims was improperly issued by Diversified. On July 10, 1964 State Auto and Diversified entered into a written contract by which Diversified was authorized to issue insurance policies on behalf of State Auto. One of Diversified's clients was Mr. Farrell Crawforth, who was insured by Diversified through another company. Desiring to change insuring companies on him, on October 1, 1965 Diversified (Mrs. Salisbury) sent a binding application of insurance for Crawforth to State Auto's regional office in Denver. On that application were listed three moving traffic citations issued to Crawforth within the preceding two years. The

application was received by State Auto's Denver branch office on October 4, 1965. On October 15, 1965 State Auto mailed the application back to Diversified, rejecting the application because of the traffic violations. Before the rejection was received by Diversified, Crawforth was involved in an accident, on October 16. Because Diversified had issued the **binder**, State Auto honored claims against Crawforth for the $19,758.54 it seeks to recover herein. The pertinent portion of the contract between the parties was: ". . . the second party shall not have binding authority as respects any risk prohibited by the underwriting guide(s) or the rate manual, or included within the prohibiting list thereof." Plaintiff, State Auto, had issued a 1964 "Prohibited List" which stated that persons who had two or more moving violations within the preceding three years were ineligible for insurance with State Auto. Did the defendant, Diversified Insurance Agency, have a duty to its principal, State Auto, which it did not discharge? [*State Automobile & Casualty Under. v. Salisbury,* 494 P.2d 529 (Utah 1972).]

binder
an insurance company's memorandum of an oral contract of insurance pending the issuance of a formal policy

8. Plaintiff, Mr. Ford, a black, visited the "Bud" Orth Real Estate Agency in Racine, Wisconsin, accompanied by his wife and infant child. The agency was owned and operated by Ellsworth C. "Bud" Orth, a licensed real estate broker. Ford asked Ken Orth, a licensed salesman on duty at the agency, to show him a particular piece of property as advertised for sale in the Racine Journal-Times newspaper. The property, owned by Donald and Joanne McMahon, was in an area of the city in which few, if any, blacks owned property or resided. Ken Orth, in the presence of Ford and his family, made a phone call to the McMahons informing them that Ford wanted to look at the property as a prospective purchaser and that he was a black. After the telephone call Orth informed Ford that the owner did not want to show the property to black persons and therefore he could not see it. Ford told Ken Orth that he was discriminating and left the agency. On August 2, 1967 Ford filed a complaint with the Wisconsin Real Estate Examining Board, alleging in substance that E. C. "Bud" Orth, a licensed broker, was guilty of racial discrimination. Was Orth, acting as an agent under the explicit instructions of his principal, the seller, guilty of discrimination? [*Ford v. Wisconsin Real Estate Examining Board,* 179 N.W.2d 786 (Wis. 1970).]

9. A bank established a securities account with plaintiff, H. Hentz & Co., stockbroker for the bank, which was styled by them "First National Bank of Grand Prairie Customers' Account." Beginning about October 1, 1970 and continuing into February, 1971, the bank forwarded various securities to the plaintiff. On December 29, 1970 Harry S. Scaling borrowed $60,000 from the bank and executed a promissory note therefor. John B. Baird owned two certificates purportedly evidencing 5,000 shares of MDC stock. With Baird's permission, Scaling "pledged and delivered" the certificates "to the Bank as collateral for the loan." In the month of January, 1971, "with the consent and authorization of the bank and Scaling," plaintiff made sales through the bank's "customer account" of 4,800 shares of the MDC stock "so pledged to the bank" for the total net price of $62,248.41. On January 8, 1971 the bank, with Scaling's authorization, delivered two purported certificates of MDC stock to plaintiff in settlements of the sales effected, and to be effected, by plaintiff.

The certificates were "forgeries and nullities." However, at the time the certificates were delivered to plaintiff, they appeared regular and negotiable in every respect, and neither the bank nor plaintiff had any notice or knowledge that they were invalid. The net proceeds of all the sales ($62,248.41) was paid by January 26, 1971. The bank retained the proceeds of the sales, applied them in full payment of Scaling's loan, and deposited the balance above the loan with the bank to the account of Scaling. The $62,248.41 paid by plaintiff to the bank was paid in reliance upon a mutually mistaken belief by plaintiff and the bank that the two certificates were genuine. The bank has been unjustly enriched to the extent of $62,248.41 by reason of the payment of such funds to the bank by plaintiff, which had lost the use thereof since February 9, 1971. The bank received no brokerage fees or benefits from the stock sales other than the repayment of the loan to Scaling. Is the plaintiff, as security broker for the bank, entitled to indemnity from the bank for losses resulting from the bank's contract? [*First Nat. Bank in Grand Prairie v. H. Hentz & Co., Inc.*, 498 S.W.2d 478 (Tex. 1973).]

10. In the case of *Chevron Oil Company v. Sutton,* 515 P.2d 1283 (N.M. 1973),[1] the court referred the case back to the trial court on the ground that the facts pleaded could result in a finding of a master-servant relationship and of apparent authority. In light of this opinion, what do you think can be done to avoid the risk of liability on the basis of master-servant relationship, and apparent authority with respect to auto repairs on the station premises?

---

[1] See pp. 245–47.

Agency and the
Law of Contracts and Torts

16

After you have read this chapter, you should be able to:

1. Explain the three things an agent must do to be protected from personal liability on a breach of contract suit.
2. Know the application of the parol evidence rule to:
   a. formal contracts with a third party and an agent.
   b. informal agency contracts with a third party and an agent.
3. Explain when an agent may agree to be held personally liable to a contract with a third party.
4. Explain an implied warranty of authorization.
5. Explain an implied warranty of capacity.
6. Define a disclosed principal and explain when he is personally liable under the agent's contract.
7. Define an undisclosed principal and explain when he is liable under the agent's contract.
8. Explain when an undisclosed principal is not liable under the agency contract.
9. Explain when a third party's payment to the agent will bind the principal; when it will not bind the principal.
10. Distinguish a servant from a nonservant agent and explain the reason for and importance of this difference.
11. Explain when the principal is liable for the torts of his agent; explain when he is not.
12. Explain why a principal is generally not liable for an agent's torts committed beyond the scope of the agent's authority.

Introduction

Agency relationships are not created to be static. Rather, what is expected is *action* which will change relationships between two persons, namely the principal and a third party.

Most often it is the law of contracts with which people are concerned in their business dealings. However, while attempting to create contracts, during the operation of the agency, the law of **torts** may come into the situation.

An agent can protect himself from assuming duties and giving rights to the principal or to third parties if he conducts himself properly in the operation of the agency.

This chapter is important because it gives you insight into how increased exposure to risk in the legal environment brought about by agency can be limited.

There are basically two substantive areas of law impacted significantly by the agency relationship. These are contracts and torts.

Contract Liability of Agents

Liability of Agent as a Party to a Contract

The agent must do the following three things to be protected from contractual liability:

1. Disclose the principal. The disclosure of the agent's capacity and the fact that he is acting on behalf of a particular principal may be expressed in any manner. The third party must be aware that the agent is acting on behalf of another.
2. Have authority to act. The agent must be authorized by the principal to act on his behalf. The authority may be express or implied, or there may be apparent authority.[1]
3. If a written contract, have it properly executed. If a written contract with the third party is signed by the agent, he must disclose his *representative capacity* on the contract. For example, if John Agent is acting for Peter Principal, a proper signature would be, "Peter Principal by John Agent." If the agent simply signed "John Agent," even though the third party knew he was acting for his principal, the *parol evidence rule* may apply and prevent verbal testimony to explain the agent's capacity.

The *parol evidence rule*[2] has the following applications:

1. **Simple contracts.** If the written contract is *simple* (i.e., not under seal, or not a negotiable instrument such as a promissory note or a check), the agent may testify concerning the fact that the third party *knew* he was acting on behalf of the principal, although the written contract does not disclose this.

tort
a civil (private)
noncontractual wrong

simple contract
a contract which need
not be in any particular
form

---

[1] See pp. 234–35 for discussion of authority and apparent authority.

[2] See pp. 162–63 for discussion of the parol evidence rule.

2. **Formal contracts.** If the contract was under seal or a commercial paper (e.g., a check), the parol evidence rule will prevent the agent from giving testimony concerning the third party's knowledge that he was acting on behalf of the principal.

formal contract
a contract which must be in a certain form

Agent May Agree to Personal Liability

The agent may agree to be held personally liable at the request of the third party. For example, in order to effect a sale and receive his commission, if T requests A to stand behind the contract, the agent may agree to be held personally liable in the event of a breach.

Agent's Implied Warranties

An agent makes two implied **warranties** on the agency contract: (1) implied warranty of authorization, and (2) implied warranty of his principal's capacity.

The agent will be held personally liable if he breaches either warranty even though he acts in good faith.

warranty
an express or implied assurance that certain facts exist

Implied Warranty of Authorization. When an agent contracts with a third party, he impliedly warrants that he has the authority to contract for the principal. If he does not have this authority, or *exceeds the scope of his authority,* he is liable to the third party for **damages** for breach of implied warranty of authority.

In the following case, a third party (T) sued his opponent's lawyers, who withdrew from the case without his client's authority, causing a loss to T. The court denied recovery because T could still recover from P, and *the lawyers had no contractual duty with T.*

damages
the money judicially awarded for another's wrongful conduct

Facts

On February 15, 1955 Harness Jones and his wife brought suit against James A. Sterling and his wife, seeking damages for the alleged wrongful death of their daughter.

On March 15, 1955 the law firm of Benton and Mosely were retained as counsel for the Sterlings. Approximately three years later they asked the court and received permission to withdraw as counsel of record for the Sterlings. As a result of this withdrawal, a default judgment was entered awarding the Joneses recovery against the Sterlings in the sum of $60,000.

Suit was initiated by the Sterlings to annul the default judgment. They claimed that the judgment was null because their attorneys, Benton and Mosely, were not authorized to withdraw as counsel. On review, the default judgment in favor of the Joneses was set aside and the matter remanded to the trial court.

In the trial court, the Joneses filed a claim seeking recovery from the Sterling's attorneys, Benton and Mosely, on the grounds that the attorneys were responsible for the annulment of the default judgment because of their unauthorized withdrawal. Did the attorneys, Benton and Mosely, owe a duty to their clients' opponent, the Joneses, not to withdraw?

Decision

No. Judgment for the attorneys.

tortfeasor
a person who has
committed a tort

Benton and Mosely owed a contractual duty to their clients, the Sterlings, but none to the Joneses. The action of the agent, lawyers, does not deprive the third party, Joneses, of their claim against the Sterlings. The Joneses could recover against the Sterlings' attorneys for an unauthorized withdrawal only if it left them with no claim against the principal **tortfeasor**, the Sterlings.

Sterling v. Jones, 249 So.2d 334 (La. 1971).

Implied Warranty of Principal's Capacity.   The agent impliedly warrants to the third party that his principal has capacity to be contractually bound. For example, if the agent acts for a dissolved corporation, it will not be liable *under the contract,* but the agent can be held liable for *breach of his implied warranty of his principal's capacity.* However, if the agent acts on behalf of a minor/ principal and does not represent that the principal has full capacity, the agent is not liable if the minor avoids the contract.

Contract Liability of Principals

Whether a principal is disclosed, undisclosed, or partially disclosed to the third person depends upon the third person's knowledge of a person as a principal and of his identity. When the third person knows that the agent is acting for a principal but he does not know the principal's identity, the latter is a partially disclosed principal. In this book, unless otherwise indicated, reference to a disclosed principal includes a partially disclosed principal.

Liability of Disclosed Principal as Party to a Contract

disclosed principal
a person known, or
who reasonably should
be known, by a third
party to be a principal
for an agent

Once the agent has **disclosed** to the third party the identity of the **principal** for whom he is *authorized to contract,* or the third person reasonably should be aware of the principal's identity, the principal becomes liable on the subsequently made contract. If the agent is not authorized, or if he exceeds the scope of his authority, the principal may ratify[3] the contract and thus become liable under the contract with the effect as though it were initially authorized. Thus, if there is a principal with contractual capacity, and the agent with authority properly executed the contract with the third party, a contract exists only between P and T.

Liability of Undisclosed Principal as Party to a Contract

undisclosed principal
a person not known, or
who is not reasonably
known, to be a
principal for an agent
by a third party

If the third party is not aware and reasonably should not be aware that the agent is acting for anyone, the principal is called an **undisclosed principal.** The parties to the contract are the agent and the third party. However, if the third party breaches his contract, his assets are available to satisfy a judgment obtained by the agent against him. Because the agent then holds such assets in trust for the benefit of his principal, the law causes the undisclosed principal to be a party

---

[3] See pp. 223–25 on the rules of ratification in agency.

also to the contract authorizedly made by the agent so that the principal's assets are available to the third party if the agent breaches the contract. So there are three parties to the contract—namely the agent, principal, and third party—unless the undisclosed principal is excluded from being a party to the contract, either expressly by the contract or by the contract being under seal or a negotiable instrument in which the principal's name does not appear. Each of the three parties is liable as a contracting party.

The following case illustrates how the court attempts to determine the parties' intent to exclude an undisclosed principal.

Facts

In August, 1969 Epstein and one Buford, the alleged agent of Cooper, executed a document entitled "Lease and Purchase and Sale Agreement." Epstein did not know Buford was acting for Cooper. This agreement was a contract to sell certain real estate. Initially, however, the property was to be leased to Buford for a period of up to 36 months for a fixed monthly rental, plus real estate taxes and insurance. Upon the cancellation of an identified **encumbrance,** the lease would automatically terminate and the sale provisions of the contract would come into effect.

The agreement contained the following nonassignment clause:

That he (Buford) will not transfer nor assign this agreement, nor let nor sublet the whole or any part of said premises without written consent of Landlord first had and obtained, such consent shall not be unreasonably withheld.

On nonpayment of the March rent and late payment of the April rent, Epstein notified Buford that he intended to cancel the contract for nonpayment.

Cooper filed a complaint for an accounting and breach of contract. He alleged that Buford was his agent and was acting in that capacity when he signed the agreement. Cooper, fearing that his credit standing might be suspect, arranged orally to have his employee, Buford, negotiate the purchase of the property. May Cooper, an undisclosed principal, bring suit?

Decision

Yes.

Reasoning

It is well settled that, absent some special exception, an undisclosed principal may sue and be sued on a contract made by his agent. Even the fact that the agent denies that there is a principal, or represents himself to be the principal, is not sufficient to preclude suit by the undisclosed principal. However, where the express terms of the contract provide that it (the contract) is to be effective only between the agent and the third party, the undisclosed principal may not enforce the contract. The undisclosed principal simply can not sue where to do so would violate a term of the written contract. Comment c to section 393 of the *Restatement of Agency* states:

Non-assignment clause. A clause in a contract against assignment does not of itself prevent the principal from bringing suit upon the contract. The existence of such a clause, however, may be considered as evidence that the parties intended to exclude an undisclosed principal. . . .

We adopt this statement of the law and, therefore, remand this cause for trial on the merits.

Cooper v. Epstein, 308 A.2d 781 (D.C. 1973).

encumbrance
a person's right in another person's property

The important point is that the agent was authorizedly *acting on behalf of the undisclosed principal* when he contracted with the third party, and the latter should stand behind the contract. When P authorizes A to purchase property on his behalf without disclosing that A is representing anyone and A, intending to act for P, authorizedly contracts with T to purchase the property in A's own name, P (as well as A) is liable under the contract.

Effect of Agent's Improper Purpose

If an agent makes a contract for his disclosed or undisclosed principal as he is authorized to do, but with an *improper purpose* of which the third party does not have notice, the principal is bound on the contract as though the agent had a proper purpose. For example, payment by the third party to the agent of funds due to the principal will bind the principal even if the agent never remits the payment. This rule applies only if the third party acted in good faith and did not know the agent would act improperly. For example, P appoints A to collect rents on his behalf. T, a tenant, paid the rent to A, who kept the money. P would have to give credit to T for the monthly rent.

The reasons for this rule are that T can not ascertain A's improper purpose, and public policy requires P to select his agent carefully for loyalty to P.

Effect of Agent's Unauthorized Misrepresentation of What He Was Authorized to Represent Truthfully

If an agent makes a contract for his disclosed or partially disclosed principal, as he is authorized to do, but he misrepresents matters in connection with the contract of which the third party does not have notice, the principal is liable on the contract and for such misrepresentations. For example, a salesman misrepresents the fabric content of a sweater sold to an innocent store customer third party. The store owner principal is liable to the customer for the agent's untruthful statement.

Tort Liability

The three-party relationship created by an agency contract frequently involves an injury arising from tort liability. If the principal directs his agent to commit a wrongful act, *the principal* is liable in tort to the injured third party. The principal is also liable for all other tortious acts committed by the agent while acting within the scope of his authority.

Even though the agent may injure the third party while acting for his principal, *the agent* may also be held liable. An agent is liable to third parties for his torts irrespective of whether or not his principal is also liable and whether or not he was acting within the scope of his authority. The injured third party may select whether he will hold the principal or the agent liable for the agent's torts committed within the course and scope of his authority. Also, it is possible that the third person may be liable *to the agent* for torts caused by his improper conduct.

While an agent is liable to a third party for his misdoing, called **misfeasance,** he is not liable for not doing anything, called **nonfeasance,** in the absence of any legal obligation for him to act. He has no duty to the third party, so he has no liability for nonfeasance. But once an agent begins to act, the law imposes a duty upon him to act carefully, as it does for everyone, and also imposes liability for misfeasance.

Principal's Liability for Torts of the Agent While Acting Within the Scope of His Authority

Let us briefly examine the *principal's* tort liability within the three-party relationship.

An agent may be a **servant** or a *nonservant* agent. We have defined an agent as a person authorized to act on behalf of another and subject to the other's control. The principal's degree of control over the conduct of the agent may vary. If the principal has the right to control, or exercises control over, the *physical conduct* of his agent, the agent is called a *servant* and the principal is called a **master.** Often courts refer to them as principal and agent. Most agents are servants.

The reason for distinguishing between servants and nonservant agents is that the principal's liability varies as the degree of his control over the conduct of the agent. Thus, a *master* is liable for the *tortious physical harm* (or loss) to third persons caused by his servant while acting within the *scope of his employment* (servants are usually called *employees*). A principal is liable for the *nonphysical* torts of his *agent* while acting within the *scope of his authority.*

For example, independent contractors who become special agents (e.g., brokers, lawyers) are nonservant agents, and because the principal does *not* control their *physical conduct,* he is not liable for their tortious physical harm to third persons. (P retains A, a real estate broker, to produce a prospective buyer of P's land. While A is driving his auto showing the land to a customer, he drives negligently and injures the customer. P is not liable for A's tortious physical harm to the customer.) (A, P's truck driver, while delivering P's goods, negligently injures a pedestrian. P is a master and liable for the tortious physical harm to the pedestrian caused by A, his servant.) Accordingly, let us first consider torts by servants and then torts by nonservant agents.

Torts by Servants. The doctrine of a master's liability for the torts of his servant committed while acting within the scope of his employment is called **respondeat superior.** "Scope of employment" is a broad phrase, but in general it means *in furtherance of the master's business.* In certain instances a master is liable even when the servant has not acted within the scope of his employment.

1. Torts committed within the scope of employment. Once *tortious physical harm* has occurred, the first step is to determine if the wrongdoer is an *agent.* If he is, the next step is to decide if he is a *servant.* If he is, then the last step is to see if he was acting within the *scope of his employment* when he committed the tort. Section 228(1) of the *Restatement (Second) of Agency*

establishes the following criteria to ascertain whether the conduct of a servant is within the scope of employment:

a. it is of the kind of conduct he is employed to perform;
b. it occurs substantially within the authorized time and space limits;
c. it is activated, at least in part, by a purpose to serve the master; and
d. if force is intentionally used by the servant against another, the use of force is not unexpectable by the master.

Notice how the court in the following tort action for unlawful arrest is concerned with the activities of the detective in determining whether his wrongful conduct was committed in the course of employment.

Facts

Stuckey, a school teacher, was shopping in Dillard Department Stores. She was arrested and accused of shoplifting by Detective Spahr, an off-duty city policeman in uniform who was employed by Dillard *to deter shoplifting and otherwise act as a security guard* within the store. Spahr testified that he saw Stuckey take a scarf and put it in a plastic bag, but when she was taken to the police station and searched no merchandise was found. After having been acquitted in municipal court, Stuckey brought suit against the store and obtained a verdict for $1,000.

Dillard urges reversal, contending that in the circumstances Spahr was compelled by statute as a policeman to make the arrest and that, inasmuch as the store did not direct or bring about the arrest, there was no agency relationship between Spahr and the department store. He acted as a policeman and not as an employee of Dillard.

Was Spahr the agent of the department store when making the arrest?

Decision

Yes. Judgment affirmed for Stuckey.

Reasoning

Dillard contends that an employer, by engaging an off-duty policeman as its agent, can immunize itself from liability for an unlawful arrest whenever the officer acts upon his own initiative. That contention, however, runs counter to the basic rule that a principal is liable for its agent's torts when committed in the course of his employment and for the principal's benefit.

Spahr was acting in the course of his employment by the store and for its benefit. The officer has worked for the store in his off-duty hours for two years. He was paid at the rate of $4 per hour. His primary duty was to deter shoplifting. Immediately after the arrest he interrogated Stuckey in the back room provided by the store. At the police station Spahr made out an "Offense Report" describing the offense as shoplifting. Thus it cannot be said as a matter of law that Spahr was acting solely as a policeman rather than as an employee of the store.

Dillard Department Stores, Inc. v. Stuckey, 511 S.W.2d 154 (Ark. 1974).

In what is known as the "independent frolic" or "detour" cases, the chief question is whether the servant's deviation from his authority is sufficient to cause his conduct not to be within the scope of his employment. Thus, the following examples of a servant's conduct at variance with his authority have been held to be within his scope of employment: the servant's unauthorized use of equipment which was not that much substantially different from what was authorized; the negligence and traffic violation of a servant truck driver when the master had instructed him to drive carefully; the servant salesperson keeping a store open a little longer than the established closing time; and the servant truck driver paying a social call requiring a slight deviation from his established service route.

2. Torts committed beyond the scope of the agent's authority. The master is not liable to the third party for torts committed by the servant when he acts beyond the scope of his employment. If the servant is no longer acting for the benefit of the master and has dealings with the third party outside his employment relationship with his master, the injured third party generally has no recourse against the master. When a servant engages in an independent frolic or detour which is not within his scope of employment, there is much difficulty and difference among the cases in determining at what point in time and space he returns into the employ of his master.

Torts by Nonservant Agents. The principal is not liable for tortious physical harm committed by a nonservant agent because he has no control over the agent's physical conduct. However, the principal is liable for the agent's nonphysical torts committed while acting within his authority or apparent authority. For example, if the agent intentionally misrepresents to a customer third party regarding the subject matter authorized, or apparently authorized, to be sold by him, the principal may be liable for the tort of deceit.

It should be noted that an agent is not liable for the torts or breach of contract committed by his principal in connection with a transaction authorizedly made by the agent. The following case is an example.

Facts

The plaintiffs, Mr. and Mrs. Dorkin, contracted with the defendant, American Express Company, for a European tour. While being transported from Antwerp to Amsterdam in Holland, Mrs. Dorkin sustained personal injuries when the tour bus in which she and her husband were riding braked abruptly, causing her to be thrown to the floor. The plaintiffs claimed that the negligence of the defendant was a failure to exercise reasonable and prudent care in providing safe equipment and careful personnel in the discharge of its contractual obligation to supply a safe, entertaining European vacation. Was American Express liable for the plaintiff's injury?

Decision

No. Judgment for American Express.

Reasoning

In the absence of agreement or acts indicating an intention of the contracting parties to superadd the responsibility of the agent, there is no such responsibility of the agent to third parties for tortious acts of the principal. Similarly, there is no liability on the part of the agent for breach of contract by the principal. In the instant case there was no breach of contract, either between the plaintiffs and the defendant agent or between plaintiffs and the bus company on whose vehicle the accident happened. American Express Company contracted on behalf of its principals, if we regard the defendant as an agent (which I do not, although I recognize that the nomenclature "travel agent" is used to designate or describe the nature of defendant's business), to provide for a planned, structured trip to Europe with a designated place of beginning and a point of termination covering a stated number of days and to provide for food and lodging and transportation between points to be visited within the context of the total trip.

Dorkin v. American Express Company, 74 Misc.2d 673 (N.Y. 1974).

Summary Statement

1. To be protected from personal liability, an agent must:
   a. disclose the principal,
   b. be authorized by the principal to act on his behalf,
   c. if there is a written contract, have it properly executed.
2. The parol evidence rule will allow an agent who signed a *simple* contract to testify that the third party with whom he contracted knew he was acting on behalf of a principal. A simple contract, as contrasted with a formal contract, is not in any required form (e.g., a check).
3. If the agent signed a *formal* contract, the parol evidence rule will prevent the agent from giving testimony concerning the third party's knowledge that he was acting on behalf of the principal.
4. If requested by the third party, the agent may agree to become personally liable on the contract.
5. The circumstances surrounding an agent's contract with a third person create an implied warranty of authorization. This means that the agent warrants he has authority and has not exceeded its scope.
6. Also, the agent impliedly warrants that his principal has capacity to be contractually bound.
7. An *undisclosed principal* is a principal not known to the third party. He has authorized the agent to act for his benefit and on his behalf. The undisclosed principal is liable to the third party under a simple contract, as is the agent also.
8. A *disclosed principal* is a principal that is known to the third party. He is liable to the third party if he has capacity and if the agent was authorized or apparently authorized to act on its behalf or if the contract was ratified by the principal.

9. If the agent makes an authorized contract for his disclosed or partially disclosed principal but with an *improper purpose,* of which the third party does not have notice, the principal is bound on the contract.

10. If the agent makes an authorized contract for his disclosed or partially disclosed principal and *misrepresents* matters in connection with the contract, of which the third party did not have notice, the principal is liable on the contract and for such misrepresentations.

11. A principal is liable for the nonphysical torts of his nonservant agent when they are committed within the course and scope of his authority or apparent authority. He is also liable for the tortious physical harm to third persons committed by his servant while acting within the scope of his employment. This rule is based on the theory that the servant, although acting wrongfully, is acting for the benefit of the principal. It is known as the doctrine of "respondeat superior."

In the following case the *master* was held not to be vicariously (substitutively) liable under the doctrine of *respondeat superior* for the negligence of its *servant.* Was the servant in this case on a *frolic of his own* (i.e., not being at all on his master's business) or on a mere *detour* (i.e., going out of his way against his master's implied commands while driving on his master's business)?

Balinovic v. Evening Star Newspaper Co.
113 F.2d 505 (1940)

Edgerton, Associate Justice. Balinovic sued the *Evening Star* on the theory that its delivery truck, negligently driven by its driver, injured him in a collision. The question is whether the district court was right in directing a verdict for the defendant because the driver had left his route, and his work of delivering papers, and was chasing a traffic violator at the command of a policeman who jumped on the running board and stayed there.

The accident occurred on June 23, 1933, before the passage of the statute which imposes liability on the owner of a car for the acts of any person who drives it with his consent, and the mere fact that the *Star* had entrusted its car to its driver did not make it liable. Balinovic urges that when an agent is sent out in charge of a car he is "impliedly authorized" by his principal to aid in law enforcement at the command of a policeman. This comes to saying that he may assume that his principal, if present, would authorize the act. That depends upon the principal's disposition, the agent's knowledge of it, and the other circumstances. Perhaps sympathy with law enforcement may be imputed to a newspaper. Perhaps this extends to a willingness to interrupt delivery of papers and risk damage to truck, driver, and public in order to chase a criminal. But the fact remains that the *Star's* business is not chasing criminals but producing and selling papers. When its driver set out to catch a criminal, he was doing the work of the District of Columbia.

When B, for his own purposes, borrows, controls, and directs A's driver, B is responsible for the driver's negligence and A is not. An express authorization from an employer to his employee to do another's work under another's direction does not make the employer responsible for the employee's negligence in doing the work; and no implied authorization can be more effective than an express one. "The master's responsibility can not be extended beyond the limits of the master's work." Whose work it is depends on "who has the power to control and direct the servants in the performance of their work."

The *Star,* by putting the driver on the road and keeping him there, did not create the risk that the criminal-catching activities of the District would injure a bystander. Whether it created the risk that those activities of the District would injure the driver, with the result that an injury to him in the course of those activities might be regarded as arising out of and in the course of his employment by the *Star,* is a question which we need not decide.

Affirmed.

Questions and Case Problems

1. Claude I. Bennett, a partner in Bennett Dairy, a partnership, executed a contract in Claude's name with Putney, who was to erect a silo on the Bennett farm and build a foundation on which the silo could be placed. Putney built the foundation but never erected the silo. Bennett Dairy alleges that it is the undisclosed principal of Claude, and it sued Putney for damages for breach of contract. May the partnership as the undisclosed principal sue on the agent Claude's contract? [*Bennett Dairy v. Putney,* 362 N.Y.Supp.2d 93 (1974).]

2. Petitioner, Mobil Oil Corporation, brings this proceeding to recover possession of a gasoline station from Burdo, lessee, based upon an alleged breach by the lessee of his lease and supply contract with the petitioner-landlord. Lessee operated a gasoline station in the Town of Huntington, State of New York, pursuant to an annual lease with petitioner. Lessee also entered into a retail dealer's contract with petitioner to sell its products. Petitioner alleges that, in violation of its supply contract with lessee, the lessee's employee adulterated its products by adding regular gas to its premium tanks and selling this combination of fuels to motorists as premium gasoline. Accordingly, petitioner asks this court to grant an order evicting the lessee and allowing petitioner to recover possession. Lessee denies the allegations but contends that, in any event, the word "adulterate," as used in the supply contract, does not include the mixing of two gasolines produced by the same supplier. Lessee contends that he did not breach his contract with petitioner since he should not be held accountable, in this instance, for the unauthorized acts of his employee. Lessee also requests this court to invoke its equity powers to prevent eviction on the grounds that it is too drastic a remedy, which would terminate the lessee's livelihood, investment, and goodwill of his customers. Was the lessee responsible for the unauthorized act of its employee? [*Mobil Oil Corporation v. Burdo,* 69 Misc.2d 153 (N.Y. 1972).]

3. Dr. Leach, a dentist, went to the Penn-Mar Shopping Center with his wife and children. Dr. Leach observed a motor vehicle driven by Labrie back out of a parking spot and into a vehicle driven by Conti. Officer DeBari, a security guard employed by Penn-Mar, said that Dr. Leach demanded the accident report as a "citizen." DeBari said he could not write the report because he

did not have police accident reports with him. Officer DeBari obtained a "Subpoena for Witness" and a State of Maryland Motor Vehicle Accident Report from the patrol cruiser. He issued the "subpoena" to Dr. Leach. Officer DeBari said that on three or four occasions, during the time he was preparing the report, he found it necessary to request Dr. Leach not to interfere with his, DeBari's, performance of his duty. According to DeBari, he placed the doctor under arrest for obstructing justice by interfering with a police officer because of Dr. Leach's persistent interference, even after prior warnings. The following city ordinance existed: "Members of the police department are held to be always on duty . . . the fact that they may be off duty shall not relieve them from taking proper police action in any matter coming to their attention. All officers shall have authority to summon witnesses." Dr. Leach was handcuffed, frisked, placed in a police vehicle, and taken before a Justice of the Peace, where he was released on $18.50 collateral. Dr. Leach complained of maltreatment by DeBari in the form of a lacerated finger, permanent injury to his right shoulder, cut gums, and a broken tooth. Dr. Leach sought and obtained medical care and treatment following his release. When the charge of obstruction of justice by interfering with a police officer was called to trial in the then People's Court, Dr. Leach was acquitted. Dr. Leach instituted suit against Officer DeBari and Penn-Mar Merchants Association, Inc. The suit charged: (a) assault and battery, (b) false imprisonment and unlawful arrest, (c) slander, (d) malicious prosecution, and (e) negligent hiring. Judgment was for Penn-Mar Merchants Association, Inc. and Dr. Leach appealed. Was Officer DeBari the agent of Penn-Mar at the time he arrested Dr. Leach? Was he acting within the scope of his employment? [*Leach v. Penn-Mar Merchants Association, Inc.*, 308 A.2d 446 (Md. 1973).]

4. Robert, the ten-year-old son of Mr. Smith, got into a fight with John, the eleven-year-old son of Mr. Burnham, who claimed Mr. Smith should pay for John's medical bills incurred as a result of this fight. Should Mr. Smith pay?

5. Some children broke an axe belonging to D while D's servant, a carpenter, was not present. Upon the carpenter's return, he discovered the breakage and assaulted one of the children. Is D liable?

6. David Hall engaged Wagner Company Realtors to sell Hall's house. Mrs. Silva was the sales agent for Wagner. Hall alleges that Silva received $1,000 earnest money from Flores, a prospective, ready, able, and willing buyer; that Silva converted $900 of the earnest money to her own use by keeping the $900; that the earnest money receipt and contract of sale reflected only $100 as the earnest money paid, and for this reason Flores rescinded the contract. Hall further alleged that, because of this, Hall's property was not sold to Flores and had to be sold to another person at a reduced price causing loss to Hall. Hall sued Wagner Company Realtors for such loss and punitive damages caused by the alleged Silva conversion of $900. Is the Wagner Company Realtor liable in punitive damages for its sales agent, Mrs. Silva's, **conversion?** [*Wagner v. Hall*, 519 S.W.2d 488 (Tex. 1975).]

conversion
the tort of intentional interference with another's right to possession, control, and dominion of a chattel

7. O, a home owner, hired C, a roofer, to repair his roof. C was a professional roofer. While C was working on the roof, he accidentally dropped a hammer, which struck M, O's mailman, on the head, injuring him. M sued O for his damages. Could M win?

8. M hired S to drive M's truck and deliver goods for his business. After S delivered the goods, he proceeded to return to M's store. On the way he stopped at his mother's house, where a children's party was in progress. The children jumped into the truck and S gave them a ride around town. While driving the children back to his mother's house, T, one of the children, who was riding on the truck fender, fell under the wheel and was injured. T sued M. Is M in this case responsible for the negligence of S?

9. Efren Gobea was employed by Desert Guild, Inc. as a handyman and delivery man. Desert rented a large air compressor and a trailer and told Gobea that he was to pick up the trailer carrying the compressor, take it home, and bring it to the job site the next day. Gobea was to use his own pickup truck to do the hauling. The next day while Gobea was driving the truck and hauling the trailer and compressor to the job site, he had a collision with an automobile driven by Anderson, plaintiff, who sued Gobea and Desert Guild, Inc., as co-defendants. Desert relies on the Arizona "going and coming to work" rule under which a workman is not in the course of his employment when going to work and returning from work. Desert claims that Gobea was not in the course of employment while hauling the trailer and compressor and, therefore, that Desert is not liable for the accident. Is Desert liable for Anderson's injuries under the doctrine of *respondeat superior*? [*Anderson v. Gobea*, 501 P.2d 453 (Ariz. 1972).]

10. The case of *Balinovic v. Evening Star Newspaper Co.*, 113 F.2d 505 (1940)[4] established that a master is liable for the torts of his agent when they are committed within the course and scope of his employment. What is the objective of this rule of law?

---

[4] See pp. 261–62.

Termination of Agency

17

After you have read this chapter, you should be able to:

1. List and explain the five methods by which agency is terminated by acts of the parties.
2. List and explain the six methods by which agency is terminated by operation of law.
3. Distinguish agency coupled with an interest in the subject matter of the agency from agency given as security.
4. Explain the effect of the principal terminating the agency without giving notice to third parties.
5. Explain the effect of terminating the agency between the principal and agent when notice is not given to third parties.

Introduction

Now that agency with its express and implied authority has been created, how is the agency and such authority terminated? Also, when apparent authority has been created, how is that terminated? Basically, how is an agent's power to act for a principal terminated so that the principal can not be made liable any longer by an agent's conduct?

If the agent knows, or reasonably should know, that if the principal knew of changed circumstances, he would not want the agent to act for him, then the agent's power is terminated. In the case of apparent authority, the same is true, if the third party so knew or reasonably should know this.

Our concern here is under what circumstances does agency, the agent's authority, and apparent authority terminate. As it is important for you to know how an agency relationship is created, it is also important for you to know how it ends.

Acts of the parties.

Termination by Acts of the Parties

Following are five ways by which agency power may be terminated by acts of the principal and agent:

Expiration pursuant to the terms of the agency contract.

Expiration of the Agency Contract

The contract between the principal and the agent may specify that it will terminate upon the happening of a certain event or at the end of a time period. For instance, a contract with a real estate broker that creates an exclusive agency to list the principal's house for sale for ninety days. At the expiration of the ninety-day period the contract is terminated, even though the purpose of the contract has not been accomplished.

Mutual agreement.

Termination by Mutual Agreement

The common law principles of the law of contracts relative to termination of a contract are applicable to terminating an agency contract.[1] Hence, the parties by mutual consent may terminate an agency contract.

Exercise of option to terminate.

Option of a Party

An agency contract, by its terms, may allow either the principal or the agent to terminate by giving advance notice to the other. Exercising this option will have the effect of a termination. For example, a life insurance agent may, under the employment contract, have the option to terminate by giving thirty days notice to the employer.

P's revocation.

"Revocation" by the Principal

Once the principal has authorized the agent to perform on his behalf, he always *retains the power* to "revoke" (terminate) the authority. Even though he may be liable to the agent for damages sustained due to *wrongful revocation,* he

---

[1] See p. 204.

Agency and Employment

nevertheless has the *power to revoke*. For example, the agency contract may provide that it can not be terminated by either party. The contract can still be revoked, although revocation will subject the principal to damages for its breach.

Unless the parties have otherwise agreed, the principal's revocation is ineffective to terminate the agency unless the agent has actually received notice of the principal's intent so to terminate, or other facts reasonably cause him to believe that revocation has occurred. (P mails a letter to A, P's agent, stating that the agency is at an end. Before A received the letter he made a contract in P's name with T pursuant to his authority. P is bound on the contract.)

In the following case a loan broker sues his principal for his commission, claiming that the principal wrongfully revoked their contract after the broker had performed in accordance with the contract. Notice how the court distinguished between the principal's *power to revoke* and his *right to revoke*.

Facts

Plaintiff, Sunshine Exploration Company, sued defendants, Manos and Muncey, doing business as Manos and Muncey Architects, a partnership, for breach of a loan brokerage contract. By a letter agreement with plaintiff, defendants offered to pay plaintiff a 1 percent commission provided he could obtain and deliver to defendants a loan within thirty days of between $560,000 and $575,000 at a rate of interest of 9.6 percent constant or better. Plaintiff claims that, as defendants' agent, he obtained a loan commitment in accordance with the contract, but defendants refused to accept it and wrongfully terminated the contract prior to the expiration of the thirty-day period provided in the contract. Did the defendants as a principal *wrongfully revoke* the agency with Sunshine?

Decision

Yes. Judgment for plaintiff, Sunshine.

Reasoning

The principal may, of course, revoke a unilateral offer, but there is a distinction between his power to revoke and his right to revoke. He may at any time before full performance revoke the authority of an agent so the agent will lose his authority to bring the principal into legal relations with a third party. However, if he has no right to revoke it, he will be liable for damages suffered by the agent by reason of the wrongful revocation.

The promise which the defendants made in this instance was such that they should have expected to induce action of a substantial nature on the part of the plaintiff. It is without dispute that the plaintiff did subsequently enter upon performance and expended at least some time and effort in attempting to negotiate the loan before defendants rescinded. Having failed to establish a right of revocation, the defendants are liable for their breach of contract.

Sunshine v. Manos, 496 S.W.2d 195 (Tex. 1973).

"Renunciation" by the Agent

The agent maintains the same power as the principal to terminate the agency contract, regardless of its terms, called a power to "renunciate" or "renounce."

If under the terms of the agency contract the agency is terminable at the will of the agent, he can renounce at any time without incurring damages for breach of the agency contract. If the principal's instructions are illegal, he has the right to renunciate.

The agent will be liable for damages for breach of the agency contract. An example is when the agency contract is for a stated period of time and the agent wrongfully renounces the contract. Thus, an exclusive ninety-day real estate listing will terminate when A notifies P two weeks after accepting the listing that he is listing the house with other brokers.

Unless the parties have otherwise agreed, the agent's renunciation is ineffective to terminate the agency unless the principal has notice, or other facts reasonably cause him to believe, that renunciation has occurred.

The following case illustrates how an "indefinite duration agency" may be terminated at the will of either the principal or the agent; however, the agent may be entitled to damages.

Facts

Plaintiff sues for an accounting for five percent commission on all business obtained for defendant within plaintiff's geographic sales area arising out of an alleged oral contract which called on the plaintiff to obtain his old business associates as customers for the defendant. The parties agreed plaintiff was to work for defendant to obtain for defendant prior customers of plaintiff; that plaintiff would have "as long as he wanted," "whatever time was necessary," and "no deadline was placed thereon"; that plaintiff would advance costs himself, and "when plaintiff succeeded in said efforts," he would get a five percent commission on the business he brought defendant; that a notice by defendant proclaimed to plaintiff's business associates that plaintiff was "now affiliated with defendant."

Plaintiff performed his obligations for seven months, brought to defendant a monthly average of $10,000 in business, and spent $3,600 in expenses. After seven months, defendant discharged plaintiff without good cause. Was this a rightful termination of the agency?

Decision

No. Judgment for plaintiff.

Reasoning

Agreements between principal and agent for an indefinite time generally may be terminated at will of either party. The agreement between plaintiff and defendant was "for an indefinite period of time, its duration was not fixed expressly or impliedly, and its expiration did not depend on the completion of a given undertaking." The agreement was therefore terminable at the will of either party, but there is a limitation on the power to terminate an agency.

Want v. Century Supply Company, 508 S.W.2d 515 (Mo. 1974).

Termination by Operation of Law

When an agency contract is terminated by *operation of law,* it ends, regardless of the parties' consent. The law brings about the result even though the principal or the agent may have another intent.

Following are six ways by which agency power may be terminated by operation of law.

Death

Since agency is a personal service contract,[2] because the agent is a fiduciary acting primarily on behalf of the principal, the authority given to him terminates without any notice to the agent upon the principal's death. The agent can not act for a nonexistent person. An ordinary contract, however, will not terminate upon the obligor's death, but rather becomes an estate obligation.[3]

However, some state statutes and a few courts take the position that the agent has power to bind the deceased principal's estate until the agent receives notice of death. Examples are statutes that relate to principals who are in the armed forces and banks that have authority to pay checks drawn by the principal or his agent before his death.[4]

The agent's death will also terminate the relationship, as is illustrated by the following case.

Facts

Commercial Nursery, the plaintiff, employed Ben Ivey as their agent to sell nursery goods to its customers. Ivey had the customers sign promissory notes payable to the plaintiff and to be paid upon delivery of the goods. Ivey was to collect on the notes and remit to the nursery the agreed fixed price with them and retain the markup he made with the customer as his commission. Ivey died and his administrator, the defendant, collected on the notes on Ivey's behalf and claimed that the proceeds belonged to Ivey's estate. Plaintiff claimed it owned the proceeds.

Decision

Judgment for plaintiff nursery.

Reasoning

The death of the agent, Ivey, terminated the agency. The notes were made payable to Commercial Nursery and were their property. Ivey had no interest in the notes except to collect them. Upon Ivey's death, the agency terminated, and his administrator had no authority to collect the notes for the nursery.

Commercial Nursery Co. v. Ivey, 51 S.W.2d 238 (Tenn. 1932).

Insanity

The principal that appointed the agent to act on his behalf must be capable of maintaining supervision over the agent. Therefore, the insanity of the principal will terminate the agency, as is illustrated by the following case.

---

[2] See pp. 185–86.

[3] *Commercial Nursery Co. v. Ivey,* 51 S.W.2d 238 (Tenn. 1932).

[4] See pp. 578–79.

Facts

The decedent, Margaret Berry, was admitted to the hospital in February 1970. On March 26, 1970 she executed a power of attorney designating her niece, Irene Montanye, as her agent. Thereafter, the decedent was discharged from the hospital. On April 29, 1970 the decedent suffered a stroke and was readmitted to the hospital. She remained in a comatose or semicomatose condition until her death on June 30, 1971. On April 30 Mrs. Montanye, acting under the power of attorney, transferred some $109,000 of the decedent's funds into a trust account in the name of the decedent in trust for Ann R. Scully, **administratrix** of this estate.

Distributees of the decedent and their assignees objected that the alleged agency created by the power of attorney was void because: the decedent did not understand what she was doing; the transfer of the funds to the trust was void as being beyond the scope of any agency created; and the transfer of the funds was void because at the time of the transfer and thereafter the decedent was mentally incompetent by reason of being in a comatose or semicomatose state and, therefore, the agency was suspended or revoked. Can an agency be terminated by the mental incompetency of the principal?

Decision

Yes. Permission is given to distributees to file verified objections to prove decedent's mental incompetency.

administratrix
a court-appointed woman not named in a will who administers the estate of a decedent

Reasoning

The Restatement of the Law of Agency, section 122, states:

The authority of the agent to make the principal a party to a transaction is terminated or suspended upon the happening of an event which deprives the principal of capacity to become a party to the transaction or deprives the agent of capacity to make the principal a party to it.

Comment (a) thereupon reads, in part:

The principal may cease to have capacity to make a contract or to subject himself to liability because of mental incompetency, as where there is a judicial determination of his insanity. . . .

Comment (b) reads:

The power of the agent terminates although he has no notice of the principal's loss of capacity or of the event causing it. It also terminates although the contingency has been provided for and it has been agreed that the authority would not thereupon terminate.

If the objectors prove that, at the time of the agent's transfer of the funds, and thereafter, the decedent was mentally incompetent or incapacitated by reason of her alleged comatose or semicomatose state, then the agency would have been suspended or revoked. The court finds that the proposed amended objections raised valid issues of law and fact and granted permission to file amended objections.

In re *Berry's Estate,* 329 N.Y.Supp.2d 915 (1972).

The agent's insanity that occurs after his appointment will terminate the agency as a matter of law. Some courts have held that, once the incapacity has been removed, the agency relationship can be restored.

Bankruptcy

Bankruptcy of P or A.

The bankruptcy of the principal will terminate the authority of the agent to act with respect to property related to the bankruptcy if the agent reasonably can believe that, because of the bankruptcy, the principal would no longer want the agent to have such authority.

The agent's bankruptcy will also, generally, terminate the relationship. The credit of the agent is frequently related to the principal's reputation in the business community, and thus the agent's authority to act will terminate if the agent reasonably can believe that, if the principal knew the facts, he would not want the agent's authority to continue.

War

War.

The outbreak of a war in the country where the agent has been authorized to transact the principal's business will terminate the agent's authority if the agent reasonably can believe that, if the principal knew the facts, he would not want the agent's authority to continue. The large number of multinational corporations and international trade could be affected by this rule. For example, if a U.S. corporation is selling its equipment in country X, and a war unexpectedly breaks out in country X, the corporate agent's authority to sell in X may terminate.

Impossibility by Destruction of the Agency Subject Matter

Supervening impossibility of performance of the agency.

If performance by the agency becomes impossible, the agent's authority is terminated. For example, a marine broker who is authorized to sell P's boat would lose his authority if the boat were destroyed by a storm.

Change of Law or Other Circumstances

Other circumstances.

The agent's authority is terminated by a change in law or other circumstances that would make performance impossible. For instance, if A, a construction contractor, must substantially change his contract because an amended building code requries fireproof material, his authority to act on behalf of P is terminated without P's specific consent.

"Irrevocable Agency"

Termination of Authority Coupled with an Interest

Authority coupled with an interest.

We have learned that agency and authority can be terminated by either the principal or the agent, and that if the termination of the agency contract is wrongful the terminating party is liable for breach of the contract. However, there are two situations when the principal can not terminate the *power* of the agent to act and affect the principal. These are often called "irrevocable agency" situations, meaning that the *power* of the agent can not be terminated by the principal, as distinguished from termination of agency and authority which the principal can do at any time.

These two situations occur when the *power* given to the agent is *security* to assure the agent that the principal will perform his promise to the agent. One is when "authority" or power is *given as security,* and the other is when the "authority" or power is *coupled with an interest in the subject matter of the agency.*

"Authority Given as Security."   When the authority is *given* by the principal *as security* to the agent *in exchange for consideration then given by the agent,* there is a *contract* between them and the principal can not revoke that authority. (On January 6, *P requests a $200 loan from A,* P promising that he will repay the loan on January 24 and that, on his default, A has authority to sell P's electric typewriter. The loan is made and there is now a *contract* between P and A. P defaulted and informs A that his authority to sell is terminated. A's power to sell is not terminated and he can sell the typewriter. P's authority to A was given in exchange for the *new* consideration of a loan of $200 made to P by A, creating a *contract* between them.) However, if *P already owes money to A* and P later gave A authority to sell P's typewriter on P's default, P's authority was not given to A in exchange for any new consideration from A; since there is *no contract* between them, P can terminate A's authority because it is *not given as security.* For there to be a contract, the authority must be given as security in exchange for consideration *then given* by A. In many states, death of the principal will not terminate this power.

"Authority Coupled with an Interest in the Subject Matter of the Agency." An agent has an irrevocable, vested *security interest* in and power over *property transferred to him* by his principal *with authority* to dispose of the property if the principal should default on an obligation owing by him to the agent. (*P owes A $200.* On February 6, P promises that he will repay the loan on February 24 and that, on his default, A has the authority to sell P's tabulator. P *delivers* the tabulator to A. A's power to sell on P's default is irrevocable by P.) A contract is not required here to make the agency irrevocable. Death of the principal will not terminate this power.

Effect of Termination of Agency and Authority

The principal's termination of agency or of the agent's authority is immediately effective *between them when the agent actually receives* notice of the principal's intent so to terminate. But what is the effect of such termination on third parties? We have learned that third parties have the duty to determine whether agency exists and the extent of the agent's authority.

If the principal (P) has represented to third persons (T) that someone (A) is P's agent, A has apparent authority to act for P within the scope of his apparent authority with the same effect as though A had authority so to act. If P wishes to terminate such apparent authority, he must give proper notice of termination of authority to those third persons to whom P had so represented creating the apparent authority.

The *extent* of such notice varies. If A is a *special agent,* P *need not give any notice to such third persons,* with certain exceptions when notice is required: (1) A is a specially accredited agent, specially accredited to deal with T on a continuing basis; or (2) P has notice that A has begun to deal with T; or (3) A has a written authorization for exhibition to T; or (4) T knows of the termination of an event on the continuance of which A's authority depends. If A is a *general agent, P must give notice of termination to such third persons.* For example, P appointed A as his agent for the purpose of selling and handling fire insurance for P. A sold a fire insurance policy of P to T. A few months later, P informed A that the agency was terminated. Subsequently T has a fire and reported it to A. Since A still has apparent authority to act as P's agent, which includes authority to receive fire reports from insured third persons, T's report to A was made to P.

The *kind* of such notice varies. If T has dealt with P *on credit,* T must receive *actual notice* of termination of authority; otherwise *reasonable notice* is sufficient "by advertising the fact in a newspaper of general circulation in the place where the agency is regularly carried on or giving publicity by some other method reasonably adopted to give the information to such third person."[5]

Summary Statement

1. An agency may be terminated by *acts of the parties*. The methods for doing so are:
   a. by contractual agreement;
   b. by mutual agreement;
   c. by option of a party in giving advance notice to the other;
   d. by revocation by the principal; and
   e. by renunciation by the agent.
2. An agency may be terminated by *operation of law*, which will end the relationship regardless of the parties' consent. The methods are:
   a. death of either the principal or the agent;
   b. insanity of either the principal or the agent;
   c. bankruptcy;
   d. war;
   e. impossibility; and
   f. change of law or circumstances.
3. When the *authority* is given by the principal *as security* to the agent in exchange for *consideration then* given by the agent, there is a *contract* between them and the principal can not revoke that authority.

---

[5] RESTATEMENT (SECOND) OF AGENCY sec. 136(3)(a)(b) (1958).

4. An agent with *authority coupled with an interest in the subject matter of the agency* has an irrevocable vested *security interest* in and power over the property transferred to the agent, with authority to dispose of the property if the principal should default on an obligation owing by him to the agent.

5. As between the principal and agent, the question of notice to third parties is of no consequence. The agent may have the *power* but not the right to act on behalf of the principal.

6. The principal's termination of agency or of the agent's authority is immediately effective between them.

7. If the agent is a *general agent,* the principal must give notice of termination to third persons.

8. If the agent is a *special agent,* the principal need not give any notice to third persons unless:
   a. A is specially accredited to deal with T on a continuing basis; or
   b. P has notice that A has begun to deal with T; or
   c. A has a written authorization for exhibition to T; or
   d. T knows of the termination of an event on the continuance of which A's authority depends.

9. If T has dealt with P *on credit,* T must receive actual notice of termination; otherwise reasonable notice is sufficient.

In the following case a hospital terminated a ten-year agency contract with its medical director which recited that it "may not be revoked or altered by The Hospital for a term of ten years." The medical director claims that the contract created an agency coupled with an interest, and the hospital has neither the right nor the power to terminate during its term.

Sarokhan v. Fair Lawn Memorial Hospital, Inc.
199 A.2d 52 (N.J. 1964)

interlocutory order
an intermediate court order pending a final decision.

Kilkenny, J.A.D. Defendants, Fair Lawn Memorial Hospital, Inc., appeal from an **interlocutory order** of the Chancery Division, restraining them from terminating plaintiff's services as medical director and director of surgery of defendant hospital, and from interfering with his rendition of such services. . . .

Defendant corporation operates for profit a private 63-bed hospital in Fair Lawn, New Jersey. The individual defendants are directors and officers thereof. . . . Plaintiff is a doctor and a surgeon. . . .

On April 19, 1962 plaintiff entered into a written agreement with defendant hospital, under the terms of which he was appointed medical director and director of surgery of the hospital for a term of ten years. No salary is specified for these services. The agreement recites that it "may not be revoked or altered by The Hospital during that period" and that plaintiff is bound to the performance of the duties undertaken by him for the ten-year term of the contract.

Until September 1963 plaintiff performed his duties without interference by the board of directors. On October 8, 1963 defendant, Nicholas DeVito, president of the hospital, wrote a letter to plaintiff inquiring why two men were not appointed assistant medical directors. A reply was received from plaintiff's counsel, stating

Agency and Employment

that plaintiff alone could appoint members to the professional staff and that under no circumstances was he to be considered the agent of the board of directors, or of the president of the hospital. The first count, alleging several acts of allegedly wrongful interference by defendants in the performance of his duties and the exercise of his contractual rights, seeks injunctive relief of the kind specified in the temporary injunction now under review.

After plaintiff instituted this suit, defendant hospital notified him that all association by him with the hospital was at an end. The hospital is dissatisfied with his services, believes that he is responsible for its poor financial condition, and it does not want him any more as its medical director and director of surgery. . . .

Defendants feel that they have just cause to terminate plaintiff's services; and, even if just cause were lacking, they have the power to terminate the agency or employment relationship, subject only to an action for damages if, in so doing, there is a wrongful breach of contract. Plaintiff's position is that defendants created an agency coupled with an interest and have neither the right nor the power to terminate during its ten-year term.

The mere fact that the appointment recites that it will be irrevocable during the term of the appointment does not preclude the principal from exercising the power to revoke it. This does not mean that the principal may breach such a contract with impunity. For a wrongful breach, the agent may sue at law and recover money damages.

The law has recognized, as an exception to the general rule, that "an agency coupled with an interest" can not be revoked by the principal during the term fixed for its existence.

Defendants concede that, if the contract herein created an agency coupled with an interest, they would not have the power to revoke it. They maintain that such an agency was not created. We agree.

If the agency is given *as security* for a debt or obligation, it is regarded as an agency coupled with an interest.

The agency herein was not given as security for some obligation due plaintiff. He had no interest in the subject matter of the power independent of the power conferred. The power conferred by defendant hospital was not one "coupled with an interest." Accordingly, it is not irrevocable, despite the terminology used by the parties.

We conclude that the contract in issue did not create an agency coupled with an interest and that defendants had and have the power to terminate it. . . . We make no determination as to whether defendants breached any contractual right of plaintiff in terminating his relationship with the hospital.

The order under review is reversed.

Questions and Case Problems

1. The defendant, Edward Morrison, is the owner of a photographic business known as Whitney Studio. Pappas was its general manager. Morrison sent a letter to the plaintiff, Gustave Fisher, its photographic supplier, stating that all future purchase orders will be signed by defendant. Gustave Fisher received Morrison's letter but continued to ship the supplies without proper signature. Is Whitney Studio liable in contract for the delivered merchandise? [*Gustave Fischer Co. v. Morrison*, 78 A.2d 242 (Conn. 1951).]

2. The plaintiff, Nathan Francis, is a co-lessee with defendant, Ted Bartlett, who managed a gravel mining operation with exclusive rights from the United States government to mine, remove, and sell all gravel deposits located on the land for a period of ten years. Bartlett gave a power of attorney to his co-lessee stating that the royalties due Francis were reduced. Francis accepted this reduction for a period of two years and now claims Bartlett had no authority to reduce their original royalty agreement. Was Bartlett correct? [*Francis v. Bartlett,* 121 So.2d 18 (La. 1960).]

3. P gave a power of attorney to A authorizing him to sell his building. The power of attorney stated that "the agency shall continue for ninety days and will not be revoked during that period." One month later P gave A notice that the agency was revoked. Sometime thereafter A made a contract with T, who knew A's agency was revoked, to sell the land to T. T brought a suit to eject P from the building. You decide the dispute.

4. P owned a building and authorized A, a real estate broker, to keep it rented and deduct a 6 percent commission on the amount collected and send the balance to P. A leased to T, who paid rent to A for several years. P died but T had no notice or knowledge of P's death. For the next year T continued to pay A the rent, with which A absconded. The executor of P's estate sued T for the year's rent due from the time of P's death. T claimed that his payment to A even after P's death is a defense. Is T correct?

5. A was the general manager of a hardware store owned by P, who was declared insane by a court. G, appointed by the court to be P's guardian, immediately terminated A, the manager and agent of P. Did G have the right to do so?

6. P, the sole proprietor of a restaurant, hired A to manage the business. P later filed voluntary bankruptcy. The bankruptcy court appointed T, as trustee in bankruptcy to manage P's assets. T told A he no longer had authority to manage the restaurant. Was T correct?

7. P owed money to A and then signed a collateral note with A secured by an automobile belonging to P, and authorized A, if the money was not paid when due, to sell the automobile and apply the proceeds to payment of the debt. P died ten days after delivery of the car to A. P's administrator sued A to regain possession of the car. Will he succeed? [*Halloran-Judge Trust Co. v. Heath,* 258 P. 342 (Utah 1927).]

8. P, a casualty insurance company, made A its general agent to write casualty insurance in P's name. A wrote T's casualty insurance on T's business. Thereafter, and without notifying T, the general agency of A was revoked by P. T later incurred a loss and notified A. T had neither notice nor knowledge of the revocation of A's authority by P. A notified P one year later and P refused to honor the claim because it was not notified by the insured, T, within a reasonable time after the loss. T sued P on the policy issued by A. Can he recover?

9. Explain the rule of law that either a principal or an agent can terminate the agency contract, but a wrongful termination will result in liability for breach of contract.

10. In the case of *Sarokhan v. Fair Lawn Memorial Hospital, Inc.*, 199 A.2d 52 (N.J. 1964),[6] the court indicates that an example of an "irrevocable agency" is an agency coupled with an interest. Irrevocable agencies are created because of the needs of justice and fairness. Why does an agency coupled with an interest meet these needs?

---

[6] See pp. 274–75.

18 Employment

After you have read this chapter, you should be able to:

1. Indicate what kind of discrimination in employment is prohibited by the federal Equal Employment Opportunity Act.
2. State those circumstances when discrimination in employment is not prohibited or unlawful under the above Act.
3. Recognize the age groups of employees which are, or are not, protected from age discrimination in employment under the federal Age Discrimination In Employment Act.
4. Explain how the federal Wage-Hour Law applies to:
   a. Child labor.
   b. Maximum daily and weekly hours of employment.
   c. Wages.
5. Discuss the common law basis for liability by an employer for injury experienced by his employees and compare it with the current basis for employer liability for such injury under state workmen's compensation statutes.
6. Explain the purpose of the federal Occupational Safety and Health Act and how business is affected.
7. Discuss and explain how the following federal programs operate under the Social Security Act:
   a. Old Age, Survivors, and Disability Insurance.
   b. Medicare.
   c. Unemployment Insurance.

Introduction

Society is concerned that people have proper and equal opportunity to obtain employment and that the terms of employment are reasonable and do not constitute an invasion of any employees' legal rights, particularly to join a union and engage in collective bargaining with employers. This area will be discussed under the heading The Employment Contract.

Another concern of society is that proper reasonable standards are established to ensure the safety and health of the employee while engaged in his work, and that reasonable compensation is provided for any injury he may sustain in his work. This area will be discussed under the heading Compensation for Injury and Protection.

Lastly, society is also concerned about the financial status of employees on their retirement, disability, hospitalization, and unemployment. This area will be discussed under the heading Social Security.

The Employment Contract

An employer's common law right of freedom of contract—basically to employ at his will and, in the absence of employment contract provision to the contrary, to fire at will—has given way to public policy in the form of federal and state legislation limiting that freedom. Judicial interpretation and enforcement of such legislation thus becomes very important to you as a present or probable employee.

Non-discriminatory Employment

Non-discrimination.

The two major federal pieces of legislation amending the federal Civil Rights Act of 1964 to ensure equal non-discriminatory opportunity for employment are the Equal Employment Opportunity Act of 1972 and the Age Discrimination In Employment Act of 1967, with their later amendments.

Equal Employment Opportunity Act (EEOA).   This federal Act applies to employers engaged in or affecting interstate commerce with fifteen or more employees for each working day in each of twenty or more calendar weeks in the current or preceding calendar year, and any agent of such person. It also applies to: state and local governments; government agencies; political subdivisions; the District of Columbia department and agencies; employment agencies; labor organizations; apprenticeship programs; and in advertising.

EEOA.

The Act prohibits employers from *unlawfully* discriminating in employment and makes it

Prohibition of discrimination on the basis of race, color, religion, sex, or national origin.

an unlawful employment practice for an employer (1) to fail or refuse to hire or to discharge any individual, or otherwise to discriminate against any individual with respect to his compensation, terms, conditions, or privileges of employment, *because of* such individual's race, color, religion, sex, or national origin; or (2) to limit, segregate, or classify his employees or applicants for employment in any way which would deprive or tend to deprive any individual of employment opportunities or otherwise adversely affect his status as an employee, *because of* such individual's race, color, religion, sex, or national origin. [Emphasis added.]

In the following first case of its kind to be decided by the Supreme Court of the United States, the court had to decide whether the difference in longevity between men and women employees could justify a valid difference in the contributions to a pension fund required to be made by those employees.

Facts

Based on a study of mortality tables and its own experience, the Los Angeles Department of Water and Power determined that its female employees would, as a class, outlive its male employees. Accordingly, the department required its female employees to make significantly larger pension fund contributions than the males, with the result that each female employee took home less pay than a male earning the same salary.

A class action suit was brought by Marie Manhart, a woman employee in the department, on behalf of all women employed and formerly employed by the department, seeking an injunction against this action by the department and retroactive relief. The federal district court and, on appeal, the federal court of appeals, decided in favor of the plaintiffs, except that retroactive relief was denied. The department, defendant, brought this matter before the Supreme Court of the United States.

Decision

Affirmed, for plaintiffs, without retroactive relief, and sent back for further proceedings.

Reasoning

The Equal Employment Opportunity Act makes it unlawful "to discriminate against any *individual* with respect to his compensation, terms, conditions, or privileges of employment, because of such *individual's* race, color, religion, sex, or national origin." The statute's focus on the individual is unambiguous. It precludes treatment of individuals as simply components of a racial, religious, sexual, or national class. Even a true generalization about the class is an insufficient reason for disqualifying an individual to whom the generalization does not apply.

An employment practice that requires 2,000 individuals to contribute more money into a fund than 10,000 other employees simply because each of them is a woman rather than a man is in direct conflict with both the language and the policy of the Act. It constitutes discrimination against every individual woman employed by the department, and is unlawful unless exempted by the Equal Pay Act of 1963 or some other affirmative justification.

City of Los Angeles Department of Water and Power, et al. v. Manhart et al., 435 U.S. 702 (1978).

The U.S. Supreme Court has made it clear in *Dothard v. Rawlinson*, 433 U.S. 321 (1977) that, in cases of alleged *unlawful* discrimination in employment on the basis of an individual's race, color, religion, sex, or national origin, there are three steps to be considered. (1) The employment standards or requirements must produce a *result* or *effect* that is discriminatory or disparate (unequal). If they do, then there *is discrimination.* Otherwise there is *no* discrimination. (2) If there is discrimination, then the employer has the burden of showing that the standards or requirements are *job-related* in that they have a definite relationship to the particular job for which they are established. If they are *not* job-related, then the discrimination *is unlawful.* (3) If they *are* job-related, then the complaining person, plaintiff, must show that *other selection devices* (other means) without a similar discriminatory effect would also serve the employer's legitimate interest in efficient and trustworthy workmanship. If the plaintiff *can* show this, then the discrimination *is unlawful.* Otherwise, the discrimination is *not* unlawful. A *discriminatory effect* together with a *discriminatory intent* results in *unlawful* discrimination.

However, it is not unlawful:

1. for an employer to employ an employee on the basis of religion, sex, or national origin in those certain instances where religion, sex, or national origin is a **bona fide** *occupational qualification* reasonably necessary to the normal operation of that particular business or enterprise;

   bona fide
   in good faith

2. for any *educational institution of learning* to employ employees of a particular religion if such institution is, in whole or in substantial part, owned, supported, controlled, or managed by a particular religion or by a particular religious corporation, association, or society, or if the curriculum of the institution is directed toward the propagation of a particular religion;

3. for an employer to apply different standards of compensation, or different terms, conditions, or privileges of employment pursuant to a *bona fide seniority or merit system,* or to a system which measures earnings *by quantity or quality of production,* or to employees who work in *different locations*— so long as such differences are not the result of an intention to discriminate because of race, color, religion, sex, or national origin. The employer may give and act upon the results of any *professionally developed ability test* so long as the test, its administration, or action upon the results is not designed, intended, or used to discriminate because of race, color, religion, sex, or national origin. However, the test must be job-related in order not to be *unlawfully* discriminatory. Also, the employer may legally differentiate on the basis of sex in determining the amount of wages or compensation if it is authorized by the federal Fair Labor Standards Act of 1938, as amended in 1974.

The EEOA further provides that *nothing* in the Act shall be interpreted to *require* any employer to grant *preferential treatment* to any individual or group because of the race, color, religion, sex, or national origin of such individual or group on account of an *imbalance* which may exist with respect to the total number or percentage of persons of any race, color, religion, sex, or national origin employed by any employer in comparison with the total number or percentage of persons of such race, color, religion, sex, or national origin in any community, state, section, or other area or available work force there. The fact that an employer has no minority people among his employees does not of itself mean that illegal discrimination has occurred. However, it raises a strong inference of such illegality. In order to dispel such an inference, many employers employ only a few minority employees so as to create an impression of nondiscrimination when, in fact, their intention is to illegally discriminate.

The Civil Rights Act establishes an Equal Employment Opportunity Commission, appointed by the President, to administer the Act. This federal commission has power to bring civil actions in federal courts against employers where there is reasonable cause to believe that an unlawful employment practice has occurred and attempts to conciliate the matter have failed. Usually states and cities have fair employment practices agencies, and if you as an employee have a complaint for illegal discrimination, you should apply to the latter agencies before the federal commission will consider the matter. In the case of illegal discrimination against *federal* employees, enforcement of the law is done by the Civil Service Commission and by the secretary of labor.

Prohibition of
discrimination on the
basis of age.

Age Discrimination in Employment Act (ADIEA). This federal Act of 1967 as amended in 1978 has for its purpose "to promote employment of older persons based on their ability rather than age; to prohibit arbitrary age discrimination in employment; to help employers and workers find ways of meeting problems arising from the impact of age on employment." Administration of the Act is the responsibility of the secretary of labor.

The Act provides in section 623(a)(1)(2) that it is unlawful for an employer engaged in an industry in or affecting interstate commerce

(1) to fail or refuse to hire or to discharge any individual or otherwise discriminate against any individual with respect to his compensation, terms, conditions, or privileges of employment, because of such individual's age;
(2) to limit, segregate, or classify his employees in any way which would deprive or tend to deprive any individual of employment opportunities or otherwise adversely affect his status as an employee, because of such individual's age.

The prohibition of age discrimination applies to nonfederal individuals who are at least 40 years of age but less than 70 years of age. Under certain conditions, the prohibition does not apply to bona fide executives or high policymakers. Nor does it apply to an employee who has attained 65 years of age but not 70 years of age who has unlimited tenure at an institution of higher learning; although this exception is repealed July 1, 1982, and then the prohibition applies to tenured faculty. Also, employees of the federal government who are at least 40 years of age are made free of any discrimination based on age. With certain exceptions, there is no maximum 70 years of age limit for federal employees. The federal Civil Service Commission is responsible for administering the federal part of the Act.

Fair Labor Standards Act
This federal Act of 1938 as amended, also known as the Wage-Hour Law, has for its purpose "the establishment of fair labor standards in employment in and affecting interstate and foreign commerce, and for other purposes." For example, if you are an employee of a manufacturer of goods which are shipped outside the state of manufacture, you are covered under the Act. It is administered by the secretary of labor. We are here generally concerned with the Act's provisions for child labor, minimum wages, and maximum hours of employment. Many states have laws in these areas.

Agency and Employment

Child Labor. The Act prohibits "oppressive child labor" as the employment of an employee under the age of sixteen years, other than by a parent under certain circumstances; or the employment of an employee between the ages of sixteen and eighteen in an occupation particularly hazardous to, or detrimental to the health and well-being of, such persons in that age group. Many states require persons below eighteen years of age to obtain a work permit.

Maximum Hours. The maximum number of hours per week that an employer can compel an employee to work is forty hours. If the employee agrees to work more than forty hours per week, the employer must pay him no less than one and one-half times the regular rate at which he is employed. However, exceptions are made in special situations, such as for employees under the terms of a collective bargaining agreement, and for wages at piece goods rates.

Many states limit the hours of work permitted for persons under sixteen years of age, with a maximum of eight hours per day and forty hours per week, although other states vary concerning the maximum weekly hours of labor.

Minimum Wages. The Act establishes a minimum hourly wage which must be paid to an employee; this amount is periodically revised by Congress. Under the Equal Pay Act amendment, wage discrimination on the basis of sex is prohibited except when such pay is made pursuant to a seniority system, a merit system, a system which measures earnings by quantity or quality of production, or a differential based on any other factor other than sex.

The term "wages" includes the reasonable cost to the employer of furnishing such employee with board, lodging, or other facilities, if they are customarily furnished by such employer to his employees. However, such cost is not included in wages to the extent that a collective bargaining agreement applicable to that particular employee excludes it as a part of wages.

Exemptions from the Above Provisions. The above maximum hourly and minimum wage provisions of the Act do not apply, with certain exceptions, to: an employee in a bona fide executive, administrative, or professional capacity, or as an outside salesman; an employee in a retail or service establishment with annual sales of less than $200,000; an employee in an amusement or recreational establishment not operating for more than seven months in a calendar year; an employee in the catching or production of fish.

Unions and Collective Bargaining
This subject is discussed in detail in chapter 34, Labor Law, to which reference should be made at this time. Beginning with the Norris-La Guardia Act of 1932, the movement to recognize and strengthen unions of employees started as an important part of the labor-management process. Subsequent federal labor legislation, discussed in chapter 34, attempted to attain a just and legal balance regarding the rights, duties, and conduct of labor and management, respectively. The various unfair labor practices by employees and unions as well as by employers are listed and discussed in that chapter.

Compensation for Injury and Protection

State Workmen's Compensation Statutes

common law
principles of nonstatutory law reflecting the customs and usages of society found in judicial decisions

Common law established various duties of employers toward their employees regarding their work. Generally, they were: to provide reasonably safe working conditions, which included reasonably safe tools and equipment; to exercise reasonable care in the selection of competent and adequate number of fellow servant employees; and to exercise reasonable care in operating the business and in the establishment of reasonable operating rules.

An employer was liable to his employees for injury caused to them *by his negligence,* with three exceptions. The first exception was the *fellow-servant rule,* when the injury to an employee was caused not by the employer's negligence but, rather, by the negligence of a fellow-servant employee. The second exception was the *servant's contributory negligence rule,* when the injury to an employee was caused by the injured employee's contributory negligence. The third exception was the *servant's assumption-of-risk rule,* when the injured employee knew of the risks of injury from the job and assumed them by entering upon the employment with such risks.

The law is different today as a result of public policy that the risks of injury to employees *arising out of, and in the course of, employment* should be that of the employer. The cost of paying for such injury should be a part of the operating expense of the business. An employee's contributory negligence and his noncompliance with his employer's rules will not preclude his recovery for his injury which arose out of and in the course of his employment.

There must be a substantial causal relationship between the employment and the injury experienced by the employee. Also, if the injury arises out of or in the course of employment, any new injury which flows from and is a consequence of the initial injury is covered by workmen's compensation.

In order to ensure that there is proper and adequate financial security to cover this risk—i.e., to indemnify the injured employee—employers must comply with state workmen's compensation laws. Usually employers are required either to take out insurance through a state insurance fund or a private insurance company, or to deposit adequate securities with the state workmen's compensation committee. Employees who are domestic servants or farm laborers usually are not covered by workmen's compensation statutes. Also, an employer is not liable for injury self-inflicted by the employee or resulting from his intoxication. Since workmen's compensation coverage must be provided by the employer, an employee can not waive such coverage. Also, since the employee is covered by workmen's compensation, in many states he can not sue his employer, although in states which permit such suit the common law defenses become available to the employer if he is sued by his employee. The employee can sue a third person who wrongfully injured him. For example, the employee can sue the driver of a vehicle for his negligence causing injury to the employee while he was transporting his employer's goods. The state laws have detailed schedules specifying the limited money amounts payable for various injuries.

Health and Safety Laws

Society is concerned about the health and safety of employees while on the job. Various state and federal laws and administrative rules and regulations have as their purpose to set standards to reduce preventable hazards to employees in the place of work and to provide for safe and healthful working conditions.

On the state level, there are departments of labor or of health which have the responsibility for determining whether an employer is complying with the state health and safety statute and administrative rules and regulations.

On the federal level is the Occupational Safety and Health Act (OSHA) of 1970 as amended, administered by the secretary of labor. The Act provides for and directs the secretary of labor to establish and publish specific mandatory and occupational safety and health standards with which employers in a business in or affecting interstate commerce must comply. The specification of standards does not relieve an employer, in the absence of a specific standard, from his duty to furnish a place of employment which will not expose employees to a recognized risk of death or serious bodily harm. The Act provides for employer record keeping of illness, injury, and death experienced by his employees and for employer reports to the secretary of labor under certain conditions.

OSHA.

The OSHA division of the Department of Labor is responsible for making inspections of an employer's business premises and working conditions and for issuing citations for alleged violation of OSHA. Employers may appeal from such citations to the OSHA Review Commission and, after exhausting their administrative remedies, they may seek judicial relief in the U.S. Court of Appeals.

Social Security

Society is further concerned about the financial impact upon employees by reason of their retirement, disability, death, hospitalization, and unemployment. These are areas of grave financial risk to an employee, and the federal and state governments participate in a program of insurance to cover this risk. The key federal law on this subject is the Social Security Act of 1935, as amended.

Old-Age, Survivors, and Disability Insurance (OASDI)

Both the employer and the employee contribute, as taxes, under the Federal Insurance Contributions Act (FICA) to help pay for: the loss of income benefits on retirement at age 65, or earlier at age 62 at a reduced benefit if early retirement is chosen by the employee; survivor benefits on death of the employee; and financial benefits to employees under 65 years of age who are physically disabled. Persons who are self-employed may financially contribute to this insurance program and thereby participate in the insurance coverage.

OASDI.

FICA.

An employer is required to withhold the necessary contributions from the employee's wages as he is paid, and the employer adds his contribution and makes deposit and payment of such funds as required by law. The basis for the employee's contribution is called the employee's *annual wage base,* which is the maximum amount of an employee's wages that are subject to the tax. For example, A's annual wage is $30,000. For 1980, the first $25,900 portion of his wages is taxable as the annual wage base, and for 1981 the annual wage base is $29,700, with increases for following years. Congress currently is reviewing the annual wage base formula. The Secretary of the Treasury has the authority to adjust the contribution and benefit base reflecting an increase in the cost of living computation.

The percentage of tax on the annual wage base is fixed by the statute. For example, for 1980 the rate is 6.05 percent, and for 1981–1985 it is 6.30 percent. When any employee has more than one job and is paid wages by two different employers, the tax is withheld from each of both wages and the *employee* is entitled to a refund for the excess tax paid by him; neither employer is entitled to any refund. Also, the employee's tax is not a deductible item on his annual federal income tax return.

Old-age, survivor's, and disability benefits are fixed by the statute, and the extent of such benefits depends on various factors. Benefits increase automatically with an increase in the cost of living of 3 percent or more between specified periods as indicated by the consumer price index, thereby also increasing the annual wage base to pay for such increased benefits. Statewide federal social security offices are available to provide all social security information to the public.

Pension plans for employees have been established by many employers. It has become very apparent that there was a need for close governmental supervision over such plans in order to ensure greater protection of the interests of employees covered by such plans. The federal Employees Retirement Income Security Act (ERISA) of 1974 serves this purpose. The Secretary of Labor has the responsibility for operation and supervision of such pension plans.

ERISA.

Medicare.

Hospital Insurance (Medicare)
The federal *Medicare Handbook* describes *Medicare* as "a health income program for people 65 and older, and some under 65 who are disabled. It is a federal government program administered by the Social Security Administration. Medicare has two parts. One part is called *hospital insurance.* The other part is called *medical insurance,*" which assists the patient in his payment of *doctor's* expenses. "Most people who have Medicare's hospital insurance do not have to make monthly payments for this protection. They have hospital insurance because of credits for work under social security." Persons who have Medicare *hospital insurance* are eligible to obtain federal *medical insurance* on payment of small monthly premiums, payable quarterly, but which rise as the cost of medical care rises.

Unemployment Insurance
FUTA.

The purpose of the Federal Unemployment Tax Act (FUTA) is to provide temporary financial assistance to a former employee with a sufficient number of credits from former employment during a period of unemployment, provided he is ready, able, and willing to take a suitable full-time job that becomes available. Refusal to take such a job which the state employment office indicates is available may well disqualify the unemployed person from receiving unemployment insurance benefits. The cost of the operation of the unemployment insurance program is administered by the federal government out of part of the tax collected, but each state and the District of Columbia administers the program in its own area.

Under FUTA, employers who are within the provisions of the Act and not exempt are taxed quarterly by the federal government. Each state also taxes the employer, although the employer can receive a credit against the federal tax. While the federal government does not require that an employee pay a tax while he is employed, a few states do impose a tax on the employee. Taxes are collected by the employer and submitted to the state, which deposits them with the federal government, where an Unemployment Insurance Fund is maintained with an account for each state and subject to withdrawal by the particular state. The tax is based on a percentage of a wage-base amount. For example, the wage base may be $6,000 and the percentage of tax 3.4 percent of the $6,000. An employer with a low rate of unemployment may benefit by having a good experience rating and thereby reduce his tax.

Summary Statement

1. The federal Equal Employment Opportunity Act (EEOA) specifies what is and what is not an unlawful employment discriminatory practice by an employer on the basis of an individual's race, color, religion, sex, or national origin. There are three steps necessary to determine when there is unlawful discrimination in employment because of an individual's race, color, religion, sex, or national origin under EEOA.
2. The federal Age Discrimination In Employment Act (ADIEA) prohibits arbitrary age discrimination in employment mainly with respect to nonfederal employees between the ages of 40 and 70 years, with certain exceptions.
3. The federal Fair Labor Standards Act (FLSA), also known as the Wage-Hour Law, establishes fair standards for the employment of child labor, maximum hours of employment, and minimum wages. Oppressive child labor is prohibited.
4. State Workmen's Compensation Statutes changed the common law basis for employer liability for injury to employees arising out of and in the course of employment.
5. The federal Occupational Safety and Health Act (OSHA) provides for specific mandatory occupational safety and health standards for employers in the workplace.
6. Irrespective of OSHA's specific standards, an employer has a duty to so maintain his workplace as not to expose his employees to a recognized risk of death or serious bodily harm.

7. The broad federal Social Security Act includes in its coverage the following:
   a. Old-Age, Survivors, and Disability Insurance (OASDI). Provision is made for financial assistance to employees on their retirement, benefits to the survivors of employees, and benefits in the event of disability.
   b. Employee's Retirement Income Security Act (ERISA). This Act serves to provide needed federal governmental supervision over pension plans for the benefit of employees.
   c. Hospital insurance (Medicare) as a health program for eligible persons 65 years of age and older, and some under 65 who are disabled.
   d. Federal Unemployment Tax Act (FUTA). This Act provides temporary financial assistance to former employees who are eligible, with sufficient credits from former employment, and who are unemployed and are ready, able, and willing to take a suitable full-time job.

In the following authoritative case, the Supreme Court of the United States clearly explained the process by which illegal discrimination in violation of the federal Civil Rights Act was determined. Observe carefully the court's approach to the question and how the burden of proof shifts from the employee, initially, and then to the employer.

Dothard, Director, Department of Public Safety of Alabama, *et al.* v. Rawlinson *et al.*
433 U.S. 321 (1977)

Mr. Justice Stewart. Appellee Dianne Rawlinson sought employment with the Alabama Board of Corrections as a prison guard, called in Alabama a "correctional counselor." . . .

I

At the time she applied for a position as correctional counselor trainee, Rawlinson was a 22-year-old college graduate whose major course of study had been correctional psychology. She was refused employment because she failed to meet the minimum 120-pound weight requirement established by an Alabama statute. The statute also establishes a height minimum of 5 feet, 2 inches.

After her application was rejected because of her weight, Rawlinson filed a charge with the Equal Employment Opportunity Commission and ultimately recieved a right-to-sue letter. She then filed a complaint in the district court on behalf of herself and other similarly situated women, challenging the statutory height and weight minima as violative of Title VII and the Equal Protection Clause of the Fourteenth Amendment. . . . [The District Court decided in her favor. Defendants brought this action before the Surpreme Court.] While the suit was pending, the Alabama Board of Corrections adopted Administrative Regulation 204, establishing gender criteria for assigning correctional counselors to maximum-security institutions for "contact positions"—that is, positions requiring continual close physical proximity to inmates of the institution. Rawlinson amended her class-action complaint by adding a challenge to Regulation 204 as also violative of Title VII and the Fourteenth Amendment.

Like most correctional facilities in the United States, Alabama's prisons are segregated on the basis of sex. Currently the Alabama Board of Corrections operates four major all-male penitentiaries. . . . The Board also operates the Julia

Agency and Employment

Tutwiler Prison for Women, the Frank Lee Youth Center, the Number Four Honor Camp, the State Cattle Ranch, and nine Work Release Centers, one of which is for women. The Julia Tutwiler Prison for Women and the four male penitentiaries are maximum-security institutions. Their inmate living quarters are for the most part large dormitories, with communal showers and toilets that are open to the dormitories and hallways. The [all-male] Draper and Fountain penitentiaries carry on extensive farming operations, making necessary a large number of strip searches for contraband when prisoners re-enter the prison buildings.

A correctional counselor's primary duty within these institutions is to maintain security and control of the inmates by continually supervising and observing their activities. To be eligible for consideration as a correctional counselor, an applicant must possess a valid Alabama driver's license, have a high school education or its equivalent, be free from physical defects, be between the ages of 20½ years and 45 years at the time of appointment, and fall between the minimum height and weight requirements of 5 feet 2 inches, and 120 pounds, and the maximum of 6 feet 10 inches, and 300 pounds. Appointment is by merit, with a grade assigned each applicant based on experience and education. No written examination is given.

At the time this litigation was in the district court, the Board of Corrections employed a total of 435 people in various correctional counselor positions, 56 of whom were women. Of those 56 women, 21 were employed at the Julia Tutwiler Prison for Women, 13 were employed in noncontact positions at the four male maximum-security institutions, and the remaining 22 were employed at the other institutions operated by the Alabama Board of Corrections. Because most of Alabama's prisoners are held at the four maximum-security male penitentiaries, 336 of the 435 correctional counselor jobs were in those institutions, a majority of them concededly in the "contact" classification. Thus, even though meeting the statutory height and weight requirements, women applicants could under Regulation 204 compete equally with men for only about 25% of the correctional counselor jobs available in the Alabama prison system.

II

In enacting Title VII, Congress required "the removal of artificial, arbitrary, and unnecessary barriers to employment when the barriers operate invidiously to discriminate on the basis of racial or other impermissible classification." . . . The district court found that the minimum statutory height and weight requirements that applicants for employment as correctional counselors must meet constitute the sort of arbitrary barrier to equal employment opportunity that Title VII forbids. The appellants assert that the district court erred both in finding that the height and weight standards discriminate against women, and in its refusal to find that, even if they do, these standards are justified as "job related."

The gist of the claim that the statutory height and weight requirements discriminate against women does not involve an assertion of purposeful discriminatory motive. It is asserted, rather, that these facially neutral qualification standards work in fact disproportionately to exclude women from eligibility for employment by the Alabama Board of Corrections. . . .

. . . to establish a prima facie case of discrimination, a plaintiff need only show that the facially neutral standards in question select applicants for hire in a significantly discriminatory pattern. Once it is thus shown that the employment standards are discriminatory in effect, the employer must meet "the burden of showing that any given requirement [has] . . . a manifest relationship to the employment in question." . . . [job related]. If the employer proves that the challenged requirements are job related, the plaintiff may then show that other selection devices without a similar discriminatory effect would also "serve the employer's legitimate interest in 'efficient and trustworthy workmanship.' "

Although women 14 years of age or older comprise 52.75 percent of the Alabama population and 36.89 percent of its total labor force, they hold only 12.9 percent of its correctional counselor positions. In considering the effect of the minimum height and weight standards on this disparity in rate of hiring between the sexes, the district court found that the 5'2" requirement would operate to exclude 33.29 percent of the women in the United States between the ages of 18–79, while excluding only 1.28 percent of men between the same ages. The 120-pound weight restriction would exclude 22.29 percent of the women and 2.35 percent of the men in this age group. When the height and weight restrictions are combined, Alabama's statutory standards would exclude 41.13 percent of the female population while excluding less than 1 percent of the male population. Accordingly, the district court found that Rawlinson had made out a prima facie case of unlawful sex discrimination. . . .

. . . we cannot say that the district court was wrong in holding that the statutory height and weight standards had a discriminatory impact on women applicants.

We turn, therefore, to the appellants' argument that they have rebutted the prima facie case of discrimination by showing that the height and weight requirements are job related. These requirements, they say, have a relationship to strength, a sufficient but unspecified amount of which is essential to effective job performance as a correctional counselor. In the district court, however, the appellants produced no evidence correlating the height and weight requirements with the requisite amount of strength thought essential to good job performance.

If the job related quality that the appellants identify is bona fide, their purpose could be achieved by adopting and validating a test for applicants that measures strength directly. Such a test, fairly administered, would fully satisfy the standards of Title VII because it would be one that "measure[s] the person for the job and not the person in the abstract." . . . But nothing in the present record even approaches such a measurement.

For the reasons we have discussed, the district court was not in error in holding that Title VII of the Civil Rights Act of 1964, as amended, prohibits application of the statutory height and weight requirements to Rawlinson and the class she represents.

III

Unlike the statutory height and weight requirements, Regulation 204 explicitly discriminates against women on the basis of their sex. In defense of this overt discrimination, the appellants rely on sec. 703(e) of Title VII, . . . which permits sex-based discrimination "in those certain instances where . . . sex . . . is a bona fide occupational qualification reasonably necessary to the normal operation of that particular business or enterprise."

The district court rejected the bona fide occupational qualification (bfoq) defense. . . .

We are persuaded—by the restrictive language of sec. 703(e), the relevant legislative history, and the consistent interpretation of the Equal Employment Opportunity Commission—that the bfoq exception was in fact meant to be an extremely narrow exception to the general prohibition of discrimination on the basis of sex. In the particular factual circumstances of this case, however, we conclude that the district court erred in rejecting the state's contention that Regulation 204 falls within the narrow ambit of the bfoq exception.

The environment in Alabama's penitentiaries is a peculiarly inhospitable one for human beings of whatever sex. Indeed, a federal district court has held that the conditions of confinement in the prisons of the state, characterized by "rampant violence" and a "jungle atmosphere," are constitutionally intolerable. . . . The record in the present case shows that because of inadequate staff and facilities, no attempt is made in the four maximum-security male penitentiaries to classify or segregate inmates according to their offense or level of dangerousness—a procedure that, according to expert testimony, is essential to effective penological administration. Consequently, the estimated 20 percent of the male prisoners who are sex offenders are scattered throughout the penitentiaries' dormitory facilities.

In this environment of violence and disorganization, it would be an oversimplification to characterize Regulation 204 as an exercise in "romantic paternalism." . . . In the usual case, the argument that a particular job is too dangerous for women may appropriately be met by the rejoinder that it is the purpose of Title VII to allow the individual woman to make that choice for herself. More is at stake in this case, however, than an individual woman's decision to weigh and accept the risks of employment in a "contact" position in a maximum-security male prison.

The essence of a correctional counselor's job is to maintain prison security. A woman's relative ability to maintain order in a male, maximum-security, unclassified penitentiary of the type Alabama now runs could be directly reduced by her womanhood. There is a basis in fact for expecting that sex offenders who have criminally assaulted women in the past would be moved to do so again if access to women were established within the prison. There would also be a real risk that other inmates, deprived of a normal heterosexual environment, would assault women guards because they were women. In a prison system where violence is the order of the day, where inmate access to guards is facilitated by dormitory living arrangements, where every institution is under-staffed, and where a substantial portion of the inmate population is composed of sex offenders mixed at random with other prisoners, there are few visible deterrents to inmate assaults on women custodians.

Appellee Rawlinson's own expert testified that dormitory housing for aggressive inmates poses a greater security problem than single-cell lockups, and further testified that it would be unwise to use women as guards in a prison where even 10 percent of the inmates had been convicted of sex crimes and were not segregated from the other prisoners. The likelihood that inmates would assault a woman because she was a woman would pose a real threat not only to the victim of the assault but also to the basic control of the penitentiary and protection of its inmates and the other security personnel. The employee's very womanhood would thus directly undermine her capacity to provide the security that is the essence of a correctional counselor's responsibility.

There was substantial testimony from experts on both sides of this litigation that the use of women as guards in "contact" positions under the existing conditions in Alabama maximum-security male penitentiaries would pose a substantial security problem, directly linked to the sex of the prison guard. On the basis of that evidence, we conclude that the district court was in error in ruling that being male is not a bona fide occupational qualification for the job of correctional counselor in a "contact" position in an Alabama male maximum-security penitentiary.

The judgment is accordingly affirmed in part and reversed in part, and the case is remanded to the district court for further proceedings consistent with this opinion.

It is so ordered.

Questions and Case Problems

1. Explain the three steps necessary to determine when there is unlawful discrimination in employment because of an individual's race, color, religion, sex, or national origin under the federal Equal Employment Opportunity Act.

2. Thirteen of the fourteen black employees at the defendant power plant brought this action, claiming that the defendant's requirement of a high school diploma or passing of intelligence tests as a condition of employment in, or transfer to, jobs at the plant was an illegal discrimination in violation of the federal Civil Rights Act of 1964. There were 95 employees at the particular plant involved. There was no proof of discriminatory purpose by the diploma and test requirements. The tests were not directed or intended to measure the ability to learn to perform a particular job or category of jobs. The requisite scores used for both hiring and transfer approximated the national median for high school graduates. Whites registered far better than blacks. The diploma and test requirements were not shown to be related to job performance. Judgment for whom? [*Griggs et al. v. Duke Power Co.*, 401 U.S. 424 (1971)].

3. Professor Scott, a black faculty member of the University of Delaware, who does not have a Ph.D. degree, brought a class action against the university, alleging illegal employment discrimination in violation of the federal Civil Rights Act of 1964, resulting in the university's failure to renew his contract. Among the various reasons for his assertion of illegal discrimination was that the university's requirement that an individual have a Ph.D. degree or equivalent to attain an assistant professorship had a disparate (unequal) impact upon blacks in the areas of hiring, contract renewal, promotion, and tenure. There was insufficient evidence to prove any intent by the university to discriminate against blacks by this requirement. He asserted that this requirement is not justified by the legitimate needs of the university. The university emphasized scholarship and the advancement of knowledge and sought people for its faculty who had "the capabilities of making significant contribution to scholarship that would bring recognition to the University." Was the Ph.D. degree or equivalent requirement related to job performance and justified by the legitimate interest of the University? [*Scott v. The University of Delaware*, 455 F.Supp. 1102 (1978).]

4. Cactus Craft of Arizona is a firm which manufactures and distributes novelty and souvenir gift items, including cactus lamps, jewelry, and numerous other items. An employee between the ages of sixteen and eighteen years of age

Agency and Employment

operated a power tool for drilling part of the time under supervision, which included shaping and forming of pieces of wood so that they could be used for lamps. The Secretary of Labor issued a regulation prohibiting employment of minors between sixteen and eighteen years of age in the operation of power-driven wood-working machines, which are defined as "all fixed or portable machines or tools driven by power and used or designed for cutting, shaping, forming (or) surfacing wood." A power tool for drilling is not specifically mentioned in the regulation. The secretary of labor contends that the defendant violated the Fair Labor Standards Act concerning child labor. Was this oppressive child labor under that Act? [*Hodgson v. Cactus Craft of Arizona*, 481 F.2d 464 (1973).]

5. Explain when wage discrimination on the basis of sex is not prohibited under the federal Equal Pay Act.

6. Sam Dell's Dodge Corp. is an automobile dealership. Salespersons received a base pay and commissions on sales of cars, trucks, accessories, etc. The company furnished many of the salespersons with demonstrator cars. These cars were used primarily in connection with the salespersons' duties at the company. The cars were parked on the lot during the day. Salespersons used them for demonstration rides for their customers. Occasionally the cars would be lent to other salespersons for the same use. Salespersons were permitted to drive the cars for personal use when not working; however, they were specifically told that the cars were not for their families. For each week that a car was provided to a salesperson, the company deducted money from that salesperson's earnings for insurance. The value of the use of the cars was not included on the salesperson's W-2 tax statements or the company's pay records. The mileage accumulated by the salespersons when driving for personal use apparently was significant when compared with business use. The secretary of labor claims that the company employer violated the minimum wage requirements of the Fair Labor Standards Act. Were the demonstration cars furnished for salespersons' use "wages" under the Act? [*Marshall v. Sam Dell's Dodge Corp.*, 451 F.Supp. 294 (1978).]

7. How did state workmen's compensation statutes change the common law liability of the employer for injuries suffered by his employees while on the job?

8. Reese was employed by Gas Engineering and Construction Company as a pipeline welder. While working under a large pipe, the scaffolding collapsed and the pipe fell, crushing Reese's left knee. This type of injury is included in the Kansas Workmen's Compensation Statute schedule of injuries for which compensation will be paid. As a result of this injury, Reese favored his left leg and now has a sore back strain and pain and skin splints in his right leg. Reese filed a claim under the Kansas Workmen's Compensation Statute, and the examiner awarded fifty weeks of temporary total disability and 40 percent permanent partial general disability. The company appealed. Should workmen's compensation for general bodily disability be awarded, such disability being a separate and distinct injury resulting from the scheduled injury under the state's workmen's compensation Act? [*Reese v. Gas Engineering and Construction Company*, 532 P.2d 1044 (Kan. 1975).]

9. Davis, the decedent, was a new employee working his fourth day with Republic Creosoting Company. He was hired to sort and stack railroad wood ties after completion of the unloading process of getting the ties off the delivery trucks. The unloader (fork lift) operator suggested to Davis that he come to the unloading so that he could help sort the ties after they had been unloaded. Davis had never witnessed the unloading operation before nor had it been described to him. However, the field superintendent, when hiring Davis, told Davis not to get around the trucks and that the unloader did all the unloading. During the entire operation of unloading, all the company's employees, other than the unloader operator, remained a safe distance from the truck, as did Davis on this occasion. The usual unloading process began with the removal of the chains holding the packages of ties onto the truck. The unloader operator then would move the unloader into position so that it supported a package of steel banded ties holding 25 to 45 ties. Only after the unloader was supporting a package did the truckdriver cut the band of the package to be unloaded. Under no circumstances would the band be cut before the unloader was in position. The unloader then removed the loosened ties from the truck.

On the day of the accident, the chains had been removed from the truck but the unloader had not yet been moved into position. Without being ordered to do so and without informing anyone of what he intended to do, Davis went up to the truck and, while standing on the ground next to the truck, cut the steel band on a package of ties with an ax. As a result, five of the ties fell on Davis, killing him.

The Secretary of Labor claimed that the company had violated the Occupational Safety and Health Act general duty clause by failing to instruct and supervise properly an untrained employee regarding the hazards of unloading railroad ties. The Occupational Safety and Health Review Commission decided that there was no violation. The secretary appealed. Did the company commit such a violation with respect to Davis? [*Brennan v. Occupational Safety and Health Review Commission*, 501 F.2d 1196 (1974).]

10. In the case of *Dothard, Director, Department of Public Safety of Alabama*, et al. *v. Rawlinson* et al., 433 U.S. 321 (1977)[1] the court had a very definite approach in the case in determining whether an illegal discrimination in violation of the federal Civil Rights Act had occurred. Explain that approach.

---

[1] See pp. 288–92.

Personal Property and Bailments

Summary

Property is something that is the subject of ownership. Personal property consists of movable things and interests in those things. A good (chattel) is a tangible, movable thing (e.g., a typewriter) and, as such, it can be transferred from one person to another in many types of business transactions.

One method of transfer is to deliver only *possession* of the goods, with the goods to be returned to the owner later. This creates a "bailment" of the goods. *Title* to the goods may be transferred in various ways, as by gift or sale, and there may be various forms of ownership.

The goods may be added to, as when a muffler is placed on an automobile. Or the goods may produce something, as when an animal produces offspring. This is a form of "accession." The goods may also be permanently affixed to land, in which case they become a part of the realty and are called "fixtures."

Warehousemen and carriers as "bailees" issue paper, called "documents of title," which acknowledge receipt of goods and contain the contract terms. This paper is personal property and capable of transfer by sale, as security, or in other ways. All bailees have duties of care with respect to the bailed goods and have varying levels of liability.

19

Personal Property

After you have read this chapter, you should be able to:

1. Define personal property, real property, and fixtures.
2. Explain why property distinctions are legally important.
3. List the methods by which property is acquired.
4. Define and distinguish accession and confusion.
5. Define gifts inter vivos and gifts causa mortis.
6. Describe the methods by which gifts are made to minors.
7. List the cases in which a purchaser from a nonowner will acquire good title.
8. List and define the different types of common ownership of property.

Introduction

Susan, a recent college graduate, made a list of the property she owned. The property included: (1) ten shares of corporate stock in Widgets International Corporation; (2) an antique dresser; (3) a valuable bookcase which Susan had attached to the wall in her apartment; and (4) an acre of farmland which Susan used for organic farming. Susan now wonders how this property would be legally classified and whether the classification would affect her rights to use or transfer the property.

If Susan acquires additional property, with her husband or with another person, additional questions will be raised. Susan might question the different methods of acquiring property. For example, is it safe to purchase goods from a merchant who might be selling goods he doesn't own? May Susan transfer property to her sister, who is a minor? What are the tax consequences of making a gift? Susan also might question the form of ownership. What is the nature of joint ownership of property? What are the special joint ownership rules in southwestern states such as California? Is joint ownership a good substitute for a will?

Susan's questions are important in our society because the answers will determine whether Susan may keep the property when her ownership is challenged by other individuals or by the government. Property classifications are especially important in determining Susan's right to use the property, to transfer the property to other persons, or to pass the property on to her loved ones when she dies.

The Meaning of Property

Property is difficult to classify because the concept of property has a number of meanings. On a broad philosophical level, property is a concept that is the cornerstone of law, for the law developed to protect property rights. According to the English philosopher Jeremy Bentham, "Property and law are born together, and die together. Before laws were made there was no property; take away laws, and property ceases."

On a more practical level, **property** means a thing or any interest or right in a thing that is capable of being owned. The owner of an interest or right in a thing is entitled to use, enjoy, or dispose of such interest or right, subject only to governmental regulations. The owner has "property."

property
a thing; also an interest or right in a thing

Property Classifications

Real and Personal Property
Real property is land or an interest or right in land and other immovable things fixed to the land, including structures on the land. Land is a tangible, immovable thing. The owner of the surface of land owns the soil beneath the surface and the air above the surface, subject to reasonable use by aircraft. Susan's acre of land is classified as real property.

real property
land and immovable things attached to land, along with interests and rights in the land

Personal property is a movable thing or an interest or right in the thing. It moves with the person, thus "personal" property. Personal property is considered to be *tangible* if it can be touched. The word **chattel** means tangible personal property. Intangible property is property which can not be touched. Susan's antique dresser would be considered tangible personal property. Her *shares* of stock would be intangible personal property because, while the certificate is tangible, the shares are interests in the corporation and can not be touched. Another illustration of intangible personal property is an account receivable. (Dan owes Charlie $100. Charlie has an account receivable—an intangible claim—against Dan for $100.)

Fixtures

The remaining item on Susan's list, the bookcase, is difficult to classify as real or personal property because it once was movable but now it is immovable, having been attached to the wall. The bookcase is considered to be a **fixture,** which is defined as a chattel which has become attached to real estate in such a way that it is considered to be real property, but is still available for chattel financing.[1]

Three tests are used to decide whether a chattel has become a fixture. *First,* is the chattel annexed to the real estate by nails, screws, glue, or other methods? It is possible that even where the property is not physically annexed, the *annexation test* will be met because of the weight of the object, as is illustrated by the following case.

Facts
A statue weighing three to four tons was erected in a courtyard in front of a house. The statue was not fastened to the real estate with clamps, cement, or by any other device. The plaintiffs bought the owner's personal property; the defendant bought the owner's real property. Plaintiffs sued defendant to determine ownership of the statue.

Decision
The court decided that defendant is the owner.

Reasoning
The statue is a fixture and therefore part of the real estate. A chattel may be annexed to real estate as much by weight as by any other device.

Snedeker v. Warring, 12 N.Y. 170 (1854).

The *second* fixture test is *adaptation*—is the article adapted to, and necessary for, the use of the real estate? A furnace installed in a house is necessary for the use of the house and would meet this test.

The *third* and most important test used by courts is *intention*—do the actions, words, purposes, and relationships of the parties show that they intended to make the property fixtures? In determining intention, the courts are not interested in the hidden or secret intention of the parties, as is illustrated by the following case.

---

[1] The fixture still retains sufficient character as a chattel. For example, a bathtub fixed in a house can be used as security for a loan. However, the brick, lumber, tile, glass in a building are not fixtures; they are a part of the structure.

Personal Property and Bailments

Facts

Green sold his house to Strain but, after the sale, Green removed a chandelier from the dining room. The chandelier had been in Green's family for fifteen years and he had moved it from house to house whenever he moved. Strain sued Green to determine whether the chandelier was a fixture.

Decision

The chandelier was a fixture and should not have been moved by Green. Judgment for Strain.

Reasoning

Even though Green always intended to take the chandelier with him, the intention was never disclosed. The court will not consider the secret intention of a party.

Strain v. Green, 172 P.2d 216 (Wash. 1946).

Reasons for Property Distinctions

Now that Susan has classified her property, she faces the question of why the classification is important. There are four reasons why property distinctions are legally important.

Transfer During Life.   If Susan wants to transfer her *real property* and fixtures attached to the real property during her lifetime, she will use a deed. A **deed** is a written document which must be in a form required by law. When Susan transfers her *personal property,* however, it is unlikely that she will use a document to transfer title, although in cases involving a substantial transfer of personal property, a document called a **bill of sale** is often used. A bill of sale is somewhat similar in form to a deed.

Transfer at Death.   The distinction between real and personal property is important in determining the transfer of property at death. Susan might have a **will,** a document which governs the transfer of her property at her death. Unlike a deed, a will has no legal significance until a person's death and can be revoked at any time before death. If Susan has a will, it probably includes separate provisions covering transfer of her real property and her personal property.

If Susan dies without a will, she is said to have died **intestate.** In such cases, state law determines the disposal of her property, and the law usually distinguishes between real and personal property. For example, if Susan died leaving a husband and one child, state law might provide that the husband will inherit one-third of Susan's real property and one-half of her personal property while the child will inherit two-thirds of the real property and one-half of the personal property. However, the law varies from state to state.

Source of the Law.   The source of the law will vary, depending on whether property is classified as real or personal. For instance, when personal property is sold, the sale is governed by the provisions of the Uniform Commercial Code, a statute which has been enacted in all states except Louisiana, where parts of it have been enacted. The law relating to the sale of real property, on the other hand, will usually be found in case decisions or in statutes other than the Uniform Commercial Code.

deed
a formal document used to transfer title to real estate

bill of sale
a formal document used to transfer personal property

will
a formal document which governs the transfer of property at death

intestate
a decedent without a will

Figure 19.1 Bill of Sale

BILL OF SALE

   I, John H. Doe, in consideration of the sum of $5000 paid by Tom J. Smith, the receipt whereof is hereby acknowledged, do grant and convey to Tom J. Smith, his executors, administrators or assigns, my Eversharp Riding Lawn Mower, serial #1007, to have and to hold forever.

   In witness whereof, I have set my hand and seal this 12th day of April, 1980.

WITNESSES:

_____   _____
                                                    John H. Doe
_____

State of_____ ⎤
                               ⎬ ss
County of_____ ⎦

   John H. Doe, being duly sworn, deposes and says that he is the vendor named in the within Bill of Sale, that he has knowledge of the facts, and that the consideration of said instrument was actual and adequate, and that the same was given in good faith for the purpose therein set forth, and not for the purpose of security, or for defrauding creditors of the vendor or subsequent purchasers.

                                                    _____

   Subscribed and sworn to before me this 12th day of ⎤
_____April_____ 1980 .   ⎥
                                                      ⎥
Notary Public, County of_____   ⎬
                                                      ⎥
State of_____   ⎥
                                                      ⎥
My commission expires_____ 19___   ⎦

Taxation.   The taxation of property varies, depending on whether the property is real or personal. Real property is normally taxed by a local governmental body, such as a city or township. Personal property is often not subject to taxation, or is taxed locally or by the state at a different rate than real property.

Methods of Acquiring Ownership

A number of methods may be used to acquire personal property. For example, an artist may acquire personal property by creating it—through painting or sculpture. A creditor may acquire personal property by obtaining a court judgment against a debtor. A person may acquire personal property by finding it, as discussed in the following chapter. And the state may acquire personal property through **escheat,** whereby property passes to the state when a person dies leaving no one to inherit the property. Four methods of acquisition, however, have special legal significance—accession, confusion, gifts, purchase.

escheat
the transfer of property to the state when a person dies without heirs

Personal Property and Bailments

Accession

Susan has decided to replace the shelving in her antique dresser. She takes the dresser to a furniture repair shop, where the new shelving is built into the dresser. This is an example of **accession**—the increase in property by what it produces or by the addition of other property to it. Examples are adding a muffler to an automobile or a horse producing a foal. Here, the shelving as property is added to other property in the form of the dresser. In such cases, Susan, as owner of the dresser, becomes owner of the shelving as well.

accession
the increase in property by what it produces or by the addition of other property to it

The situation becomes more complicated when the new shelving is installed by an innocent third party to whom the shopowner has wrongfully sold Susan's dresser or by a thief who steals the dresser from Susan. If the shelving can not be removed without damaging the dresser, the general rule is that Susan may recover from the thief either the dresser or damages based on the value of the dresser as repaired. The result would be the same if Susan sued the innocent third party, with two major qualifications. First, Susan would not be allowed to recover the dresser if the innocent purchaser substantially altered the dresser to such an extent that it is in reality a different and more valuable dresser than the one which Susan originally owned. Second, in a suit for damages against the innocent purchaser, value would be based upon the value of the dresser when Susan owned it rather than its value with the new shelves, as is illustrated by the following case.

Facts
On Christmas Eve, 1918 Ochoa's Studebaker truck was stolen. Eventually it was sold to Rogers as "junk"—a pile of broken parts—for $85. Rogers used the parts to construct a delivery truck at an expense of $800. In 1920 Ochoa spotted the truck and recognized the parts. Ochoa sued Rogers for return of the truck or for the present value of the truck, $1,000.

Reasoning
Rogers was an innocent party who made improvements to the property which exceeded the value when Rogers acquired the property. In such cases, the innocent purchaser is liable only for the market value at the time he acquired possession.

Ochoa v. Rogers, 234 S.W. 693 (Tex. 1921).

Decision
Judgment for Ochoa for only $85.

Confusion

Confusion occurs when chattels of different persons are mixed so that the chattels of one person can not be distinguished from the chattels of the other persons. Fungible goods, discussed later in this chapter, are like units of goods (e.g., wheat), and are the most common kind of goods confused. Confusion is different from accession.

confusion
the mixing of chattels of like kind of different persons so that the chattels of one person can not be distinguished from the chattels of the other persons

In most cases, confusion of personal property is not complicated in legal terms. For instance, assume that Susan grows wheat on her real estate and stores her wheat at a local grain elevator, where it is mixed with the wheat of the elevator operator. If the wheat is of the same quality, it can easily be divided when Susan decides to sell her share of the wheat.

The problem becomes more complex, however, when Susan's high-grade, expensive wheat is mixed with the owner's low-grade, cheap wheat. If Susan consented to the mixture of the two grades of wheat, she would have no cause to complain and would be entitled to remove only her proportionate share of the mixture. However, if the owner of the elevator intentionally mixed Susan's high-grade wheat with his low-grade wheat without Susan's knowledge, most courts would place the burden on him to prove that the wheat could be separated. If it is impossible to divide the wheat, Susan would receive all of the wheat or, as in the following case, a share of the mixture.

Facts

Troop personally owned one oil and gas lease, and he and his partner Rust owned another oil and gas lease. Troop mixed oil from the two leases. After Rust's death, his executor claimed that the estate was entitled to his share of the total oil from both leases.

Decision

Rust is entitled to his share of the oil from both leases. Judgment for Rust's executor.

Reasoning

Under the confusion doctrine, where goods are mixed together, the person who commingled the goods must prove the correct proportions. In this case Troop could not prove whether the oil came from his lease or the partnership lease.

Troop v. St. Louis Union Trust Co., 166 N.E.2d 116 (Ill. 1960).

Gifts

Gift Inter Vivos. A **gift** is a voluntary transfer of a chattel by a **donor** who is not to receive anything in exchange from the person receiving the chattel, the **donee.** As discussed below under Estate Planning,[2] a gift after the death of a person is accomplished by the use of a will. A gift during life, an *inter vivos* gift, is somewhat more complicated than after-death gifts because two requirements must be met: (1) the donor must have intended to make a gift, and (2) there must be delivery of the chattel to the donee.

The *intent* requirement means that the donee needs to prove more than mere possession of the chattel to prove a gift. In many cases, the intent of the donor is clearly spelled out in a letter or other writing. In other cases, courts will infer intent to make a gift because of factors such as the relationship between the parties and the size of the gift.

The *delivery* requirement is met when the donor transfers the chattel to the donee in such a manner that the donor relinquishes all right to and control over the chattel. Delivery may be *actual,* as when the donor delivers a new automobile to the donee, or *symbolic,* as when the donor delivers the keys to the car to the

gift
a voluntary transfer of a chattel by someone who is not to receive anything in return

donor
the person who makes a gift

donee
the recipient of a gift

---

[2] See p. 310.

donee instead of delivering the car itself. Additionally, the delivery may be made to a third party who is to hold the property for the donee, or to a person already in possession of the chattel who is to keep it as a gift. In the following case delivery was made to donees by delivery to their agent.

Facts

Aunt Jessie sent her nephew, Joseph, $5,000 and later sent him a letter which stated that, at her death, the money was to be divided among Joseph, his brother, and his sisters. On Jessie's death, her executor sued Joseph, claiming that the money should go to Jessie's estate because a valid inter vivos gift had not been made.

Decision

This was a valid inter vivos gift. Judgment for Joseph.

Reasoning

Jessie's intention to make a gift is proven by the letter. The delivery requirement was met when Jessie relinquished control by delivery to Joseph as agent for the donees.

In re *Gorden's Will*, 27 N.W.2d 900 (Iowa 1947.)

Gift Causa Mortis.   Gift cases are not difficult to resolve when the required intent and delivery exist and when the donor makes an *unconditional* gift to the donee. The cases are more difficult when the donor places a condition on the gift, such as, "This stereo is yours if I do not return from my trip to Boulder." In this case there is not a valid gift because it is not a *present* gift but, instead, an attempted future gift. This is true even if the condition is met.

The major exception to the conditional gift rule is the case where a donor facing imminent death from a present illness or impending peril makes a conditional gift to a donee which is to be *effective immediately*. The donor may revoke the conditional gift anytime before his death from that illness or peril, and revocation occurs automatically if either the donor recovers or the donee predeceases the donor. However, the gift is valid if not revoked. This is a **gift causa mortis.**

gift causa mortis
a conditional, revocable gift by someone facing imminent death from a present illness or impending peril

Gift to a Minor.   Susan wants to make a gift of $100 and a share of stock to her sister Sally, aged ten, but feels that Sally is too young to manage the property. How should Susan make the gift?

The answer is found in the Uniform Gifts to Minors Act which has been adopted in 48 states. Under the Act, Susan could open a bank account under her own name "as custodian for Sally." Under the Act, Susan has now made a completed gift although she may use the property for the support, benefit, and education of Sally. The property must be delivered to Sally at age 18 or 21, depending on state law.

Gift Tax.   The federal government imposes a gift tax on a donor and an estate tax on an estate at death. At one time it was advantageous for a person to give away property before death because the gift tax was three-fourths of the estate tax. However, the Tax Reform Act of 1976, which became effective on January 1, 1977, created a unified tax schedule for gift and estate taxes. Even after the tax reform, gifts are popular because no tax is levied for gifts which do not exceed $3,000 per year. For instance, a person with five children could give them each $3,000 a year for thirty years without paying estate or gift taxes.

Purchase

The last method of acquiring property is by purchase. The sale and purchase of *goods* under the Uniform Commercial Code is the subject of Part 5, Sales. The most troublesome area in the purchase and sale of chattels in general is the case where a nonowner sells the chattel.

Assume, for example, that a thief, Clyde, steals Susan's bookcase and sells it to an innocent third party, Rudolph. If Susan sues Rudolph to recover the dresser, the difficult question the law faces is deciding which innocent party, Susan or Rudolph, must suffer the loss. The cases generally fall into one of the following four categories.

Void Title. If the person selling property had *void title,* which is no title at all, the purchaser acquires no title. Thus, in our example, Susan would win the case because the thief, Clyde, having no title of his own, had no title to transfer to Rudolph.

Voidable Title. In many cases a person will acquire title to goods that may be avoided by the seller. For instance, if Susan were a minor and sold the bookcase to Clyde, Clyde would have *voidable title. Susan* could avoid her contract *with Clyde* any time before reaching the age of majority. In such cases, however, *Rudolph* would win if sued by Susan because, under sec. 2–403(1) of the Uniform Commerical Code, a person with a *voidable title* to goods, such as Clyde, has the *power* to transfer a good title to a good faith purchaser who pays value.

Entrustment. Whenever an owner entrusts goods to a merchant who deals in similar goods, the merchant has the power to sell the goods to a buyer in the ordinary course of business. If Sally delivered a valuable antique necklace to a dealer in jewelry for repairs, and the jeweler sold the necklace to Rudolph, Rudolph would be the owner of the necklace. Sally's only recourse would be to sue the jeweler either for **damages** for breach of the bailment contract, or for the tort of **conversion** for the value of the necklace.

Estoppel. If the owner of goods indicates to a third party that someone else owns the goods, and the third party, in reliance on the statement, buys the goods from the nonowner, the third party may keep the goods under the principle of law called **estoppel.** This principle prevents a person from denying what he had represented (held out) previously to another person if, meanwhile, the other person had changed his position materially in reasonable reliance on the representation.

In the following case the court held that allowing a nonowner to act as if he were the owner is a holding out resulting in an estoppel.

damages
the money judicially awarded for another's wrongful conduct

conversion
the tort of intentional interference with another's right to possession, control, and dominion of a chattel

estoppel
a principle of law that when one person "holds out" (represents) a material fact to another person, who changes his position materially to his prejudice in reasonable reliance on the holding out, the first person is "estopped" (prohibited) to deny what he asserted previously

Facts

Harry Winston, Inc., a diamond merchant, owned a diamond ring. Winston delivered the ring to Brand who, with the knowledge and approval of Winston, offered the ring for sale. Brand sold the ring to Zendman for $12,500 but, before paying Winston, Brand declared bankruptcy. Zendman now sues Winston to determine ownership of the ring.

Decision

Judgment for Zendman.

Reasoning

Winston is estopped from asserting ownership. Winston allowed the nonowner, Brand, to act as if he were the owner of the ring, and Zendman relied on the apparent ownership of Brand.

Zendman v. Harry Winston, Inc., 111 N.E.2d 871 (N.Y. 1953).

Forms of Ownership

Ralph and Betty are engaged to be married. Before the marriage they decide to purchase personal property (a car) and real property (a summer cottage on a lake). If either Ralph or Betty purchase the property as individuals, the form of ownership would not be complicated in legal terms because the title would be in the name of only one of the two. However, whenever two or more persons join together to purchase property, they must decide whether to purchase the property as joint tenants, tenants by entirety (or the entireties), or tenants in common. Each of these methods will result in different legal consequences.

Joint Tenancy

Ownership in **joint tenancy** is ownership of property by more than one person with the right of survivorship. When one person dies, the other surviving person or persons automatically become the sole owner or owners because this is what the parties intended in using joint tenancy. If Ralph and Betty purchased the car and cottage as *joint tenants,* on Betty's death the property would be owned by Ralph alone without the necessity of probate (proof of a will) court proceedings, which are usually necessary when a person dies.

Four requirements must be met if there is to be a joint tenancy between two or more persons such as Ralph and Betty. First, Ralph and Betty must acquire their interests at the *same time.* Second, they must acquire their interests in the *same conveyance;* that is, their title must be the same. Third, they must have an *equal interest* in the property. And fourth, they must have the right to *equal possession* of the property.

If any one of these requirements is missing, most courts will decide that there is a "tenancy in common" (discussed later) rather than a joint tenancy. For example, if Ralph owned the cottage and deeded it "to Ralph and Betty as joint tenants" a joint tenancy would not be created because Ralph originally acquired his interest at an earlier time and in an earlier conveyance than Betty. In order to create a joint tenancy, Ralph would have to deed the cottage to a third party, usually Ralph's attorney, who would then deed the cottage to Ralph

joint tenancy
a form of ownership of property by more than one person with the right of survivorship

and Betty. In recent years, however, many states have decided that this procedure should not be required and, therefore, as an exception to the first requirement, allow a direct conveyance to Ralph and Betty.

Severance. A joint tenancy will be *severed,* that is, the interest of the parties will be separated, whenever one of the four requirements is destroyed. A joint tenancy interest, however, can not be severed or transferred by a will. There are four common methods of severance: conveyance, divorce or dissolution of marriage, partition, or murder.

Conveyance. A conveyance by one of the joint tenants will sever the joint tenancy. For instance, if Ralph and Betty own the cottage as joint tenants and Betty sells her interest to Steve, Ralph and Steve would own the property as tenants in common, not as joint tenants. The same result is reached in cases of involuntary conveyance where a sheriff sells Betty's interest in order to pay her creditors. If *three* persons, A, B, and C, own as joint tenants and C sells his interest to D, the relationship between A and B is still a joint tenancy but, with respect to D, they are tenants in common.

Divorce/Dissolution of Marriage. If Ralph and Betty own property as joint tenants as a married couple, severance occurs when they are divorced. In some states, however, the divorce judgment must specifically order severance, and if the property is not specifically mentioned in the divorce judgment, the joint tenancy continues after the divorce.

partition
a division of property
between joint owners

Partition. A **partition** takes place when Ralph and Betty divide their property either voluntarily or by court order. If a court handles the partition, a physical division of the property is preferred. It is not possible, however, to physically divide a cottage or a car, and in such cases a court will order that the property be sold and the proceeds divided between Ralph and Betty.

Murder. Assume that Ralph murders Betty while they hold property as joint tenants. Should Ralph be allowed to take the property as the survivor? This has been a difficult question for the courts, and three different approaches have developed. The first approach is to decide that Ralph receives the property as survivor despite the murder. The second approach would be that the property passes to Betty's estate, with Ralph receiving nothing. The third approach would be to give Ralph half the property and Betty's estate the other half.

Tenancy by Entirety

A **tenancy by entirety** (or by the entireties) is identical to a joint tenancy with the following three qualifications.

tenancy by entirety
a form of co-ownership
between husband and
wife with the right of
survivorship

Husband and Wife. A tenancy by the entirety can only be created between a husband and wife, and the couple must have been husband and wife at the time the property was acquired. Notice how the court in the following case got around the problem of an illegal marriage and considered the intention of the parties as though they were married in order to achieve a joint tenancy.

Facts

Alejo married Soledad. He then married Helen before divorcing Soledad and, with Helen, they purchased real estate as tenants by the entirety. Later he divorced Soledad and married Helen again. On Alejo's death, a question arose concerning Helen's interest in the real estate.

Reasoning

Helen and Alejo were not legally married when the real estate was purchased. However, because there clearly was an intent that the property pass to the survivor, the property was held in joint tenancy.

Lopez v. Lopez, 243 A.2d 588 (Md. 1968).

Decision

Helen takes the real estate as a joint tenant, not as a tenant by the entirety.

Severance. A joint tenancy can be severed when *one* of the owners sells his interest. However, a tenancy by entirety can be terminated only when *both* husband and wife agree to the sale. We might assume that Ralph and Betty, now married, purchase a house as tenants by entirety. After the purchase, Ralph leaves Betty and moves to a different state. A few years later, Ralph's creditors contact Betty and tell her that if she does not pay Ralph's debts they will ask the sheriff to sell the house and use the proceeds to pay the debts. The creditors will not be allowed to force a sale of the house for the reason that the debts were Ralph's alone, and one party's interest in a tenancy by entirety can not be conveyed.

Control. In most states both the husband and the wife have equal right to control and possess the property held as tenants by entirety. However, in some states, following an older view of the marriage relationship, the husband has the exclusive right to control and possession.

Tenancy in Common

A **tenancy in common** is distinguished from the joint tenancy and tenancy by entirety by the fact that in a tenancy in common, when one person dies, his interest passes to his estate rather than to the surviving tenant. A tenant in common is free to convey his interest or seek a partition by agreement or by court proceedings.

tenancy in common
a form of ownership of property by more than one person without survivorship

Community Property

If Ralph and Betty settle in one of eight states in the Southwest and West, much of their property would be considered **community property.** These states are Arizona, California, Idaho, Louisiana, New Mexico, Nebraska, Texas, and Washington.

Although community property laws often vary from state to state, the law generally provides that all property acquired through the efforts of the husband and wife during their marriage is considered to be community property. All other property—property acquired before marriage, by gift, or by inheritance during marriage—is the separate property of the husband or wife.

community property
a form of ownership by husband and wife of property acquired by their efforts during their marriage

As a general rule, the husband has the right to manage and control community property,[3] although both husband and wife must sign the deed when community real property is sold. When one spouse dies, the decedent's one-half interest will pass according to the terms of the will or, if there is no will, according to state law. The surviving spouse retains a one-half interest in the property.

Joint Ownership and Estate Planning

A person establishes an *estate plan* in order to arrange for the orderly transfer of property to loved ones after death. Most estate plans include the use of a will and a trust. The **trust** involves the transfer of property before or after death to a *trustee,* often a bank, which will hold and invest the property for the trust **beneficiaries.**

In recent years it has become popular to avoid the use of a will and trust by placing property in joint tenancy or tenancy by entirety. The reason for not using a will is that wills must be "probated"—that is, proven to be legally valid in a **probate court**—and probate court proceedings often are time-consuming and expensive. If property is held jointly, the survivor automatically becomes the sole owner without the approval of probate court.

While joint ownership is a useful estate planning device, it should not be used exclusively, but, instead, should be used along with a will and a trust. For example, Ralph and Betty have two young children and own assets worth $100,000, all of which are held in joint ownership. When Ralph dies, Betty automatically becomes the sole owner of the property without probate court proceedings. However, what will happen if Ralph and Betty die together in an automobile accident? Who would receive their property? Who would be named guardian for their children? Do they want their children to receive all of the property when they become adults, which in most states would be at the age of eighteen? Who will manage the property until the children are to receive it? In order to resolve these questions, Ralph and Betty should execute wills which name an **executor** who will manage the property and which name a **guardian** for the children. Additionally, if they do not want the children to receive the property at age eighteen, they should enter into a trust agreement with a bank or a friend and provide in the agreement that the property is to pass to the children at a specified age.

The need for a will and a trust becomes more important later in life after Ralph and Betty have accumulated substantial assets. By setting up the trust in the proper manner, thousands of dollars in estate taxes will be saved at their death.

trust
a legal device whereby legal title to property is held by one person (a trustee) for the benefit of a beneficiary

beneficiary
a person who receives a benefit

probate court
a court which has jurisdiction over the estate of a deceased person

executor
a man who is named in and administers a will

guardian
a person legally entrusted with custody and/or property of another

---

[3] But in some states, such as California, there is equal control by husband and wife.

Summary Statement

1. The distinctions of real property, personal property, and fixtures are important in matters such as transfer of property and taxation.
2. Accession involves the addition of property; confusion involves the mixing of chattels of different owners.
3. Gifts may be made during life if there is intention and delivery. A conditional gift is not valid unless it is made causa mortis.
4. In making a gift to a minor, the donor must meet the requirements of the Uniform Gifts to Minors Act.
5. A good-faith purchaser for value will acquire good title from a nonowner if the nonowner: (1) has voidable title; (2) is a merchant dealer of goods to whom similar goods have been entrusted; or (3) has been held out as the owner by the real owner under the principle of estoppel.
6. When property is acquired by more than one person, it may be held in (1) tenancy in common, (2) joint tenancy, or (3) tenancy by entirety. In the Southwest and West, *community property* represents another form of ownership of property.

The following case has been chosen because it illustrates the difficult decision courts face when one joint tenant murders another.

Bradley v. Fox
129 N.E.2d 699 (Ill. 1955)

Lawrence Fox murdered his wife, Matilda, with whom he owned property in joint tenancy. After the murder a question arose concerning ownership of the property.

Davis, Justice. In this category of cases the courts have differed as to whether the murderer should be allowed his survivorship rights. Those courts which hold that he is entitled to the entire property as surviving joint tenant predicate their conclusion on the legal fiction incident to the concept of joint tenancy, whereby each tenant is deemed to hold the entire estate from the time of the original investiture, and reason that the murderer acquired no additional interest by virtue of the felonious destruction of his joint tenant, of which he can be deprived. . . . Other courts, however, concerned with the equitable principles prohibiting a person from profiting from his own wrong, and with the realities of the situation, have abandoned the Common Law fictions, and have either divested the killer of the entire estate . . . or have deprived him of half the property . . . or have imposed a constructive trust on the entire estate held by the murderer for the benefit of the heirs of the victim . . . or a constructive trust modified by a life interest in half the property.

In joint tenancy the contract that the survivors will take the whole necessarily presupposes that the death of either will be in the natural course of events and that it will not be generated by either tenant murdering the other. One of the implied conditions of the contract is that neither party will acquire the interest of the other by murder. It is fundamental that four coexisting unities are necessary and requisite to the creation and continuance of a joint tenancy; namely, unity of interest, unity of title, unity of time, and unity of possession. Any act of a joint tenant which destroys any of these unities operates as a severance of the joint tenancy and extinguishes the right of survivorship. . . . It is our opinion, therefore, that it would be unconscionable for defendant Fox, as murderer of his joint tenant, and for defendant Downey, as transferee [of the property from Fox] with full knowledge of how Fox acquired the sole legal title to the property and of the fact that the conveyance was in fraud of creditors' claims, to retain and enjoy the beneficial interest in the property. It is our conclusion that Fox, by his felonious act, destroyed all rights of survivorship and lawfully retained only the title to his undivided one-half interest in the property in dispute as a tenant in common with the heir-at-law of Matilda Fox, deceased.

Questions and Case Problems

1. The Premonstratensian Fathers purchased a supermarket and leased it back to the prior owners. The building contained five coolers, valued at over $23,000. The cooler walls constituted the walls of other rooms, and the coolers were attached to a hardwood floor which was attached to concrete. When the coolers were destroyed by fire, the insurance company refused to pay on the grounds that they were not fixtures and therefore were not covered by fire insurance on the building. Is the company correct? [*The Premonstratensian Fathers v. Badger Mutual Insurance Co.*, 175 N.W.2d 237 (Wis. 1970).]

2. Roberts constructed an above-ground swimming pool on his property which was valued at $5,000. The pool could easily be taken down and removed to another location and was not attached to the real estate. Because of the pool, Roberts' real estate tax assessment was increased, and he sued to cancel the assessment. Decision? [*Roberts v. Assessment Board of Review of the Town of New Windsor*, 84 Misc.2d 1017 (N.Y. 1975).]

3. Sligo Furnace Co. owned timberland. Hobart-Lee Tie Co. trespassed on the land, cut down timber and used it to make railroad ties. Sligo sues Hobart-Lee to recover the value of the ties, claiming that, under the law of accession, a willful trespasser is liable for the value of the timber as improved. Decision? [*Sligo Furnace Co. v. Hobart-Lee Tie Co.*, 134 S.W.585 (Mo. 1911).]

4. A mother, using her own money, purchased securities in her name and the name of her daughter as joint tenants with the right of survivorship. The mother retained possession of the certificates. A dispute arose regarding dividends, and the mother brought suit against the daughter claiming that the daughter had no interest in the securities. Decision? [*Kinney v. Ewing*, 492 P.2d 636 (N.M. 1972).]

5. Closter lived in the same rooming house with his friend Schutz. Closter owned a note for a debt owed him by a third party. One day Closter went to his room, indorsed the note to Schutz, placed the note on a table and shot himself. Schutz entered the room and took the note while Closter was unconscious but before death. Did Closter make a valid gift to Schutz? [*Liebe v. Battman*, 54 P. 179 (Or. 1898).]

6. Montgomery, a career soldier, had a savings account in a bank. Before going to Germany, he delivered the savings account passbook to his first cousin, Mrs. Stone, and stated: "If I happen to crap out, it is all yours." Montgomery died in Germany. Does Mrs. Stone own the savings account? [*Guest v. Stone,* 56 S.E.2d 247 (Ga. 1949).]

7. Mosely purchased a car from a used car dealer and installed a sun visor, gasoline tank, and seat cover. The car had been stolen from Grunwell and the thief had installed a new engine. Grunwell's insurance company now sues to recover the car from Mosely. Decision? [*Farm Bureau Mut. Automobile Ins. Co. v. Moseley,* 90 A.2d 485 (Del. 1952).]

8. A husband and wife own a home as tenants by entirety. After 35 years of marriage, they become estranged and husband refuses to allow the wife into the home. May the husband exclude his wife from the home? [*D'Ercole v. D'Ercole,* 407 F.Supp. 1377 (Mass. 1976).]

9. A husband and wife lived in a community property state. Husband owned two restaurants as separate property. Through the husband's efforts during the marriage, the restaurants were income-producing. Is this income community property? [*Steward v. Torrey,* 95 P.2d 990 (Ariz. 1939).]

10. In *Bradley v. Fox,* 129 N.E.2d 699 (Ill. 1955),[4] the court held that it would be unconscionable for Fox to profit from his criminal conduct by taking, as a joint tenant, property by surviving his victim. How does this decision evidence the complementary nature of the various areas of the law and a limit to the concept of property?

---

[4] See pp. 311–12.

20 Bailments

After you have read this chapter, you should be able to:

1. List at least five situations where bailment law personally affects you.
2. Define a bailment.
3. Describe the duties of a bailee in the three types of bailments.
4. Decide whether a bailee may disclaim liability.
5. Determine who bears expenses that arise when the bailee uses goods.
6. Describe the rights of a person who finds lost or mislaid goods.

Introduction

On both an individual and a professional level, every person is affected by the law of bailments on almost a daily basis. It is, therefore, surprising that few persons can define a bailment or understand the rights and liabilities that arise under bailment law. Briefly, a bailment occurs when goods are delivered and are to be later returned pursuant to agreement between the parties.

To illustrate the importance of bailment law, let us assume that Harry recently purchased a new suit which he planned to wear while interviewing with companies visiting campus. A week before his first interview he delivered the suit to Quick'N Clean Dry Cleaners to have the suit dry-cleaned. Quick'N Clean gave Harry a receipt for the suit and told him the suit would be ready within one week. The morning of his first job interview Harry went to Quick'N Clean, presented his receipt, but was told by the owner: "I'm sorry, I can't seem to find your suit." When Harry demanded that the owner pay for the suit, he refused, claiming that he and his employees were always careful with customers' property and that the loss could not have been their fault.

Harry at first might think that his dispute would be classified as a contract or tort problem. However, because of historical reasons and because in many bailments the elements of a contract such as mutual assent or consideration are not present, the principles of contract law do not govern this situation. For example, one person may hold goods as a favor to the owner. And tort law, while relevant to the solution, does not control because the cleaners may have a greater duty of care than would normally be the case and, additionally, the law might impose a stronger burden of proof on the cleaners. As a result this case falls within the law of bailments.

The law of bailments is obviously important to individuals such as Harry. In one day Harry may park his car in a parking lot, deposit his books in a locker at the entrance to a bookstore, hang his coat in a restaurant cloakroom, lend his stereo to a friend for a party, and ask another friend to watch his belongings in the library while he takes a study break. In each situation it is possible that Harry has created a bailment.

Bailment law is also of extreme importance to persons in business, especially when, unaware of potential liability, they fail to purchase adequate insurance to cover losses. For instance, a person who owns a hotel should be aware of the consequences when his employees park guests' cars in the hotel lot, hang guests' coats in the cloakroom of the hotel restaurant, and store guests' valuables in the hotel safe.

Bailment Defined

A **bailment** may be defined generally as the delivery of goods (or chattels) by one person, the **bailor,** to another person, the **bailee,** for a particular purpose, with the understanding that at a future time the goods are to be redelivered to the bailor or delivered to a third person as directed by the bailor in accordance

bailment
a delivery of goods by a bailor to a bailee which are to be returned to the bailor or as he directs in accordance with the bailment agreement

bailor
the person who bails goods

bailee
the person to whom goods are bailed

with the bailment agreement. For example, a seller (bailor) delivers goods to a railroad (bailee) for delivery to a buyer. Another example is the commercial bailment (for hire)—e.g., the rental of office furniture, equipment, or machines, which are to be returned at the end of the rental period.

The word bailment is derived from the French word *bailler* meaning "to deliver," and the key to the creation of any bailment is *delivery* of *goods* and their *return*. The courts interpret *delivery* as a combination of a voluntary transfer of *physical possession* coupled with the bailee's *intention to control* the property. This combination will be further explored in the applications which follow.

Using the general definition of a bailment, two related transactions may be distinguished, a **lease** of space and a *sale*. When a person leases a locker or a parking space and deposits goods in the locker or parks a car in the space, a bailment is not created because the *goods* have *not been delivered* to the lessor. Instead, the owner of the goods has retained possession and control of his goods. However, a *lease of goods* creates a bailment.

A **sale** is distinguished from a bailment in that the purchaser acquires *title* to the goods and is under no duty to return the goods, although it is possible that the purchaser will deliver other goods to the seller as payment. For example, if Nick leases his farm and cows on the farm to Alexandra for one year, and if the lease provides that Alexandra is to return *cows of equal quality* at the end of the year, there has been a sale of the cows to Alexandra. As a result, she is free to dispose of the cows as she pleases, and her creditors may force a sale of the cows to satisfy her debts.

Applications

To illustrate the application of bailment principles, we will examine three situations where bailment law has been especially troublesome to courts.

The Cloakroom

A common bailment issue arises when a person hangs his coat in a cloakroom in a theater, restaurant, or store. To illustrate the application of bailment law to the cloakroom setting, we might assume that three students—Tom, Dick, and Harry—visit a clothing store to shop for sweaters. Tom takes off his coat, lays it across a clothes rack, and begins to try on sweaters. A clerk helps Dick remove his coat and lays it next to Tom's coat. Harry leaves his coat on a hook in a changing room before trying on the sweaters. A thief steals all three coats, and the question arises whether the store is liable for the coats as a bailee.

In all three cases the coats were left on the store's property, and consequently the store potentially had the power to physically control the coats. But was the other requirement met? Did the store show an *intention to control* the coats? Most courts would agree that there was no intention to control Tom's coat. There is no proof that the store even knew that Tom had laid down his coat. A clerk physically removed Dick's coat, however, and this act implies an intention to control. Thus the store would be a bailee of Dick's coat but not of Tom's coat.

lease
a form of contract giving one person, the tenant, the exclusive right to occupy for a period the property of another, the landlord

sale
the transfer of title from seller to purchaser for a price

Harry's coat presents the greatest legal difficulty. On the one hand, it is generally held that a store does not become a bailee merely because there are hooks on the wall for customers' garments, for the reason that the store offers this as a service to the public and makes no attempt to supervise the clothing. On the other hand, a bailment would exist if a coat is *checked* with a person in a restaurant cloakroom, or if the coat is left in a *private* room or office, as is illustrated in the following case concerning a clothes closet in a doctor's office used for patients' clothing.

Facts

A woman visited her psychiatrist wearing a fur coat worth $1,725. Upon entering the office, she deposited her coat in a clothes closet in the reception room. After her consultation with the psychiatrist she discovered that her coat was missing, and she sued the psychiatrist, claiming that he was liable as a bailee.

Decision

The psychiatrist is a bailee.

Reasoning

By maintaining the closet, the psychiatrist was impliedly inviting his patients to leave their coats there under his control. He also should know that patients normally must remove their coats before their consultation.

Laval v. Leopold, 47 Misc.2d 624 (N.Y. 1965).

The Parking Lot

Let us assume that, upon leaving the store without their coats, Tom, Dick, and Harry proceeded to their respective cars. Tom had parked his car in an unfenced, unguarded lot. He had paid the attendant upon entering the lot, kept the keys to the car, and was free to pick up his car and to leave at any time. Dick had parked his car in a lot where an attendant had taken the key to his car, had parked it for him, and had retained the key. Harry parked his car in the type of lot commonly found at airports. He entered the lot by removing a ticket from a machine and, in order to leave the lot, he must produce the ticket and pay an attendant. Upon arriving at the three lots from the store, Tom, Dick, and Harry discover that thieves have stolen their cars and, once more, they question whether a bailment has been created.

In Tom's case, clearly a bailment has not resulted, because Tom has retained control of the car. Dick clearly has created a bailment because, in delivering the key to the attendant, he also delivered physical possession, and the attendant, by taking the key, showed the required intent to control the car. In other words, in many cases the key to determining whether a bailment exists is the possessor of the key!

Harry's case is more difficult. In cases involving airport lots, most courts hold that a bailment relationship is not created because the parking lot owner does not control vehicles parked in the lot. The following case is illustrative.

Facts

At the parking lot at O'Hare Airport in Chicago motorists enter through automatic gates and receive a ticket that notes the time and date of arrival. They then park their own cars and retain the keys. When they are ready to leave, they pick up their own cars and, at an exit, give the ticket to an attendant who collects the parking charges. An automobile was stolen from the lot, and the parking lot company was sued as a bailee.

Decision

The parking lot company is not a bailee.

Reasoning

The company never accepted control of the vehicle. Motorists retained actual control by locking their cars and taking the keys.

Wall v. Airport Parking Co. of Chicago, 244 N.E.2d 190 (Ill. 1969).

If we assume that Dick can recover the value of his car because of the bailment relationship, can he also recover the value of a CB radio which he had installed in the car and the value of his tennis racket which was in the trunk of the car? Under the **closed container rule,** the bailment of the automobile includes only those items of which the parking lot attendant has actual notice or which the parking lot attendant should have known were in the car. Thus, if Dick did not give the attendant actual notice that the CB and the racket were in the car, the bailment would cover only the CB, because the attendant should have seen the CB when he parked the car. The bailment would not include items in the "closed container," the trunk, such as the tennis racket, but would include the spare tire, the jack, and other ordinary accessories, because people generally are aware of their presence in a car trunk.

closed container rule bailee is not responsible for the contents of a closed container unless he knows or should know the contents

Safe Deposit Box

Joan has rented a safe deposit box at a local bank. In order to gain access to the box, Joan must sign a signature card and produce a key to the box. A bank employee will then produce a second key and proceed to the vault with Joan to open the box. After entering the vault, the safe deposit box can be opened only by using both keys. One day Joan discovered that some valuable coins had been removed from the box. Is the bank liable as a bailee?

The bank, of course, will argue that, if there is a bailment relationship, it is the bailee only of the box itself and not of the contents because of the "closed container" rule. Courts have generally decided, however, that the bank is also bailee of the contents of the box because banks should know that customers use the boxes to store valuable possessions. In many states court decisions have been overturned by statutes which provide that the rental of the box is a lease of the box but not a bailment of its contents, and which allow a bank to limit its liability to a certain amount.

Rights and Duties

Bailee's Duty to Return Identical Property

At the conclusion of the bailment, the bailee must return the identical property to the bailor, or to a third person, as directed by the bailor or as previously agreed. If there is no duty to return identical property, the transaction is a sale rather than a bailment. A major exception to this rule exists when the goods are **fungible,** that is, goods which are the equivalent of other goods. For instance, Farmer Brown and Farmer Green might each store 10,000 bushels of wheat in a local grain elevator. Since the wheat will be mixed together, it will be impossible for the elevator operator, the bailee, to return the identical wheat to each farmer. However, because of the commercial importance of such transactions, coupled with the intentions of the parties, a bailment has been created and, while the wheat is in the elevator, both farmers are considered to be bailor tenants in common and the elevator operator becomes the bailee. Thus, if the elevator operator becomes insolvent, the farmers are entitled to the return of their wheat.

fungible goods
every unit of goods is the equivalent of any other like unit, either actually or by contract

Bailee's Duty to Return to Bailor

In most cases the bailee must return the goods to the bailor, even if the bailor is not the owner. However, in the following two cases the bailee is excused from this duty.

First, the bailee might be under a court order to deliver the goods to a legal officer who has a **writ of execution** which authorizes him to take possession of and sell the goods to satisfy a judgment. Although the bailee must deliver the goods to the officer, he should make every effort to contact the bailor so that the bailor may take appropriate action to recover the goods.

writ of execution
a court order authorizing a sheriff to seize tangible property to satisfy a court judgment

Second, a situation might arise where the bailor is not the owner of the goods or, at least, his rights to possession are subordinate (inferior) to those of a third person. If the real owner or the person with a superior right to possession appears and claims the goods, the bailee must deliver the goods to that person. However, any action by the bailee is risky. For example, assume that Tinkers, the bailor, delivers his car to a repair shop run by Evers, the bailee. A few days later Chance contacts Evers and states that he, not Tinkers, owns the car and demands that Evers return it. If Chance is telling the truth, then Evers must deliver the car to him and if, instead, Evers returns it to the bailor, Evers must pay damages to Chance. If Chance is not telling the truth, or if he does not have the right to possession, having previously loaned the car to Tinkers, then Evers must return the car to Tinkers or pay damages to him for not doing so. In such cases the safe approach would be for Evers to commence a court action against both Tinkers and Chance so that the court could determine to whom the car belongs. This remedy is called **interpleader.**

interpleader
an equitable remedy of a person who has some thing but does not claim any interest in it, requesting the court to decide who, as between two or more claimants, is entitled to the thing

Bailee's Duty of Care

A bailee is not liable as an insurer of the goods. That is, a bailee is not liable in all cases when goods within his control are damaged or destroyed. Instead, the bailee is only responsible when he is *negligent* in that he does not exercise the proper degree of care, which will vary depending on the facts of each case. However, in all cases the burden of proving that the requisite degree of care was met is on the bailee since, because of his possession and control of the goods, he is in the best position to explain why they were damaged or destroyed.

To illustrate the different degrees of care required of a bailee, we might assume that Jimmy owns a pair of tennis shoes, a tennis racket, and a can of tennis balls. In preparation for a trip, Jimmy asks his good friend Able to do him a favor and keep his tennis shoes for him. Jimmy then delivers his tennis racket to Baker, who is to restring the racket for $10. And Chance borrows Jimmy's tennis balls for use in a local tournament. Three different types of bailment have been created. The bailment of the tennis shoes is a *bailment for the sole benefit of the bailor,* Jimmy, and the bailee only owes a duty of *minimal care* in looking after the shoes. The bailment of the tennis racket is a *bailment for mutual benefit* in that Jimmy benefits by having his racket restrung and Baker benefits by being paid. In such cases the bailee owes a duty of *ordinary care.* The bailment of the tennis balls is for the *sole benefit of the bailee,* Chance, who must exercise *extraordinary care* in looking after them.

A bailee who uses the goods for his own purposes without the permission of the bailor is liable for any loss. For example, if Baker, after stringing Jimmy's racket, had used it in a tournament and, during the tournament, an armed robber stole the racket, Baker would be liable for the loss even though he exercised reasonable care under the circumstances.

Contractual Modification of the Duty

The bailor and the bailee may decide to modify the legal duty of care of the bailee when they negotiate the bailment contract. In some cases the bailee will assume a greater duty. For example, the contract might provide that the bailee is an insurer of the goods, or that the bailee has a duty either to return or to pay for the goods. This agreement is legally valid.

A more common type of contractual modification is a **disclaimer** of liability by the bailee. For example, when you deliver a car to a garage for repairs, a sign on the wall might provide: "The garage is not responsible for loss or damage to cars"; or when you deliver your coat to a restaurant cloakroom attendant, there might be a provision on the back of the claim check: "The restaurant is not responsible for any loss or damage to articles."

disclaimer
denial of an obligation or a claim

Figure 20.1 Parking Ticket with Disclaimer

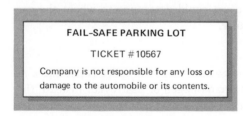

Personal Property and Bailments

A bailee using these disclaimers faces two major legal problems. *First,* since the disclaimer involves a contractual agreement, the bailee must prove that the bailor agreed to the terms of the contract. A bailor who was unaware of the sign or the language on the *back* of the claim check will not be bound by the disclaimer. Furthermore, courts generally do not favor disclaimers and will not uphold them unless the language is clear. In the following case the disclaimer did not specifically cover negligence.

Facts

A corporation which was engaged in commercial photography purchased several rolls of Kodak film which it used to shoot movies in Alaska. After the movies were taken, the film was sent to Kodak for processing. However, as a result of Kodak's negligence, a substantial portion of the film was damaged. The corporation sued Kodak for over $1,500, expenses incurred in refilming. Kodak's defense was that the box containing the film noted that, except for replacement of film, the sale "is without warranty or other liability of any kind."

Decision

Kodak is liable.

Reasoning

The law disfavors disclaimers of liability especially when, as in this case, the disclaimer does not specifically cover negligence.

Willard Van Dyke Productions v. Eastman Kodak Co., 189 N.E.2d 693 (N.Y. 1963).

The *second* problem is that many courts have decided that, on the grounds of public policy, a bailee may not disclaim liability for his own negligence. The public policy reasons are especially strong when the person receiving the goods is in the bailment business and when the bailor has little bargaining power. For instance, Waldo wanted to park his car in a major city, and all of the parking lots had signs disclaiming liability for damage to cars. When Waldo tried to negotiate with the lots by offering to pay more if they would remove the disclaimer, they all refused and, in effect, told him, "Take it or leave it." Most courts would hold that Waldo would not be bound by the disclaimer because it was forced on him by the party offering an essential service. However, the result would be different when the bailor is a large corporation with strong bargaining power of its own or when Waldo is negotiating with a friend who wants to rent his stereo. In such cases the disclaimer will probably be upheld because the bargaining power is equal.

Compensation and Expenses

In most cases involving a bailment for mutual benefit one of the parties must compensate the other, and the amount of the compensation will normally be decided in advance. For example, if Clyde, the bailee, rents a moving van from Do-It-Yourself Van Company, the contract will provide the compensation due the company. If the compensation is not agreed upon in advance, then reasonable compensation must be paid. Thus, if Susan takes her car to a garage for a new transmission, she must pay reasonable compensation if the cost of the service is not determined in advance. If the goods are destroyed through no fault of the bailee after the service has been performed, the bailee is still entitled to compensation. That is, if the transmission were installed and the car destroyed by lightning before Susan could pick it up, she would still have to pay for the transmission.

In addition to compensation, one of the parties to a bailment contract will be liable for expenses which arise in using the goods. If Clarence rents a car for two weeks from We-Try-Harder Rentals, and during the two weeks the car needs a quart of oil and a new transmission, who is liable for these expenses? The general rule is that the bailee is responsible for ordinary maintenance, in this case for the oil, while the bailor must pay for extraordinary expenses—e.g., the transmission work.

Bailor's Liability

warranty
an express or implied assurance that certain facts exist

In the most common bailment situation, *the bailment for mutual benefit,* the bailor traditionally was required to exercise *reasonable care* in checking the goods for defects and in warning the bailee of potential damages. However, several recent court decisions have gone beyond the traditional rule in deciding that a bailor is liable even when he exercised the greatest degree of care in trying to protect the bailee. In such cases the bailor has been held liable on the theory that a bailor in the business of leasing goods gives an *implied* **warranty** that the goods are fit for ordinary use. In other cases courts have used the tort theory of *strict liability* (absolute liability), as illustrated by the following case involving a defective ladder.

Facts
A company leased from Shell Oil Co. a gasoline tank with a movable ladder mounted on the tank for use in refueling airplanes. An aircraft mechanic employed by the company was seriously injured while climbing the ladder when both of the ladder's legs split. He sued Shell for damages.

Decision
Shell is liable on the theory of strict liability.

Reasoning
The purpose of strict liability is to require manufacturers who put products on the market to bear the cost of injuries caused by the products rather than place this burden on innocent consumers. The purpose applies equally to bailors who put goods on the market by means of a lease.

Price v. Shell Oil Company, 466 P.2d 722 (Cal. 1970).

Lost, Mislaid, and Abandoned Personal Property

Finder's Rights

In leaving class one day Ray discovered someone's business law book. Ray is legally considered a *finder,* and his rights depend upon the legal status of the book.

The book might be considered **abandoned property,** discarded goods in which the owner has voluntarily relinquished all his interest. If the book was found in a wastebasket, it is likely that the book would be considered *abandoned,* and Ray, the finder, would now own the book.

But the book might also be classified as **lost property,** goods in a place where they were not intentionally put by the owner, who does not know where they are. If the book were accidentally dropped in the hall by the owner, it would be considered *lost* property. The book might also be considered **mislaid property,** goods which the owner has voluntarily laid down and forgotten where they were laid. If the owner laid the book on a windowsill and then forgot where it was laid, it would be considered *mislaid* property. With both *lost* and *mislaid* property, the owner retains his right to the goods.

However, the finder, as an *involuntary* bailee,[1] has a right to the goods which is superior to everyone in the world except that of the owner. If the owner never reclaims the goods, the finder may keep them. In other words, the rule is "finders keepers," although the losers are not weepers if the losers reclaim the goods! In the following case the finder of jewelry prevailed over a person to whom the finder bailed the goods, who refused to return the goods to the finder.

abandoned property
discarded goods in which the owner has voluntarily relinquished all interest

lost property
goods in a place where they were not put by the owner who does not know where they are

mislaid property
goods which the owner has voluntarily laid down and forgotten where they were laid

Facts
A chimney sweep found a piece of jewelry. He delivered it to a jeweler to have it appraised. The jeweler's apprentice removed the jewels and refused to return them to the chimney sweep. The chimney sweep sued the jeweler for the value of the jewels.

Decision
The chimney sweep wins.

Reasoning
A finder has rights of ownership against everyone but the real owner.

Armory v. Delamire, 1 Strange 505, 93 Eng. Rep. 664 (1722).

Owner of the Locus in Quo
Although as a general rule the finder's rights to the goods are superior to all but the owner, the rule often has no effect when the goods are discovered on private property. The owner of the private property is called the owner of the **locus in quo,** which means the "place in which" the goods are found. If the owner of the *locus* can prove any one of five tests, he will be considered the *involuntary* bailee and, if the owner never appears, will keep the goods.

locus in quo
the place in which

First, the owner of the *locus* will prevail if the goods are found in a *private area* on the property. The reason for this rule is that the owner of the *locus* is considered to have taken constructive possession of the goods in the private area. For example, if goods are found in a bank in a private room used to open safe deposit boxes, the bank has the better right to possession of the goods. But if the goods are found in an area open to the public, such as the bank lobby, the finder has the better right to possession.

---

[1] While a finder is not a bailee because the goods have not been delivered to him and there is no understanding with the owner, nevertheless, the law imposes a duty upon him involuntarily to exercise the care of a bailee.

Second, if the finder is an *employee* with a duty to turn goods over to the employer, the employer will have the superior right to possession, as is illustrated by the following case.

Facts

A chambermaid in a hotel discovered eight $100 bills hidden beneath the paper lining of a dresser drawer. She turned the bills over to the owner of the hotel. When the owner of the money could not be located, the chambermaid asked the hotel owner to return the bills and, when he refused, she sued him.

Decision

The hotel owner wins.

Reasoning

The chambermaid, as an employee of the owner of the *locus,* was simply performing her duties in turning the money over to her employer. She had been expressly instructed to take such property to the desk clerk.

Jackson v. Steinberg, 200 P.2d 376 (Or. 1948).

Third, courts generally hold for the owner of the *locus* if the goods are *mislaid.* The reason for this rule is that the owner of the goods is likely to remember where he left mislaid property and to return to that spot. If he does, the owner of the *locus* would be holding it for him. This principle could have been used to decide the *Jackson* case above.

Fourth, courts will hold for the owner of the *locus* if the property has been buried in the ground. In some states, however, if the property is **treasure trove,** the finder will have the superior right to possession. *Treasure trove* is defined as buried treasure such as gold, silver, or money. The following case involving buried property was decided in favor of the owner of the *locus.*

treasure trove
buried treasure

Facts

Plaintiffs, while swimming in the Chariton River, discovered a twenty-seven foot prehistoric Indian canoe, one-third of which was embedded in the soil. They sued the owner of the *locus in quo* to recover possession of the canoe.

Decision

The owner of the *locus in quo* wins.

Reasoning

The canoe is considered to be property embedded in the soil. In such cases the finder has no rights in the property.

Allred v. Biegel, 219 S.W.2d 665 (Mo. 1949).

Fifth, courts will hold for the owner of the *locus* if the finders are *trespassers.* This rule is discussed in the *Bishop v. Ellsworth* case at the end of this chapter.

Personal Property and Bailments

Summary Statement

1. Bailment law is important both to business and the consumer. Bailment questions often arise when you park a car in a parking lot, leave goods in a safe deposit box, or hang your coat in a store or restaurant.
2. A bailment is a delivery of goods by one person, bailor, to another person, bailee, with the understanding that the bailee is to return the goods to the bailor or deliver them to a third person, as directed by the bailor or as previously agreed.
3. If a bailment is for the sole benefit of the bailor, the bailee owes a duty of minimal care of the goods. A bailee in a bailment for mutual benefit owes a duty of ordinary care. In a bailment for the sole benefit of the bailee, the bailee must exercise extraordinary care.
4. A bailee may disclaim liability only if the bailor agreed to the disclaimer, the language of the disclaimer is clear, and the disclaimer does not violate public policy.
5. A bailee must bear the cost of ordinary expenses while the bailor must pay for extraordinary expenses, unless the contract provides otherwise.
6. The finder of lost or mislaid goods has superior right to the goods against everyone but the true owner. However, if the goods are found on someone else's property, the owner of the property will usually have rights superior to the finder.

In the following well-reasoned case the court discussed several of the issues noted in the text regarding the right to lost property. The court also summarized a typical state statute which can often be used by a finder to obtain rights which are superior to those of the person who lost the property.

Bishop v. Ellsworth
234 N.E.2d 49 (Ill. 1968)

Stouder, Presiding Justice. Dwayne Bishop, plaintiff, filed a complaint alleging that on July 21, 1965, defendants, Mark and Jeff Ellsworth and David Giboon, three small boys, entered his salvage yard premises at 427 Mulberry Street in Canton, without his permission, and while there happened upon a bottle partially imbedded in the loose earth on top of a landfill, wherein they discovered the sum of $12,590.00 in United States currency. It is further alleged that said boys delivered the money to the municipal chief of police, who deposited it with defendant, Canton State Bank. The complaint also alleges defendants caused preliminary notices to be given as required by Ill. Rev. Stat., Chap. 50, Subsections 27 and 28 (1965), but that such statute or compliance therewith does not affect the rights of the plaintiff. The complaint then prays that the court appoint a **guardian ad litem** for the minor defendants and adjudicate "the rights of the parties hereto with respect to [the] currency hereinabove mentioned." To this complaint, an attorney, on behalf of the next friends and natural guardians of the minor defendants, filed a motion to dismiss on the grounds that no cause of action is stated. The trial court, after hearing arguments, sustained this motion, and after ascertaining, at the same time, that plaintiff admitted to no claim except as theretofore set forth in the

guardian ad litem
guardian for the legal action, appointed by a court

complaint, denied him leave to amend. Plaintiff has perfected this appeal from the order dismissing his complaint and denying his request for leave to amend.

It is plaintiff's contention that an owner or person in possession of land has a right of possession also to all property in, on and under it, against all but the rightful owner, and that the complaint herein, alleging that defendants, as trespassers, took the money from plaintiff's private grounds, is sufficient in law to state a claim to the possession of the discovered property. It is defendant's contention that the provisions of Ill. Rev. Stat., Chap. 50, Subsections 27 and 28 govern this case. The relevant portions of this statute are as follows:

27. Lost goods. . . . If any person or persons find any lost goods, money, bank notes, or other choses in action, of any description whatever, such person or persons shall inform the owner thereof, if known, and shall make restitution of the same, without any compensation whatever, except the same shall be voluntarily given on the part of the owner. If the owner be unknown, and if such property found is of the value of $15 or upwards, the finder . . . shall, within five days after such finding . . . appear before some judge or magistrate . . . and make affidavit of the description thereof, the time and place when and where the same was found, that no alteration has been made in the appearance thereof since the finding of the same, that the owner thereof is unknown to him and that he has not secreted, withheld or disposed of any part thereof. The judge or magistrate shall enter the value of the property found as near as he can ascertain in his estray book together with the affidavit of the finder, and shall also, within ten days after the proceedings have been entered on his estray book, transmit to the county clerk a certified copy thereof, to be by him recorded in his estray book and to file the same in his office. . . .

28. Advertisement. . . . If the value thereof exceeds the sum of $15, the county clerk, within twenty days after receiving the certified copy of the judge or magistrate's estray record shall cause an advertisement to be set up on the court house door, and in three other of the most public places in the county, and also a notice thereof to be published for three weeks successively in some public newspaper printed in this state and if the owner of such goods, money, bank notes, or other choses in action does not appear and claim the same and pay the finder's charges and expenses within one year after the advertisement thereof as aforesaid, the ownership of such property shall vest in the finder.

Defendants assert that their initiation of proceedings in accord with the foregoing statute, which is admitted in the complaint, establishes the superiority of their claim, as a matter of law. Defendants also argue that the Common Law and majority of jurisdictions adhere to the rule which favors the finder of personal property against all others but the real owner.

We think it apparent that the statute to which defendants make reference provides a means of vesting title to lost property in the finder where the prescribed search for the owner proves fruitless. This statute does not purport to provide for the disposition of property deemed mislaid or abandoned nor does it purport to describe or determine the right to possession against any party other than the true owner. The plain meaning of this statute does not support plaintiff's position that Common Law is wholly abrogated thereby. The provisions of the statute are designed to provide a procedure whereby the discoverer of "lost" property may be vested with the ownership of said property even as against the true owner thereof, a right which theretofore did not exist at Common Law. In the absence of any language in the statute from which the contrary can be inferred, it must be assumed that the term "lost" was used in its generally accepted legal sense and no extension of the term was intended. Thus the right to possession of discovered property still depends upon the relative rights of the discoverer and

Personal Property and Bailments

the owner of the locus in quo and the distinctions which exist between property which is abandoned, mislaid, lost or is treasure trove. The statute assumes that the discoverer is in the rightful possession of lost property, and proceedings under such statute is not a bar where the issue is a claim to the contrary.

There is a presumption that the owner or occupant of land or premises has custody of property found on it or actually imbedded in the land. . . . The ownership or possession of the locus in quo is related to the right to possession of property discovered thereon or imbedded therein in two respects. First, if the premises on which the property is discovered are private, it is deemed that the property discovered thereon is and always has been in the constructive possession of the owner of said premises, and in a legal sense the property can be neither mislaid nor lost. . . . Second, the question of whether the property is mislaid or lost in a legal sense depends upon the intent of the true owner. The ownership or possession of the premises is an important factor in determining such intent. If the property be determined to be mislaid, the owner of the premises is entitled to the possession thereof against the discoverer. It would also appear that if the discoverer is a trespasser, such trespasser can have no claim to possession of such property even if it might otherwise be considered lost. . . .

. . . The facts as alleged in substance are that the plaintiff was the owner and in possession of real estate, that the money was discovered in a private area of said premises in a bottle partially imbedded in the soil, and that such property was removed from the premises by the finders without any right or authority and in effect as trespassers. We believe the averment of facts in the complaint substantially informs the defendants of the nature of and basis for the claim and is sufficient to state a cause of action.

The judgment of the Circuit Court of Fulton County is reversed and the cause is remanded with directions to proceed in accordance with this opinion.

Judgment reversed and remanded with directions.

Questions and Case Problems

1. The plaintiff left his car with the defendant parking lot, a bailee. The plaintiff's golf clubs were in the trunk of the car but plaintiff did not tell defendant of their presence. The car was stolen and later recovered but the golf clubs were missing. Is the defendant bailee liable for the clubs? [*Allen v. Houserman*, 250 A.2d 389 (Del. 1969).]

2. Baer shipped merchandise to Slater, a salesman, who was to sell the merchandise. Baer later directed Slater to return the merchandise to Baer. Slater delivered the merchandise to a person dressed in an American Railway Express uniform who gave Slater a receipt and who was to deliver the goods to Baer. The person was an imposter who left with the goods and has not been seen again. Is Slater liable to Baer for the goods? [*Baer v. Slater*, 158 N.E. 328 (Mass. 1927).]

3. The Freeds delivered their household furniture to Barrett for storage at 618 I. Street, Washington, D.C. Barrett later moved the goods to another address, where they were destroyed by fire. Barrett was in no way negligent. The warehouse receipt which Barrett gave the Freeds stated that he would not be liable for loss by fire. Is he liable for the loss? [*Barrett v. Freed*, 35 A.2d 180 (D.C. 1943).]

4. The plaintiff delivered his registered Tennessee Walking mare, a show horse, to the defendant's stables for breeding. The defendant was warned that the mare was skittish and would kick. The defendant placed the mare in a stall next to a stallion. After she was left unattended for 18 minutes, the mare was found steaming wet and breathing hard. Her leg was broken and she had to be destroyed. No one knew how the injury occurred. Is the defendant liable? [*David v. Lose,* 218 N.E.2d 442 (Ohio 1966).]

5. Healy checked his handbag in the parcel room of a railroad company. He was given a receipt which stated that the company would not be liable for any loss or damage in excess of $10. The wording on the receipt was not pointed out to Healy, and he put the receipt in his pocket without reading it. The clerk later mistakenly gave Healy's handbag, which was worth $70, to another person and it was not recovered. Is the railroad liable for $70? [*Healy v. New York Cent. & H.R.R.,* 138 N.Y.Supp. 287 (1912), aff'd 105 N.E. 1086 (1914).] (1914).]

6. A motorist parked her car in a parking lot and was instructed by an attendant to leave her keys in the car so that it could be moved. The motorist was given a ticket which stated that the parking lot would not be liable for any loss, regardless of the cause. The motorist was not warned of the printed condition on the parking ticket. The car was stolen and was later recovered in a damaged condition. Is the parking lot company liable for the damages? [*Agricultural Insurance Co. v. Constantine,* 58 N.E.2d 658 (Ohio 1944).]

7. A student enrolled in a flight school. While on a practice flight at 900 feet, the student discovered that a rudder was stuck and that he could not straighten the plane. The plane struck the ground at a 45-degree angle and the student was seriously injured. It was later discovered that a screwdriver had been left in the plane below the floorboard and had caused the rudder to stick. Is the flight school liable? [*Aircraft Sales & Service, Inc. v. Gantt,* 52 So.2d 388 (Ala. 1951).]

8. In 1622 a Spanish treasure galleon, the "Nuestra Senora de Atocha," sank and came to rest on the continental shelf outside the territorial waters of the United States. Private treasure finders recently discovered the ship, but the United States filed a claim under statutes which give the United States jurisdiction over the continental shelf. Who is entitled to the ship? [*Treasure Salvors, Inc. v. Unidentified Wrecked and Abandoned Sailing Vessel,* 569 F.2d 330 (1978).]

9. The plaintiff rented a safe deposit box from a bank. One day she visited the bank, removed the box, and entered a private booth in a restricted area. In the booth she discovered a $100 bill tucked in an advertising folder which she removed from a rack. She turned the bill over to the bank and it was never claimed. Who is entitled to the money? [*Dolitsky v. Dollar Sav. Bank,* 118 N.Y.Supp.2d 65 (1952).]

10. In *Bishop v. Ellsworth,* 234 N.E.2d 49 (Ill. 1968),[2] the court refused to give ownership of found property to trespassers. How does this result illustrate the complementary nature of substantive areas of law?

---

[2] See pp. 325–27.

Personal Property and Bailments

Carriers, Documents of Title, and Innkeepers

21

After you have read this chapter, you should be able to:

1. Discuss the liability of a common carrier.
2. List five exceptions to the general rule governing liability of the common carrier.
3. Determine when the exceptional liability of the common carrier begins.
4. Define the term "document of title."
5. Discuss the rights of a purchaser of a document of title after due negotiation.
6. Summarize the liability of a common carrier to passengers.
7. Compare the liability of a common carrier to that of an innkeeper.

Introduction

The general principles of bailment law were discussed in chapter 20. While bailment law affects each of us personally, certain bailment situations are especially important to the person in business.

In this chapter, three of these business bailments are examined—those involving delivery of goods to a common carrier, to a warehouseman, and to an innkeeper. These bailments are unique for two major reasons. *First,* under the common law, the common carrier and the innkeeper were absolutely or strictly liable as insurers for lost or damaged property. Exceptions to this rule and statutory modification will be explored below.

Second, it is usual for common carriers and warehousemen to issue receipts, called *documents of title,* when they receive goods. These receipts are of special legal importance because they represent the contract between the bailor and bailee, and often the purchaser of the document acquires greater rights than the seller. Two documents of title, the bill of lading and the warehouse receipt, are discussed in this chapter.

These bailments are a necessary part of everyday business experience, and the law covering them is, therefore, important.

Common Carrier of Goods

Defined

After graduating from college, Rollo accepted a job in Chicago and began to make arrangements for moving his personal belongings. Eventually Rollo discovered that he had two options for moving his goods: (1) he could hire a professional moving company, or (2) his friend Sam could move the goods in his pickup truck free.

common carrier
a carrier which offers its services to the general public for a fee

private carrier
a carrier which does not offer its services to the general public

In legal terms, Rollo must choose between a **common carrier** and a **private carrier,** and his choice will become important if the goods are lost or destroyed enroute. A common carrier is a carrier which offers its services to the public and charges a fee; if either of those two elements is missing the carrier is considered to be a private carrier. Thus, Rollo's friend would be classified as a private carrier, while the moving company would be considered a common carrier.

Liability

There are two reasons why the distinction between common and private carriers is important. First, a *common carrier must* accept and deliver goods of the type it normally ships from any member of the public, while a *private carrier* is *free* to pick and choose its customers. Second, and more important, a *private carrier* is liable only for loss caused by its *negligence,* as an *ordinary bailee.* The *common carrier,* however, is said to be absolutely liable as an *insurer* of the goods and will be held liable for *any* loss unless it can prove one of the following five exceptions to liability.

Act of God. If the goods are destroyed by an act of God, the carrier will not be liable. An **act of God** is generally defined as an unexpected force of nature, such as an earthquake or lightning which can not be prevented or avoided. However, if the loss resulted from a combination of an act of God and *human* error, the carrier remains liable as an insurer. In the following case the common carrier was liable for damage caused by human error.

Facts

A shipper contracted with a common carrier for the shipment of cucumbers from Nogales, Arizona to Los Angeles, California. The produce was damaged when the shipment was delayed as the result of unusually heavy rains. The carrier waited for one week after the rainfall before it dispatched an employee to inspect the track on January 25. He discovered that certain railroad bridges had fallen into the water. By January 28 the damage was repaired and the cucumbers then departed for Los Angeles. The shipper claims that the carrier is liable for over $10,000 because the cucumbers were not delivered within the usual time.

Decision

The carrier is liable.

Reasoning

The carrier's delay for one week in dispatching the employee to avoid the consequences of the rainfall contributed to the loss. Also, the carrier offered no proof that the rainfall was of such unusual intensity or duration as to be considered an act of God.

Southern Pacific Company v. Loden, 508 P.2d 347 (Ariz. 1973).

Act of Public Enemy. A carrier is not liable for the acts of a public enemy. The term *public enemy* is defined narrowly to include only a foreign nation at war with the United States, pirates on the high seas, and in some cases rebels in insurrection against the government. Today piracy would probably include piracy by aircraft. The following case held that domestic criminals are not public enemies.

Facts

A shipper delivered goods to a common carrier. While the goods were being shipped, the truck on which they were loaded was hijacked on the streets of New York City. The shipper claims the carrier is liable for the loss. The carrier's defense is that the loss resulted from the act of a public enemy.

Decision

The shipper wins.

Reasoning

Domestic criminals are not public enemies under the exception to common carrier liability, even when they have been designated "public enemies" by the F.B.I.

David Crystal Inc. v. Ehrlich-Newmark Trucking Co., 64 Misc.2d 325 (N.Y. 1970).

Act of the Shipper.   Widget Corporation has just received an order for 1000 crystal widgets, which are to be shipped by railroad. An employee of Widget carelessly packs the crystal widgets so that they all are shattered while being shipped by the railroad. Widget Corporation now claims that the railroad is liable as an insurer on the **consignment.**

As a general rule a common carrier, the railroad, is not liable for losses caused by the acts of the shipper—the **consignor.** However, there are two long-recognized exceptions to this rule. *First,* if the loss was caused in part by the negligence of the common carrier, the carrier must bear the full loss. The fact that the shipper was contributorily negligent is irrelevant because the carrier is not being sued for committing the tort of negligence but, instead, as an insurer. In our case, if the engineer accidentally stopped the train too quickly and, as a result, the poorly packed widgets were damaged, the carrier would be liable. *A common carrier is liable for loss caused by its negligence as well as for loss as an insurer.*

Second, common carriers are liable as insurers in cases when they *know* that the shipper has been careless in packing or loading the goods. Thus, if the railroad has inspected the boxes and knew that they were defectively packed or if the railroad knew that Widget Corporation was careless in loading the boxes, the carrier would be absolutely liable for resulting losses.

Inherent Nature of the Goods.   In many cases the inherent nature of the goods will result in damage or destruction while the goods are being shipped. For instance, goods such as molasses will be damaged through natural fermentation, certain metals will become rusted or corroded, perishable fruits will deteriorate, and animals will die during shipment. In each of these cases the common carrier will not be liable unless the carrier's own negligence was a contributing factor. In the following case the damage to goods was not caused by the inherent nature of the goods.

Facts
A shipper shipped crates of honeydew melons from Rio Grande City, Texas to Chicago, Illinois. The melons were in good condition when they were delivered to the common carrier, but 640 crates of melons were damaged upon arrival in Chicago even though the carrier was not negligent. The shipper now claims that the carrier is liable for the loss.

Decision
The carrier is liable.

Reasoning
The carrier bears the burden of proving the cause of the loss. In this case, the carrier did not prove that the loss resulted from the inherent nature of the goods.

Missouri Pacific R.R. v. Elmore & Stahl, 377 U.S. 134 (1964).

Act of Public Authorities.   A common carrier is not liable for failure to deliver the goods because of the act of a public authority. For example, *a writ of execution* is a court order which authorizes a sheriff to seize property in order to satisfy a court judgment. If a sheriff seizes property from the carrier because the shipper has failed to pay a court judgment, the carrier would not be liable. However, the carrier should notify the shipper of the execution so that the shipper may take appropriate legal action to defend itself.

Scope of Carriage

Beginning of Carriage.   A **warehouseman** is a person who stores goods in a warehouse in return for compensation. When goods are stored in a warehouse, a bailment for mutual benefit is created and the warehouseman has a duty of ordinary care. In many cases a common carrier will act as a warehouseman in storing goods either before or after shipment and, as such, will be liable as a bailee rather than as an insurer.

> **warehouseman**
> a person in the business of storing goods for a fee

To illustrate, Mary works for a banana company and wants to ship 1000 crates of bananas from Tampa to a buyer, Tom, in Phoenix. She delivers 600 crates to the common carrier, a railroad, and asks the carrier to delay shipment until she delivers the other 400 crates. Before she completes the delivery, the 600 crates are stolen by thieves. If the railroad proves that it exercised ordinary care, is it still liable as an insurer?

The test to be applied in such cases is: Must the shipper do something else before the goods can be shipped? If so, the carrier is only liable as a bailee. But if the shipper has done everything necessary for shipment, the carrier is liable as an insurer. Thus, where the shipper has not yet told the carrier where the goods are to be shipped or, as in Mary's case, the shipper has not yet completed delivery of the goods to the carrier, the carrier is a warehouseman-bailee and is liable only for not exercising ordinary care. When goods are delivered to a common carrier for *immediate shipment,* there is a **shipper-carrier** relationship between the shipper and the carrier, who is now liable as an insurer.

> **shipper-carrier**
> a legal relationship between the shipper and the common carrier when goods have been delivered to the carrier for immediate shipment

Termination of Carriage.   A similar problem exists after the goods have arrived at the destination point. If the 1000 crates of bananas arrived in Phoenix but, before the buyer, Tom, could pick them up, they were stolen from the carrier by thieves, would the railroad be considered an insurer or a warehouseman-bailee?

The answer usually depends on the contract in each case. If the contract is silent, or if the contract specifies that delivery is to be made *to Tom's company,* the railroad would be liable as a carrier until the goods are delivered to Tom or, at least, until the carrier has made reasonable efforts to deliver the bananas to Tom.

However, if the contract or the local business custom dictates that Tom is *to pick up* the goods at the station, the carrier must unload the crates in the depot so that they are ready to be picked up by Tom. In a few states, once this has been done, the railroad's liability is that of a bailee. However, most state courts have decided that the railroad does not achieve bailee status until the **consignee** has had a reasonable chance to pick them up or until the railroad notifies the consignee that the goods have arrived and the consignee has had an opportunity to pick them up.

> **consignee**
> one to whom goods are shipped

Limitation of Liability

If goods are shipped *interstate,* the *federal* Interstate Commerce Act governs attempts by the common carrier to limit its liability. Under this Act carriers may not limit their liability, with two exceptions: (1) liability may be limited for damage to *baggage* carried on passenger trains and boats; and (2) a carrier may establish *rates* which are dependent upon the value of the goods being shipped. The second exception has the effect of limiting liability because the shipper will only be allowed to recover *up to* the value *declared* by him if the goods are lost or damaged. For example, if the declared value is $1000 and the loss or damage is $600, the carrier will be liable only for $600.

If the goods are not shipped interstate, the *state* rule in most cases is found in section 7–309 of the Uniform Commercial Code. Under this section, a common or private carrier who issues a bill of lading—which will be discussed below under Documents of Title—must at least act with reasonable care. However, as under federal law, the carrier may limit damages by providing that its liability is limited to the value stated by the shipper, provided that rates are dependent on value and that the shipper is given the chance to declare a higher value. In the following case the shipper did not declare any value and could recover only for the common carrier's maximum fixed rate for goods which were stolen from the carrier.

Facts

A suitcase was delivered to a common carrier in New York City for delivery in Jacksonville, Florida. The shipper selected the lowest freight rate available, with a maximum carrier liability of $10. The contents of the suitcase were stolen enroute, and the shipper sought to recover from the carrier the actual value of the property.

Decision

The carrier was liable only for $10.

Reasoning

Carriers may limit their liability by establishing rates based on valuations. Classifications and tariffs filed by carriers with the Interstate Commerce Commission have the force of law and, therefore, shippers are presumed to know the relation between the values and the rates charged.

Kaufman v. Penn. R.R., 47 N.Y.Supp.2d 639 (1944).

Documents of Title

Definition

warehouse receipt
a document issued to the bailor by a warehouseman

bill of lading
a document issued to the shipper by a carrier

document of title
a document evidencing that the person possessing it is entitled to receive, hold, and dispose of the document and the goods it covers

If Herman delivers his furniture to a warehouseman for storage, the warehouseman will give him a receipt for the furniture called a **warehouse receipt.** If Herman delivered the goods to a carrier for shipment, he would receive a receipt called a **bill of lading.** Both the warehouse receipt and the bill of lading are **documents of title** and, as such, are more than mere receipts. Documents of title normally spell out the terms of the contract between Herman and the bailee, and in many cases a person who has possession of the document is the only one entitled to recover the goods from the bailee.

Personal Property and Bailments

Figure 21.1 Negotiable Bill of Lading (Front)

FORM 1585

(Uniform Domestic Order Bill of Lading, adopted by Carriers in Official, Southern, Western and Illinois Classification Territories, March 15, 1922, as amended August 1, 1930, and June 15, 1941.)

9-66— 15M Sets
1st SHEET

UNIFORM ORDER BILL OF LADING
ORIGINAL

Shipper's No._____

Agent's No. _____

UNION PACIFIC RAILROAD COMPANY

RECEIVED, subject to the classifications and tariffs in effect on the date of the issue of this Bill of Lading,

at_____ 19____

from_____

the property described below, in apparent good order, except as noted (contents and condition of contents of packages unknown), marked, consigned, and destined as indicated below, which said company (the word company being understood throughout this contract as meaning any person or corporation in possession of the property under the contract) agrees to carry to its usual place of delivery at said destination, if on its own road or its own water line, otherwise to deliver to another carrier on the route to said destination. It is mutually agreed, as to each carrier of all or any of said property over all or any portion of said route to destination, and as to each party at any time interested in all or any of said property, that every service to be performed hereunder shall be subject to all the conditions not prohibited by law, whether printed or written, herein contained, including the conditions on back hereof, which are hereby agreed to by the shipper and accepted for himself and his assigns.

The surrender of this Original ORDER Bill of Lading properly indorsed shall be required before the delivery of the property. Inspection of property covered by this Bill of Lading will not be permitted unless provided by law or unless permission is indorsed on this Original Bill of Lading or given in writing by the shipper.

Consigned to **ORDER OF**_____

Destination_____ State of_____ County of_____

Notify_____

At_____ State of_____ County of_____

Route_____

Delivering Carrier_____Car Initial_____Car No._____

No. Packages	DESCRIPTION OF ARTICLES, SPECIAL MARKS, AND EXCEPTIONS	*WEIGHT (Subject to Correction)	CLASS OR RATE	CHECK COLUMN	
					Subject to Section 7 of conditions, if this shipment is to be delivered to the consignee without recourse on the consignor, the consignor shall sign the following statement:
					The carrier shall not make delivery of this shipment without payment of freight and all other lawful charges.
					(Signature of Consignor)
					If charges are to be prepaid, write or stamp here, "To be Prepaid."
					Received $_____ to apply in prepayment of the charges on the property described hereon.
					Agent or Cashier.
					Per_____
					(The signature here acknowledges only the amount prepaid.)
					Charges Advanced:

*If the shipment moves between two ports by a carrier by water, the law requires that the bill of lading shall state whether it is "carrier's or shipper's weight."
NOTE—Where the rate is dependent on value, shippers are required to state specifically in writing the agreed or declared value of the property.
The agreed or declared value of the property is hereby specifically stated by the shipper to be not exceeding

$_____

_____ per _____

_____Shipper. _____Agent

Per_____ Per_____

Permanent postoffice address of shipper_____

COURTESY, SAFETY AND RELIABLE SERVICE

Figure 21.2   Non-negotiable Warehouse Receipt (Front)

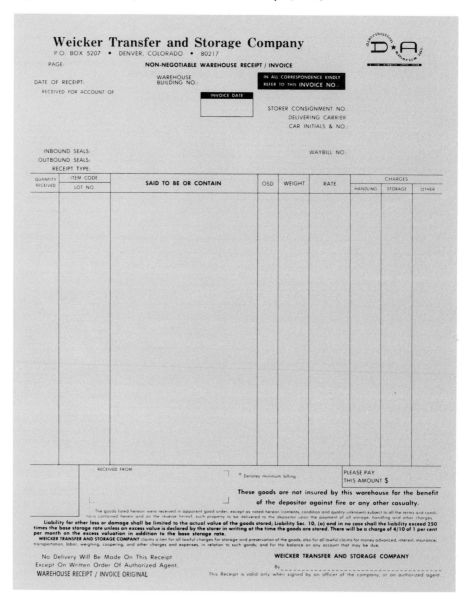

Personal Property and Bailments

Negotiation

Documents of title fall into two categories—they are either negotiable or non-negotiable. A **negotiable document** *of title* is one which states that the goods are to be delivered either to *bearer,* meaning any person in possession of the document, or to the *order* of someone. If neither of these requirements is met, the document is non-negotiable. Thus, if the warehouse receipt stated that the goods are to be delivered "to the order of Herman," it is negotiable. If it states that the goods are to be delivered "to Herman," it is non-negotiable.

The difference between a negotiable and a non-negotiable document of title has an important consequence for the bailee. If the document is negotiable, the goods must be delivered to the *holder* of the document—namely, the person who has possession of the document which flows to him either originally or by indorsement. If the document is non-negotiable, the goods must usually be delivered to the person named in the document.

Furthermore, if Herman's document of title is negotiable, Herman must follow certain procedures to *duly negotiate* it to his friend Fred. If the document is **bearer** paper, it is negotiated by simple delivery to Fred. If the document is order paper, Herman must first indorse the document and then deliver it to Fred. In either case, Fred must purchase the document as a holder in good faith without notice of any claim or defense to the document and must pay value in order to claim **due negotiation.** If Fred were to purchase the document as payment for a *past money debt* owing to him by Herman, Fred would not be giving value. Fred must also purchase the document in the regular course of business or financing.

If there is due negotiation, the holder usually takes the document, and the goods, free of claims and defenses, raised by the bailee or third persons. However, there are two major exceptions to the protection given to the purchaser of a document of title. *First,* the bailee is entitled to compensation for transportation or storage charges, which is usually specified on the document or in tariffs filed by the carrier. *Second,* the holder will not be entitled to the goods in cases where the *bailor* had no authority to deliver the goods to the bailee carrier or warehouseman. For example, if a *thief* stole Herman's furniture, delivered it to a warehouseman, and then duly negotiated the warehouse receipt to Fred, Herman would still have a right to the furniture superior to that of Fred. The reason is that *Herman* never put the goods in the stream of commerce. The second exception does not apply in cases where *Herman* delivered the goods to the warehouse and received a warehouse receipt which a thief then stole from Herman and duly negotiated to Fred. Under the Uniform Commercial Code, section 7–502(2), rights acquired by a holder after due negotiation are not impaired even though a prior "person has been deprived of possession of the document by misrepresentation, fraud, accident, mistake, duress, loss, theft or conversion."

Nonconformity of Goods to the Receipt

Clara has just purchased a bill of lading from the consignee, the person to whom goods are shipped. The bill of lading describes the goods being shipped as "5 packages of class B Widgets." When Clara delivers the bill of lading to the carrier, she is advised that only four packages were shipped. May Clara recover damages from the carrier for the value of the missing package?

The answer to this question will vary, depending on the circumstances. In most cases, a good-faith purchaser for value may recover damages from the bailee unless the document indicates that the bailee does not know whether the goods were received or conform to the description. Consequently, Clara could not recover if the bill of lading states "contents unknown" or "said to contain" or "shipper's load, weight and count" if these statements were, in fact, true. In the following case the common carrier was not liable for damage to goods on a shipper's load and count movement.

Facts
A shipper delivered goods to a carrier for delivery to a buyer. The carrier gave the shipper a "clean" bill of lading—that is, the bill of lading contained no mention that the goods were damaged. The shipment was a shipper's load and count movement. The goods arrived in a damaged condition and the shipper claims that the carrier is liable.

Decision
The carrier is not liable.

Reasoning
The shipper never proved delivery of goods to the carrier in good condition. This was a shipper's load and count movement and, in fact, the carrier had no knowledge of the contents or condition of the goods.

United Steel & Strip Corp. v. Monex Corp., 310 So.2d 339 (Fla. 1975).

The result might be different, however, if the bailee issued a correct document of title which is later *altered* by someone without authority. If a *bill of lading* is filled in or otherwise altered without authority, the carrier is liable only according to the *original terms* of the document, *irrespective* of whether it is negotiable or non-negotiable. The same rule is true for warehouse receipts except that when a *blank* is filled in on a *negotiable warehouse receipt,* a purchaser for value may enforce the receipt *as completed,* even though it was completed without authority.

Sale by the Bailee
Suppose that Herman delivered his furniture to a warehouse and the warehouseman, without permission, sold Herman's furniture to Claude and then left the country. May Herman recover his furniture from Claude? In most cases, the bailor, Herman, will win because the bailee had no title to convey to Claude. There is one exception to the rule under the Uniform Commercial Code, section 7–205, which provides that, when a buyer in the ordinary course of business purchases *fungible* goods from a warehouseman who is in the business of buying and selling such goods, the buyer takes free and clear of all claims under a warehouse receipt. Thus, if Herman had delivered grain for storage to a warehouseman who deals in grain and Claude had purchased Herman's grain from

the warehouseman, Claude would prevail even against a person to whom the warehouse receipt has been duly negotiated. The dealer has been given the appearance of being an owner, and his sale to the innocent purchaser transfers the title.

Liens

A **lien** is a legal right in another's property as security for the performance of an obligation. It includes the right of a creditor to have a debt paid from the proceeds of the sale of property. A carrier is given a specific possessory *lien* on the goods described in the bill of lading as security to assure payment for storage and transportation charges. A warehouseman has a *lien* on the goods described in the warehouse receipt as security to assure payment for storage and transportation charges as well as insurance and labor expenses. A *possessory lien* is a lien which includes the right to *possession* of the property which is subject to the lien. A *specific lien* is a lien only on *specific* property for services rendered *to that* property.

Under UCC 7–210 and 7–308 both the carrier and the warehouseman may enforce the lien by public or private sale of the goods in a commercially reasonable manner after notifying all persons known to claim an interest in the goods. Additionally, in cases where the bailor is not a merchant, the warehouseman must also publish an advertisement of the sale once a week for two consecutive weeks in a newspaper in the place where the sale is to be held, and the sale must take place at least fifteen days after the first publication. If the sale of goods brings more than the amount due the bailee, the bailee must hold the balance for the person who was to have received the goods.

lien
a legal right in another's property as security for the performance of an obligation

Warranties

When a person sells a document of title, by law he gives the purchaser the usual warranties made when someone sells goods, discussed in Part 5, Sales. But additionally, the seller warrants that: (1) the document is genuine; (2) the seller knows of no fact that impairs its validity or worth; and (3) the negotiation is rightful and effective. However, an intermediary which is entrusted with a document of title, such as a collecting bank, warrants only that it is acting in good faith with authority.

Common Carrier of Passengers

The common carrier of passengers faces two main legal concerns. *First,* the carrier faces possible liability for injuries to passengers during the course of the journey. The general rule is that the carrier is not liable as an insurer for every injury suffered by passengers, but the carrier does owe the highest degree of care to passengers. In the following case a woman was a "passenger" while walking on the station platform to the train.

Facts

A woman waited on an elevated platform for a train. As the train arrived, she walked toward the train but fell when the heels of her shoes caught in spaces between the wooden planks of the platform. The woman claims the railroad is liable for damages of $27,500. The railroad defends by claiming that it owed only a duty of ordinary care, which was met here since the railroad had no knowledge of the condition which caused the injury.

Decision

The woman won.

Reasoning

The railroad owed the highest degree of care to the woman, who was a passenger. A person does not have to be in physical contact with a vehicle in order to be a passenger. The purpose of the law is to increase the duty of care as the danger increases.

Katamay v. Chicago Transit Authority, 289 N.E.2d 623 (Ill. 1972).

Second, the common carrier faces liability as an insurer in cases where a passenger's baggage is lost or damaged. However, in order to recover, the passenger must prove that there was a *bailment* of the baggage. If the passenger retained possession of the baggage during the trip, there would be *no bailment* because the *delivery* requirement is missing. Furthermore, even when there is delivery to the carrier, the carrier is normally not liable for the contents of the baggage unless the contents were for the personal use and convenience of the passenger. This rule prevents unexpected liability on the part of the carrier when a passenger attempts to ship valuables, such as paintings or rare china, as baggage without paying the customary rates for goods of higher value and greater risk to the carrier.

Innkeepers

innkeeper
operator of an establishment engaged in making lodging accommodations available to transients

An **innkeeper** is an operator of a hotel, inn, motel, or any other establishment engaged in making lodging accommodations available to transients.

At common law, the liability of an innkeeper for lost or damaged goods was similar to that of the common carrier: the innkeeper was liable as an insurer of the goods, unless an exception applied, such as loss resulting from an act of God, an act of a public enemy, an act of a public authority, or the inherent nature of the goods.

In most states the common law rule has been changed by statute. Although the statutes vary from state to state, the Florida statute illustrates the extent of statutory modifications of the innkeeper's duty. Under the Florida Statutes, section 509.111, an innkeeper is liable only when the loss resulted from the negligence of the innkeeper or his agent. However, even when the innkeeper is negligent, liability is limited to $100 unless: (1) the guest files an inventory of his property with the innkeeper before the loss, in which case the innkeeper will be liable for up to $500; or (2) the guest deposits goods with the innkeeper for safe keeping, although the innkeeper is allowed to limit his liability to $1000 for such property by inserting a notice in the receipt given the guest. In many states an innkeeper may provide a safe place for valuables and, if notice is given of such facility, the innkeeper's liability for valuables left in that place is as an insurer, but he is liable only as bailee for valuables left in a guest's room. The common law liability of an innkeeper, and the statutory modifications, do not apply when a room is rented to a permanent lodger. A permanent lodger may recover damages only when the owner of the boarding house is negligent.

In order to be protected by statute, the bailee must, in fact, be an innkeeper. In the following case the bailee restaurant was not an innkeeper and, therefore, not protected by the Georgia statute applicable to innkeepers.

Facts
Several persons visited a restaurant. Their car was delivered to a restaurant employee, who parked it in the restaurant parking lot. Several items were removed from the car, and it was claimed that the restaurant was liable. The restaurant claimed that, under a Georgia statute, the liability of an innkeeper was limited to $100.

Decision
The restaurant lost.

Reasoning
The Georgia statute applies only to places which furnish lodging to a guest. A person who only operates a restaurant and bar is not protected by the statute.

Diplomat Restaurant, Inc. v. Townsend, 165 S.E.2d 317 (Ga. 1968).

Summary Statement

1. The liability of a common carrier is unique in bailment law in that the carrier is liable in most cases as an insurer of the goods.
2. A common carrier is not liable for (a) an act of God, (b) an act of a public enemy, (c) an act of the shipper, (d) a loss resulting from the inherent nature of the goods, and (e) an act of public authorities.
3. A common carrier is liable as an ordinary bailee until the shipper has done everything necessary to make the goods ready for shipment (thereby creating a *shipper-carrier relationship*), the carrier then becoming liable as an insurer.
4. A document of title is a receipt given by a warehouseman or common carrier which also serves as the contract between the bailor and the bailee.
5. In most cases, when a document of title has been duly negotiated, the purchaser takes the document free and clear of defenses which could have been raised by the bailee against the bailor, and also free and clear of claims to the document and to the goods by third persons.
6. A common carrier is not liable as an insurer of the safety of passengers; however, the carrier does owe passengers the highest degree of care.
7. Under the common law, an innkeeper was liable as an insurer for guests' belongings which were damaged or destroyed. This liability has been changed by statute in most states.

In the following case the court discussed the common law liability of the innkeeper and problems which arise in interpreting modern statutes.

Federal Insurance Co. v. Waldorf-Astoria Hotel
60 Misc.2d 996 (N.Y. 1969)

Hilda G. Schwartz, Judge. Defendant hotel moves for summary judgment under Section 200 of the General Business Law which provides that the proprietor of a hotel is relieved from liability for loss to a guest of his money, jewels, ornaments, bank notes, bonds, negotiable securities or precious stones, if the hotel provides a place of safekeeping and patrons do not avail themselves of it. Defendant argues that the gold cuff-links lost by plaintiff's subrogors [the original complainants whose claim the plaintiff insurance company acquired by subrogation] satisfied the definition of "jewels" under Sec. 200.

Plaintiff makes a cross-motion for summary judgment, arguing that the articles lost were not "jewels," "ornaments" or "precious stones" within the meaning of Sec. 200, but were articles of ordinary wear carried for use and convenience and not for ornamentation. Plaintiff refers to Sec. 201, General Business Law, which places certain limits, not applicable here, on the common law liability of a hotel keeper for loss of his guests' property.

Both parties agree that . . . the sole question to be determined is whether the missing cuff-links come within the meaning of the words "jewels," "ornaments" or "precious stones" in the statute.

It is not disputed that plaintiff's subrogors were guests of the hotel on May 18 and 19, 1968 and that, at some time between the evening of May 18 and the morning of May 19, they discovered that a nightcase in their hotel room had been opened and a pair of gold cuff-links with a 9 mm. pearl in each, valued at $175, were missing.

At common law, an innkeeper was liable as an insurer of the property of his guests unless the loss was occasioned by the negligence or fault of the guest. . . .

The purpose of Sec. 200, in providing that the hotelkeeper shall not be liable for money, jewels, ornaments, and precious stones if they are not deposited in the hotel safe provided, is to protect the hotel from an undisclosed excessive liability. . . .

Section 200 of the General Business Law, being in derogation of the common law relative to the liability of innkeepers, is strictly construed. . . . The exemption is limited to the particular species of property named and, being strictly construed, cannot be extended in its application by doubtful construction so as to include property not fairly within its terms. "Property . . . which is useful or necessary to the comfort and convenience of the guest, that which is usually carried and worn as a part of the ordinary apparel and outfit . . . is left, as before the statute, at the risk of the innkeeper." . . .

In the *Ramaley v. Leland* case, . . . the plaintiff's gold watch with chain, seal and key attached and fifty dollars in money were stolen from his hotel room. A hotel safe had been provided and a notice posted. As to the money, the Court of Appeals held the defendant not liable. But the defendant hotel was held liable for the loss of the gold watch, chain, seal and key on the ground that a watch is neither a jewel or ornament. A watch is neither a jewel or ornament, as these words are used and understood, either in common parlance or by lexicographers. It is not used or carried as a jewel or ornament, but as a timepiece or chronometer, an article of ordinary wear by most travelers of every class, and of daily and hourly use by all. . . . It is carried for use and convenience and not for ornament.

In *Jones v. Hotel Latham Co., . . .* the Appellate Term held that a watch, chain, purse and rosary, being each an article of use and not worn for ornament, are not "jewels" or "ornaments" within the meaning of the statute. In *Briggs v. Todd, . . .* the court held that silver table forks, a silver soup ladle and an heirloom gold watch were not jewels or ornaments under the statute, and the fact that a state coat of arms was engraved on the watch and a portrait appeared on the inside of the case did not convert it into a jewel or ornament.

A traveling bag finished with a silver mounted set and other silver articles was held not to be an ornament. . . . In *Hart v. Mills Hotel Trust, . . .* it was held that a watch, a gold chain and knife were not jewels or ornaments, within the meaning of Sec. 200 of the General Business Law, and as to them, the defendant hotel was at all times an insurer.

In *Kennedy v. Bowman Biltmore Hotel Corporation, . . .* the article lost from the hotel guest's room was a wrist watch ornamented with diamonds. The court said, "The watch involved while ornamented with diamonds was primarily an article of daily use and not a jewel, ornament or precious stone within the meaning of Section 200 of the General Business Law. . . . Nor would the fact that a broken clasp made it unsafe to wear the watch on the day of its loss change the nature of the article." . . .

By analogy, the cuff-links in suit, even though fashioned of gold and ornamented with a pearl in each, cannot be considered as jewels or ornaments, as these terms are used and understood in common parlance. Black's Law Dictionary defines "jewels" as "an ornament of the person, such as earrings, pearls, diamonds, etc. prepared to be worn . . . , an ornament made of precious metal or a precious stone." Cuff-links are not used as jewels or ornaments but to close the cuffs, otherwise buttonless, of shirts. They are articles of utilitarian and ordinary wear in daily use, on all occasions, with business clothes as well as clothes designed for leisure, in the daytime as well as the evening. They are carried principally for use and convenience and not for ornament. Cuff-links, as with watches and other articles of ordinary wear, may be made of precious metals, and even made more elaborate with precious stones, but these do not change their essential description as articles of ordinary wear.

Section 200 of the General Business Law has modified the hotelkeeper's liability only as to the articles named. Cuff-links, even though made of gold and decorated with a pearl, are articles of use and are not jewels or ornaments within the meaning of Section 200. The defendant hotel is therefore not relieved of liability for their loss despite the failure of the guests to deposit them in the hotel safe provided.

Questions and Case Problems

1. A shipper shipped packaged jewelry from Dallas to New York City on Delta Air Lines. The shipper told Delta that the package contained "printed matter," and the package was not wrapped in accordance with Delta's regulations covering jewelry shipments. The jewelry was lost during shipment, but Delta claims it is not liable because of the shipper's misdescription and improper packaging. Is Delta liable? [*Travelers Insurance Co. v. Delta Air Lines, Inc.*, 498 S.W.2d 443 (Tex. 1973).]

2. A shipper delivered pine seed to a common carrier in Birmingham, Alabama for transport to New Orleans, Louisiana. However, the shipment was delayed when Hurricane Betsey struck New Orleans and later the shipment could not be located. The seed finally turned up at the carrier's home office in Hattiesburg, Mississippi. As a result of the delay, the seed was commercially worthless. Is the carrier liable? [*West Bros. Inc. v. Resource Management Serv., Inc.*, 214 So.2d 431 (Ala. 1968).]

3. A common carrier contracted with a shipper to ship 100 bales of cotton. The shipper delivered 29 bales to the shipping platform and advised the carrier that the remaining 71 bales would be delivered within a few days. A fire destroyed the 29 bales on the platform. Is the carrier absolutely liable for the cotton? [*Rio Grande City Ry. Co. v. Guerra*, 26 S.W.2d 360 (Tex. 1930).]

4. Waldo was moving from Slippery Rock to Pebble Beach. He delivered all of his furniture to a common carrier on Tuesday with instructions to deliver the furniture to Pebble Beach. The carrier advised Waldo that the next shipment to Pebble Beach would leave on Thursday and that the furniture would be placed on that shipment. On Wednesday night the furniture, while on the shipping platform, was destroyed by vandals. Is the carrier liable?

5. A passenger checked a bag and contents worth $2,190 at a room in the railroad station at Portland, Oregon. A railroad employee gave him a receipt which limited the railroad's liability to $25, unless the passenger paid a higher rate. The passenger was unaware of the limitation. When the passenger returned, the bag could not be found. The railroad claimed that the limitation of liability was valid because the rules and regulations governing carriers allowed such contracts. Is the carrier correct? [*Allen v. Southern Pacific Co.*, 213 P.2d 667 (Utah 1950).]

6. A construction company entered into a contract with a railroad to build a section of track. The railroad agreed to ship materials needed for construction to the company at a special rate, but their contract also provided that the common carrier would not be liable for any losses. Is the exemption from liability valid? [*Santa Fe, P. & P. Ry. Co. v. Grant Bros. Const. Co.*, 228 U.S. 177 (1913).]

7. A seventy-year-old passenger was riding on a streetcar. The motorman of the streetcar, in driving through an intersection, had to stop quickly because of an approaching vehicle. The passenger fell to the floor and fractured two vertebrae. Is the streetcar owner liable? [*Dolan v. New Orleans Public Service Inc.*, 317 So.2d 688 (La. 1975).]

8. A seaman was riding on a bus. Four drunken youths entered the bus and sat behind the seaman. They tried to pick his pocket and asked him for money. When he refused, they began to punch and kick him. The driver then stopped the bus, called the police, and ordered the youths off the bus. Is the bus company liable for the seaman's injuries? [*Orr v. New Orleans Public Service Inc.,* 349 So.2d 417 (La. 1977).]

9. The wife of an army general who had no permanent home was residing with him at a hotel. She expected to stay at the hotel from November until the next spring or summer, and they were given a special rate for room rent. The wife's belongings were stolen from her room, and she claimed that, under the common law rule, the innkeeper was liable. Is the innkeeper liable? [*Hancock v. Rand,* 94 N.Y. 1 (1883).]

10. In *Federal Insurance Co. v. Waldorf-Astoria Hotel,* 60 Misc.2d 996 (N.Y. 1969),[1] the court indicated that the statute is in derogation of the common law and must be strictly construed. How does this approach provide flexibility to meet the needs of commerce?

---

[1] See pp. 342–43.

Summary

The legal area of "sales of goods" has come a long way in its development and is still in a developing stage. The factors involved in this development today are: Article 2 on Sales of the Uniform Commercial Code; consumer legislation, both federal and state; and federal and state judicial decisions interpreting and applying the Code and consumer legislation. The Code establishes guidelines and rules of interpretation for merchants and consumers in their sales transactions, in the absence of their agreement to the contrary. In some instances the Code does not permit variation and establishes fixed rules. The first four chapters discuss the history and objectives of the Code and the formation, performance, breach, and remedies in connection with the sales contract for goods. Many changes in the common law of contracts are made by the Code.

However, Article 2 is not enough to reflect the protection needed by the consumer in his dealing with merchants, and particularly in establishing manufacturer liability for defective products. A whole new body of consumer law has exploded suddenly into reality making a startling change in consumer/retailer/manufacturer relations. Chapter 26, Consumer Law, discusses this breakthrough in consumer protection, particularly with respect to the area called "product liability."

22

Introduction to the Uniform Commercial Code

After you have read this chapter, you should be able to:

1. Give the reasons for having a uniform commercial code.
2. Define a code.
3. State the purposes of the UCC.
4. Define the term "merchant."
5. In a short paragraph describe:
   a. the contributions of Professor Karl Llewellyn to the formulation of the UCC.
   b. "goods" and distinguish goods from items or commercial circumstances not covered by Article 2.
   c. the standard of conduct required by Article 2 and explain how this standard of conduct is to be "found" in many cases.
6. Define the statute of frauds and the parol evidence rule under Article 2, and then explain how they apply in real-life situations.

Introduction

Most American automobiles are manufactured in the state of Michigan from parts made in Pennsylvania, Ohio, Minnesota, and other states and then shipped to all states, where they are sold to consumers. If each state had its own different set of commercial rules applicable to the sale of **goods** within its borders, then the thousands of transactions required to produce an automobile would be governed by at least fifty sets of state rules. If this were the case, then our economy and standard of living would not be what they are today. The numerous transactions required to produce an automobile and other complex goods demand that only one set of commercial rules apply to most of the transactions. Such a single set of commercial rules has been formulated and is entitled the Uniform Commercial Code. The Code has been adopted by all the states except Louisiana.[1] It is a response to a business need.

goods
tangible movable things

The Uniform Commercial Code (UCC) has nine substantive Articles. Part 5 of this book will focus primarily upon Article 2, Sales, and will include some explanation of Article 1, General Provisions, and Article 6, Bulk Transfers. Part 6 is concerned with Article 3, Commercial Paper, and Part 10 covers Article 9, Secured Transactions, Insurance, and Bankruptcy. Article 5 of the UCC, Letters of Credit, is not covered in this book because it is so specialized.

The Concept of a Code

There is a distinct difference between a code and other statutory enactments. A **code** is a comprehensive, systematic collection of statutes in a particular legal area. The Uniform Commercial Code contains and governs much of the law applicable to ordinary commercial transactions. A code, because of its comprehensive and integrated character, is its own best reference for interpretation. Noncode enactments are often fragmentary, and interpretation of them varies widely.

code
a comprehensive, systematic collection of statutes in a particular legal area

The purposes of the Uniform Commercial Code are set out in one of its initial passages. These purposes are as follows:

(a) to simplify, clarify and modernize the law governing commercial transactions;
(b) to permit the continued expansion of commercial practices through custom, usage and agreement of the parties; [and]
(c) to make uniform the law among the various jurisdictions.[2]

In short, the basic philosophy of the UCC is to facilitate commercial transactions through the twin objectives of simplicity and uniformity while allowing for reasonable growth and change in commercial practices.

---

[1] Louisiana has adopted only Articles 1, 3, 4, and 5 of the UCC.

[2] UCC 1–102(2).

History of the UCC

Creation of the Uniform Commercial Code and its adoption by the states.

Proposals for uniform legislation for sales of goods have been made since the 19th century. One of the UCC's sponsors, the National Conference of Commissioners on Uniform State Laws, has been in existence since 1892 and has drafted approximately 170 Uniform Acts.[3] A *Uniform Sales Act* was promulgated by this commission in 1906 and was adopted in 37 jurisdictions before it was supplanted by the UCC. In 1940 this commission adopted a resolution to expand coverage of the Uniform Sales Act and update its key features. The American Law Institute—an organization composed of over 1,500 law professors, judges, and leading attorneys—joined the National Conference in this endeavor, and between 1945 and 1952 numerous drafts and redrafts of the UCC were debated. In October of 1952 the first official edition of the Code was published, and Pennsylvania became the first state to adopt its provisions without amendment, effective July 1, 1954. Since that time all the states (except Louisiana) have adopted most of its Articles. Many of the states have made a few small changes when adopting the Code, but it is essentially the same Code.

Each of the two sponsoring organizations of the Code has five representatives on a permanent editorial board. The Code has been amended only four times. In this book we will refer to the 1978 Official Text and its Comments.

The Legal Philosophy of Karl Llewellyn

Perhaps the single most influential person in the drafting of the UCC was its "chief reporter," Karl Llewellyn, a law professor at the University of Chicago Law School. He determined which subjects the UCC would cover and in what order. He was the principal draftsman of Articles 1 and 2. Of greater importance, however, was the fact that much of the language of Articles 1 and 2 reflected notions Professor Llewellyn held as a result of his commitment to "legal realism."

Legal realism.

Legal realism is a phrase used to designate a school of jurisprudential thought which maintains that the "law" should not be viewed as one large complex body of internally consistent and logical rules. Rather, "law" is embedded fundamentally in situations or the everyday transactions of life. *The rules should reflect what is socially desirable in "reality."* No rule should be made for its own sake or merely because it is a logical extension of another rule. Thus, when one applies this notion to the development of a commercial code for the sale of goods as Professor Llewellyn did, one should appreciate the fact that the rules are an attempt to *state simply* and *make uniform* much of the changing *current* commercial practices. Llewellyn believed commercial law is to reflect the most desirable practices of business people.[4]

---

[3] For a fine but short history of the UCC, see W.D. Malcolm, "The Uniform Commercial Code," reprinted in *Uniform Commercial Code Handbook* (Chicago: American Bar Assoc., 1964), pp. 1–19.

[4] See Danzig, "A Comment on the Jurisprudence of the Uniform Commercial Code," 27 STANFORD L. REV. 621–35 (1975).

In our study of Articles 1 and 2 we should be mindful of the fact that the *words* of these Articles are but a *starting point* for our study. In many key instances the words direct us to current commercial practice to establish the standards for a transaction. No better example of this manifestation of Llewellyn's legal philosophy can be found than section 1–204(2), which provides:

What is a reasonable time for taking any action depends on the nature, purpose and circumstances of such action.

In addition, the official comments to section 2–302 on **unconscionable** contracts, one of the most important sections of Article 2, provides in part:

The basic test is whether, *in the light of the general commercial background and the commercial needs of the particular trade or case,* the clauses involved are so one-sided as to be unconscionable under the circumstances . . . [emphasis added]

unconscionable offends the conscience, immoderate, too one-sided

The genius of this approach to law accommodates the seemingly inconsistent needs of our commercial society. On the one hand, our commercial society demands consistency, regularity, and stability in its rules. On the other hand, because our commercial society is very dynamic, we must provide for change and development of the rules. The required measure of stability is provided by the fact that so many state legislatures have adopted the UCC and the fact that these state legislatures are discouraged from amending the UCC. However, a means for growth is provided by the fact that in interpreting and applying the words of the UCC, especially Articles 1 and 2, attorneys and courts are directed to current commercial standards of performance.[5] As the standards change, so do the meanings of some of the key words of the Sales Article.

Evaluation of the UCC

In general, has the Code been successful? A few legal scholars lament the soft structure and loose wording of the Code,[6] but because of its wide adoption and the growing amount of litigation (especially involving the provisions on warranties and unconscionability[7]), indicating developing definitions of key words, many scholars believe the Code has been successful in achieving its objectives. Indeed, one authority has called the UCC "the most spectacular success story in the history of American law."[8]

---

[5] The words "reasonable" and "unreasonable" appear at least 97 times in Article 2. See Bonsignore, *Existentialism, The Rule of Law and Article 2 of the Uniform Commercial Code,* 8 Am. Bus. L. J. 133 at 147 (1970).

[6] See Mellinkoff, *The Language of the Uniform Commercial Code,* 77 Yale Law Rev. 185 (1967).

[7] See White, *Evaluating Article 2 of the Uniform Commercial Code: A Preliminary Empirical Expedition,* 75 Mich. Law Rev. 1262 (1977).

[8] J. White and R. Summers, *Handbook of the Law Under the Uniform Commercial Code* (St. Paul: West Pub. Co., 1972), p. 5.

Introduction to Article 2: Transactions Covered

We now proceed to focus primarily upon Article 2, with occasional references to Article 1. Article 1 is primarily definitional in character, but it also sets the background for the coverage of the UCC by including provisions on the purposes of the UCC, rules of construction of statutory language, the territorial application of the UCC, and the definitions of "good faith," "reasonable time," etc. These provisions will be mentioned only as they apply to Article 2.

Article 2 applies to *transactions in goods*.[9] A transaction is usually interpreted to mean a *sale* of goods and does not include transactions where only a **security interest** is transferred or where a *gift* or a *lease* of goods is involved. In the following case the court distinguished a sale from a lease.

security interest
"an interest in personal property or fixtures which secures payment or performance of an obligation" UCC 1-201(37)

Facts
Plaintiff was a passenger in a truck rented by his employer from Hertz. It was alleged that the truck had defective brakes and the plaintiff was injured as a result. Should the plaintiff's claim against the defendant, Hertz, be determined by Article 2?

Decision
No.

Reasoning
The court held that no "sale" was involved, so Article 2 was not to be applied directly. However, the appellate court did find in the plaintiff's favor by relying both on the common law and the general policy embedded in the warranty provisions of the UCC. It held that the offering to the public of trucks and pleasure vehicles for hire necessarily carries with it a representation or implied warranty that they are fit for operation.

Cintrone v. Hertz Truck Leasing & Rental Service, 212 A.2d 769 (N.J. 1965).

lease
a form of contract giving one person, the tenant, the exclusive right to occupy for a period the property of another, the landlord

The case above makes two important points. The first is that the UCC does not apply to **leases** of goods. The second is that just because the UCC is not directly applicable does not mean it can not be used as a general reference to shape the rights and duties of parties to nonsales transactions. A central point of this chapter is that the UCC and Article 2 are more than an isolated grouping of statutes; they are a comprehensive treatment of commercial law enacted by almost all the states and represent the major policy statements regarding commercial transactions. The impact of the UCC in shaping commercial law may go far beyond its "technical" applications.[10]

While the distinction between a sale and a lease of goods may appear somewhat artificial, the distinction between goods (movable things which can be identified), on the one hand, and services and nonmovable things, on the other, is not. Goods are those things which must be dealt with *uniformly* by the states, or the value they have because they can be shipped and used elsewhere will be

---

[9] UCC 2–102.

[10] R. J. Nordstrom, *Handbook of the Law of Sales* (St. Paul: West Pub. Co., 1970), pp. 43–44.

impaired. **Services**—such as those rendered by an accountant, a doctor, an architect, or a plumber—are peculiarly local in nature, and the necessity for uniform treatment by states is not as apparent. The same is true for land and things so fastened to the land that they can not be moved. Of course, what is movable and what is not movable depends on the effort someone is willing to exert.[11] Even London Bridge was moved! Generally, however, Article 2 was intended to apply not to items of an extraordinary character, like London Bridge, but to things which normally can flow in commerce and can be reasonably identified.

Growing crops and timber are goods (2–105); and so are minerals (including oil and gas) and other substances or structures *in* the land if they are to be mined, extracted, or severed by the *seller*.[12] If minerals or structures in the land (not crops or timber) are to be mined or severed by the *buyer,* then the contract is viewed as a sale of an interest in *land* and is not covered by Article 2. The reason that minerals, etc. to be severed by the *buyer* are not covered by Article 2 is not explained clearly in the Code, but it seems that this is the traditional distinction recognized by the common law. That is, a lease of land to an oil company to extract oil and gas has always been treated as a lease of real property; and a sale of coal to be mined by the seller has always been treated as a sale of goods and not a sale of an interest in land. The UCC maintains this distinction.

Investment securities (e.g., certificates of stock, bonds) traditionally have been regulated separately (separately, that is, from goods), so they are excluded from Article 2. They are discussed in chapter 43, Corporate Stock and Shareholders.

The most difficult distinction to make, however, is whether Article 2 applies to transactions involving *both* the sale of goods and the sale of services or labor. The "test" used to determine the applicability of Article 2 in this circumstance is clearly defined in the following case.

service
usually labor rendered by one person for another

Facts

The defendants, the Cox brothers, had operated a bowling alley for twenty years in Missouri Valley, Iowa. In February 1968 it was gutted by fire and they contracted with the plaintiff, Simek, to "rebuild" the bowling alley with "used" equipment. Some of the used equipment furnished did not operate properly, and before the job was completed and the liabilities for the faulty equipment established,

Simek died. The defendants hired someone else to complete the work, and the representative of Simek's estate sued the Cox brothers for breach of contract. Should the obligations of the parties be determined by Article 2 of the UCC?

Decision
Yes.

---

[11] Id. at 45.

[12] UCC 2–107.

Reasoning

The court held that Article 2 did apply even though the contract involved "substantial amounts" of labor. The test, it held, is not whether the contract involves a service too, but, granting that it does, "whether the predominant factor, the thrust, the purpose, reasonably stated, is the rendition of service with goods incidentally involved (e.g., contract with an artist for a painting . . .) or is a transaction of sale, with labor incidentally involved (e.g., installation of a water heater in a bathroom . . .)."

Bonebrake v. Cox, 499 F.2d 951 (1974).

By applying the test above in other cases, courts have held that an operation requiring the transfusion of blood and a beauty parlor treatment requiring the sale of hair dye did not involve the sale of goods.

If a transaction in goods exists, then Article 2 applies irrespective of whether or not the goods are in existence at the time the contract is made. In a later chapter we will discuss the consequences of distinguishing between "'existing" and **"future" goods.** For the present, it is important just to note that, if the predominant factor in a transaction is the sale of goods, then Article 2 applies even though the goods are to be made in the future.[13]

future goods
"goods which are not both existing and identified"
UCC 2-105(2)

Standard of Conduct Under Article 2

Good Faith

Article 2 preserves our fundamental American notions about freedom of contract by allowing the parties to vary the effect of Code provisions or determine standards of performance by their agreement. These standards of performance will be upheld as long as they are not "manifestly unreasonable."[14] One standard of performance which may not be waived or altered by agreement because it would be unreasonable is the requirement that "every contract" covered by the Code must be entered into and conducted in good faith.[15] *Good faith* is defined as "honesty in fact in the conduct or transaction concerned."[16] Almost every contract involves the exercise of some discretion. It is these discretionary elements which must be governed by the concept of good faith. The court found bad faith in the following case.

Facts

The plaintiff, seller, contracted to plant and cultivate 28 acres of beans. The defendant, buyer, was to use its own judgment as to when the beans would be ripe and was then to send its crew in to pick the beans. A severe drought in the area made the time for picking the beans very critical. The plaintiff notified the defendant that they should be picked by Tuesday, July 1. An agent for the buyer inspected the crops on June 30 and indicated they would be picked after Ennis' crop, which had been planted earlier than plaintiff's. The pickers finished Ennis' crop on July 2 but were directed by defendant to go elsewhere because the crops were of better quality.

---

[13] UCC 2–105(2), 2–106(1).   [14] UCC 1–102(3).   [15] UCC 1–203.   [16] UCC 1–201(19).

Defendant began picking plaintiff's crops on July 4, but stopped after a short while because the beans were of "unacceptable" quality. Did the defendant fail to meet its standard of performance?

Decision

Yes.

Reasoning

The trial court found for the plaintiff, and the appellate court affirmed this. The court held that matters of judgment in contractual understandings must be exercised honestly and in good faith. In this case, there was evidence which could demonstrate that the buyer's decision to delay harvesting the crop was not made in good faith. "To begin with there was testimony that the effect of hot temperatures and drought on any snap beans is not only to accelerate the maturing process but also to dehydrate the crop. . . . Since this type of crop, even under normal weather conditions, must be harvested within a few days of when it ripens, a three-day delay during a drought is evidence from which a jury may conclude bad faith was exhibited."

Dorsey Bros., Inc. v. H. Anderson, 287 A.2d 270, at 272 (Md. 1972).

Merchants

In the following chapters of Part 5 we will see that in some instances Article 2 imposes on **merchants** more rigid standards of performance than on nonmerchants. The common law of contracts did not recognize a difference between someone who sells goods only occasionally (e.g., selling a lawnmower at a garage sale) and someone who sells goods of a particular kind for a living (e.g., retailer). However, it seems obvious that someone who holds himself or herself out as a seller of goods of a particular kind should have a certain "expertise" in the sale of those items. Thus, a "professional" seller or merchant should be held to a higher standard of care in some instances. This "realistic" view of some sales transactions is another example of the contributions of Professor Llewellyn.

merchant
"a person who deals in goods of the kind or otherwise by his occupation holds himself out as having knowledge or skill peculiar to the practices or goods involved in the transaction. . . ." UCC 2-104(1)

Article 2 and the Common Law of Contracts

The fact that Article 2 imposes more rigid standards of performance on merchants than on nonmerchants when the **common law** did not do this highlights the fact that Article 2 does change some of the contract law you studied in Part 2. In general, the purpose of the Code changes was to recognize circumstances of current commercial practice not recognized by the common law of contracts. More specifically, Article 2 differs from "contract" law and embodies notions of current commercial practice in the following important areas (in addition to the distinction made for merchants noted above):

common law
principles of nonstatutory law reflecting the customs and usages of society and found in judicial decisions

> statute of frauds;
> firm offers;
> additional terms in acceptance;
> modification;
> unconscionable contracts.

Some of these changes were noted in chapters 5–13, on contract law. However, here in Part 5 we will go into greater detail on these changes. Of course, in those areas of commercial law not covered by Article 2 (lease of goods, sale of an interest in land, contracts for services, etc.), the common law of contracts still controls.

It is impossible in such a complex area as the commercial sale of goods to enact a code which will stand alone in its application to appropriate factual situations. The Code was not intended to be read in isolation, but together with and relying upon other areas of the law. It is very important to observe that other areas of the law—e.g., the common law of contracts—*supplement* the Code which governs these areas. For example, to make a sale, we have to make a contract, and *the common law of contracts applies, except as the Code changes the law of contracts or adds to it.*[17] The following case illustrates why this reliance is necessary.

damages
the money judicially awarded for another's wrongful conduct

incidental damages
the money judicially awarded for expenses reasonably incurred by the nonbreaching party on the other party's breach

consequential damages
the money judicially awarded for loss which the breaching party reasonably could foresee would be a consequence of his breach

Facts

The plaintiffs contracted with the defendants to take photographs of their wedding for $110, but the photographs were never delivered because of the negligence and carelessness of the defendant. The plaintiffs asked for **damages** in excess of $10,000. This amount includes the present cost to restage the wedding and to photograph it, additional amounts for loss of sentimental value for failure to photograph the actual wedding, and emotional distress. The action was brought in federal court, which required that the damages alleged could reasonably exceed $10,000. The trial court dismissed the case and the plaintiffs appealed, claiming that the UCC allows the buyer of goods both incidental and consequential damages for a seller's breach of contract. Do the words **"incidental"** and **"consequential" damages** include damages of the kind sought here?

Decision

Judgment affirmed for the defendants.

Reasoning

The UCC itself does not answer this question. The court held for the

defendants because the damages alleged could not possibly exceed $10,000. The court notes that this contract is one for the sale of goods and, therefore, must be covered by Article 2. However, whether the Code language of "incidental" and "consequential" damages would limit the plaintiff's measure of damages here is not clear. So the court relies on Pennsylvania common law to give meaning to the UCC provisions. Pennsylvania common law provides that damages are recoverable for losses caused, or for profits or other gains lost, by the breach only to the extent that the evidence affords a sufficient basis for estimating their amount in money with reasonable certainty. The court agrees with the plaintiff that there is no market value or replacement value for the photographs, and these values usually help determine "incidental" and "consequential" damages. The only arguable cost-related measure of damages would be the estimated cost of restaging the wedding, and even the plaintiffs agree this alone would not cost $10,000.

Carpel v. Saget Studios, Inc., 326 F.Supp. 1331 (1971).

---

[17] UCC 1–103.

Statute of Frauds

In chapter 11, on the common law of contracts, we observed that an enactment by the English Parliament in 1677 called the Statute of Frauds stated which promises had to be evidenced by a writing before they would be *enforced* by a court. Both the present-day law of contracts and the UCC retain the use of the phrase "statute of frauds" to designate those enforceable promises which must be evidenced by a writing.

Enforceability of sales contracts.

Article 2 adds to the list of transactions under the law of contracts, to which the statute of frauds applies. It provides that a contract for the sale of goods for the *price* of $500 or more is not enforceable unless there is some writing recognizing the contract and stating the quantity of goods involved, and it is signed by the party against whom enforcement is sought.[18] There is a distinction between saying *the contract must be in writing* and stating that the promises must *be evidenced* by a writing. Article 2 requires only the latter. For example, if S orally agrees to sell his car to P for $1,000 and S then refers to this fact in his letter to Q, P's sister, S may not assert the statute of frauds as a defense if P should sue for breach of the promise because the letter, if signed by S, is sufficient evidence of the promise to sell. This would be true even if the letter incorrectly stated one of the terms, but the promise would not be enforceable beyond the *quantity* of the goods referred to in the letter. Office memos, minutes of a board of directors' meeting, and the like may be used in addition to letters.

The purpose of the statute of frauds is to protect an innocent party against others who might *fraudulently* assert that the innocent party had promised to perform. The opportunity for fraud is minimized when there is some evidence that a party who made an oral promise has begun to perform. Article 2 recognizes this and provides that an *oral promise is enforceable without a writing* when: (1) goods are to be specially manufactured for the buyer, and they are not suitable for sale to others in the ordinary course of the seller's business, and the seller has made either a substantial beginning of their manufacture or commitments for their procurement;[19] or, (2) if the party being charged admits in its pleadings or testimony in court that a contract was made;[20] or, (3) if the party being charged has either paid for the goods in question or accepted the goods.[21] It should be obvious that, in these three circumstances, the *actions* of the party being charged with having made a contract have themselves minimized the chance for fraud: the party has either paid for or accepted the goods, admitted the contract, or begun work on goods requested.

Finally, Article 2's version of the statute of frauds recognizes a different standard of performance for merchants and in so doing substantially changes the older common law interpretations. It provides that if a *written* **confirmation** of the contract is sent by one *merchant* to another *merchant* within a reasonable time of the exchange of oral promises and the receiver has reason to know its contents, it satisfies the writing requirement for both the sender *and* the receiver

confirmation
an assuring expression of understanding

---

[18] UCC 2–201(1).   [20] UCC 2–201(3b).

[19] UCC 2–201(3a).   [21] UCC 2–201(3c).

even though not signed by the receiver, unless the receiver objects to its contents within ten days of receipt.[22] This provision again shows the perceptions of Professor Llewellyn, who recognized that much of today's business is conducted by one merchant's merely filling in a few blanks on a form and sending it off to another merchant. This section of the statute puts a duty on merchants to read their mail! If the merchant receiving the form or confirmation has no intent to contract with the sending merchant and has reason to know the contents of the form, then the receiving merchant must reject the form within ten days. Otherwise, he can not successfully defend a suit on the grounds that he has not signed a written order.

In general, Article 2 is fairly liberal in allowing evidence of an oral contract. The Code Comments to the statute of frauds section make it clear that, when a writing is required, it need not state the price, time, or place of payment or delivery, nor the general quality of the goods. Business people frequently base their agreement as to price on a price list or catalogue known to both of them. Therefore, the only three essential ingredients of the required writing are that (1) it must refer to a contract for the *sale of goods* between the parties, (2) it must specify the *quantity* of goods, and (3) it must be *signed by the party* to be charged.

A diagram of Article 2's statute of frauds (2–201) might appear as in figure 22.1.

In applying section 2–201 to a factual situation, we must keep the position of the parties in mind. In a case where the plaintiff alleges that the defendant orally promised to sell or buy goods, it is highly unlikely that the plaintiff's claim is untrue. *Usually* the plaintiff is asserting the existence of an agreement with the defendant and the fact that the defendant did not perform in some respect. The plaintiff, then, is met with a defense. It is a defense which does not go to the merits of the case but which is intended to clarify preliminary matters about precisely what was agreed upon, if anything, and to minimize the chances of fraud.[23] The defense asserts that the statute of frauds requires a signed writing by the party asserting such defense (unless the parties are merchants) sufficient to allow the plaintiff to continue with the proof, and no such writing exists. At this point the court focuses upon the sufficiency of the writings, if any, or other facts required by the statute of frauds. If these requirements are not met, the court will hold that a good defense exists and dismiss the case for lack of proof that a contract was made by the person asserting the defense. However, if the requirements are met, then this simply means the plaintiff must proceed with proof of the contents of the contract, its breach, and loss. Because the defense of the statute of frauds is overcome, do not assume that the plaintiff has won. Substantial problems of proof may remain. The plaintiff must still prove that there was an offer and acceptance, consideration, breach, damages, etc.

---

[22] UCC 2–201(2).

[23] R. J. Nordstrom, *supra* note 10, at 54.

Figure 22.1   Diagram of UCC 2-201—Statute of Frauds

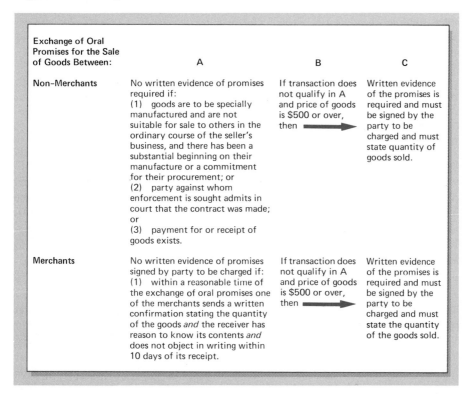

Exchange of Oral Promises for the Sale of Goods Between:	A	B	C
Non-Merchants	No written evidence of promises required if: (1) goods are to be specially manufactured and are not suitable for sale to others in the ordinary course of the seller's business, and there has been a substantial beginning on their manufacture or a commitment for their procurement; or (2) party against whom enforcement is sought admits in court that the contract was made; or (3) payment for or receipt of goods exists.	If transaction does not qualify in A and price of goods is $500 or over, then ▬▶	Written evidence of the promises is required and must be signed by the party to be charged and must state quantity of goods sold.
Merchants	No written evidence of promises signed by party to be charged if: (1) within a reasonable time of the exchange of oral promises one of the merchants sends a written confirmation stating the quantity of the goods *and* the receiver has reason to know its contents *and* does not object in writing within 10 days of its receipt.	If transaction does not qualify in A and price of goods is $500 or over, then ▬▶	Written evidence of the promises is required and must be signed by the party to be charged and must state the quantity of the goods sold.

Parol or Extrinsic Evidence

An issue often perceived as closely related to the application of the statute of frauds—but, in reality, quite different—is the use of oral testimony (**parol evidence**) or written evidence to clarify a *written* understanding. The usual position of the parties when we see the **parol evidence rule** asserted is that the plaintiff has introduced as evidence a *writing* which purports to be "the understanding" between the parties. The defendant admits the existence and signing of the document but counters with an assertion that one of the terms of the writing was varied or modified by a *prior* oral understanding or other evidence. For example,[24] buyer and seller exchange memoranda confirming a telephone conversation in which buyer agreed to purchase goods for "$35 per hundredweight." Seller ships the goods, and buyer now claims that, during the initial phone conversation, seller agreed to give the buyer a 2 percent discount if payments were made within ten days of the invoice date. The seller claims that the parol evidence should not be admitted because it would vary or contradict their memoranda. Should the parol evidence be admitted?

parol evidence
oral testimony

parol evidence rule
a rule of law which provides that, when there is a written contract, it can not be contradicted (added to or varied) by any prior or contemporaneous oral agreement or by a prior written agreement

---

[24] Id. at 164.

Article 2 attempts to cover this rather common situation by providing:

Terms with respect to which confirmatory memoranda of the parties agree or which are otherwise set forth in writing intended by the parties as a final expression of their agreement with respect to such terms . . . may not be contradicted by evidence of any prior agreement or of a contemporaneous oral agreement but may be explained or supplemented:

(a) by course of dealing or usage of trade . . . or by course of performance . . .; and

(b) by evidence of consistent additional terms unless the court finds the writing to have been intended also as a complete and exclusive statement of the terms of the agreement.[25]

The key features of this section direct a court to first find whether or not the parties intended their *writing,* namely the memoranda in question, to be a "final" expression of their agreement with respect to the "term" in question. If a court so finds, then any oral (parol) or other evidence of an agreement between the parties which occurred *before,* and any oral agreement which occurred *contemporaneously* with, the writing will not be admitted if it *contradicts* the writing. Before proceeding with the application of this section to our example, we should note that oral agreements made *after* the confirmatory memoranda will be admissible as evidence unless the statute of frauds requires their exclusion.

In our example above, if a court finds from the evidence that the parties intended their memoranda as a final expression of their agreement, then it must decide if the evidence of a discount *contradicts* the price term or not. Whether it does so in our example is not perfectly clear. The UCC definition of the word "term" is ". . . that portion of an agreement which relates to a particular matter."[26] If the words "particular matter" are interpreted to mean "price," then a court could exclude the oral testimony about the discount. Perhaps this is the best result, because "discounts" are very directly related to "price." However, if a court recognizes that within a given industry discounts are customarily given, and have been given between the two parties in the past, then it might decide to admit the oral evidence on the basis that there is no contradiction but a mere explanation of the term. Evidence which *explains* and does not contradict will be admissible. The parol evidence rule will not be applied in situations where one of the parties is alleging that contractual capacity was lacking, or that the agreement was procured through fraud, duress, or illegality.

We can see from our study of both the statute of frauds and the parol evidence sections how Article 2 attempts to achieve the main objectives of the UCC. Both sections require merchants and others to meet certain minimum standards in the statement and modification of their agreement for the sale of goods. Yet, in defining these standards, the parties are allowed a large measure of flexibility. This flexibility is intended to reflect changes in custom and commercial usage of documents dictated by an ever-changing commercial world.

---

[25] UCC 2–202.

[26] UCC 1–201(42).

Summary Statement

1. The purposes of the Uniform Commercial Code are to simplify, clarify, and modernize the law governing commercial transactions; to permit the growth of commercial law; and to make uniform the commercial law of the various states.

2. Article 2 of the UCC was drafted by Professor Karl Llewellyn, who believed that the best commercial rules were those that reflected the best parts of current commercial practice. Article 2 uses such words as "reasonable" and "good faith" so that courts may update the Article by continuing to focus on the best commercial conduct as defining what is "reasonable" and so forth.

3. Article 2 applies to transactions in *goods* and does not apply to leases, gifts, the sale of an interest in land (and other nonmovables), investment securities, and services.

4. Every transaction for the sale of goods covered by Article 2 must be conducted in good faith.

5. Even though Article 2 changes some of the rules of the common law of contracts, the latter still supplements the UCC and is applicable in cases where Article 2 or the UCC do not provide the answer to a legal question.

6. Article 2's statute of frauds provision provides that a contract for the sale of goods for the price of $500 or more is not enforceable unless there is some writing recognizing the contract and stating the quantity of goods involved, and it is signed by the party against whom enforcement is sought. No writing is needed when:
   a. the goods are to be specially manufactured for the buyer, they are not suitable for sale to others in the ordinary course of the seller's business, and the seller has made either a substantial beginning of their manufacture or commitments for their procurement; or
   b. the party being charged admits in court a contract was made; or
   c. the party being charged has paid for or accepted the goods.

7. If a written confirmation of the contract is sent by one *merchant* to another *merchant* within a reasonable time of the exchange of oral promises, and the receiver has reason to know its contents, it satisfies the writing requirement for both the sender and receiver even though not signed by the receiver, unless the receiver objects to its contents within ten days of receipt.

8. The parol evidence rule is a rule of evidence which excludes testimony of an oral agreement made prior to or contemporaneously with a written agreement, or a prior written agreement, which would contradict the written agreement.

9. The following case is a good example of how the Code's statute of frauds is applied to merchants.

Campbell v. Yokel
313 N.E.2d 628 (Ill. 1974)

The plaintiffs, owners and operators of the Campbell Grain and Seed Company, alleged that they had reached an oral agreement on February 7, 1973 with the defendant group of farmers to purchase 6,800 to 7,200 bushels of yellow soybeans at a price of $5.30 per bushel. After the conversation between the plaintiffs and the defendants on February 7, the plaintiffs signed and mailed a written confirmation of the oral agreement. Defendants received the written confirmation but did not sign it or give any notice of objection to its contents to the plaintiffs. The defendants refused to deliver any soybeans to the plaintiffs and, on April 30, 1973 informed the plaintiffs that, since the defendants did not sign the written confirmation, they were not bound by it. They also stated that it was their understanding that the agreement was tentative and was not to be binding unless a written contract was signed.

The plaintiffs rely on UCC 2-201(2), the Statute of Frauds, which provides that there is no writing required if:

Between merchants if within a reasonable time a writing in confirmation of the contract and sufficient against the sender is received and the party receiving it has reason to know its contents, it satisfies the requirements of subsection (1) against such parties unless notice of objection to its contents is given within 10 days after it is received.

The first issue the court had to decide was whether or not the defendants were merchants. The court noted that some state courts have held that farmers were not merchants but that the better reasoned opinions held that farmers were merchants, especially with regard to an agreement to sell growing crops. UCC 2-104(1) defines a merchant as

. . . a person who deals in goods of the kind or otherwise by his occupation holds himself out as having knowledge or skill peculiar to the practices or goods involved in the transaction or to whom such knowledge or skill may be attributed by his employment . . .

The defendants admitted in discovery depositions that they had grown and sold soybeans and other grains for several years. The court concluded that "we believe that a farmer who regularly sells his crops is a person who 'deals in goods of that kind.' " Placing this small burden upon farmers in instances lessens the possibility that the Statute of Frauds would be used as an instrument of fraud. For example, assuming that an oral agreement had been reached, . . . that the farmers had received written confirmation signed by the plaintiffs, and that the farmers were not "merchants," the farmers would be in a position to speculate on a contract to which the grain company was bound. If the market price fell after the agreement had been reached, the farmers could produce the written confirmation and enforce the contract. If the market price rose, the farmers could claim the protection of the Statute of Frauds and sell their crops on the open market.

The court concluded, "Our decision is not tantamount to a finding that a contract did exist between plaintiffs and defendants. We hold merely that since the defendants were merchants Section 2-201(2) operates to bar the defendants from asserting the defense of the Statute of Frauds. The burden of persuading the trier of fact that an oral contract was in fact made prior to the written confirmation is unaffected."

Questions and Case Problems

1. In your own words, write a short but complete paragraph describing the need for a uniform commercial code, the purposes of the UCC, and the basic philosophy underlying many of Article 2's key provisions.

2. Make up an example of a sales transaction involving both goods and services. Then state the "standard" or "test" a court would use in determining whether or not Article 2 would apply. Finally, state your conclusion as to whether or not Article 2 would apply. In reaching this conclusion, be sure to integrate the proper facts from your example with the stated standard or test used.

3. Review the material in Part, Contracts, and then write down all of the kinds of promises which must be "evidenced" by a writing to be enforced by courts.

4. Review the material in Part 2, Contracts, on the parol evidence rule and then, in a concise series of paragraphs, explain the circumstances when a prior or contemporaneous oral understanding may be used as evidence when one of the parties is relying upon a written agreement.

5. Define the circumstances studied so far in which Article 2 distinguishes between merchants and nonmerchants. What is the reason for this distinction?

6. Indicate without stating any reasons which, if any, of the following transactions and legal disputes arising therefrom would be governed by the sections of Articles 1 and 2 of the UCC:
   a. a written contract in which S agrees to manufacture special parts for P which are not currently in existence;
   b. an oral contract for the sale of a used car from one neighbor to another for $450;
   c. an oral contract to paint your neighbor's house for $800;
   d. a contract to sell an **easement** over your farm so a neighbor may water his cattle in your stream;
   e. a written contract to sell your house;
   f. a written agreement to buy a TV set from Sears;
   g. an agreement made with an oil drilling company to drill for oil on your land;
   h. a written agreement to sell your fall crop of apples, which will be picked by you;
   i. an agreement to lease your sailboat to a friend for the summer;
   j. an oral agreement you make to purchase, cut, and haul away all of the dead trees in a large forest owned by a farmer for $600.

easement
a right to the limited use of another's land which can not be revoked by the latter owner

7. The plaintiff bought a used car from the defendant, a car dealer. The plaintiff signed a contract which clearly stated there were no warranties made by the seller beyond the manufacturer's new car warranty insofar as it may be applicable. Several weeks after the purchase, the plaintiff alleges, the paint on the car developed "defects." The plaintiff sues the defendant for the value of a new paint job and attempts to state at the trial that the defendant's agent made certain oral representations about the condition of the car (and paint) at the time of the sale. Should oral testimony of the representations or warranties of the seller's agent be admissible? [*Tracy v. Vinton Motors, Inc.*, 296 A.2d 269 (Vt. 1972).]

consignment
the shipment of goods
from one person to
another

8. The plaintiff, Lipschutz, a large New York wholesaler of diamonds, sends a **consignment** of diamonds to the defendant, Linz, retailer of diamonds. The defendant acknowledges receipt of the diamonds by sending the following "all risk" memorandum to the wholesaler:

> Received on consignment from Lipschutz & Gartwirth Co., 630 Fifth Avenue, New York City, the following goods pursuant to the following agreement:
> The goods described and valued as below are delivered to undersigned Linz Bros. for examination, . . . and shall be at once returned to you on demand. The undersigned assumes full and unqualified responsibility for the absolute return of the said property, or the cash proceeds to you on demand, without any excuse or defense whatsoever.
> . . .

After receipt of the diamonds there was a robbery at Linz in which merchandise valued at $1.5 million (retail value) was taken; of this amount, Lipschutz owned $700,000. The insurance policy of Linz did not cover the entire *retail* value of the loss. The plaintiff asserts the defendant Linz is liable for the full *retail* market value of its diamonds, $700,000. The defense argues that custom and trade usage in the diamond business establish that where the loss is the result of a robbery and there is insufficient insurance, the consignee is liable not for the *retail value* of the diamonds, but the consignor's *actual cost* plus a small percentage to cover the costs of handling the diamonds. Should oral and other evidence be admitted to substantiate the defendant's arguments? [*Lipschutz v. Gordon Jewelry Corp.,* 373 F.Supp. 375 (1974).]

9. P, a store owner, entered into a written contract with S, an air conditioning company, to purchase an air conditioning system and to have it installed in the store. The contract referred to a sale and installation of an "air conditioning apparatus." The total contract price was $1,200. The contract contained this statement: "This contract contains the entire agreement of the parties, and no representations or promises or warranties of any kind and no other agreements written or oral exist except as contained in this written agreement."

   a. In a dispute between P and S which centers on the sufficiency of the "air conditioning apparatus," will S be allowed to introduce oral or extrinsic testimony to prove that it was the parties' intent to have installed a G.E. air conditioning unit #L.B. 4 and not a larger model as P argues? How will this dispute be resolved?

   b. Disregard the "a" paragraph and assume that, three days after P receives the written contract, P decides to purchase the unit and have the employees of *P* install it. P telephones S and S agrees to sell an air conditioning unit to P for $900 and not to provide the installation. A dispute between P and S develops, and P sues S. May S successfully assert the parol evidence rule to defeat P's attempt to introduce evidence of the oral modification? Does S have another defense?

10. In the case of *Campbell v. Yokel,* 313 N.E.2d 628 (Ill. 1974),[27] a farmer was held to be a merchant. Discuss how a farmer may not be a merchant.

---

[27] See p. 362.

Formation and Interpretation of the Sales Contract

23

After you have read this chapter, you should be able to:

1. Describe the general circumstances in which merchants contract.
2. State in a paragraph or two how the UCC altered the common law of offer and acceptance in the creation of a sales contract.
3. Describe how section 2-207 resolves some of the problems created by the fact that most merchants do business by exchanging forms.
4. Define "course of performance," "course of dealing," and "usage of trade" and then clearly state how these terms are used by courts to help them ascertain the parties' intended meanings of words used by them.
5. State how the UCC allows merchants to modify a contractual agreement and state the circumstances in which a court might decide that a party has "waived" a contractual provision.
6. Define an insurable interest; describe when an insurable interest is created in a buyer; then define when the "risk of loss" for damage to or destruction of goods passes to the buyer; and, finally, be able to differentiate between the creation of an insurable interest and passage of the risk of loss.
7. Describe the significance of "title" under Article 2 of the UCC and determine how and when title is transferred.

Introduction—How to Think About Commercial Transactions

Let us first think about the concepts and ideas involved in making a sales contract. There is more to this than just buying or selling a typewriter, for example. After we have examined the concept of how large corporate merchants bargain and negotiate in order to have a sales contract, then we can get to what really matters—what actions or words make a sale, what a sale really is, and all of a sale's important implications and effects. It is necessary to do this so that you may better understand the marketplace, why and how sales of goods occur, and thereby be a more knowledgeable business person and consumer.

Well regarded social commentators such as John Kenneth Galbraith[1] and Kenneth Boulding[2] believe that, to understand current social phenomena such as law, we should not focus exclusively on the events (laws) themselves. We must, they argue, also focus on our own conceptual base which is used to organize our knowledge about these events. Galbraith uses the term "conventional wisdom" to refer to the conceptual base of large groups of persons. Boulding uses the term "image" to define the key operational concept governing individual human behavior.

Thus the conceptual framework that each member of your law class has with regard to law is used to help the members understand and know new information about the law. These collective conceptual structures are the conventional wisdom of the class and most probably reflect the conventional wisdom of the society as a whole. Closely connected to this collective thought pattern is the individual thought pattern or image one has of the law.

Where is this theoretical discussion leading—especially in a chapter on commercial law? Boulding and Galbraith emphasize that the abstract images we use to interpret reality change much more slowly than does reality. In order to understand today's rapidly changing world, we must modify our collective and individual images of reality. We can not, obviously alter the reality. That the conventional wisdom about the law, its rules, its functions, and its value lags behind the fast-moving sociological and economic events of our day is a point seldom stressed in undergraduate courses. Yet it appears to be fact. A good illustration of this can be found by pointing out that it is a common belief (the conventional wisdom) that consumers "contract" in the traditional sense when they purchase consumer goods from a merchant. At the heart of our conventional wisdom about "contracting" is the notion that the parties **bargain** or **negotiate.** This implies that they are each aware of all unfavorable and favorable terms, and they consciously select those that best serve their interests.

Yet this image does not reflect reality, and it misleads us in our study of the law. When was the last time you made a "bargain" or "negotiated" the terms of a sale as a consumer? The belief that one "bargains" with Standard Oil, Sears, General Motors, a McDonald's restaurant, the Adidas sports shop, or a utility such as your local electric or gas company and almost all merchant-sellers

bargain or **negotiate** terms used to indicate that both parties to a sales contract are aware of all the terms of the contract and that both parties exchanged value to establish the terms

---

[1] J. K. Galbraith, *The Affluent Society* (Boston: Houghton Mifflin, 1958).

[2] K. E. Boulding, *The Image* (Ann Arbor: Univ. of Michigan Press, 1956).

of goods persists today despite the fact that many of the notions you have learned about "contracting" are not applicable.[3] You may shop around and choose from several alternatives, but when the "bargain" is struck, you as a consumer take what is *given!*

In short, despite the conventional wisdom of the central place of contract law and the value of a "bargain" in our economy (a belief perpetuated by many professors and textbooks), you as a consumer usually do business on the *seller's terms* or not at all! Have you ever tried to vary so much as one word in the written, contractual language found on your Standard Oil, Sears, or other charge card?

The disparity between how one *imagines* contracting is done and how it *is,* in fact, done is greatest with regard to the sale of goods from a merchant to a consumer. The standardized contract produced by the thousands or, in the case of very large merchants, by the millions, is the rule of the day. Moreover, it is reasonable to expect that such contracts are more favorable to their authors than to the other party to the transaction.

Highlighting this disparity between how one imagines commercial contracting is done and how it is done in reality serves as a basis for understanding *why* the "consumer movement" developed. Simply put, the conventional wisdom was that our commercial law, and particularly the UCC, is a *neutral* body of legal principles protecting equally the interests of merchants and consumers. However, this view failed to account for a political reality. As merchants have become larger and larger economic units, their impact on state legislatures has grown proportionately. When the UCC was adopted, the interests of merchants vis-à-vis consumers were predominant.[4] This predominance and the resulting bias in the UCC has only recently been perceived, and the response has been a piecemeal effort to redress the imbalance.

The remedy has not been to change the UCC, since the merchants want to maintain uniformity of the UCC. Rather, the remedy has been for both the federal government and state legislatures to pass laws giving consumers remedies *outside* the UCC. It is very difficult in such a short space to assess adequately the reasons for the "consumer" movement. Some of the reasons and a more general inquiry into "consumer" law can be found in chapter 26, Consumer Law.

We only wish to emphasize at this point that it is useful to imagine at least two general patterns of commercial conduct (with numerous variations) and, consequently, two broad categories of commercial law. On the one hand, we have commercial activity in large economically concentrated markets in which, generally, *merchants deal with merchants.* On the other hand, we have the retail level of those same markets in which large, *powerful merchants contract with consumers.*

The inadequacy of commercial law and the pressure of consumer groups resulted in legislation providing further consumer relief in sales transactions.

---

[3] On the diminished role of contract law generally, see L. M. Friedman, *Contract Law in America: A Social and Economic Study* (Madison: Univ. of Wisconsin Press, 1965), and G. Gilmore, *The Death of Contract* (Columbus, Ohio: State University Press, 1974).

[4] On this point generally, see J. W. Hurst, *Law and Economic Growth, the Legal History of the Lumber Industry in Wisconsin* (Cambridge: Belknap Press of Harvard Univ. Press, 1964).

Since the reality is that we have at least these two general commercial patterns and two categories of legal principles, we have separated the remaining material on the UCC into two broad categories. This chapter and the two that follow, chapters 24 and 25, are largely based on an image of the parties involved *both* being merchants. Chapter 26, then, the final one of Part 5, is on consumer law. As you read this and the following chapters on Article 2, we ask you to keep in mind this central image of two merchants dealing with one another, but do not be misled into believing that Article 2 applies *only* to merchants.

A General Pattern of Commercial Conduct

Today dealings between merchants, especially the large corporate merchants, are often conducted by employees at a low level in the corporate organization who use standardized forms provided by their legal departments or management. These employees do not think of themselves as "contracting," but they do realize that they place and receive "orders" or "confirmations," using "order forms," "quotation forms," or any of a series of forms provided for use.

Very often a supplier will provide a catalogue with prices and descriptions of goods, and the first response from a merchant purchaser may be by telephone, asking for clarifications of price or credit terms. If the response is satisfactory, the purchaser's employee will take a form from a drawer and, in the blank spaces, either write or type the price, description of the goods, quantity, delivery time and means of transportation, and credit terms. When the seller receives the form, an employee will usually transfer the crucial information from the filled-in blanks (after perhaps varying some terms) to his company's "confirmation" form and send it back to the purchaser. If the "contract" is a complex one, as for the construction of a large machine or the sale of complex goods over a period of years, it is highly likely that the exchange of forms was preceded by "negotiations" at several levels within the two corporate organizations.

Moreover, after the exchange of forms, there may be numerous further changes or modifications as the economic, technological, or political environment changes. In addition to the forms, there may be telephone calls, letters, resolutions from the board of directors, intracorporate communications, standard operating procedures, and other similar pieces of evidence, *all of which* reflect the understanding of the parties.

If one were to attempt to apply the common law contract rules of offer and acceptance to this typical situation, then a court would be compelled to hold that *no* contract existed because a few essential terms in the offer or acceptance varied. Under the common law, an acceptance was effective only if it mirrored the offer by *completely* complying with the offer, the terms of the acceptance being identical to the terms of the offer. Given the common actual pattern of commercial activity as sketched above, this result would be absurd, especially when one considers that it was the *terms* and not the *general intent* which had been varied. The authors of the UCC recognized this and drafted Article 2 to reflect reality.

The remaining portion of this chapter will focus upon contract formation and interpretation and the various ways merchants may protect themselves from loss caused by damage or destruction to the goods. We will use the above general factual pattern to establish an image of current commercial realities.

Contract Formation—Offer and Acceptance

Article 2 substantially changes the common law doctrines of contract formation. It provides that a contract for the sale of goods may be made in *any* manner sufficient to show *agreement* by the parties.[5] This includes *conduct* by both parties that recognizes the existence of a contract. Moreover, it states that a contract for the sale of goods may be found to exist even though the moment of its making is undetermined or one or more terms are left open, so long as a court could find the general *intent to contract* and there is a reasonably certain basis for giving an appropriate remedy for its breach.[6] The Official Comments to section 2–204 add that commercial standards on the degree of "indefiniteness" should be applied and that, generally, the more terms the parties leave open, the less likely it is they have intended to be bound, but that their actions may be frequently conclusive on the matter despite the omissions. This is illustrated by the following case.

Facts

The plaintiff, Admiral, ordered three specially designed machines from the defendant, Trueblood. The chief engineer for the plaintiff, Paul Marcus, was told by the defendant at the time of the initial contact that the defendant had never made machines of the type ordered but would consider doing so if Admiral would provide the specifications. Based upon preliminary specifications and Marcus' oral discussions with the defendant, the defendant quoted a price to the plaintiff on May 24, 1966 of $39,750 per machine. At this point Marcus orally ordered three machines and promised that a down payment, a written order form, and the specifications would be sent.

Not until July 20, 1966 did the defendant receive from Admiral a check for $29,812.50 as a partial payment as well as a set of specifications and a purchase order.

The purchase order provided that the delivery dates for the three machines were to be November 1, November 15, and December 1, 1966. In late August, Marcus visited the defendant's plant and expressed concern that the construction had not started. Marcus was informed that there were discrepancies between the specifications as submitted and Marcus' earlier discussions and that revised specifications were needed. On September 9, 1966 revised specifications were received by the defendant, but they were inadequate in some respects. On November 11, 1966 and again on December 1, 1966 an agent of Admiral visited the defendant's plant to observe the machines in operation and found that the basic welding on only one machine had been done. The defendant never did sign the purchase order form. On

---

[5] UCC 2–204(1).   [6] UCC 2–204(3).

December 8, 1966 the plaintiff informed the defendant that there was a default and the plaintiff was initiating suit. No machines were ever delivered, and the defendant did not return the $29,812.50 paid, stating that this did not even cover its expenses. Was there a contract?

Decision

The court rendered a partial judgment for the plaintiff.

Reasoning

The trial court found that there was a contract followed by mutual rescission. The appellate court affirmed this. The court relied upon UCC 2–204 and said, in part, that "a contract for sale of goods may be made in any manner sufficient to show agreement, including conduct by both parties which recognizes the existence of such a contract [and] . . . a contract for sale does not fail for indefiniteness if the parties have intended to make a contract and there is a reasonably certain basis for giving an appropriate remedy." In the designing and producing of special machines, it is understandable that certain terms were to be left unspecified and that difficulties would be encountered.

The court emphasized that the nature of the contract made it imperative that both parties cooperate to the fullest extent in order for the machines to be successfully designed and built. Both parties failed to act in good faith and failed to cooperate. There was evidence that Admiral was delinquent in furnishing the specifications, as was the defendant in failing to pursue its obligations.

The court concludes by noting that the UCC does not provide a remedy for the specific situation of a *mutual* breaching of contract, so it turns to "other . . . principles of law and equity." The court dismissed the defendant's counterclaim and ordered the return of the plaintiff's down payment.

Admiral Plastics Corp. v. Trueblood, Inc., 436 F.2d 1335 (1971).

The above case reveals that in complex commercial transactions not all details of the transaction can be spelled out at the time the parties become bound. Article 2 clearly accounts for this reality and rejects many of the technical requirements of contract formation developed by the common law. However, while such common law formalities as the effect of a seal on a document today have no legal effect under Article 2 (2–203), the *method of analysis* for finding the existence of an agreement that courts will enforce remains intact. That is, courts still *search for an offer and a response thereto, indicating an intent to be bound, called an acceptance.* Also, the promise of the parties must *manifest a desired exchange of value.* This exchange of value was defined as "consideration" in the chapters on the common law of contracts, and this concept retains its vitality in Article 2 with some notable exceptions. We will discuss one exception here and another one when discussing modification, rescission, and waiver.

At common law, if an offeree wanted to be sure that an offeror would hold his offer open for a given length of time, the offeree was bound to give something of value (consideration) to the offeror. As you read in Part 2, Contracts, when such value was given, a contract was formed to keep the main offer open for a time, which became an **option.** While Article 2 does not eliminate the option in

option
the irrevocable offer in an option contract

a transaction for the sale of goods, it adds a new term, **firm offer**, which has the same effect as an option, but value is *not required* to keep an offer open for a limited time. Article 2 provides that when a *merchant* gives his *signed written assurance* in an offer that it will be held open for a stated time, then it is not revocable for lack of consideration.[7] If no time is stated, then the courts will infer that a reasonable time was intended, but in no event shall the period of the open or "firm" offer exceed *three months*. This provision of the UCC is still consistent with the older notion that an offeror controls the offer. In this case the law simply attaches legal significance to the offeror's announced intent to hold an offer open. A firm offer and an option may exist at the same time. For example, a merchant's signed, written offer to be kept open for five months on the offeree's giving value is valid as a *firm offer* for three months and as an *option* for five months.

It is interesting to note that Article 2 does not *expressly* require an offer or consideration in a contract for the sale of goods but, obviously, they are required by implication. This was not an oversight on the part of the drafters. As we pointed out in the last chapter, many of the fundamental, nontechnical rules developed over several centuries of mercantile conduct are applicable to Article 2 by section 1–103, which provides:

Unless displaced by the particular provisions of this Act, the principles of law and equity, including the . . . law relative to capacity to contract . . . estoppel, fraud, misrepresentation, duress, coercion, mistake . . . shall *supplement* its provisions. [Italics added.]

Generally, offers may be made in any way that reveals an intent to be bound by the promises contained in the offer, and an acceptance shall be made in any manner and by any medium reasonable in the circumstances.[8] What did the drafters of Article 2 do to the famous **"mail box rule"**?[9] At what point does an acceptance become effective? This very question was not of great importance to the drafters. In one sense they minimized its importance by providing that a court could find that a contract existed even though the time of its "making" was uncertain, and by adding that acceptance could be by any reasonable means. Moreover, in the comments to section 2–206, they provide that "former technical rules as to acceptance, such as requiring that telegraphic offers be accepted by telegraphic acceptance, etc., are rejected and a criterion that the acceptance be, 'in any manner and by any medium reasonable under the circumstances,' is substituted." Of course, if the offer requires a specific medium for acceptance, an acceptance is to occur by that medium.

---

[7] UCC 2–205.

[8] UCC 2–206(1)(a) and (b).

[9] Under the common law of contracts, if A mailed an offer to B and B received it on September 15 and then sent an acceptance by mail the same day, a contract was formed as of the time B posted the letter of acceptance. A later attempt by A to revoke his offer and a later attempt by B to revoke his acceptance are not effective.

firm offer
a merchant's signed irrevocable offer to buy or sell goods, giving assurance that it will be kept open; consideration is not required, and its maximum time is three months

mail box rule
the rule in *Adams v. Lindsell:* an acceptance is effective when it is sent if the means of sending it were impliedly authorized by, for example, the offeror's use of the mails to send the offer

There persists in some cases, nevertheless, a search for the time of contracting, compelled by the conventional assumption that an agreement must arise at some point in time. The better authorities suggest that, if the circumstances demand it, courts are still free to use the mail box test even when applying section 2–206.[10] In short, under the UCC an acceptance is effective when it is sent if the means of sending it are reasonable under the circumstances, in the absence of requirements specified in the offer.

Article 2 recognizes the distinction between bilateral contracts and unilateral contracts by providing that an order or other offer to buy goods for prompt shipment shall be construed as inviting acceptance either by a prompt promise to ship (forming a bilateral contract) or by the prompt shipment of conforming goods (forming a unilateral contract). If the offer requests prompt shipment, then a contract for sale is formed upon the prompt shipment by the seller even though the goods shipped are non-conforming.[11] The drafters thought it would expedite commerce by recognizing that the shipment of non-conforming goods was an acceptance. In this case, although technically a contract exists upon shipment of non-conforming goods, the contract has been breached, and the purchaser has a remedy for the breach (paradoxically, the act of shipping non-conforming goods may be both an acceptance and a breach).

If a seller realizes that the goods shipped are non-conforming and ships them anyway to "accommodate" the buyer, then the act of shipment may not be an acceptance so long as the seller notifies the buyer that the goods are being shipped only as an "accommodation." For example, assume that P Co. orders for prompt shipment a large quantity of #10 *aluminum* wood screws from S Co. Upon receiving the order, the agent for S Co. realizes that it has no #10 aluminum wood screws but can ship immediately #10 steel wood screws. If S Co. ships the steel wood screws, there is an acceptance of the offer and a contract results, but P Co. may have a remedy for breach of the contract. However, the proper response here would have been for S Co. to notify P Co. that it was out of the aluminum screws and, if the steel screws would suffice, they would be sent as an accommodation to P Co.[12] In this case, no contract for the sale of aluminum wood screws would result and, therefore, there could be no breach of contract. If P Co. assents, there would be a contract for the sale of #10 steel wood screws.

Finally, section 2–206 protects the offeror by adding that where the beginning of a requested performance is a reasonable mode of acceptance, the offeree must notify the offeror that performance has begun. If the offeror is not notified within a reasonable time, the offeror may treat the offer as having lapsed before acceptance.[13] This section of the Code recognizes a basic fact of commercial life: both buyers and sellers are looking forward to performance, and usually the sooner the better. If an "offer" form or "order" form requests prompt shipment,

---

[10] R. J. Nordstrom, *Handbook of the Law of Sales* (St. Paul: West Pub. Co., 1970).

[11] UCC 2–206(1)(b).

[12] Nordstrom, p. 88.

[13] UCC 2–206(2).

then, to protect the offeree, an acceptance occurs when the requested performance begins so long as some notification is sent to the offeror. This notice must be sent within a reasonable time or the offeror may treat the offer as having lapsed. What is a reasonable time? When a merchant makes such an offer, it is usually to some other merchant from whom goods have been received in the past. It is the past conduct or, in the absence of this conduct, current commercial practice which will establish whether or not the notice of the beginning of performance was sent within a reasonable time.

The Battle of the Forms and Section 2–207

Recall now the fact pattern we discussed at the beginning of this chapter to show how many commercial contracts are formed. We have an exchange of forms together with prior and subsequent agreements. What is "the contract"? Before we begin our analysis of "the contract," we should reemphasize that any statute of frauds or parol evidence problems should first be evaluated. They have been treated in chapter 22, Introduction to the Uniform Commercial Code. With this out of the way, we then proceed to the key section, 2–207. Following our discussion of this section and a case to reveal its application, we will discuss two more aspects of the problem created by the battle of the forms: first, how "course of performance" is used to interpret contracts; and second, a word about modification, rescission, and waiver of the contract.

The difficulty of interpreting the terms in the forms used by seller and buyer in order to determine their intentions as to whether they have agreed, creating a sales contract.

Section 2–207 provides:

(1) A definite and seasonable expression of acceptance or a written confirmation which is sent within a reasonable time operates as an acceptance even though it states terms additional to or different from those offered or agreed upon, unless acceptance is expressly made conditional on assent to the additional or different terms.

(2) The additional terms are to be construed as proposals for addition to the contract. Between merchants such terms become part of the contract unless:
(a) the offer expressly limits acceptance to the terms of the offer;
(b) they materially alter it; or
(c) notification of the objection to them has already been given or is given within a reasonable time after notice of them is received.

(3) Conduct by both parties which recognizes the existence of a contract is sufficient to establish a contract for sale although the writings of the parties do not otherwise establish a contract. In such case the terms of the particular contract consist of those terms on which the writings of the parties agree, together with any supplementary terms incorporated under any other provisions of this Act.

It should be obvious from the first paragraph above that section 2–207 shatters the mirror-image requirement of an acceptance that prevailed at common law, so long as the acceptance is *definite* and timely *and* the acceptance was not made *expressly* conditional on assent to the additional terms.

Section 2–207 reflects this approach of the Code: *is there a bargain between the parties;* do their forms agree on *anything?* If they do, then there is a contract on what they agree upon, unless the offer clearly indicates that acceptance can

The search for a bargain from the forms of the parties.

be *only* in compliance with the offer's terms. The Code is saying: speak up clearly to indicate your intent, for if you do not do so, this is how the UCC will interpret your expression or silence or conduct in order to determine your intent and its legal effect.

In the battle of forms context, then, the starting point is that there is a contract that consists of the *terms on which the forms agree,* unless it is expressly stated in the acceptance that the acceptance is a counteroffer.

With regard to terms in the forms that vary, section 2 provides two lines for analysis depending upon the character of the parties. *If one or both of the parties are not merchants,* then the additional terms are to be construed as *proposals for additions to the contract.* This means they are *not* part of the contract unless the offeror agrees to them. This provision protects the offeror by allowing courts to find that a contract exists but essentially on the offeror's terms. However, the offeree is also not without protection. If the *offeree* intends to be bound *only* if *all* of its conditions are met, then it must conspicuously state this, in which case the offeree's form will not appear as a definite and seasonable expression of acceptance. It will be a *counteroffer,* and no contract will result until the offeror accepts the offeree's terms.[14]

However, section 2–207 contemplates our given factual pattern involving merchants and provides a second and more significant line of analysis. If both the parties are merchants and the acceptance does not expressly state it is a counteroffer, then the added terms of the offeree in the acceptance *become part of the contract* unless (1) the offer form expressly limits acceptance to *its* terms, or (2) they materially alter the offeror's form, or (3) notification of objection to them is given within a reasonable time after notice of them is received.

Although neither of the merchants in our factual pattern may have read the other's form, the law properly assumes that they should. Again, section 2–207 seems to favor the merchant offeror by making its document controlling if it limits acceptance to its terms only. If the offering form does not so limit acceptance, then the offeree's additions become part of the contract (again, on the assumption that the acceptance can not be termed a counteroffer) unless the offeror objects to them within a reasonable time after notice of them is received *or* they materially alter the offeror's form.

This brings us to the crucial question of what is a material alteration? The comments to section 2–207 state that a material alteration is one that would result in unreasonable surprise or hardship to the other party. Comment 4 gives (in part) the following general examples of additions that would materially alter an offer:

1. "a clause negating . . . standard warranties"; and
2. "a clause reserving to the seller the power to cancel upon the buyer's failure to meet any invoice when due."

Another example is a clause requiring one of the parties to meet a much higher standard of performance than is accepted in the trade generally.

---

[14] For a thorough review and analysis of 2–207, see Barron and Dunfee, *Two Decades of 2–207: Review, Reflection and Revision,* 24 Clev. St. L. Rev. 171, 182 (1975).

When the terms in the forms agree.

When the terms in the forms vary.

If one or both parties are not merchants.

If both parties are merchants.

Offeree's terms materially altering offeror's terms.

Comment 5 suggests alterations that would not materially alter an offer. They are (in part):

1. "a clause setting forth and perhaps enlarging slightly upon the seller's exemption [from liability] due to supervening causes beyond his control";
2. "a clause fixing a reasonable time for complaints within customary limits";
3. "a clause providing for interest on overdue invoices . . . where they are within the range of trade practice".

By comparing the above suggestions on defining materiality, one may discern the central policy of this section. It is, stated briefly: *where either of the parties attempts to vary standard or accepted commercial usage, they should bring this to the attention of the other party and make it a subject of negotiation.* If such a variation is not negotiated, then a court may find that such a provision is not part of the contract.

A simple approach to the complexities created by doing business through standardized forms is to provide large spaces for the parties either to write or type in all key features of the understanding. Where trade usage is being varied (not merely clarified), this should be typed or written in and the offeror's approval of it should be sought. The UCC provides that, where express terms in a contract conflict with a course of performance or usage of trade, the express terms will control.[15] In the following case there was no express consent to a disclaimer of consequential damages, so it did not become part of the contract.

Use of spaces in the forms.

Facts

The plaintiff, Air Products and Chemicals, Inc., purchased from the defendant, Fairbanks Morse, Inc., ten large electric motors ranging from 800 to 1700 horsepower. The negotiations formally began on April 15, 1964 when the plaintiff orally ordered some of the motors which were to become the subject of this controversy. On April 21, 1964 the plaintiff sent its "purchase order" confirming its verbal order of April 15. On April 30, 1964 the defendant returned an executed copy of the plaintiff's purchase order together with the defendant's "Acknowledgment of Order" form. After the motors were constructed, shipped, and installed, the plaintiff alleged that they failed to perform as promised and sued the defendant for more than $31,000.

In this case there were numerous issues of law and fact to be decided, and just one of them was whether the plaintiff could sue for damages beyond what it cost to have the motors repaired to perform properly. These damages, called consequential damages, may be awarded if they are a foreseeable event at the time the contract is made and the other party is aware of them. In this case the plaintiff was asking for consequential damages because of work stoppage and lost profits.

The plaintiff's purchase order form stated, in part:

Seller recognizes that failure to make delivery of . . . equipment conforming to the requirements of this purchase order . . . will subject buyer to substantial damages due to delay and disruption of work schedules, inefficient use of manpower and other reasons. . . .

---

[15] UCC 1–205(4) and 2–208(2).

In response to the purchase order, the defendant sent its "Acknowledgment of Order" form, which read, in part:

We thank you for your order as copied hereon, which will receive prompt attention and shall be governed by the provisions on the reverse side hereof unless you notify us to the contrary within 10 days or before shipment whichever is earlier. . . .

On the reverse side of the acknowledgment form it stated, in part:

The Company nowise assumes any responsibility or liability with respect to use, purpose, or suitability, and shall not be liable for damages of any character, whether direct or consequential, for defect, delay, or otherwise. . . .

Was there a "contract"? If so, which contract provision controls the question of whether the plaintiff may seek damages for the delay caused by the improper performance of the motors?

Decision
Judgment for the plaintiff.

Reasoning
The appellate court held that the plaintiff could sue for consequential damages caused by the delay. The court held that a contract existed because the "Acknowledgment of Order" form stated that the provisions contained there "form part of the order acknowledged and accepted on the face hereof," and, this form contained no express provision making assent to its different or additional terms necessary. The remaining issue was whether the additional or different terms of the "Acknowledgment of Order" form were material. On this point the court held that a disclaimer for consequential loss that has the effect of eliminating millions of dollars in damages is sufficiently material to require that a waiver or alteration of it be expressly consented to by the party affected.

Air Products & Chemicals, Inc., v. Fairbanks Morse, Inc., 206 N.W.2d 414 (Wis. 1973).

Section 2–207 makes another important change in the common law of contracts. Under that law, a confirmation is not an acceptance because it does not assent to the offer; it only confirms receipt of the offer. Section 2–207 provides that a *written* confirmation is an acceptance, the above discussion being applicable to it. Of course, if the confirmation specifies that it is not an acceptance, then it is not an acceptance.

The confirmation as an acceptance.

Interpretation of the Sales Contract

The Significance of "Course of Performance," "Course of Dealing," and "Usage of Trade"

Interpreting the intent of parties by focusing on their exchange of *words* may not be a good way to arrive at the parties' understanding but, as one commentator remarked about democracy, "Show me something better." Words, although used precisely, lack precision. Yet they are the single best starting point for an analysis of the parties' "contract."

The UCC read with the common law of contracts helps to determine what evidence can be used by a court to give meaning to words. One of these rules of evidence, the parol evidence rule, was presented in chapter 22, the *first* chapter on Sales, because it is a general guide for courts to use in ascertaining the parties' intent. We have just completed an analysis of the sections that tell us which *words* should be controlling when forms are exchanged.

The UCC provides us with two more lines of analysis to help us in arriving at a fair interpretation of the parties' contractual intent. One is on course of performance, course of dealing, and usage of trade; the other is on modification, rescission, and waiver.

Comment 1 to section 1–205 sets out the general rule that "the meaning of the agreement of the parties is to be determined by the language used by them and by their action, read and interpreted in the light of commercial practices and other surrounding circumstances." Of course, the terms of the agreement and any course of performance, **course of dealing** and usage of trade are to be construed as consistent with each other whenever reasonable.[16]

course of dealing "a sequence of previous conduct between the parties to a particular transaction which is fairly to be regarded as establishing a common basis of understanding for interpreting their expressions and other conduct" UCC 1–205(1)

When there is conflict between events such as just mentioned, the UCC provides this order of priority of controlling events:

1. express terms of an agreement,[17]
2. course of performance,[18]
3. course of dealing,
4. usage of trade.

The distinction between course of performance and course of dealing is directly related to the time in the transaction when the conduct occurs. Conduct *after* the particular agreement is made and which is a result of the agreement is a "course of performance"; conduct of the parties *prior* to the particular agreement is a "course of dealing."[19]

Usage of trade is defined by the conduct of "the great majority of decent dealers, even though dissidents ready to cut corners do not agree" and is not defined solely by the parties themselves.[20] The following case is concerned with an industry-wide practice as a usage of trade.

usage of trade "any practice or method of dealing having such regularity of observance in a place, vocation or trade as to justify an expectation that it will be observed with respect to the transaction in question" UCC 1–205(2)

Facts

During February 1973 a general contractor telephoned a supplier of concrete and inquired about the price and terms for the sale of concrete. The supplier said that the stated price would be "adhered to for the year." The supplier provided concrete for the general contractor from February 1973 through March 1974. The price remained the same from February 1973 until December 30, 1973. These deliveries were paid for by the general contractor. The general contractor was notified of a price increase effective

---

[16] UCC 1–205(4), 2–208(2).

[17] UCC 1–205(4).

[18] UCC 2–208(2).

[19] Nordstrom, p. 152.

[20] UCC 1–205, comment 5.

January 1, 1974 but believed that since "the contract" was for "the year" they would not be effective regarding him until the end of February 1974. Deliveries were made by the supplier to the general contractor during January and February 1974. When billed for these at the increased price, the general contractor offered to pay only at the 1973 price. Was the initial oral contract, neither of which the parties deny, for the delivery of concrete at a stated price for "the year" to run for one year from the date of its making or to run until the end of the calendar year?

Decision
Judgment for the supplier.

Reasoning
The court pointed out that the words used, the course of performance, and course of dealing were not helpful in giving meaning to the words "the

year." The court relied on three other reasons. The first is that both parties agreed the words were "the" year and not "a" year. Seeing no circumstances surrounding the contract formation or the subsequent conduct of the parties which would lead it to believe the parties intended anything other than the normal and natural meaning, the court concluded that when one uses the words "the year," the calendar year is contemplated.

Secondly, the court noted that it was an industry-wide practice to make price increases effective on January 1, and the general contractor could be charged with notice of this.

Finally, the court said that, in fact, the general contractor had actual notice of the price increase.

Loizeaux Builders Supply Co. v. Donald B. Ludwig Co., 366 A.2d 721 (N.J. 1976).

Contract Modification, Rescission, and Waiver

If an offeree agrees to most of the terms in an offer but conspicuously notes additional terms in its form and makes acceptance *conditional* upon them and they are agreed to by the offeror, then, technically, there is a contract on the *first* set of terms and a *modification* of the contract by the offeree's terms. *Such a modification needs no consideration to be binding.*[21] Again, the UCC de-emphasizes the technical requirements of the common law and makes the manifested intent of the parties controlling. Certain "adjustments" to contractual understandings are inevitable, and these are recognized and given effect—so long as they are done in good faith. Comment to 2–209 expressly provides that a "modification" without legitimate commercial reason is ineffective as a violation of the duty of good faith.

For example, many contracts for the purchase of raw materials such as coal or minerals may be for periods of five years or longer. In some cases a buyer may have rearranged his business to depend upon raw materials from a particular supplier with whom a long-term contract has been negotiated. As the dependency upon a certain seller by the buyer increases, the seller gains bargaining power and may be tempted to assert that the buyer agreed to a modification of the contract price. Such an assertion by the seller would not be in good faith. Since

---

[21] UCC 2–209(1).

no new consideration is needed to support this "alleged" new promise, courts will police such agreements looking for commercial circumstances which would be somewhat beneficial to both parties if a modification were made.

There are two potential problems with modification which were contemplated by the drafters of the UCC. The first is that they recognized the commercial necessity for modification, but they perceived that many merchants would attempt to protect themselves against fraudulent oral modifications[22] by putting in their forms that no modification will be effective unless it is signed by the parties. If such a provision is in a merchant's form, then section 2–209(2) states that a requirement compelling a written modification must be separately signed by the party *not* supplying the form. For example, if a merchant-*seller's* form states that it can not be modified or rescinded except by a signed writing, then, to be effective, the purchaser must separately sign or initial this requirement. The UCC requires the merchant who is not the author of the form to sign separately this provision in the form because such a provision may vary trade usage with regard to modification.

A second and related problem may involve the application of the statute of frauds. If the contract as modified (a change of price from $600 to $550, for example) is within the statute, then a signed writing by the party to be charged is needed. In the following case, while the oral modification was within the statute of frauds, nevertheless, since the statute was not pleaded, it was unavailable as a defense. Also, the court held that a modification did not require consideration to be binding.

Protection against fraudulently alleged oral modification.

Modification and the statute of frauds.

Facts

The purchasers of an airplane sued the sellers for the return of the airplane which was repossessed by the sellers on the alleged default of the buyers. On October 3, 1959 the plaintiffs purchased an airplane from the defendants, taking possession of the plane and promising to make payments of $200 per month over a period of 24 months with a final payment of $353.34. Prior to the due date of the first payment, the airplane developed engine trouble, to repair which required either the rebuilding of the engine or the installation of a new one for $1,400. This imposed a financial burden on the plaintiffs which they were unable to bear. They offered to return the unrepaired plane without charge in exchange for a cancellation of all agreements. But the defendants orally agreed that for the first year of the installment contract the payments were to be reduced from $200 to $100 per month. The plaintiffs agreed to this. The defendants derived no benefit from this oral modification other than that the plane was not returned.

This modification was suggested in October and begun in November 1959. In March 1960 the defendants told the plaintiffs the payments would

---

[22] The circumstance contemplated here is when the seller tells the buyer after a substantial down payment has been made, "I can not possibly produce for the contract price, I must have ten percent more." Understandably, purchasers desire protection when it is asserted fraudulently by the seller that they agreed to the modification. See J. White and R. Summers, *Handbook of the Law Under the Uniform Commercial Code* (St. Paul: West Pub. Co., 1972), p. 40.

have to be increased to $200 per month. When the plaintiffs refused this, the defendants took possession of the plane. The trial court rendered judgment for the plaintiffs. The defendants appealed. Was the contract of purchase modified, thus rendering the repossession wrongful?

Decision
Judgment for the plaintiffs.

Reasoning
The court discussed three major issues, only two of which are important here. First, the defendants argued *on appeal* that the statute of frauds rendered the modification unenforceable. The appellate court noted that since the statute of frauds was not pleaded at the trial stage as a first item of defense, it was not available as a defense later in the litigation. Second, the defendants argued that they received no consideration whatsoever when they agreed to modify the terms of the installment contract. The court found this an obvious situation for application of section 2-209(1), which states that an agreement modifying a contract needs no consideration to be binding. Thus, there was no breach of the modified contract by the plaintiffs and the repossession of the plane was wrongful.

Skinner v. Tober Foreign Motors, Inc., 187 N.E.2d 669 (Mass. 1963).

The opinion in the case above notes that, under the written agreement, the payments were due on the 15th of every month. They were, in fact, made between the 15th and 18th, but the defendants never protested. Also, the defendants never protested the fact that the plaintiffs failed to carry insurance on the plane for short periods of time, also in breach of the written agreement. Although the defendants in this case did not make these circumstances the subject of their arguments, could they have relied upon them as evidence of a breach? This is doubtful. A court may hold that failure to object to conduct varying from that required by a written contract is a *waiver* of the written provisions. The UCC does not define waiver but does recognize that waivers may exist where modifications or rescissions do not. Section 2–209(4) states that, although an attempt at modification or rescission does not satisfy the signed writing requirements of a modification or of the statute of frauds, it can operate as a waiver. In the above case, if waiver of the statute of frauds had not occurred, the modified contract would be within the statute and unenforceable without a proper writing.

In conclusion, section 2–209 cautions both the parties to a contract and the courts about the need for a writing to support oral modifications of written contracts, but the section allows a court the flexibility to find that a party has waived a right if the court is convinced the party knowingly relinquished it and the other party has relied upon this. Waiver is used more often in situations where estoppel would have been pleaded at common law.

The Exchange of Property Interests in a Sales Transaction

property
a thing; also an interest or right in a thing

The nature of property merits our attention as another dimension to our image of a typical sales transaction between merchants. **Property,** as the word is conventionally used, refers to things, such as goods or land, which are tangible, and rights of action (e.g., accounts receivable) which are intangible. However, the law and the UCC in particular recognize numerous different legal rights in property often called **property interests.** This accumulation of property interests, usually likened to a bundle of sticks, should be the object of our attention together with the physical item that is the object of the contract. In other words, we are talking about a thing and an interest in that thing. For example, if you own a typewriter, the typewriter is the thing and your title is the interest in the thing. The contract of sale is merely the legal device by which these property interests are shifted—sometimes one at a time, sometimes in bunches—from one party to another.

property interest
a legally recognized and protected right in property

The UCC recognizes many different property interests. Article 3, for example, sets out the law on commercial paper, the use of which, among other things, shifts property interests in checking accounts. Also, all of Article 9 is devoted to the creation, transfer, enforcement, and destruction of a property interest called a "security interest." This property interest allows the holder of it to claim possession of goods under certain circumstances—usually when a buyer defaults in payment of the purchase price to the holder of the interest.

In this part of the chapter we analyze a very important property interest recognized by Article 2, the "insurable interest." Following this we analyze a related notion, risk of loss of an interest. And finally, we discuss briefly the concept of title under Article 2.

Insurable Interest

One of the most important things in the minds of contracting merchants is how to protect themselves from some unforeseeable event which might cause damage or destruction to goods that are the subject of the contract. Section 2–501 was drafted specifically to cover this concern of the parties. It is one of the least complicated sections of Article 2, so spelling it out is the best way to begin our analysis of it. It provides:

insurable interest
a person's interest in property or life which can be insured against loss or death

(1) The buyer obtains a special property and an insurable interest in goods by identification of existing goods as goods to which the contract refers even though the goods so identified are non conforming and he has an option to return or reject them. Such identification can be made at any time and in any manner explicitly agreed to by the parties. In the absence of explicit agreement identification occurs
(a) when the contract is made if it is for the sale of goods already existing and identified;
(b) if the contract is for the sale of future goods . . . when goods are shipped, marked or otherwise designated by the seller as goods to which the contract refers. . .
(2) The seller retains an insurable interest in goods so long as title to or any security interest in the goods remains in him and where the identification is by the seller alone he may until default or insolvency or notification to the buyer that the identification is final substitute other goods for those identified.
(3) Nothing in this section impairs any insurable interest recognized under any other statute or rule of law.

Possession of an insurable interest in goods enables the possessor to obtain insurance on the goods to cover the risks of damage to, or loss of his interest in, the goods. *An insurable interest exists independently of which party has title, and of which party has the risk of loss; and, it may exist in duplicate so that both the seller and buyer may have insurable interests in the same goods.*[23] For example, when a seller identifies goods as those which will fill a specific contractual obligation, then an insurable interest passes to the buyer (unless the contract provides otherwise). If the goods are destroyed while still in the possession of the seller, the buyer, if it had insurance, could recover the value it lost (usually the downpayment) and the seller, assuming it still had an insurable interest and in fact had insurance, could recover the value of its loss.

The crucial inquiry is: when is the earliest possible moment that a buyer can acquire an insurable property interest in goods for which the buyer may have already made a substantial payment? The answer is: as soon as the seller (or in some cases the buyer) *identifies* the goods—designates those goods for that contract. *The act of identification* may be defined by the agreement of the parties and, if it is not, then it occurs according to subsections (a) and (b) above. The following case illustrates that an insurable interest passed to the purchaser when the contract was made since the goods were existing and could be identified then.

Facts

The Missouri Pacific Railroad sold to the firm of Carrow and McGee all of its equipment located in five buildings in DeSoto, Missouri, on April 21, 1966. Carrow and McGee were to remove all of the equipment, and the best reading of the contract for sale was that title to the equipment was to pass when the equipment was removed. Before removal of the equipment, Carrow and McGee sold a large compressor on the property to Davis, who some weeks later sold it to the National Compressor Corporation for $12,000, which was paid. A fire destroyed the compressor before its removal.

The National Compressor Corporation sued numerous parties alleging that *its* compressor was destroyed by the fire which was negligently caused by the various parties involved in cleaning up the property. The defendants moved to have the plaintiff, National Compressor Corporation, dismissed from the suit because it had no property interest in the compressor.

Decision

Judgment for the plaintiff.

Reasoning

The court held that the passage of title to the compressor was *not* controlling because the plaintiff had a "special property" or insurable interest in the compressor. This property interest passed at the time the contract for sale was made because the compressor was existing and had been identified at that time.

National Compressor Corporation v. Carrow, 417 F.2d 97 (1969).

---

[23] Nordstrom, pp. 383, 387.

If the contract is for the sale of *future goods*, then an insurable interest passes to the buyer when the "goods are shipped, marked or otherwise designated by the seller as goods to which the contract refers." This "designation" by the seller requires some overt act by the seller which comes at a time when those goods are so far assembled that they would be considered "existing" in the common understanding of those in commerce.[24] Under section 2–501 all doubts are resolved in favor of identification. Providing for early identification by resolving all doubts in favor of identification does not give the buyer a windfall because only the loss suffered can be recovered from an insurance company.

Fungible goods are goods (such as grain or oil) in which every part of the goods is perfectly substitutable, or is so treated by the sales contract. Under section 2–501(1)(a), the mere making of a contract for the sale of existing fungible goods is sufficient identification to effect an identification.

Risk of Loss

Article 2 has two sections directly applicable in determining which party has the risk of loss. The underlying theory of both of these sections is that the risk of loss should shift according to the agreement of the parties. If the agreement is silent, then the point at which the risk shifts depends upon whether the seller has completed its performance and whether the seller breaches the agreement by tendering non-conforming goods. That is, the drafters of Article 2 did not think it fair that the seller, who is assumed to have the risk of loss, could shift the risk to the buyer by tendering goods that failed to conform to the contract. So, two sections were devised: one to operate in the absence of a breach, the other to operate when there has been a breach by either party.

First, in the absence of a breach by the seller and in the absence of a contractual provision to the contrary, the *risk of loss shifts, generally speaking, when the seller completes its performance with regard to the goods.* So, where the contract requires the seller *to ship the goods by carrier,* the risk of loss passes to the buyer when the goods are duly delivered[25] to the carrier[26] or, if the contract requires *delivery at a particular destination,* the risk of loss passes at the destination when the goods are so tendered to enable the buyer to take delivery.[27] In the following case the seller was to ship the goods by carrier and, on doing so, the risk of loss shifted to the buyer.

Risk of loss without breach of contract.

---

[24] Id., p. 386.

[25] The words "duly delivered" are meant to incorporate the tender requirements of a shipment contract (set out in 2–504) which are that the seller must (1) put the goods in the possession of such a carrier as is reasonable; (2) make a reasonable contract for their transportation; and (3) obtain and promptly deliver the necessary documents and notify the buyer of shipment. See section 2–509, comment 2.

[26] UCC 2–509(1)(a).

[27] UCC 2–509(1)(b).

Facts

A manufacturer of men's clothing in Los Angeles contracted with the owner of a men's clothing store located in Westport, Connecticut for the sale of a variety of clothing for the sum of $2,216. The contract stated that the shipment was to be "F.O.B. Los Angeles." The manufacturer made arrangements for the shipment via carrier from Los Angeles to Connecticut. When the goods were delivered to the purchaser's place of business, the purchaser's agent refused to unload the clothes. The carrier's agent likewise refused to unload the truck, saying that it was the purchaser's obligation to unload. The carrier left with the shipment, which was either destroyed, lost, or stolen from the carrier. It simply disappeared or was beyond the power of the parties to reclaim it. The manufacturer sued the purchaser for the contract price alleging the risk of loss had passed to the purchaser at the time of the delivery of the clothes to the carrier.

Decision

Judgment for the plaintiff manufacturer.

Reasoning

The risk of loss passes from the seller to a purchaser when the seller completes its performance with regard to the goods. The use of the phrase "F.O.B. (meaning free on board) Los Angeles" in the contract is a delivery term. Where the term is F.O.B. place of shipment (Los Angeles), the seller must at that place put the goods into the possession of a carrier and pay the expense and bear the risk *to that point*. From this point, the purchaser bears the expense and the risk of loss. The seller's duties ended upon proper delivery of the goods to a carrier in Los Angeles and so did its liability for loss or damage to the goods. The carrier became the agent of the purchaser, and any liability for loss must be resolved between these two parties.

Ninth Street East, Ltd. v. Harrison, 259 A.2d 772 (Conn. 1968).

---

bailee
the person to whom goods are bailed

bailment
a delivery of goods by a bailor to a bailee which are to be returned to the bailor or as he directs in accordance with the bailment agreement

When the goods are in the possession of a **bailee**—a warehouseman for example—and they are to be delivered without being moved, then the risk of loss again passes when the seller completes its performance under the contract by passing the right to control the goods to the buyer. This may occur (a) when the seller delivers a *negotiable document of title* to the buyer for the goods; or (b) when *the bailee acknowledges* the buyer's right to possession of the goods; or (c) after the buyer receives, and does not object to, a non-negotiable document of title or written direction of the seller for the bailee to deliver the goods.[28] The buyer is entitled to (a) or (b) above; he does not have to accept (c).

Finally, in circumstances in which the seller is not required to ship and the goods are not in the possession of a bailee, the risk of loss passes to the buyer *on receipt* of the goods *if the seller is a merchant;* otherwise the risk passes on tender of delivery of the goods.[29]

---

[28] UCC 2–509(2).

[29] UCC 2–509(3).

Second, obviously, the seller should not be able to shift the risk of loss to the buyer when the seller has breached the contract, as by tendering non-conforming goods or otherwise failing to fulfill its obligations. This result is reached by section 2–510, which provides that the risk does not shift when the goods fail to conform until the seller **cures** the defect or the buyer accepts the goods. If the goods have been accepted by the buyer and then the buyer discovers a defect that would be a breach of contract by the *seller,* or if the *buyer* breaches the contract while the goods are still in the possession of the seller and the goods are damaged or loss occurs, then the one suffering the loss may recover any amounts not covered by its insurance from the other party. The UCC comments state this rule this way: "In cases where there has been a breach of the contract, if the one in control of the goods is the aggrieved party, whatever loss . . . may prove to be uncovered by his insurance falls upon the contract breaker . . ."[30] For example, if the buyer repudiates the contract *after* the seller has identified conforming goods to the contract but *before* shipment, and the goods are damaged through no fault of its own, the seller may collect the loss not covered by its insurance from the buyer. In short, the wrongdoer suffers the loss.

In conclusion for this part on insurable interest and risk of loss, one should understand that these are special property interests which may exist independently, although there are circumstances in which both will pass to the buyer at the same time. One example of an insurable interest in the buyer being significant—without risk of loss passing—would be when the buyer contracts for the construction and delivery of a large, complex machine. After the machine has been identified to the contract in the seller's plant, it is destroyed by fire that consumed the entire plant. The buyer, let us assume, had paid $10,000 at the time the contract was formed on a total price of $50,000. Further, let us assume the seller is now insolvent and had not carried sufficient insurance to cover the loss of the machine. The risk of loss may still be on the seller because it has not delivered the machine, but if the buyer had been prudent, it should have insured its interest in the machine, which would have been at least $10,000. The buyer could have done so because an insurable interest (its contract right to the machine) passed to the buyer when the machine was identified to the contract.

Transfer of Title Under Article 2
In pre-UCC law, the predominant property interests in goods were all linked to the concept of title to the goods. But the abstract notion of who had title became confusing as merchants entered into increasingly complex commercial transactions. The drafters of the UCC realized that what the parties were essentially interested in, when they referred to title, was who could get insurance on the goods and who would suffer damage due to loss if the goods were destroyed. Therefore they drafted Article 2 to deal specifically with these circumstances, which were discussed above.

---

[30] UCC 2–510(2)(3), comment 3.

cure
a seller's correction of his failure to deliver conforming goods under a contract for sale before the due date has expired

The drafters realized that problems concerning "the rights, obligations and remedies of the seller, the buyer, purchasers or other third parties"[31] could not be resolved by the single all-governing concept of who had the title. Accordingly, the Code provided separate, specific provisions to apply to such rights, obligations, and remedies "irrespective of title to the goods except where the provision refers to such title." When situations arise which are not covered by the Code, and when title becomes material, section 2–401 established rules for the transfer of title.

Before we proceed to an examination of ownership or title problems created by a "faulty title" or entrusting goods to another, we will consider *when* and *how* title is transferred to a buyer.

Existing and identified goods at the time the contract is made.

When Title Can Pass Under Article 2. Title to goods can not pass prior to the time *goods exist and are identified to the contract.* If the goods exist and are identified to the contract *at the time the contract is made,* then the passage of title will depend upon the express or implied intention of the parties. If the agreement *expresses* when title is to pass, it will pass at that time. However, if the agreement contains no expression of intent, then title will pass at the moment the seller *commits* those goods to the contract.[32] Under the Code, committing goods to the contract depends on whether or not *delivery* is to be made by moving the goods. When delivery is to be made *without moving the goods* (seller says, pick up the goods at my warehouse or from a third party), then:

Delivery without movement of the goods.

(a) if the seller is to deliver a document of title, title passes at the time when and the place where he delivers such documents; or
(b) if the goods are at the time of contracting already identified and no documents are to be delivered, title passes at the time and place of contracting.[33]

Delivery by movement of the goods.

When delivery is to be made *by moving the goods,* title passes at the time and place at which the seller completes *its performance* with reference to the physical delivery of the goods.[34] Determining when this performance has been completed is aided by using certain shipment abbreviations.

If the seller is *to ship* the goods, then when the title passes depends on whether the seller is to "send" the goods—namely, "F.O.B. shipping point"—or the seller is to "deliver" the goods at a destination—namely, "F.O.B. destination." If "F.O.B. shipping point," then there is no expense to the buyer until the goods are delivered to the carrier. If "F.O.B. destination," then there is no expense to the buyer until the goods are tendered at the destination point. *If F.O.B. shipping point, title passes at the time and place the goods are delivered to the carrier. If F.O.B. destination, title passes when the goods are tendered at the destination.* Delivery may be of the actual goods, or of a negotiable bill of lading covering them. The form of the bill of lading, whether negotiable or non-negotiable, and irrespective of who the consignee is, has no effect on the transfer of title.

[31] UCC 2–401, opening paragraph.

[32] UCC 2–401.

[33] UCC 2–401(3)(a) and (b).

[34] UCC 2–401(2).

When, pursuant to the contract, goods are shipped C.O.D., meaning "collect on delivery," the carrier is to collect the purchase price before delivering the goods. C.O.D. has no effect on the transfer of title. It defers the buyer's right to inspect the goods before accepting them.

It should be noted that, in a "sale on approval," neither title nor risk of loss passes until the buyer approves. However, in a "sale or return," title and risk of loss pass to the buyer subject to his right to return the goods instead of paying the purchase price. If the intention of the parties is unclear as to which of these it is: if the goods are acquired *primarily for use,* it is a sale on approval; if *primarily for resale,* it is a sale or return.[35]

The above discussion of *when* title could pass under Article 2 was premised on the fact that the goods existed and were identified at the time the contract was made. If the goods do not exist and are therefore not identified to the contract (for example, a contract to sell a machine to be built), they are "future goods." A contract for future goods is enforceable, but title can not pass until the goods are identified to the contract in accordance with the intention of the parties.

Future goods at the time the contract is made.

How Title Can Be Transferred Under Article 2. The general rule is that a *person can transfer only what he has.* So a seller can not pass to a buyer a "better" title than the seller had. (T stcals O's goods and sells them to B, a **good faith** purchaser for value. B got what T had and, since T got nothing from O, then O still owns the goods.) Section 2–403 recognizes this rule, but adds to it that in three instances the seller has a "power" to transfer a better title than the seller has. These three instances are the result of conduct by the owner which is unfair to the buyer causing the buyer to obtain the owner's title.

good faith
"honesty in fact in the conduct or transaction concerned"
UCC 1-201(19)

The transferee gets only what the transferor has or has power to transfer.

1. *Estoppel.* When one person *holds out* (manifests) to another person that something is or is not so, and the other person *materially changes his position in reasonable reliance on the holding out,* the first person is "estopped" (precluded, stopped, prevented) from asserting the reverse of what he held out. (T steals your goods and tells B that he, T, owns the goods and will sell them to B. B then telephones you, describes the goods, tells you that he, B, is about to buy the goods from T, and asks you if they are your goods. You say they are not your goods. B then, for value and innocent of thc theft, buys the goods from T. Later you demand the goods from B. You are estopped to assert that the goods belong to you because you had held out to B that they did not belong to you and B then materially changed his position in reasonable reliance on your statement when he bought the goods from T. T had the "power" to transfer your title to B because of your conduct creating **estoppel,** and B gets your title to the goods.)

estoppel
(UCC Sales) a holding out by the owner and a material change of position by the buyer in reasonable reliance on the owner's holding out

2. *Voidable title transfer.* If the seller has a voidable title, he has the "power" to transfer a good title, free of the power of avoidance, to a "good faith purchaser for value." (S fraudulently induced you to sell your goods to S, thereby creating a voidable contract voidable by you. S has a voidable title to the goods.

Voidable title transfer, and a "good faith purchaser for value."

---

[35] UCC 2–326(1). But, with one exception, if the goods are delivered to a person for sale who has a place of business under a name other than that of the person selling him the goods, then, solely with respect to the buyer's creditors, the transaction can be only a sale or return and not a sale on approval irrespective of the intentions of the parties. UCC 2–326(3).

S sells the goods to B, a good faith purchaser for value. You could have exercised your power of avoidance *before* S's sale to B and, since S would no longer have title to the goods, S could not later pass any title to B. Since you did not do this before B's innocent purchase, your power to avoid as to B ceases to exist, T now has the "power" to transfer your title to B, and B gets the title.)

3. *Entrusting goods to a merchant who deals in goods of that kind.* UCC 2–403(2) provides:

> Any entrusting of possession of goods to a *merchant* who deals in goods of that kind gives him power to transfer all rights of the entruster to a buyer in ordinary course of business. [Emphasis added.]

When the owner of goods "entrusts" (delivers) them to a merchant who deals in goods of that kind, the owner clothes the merchant with the appearance of being the owner of the goods. The merchant's unauthorized sale of the goods to a buyer in ordinary course of business transfers a good title to such buyer. (You deliver your watch for repair to a jeweler, J, who *sells* watches. J sells your watch for $100 to B, who believes J owns the watch. B gets title to your watch. You may recover the reasonable value of the watch from J because of his tort of **conversion** by his unauthorizedly exercising control and dominion over your watch as the owner without authority to do so, but B will have title to the watch.)

A problem of "value" arises under the "entrusting" rule above. You have learned in Part 2, Contracts, that under contract law a past debt is not consideration for a promise so that such a promise is not a contract. However, under the Code, which reflects the law merchant, "value" for a promise is a past debt as well as consideration. In the watch example above, if B had previously loaned money to J and J now promised to deliver the watch to B in satisfaction of that debt, J's promise under the law of contracts would not be a contract. However, since J is *selling goods* (a watch) to B, J's promise comes under Article 2 of the Code and *ordinarily* is "value" and enforceable. *But there are two exceptions under the Code when a past debt is not value.* One is in the case of a "duly negotiated holder" of a negotiable document of title, previously discussed in chapter 21, Carriers, Documents of Title, and Innkeepers. The other is for the "entrusting" rule above. Since B paid $100 as consideration for the watch, he is called a **buyer in ordinary course of business,** signifying that he is a good faith purchaser *who paid consideration* and not a past debt for that watch. If B had taken the watch for a past debt, he would not have paid value and you would have the right to regain the watch from B.

The reason for these three exceptions to the general rule of transfer of title is to protect and encourage the free flow of commerce. However one may rationalize these exceptions, it does appear that they represent an assertion on behalf of our collective society at the expense of individual property rights.

Today one of the most important reasons for establishing which party has title to goods is to determine which party may be subject to various forms of state taxation. Inventory taxes, sales taxes, personal property taxes, and the like may be assessed depending on which party has title.

Entrusting goods to a merchant who deals in goods of that kind, and a "buyer in ordinary course of business."

conversion
the tort of intentional interference with another's right to possession, control, and dominion of a chattel

buyer in ordinary course of business
"a person who, in good faith and without knowledge that the sale to him is in violation of the ownership rights or security interest of a third party in the goods, buys in ordinary course from a person in the business of selling goods of that kind but does not include a pawnbroker"; buying does not include a transfer for a past debt
UCC 1–201(9)

Under the Code, but not under contracts, a past debt is value, with two exceptions.

Summary Statement

1. In your study of this chapter and the next two chapters, imagine two large corporate merchants doing business; usually they "contract" by exchanging various form documents.
2. A contract for the sale of goods may be made in any manner sufficient to show agreement.
3. When a merchant gives his signed, written assurance in an offer that it will be held open for a stated time, it is not revocable for lack of consideration.
4. Generally offers may be made in any way that reveals an intent to be bound, and an acceptance shall be made in any manner and by any medium reasonable in the circumstances.
5. A shipment of non-conforming goods may be an acceptance, and so may the beginning of a requested performance if it is a reasonable mode of acceptance.
6. An acceptance sent within a reasonable time is effective even though it includes additional or different terms from those offered unless the acceptance is expressly made conditional on assent to the additional or different terms. Additional terms are to be construed as proposals for additions to the contract and, as between merchants, they become part of the contract unless:
   a. the offer expressly limits acceptance to the terms of offer;
   b. they materially alter it; or
   c. notification of the objection to them has been given or is given within a reasonable time after notice of them is received.
7. Express terms of an agreement together with course of performance, course of dealing, and usage of trade are all used to ascertain the parties' contractual intent.
8. The parties to a sales contract may modify their contractual understanding without consideration.
9. An insurable interest in the goods may pass to the buyer independently of the passage of the risk of loss or title to the goods; it passes when goods are identified to the contract. If the goods are existing, then identification occurs when the contract is made; if the contract is for the sale of future goods, then they are identified when they are shipped or otherwise designated by the seller as goods to which the contract refers.
10. The risk of loss for the goods passes from seller to buyer when the parties agree it will pass. If they have not so agreed, then the risk of loss shifts when the seller completes its performance with regard to the goods. But if the seller tenders non-conforming goods, then the risk shifts when the seller cures the defect or the buyer accepts the goods.
11. Goods must exist and be identified to the contract before title can pass, depending on the intention of the parties. If no intent is expressed, then the Code establishes the rules for the implied intent.
12. Generally, a seller can not pass to a buyer a better title than the seller itself has. However, the doctrines of estoppel, voidable title, and the entrusting of goods section of Article 2 make it possible for a seller to have the power to transfer a better title than he has.

The following very long appellate case presents a typical, complex commercial dispute and its resolution by Article 2. The court's opinion is very clear and educational, tying together the common law of contracts concerning offer and acceptance and the need for Article 2, particularly section 2–207. The case is well worth reading, even though it is long.

d/b/a
doing business as

Dorton & Castle, d/b/a The Carpet Mart v. Collins & Aikman Corp.
453 F.2d 1161 (1972)

The plaintiff, a carpet dealer doing business under the name of The Carpet Mart, sued the defendant, Collins & Aikman, a carpet manufacturer. Between 1968 and 1970 the plaintiff and defendant entered into more than 55 transactions involving the purchase and sale, respectively, of substantial quantities of carpeting. In 1970 the plaintiff learned that some of the carpeting purchased from the defendant was not 100 percent Kodel polyester fiber, as ordered, but was made of cheaper carpet fiber. The plaintiff sued for $450,000 based upon fraud and misrepresentation. Before the trial court could reach the merits of the case, the defendant moved to stay the proceedings based upon the allegation that its printed "sales acknowledgment" form *compelled* the parties to arbitrate their agreement if a dispute should arise. Before proceeding to an account of how the court resolved the issue about whether the parties were compelled to arbitrate, it is instructive to consider this factual background recounted by the court:

In each of the more than 55 transactions, one of the partners in The Carpet Mart, or on some occasions, Collins & Aikman's visiting salesman, telephoned Collins & Aikman's order department in Dalton, Georgia, and ordered certain quantities of carpets listed in Collins & Aikman's catalog. There is some dispute as to what, if any, agreements were reached through the telephone calls and through the visits by Collins & Aikman's salesman. After each oral order was placed, the price, if any, quoted by the buyer was checked against Collins & Aikman's price list, and the credit department was consulted to determine if The Carpet Mart had paid for all previous shipments. After it was found that everything was in order, Collins & Aikman's order department typed the information concerning the particular order on one of its printed acknowledgment forms. Each acknowledgment form bore one of three legends: "Acknowledgment," "Customer Acknowledgment," or "Sales Contract." The following provision was printed on the face of the forms bearing the "Acknowledgment" legend: "The acceptance of your order is subject to all of the terms and conditions on the face and reverse side hereof, including arbitration, all of which are accepted by buyer; it supersedes buyer's order form, if any. . . ."

The small print on the reverse side of the forms provided, among other things, that all claims arising out of the contract would be submitted to arbitration in New York City. Each acknowledgment form was signed by an employee of Collins & Aikman's order department and mailed to The Carpet Mart on the day the telephone order was received or, at the latest, on the following day. The carpets were thereafter shipped to The Carpet Mart, with the interval between the mailing of the acknowledgment form and shipment of the carpets varying from a brief interval to a period of several weeks or months. Absent a delay in the mails, however, The Carpet Mart always received the acknowledgment forms prior to receiving the carpets. In all cases The Carpet Mart took delivery of and paid for the carpets without objecting to any terms contained in the acknowledgment form.

Before the court reached the application of section 2-207 to these facts, it stated the following about the intended purpose of section 2-207:

. . . [I]t is clear that section 2-207, and specifically subsection 2-207(1), was intended to alter the . . . "mirror" rule of common law, under which the terms of an acceptance or confirmation were required to be identical to the terms of the offer or oral agreement. . . . Under the common law, an acceptance or a confirmation that contained terms additional to or different from those of the offer or oral agreement constituted a rejection of the offer or agreement and thus became a counteroffer. The terms of the counteroffer were said to have been accepted by the original offeror when he proceeded to perform under the contract without objecting to the counteroffer. Thus, a buyer was deemed to have accepted the seller's counteroffer if he took receipt of the goods and paid for them without objection.

Under section 2-207 the result is different. This section of the Code recognizes that in current commercial transactions, the terms of the offer and those of the acceptance will seldom be identical. Rather, under the current "battle of the forms," each party typically has a printed form drafted by his attorney, containing as many terms as could be envisioned to favor that party in his sales transactions. Whereas under common law the disparity between the fineprint terms in the parties' forms would have prevented the consummation of a contract when these forms are exchanged, section 2-207 recognizes that in many, but not all, cases the parties do not impart such significance to the terms on the printed forms. . . . [U]nder subsection (1), a contract is recognized notwithstanding the fact that an acceptance or confirmation contains terms additional to or different from those of the offer or prior agreement, provided that the offeree's intent to accept the offer is definitely expressed . . . and provided that the offeree's acceptance is not expressly conditioned on the offeror's assent to the additional or different terms. When a contract is recognized under subsection (1), the additional terms are treated as "proposals for addition to the contract," under subsection (2), which contains special provisions . . . such additional terms are deemed to have been accepted when the transaction is between merchants. Conversely, when no contract is recognized under subsection 2-207(1)—either because no definite expression of acceptance exists or, more specifically, because the offeree's acceptance is expressly conditioned on the offeror's assent to the additional or different terms—the entire transaction aborts (stops) at this point. If, however, the subsequent conduct of the parties— particularly, performance by both parties under what they apparently believe to be a contract—recognizes the existence of a contract, under subsection 2-207(3) such conduct by both parties is sufficient to establish a contract, notwithstanding the fact that no contract would have been recognized on the basis of their writings alone. . . .

The appellate court remanded this case back to the trial court for further findings of fact and suggested a method for resolving the issue of whether or not the parties had "agreed" to arbitrate the dispute. First, it said the court should find if the agreement was composed of the plaintiff's oral order and the defendant's acknowledgment. Second, if it was, was the arbitration provision an addition to or a term different from the offer? Third, if the arbitration provision was additional or different from the offer, was the acceptance expressly made conditional on assent to the additional terms so that 2-207(1) would be applicable? On this point the court advised that merely stating that the acceptance was "subject to all of the terms and conditions on the face and reverse side hereof including arbitration, all of which are accepted by the buyer," might not be sufficient to meet the requirement of 2-207(1). It suggested: "In order to fall within this proviso (2-207(1)), it is not enough that an acceptance is expressly conditional on additional or different terms; rather an acceptance must be *expressly* conditional on the offeror's assent to those terms."

Fourth, if on remand the trial court were to find that the acceptance was not expressly made conditional on assent to the additional terms, then the court must find there was a contract and, finally, the term compelling arbitration would bind both of the parties unless it materially altered the parties' understanding. This finding of materiality was the final point demanding the trial court's opinion.

Questions and Case Problems

1. State the three methods in which section 2-206 allows offerees to accept an offer.

2. In a paragraph or two, explain how section 2-207 of the UCC would resolve a conflict which centered upon the terms in forms of merchants.

3. Courts often must go beyond the terms of a written contract to give the words used some meaning. Clearly state what items of evidence or circumstance they may use in this inquiry and state the relative weights that must be given to each; that is, which bits of evidence are to control over others when there is a conflict?

4. An item of great importance to any sales contract is the question of which party is to bear the risk of loss for damage or destruction of the goods. Describe the point at which the risk of loss passes from the seller to the buyer, and how and when a buyer can protect itself from suffering a loss due to damage or destruction of the goods.

5. Roto-Lith, Ltd. is a corporation engaged in manufacturing cellophane bags for packaging vegetables. It ordered a drum of N-132-C emulsion from F.B. Bartlett & Co. on October 23, 1969 for the stated purpose of making wet pack spinach bags. In response to Roto-Lith's order form, the seller sent its "acknowledgment" form and the goods were shipped. The acknowledgment form and the invoice accompanying the goods both stated in conspicuous language, "all goods sold without warranties, express or implied. . . ." Further, on the back of the acknowledgment there was this statement, "If these terms are not acceptable, buyer must so notify seller at once."

   Roto-Lith did not protest the waiver of the warranties; it received, paid for, and used the emulsion. The emulsion was defective and Roto-Lith sued F.B. Bartlett for breach of contract (warranties). Article 2 states that, in every contract for the sale of goods, the seller makes a warranty that the goods sold were fit for the use for which the goods were sold. These "implied" warranties exist unless *the contract* between the parties waives these warranties. What was the contractual understanding between these parties with regard to the warranties? [*Roto-Lith Ltd. v. F.P. Bartlett & Co.,* 297 F.2d 497 (1962).]

6. Blue Rock Industries, a seller of sand, contracted with Raymond International to deliver large quantities of sand for road construction in Maine. The initial contract between the two stated that Blue Rock's price was to be as follows:

   . . . for truck measured sand delivered to the job site as you require:
   $2.75 per cubic yard delivered to the north side of the project;
   $2.60 per cubic yard delivered to the south side of the project.

Assume that the sand delivered may be measured in at least two ways. One way is to fill a five-yard dump truck up to the top; another is to figure what one yard of sand weighs, then weigh the sand (in the truck) and compute the price on this basis. That is, one method is to price the sand by volume, and one by weight.

   a. Looking at the contract, which method was contemplated?
   b. If a dispute arose between the two parties over these two varying methods of measuring sand, how would a court resolve it?

7. The firm of Bowman Hydro-Vat owned an airplane which they agreed to sell to Hemmer on December 12, 1970 for a price of $18,500. On that date $15,000 was paid down and the balance of $3,500 was to be paid later. Both parties agreed that title was to pass when "the necessary paperwork" was completed. A formal document of title was requested from the Federal Aviation Administration (FAA), and meanwhile Hemmer began using the airplane. The formal document was received by the seller on December 18, 1970 and was put in the mail on that date to Hemmer. On that same day, while Hemmer was piloting the aircraft, the tip of the wing caught a snow bank on takeoff, resulting in extensive damage. According to FAA regulations, the purchaser of an aircraft had to sign the title document received from the seller and then send it to the FAA, which would issue a title to the purchaser.

   a. Can the seller, Bowman Hydro-Vat, recover for the damage from its insurance company, provided that premiums were paid and the policy had not been cancelled?
   b. Could the purchaser have purchased insurance on the aircraft on December 12, 1970? [*Bowman v. American Home Assurance Company,* 213 N.W.2d 446 (Neb. 1973).]

8. Purchaser orders $10,000 worth of goods from seller and pays $5,000 down. The contract said that the seller was "to ship" the goods to the purchaser's plant. The parties did not otherwise agree on who was to bear the risk of loss, and the contract did not state that the shipment was to be F.O.B.

   a. When does the purchaser have an insurable interest?
   b. If the goods are placed on board a carrier by the seller and the goods conform to the contract and a reasonable contract for their shipment is made and the goods are destroyed in transit, which party bears the loss?
   c. Would the result in (b) above change if the goods placed on board the carrier by the seller were non-conforming? If so, how?

9. F fraudulently induced O, the owner of goods, to sell and deliver certain goods to F. F then sold and delivered the goods to G, a good faith purchaser, for value without notice of the fraud. G made a gift of the goods to D, who also is innocent of the fraud. O now discovers the fraud and demands the goods from D. Who gets the goods?

10. In the case of *Dorton & Castle, d/b/a The Carpet Mart v. Collins & Aikman Corp.,* 453 F.2d 1161 (1972),[36] the court discussed the impact of UCC 2-207 on that part of the law of contracts concerned with offer and acceptance. How would you explain that impact?

---

[36] See pp. 390–92.

24

Performance of the Sales Contract

After you have read this chapter, you should be able to:

1. Define how performance obligations of the parties are determined.
2. List and define the performance obligations of the seller and buyer in a typical sales transaction and be able to define the terms "F.O.B.," "F.A.S.," "C.I.F.," "C.F.," and "C. & F." and state the legal consequences of using them.
3. State what is meant by "perfect tender" of goods and documents and then state two circumstances in which the requirement of perfect tender is lessened.
4. Define what is meant by payment and state when and under what circumstances it is due.
5. Describe two special circumstances in which both the seller and buyer have performance obligations to one another and, in one case, obligations to creditors of the seller.
6. Define and explain three exceptions to the general rule that the parties must perform as promised.

Introduction

This chapter presents the key sections of Article 2 governing performance by the parties to a sales contract. As you study this chapter, imagine two *merchants* in cities some distance apart doing business. The "contract" between these parties is evidenced by one or more pieces of paper or one or more conversations exchanged by the parties. Based upon the material in chapters 22 and 23, you should be able to determine *the parties' contractual intent* when several documents or conversations or a mixture of both are present.

Generally, *it is this manifested intent that will determine the performance of the parties to the agreement.* That is, in almost all cases in which the *parties have reached* agreement about performance, this agreement will control. Where the parties *have not* reached agreement, because nothing was said or clearly understood about a particular performance obligation, then *Article 2 and the sections discussed* in this chapter *will control* the parties' performance.

Article 2, then, is valuable for our study of performance obligations for two important reasons: it will control when the agreement of the parties does not; and, even though the agreement may control in any given case, Article 2 will probably reflect how most of the agreements may allocate performance obligations.

> The express and implied contractual intent of the parties under the Code regarding their performance of the sales contract.

Performance Obligations of the Seller

Tender Obligations of the Seller

The general obligations of both parties to a sales contract are set out clearly in section 2–301. It provides:

> The obligation of the seller is to transfer and deliver and that of the buyer is to accept and pay in accordance with the contract.

> **tender**
> to proffer, make available

This section creates a set of **concurrent conditions—conditions** which must occur at the same time. The seller must duly tender the goods as a condition to the buyer's duty to accept and pay,[1] and the buyer must offer payment as a condition to the seller's duty to tender and complete delivery of the goods.[2] One of the parties must manifest an intent to perform (by either tendering the goods or payment) before the other party can be put in default. To put a buyer in default, *the seller must tender the goods in accordance with the contract,* and, if the buyer does not respond with payment, then a breach exists.

Conversely, to put the seller in default, *the buyer must tender payment.* Theoretically, if a substantial period of time passes after the date for performance and neither party comes forward to put the other in default by tendering performance, then courts may conclude that the parties have treated the contract as having expired. What usually happens, however, is that one of the parties will tender.

> **condition concurrent**
> a condition which must occur at the same time as another condition
>
> **condition**
> an uncertain event on the occurrence of which a contractual obligation is made contingent or dependent

---

[1] UCC 2–507(1).

[2] UCC 2–511.

Remember that both parties are under a fundamental duty to *perform in good faith*. We must proceed then on the assumption that, unless otherwise agreed, the parties will *begin* their performance after the agreement is made by the seller making plans for delivery of goods and the buyer making plans for payment.

Let us first examine what is meant by the seller's performance and start with the seller's *obligation to tender*. Under section 2–503 (in part):

(1) Tender of delivery requires that the seller put and hold **conforming goods** at the buyer's disposition and give the buyer any notification reasonably necessary to enable him to take delivery. The manner, time and place for tender are determined by the agreement and this Article, and in particular

(a) tender must be at a reasonable hour, and if it is of goods they must be kept available for the period reasonably necessary to enable the buyer to take possession; but

(b) unless otherwise agreed the buyer must furnish facilities reasonably suited to the receipt of the goods.

Methods of seller's tender of delivery.

The section above provides that the seller is to "put and hold conforming goods at the buyer's disposition," but it does not state *where* this is to take place. If the seller is to *ship* the goods, there are at least *three* possible places, depending on the circumstances. Usually the contract of the parties will *state* either where the *seller* is to ship the goods or where tender is to take place.

The *first common circumstance concerned with tender* is where the contract provides that the goods are to be shipped F.O.B. or F.A.S. *destination*. If, for example, a seller in Chicago agrees to tender the goods in Los Angeles, or at *any particular destination not in the seller's town,* then the seller must make all shipment arrangements and tender, through an agent of some sort, *at that destination*. This obligation is *usually* imposed upon the seller by the use of the term "F.O.B." (e.g., "F.O.B. Los Angeles" and the seller is in Chicago), or "F.A.S." followed by the name of a vessel and a port.

In the first instance (F.O.B. Los Angeles), tender is to take place in Los Angeles and the seller must, at its own expense and risk, transport the goods there to an address provided by the purchaser and there tender the goods.[3] If the term used is "F.O.B. Los Angeles" and the *port* and a *vessel* are named, then the *seller* must, again at its own expense and risk, transport the goods to Los Angeles and *load* the goods on board the vessel.[4]

F.A.S.
free alongside

If the term "**F.A.S.**" followed by a named port and vessel is used, the seller must deliver the goods at its own expense and risk *alongside* the vessel and there tender documents to an agent of the buyer.[5]

A *second common circumstance concerned with tender* is that the contract will state F.O.B. "place of shipment," "seller's town," or "seller's factory" (e.g.,

---

[3] UCC 2–319(1)(b).

[4] UCC 2–319(1)(c).

[5] UCC 2–319(2)(a).

"F.O.B. Chicago" if the seller is in Chicago), or will merely state that the seller is "to ship" the goods. In this case the seller must, in *its town or place of business,* put the goods in the possession of such a carrier and make such a contract for their shipment as may be reasonable, having regard for the nature of the goods, and then promptly notify the buyer of the shipment.[6] The seller will obtain from the carrier a document, e.g., **bill of lading,** which is sufficient to enable the buyer to obtain possession of the goods, and the seller must then deliver or tender this document to the buyer.[7]

bill of lading
a document issued to the shipper by a carrier

The terms "F.O.B." and "F.A.S." are not intended to be used in pricing goods, but are intended to be used to determine *performance with regard to delivery and tender.* However, merchants often use the term **"C.I.F."** when they do not use the terms F.O.B. or F.A.S. When they use this term they intend that the price quoted is a lump sum which includes the cost, insurance, and freight to a named destination. If they use the term **"C. & F."** or "C.F.," it means that the price includes the cost of the goods plus freight to the named destination. The obligations imposed on the seller when the term "C.I.F. *destination*" is used are to load the goods onto a carrier, make a contract for their shipment, and pay for the freight and insurance. (The insurance is purchased for the benefit of the buyer since the risk of loss passes upon the loading of the goods.) Finally, the seller must obtain a document enabling the buyer to obtain possession of the goods from the carrier and must deliver it or tender it to the buyer.[8] Under the terms C. & F. or C.F., the seller is obligated to do the same except that insurance is not purchased.

C.I.F.
cost, insurance, freight

C. & F.
cost plus freight

The main distinction between using F.O.B. or F.A.S., on the one hand, and C.I.F. or C. & F. or C.F., on the other, will be discussed later in this chapter. The important point to remember here is that the terms F.O.B., or "F.A.S. vessel," followed by either the town of the point of shipment or the town of destination *indicate where the seller is to tender the goods* and, consequently, where the risk of loss passes.

A third circumstance establishing the seller's obligation to tender at a specific place occurs when the agreement states nothing about delivery—the terms F.O.B., F.A.S., C.I.F., etc. are not used. When this occurs, the place for delivery is the seller's place of business,[9] if that is where the goods are located. If the goods are located at some other place at the time of the contract and if the goods are identified, then the delivery is presumed to be wherever the goods are located.[10] In the following case the seller's place of business was the place for delivery, the goods being located there.

Place of tender in the absence of express agreement.

---

[6] UCC 2–504(a)(c).   [9] UCC 2–308(a).

[7] UCC 2–504(b).   [10] UCC 2–308(b).

[8] UCC 2–320.

Facts

Bodge Lines, Inc. agreed to purchase from Parker Truck a new 1969 G.M.C. Model 30T tractor. As part of the purchase price, Bodge agreed to trade in a 1966 Mack tractor which it owned. Part of the contract for sale was oral and part was written. Neither agreement said anything about delivery of the new or used tractors (trucks). Bodge was to replace some tires on the older tractor before the trade-in. Some agents of Parker arrived at the Bodge shipping terminal to pick up the older tractor, but the tires were not changed. An agent of Bodge then volunteered to drive the trade-in vehicle to Parker Truck after the exchange of tires. During this trip the truck was involved in an accident. In a dispute over which insurance company should pay (Bodge's or Parker's), the issues of who owned the 1966 Mack tractor and which party had the obligation of delivery arose. Who did own the 1966 truck at the time of the accident, and what were the parties' obligations to deliver the respective goods?

Decision

The appellate court held that Parker's insurer must suffer the loss since Parker was the owner of the 1966 truck and Bodge had no duty to deliver it.

Reasoning

The court first relied upon section 2–401, which provides (in part) that title passes at the time and place at which the seller completes his performance with reference to the physical delivery of the goods even though a document of title is to be delivered at a different time or place. Secondly, the court concluded that, unless otherwise agreed, the place for delivery is the seller's place of business (section 2–308). In this case we have two sellers, and the seller of the 1966 tractor was Bodge, so the place of delivery was its place of business. Although the tractor was being driven by Bodge's employee at the time of the accident, the truck was owned by Parker, and a technical delivery had taken place at Bodge's place of business.

Home Indemnity Company v. Twin City Fire Insurance Company, 474 F.2d 1081 (1973).

Did the court decide this case properly by focusing on the time of the passage of ownership (title) rather than focusing upon the passage of the risk of loss? In this case, the risk of loss would have passed on tender of delivery,[11] and the place of delivery was the seller's place of business.[12]

In summary, we think of three different circumstances in which the seller meets its obligation of *tendering*. Two of them involve moving the goods—either to a carrier in its town to be shipped or to some other destination where the seller is to tender. One does not involve moving the goods—the seller must simply inform the buyer how and where to pick up the goods.

Moving the goods—or not, as the case may be—is not the final event of tendering. When the goods are to be shipped from the seller's town or when the goods are in the possession of a bailee, *the seller must send to the buyer the proper documents* enabling it legally to gain possession of the goods.[13] But is the

---

[11] UCC 2–509(3).   [13] UCC 2–503(3)(4)(5).

[12] UCC 2–308.

seller required to tender the goods *and* send the documents entitling the other party to possession without first being paid? The answer is yes! Unless the agreement provides otherwise, payment must be made when the obligations of tender are met. But does this not put the seller at a slight disadvantage? The seller does not want to give up possession of the goods until it is paid, nor, really, does the buyer want to pay until the goods have been properly shipped and tendered. How is this difficulty of both parties dealt with in practice?

Although there are many ways of dealing with this circumstance, a usual one might be as follows. Let us assume that a manufacturer of steel desks near Chicago, Illinois contracts to sell 100 of them "F.O.B. Los Angeles, California" for a total price of $10,000. The seller has the duty to deliver them to Los Angeles, California and, unless the agreement specifies otherwise, the seller is to tender, usually at the carrier's terminal in Los Angeles, in accordance with the terms set out in section 2–503, already discussed. The seller crates the desks and delivers them to the railroad and receives a bill of lading from the railroad. For purposes of this discussion, a bill of lading is a document issued by the carrier entitling the holder of it to the physical possession of the goods. The seller takes the bill of lading to its bank in Chicago and there signs a money instrument called a "draft." A draft is simply an instrument ordering the buyer to pay the sum of $10,000 to the Chicago bank. The seller then usually indorses (signs) the bill of lading over to the buyer and asks his Chicago bank to send the bill of lading and the draft to a Los Angeles bank which the Chicago bank knows and trusts. The Chicago bank then indorses the draft, stating thereon, "Pay to the order of any bank." What has happened so far is that the seller has asked its bank to be a collecting agent, and the bank has, by its indorsement, empowered a bank in Los Angeles to be its (the bank's) collecting agent. Both the draft and the bill of lading are then mailed to a Los Angeles bank. The two items together are called a **documentary draft.**

When the documentary draft arrives in Los Angeles (before, we assume, the goods arrive), the buyer is notified and an employee of the buyer will go to the Los Angeles bank and make arrangements for payment. Before the actual payment is made, the buyer has a right to inspect the goods. After the goods arrive and while they are still in the possession of the carrier, they are inspected, and then the employee goes to the bank to complete the transaction. The employee pays at the bank and then receives the bill of lading. The employee delivers the indorsed bill of lading to the carrier and receives the desks. The $10,000, through various bank transfers, will be credited to the seller's account in the Chicago bank. This use of banks as agents enables both the seller and buyer to be more comfortable with the transaction. The seller was able to retain control of the goods until the price was paid (its agents had the bill of lading), and the buyer was not required to pay until it was assured that the goods were on the carrier, shipped to it, and inspection had been completed.[14]

documentary draft
"any negotiable or non-negotiable draft with accompanying documents, securities or other papers to be delivered against honor of the draft" UCC 4-104 (f)

---

[14] See R. J. Nordstrom, *Handbook of the Law of Sales* (St. Paul: West Pub. Co., 1970).

The mechanics of tender, then, usually involve two separate events. One is the tendering of the goods, and a second is tendering the proper documents to the buyer. These mechanics are greatly simplified if tender is to be at the seller's plant.

Standard of Performance by the Seller

We have just discussed the mechanics of *where* and *how* the seller is to tender. *What* he is obligated to tender are the *exact goods* required by the agreement of the parties.

Under the common law of contracts the seller was required "substantially" to perform its obligations before triggering the buyer's obligation to pay. Article 2 has changed this and now requires that the seller perform in *every respect*. More particularly, Article 2 provides that if either *the goods* or the *tender of delivery* fail in *any respect* to conform to the contract, then the buyer may: reject the whole; accept the whole; or accept any **commercial unit** or units and reject the rest.[15] This section imposes on the seller the requirement of a perfect tender[16] of both the goods and any documents needed to make the mechanics of tender good.[17] At first, this requirement may seem burdensome. Certainly it would have been burdensome in the late 19th and early 20th centuries before our manufacturing processes could warrant uniform quality of a single line of products. Today, however, when a large merchant seller represents that goods will be exactly as they appear in either a catalog or a sales presentation where models are used, the seller is not unduly burdened by a requirement that the goods tendered be exactly like those originally represented to the buyer. In the following case the court held that the buyer could reject non-conforming goods.

> **commercial unit**
> "such a unit of goods as by commercial usage is a single whole for purposes of sale and division of which materially impairs its character or value on the market or in use"
> UCC 2-105 (6)

Facts

Maas, a large commercial grower of wheat and corn, agreed to purchase a large silo and other needed equipment for the storage of grain. The contract stated that there was a "one year warranty of customer satisfaction." The silo was constructed on Maas property in October of 1966. There was some evidence that the equipment and the construction of the silo were not exactly as they should be. From time to time the equipment would fail and, it was alleged, several hundred bushels of corn out of 3,000-plus spoiled. In August of 1967 Maas wrote the seller saying it was rejecting the silo and the equipment. Rather than ask for damages, Maas requested the seller simply to remove all of the items provided from his property. Did Maas accept the goods sold, or could he still reject them because they failed to conform? Also, to what standard of performance should the seller be held in this case?

---

[15] UCC 2–601.

[16] Nordstrom, p. 308; and see comment 2, section 2–106, defining "conforming goods" wherein it is stated it is the policy of Article 2 to require "exact performance" by the seller.

[17] This discussion assumes that the goods sold are *new* and not used. When used goods are sold, the term "as is" is usually used to describe them, and the use of such a term requires the seller to deliver the goods in the used condition as they exist.

Decision

The appellate court found in favor of Maas.

Reasoning

The court held that the one-year warranty of customer satisfaction gave the buyer, Maas, the right to reject the goods one year from the date of installation. With regard to the standard of performance, the court recognized that courts follow one of two rules. The first is that the test of the buyer's satisfaction is his own personal judgment (which must be exercised in good faith). The second is that the purchaser is bound to be satisfied with the goods if a reasonable person would be satisfied with them. Since section 2-601 states, "If the goods or the tender of delivery fail in *any respect* to conform to the contract. . .", the first standard must be used. The court concluded that so long as the rejection was done in good faith and not capriciously, the jury in the trial court could have properly found for Maas. The seller was required to remove all of the equipment and the silo.

Maas v. Scoboda, 195 N.W.2nd 491 (Neb. 1972).

There are two important instances in which the impact of this requirement of a perfect tender on the seller's obligations may be *lessened.*

The first instance gives the seller, following an initial defective tender, an opportunity to tender again, or to *cure* the original defective tender of goods or documents *when there is time.* Section 2–508 provides:

(1) Where any tender or delivery by the seller is rejected because non-conforming and the time for performance has not yet expired, the seller may seasonably notify the buyer of his intention to cure and may then within the contract time make a conforming delivery.

(2) Where the buyer rejects a non-conforming tender which the seller had reasonable grounds to believe would be acceptable with or without money allowance the seller may if he seasonably notifies the buyer have a further reasonable time to substitute a conforming tender.

The *first paragraph* above is fairly clear. Assume that a contract calls for delivery on September 1. If there is a tender *before* that date and it is rightfully rejected, and there is time remaining in which to perform, the seller is given the opportunity to do so as long as reasonable notice is given to the buyer. In the case just described, Maas did give the seller of the equipment an opportunity to make it perform properly, but apparently this was not sufficient to meet Maas' satisfaction.

The *second paragraph* of section 2–508 attempts to protect the seller from a surprise rejection.[18] The surprise rejection may arise from a rejection of *goods or documents* which the seller had reasonable grounds to believe would be acceptable. For example, assume that a seller agrees to sell 1,000 mini-calculators, model A-500, for $50 each. Only 950 of model A-500 can be conveniently located,

---

[18] UCC 2–508, comment 2.

so the seller decides to send along, for the same price, 50 of its newest model, A-502, which has two more functions than the A-500 and which would normally sell for $60. It seems that the seller should be given an opportunity to cure and tender the remaining 50 of model A-500 if the buyer objects to the imperfect tender. Or, assume that the buyer includes in his form standards for tender of documents that vary the prior course of dealing, course of performance, or usage of trade of which the seller was not seasonably notified or could not reasonably foresee. The seller should be given an additional reasonable time to "cure" his tender of the documents so long as he notifies the buyer and acts within a reasonable time.[19]

installment contract
"one which requires or authorizes the delivery of goods in separate lots to be separately accepted"
UCC 2-612 (1)

The *second instance* in which the impact of perfect tender on the seller's obligations is *lessened* occurs when the parties have agreed to an **installment contract.** If the goods are to arrive in separate lots, then the buyer may reject any such lot only if it *substantially impairs* the value of that installment and can not be cured.[20] The Uniform Commercial Code generally favors any reasonable legal standard that attempts to keep goods moving in commerce. When parties contract for a one-time sale, the standard of the seller's performance, as we have seen, is that it must tender precisely what the contract calls for. When, however, the parties have contracted for a series of deliveries over a period of some months or years, Article 2 lessens the perfect tender requirement and allows the buyer to reject the goods only if the non-conformity *substantially impairs* the value of that installment. This is true even if the contract states that "each delivery is a separate contract." The drafters apparently intended to provide some flexibility for the parties in installment contracts.

We assume that if the tender of an installment did not *exactly* meet the standards of the contract but the defect *did not substantially* impair its value, there would be some readjustment in price. If the defect in tender does substantially impair the value of that installment, the seller is given the opportunity to cure. If the seller can not cure within a reasonable time and if the defect would substantially impair the value of the *whole* contract, there may then be a breach of the *whole* contract.[21] This is illustrated by the following case.

Facts

Holterbosch was an American importer and distributor of Lowenbrau beer. It applied for and received permission to operate a Lowenbrau Pavilion at the 1964 New York World's Fair. It contracted with Graulich Caterer, Inc. to provide quality food for the pavilion. The quality of the food was to be equal to that presented to the agents of Holterbosch at a meeting on March 17, 1964 in which eight different platters of food were displayed and sampled. The initial contract was for about 1,000,000 units of food to be delivered over a one-year period. The first delivery of food on April 23, 1964 did not, according to Holterbosch's employees, in any way match the contract samples presented on March 17. The first 955 unit installment was rejected as unacceptable. Holterbosch

---

[19] UCC 2–508, comment 2.   [21] UCC 2–612(3).

[20] UCC 2–612(2).

agreed that it would allow Graulich to tender another batch of food. On April 25, 1964, 2520 units were delivered. Out of this number, between 500 and 700 were distributed among employees of Holterbosch and patrons at the exhibit. The complaints in response to this food were numerous. Generally, Holterbosch complained that the food was not German in character and was of such inferior quality that it could not be served. Holterbosch cancelled the contract.

Graulich sued Holterbosch for out-of-pocket loss of $29,937 spent on platters, trays, and doilies, and for the amount of profit lost, $35,950. Was Holterbosch liable for cancelling the entire contract?

Decision

No! The appellate court found in favor of Holterbosch.

Reasoning

The appellate court relied on the trial court's conclusion that the tenders of food on April 23 and 25 did not conform to the samples provided on March 17. This conclusion was reached by the jury, who observed the testimony and demeanor of the witnesses for both sides.

The key question was, however, did the non-conforming tenders substantially impair the value of the whole contract? The court said that the failure of the second delivery to be acceptable left Holterbosch without food for one week. Time was critical, and Graulich knew that platters of maximum quality German food were required on a daily basis. So, because of Holterbosch's immediate need for quality food and the failure of Graulich to cure and the non-conformity of the second delivery, the court found a substantial impairment of the value of the whole contract and allowed the buyer to cancel.

Graulich Caterer, Inc. v. Hans Holterbosch, Inc., 243 A.2d 253 (N.J. 1968).

The discussion in the chapter thus far is intended to outline the general performance obligations of *the seller* in tendering goods and meeting its standard of performance. The mechanics of the tender obligations of the seller are relatively simple. A much more complex set of issues was presented in this standard-of-performance section. Whether or not the goods provided are in "accordance with the contract"[22] is itself an issue often as complex as the nature of the goods sold.

For example, ascertaining whether a carload of construction lumber is in accordance with the contract is easy compared to ascertaining whether or not a Boeing 747, a supertanker, or a new model computer is in accordance with the contract. In many instances, issues involving the failure of such complex goods are resolved by a breach of warranty analysis. We point this out here simply to illustrate that the seller's performance obligations to tender goods exactly as they were promised are subject to at least two methods of analysis. The *first*—whether the goods conformed to the contract *at the time of delivery*—is relatively easy. Only obvious defects will be revealed at this point. However, failure of goods *during the time of its use* requires a second method of analyzing a seller's obligation to provide the quality of goods promised. This *second* method of analysis relies on a breach of warranty analysis and will be found in chapter 26.

---

[22] UCC 2–106(2).

Performance Obligations of the Buyer

The performance obligations of the buyer, not as complex as those of the seller, may be divided into two classifications. The first classification of performance obligations of the seller is technical and exists only if the contract for sale *does not* establish the order for performance by the buyer and seller. Recall that we said that the seller's and the buyer's obligations are, technically, *concurrent*. This means that the seller must tender the goods in order to trigger the buyer's obligation to pay, and the buyer must tender payment in order to trigger the seller's obligation to deliver the goods.

The effect of this approach is to make it relatively easy for a court to determine when a breach of the sales agreement has taken place. In order to maintain a lawsuit based on a breach of a sales agreement, the complaining party must allege and prove that it was willing and able to discharge its performance obligations but the other party was not. Therefore, unless the agreement provides another order of performance, and if the buyer wishes to put the seller in default, the buyer must perform first by tendering payment.[23] This, then, is the first classification of performance obligations for the buyer.

Payment by the Buyer

Obviously the buyer is to pay, but what are the specifics of this obligation? What is payment? When and where must it (usually) be made? Tender of payment is sufficient when it is made by any means current in the ordinary course of business.[24] Unless the agreement provides otherwise, this means that the full price must be tendered in cash or check. If the payment tendered is by check and the seller demands cash, the buyer will be allowed an extension of time reasonably necessary to procure the cash.[25] Credit or a delay in payment is available only if the parties have agreed to it.

Also, the parties may agree to exchange something other than cash for goods. Goods, for example, may be exchanged for goods,[26] and such a "barter" transaction is a sale for purposes of Article 2. The parties need not have agreed upon a price or payment, but as long as there is evidence that *the parties intend to be bound,* a court may find that an enforceable agreement exists. In this case, the amount of the price is to be a reasonable one.[27] In the following case, the court found from the evidence that the parties intended to be bound even though they had not reached agreement on payment.

(margin note: Tender of payment by the buyer.)

(margin note: Tender of payment by cash, check, or other property.)

---

[23] UCC 2–511(1).   [26] UCC 2–304(1).

[24] UCC 2–511(2).   [27] UCC 2–305(1).

[25] UCC 2–511(2).

Facts

Southwest Engineering Company, Inc. was engaged in general contracting work and wanted to bid on the construction of runway lighting facilities, for which they needed large electrical generators. They asked Martin Tractor Company (Martin) for a bid on the type of generator needed, and this bid was received in the amount of $18,500 on April 13, 1966 over the phone. Southwest's bid was accepted on April 14, and it relied on the price of $18,500 for the generator in making its bid. When the parties met on April 28 to "firm up" the deal, the price was renegotiated to $21,500 and the detailed specifications of the generator were discussed and a "memorandum" satisfying the statute of frauds was signed by Martin. Toward the end of the meeting Martin's agents testified that they said they wanted payment as follows: 10 percent with the order, 50 percent on delivery, and the balance upon acceptance. Southwest's agents testified that they thought payment was to be 20 percent down and the balance on delivery, while there was testimony that the way payment was usually made was 90 percent on the 10th of the month following delivery and the balance on final acceptance.

No payment was made when the order was placed; and when Southwest demanded performance, Martin denied that there was an enforceable agreement because, among other things, the parties had never agreed on the terms of payment. The signed memorandum did not mention a specific term of payment. Was there an enforceable contract?

Decision

Yes. The appellate court affirmed a decision for Southwest.

Reasoning

The court concluded from the conflicting testimony that the parties had reached no agreement on payment. They found from other evidence, however, that the parties intended to contract and that there was a reasonably certain basis for giving an appropriate remedy. The time for payment is supplied by section 2-310, which states, "Unless otherwise agreed (a) payment is due at the time and place at which the buyer is to receive the goods. . . ." The buyer was ready and willing to perform at this point, and so the court found for it.

Southwest Engineering Company, Inc., v. Martin Tractor Company, 473 P.2d 18 (Kan. 1970).

When and where must the tender of payment be made? Generally the buyer is to tender payment at the time and place at which the buyer is *to receive* the goods.[28] This clearly means that the *seller must complete all obligations of shipment and delivery* and must wait until the buyer has received the goods before it can expect payment. In the absence of the need for the buyer to establish a breach of the agreement, the delivery and receipt of the goods is a precondition and not a concurrent condition.[29]

Tender of payment, when and where.

---

[28] UCC 2–310(a).

[29] J. White and R. Summers, *Handbook of the Law Under the Uniform Commercial Code* (St. Paul: West Pub. Co., 1972).

The buyer's right to
inspect the goods
before tendering
payment, unless
otherwise agreed.

Inspection by the Buyer

A second significant precondition to payment is the buyer's right to inspect the goods. The buyer has a right to inspect the goods after they have been identified to the contract for sale or after tender or delivery (or whenever the seller completes its performance) and *before* payment.[30] The time, place, and manner of inspection must be reasonable, and the expenses of inspection must be borne by the buyer but may be recovered from the seller if the goods do not conform and are rejected.[31]

In some instances, especially when the buyer is not well known to the seller and is a great distance from the seller, the seller may fear that the buyer will abuse this right to inspect before payment. So, the seller may ask for payment *against a tender* of *documents* entitling the buyer to possession. In most cases this is accomplished by using the terms C.I.F. or C.O.D. The term C.I.F. is a pricing term (already discussed) which creates some performance obligations for the seller. In addition, however, when used, it entitles the seller to payment *before* inspection.[32] When the terms F.O.B. or F.A.S. are used, the buyer has a right to inspect before the payment. The buyer's waiver of the right to inspect when the C.I.F. term is used is a chief distinction between that term and F.O.B. followed by some destination (not the seller's city).

The performance obligations of inspection and payment are easily understood when the buyer is to pick up the goods from the seller's plant or warehouse or from a bailee. Let us consider two additional circumstances.

First, if the sales agreement includes the words "F.O.B. *Buyer's* City," then, as we learned from previous discussion, the risk of loss does not pass and the obligations to inspect and pay do not arise until the goods arrive in the buyer's city and are there so tendered as to enable the buyer to take delivery. This usually means that the carrier notifies the buyer that the goods can be picked up. The seller may instruct the carrier that the buyer may inspect the goods, but usually formal possession of the goods—moving them from the carrier—does not take place until inspection and payment are made. The interests of both parties are best protected by using bank agents as previously described for purposes of collecting payment and surrendering possession. When this occurs, the buyer would usually be given an opportunity to inspect *before* making payment.

A *second* and potentially confusing circumstance involves the buyer's performance obligation of payment when the contract either states that the seller "will ship" the goods or contains the terms "F.O.B. *Seller's* City." In this instance the seller is required to tender the goods to the buyer in *its* (seller's) *city,* and it is at this point that the *risk of loss* will pass. It is likely that an insurable interest passed much earlier, when the goods were identified. Title to the goods may also have passed earlier. Although the seller may have completed its performance by making a reasonable contract for the delivery of the goods,

---

[30] UCC 2–513(1).

[31] UCC 2–513(2).

[32] UCC 2–513(3).

it is not entitled to payment until the goods have been *received and inspected* by the buyer. But what if the goods were lost in transit and can not then "be received." Is the seller entitled to payment? Yes! The section requiring receipt and inspection of the goods before payment was written on the assumption that the goods would arrive in due course.[33] If they do not, the section can not be used to defeat the specific Article 2 section on risk of loss and, consequently, the buyer's obligation to pay.

Acceptance by the Buyer

Finally, Article 2 requires that the buyer accept the goods. This is a technical performance obligation and occurs when the buyer

> The buyer must accept conforming goods tendered pursuant to the contract.

(a) after a reasonable opportunity to inspect the goods signifies to the seller that the goods are conforming or that he will take or retain them in spite of their non-conformity; or

(b) fails to make an effective rejection . . . but such acceptance does not occur until the buyer has had a reasonable opportunity to inspect them; or

(c) does any act inconsistent with the seller's ownership. . . .[34]

Acceptance is important because, once it occurs, the *seller* is given an additional remedy in the case of a breach of the sales contract. Generally, before acceptance the seller's chief remedy upon the breach by a buyer is to stop shipment, recover the goods, or sue for lost profit. *After acceptance,* the buyer may not reject the goods[35] and the seller has the additional remedy of suing for the entire purchase price.[36]

In summary, the buyer's obligations, generally speaking, follow those of the seller to ship or deliver the goods. Upon receipt of the goods, the buyer is to inspect, pay, and accept them.

Performance Obligations in Special Circumstances

Article 2 has more performance obligations of the parties than we present here. However, this text on commercial law is intended to be as thorough as possible given space constraints. Of necessity, some of the provisions of Article 2 must be left for explanation and analysis in later courses on commercial law. Two sets of performance obligations are so important, however, that they merit special attention. The first set arises from Article 2 itself. The second arises from Article 6, Bulk Transfers. First we present the additional performance obligations of Article 2.

---

[33] Nordstrom, pp. 345, 365.

[34] UCC 2–606.

[35] UCC 2–607(2).

[36] UCC 2–709.

The Obligation to Provide Adequate Assurance
of Performance When Demanded

Impairment of one party's expectation of another party's performance, and the right to additional adequate assurance from the other party that the expected performance from the other party will occur.

When they become legally bound, the parties to a contract for the sale of goods contemplate *performance* and not breach or the right to sue. So, if either the willingness or the ability of a party to perform declines materially between the time of contracting and the time of performance, the other party is threatened with the loss of a major part of what has been bargained for.[37] Article 2, section 2–609(1) attempts to protect both parties by providing these additional obligations of the parties:

> (1) A contract for sale imposes an obligation on each party that the other's expectation of receiving due performance will not be impaired. When *reasonable grounds* for insecurity arise with respect to the performance of *either* party the other may in writing demand *adequate assurance* of *due performance* and until he receives such assurance may, if *commercially reasonable,* suspend *any performance* for which *he has not already received the agreed return.* [Emphasis added.]

The italicized words in the section above are the key ones. Between merchants, they are defined according to current commercial standards[38] and the general obligation of acting in good faith. From the seller's point of view—and this is especially true if it is selling on credit—any information that the buyer is **insolvent** or in financial difficulty should cause the seller to demand in writing that the buyer clarify its financial condition. A mere rumor of insolvency is not sufficient grounds upon which the seller may refuse to perform;[39] however, if the rumor is true, or if the seller learns by inquiring from the buyer that there are reasonable grounds to believe that the buyer may be insolvent, the seller may refuse to deliver except for cash.[40]

insolvency
when the debtor "either has ceased to pay his debts in the ordinary course of business, or can not pay his debts as they become due, or is insolvent within the meaning of the federal bankruptcy law" (assets are less than liabilities) UCC 1-201(23)

If either party receives a written demand for adequate assurance of performance and does not respond with an adequate assurance within a reasonable time—in any event, not longer than thirty days—then the demanding party may treat this as a repudiation of the contract.[41] In short, if reasonable grounds for insecurity exist, the party owing the obligation to perform may: (1) suspend performance; (2) demand in writing an adequate assurance of performance from the other party; (3) await a reply for a reasonable time, which is not over thirty days; and (4) if there is not an adequate reply, view the contract as repudiated by the other party. In the following case, since adequate assurance was demanded by the seller and not given, there was justifiable ground for the seller's suspended performance.

---

[37] UCC 2–609, comment 1.

[38] UCC 2–609(2).

[39] Nordstrom, p. 495.

[40] Id.

[41] UCC 2–609(4).

Facts

Gestetner sold goods on credit to Turntables, Inc. After delivery of some of the goods, Gestetner found out that Turntables' "Fifth Avenue Showroom" address was a telephone answering service, that its "Island Park factory" was someone else's premises and Turntables had no leased space, and that they had a "bad" reputation for performance. Gestetner demanded adequate assurance for future performance (payment on delivery, we assume) even though the sales were to be on credit. Turntables was not insolvent at the time even though Gestetner believed it to be so. Adequate assurance was not given, so Gestetner refused to make more deliveries required by the contract. Turntables, Inc. sued Gestetner for failure to perform.

Decision

The appellate court entered judgment for Gestetner.

Reasoning

The facts of the case, not disputed by Turntables, do reveal reasonable grounds for insecurity, and section 2-609 allows such a party having reasonable grounds for insecurity to suspend performance for which he has not already received an agreed exchange.

Turntables, Inc. v. Gestetner, 382 N.Y.Supp.2d. 798 (1976).

Performance Obligations Imposed When Bulk Sales are the Subject of the Contract

The image of a complex commercial sale of goods we suggested in the last chapter was based upon the assumption that the seller was a manufacturer of some kind. Most manufacturers buy materials, usually on credit, and then add value to the materials by constructing either a final product or one that is not completely finished but is used by another manufacturer. Many of the suppliers who sell raw materials to the seller in our typical example rely on the fact that they will be paid out of the proceeds of what our seller transfers to others.

Article 2 is premised on the notion that a seller is offering goods in the *ordinary course of its business*. When a seller of goods decides either to change the nature of its business or to sell out completely by selling a major part of all of its materials, supplies, or other inventory, then there is a potential for commercial injury to those who normally rely on the fact that the seller will continue in operation. Those persons who could be commercially injured are the creditors of the seller.

For example, assume that a merchant seller of goods is barely solvent, and insolvency seems imminent. Such a seller might desire to sell its inventory to a friend for less than it is worth, pay the creditors less than is owed them, and some time later reenter the business by getting a loan from the friend. Or the seller might simply sell the inventory, pocket the proceeds, and disappear.[42] So, to protect the creditors of the seller, Article 6 of the Uniform Commercial Code was drafted and has now been adopted by most of the states. However, Article 6 does provide the same general type of protection as the Uniform Fraudulent

> **bulk transfer**
> "any transfer in bulk and not in the ordinary course of the transferor's business of a major part of the materials, supplies, merchandise or other inventory of an enterprise subject to Article 6"
> UCC 6-102(1)

---

[42] UCC 6–101, comment 2.

Conveyance Act, so some states have not adopted Article 6; or if they have adopted it, they may have substantially changed some of its provisions.[43] Nevertheless, it is important to realize that in many states the sellers and buyers involved in bulk transfers have certain performance obligations which run to the creditors of the seller.

Article 6 defines a bulk transfer as one that is a transfer of *a major part* of the materials, supplies, merchandise, or other inventory not in the ordinary course of the **transferor's** business. Under that Article, the transferor's business must be principally in the sale of merchandise from stock, including a manufacturer seller, although this has been modified in some of the states. Generally, if a bulk transfer is made for purposes of securing a loan, or is a general assignment for the benefit of all creditors, or is a sale subject to judicial order, then it is excepted from coverage by Article 6.[44]

The Article does not clearly define what a "*major part*" of the materials, supplies, etc. is. It has been suggested by prominent authorities that a "major part" refers to *value* and not *quantity* of the materials or inventory, and that certainly a transfer of *45 percent* of the total value should be a "major part."[45] Some courts have recognized a sale of 25 percent of a merchant's inventory as a major part.[46]

Generally there are four performance obligations required of the transferor (seller) and the transferee (buyer). The *first* is that, before the actual transfer takes place, the **transferee** must demand and receive a list of creditors of the transferor together with a schedule of the property sufficient to identify it. The transferee must preserve the schedule for six months and permit inspection of it by any creditor of the transferor during this period.[47]

Second, at least ten days before the *transferee* is to take possession of the goods or is to pay for them (whichever happens first), *it* must give notice of the transfer to creditors of the transferor.[48]

Third, this notice must state, among other things:[49]

1. that a bulk transfer is about to be made;
2. the names and business addresses of the transferor and transferee . . . ;
3. whether or not all the debts of the transferor are to be paid in full as they fall due . . . ; [or, if not],
4. the location and general description of the property to be transferred and the estimated total of the transferor's debts. . . .

---

[43] For example, only eighteen states had adopted section 6–106 of the Article as of 1972. See White and Summers, p. 644.

[44] UCC 6–103.

[45] White and Summers, p. 646.

[46] See *Danning v. Daylin, Inc.,* 488 F.2d 185 (1973).

[47] UCC 6–104.

[48] UCC 6–105.

[49] UCC 6–107.

transferor
one who has transferred some thing to another

transferee
one to whom another has transferred some thing

Finally, this notice must be either delivered personally or sent by registered or certified mail to all persons shown on the list provided by the transferor.[50]

The failure to comply with the above four obligations renders the bulk transfer ineffective.[51] In such cases, the creditor of the seller will be able to assert whatever legal rights it has in the goods. The purpose of Article 6 is not to protect the creditors of a transferor in all cases in which a bulk transfer occurs; the purpose is to *alert* these creditors that a bulk transfer of goods in which they *may* have some property interest is about to take place. If their interests are not legally jeopardized by the proposed transfer, then the creditors can not object.

The central point to remember is that, in certain cases, a buyer of a major part of a seller's inventory may have to relinquish possession of the goods if the performance obligations of Article 6 are not met. In the following case the buyer did not comply with the notice requirements, and the bulk sale was declared ineffective.

Facts

Pastimes was a publisher of books and on August 23, 1968 sold its entire inventory of books to Saalfield for $27,000. At this time Pastimes owed Midland $34,000 and owed other unsecured creditors substantial sums. No notice of the sale was sent to the creditors of Pastimes. The entire proceeds of the sale were credited to Midland. The other creditors of Pastimes objected, and litigation resulted. What are the remedies of the unsecured creditors of Pastimes against Saalfield and Midland?

Decision

The appellate court declared the sale ineffective and affirmed a judgment in favor of the unsecured creditors of Pastimes on a pro rata basis.

Reasoning

The court held that a bulk sale was made and that the failure to meet the notice requirements of Article 6 resulted in a violation. Article 6 itself provides no specific remedies for unsecured creditors of bulk-sale sellers except to provide that the sale is ineffective. Under Illinois law, the unsecured creditors of Pastimes could recover the inventory sold or, at their option, divide the proceeds of the sale. The creditors opted to divide the proceeds, and this had to be done on a pro rata basis. The credit of the entire proceeds to Midland was inappropriate since the amount credited arose from an ineffective transfer.

Pastimes Publishing Co. v. Advertising Displays, 286 N.E.2d 19 (Ill. 1972).

Most courts would allow judgment creditors of a bulk-sale seller to recover possession of the goods sold, but there would be little value in this if the goods were sold at a fair market price. The easiest remedy would be to levy on the proceeds of the sale as the creditors did in the case above.

---

[50] UCC 6–107(3).

[51] UCC 6–105.

Circumstances Excusing Performance of the Parties

Almost the entire body of our commercial law is built upon the assumption that parties to a commercial agreement intended and contemplated *performance*. The strength and value of our contract and commercial law are directly dependent upon the extent to which the law facilitates the parties' intent to perform pursuant to their agreement. Even when there is a failure of performance or a breach of the agreement, the law responds by providing a measure of damages calculated to put the injured party in the same position it would have been in *had there been performance.*

In a sense, the commercial law is weakened in each instance in which the law recognizes an exception to the general rule that parties *must* perform when they have promised to do so. In some circumstances, however, there are good reasons for such exceptions. Generally, the reasons for excusing one or both of the parties from their agreement are based upon *the occurrence of events which neither party could reasonably foresee, given the current commercial realities.*

Article 2 recognizes four important circumstances in which a court will excuse performance. Three of these will now be considered. A fourth, involving "unconscionable contracts," will be discussed in chapter 26, Consumer Law. As you read this final part of the present chapter, remember that, generally speaking, exceptions to the fundamental obligations of performance are narrowly defined and are recognized only where our *notions of fairness override the necessary emphasis on performance.* Note also that since the seller usually has the first obligation to perform, it is generally the seller who is excused from performance.

Excused
nonperformance by
reason of total
destruction of the
identified goods.

First: Excuse by Casualty to Identified Goods

A contract for the sale of goods contemplates the delivery of specific, identifiable goods, so their *total* destruction through no fault of either party will excuse *both* parties from their performance obligations. Section 2–613 provides:

no arrival, no sale
a term used by a seller
when it or another is
shipping goods and
does not want to be
liable if the goods do
not arrive at their
destination

Where the contract requires for its performance goods identified when the contract is made, and the goods suffer casualty without fault of either party before the risk of loss passes to the buyer, or in a proper case under a **"no arrival, no sale"** term . . . then

(a) if the loss is total the contract is avoided; and

(b) if the loss is partial or the goods have so deteriorated as no longer to conform to the contract, the buyer may nevertheless demand inspection and at his option either treat the contract as avoided or accept the goods with due allowance from the contract price for the deterioration or the deficiency in quantity but without further right against the seller.

There are four important conditions that must be satisfied before the seller is excused from performance because of casualty to the goods.

1. The first condition is that the goods must be "identified when the contract is made." The precise meaning of this phrase is not made clear in Article 2. The comments to this section do state that the section is intended to excuse performance (a) when the identified goods were destroyed *before* the contract

was made and neither party was aware of this when they "contracted," or (b) when the goods were to be manufactured *after* the contract was made and they were destroyed *after* manufacture and identification but *before* delivery.[52] In either case, the goods, technically speaking, could not be "identified" as existing when the contract was made. So the term "identified" must mean that *they could be reasonably specified* or *described* at the time of the contract. Specification or description means that the goods can be separated from others when made or when the contract is formed; e.g., *that one* generator and no other, or *that machine* to be built and no other.[53]

2. The goods must be *totally* destroyed. If the goods are only partially damaged, the seller should notify the buyer and, if the buyer desires, the buyer may demand tender and inspection and may accept the goods with an allowance in price for the diminution of value. If the buyer chooses this option, however, it may not sue the seller for failure to deliver conforming goods.

3. The casualty must not have been caused by either party.

4. The risk of loss must not have passed to the buyer.

While these four conditions are necessary to excuse the seller *and* buyer *from their performance obligations*, which one will suffer the *loss*? If the casualty to the goods occurs *before* the risk of loss passes to the buyer, although the seller is excused from his performance obligation, he will suffer the loss. He is excused from having to tender new goods or a set of goods. If the casualty occurs *after* the risk passes to the buyer, the parties are not excused from their performance obligations, and the buyer suffers the loss.

Second: Excuse by Failure of the Manner of Delivery, or Failure of the Means or Manner of Payment

Failure of the Manner of Delivery. When neither party is at fault and the agreed *manner of delivery becomes commercially impracticable,* if there is a reasonable *substitute,* it must be tendered and accepted.[54] The "excuse" provided by this section is not a total one. From the *seller's* point of view, the excuse is from the *agreed* manner of delivery. *Delivery is still required,* but a reasonable substitute for the agreed manner of delivery may be used. The words "commercially impracticable" are not defined in Article 2, although section 2–614(1) gives the following illustrations: "the agreed berthing, loading, or unloading facilities fail or an agreed type of carrier becomes unavailable." Generally "commercially impracticable" means something more than simply "more expensive." If the agreed means of delivery becomes tremendously more expensive, then the seller will probably seek application of the next section below for "excuse by failure of presupposed conditions."

Excused nonperformance by reason of failure of the manner of delivery, or failure of the means or manner of payment.

---

[52] UCC 2–613, comment 2.

[53] Nordstrom, p. 327.

[54] UCC 2–614 (1).

Failure of the Means or Manner of Payment. The *buyer* is also protected by this section. If the agreed means or manner of payment *fails* because of a domestic or foreign governmental regulation, then the buyer may provide payment by a means which is a substantial equivalent.[55]

Third: Excuse by Failure of Presupposed Conditions

At a very basic level, the law of contracts and Article 2 of the UCC are intended to protect and enforce the intention of parties to an agreement when they consciously allocate business risks. Simply put, if a seller agrees on January 1 to deliver 100 cases of tennis balls, "F.O.B. Buyer's City" on May 30 for $80 per case, then the seller has assumed the risk that on May 30 the same tennis balls could be sold for the higher price of $100 per case. Any time an agreement calls for future performance (and most do), there are certain price, delivery, and product risks. The very reason for our commercial law is to enforce the allocations of these risks. So if the price of tennis balls in the buyer's city is $100 per case on the date of delivery, our seller has lost $20 per case because the same balls could have been sold there for the higher price. The law, however, requires the seller to perform or pay damages, because it assumed this risk.

The buyer also assumed some risks back in January. It assumed the risk that the price for the tennis balls in its city would be at least $80 per case. If it were less (say, $50 per case) on the date of delivery, then it would lose $30 per case, but it *must perform* its obligations to the seller at $80 per case on that date or pay damages. The general rule is that *the law will not excuse performance merely because a transaction may have become unprofitable.* A rise or a collapse in the market for goods is not in itself a justification for excuse of performance; that is exactly the type of business risk that business contracts made at set prices are intended to cover.[56] There are thousands, perhaps millions, of transactions each day that result in losses to one or both parties. There is no excuse from such performance unless a court can be convinced that the parties *did not consciously allocate the risk of an event that occurred.*

This notion of the parties not *consciously* allocating the risks associated with an event that occurred and the resulting excuse of performance by the seller is expressed this way (in part) in section 2–615:

(a) Delay in delivery or non-delivery in whole or in part by a seller . . . is not a breach of his duty under a contract for sale if performance as agreed has been made impracticable by the occurrence of a contingency, the non-occurrence of which was a basic assumption on which the contract was made or by compliance in good faith with any applicable foreign or domestic governmental regulation or order whether or not it later proves to be invalid.

---

[55] UCC 2–614(2).

[56] UCC 2–615, comment 4.

Again we emphasize that increased cost to the seller does not by itself excuse performance so long as the increased cost reflects only *normal* business risks. Some of the basic assumptions made by parties when they contract are that there will be no catastrophic storms, crop failures, unforeseen bankruptcies of major suppliers, unforeseen embargoes or wars, and so forth. When one of these events does occur, causing a *drastic* or *unusual* change in price, then the seller must first give notice to the buyer that there will be a delay or nondelivery[57] and may then attempt to "renegotiate" the contract with the buyer. However, if the parties can not agree, the final arbiter will be a court. Whether the court will classify the event as a normal business risk or a totally unforeseen contingency altering the essential nature of the performance obligation is not certain. In the following case the court found a normal business risk and imposed liability for nonperformance by the seller.

Facts

Wegematic Corporation designed and produced a small computer known as the ALWAC III-E, which enjoyed considerable success. Wegematic designed in a preliminary way the ALWAC 800, which was characterized as a "truly revolutionary system," and submitted a proposal to the Federal Reserve Board for the production of the ALWAC 800 computer. The proposal was submitted as a competitive bid and was selected by the Federal Reserve Board. The parties agreed that the ALWAC 800 would be delivered on June 30, 1957 at a cost of $231,000. The board emphasized the importance of delivery on time, and the parties agreed that Wegematic would pay the board $100 per day for each day the delivery was late.

In March of 1957 Wegematic requested a postponement of the delivery date to late summer. In April they requested an October 30 delivery date because of design difficulties. And in mid-October Wegematic announced that it had become

impracticable to deliver the ALWAC 800 due to engineering difficulties. They requested a cancellation of the contract with the board and a waiver of damage claims.

In October, 1957 the Federal Reserve Board set out to purchase comparable equipment and then sued Wegematic for a total of $235,806, which included damages for delay and the increased price they had to pay another computer firm for the same goods. Wegematic argued that to produce the ALWAC 800 would have taken an additional $1 million to $1.5 million and between one or two years full-time research. It argued that the agreement had become commercially impracticable because of the occurrence of events it could not predict in the fields of electronic engineering and rapidly developing computer technology.

Should the seller be excused from performance and the payment of damages because it was involved in a high risk field where developing new products was uncertain and hazardous?

---

[57] UCC 2–615(c).

Decision

No! The court awarded judgment to the government for $235,806 plus interest.

Reasoning

The court acknowledged that section 2–615 is the controlling section and lamented the "somewhat complicated" way it states the rule. If one of the parties expressly assumed the risk attendant to some promised performance, then it must suffer the consequences. The court stated, "We see no basis for thinking that when an electronics system is promoted by its manufacturers as a revolutionary breakthrough, the risk of the revolution's occurrence falls on the purchaser." Even in fields of new and rapidly developing technology, a seller of a product should not be able to transfer the risks accompanying development to the purchaser. Sellers should not be free to gamble on mere probabilities of development without any risk of liability.

United States v. Wegematic Corporation, 360 F.2d 674 (1966).

The best method for determining which of the parties assumed which risks is to read the agreement, or, where there is no written agreement, ascertain the oral understanding of the parties. Course of performance, course of dealing, and usage of trade are also important in ascertaining which risks the parties allocated in the absence of an expressed statement in the agreement.

Also, it is important whether the seller owns the goods at the time of the contract. For example, if a seller agreed to deliver oranges from groves located in two Florida counties and could not because an unanticipated freeze destroyed the crop, the first issue a court would have to determine would be whether the oranges were the seller's and could be identified when the contract was made. If this were so, section 2–613 (on casualty to identified goods) would excuse performance. However, if the seller could not identify the oranges at the time of the contract and was merely to buy oranges from growers to meet its own performance obligation, then it would be under a duty to buy whatever oranges were available in the two counties and supply them to the buyer on the date for delivery even though it would suffer a loss. If there were no oranges available in the two counties and the agreement or surrounding circumstances revealed that the seller assumed the risks of a freeze, it would be required to pay damages. If it did not assume such a risk, the seller could then attempt to assert section 2–615.[58]

Section 2–615 does not use the word "mistake" and, in fact, there are no specific Article 2 sections directly applicable to circumstances in which one or both of the parties makes a mistake of calculation, typing, or the like. However, the common law rules on mistake are to supplement Article 2 (1–103), so the rules you learned in Part 2, Contracts, on mistake are applicable in appropriate circumstances and may be argued using the language of section 2–615.[59]

Finally, we must emphasize that the defenses of mistake, excuse of performance, duress, coercion—or the existence of an unconscionable provision or

---

[58] See *Holly Hill Fruit Products Co. v. Bob Staton, Inc.,* 275 So.2d 583 (Fla. 1973).

[59] Nordstrom, p. 334. See pp. 110–11.

contract (discussed in chapter 26, Consumer Law)—are recognized and have legal significance *only* when courts declare them to be applicable. An assertion by one of the contracting parties that these circumstances excuse performance is not effective until and unless a court or the other party agrees.

Summary Statement

1. Generally, it is the parties' intent as expressed in their contractual documents that will determine the performance obligations of the parties.
2. The obligation of the seller is to transfer and deliver the goods and that of the buyer is to accept and pay for them in accordance with the contract.
3. The seller must tender the goods to the buyer in a manner and at the time and place as set in the agreement. The use of the terms F.O.B. or F.A.S. followed by a destination (e.g., the name of a distant town) require the seller at its own expense and risk to transport the goods *there* and tender them. If the terms used are F.O.B. or F.A.S. seller's town, or if the seller is "to ship" the goods, then the seller must put the goods in the possession of a carrier in *its* town and make a reasonable contract for their shipment and then notify the buyer.
4. If the term C.I.F. is used (e.g., C.I.F. Austin, Texas, when the seller is in Lansing, Michigan), the seller is to load the goods onto a carrier, make a contract for their shipment, and pay for the freight and insurance.
5. Where the agreement states nothing about the place for delivery, the place for delivery is the seller's place of business, but if the goods are somewhere else, then delivery is where the goods are located.
6. The goods tendered by the seller must conform to the contract in every respect; if they do not, the buyer may reject them but the seller may cure its tender if there is time or if the seller reasonably thought the goods would be accepted.
7. The obligations of the buyer are to inspect, pay for, and accept the goods. The buyer is to tender payment at the time and place at which the buyer is to receive the goods.
8. A party has an obligation to provide an adequate assurance of performance when demanded if there are reasonable grounds for insecurity with respect to the party's performance.
9. In some states the sellers and buyers involved in bulk transfers have performance obligations to inform the creditors of the seller of the transfer.
10. The parties to a sales agreement may be excused from their performance obligations when:
    a. the goods are totally destroyed through no fault of either party before the risk of loss passes to the buyer;
    b. the manner of delivery or the manner of payment fails; however, a reasonable substitute must be tendered;
    c. an event occurs which neither party could foresee and the risk for which was not allocated between the parties.

In the following case the question of who was to bear the risk of loss was determined by the seller's *typing* overruling the contrary *print* on the seller's forms of acknowledgment which were the basis of their contract.

National Heater Company, Inc. v. Corrigan Co. Mechanical Contractors, Inc.
482 F.2d 87 (1973)

National Heater, the seller, offered on March 1, 1969 to sell certain heating units to be used in the construction of the Chrysler automobile plant in Fenton, Missouri. The original offer of the seller stated that the price quoted was for the merchandise "F.O.B., St. Paul, Minnesota." The buyer, Corrigan Company, sent its "purchase order" back to the seller with the statement that the price was "$275,640—Delivered." The seller then mailed to the buyer an "Acknowledgment of Purchase Order" bearing the printed words "Sale Price Total" followed by typed-in wording "$275,640, Total Delivered to Rail Siding." In another of the seller's acknowledgment forms were the printed words "delivery of equipment hereunder shall be made F.O.B. point of shipment unless otherwise stated."

The heating units were shipped by the seller but were damaged in transit. The buyer received the goods and accepted them subject to a reduction in the sales price. The full contract price was not paid and the seller sued the buyer for the balance. The buyer counterclaimed, arguing that the risk of loss due to shipment damage was on the seller until delivery to the construction site in Missouri. The seller argued that the risk of loss was on the buyer once a reasonable contract for the delivery of the heaters was made in St. Paul. At the trial it was shown that both parties contemplated a Fenton, Missouri "rail siding" when the words "rail siding" were used.

When did the agreement of the parties state that the risk of loss was to pass? Judgment for the buyer, Corrigan Company. Seller appeals.

The intention of the parties is to control in determining the allocation of the risk of loss. When a written contract is partly written or typewritten and partly printed, any conflict between the printed portion and the typewritten portion will be resolved in favor of the latter. Also, any ambiguity in a party's form will be construed against that party since they drafted it and should not be allowed to take advantage of their own ambiguous draftsmanship. The seller's form stated in print that delivery was to be F.O.B., point of shipment, unless otherwise stated. It was "otherwise stated." The seller had typed in the words "$275,640, Total Delivered to Rail Siding." There was uncontradicted evidence that the rail siding referred to was the one at the construction site in Fenton, Missouri. The seller's obligations were to deliver to that point, and there the risk of loss would pass to the buyer.

Affirmed for the buyer, Corrigan Company.

Questions and Case Problems

1. Explain how banks are sometimes used in commercial transactions to facilitate the surrendering of possession of goods, the inspection of the goods by the buyer, and payment.

2. If one of the parties to a sales transaction has reasonable grounds to believe that the other party may not be able to perform, what are its remedies?

3. S, seller, has just sold $14,000 worth of chains, sprockets, and steel tubing to B, buyer, on credit. B has a business in which it manufactures bicycles for the retail market. You are interested in starting a bicycle manufacturing operation and agree with B to buy 40 percent of his inventory of parts. Explain the performance obligations imposed on your transaction with B by Article 6 of the UCC (Bulk Transfers). If these obligations are not met, what are the remedies available to S if S is not paid?

4. Write a short paragraph explaining the principle of commercial impracticability.

5. S agreed to sell to B 50 crates of machine parts for $300 per crate. The agreement stated nothing about the place of delivery nor the place or manner of payment. Several months after the agreement, B demanded that S deliver the machine parts to B's place of business in a town 150 miles from S's place of business. S countered by demanding that B pay for and pick up the crates of machine parts which had been identified and were at S's warehouse. How is this dispute resolved by Article 2? Where is delivery and tender to take place? What must both parties do to place the other in default?

6. S contracted to sell to B 1,000 bushels of apples at $6 per bushel, "to be shipped in September" to B in B's city. On September 20, 850 bushels were shipped to B and they arrived on September 25, when the price of apples in B's city was $5 per bushel. The usual time of shipment was three to seven days. B refused the delivery after inspection because it found there were only 850 bushels. On September 26, S was notified and on that date shipped the remaining 150 bushels. What are the rights and obligations of the parties?

7. A agreed to sell and B agreed to purchase 1,000 small electric motors for $85 each, "F.O.B., Lansing, Michigan," the buyer's place of business. Nothing else in the agreement defined the delivery or payment obligations. The seller's place of business is Mobile, Alabama. What are the performance obligations of A and B?

8. In the fact pattern of question 7 above, assume that after B took possession of the motors, it is discovered that 20 percent of the motors would not perform according to the specifications supplied to A by B. What should B do? If there is sufficient time, what course should A follow? How would the performance obligations differ if the parties had negotiated an "installment contract?"

9. Neal-Cooper, buyer, was engaged in the business of selling grain and fertilizer. They used large quantities of phosphates and potash, most of which were supplied by Texas Gulf Sulphur Co., seller. For several years prior to 1969 these two parties conducted business on an order basis without written contracts. Usually a phone call was made by the buyer stating the quantity needed; the seller stated a price and when and where the shipment would arrive. On November 20, 1969 the buyer received from the seller some printed form contracts which they were to use in making future orders. Two of the

forms already bore the signature of the *seller's* general sales manager. The buyer was asked to fill in the quantities needed, sign the forms, and return them to the seller.

The buyer's agent agreed to buy 10,000 tons of coarse potash and 2,000 tons of granular potash for the period November 1, 1969 through June 30, 1970. All deliveries were to be "F.O.B. cars seller's plant, Potash, Utah." The printed form stated that the price was to be in accordance with the "seller's attached price list." No price list was attached but at the bottom of the agreement were the typed words:

> Coarse at 21¢ per unit through January 31, 1970
> Granular at 23¢ per unit through January 31, 1970.

exculpatory clause
a clause which
relieves one from
liability

Furthermore, the printed form stated that the contract would not be binding upon the seller until duly accepted at its New York office. The seller's form also had a provision enabling the seller to institute a price increase during the life of the contract effective fifteen days after receipt by the buyer of a "revised TGS price list." Finally, the form contained an **exculpatory clause** excusing the parties from performance caused by, among other things, the operation of statutes or law.

Between November 12 and December 4, 1969 the seller shipped three shipments of potash to the buyer at the price stated in the form contract. On December 2, 1969 the buyer placed a large order for potash to be delivered in January. The seller refused to fill the order because (among other things): (1) the original contract was never formally accepted in New York so there was no "enforceable" agreement; (2) the Canadian government passed regulations which controlled the seller's production and price of potash so they were unable to promise any fixed tonnage for shipment in the future. (The Canadian regulations were intended to limit the production of potash and to set a minimum price of 33.75¢ (Canadian) per unit.) The seller argued that the agreement, if there was one, was thus rendered commercially impracticable, thereby excusing performance under section 2-615 of the UCC.

At the trial there was testimony that the Canadian source was the primary source of the seller's potash but not the only source. The seller did have potash mines in the U.S. [*Neal-Cooper Grain Co. v. Texas Gulf Sulphur Co.,* 508 F.2d 283 (1974).]

a. Was there an enforceable agreement? Why?
b. What was the price? Could the seller change its price during the life of the agreement?
c. Was the seller excused from performance?
d. If the buyer had ordered all 10,000 tons of coarse and 2,000 tons of granular potash for January delivery, would the seller have an excuse for not shipping all of it at that time?

10. In the case of *National Heater Company, Inc. v. Corrigan Co. Mechanical Contractors, Inc.,* 482 F.2d 87 (1973),[60] if you were the seller, what would you have done to avoid the risk of loss which the seller had in that case?

---

[60] See p. 418.

Breach of the Sales Contract, Courses of Action, and Remedies

25

After you have read this chapter, you should be able to:

1. Describe the buyer's courses of action if the seller defaults before its date of performance; then describe the seller's courses of action if the buyer defaults before its performance is due.
2. List and then define the various monetary remedies available to buyers and sellers upon the breach by the other party.
3. Describe the differences between incidental and consequential damages, give an example of each, and state the circumstances in which the court will award consequential damages.
4. List and then describe the circumstances in which the buyer may recover the goods contracted for from the seller and the circumstances in which the seller may recover the goods it has delivered to the buyer.
5. Discuss the circumstances in which the parties may limit the damage recovery of the opposing party.
6. Define what is meant by a statute of limitations and describe when the time period of this statute usually begins and ends in sales transactions.

Introduction

Courts and "the law" must attempt to put the non-breaching party in the same position it would have been in had there been full performance.[1] Any remedy or measure of damage which strives to achieve something less than this creates an incentive *not* to perform exactly as promised. The entire body of our commercial law is premised on the notion that the parties to a commercial transaction desire performance. Protecting the full *value* of that performance to the non-breaching party is the chief objective of the sections on remedy. If the remedy sections do not achieve this objective, the value of all other sections is diminished. It is for this reason that the principles of breach and remedies are so important.

We suggested in chapter 23, Formation and Interpretation of the Sales Contract, that your comprehension of this sales material might be facilitated by focusing on two different patterns of commercial conduct. One pattern, that of two large corporate merchants doing business, has been the focus of the preceding two chapters and will be the focus of this one. The other pattern, that of a consumer doing business with a merchant, we will analyze in the following chapter. Perhaps the most substantial area of overlap in these two patterns is the area of analysis involving a remedy for a breach of **warranty**—an assurance that goods will meet a certain standard of performance or quality. Large corporate merchants make warranties to one another *and* to consumers also. We will present breach of warranty and damage material in the following chapter, Consumer Law, because the most rapid expansion of litigation in this area involves, usually, a consumer suing a merchant. However, you should remember that merchants may also sue one another for breach of warranty.

The subject of **unconscionable contracts** will also be analyzed in the next chapter. Most parties who successfully assert that their contract or a clause of it was "unconscionable" at the time it was made, and almost all of the reported cases interpreting the unconscionability provision of Article 2 (2–302), are concerned with consumers.[2] Thus, it logically belongs in the discussion of commercial patterns involving merchants and consumers.

This chapter presents an analysis of both the buyer's and seller's courses of action once they have learned of a breach by the other party and their various remedies. The material is best read based upon the central image of two corporate merchants who have entered into an enforceable sales agreement.

warranty
an express or implied assurance that certain facts exist

unconscionable contract
a contract in which one of the parties is in too unequal or one-sided a bargaining position

Breach of the Sales Contract by the Seller

Buyer's Courses of Action Without Bringing a Lawsuit
One of the most difficult problems which arise from commercial conduct is the judgment about the other party's anticipated performance. When a doubt about the seller's performance is created in the mind of the buyer, for example, what should the buyer do? Below we consider first the possible courses of action of the

---

[1] UCC 1–106(1).

[2] J. White and R. Summers, *Uniform Commercial Code,* 114 (1972).

buyer; then we analyze the remedies and measures of damage available to the buyer when the seller breaches. We start with the buyer's courses of conduct and remedies because, generally, the buyer faces a tougher problem in assessing the nature of the seller's performance than does the seller in assessing whether or not the buyer has paid or will pay.

The discussion of the various courses of action analyzed below is based on the assumption that the opposing party is *not* perfectly clear about repudiating its performance obligations. If a party is clear about repudiating, then the course of conduct is clear. For example, if the seller writes to the buyer that it has no intention of performing at all, this is called an *anticipatory repudiation,* and the buyer may select one of two courses of action. (1) It may, for a commercially reasonable time, await performance (to see if the seller changes its mind), or (2) it may suspend its performance obligations and resort to any of the remedies for breach discussed below.[3] In essence, the problem of breach is solved, and the buyer need not concern itself with many of the courses of action because the seller's acts are not ambiguous.

Also, remember that the *buyer's* acts should not be ambiguous. Article 2 (2–301) imposes on the parties *mutual* obligations of performance. Until the buyer is convinced of the seller's intent not to perform, or to perform partially, it should remain ready to accept and pay for the goods.

The Buyer's Right to Adequate Assurance of Performance.   If reasonable grounds appear which cause the buyer (or seller) to feel insecure about the seller's (or buyer's) performance, then the buyer should (1) suspend performance, (2) demand in writing an adequate assurance of performance, and (3) await a reply for a reasonable time, which is not over thirty days. If there is no adequate reply, then the buyer may treat the contract as repudiated by the seller.[4] Section 2–609 was intended to provide a course of action to a party when the other party's actions were ambiguous or cast doubt on its ability to perform. Obviously, it was intended to apply to circumstances *before* the date of performance of either party. This section was discussed more fully in chapter 24, Performance of the Sales Contract.

Demand adequate assurance of performance by the seller.

The Buyer's Right to Reject or Accept the Goods.   Generally, at the time of the seller's tender of the goods, it is the obligation of the buyer to inspect the goods and either accept or reject them. It *must* accept and pay for them if they conform to the contract. If, however, the goods fail *in any respect,*[5] then the buyer may reject the whole, or accept the whole (with, we assume, an allowance

Rejection of the goods.

---

[3] UCC 2–610.

[4] UCC 2–609.

[5] This is the language of the Code creating the requirement of a "perfect" tender discussed in chapter 24. Although the Code itself states that "exact performance" is required (see section 2–106, comment 2), some legal scholars have concluded that "substantial" performance is all that is required. See White and Summers, p. 256. This view seems to contradict the expressed intent of the drafters.

in the price for the defect), or accept any commercial unit or units and reject the rest.[6] This duty was also discussed in chapter 24, so we will not pursue its exceptions (for installment contracts, for example) and meaning here.

Let us assume that the buyer has ordered one shipment of goods and it has arrived and the buyer desires to *reject* the shipment. How is an effective rejection made? The rejection:

1. must be made within a reasonable time after the delivery or tender of the goods (but before acceptance), and
2. is effective when the buyer seasonably notifies the seller of the rejection.[7]

These requirements of an effective rejection demand that the buyer act *promptly*. The words "reasonable" and "seasonably" are not defined in this section, so a court is left free to define them in relation to the circumstances of the case. The buyer's actions must be precise when rejecting goods. Any exercise of ownership of the goods by the buyer is wrongful against the seller and may cause a court to conclude that the buyer has waived its rejection.

After notice of rejection is sent, the buyer's course of action will depend on whether it has paid anything for the goods received. If the buyer *has not* paid anything for the goods, it is under a duty to hold them with reasonable care for disposition by the seller.[8] If the seller has no agent or place of business at the place where the rejection takes place, then a merchant buyer must follow any reasonable instructions from the seller. In the absence of such instructions, and if the goods are perishable or will quickly decline in value if not sold, the buyer *must* make reasonable efforts to sell the goods for the account of the seller, deducting from the sales price its reasonable expenses for caring for and selling the goods.[9]

If the buyer *has paid* something for them, whether it is the full price or just a partial payment, the buyer has a property interest in the goods in its possession or control, called a security interest, for the amount paid *and* expenses reasonably incurred in their inspection, receipt, transportation, care, and custody.[10] This property interest in the goods enables the buyer to sell the goods in good faith and in a commercially reasonable manner. The buyer must account to the seller for any excess money received over the amount of the security interest.[11]

Acceptance of the goods.

The alternative to rejecting the goods is to accept them. Acceptance occurs (1) after a reasonable opportunity to inspect and when the buyer signifies to the seller that the goods are conforming or that he will take them in spite of their non-conformity; or (2) if the buyer fails to make an effective rejection (after a reasonable opportunity to inspect); or (3) if the buyer does any act inconsistent with the seller's ownership.[12] Acceptance of a part of any commercial unit is acceptance of that entire unit.[13]

---

[6] UCC 2–601.   [10] UCC 2–711(3).

[7] UCC 2–602(1).   [11] UCC 2–706(6).

[8] UCC 2–602(2)(b).   [12] UCC 2–606(1).

[9] UCC 2–603(1)(2).   [13] UCC 2–606(2).

Acceptance of the goods has three important consequences. (1) Acceptance obligates the buyer to pay for the goods at the contract rate.[14] (2) Acceptance gives the *seller* an additional remedy for a breach by the buyer. (3) Of more importance to our inquiry into breach and damages, acceptance shifts the burden of proof for establishing non-conformity from the seller to the buyer. A rejection of the goods by the buyer results in the seller bearing the burden of proving that the goods were conforming. However, if acceptance takes place and then an alleged non-conformity is detected, it is the burden of the buyer to establish the nature of the seller's breach.[15]

The Buyer's Right to Revoke Its Acceptance.　　We must assume that many, if not most, of the breaches by a seller for tendering non-conforming goods are discovered after acceptance. The complexity of goods manufactured today makes it difficult to discover whether goods tendered are non-conforming by mere visual inspection or even sampling their performance. The Code recognizes this and provides a course of action for the buyer when it discovers a non-conformity after acceptance. Section 2–608 allows a buyer to *revoke acceptance*. It provides:

Revocation of acceptance.

(1) The buyer may *revoke his acceptance* of a lot or commercial unit whose non-conformity *substantially impairs its value to him* if he has accepted it
 (a) on the reasonable assumption that its non-conformity would be cured and it has not been seasonably cured; or
 (b) without discovery of such non-conformity if his acceptance was *reasonably induced* either by *the difficulty of discovery before acceptance* or by the seller's assurances.
(2) Revocation of acceptance must occur *within a reasonable time* after the buyer discovers or should have discovered the ground for it and before any substantial change in condition of the goods. . . . It is not effective until the buyer notifies the seller of it.
(3) A buyer who so revokes has the same rights and duties with regard to the goods involved as if he had rejected them. [Emphasis added.]

Rejection and revocation of acceptance have some similarities and some substantial differences. If the revocation is effective, then, as in rejection, the goods will be treated as if they were the seller's, and the buyer has the same courses of action open to it, including the right to sell the goods it possesses. Unlike a rejection, which is available in *single delivery contracts* for *any* non-conformity, a revocation of acceptance is permitted only where the non-conformity *substantially impairs* the value of the goods to the buyer. This substantial impairment of value can be asserted by the buyer only where the buyer noted an earlier non-conformity which was not seasonably cured, or where detection of the non-conformity was reasonably induced either by difficulty in discovery or by the seller's assurances. The right to revoke acceptance may be lost unless it is asserted within a reasonable time after the discovery of the non-conformity (or the passage of time within which the buyer should have discovered it). If the

---

[14] UCC 2–607(1).

[15] UCC 2–607(4).

buyer uses the goods after an attempted revocation, courts will most likely hold that such use bars the assertion of the revocation, with the result that the buyer would retain the goods.[16]

In the following case, the non-conformity of the goods did not substantially impair the value of the goods to the buyer, who was not permitted to revoke its acceptance.

Facts

The plaintiffs, Kearney & Trecker, were sellers of sophisticated industrial equipment used to make metal parts. On July 1, 1970 they agreed to sell to Fargo Machine & Tool Co. for $153,725 a metal-shaping machine with additional parts that made the machine adaptable for a number of tasks. Delivery and installation were completed in September, 1971. The machine did not operate to the full satisfaction of the buyer, and numerous service calls followed. As of January, 1972 Fargo Machine had paid $75,000 on the machine and was not content with the machine's performance but agreed to pay an additional $28,868, reducing the balance to $50,000 in return for Kearney's promise to correct specified deficiencies. In June of 1972 Kearney advised Fargo that the deficiencies had been remedied and requested prompt payment of the balance. Fargo refused to pay, stating that new deficiencies were noticed all the time. In April of 1973 the seller, Kearney & Trecker, filed suit for the balance. The buyers, Fargo Machine & Tool Company, counterclaimed by asserting that they wished to revoke their acceptance of the machine. Can the buyer revoke its acceptance?

Decision

The court held that the buyer could not revoke its acceptance but did allow the buyer to offset specified items of damage against the seller's claim for the balance.

Reasoning

The court relied on section 2–608 and the requirement that a non-conformity must substantially impair the value of the goods to the buyer before revocation of acceptance will be ordered. The court stated that although the impairment in value is a subjective issue, requiring the court to focus on the impairment of value to the particular buyer before the court, it is to be resolved based upon the objective facts of the case and not based upon personal beliefs of the buyer. The "facts" the court found persuasive were: (1) the buyer made a $28,000-plus payment after acceptance and had a reasonable opportunity to use the machine; (2) in the first two years of operation there was only one period when the machine went down, and there were no incidents where a work piece was defectively machined or finished late; and (3) in the nearly 5½ years that Fargo operated it, the machine was used to at least the same productive extent as is normally expected of such a machine. The court concluded that Fargo's extensive use of the machine is a clear indication that the effect of the malfunctions on the user was not substantially adverse. The court awarded the plaintiff $46,260, allowing the defendant to offset over $4,000 of damages for lost profits and repairs.

Fargo Machine & Tool Co. v. Kearney & Trecker Corp., 428 F.Supp. 364 (1977).

---

[16] R. J. Nordstrom, *Handbook of the Law of Sales* (St. Paul: West Pub. Co., 1970).

In summary, the buyer's courses of action should be determined, first, by reading the sales contract. The right to inspect the goods, reject or accept, etc. may be defined in the sales contract, and this will control. Remember the case in the last chapter[17] involving Maas, a large commercial grower of wheat and corn who ordered a large silo and related equipment for the storage of grain. The sales contract stated that the buyer was to have a "one-year warranty of customer satisfaction." The court held that this gave the buyer the right to reject the goods (not revoke acceptance) within the one year. Without such a provision in the contract, buyers do not have this long to reject.

In the absence of a controlling provision in the sales contract, and if the time for tender has not arrived, the buyer may, under appropriate circumstances, demand adequate assurance of performance by the seller. At the time and place of tender, the buyer may inspect the goods (unless this right has been waived by, for example, agreement to pay C.O.D.). After inspection, the buyer may either reject or accept. If the buyer accepts, it may later revoke acceptance if the requirements of section 2–608 are met.

In most situations where the goods do not conform to the contract, the buyer and seller, guided by their own notions of good faith action, and perhaps by the thought of doing business in the future, will attempt to work out an adjustment of the price for the non-conformity. If such an adjustment is not possible and the buyer has followed one of the courses of action just described and, further, desires a legal remedy for breach, then the buyer *must notify* the seller that it is claiming a breach of the agreement.[18] Upon breach of the sales agreement by the seller, the buyer may select one or more of the court-awarded remedies discussed next.

> Buyer must notify seller of a breach.

Buyer's Remedies in the Courts

Buyer's Monetary Recovery. The law must attempt to compensate the non-breaching party so that it is put as close as possible to the position it would have been in had there been performance. Courts, as a general guide to awarding remedies, recognize three basic principles which are usually phrased in terms of the non-breaching party's *interests* in the transaction. They are, in order of importance, the expectation, reliance, and restitution interests.

No single legal principle will provide a guide for action in every situation involving a breaching party. However, given the general objective of compensation, the best principle to begin with is that courts should give the non-breaching party what it *expected* from the other party's performance. In some cases an award of money damages will do this, and in other cases an order to the seller to convey the goods will do this. The fundamental notion, though, is to give the buyer the *gain* that it had expected. When such a *gain* is given to the non-breaching party, a court is protecting the *expectation interest* of that party.

In some circumstances, however, a buyer may have incurred expenses in reliance upon the expected performance which exceed the gain from the particular breached performance. For example, a manufacturer of small steel products

---

[17] See pp. 400–401.   [18] UCC 2–607(3)(a).

may have spent $1,000 for cement footings and supporting structures for a large steel stamping machine it ordered from the seller. Assume that the seller repudiates the contract and the buyer finds that it can purchase a similar machine for the same price it was to pay the first seller. However, the new machine required *new* cement footings, which cost another $1,000, and the old ones had to be removed at a cost of $500. This buyer incurred expenses of $1,500 in *reliance* on the first seller's promise and should be able to recover that amount even though the measurable *gain* to the buyer had there been no breach may have been less.

In a few cases the anticipated gain may be too speculative to measure and there may be no amounts expended by the non-breaching party in reliance on the breached promise, but the *breaching* party may have experienced a gain as a result of the transaction. In this case the courts will measure the amount of loss to the non-breaching party by allowing it to recover the breaching party's gain. Courts are protecting the **restitution** interest of the buyer in this instance. The best example of this measure of damage is a case in which the buyer pays $3,000 down on a $5,000 contract and there is a breach by the seller. For a number of reasons the buyer is unable to prove its gain had there been performance and can not show damage caused by reliance on the breached promise (assume, for example, that a mountain ski resort had ordered a large snow-making machine the fall before a winter in which there were record snowfalls). Courts would order the return of the $3,000.

Protecting the expectation, reliance, and restitution interests of the non-breaching party is accomplished by the law's recognizing one or more of the following remedies of the buyer: (1) the right to cover (buying substitute goods); (2) the right to sue for damages for nondelivery or repudiation; (3) the right to accept the goods and either deduct damages from the price or sue for damages resulting from the accepted goods; and (4) the right to require the seller to convey the goods contracted for. In this section we analyze the different types of the buyer's monetary recovery (the first three listed remedies). In the next major section we analyze the fourth category of remedies, the right to goods.

Before the buyer claims one of the first two remedies discussed below, it must give the breaching seller notice that it is claiming a breach, and it may also demand the return of any money paid the seller under the breached contract. If this money paid is not returned, it may be made part of the damage claim.

1. The Buyer's Right to **Cover** (Procure Substitute Goods). One of the innovations in Article 2 is the buyer's remedy of "covering." After a breach (nondelivery of the goods) by the seller and notice to the seller that the buyer is claiming such a breach, the buyer may, in good faith and without unreasonable delay, make a reasonable purchase of goods in substitution for those due from the seller.[19] If the goods cost more than the buyer had agreed to pay, it may sue the seller for this added cost plus any incidental or consequential damages, but less any expenses saved in consequence of the seller's breach.[20] The section on

---

[19] UCC 2–712(1).   [20] UCC 2–712(2).

restitution
a legal remedy restoring one to his original position prior to the particular transaction

cover
to seek a substitute performance

"covering" was intended by the draftsmen of the Code to be the primary remedy of the buyer, but the buyer is not "forced" to cover (it may select any appropriate remedy). In the following case, the buyer chose to cover.

Facts

The plaintiff, Owens, agreed to buy 143,500 feet of 6-inch pipe and 103,000 feet of 3-inch pipe from the defendant, Clow. The defendant did not make several deliveries on time, and the plaintiff suffered some damage as a result. When it appeared that the defendant would not be able to make future deliveries on time, the plaintiff "cancelled" the contract with Clow, bought the required pipe elsewhere for more than it was required to pay Clow, and sued Clow for the difference. Clow admitted that it could not fully perform the contract but argued that Owens was required to buy all the pipe Clow had before buying the pipe from another source. Was the defendant correct?

Decision

No. The appellate court affirmed a trial court finding in favor of the plaintiff, Owens.

Reasoning

In reviewing Owens' action in claiming a breach and covering, the court noted that whether it was reasonable for Owens to purchase elsewhere, after his agreement with Clow caused him damaging delays, was a classic jury issue. The court affirmed the charge to the jury on the law and quoted it as follows:

. . . if you are reasonably satisfied from the evidence that defendant, Clow, . . . failed to furnish the materials as agreed or within a reasonable time, then Owens would be entitled to cancel the contract with Clow and purchase other materials from another supplier and set off the difference in cost against. . . Clow, provided such purchase was or were reasonably necessary and were made in good faith without any unreasonable delay.

Owens v. Clow Corporation, 491 F.2d 101, 104 (1974).

Note that the court did not say that the law required Owens to purchase the supply of pipe Clow had on hand before covering.

The Code provision for covering reads simply, but applying its provisions to a factual pattern may be complicated by the nature of the goods contracted for and the buyer's plans for the goods when received. Let us start with a simple example. Assume that B contracted to buy a quantity of apples for $5,000, payment due on delivery. S, seller, breaches and the buyer buys elsewhere the same quantity and quality apples for $4,500. This is one of those rare situations where there has been a breach but no **damage.** In such cases the court would award **nominal damages** of $1 to B should B desire to sue. The more realistic situation is one in which B must pay $6,000 for the same apples (or reasonable substitutes). In this case B could buy the apples and sue S for $1,000.

Now let us change from apples to a complex piece of machinery and assume that there are very few sellers of such machinery. If there is only one seller of such machinery, then B would attempt to get the machine itself (if it had been constructed) and would not have opted to cover. If there are a few sellers, good commercial practice would dictate that B get price quotes from them for the machinery. The identical machine need not be ordered, but the Code requires

damage
loss or harm

nominal damages
the money judicially awarded when no damage has occurred from another's wrongful conduct

that the substitute be "commercially usable as a reasonable substitute under the circumstances of the particular case."[21] What is meant by "commercially usable as a reasonable substitute" can not be defined without the facts of a particular case. Ultimately who defines such terms is the trier of fact (either the jury or the judge sitting without a jury). If B finds a machine which is commercially usable as a reasonable substitute, he may buy it and sue S for any added cost.

Another factor (besides the nature of the goods) which complicates the calculation of monetary damages for the buyer is what the buyer intended to do with the goods. At this point we are going to emphasize a basic distinction in the types of monetary damages. This distinction is between incidental and consequential damages.

Obviously, the buyer should be able to recover all of its *expenses resulting from the seller's breach*. So, if there are added expenses in covering for inspection, receipt, transportation, care or custody of the goods rejected or later purchased, these may be recovered. These "reasonable expenses" associated with breach, Article 2 calls "incidental damages."[22] **Incidental damages** are essentially unplanned-for reliance losses and they must be *caused* by the seller's breach. In our apple example above, if B had agreed to send his truck (at a cost of $100) for the apples, and S refused to deliver the apples when the truck arrived, and it cost B an *additional* $75 to get substitute apples, then B should be able to recover the $75. B should not be able to recover as incidental damages the $100 it had planned to spend to get the first load. The breach did not cause the $100 expenditure; it did cause the $75 expenditure.[23] If B decided not to purchase substitutes, then the $100 may be recovered because the truck made the trip to S's place.

B, however, may have incurred an additional item of damage. If B had one contract to purchase apples for $5,000 before S breached and then made another to sell them for $5,800, B was *expecting* an $800 *gain* from the two transactions. This gain is an item of **consequential damages** and *may* be recovered from S so long as *S knew or had reason to know that the apples were being purchased for resale at the time B and S contracted*. Consequential damages are those resulting from the breach and the buyer's inability to fulfill general or particular requirements for which the goods were needed. Usually in a sales contract case, consequential damages refer to the lost gain or lost expectation of the parties.[24] Recovery of this gain in proper circumstances is important, and it is for this

incidental damages
the money judicially awarded for expenses reasonably incurred by the non-breaching party on the other party's breach

consequential damages
the money judicially awarded for loss which the breaching party reasonably could foresee would be a consequence of his breach

---

[21] UCC 2–712, comment 2.

[22] UCC 2–715(1).

[23] See Nordstrom pp. 464–465. Is there a conflict between this example and the one mentioned earlier in the chapter where a buyer was allowed to recover $1,500 for cement footings prepared for a machine not delivered? No! In the latter case the buyer was willing to spend $1,000 to properly seat the machine. As a result of the breach it spent $500 to remove unsuitable footings and $1,000 more to create new ones. The recovery should be for $1,500 because these were the expenses *caused by the breach*.

[24] In a breach of *warranty* case, they also refer to damage to person or property proximately resulting from the breach.

reason we said that what the buyer of goods plans to do with the goods is a complicating factor in our analysis of monetary damages.

When someone asserts that he is entitled to consequential damages, he faces a relatively tough matter of proof. He must first prove that it is more probable than not that the breaching party knew or had reason to know at the time the contract was formed the general or particular requirements for the goods which were not fulfilled. This is relatively easy to do where the buyer is a known "middleman" whose sole purpose for being in business is to purchase and resell goods. It is also relatively easy to do where the contract states that the goods are for resale. But what test should be applied by a court where these circumstances are not present? How much and what kind of "knowledge" must the seller possess to make it liable for consequential damages?

The majority of courts seem to be utilizing the same test announced in the classic case of *Hadley v. Baxendale*,[25] summarized by Professor Corbin in his classic treatise on contract law. He stated that a plaintiff may recover consequential damages if it can prove that "it is one that ordinarily follows the breach of such a contract in the usual course of events, or [is one] that reasonable men in the position of the parties would have foreseen as a probable result of breach."[26]

Another troublesome part of proving consequential damages is proving that it is more probable than not that the exact amount asserted by the plaintiff would have been lost had there been performance. If the buyer can prove that a particular resale contract was for the very goods which were to be supplied by the breaching seller, then its burden of proof is lessened. But this is not always the case. While the Code does not require "mathematical precision" in the proof of loss,[27] it does require that the buyer prove that it is more probable than not that the amount lost and claimed as consequential damages would have been gained had there been performance. Like so many other issues, this one must be left for the jury or a judge sitting as a fact finder. The following case illustrates the proof necessary for a court award of consequential damages.

Facts

The plaintiff, Great American Music Machine, Inc., contracted with the defendant, Mid-South Record Company, to press some record albums from a tape made by Ralph Harrison, an unknown songwriter and singer. The plaintiff planned to have Harrison's records distributed and promoted and at the same time planned to raise additional capital through a public offering of its stock.

On April 3, 1972 the plaintiff received the first shipment of records and, upon inspection, discovered that they were warped, pitted, and blistered and produced excessive surface noise. The plaintiff immediately contacted the defendant but was told that 8,000 of the records had already been distributed. In the meantime the plaintiff had contacted a brokerage firm to underwrite some of its stock.

---

[25] 156 Eng. Rep. 145 (Ex. 1854).

[26] A. Corbin, *Corbin on Contracts* 79 (1964), quoted in White and Summers, p. 316.

[27] UCC 2–715, comment 4.

The brokerage firm agreed to underwrite $500,000 worth of the plaintiff's securities if it could get the Harrison record album "up and going." The plaintiff alleged that the defective pressing of the records virtually destroyed the market for Harrison's records and caused the failure of the brokerage firm to underwrite its stock. Can the plaintiff recover the capital lost from the projected underwriting as a measure of damages for the defendant's breach?

Decision

No. On the issue of the consequential damages, the court found for the defendant.

Reasoning

The court says that although there was "some mention" between the plaintiff and defendant of the stock offering, it does not appear from the proof that this matter was discussed in sufficient detail so that the defendant had *any idea* it might be held liable for the failure of the underwriting. Also, the court rejected the $500,000 claim because the proof was not sufficient to establish that the underwriting failed as a result of the defective record pressing.

American Music v. Mid-South Record Company, 393 F.Supp. 877 (1975).

Mitigation of damages.

We have explained incidental and consequential damages because they are available in almost all cases where either party is claiming monetary damages. We should emphasize that many merchant-seller's form agreements attempt to limit recovery for consequential damages. This attempted limitation of damages will be discussed near the end of this chapter.

The common law required the parties to mitigate their damages. This means that a non-breaching party had to choose a course of action upon breach which would limit rather than compound the damages. This policy of the law is continued in Article 2 in the requirement that a buyer can recover consequential damages under the general remedy of "covering" only where that consequential loss could not have been reasonably prevented by covering.[28]

In summary, the buyer's primary monetary remedy is to "cover" by making a good faith purchase of substitute goods and then to sue the seller for the difference between the cost of cover and the contract price plus incidental and consequential damages less expenses saved when covering.

Sue for damages.

2. The Buyer's Right to Sue for Damages for Nondelivery or Repudiation. The buyer is free to choose between the cover remedy just discussed and suit for damages for nondelivery under section 2–713.[29] It may not, however, "cover" *and* sue for damages under section 2–713.[30] Section 2–713 permits a buyer who has not accepted or received the goods to sue a repudiating seller for an amount of money determined by the difference between the market price of the goods at the time the buyer learned of the breach and the contract price, together with any incidental or consequential damages and less expenses saved. The place

---

[28] UCC 2–715(2)(a).

[29] See UCC 2–712, comment 3.

[30] See UCC 2–713, comment 5.

where market price is to be determined is the place where the goods were to be tendered; or, in cases of rejection or revocation of acceptance, at the place of arrival.[31]

Assume that on April 10, B agreed to pay $5,000 to S for a quantity of apples, "F.O.B. S's orchard" in Holland, Michigan, for delivery September 10. On August 10, S repudiates the contract. Further, assume that on August 10 the price for the same quantity and quality apples in Holland, Michigan (a noted apple-growing region) is $6,000. B may sue S for $1,000 plus any incidental or consequential damages, less expenses saved in consequence of the breach.

3. The Buyer's Right to Accept the Goods and Either Deduct Damages from the Price or Sue for Damages. As a last remedy for monetary recovery, the buyer may accept the goods and either (a) notify the seller of the breach within a reasonable time after he discovers or should have discovered the breach, and recover damages for loss as well as incidental and consequential damages; or (b) notify the seller of his intention to deduct from the purchase price due to the seller the damages resulting from the seller's breach.

> Accept the goods and either deduct or sue for damages.

The Buyer's Right to Recovery of the Goods. 1. The Buyer's Right to Specific Performance. Section 2–716(1) directs a court to award **specific performance** "where the goods are unique or in other proper circumstances." Specific performance is an order from a court decreeing that a party to a contract should perform as promised or face contempt of court charges. The old common law of contracts provided that specific performance should be decreed only where the remedy at law (usually the award of money damages) was inadequate. Recall that contracts for the sale of land were assumed to be contracts of such a special type that the remedy at law was deemed inadequate and specific performance was awarded in almost every case.

> **specific performance** the exact performance of a contract by a party as ordered by a court

Contracts for the sale of priceless works of art or heirlooms were, at common law, and remain under Article 2, appropriate cases for the award of specific performance.[32] However, the drafters wanted section 2–716 to be read more broadly and they admonished that "this Article seeks to further a more liberal attitude than some courts have shown in connection with the specific performance of contracts of sale."[33] The only requirement is that the goods be "unique." Certainly this means that the goods could not be purchased in a reasonable fashion or for a reasonable price elsewhere.

Where one large merchant agrees to buy all of its requirements for goods for a stated period of time from a "peculiarly available source," then a court may award specific performance.[34] The court may also order such payment of damages or other relief for the non-breaching party as it may deem just.[35]

In the following case, the court found that the circumstances merited a decree of specific performance.

---

[31] UCC 2–713(2).

[32] See UCC 2–716, comment 2.

[33] See UCC 2–716, comment 1.

[34] See UCC 2–716, comment 2.

[35] UCC 2–716(2).

Facts

The plaintiff, Mitchell-Huntley Cotton Co., agreed to buy from a group of merchant-farmers all of the cotton planted, produced, and ginned by the defendants through December 15, 1973. The plaintiff was engaged in the business of buying cotton from large commercial growers and selling and delivering it to textile mills and others. The contract was made on February 15, 1973 and the basic price to be paid for the cotton was $.30 per pound. Shortly after the contract was made, a drastic shortage of cotton developed, and the price for cotton increased to over $.80 per pound by the late summer of 1973. The defendants claimed that the contract was unenforceable since they could wait until after December 15, 1973 to have their cotton ginned and were thus not required to perform. The plaintiff sued the defendants for breach of the contract and requested the court to order the defendants to specifically perform. Should the plaintiff be awarded the remedy of specific performance?

Decision

Yes. The court entered judgment for the plaintiff.

Reasoning

The court found that since the tradition and trade custom was to gin cotton promptly upon its maturity, the defendants were under an obligation of good faith performance to so gin all their cotton which matured prior to December 15, 1973. The court further found that, as of the fall of 1973, the "majority" of all cotton to be produced in the U.S. for 1973 had been sold, and that there were no merchantable grades of cotton in storage in the U.S. So, as of February 25, 1974 the court ordered the defendants to harvest their cotton, have it ginned and deliver it to the plaintiffs.

Mitchell-Huntley Cotton Co., Inc. v. Waldrep, 377 F.Supp. 1215 (1974).

Sue to get the goods.

2. The Buyer's Right to the Goods When the Seller Becomes Insolvent, and the Buyer's Right to Replevin. The buyer may attempt to get the goods contracted for under the authority of two more Code sections in addition to the specific performance action. We will examine first the one which is more likely to be used.

The buyer is very much interested in receiving the goods from the seller when it has made a substantial prepayment to the seller and then finds out that the seller is insolvent. In this case any later court judgment for money damages against the seller will probably remain unpaid (or the buyer will be paid just a fraction of what its judgment is worth). Section 2–502 allows the buyer to recover the goods contracted for if the following conditions are met:

a. The goods must have been identified to the contract so that a "special property" interest in them passes to the buyer. (This happens when the contract is made, if the goods are existing and can be identified at the time the contract is made. If the goods are not existing, it happens when the seller designates which goods are for the particular contract. You may want to review section 2–501 here.)

b. The buyer must have paid all or a part of the purchase price.

c. The buyer must remain willing to pay any balance owing.

d. The seller must become insolvent within ten days after receipt of the first installment payment.

Meeting the conditions of section 2–502 is difficult—especially the last one. Attempting to prove the very day of insolvency has been described as a "venture into foolhardiness"[36] which has compelled some scholars to assert that this section is of questionable value to the buyer.[37] Even if the buyer can qualify under this section, there is the chance that the federal bankruptcy Code will take precedence in any case where it is properly invoked.

Another section of limited application recognizes the common law right to **replevin.** Section 2–716(3) allows the buyer the right to replevy the goods from the seller if:

replevin
a common law form of action to regain possession of specific chattels

a. the goods are identified to the contract (see the section just above for a definition of "identification" or see UCC 2–501); *and*

b. the buyer has made a reasonable effort to cover and has not been able to do so, or the circumstances are such that an effort to cover would be unavailing; or

c. the goods have been shipped under reservation, and satisfaction of the security interest in them has been made or tendered.

If the goods have been identified to the contract but not delivered and the seller refuses to deliver the goods and cover is not a reasonable alternative, then the situation may involve one of two circumstances. The first is that the goods may be unique (what else could they be if cover is not reasonable?) and the seller is withholding delivery in bad faith. In this instance a claim for specific performance would be appropriate. The second circumstance is that the seller is near insolvency and has been advised by its attorney not to ship the identified goods. This circumstance gives the buyer some limited protection against other creditors of the seller and makes sense because the goods should be of greater value to the buyer than to other creditors. Moreover, the other creditors of the seller would probably rather have money (the purchase price) in the place of the goods.

The third condition allows the buyer to replevy the goods once shipped even though the *seller* has reserved a security interest in the goods by the buyer's tendering payment. Again, this condition seems to contemplate a potential conflict between the buyer and creditors of the seller who may be trying to reach shipped goods, and it favors the buyer.

In conclusion, we should emphasize that in almost all cases performance is preferred over a breach and remedy. In very few instances do the remedies provided by this Code or any other *really* put the non-breaching party in the *same* position it would have been in had there been performance. This, however, is the appropriate aim of the remedies of the buyer. The primary remedies of

---

[36] Nordstrom, p. 485.

[37] Id., p. 484.

"cover" and suit for damages for nondelivery should be the first alternatives explored by a buyer. The buyer's other remedies discussed above are of less significance but may be awarded by a court when the proper conditions are satisfied.

Breach of the Sales Contract by the Buyer

Seller's Courses of Action Without Bringing a Lawsuit

In most instances when a buyer's performance becomes doubtful, the seller's courses of action are going to depend upon an assessment of the buyer's solvency. The seller has contracted for *payment*, and potential insolvency threatens this promised performance. In many commercial transactions it is the tradition to pay sometime after receipt of the goods. Often the seller will have lost control of the goods when the seller learns of the buyer's insolvency or other breach. Therefore, we can imagine at least three courses of conduct based upon *who has the goods:* the seller, the buyer, or perhaps a third party to whom the buyer has transferred the goods. The courses of action discussed below assume that the seller still has control of the goods. Generally, where a seller has relinquished control of the goods, it must seek the assistance of a court order (a remedy) to regain them.

The Seller's Right to Adequate Assurance of Performance. If the seller still has the goods and if reasonable grounds for insecurity exist, then he may (1) suspend performance, (2) demand in writing an adequate assurance of performance, and (3) await a reply for a reasonable time, which is not over thirty days.[38] If the assurance—the reasonableness of which is to be determined according to prevailing commercial standards—is not adequate under the circumstances, then the buyer has repudiated the contract, and the seller may choose one of the remedies discussed below.[39]

The Seller's Right to Receive Cash Payment Upon Discovery of the Buyer's Insolvency. If the seller should discover that the buyer is insolvent, then, even if the buyer is not required by the sales contract to pay cash, the seller may refuse delivery unless he is paid in cash. The seller may also ask for cash for goods already delivered and, if the goods are in transit, stop the delivery of them unless he is paid in cash.[40] If the buyer refuses to pay cash, it is in default. Section 2–702 also outlines one of the seller's *remedies* upon the discovery of the buyer's insolvency. It will be analyzed in the next section.

The Seller's Right to Withhold Goods and Stop Delivery of Goods in Transit or Otherwise. Where the buyer repudiates the contract before delivery, or fails to make a payment due on or before delivery, or wrongfully rejects or revokes acceptance of the goods, or becomes insolvent before its performance is due, the seller may withhold the goods.[41] If the goods are in the possession of *any* carrier or bailee, the seller may order the goods withheld when he discovers the buyer

Demand adequate assurance of performance by the buyer.

Get cash on the buyer's insolvency.

Withhold the goods; regain them if they are in transit.

---

[38] UCC 2–609.   [39] UCC 2–609(4).   [40] UCC 2–702(1).   [41] UCC 2–703(a).

to be *insolvent;* in other instances of breach such as a repudiation or failure *to make a payment due,* the seller may withhold or stop delivery *only* if the goods are shipped by the carload, truckload, planeload, or are in larger shipments of express or freight.[42] Stoppage of a shipment is a burden to carriers. However, it is permitted in all cases of the buyer's insolvency—a crucial event for the seller because, if the goods are tendered to the buyer and it accepts, creditors of the buyer may have a claim against them. In other cases of breach by the buyer, stoppage is allowed only if the shipment is large. Stoppage is effected by notifying the carrier (a bailee) with reasonable diligence.[43] Once the goods are stopped, the seller may direct the carrier to deliver them to any destination.

On stoppage, the seller then pays the cost of transporting the goods in another direction other than to the buyer consignee. However, if a *negotiable* bill of lading is outstanding (see chapter 21), the carrier is not obligated to stop the goods in transit without surrender of the negotiable bill.

Seller's Remedies in the Courts

Seller's Monetary Recovery. Some of the courses of action discussed above may be thought of as "remedies" in that they are attempts to minimize the seller's damages and thus, to a limited degree, compensate the seller. However, usually more is needed to compensate the seller. In this section we present the affirmative causes of action which a court would recognize in attempting to put the damaged seller in the same position it would have been in had there been performance. These remedies are presented in two broad classifications: the seller's right to monetary recovery; and the seller's right to reclaim the goods under certain conditions, discussed in the next section. The Code recognizes that there may be instances in which more than one remedy would be appropriate and specifically sanctions this by rejecting any doctrine requiring the seller to "elect" one remedy to the exclusion of another.[44]

In applying the remedies discussed below, courts will attempt to protect the expectation interest of the seller, and where this is not adequate, the reliance interest and the restitution interest. Before focusing on these general guides to a remedy, a court must find that the buyer has defaulted. A default may be established by proving that the buyer: (1) wrongfully rejected the goods; or (2) wrongfully revoked acceptance; or (3) failed to make payment which was due on or before delivery; or (4) repudiated with respect to a part or the whole of the contract.[45] If a *buyer* "rightfully" rejects or revokes acceptance, this establishes a breach by the seller. A "wrongful" rejection or a "wrongful revocation of acceptance" establishes a breach by the buyer and is proved by showing that the buyer has refused to accept or retain conforming goods properly tendered.[46] This is illustrated by the following case of a wrongful rejection by the buyer.

---

[42] UCC 2–705(1).

[43] UCC 2–705(3)(a).

[44] See UCC 2–703, comment 1.

[45] UCC 2–703.

[46] See UCC 2–602, comment 3.

Facts

The plaintiff, E. H. Thrift Air Conditioning, Inc. contracted on October 13, 1967 with the defendant subcontractor, R. R. Waites Co., to construct large air ducts for installation in a Ramada Inn. The plaintiff was furnished with the detailed plans for the air ducts and fabricated them exactly as the plans indicated. In December of 1968 the goods were received by the defendant, and a few days later the defendant informed the plaintiff that the goods could not be used because there was an error in the defendant's construction plans. The defendant said that it was shipping the goods back; the plaintiff informed the defendant that it should keep the goods, pay the price, and the plaintiff would help the defendant resell the goods. In May, 1969 the defendant shipped the goods back to the plaintiff and refused to pay for them. The plaintiff brought an action for the full price. Should it recover?

Decision

Yes. The appellate court affirmed a decision for the plaintiff for the full price.

Reasoning

An agent of the defendant corporation testified that the delivered air ducts conformed in all respects to the plans given to the plaintiff. A tender by the seller of goods which conform to the contract in all respects gives rise to a positive duty on the buyer to accept and pay in accordance with the contract. If the goods conform to the contract, the buyer has no other option than to pay. A failure to do so gives rise to a *wrongful rejection,* which gives the seller immediate remedies for breach. The court allowed the plaintiff to recover the full contract price and said nothing about the plaintiff returning the goods to the defendant, purchaser. [We must assume, therefore, that their market value was zero.]

R. R. Waites Co., Inc. v. E. H. Thrift Air Conditioning, Inc., 510 S.W.2d 759 (Mo. 1974).

Resell.

1. The Seller's Right to Resell and Recover the Difference Between Resale Price and Contract Price. When the buyer wrongfully rejects or revokes acceptance or fails to make a payment due, the seller may resell the goods concerned and, if the sale is made in good faith *and* in a commercially reasonable manner, recover the difference between the resale price and the contract price together with incidental damages, but less expenses saved.[47] In our simple example involving the sale of apples for $5,000, if we assume a breach by the buyer before delivery, and a resale price of $4,200 and an added expense of $50, the seller should be able to recover $850 from the buyer. If the apples were resold for $5,500, then the seller suffered no damage and may keep the profit.[48]

Today's commercial transactions are rarely this simple, however. Assume that the seller of the apples could prove that it had reasonable expenses of $4,200 in growing the apples and would have made a profit of $800 in the transaction. Assume further that all of its apples were not sold at the time of breach. Therefore, the "resale" remedy would not be adequate because the purchaser of the

---

[47] UCC 2–706(1).

[48] UCC 2–706(6).

"resale" apples would have purchased some of the unsold apples, and the seller would have made $1,600 on the two transactions ($800 on the sale to the breaching buyer and $800 from the resale buyer). So the "resale" remedy will not give the seller its expectation value where the seller has a relatively limitless inventory of goods to sell.[49] The lost profit may be recovered under section 2–708(2). The point is that the appropriateness of section 2–706's applicability may be determined by an evaluation of the seller's potential to sell other goods on hand (its inventory) and the market conditions (could two sales really have been made?) together with the nature of the product (is it unique or standard?).

Other complicating circumstances are the nature of the goods and the time of breach. Assume that the buyer repudiates just as the seller is assembling the parts to a complex specially designed machine. In this case Article 2 provides the seller great flexibility. If the goods are not identified to the contract but are finished, the seller may identify such goods and then resell them. If the goods are not finished, it may, in the exercise of reasonable commercial judgment, either: complete the goods, identify them to the contract, and then resell them; or it may cease manufacture of them and resell the pieces for scrap or salvage value and sue for the contract price less the resale price; or it may proceed in any other reasonable manner.[50]

Article 2 has rather lengthy provisions governing the *resale* of goods. For our purposes, however, it is sufficient to point out that the remedy of resale[51] is premised on the assumption that the resale will be in good faith and will minimize (not maximize) the seller's losses. The resale price is assumed to be a reflection of the reasonable value of the goods in the seller's possession. The contract establishing the price may be made at a "public sale" (an auction) or a "private sale," but the latter is permitted only where the seller has given the buyer reasonable notification of the intention to resell.[52]

2. The Seller's Right to Sue for Damages for Nonacceptance or Repudiation. The seller may desire not to resell the goods identified to the contract and is not compelled to do so. For example, if the seller has agreed to sell apples in March but finds that, after a buyer breaches in September, it can make more money by converting the apples to applesauce or apple cider, then it may do so. In this instance, and in any instance where the seller does not accept the goods or repudiates, the seller may sue the buyer for the difference between the market price at the time and place for tender and the unpaid contract price, together with any incidental damages but less expenses saved in consequence of the buyer's breach.[53]

Sue for damages.

---

[49] Such a seller has been labeled a "lost volume seller." See Harris, *A Radical Restatement of the Law of Seller's Damages: Sales Act and Commerce Code Results Compared,* 18 STAN. L. REV. 66 (1965); Harris' analysis is summarized and supported in White and Summers, pp. 226–27.

[50] UCC 2–704.

[51] UCC 2–706.

[52] UCC 2–706(3).

[53] UCC 2–708(1).

The most obvious problem with this remedy is with the seller's burden of proving what the market price of the goods was at the time and place for tender. This is not so troublesome if the contract is for common agricultural products, typical consumer goods, or other standardized products for which there often are daily or weekly quoted prices in various geographical locations. In the case of nonstandardized products, a market price may be established by evidence which in the commercial judgment or the usage of trade of those in the market for the goods would serve as a reasonable substitute.[54] As is so often the case, what is a reasonable market price or a reasonable substitute for it is a matter for the finder of fact.

If the seller wishes to sue before the date of tender, it may do so. In this instance the market price for the goods will be determined at the time when the seller learned of the repudiation.[55]

If the measure of damages as calculated by the contract-price-minus-market-price formula is inadequate to compensate the seller for its expected gain, it may sue for the lost profits it would have made from full performance plus incidental damages.[56] The calculation of "lost profits" is usually measured by taking the seller's cost from the seller's list price or contract price. Utilization of this measure is appropriate only to put the seller in the same position it would have been in had there been performance. It can not put the seller in a better position. For example, if a seller had constructed a machine at a cost of $7,000 and contracted to sell it for $8,000 and, following a breach by the buyer, realized $7,800 on resale of it, the seller's recovery is limited to $200 (plus incidental damages). It may not recover $1,000 unless it proves that it is more probable than not that it could have sold two machines (one to the breaching buyer and one to the resale buyer).

Sue for the contract price.

3. The Seller's Right to Sue for the Full Contract Price. The seller's right to sue for the full contract price can be viewed as a parallel remedy to the seller's cause of action for specific performance. Like the buyer's cause of action for specific performance, this right of the seller is limited rather substantially. It is available in only three circumstances. If the buyer has failed to pay the price as it becomes due, the seller may recover the price, together with any incidental damages, where:

a. the goods have been delivered and accepted by the buyer;[57] or
b. conforming goods were lost or damaged within a commercially reasonable time after risk of their loss has passed to the buyer;[58] or
c. the seller is unable, after a reasonable effort, to resell goods identified to the contract at a reasonable price, or the circumstances reasonably indicate that such effort will be unavailing.[59]

---

[54] UCC 2–723(2).   [57] UCC 2–709(1)(a).

[55] UCC 2–723(1).   [58] UCC 2–709(1)(a).

[56] UCC 2–708(2).   [59] UCC 2–709(1)(b).

The first circumstance, above, is so clear it needs no explanation. The second circumstance requires the seller to prove that the goods were conforming and that the risk of their loss had passed to the buyer before they were lost or damaged. If the seller can show that it shipped goods which were manufactured in the usual manner, this should raise a presumption that the goods lost or damaged were conforming. It then becomes the buyer's burden to prove that the goods were not conforming before the damage or loss. The buyer can not assert that the damage or loss prevented its inspection since in most cases the risk of loss passes before the right to inspect.

The third circumstance may at first seem complex, but ask yourself, how many instances are there in which the goods can not be resold after a reasonable effort? These relatively rare instances may occur when the seller is in a specialty market of some sort (for example, making silverware heavily embossed with a unique family crest).[60] When this alternative is selected, the seller must hold the goods for the buyer if they are identified to the contract and within his control. If an opportunity to resell develops while he still has the goods, he may resell the goods any time before judgment, crediting the buyer with the proceeds.[61]

The Seller's Recovery of the Goods from an Insolvent Buyer. In most commercial transactions between merchants, at least three Articles of the UCC may apply. This is especially true in the common situation where a seller sells goods on credit. Depending upon the nature of the breach and the damages sought, Article 2, Sales, may control or Article 3, Commercial Paper, may control or Article 9, Secured Transactions, may control.

Sue to get the goods.

When a seller delivers goods and demands payment and payment is made by a check which is later dishonored, the seller may use one of the remedies provided in Article 3 and bring suit "on the check." These remedies are discussed in Part 6, Commercial Paper.

When a seller contracts to sell goods, it may agree to deliver the goods with payment in thirty, sixty, or ninety days after delivery. To protect itself, the seller may create an enforceable security interest in itself by complying with the requirements of Article 9. Such a seller is a "secured" party and may recover (upon breach of the security agreement) the goods delivered to the buyer by following the procedures outlined in Article 9. Article 9 is the subject of chapters 48 and 49 and will not be discussed here.

This section focuses upon "unsecured" sellers and the right to reclaim goods under Article 2. An unsecured seller is one who has no agreement with the buyer creating a security interest in the goods sold. Such a seller has merely a promise to pay for the goods delivered, either upon acceptance or sometime thereafter. Except for instances in which the buyer is insolvent, Article 2 contains no section which gives the unsecured seller a right to reclaim the goods.

---

[60] Nordstrom, p. 545.

[61] UCC 2–709(2).

Section 2–702(2) provides:

> Where the seller discovers that the buyer has received goods on credit while insolvent he may reclaim the goods upon demand made within ten days after the receipt, but if misrepresentation of solvency has been made to the particular seller in writing within three months before delivery the ten day limitation does not apply.

The applicability of the first part of this section is limited substantially. Recall that if the seller knows of the buyer's insolvency before delivery, it may refuse to deliver unless it is paid in cash.[62] So the section above would probably apply only if the seller did not know of the buyer's insolvency upon delivery but found out within ten days of the receipt of the goods. In such a case the seller may reclaim the goods. This ten-day limitation does not apply, however, if the seller has received during the three months before delivery, in writing, a representation by the buyer that it is solvent. Just how long the seller has to reclaim the goods if it has received a writing which makes representations about solvency dated within three months of the delivery is not mentioned in Article 2.

Finally, the unsecured-credit seller always runs the risk that the buyer will sell the goods delivered, or transfer a security interest in them, to someone else. If the buyer sells the goods to a buyer in the ordinary course of business or to some other good faith purchaser, then the seller may not reclaim the goods.[63] If, however, the buyer has transferred a security interest in the goods which are subject to reclamation by a third party, the judgment of which party gets the goods will be made by a court or a trustee in bankruptcy applying the appropriate state or federal law.

It should be obvious that unsecured-credit sellers take substantial risks. Usually such sales are made only to buyers who are well known and trusted by the sellers.

Limitation of Remedies and Damages

We have made several assumptions which seem reasonable in presenting this material on sales law. One is that the material is best learned by contemplating how large corporate merchants do business. A central feature of the image we suggested that you keep in mind is the fact that these merchants do business by means of exchanging their own forms. It is quite natural to assume that a seller's form will contain not only price, quantity, and delivery terms, but also clauses which attempt to limit the damage recovery of the buyer or, more generally, to limit the buyer's remedies. The buyer's printed form will similarly attempt to limit the seller. The determination of which form is "the contract" of the parties is made according to the principles discussed in chapter 23, Formation and Interpretation of the Sales Contract. In this section we just review the types of limitations which are possible.

---

[62] UCC 2–702(1).

[63] UCC 2–702(3).

Courts have long respected attempts by the parties to agree in advance what the damages will be upon breach. Where such a limitation is attempted in "the contract," the amount of damages stated is called **liquidated damages.** These liquidated damages will be awarded to a non-breaching party only if they are reasonable. The reasonableness of the amount is to be determined as of the time the contract is made. Courts also will consider (1) the anticipated or actual harm caused by the breach; (2) the difficulties of proof of loss; and (3) the inconvenience or nonfeasibility of otherwise obtaining an adequate remedy. In the following case, the court held that the agreement for liquidated damages is to be considered as of the time the agreement was made.

liquidated damages the money judicially awarded in the amount as agreed to by the parties as reasonable compensation for damage which may be caused by the wrongful conduct of one of the parties in the future

Facts
The plaintiff, Bethlehem Steel Company, agreed on December 21, 1961 to furnish steel and construction crews to erect part of the defendant's (the City of Chicago) "South Route Superhighway." The contract price was for $1,734,200. The critical clause of the contract provided for $1,000 "liquidated damages" for each day of delay. The work was to have been completed on or before July 29, 1962, but that date was later extended to September 20, 1962. The work was actually completed 52 days late, on November 21, 1962, thus creating an alleged breach of the agreement. The defendant withheld $52,000 as its liquidated damages from the final payment due the plaintiff, and the plaintiff sued for this and other amounts allegedly due from the city. The plaintiff alleged that the city *actually* sustained no damage, that the highway was completed "substantially on time" (even though the contract said "time was of the essence"), and that the $52,000 withheld amounted to a penalty. Should the plaintiff recover the $52,000?

Decision
No. The court found in favor of the defendant, City of Chicago, thus enforcing the liquidated damages provision of the contract.

Reasoning
The court stated that it made no difference whether or not actual loss followed from the breach because the validity of the liquidated damages stipulation must be judged as of the time when the contract was entered into. At the time the contract was entered into the damages resulting from the plaintiff's breach were difficult if not impossible to ascertain. Moreover, the court emphasized that the law should look with favor "upon such provisions in contracts when deliberately entered into between parties who have equality of opportunity for understanding (because such provisions promote) . . . prompt performance of contracts and . . . adjust . . . in advance, and amicably, matters the settlement of which through courts would often involve difficulty, uncertainty, delay, and expense."

Bethlehem Steel Company v. City of Chicago, 234 F.Supp. 726, 730 (1964).

An attempt to fix an unreasonably large liquidated damage may be declared void as a penalty.[64]

---

[64] UCC 2–718(1).

Facts

The plaintiff sold the defendant a fire detection system for $498. The contract provided that one-third of the contract price was to be paid in the event the defendant cancelled. The day after the contract was signed, the defendant cancelled the contract. Can the plaintiff recover one-third of the contract price?

Decision

No. The court affirmed a judgment for the plaintiff in the amount of $1.

Reasoning

The trial court found that the agreement was cancelled before the plaintiff did anything in respect to the work it was to perform. There was no evidence of actual damage suffered by the plaintiff, so the court held the stipulated sum was unreasonably and grossly disproportionate to the real damage and enforcing it would be a penalty against the defendant.

Security Safety Corp. v. Kuznicki, 213 N.E.2d 866 (Mass. 1966).

The parties may also agree that remedies in addition to, or in substitution for, those in Article 2 (arbitration, for example) are to be utilized in the case of breach.[65] In this area, Article 2 expressly provides that both of the parties are to have some "minimum adequate remedy"[66] and that courts should police attempts at waiver of remedies by using their power to declare such a waiver unconscionable. As between bargaining merchants, a limitation of consequential damages may be binding. But where a merchant attempts to limit a consumer to suing for damages for defective goods (and excluding damages for personal injury), a court may declare the limitation unconscionable.[67]

Statute of Limitations

statute of limitations
a statute limiting the time in which a claim may be asserted in court; expiration bars enforcement of the claim

A **statute of limitations** exists for all areas of the law—criminal law, tort law, contract law, and sales law. These statutes express a policy judgment by state legislatures that for the "efficient" administration of justice, plaintiffs should bring their claims to court as soon as it is reasonably possible to do so. They achieve this by simply stating in a "statute of limitations" that if the action is not commenced within a number of years, the action is barred; the legal cause of action is thus extinguished.

Article 2's statute of limitations is not complicated, so it surprised legal scholars when they found recently that of all the reported appellate cases, section 2–725, statute of limitations in contracts for sale was one of the most frequently litigated sections.[68] The heart of the statute provides:

---

[65] UCC 2–719(1)(a).

[66] See UCC 2–719, comment 1.

[67] UCC 2–719(3).

[68] The subject litigated most in the reported appellate cases was attempted disclaimers of warranties. White, *Evaluating Article 2 of the Uniform Commercial Code: A Preliminary Empirical Expedition*, 75 MICHIGAN L. REV. 1262 (1977).

An action for breach of any contract for sale must be commenced within four years after the cause of action has accrued. By the original agreement the parties may reduce the period of limitation to not less than one year but may not extend it.[69]

In most cases the four-year period begins to run from the date when a breach is *announced* by a party or the date the breaching party fails to perform.[70] For a breaching seller, this is the date of tender; for a breaching buyer, the date payment is due. But what happens when there is a breach of warranty after both parties have performed? The Code attempts to deal with this difficult problem by providing:

. . . A breach of warranty occurs when tender of delivery is made, except that where a warranty explicitly extends to future performance of the goods and discovery of the breach must await the time of such performance the cause of action accrues when the breach is or should have been discovered.[71]

The words "cause of action accrues" mean that the four-year period begins on that date. The difficulty courts have had with the section is based on the fact that almost all warranties contemplate future performance. So, under what circumstances does a warranty *explicitly* extend to future performance? We will learn in chapter 26, Consumer Law, that Article 2 creates some warranties—it simply "places" the warranties in a sales transaction. The statute of limitations would begin to run for a breach of these warranties on the date of tender. Thus, the warranty of title created by Article 2 is breached on delivery of the goods. However, if a seller "explicitly" extends a warranty to future performance (for example, a merchant seller gives a "lifetime guaranty" or promises that a machine will last for 10,000 hours), then it seems that if a breach occurs during this period, the buyer has four years to bring suit from the date of that breach.[72]

In the following case, the court held that the statute of limitations had run on the plaintiff's claim from the time the defective machine was installed. However, the court sent the case back for trial because of the plaintiff's allegation that the defendant had fraudulently concealed the defect.

Facts

The plaintiff, Gates Rubber Company, ordered a large lead extrusion press from the defendant, USM Corporation. The press was installed in early 1964, a failure in the press occurred on July 23, 1968, and the plaintiff initiated suit on March 16, 1971. Illinois, the state in which this action was commenced (but in a federal court), had a five-year statute of limitations (states are free to change portions of the UCC from that originally proposed by the drafters). The trial court dismissed the plaintiff's claim for $67,000 for direct damage to property and $650,000 for damage caused by interruption of production schedules because the suit was not brought within five years from the date of installation. Was this decision correct?

---

[69] UCC 2–725(1).   [71] UCC 2–725(2).

[70] UCC 2–725(5).   [72] White and Summers, p. 342.

Decision

The appellate court essentially agreed with the trial court but remanded the case because the plaintiff did properly allege factual issues which should have been submitted to the jury.

Reasoning

The court noted that statutes of limitations are intended to accomplish two quite different policies. First, they are intended to protect defendants from false claims that might be difficult to disprove if brought after all relevant evidence has been lost or destroyed and witnesses have become unavailable. Second, our society has an interest in the efficient administration of commercial transactions, and therefore it is desirable to simply cut off possible liabilities at specific points in time. If goods are negligently made, the cause of action for such negligence accrues as of the date of the negligent act—this is the date of acceptance of the goods, not the date the injury occurred. In most cases, such as this one, the cause of action accrued at the time the defective press was installed. However, Illinois recognizes an exception to this rule. If a person liable in such a case fraudulently conceals the defect, then the cause of action may be commenced within five years from the date of discovery of the defect. In this case the defendants stated that the part which ultimately failed was designed for "low loading stress" when its engineers knew and had calculated that the part was actually "fairly highly stressed." The court held that this was a sufficient allegation of an intentional misrepresentation to warrant the submission of evidence to the jury, and dismissal of the plaintiff's claim without hearing evidence was error.

Gates Rubber Company v. USM Corporation, 508 F.2d 603 (1975).

Overview of Article 2

In chapter 26, Consumer Law, the final chapter of this part, Sales, we lift our focus from Article 2 of the UCC and examine the broad range of remedies available to consumers when they have been financially damaged or personally injured from defective consumer goods. Since we are leaving our primary discussion of Article 2, we will summarize here some of the main points we have made about Article 2 of the UCC.

More than any other single person, Karl Llewellyn was responsible for the thrust and the general intent of Article 2. This intent was to have the commercial law governing contracts for the sale of goods reflect the best commercial practices of our society. This was, and is, achieved through a liberal use of the word "reasonable" and similar words which give courts wide discretion when instructing juries on how they are to apply the law. This approach keeps the commercial law flexible and capable of change in an industrial society in which change seems to be accelerating.

Another substantial contribution of Llewellyn and Article 2 is the clear statement of consequences which flow from legally operative "facts."[73] The important operative "facts" are the *performance obligations* of the parties. Of

---

[73] Peters, *Remedies for Breach of Contracts Relating to the Sale of Goods Under the Uniform Commercial Code: A Roadmap for Article Two,* 73 YALE L.J. 199 (1963).

course, these are to be determined by, first of all, focusing on "the contract" of the parties. Where there is no contract or where it is not clear, then Article 2 controls. These legally operative facts (e.g., identification of goods to the contract, making a contract for delivery, shipment, tendering, etc.) reveal when certain "special" interests or property interests shift and the circumstances in which one party may (in most cases *must*) put the other party in default. It is the *demonstrable realities* of the particular transaction, and not some legal abstraction (e.g., which party has title) which will control the rights and duties of the parties.

The strength of the commercial law is in its uniformity of application—thus assuring, so far as possible, that all merchants will know what the commercial law is—and its remedies. Although the parties to a commercial transaction contemplate and desire performance, when the other party breaches, the damaged party must be put as close as possible to the position it would have been in had there been performance. There are a number of courses of action and remedies available to a non-breaching party under Article 2. At first this wide selection of choices may mislead one. Upon close study of these remedies you will see a series of steps which must occur in a certain order.[74] Some remedies are available only if others will not achieve the law's objective.

Summary Statement

1. Generally the damage remedies of buyers and sellers must attempt to put the non-breaching party in the same position it would have been in had there been full performance.
2. The courses of action of a buyer when it learns of a breach or potential breach are to:
   a. demand an adequate assurance of performance if the goods have not been delivered; or
   b. reject non-conforming goods; or
   c. accept the goods; or
   d. revoke acceptance of a lot or commercial unit whose non-conformity substantially impairs its value to him; and
   e. in all cases, if the buyer wishes to pursue its legal remedies for damages, it must notify the seller that it is claiming a breach of the agreement.
3. In awarding damages to a non-breaching party, a court will attempt to protect the party's expectation, reliance, or restitution interests.
4. The buyer's possible remedies for breach of the sales agreement by the seller are:
   a. the right to cover; or
   b. the right to sue for damages for nondelivery or repudiation; or
   c. the right to accept the goods and either deduct damages from the price or sue for damages resulting from the accepted goods; or
   d. the right to require the seller to convey the goods contracted for (specific performance); or
   e. the right to the goods when the seller becomes insolvent and replevin.

---

[74] Id., p. 285.

5. Incidental damages are money amounts awarded by a court for *expenses* reasonably incurred by the non-breaching party; consequential damages are money amounts awarded by a court for loss which a breaching party reasonably could foresee would result from its breach.

6. The courses of action of a seller when it learns of a potential breach or a breach are to:
   a. demand an adequate assurance of performance;
   b. demand and receive cash payment upon the discovery of the buyer's insolvency;
   c. withhold the goods or stop delivery of goods in transit.

7. The seller's possible remedies for breach of the sales agreement by the buyer are:
   a. The right to resell the goods and recover the difference between the resale price and the contract price; but, if this is inadequate, to put the seller in as good a position as performance would have; then the measure of damages is the profit which the seller would have made from full performance by the buyer together with any incidental damages; or
   b. the right to sue the buyer for damages for nonacceptance or repudiation; or
   c. the right to sue for the full contract price; or
   d. the right to recover the goods from an insolvent buyer.

8. The buyer and seller may, in their agreement, limit the remedies available to the other party and the damages they may be liable for. Such limitations are enforceable so long as they are reasonable.

9. An action for breach of any contract for sale must be commenced within four years after the cause of action has accrued.

10. The time when a breach of warranty occurs is when tender of delivery is made, except that where a warranty explicitly extends to future performance, and discovery of the breach must await the time of such performance, the cause of action accrues when the breach is or should have been discovered.

In the following case involving two large corporations, the court first examined the nature of a "requirements contract" and then passed judgment on the claim for specific performance and the defense of commercial impracticability.

Eastern Air Lines, Inc. v. Gulf Oil Corporation
415 F.Supp. 429 (1975)

The plaintiff, Eastern Air Lines, Inc. (Eastern), had been purchasing some of its aviation fuel in the south from the defendant, Gulf Oil Corporation (Gulf), for over thirty years. On June 27, 1972 Eastern and Gulf agreed that Gulf would furnish jet fuel to Eastern at certain specific cities in the Eastern system until January 31, 1977. The contract was one of Gulf's "standard form aviation fuel contracts," which was similar to contracts in general use in the aviation fuel trade. It was signed after "substantial arm's length negotiation" between the parties and considered to be favorable to both. The agreement was a "requirements contract," which provided Eastern the opportunity to demand and receive aviation fuel as their requirements dictated at the various sites. Eastern gave up the right to buy fuel from other suppliers at these locations. The "requirements" agreement provided Gulf with a long-term outlet for their jet fuel, which was needed because of the construction of a new refinery. Gulf had to be prepared to supply Eastern's reasonable good faith demands at these locations. The price of the fuel was to be set according to an indicator which was directly dependent upon the price of *domestic* crude oil. Both parties knew at the time of contract negotiations that increases in crude oil prices would be expected and were "a way of life."

The major Arabian countries producing oil (OPEC) increased their crude oil prices 400 percent between September 1973 and January 1974. The price of a portion of the U.S. domestic production also increased by this amount, but much of the domestic production was covered by a U.S. government pricing system which kept the price relatively low. The contract price of the Eastern-Gulf agreement was set by the government pricing system. As the price of aviation fuel began to climb dramatically, Eastern began buying more and more fuel from Gulf. In a requirements contract there almost always is a large measure of discretion exercised by the purchaser. In this case Eastern could fill its planes from several different suppliers, each at a different location. As the terms of the Gulf agreement became more favorable to Eastern, it ordered that more of its planes fill up at the cities served by Gulf. This practice was called "fuel freighting."

On March 8, 1974 Gulf informed Eastern that it was increasing its price for aviation fuel beyond that provided for by the price indicator in their agreement, and that if Eastern would not agree to this, Gulf would shut off Eastern's supply of jet fuel within fifteen days. Eastern responded by filing a complaint in court alleging that Gulf had breached its contract and requesting the court to enter an order of specific performance. Gulf replied by arguing three major points. (1) Eastern's practice of fuel freighting was not performance in good faith and was a breach of the agreement. (2) If the court found against it on the first point, then Gulf argued that the agreement was unenforceable because it had become commercially impracticable within the meaning of the UCC. (3) An order for specific performance was not appropriate.

The court stated that the UCC specifically approves requirements contracts. Section 2-306 (1) states:

A term which measures the quantity by the output of the seller [called an "output" contract] or the requirements of the buyer [called a "requirements" contract] means such actual output or requirements as may occur in good faith, except that no quantity unreasonably disproportionate to any stated estimate or in the absence of a stated estimate to any normal or otherwise comparable prior output or requirements may be tendered or demanded.

Was Eastern's practice of "fuel freighting" performance in good faith? The court found that it was because it was consistent with established commercial practice. The fuel taken on by a plane depends upon the price, the weather, schedule changes, aircraft load, ground time, and many other factors. The court found these factors have been known to oil companies and have been taken into account by them in drafting their fuel contracts. "Fuel freighting" is an established industry practice inherent in the nature of the business and is not performance in bad faith.

Breach of the Sales Contract, Courses of Action, and Remedies

The court responded to Gulf's second argument by pointing out that the UCC states that increases in price alone do not excuse performance unless the rise in cost is due to some unforeseen contingency which alters the essential nature of the performance. Both parties knew that the price of fuel was going to rise, and they agreed on a formula to account for this. The court used these words to find for Eastern on this issue:

We will not allow a party to a contract to escape a bad bargain merely because it is burdensome. The buyer has a right to rely on the party to the contract to supply him with goods regardless of what happens to the market price. That is the purpose for which such contracts are made. [Emphasis added.]

In addition, the court stated that it could not approve the defense of commercial impracticability where Gulf had tendered no evidence on how much it cost Gulf to produce jet fuel. For all the court knew from the evidence, Gulf might still be selling jet fuel to Eastern at a profit. Indeed, the court noted that in 1973, the year in which the "energy crisis" began, Gulf had its best year ever, recording $800 million in net profits after taxes.

Finally, the court awarded specific performance to Eastern because the UCC directed courts to take a more liberal attitude toward this remedy. A party was no longer required to prove that the money damage remedy would be inadequate. In this case the issues were squarely framed and clearly resolved in Eastern's favor, and it would be a "vain, useless and potentially harmful exercise" to declare that Eastern had a valid contract but then leave it to bring another suit to determine its past and future damages.

The court found in favor of Eastern and entered an order for specific performance of the agreement.

Questions and Case Problems

1. B, buyer, has just received a large metal-working machine from S, seller. B has visually inspected the machine but it will not be ready for operation until it is installed. If B detects a defect in the machine upon visual inspection at the time of installation (assume that there is a crack in the metal casing), what should B do? If B installs the machine and it does not appear to work properly, what may B attempt to do? In what circumstances will B be successful in choosing a course of action?

2. In question 1. above, assume that B lost twenty days' production because the machine did not function properly. In what circumstances may B recover consequential damages?

3. If B, buyer, buys from S, seller, ten dozen electronic staplers for his business-supply company to resell, and S phones B before delivery that it will not perform, carefully describe at least two of the remedies available to B.
    a. In what circumstances can B "force" S to deliver the staplers?
    b. Assume that B properly accepted the staplers once they were delivered but discovered later that they were defective. What is the measure of B's damages?

4. S, seller, has contracted with B, buyer, to sell 100 finished picture frames of various sizes and made from various kinds of rare hardwood. Describe the

courses of conduct and/or remedies of S in each of the circumstances below:

a. S has received word that B is insolvent.

b. S has completed some and has shipped some (which are in the possession of a carrier) when it is informed by B that B is repudiating the contract.

c. S can prove that it would have spent $2,500 to make the frames, and the contract price was $3,700. In what circumstances may it recover the lost profit?

5. M, manufacturer, manufactures small tent-campers. These are nothing but aluminum boxes placed on wheels and towed by car owners. When the owners wish to stop and camp, they unfold a tent which springs up from the aluminum box. M contracted to sell fifteen of these units for $800 each to R, retailer. M produced the units for $675 each and usually kept such a large supply of these tent-campers on hand that it could fill any order. Five days before M was to deliver the tent-campers, R telephoned M and explained that it was having trouble moving its inventory and was "reconsidering" its order.

a. What should M do?

b. On the date for M's performance, it tenders the goods and R refuses, saying that it is "cancelling" the order. What are M's remedies and measures of damage?

c. Assume that M resells the very tent-camper units it had identified for the contract with R for $800 each. Has M suffered any damage? If so, what amount?

6. A large state university in the midwest attracted two of the best high school basketball players in the country. In their freshman year these players led their team to the first conference basketball title won by the university since the 1940s. The basketball games were played in a very old gymnasium. There was a tremendous amount of pressure to refurbish the old gymnasium and increase the seating capacity. The pressure came from the fact that there was great demand for tickets to see this basketball team; the university could easily sell twice the tickets it did. Also, there was much talk about the two stars turning pro before they graduated.

In the winter of 1978 the university (U) contracted with S to supply 5,000 new seats. The seats were to be installed by U's maintenance department. The contract provided that the seats were to be delivered by November 1, 1978 so that they could be installed by the time of the first home game for the 1979–80 season, which was to be played December 12, 1979. The contract stipulated that "time was of the essence" since the 1979–80 season was the last the basketball stars would probably play, and their presence assured a sell-out crowd for each home game.

a. If S breached the contract by delivering the seats on December 10, 1979, thus causing U to play six home games elsewhere, how would the measure of damages be calculated? What problems do you foresee with this calculation?

b. If the contract stated that S would pay $50,000 as "liquidated damages" for each home game missed because the seats were not delivered, would a court award U $300,000 as damages?

7. S agreed to manufacture and deliver twelve snowmobiles to P on November 1, 1974. They were delivered on that date, inspected, and paid for by P. On the packaging, in the sales contract, and in the instructions for the snowmobiles, S stated that it would warrant that the snowmobiles would perform properly for one year from the date of delivery to P. In December 1974 P sold three of the snowmobiles to A, B, and C, individually, who received the same warranty from S. The snowmobiles of A, B, and C all malfunctioned, and S denied any liability. A filed a lawsuit against S on October 30, 1978, B filed suit exactly one year later, and C filed one year after that (October 30, 1980). Can these legal actions be maintained? Why or why not?

8. For purposes of review, this question and the one that follows contain some fundamental legal issues discussed in chapters 22-24.

   W, an oil well drilling company, contracted with S, a southwest oil company, to explore a small region of Texas for oil formations and to drill if the formations appeared to be of the type that might yield oil. The "contract" which was made was oral and provided that W would be paid expenses for exploring, would be paid $10 per foot for drilling, and would be paid what it cost W for the piping needed. W and S were to share the profits if any oil was found. W explored for oil for three weeks and found a promising location and began drilling. After it had been drilling for a week and reached a depth of 500 feet, S informed W that as far as it was concerned no contract was ever formed and it did not intend to pay W for exploration and drilling expenses. W had received several letters from S during the one month of its operation referring to their agreement. What legal problems does W have?

9. The L Corporation was engaged in the business of building lobster boats. The Maine Lobstermens' Cooperative Association, Inc. (M) ordered three lobster boats from L. M's order form stated a price of $50,000 per boat, a delivery date of April 1, 1980, and other technical information relating to the specifications and performance capabilities of the boats. L's acknowledgment form agreed in all important particulars with M's except that printed on it in large letters were the words "The parties hereby expressly agree that L will not be liable for consequential damages." Agents of M had signed L's form and returned a copy of it to M. The boats were delivered on time and, during one of the first voyages of one of the boats, the engine malfunctioned because it was not properly installed in the boat. It was out of line, and the shaft and bearing overheated and broke. The boat was swept upon the rocks and destroyed. Miraculously, the crew of the boat was saved, but there were injuries. M sued L for the value of the destroyed boat, and the injured crew sued for their injuries. What arguments would you expect from L, and do you think they will be successful?

10. In the case of *Eastern Air Lines, Inc. v. Gulf Oil Corporation*, 415 F.Supp. 429 (1975),[75] why was the court reluctant to consider the commercial impracticability defense of Gulf? Why was an order for specific performance more appropriate than a remedy for money damages?

---

[75] See pp. 448–50.

Consumer Law

26

After you have read this chapter, you should be able to:

1. Define the various possible types of warranty which can be made by a seller in a sales transaction and list the elements of each or the conditions in which each is made.
2. Describe the circumstances in which each of the warranties made by a seller or merchant may be excluded or modified.
3. Write a paragraph explaining the reasons for the doctrine of unconscionability and then describe the circumstances in which this legal principle is usually applied.
4. Define the two general categories of negligence which provide remedies for injured consumers and explain how the legal device of "res ipsa loquitur" works.
5. Make a list of all the major defenses which can be asserted by a manufacturer in a case by an injured consumer-plaintiff and briefly describe each.
6. Write a paragraph on the need for the tort theory of strict liability and describe this theory and the key elements of proof required for its application.
7. Make a short list of the recent major federal and state items of legislation affecting both product safety and undesirable merchant behavior and describe the general objective of each.

Introduction

In this final chapter in Part 5, Sales, we shift our focus from the situation in which a merchant contracts with a merchant to *a merchant contracting with a consumer*. The word "merchant" has already been defined, but we give the Code definition, in part, here because it is important to the subject of this chapter. A merchant is any seller

who deals in goods of the kind [sold] or otherwise by his occupation holds himself out as having knowledge or skill peculiar to the practices or goods involved in the transaction. . .[1]

consumer
a person who buys goods for use primarily for personal, family, or household purposes

A **consumer** is a person who buys goods for use primarily for personal, family, or household purposes.[2] In short, a merchant is a person who is in business to sell goods or leads others to believe it has special knowledge about the goods sold, and a consumer is the one who buys goods for his own or other's use (but not for resale).

Although we are suggesting a different image for you to think about when studying the law in this chapter, we emphasize that almost all of the law studied so far in Part 5 is applicable to the merchant-consumer relationship, and most of the law presented in this chapter is applicable to a merchant-merchant transaction. Why, then, suggest the differing images? It makes sense to do so because the way the legal principles are applied in reality suggest this distinction. For example, when you learned about the seller's obligations to ship and tender goods; or the seller's right to sell and sue for the difference between the market price received and the contract price; or the buyer's right to withhold performance until an adequate assurance of performance was given; or the buyer's right to cover—it is easier to understand if you think of large corporate merchants contracting with one another. Consumers also have a right to demand from merchants, in appropriate circumstances, an adequate assurance of performance, but it just does not make much sense to think of this right that way.

A key to understanding the legal principles used today to resolve a merchant-consumer dispute is to realize that this transaction is probably evidenced by a form contract drafted by the merchant-seller. We emphasized in this Part that consumers no longer bargain in the traditional sense. They may choose from a limited variety of alternatives offered by a few merchant-sellers, but when it comes time to transact the sale, the terms are spelled out by the seller on its form, drafted, we must assume, to benefit it. This reality aids us in understanding why some of the consumer remedies discussed in this chapter grew from *outside* contract law.

Today the words "consumer law" denote a wide variety of consumer remedies based upon state and federal statutory law and common law. These remedies may be divided into two broad categories depending upon the nature of the damage suffered by the consumer. The first and major subsection of this chapter

---

[1] UCC 2–104(1).   [2] UCC 9–109(1).

presents the remedies available to a consumer who suffers *economic loss* or *personal injury* caused by a defective product. The second subsection of this chapter offers an explanation of remedies available to a consumer who suffers *economic loss* caused by an *illegal credit transaction.* The last subsection of this chapter analyzes the Uniform Consumer Credit Code (UCCC) and "truth-in-lending" statutes and related developments.

Excluded from this chapter is a full analysis of liability for the sale of a *service.* Although the services segment of our economy is growing more rapidly than the industrial segment, space simply does not permit a presentation of, for example, the liability of doctors, attorneys, accountants, and related service-oriented professions.

Products Liability

Products liability is an area of civil law imposing damages upon producers and sellers of goods for both economic loss and personal injury caused by a defective product. The legal principles which create this liability have evolved since the early 1900s and today are as varied and as complex as the goods sold in our consumer markets.

Liability for defective products in the mid-to-late 1800s was almost unknown. There are two reasons for this. The first is that such liability was conceived of as a "commercial circumstance"; thus the principles creating liability should arise from contract law, not from other areas of civil liability such as negligence. Many of the appellate cases from this period held that an injured person could not even bring an action against a producer or seller unless it was in **privity** with that producer or seller. The notion that privity was needed to maintain an action served the industrial interests of the period and most probably eliminated numerous suits. However, under an exception to the general rule requiring privity, one could recover (if there were no privity) if the goods causing the injury were "inherently dangerous." The class of goods which were "inherently dangerous" in the mid-to-late 1800s and early 1900s included mislabeled poison, a defective scaffold ninety feet high, and a defective bottle of aerated water. The severe result of invoking the requirement of privity was lessened shortly after the turn of the century when an appellate court held that a Buick automobile[3] was negligently manufactured and, therefore, allowed an injured plaintiff consumer to maintain an action for personal injury against a defendant corporate manufacturer with whom the plaintiff had *not* contracted. We will learn in a later portion of this chapter how the classification of "inherently dangerous" goods grew into a significant element of one of the major theories of products liability today.

A second reason for the relatively slow development of products liability law in the late 1800s and early 1900s was the doctrine in our jurisprudence of **caveat emptor.** This phrase expresses a general policy recognized by courts that the one who buys a defective product should, as against the producer or seller, suffer the

privity
a mutuality of relationship between persons or between persons and a particular transaction

caveat emptor
a Latin phrase meaning "let the buyer beware"

---

[3] *MacPherson v. Buick Motor Co.,* 111 N.E. 1050 (N.Y. 1916).

loss. This is a less precise notion than privity and arose from the social and economic climate of the times. Caveat emptor denotes a general behavior of courts rather than a precise legal principle.

At a time when manufactured goods were relatively simple, it was judged best to let the consumer choose the appropriate product—even try it out—and if a purchase of a product were made, then the consumer should be stuck with it even if it were defectively made. This was good policy because, in an economic system which encouraged the presence of numerous sellers in the market for goods, over time the producer of faulty products would go out of business as word spread about the quality of its product. However, with the increasing complexity of goods and with the trend toward concentration (fewer producers) in almost all major industrial markets, the doctrines of privity and caveat emptor were perceived as increasingly unjust. The response of the law has been literally explosive. Today, in most jurisdictions, privity is no longer referred to, and many legal scholars would characterize products liability law as based on the premise of "seller beware." The predominance of these doctrines for decades, though, shaped the legal environment of today's products liability law.

The remedies available to an injured consumer today may come from one of three general areas: from the *warranties* provided for in Article 2 of the UCC; from the *common law of torts* (here there are two chief theories of remedies based upon negligence theory and strict liability theory); and, from miscellaneous *federal and state statutory provisions* creating liability for sellers who sell defective products or deceive consumers.

In a particular circumstance, an injured consumer-plaintiff may argue theories of relief from all of the categories just mentioned. There is no inconsistency in arguing that, for example, liability may be based upon one or more of the warranties provided for in Article 2 of the UCC, upon negligent design, and also upon strict liability. The circumstances will usually favor one theory over another, however. We will explain these circumstances in the sections that follow.

The Warranties of Article 2 of the UCC

Five elements are essential to establish a claim for damages caused by a defective product using **warranty** theories. They are (1) establishing the existence of a warranty; (2) establishing the fact that the goods did not conform to the warranty at the time the sale was made; (3) establishing that the defect caused the injury; (4) establishing the amount of damages suffered as a result of the breach of warranty; and (5) establishing facts that may be needed to overcome any defenses asserted. Items (2), (3), and (4) are matters of proof and vary with each case, so they will not be explained here. In this section we will first explain how and what types of warranties are made by sellers and/or merchants and then examine some of the possible defenses.

Since warranties are essentially based upon our notions of contract law, it has long been held that the parties to a sales transaction may bargain away, waive, disclaim, or modify warranties. The questions arising from whether a warranty was so changed by the "bargaining" of the parties present the chief

warranty
an express or implied assurance that certain facts exist; (sales of goods) generally, a promise made by a seller or manufacturer of goods, or a promise implied in a sales transaction by law, that the goods sold are of a certain quality or will perform in a certain manner

defenses or challenges to a warranty claim. If it is established that a warranty was so waived or modified as to affect the plaintiff's case, then, in appropriate circumstances, the plaintiff may argue that the waiver or modification was "unconscionable." Because the issue of whether an "agreement" was unconscionable usually is litigated in this circumstance,[4] we will analyze unconscionability at the end of this section.

There are three classifications of warranties made by sellers or merchants; they are express warranties, implied warranties, and warranties of title and against infringement of **patent** or **copyright**. Express and implied warranties are much more significant than warranties of title and against infringement, so they will be analyzed first.

Express Warranties. A seller makes **express warranties** by:

a) Any affirmation of fact or promise made . . . to the buyer which relates to the goods and becomes part of the basis of the bargain. . . .
b) Any description of the goods which is made part of the basis of the bargain. . . .
c) Any sample or model which is made part of the basis of the bargain. . . .[5]

This warranty must, simply put, be *expressed*—that is, *outwardly stated*—by the seller as an affirmation of fact or promise, or by the seller's providing a description, model, or sample. It is not necessary that the words "warrant" or "guarantee" be used or that the seller have an intention to make a warranty.[6]

The expression which the seller must make may be found in the sales agreement, in advertising, in plans or instructions furnished with the goods, in packaging, or may be made orally. This expression, however, must be more than a statement of opinion. The statement that "this car is tuned like an orchestra and will provide good service and will get 32 miles per gallon when driven at 50 miles per hour" contains just one expressed warranty—the mileage-per-gallon phrase. You should be able to see the express warranty portion. The opinion portion is labeled "puffing" by the courts and creates no liability for the seller. One of the vestiges of the doctrine of caveat emptor is that a buyer should be able to tell the difference between fact and opinion and is allowed to rely only on the former.

Section 2–313 also requires that the statement of the seller creating the express warranty become part of the *basis of the bargain.* The "basis of the bargain" phrase is not defined in the UCC, and its definition has not been clarified by case law. The comments to section 2–313 state that "no particular reliance on such statements (affirmations of fact) need be shown in order to weave them into the fabric of the agreement."[7] In all probability, in a case involving a consumer plaintiff and a merchant defendant, all the plaintiff need do is allege that it relied on an express warranty in making a purchase, and this should be

patent
a governmental grant of protection of an invention

copyright
a governmental grant of protection of original works in a tangible medium of expression

express warranty
a warranty expressed by a party

---

[4] J. White and R. Summers, *Uniform Commerical Code,* 114 (1972).

[5] UCC 2–313(1).

[6] UCC 2–313(2).

[7] UCC 2–313, comment 3.

sufficient to submit the issue of the existence of the express warranty to the jury.[8] The facts in the following case were such that the court held there was no express warranty.

Facts

The plaintiff, Myrtle Carpenter, purchased some hair dye from a local drug store. When she used the hair dye, she suffered an adverse skin reaction and sued both the local drug store and the manufacturer of the hair dye, Alberto Culver Company. She alleged that while she was viewing the various hair-dyeing products in the store she was offered assistance by one of the sales clerks. She claims the clerk indicated that several of her friends had used the hair-dyeing product in question and that her own hair came out "very nice" and "very natural." Also, the plaintiff stated that the clerk told her she "would get very fine results."

The package containing the solution and the bottle had cautionary instructions. They instructed the user to first make a preliminary skin test (called a patch test) to determine if the buyer would be unusually susceptible to the product. The plaintiff claimed that she did this and suffered no adverse reaction but did admit that she had suffered adverse reactions from other hair dyes in the past. Does the evidence presented indicate that the seller made an express warranty?

Decision

The appellate court held that the trial court properly refused to submit the express warranty issue to the jury. As a matter of law, no express warranty was made.

Reasoning

The appellate court stated that in determining whether a statement of the seller is to be deemed a warranty, it is important to consider whether, in the statement, the seller asserts a fact of which the buyer is ignorant or merely states an opinion or judgment upon a matter of which the seller has no special knowledge and on which the buyer may be expected also to have an opinion and to exercise her judgment. Representations which merely express the seller's opinion, belief, judgment, or estimate do not constitute a warranty. From the context in which the statements were made in this case, coupled with the cautionary instructions, no express warranty existed.

Carpenter v. Alberto Culver Company, 184 N.W.2d 547 (Mich. 1970).

implied warranty
a warranty imposed by law

Implied Warranties. **Implied warranties** are those imposed on a sales transaction by statute or court decision. If certain circumstances exist, there is a tradition in our jurisprudence which compels courts to assert that a seller has made implied warranties *whether the seller intended them or not.* Given this broad definition of implied warranties, one may conclude that Article 2 creates three classes of implied warranties: those of merchantability, fitness for a particular purpose, and title. The last warranty is not traditionally thought of as an implied warranty, nor is it labeled as such in Article 2, so it is explained in a separate section.

---

[8] R. J. Nordstrom, *Law of Sales* 204 (1970).

1. Implied Warranty of Merchantability. This warranty, imposed on all merchants, implies a promise by the selling merchant that the goods are *fit for the ordinary purposes for which such goods are used.*[9] This warranty may be excluded or modified by the agreement as discussed in a section below.

There are no "technical" requirements to proving the existence of this warranty other than proving that the seller is a merchant with respect to goods of the kind sold. The sale of food items *not to be consumed on the premises* (from, say, a grocery store) has traditionally been thought of as a sale of goods, hence subject to the imposition of implied warranties for the sale of goods. However, under the pre-Code law, the sale of food to be consumed *on the premises* (from a restaurant, for example) was held to be the sale of a service and thus the transaction was not subject to the imposition of implied warranties for the sale of goods. Article 2 changed this by providing that, ". . . the serving for value of food or drink to be consumed either on the premises or elsewhere is a sale."[10]

If a consumer buys a TV set, a camera, a washing machine, an auto, or whatever from a merchant, there is imposed on the sales transaction, unless waived or modified, a warranty that the goods are of a quality comparable to that generally acceptable in that line of trade. Certainly the goods must perform for the purposes for which they were intended. A TV set must show a picture, a camera must take a picture, etc.

2. Implied Warranty of Fitness for a Particular Purpose. Section 2–315 states:

Where the seller at the time of contracting has reason to know any particular purpose for which the goods are required and that the buyer is relying on the seller's skill or judgment to select or furnish suitable goods, there is unless excluded or modified . . . an implied warranty that the goods shall be fit for such purpose.

This implied warranty is imposed on *any seller* (not just merchants) but requires two elements of proof: (1) that the seller *knew the particular purpose* for which the goods were bought, and (2) the buyer *relied* on the seller to select the goods. *Actual* knowledge of the particular purpose is not required so long as the circumstances of the purchase are such that the seller *should* have reason to know the purpose.[11] This implied warranty usually arises when a consumer asks a merchant seller to provide goods for a specific task which is beyond the consumer's general knowledge. For example, a consumer may hire a heating and cooling firm to air-condition his or her home to 75 degrees during the summer months. If the equipment fails to cool the home as provided in the contract, then this warranty is breached. Note that the air-conditioning system installed may work properly and therefore be "merchantable" but does not fulfill the particular purpose for which it was purchased.

---

[9] UCC 2–314(2)(c).

[10] UCC 2–314(1).

[11] UCC 2–315, comment 1.

Also, this implied warranty is significant in a large commercial transaction between merchants when the buyer submits some rough plans or basic specifications and relies on the seller to design and then manufacture an item. In the following case, the two elements necessary for an implied warranty of fitness for a particular purpose were present.

Facts

The plaintiff, Michael Catania, entered the defendant's retail paint business and asked the defendant to recommend a paint to cover the exterior stucco walls of the plaintiff's house. The defendant was told that the stucco was in a "chalky" and "powdery" condition. The defendant advised the plaintiff to "wire brush" any loose particles which were "flaky" or "scaly" before applying any paint. The defendant recommended and sold to the plaintiff a paint known as Pierce's shingle and shake paint and told him to mix two or three gallons of the paint in a container and to add a thinner. The plaintiff followed the instructions, and five months after the date of the purchase, the paint on the exterior walls of the plaintiff's house began to peel, flake, and blister. Did an implied warranty of fitness for a particular purpose exist?

Decision

Yes. The appellate court affirmed a decision by the trial court that such a warranty existed.

Reasoning

In creating an implied warranty of fitness for a particular purpose, the court acknowledged that two requirements must be met: (a) the buyer must rely on the seller's skill or judgment to select or furnish suitable goods; and (b) the seller at the time of contracting must have reason to know the buyer's purpose. In every case it is a matter of fact whether these requirements are met. In this case the jury found that these facts existed, so a decision in the plaintiff's favor was proper.

Catania v. Brown, 231 A.2d 668 (Conn. 1967).

One factual pattern or circumstance may create all three of the warranties discussed thus far. If a buyer informs a seller of a purpose for the purchased goods and relies on the seller to select it and the seller goes on to say, "These goods will fit your needs," or similar language, the statement may be an express warranty.[12] If the intended use of the goods was an *ordinary* use of the goods and the product failed to operate for this use, both the express warranty and the warranty of merchantability may have been breached. If the intended use was not an "ordinary" one and the product failed to perform, then a breach of the warranty of fitness may be argued. Article 2 recognizes that more than one of the warranties may exist and states that they may be cumulative so long as they can be construed as consistent with each other.[13] If there is an inconsistency in cumulating the warranties such that it appears unreasonable, then the intention of the parties is to prevail over the implied warranties created by Article 2. For example, express warranties will be favored over implied warranties of merchantability.[14]

---

[12] Nordstrom, p. 243.   [13] UCC 2–317.   [14] UCC 2–317(c).

Warranty of Title. When a seller contracts to sell goods, Article 2 provides that there is a warranty that the title to the goods shall be good and its transfer rightful and that the goods shall be delivered free from any security interest or other **encumbrance** of which the buyer at the time of contracting has no knowledge.[15] This provision requires the seller to defend any lawsuit against the purchaser that involves claims of ownership of the goods sold. The seller must also defend against any claims that it, the seller, infringed any patent or trademark in producing or selling the goods if it is a dealer in those goods.[16]

Exclusion or Modification of Warranties and Limitation of Damages for Breach of Warranty. Perhaps the most fundamental notion in American contract law is that there should be "freedom of contract." Generally this means that the parties to a contract should be free to work out the terms of their agreement and courts should not interfere with the bargaining process or the terms of the contract. The function of courts should be to enforce the parties' contractual intent! As we have seen, ascertaining that intent is not always an easy task. However, if the parties intend, as evidenced by their written agreement or otherwise, to waive warranties implied by Article 2, then courts should enforce this intent. One place we find this freedom-of-contract notion in Article 2 is in section 2–316, which permits the parties to exclude altogether or modify the warranties just explained above. First we will describe how each of the warranties above may be waived or modified, and then we will examine some circumstances which reveal how merchants have taken advantage of the "freedom to contract" notion. The material which follows outlines some of the possible legal defenses by merchants to products liability claims of consumers.

Express warranties are supposed to arise from the negotiated or dickered terms of the parties. Words or conduct which create express warranties and words or conduct tending to limit such warranties are to be construed as consistent with one another. When the words or conduct of limitation are *unreasonable,* they are *inoperative* as a waiver of modification.[17] So a seller may describe goods in one clause of an advertisement or contract and then state elsewhere that no express warranties are made. A reasonable interpretation of this would be that the disclaimer was intended to apply to qualities of the goods not stated or implicit in the description.[18] The attempted disclaimer *could not* be read to waive the express warranty created by the description. In short, any attempt by a seller to first make an express warranty and then later deny making it should be labeled as unreasonable conduct and will be inoperative. The way around this for the merchant is, of course, to make no express warranties but to rely on the seller's right to "puff" to make a sale.

The *implied warranty of merchantability* may be excluded or modified (1) if any part of the language mentions the word "merchantability"; and (2) if the language is written, it must be conspicuous.[19] Language is conspicuous if it is so

---

[15] UCC 3–312.
[16] UCC 2–312, comment 3.
[17] UCC 2–316(1).
[18] Nordstrom, p. 286.
[19] UCC 2–316(2).

written that a reasonable person against whom it is to operate ought to have noticed it. If the language is in the text of a form contract, it is conspicuous if it is in larger or contrasting type or color.[20]

The implied *warranty of fitness for particular purpose* may be waived or modified (1) by a writing and (2) by conspicuous language of waiver or modification in the writing. This warranty may be waived by, for example, conspicuous language which states that "there are no warranties which extend beyond the description on the face hereof."[21]

In addition, both implied warranties may be excluded if the goods are said to be sold "as is" or "with all faults" or if other language calls the buyer's attention to the exclusion of warranties and makes plain that there is no implied warranty.[22] Also, when the buyer has examined the goods *before* entering into the contract or has refused the seller's demand to examine the goods if given an opportunity, there is no implied warranty with regard to defects which such an examination ought (in the circumstances) to have revealed.[23] In some cases where the intent of the parties is not clear,[24] course of dealing or course of performance or usage of trade may result in a waiver or modification of an implied warranty.[25]

The *warranty of title* may be excluded or modified by specific language of waiver or modification or by circumstances which give the buyer reason to know that the person selling does not claim title.[26]

There can be no doubt that the sections of Article 2 providing for waiver or modification of warranties are powerful and significant when a merchant sells to a consumer. When merchants deal with one another, the warranty provisions in the sales contract, or the attempted waiver or modification of implied warranties, will be the subject of close scrutiny and negotiation. But when *you* as a consumer make a purchase from a merchant, how often do you read the seller's agreement for warranty provisions? If you did read the agreement, what would you find? And if you found conspicuous language which waived or modified the implied warranties, what could you do about it?

It is impossible here to review the content of many merchants' sales contracts to determine how they attempt to waive or modify warranties. We will, however, single out just a few for analysis to illustrate how merchants may take advantage of section 2–316, "Exclusion or Modification of Warranties." The fact that many merchants do take advantage of section 2–316 and the fact they are successful helps to explain why so many different remedies for damage caused by defective products have developed *outside* the context of contract law.

Long ago Karl Llewellyn pointed out that there is a practice among business lawyers to do what no intelligent engineer would think of doing. Business lawyers,

---

[20] UCC 1–201(10).

[21] UCC 2–316(2).

[22] UCC 2–316(3)(a).

[23] UCC 2–316(3)(b).

[24] Nordstrom, p. 271.

[25] UCC 2–316(3)(c).

[26] UCC 2–312(2).

he said, tend to draft to the edge of the possible, not to within a *margin of safety*,[27] as intelligent engineers would. Engineers allow for a margin of safety. This is explained by the fact that lawyers are advocates and are trained to push for their clients' interests to the absolute limit. When drafting a form sales contract, lawyers attempt to protect the merchant seller by waiving all possible warranties, or at least waiving or modifying such warranties as the courts will permit.

Many form contracts of merchants first state clearly which warranties are made and then state that all other warranties are excluded. Most, in addition, *attempt to limit liability for a breach of the warranty*. Recall that in chapter 25 we explained that damages may be limited by agreement of the parties.

Consider, for example, the warranty and limitation of damages provided for on the package of Sears "Early One" Smoke and Fire Detector. This is a typical smoke and fire alarm which sells for under $20 and is intended for home installation. On the box there is the language:

FULL ONE YEAR WARRANTY ON SMOKE DETECTOR
For one year from the date of purchase, Sears will repair or replace this smoke detector free of charge, if defective in material or workmanship. This warranty shall not apply to the batteries, which are expendable. To obtain warranty service, simply return the smoke detector to your nearest Sears store throughout the United States.

In heavy black letters there follows this language:

LIMITATION ON LIABILITY
Sears will not be liable for loss or damage to property or any incidental or consequential loss or expense from property damage due directly or indirectly to occurrences which the smoke detector is designed to detect.

Sears makes a rather generous warranty on the detector! But what would happen if the alarm failed to operate and, as a result, a home was destroyed by fire and, in addition, substantial personal injury was suffered? Damage to the property and persons in this case would be consequential damage, and a court would have to judge whether the limitation on the damages was effective. In some states there are statutes prohibiting this, or courts have held that such a limitation is "unconscionable" and have not enforced the limitation provision. Sears does note this on the box by adding:

Some states do not allow the exclusion or limitation of incidental or consequential damages, so the . . . limitation or exclusion may not apply to you.

It is not our purpose here to explain why merchants respond to the UCC as they do, nor is it our purpose to analyze the fairness of Sears' limitation in this case. They are, after all, faced with tremendous potential liability from selling such an item; and perhaps the public is best served by allowing Sears to make such limitations. We must assume that most of the detectors will work properly and that damage to property and persons will be averted.

---

[27] See New York Law Revision Commission Hearings on the Uniform Commercial Code (1954).

Before we begin our explanation of the legal doctrine of unconscionability, let us set out another typical but more complex example of merchant language which attempts to waive or modify warranties and limit damages. Automobiles and most trucks are sold, technically, by manufacturers to dealers, who then sell to the public. A "retail order" for a 1978 Ford Van which was purchased from a Ford dealer reads as follows:

All warranties, if any, by a manufacturer or supplier other than dealer are theirs, *not* dealer's, and only such manufacturer or other supplier shall be liable for performance under such warranties. Unless dealer furnishes buyer with a separate written warranty or service contract made by dealer on its own behalf, dealer hereby disclaims all warranties, express or implied, including any implied warranties of merchantability or fitness for a particular purpose: (A) on all goods and services sold by dealer, and (B) on all used vehicles which are hereby sold "as is—not expressly warranted or guaranteed."

And, on the back of the "retail order," under the heading "Additional Terms and Conditions," there is this language:

Purchaser shall not be entitled to recover from dealer any consequential damages, damages to property, damages for loss of use, loss of time, loss of profits, or income, or any other incidental damages.

It is clear that the dealer is attempting to exempt itself entirely from any warranty liability or damage claims—unless, of course, a consumer could prove that a salesperson made an oral express warranty or, as the language reveals, the dealer provides a separate written warranty contract. In the package of materials a consumer receives from the dealer at the time of purchase there is a manufacturer's "Warranty Facts Booklet." In this booklet we find this statement:

Ford warrants for its 1978 model cars and light trucks operated under normal use in the U.S. or Canada that the Selling Dealer will repair, replace, or adjust free any parts, except tires, found to be defective in factory materials or workmanship within the earlier of 12 months or 12,000 miles from either first use or retail delivery.

In larger and bolder type it further provides:

There is no other express warranty on this vehicle. To the extent allowed by law:
  1. Any implied warranty of merchantability or fitness is limited to the 12-month or 12,000 mile duration of this written warranty.
  2. Neither Ford nor the selling dealer shall have any responsibility for loss of use of the vehicle, loss of time, inconvenience, commercial loss or consequential damages.
Some states do not allow limitations on how long an implied warranty lasts or the exclusion or limitation of incidental or consequential damages so the above limitations may not apply to you.

If the language above were applied literally, then a consumer who was injured because his or her new car failed to stop due to defective brakes could not sue the manufacturer of the car based on a contract or sales theory of liability and recover damages for the personal injury. Fortunately for the consumer, some courts have found a way to deal with this language.

The Unconscionable Contract or Clause

Certainly the most potent weapon a consumer plaintiff has to support an assertion that a clause of a contract or an entire contract with a merchant is basically unfair is section 2–302. It provides:

If the court as a matter of law finds the contract or any clause of the contract to have been unconscionable at the time it was made the court may refuse to enforce the contract, or it may enforce the remainder of the contract without the unconscionable clause, or it may so limit the application of any unconscionable clause as to avoid any unconscionable result.[28]

This section gives the judge, not the jury, the right to "police" sales contracts for fundamental fairness. According to one legal scholar, what Karl Llewellyn had in mind when he first drafted section 2–302 was the development of an open and direct attack upon one-sided, unbargained-for, small-print clauses in standardized form contracts.[29]

The official comments to this section state that the basic test or definition is whether "in the light of the general commercial background and the commercial needs of the particular trade or case, the clauses involved are so one-sided as to be unconscionable under the circumstances existing at the time of the making of the contract."[30] Aside from the obvious vagueness, this attempted definition is noteworthy because the scholars who drafted it violated a basic rule of clear expositive writing: they used the term they were attempting to define in the definition itself!

Section 2–302 is one of those sections, similar to those which use the words "reasonable" or "unreasonable," which permit courts to change the meaning of the written words of the law as our commercial society changes. Courts have traditionally had the power to declare sales agreements unenforceable because they were fundamentally unfair, but they did this by varying the definition of such concepts as "misrepresentation," "illegality," "consideration," or by declaring an agreement "void" because it violated "public policy." In fact, two states which adopted other sections of the Code did not adopt section 2–302.[31] Apparently the courts in these states still rely on their traditional equity powers to police sales agreements.

We can best understand the notion of unconscionability by reexamining how courts respond to what could be labeled "unfair" sales agreements between a merchant seller and a merchant buyer on the one hand, and a merchant seller and a consumer on the other hand.

---

[28] UCC 2–302(1).

[29] W. Zelermyer, *The Unconscionable Contract,* a paper read at the American Business Law Association Annual Meeting, College Park, Maryland, August 18, 1978.

[30] UCC 2–302, comment 1.

[31] These states are California and North Carolina; White, p. 114, n. 9.

A sales agreement between merchants is intended to shift certain business risks. If a court is convinced that the merchants "bargained" for the provisions of the sales agreement, the provisions will be enforced even if the result is to cause severe economic loss. In the following case the court held that a price rise of goods did not, of itself, make the enforceability of a contract unconscionable.

Facts

The plaintiff, a textile manufacturer, agreed in the spring of 1973 to buy all of the cotton produced by the seller for $.32 a pound. In the fall of 1973 on the date when the seller's performance was due, the market price of cotton was over $.80 a pound. The seller refused to perform, and the buyer sued it, seeking specific performance. The seller asserted as a defense that the contract for the sale of its cotton is now unconscionable and should not be enforced by the court. The seller further argued that the plaintiff had a "peculiar knowledge" that the price of cotton would spectacularly rise even though it admitted that the contract price was not substantially out of line with the market price of cotton at the time the contract was made. Was the contract unconscionable?

Decision

The court found in favor of the plaintiff and as a matter of law would not allow the defendant to argue unconscionability.

Reasoning

The court said that "unconscionability" must be defined as an absence of meaningful choice on the part of one of the parties together with contract terms which are unreasonably favorable to the other party. The presence of a meaningful choice can only be determined by consideration of all the circumstances surrounding the transaction. Such circumstances as gross inequality of bargaining power, the education of each party, and the nature of the language used are usually significant. The general rule that one who signs an agreement is bound by its terms should be followed unless one or more of these circumstances existed at the time the contract was made. In this case, there was no issue of fact which could be used to establish unconscionability.

West Point-Pepperell, Inc. v. O. W. Bradshaw, 377 F.Supp. 154 (1974).

Almost all instances in which there has been a successful assertion at the appellate level that a contract or clause of a contract is unconscionable involve consumers *and merchants* as the two parties.[32] The following classic case is such a successful assertion.

Facts

Mr. Henningsen purchased a new Plymouth from Bloomfield Motors as a Mother's Day gift for his wife. Ten days after getting the car, Mrs. Henningsen was driving when she heard a "crack" under the hood of the car, the steering wheel spun in her hands and the car veered 90 degrees from its path into a brick wall. The car, with 468 miles on it, was totally

---

[32] White, p. 114.

destroyed and Mrs. Henningsen was injured. Mr. and Mrs. Henningsen sued Bloomfield Motors and Chrysler Corporation for personal and property damage based, among other things, on a breach of warranty theory.

The purchase order signed by Mr. Henningsen contained this language (in part):

The manufacturer warrants each new motor vehicle . . . chassis or parts . . . to be free from defects in material or workmanship under normal use and service. Its obligation under this warranty being limited to making good at its factory any part or parts thereof which shall within ninety (90) days after delivery . . . or before such vehicle has been driven 4,000 miles, whichever event shall first occur, be returned to it with transportation charges prepaid and which its examination shall disclose to its satisfaction to have been thus defective; this warranty being expressly in lieu of all other warranties expressed or implied and all other obligations or liabilities on its part.
. . .

The defendants argued that the last clause of the above "warranty" barred the plaintiff, Mrs. Henningsen, from asserting a claim for personal injuries. The jury returned a verdict for the plaintiffs and the defendant appealed. Should the "warranty" language apparently modifying or limiting the plaintiffs' right to sue for personal injuries be a bar to the plaintiffs' claim?

Decision
The appellate court agreed with the trial court and affirmed the verdict for the plaintiffs.

Reasoning
The court said that the terms of the warranty are a "sad commentary" upon the automobile manufacturers' marketing practices. The manufacturer agrees to replace defective parts for 90 days or 4,000 miles, whichever occurs first, if the part is sent to the factory, transportation charges prepaid, and if examination discloses to its satisfaction that the part is defective. It is difficult to imagine a greater burden on the consumer or a less satisfactory remedy, said the court. It added that, aside from imposing on the buyer the trouble of removing and shipping the part, the manufacturer has sought to retain the uncontrolled discretion to decide the issue of defectiveness. The court called the security provided to the buyer by the warranty illusory in character and then concluded that the warranty, even though apparently agreed to by the parties, should not be enforced. It said:

The status of the automobile industry is unique. Manufacturers are few in number and strong in bargaining position. In the matter of warranties on the sales of their products, the Automotive Manufacturers Association has enrolled them to present a united front. From the standpoint of the purchaser, there can be no arms length negotiating on the subject. Because his capacity for bargaining is so grossly unequal, the inexorable conclusion which follows is that he is not permitted to bargain at all. He must take or leave the automobile on the warranty terms dictated by the maker. He cannot turn to a competitor for better security.

The attempted exclusion of all obligations except those specifically assumed by the express warranty are a studied effort to frustrate the protection given to consumers by the warranties created by law. The attempted disclaimer is so inimical to the public good as to compel an adjudication of its invalidity.

Henningsen v. Bloomfield Motors, Inc. and Chrysler Corporation, 161 A.2d 69, 94 (N.J. 1960).

This case was decided before the UCC was adopted in New Jersey. However, the court's reasoning is a classic statement of the need for the doctrine of unconscionability.

Although the above case makes clear the "policy" reasons for the doctrine of unconscionability, it does not clearly define the doctrine itself. Such a definition is difficult and varies from state to state and case to case. Generally, in finding that a contract or clause is unconscionable, courts consider these circumstances important: (1) the background of the party asserting unconscionability—such facts as age, education, economic status, etc.; (2) the "hidden" or complex nature of the language used; (3) the degree of inequality in bargaining position; and (4) the number of "meaningful choices" available to the party asserting unconscionability.

Privity Under Article 2 and Other Defenses to a Products Liability Claim

Defenses to product liability.

Privity Under Article 2.   The liability of a seller of goods for economic loss or personal injury caused by a defective product is still limited by privity in many jurisdictions today. This limitation can best be described by dividing privity issues into two major classifications: horizontal privity and vertical privity.

1. Horizontal Privity. Issues which involve who is a *proper plaintiff* in a products liability case based on breach of warranty are labeled *horizontal privity cases*. These cases involve the question "to whom is the warranty made?" Typically, a consumer buys goods and either takes them home or gives them as a gift and someone else is then injured as a result of the defect. Should this injured person recover? Article 2 provides *some* guidance in answering this question. The 1978 Official Text of Article 2 provides three alternative sections which may be adopted by states. The alternative adopted by most of the states provides:[33]

A seller's warranty whether express or implied extends to any natural person who is in the family or household of his buyer or who is a guest in his home if it is reasonable to expect that such person may use, consume or be affected by the goods and who is injured in person by breach of the warranty. A seller may not exclude or limit the operation of this section.[34]

Thus, the UCC has expanded the traditional definition of privity, but there is still confusion resulting from courts applying this section. Some have held that this section states once and for all the *entire* group of plaintiffs who may be allowed to recover for a breach of warranty. Other courts—and this view is preferred by some scholars—have held that section 2–318 was intended to set the *minimum* boundaries on the class of those who could sue for a breach of warranty.[35]

---

[33] Four states have adopted a more liberal version, Alternative B, and at least eight states have adopted the most liberal version, Alternative C. See White, p. 331.

[34] UCC 2–318, Alternative A.

[35] Nordstrom, p. 280.

Horizontal privity, then, is a legal defense which is of varying vitality depending upon what the supreme court of the state in which the suit is brought has held on this issue.

2. Vertical Privity. There seems to be more agreement in state appellate decisions about *vertical privity*. This class of issue refers to which party in the chain of distribution—the manufacturer, the wholesaler, the distributor, or the retailer—is the proper defendant when facing a plaintiff injured by defective goods and who is relying on a breach of warranty theory. In most cases where a consumer is suing a *manufacturer,* there is no technical privity. Usually, the plaintiff is in privity only with a retailer. In most of the recent cases, the need for this privity has been discarded when a defendant higher up in the chain of distribution is sued by a consumer. There are several reasons for this. (1) It is usually the manufacturer who, through mass advertising campaigns, has created the demand for the goods, thus, it is "fair" that it be liable for injury caused by a defect. (2) If such privity were required, it might result in hardship to the plaintiff if the retailer were insolvent. (3) Requiring this technical privity would result in a multiplicity of lawsuits where the consumer sues a retailer, the retailer sues the wholesaler, etc.

Other Defenses to Products Liability. It is beyond the scope of this material to explain in detail all of the possible legal defenses of a merchant to a claim for damage caused by a defective product. We will just briefly and generally define each.

A significant category of defenses is directed at what may be called the *plaintiff's misbehavior in using the product.* These defenses are **contributory negligence** *of the plaintiff,* **assumption of a known risk,** *misuse, hypersensitivity,* and *lack of* **proximate causation.** The use and application of these defenses varies so widely from state to state that generalization about them is almost impossible. Some states, for example, have adopted the position that contributory negligence is *not* a defense to a claim for damage based upon a breach of warranty theory, while some other state supreme courts have held that it is an absolute defense.[36] Moreover, some states might hold that, where a woman uses a hair dye when she knows she experiences severe skin reactions to hair dyes, a vague doctrine of "hypersensitivity" would preclude her recovery for damage. Some courts might hold that similar "misconduct" tended to prove a lack of proximate causation in that it was the plaintiff's own acts which were the primary cause, not the product. Whatever the label used, where an injured plaintiff voluntarily and unreasonably proceeds to encounter a known danger or a danger that would be known to a reasonable person, or where the plaintiff uses a product in a manner for which it was not intended, the plaintiff will most probably encounter some form of defense. The "reasonableness" of the plaintiff's conduct ultimately will be decided by the jury.

Finally, recall that law requires that any claim for a breach of warranty be brought within, usually, four years from the date of tender of delivery (section 2–725(1)(2)) unless there is a warranty explicitly extending this period. Many

contributory negligence
plaintiff's conduct which falls below the standard to which he should conform for his own protection and which is a legally contributing cause with the defendant's negligence causing the plaintiff's harm

assumption of risk
voluntarily assuming a known risk of harm

proximate cause
the cause of an injury without which the injury would not have occurred

---

[36] White, p. 336.

injured plaintiffs must use a tort theory of liability because their sales-theory claim has been barred by this statute of limitations.

A closely related notion is that Article 2 imposes on a buyer the obligation to notify the seller of *any breach* within a reasonable time after it discovers or should have discovered the breach.[37] If a buyer fails to give this notice, it is barred from any remedy. This provision is applied liberally to the merchant-consumer transaction, but there are cases denying a plaintiff recovery because of failure to give notice of breach so that a merchant-defendant may act to preserve evidence essential for its defense.

Tort Theories of Products Liability

tort
a civil (private) noncontractual wrong

Our American "civil" law is traditionally divided into the two broad categories of contract law and tort law. **Tort** law is further divided into three categories: intentional torts, negligence, and strict liability. Establishing liability based upon an intentional tort theory requires proof of the defendant's *intent* to commit a wrongful act. This theory is almost never used in products liability cases because manufacturers and sellers *intend* no harm by the sale of their product. Negligence and strict liability are today, however, widely accepted theories of products liability.

This has not always been true. As we pointed out earlier in this chapter, until the second or third decade of this century, most courts would bar a plaintiff from asserting a claim against the manufacturer or seller unless the plaintiff could prove privity with the defendant. An exception to this general rule allowed an injured plaintiff to recover on a negligence theory if the defective goods were "inherently dangerous." During the 1960s, courts so expanded the classification of goods which were "inherently dangerous" that today one need not prove that the goods were "inherently dangerous." However, some courts may not have freed themselves entirely from this requirement and thus demand that the plaintiff at least allege that the defective goods were inherently dangerous.

Today negligence and strict liability are two independent legal theories upon which an injured plaintiff may base its product liability claim. They may be alleged and proved in the *same case* in which a breach of warranty theory is argued or they may serve as the sole basis for liability. Obviously these theories can not be defeated by an assertion that there was no privity. Nor are any arguments based upon a waiver or modification of a warranty relevant.

A chief reason for using tort theories of liability is that although the statute of limitations for personal injury is usually shorter—most jurisdictions have a three-year statute of limitations on personal *injury* claims—the time period begins to run from the date of injury, not the date of delivery. A disadvantage of using these theories is that most courts will not permit recovery for economic loss *alone,* such as lost profits or damage to the goods. To recover from economic loss, the plaintiff must also show *personal injury.*[38] Providing a remedy in the

---

[37] UCC 2–607(3)(a).

[38] See D. Noel and J. Phillips, *Products Liability in a Nutshell* (St. Paul: West Pub. Co., 1974), p. 10.

form of money damages to one who has suffered personal injury is the real purpose of our tort law.

Negligence.   To establish "**negligence**" in a products liability case, the plaintiff must prove that the defendant's conduct in either manufacturing or designing goods produced a risk of harm greater than society is willing to accept in light of the benefits to be derived from that activity. Simply put, the risk of harm must be unreasonable.[39] In almost all negligence cases the issue of the "reasonableness" of the defendant's conduct is an issue for the jury to decide. That is, most of these cases present problems of proof rather than issues of substantive law.

negligence
(conduct) failure to use the degree of care demanded by the circumstances; (the tort) negligence proximately causing injury to another person's interest

The negligence cases, however, may require differing elements of proof. If an injured plaintiff is attempting to establish the negligent manufacture of goods, it must prove that the goods were *defective* and the defendant acted unreasonably in its manufacture of the goods. If the plaintiff is attempting to establish the negligent design of a product, then it must prove that the injury was *foreseeable* for a "reasonable" manufacturer at the time it was designed.

Proving that goods were defective is no easy task. Without the help of an additional legal device, it would be impossible to prove if the goods were destroyed as a result of the defect. This legal device is designated by the Latin phrase **res ipsa loquitur,** which, literally translated, means "the thing speaks for itself." This device is properly used where there is a *gap* in the plaintiff's proof of negligence caused simply by the circumstances of the case. If the plaintiff can show that (1) the injury complained of *does not normally happen* in the absence of negligence, and (2) the defendant has *exclusive control* of the thing causing the injury at the *time of the alleged negligent act*—the time of the manufacture of the goods, not the time of injury—then res ipsa loquitur will cause the judge to state that the plaintiff has filled the gap in its evidence, and an inference of negligence will be created. It is then up to the defendant to rebut that inference. The following case illustrates the use of res ipsa loquitur.

res ipsa loquitur
the thing speaks for itself

Facts

The plaintiff, a waitress in a restaurant, was severely injured when a bottle of Coca Cola exploded in her hand. She sued the bottler and alleged that it either negligently bottled the Coke (put it under too much pressure) or negligently manufactured the bottle. She was unable to show any specific acts of negligence. The bottler defended by introducing evidence that it bottled Coke in a manner all bottlers used and was therefore not acting unreasonably—that is, was not negligent. The defendant also argued that it was the plaintiff who must have mishandled the bottle. The jury returned a verdict for the plaintiff. On appeal, the defendant argued there was not sufficient evidence of negligence to submit the issue to the jury. Should the plaintiff's verdict be reversed?

Decision

No. The appellate court found in favor of the plaintiff.

---

[39] J. Henderson and R. Pearson, *The Tort Process* (Boston: Little, Brown, 1975), p. 268.

Reasoning

The appellate court held that the doctrine of res ipsa loquitur applies in a negligence case if the plaintiff alleges and the proof could reasonably show that (1) the defendant had exclusive control of the thing causing the injury and (2) the injury is of such a nature that it ordinarily would not occur in the absence of negligence by the defendant. The plaintiff also alleged that the bottle had not changed since it left the defendant's possession and that she was using due care at the time the bottle exploded. The court concluded that the evidence was sufficient to support a reasonable inference that the bottle was in some manner defective at the time it left the defendant's possession. The jury could properly rely on this inference in finding for the plaintiff.

Escola v. Coca Cola Bottling Co., 150 P.2d 436 (Cal. 1944).

A second significant line of cases applying the theory of negligence centers on the *negligent design of a product.* In these cases there is no defect in the goods in that they operate as they are intended to operate. The conduct that is "unreasonable" is the *failure to design a safe product* when injury of the type complained of occurs and is foreseeable by the manufacturer.

Facts

The plaintiff was driving a 1963 Chevrolet Corvair when the car was struck head-on by another car. The plaintiff was severely injured when the steering column was thrust into his head. The car was so designed that the steering column was one piece of steel all the way from a position directly in front of the driver to a point 2.7 inches in front of the leading surface of the front tire. The plaintiff did not contend that the design caused the accident but that, because of the design, he received injuries he would not otherwise have received. The defendant, General Motors, the designer and manufacturer of the car, argued that it has no legal duty to produce a vehicle in which it is safe to collide or which is accident-proof. The trial court dismissed the plaintiff's claim, and the plaintiff appealed. Did the plaintiff state a proper case based upon negligent design?

Decision

Yes. The appellate court reversed the trial court and held that the plaintiff did state a good cause of action based upon negligent design.

Reasoning

The court reasoned that under the present state of the art, an automobile manufacturer is under no duty to design an accident-proof vehicle, but such manufacturer is under a duty to use reasonable care in the design of its vehicle to avoid subjecting the user to an unreasonable risk of injury in the event of collision. Collisions with or without fault of the user are clearly foreseeable by the manufacturer and are statistically inevitable. The injury of the type complained of in this case was foreseeable as an incident to the normal and expected use of an automobile, given the fact that the steering column was designed as it was. The normal risk of driving must be accepted by the user, but there is no need to further penalize the user by subjecting him to an unreasonable risk of injury.

Larsen v. General Motors Corporation, 391 F.2d 495 (1968).

In a products liability case based upon negligence, the retailer or immediate seller (if there is one) is not held liable unless it has reason to know of the defect or dangerous design and fails to warn the purchaser. To find liability, each of the defendants must have acted negligently.

The defenses of contributory negligence, assumption of risk, and lack of proximate causation are defenses available to the defendant. Also, the defendant may meet the plaintiff's case with proof that its conduct is not unreasonable because it conforms to the generally accepted standards of performance in the particular area of conduct. For example, Coca-Cola attempted to counter the plaintiff's case in Escola by introducing evidence that the industry standard of taking a sample bottle every three hours from the manufacturing mold (this is approximately one out of every 600 bottles) and subjecting it to an internal pressure of 450 pounds per square inch, sustained for one minute, is "pretty near" infallible in guarding against defectively manufactured bottles. The Escola case presented some difficult factual issues for the jury. It was a very close case. The original fact finder in that case simply believed the plaintiff's evidence, but many negligence cases on similar evidence result in verdicts for the defendant.

Strict Liability. **Strict liability** as a tort theory used in products liability cases is of recent and increasing significance. If it has not become so already, it soon will be the dominant theory in products liability cases. A manufacturer may be strictly liable when it:[40]

strict liability absolute liability irrespective of the absence of negligence or fault

. . . sells any product in a defective condition unreasonably dangerous to the user or consumer or to his property and is subject to liability for physical harm thereby caused to the ultimate user or consumer, or to his property, if
  a) the seller is engaged in the business of selling such a product and
  b) it is expected to and does reach the user or consumer without substantial change in the condition in which it is sold.

The basic reason for the increasing use of this theory is that, for the reasons already stated, warranty theory and negligence theory still permit the successful assertion of defenses when a plaintiff may be injured by a product through no fault of its own. Strict liability is based on the notion that, as between an innocent injured plaintiff and a merchant, the latter should pay for an injury caused by a defect.

The Escola case discussed above was so close on the negligence issue that Judge Traynor, a famous California jurist, would have applied the theory of strict liability in that case. In a concurring opinion, he clearly stated the policy reasons for strict liability as follows:

Even if there is no negligence, . . . public policy demands that responsibility be fixed wherever it will most effectively reduce the hazards to life and health inherent in defective products that reach the market. It is evident that the manufacturer can anticipate some hazards and guard against the recurrence of others as the public cannot. Those who suffer injury from defective products are unprepared to meet its consequences. The cost of an injury and the loss of time or health may be an

---

[40] RESTATEMENT (SECOND) OF TORTS sec. 402A (1965).

overwhelming misfortune to the person injured, and a needless one, for the risk of injury can be insured by the manufacturer and distributed among the public as a cost of doing business. It is to the public interest to discourage the marketing of products having defects that are a menace to the public. If such products nevertheless find their way into the market it is to the public interest to place the responsibility for whatever injury they may cause upon the manufacturer, who, even if he is not negligent in the manufacture of the product, is responsible for its reaching the market. However intermittently such injuries may occur and however haphazardly they may strike, the risk of their occurrence is a constant risk and a general one. Against such a risk there should be general and constant protection and the manufacturer is best situated to afford such protection. [*Escola v. Coca-Cola Bottling Co.,* 150 P.2d 436, 440–41 (Cal. 1944).]

To state a claim in strict liability, the plaintiff must allege and prove that the defendant sold the goods in a *defective condition* and that it was *unreasonably dangerous*. The types of products which are "unreasonably dangerous" if defective vary from case to case and state to state. Some states have been slow in expanding this category of goods much beyond those which are "inherently dangerous" if defectively made—autos, power tools, ladders, and the like. Many states have taken a more liberal position. The following case is fairly typical.

Facts

Benjamin E. Dunham, the plaintiff, was using a hammer manufactured by Vaughan & Bushnell Manufacturing to drive a pin into the connector between his tractor and a manure spreader. A chip from the beveled edge of the hammer broke off and struck him in the right eye, resulting in the permanent loss of sight in that eye. The hammer was about eleven months old and had been used for ordinary tasks around the plaintiff's farm. The defendant argued that the plaintiff's reliance on strict liability was not appropriate because the evidence did not show that there was a defect in the hammer when it left the manufacturer's control. The defendant also argued that everyone knows metal "tires" with age and use and is subject to failure. No manufacturer should be expected to produce a hammer which would last forever. The trial court found in favor of the plaintiff, and the defendant argued, on appeal, that strict liability was not proved in the trial court.

Decision

The appellate court affirmed a verdict for the plaintiff.

Reasoning

The court acknowledged that there must have been a defect in the goods and it must have existed when the goods left the custody of the manufacturer; this does not mean, however, that the defect must manifest itself at once. On this issue the court relied on another case in which a defective brake linkage bracket on a tractor broke over three years after it was installed in the tractor. The court also concluded that the jury could find that a defect existed because the definition of a defect rests on the premise that those products are defective which are dangerous because they fail to perform in the manner reasonably to be expected in light of their nature and intended function. A defect may be a "condition" not contemplated by the ultimate consumer, which would be unreasonably dangerous to him.

Dunham v. Vaughan & Bushnell Mfg. Co., 247 N.E.2d 401 (Ill. 1969).

Recent Federal and
State Consumer Protection Legislation—Products

Almost ten years ago a major study of consumer product safety sponsored by the federal government found that twenty million Americans were injured each year as a result of incidents connected with consumer products.[41] Of this total, 110,000 were *permanently disabled* and 30,000 were killed. It estimated that the annual cost to the nation of product-related injuries might exceed $5.5 billion.[42] These statistics *excluded* injuries caused by food, drugs, cosmetics, motor vehicles, and some other categories of consumer injury.

In a more recent publication the federal government listed the number of consumer products injuries[43] by product group.

Figure 26.1   Consumer Products Injuries by Product Groups

Estimated Number of Injuries Associated with Consumer Products
Requiring Emergency Room Treatment . . .
September 1, 1977–August 31, 1978
(A Partial Listing)

Product Group	National Estimate in Thousands
Stairs — (including folding stairs)	572
Bicycles and Bicycle Accessories	430
Football, Activity and Related Equipment	403
Baseball, Activity and Related Equipment	401
Nails, Carpet Tacks, Screws and Thumbtacks	265
Glass Doors, Windows and Panels	186
Playground Equipment	151
Glass Bottles and Jars	106
Power Lawn Mowers	69
Power Home Workshop Saws	68
Chain Saws	48
Miscellaneous Household Chemicals	29
Television Sets	17
Refrigerators and Freezers	16

(1979 Annual Report, Part Two, U.S. Consumer Product Safety Commission, Appendix D, pages 47-53.)

[41] The term "consumer products" in this context includes all retail products used by consumers in and around the household *except* foods, drugs, cosmetics, motor vehicles, insecticides, firearms, and cigarettes.

[42] *Final Report of the National Commission on Product Safety,* Washington, D.C.: U.S. Government Printing Office, June 1970, p. 1.

[43] "Consumer products" were defined as in note 41.

The fact that 430,000 Americans were estimated to have been injured during the time period by bicycles is not as noteworthy as the estimated 106,000 injuries from glass bottles and jars, 17,000 injuries from TV sets, and 16,000 injuries from refrigerators and freezers. We all know of the dangers and risks involved in riding a bicycle, but the threat to us from glass bottles and jars, TV sets, refrigerators, and freezers is less foreseeable. The statistics reveal that almost every consumer product may be dangerous if it is not properly made and/or if it is not properly used. A crucial question is whether the traditional legal theories of breach of warranty, negligence, and strict liability, together with the forces which economic theory has assumed to be at work in the retail market place, provide our society with reasonably safe products. If we consider the activity of both federal and state governments in the areas of consumer product safety, the answer to this question must be a resounding NO! Why?

First, an injured consumer must be aware of his or her legal right to sue the sellers and producers of a defective product. Second, he or she must have sustained sufficient damage so that an attorney will find the promise of an adequate fee in the case. Probably the most serious limitation on recovery of damages to consumers is the cost of trial. Some experts say it hardly pays to go to trial for less then $5,000 to $10,000.[44] Moreover, at the trial the plaintiff usually runs a substantial risk that one of the defenses available to the seller or manufacturer may be successfully asserted. Even in the best of circumstances, a products liability case is a financially bruising, onerous undertaking for both client and lawyer.[45]

Only the most serious products liability cases are litigated. A survey of 276 persons in Denver and Boston who had reported injuries to the Food and Drug Administration showed that only 4 percent contacted an attorney to investigate initiating a claim for injury.[46] Another study revealed that *some* manufacturers do not even respond to letters claiming compensation because they know that over two-thirds will never pursue their claim further.[47] As for the others, let us assume that a plaintiff does recover a substantial judgment for injury due to a defective power saw. How does the manufacturer respond? More likely than not, the manufacturer will have insurance which will cover most, if not all, of the claim and thereby lessen some of the incentive to design a safer product.

Even where there is money recovery there is no coherent or organized effort to publicize the name of a manufacturer held liable so that consumers could *in the future* select safer products over those produced by manufacturers with bad safety records.

The legal theories discussed thus far in this chapter provide legal remedies for only a few of the most seriously injured consumers. These remedies do little

---

[44] Final Report of the National Commission on Product Safety, p. 74.

[45] Id., p. 73.

[46] Id., p. 74.

[47] Id.

to assure us that in the future we will be able to select safer products. For these reasons, Congress and most state legislatures have passed consumer product legislation, the significant features of which are discussed in the following sections.

Since 1966 Congress has passed six Acts which govern some aspect of product safety or product design. Also, the Federal Trade Commission and the Consumer Affairs Section within the Antitrust Division of the Justice Department have become much more active in pressing the interests of consumers. In this section we will briefly explain some of the recent federal legislation.

The Consumer Product Warranty and Federal Trade Commission Improvement Act (Also Called the Magnuson-Moss Warranty–Federal Trade Commission Improvement Act)

Federal legislation.

This Act,[48] which became law on July 4, 1975, was prompted in part because consumers were dissatisfied with their "protection" afforded by the UCC warranties. "Warranty abuse" was a phenomenon substantiated in 1974 when a congressional subcommittee reviewed 200 warranties from 51 major companies and found only one which offered a warranty free of ambiguous phrases, exemptions, and disclaimers.[49] This Act seeks to make warranty enforcement a reality by providing to the consumer the information needed to pursue a claim for a breach. The Act does not alter the warranties of merchantability or fitness for a particular purpose. The provisions of the Act do not compel a merchant to make a warranty; but general provisions of the Act do apply when a *written* warranty is made *and* the cost of the item purchased exceeds $15.00, as provided by Federal Trade Commission regulation. The one who makes a warranty (called a "warrantor") is required by the Act to fully and conspicuously disclose the terms and limitations of the warranty to the consumer *before* the sale. Some of the items which warrantors should disclose are:

1. The names and addresses of the warrantors.
2. The product or parts covered.
3. A statement of what the warrantor will do upon breach of the warranty, at whose expense the work will be done, and the period of time the warranty will last.
4. The step-by-step procedure consumers must take in order to obtain performance of any obligation under the warranty.
5. A brief summary of the legal remedies available to the consumer upon breach.

The Act allows warrantors to make either "full" warranties or "limited" warranties but, regardless of the label used, the Act allows a warrantor to limit or exclude consequential damages if it is done conspicuously in the same writing that makes the warranty.

---

[48] 15 U.S.C.A. sec. 2301 et seq.

[49] W. Haemmel, B. George, and J. Bliss, *Consumer Law* (St. Paul: West Pub. Co., 1975), p. 285.

Perhaps the most significant provision of the Act limits the use of written warranties to disclaim the implied warranties created in law by the UCC. A written warranty may not be used to impose any duration on the implied warranties, but if a written warranty of reasonable duration is made, an implied warranty may be limited by the warrantor to that period.

Responsibility for enforcement of the Act's provisions is divided between consumers and the Federal Trade Commission. Consumers must report violations to the FTC in Washington or to one of its regional offices. The FTC may sue repeated violators and request an injunction against violations of the Act or a civil penalty not exceeding $10,000. Only if consumers and the FTC accept the responsibilities of reporting and prosecuting violators will the Act achieve its objectives of attempting to hold warrantors liable for the warranties made by them or by law.

The Consumer Product Safety Act of 1972

The Consumer Product Safety Act of 1972[50] created the Consumer Product Safety Commission (CPSC), which is becoming one of the most powerful regulatory agencies in the federal government. This commission has jurisdiction over every consumer product *except* automobiles, food, and a few other items regulated by older agencies of government. The basic idea behind the creation of the CPSC was to bring order to an increasingly confusing mish-mash of federal and state consumer regulatory bodies. The commission is to collect and disseminate information relating to injuries and to conduct investigations and tests on consumer products and their use. When a consumer product creates a hazard of injury or illness, the CPSC may develop consumer product safety standards. These standards must be set forth in performance requirements. If the CPSC finds that an unreasonable risk exists and that no standard will provide protection, it may ban a product. Recently it banned such products as garments containing asbestos, some baby cribs, some drain cleaners, assorted types of fireworks, furniture painted with lead paint, some kinds of lawn darts, and self-pressurized products containing vinyl chloride.[51] While the basic idea of CPSC was to disseminate information about product safety and attempt to get products redesigned in light of the consumer's foreseeable ignorance, consumer misbehavior or misuse was noteworthy, and the performance of CPSC has been less than spectacular. After two years of operation, one source reported that there has been no notable reduction in consumer-product related injuries.[52]

Motor Vehicle Safety Legislation.   Motor vehicle safety legislation has been on the books since 1966, but only recently have the various enforcement activities established the legislation as noteworthy. Although the National Traffic and

---

[50] 15 U.S.C.A. sec. 2051 et seq.

[51] U.S. Consumer Product Safety Commission, *1979 Annual Report,* Appendix L.

[52] "The Hazards of Trying to Make Consumer Products Safer," *Fortune Magazine,* p. 103 at 104, July 1975.

Motor Vehicle Safety Act of 1966[53] and the Highway Safety Act[54] have been amended or altered by legislation or executive order almost every year since their adoption, they are some of the more successful attempts to regulate product safety. It has been estimated that 150,000 lives have been saved during the period 1967 to 1977 due to automobile safety legislation and the reduced speed limit necessitated by the oil shortage of 1973.[55]

The National Traffic and Motor Vehicle Safety Act of 1966 created the National Highway Traffic Safety Administration. It has the authority to promulgate rules for traffic safety, conduct research, disseminate information about vehicle safety, and, if a manufacturer will not voluntarily comply, initiate procedures resulting in the recall of automobiles which pose a threat to the public.

Food Quality and Packaging Legislation
Under the Fair Packaging and Labeling Act,[56] passed in 1966, often called the Truth-In-Packaging Act, the Federal Trade Commission and the Food and Drug Administration were to establish and regulate standards regarding contents information to be shown on packages and to encourage the voluntary development of standards for package sizes. The Wholesale Meat Act[57] passed in 1967 strengthened and updated the federal standards of meat inspection and provided states with assistance so that local standards might be "at least equal" to federal standards.

Attempts by the federal government to legislate standards for merchants and products performance have been, at best, mildly successful. It now appears that because of two related developments at the state level, a consumer remedy of true value is beginning to emerge for consumers who are plagued by merchant misconduct. Now over 39 states[58] have legislation which attempts to correct much of the consumer abuse caused by the more unscrupulous merchants. This legislation, plus the fact that many states allow consumer-related complaints to be filed without an attorney's help in small claims courts, provide remedies within the reach of many consumers. For example, Michigan law provides that "unfair, unconscionable or deceptive methods, acts or practices in the conduct of trade or commerce are unlawful."[59] The legislation defines 29 unlawful acts. It also provides that a person who suffers loss as a result of a violation of one of the 29 acts may bring an action to recover actual damages or $250, whichever is greater.

State legislation.

---

[53] 15 U.S.C.A. sec. 1381 et seq.

[54] 23 U.S.C.A. sec. 401 et seq.

[55] *Motor Vehicle Safety 1977,* Annual Report, U.S. Department of Transportation.

[56] 15 U.S.C.A. secs. 1451 et seq.

[57] 21 U.S.C.A. sec. 601.

[58] Haemmel, p. 36.

[59] 14 *Mich. Stat. Ann.* secs. 19.418 (3) et seq.

This legislation does not provide a remedy for the recovery of substantial amounts for personal injury as a result of a defective product but does allow recovery for minor amounts. For example, a student at Michigan State University was recently awarded $250 when he showed in the local small claims court that he was told his defective stereo speaker was covered by warranty. When he went to pick up the speaker from the merchant, he was told that it would cost him $60. He paid the amount under protest and then filed his claim.

Recent Federal and State Consumer Protection Legislation—Credit

Closely related to the actual sale of goods (or real property) is the manner in which the buyer pays. Quite often the buyer pays a small portion of the purchase price and then promises to pay the balance plus interest on this outstanding balance until the full amount is paid. When a seller relies on a buyer's promise to pay in the future, it is extending credit to the buyer.

Often it is difficult for a consumer to assess the exact amount that will be paid for goods when credit is involved, and just as difficult is the computation of the cost of credit itself. Recently both Congress and state legislatures passed legislation to provide the consumer with knowledge about his or her credit transactions.

The Consumer Credit Protection Act

Federal legislation.

The Consumer Credit Protection Act[60] (also called the Truth-In-Lending Act) is administered by the Federal Reserve System and has been in force since 1969, when the Federal Reserve Board adopted regulations for conduct. These regulations reach all extensions of credit for personal, family, household, or agricultural purposes. The applicability of the Act is suspended if there is state legislation covering similar transactions and the requirements for disclosure are substantially similar to those imposed by the Act.

Under the 1969 regulations, the lender must furnish to the borrower, before the credit is extended, a written disclosure statement which sets forth (1) the cash price, (2) the down payment, (3) the total amount financed, (4) the dollar amount the loan will cost, (5) the approximate amount of the true annual interest rate, and (6) an explanation of the delinquency and default charges. The Act does not set any ceiling on finance charges or interest rates, nor does it affect state **usury** laws.

usury
charging a rate of interest on a loan higher than that permitted by statute

A violator of the Act may incur both civil and criminal liability. If a creditor fails to disclose the required information, the debtor can bring a civil action and seek to recover double the amount of the finance charge (limited to a minimum of $100 and a maximum of $1,000 plus attorney's fees and court costs). Under an amendment to the Act, if a creditor gives false or inaccurate information, it is a criminal offense punishable by a fine up to $5,000 or a year in jail or both.

---

[60] 15 U.S.C.A. sec. 1601 et seq.

Today the Act is enforced by a number of federal agencies, such as the Director of the Bureau of Federal Credit Unions, the Federal Home Loan Bank Board, and a few others. Also, the coverage of the Act has been extended by enactment of the Fair Credit Reporting Act of 1970,[61] which covers credit-card transactions. This amendment limits the liability of new credit-card holders to $50 if this liability is incurred by someone using the owner's lost or stolen credit card.

The Uniform Consumer Credit Code (UCCC)

State legislation.

The Uniform Consumer Credit Code (UCCC), like the Uniform Commercial Code, was drafted by the National Conference of Commissioners on Uniform State Laws and was published in 1968 for adoption by the states. This legislation has been controversial. By 1974 it had undergone six redrafts and only nine states had adopted it.[62]

As in the Truth-in-Lending Act, the annual percentage rate for the credit and the difference between the cash price and the credit price must be disclosed in every transaction involving retail installment sales, consumer credit, or small loans.

Additionally, there are four major features of this legislation. (1) It prohibits a seller from taking a negotiable instrument other than a check in a consumer credit sale. This thwarts the practice of some unscrupulous sellers of taking a negotiable promissory note for worthless goods, negotiating the note to a good faith "holder in due course," and leaving town. (2) The Act prohibits "balloon" payment provisions which require a debtor to pay the full amount due plus a penalty if he misses just one payment. (3) It prohibits debtors from assigning their earnings as part of a credit transaction. And (4) it gives a credit buyer the right to cancel a home solicitation sale until midnight of the third day after the day the buyer signed the agreement.

Conclusion

This chapter has traced the growth of a significant area of our substantive law. The conventional wisdom has been that our standard of living has been due in large part to our capitalistic economy, which is based on our historical notions of private property and the inherent "rightness" of measuring economic activity by standards of efficiency and profit. Property interests were protected by the general notion of freedom of contract. This doctrine is based on the assumption that the parties to a contract are roughly equivalent in terms of knowledge and economic power. When this is true, the warranty provisions of Article 2 and the sections allowing modification and waiver of warranties and limitation of damages make sense and seem fair. However, where the parties are not roughly "equal" in terms of knowledge and economic power, deciding claims by the

---

[61] 15 U.S.C.A. secs. 1642, 1643, and 1644.

[62] Haemmel, p. 119.

weaker against the stronger based on a doctrine premised on a nonexistent "freedom" has become increasingly uncomfortable for the courts. So we see the courts relying more and more on either the doctrine of unconscionability or tort law to shape new remedies for injured consumers and others.

At first the doctrine of unconscionability and the relatively new remedies of negligent design and strict liability were thought adequate; but they were remedies sought after the fact. These legal doctrines held little promise as a permanent solution to the perceived threat to society of an incredible array of complex and potentially dangerous products. The 1970s have seen a substantial shift from "private litigation" as a permanent solution to "public legislation." The effect of the numerous federal and state regulatory bodies applying product-safety legislation on this perceived threat is now being debated. The change has been so rapid that the contours of the next change are almost impossible to see. However, the general direction of the movement of the law is apparent. The area of products liability law, like the law providing remedies to injured employees (Workmen's Compensation Laws) and, more recently, the law providing remedies to those injured by another automobile, is moving toward a reality of compensation without regard to either contract law or negligence and their underpinning philosophies of "breach" and "fault." The direction toward "no fault" recoveries in the area of products liability is well on its way.

Summary Statement

1. Briefly, a merchant is one who deals in goods or by his occupation holds himself out as having knowledge or skill peculiar to the sale of goods. A consumer is one who buys goods for use primarily for personal, family, or household purposes.
2. The doctrines of privity and caveat emptor kept our law from developing remedies for consumers injured by defective products until the midpoint of this century and after.
3. In Article 2 there are provisions for the creation of four kinds of warranties. Each serves a different purpose and is made in different circumstances. These warranties are express warranties, implied warranties of merchantability, implied warranties of fitness for a particular purpose, and warranties of title including warranties against infringement of patent or copyright.
4. Each of the four kinds of warranties may be modified or waived by the agreement of the parties. Like the creation of these warranties, their modification and waiver each requires different circumstances.
5. In many instances, when a large merchant seller attempts to modify or waive warranties or consumer remedies in a sales contract with a consumer, a court may declare such an attempt "unconscionable" and refuse to enforce it. An unconscionable clause or contract is one that, in light of the general commercial background and the commercial needs of the particular trade or case, appears so one-sided at the time the contract was made that a court in good conscience can not enforce them.

6. Major legal defenses used by merchant sellers in a defective products liability claim include the lack of horizontal privity, contributory negligence, assumption of a known risk, misuse of the product, hypersensitivity, and lack of proximate causation.

7. A consumer injured by a defective product may also use the tort theories of negligent manufacture or negligent design of a product to establish liability. In appropriate cases, the legal device of *res ipsa loquitur* may help the plaintiff in establishing a prima facie case of negligence.

8. If personal injury is suffered by a consumer because goods were sold in a defective condition and this made the goods unreasonably dangerous, the injured consumer may sue the seller using the tort theory of strict liability.

9. Litigating a products liability case is very expensive and very time-consuming and may not always result in safer products being produced. So both federal and state legislatures have passed statutes which are intended to result in the production of safer products or better remedies for injured consumers. Some of the important statutes are:
   a. the Consumer Product Warranty and Federal Trade Commission Improvement Act (also called the Magnuson-Moss Warranty–Federal Trade Commission Improvement Act),
   b. the Consumer Product Safety Act of 1972,
   c. motor vehicle safety legislation,
   d. food quality and packaging legislation.

10. Recently there have been a number of attempts at both the federal and state levels to protect consumers in the area of credit buying. Some of the important statutes passed in this area are:
    a. the Consumer Credit Protection Act (also called the Truth-in-Lending Act),
    b. the Uniform Consumer Credit Code.

The following case was passed upon in some respects, on four different occasions, by two different trial courts, the Florida Supreme Court, and by the United States Fifth Circuit Court of Appeals. Ultimately, the Fifth Circuit decided the case (409 F.2d 1166 (1969)) based upon Judge Simpson's dissenting opinion in an earlier appeal of the case, which is summarized below. Liability was not imposed upon the defendant for the decedent's lung cancer.

Green v. American Tobacco Company
391 F.2d 97 (1968)

In December 1957 Edwin Green, Sr. as plaintiff brought suit against the American Tobacco Company, claiming that he had incurred lung cancer as a result of smoking the defendant's product, Lucky Strike cigarettes, for almost 31 years. On February 25, 1958 Mr. Green died, and the administrator of his estate and his widow pursued his original claim. The jury in the first trial found as fact that Mr. Green had primary cancer of the lung, that this was the cause or one of the causes of his death, and that smoking Lucky Strike cigarettes was a proximate cause or one of the proximate causes of the cancer. This finding was based upon the plaintiff's expert witnesses, who testified that one out of nine or ten heavy cigarette smokers die of lung cancer; that 30,000 or 35,000 deaths yearly in the United States are caused by lung cancer caused by cigarette smoking; and that there is a much greater incidence of lung cancer in the half of the adult population that smokes.

The plaintiffs argued that liability for Mr. Green's death should be imposed on the defendant based upon a breach of implied warranty of merchantability theory and negligence. In the first trial the jury concluded that there was no developed human skill or foresight which could have afforded the manufacturer a knowledge of the harmful effects of smoking. So the jury initially found for the defendant.

As a result of this jury finding, the negligence theory was deemphasized in an appeal of the case, and the subsequent appeals and rehearings focused on whether cigarettes which cause lung cancer which result in death are "merchantable." The attorneys for the plaintiffs argued that the concept of "merchantability" imposes a form of strict liability on the defendant, and all the plaintiff need prove is that the product caused the injury complained of.

In response to this, the defendant argued that the cigarettes were merchantable since they were fit for the ordinary purposes for which such goods were sold—namely, smoking. They admitted that cigarettes would not be merchantable if they contained some foreign matter such as a mouse's ear or glass; but as long as they were essentially identical to other cigarettes that pass in the trade under the label "cigarettes," they are merchantable. Should a jury verdict for the defendant be affirmed? If so, on what ground?

The court noted that there never had been any evidence presented which would tend to show Lucky Strikes were more dangerous or had a greater propensity to cause lung cancer than cigarettes bearing other brand names. Nor was there any evidence that the cigarettes which Mr. Green smoked contained any foreign substance or any spoiled, contaminated, or other substandard ingredient which caused injury. The concept of merchantability does not impose *absolute* liability on the defendant when the product is shown to cause injury. It may impose a form of strict liability on the defendant in that liability will be established without regard to the defendant's intent or carefulness, *but* a defect in the goods must be proved. In this case there was no defect! The court found that the Lucky Strike cigarettes were exactly like all others of the particular brand and virtually the same as all other brands on the market.

Moreover, the court reasoned, if it adopted the plaintiff's reasoning, a seller of butter could be liable to a plaintiff damaged when his or her cholesterol count rose dangerously; or the seller of whiskey might incur liability to everyone who could prove the overconsumption of whiskey contributed to injury or death.

[The United States Fifth Circuit Court of Appeals overruled an earlier decision of its own, and in a final hearing en banc (all of the judges of the circuit sitting on the case), essentially affirmed a jury decision for the defendant.]

Questions and Case Problems

1. Write a paragraph in which you define and then explain the impact of both privity and the general doctrine of caveat emptor upon our legal system.

2. Define each of the following and then explain the differences between them; include a statement of the circumstances in which each may be excluded or modified:
   a. express warranty,
   b. implied warranty of merchantability,
   c. implied warranty of fitness for a particular purpose,
   d. warranty of title.

3. In a series of short paragraphs explain in your own words why the tort theories of negligence and strict liability have seen such rapid growth in their application to products liability cases. Why would an injured plaintiff prefer these tort theories over a claim for damages based upon warranty theories?

4. John wanted to buy a new electric drill. He saw an advertisement in the local newspaper which said that Sears was having a special sale on "½ inch electric drills, reduced 20% to $15." John went to Sears to buy the drill but was very interested in whether or not the drill was double-insulated. This meant that the drill had special wiring in it so that if a short developed the drill would not shock the user. John was interested in this feature because he often worked in his basement, where the floor was damp as the result of leaky plumbing, and there was a substantial risk of electrocution. John asked the salesperson at Sears, "Do you have double-insulated drills?" The salesperson replied, "We have just what you want," and got for John one of the drills on sale. She said, "This drill is double-insulated." John then said, "Fine, I'll take it," and handed her his Sears credit card. The salesperson made out the appropriate sales slip and John left with the drill.
   Answer the following questions in a series of short paragraphs by first defining the legal principle used and then picking out the circumstances of the factual pattern which would be appropriate for applying the principle.
   a. Did Sears make an express warranty?
   b. Did Sears make an implied warranty of merchantability?
   c. Did Sears make an implied warranty of fitness for a particular purpose?
   d. Did Sears make any other warranties?

5. In question 4 above, assume that John took the drill home and one day his daughter was using it in the basement and was injured because the drill was not double-insulated. If Sears were sued for the injuries based upon a warranty theory, what might Sears argue? Would Sears be successful? Assume that John, before using the drill, had sold it to a friend visiting from another state and the friend was injured in his (the friend's) home because the drill was not double-insulated. What would Sears argue in response to a claim for injury based upon warranty theories? Would Sears be successful this time?

6. In questions 4 and 5 above, the packaging for the drill which John purchased and the instructions said in plain and conspicuous language:

For one year from the date of purchase, Sears will repair or replace this drill free of charge if defective in material or workmanship.

And, in larger type, it added:

Sears will not be liable for loss or damage to property or any incidental or consequential loss or expense from property damage due directly to defects in the drill.

Assume that all of the information in question 4 above is true, and that after John purchased the drill, he was severely injured when using the drill in his basement, which at the time was dry. You may also assume that the drill was not properly double-insulated. As a result of this defect, the drill exploded and caused John's basement to catch fire, resulting in $5,000 damage to the basement and personal injury to John. Does the above language on the packaging and directions limit John's measure of recovery to the value of the drill? What additional circumstances might help John's case?

7. Assume the facts in questions 4 and 5 above to be true; what theories of liability should John argue and which would he probably be successful with?

8. Walker-Thomas Furniture Company operated a retail furniture store in the inner city of the District of Columbia. From 1957 to 1962 it contracted with Williams for the "purchase" of household items. The "agreement" of the parties read in such a way that Walker-Thomas was supposedly leasing each item to Williams for a stipulated monthly rent. It also provided that title to the goods would remain in Walker-Thomas until the total of all the monthly payments had been made on all items purchased. Also, an obscure provision added that all payments now and hereafter made shall be credited pro rata on all outstanding "leases," bills, and accounts. The effect of this last provision was to keep a balance due on every item purchased until the balance due on all items, whenever purchased, had been fully paid. This resulted in the debt created by any new credit purchase being secured by the right to repossess all items previously purchased by that purchaser. On April 17, 1962 Williams bought a stereo set for a stated value of $514.95, but she soon defaulted in her payments. Walker-Thomas seeks to repossess all items purchased by her since December 1957. What legal argument would you expect Williams to make in her defense? What circumstances might be important in establishing this defense? [*Williams v. Walker-Thomas Furniture Company,* 350 F.2d 445 (1965).]

9. The plaintiff, Philip Schemel, was a passenger in a car which was being driven within the 55 mph speed limit when it was struck from behind by a 1960 Chevrolet Impala travelling at a speed of about 115 mph. The plaintiff was injured and sues General Motors, the manufacturer of the Impala, alleging the following items:
   a. The defendant knew or should have known that there was no useful purpose in designing an automobile which could be driven at excessive speed.

b. The defendant should have foreseen that the automobile would, in fact, be driven by someone at an excessive and unlawful speed, to the risk of the public in general.
   c. The defendant advertised the speed at which its automobile could be driven, thereby encouraging irresponsible persons to exceed lawful and reasonable speed limits.
   d. The defendant has a duty basically the same as that of any member of our society—the duty to act with reasonable care.
   e. Therefore, General Motors should be liable because they negligently designed an automobile which they knew was capable of violating, and in fact would probably violate, the expressed social policy of traveling no faster than 55 mph; and the injury of the kind complained of was therefore reasonably foreseeable, given the design features of the Impala.

The driver of the speeding car is not a party to the lawsuit, and nowhere does the plaintiff argue that the Impala was defective. Based on the material you read in this chapter, should a court dismiss the plaintiff's claim for failure to state a legally recognizable claim? [*Schemel v. General Motors Corporation,* 384 F.2d 802 (1967).]

10. In the case of *Green v. American Tobacco Company,* 391 F.2d 97 (1968),[63] explain how you would try to prove *today* the defendant's cigarettes to be unmerchantable in view of the movement toward decreased nicotine content and the required labeling of cigarette smoking as dangerous to health.

---

[63] See pp. 483–84.

Commercial Paper

Summary

Over the centuries it was recognized that it was much more convenient, and in many ways safer, to use paper which could transfer *rights to payment* than to use money. If the paper qualified as "negotiable" as opposed to "non-negotiable," it could pass to an innocent purchaser *greater rights* than are normally transferred to another by assignment. "Commercial paper" under Article 3 of the Uniform Commercial Code may be either negotiable or non-negotiable. Our main concern in Part 6, Commercial Paper, is with that kind of commercial paper called the "negotiable instrument." A negotiable instrument is a signed writing, containing an unconditional promise or order to pay, a sum certain in money, on demand or at a definite time, to the order of someone or to the bearer of the instrument. If any of these elements is missing, the paper is non-negotiable. Keep in mind that the paper is still legal and enforceable as a contract, but it is simply not negotiable.

Negotiable instruments are in the form of checks, drafts, promissory notes, and certificates of deposit. Some instruments—payable to bearer in form—can be "negotiated" by their delivery to a "holder." Other instruments—payable to order in form—require for their negotiation an indorsement coupled with delivery. If the indorsement is not proper, the recipient will be only a **transferee**, not a holder. A mere transferee can not be a holder in due course with rights superior to those of an assignee.

The holder in due course is a holder who takes the instrument "in due course"—i.e., for value, in good faith, and without notice of various improper things which would destroy the justification for conferring greater rights in the holder.

We will see that parties to negotiable instruments and those holding such instruments have rights and duties toward each other.

Banks have an important role in the collection of checks. They have rights and duties toward each other and toward their customers.

transferee
one to whom another has transferred some thing

27

Introduction to Commercial Paper and Banking Operations

After you have read this chapter, you should be able to:

1. Understand the concept of negotiability.
2. Recognize practical applications of negotiable instruments.
3. Relate the flow of commercial paper to banking operations.
4. Identify the various types of negotiable instruments.
5. Discuss the formal requirements of negotiable instruments.

Introduction

Most people take negotiable instruments for granted, and there are very good reasons for this. Each time someone writes a check for the purchase of goods and services, or signs a promissory note for a loan or for a purchase on credit, in all likelihood that person has created a negotiable instrument.

The **negotiable instrument** is a formal written contract used extensively in everyday business transactions. It is a means by which a person called a "holder in due course" can get "greater rights" against the party who made or drew the instrument than would be the case if liability depended simply on the law of contracts. Accordingly, it becomes extremely important to learn about negotiable instruments as a kind of commercial paper.

Negotiation and Assignment Compared

A familiar illustration can quickly identify and compare the qualities of negotiation with an *assignment,* a legal concept that was introduced in Part 2, Contracts. Suppose that Mary buys for business use a $600 electric typewriter from Pete on credit. The sales contract may allow her a period of time—six months, for example—before she is required to pay the purchase price. Prior to the due date, however, Pete is entitled to sell or assign his rights in the contract to a third party.

Assume that Pete sells his rights in the $600 contract to Community Bank for $500 cash—a $100 discount. In this event, Community, the assignee, simply steps into the shoes of Pete, assignor. Community receives all of Pete's rights, but it is also subject to all of the defenses against Pete which Mary might raise under the original contract. If, for example, Pete had warranted the typewriter and the warranty is breached, Mary's defense in refusing to pay under the original contract will be valid against Community just as it would be against Pete if he had never made the assignment. Community may then recover from Pete under the terms of the assignment contract or on the basis of an implied warranty.

Now, consider the difference in outcome if the credit terms of the sale to Mary are embodied in the form of a negotiable promissory note[1] payable to the order of Pete. Mary would be the "maker"[2] of the note and Pete the "payee" to whom it was payable. He could then indorse and transfer the note in a manner that would create in the Community Bank the rights of a **holder in due course**[3] (HIDC).

If the note was not voluntarily paid at maturity, Community could enforce it against Mary despite the breach of warranty defense mentioned above and most other defenses that she could raise.[4] Mary would then be compelled to bring a warranty action against Pete to rescind the contract or to recover money damages for getting the typewriter fixed.

In either event, notice that the responsibility for the breach ultimately falls on Pete, as it should. However, when a negotiable promissory note is used as a

---

[1] UCC 3–104(1).   [2] UCC 3–413(1).   [3] UCC 3–302.   [4] UCC 3–305.

negotiable instrument
a writing signed by the maker or drawer containing an unconditional promise or order to pay a sum certain in money payable on demand or at a definite time to order or to bearer

A negotiable instrument as a credit device.

holder in due course (HIDC)
the holder of a negotiable instrument who takes it for value, in good faith, and without notice that the instrument is overdue or has been dishonored or of any defense against, or claim to, the instrument by any person

credit instrument, HIDCs like the bank can be confident of getting a judgment against the primary party-maker, Mary, or, as will be discussed later, against the secondary party-indorser,[5] Pete.

The HIDC Concept

From the point of view of HIDCs then, negotiable instruments are a great advantage over mere assignment. Greater rights can be obtained by an HIDC of a negotiable instrument than by an assignee of a contract right. Indirectly they benefit debtors too, because many sales would not be made unless the seller-payee could depend on negotiating the instrument for cash to some third party, typically a bank or finance company.

Discounting.

This transaction is known as *discounting*. The seller-payee will normally receive less than face value for the note—e.g., a $1,000 note may sell for $980 (a low discount) or for $800 or less (a high discount).

The difference between face value and the discount price is the margin or yield. The purpose of this margin is to compensate the third party for its risk. This will vary, depending on the credit rating of the debtor, the length of time until maturity, and the security or collateral which stands behind the instrument in the event of default.

Negotiable Instruments as a Substitute for Money

Negotiable instruments can be used as substitutes for money just as, in the previous example, a promissory note was used as a credit device. The *check*, which is a form of a **draft** drawn on a bank and payable on demand, is the most familiar illustration.[6]

draft
a negotiable instrument containing an unconditional order, e.g., "pay"

check
"a draft drawn on a bank and payable on demand"
UCC 3-104 (2)(b)

drawee
the person on whom a draft is drawn and ordered to pay

Assume that David, who has money on deposit in a checking account with Hometown Bank, draws a $25 **check** payable to the order of Pineville Bookstore, payee, for the purchase of textbooks. An authorized agent of the bookstore, usually the cashier who handles the transaction, will indorse on the back of the check with a rubber stamp: "Pay to Community Bank, For Deposit, Pineville Bookstore."[7]

As a routine matter, this check, along with other items,[8] will be placed in Pineville's depositary bank,[9] Community. Pineville Bookstore will be given a $25 provisional credit[10] in its checking account, and the check will be forwarded through bank channels to David's Hometown Bank, known as the **drawee,** payor bank.[11]

---

[5] UCC 3–414(1).

[6] UCC 3–104(2)(b).

[7] This indorsement is "special," UCC 3–204(1), because it names the person to whom it is indorsed; it is also "restrictive," 3–205(c), because it limits the things that the indorsee Community Bank can do with it. The bank can place this for deposit only in the Pineville Bookstore's account and forward the check for collection.

[8] UCC 4–104(1)(g). [10] UCC 4–201(1).

[9] UCC 4–105(a). [11] UCC 4–105(b).

If there are sufficient funds on deposit in **drawer** David's checking account, the item will be debited, or charged, against his balance. Periodically David will receive through the mail a statement of his account and his cancelled checks.

The provisional credit that **payee** Pineville Bookstore received at Community becomes final since the check was paid from David's account by Hometown. Pineville Bookstore can now draw on that account as it wishes—e.g., to pay its bills, replenish its inventory, or expand its operations.

drawer
the person who initially draws or creates and signs a draft

payee
the person to whose order the instrument is originally written

Figure 27.1   Check Flow Chart

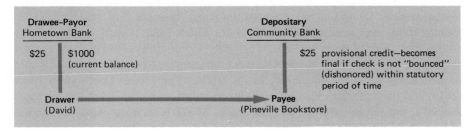

Figure 27.2   Sample Check

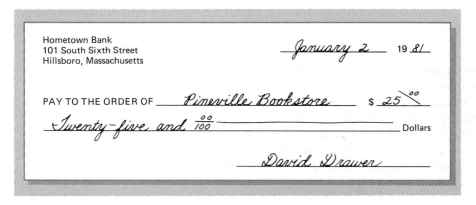

Figure 27.3   Deposit Stamp on Back of Check

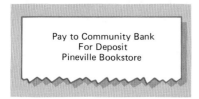

If David did not have sufficient funds on deposit with Hometown, the drawee-payor bank, or if for some reason David stopped payment on his check,[12] the check would be returned through channels to Community. Community would then reverse the provisional credit with an offsetting debit entry and return the check to Pineville Bookstore.

At this stage Pineville would have to collect on the check from David, perhaps resulting in a lawsuit. Keep in mind that the payment of debts with checks or notes is conditional payment only—conditioned on the instrument being paid.[13]

You can see that an assignment of contract rights would be very awkward in this situation. Checks, however, are tailor-made for such transactions. With very little change, if Community Bank permitted Pineville to withdraw the funds represented by David's check prior to its being "bounced," or returned, Community Bank may become an HIDC of the check since it paid value for it by advancing money to Pineville. In that capacity, Community could proceed against David, the drawer, on the check, and most defenses that David could raise would be ineffective against Community as an HIDC. The HIDC Community Bank could, and probably would, first make every effort to collect from its customer Pineville, the payee-indorser, but the status of HIDC is very valuable because it practically assures Community of a judgment against David.

Types of Negotiable Instrument—Notes and Drafts

Many new terms were introduced during the previous discussion of the concept of negotiability. In this part of the chapter we will elaborate on these terms and observe further the importance of negotiability as we discuss

1. the types of instrument,
2. the parties and banks that deal with them, and
3. the form which all instruments must have in order to be negotiable.

Notes are promises, drafts are orders.

Notes are two-party instruments.

Drafts are three-party instruments.

All instruments are either notes or drafts.[14] Notes *promise* payment and are promissory instruments, while drafts *order* payment and are order instruments. Notes are *two*-party instruments in which a maker, such as a credit purchaser or borrower, promises to pay money to a payee. A certificate of deposit is a particular kind of note in which a bank acknowledges receipt of money and engages to repay it.

Drafts are *three*-party instruments in which a drawer orders the drawee to pay to a payee. A check is a special form of a draft which is *drawn on a bank*, drawee. The drawee bank is ordered to pay the money *on demand*.

Notes and drafts may or may not be negotiable. If not negotiable, they are still legal and enforceable as contracts, and they may be transferred by *assignment;* but they cannot be negotiated.

---

[12] UCC 4–403.

[13] UCC 3–802(1)(b).

[14] UCC 3–104(2).

Figure 27.4 Certificate of Deposit

CERTIFICATE OF DEPOSIT

NO INTEREST PAID AFTER DUE DATE INVESTMENT—SAVINGS **No. 2382**

HILLSBORO, MASSACHUSETTS ____________________

THIS CERTIFIES THAT ____________________

HAS DEPOSITED WITH

Hometown State Bank HILLSBORO, MASSACHUSETTS $__________

____________________ DOLLARS

PAYABLE __________ DAYS-MONTHS AFTER DATE IN CURRENT FUNDS ON RETURN OF THIS CERTIFICATE PROPERLY ENDORSED WITH INTEREST AT THE RATE OF __________ PER CENT PER ANNUM.

THIS CERTIFICATE SHALL BE CONSIDERED RENEWED AUTOMATICALLY FOR THE SAME LENGTH OF TIME AND INTEREST RATE FROM ITS ORIGINAL MATURITY AND THEREAFTER FOR SUCCESSIVE PERIODS OF TIME OF THE SAME LENGTH, UNLESS PRESENTED FOR REDEMPTION WITHIN TEN (10) DAYS AFTER THE END OF THE ORIGINAL TERM OR ANY SUBSEQUENT TERM. THE BANK MAY REDEEM THIS CERTIFICATE AT ANY ORIGINAL OR SUBSEQUENT MATURITY DATE BY TEN (10) DAYS WRITTEN NOTICE TO THE PAYEE AT HIS ADDRESS SHOWN BY THE BANK'S RECORDS. IF SUCH NOTICE IS GIVEN, THIS DEPOSIT WILL NOT BEAR INTEREST AFTER THE REDEMPTION DATE. SUBJECT TO THE FOREGOING, THIS CERTIFICATE IS CONTINUOUS; NO RENEWAL NECESSARY.

TAX I.D. NO. ADDRESS

☐ DEPOSIT INTEREST TO ACCOUNT

☐ ADD INTEREST TO PRINCIPAL UPON RENEWAL

____
EXEC. ASSISTANT CASHIER—VICE PRESIDENT

NOT SUBJECT TO CHECK

Negotiability Is a Matter of Form

The form which notes and drafts must assume in order to qualify as negotiable will be discussed in detail later, but, to aid in understanding the various types of commercial paper, notice that all negotiable instruments must comply with the following requirements:

1. The instrument must be in writing and signed by the maker or drawer.
2. Each instrument must contain an unconditional promise or order to pay a sum certain in money.
3. The time of payment must be on demand or at a definite time.
4. Each instrument must be payable to order or to bearer.[15]

Negotiable Promissory Notes

Recall the previous hypothetical situation in which Mary purchased a typewriter on credit and financed the unpaid balance by creating a $600 negotiable promissory note to the order of Pete, payee. The note had two parties, **maker** and *payee,* and a promise to pay. The instrument gave a definite time before the maker, Mary, was required to pay.

maker
the person who initially makes and signs a promissory note

This illustrated the use of a negotiable note as a credit device.[16] If the terms had called for payment on demand,[17] Pete could have required payment at any

[15] UCC 3–104(1). [16] UCC 3–109. [17] UCC 3–108.

Figure 27.5 Promissory Note

PROMISSORY NOTE

NAME __John Robinson__ NO. __471-00-3322__ $ __1000.00__

DUE __Demand__ SECURITY __Signature__ **HILLSBORO, MASSACHUSETTS** __Current Date__ ,19 ____

On demand, or if no demand is made, then ___Six Months___ *after date, without grace,*

I, we or either of us, as principals, promise to pay to the order of Hillsboro State Bank, Hillsboro, Massachusetts,

the sum of __One Thousand Dollars & 00/100 —————————————————————————————* Dollars*

with interest at the rate of __10%__ *percent per annum from date until paid, at its offices in Hillsboro, Massachusetts.*
  And in the event default is made in the payment of this note at maturity and it is placed in the hands of an attorney for collection, or suit is brought on same, then a reasonable additional amount shall be added as attorney's and collection fees.
  The makers and endorsers hereof hereby severally waive all notices, demands for payment, presentation hereof for payment, protest in case this note is not paid at maturity, and agree to all extensions and partial payments before or after maturity without prejudice to holder, and further agree that any one of them, acting individually, may renew this note and thereby extend the time for payment of any portion of the principal and accumulated interest due and agree to pay an interest rate to be determined at the time of such renewal. Makers agree that each of them shall be and remain obligated as principals during any such extended period for payment. The death or loss of capacity of any of the makers hereof shall not revoke or terminate, as to the other makers, the authority of each to renew and extend this note for and on behalf of all other surviving or non-incapacitated makers.

(signed) *John Robinson* *Address* __Hillsboro, Mass.__
(signed) *Larry Cox* *Address* __Hillsboro, Mass.__
(signed) *Richard Nelson* *Address* __Hillsboro, Mass.__
Form 77B Revised

Promissory Note

1. Which party or parties occupy a position analogous to that of Mary in the textbook example?
2. Which party most closely resembles Pete, the person who sold Mary the car?
3. If John Robinson receives the entire $1000, what function do the signatures of Cox and Nelson serve?
4. What is an acceleration clause? Does this instrument have an acceleration clause?
5. Since three parties have signed this note payable to the order of the bank, does that fit the definition of a note as a TWO PARTY instrument and a PROMISE to pay?

time after the note was issued to him.[18] This would not have suited the needs of the parties quite as well, but on some occasions the only way a maker can induce the payee to lend money or to sell on credit is by promising to pay on demand.

Mary, the maker of the note, is undertaking a direct and personal obligation to pay Pete the $600 at maturity. No one else is being ordered to pay on her behalf. Since the maker is absolutely liable, she is described as a "primary party."[19]

Negotiable Drafts

If the terms of an instrument include three parties—a *drawer* who orders a *drawee* to pay money to a *payee*—the instrument is a draft. Suppose that a draft is used to finance the credit sale of $1,000 worth of goods. The seller may draw a six-month time-draft on the *buyer-drawee* ordering the buyer to pay $1,000 to a payee. The payee may be the seller himself, the seller's bank, or any person designated by the seller.

---

[18] UCC 3–122(1)(b).   [19] UCC 3–413(1).

Figure 27.6 Envelope Draft

Customer's Draft

Hillsboro State Bank

On Demand/at Sight

HILLSBORO,
MASSACHUSETTS   Current Date   19 ____

PAY TO THE
ORDER OF ____ **Payee-Seller** _____ $ _1,000.00_

One Thousand Dollars and No/100 ——————————————————— DOLLARS
VALUE RECEIVED AND CHARGE TO ACCOUNT OF   WITH EXCHANGE

ENCLOSURES Invoice in triplicate airway bill of lading; marine and war risk insurance;
            non-negotiable airway bill of lading.

TO ____ Drawee-Buyer _____

THROUGH ____ Seller's Bank _____   Drawer-Seller _____

FORM 163

Envelope Draft

1. This draft is in the form of an envelope that will enclose the invoice, insurance policies, and bill of lading. The drawee-buyer is entitled to examine these documents before paying the $1000.
2. This draft is payable *on demand* or *at sight*. While the buyer can examine the enclosed documents to see that they are in proper order, he must not use them to pick up the goods at the carrier's depot until he has paid the draft.
3. A trade acceptance is a draft that would have given the buyer a *credit period* after his signature or acceptance of the draft. The time period would be, for example, six months after date. There is no place for the drawee-buyer's signature on this draft, but on the typical trade acceptance there will be a designated line.
4. A bank acceptance is a draft resembling a trade acceptance, except, by prior arrangement, the buyer's bank agrees to become the drawee-acceptor and to sign or accept on behalf of its customer.

This type of draft is known as a *trade acceptance.* When the instrument is drawn by the seller ordering the buyer to pay and it is signed as accepted by the *buyer,* the buyer becomes an **acceptor,** and he is a *primary party* with liability on the instrument similar to that of the maker of a note.[20] Primary parties are directly liable on the instrument they sign; unlike secondary parties, they do not expect someone else to pay on their behalf.

acceptor
the drawee on a draft who has asserted in writing on the draft to pay it

If the *bank* accepts the draft—usually by prior arrangement between the buyer and his bank—the instrument is known as a *banker's acceptance.*

The importance of this distinction becomes apparent if you visualize a situation in which the payee needs cash before the instrument matures in six months. If he should decide to **negotiate** the instrument—i.e., indorse and discount the draft for as much cash as it will bring on the market—do you suppose the payee will receive a higher price (low discount from face value) if it has been accepted by a bank rather than accepted by the buyer alone? Chances are that a purchaser of the paper will pay more for a banker's acceptance. Other things

negotiate
to deliver a negotiable instrument to a holder

---

[20] UCC 3–413(1).

Introduction to Commercial Paper and Banking Operations

being equal, the bank's financial status and reputation will make this instrument more desirable than a trade acceptance.

Of course, most buyer-drawees will discharge their liability at maturity by full payment, but the financial reputation of the party who accepts can make an important difference. If a seller-payee wants to assure himself of a ready and willing market for the draft, and also a high price (low discount), a banker's acceptance normally is preferable to him.

Not all drafts are time drafts with a definite maturity date. Some are sight drafts payable "at sight" or "on demand" when presented to the drawee.

A check is the most common example of a draft payable on demand. Remember that a check is a special form of draft that is always drawn on a bank.[21] In the normal course of things it is expected that the drawee bank will pay on demand the amount designated in the check. Then the bank will charge or reduce the drawer-depositor's account by that amount.

cashier's check
a check drawn by a bank on itself and payable to the order of a payee

Other forms are the **cashier's check** and the *traveller's check*. A cashier's check is drawn by a bank officer (cashier) on the bank itself as drawee and payable to the order of a payee. It resembles a note since the one drawing the draft (the drawer) and the one expected to pay (the drawee) are the same party. The bank drawer of a cashier's check can not stop payment on it, as is illustrated by the following case.

Facts
Reinhard purchased goods from the plaintiff, Moon Over the Mountain Ltd., and paid for them by delivering to the plaintiff's agent a cashier's check which he had purchased from the defendant, Marine Midland Bank, where he was a customer. The check was drawn by the defendant payable to the plaintiff's agent, who indorsed and delivered it to the plaintiff. It was then deposited for collection in the bank where plaintiff had its account. Meanwhile, Reinhard decided to stop payment on the check and directed the defendant to do so. The check was returned to plaintiff's bank marked "Payment Stopped." Plaintiff sued the defendant on the check and obtained a judgment. Defendant appealed.

Decision
Affirmed for plaintiff.

Reasoning
Since under UCC 3-802(1)(a) the payee loses its right against its debtor when a cashier's check is taken in payment of an underlying debt, the bank drawer can not refuse payment on the instrument. The bank here has drawn and issued the cashier's check; it is primarily liable thereon and cannot stop payment.

Moon Over the Mountain Ltd. v. Marine Midland Bank, 87 Misc.2d 918 (N.Y. 1976).

A traveller's check may name as drawee a financial institution that is not a bank. Strictly speaking, then, it is not a check at all, but a draft.

In its original form, the traveller's check does not name a payee. The payee will be specified later when the owner or "traveller" decides to use or cash the

---

[21] UCC 3–104(2)(b).

check; he will then insert the name of the payee. The "traveller" will also be required to sign the instrument when it is used. This gives the recipient payee, perhaps a hotel or airline, an opportunity to verify the owner's written signature at that time by comparing it with his written signature on the instrument as it was originally issued.

A *letter of credit* is neither a draft nor a note. It is a promise by a bank or other person to honor or to pay drafts drawn in accordance with its terms. For example, a Texas merchant who is not well known beyond the borders of his home state may bargain with his bank to guarantee payment of drafts drawn upon it by Mexican or Japanese exporters. This will allow the Texas businessperson to make purchases of goods that would not have been sold to him on the strength of his credit alone.

Parties

By this time most of the parties and banks that deal with negotiable instruments have been introduced. To review and reenforce one's knowledge of this material, it will be discussed in more detail under the subheadings "Primary Parties," "Secondary Parties," and "Other Parties," including banks.

Primary Parties

Primary parties are *makers* of *notes* and *acceptors* of *drafts*.[22] The party or parties who purchase on credit or borrow money and sign promissory notes as makers are primary parties. Acceptors of drafts—such as drawee banks that certify checks[23] or buyer-drawees that agree to be bound on trade acceptances by signing and accepting them[24]—are primary parties also.

These parties promise to pay the instrument according to its tenor or terms at the time the instrument is created or the time of acceptance. If the instrument is incomplete at the time of acceptance, a person takes a risk in accepting it. If the instrument is later filled in properly, there is no problem.[25] For example, if a buyer-drawee on a trade acceptance accepts it with his signature and authorizes the seller to fill in the blank space with the amount of the purchase price, the acceptor has no ground for complaint when the correct amount is inserted as authorized. If an excessive, unauthorized amount is filled in, however, the acceptor will be liable for that sum to a subsequent HIDC.[26] The acceptor is responsible for the incompleteness since he gives the wrongdoer a golden opportunity to materially alter the instrument. After paying the HIDC, the acceptor has a right of recovery against the wrongdoer.

primary parties
parties (maker and acceptor) on a negotiable instrument who are absolutely liable for its payment according to the terms at the time they sign

---

[22] UCC 3–413.   [25] UCC 3–115(1).

[23] UCC 3–411.   [26] UCC 3–407(3).

[24] UCC 3–410.

Figure 27.7   Letter of Credit

<table>
<tr><td>CABLE ADDRESS
HILLSBANK</td><td colspan="2" align="center">HILLSBORO STATE BANK
HILLSBORO, MASSACHUSETTS</td><td align="center">IRREVOCABLE
COMMERCIAL CREDIT</td></tr>
</table>

HILLSBORO,   NO.   A-524
MASSACHUSETTS   UP TO $10,186.50

SELLER'S NAME Po Lung-Yu
Tachibana Bldg., 1083 Ikebukuro,
2-chome, Toshima-ku, Tokyo, Japan   DATE OF ISSUE

GENTLEMEN:

    WE HEREBY AUTHORIZE YOU TO DRAW ON HILLSBORO STATE BANK

FOR ACCOUNT OF NAME OF BUYER-CUSTOMER OF HILLSBORO STATE BANK, HILLSBORO, MASS. 86543

UP TO AN AGGREGATE AMOUNT OF **TEN THOUSAND ONE HUNDRED EIGHTY SIX AND 50/100***

AVAILABLE BY YOUR DRAFTS AT Sight

ACCOMPANIED BY Airbill, marked Freight Prepaid; Commercial Invoice, signed in
triplicate; Packing List in Triplicate; Insurance policy or certificate endorsed
in blank, for 110% of the invoice cost including: The Institute War Clauses, and
the Institute Cargo Clauses (All Risks) and the Institute Strikes, Riots and
Civil Commotions Clauses. Claims to be payable in the United States of America in
the currency of drafts. Airbill should be made out to order and blank endorsed
and marked "Notify the above mentioned applicant."

No partial shipments allowed.

Shipping Expiration: 60 days.

Document Negotiation: 90 days.

Bank: Dai-Ichi Kangyo Bank, Tokyo, Shinbashi Branch

Reference: Attached copy of Refiners & Producers Marketing, Inc. purchase order
which becomes a part of this Letter of Credit.

    DRAFTS MUST BE DRAWN AND NEGOTIATED NOT LATER THAN Expiration Date of Letter . EACH DRAFT
MUST BE MARKED "DRAWN UNDER LETTER OF CREDIT NO.   A-524   OF HILLSBORO STATE
BANK, HILLSBORO, DATED   Date of Issue   " AND THE AMOUNT OF EACH DRAFT SO DRAWN ENDORSED
BY THE NEGOTIATING BANK ON THE REVERSE SIDE HEREOF. WHEN PRESENTED BY THE MAKER DIRECT TO THE DRAWEE
BANK, THE DRAFTS MUST BE ACCOMPANIED BY THIS LETTER OF CREDIT FOR THE PURPOSE OF SUCH ENDORSEMENTS
BEING MADE THEREON.
    WE HEREBY AGREE WITH THE DRAWERS, ENDORSERS AND BONA FIDE HOLDERS OF DRAFTS DRAWN UNDER AND IN
COMPLIANCE WITH THIS CREDIT THAT SAME SHALL BE DULY HONORED UPON PRESENTATION TO THE DRAWEE BANK AS
SPECIFIED ABOVE.
                  YOURS VERY TRULY

SIGNATURE OF BANK OFFICIAL
_____
AUTHORIZED SIGNATURE

Secondary Parties

If a person's signature on a negotiable instrument is *other than as maker or acceptor,* that person is a **secondary party.**

Drawer. It is easy to be trapped by the comparison of a secondary party-drawer who initiates a draft with a primary party-maker who initiates a note. Be careful—the analogy is misleading.

In the normal course of events, the *drawer* of a draft or check expects the drawee to pay. When a person writes a check, it is an *order* from the drawer to the drawee bank to pay out of the money on deposit in the drawer's checking account. When the maker of a note borrows money, however, or purchases on credit, he does not order someone else to pay,[27] he himself *promises* or undertakes to pay.

A drawer does obligate himself to pay the instrument *if* the holder takes the proper three steps:

1. *Presentment.* The instrument is properly presented to the drawee for payment.
2. *Dishonor.* The instrument is dishonored by the maker's or drawee's refusal to pay it.
3. *Notice.* The drawer is given proper notice of nonpayment or dishonor.[28]

The drawer may avoid or disclaim this liability by drawing the draft "without recourse."[29] However, it is difficult to find people who are willing to do business with a drawer on this basis because they do not have recourse—i.e., do not have the right of recovery—against the drawer on his signature if the draft is dishonored by the drawee.

Indorser. **Indorsers** are secondary parties who sign notes and drafts in the process of negotiation. They do not sign as makers or acceptors. Generally speaking, every indorser makes a conditional or secondary promise that he will pay the holder of the instrument if the usual three steps of presentment, dishonor, and notice are followed. Qualified indorsers ("without recourse" indorsers)[30] disclaim their signature as indorsements with secondary liability if the instrument is dishonored, but they are exceptions to the rule.

Discharge of Secondary Parties for Failure to Observe the Conditions of Presentment, Dishonor, and Notice of Dishonor.

These preliminary three steps are conditions for holding an indorser secondarily liable. They are the same as those for holding a drawer secondarily liable, but there is a very important difference. If these conditions do not occur, the indorser is completely discharged,

secondary parties
parties on a negotiable instrument who are liable on the instrument only if certain conditions occur

indorser
the person who signs on an instrument (or on a paper attached to it) other than as a maker, drawer, or acceptor

---

[27] Some states have adopted UCC 3–121, Alternative A, which makes a note payable at a bank "the equivalent of a draft drawn on the bank payable when it falls due out of any funds of the maker or acceptor for such payment."

[28] UCC 3–501.

[29] UCC 3–413(2).

[30] UCC 3–414(1).

but the drawer is discharged only if the drawee becomes insolvent *during the delay* in *presentment for payment* or *notice of dishonor.*[31]

If the drawee does become **insolvent,** the drawer is discharged to the extent that his claim against the drawee is reduced. For example, assume that a $100 check would have been paid by the drawee if the instrument had been properly presented. However, if the holder of the check is late in presenting it to the drawee for payment, and the drawee becomes insolvent during the delay, then the drawer is discharged from any further liability by assigning all of his rights to the holder. The holder may be able to recover a fraction of the $100 check from the insolvent drawee. Thus, if the drawee's creditors eventually receive twenty cents on the dollar, the holder of the check will be entitled to collect $20.

Other Parties

Payee. The *payee* is the person to whose order the instrument is originally written. This person must be identified with reasonable certainty.[32] The payee normally becomes an indorser-secondary party when he signs on the instrument so that it can be negotiated to some other person.

Indorsee. The **indorsee** is the person named in the **indorsement**—e.g., "Pay to A [indorsee], [signed] B [indorser]"; or "Pay to Community Bank [indorsee], [signed] Pineville Bookstore [indorser]."[33]

For the time being, please note that these indorsements which *name* the indorsee are called *special indorsements*—the indorsement is to a "special" person. If the last or only indorsement of an instrument is a special indorsement, the instrument is *order paper.* This means that the indorsee *must* indorse before the paper can be further negotiated.[34]

An additional point to observe here is that the word "order" does not necessarily have to appear in the special indorsement. If not present, it is simply assumed to be there—i.e., the indorsement is read as if the word *order* appeared in it as follows: "Pay to [the order of] A, [signed] B."

Remember that we are speaking here of an *indorsement.* If words of negotiability—that is, "order" or "bearer" or their equivalents—do not appear on the *face* or front of the instrument, it is not negotiable to begin with.

Holder. A **holder** is a person who is in *possession* of an instrument which has been originally drawn or issued to him or his order, or later specially indorsed to him.[35] Merely *naming* someone as payee or indorsee is not sufficient to make the person a holder. That person must be *in possession* of the instrument as well.

Further, a holder may be a person who is in possession of an instrument which is bearer paper *originally,* e.g., on the face of the paper it reads "Pay to the order of *Bearer,*" or "Pay to the order of *Cash.*" Another possibility is that the holder may be in possession of an instrument that was *originally* order paper,

---

[31] UCC 3-502(1).   [33] UCC 3-204(1).   [35] UCC 1-201(20).

[32] UCC 3-110(1).   [34] UCC 3-204(1).

insolvent
"a person is insolvent who either has ceased to pay his debts in the ordinary course of business or cannot pay his debts as they become due or is insolvent within the meaning of the federal bankruptcy law" UCC 1-201(23)

indorsee
the person named by an indorser on an instrument to whom it is to be paid

indorsement
the indorser's signature on an instrument (or on a paper attached to it)

holder
the person in possession of an instrument which flows to him either initially or by indorsement

but which has become bearer paper because the last or only indorsement is a *blank* indorsement—e.g., the indorser simply signs his name, "Jarrett Hudnall," but does not name an indorsee. A blank indorsement is an indorsement without any accompanying words. Because of the risk of a bearer instrument being lost or stolen and getting into the hands of a holder who can then collect on the instrument, one should be very careful when indorsing an instrument in blank.

Bearer.[36]   A **bearer** is a holder who is in possession of an instrument which is bearer paper on its face—i.e., it is made out to "Bearer," or to "Cash," or to the equivalent of these, discussed later. A bearer may also be a person who is in possession of an instrument on which the last or only indorsement is a blank indorsement.

bearer
the person in possession of an instrument payable to bearer or indorsed in blank (a signature without additional words)

Holder in Due Course (HIDC).   An HIDC must first qualify as a holder. In addition, this holder must purchase for value, in good faith, and without notice that the instrument is overdue, has been dishonored, or that there is an outstanding claim of ownership on or defense against the instrument.[37] A bank can become an HIDC, as is illustrated by the following case.

Facts
Defendant, Sidney Pazol, drew a check for $49,000 on the drawee bank, payable to the order of Eidson & Seiden, the payee. The payee deposited the check with the plaintiff-depositary bank, Citizens National Bank. The payee omitted to indorse, so Citizens indorsed on behalf of the payee. Citizens allowed the payee, its customer, to withdraw the full amount immediately. The check "bounced" (dishonored) because the defendant placed a stop payment order with the drawee. Citizens decided to sue the drawer rather than to pursue its customer, the payee.

Decision
Judgment for plaintiff.

Reasoning
A depositary bank is entitled to indorse items on behalf of its customers (UCC 4-205(1)). The bank then qualified as a holder—one in possession of an instrument indorsed to it (UCC 1-201(20)). Citizens gave value for the instrument to the extent that it held a security interest (UCC 4-209); and a bank has a security interest in "an item deposited in an account to the extent to which credit given for the item has been withdrawn or applied" (UCC 4-208(1)). Since the plaintiff bank met all of the other requirements, it was entitled to proceed as an HIDC.

Pazol v. Citizens National Bank of Sandy Springs, 138 S.E.2d 442 (Ga. 1964).

Special Relationships

Accommodation Party.   An accommodation party may be primarily or secondarily liable. This depends on whether he signs as an accommodation maker, accommodation drawer, accommodation acceptor, or accommodation indorser.[38]

---

[36] UCC 1–201(5).   [38] UCC 3–415(2).

[37] UCC 3–302.

The purpose of such a signature is to lend the name and financial resources of the accommodation party to the instrument. The accommodation maker and acceptor are primarily liable. The accommodation drawer and indorser are secondarily liable.

An accommodation *maker,* for example, signs as an inducement to a third person to make a loan or to sell on credit to the one who is actually receiving the benefit of the transaction. The signature of an accommodation maker is part of the consideration received by the third person to encourage him to enter into the transaction. There are many variations on this theme. Suppose D wishes to buy goods on credit from C, but D's credit is poor. A's credit is good. C wishes to have A liable on the note as an accommodation maker for D, and to have D liable as the payee indorser as well. So A signs as an accommodation maker of a note with D as the payee. D indorses and delivers the note to C, who now sells the goods on credit to D.

The instrument may be signed by an accommodation *indorser* along with a payee who indorses, or along with a subsequent indorser. The purpose of the accommodation indorsement is to promote the acceptability or marketability of the instrument because of the accommodation indorser's liability on the instrument. Other things being equal, an instrument with an accommodation indorsement is more attractive to potential purchasers than one without such an indorsement. It supplies an additional secondary party to whom the holder may turn following presentment, dishonor, and notice.

The accommodation party is never liable to the party accommodated.[39] In the event an accommodation maker is required to pay the instrument, he can recover from the *accommodated* party.

The same is true of an accommodation indorser. If he is required to pay the instrument, he has a right to recover such payment from the accommodated indorser or from any prior person who has become liable as a secondary party.

Guarantor. One who uses the words "payment guaranteed" or an equivalent phrase with his signature is bound according to the terms of the instrument if it is not voluntarily paid at maturity. There is no need for the holder to pursue or to give notice to any other party.[40]

A person may undertake a less demanding guaranty obligation by merely guaranteeing collection. "Collection guaranteed" obligates the signer only if the primary party is insolvent or if the holder has gone into court and received a judgment on the instrument and is now unable to collect on the judgment.[41]

Words of guaranty will be interpreted to mean that *payment* is guaranteed unless collection is specified. Any words of guaranty make unnecessary presentment, dishonor, and notice, which are normally required before secondary parties become liable on their indorsement contracts.[42]

---

[39] UCC 3–415(5).   [41] UCC 3–416(2).

[40] UCC 3–416(1).   [42] UCC 3–416(5).

The Banking Process

Depositary Bank

The *first* bank in which one deposits a check to *begin* the collection process is the **depositary bank.**[43] The first bank may also be the drawee-payor bank. The depositor will receive a provisional or temporary credit in his checking account, and the item will be forwarded to the next bank for collection. If the check does not bounce within a prescribed deadline—i.e., if it is not returned to the depositary or if notice is not sent to the depositary that there are "not sufficient funds" to pay the check or that payment has been "stopped"—the provisional credit will be made final. If the check is properly returned or if notice is sent within the deadline, the depositary bank will reverse the provisional credit.

Remember, from the depositor's point of view, the depositary bank is his drawee bank. Whenever this depositor writes a check, he will be drawing on this account and ordering his drawee bank to pay money to a payee.

The depositary bank could give value and perhaps become an HIDC if it allowed its customer-depositor to cash another person's check or to withdraw funds represented by another's check before the collection process was completed. Of course, the depositary bank would have to meet all the requirements for becoming an HIDC in addition to giving value. This could become very important if the other person's check bounced and, instead of proceeding against its own depositor-customer, the bank chose to pursue the drawer. (See the *Pazol* case, p. 503.)

depositary bank
"the first bank to which an item is transferred for collection even though it is also the payor bank"
UCC 4-105(a)

Payor Bank

In the check collection process, items are transferred from the depositary bank through intermediary banks to the **payor bank.** The payor bank holds the checking account of the drawer. From the point of view of the drawer, the payor bank is synonymous with the drawee.[44]

Assuming that there are sufficient funds on deposit in the drawer's account, the item will be paid and the depositor's account will be debited or charged. If funds are not sufficient or if payment has been stopped, the item will be returned to the depositary bank.

When a check reaches the payor bank through collection channels, it has until the midnight deadline[45]—midnight on the next banking day following receipt of an item—to decide whether to pay or to return the check. If the payor bank fails to examine its customer's account within the allotted time, and it discovers after the midnight deadline has passed that there are not sufficient funds to pay the check, the payor bank will be accountable for the amount of the item to the collecting banks.[46] It is penalized for failing to act within the prescribed time limits established by law. The payor bank then has recourse against its customer, the person who overdrew his account.[47]

Keep in mind that some drafts are not drawn on bank-drawees—e.g., a trade acceptance. In that case the payor may be an individual or a business firm.

payor bank
"a bank by which an item is payable as drawn or accepted"
UCC 4-105(b)

---

[43] UCC 4-105(a).   [45] UCC 4-104(h).   [47] UCC 4-401(1).

[44] UCC 4-105(b).   [46] UCC 4-302(a).

Collecting Banks

This term includes all banks, even the depositary bank, forwarding a check for collection to a payor bank.[48] It does not include the payor bank.

Presenting Bank

This is the last bank in the collection process. It turns the check over to a payor bank for final disposition.[49]

Intermediary Bank

Intermediary banks are "in between" the depositary and the payor banks. Neither the depositary nor the payor bank is included, but the presenting bank does fall within the definition.[50]

Figure 27.8 Diagram of Check Collection Process

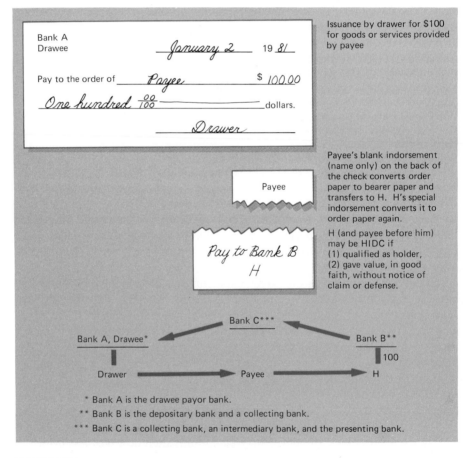

Issuance by drawer for $100 for goods or services provided by payee

Payee's blank indorsement (name only) on the back of the check converts order paper to bearer paper and transfers to H. H's special indorsement converts it to order paper again.

H (and payee before him) may be HIDC if
(1) qualified as holder,
(2) gave value, in good faith, without notice of claim or defense.

* Bank A is the drawee payor bank.
** Bank B is the depositary bank and a collecting bank.
*** Bank C is a collecting bank, an intermediary bank, and the presenting bank.

---

[48] UCC 4-105(d).   [49] UCC 4-105(e).   [50] UCC 4-105(c).

Formal Requisites of Negotiable Instruments

"Commercial paper" may be negotiable or non-negotiable. We are primarily interested in the negotiable instrument. If the instrument is not negotiable, it is still valid and enforceable as a contract, but no one can become an HIDC.

The basic elements that are common to all negotiable instruments were introduced briefly in the discussion of the various types of instrument. The final portion of this chapter will deal with each of these components in detail:

1. *Written and signed.* The instrument must be in writing and signed by the maker or drawer.
2. *Unconditional promise or order—sum certain in money.* Each instrument must contain an absolute, unconditional, ironclad promise or order to pay a sum certain in money.
3. *Demand or definite time.* The time of payment must be on demand or at a definite time.
4. *Order or bearer.* Each instrument must be payable to order or to bearer.[51]

Formal requisites.

Written

Oral contracts to pay money may or may not be enforceable, depending on the statute of frauds and its exceptions. Negotiable instruments, however, must be in writing.

Writing includes printing, typewriting, handwriting, or any other method of committing words to paper. The UCC permits the writing to be on anything, but as a practical matter, the writing will be on a convenient-to-handle printed form. Writing in pencil is permissible, but most prudent people will guard against that because of the opportunities for fraudulent material alteration of the instrument.

The writing.

Signed

The signature of the maker or drawer may be written at any place on the instrument. Usually it appears at the bottom-right of the paper, but it may be incorporated in the language of the instrument itself. For example, a *handwritten* negotiable note may recite that "I, Jay Rhymes, promise to pay $100 to bearer on demand." Here Rhymes is clearly identified as the maker who engages or undertakes to pay. Unless clearly identified as a maker, drawer, or acceptor, the person who signs will be treated as a secondary party indorser.[52]

The signature may consist of any mark, stamp, or symbol adopted by a party with a present intention to authenticate the writing.[53] It could be an X mark, for example, if it is the genuine intention of the signer to use such a symbol for this purpose.

Marks and symbols present practical problems. All X marks are basically alike, whereas a signature is a highly individualized symbol associated and identified with only one person. A payee of a note or draft may be quite satisfied upon witnessing Wayne Mondy, as maker or drawer, authenticate an instrument

Signed.

---

[51] UCC 3–104(1).   [52] UCC 3–402.   [53] UCC 1–201(39).

with an X. However, if the payee attempts to negotiate such an instrument to a third party, particularly one who was not present at the original transaction, that party may decline to pay out hard-earned cash for an instrument signed with an X.[54] If you were the third party, would you have any reluctance?

Signature by Authorized Agent or Representative. A person's signature may be placed on the instrument by an authorized agent in a manner that obligates only his principal. If it is the intention of an agent operating within the scope of his authority to obligate the principal alone, he should do one of the following:

1. Sign the name of the principal, but not his own name.
2. Disclose the principal and clearly show that he is signing in a representative capacity.[55]

For example, if Lane Feazel is the authorized agent of World Services, Inc., he can obligate *only* his employer by signing in these examples:

1. "World Services, Inc."
2. "World Services, Inc., by Lane Feazel, Secretary-Treasurer," or "Lane Feazel, Secretary-Treasurer for World Services, Inc."[56]

One can feel confident that personal liability is avoided by following alternative 1 above because a *person can not be held liable on the instrument unless his signature appears on it.*[57]

If a signature appears, even though it may be forged or unauthorized, the actual signer is personally liable. Forgers and unauthorized signers are, thus, personally liable even though their *real* signatures do not appear at all;[58] the improper signature becomes that of the person who wrongfully signed. For example, if the payee is Jones, and Smith forged Jones' signature as indorser, Smith is now liable as an indorser.

If the authorized agent follows alternative 2 above, he can obligate his principal only by disclosing the name of the principal before or after the name and office of the agent. When an agent puts his own name on an instrument, he simply invites problems upon himself unless he both (a) discloses the principal and (b) clearly shows his representative capacity. In the event he does only one of these things, the agent may prove his representative capacity by parol evidence if he is being sued by an "immediate party"—e.g., a payee.[59]

No such opportunity for defense will be available against one who is not an immediate party. The reason for this rule is that these parties, who were not present at the original transaction, are entitled to assume that there are two parties liable on the instrument—the principal, and the agent who did not take appropriate steps to show that he is operating in a representative capacity.

---

[54] Some states require that a person who is capable of signing place his or her signature on the instrument as a witness.

[55] UCC 3–403(2)(b).

[56] UCC 3–403(3).

[57] UCC 3–401(1).

[58] UCC 3–404(1).

[59] UCC 3–403(2)(b).

As a practical matter, it makes a great deal of sense to take precautionary measures that can avoid a lawsuit in the first place. Even those suits that are eventually won expend a great deal of time, money, and anxiety in the process.

The Promise or Order

The Promise. The promise contained on the face of a note to pay money simply discloses an intention to be bound or an engagement to pay. Synonyms such as "undertake" or "obligate" or "engage" would do just as well,[60] but when important sums of money are in the balance, why invite litigation by using such unusual terms?

The promise.

Since most of the instruments that you will be called upon to sign are printed forms anyway, this does not present much of a problem. The word "promise" is typically used, and there is no necessity to discuss the matter.

Remember, however, that a mere acknowledgment of a sum due or payable in the future—"IOU $100, [signed] John Bonhomme"—while legal, enforceable, and assignable under the law of contracts, is not a sufficient promise under the Code and can not be a negotiable instrument.

The Order. An order is an instruction or direction to pay, issued by the drawer to the drawee.[61] For example, in every check the drawer orders the drawee bank to pay money. The drawer is entitled to do this because the relationship between the depositor and the drawee bank is creditor/debtor. The drawee is the drawer's debtor to the extent of the drawer's checking account balance. The contractual arrangement was agreed to when the drawer-depositor first opened that checking account.

The order.

The instruction, direction, or order must be more than a mere request or authorization. In other words, it must leave nothing to the discretion of the drawee. For example, on a check the first word addressed to the drawee bank is "Pay." The drawee must be identified with reasonable certainty, and may be addressed with words of courtesy, e.g., "Please pay." The instrument in the following case was not payable to order or to bearer and, therefore, the holder could not be an HIDC.

Facts

Plaintiff, a law partnership, claims to be an HIDC of a negotiable instrument in the form of a letter given to it by a former client. The letter read in part as follows: "I agree to pay to your firm as attorney's fees for representing me in obtaining property settlement (and other matters), the sum of $2,760 (payable in installments). [signed] Barbara Hall Hodge." The defendant responded with defenses that are effective against plaintiff unless (a) the instrument is negotiable and (b) the plaintiff is an HIDC.

Decision

Judgment for defendant.

---

[60] UCC 3–104, comment 5.

[61] UCC 3–102(1)(b).

Reasoning

"One of the requirements of a negotiable instrument is that it contain the time honored 'words of negotiability,' such as pay to the order of or pay to bearer. This was inherent in our law prior to the enactment of the Commercial Code. . . . The Commercial Code continues this practice by now stating: 'Any writing to be a negotiable instrument within this Article must . . . be payable to order or to bearer.' 3-104(1)(d). . . . In the absence of such language, [the letter] would not be a negotiable instrument. . . .

"Furthermore, even a holder in due course takes the instrument free of all defenses *only* 'of any party to the instrument with whom the holder has not dealt.' 3-305(2). . . . Here, the plaintiffs failed to show they occupied the status of a holder in due course, or to establish they were not a party with whom the defendant dealt in this transaction."

Hall v. Westmoreland, Hall & Bryan, 182 S.E.2d 539 (Ga. 1971).

The promise or order must be unconditional.

Unconditional. The promise or order must be absolute, unconditional, iron-clad. It must be a general and unreserved commitment on the maker's or drawer's resources—no condition, escape clauses, or cop-outs.

Anything less than a full and total dedication of the maker's or drawer's financial strength would destroy the instrument's unique capacity to function as a substitute for money or as a credit device. It is obvious that potential purchasers of commercial paper would be less willing to spend their money on instruments that are hedged with excuses and alibis than on instruments that are not so limited.

Only *express* conditions destroy negotiability. Implied conditions do not.[62] Nor is negotiability affected by the mere mention of, or reference to, the underlying consideration which supports the original contract.[63]

For example, "I promise to pay $1,000 to the order of J. T. Bain on demand, subject to his faithful performance of Contract #61382. [signed] Merrill Goodwyn." The express condition, "subject to his faithful performance of Contract #61382," makes the promise conditional and destroys negotiability.

One must be able to determine *from the face of the instrument* whether the commitment to pay is absolute and unconditional.[64] The above promise does not measure up to the standard of negotiability because the maker is entitled to avoid payment if the contract is not performed, and whether or not performance has occurred *cannot be determined from the face of the instrument*. The fact that Bain may have actually performed the contract does not make the instrument negotiable because that fact *can not be determined by examining the instrument*.

---

[62] UCC 3–105(1)(a).

[63] UCC 3–105(1)(b)(c).

[64] If an instrument states that it is void if drawn for more than a particular amount or void if presented for payment after a particular date, negotiability is *not* destroyed because that condition can be determined from the face of the instrument.

Consider, however, a modification of the above note which simply mentioned that it was given in return for, or in consideration of, or in reference to, Contract #61382. One might say there was an implied condition that the maker not be liable contractually if Bain failed to perform, but this does not destroy negotiability.

If Bain does not perform the underlying transaction referred to, that is a matter to be taken up *outside* the scope of the negotiable instrument. The maker or drawer is absolutely committed *on the instrument* despite the implied condition that the payee may not perform and the maker or drawer may later have to sue the payee for breach of contract. In the following case the court held that an instrument was negotiable even though it referred to the transaction which gave rise to the instrument.

Facts

Defendant, Wellbanke, was being sued by Federal Factors, plaintiff, on grounds that the defendant had accepted a trade acceptance but failed to pay it at maturity. The defendant bought goods from Chemical Products, the drawer-payee of the draft and, following the defendant-drawee's signature or acceptance of the trade acceptance, Chemical Products indorsed and transferred the instrument to the plaintiff, Federal Factors. Wellbanke contends that he has a valid "breach of contract" defense against Federal Factors because of a sentence in the draft that made it non-negotiable: "The transaction which gives rise to this instrument is the purchase of goods by the acceptor from the drawer."

Decision

Judgment for plaintiff, Federal Factors.

Reasoning

Mere reference to the contract or underlying transaction for which the draft was given does not affect negotiability of the instrument. Only express conditions, not implied ones, destroy negotiability. Since Federal Factors is a holder of the instrument, and since it was purchased for value, in good faith, and without notice of claim or defense to the trade acceptance, it is an HIDC and is entitled to a judgment against Wellbanke despite the payee's breach of contract.

Federal Factors, Inc. v. Wellbanke, 406 S.W.2d 712 (Ark. 1966).

A statement in an instrument that it is secured—by a mortgage or in some other way—does not destroy negotiability.[65] This operates to the creditor-holder's benefit and simply adds to the salability or marketability of the instrument.

If, for purposes of bookkeeping convenience, the instrument mentions a particular fund to be debited or charged, negotiability is not affected.[66] This rule favoring negotiability holds true for commercial paper that is limited to a particular fund backed by a governmental unit or limited to payment from the entire assets of a partnership, unincorporated association, trust, or estate.[67] It is assumed that instruments issued by these entities will carry sufficient assurance of payment to encourage their acceptability.

---

[65] UCC 3–105(e).   [66] UCC 3–105(f).   [67] UCC 3–105(h).

Keep in mind that instruments *expressly* made *subject* to, or *governed* by, some other agreement—e.g., subject to Contract #61382—are not negotiable. Neither are instruments that are strictly limited to payment out of a particular fund.[68]

To illustrate: if Jack Sorenson limits or restricts payment of his note to "the proceeds from next year's corn crop," the instrument would be non-negotiable. His general credit is not committed to payment, and no one can tell from examining the *face* of the note whether "next year's corn crop" will even be planted, much less whether it will be sufficient to pay the note.

A governmental unit can limit its obligation to payment out of a particular fund without affecting negotiability because it is assumed that tax revenues will always be sufficient. A similar exception is made in favor of instruments by partnerships, unincorporated associations, trusts, and estates when all their assets are committed.

Sum Certain in Money

The sum certain.

Sum Certain. The reason for this requirement is obvious. Every potential purchaser will insist on knowing how much money will be received at maturity. No serious buyer or investor wants to play guessing games on the amount of money involved.

As a general rule, the sum is sufficiently certain if, *at the time of payment,* it can be computed from the information that appears on the face of the instrument.[69] This means that the sum certain is *unaffected* by:

1. payment with interest or in installments;
2. payment with interest at different rates before and after default;
3. payment with a discount before a fixed date or with an addition afterward;
4. payment with (or less) foreign exchange rates to protect the constant value of an instrument;
5. payment with collection or attorney's fees in the event of default in payment.[70]

Keep in mind that the crucial time is the *time of payment,* and the computations must be made from what appears on the *face* of the instrument. It can not be known at the time of issuance whether there will be a default, whether payment will be accelerated, or whether an attorney or collection agency will be needed, but these facts will be available at the time of payment.

An instrument with interest payable at the *legal rate or judgment rate, as fixed by state law,* is negotiable even though the actual rate of interest is not specified. An interest term which calls for application of the *bank rate or current rate,* however, does not satisfy the requirement of sum *certain.*

---

[68] UCC 3–105(2).   [70] UCC 3–106(1).

[69] UCC 3–106, comment 1.

Money.   Money means a medium of exchange authorized or adopted by any government as part of its currency.[71] The medium of exchange must qualify as money *at the time the instrument is issued.* The reason for this, of course, is to give assurance to a potential purchaser right from the start that the instrument will be paid in the currency of a recognized government.

Keep in mind that for *certainty of sum,* the important time is the *maturity date.* For the purpose of *qualifying as money,* however, the important time is *when the instrument is issued.*

Note here as well that negotiable instruments are not the equivalent of money, and that a person can not compel another to take commercial paper in payment of debts. Generally speaking, negotiable instruments are *conditional payment* contingent upon being honored at maturity. The *obligation* on the basis of which the instrument was given is suspended pending payment of the instrument on the due date. If not paid when due, then suit may be based on the *instrument* or on the *obligation* for which the instrument was given.[72]

Unless the instrument requires otherwise, a promise or order to pay in foreign currency may be satisfied by payment at maturity of the *dollar* amount that the foreign currency will buy at the exchange rate. For example, an instrument payable in Belgian *francs,* Japanese *yen,* or Chilean *pesos* may be satisfied with the number of U.S. dollars that the foreign currency could buy at current exchange rates. If the instrument *requires* payment in the foreign currency, an attempt to discharge one's obligation in U.S. dollars will not be sufficient.[73]

No other promise or order *except payment of money* is sufficient to establish negotiability. Promises or orders of payment in seal skins, wampum, or gold dust destroy negotiability because they are not money; the money value is not readily apparent on the *face* of the paper. Certain other promises are permitted, without affecting negotiability, because of one thing in common—they promote acceptability and marketability of the paper.

As an example, some instruments include a term that allows the holder or creditor to **confess judgment** against the debtor when an instrument is not paid at maturity.[74] This strengthens the creditor's position by expediting enforcement of the paper upon default. The creditor can get a judgment on the unpaid instrument without giving notice of the proceedings to the debtor. Whether or not a confession of judgment is illegal has no effect on the *negotiability* of the instrument.

confession of judgment
a party's consent to jurisdiction and judgment of a court without a trial in a civil case

Promises that give collateral security to an instrument, promises to protect or increase collateral should it decline in value, and promises that relinquish the benefit of debtor protection laws—all add to the advantage of the holder.[75] Since they encourage and promote the flow of negotiable paper rather than impede it, the law permits these extra promises to be made.

---

[71] UCC 3–107(1).

[72] UCC 3–802(1)(b).

[73] UCC 3–107(2).

[74] UCC 3–112(d). A note with such a term is called a "cognovit note."

[75] UCC 3–112(b)(c)(e).

Time of Payment

If a prospective user of a negotiable instrument can not tell from the face of the paper when it is due, this naturally will diminish its acceptability. To encourage a ready and open market for commercial paper then, a negotiable instrument must be made payable *on demand* or *at a definite time*.

On Demand. An instrument is payable on demand if it expressly states that it is payable on demand, if it calls for payment at sight or presentation, or if no time for payment is stated.[76]

A check falls into the last category—no time for payment is stated. It normally contains the date of issue but no maturity date. It is the absence of a maturity date that makes it payable on demand.

From the point of view of the *maker or drawer* of an instrument, the time of payment is not certain, but that is not the controlling factor. The *prospective buyer* or holder is the one that the law wants to encourage, and it seeks to do that by allowing him to collect on demand. It was held in the following case that blank spaces for installment payments on a note did not cause the note to be non-negotiable for failure to state a definite time when it was payable; it was payable on demand.

Facts

Defendant, Zimmerman, was being sued on a note that he admittedly executed in the face amount of $9,747. The blank spaces in the note which would normally be filled in with the amount of each monthly installment were left vacant. A question then arose whether the instrument was payable at a definite time. The only date on the note was not a maturity date, but the date of issue. Defendant claimed the note was not negotiable.

Decision

Judgment for plaintiff.

Reasoning

The note is not rendered defective because the blanks for alleged installment payments appear unused. On its face the note designates a principal sum of $9,747. The failure to fill in the monthly installment blanks does not indicate that no principal sum was intended. The UCC provides in 3–108, "Instruments payable on demand include those payable at sight or on presentation and those in which no time for payment is stated." Under this section, the note in question is a demand note, due and payable immediately.

Master Homecraft Company v. Zimmerman, 222 A.2d 440 (Pa. 1966).

Definite Time. The common link among each of the following requirements for definite time is *the face of the paper*. Time of payment is definite if it can be determined from the terms appearing on the instrument itself.

The requirement of definite time is met if the instrument is payable on a fixed date, before a fixed date (frequently these are combined as "on or before

---

[76] UCC 3–108.

31 December 1999," for example), or a fixed period after a fixed date (one year from the date of the instrument).[77] A term which recites that the paper is payable "on or before the expiration of one year from the date of issue" sets a maximum length of time but allows the *maker or drawer* to make payment before the end of a full year and thereby save money on interest.

The requirement for certainty of time is also satisfied if the instrument is payable "a fixed period after sight" or "a fixed period after acceptance."[78] This can be very useful in a sales transaction that allows an extended credit period to the buyer—i.e., the drawee on a trade acceptance drawn by the seller. The draft will be presented to the buyer-drawee by the seller or the seller's agent; if the buyer properly "accepts" the instrument by signing it and returning it to the seller, the goods will be delivered to him. The seller keeps possession of the negotiable instrument, then, when the fixed period after sight or acceptance expires, presents the instrument to the buyer for payment.

If maturity of an instrument is made to depend on an act or event uncertain as to time of occurrence, the time requirement is not satisfied even though the event has later occurred.[79] Examples are: promises to pay when a person attains a stated age, when a certain building is built, or on the death or marriage of a certain person. The standard, once more, is the *face* of the paper. If time is not certain on the face of the instrument, then time is not certain for purposes of negotiability.

Acceleration Clauses. The Code approves of a definite time subject to *any acceleration.*[80] Normally the holder of an instrument is given the option of accelerating time of payment if the debtor defaults on an installment. The reason behind this rule is that the debtor "brings it upon himself" by not living up to his agreement and this is a reasonable way of assuring the creditor that he can take appropriate action now to protect himself.

Acceleration clauses.

Other acceleration clauses allow the *holder* to declare the full amount to be due and payable at any time he in good faith deems himself to be insecure.[81] This term is not particularly advantageous to the debtor, but he may not be given any choice in the matter—take it or leave it, the creditor tells him. For purposes of negotiability, such acceleration clauses do not destroy certainty of time.

Extension Clauses. Clauses which give the debtor an additional period of time for payment are extension clauses and are just the opposite of acceleration clauses. They are permitted on the following terms:

Extension clauses.

1. At the option of the *holder* (this simply means that the creditor-holder can give the debtor more time to pay if he so chooses).
2. At the option of the *maker or acceptor* to a further definite time (except for this limitation, enforceability of the paper could be frustrated indefinitely).
3. Automatically upon the happening of a specified event (e.g., "maturity shall be extended by one year, if crop yields fall below eighty bushels per acre").[82]

---

[77] UCC 3–109(1)(a).   [79] UCC 3–109(2).   [81] UCC 1–208.

[78] UCC 3–109(1)(b).   [80] UCC 3–109(c).   [82] UCC 3–109(1)(d).

The Words of Negotiability: To Order or To Bearer

Unless an instrument contains one of the "magic words" of negotiability— "to *order* of," "to *bearer*," or the equivalent—it is not negotiable and can be transferred only by assignment. "Pay to the order of A" is different from "Pay to A," the latter phrase causing the instrument to be non-negotiable.

To Bearer. An instrument is payable to *bearer* when the terms specify "bearer," or "the order of bearer."[83] The latter phrase, "the order of bearer," normally occurs on a form that is printed to read "Pay to the order of _____," and the word "bearer" is inserted in the blank space. Until the space is filled in, the paper is incomplete in a necessary respect and, therefore, is non-negotiable and unenforceable.[84]

The instrument is payable to bearer if the paper reads "Pay to Cash," or "Pay to the order of Cash," or any other word besides "cash" that does not designate a payee capable of making a signature.[85] An instrument which reads "Pay to the order of One Keg of Beer" or "Pay to Two Crates of Pop" shows that the maker or drawer is not interested in having a "payee" indorse! If the "payee" or the object designated instead of a payee is not capable of indorsing, then the instrument becomes payable to bearer.

Another illustration of bearer paper is one which names "a specified person or bearer" as payee.[86] The bearer provision takes precedence, and it is a bearer instrument; e.g., "Pay to the order of John Jones or bearer."

When an instrument is *order* paper either on its face, or because of a special indorsement, e.g., "Pay to A, [signed] Payee," a subsequent blank indorsement, which consists only of the signature of the indorser, e.g., "A," changes the instrument to bearer paper.[87]

To order.

To Order. An instrument meets this requirement when it is payable to the order, or to the assigns, of *any person reasonably identified,* or to him or his order.[88] For example, "Pay to the order of A," or "Pay to A or his order." This indicates that the maker of the note or drawer of the draft intends that the payee be able to negotiate the instrument to some other party. An instrument on its face reading "Pay to Lee Young" is non-negotiable; the words "order of" or "bearer" are missing.

On all *drafts,* the drawer first *orders* the drawee to pay money. To take the process a second step, the drawee may be ordered to pay not merely to Rich Soland alone, but "to the order of Rich Soland"—i.e., to the named payee Rich Soland or to whomever the payee may indicate in his indorsement.

If Rich Soland to whom the instrument flows indorses in blank with only his name, then the drawee will be directed to pay the bearer, i.e., the holder, of the instrument. If he indorses specially, "Pay to Fran Zappa, [signed] Rich Soland," the drawee will be directed to pay the named indorsee.

---

[83] UCC 3–111(a). [86] UCC 3–111(b).

[84] UCC 3–805. [87] UCC 3–204(2).

[85] UCC 3–111(c). [88] UCC 3–110(1).

Instruments may be made payable to the order of the following payees:

1. The maker or drawer; e.g., the seller who is the drawer of a trade acceptance may name himself as payee, or the drawer of a check may name himself as payee.
2. The drawee; e.g., the drawer of a check in paying a debt that he owes to the drawee bank will name the drawee bank as payee.
3. A payee who is not a maker, drawer, or drawee (this covers the great majority of transactions).
4. Two or more payees *jointly*—e.g., A *and* B—or two or more payees in the *alternative*—e.g., A *or* B.
5. An estate, trust, or fund (in this event, the instrument is payable to the order of the representative—e.g., a check payable to the order of United Fund would be treated as payable to the order of its authorized agent, perhaps the treasurer, who would indorse on behalf of the fund).
6. An office or officer by his title, in which event it is payable to the incumbent officer or his successor; e.g., Travis County Tax Collector.
7. A partnership or unincorporated association.[89]

An instrument made payable both to order *and* to bearer is payable to order unless the "bearer" word is handwritten or typewritten. The reason for this is that on a printed form, "Pay to the order of _____ or bearer," the word "bearer" is likely to be overlooked when the name of a payee is inserted. To avoid an unintended result, the paper will be bearer paper only if the drawer or maker has shown that that is the desired objective by writing in the word "bearer."[90]

Summary Statement

1. Negotiable instruments are either notes or drafts. Notes are two-party instruments in which a maker-primary party promises to pay money to a payee. Drafts are three-party instruments in which the one who creates it, the drawer, orders the drawee to pay money to a payee.
2. A certificate of deposit is a special kind of note in which a bank borrows money from a customer, acknowledges receipt of it, and promises to repay. This is a reversal of the norm because usually the customer is borrowing from the bank.
3. A check is a special kind of draft which is drawn on a bank and payable on demand.
4. Frequently you come across a trade acceptance and banker's acceptance in the financing of sales transactions. These are simply drafts drawn by the seller on the drawee, who is either the buyer or the buyer's bank, payable to the order of a payee. These drafts usually give the buyer some time or credit period in which to pay. Typically, the buyer or the buyer's bank will accept by signing the draft and returning it to the seller; the goods which

---

[89] UCC 3–110(1).   [90] UCC 3–110(3).

are being sold on credit will be turned over to the buyer at that point, and at the end of the credit period the instrument will be presented to the acceptor for payment.

5. Notice that the drawee becomes a primary party when the drawee accepts the instrument by signing it. A check will have the drawee bank as a primary party only if the bank certifies the check.

6. Primary parties are makers of negotiable notes and acceptors of drafts. As a general rule, everyone else who signs an instrument is a secondary party.

7. Watch out for accommodation parties, however! An accommodation party may be an accommodation maker or an accommodation acceptor, in which event he would be a primary party; or he may be an accommodation drawer or indorser, in which event he would be a secondary party.

8. Primary parties are absolutely liable on the instrument according to its terms. Secondary parties expect to be called upon to pay only if, at maturity, the instrument is properly presented, dishonored, and notice of dishonor is given to the secondary party.

9. Other important parties are the *bearer* (a person in possession of bearer paper) and the *holder* (a person who must be in possession of an instrument that has been drawn, issued, or indorsed to him or her, or who is in possession of bearer paper). HIDCs are holders who have, in addition, given value, in good faith, and without notice of a claim or defense, or that the instrument is overdue or has been dishonored.

10. In the collection process, the banks with which one most frequently comes in contact are depositary banks—the first bank to receive a check and initiate the bank collection process—and the payor-drawee bank. The payor-drawee is the bank at the end of the line. It pays the check if its customer-depositor has sufficient funds on account and has not issued a stop-payment order; otherwise it returns the check by its midnight deadline to avoid being held accountable for it.

11. It is important to remember that any kind of writing will do—pen, pencil, typewriter, or some other form. The signatures can be written by an authorized representative as well as by the person who actually becomes a party on the instrument. It is crucial, however, that the signature, whether it be in the form of an X mark or a written name, actually be intended to validate the paper.

12. The instrument must not have any express conditions to the liability of the person creating it. Otherwise no one is likely to be willing to accept it as a credit device or as a substitute for money. Keep in mind that the holder must be able to determine from the *face* of the instrument that the person who issued it has absolutely committed his general credit to payment at maturity.

13. The money that is designated on the draft or note must be backed up by a recognized government, and the amount must be certain. The reason for this is to assure the prospective purchaser that he is receiving something of value.

14. From the *holder's* point of view, the time of payment must be certain. This requirement can be satisfied by maturity on a fixed date, before that date, a fixed time after a fixed date, a fixed date subject to *any* acceleration, and

a fixed date with *some* extensions of time. It may be a bit confusing that demand instruments satisfy the time requirement, but remember, it is the holder who must be induced to accept these instruments. From that perspective, time is certain, and the person who issued the instrument must simply contend with this feature.

15. Every negotiable instrument must contain the "magic" words of negotiability—"to order," "to bearer," or their equivalents. This permits the payee or the holder to whom the instrument is first issued to negotiate it to some other party. That party may subsequently hold the instrument to maturity or further negotiate it to someone else.

We have read that there is a difference between a formal contract and a simple contract. The following case illustrates an aspect of the basic difference between these two types of contract.

Perry v. West
266 A.2d 849 (N.H. 1970)

Kenison, C. J. The issue in this case is whether a municipality can be compelled to accept a bid [at a tax sale of property] accompanied by a bank draft or cashier's check when the municipal ordinance and the announced terms of the auction sale require the bid to be accompanied by "cash or certified check."

Plaintiff, Perry, submitted the highest bid at an auction sale of certain property within the City of Concord conducted by George M. West, Tax Collector. . . . The city had previously acquired the property by tax sale.

The newspaper advertisements required that all bids be accompanied "by cash or certified check in an amount to at least 10% of the bid price."

Plaintiff's high bid was accompanied by a bank draft of the New Hampshire Savings drawn on the Mechanics National Bank and payable to George West, Tax Collector. The second high bid, submitted by Henry J. Love, was accompanied by a cashier's check of Concord National Bank payable to the City of Concord. The third highest bid was submitted by Pasquale Alosa and accompanied by U.S. currency. Lockwood Realty Co. submitted the fourth highest bid accompanied by its check certified by the Mechanics National Bank.

On the day of the auction, defendant West, on the advice of the City Solicitor, sent a letter to Alosa and to [the plaintiff] Perry advising them that Alosa was the successful bidder.

Perry instituted this action challenging the decision of the City of Concord, and the other bidders were joined as parties to the suit.

The plaintiff contends that the bank draft submitted with its bid was "cash" within the modern usage of the term and therefore his bid complied with the terms of the auction.

Although the meaning of "cash" may vary with the context of its use, the common meaning is U.S. currency. Nothing in the present case indicates that the City Council intended to expand this meaning. Indeed the term "certified check" would be unnecessary if "cash" were to include various forms of commercial paper in addition to currency.

The various commercial instruments involved in this case have definite and distinct meanings. A bank draft is merely the instrument of one bank drawing upon

Introduction to Commercial Paper and Banking Operations

its deposits with another bank. A cashier's check is the instrument of a bank drawing upon its own funds. Certification of a check is acceptance by the drawee.

For this case the important distinction among these instruments is the number of parties liable on the instrument. Bank drafts and cashier's checks are "one-name paper." Only the drawer bank is liable on a bank draft until accepted by the drawee. Although a cashier's check is accepted upon issuance, there is only one bank involved and therefore only one party bound on the instrument. However, both the drawer and drawee are bound on a certified check when the certification is obtained by the drawer.

There are, therefore, accepted and reasonable distinctions among "cash," "certified check," "bank draft," and "cashier's check" upon which the City Council could base its preference for cash or certified check. Within the context of the auction of property sold for taxation, the phrase "cash or certified check" had a definite, unambiguous and accepted commercial meaning.

Pasquale Alosa, the highest bidder who conformed to the terms of the auction, is therefore entitled to the property upon full payment of his bid price.

Questions and Case Problems

1. Defendant, McManus, signed a note of the corporation that employed him. His signature and that of another officer followed the stamped name of the corporation, but there was no designation of a representative capacity. McManus is being sued personally by the payee. Discuss the outcome. Would your answer be the same if McManus were being sued by an HIDC who took the instrument by negotiation from the payee? What if the payee negotiated the note to someone who did not qualify as an HIDC? Could that person get a judgment against McManus? [*Leahy v. McManus*, 206 A.2d 688 (Md. 1965).]

2. Assume that Jessica Savage sees a $100 coat that she wants to purchase at Foxy Fashions. When she opens her personalized check book supplied by her bank, Capital State, she discovers that there are no more blank checks left in the book. Before the sales clerk can object, Jessica simply writes on a piece of scratch paper as in figure 27.9. The sales clerk consults the manager, who refuses to accept Jessica's "check."

Figure 27.9 "Handmade" Instrument

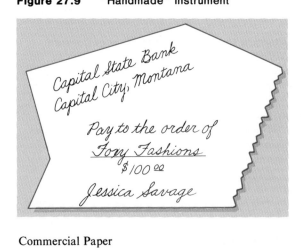

Commercial Paper

a. Is this really a check?

b. Is it negotiable?

c. Is it enforceable—on the assumption that someone will take it—even if it is not negotiable?

d. What is the effect on negotiability of the omission of a date on it?

e. When is the instrument payable?

f. What is the effect on negotiability of Jessica's failure to spell out $100 in words in addition to putting it into figures?

g. If the instrument is negotiable, can Jessica legally compel Foxy to take the instrument in payment for the coat?

h. Is this instrument really a check or a draft?

i. On the assumption that this instrument is negotiable, will Foxy Fashions' indorsement be necessary to negotiate it?

j. Is Capital State properly classified as a depositary, presenting, drawee, or payor bank?

3. A note was drafted in duplicate. The original was signed by the maker and, with the use of carbon paper, the maker's signature was impressed on the duplicate copy. Since the original cannot be found, can the payee enforce the duplicate with a carbon copy of the maker's signature as a negotiable instrument? [*Chrismer v. Chrismer*, 144 N.E.2d 494 (Ohio 1956).]

4. Richard Donohoe sought to collect on the instrument illustrated in figure 27.10 from the estate of Cecelia W. Donohoe.

a. Is this instrument negotiable?

b. Is Richard Donohoe entitled to a judgment against the estate?

c. Would your answer be the same if the note did not include the word "order"? [In re *Donohoe's Estate*, 115 A. 878 (Pa. 1922).]

5. Defendant, Samuel Feinberg, signed a promissory note personally and as the representative of Sain Builders, Inc., which is now involved in bankruptcy proceedings. Feinberg argues that the phrase "as per contract" contained in the note destroys the requirement of an unconditional promise and that the plaintiff-indorsee, D'Andrea, is not an HIDC because he must have been aware

---

Figure 27.10 Instrument

$13070.86   August 30th, 1910

I, *Cecelia W. Donohoe*, after date, August 30, promise to pay to the order of *Richard Donohoe*, *Thirteen thousand and seventy & 86/100* ——— dollars.

Witness my hand and seal.

Hester Johnson
HESTER JOHNSON (seal)
Notary Public

Introduction to Commercial Paper and Banking Operations   521

of the underlying contract between Sain Builders and payee. Judgment for whom and why? [*D'Andrea v. Feinberg*, 45 Misc.2d 270 (N.Y. 1965).]

6. An instrument in all other respects negotiable related in part as follows: "It is agreed that this note is to be paid in Elks Club #8 Second Mortgage real estate bonds." Does this sentence render the entire note non-negotiable? Why or why not? [*Moore v. Clines*, 57 S.W.2d 509 (Ky. 1932).]

7. A note provides that it is payable in sixty days, or sooner if certain property is sold. Is the note negotiable or does this acceleration provision destroy certainty of time? [*Fox v. Morris*, 496 P.2d 158 (Nev. 1972).]

8. A note with a definite maturity date provided that the holder could accelerate payment at any time he felt insecure. When the holder accelerated on the basis of this term, the maker of the note defended on grounds that there was no reason for the holder to feel insecure. Result?

9. Defendant, South Sea Apartments, Inc., issued a note to the order of payee in return for services that were to be performed by payee in the future. At the time payee negotiated the note to plaintiff it was not disputed that plaintiff knew of this agreement. Since the agreement was later breached by payee, defendant refuses to pay at maturity and claims that the plaintiff's knowledge of the agreement imports a condition which destroys negotiability of the note. In the alternative, defendant asserts that plaintiff's knowledge of the agreement either destroys its good faith or puts it on notice of a defense, and as a result plaintiff is a mere holder, not an HIDC. Evaluate these defenses. [*Gordon Supply Co. v. South Sea Apts., Inc.*, 257 N.Y.Supp.2d 237 (1965).]

10. In *Perry v. West*, 266 A.2d 849 (N.H. 1970),[91] the court held that the attempted acceptance of an offer, which looked to the formation of a unilateral contract, by the tender of a bank draft or a cashier's check would not create the simple contract when the terms of the offer required cash or a certified check. When can commercial paper act as a substitute for cash? What does this tell us about the relationship between a simple contract and a formal contract?

---

[91] See pp. 519–20.

Transfer and Negotiation

28

After you have read this chapter, you should be able to:

1. Speak confidently of the meaning and importance of "negotiation."
2. Be familiar with the methods of negotiating a negotiable instrument.
3. Recognize the types of indorsements, their common features, and the legal consequences of each.
4. Illustrate the "shelter provision" and its exceptions.
5. Explain the legal effect of reacquisition of an instrument by a prior owner.
6. Understand the importance of warranty liability and its relationship to indorsement liability.
7. Determine the legal effect of forged instruments, forged indorsements, and the signatures of impostors.
8. Discover when payment of an instrument is "final."

Introduction

We noted in chapter 27, Introduction to Commercial Paper and Banking Operations, that a negotiable instrument, which is a type of formal contract, has the potential of conferring upon another "greater rights" than could be obtained under a simple contract by assignment. This chapter is important because it tells you *how* these greater rights become vested in another. It is not enough to know that these greater rights exist. If *you* are to derive the benefits or avoid the burdens associated with commercial paper, you must know how to use the law of commercial paper effectively.

Negotiation

negotiation
the delivery of
negotiable paper to a
person who thereby
becomes a holder

At the outset of this inquiry it is important to fix firmly in mind that "order" paper requires an indorsement and delivery for a **negotiation.**[1] However, no indorsement is necessary for the negotiation of "bearer" paper it can be negotiated by delivery alone.[2]

Order and Bearer Paper

Identification of Order Paper
An instrument can be identified as order paper:

1. if it names a payee that is capable of indorsing—e.g., "Pay to the order of Greenery USA"[3]—or
2. if the last or only indorsement is a special indorsement (one that names an indorsee)—e.g., "Pay to Ruston State Bank, [signed] Charles Ogden."[4]

In each of these illustrations the named party, *Greenery USA* or *Ruston State Bank,* must indorse and deliver the instrument be fore it can be further negotiated by the holder.

Identification of Bearer Paper
Bearer paper expressly states that it is payable to bearer, to the order of bearer, or it names no payee that is capable of making an endorsement, e.g., "Pay to *Bearer,*" "Pay to the order of *Bearer,*" or "Pay to the order of *Cash.*"[5] Order paper may even be converted into bearer paper if the last or only indorsement is in blank (blank indorsements consist of the signature of the indorser only; no indorsee is named).[6]

While the holder of bearer paper can legally negotiate it without further indorsement, people who are willing to receive negotiable paper normally require

---

[1] UCC 3–204(1).   [4] UCC 3–204(1).

[2] UCC 3–204(2).   [5] UCC 3–111(2)(6).

[3] UCC 3–110.   [6] UCC 3–111(c), 204(2).

Figure 28.1   Check

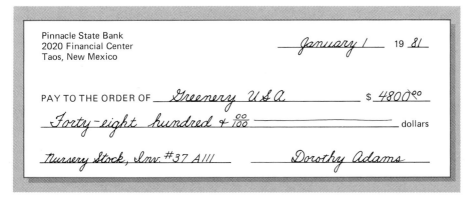

```
Pinnacle State Bank                    January 1      19 81
2020 Financial Center
Taos, New Mexico


PAY TO THE ORDER OF    Greenery USA              $ 4800⁰⁰

Forty-eight hundred & ⁰⁰/₁₀₀ ——————————————— dollars


Nursery Stock, Inv. #37 A///        Dorothy Adams
```

an indorsement. This will facilitate recovery against the indorser on the instrument in the event of later dishonor of the instrument. Also, a person who negotiates without an indorsement makes certain transfer warranties, but only to the *immediate recipient*. If the recipient indorses and transfers the instrument, he then incurs indorsement liability as well as warranty liability.[7]

Order and Bearer Paper in Action

To put this in a realistic focus, assume that Dorothy Adams, owner of a landscape firm, purchases a selection of plants from *Greenery USA*. By way of payment, she draws and issues a $4,800 check on her drawee bank, Pinnacle State, payable to the order of Greenery, the payee-supplier (figure 28.1).

Greenery may either deposit the check for credit in its account, use the check to pay off its trade creditors, or discharge an obligation on a loan. The possibilities are far too numerous to pursue, but, for purposes of illustration, suppose that an authorized representative of Greenery indorses it "Without Recourse, Greenery USA, by Jack Ingram, President" and donates it to United Fund. "Without recourse" is discussed later; briefly, it means that the indorser will not be liable as an indorser if the instrument is not paid when due.

In all likelihood United Fund will indorse the check for deposit in its bank—e.g., "For deposit, Pay to Ruston State Bank, [signed] United Fund, by Tamila Jackson, V.P." (figure 28.2)—and the bank will then forward the check through collection channels to Pinnacle State. If funds are sufficient and no stop-payment order has been issued by Dorothy Adams, the check will be paid by the drawee-payor bank, Pinnacle State Bank.

---

[7] UCC 3–417(2).

Figure 28.2 Indorsements on Check

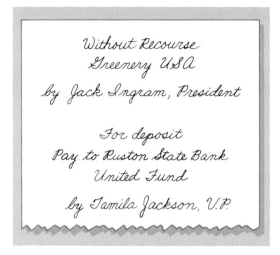

Without Recourse
Greenery USA
by Jack Ingram, President

For deposit
Pay to Ruston State Bank
United Fund

by Tamila Jackson, V.P.

Indorsements

All Indorsements are Multifaceted

Dorothy Adams' first delivery ("issue")[8] of her check to Greenery makes it a holder.[9] A close look at the indorsements placed on the instrument by Greenery and United Fund will be helpful in illustrating certain elements that are common to all indorsements.

All indorsements, from the simplest to the most complex, are hybrid in nature and may be analyzed on the following basis:

1. blank or special—determines the method to be used in subsequent negotiations;
2. restrictive or nonrestrictive—determines the type of interest being transferred;
3. qualified or unqualified—determines the liability of the indorser.

Blank Indorsement

blank indorsement
an indorsement which does not specify any particular indorsee

A **blank indorsement** consists simply of the indorser's signature.[10] For example, in figure 28.3 the payee's signature, Greenery USA, appears on the instrument without naming an indorsee.

Since a business firm can act only through its agents, the fact that Greenery's signature was placed there by Jack Ingram does not change things in the least. Nor, for that matter, does the qualifying phrase "Without Recourse" (see the discussion below on qualified indorsements).

The instrument is now bearer paper because the last or only indorsement is in blank. United Fund can negotiate it by delivery alone. Since a bearer instrument which is lost or stolen may get into the hands of an HIDC, a cautious party

---

[8] UCC 3–102(1)(2).   [9] UCC 1–201(20).   [10] UCC 3–240(2).

Figure 28.3 Blank (and Qualified) Indorsement

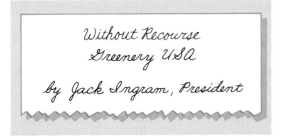

Without Recourse
Greenery USA

by Jack Ingram, President

Figure 28.4 Special (and Restrictive) Indorsement

For Deposit
Pay to Ruston State Bank

United Fund

by Tamila Jackson, V.P.

will be well advised to write above the signature of Greenery "any contract consistent with the character of the indorsement."[11]

To illustrate, United Fund may write above Greenery's blank signature "Pay to United Fund." This converts Greenery's blank indorsement into a "special" one because it now names a special indorsee. If the instrument then is lost or stolen, it can never get into the hands of an HIDC because nobody can be a holder without the indorsee's indorsement. The instrument can not *flow* to anyone as a holder without such indorsement.

No title or ownership can be transferred by a forgery of a required indorsement. While C, an innocent party, may purchase an instrument in good faith and without notice of a forgery of a required indorsement, C can not be an HIDC because he is not, first, a holder. To qualify as a holder, C would have to be in possession of an instrument *indorsed* to him or in blank—that means a genuine indorsement, not a forgery. (P is the payee of a check. T stole it, forged P's blank indorsement, and delivered it to you. Although you possess the check, ownership can not flow to you without P's indorsement.)

Usually an indorsement (or other signature) by a mark—e.g., "X"—must be witnessed by two or more people and signed by them as witnesses.

Special Indorsement

A **special indorsement** names the indorsee.[12] For example, when United Fund indorsed "Pay to Ruston State Bank," it named the bank an indorsee and, therefore, the indorsement is special (figure 28.4). A special indorsement need not use the word "order"; it will be implied.[13]

The fact that the "For Deposit" language limits or restricts the use of the instrument has no bearing on the issue of special versus blank indorsements. Nor is it relevant to special or blank indorsements that the signature was made by an agent, Tamila Jackson, Vice President.

Before the instrument can be further negotiated, the special indorsee must indorse. If joint payees or indorsees are named ("A and B"), both must indorse; if payees or indorsees are named in the alternative ("A or B"), either may indorse.[14]

special indorsement
an indorsement which specifies a particular indorsee

---

[11] UCC 3–204(3).   [12] UCC 3–204(1).   [13] UCC 3–204(1).   [14] UCC 3–116.

Blank and Special Indorsements: A Summary

All indorsements are either blank or special. If an indorsement consists of the indorser's name without designating an indorsee, it is a blank indorsement.

Do not be in the least bit surprised to find that the blank or special characteristics of an indorsement exist alongside the restrictive/nonrestrictive and qualified/unqualified elements of the same indorsement. An analysis of any indorsement will reveal each of these components, which will now be discussed.

Restrictive Indorsement

Keep in mind that a **restrictive indorsement** determines the type of interest being transferred. It will either *condition* the indorser's liability on the instrument (transfer a conditional interest) or *regulate* the things that the recipient, who may be an agent or trustee, can do with the instrument (transfer a limited interest).[15]

Restrictive Indorsements That Impose Conditions. It is important to point out that *no* indorsement destroys the negotiable character of a negotiable instrument. While the original promise or order on the *face* of a negotiable instrument must be absolute and unconditional, an indorser may make his indorsement contract depend on the performance of an express condition.[16] The right to impose a condition makes the instrument more adaptable to the indorser's needs. For example, the payee may indorse "Pay to Del Wells upon performance of contract #61387, [signed] David Reitzel."

Notice that the indorsement is special as well as restrictive, so Del Wells must indorse before the instrument can be further negotiated. The fact that the indorsement is both special and restrictive simply reenforces the earlier observation that all indorsements are hybrid in nature. All parties including depositary banks (but not intermediary or drawee-payor banks)[17] must recognize the existence of the condition.

In order to become an HIDC, the person who receives such an instrument must pay in accordance with its terms.[18] In other words, you could not become a holder *for value*—one of the requirements of an HIDC—if you do not pay consistent with this indorsement.

An exception was noted above for nondepositary intermediary and drawee-payor banks.[19] These banks simply handle too many thousands of checks daily in the clearing-house or collection process to be responsible for this type of indorsement. They must, however, obey the terms of the indorsement of the bank that forwarded the item for collection.

To make certain that payment at maturity discharges the person who pays from further liability on the instrument, the condition must be obeyed. If the instrument that the payee, Reitzel, indorsed restrictively to Wells was a $1,000

---

[15] UCC 3–205. [17] UCC 3–206(2), 4–205(2). [18] UCC 3–206(3).

[16] UCC 3–205. See pp. 505–6 for definitions of these banks. [19] UCC 3–206(2), 4–205(2), 4–105(a)(c).

note that you had issued, you could discharge your liability on the instrument only by paying the holder, Wells, in a manner "consistent with the terms of such restrictive indorsement."[20]

This restrictive indorsement should be a warning signal to you, the maker-primary party. If you expect to be fully discharged by your payment to Wells, you should inquire of the payee, Reitzel, to determine whether contract #61387 has been performed. If it has not been performed, payment should be withheld. Otherwise you may be compelled by the payee, Reitzel, to pay a second time.[21]

Restrictive Indorsements That Purport to Prohibit Further Negotiation. The indorsement "Pay A only, [signed] Indorser" *purports* to prohibit further transfer or negotiation of the instrument, but the UCC does not give it that legal effect.[22] It is treated as if it were a special *and* nonrestrictive indorsement instead.

By way of justification of this rule, you may keep in mind that it is really none of the indorser's business what the indorsee, A, does with this instrument. It may be convenient for A to collect it directly from the maker, drawee, or acceptor. But what if A is in Maine and the maker of the note is in California? Why shouldn't A be permitted to put the instrument in the hands of an agent for collection, or do anything else that he might want to with it? The UCC gives A that freedom despite the word "only" in the indorsement.

Restrictive Indorsements for Deposit and Collection. The most frequent type of restrictive indorsement is one which reads "For Deposit" or "For Collection" along with the indorser's signature.[23] That is what the agent of United Fund did with the check received from Greenery USA (figure 28.5).

If you will consult the back of the cancelled checks your drawee-payor bank sends to you each month (a statement of your account will accompany these checks), you will find another common form of restrictive indorsement: "Pay any bank" or "Pay any bank, banker, or trust co."[24] These are placed on the check by depositary and collecting banks, and they are the only indorsements to which banks in the collection process have to pay any attention.[25]

Figure 28.5 Restrictive Indorsement

For Deposit
Pay to Ruston State Bank

United Fund
by Jamila Jackson V.P.

---

[20] UCC 3–603(1)(6).　　[22] UCC 3–205(b), 3–206(1).　　[24] UCC 3–205(c).

[21] UCC 3–603(1).　　[23] UCC 3–205(c).　　[25] UCC 3–206(2), 4–205(2).

Once these indorsements have locked an instrument into bank collection channels, "outsiders" are put on notice. No one can become a holder for value unless payment for the instrument is applied consistent with this indorsement, i.e., the money is deposited into the account of the indorser.[26] In the following case the drawee-payor bank was held liable for not complying with the restrictive indorsement.

Facts

Mrs. O, the plaintiff-payee, was advised by her attorney to indorse a check specially to the estate of O, which she did. In her absence, the attorney indorsed the check "Estate of O—For Deposit, [signed] Harold Breslow, Trustee" and placed the funds in his general account. The defendant bank did not inquire into the authority of Breslow to indorse for the estate; actually, only Mrs. O was qualified to do this. Since Breslow has withdrawn all the funds, she seeks recovery from the bank.

Decision

For Mrs. O.

Reasoning

Since the check had been indorsed specially to the estate of O, it could only be negotiated by a legitimate and authorized indorsement of the estate.

Breslow was not properly authorized to act for the estate. The bank should have inquired into the extent of his authority and, having failed to act reasonably, it is liable to Mrs. O for the loss caused by its negligence. Payment of a check following a forged or unauthorized indorsement is a conversion. UCC 3–419(1)(c).

Furthermore, the defendant bank did not apply the funds consistent with the restrictive indorsement *for deposit into the estate of O*. Therefore, even if Breslow had been authorized, the defendant bank would still be liable because it placed the funds in Breslow's general account rather than an estate account. UCC 3–206(3).

Salsman v. National Community Bank of Rutherford, 246 A.2d 162 (N.J. 1968).

Restrictive Indorsements in Trust. A restrictive indorsement may establish a trust for the use or benefit of the indorser or some other person.[27] For example, the indorsements "Pay to T for the use of P, [signed] P" and "Pay to T in trust for M, [signed] P" establish T as the trustee for a beneficiary, who is either the indorser, P, in the first instance, or some other person, M, perhaps a minor child, in the second instance.

The party who receives the instrument from T—i.e., the "first taker" following such an indorsement—must pay or apply the money consistent with the indorsement. If this is done, and if all of the other requirements are met, the first taker may qualify as an HIDC. Subsequent parties are not in any way affected or given notice by such an indorsement, unless they have actual knowledge that the trustee, T, has violated his duty in negotiating the instrument.[28]

---

[26] UCC 3–206(c), 4–201(2).   [28] UCC 3–206(4), 3–304(2).

[27] UCC 3–205(d).

Qualified Indorsements or Indorsement Without Recourse

Whenever a person transfers an instrument for consideration, the transferor makes certain implied transfer warranties,[29] discussed later. If the transfer is made with an indorsement, the holder receives, in addition to the implied warranties, a right of recourse against the indorser if the following steps are taken:

1. Presentment: the instrument is properly presented for payment or acceptance.
2. Dishonor: payment or acceptance is refused.
3. Notice of dishonor: the indorser is given timely notice of dishonor.[30]

It is possible for the indorser to avoid this conditional liability under the indorsement contract *if he so indicates expressly on the instrument.* The use of the phrase "without recourse" along with the indorser's signature has this effect.[31] The phrase means that, in the event of dishonor, no recourse can be made against that indorser because of such dishonor. The implied transfer warranties of such an indorser are now comparable to those of an assignor under the common law.

From the indorser's point of view, "without recourse" is an excellent way of escaping the normal liability that accompanies one's signature as an indorser on a negotiable instrument. The difficulty is in finding someone who will take such an indorsement.

You should be cautious in receiving instruments indorsed in this manner. If the holder is not able to collect from the debtor at maturity, he must rely on breach of implied warranty by the transferor.

Assume that P receives a check from D in return for the sale of merchandise. P indorses "without recourse" to H and delivers the check to H. Then D notifies the drawee bank to stop payment on the check (a stop-payment order). H will be able to recover from P only if H can prove some breach of the implied transfer warranties by P.

If H sued P on the basis of P's transfer warranties to H, H would attempt to prove that:

1. P did not have good title to the instrument. (*But he did!*)
2. Signatures were not genuine or authorized. (*But they were!*)
3. The instrument has been materially altered. (*But it was not!*)
4. P had knowledge of some defense. (*Assume that P did not.*)
5. P had knowledge of D's insolvency. (*Assume that D was not insolvent or that P had no knowledge of it.*)[32]

In many situations H will simply be unable to recover a single penny from P. However, H may proceed against D. The stop-payment order does not mean that D is certain to be successful in a suit by H. In the following case a qualified "without recourse" indorsement did not prevent the qualified indorser from being liable for breach of warranty of no knowledge of any defense good against him.

---

[29] UCC 3–417(2). [31] UCC 3–414(1).

[30] UCC 3–414(1). [32] UCC 3–417(2)(3).

Facts

Prior litigations before this court invalidated a loan entered into in violation of the District of Columbia Loan Shark Law provisions against usury. The effect of the decision was to render uncollectible the unpaid balance of approximately $79,000. The present case involves a dispute as to bearing the loss.

Walker & Dunlop, Inc. loaned Suburban Motors a sum of $100,000. The loan, evidenced by a promissory note, was secured by a deed of trust on real property owned by Suburban. Walker & Dunlop, Inc. transferred the note and deed of trust to Hartford Life Insurance Co., indorsing the note "without recourse." Since the note was later invalidated, Hartford sued Walker & Dunlop, Inc. for $79,000.

Decision

For Hartford Life Insurance Co.

Reasoning

A "without recourse" indorsement is a qualified indorsement but it does not eliminate all obligation owed by the transferor of an instrument to his transferee. By the term "without recourse," Walker & Dunlop, Inc. warranted to Hartford that it had no knowledge of any fact which would establish the existence of a good defense against the note. Walker & Dunlop, Inc. breached the warranty. At all times it was fully aware that the note was unenforceable because of the illegality of the underlying loan. Walker & Dunlop, Inc.'s ignorance of the law was no excuse. Although Hartford had full knowledge of the same facts as Walker & Dunlop, Inc. and made the same "mistake" of law, it did not know when it accepted the note that a good defense existed against it. Therefore, it is entitled to coverage of warranty.

Hartford Life Insurance Company v. Walker & Dunlop, Inc. 520 F.2d 1170 (1975).

Qualified indorsements are most likely to be used when the indorser has no personal interest in the instrument—e.g., the instrument has been made payable to an agent rather than to the principal (the agent's employer) and the agent simply indorses it over to his principal—or when the recipient has no bargaining power—e.g., the instrument is conveyed as a gift, such as the one by Greenery USA to United Fund (figure 28.6).

Irregular Indorsements

A bit of confusion can arise when a negotiable instrument is "assigned" (figure 28.7).

Beware of the obvious temptation to consider Rosemary's indorsement as having the same legal effect as either of the following:

1. the assignment of a non-negotiable contract, or
2. the indorsement of a negotiable instrument without recourse.

If Rosemary's indorsement were considered as being either 1 or 2, then Wallflower would have no recourse against her except for breach of implied transfer warranties. That is not the result, however. Wallflower has recourse against Rosemary as an *indorser* as well as a *warrantor*.

Figure 28.6 Qualified Indorsement
Figure 28.7 Irregular Indorsement

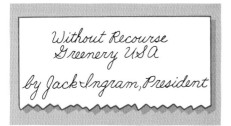

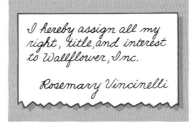

Words of assignment do not affect the character of Rosemary's signature as an indorsement.[33] The language which prefaces Rosemary's indorsement to Wallflower is not sufficient to *warn* the indorsee or to put it *on notice* that it is receiving something less than full recourse against Rosemary.

Transfers

Transfers Without Indorsement

By way of review, recall the manner in which negotiable paper is negotiated: bearer paper by delivery; order paper by indorsement and delivery. On some occasions, and normally because of forgetfulness, order paper will be transferred without an indorsement. For example, you may rush into a familiar store on the way to school or work to cash a payroll check or pay a bill and forget to indorse the instrument. In situations like these, the transferee or recipient is entitled to your unqualified indorsement.[34] The negotiation takes place when you finally indorse. *At that time* the store becomes a holder and, if all the other requirements are met, an HIDC.

Transfers for Less Than the Full Amount

An indorsement can be effective as a negotiation only if it conveys the full amount of the instrument or the unpaid balance. A $1,000 instrument indorsed $400 to A and $600 to B is quite legal and enforceable, but neither of the parties would qualify as a holder. They would be treated instead as assignees of the indorser's interest.[35]

Shelter Provision

The transfer of a negotiable instrument conveys to the recipient-transferee all the rights of the transferor.[36] If, for example, the transferor was an HIDC, the transferee would receive all the rights of an HIDC; he can claim through the

shelter concept
obtaining rights by claiming "through" or "under"

---

[33] UCC 3–202(4). [35] UCC 3–202(3).

[34] UCC 3–201(3). [36] UCC 3–201(1).

HIDC using the HIDC as a shelter. This result will follow even though the transferee could not meet all the requirements for being an HIDC.

When Greenery USA donated a check to United Fund, United Fund could not qualify as an HIDC because it did not give value. Nevertheless, United Fund received the rights of Greenery, and, if Greenery qualified as an HIDC, United Fund would be entitled to exercise those rights as well.

The same result follows despite the fact that the transferee takes the instrument either:

1. after it is overdue;
2. with notice of its previous dishonor;
3. with notice of a claim to it; or
4. with notice of a defense against it.

For example, if a draft or note payable to the order of P, payee, is negotiated to an HIDC, the rights of the HIDC pass to the transferee, X, even though:

1. X gave no value; or
2. X received the instrument after it was overdue; or
3. X had notice of a defense against the instrument, such as fraud by the payee on the maker or drawer of the instrument; or
4. X had notice that the instrument had been previously dishonored, such as by the drawee-payor or maker refusing to honor the instrument.

There are two easily recognized exceptions to this shelter provision. The transferee does not receive the transferor's rights:

1. where the transferee was a *party* to fraud or illegality affecting the instrument, or
2. where the transferee as a *prior holder* had notice of a claim or defense.

The justification for these exceptions is readily apparent.

   a. A wrongdoer should not benefit from his wrongdoing. Therefore, if X collaborated with P in the fraud illustration above, X should not subsequently profit from the shelter provision by claiming through the HIDC.
   b. If X was a prior holder before the HIDC—e.g., if the instrument went from M to P to X (assume that X knew of P's fraud or illegality with regard to M although he played no part in it), and then *from X to an HIDC before coming back to X*—X can not improve his status as a mere holder and he can not claim through the HIDC. In other words, a *reacquirer* can not "whitewash" or "launder" the instrument by running it through the hands of an HIDC.

Reacquirers

Generally speaking, when a party reacquires an instrument that he formerly held, he may reissue or further negotiate it.[37] For example, a negotiable note issued by Mackey, the maker, to Peterson, the payee, could be negotiated initially to Arturo and then back to Arturo with the following indorsements as shown in figure 28.8.

Arturo is a reacquirer. Even if the note is now overdue, he can still negotiate it. On the assumption in the above example that he further indorses and negotiates it to X, the liability of Bingham and of Carlin is discharged (1) against Arturo, the reacquiring party, and (2) against subsequent holders *not* in due course.[38] It would be foolish not to discharge Bingham and Carlin because, if Arturo or a subsequent holder *not* in due course collected from one of them, the one who paid would in turn proceed back against Arturo, as diagrammed in figure 28.9.

The reacquiring party can cancel any indorsement which is not necessary to his title or ownership.[39] If so inclined, Arturo could mark out the special indorsements of Bingham and Carlin. This would leave only Peterson's special indorsement and Arturo's blank one. If Arturo then negotiated the instrument to anyone who qualified as an HIDC, Bingham and Carlin would not be liable as indorsers. In effect, Arturo has made a gift to Bingham and Carlin by discharging them from further liability.[40]

Figure 28.8 Reacquired Instrument by Arturo

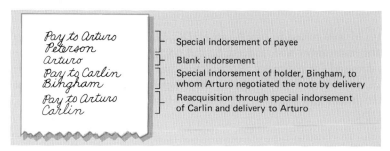

Figure 28.9 Instrument Renegotiated to Arturo

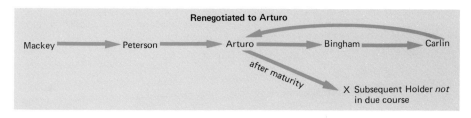

[37] UCC 3–208. [39] UCC 3–208.

[38] UCC 3–601(3)(a). [40] UCC 3–605(1)(a).

Forgeries and Unauthorized Signatures

Nobody is liable on a negotiable instrument unless his signature is on the instrument. The forgery of a signature or the unauthorized use of a signature (by an agent, for example) does not obligate the party whose name is wrongly used unless:

1. he ratifies the transaction (after learning all the facts, he OK's the transaction by word or other conduct); or
2. he is precluded or estopped from denying it (engaged in conduct that makes it unfair for him to avoid or disown the transaction).[41]

To illustrate each of the above, (1) a mother might ratify the forgeries of her signature on checks by a daughter, and (2) an employer might be precluded or estopped by its negligent supervision of a check-writing machine from disclaiming the conduct of an agent who abused his position and wrongfully placed the employer's signature on a company blank check.

You will want to make a distinction between two types of forgeries: (a) instruments that are completely forged from the very outset—e.g., X forges D's signature as drawer on a check; and (b) forged indorsements—e.g., X steals a check drawn originally by D to the order of P and X forges P's blank indorsement. The first of these forged instruments (a) can be negotiated to innocent HIDCs. Forgery of a *drawer's* signature does not prevent the otherwise negotiable instrument from being negotiable. The instrument *is* signed, although the drawer whose signature is forged is not liable thereon. However, following a forged required *indorsement* (b), no title passes, and no one can become a holder or an HIDC.

At maturity, M will refuse to pay A, an HIDC, because M's signature does not appear on the instrument and, indeed, he did not know of its existence prior to the HIDC's demand for payment. No *contract* has ever existed between *M*, on the one hand, and either X, P, or A, on the other hand; therefore, M is not liable on the instrument and has a "real" defense which is valid against anyone, including an HIDC.

Figure 28.10 Forged Instrument

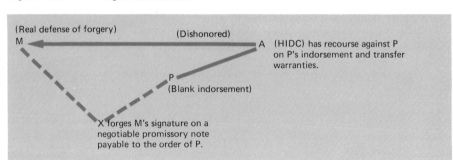

(Real defense of forgery)
M (Dishonored) A (HIDC) has recourse against P on P's indorsement and transfer warranties.

P
(Blank indorsement)

X forges M's signature on a negotiable promissory note payable to the order of P.

---

[41] UCC 3–404, 3–406.

M would be liable if he ratified X's forgery or if he negligently supervised X's use of a check-writing machine. However, as matters stand, A, the HIDC, must seek recovery against P or X; but since M did not sign the instrument, M is not liable on the instrument. As a rule, the loss will fall upon the person who dealt with the forger unless the forger can be found and made to pay.

An unauthorized signature operates as the signature of the unauthorized signer; *he* did sign it. So X's forgery of M's signature causes X to be liable as the maker; if X had forged P's indorsement, X would also be liable as an indorser.[42]

The fact that A is an HIDC does not assist him in these collection efforts. He will be pursuing X on his liability as a *maker,* and P as an *indorser* and as a *warrantor.* Accordingly, while X's real name does not appear on the instrument, the forgery obligates him nevertheless. In the following case the court held that the drawee bank can not charge its depositor drawer's account when the latter's signature was forged on the check.

Facts

Plaintiff, Mortimer Agency, Inc., a depositor in Underwriters Trust Company (drawee), sued to recover $4,000 paid out of plaintiff's account by Underwriters on a forged check. The plaintiff's signature as drawer was forged. Underwriters in turn proceeded against both Chemical Bank and Rego Trading Company, asserting: (1) that the signature of the payee as indorser was also forged; and (2) that Chemical as the collecting bank, and Rego as a purchaser of the check, violated their respective warranties with regard to the forged indorsement of the payee and should be held ultimately responsible if Underwriters is found liable in the original action.

Some unknown individual forged a check in the name of the plaintiff by a rubber stamp and submitted a letter to Underwriters requesting that the check be certified. The letter was of suspicious appearance, and also misspelled the plaintiff's name. The check was certified by Underwriters. Rego bought the check for cash, and deposited the check for collection with its bank, Chemical. Chemical

forwarded the check for collection to Underwriters, which honored the check and remitted the money to Chemical. Mortimer, on receiving its bank statement, informed Underwriters of the forgery of its signature.

Decision

For plaintiff, Mortimer, against Underwriters. Action of Underwriters against Chemical and Rego dismissed.

Reasoning

The court found that Mortimer was not negligent because the forgery scheme (involving theft of check blanks) was too complicated for its security control. However, it found Underwriters negligent for not making further inquiries into the peculiar appearance of the check—rubber stamped signature, misspellings, and an uncommonly large sum.

A drawee, such as Underwriters, that certifies or pays an instrument on which the signature of the drawer is forged is bound on its acceptance and cannot recover its payment, according to UCC 3–418. Normally persons who obtain payment (both Chemical and Rego obtained payment) or

---

[42] UCC 3–404(1).

acceptance, and any prior transferors, warrant to a drawee who in good faith pays or accepts that all previous indorsements are authentic. However, these checks were never at any time valid subsisting orders; they were fakes or forgeries right from the very beginning. Furthermore, the forged indorsement put the defendant in no worse position than it would be in if the indorsements were genuine. Why? Because Underwriters was supposed to recognize the signature of its depositor Mortimer and failed to do so. Finally, the defendant's certification set these events in motion and had much to do with Rego's decision to take the instrument. It would be anomalous now to hold Rego responsible to a party (Underwriters) whose conduct induced it to receive the check to begin with.

Mortimer Agency, Inc. v. Underwriters Trust Co., 341 N.Y.Supp.2d 75 (1973).

Figure 28.11   Forged Indorsement

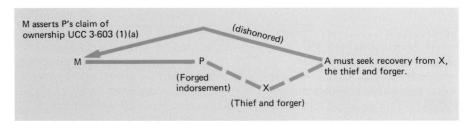

As shown in the above figure 28.11, M signs a negotiable promissory note with P as the payee. X steals the note, forges P's blank indorsement, and transfers the note to A, who, *except* for the forgery, meets the requirements for being an HIDC. At maturity, M refuses to honor the note, asserting P's claim to the note. (UCC 3–603(1)(a))

In this situation, A is neither a holder nor an HIDC. A is in possession of an instrument, but it has not been properly indorsed so as to flow to him so he can not become a holder nor an HIDC even if he met all of the other requirements. A can proceed against X on the forged indorsement and on the breach of transfer warranty, but P still owns the instrument.

If P is sued as an indorser by A or a subsequent party that has received the instrument through A, the forgery operates as a *real defense* for P, if we assume no ratification or estoppel by P. On the other hand, if P decides to take the initiative, he could assert a *claim of ownership* against A or anyone else to recover possession of the instrument.

Impersonation.

Impostors

When an impostor payee induces issuance of an instrument, anyone can indorse in the payee's name. Thus, if X impersonates P and induces M to issue a negotiable instrument to the order of P (the person who is being impersonated),

Figure 28.12 Impersonator Receives an Instrument

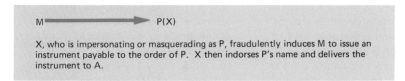

X, who is impersonating or masquerading as P, fraudulently induces M to issue an instrument payable to the order of P. X then indorses P's name and delivers the instrument to A.

Figure 28.13 Indorsement by Impersonator

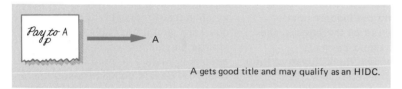

A gets good title and may qualify as an HIDC.

anyone can indorse in P's name. X's indorsement of P's name is not treated as a forgery. In other words, X can indorse P's name and negotiate such an instrument to A, who may qualify as an HIDC. The HIDC as a plaintiff will prevail against M if M refuses to pay the instrument at maturity.[43] While M is guilty of no wrongdoing, he nevertheless intended to create a negotiable instrument despite the trickery of X. This led to the purchase of the instrument by a completely innocent person, A, who had no opportunity to prevent or detect the original fraud. By way of justification of this rule, it can be said that, when one of two innocent persons must suffer (M or A), the loss falls on the one who had an opportunity to detect the wrongdoing or the opportunity to insure against it. Furthermore, A has the right to proceed against the wrongdoer, X. A can not collect from P, the party who has been impersonated, because P's signature never really appeared on the instrument.

This same result will follow: (1) if an employee supplies the maker or drawer with the name of a real or fictitious payee that the employee does not intend should have any interest in the instrument; or (2) if an agent with authority to sign does sign on behalf of his employer but with the intention that the real or fictitious payee have no interest.[44]

What the employee or agent really intends is to take the instrument which has now been made out to a phony supplier-creditor or to a fictitious name added to the payroll list, indorse the payee's name, and pocket the cash. The innocent purchaser of such an instrument is protected, and once again the loss falls on the person who had an opportunity to prevent the deception, or to insure against it. Here, that person would be the employer.

However, if the person who deals with the impersonator acts negligently in cashing the checks, he may be liable instead of the employer. This is illustrated in the following case.

---

[43] UCC 3–405(1)(a).   [44] UCC 3–405(1)(b)(c).

Facts

A Board of Education employee, Ms. Rich, had a duty to prepare checks to be issued by the plaintiff, Board, for scholarships and other payments to students, to have them signed by authorized personnel, and to send the checks to their recipients. With the intention of committing fraud, she prepared a number of checks, had them signed, but instead of sending the checks, Ms. Rich retained them. She then forged the indorsement of the named payees on the checks she retained and cashed them at defendant Chemical Bank. Some of the checks were drawn on plaintiff's account at Chemical Bank, others on its account at Bankers Trust. After discovery of the forgeries, the plaintiff demanded that its accounts be credited. Defendants refused. Both defendants requested a summary judgment. [A summary judgment, compared with a jury trial, is brief and uncomplicated. It is a judgment on the pleadings without a trial on the facts. It may be granted when there are questions of law only but no factual disputes. Cases involving documentary evidence—notes and drafts—present an excellent opportunity for a summary judgment. However, if fact issues, such as negligence, are present, a summary judgment will be denied.]

Decision

Summary judgment was denied for Chemical Bank but granted for Bankers Trust.

Reasoning

The Board of Education employee cashed checks at Chemical Bank without ever being asked for identification or authorization. They were familiar with her and knew she was not a named payee, but she often obtained cash for checks made to several different payees. This was in itself against Chemical Bank's policy. With respect to the checks it cashed, Chemical Bank, as drawee bank, had an obligation to plaintiff to exercise due care, and it had authority to charge plaintiff's account only for checks it cashed in good faith. Since Chemical Bank's conduct raised the issue of negligence in cashing the checks, summary judgment was denied.

In the case of Bankers Trust, the facts are quite different. The checks honored by Bankers Trust were paid and contained effective indorsements. UCC 3–405 states that indorsements are effective where an employee of the maker or drawer has supplied the drawer with the name of the payee, intending the latter to have no such interest. Thus, Bankers Trust was granted a summary judgment on grounds that the checks it cashed had effective indorsements, and the plaintiff made no allegations of negligence or bad faith on the part of Bankers Trust in making payments.

Board of Higher Education of The City of New York v. Bankers Trust Company, 383 N.Y.Supp.2d 508 (1976).

Warranties

Various warranties implied by law under the Code are made by persons transferring a negotiable instrument and by persons who obtain payment or acceptance of the instrument.

Figure 28.14 Negotiable Promissory Note Indorsed in Blank by P, Payee, and Delivered to A, to B, to H

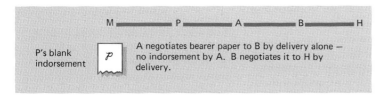

P's blank indorsement

A negotiates bearer paper to B by delivery alone — no indorsement by A. B negotiates it to H by delivery.

Transfer Warranties

Transfer warranties.

If M issues a negotiable instrument payable to the order of P, P may indorse and deliver it to a holder, A, in payment for goods or services. In this situation, P becomes conditionally or secondarily liable on his indorsement contract to the holder, A. P impliedly agrees that the instrument will be honored. If M refuses to pay the note at maturity and A gives timely notice of dishonor or nonpayment, P is liable to A for the face amount. This is the liability of an indorser *as a secondary party*.

P may be liable to A for breach of implied *transfer warranties* as well. When a person transfers an instrument and receives a consideration, certain implied transfer warranties are created automatically or by operation of law. If the transferor has indorsed the instrument, these warranties extend to all subsequent transferees. However, if bearer paper is negotiated by delivery alone, transfer warranties are made to the immediate recipient only.[45] In other words, for the situation diagrammed in figure 28.14:

1. P's transfer warranties extend to A, B, and H.
2. A's transfer warranties extend *only* to B, not to H.

   Transferors warrant as follows:

   a. The transferor has good title or is authorized by the owner to collect.
   b. All signatures are genuine or authorized.
   c. No material alterations.
   d. No defense of any party is valid against the transferor.
   e. No *knowledge* of insolvency proceedings against the drawer of an unaccepted instrument (secondary party) or against the maker or acceptor (primary party).[46]

In the following case the collecting bank was held liable for breach of its warranty of genuine indorsements.

---

[45] UCC 3–417(2).

[46] UCC 3–417(2) (a)–(e).

Facts

Jensen Movers drew a check on Union Bank payable to the order of Lewittes Furniture Enterprises, Inc., plaintiff, and delivered it to plaintiff. A thief, Joel Simpson, stole the check, forged Lewittes' indorsement, and transferred it to Margaret Marino. She deposited the check, containing plaintiff's forged indorsement, into her joint account with Peter Marino at Bankers Trust, defendant. Bankers presented the check to Union and it was paid. Plaintiff sued the defendant for recovery of the proceeds of the check.

The plaintiff's case was based on its rights as assignee of the drawee bank to go against defendant collecting bank for breach of its implied (statutory) and express warranties of the genuineness of prior indorsements.

Decision

For defendant on other grounds (statute of limitations).

Reasoning

The warranty of genuineness of prior indorsements is spelled out in UCC sections 3–417 and 4–207. Besides these implied (statutory) warranties, the defendant here also expressly warranted to the same effect by its stamped notation on the reverse side of the check, "Pay any bank—P.E.G." P.E.G. means "prior endorsements guaranteed." The drawee's (Union's) responsibility upon presentment of the check is to determine the genuineness of the drawer's signature; but as to all other indorsements, it is entitled to rely upon defendant collecting bank's warranty, and this warranty was obviously breached.

Lewittes Furniture Enterprises, Inc. v. Bankers Trust of Suffolk, 372 N.Y.Supp.2d 830 (1975).

Typically, a party's indorsement liability and warranty liability will overlap. Suppose that X forged M's signature as maker of a negotiable promissory note with X as the payee; X then indorsed and negotiated the note to A, and A subsequently indorsed and delivered the note to H. M is justifiably entitled to refuse payment to H (assuming no ratification or estoppel by M). Given timely notice of dishonor by H, A is liable to H on his indorsement contract. A would be liable also as warrantor because M's signature is not genuine.

Figure 28.15 Overlap of Indorsement Liability and Warranty Liability

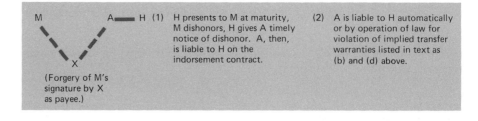

M   A——H   (1) H presents to M at maturity, M dishonors, H gives A timely notice of dishonor. A, then, is liable to H on the indorsement contract.

X

(Forgery of M's signature by X as payee.)

(2) A is liable to H automatically or by operation of law for violation of implied transfer warranties listed in text as (b) and (d) above.

If A negotiated bearer paper by delivery alone, or if A indorsed but H failed to properly present for payment or give notice of dishonor following A's indorsement, H would have to rely solely on breach of implied transfer warranty. Warranty liability, therefore, has a value over and above indorsement liability.

Keep in mind also that, if A indorses "Without Recourse," he is not liable as an indorser but he is liable on transfer warranties. In that case the transfer warranties are modified somewhat. The qualified indorser warrants that he has *no knowledge* of a defense that is valid against him.[47] All other indorsers warrant against valid defenses rather than no knowledge of defenses.

Presentment Warranties

Presentment warranties.

When an instrument is presented to the proper party at maturity for payment or acceptance (certification), the person presenting warrants:

1. he has good title or is authorized to collect for the owner;
2. he has *no knowledge* that the signature of the maker or drawer is forged or unauthorized; and
3. the instrument has not been materially altered.[48]

The general rules are basically straightforward and easily justified. For example, M makes a promissory note. X steals it from the payee, P, forges the payee's blank indorsement, and sells and delivers it to A. A does not have good title to the note. If M innocently pays A, then M should be able to recover from A.[49] After all, A is not the holder nor the owner of the instrument. The payee is still the owner and is entitled to payment from M.

The instrument has been "converted"[50] (explained later) if M pays following a forged indorsement. M is liable to P, so M should be entitled to recover from A any mistaken payment that M has made to A. The following case illustrates, in the case of a check, the liability of a depositary collecting bank on its warranty of title to the payor bank.

Facts

Fred Rzepka drew two checks on plaintiff, Society Bank, payable to ABS Company and delivered them to an agent (Mishler) of payee company. Mishler forged the indorsement of ABS on the two checks, delivered them to Society, and in exchange obtained two cashier's checks from Society payable to ABS. Mishler then forged ABS's indorsement on them also. He deposited both cashier's checks in his account at Capital National Bank, defendant, and, through the clearing house, Society Bank paid them.

Rzepka notified Society of the forgeries and Society reimbursed his account. Society then brought suit against defendant Capital National Bank to recover the amount paid.

---

[47] UCC 3–417(3).   [49] UCC 3–417(1)(a).

[48] UCC 3–417(1).   [50] UCC 3–419(1)(c).

Decision

For plaintiff.

Reasoning

In issuing cashier's checks, Society rather than Rzepka became primarily liable on them. Banks such as Capital National that forward and present items for payment or acceptance make certain warranties to the payor-drawee bank. These warranties include good title to the instrument or authority to obtain payment or acceptance on behalf of one who has a good title (UCC 3-417). The reason for not holding the payor-drawee bank liable where there is a forged indorsement is that the drawee "has ordinarily no opportunity to verify an indorsement." In reference to warranty of good title, a forged indorsement will break the chain of title and, after the forgery, good title to order paper cannot be passed.

Society National Bank of Cleveland v. Capital National Bank, 281 N.E.2d 563 (Ohio 1972).

Implicit in the second presentment warranty—no knowledge of a forged maker's or drawer's signature—is the thought that the one who is paying (the maker, acceptor, or drawee) is in a better position to recognize a forgery than the presenter.[51] If the maker's signature has been forged on a note but that person does not recognize the forgery when the instrument is presented at maturity for payment, the money can not be recovered from the innocent HIDC who received payment. Similarly, the drawee or acceptor who pays a check or draft on the drawer's behalf, despite the forgery of the drawer's signature, is penalized because of this negligence or carelessness. Such persons do have the right to pursue the wrongdoer, however.

Material alteration,[52] which will be discussed in a later chapter, is a "real" or "universal" defense that is valid even against a holder in due course. The thought behind this rule is that a contracting party on an instrument should not be liable for more money than he has originally agreed to pay.

Carefully note the exceptions to presentment warranty rules—(1) no knowledge, and (2) material alterations—in favor of an HIDC acting in good faith. To summarize these exceptions, an HIDC who is acting in good faith—i.e., one who continues to be innocent of any knowledge of a forged maker's or drawer's signature or a material alteration when he presents for payment or acceptance— does not always make these warranties. Therefore, he is entitled to keep the money—the one who pays has recourse against the wrongdoer.

Finality of Payment or Acceptance

Payment or acceptance of an instrument is "final" in favor of an HIDC *or* one who in good faith changes his position in reliance on payment.[53] This rule is easily enough understood in its protection of an HIDC. However, if a person has

---

[51] UCC 3–417(1)(b)(i)—(iii).   [53] UCC 3–418.

[52] UCC 3–417(1)(c).

not given value or does not otherwise qualify as an HIDC but has made some irrevocable commitment on the strength of this payment, then it is made final in his favor as well.

There are two exceptions to this rule. Payment may be recovered if a presentment warranty has been breached,[54] and if certain provisions of the Article on Bank Deposits and Collections are violated.[55]

Conversion

An instrument is **converted**—controlled by someone other than the rightful owner—when it is cashed on a forged indorsement.[56] If X steals from P a $1,000 check drawn payable to the order of P, forges P's indorsement, and passes it to an innocent party, A, who collects on it from the drawee, the drawee has converted P's instrument. If P acts within the time limits, he can assert his claim of ownership against the drawee for $1,000.[57] P can proceed against X and A as well in order to obtain a full recovery.

Since the drawee did not know what the payee's signature looked like (it has a copy of the drawer-customer's signature, which it is supposed to recognize, but not the payee's), it is entitled to charge back against collecting banks for breach of the presentment warranty of good title.[58]

If a forged signature of a drawer-customer is not detected, the bank is not likely to recover on grounds of a presentment warranty. It is penalized for its negligence or oversight, and as a rule, the drawee can recover from the wrongdoer only.[59]

Agents or representatives, including depositary and collecting banks, may advance checks through bank channels following a forged indorsement of the true owner's signature. If they have acted in good faith and in accordance with reasonable business standards, they are not liable to the true owner beyond the amount that remains in their hands.[60] For example, if X steals P's $1,000 check, forges P's indorsement, and transfers the check to A, A may indorse it for collection to the depositary bank (not the payor-drawee bank) and withdraw $500 before P discovers the theft and forgery. In such an event, the depositary bank is liable to P for the remaining $500. It may also have to account to the drawee bank for breach of the presentment warranty of good title.[61] (See *Lewittes v. Bankers Trust*,[62] in which the drawee assigned to the payee its right to proceed against a collecting bank.)

conversion
the tort of intentional interference with another's right to possession, control, and dominion of a chattel

chattel
a tangible, movable thing

---

[54] UCC 3–417(1).

[55] UCC 4–213, 4–301.

[56] UCC 3–419(1)(c).

[57] UCC 4–406(4).

[58] UCC 3–417(1)(a), 4–207(1)(2).

[59] UCC 3–417(1)(b), 4–207(1)(b).

[60] UCC 3–419(3).

[61] UCC 3–419, comment 6.

[62] See p. 542.

Summary Statement

1. Bearer paper is negotiated by delivery alone. Order paper is negotiated by indorsement and delivery.
2. To identify bearer paper, examine its face. If the face of the paper expressly states that it is payable "to Bearer" or "to Order of Bearer," or it names no payee capable of making a signature—e.g., "Cash"—then it is bearer paper. Don't stop there, however. If the instrument has been indorsed, examine the last (or only) indorsement. A blank indorsement means that the instrument is still bearer paper. A special indorsement converts it to order paper.
3. Order paper will name as payee on the face of the instrument a natural person—e.g., Willie Nelson—or some legal entity that is capable of making a signature through an agent—e.g., Ruston State Bank. Examine the reverse side of the instrument as well as the face, however. If the last or only indorsement is special, the instrument continues to be order paper. If the last or only indorsement is in blank, the instrument becomes bearer paper. If it was bearer to begin with, the special indorsement converts it into order paper.
4. All indorsements are hybrid in nature. Each one will contain elements of the following:
   a. Blank or special. These indorsements determine the method to be used in subsequent negotiations.
      Delivery alone if the last or only indorsement is blank; indorsement plus delivery if the last or only indorsement is special.
   b. Restrictive or nonrestrictive. These indorsements determine whether the interest conveyed is conditional or limited.
      One form of restrictive indorsement contains an express condition—e.g., "Pay to A when he finishes painting my house, [signed] P." The other important form makes the indorsee an agent or trustee—e.g., "Pay to ABC Bank for deposit, [signed] P," or "Pay to T in trust for M, [signed] P."
   c. Qualified or unqualified. These indorsements determine the liability of the indorser.
      When one indorses qualifiedly or without recourse and transfers for a consideration, he makes certain warranties but is not liable as an indorser.
5. The "shelter provision" transfers to the recipient of the instrument all the rights that the transferor had to convey. If the transferor was an HIDC, the transferee gets the rights of an HIDC. This rule opens up the market for commercial paper and makes it easier to sell. However, where the transferee was a party to fraud or illegality affecting the instrument, or where the transferee as a holder *prior* to the HIDC had notice of a claim or defense, the shelter provision rule is ineffective.
6. Forgeries and unauthorized *signatures* do not obligate the party whose name was wrongly used, unless he ratifies the signature or is precluded or estopped from denying it. *Forged instruments* can get into the hands of HIDC's, but the forger and all indorsers incur signature liability as well as warranty

liability. If a *required indorsement* is *forged,* no subsequent party can become a holder or an HIDC. The forger and all indorsers that follow do incur signature and warranty liability, however, and the true owner of the instrument will have a valid claim against the person in possession of the instrument.

7. An impersonator's signature of the name of the individual being impersonated is not a forgery. It operates as a valid signature and subsequent holders can qualify as HIDCs. The wrongdoer is responsible for his conduct but, if recovery against him is not practicable, the party who issued the instrument to the impersonator is liable for it.

8. Each time an instrument is *transferred* for a consideration, and each time one is *presented* and payment or acceptance is obtained, certain warranties are made. If the instrument is indorsed by the transferor, the warranties run in favor of all subsequent parties; if the instrument is negotiated by delivery alone, the transfer warranties extend only to the immediate recipient.

9. Warranty liability is different from indorsement liability but is compatible with it. Indorsement liability is discharged if the instrument is not presented for payment at the proper time or if timely notice of dishonor is not given. Warrantors continue to be liable, however. Their obligation is not conditioned on presentment, dishonor, and notice of dishonor.

10. A bank is supposed to know the status of its customers' accounts. When it honors a check—even one creating an overdraft—payment is, generally speaking, *final* in favor of an HIDC or one who in good faith changes his position in reliance on payment.

11. If an *indorsement* has been forged, the drawee bank that pays the check is liable to the true owner. Then it may proceed against a collecting bank for violation of a presentment warranty. If a *customer-drawer's signature* is forged, the bank should detect it. Payment of such a forged instrument makes the payor bank liable to its customer. The bank may then proceed against the wrongdoer, but not against collecting banks.

This chapter has emphasized the various rights and duties that can arise when commercial paper is negotiated. The following case presents us with an example of how the principles of law (one is that a bank is required to know its depositor's signature) can be modified by equitable considerations (contributory negligence by one innocent party causing another innocent party to suffer loss).

Terry v. Puget Sound National Bank
492 P.2d 534 (Wash. 1972)

Per curiam [by the court]. Plaintiffs, partners in a Tacoma barber shop, have maintained a partnership checking account with the defendant, Puget Sound National Bank, since October 1964. The signatures of both partners were required for withdrawal from the account. Mr. Nash, a longtime employee of the plaintiffs, was occasionally left alone and in charge of the barber shop. He had no formal managerial responsibilities and no authority to write partnership checks. Between September 16, 1968 and January 3, 1969, Mr. Nash forged plaintiffs' signatures on numerous checks. Defendant bank honored these checks. In early January of 1969, plaintiffs discovered the forgeries. This action was then commenced to recover the monies paid.

The bank asserted plaintiffs' negligence as an affirmative defense under UCC 3-406 and 4-406. . . . On appeal from a jury verdict and judgment for defendant, plaintiffs contend that the affirmative defense should not have been submitted and that the bank should have been held liable as a matter of law.

The record shows that the check blanks were left in an unlocked drawer on the barber shop premises, easily accessible to Mr. Nash. Plaintiffs never inquired of one another about missing check blanks. For about four years, on a regular monthly basis, defendant sent statements and cancelled checks to plaintiffs' place of business. Plaintiffs regularly examined the cancelled checks and bank statements upon receipt. The monthly statements sent in October, November, and December of 1968 were intercepted by Mr. Nash and not received by plaintiffs. Plaintiffs did not inquire of the bank nor discuss between themselves this unusual absence of statements and cancelled checks. It was only when they received notice late in December that the account was overdrawn that they went to the bank and then discovered the forgeries.

These facts constitute substantial evidence of negligence on the part of the plaintiffs. Plaintiffs suggest that negligence is insufficient to support the affirmative defense afforded by these statutes in a forgery case, since forgery is a crime involving specific criminal intent. The statutory language contradicts this assertion. Under the statutes, the customer is precluded from asserting his unauthorized signature against the bank when he has failed to exercise reasonable care. Criminal activity is not a measure; negligence substantially contributing to the unauthorized signature is plainly sufficient. The issues of negligence and substantial contribution to the forgeries were properly submitted to the jury. The verdict will not be disturbed on this ground.

Plaintiffs also argue that they were entitled to a directed verdict in that they had established by their evidence a lack of ordinary care on the part of the bank as a matter of law, thus preventing application of the affirmative defense. . . . However, plaintiffs would be entitled to a directed verdict only if there is no evidence or reasonable inference therefrom to support the bank's position that it had acted in good faith and with reasonable care. We have reviewed the record and find therein testimony which, if believed by the jury, would establish that the bank had cashed no checks not bearing the names of both plaintiffs; that the tellers checked the signatures against the formal signature card until they were familiar with Mr. Nash and with the signatures; and that the forgeries were so skillful as to escape detection. The record does not support plaintiffs' assertions to the contrary. Under these circumstances, the trial court's denial of plaintiffs' motion for a directed verdict was correct.

Judgment affirmed.

Questions and Case Problems

1. A negotiable instrument was indorsed in blank by P, the payee, and negotiated to A. The indorsement of A was placed on the instrument by an unauthorized party and then the instrument was transferred to P. Does P qualify as a holder? [*Westerly Hospital v. Higgins,* 256 A.2d 506 (R.I. 1969).]

2. P, the payee of a negotiable promissory note originally issued by M, indorses it as follows: "Pay to T in trust for my niece Velma, [signed] Payee." T discounts the note with A, purportedly to get enough money to pay Velma's tuition, books, and other expenses; actually, T pockets the cash. A negotiates the instrument to B, who is, of course, aware of the restrictive indorsement by P. When it is discovered that T has misappropriated the funds, Velma (represented by her Uncle, P) brings an action to recover the instrument from B. Is she likely to be successful? Discuss the possibilities.

3. Cole drew a check on Buffalo Bank payable to the order of Wyoming Homes. An agent for Wyoming Homes deposited it in a Gillette bank without an indorsement. The bank stamped the check "First National Bank, Gillette, Wyoming, For Deposit Only" and collected it for the payee, Wyoming Homes. Buffalo Bank charged Cole's account. Cole then proceeded against the First National Bank of Gillette, contending that it was only a transferee of the check (not a holder or an HIDC) and that it took the check subject to Cole's defenses of fraud and failure of consideration against Wyoming Homes. Decision? [*Cole v. First National Bank of Gillette,* 433 P.2d 837 (Wyo. 1967).]

4. A negotiable note was created by the defendant-maker payable to the order of "Greenlaw & Sons Roofing & Siding Co." and indorsed in blank "Greenlaw & Sons." The plaintiff is confronted with the defense that since the note was not properly indorsed, the plaintiff can not be a holder or a holder in due course. If the defendant is correct—he points to UCC 3–203 and 3–307 to substantiate his argument—any defense will be sufficient to defeat plaintiff's claim. Discuss. [*Watertown Federal Savings & Loan Association v. Spanks,* 193 N.E.2d 333 (Mass. 1963).]

5. M-Buyer purchased a car and issued to L.A. Auto-Sellers a $2,000 negotiable note payable to the order of CASH. Auto-Sellers indorsed it specially to Grimley Supply in payment of a debt. Before maturity, Grimley sold the note to Ace Finance Co. without indorsing it. M-Buyer dishonored the instrument at maturity. In an action by Ace against M-Buyer, can the defendant successfully assert breach of warranty on the used car?

6. A check was made payable to the order of payees A and B. After the check was certified by the drawee bank, it was indorsed by B only and cashed. When the check was eventually presented to the drawee bank, it refused payment because A did not indorse. Was the bank justified in its refusal to pay? [*Clinger v. Continental National Bank et al.,* 503 P.2d 363 (Colo. 1972).]

7. Feldman Construction Company drew a check on Union Bank (defendant-drawee) payable to the order of "A Corp. and B Supply." A Corp. indorsed and cashed the check at Union Bank without B Supply's indorsement. Since B Supply was not paid, it filed a lien against Feldman's property. Feldman satisfied B Supply's lien and then proceeded against Union on the ground that the check had not been properly indorsed. Decision? [*Feldman Construction Co. v. Union Bank* 104 Cal.Rptr.912 (1972).]

8. D issues a $100 check to P. P raises the check to $1,000 (a material alteration) and has it certified by the drawee bank. P then indorses the check "Pay to H, [signed] P" and negotiates it to H. H, an HIDC, cashes the check for $1,000. When D discovers these facts (immediately upon examining his monthly bank statement and cancelled checks), he compels the drawee to reinstate his account for $900. UCC 4–401(2)(a). Can the drawee bank recover the $900 from H? If not, can it recover from P? Discuss the application of UCC 3–417 to this fact situation.

9. D draws a $1,000 check on D-Bank payable to the order of P. X steals the check and forges P's blank indorsement. A receives the check from X for value, before maturity, and without knowledge of the forgery. A deposits the check in A-Bank, which forwards it to D-Bank for collection. D-Bank pays the check and returns it to D at the end of the month. P then discovers the wrongdoing and notifies D. Discuss P's rights against D, D-Bank, A-Bank, A, and X.

10. In *Terry v. Puget Sound National Bank,* 492 P.2d 534 (Wash. 1972),[63] why did the court not hold the bank responsible for not knowing its depositor's signature? When is the bank responsible for knowing its depositor's signature?

---

[63] See pp. 547–48.

Holder, Holder in Due Course, and Defenses

29

After you have read this chapter, you should be able to answer the following questions:

1. What is a holder? What are the rights of a holder?
2. What is a holder in due course? What are the rights of a holder in due course?
3. What is "value"? Is value the same thing as consideration?
4. Is "notice" of a claim or a defense the same thing as "knowledge" of a claim or defense?
5. What does the phrase "good faith" mean? Can a person be in good faith if he or she has notice of a claim or a defense?
6. What is the difference between a claim and a defense?
7. What claims or defenses are valid against a holder? Are these valid against a holder in due course as well?

Introduction

Chapters 27 and 28 illustrate the possibility of obtaining "greater rights" in a negotiable instrument by its negotiation. This chapter centers on the person who occupies the most favored position, namely, the *holder in due course* (HIDC). Therefore, since the negotiable instrument is used so commonly in business as *the* means of payment, and since many defenses cannot be asserted against a person who is an HIDC, it becomes necessary to fully understand how you can become an HIDC. HIDC status gives you as much protection as possible in being able to enforce payment on the instrument.

Holder and Holder in Due Course

An HIDC must first be a holder.

A *holder* is a person in possession of a negotiable instrument "drawn, issued, or indorsed to him or to his order, or to bearer, or in blank."[1] The holder may qualify as an HIDC if the instrument is taken (1) for value, (2) in good faith, and (3) without notice of any claim or defense or that it is overdue or has been dishonored.[2]

A payee may qualify as an HIDC,[3] but, if there is any defense on the instrument, normally the payee will know about it. For example, if a retailer-payee has sold defective merchandise to a consumer, he probably will not qualify as an HIDC because of bad faith and notice of a defense—e.g., breach of contract, failure of consideration.

Even on the assumption that the payee did meet all the requirements of an HIDC, HIDCs are subject to the assertion of defenses—real or personal—of those parties with whom they have dealt.[4] While a seller-payee may be in good faith and quite innocent of any notice of a defense at the time of the sale, the purchaser-drawer could still assert that defense against him at a later time.

As a practical matter, the payee can benefit from the HIDC status only if he is somehow insulated from the transaction which gives rise to the defense of the maker or drawer of the instrument. Assume that D draws a $1,000 check without inserting the name of a payee. If he entrusts the check to his agent, A, to deliver it to XYZ Corporation, but instead A inserts the name of one of his personal creditors (P), P may become an HIDC if he meets all of the requirements.[5] The following case is an illustration.

Facts

The plaintiff imported steel coil from Japan. It was damaged on arrival, and the plaintiff's insurer advertised and sold it "as is, where is." The defendant steel company purchased the coil and, as part of the purchase price, named the plaintiff importer as payee of a negotiable promissory note. Later the defendant complained that it was the victim of a fraudulent switch or substitution of inferior goods. It asserts this fraud as a defense against the plaintiff, who claimed to be an HIDC.

---

[1] UCC 1–201(20). [3] UCC 3–302(2). [5] UCC 3–302, comment 2(g).

[2] UCC 3–302(1). [4] UCC 3–305(2).

Decision

For the plaintiff-payee (HIDC).

Reasoning

There is no suggestion that plaintiff played any knowing role in the fraud. The insurer took over matters instantly on complaint by the plaintiff and arranged for the salvage sale without any participation by the plaintiff. As a technical matter, the insurance company and its surveyor were acting as agents of the plaintiff in arranging for the plaintiff to receive a negotiable promissory note from the defendant, but this was solely for the purpose of implementing the transfer and makes no difference in the outcome.

Saale v. Interstate Steel Co., Inc., 228 N.E.2d 397 (N.Y. 1967).

The Status of a Holder Is Fixed at the Time He Becomes a Holder

If he becomes a holder in due course and *later learns* of facts which, if known before he became a holder, would have prevented him from becoming an HIDC, he *continues* as an HIDC.

Value

For value.

Consideration is a "bargained for" exchange—a legal detriment that a promisee gives or promises to give in return for the promisor's promise. If A has promised to sell B a $400 Honda on credit, and B accepts, then B's consideration is his promise to pay. Until B has actually paid, his promise is executory, i.e., it has not been executed or fulfilled.

When the word "value" is used in connection with the law of negotiable instruments, it means *consideration* that has been performed,[6] and also a *past debt.* In the illustration above, if a negotiable promissory note is substituted for the Honda, B becomes a holder for value when he pays the $400. If he makes only partial payment, he becomes a holder for value to the extent actually paid.

If the $400 note was being sold at a discount—say, for the price of $387— B would be a holder for full face value upon payment of the agreed sum, $387. On the assumption that all the other requirements were met, B would qualify as an HIDC as well.

However, if B has paid only $200 of the $387 discount price, and then receives notice of a defense, he could not qualify as an HIDC for the remainder. B would be limited in his HIDC status to $200. He is not required to pay the additional $187 because he is not getting what he originally bargained for.

security interest
"an interest in personal property or fixtures which secures payment or performance of an obligation"
UCC 1-201 (37)

One who acquires a **security interest** in an instrument may become a holder for value.[7] For example, P, the payee of a $1,000 note due in one year, may need cash immediately. Instead of selling the note at a steep discount, the payee may pledge it as collateral security for a $600 loan. In that event, the one who advances the $600 on the security of P's $1,000 note is a holder for value to the extent of the loan.

---

[6] UCC 3–303(a).

[7] UCC 3–303(a), 4–209.

cancellation
the nullification of a
contractual obligation

A holder may give value if an instrument is taken for an antecedent or preexisting claim whether the claim is due and matured or not. An easy illustration of this is the payment of a debt with a check. The **cancellation** of the debt in return for the check constitutes value.[8]

Keep in mind that "payment" with negotiable instruments is really only "conditional" payment. That is, the debt is considered paid only if the instrument is honored or paid. If the check "bounces" (is dishonored and returned) or the note is not paid at maturity, the debt is now enforceable in the courts.[9] A full discharge from an obligation occurs only in those situations where a *bank* is a maker, drawer, or acceptor of an instrument and the party who uses it to satisfy the obligation does not indorse.[10] For example, if Bert Jones purchased athletic equipment from Spaulding Company and paid for it with a cashier's check issued by Baltimore Trust Company payable to the order of Spaulding, Jones would not be liable on the instrument if he did not indorse it. The debt is solely that of Baltimore Trust, the primary party.

Value is given if negotiable instruments are exchanged—e.g., if a check is given in purchase of a note, or if an irrevocable commitment is made to a third party in return for an instrument.[11] The latter is illustrated by the issuance of a letter of credit by a bank in return for a note or check of its customer.

Banks give value, and may become HIDCs upon meeting the other requirements, to the extent they acquire a security interest.[12] Security interests arise to the extent that the credit given for an item has been withdrawn.[13] For example, if a bank that is in the process of collecting a $1,000 item for its customer-depositor allows the immediate withdrawal of $500, it will be a holder for value for $500 if the check later bounces.

A bank may give its customer an unreserved right of withdrawal prior to the time an item is collected. In this event, the bank is an HIDC for the full amount even if none of the credit has been drawn upon[14] because of the customer's right of immediate withdrawal and contingent liability of the bank. This is illustrated in the following case.

Facts

Mr. Maisto purchased a "cashier's check" from the defendant, City Bank, for $3,446 with two checks plus cash. One check was for $2,585.50 drawn on account no. 0-41190-6 (Tony's Sunoco) maintained with Laurel Bank, the plaintiff. Upon the issuance of the "cashier's check," an officer of the defendant, City Bank, phoned the plaintiff, Laurel, and was told by some unidentified person in bookkeeping that the check "was good at this time."

On the same day, Mr. Maisto deposited the cashier's check for $3,446 with other items for a total deposit of $9,501 in account no. 0-41233-3 (B & D Automotive), which was also maintained with plaintiff Laurel Bank. This account, at time of deposit, was overdrawn by

---

[8] UCC 3–303(b).
[9] UCC 3–802(1)(b).
[10] UCC 3–802(1)(a).
[11] UCC 3–303(c).
[12] UCC 4–209.
[13] UCC 4–208(1)(a).
[14] UCC 4–208(1)(b).

$21,079.43. The deposit was provisionally credited by plaintiff to the B & D Automotive account and the overdrawn balance was reduced by that amount. The plaintiff later "bounced" (dishonored) the $2,585.50 check—returned it to the defendant, City Bank, because of insufficient funds. When the plaintiff, Laurel, then presented the cashier's check for $3,446 to the defendant, City Bank, it was dishonored.

The trial court concluded (1) that the plaintiff was a mere holder of the cashier's check because it did not establish that it took the check for value, and (2) that the defendant, City Bank, established a defense of want of consideration because the $2,585.50 check, which was one of the items used to purchase the cashier's check, was subsequently dishonored. The court rendered judgment for the plaintiff in the amount of only $860.50, the difference between the checks. The plaintiff then appealed.

Decision

For the plaintiff; new trial.

Reasoning

Defendant established want of consideration, which is a valid defense against a holder but not against an HIDC. The trial court held that no value was given because credit against the Maisto account was not irrevocable. Since Maisto's account B was overdrawn, the plaintiff, Laurel Bank, did give value through an antecedent claim. The provisional basis of credit in no way hinders the value given to determine one's HIDC status. The plaintiff's action in provisionally crediting a $9,501 deposit to the antecedent debt of Maisto was an exercise of its common law right of set-off. The plaintiff was an HIDC as far as value given is concerned. The judgment of the lower court is set aside and the matter remanded for trial limited to the issue of whether the plaintiff took the cashier's check in good faith and without notice of its being overdue, of dishonor, defect, or defense.

Laurel Bank and Trust Company v. The City National Bank of Connecticut, 365 A.2d 1222 (Conn. 1976).

Good Faith

Good faith.

There is a simply stated test for the good faith of a holder—"honesty in fact in the conduct or transaction concerned."[15] The test is entirely subjective in nature, i.e., the holder is not judged by an objective standard of reasonableness or anything else. Even though a reasonable person would or should have suspected some defense or claim, if the holder honestly did not, he can satisfy the good faith test.

The good faith test, sometimes characterized as "empty head–honest heart," means that a holder can meet this criterion even though he negligently or carelessly turns a deaf ear to facts and circumstances that would put a reasonable person on notice of a defense. Such disregard for suspicious circumstances, however, may cause one to flunk the "notice"[16] test. In the following case the court held that the carelessness of the holder did not constitute bad faith.

---

[15] UCC 1–201(19).

[16] UCC 1–201(25).

Facts

The defendant, Leo's Used Car Exchange, Inc. (Leo), is being sued for stopping payment on two checks totaling $15,150 which were issued to payee, Villa's Auto Sales, Inc., in payment for two cars. An authorized agent of Villa's indorsed the checks and cashed them at the plaintiff bank, Industrial National. Normal procedure at Industrial National calls for the manager to approve corporate checks drawn on another bank. The manager would approve if he knew the person cashing the check and knew his business. But these two checks were cashed by a teller at National Industrial Bank without the manager's approval being sought. The plaintiff bank will qualify as an HIDC and be successful in its suit against Leo if it purchased the two checks in good faith.

Decision

For the plaintiff, Industrial National.

Reasoning

The defendant argued that the plaintiff failed to exercise ordinary care by violating its own rule of management, and that this is evidence of lack of good faith. However, good faith only requires "honesty in fact in the conduct or transaction concerned." Nothing in the definition suggests that, in addition to being honest, the holder must exercise due care as well. In those situations where the UCC has required more than "honesty in fact," it has explicitly so stated.

This is not to say that negligence has no role in the determination of one's HIDC status. Evidence of negligence goes to the notice requirement, however; it is not relevant to the issue of good faith.

Industrial National Bank of R.I. v. Leo's Used Car Exchange, Inc., 291 N.E.2d 603 (Mass. 1973).

Notice.

The Notice Requirement

If a holder takes an instrument with notice that there is a claim or defense against it, or that it is overdue or has been dishonored, then he can not qualify as an HIDC.[17] A holder has notice of one of these facts if:

1. he has actual knowledge of it; or
2. he has received[18] a notice or notification of it; or
3. from all the facts and circumstances *known to him at the time in question,* he has *reason to know* that it exists.[19]

Effective notice must allow a reasonable time to act.[20] To illustrate, assume that H is in good faith—i.e., that he honestly does not know that M, the maker of a note, has a defense of fraud against P, the payee. If H has received notification of this defense through the mails, and, while it has not actually come to his attention, the letter has been delivered to his business address in ample time for receipt of such communications,[21] then H has legal notice of the defense and can not qualify as an HIDC.

Next—and still on the assumption that H is in good faith—suppose that two days before maturity he pays $100 for a $1,000 note which has been in circulation, with interest compounded, for ten years. The reason P, the payee, is

---

[17] UCC 3–302(1)(c).   [19] Ibid.   [21] UCC 1–201(26).

[18] UCC 1–201(25).   [20] UCC 3–304(6).

willing to sell the instrument so cheaply is that he has defrauded the maker. Since H honestly does not know of the fraud, will he qualify as an HIDC? Not likely. The sale of this instrument at *such a large discount* is a fact "known to him at the time in question" and will probably be sufficient to give H "reason to know" that some defense exists.[22]

Claims exist when the owner has been wrongfully deprived of the instrument. In the above illustration, H would not qualify as an HIDC if, at the time he became a holder, he had notice of a *claim* rather than notice of a *defense*. The owner of an instrument would have a claim if it were stolen by someone and transferred to H. On the assumption that the instrument was *bearer* in form at the time it was stolen, H could be an HIDC if he had no notice of the owner's claim, and if all the other requirements were met.

If the instrument was *order* in form, however, the thief would have to forge the owner's indorsement, and in that event, H could not become an HIDC because he would not be a holder—the instrument did not flow to him by indorsement. Even in those situations where H is in good faith and has no notice of the forgery, title does not pass to him through the unauthorized indorsement of the forger.[23]

Notice of a Claim or Defense. The following are illustrative of those events that will give notice of a claim or defense and prevent a holder from becoming an HIDC:[24]

1. Visible evidence of forgery, alteration, or other irregularity (such as wholesale incompleteness) that calls into question the validity, terms, or ownership of the instrument.
2. Information that the obligation of some party is voidable—e.g., the party was induced by fraud or mistake to sign the instrument—or, information that all parties have been discharged—e.g., all signatures have been cancelled or the instrument has been paid.
3. Knowledge that the **fiduciary** has negotiated in breach of duty—e.g., an instrument indorsed "Pay to T in trust for P, [signed] P" was negotiated by T to H in payment of T's personal debt.

fiduciary
a person with a duty to act primarily for the benefit of another

In the following case the drawee bank was held to be on notice of the payee's agent acting contrary to his fiduciary duty, thereby precluding the drawee from being an HIDC.

Facts

The Mott Grain Company had signed an agreement with the First National Bank & Trust Co. of Bismark to allow any one of three of Mott's men to indorse the checks received by the company and have them deposited in the company's account at the bank. One of these men, Vernon Baszler, indorsed some $40,520.93 of such checks and, instead of having them placed in the company's account, he had them placed in his own account at the same bank. Vernon Baszler was later convicted of criminal charges, and the Mott Grain Company sued to get its money back from First National.

---

[22] UCC 1–201(25)(c).   [23] UCC 3–404.   [24] UCC 3–304(1)(2).

Decision

For the plaintiff, Mott Grain Company.

Reasoning

The court held that Baszler was depositing third-party checks payable to the grain company in his personal account and thus "for his own benefit." Thus, the bank did have notice and does not qualify as a holder in due course. The purchaser has notice of a claim against an instrument when he has knowledge that a fiduciary has negotiated the instrument in payment of or as security for his own debt or in any transaction for his own benefit or otherwise in breach of duty.

Mott Grain Company v. First National Bank & Trust Co. of Bismark, 259 N.W.2d 667 (N.D. 1977).

Notice That the Instrument Is Overdue or Dishonored.   A purchaser is given notice that an instrument is overdue or dishonored if he has *reason to know:*

principal
(in money) the capital sum of a money debt

default
a failure to perform a legal duty

1. that the **principal,** or any part of it, is overdue, or that there is an uncured **default** in payment of another instrument of the same series; or
2. that acceleration of the instrument has been made; or
3. that a demand instrument is being taken after a previous unsuccessful demand for payment, or after an unreasonable length of time following issuance (a reasonable period of time for an uncertified check drawn and payable in the U.S. is presumed to be thirty days).[25]

There are some events which do not convey notice. The public filing or recording of a document which relates to a negotiable instrument does *not* give notice sufficient to prevent a purchaser from becoming an HIDC.[26] Nor does knowledge of the following facts give notice of a claim or defense:[27]

1. the instrument was antedated or postdated;
2. the instrument was issued in exchange for an executory (unperformed) promise;
3. the instrument has an accommodation signature;
4. completion of an incomplete instrument, without notice of impropriety;
5. negotiation by a fiduciary but without knowledge that the fiduciary is breaching a duty;
6. default in payment of interest on the instrument or in payment of another instrument (except a default on an instrument of the same series).

Rights of a Holder in Due Course

If a holder qualifies as an HIDC, he takes the instrument

1. free of *all claims*—e.g., the true owner of lost or stolen bearer paper cannot reclaim it from an HIDC;
2. free of all defenses, except real or universal defenses and defenses of those parties who dealt with the HIDC.[28]

---

[25] UCC 3–304(3).   [26] UCC 3–304(5).   [27] UCC 3–304(4).   [28] UCC 3–305.

Real or Universal Defenses

While a negotiable instrument is, for all appearances, a formal written contract, it may not be *contractually* binding on various parties because either they don't have the capacity to contract, or they assert other defenses which preclude or relieve them of contractual liability on the instrument.[29] Defenses to *contractual* liability on an instrument are called **real** or **universal defenses.** The following are examples of real defenses.

real or **universal defense**
a defense to *contractual* liability on an instrument

Minority

This defense is allowed against an HIDC to the same extent that state law will allow it against anyone else.[30] For example, in most states a minor has the option to disaffirm any contract made with an adult. If the minor disaffirms the purchase of a *necessary* item, he is liable for the reasonable value. For *nonnecessaries,* the minor simply returns or offers to return what is left of the item (if anything) and is entitled to receive back all of the money he paid for the item. The adult is generally not permitted to retain any part of the money for wear and tear, damage, or depreciation.

Those states which follow the majority view outlined above would allow the minor a full defense against an HIDC if the minor purchased nonnecessaries. The HIDC would have to recover from other parties to the instrument on their indorsement contracts or their transfer warranties.

If the minor purchased a necessary item, he would be liable to the HIDC for an amount equaling the reasonable value of the item. For the amount between the reasonable value and the larger amount on the face of the instrument, the HIDC would have to pursue other parties to the instrument.

Insanity or Duress Precluding Contractual Liability

A person who has been judicially committed to a mental institution has been **adjudicated** not to have capacity to contract. He can not be contractually liable as a party to a negotiable instrument. If he made or drew such an instrument, which was later negotiated to an HIDC, he could assert the real defense of lack of capacity.

adjudicate
to determine by judicial authority

The effect of **duress** (coercion) in influencing someone to sign a negotiable instrument depends upon the law in each particular state. In some instances the duress causes the contract to be voidable, in which case duress is a "personal defense" (discussed later) not assertable successfully against an HIDC. In other instances the duress prevents the transaction from being a contract, in which case it is a real defense assertable successfully against all parties. For example, T threatens D that, if D doesn't sign the check as drawer, T will urge the district attorney to prosecute D's wife for the commission of an alleged crime. D signs

duress
wrongful inducement to do that which a reasonable person would have been unable to resist

---

[29] UCC 3–305(2)(a)–(e).   [30] UCC 3–305(2)(a).

the check. D is liable on the check as a voidable contract, which he can avoid; he has a "personal defense." However, if T pointed a loaded gun at D's head, compelling D to sign the check, while the instrument is negotiable on its face, it is *not a contract* binding *D* as a party to it because D did not intentionally or voluntarily create it. This is a form of duress precluding contractual liability; it is a real defense, and D is protected from any liability on the check. But the instrument can be negotiated by P to an HIDC, and *P* would be liable thereon as a contracting party. The HIDC will have to recover from the wrongdoer or some indorser or transferor subsequent to the wrongdoer.

Illegality

Illegality also may be a real defense. For example, some states prohibit the enforcement of any contract or instrument given in connection with a gambling transaction. These obligations are treated as **null** and void because gambling is thought to be inimical to the public interest and, therefore, contrary to public policy. In such a state, an HIDC would be confronted with a real defense if the maker or drawer of an instrument can prove that it was issued in payment of a gambling debt.

Another common illustration of illegality as a real defense is **usury.** Some states penalize the charging of an excessive rate of interest on a loan by absolutely denying the enforcement of usurious instruments. The remedy of an HIDC in such cases is against the indorser or warrantor.

In each of these examples the nature of the defense—whether or not it is a real defense—depends on state law. In some states—Nevada for instance—gambling may be no defense at all. In some states illegality merely makes the contract voidable. Accordingly, where illegality makes the transaction *void,* it is a *real defense.* When illegality makes the transaction *voidable,* it is a *personal defense.*

In the following case, the maker of a negotiable promissory note issued it in violation of a court injunction, but, since the basis on which the maker issued the note was not illegal by statute, the maker did not have a real defense on the ground of illegality.

null
of no legal effect

usury
charging a rate of interest on a loan higher than that permitted by statute

Facts

The Berenyi's, defendants, bought carpeting from Kroyden Industries. The sales representative offered to *give* the Berenyi's the carpeting, valued in the contract at $44 per square yard, without making any payments on their $1,520 note as long as they referred prospective customers to Kroyden. At the time of this offer, Kroyden was under an injunction to refrain from making such offers. The Berenyi's signed a negotiable promissory note for $1,520, which was later negotiated to the plaintiff, New Jersey Mortgage and Investment Corp., who sued the defendants on the note.

Decision

For plaintiff, New Jersey Mortgage.

Reasoning

The plaintiff took the note with no knowledge of the action against Kroyden or that Kroyden had violated the injunction. The plaintiff qualified as an HIDC. The question here is whether the defense is "real" or "personal," since only "real" defenses are available against an HIDC. UCC states that an HIDC takes an instrument free from all defenses of any party to the instrument with whom the holder has not dealt, except incapacity, duress, or illegality of the transaction, as renders the obligation of the party a nullity. But the fact that it was illegal for *Kroyden* to enter the transaction did not render the *Berenyi's* obligation under the note a nullity. Since there is *no statute* that makes a note obtained in violation of an injunction void and unenforceable, the illegality involved is not a "real" defense. Therefore, the note is enforceable in the hands of an HIDC who had no knowledge of the injunction.

New Jersey Mortgage and Investment Corp. v. Andrew and Anna Berenyi, 356 A.2d 421 (N.J. 1976).

Fraud in the Procurement

A person who has signed an instrument has a real defense if he has been deceived to the extent that

1. he *does not know* that he signed *an instrument, or* he *knows* that he signed an instrument, but is completely *tricked and deceived* regarding its essential *terms, and*
2. this person has not acted negligently or carelessly.[31]

If a country-western music fan rushes up to Willie Nelson to get his autograph, Willie will have a real or universal defense against a subsequent HIDC if that signature was placed on a negotiable note cleverly hidden in an autograph pad. It is clear that Willie did not intend to create the note, and, on the assumption that under these circumstances he was not negligent, he will be protected if the "fan" negotiates the instrument to an HIDC.

This defense would arise as well if the person who knowingly and intentionally signed an instrument did not have knowledge or reasonable opportunity to obtain knowledge of its essential terms. For example, assume that M is given one note to read and become familiar with while the salesman is filling in the blanks of a supposedly identical note. Actually there are new and unfavorable terms in the salesman's note, but M has been told that they are identical. Finally, the salesman switches notes with M, and M innocently signs the one with the unfavorable terms. This will give M a real defense even if the salesman negotiates the note to an HIDC.

The common features in these two examples of the real defense of fraud—sometimes called fraud in the *procurement* or *factum*—are

1. no intent to create a negotiable instrument, *or* no knowledge of the terms, *and*
2. no negligence.

---

[31] UCC 3–305(2)(c).

In effect, *no contract has been created,* so there is no legal ground for liability.

If, on the other hand, a person really intends to create a negotiable instrument but has been *induced* to do so by P's fraud and deceit—e.g., P has lied to M regarding some essential component of a stereo unit—M would have only a personal or limited defense, which would not be valid against an HIDC. Such a defense of fraud in the inducement would be successful against a mere holder or assignee but not against an HIDC, who could get a judgment against M. M would then have to seek recovery against P, the person who defrauded him. This "personal" or "limited" defense of fraud—where M really intends to create the instrument and is not so defrauded that he does not know what he is signing—is known as *fraud in the inducement* or *fraud in the execution.*

Unauthorized Signatures

A forgery or unauthorized signature does not obligate the person whose name has been wrongfully used, unless that person ratifies the signature or is precluded by his negligence from denying the signature.[32] The rationale for this rule is obvious. Since the person whose name has been forged had no intention of creating the instrument or parting with ownership, he is not obligated by the forgery. He has not agreed to any contract, and he is not liable on the instrument because his signature does not appear thereon. If the real owner's *indorsement* has been forged, he still has a claim to the instrument. The recipient of such an instrument, which is later reclaimed by the true owner, can attempt to recover from the wrongdoer on the forged indorsement[33] or on the transfer warranties.[34] In the following case, the drawer/drawee was held liable on its draft to one of the payees whose indorsement was forged.

Facts

The plaintiff, Naoma Lee, appealed from an order dismissing her complaint against the American National Life Insurance Company. The plaintiff had sued the insurance company for a fire loss covering the premises which she and another had contracted to sell to Murl and Adeline Skidmore. In her complaint, the plaintiff alleged that a contract of insurance was procured from the defendant by the parties pursuant to a land contract. The Skidmores and Naoma Lee were the named insureds.

On September 10, 1974 the property covered by the policy was partially destroyed by fire. The plaintiff maintained that the defendant company was notified of the fire but failed to indemnify her for the loss, which she alleges was $2,500. The company contended that it issued a draft on October 14, 1974 in the sum of $2,125 in the name of the land contract buyers (Skidmores) *and* plaintiff Lee to cover the fire damage. It maintained that, by issuing this instrument, which was apparently cashed by the Skidmores over plaintiff's forged indorsement, it has satisfied its obligation to plaintiff. Lee never got any of the money.

---

[32] UCC 3–404, 406. [34] UCC 3–417(2).

[33] UCC 3–404(1).

Decision

Judgment for plaintiff.

Reasoning

"Under the Ohio statute, an instrument payable to the order of two or more persons . . . if not in the alternative is payable to all of them and may be negotiated, discharged, or enforced only by all of them." The draft in question was not payable in the alternative, and therefore it could not be properly negotiated nor discharged following the unauthorized and forged indorsement. As the defendant was both the drawer and drawee of the draft, it was obligated to make payment to the named payees therein, or other proper holders.

The payment of the draft through a forged indorsement failed to discharge the instrument as to the plaintiff, and such a payment by the drawer-drawee constitutes a conversion of that instrument for which it must respond in damages.

Lee v. Skidmore, 361 N.E.2d 499 (Ohio 1976).

Remember to distinguish *forgery* from the signature of an *impostor,* because the signature of an impostor does pass good title to the holder. The holder may even qualify as an HIDC, but there can never be a holder or an HIDC following a required indorsement which has been forged.

Material Alteration

The real or universal defense of **material alteration** can best be understood by considering, first, its definition, then its general effect, and finally its effect on an HIDC.[35] Keep in mind, however, that a defendant's *negligence* can deprive him of this defense just as it can deprive one of the defense of forgery,[36] and further that any party may assent to or *ratify* a material alteration.

Any change in the contract of any party to the instrument in *any* respect is a material alteration. It may be only a slight change such as the addition of one cent to the amount payable or an advance of one day in the date of payment.[37] This definition includes, but is not limited to, unauthorized filling in the blanks on an incomplete instrument as well as adding to or deleting from the instrument.

For example, an incomplete instrument may be issued to a payee-creditor with instructions to fill in the amount with the balance due. If this *holder* fills in an excessive amount, that would be a material alteration. It would be a material alteration as well if this person added, changed, deleted, or in any way modified terms of a complete instrument to which the issuer previously had become bound. In the following case, the unauthorized completion of an incomplete instrument in the amount payable was a material alteration not assertable against the HIDC.

material alteration
"any alteration of an instrument which changes the contract of any party thereto in any respect"
UCC 3-407 (1)

---

[35] UCC 3-407.

[36] UCC 3-406.

[37] UCC 3-407, comment 1.

Facts

Elias Saka, defendant, gave Weaver Levy a signed check that was blank regarding the amount. Levy was instructed to complete it for $800 and make payment to the payee, Sahara Hotel, plaintiff, on a $3,046.03 bill charged to Affinity Pictures, Inc. Instead, Levy completed the check for the full amount of $3,046.03 and delivered it to the Sahara. Saka stopped payment on the check, and this suit was instituted by Sahara for the full amount. Saka alleges by way of defense (1) that the payee Sahara is not an HIDC because it had notice that the charges were disputed and (2) that the completion of the check by Levy in a different handwriting from that of the drawer, Saka, was sufficient to put Sahara on notice of irregularity.

Decision

Judgment for Sahara.

Reasoning

A payee may be an HIDC, UCC 3-302(2), but, as a practical matter, this is the exception rather than the rule. Since the payee is an immediate party to the underlying transaction, under normal circumstances he cannot claim this status because he necessarily knows of any defenses to the contract. However, Saka's evidence was not sufficient to raise the issue that the hotel had notice of a dispute.

The fact that the body of the check was completed in a different handwriting from that of the drawer's signature did not impose on Sahara the duty to make further inquiries, nor did it destroy Sahara's good faith because UCC 3-304(4)(d) provides that knowledge that an incomplete instrument has been completed by another does not of itself give the purchaser notice of a claim or defense unless the purchaser has notice of any improper completion.

Elias Saka v. Sahara-Nevada Corporation, 558 P.2d 535 (Nev. 1976).

The next inquiry concerns the *effect* of a material alteration. If a *holder* makes a material alteration *and* if it is made with a fraudulent purpose, any party whose contract is thereby changed receives a discharge from any further liability on the instrument. This means that, if the payee of an instrument raised the amount from $100 to $1,000, the maker or drawer is fully discharged.

If this instrument was issued by a buyer for merchandise, the buyer could retain the goods without making further payment to the seller payee-creditor. The payee-creditor is penalized for his fraud. To carry this example one step further, the payee and the issuer would be discharged if the material alteration was made by a *subsequent* holder. Those persons on the instrument *prior* to the material alteration are the ones whose contract and liability on the instrument are so affected.

Alterations that are not made by *holders,* or alterations that are made by holders *without any fraudulent intent,* do not discharge anyone. To illustrate: if a holder extended the time of payment with the purpose and effect of benefiting the debtor, there would be no material alteration, and the debtor would not be discharged. Nor would anyone be discharged if the change was made by a person who did not qualify as a holder.

In the following case, it was held that the alteration was not material nor fraudulently made.

Facts

The plaintiff, William C. Thomas, filed suit alleging that the defendants, Mr. and Mrs. Osborn, as makers of a note payable to the plaintiff, refused to pay the note when due. After the note was signed, the plaintiff had a notary public who had seen James Osborn sign the note, but had not witnessed Mrs. Osborn's signature, add an acknowledgment and notarize the signature of James. The defendants denied the plaintiff's claim and asserted that the note was obtained by misrepresentation. They also counterclaimed for damages claimed to have resulted when the plaintiff added an acknowledgment to the note and when the note was recorded. The court entered judgment for the plaintiff.

The defendants challenged the decision of the trial court. They claimed that the acknowledgment, notarization, and recording of the note was fraudulent and a material alteration under UCC 3–407.

Decision

Affirmed, for plaintiff.

Reasoning

The Osborns contended that the recording of the note added the relationship of mortgagor-mortgagee to that of maker-payee and, therefore, there was a material alteration of the note. However, the note cannot be taken as a mortgage, for it does not contain the expression of an intent to impose a lien upon the property. The note includes the legal description of the real property because the terms of the note provide for payment in full on sale of the property and not because of the granting of a security interest which might be looked to in case of default. According to UCC 3–407, an alteration may be material if it involves a change in "the number or relations of the parties." In this case, the instrument could not be construed as a mortgage, and thus it did not change the relations of the parties.

The Code says that "alteration by a holder which is both fraudulent and material discharges any party whose contract is thereby changed . . ." 3–407(2)(a). Neither the recording of the instrument nor the addendum changed the relationships of the parties, or materially affected the form of the document, the time of payment, or the sum payable. Thus the change is not material. Finally, the plaintiff did not act fraudulently. The plaintiff's purpose for recording the note was to achieve security for payment of the debt; his intent was "misguided" rather than fraudulent.

Thomas v. Osborn, 536 P.2d 8 (Wash. 1975).

Material alterations do not deprive a subsequent HIDC of the right to enforce the instrument for the *original amount,* or *for the amount that was fraudulently inserted on an incomplete instrument.* If a payee raised a $100 instrument to $1,000 or improperly filled in the amount of $1,000 on an incomplete instrument, the issuer would be liable to an HIDC for $100 on the *raised* instrument, and for $1,000 on the *improperly completed one.*

Discharge

If at the time the instrument is received the HIDC has notice that a party has been discharged, the discharge will operate as a real defense against the HIDC. Discharge in insolvency proceedings is a real defense even if the HIDC has no notice of it.

Personal or Limited Defenses

Defenses which seek to *avoid* liability on the instrument (*voidable* contract) are called **personal** or **limited defenses.** Such defenses can not be asserted successfully against an HIDC. Examples are:

1. fraud inducing the making of an instrument;
2. failure of consideration;
3. want of consideration;
4. defenses to liability on a contract, a valid claim to the instrument by anyone;
5. nonperformance of any condition precedent;
6. nondelivery of the instrument;
7. delivery for a special purpose which has not occurred and the instrument was unauthorizedly delivered; and
8. generally other defenses which are not real defenses, just discussed.

To illustrate: suppose D issues his check to P to pay for goods which P promised to deliver to D. P never delivered the goods and never intended to do so. D has the personal defenses of fraud and failure of consideration, which D can assert successfully against P and later holders but not against a subsequent HIDC. If D issues a check to P as a gift, there is a *want* of consideration.

HIDC and the Federal Trade Commission

The FTC issued a rule in 1976 that has the effect of denying the rights of an HIDC to a holder who receives an instrument given in a *consumer credit transaction.* The rule declares that it is an unfair and deceptive practice within section 5 of the Federal Trade Commission Act for the credit-seller of personal, family, or household goods or services to natural persons to use *any* method of financing that separates the seller's duty to perform from the buyer's duty to pay.

In at least ten-point boldface type, the seller must include the following *notice #1* in any consumer credit contract executed by the buyer, and *notice #2* in any direct loan financing agreement which the seller arranges for the buyer.

Notice #1
ANY HOLDER OF THIS CONSUMER CREDIT CONTRACT IS SUBJECT TO ALL CLAIMS AND DEFENSES WHICH THE DEBTOR COULD ASSERT AGAINST THE SELLER OF GOODS OR SERVICES OBTAINED PURSUANT HERETO OR WITH THE PROCEEDS HEREOF. RECOVERY HEREUNDER BY THE DEBTOR SHALL NOT EXCEED AMOUNTS PAID BY THE DEBTOR HEREUNDER.

Notice #2
ANY HOLDER OF THIS CONSUMER CREDIT CONTRACT IS SUBJECT TO ALL CLAIMS AND DEFENSES WHICH THE DEBTOR COULD ASSERT AGAINST THE SELLER OF GOODS OR SERVICES OBTAINED WITH THE PROCEEDS HEREOF. RECOVERY HEREUNDER BY THE DEBTOR SHALL NOT EXCEED AMOUNTS PAID BY THE DEBTOR HEREUNDER.

The rule covers sellers who in the ordinary course of business sell or lease goods or services to consumers. It does not include the following:

1. sales for industrial or commercial uses;

2. transactions by legal entities other than natural persons;
3. purchases of realty, commodities, securities, farm equipment, or services of public utilities;
4. consumer goods or services where the purchase price is more than $25,000.

To illustrate: assume that a consumer enters into a credit purchase of a stereo with a local retailer. Prior to the FTC rule, the consumer may have been required to sign a negotiable promissory note for the unpaid balance, and the note may have been negotiated to an HIDC. If so, the HIDC could get a judgment against the consumer who defaulted upon payments even though the stereo never functioned properly.

Today the consumer preserves all his defenses, and these defenses may be asserted against the retailer or against a third party who, except for the FTC rule, would have had the rights of an HIDC. The third party is treated as an *assignee* of the retailer-assignor's rights. The third party assignee or transferee simply stands in the shoes of the retailer and is subject to all the defenses that are available against the retailer.

Summary Statement

1. An HIDC is a holder who has given value for a negotiable instrument in good faith and without notice of a claim or defense to the instrument or that the instrument is overdue or has been previously dishonored. A payee may qualify as an HIDC. Personal defenses can not be asserted successfully against an HIDC, but real defenses can be asserted against the HIDC. However, even an HIDC is subject to the defenses (real or personal) of a party *with whom he has dealt.*
2. *Value* means that the consideration promised in exchange for an instrument has been executed or performed. It may also consist of an antecedent (preexisting) claim (past debt), whether the claim is due or not, or of a security interest acquired by any party (including a bank). Value is given when negotiable instruments are exchanged and when one party makes an irrevocable commitment to another in reliance on a negotiable instrument.
3. The *good faith* required of an HIDC simply means that he must have acted *honestly in fact* in the transaction in which he purchased the instrument. This standard is completely *subjective* and is applied on a case-by-case basis.
4. *Notice* of a claim or defense to the instrument, or that the instrument is overdue or previously dishonored, is a more rigid or *objective* standard than good faith. A holder has notice of one of these and is prevented from becoming an HIDC: (a) if he has actual knowledge; or (b) if he has received notice even though he has not actually read it within a reasonable time after receipt; or (c) if from all the facts and circumstances *known to him at the time in question* the holder has *reason to know* that one of these defects exists.
5. One may be confronted with notice of a claim or a defense, or that an instrument is overdue or dishonored, by information which appears on the

face of the instrument or from outside sources. However, *no notice* is conveyed: (a) by the filing of a document which affects the instrument; (b) by antedating or postdating; (c) by issuance of the instrument for an executory promise; (d) by knowledge of accommodation signatures; (e) by completion of an incomplete instrument; (f) by the negotiation of a fiduciary (T negotiates to you an instrument previously indorsed restrictively, "Pay to T in trust for X, [signed] Billy Carter," and you are without knowledge of any breach of trust by T); or (g) by default in payment of interest or in payment of another instrument.

6. Basically, a mere holder takes an instrument subject to all claims and defenses that may exist, but an HIDC is free from all claims and free from all defenses *except* real defenses and defenses of parties with whom he has dealt. Real defenses arise when the basic obligation for which the instrument was originally issued is *null* and *void*. This may be because the initial transaction—e.g., gambling "contracts" in some states—was completely illegal and prohibited by statute, or because a "contract" never really existed in the first place—e.g., extreme duress or other lack of capacity, fraud in the procurement or factum, forgery, or fraudulent material alteration. A discharge in insolvency proceedings is a real defense, and the same is true of any other discharge that the HIDC has notice of when he takes the instrument.

7. The Federal Trade Commission has adopted a rule which has the effect of eliminating HIDCs from consumer credit transactions. Those parties who would normally qualify as HIDCs under the UCC are subjected to the same defenses as a retailer who has made a credit sale of personal, family, or household goods or services to a consumer.

This chapter has emphasized the benefits of the status of a holder in due course. The following case illustrates how this status can be ignored by the court in the absence of legislation when the court senses that it is being abused and justice and equity demand such action.

Matthews v. Aluminum Acceptance Corp.
137 N.W.2d 280 (Mich. 1965)

Fitzgerald, Judge. If ever the elements of a classic case involving an aluminum siding company and its subsequent assignee were before an appellate court, that case unravels here. It could be drawn from the files of almost any practising lawyer, or it might be the complaint of the next client in the waiting room.

In this action to enjoin defendant from enforcing any claims against plaintiffs and from foreclosing the mortgage upon plaintiffs' home, the questions on appeal are whether constructive forgery or fraud was established and whether the entire transaction was shot through with usury.

In April of 1962, plaintiffs Robert and Katherine Matthews were approached by representatives of All-Style Builders, aluminum siding applicators. They allege that All-Style indicated that their modest home had been chosen as a demonstration site for aluminum siding for that area. New siding was to be applied over the tar paper on their home, and in addition they were to be given a loan of $650 in cash to fix their tractor, and the total price of this was to be $3,250.

Further, they were to receive $100 to apply against their contract for each potential customer which All-Style brought to view their newly sided home.

To the Matthews, the alleged inducements were sufficiently alluring that they signed up for the package. The siding was applied, they were given $650, but to time of trial no one had even shown up to view the siding as a potential customer.

When the smoke cleared, so to speak, the Matthews learned that the instrument they had signed included a promissory note and mortgage calling for 84 equal monthly installments at the rate of $61.04 per month for a grand total of $5,127.36, not the $3,250 they had anticipated, and the instruments had been assigned to defendant Aluminum Acceptance Corporation, a firm specializing in financing siding application.

All-Style Builders is not a party to this suit, and defendant Aluminum Acceptance claims it is a bona fide holder of the paper, denies fraud, and further claims that the instruments are not usurious because the agreement provided for a cash price, whereas the note and mortgage represent a "time price" and a discount transaction.

As to the transaction itself, Mr. Matthews says that he was unable to read any but the largest print, and that only with difficulty, and Mrs. Matthews was able only to read the printed portion with her glasses and that the papers were stacked one on top of another at the time of signing and with the upper portions covered, leaving visible only the area to be signed. The papers, they further allege, were blank at the time of signing.

Plaintiffs made only one payment and now seek to enjoin foreclosure of the mortgage, and defendant counterclaims seeking foreclosure, deficiency, and such other relief "as shall be agreeable to equity and good conscience."

The latter phrase is a little difficult to digest when the record is studied closely.

Judgment was entered canceling the mortgage and giving defendant judgment on its counterclaim in the sum of $3,250. Aluminum Acceptance Corporation appeals this judgment. The rule in Michigan is that a signature deceptively procured is in law a forgery, and those who subsequently acquire interest under the forged instrument are in no better position than if they had purchased with notice.

Appellant corporation also urges that if, as the defendant, it is a holder in due course, it is immaterial whether or not there was fraud in the inducement with respect to the promissory note.

The agreement gave defendant notice of the agreed contract price of $3,250 while the note and mortgage stated the sum of $5,127.36. Such a disparity furnishes ample notice of the infirmity of the instrument and that it was usurious, rendering it impossible for defendant to be a holder in due course and to avail itself of such defenses as a holder in due course might have.

The judgment of the court is affirmed.

Questions and Case Problems

1. Defendant, Arena Auto Auction, Inc., created a problem by twice mailing checks to the wrong payee. After the wrong payee received the first check, he indorsed it in the name of the named payee and cashed it with the plaintiff, Park State Bank. Park State knew the wrong payee, had cashed his checks

and loaned him money in the past, and allowed him to withdraw the money before the check cleared.

Payment on the check was stopped, but, instead of correcting its error, the drawer-defendant (Arena Auto Auction) innocently issued another check to the same wrong payee. He attempted to cash it as well, but when Park State refused to cooperate, he hastily left town.

Is Park State liable for the amount of the first check because it dealt with a forger, or not? Discuss.

2. Temple drew a draft payable to the order of Yin-Li. Yin-Li indorsed in blank and lost it. The draft was found by Vasquez, who indorsed specially to Robel and negotiated it to Robel who gave value, in good faith, before maturity, and without knowledge of the preceding facts.
   a. Does Robel qualify as an HIDC?
   b. If Robel is an HIDC, is he subject to any valid claims or real defenses?
   c. If Vasquez retained the instrument, would he be a holder, HIDC, and subject to any claims or defenses?
   d. If Vasquez stole the instrument instead of finding it, discuss Robel's rights against Temple. All other facts remain as stated.

3. Defendant-maker issued a ninety-day $1,200 negotiable promissory note at 8.5 percent to the payee for the purchase of auto-parts inventory. Payee negotiated to an HIDC, who sold the instrument to A three days before maturity at a substantial discount. When A presented for payment at maturity, the defendant dishonored the instrument, alleging, among other things, that A was not an HIDC because he (A) had notice that payee never delivered the inventory. Result?

4. At the request of her attorney, 61-year-old Mrs. Frances MacDougal signed her name twelve times in the lower right-hand corner of designated pages fastened together at the top in tablet form. She glanced at the first few items, found them to be uniformly dull and unintelligible, and signed the remaining sheets without question. Her attorney, who was at all times present and had represented her in other legal matters over a period of eight years, volunteered no information except that her signature was needed to "expedite the performances of several contracts and for year-end tax purposes."

One of the items which she signed turned out to be a $4,000 negotiable promissory note to the attorney's order. He discounted it at a local bank before absconding with other embezzled funds from numerous other clients. On the assumption that the bank is an HIDC, is Mrs. MacDougal liable to it?

5. While burglarizing Drover's home, Cassidy stole, among other things, personalized check blanks that had been provided to Drover by his bank, the Sundance National Bank of Wyoming. Later, Cassidy used one of the blanks and drew a $250 check payable to the order of Great Western Hardware in Laramie. He identified himself as Drover with a fake I.D. prepared with the aid of pictures and other items taken from Drover's residence at the time of the burglary.

Great Western deposited the check in a Laramie bank for collection and it was paid by Sundance National. Drover detected the forgery when the cancelled check was returned to him at the end of the month along with a statement of his account. He insists that someone—either the Sundance Bank, the Laramie Bank, or Great Western—is responsible to him for the $250 since Cassidy disappeared. Discuss.

6. A drawee bank was sued by one of its depositors on a check originally drawn in payment for services in the amount of $1.25. Actually, the depositor allowed the payee to fill out the amount of the check for her signature. Given this opportunity, the payee wrote the figures of $1.25 far to the right side so that the number 684 could be added to the left of $1.25, and the words "One 25/100" were written close to the printed word "dollars" on the check blank so that "Six Thousand-Eight hundred-Forty" could be inserted ahead of the words, causing the check to read $6,841.25. The drawee honored the check for $6,841.25. Must the drawee reimburse the customer's account for the full (or any) amount? Discuss. [*Williams v. Montana National Bank of Bozeman*, 534 P.2d 1247 (Mont. 1975).]

7. Jesse Abrams issued a note when he borrowed money from the Peoples Credit Union of Long Island to purchase a stereo. He received a draft drawn by the credit union on the Chase Bank and deposited it in Webster Trust Co. Then he bought the stereo from Sound-City and gave his personal check drawn on Webster. The stereo proved defective. Sound-City refused to honor its warranty and is now insolvent. Abrams proceeded against Peoples Credit Union to cancel the note on the basis of FTC's 1976 rule "eliminating" HIDCs in consumer credit transactions. The note Abrams signed did not recite in ten-point bold face print the legend that the consumer-debtor retained all defenses which he could normally assert against the retailer. Discuss.

8. Carolyn Brazil entered into a contract with the payee of her check to make certain home improvements. The payee made false representations to her regarding the purchase of construction materials for the job and cashed the check that same day. When she discovered the deception, she stopped payment by the drawee. The plaintiff-depositary bank, Citizen National, which is acknowledged to be an HIDC, instituted this action against Brazil. Result? [*Citizens National Bank of Quitman v. Carolyn Brazil*, 233 S.E.2d 482 (Ga. 1977).]

9. Defendant Blackburn issued a check to Vanella for the purchase of a used car. Vanella deposited the check in plaintiff bank and received cash and credit. Blackburn stopped payment when he learned that Vanella misrepresented that the automobile was free of liens. Plaintiff received partial repayment of the value it advanced to Vanella and brings this action against Blackburn to recover the balance. It is conceded that the plaintiff bank is an HIDC. Discuss. [*Marine Midland Trust Co. of Rochester v. Blackburn*, 50 Misc.2d 954 (N.Y. 1966).]

10. In *Matthews v. Aluminum Acceptance Corp.* 137 N.W.2d 280 (Mich. 1965),[38] why did the defendant feel it was a holder in due course and on what basis in law, not equity, did the court refute this contention?

---

[38] See pp. 568–69.

30 Banks, Checks, and Customer Relations

After you have read this chapter, you should be able to:

1. Recognize the contractual relationship between the bank and its customers.
2. Assess a bank's liability for the wrongful dishonor of an item.
3. Determine when a bank may charge a customer's account.
4. Understand the importance and effectiveness of stop-payment orders.
5. Appreciate the customer's duty to examine cancelled checks and the risk involved in failing to do so.
6. Explain the bank's alternatives when confronted with stale checks and checks issued by customers who later become deceased.
7. Compare certified with uncertified checks.
8. Examine bank collection indorsements and checks with missing indorsements.

Introduction—The Nature of a Check

As individuals conducting personal business and transacting business for proprietorships, partnerships, and corporations, we will write checks and deal with banks. It is important to recognize that there is a body of law that governs banks and that has its impact on negotiable instruments. Our study of commercial paper would be incomplete, therefore, without an examination of the law of banking to the extent that it relates to checks and drafts.

The relationship between a drawee bank and its customer is debtor/creditor. The customer's check is a draft on the bank for the amount the bank owes the customer. A check is simply a "draft drawn on a bank and payable on demand."[1] It is assumed that there are sufficient funds on deposit with the drawee bank to cover any check which is issued; no such assumption is made with other drafts.

The demand nature of a check may be altered by postdating, but this does not affect its negotiability.[2] Since the drawee bank is under contract to follow orders of the depositor-drawer, it must not pay the check until the date arrives. The effect, then, of postdating is to change a check into a time draft.

A check does not operate as an assignment of funds in the hands of the drawee for payment of the holder. In fact, the holder has no rights against the drawee at all unless the drawee has accepted or certified the instrument.[3] If the drawee wrongfully dishonors an uncertified instrument, the holder can only pursue prior parties on their indorsements and warranties.

The Contract Between the Bank and Its Customer

When a check is deposited for collection, the bank becomes the agent or subagent of the owner; any settlement given for the item is provisional and may be charged back until the check is finally honored by the payor bank.[4] The bank must use ordinary care in forwarding any item for collection.[5] If it does, the bank will not be liable for the insolvency, neglect, misconduct, mistake, or default of another bank or person or for loss or destruction of an item in transit or in the possession of others.[6]

These and all other provisions of Article 4, Bank Deposits and Collections, can be changed by agreement of the bank and its customer. However, no agreement can disclaim the bank's liability for its lack of good faith or failure to exercise ordinary care; nor can an agreement limit the measure of damages for such lack of good faith or failure to exercise ordinary care. The bank and its customer may agree on reasonable **standards** of responsibility by which the conduct of the bank is to be judged.[7] In the following case, the court used the common law principle of estoppel as supplementary to the Code provisions in establishing a standard of responsibility.

standard
an established
measure

---

[1] UCC 3–104(2)(b).

[2] UCC 3–114(1).

[3] UCC 3–409(1). No one is liable on a negotiable instrument unless his signature is on it. UCC 3–401.

[4] UCC 4–201(1), 4–212.

[5] UCC 4–202(1).

[6] UCC 4–202(3).

[7] UCC 4–103(1).

Facts

Mr. Ulibarri operated a retail jewelry business in Denver and conducted his banking business with the First National Bank of Denver. He called the bank to inquire about the validity of a check issued to him by a customer in the amount of $3,500 and drawn on the First National for the purchase of a diamond ring. The reason for Mr. Ulibarri's call was to confirm the check's validity before releasing the ring to the customer. After talking to an officer of the bank and being assured that the check was genuine and the account sufficient to cover the amount, Mr. Ulibarri released the ring. However, when the check was presented for payment, the bank returned it marked, "No Account." Mr. Ulibarri contacted the bank but could not receive an adequate explanation, so he refused to repay the proceeds which the bank had advanced him on the check. The First National Bank of Denver then instituted the action against Ulibarri.

Decision

For Ulibarri.

Reasoning

Since Mr. Ulibarri suffered a loss by relying on the bank's assurances, the First National Bank of Denver was **estopped** from charging back the amount of the check against him. The Code states that, unless displaced by a particular section, the principles of law and equity including the law relative to estoppel shall supplement its provisions. UCC 1-103.

"The effect of the provisions of this Article may be varied by an agreement except that no agreement can disclaim a bank's responsibility for its own lack of good faith or failure to exercise ordinary care or can limit the measure of damages for such lack or failure . . ." UCC 4-103(1).

First National Bank of Denver v. Ulibarri,
557 P.2d 1221 (Colo. 1976).

Banks that participate in the collection process are supposed to take proper action on an item before the midnight deadline.[8] A bank acts seasonably or within the midnight deadline if it does so by midnight on the banking day following the one on which it receives the item.[9] Failure to act within this time limit can make the bank accountable for the face amount of an item.[10]

When an item has been finally paid or honored by the payor bank,[11] the relationship between the depositary bank and its customer becomes that of a debtor to its creditor. The bank is the debtor of its depositor to the extent of the money held on account. This is the basis of the customer's right to "order" its bank to pay one person or another.

Wrongful Dishonor

A bank is not liable on a check or other draft unless it certifies or accepts.[12] At that time it becomes a primary party and agrees to pay a holder according to the terms of the instrument.[13] Holders can not compel the drawee bank to honor

---

[8] UCC 4–202(2). [11] UCC 4–213.

[9] UCC 4–104(h). [12] UCC 3–410, 4–411.

[10] UCC 4–302. [13] UCC 3–413(1).

an uncertified or unaccepted instrument however; their recourse is against prior parties on the instrument.

If the drawee bank does refuse to honor a properly payable item—i.e., refuses to pay a check that has not been stopped, that is regular in form, and one for which there are sufficient funds on deposit—then the customer is entitled to recover from the drawee bank for damage proximately caused to the customer by the wrongful dishonor.[14]

The customer must prove the extent of his damages, just as he must prove the other facts of his case. This may include an amount for his arrest or prosecution or other consequential (indirect) damages. To illustrate: the direct damages proximately caused by wrongful dishonor might be the loss of profit on a transaction; consequential damages could be the permanent loss of that customer or damage to one's reputation. This is illustrated in the following case.

Facts

Depositor, Palmer, brought action against his bank to recover for the alleged wrongful dishonor of several checks. Jury found for the plaintiff and awarded actual and punitive damages, and the defendant appealed.

The trial court jury answered several issues, which were: (1) that someone forged Palmer's signature as an indorser on a $275 check; (2) that thereafter the bank intentionally refused payment of checks written by Palmer; (3) that the bank attempted to collect an overdraft resulting from the charge back against the account of the $275 check, and for insufficient check fund charges resulting from its dishonor of Palmer's checks after it knew or should have known that the indorsement was a forgery; (4) that Palmer had suffered actual damages of $2,000; (5) that Palmer was entitled to punitive damages of $3,500; and (6) that the dishonor of the checks was not the result of a mistake.

Decision

For Palmer.

Reasoning

The amount of actual damages included the $275 wrongfully charged against the account, plus subsequent checks written by Palmer which the bank "bounced," $15 service charges on these dishonored checks, plus the week's time he lost from work and school as a result. He is also entitled to damages for his mental anguish—embarrassment, humiliation, and being turned down for credit for the first time in his life.

If the failure of the bank to honor Palmer's checks had been a result of an honest mistake made in good faith, the actual damages in the amount of $2,000 would have been all he would receive. The trial court found, and the appellate court affirmed, that the bank had not acted in good faith and had wrongfully and maliciously refused payment on Palmer's checks even after they knew that Palmer's indorsement had been forged on the $275 check. The appellate court ruled that this lack of good faith and malicious action of the bank made it liable to punitive damages in the amount of $3,500.

Northshore Bank v. Palmer, 525 S.W. 2d 718 (Tex. 1975).

---

[14] UCC4–402.

When a Bank May Charge a Customer's Account

A bank may charge against its customer's account any item that is properly payable. This is true even though the charge creates an overdraft, because the issuance of the check itself carries authority to pay and the implied promise to reimburse the bank.[15]

Since the bank is under a contract with its depositor, it is supposed to know and record the status of each account and to follow its depositor's orders. When an overdraft is paid, the recipient is protected and the drawee is repaid by its customer. Except for recovery of bank payments[16] and for violation of presentment warranties,[17] the rule to remember is that payment is *final* in favor of an HIDC and those who have in good faith substantially changed their position in reliance on the payment.[18]

In keeping with the protection of an HIDC (see Real or Universal Defenses in chapter 29), a bank which in *good faith* makes payment to a *holder* may charge its customer's account for

tenor
what is stated as meant

1. the original **tenor** or amount of a materially altered item, or
2. the final or completed tenor of an item that was originally issued incomplete, unless the bank has notice that completion of the item was improper.[19]

To give an example, if the drawee-payor bank innocently charges a customer's account with an uncertified check that has been materially altered from $100 to $1,000, the customer can compel the bank to reimburse the account for $900. Material alteration is a real defense against an HIDC to the extent of the $900 alteration.[20] Since banks in the collection channel make transfer and presentment warranties, the drawee-payor bank would then be entitled to charge back against the presenting bank $900 for breach of material alteration warranty.[21]

If the bank in good faith pays an item that was originally issued incomplete, it can charge the customer for the full amount. In the absence of notice to the bank of improper completion, the customer takes responsibility for these instruments.

Stop-Payment Orders

A customer may order its bank to stop payment on a check, but the bank must be given a reasonable time to put the order into effect.[22] In the following case, the court found one and a half hours to be a reasonable time.

---

[15] UCC 4–401(1).

[16] UCC 4–213, 4–301.

[17] UCC 3–417(1), 4–207(1).

[18] UCC 3–418.

[19] UCC 4–401(2).

[20] UCC 3–407.

[21] UCC 3–417, 4–207.

[22] UCC 4–403(1).

Facts

The plaintiff, Tusso, delivered a check to the payee for the sum of $600 on July 24, 1972. The following morning at 9:00 a.m. the plaintiff appeared and placed a stop-payment order on the check. The same morning at 10:30 a.m. the payee appeared at the defendant Security National Bank, the same bank where the plaintiff had placed the stop order, and had the check certified. The bank charged the plaintiff's account immediately. Plaintiff sued to have the defendant Security National Bank reimburse his account.

Decision

For plaintiff Tusso.

Reasoning

Payment of a check in violation of a stop-payment order is a direct violation of the agreement between the customer and the bank. Therefore, the bank must recredit the plaintiff's account. The bank's claim that it was not given a reasonable amount of time in order to act on the order is denied. The court felt that any reasonable person would judge one and one-half hours to be a reasonable time to act on the stop-payment order.

Tusso v. Security National Bank, 76 Misc. 2d 12 (N.Y. 1973).

An oral stop order is effective for fourteen *calendar* days. Written orders or written confirmations of oral ones are valid for six months and may be renewed.[23]

If the bank pays despite a valid stop order, the customer can compel the bank to reimburse the account by proof of the fact and amount of the loss.[24] The bank is then **subrogated** to the customer's rights against the payee or any other holder of the check.[25] If this approach does not prevent unjust enrichment of the drawer-customer at the expense of the bank, the bank is subrogated to the rights of an HIDC, holder, or payee against the *drawer*.

subrogate
to substitute one person for another with reference to a claim or a right

Assume that D purchases merchandise from P and issues a $45 check on ABC Bank (drawee) in payment. If, without any legitimate reason, D simply decides not to pay and issues a valid stop order to ABC Bank, P would be successful in a lawsuit against D. D has made a contract with P and has no legal grounds to avoid payment.

If ABC Bank paid the check despite the stop order, its customer, the drawer, could not compel ABC Bank to reimburse his account because he has suffered no loss. Even if the bank initially reimbursed the account to appease its customer, it could subsequently charge back. Remember that the bank is subrogated to the rights of an HIDC, holder, or payee against the drawer to avoid a loss and prevent the drawer from being unjustly enriched. After all, there is no good reason to allow D to keep the merchandise and, simply at his whim, stop payment on the check issued to pay for it.

On the assumption that D has legal grounds for stopping payment—e.g., P never delivered the merchandise to D—the bank's negligence in paying despite the order will cause D a loss. In this event, D can compel ABC Bank to reimburse his account, and ABC will be subrogated to D's rights against P.

---

[23] UCC 4–403(2).   [25] UCC 4–407(c).

[24] UCC 4–403(3).

However, if P negotiated to an HIDC, the bank's conduct (negligent or not) in paying the check would not be the cause of D's loss. D had a personal defense only—failure of consideration—and an HIDC would have succeeded in an action against D in spite of this defense. Thus the bank would be subrogated to the HIDC's rights and could charge D's account. On the other hand, if D could prove a real defense, the bank's conduct in paying the check would cause D to suffer a loss, so it would have to reimburse D's account.

Stale Checks

When an uncertified check has been in circulation more than six months, the drawee is *not obligated* to pay it. Normally it will consult its depositor on such checks, but it has the option to pay them without consultation if it acts in good faith.[26] For example, the check may be issued in payment of dividends by one of the bank's corporate customers and held by one of the stockholders for more than six months. This check could be paid in good faith without consultation with the corporate issuer. In the following case it was held to be proper for the drawee bank to honor a check, in good faith, without consulting the drawer, fourteen months after the date of the check.

Facts

Advanced Alloys, Inc., plaintiff, wrote a check payable to Sergeant Steel Corp. For some reason, this check was not presented for payment until fourteen months later. The drawee, Chase Manhattan Bank, honored this stale check, and Advanced Alloys sued the bank, contending that it should have inquired of its depositor before honoring such an instrument, especially since the plaintiff had issued a written stop-payment order.

Decision

For the bank.

Reasoning

According to UCC 4-404, the bank, while not obligated to do so, may pay a stale check so long as it does so in good faith, and it is under no duty to make any inquiry of the depositor before doing so. The stop-payment order was good only for six months and the plaintiff had not renewed it. The question the court had to decide was whether or not the bank had acted in good faith as required by UCC 4-404. UCC 1-201(19) defines "good faith" as "honesty in fact in the conduct of the transaction concerned." Under this definition, it appears that the payment of a stale check, even without making inquiry, constitutes a payment "in good faith."

Advanced Alloys, Inc. v. Sergeant Steel Corp., 72 Misc.2d 614 (N.Y. 1973).

Death or Incompetence of a Customer

Neither death nor adjudication of incompetence of a customer of either a collecting or payor bank affects that bank's authority to accept, pay, or collect an item or to account for its proceeds until the bank *knows* of the death or adjudication and has a *reasonable opportunity to act* on it.[27] Even with knowledge

---

[26] UCC 4-404.   [27] UCC 4-405(1).

of the death of a customer, a bank may certify or pay checks (but not other items) for a period of *ten days after death*.[28] A person claiming an interest in the account—e.g., a relative or the executor of the decedent's will—may order the bank to stop further payment. The reason for this exception is that "there is almost never any reason why they should not be paid, and that filing in probate is a useless formality, burdensome to the holder, the executor, the court and the bank."[29]

Customer's Duty to Examine Cancelled Checks

Periodically the bank will send to each customer a statement of account supported by the cancelled or paid items that have been charged (debited) to the account. The customer must then exercise reasonable care and promptness in examining the materials for unauthorized signatures and for alterations. The bank is entitled to prompt notice if any irregularities are discovered.[30]

The bank is protected, and the customer must pursue other means of recovery, when an item bearing his unauthorized signature or an alteration is paid if all of the three following conditions are satisfactorily proved:

1. the bank establishes that the customer failed in his duty to examine the checks and report his unauthorized signatures or alterations;[31] *and*
2. the bank establishes that it suffered a loss because of the customer's breach of duty;[32] *and*
3. the customer is not able to show that the bank failed to exercise ordinary care in the payment of these items.[33]

If the bank fails to establish either 1 or 2 above, or if the customer is able to establish the bank's failure in 3, then the bank is liable for the unauthorized signature or the altered item. This is exactly what one would expect. After all, the bank is under contract with its customer, it has a copy of the customer's signature, and it is supposed to follow the customer's orders—no forgeries or alterations, please. Since a certain number of these are bound to occur, the bank must train its employees to detect as many of these items as possible, and it must absorb the loss or losses that do materialize or insure against them.

If the same wrongdoer undertakes *subsequent* forgeries, unauthorized signatures, or alterations which the bank pays in good faith after the first check (or "first batch," if two or more items are involved) has been forwarded to its customer, the bank is once more protected. The customer must pursue other means of recovery if he failed within a reasonable period of time (not exceeding fourteen calendar days) to detect the "first batch" of irregularities and notify the bank. In this way the customer is penalized for his breach of duty in not promptly examining his checks and reporting irregularities.[34] The bank is not protected, however, and the customer may recover if the bank did not exercise ordinary care in paying the "second batch."[35]

---

[28] UCC 4–405(2).

[29] UCC 4–405, comment 2.

[30] UCC 4–406(1).

[31] UCC 4–406(1).

[32] UCC 4–406(2)(a).

[33] UCC 4–406(3).

[34] UCC 4–406(2)(b).

[35] UCC 4–406(2)(b), (3).

Without regard to the exercise of reasonable care by either the customer or the bank, there is a statute of limitations on the customer's right to assert these irregularities against the bank. For unauthorized customer-drawer signatures and for alterations, the period is one year from the time the statement of account and supporting items are made available to the customer. Since the customer is not likely to recognize the forged or unauthorized signature of an indorser, the statute of limitations is three years, rather than one, from the time the materials are made available to the customer.[36] In the following case, the court held that the drawee bank's limit of ten days in which the drawer is to notify the drawee of an alteration on the check was unreasonably short.

Facts

A check was drawn upon an account by the state for $54. The bank of the payee improperly encoded the check for $10,000 more than the actual amount. The drawee bank's computer paid the overstated amount. The bank's statement in which the check was sent stated that, if not notified otherwise within ten days, the statement would be assumed to be correct. Seven and a half months later, during a routine audit, the mistake was found, the bank was notified, and a claim for the overstatement was made.

Decision

For the state.

Reasoning

While it is the customer's duty to examine the bank statement, violation of the ten-day limit contained in the statement will not absolutely discharge the bank. Discharge of the bank's liability is a question to be determined upon the circumstances in each case.

The check was mailed to the right person, it was the payee's bank that improperly encoded the check, and then the drawee bank improperly charged the improper amount.

The time frame set out by the Code to discover the error is one year, which is longer than the state took and much longer than the bank demanded. The loss was not due to the negligence of the state, and it has not been shown that an earlier notice would have prevented or reduced the amount of loss. Under UCC 4–406 a customer must exercise reasonable care and promptness to examine the statement to discover any alteration and then must promptly notify the bank of the error. If notice comes within one year, however, and if the bank suffers no loss on account of the delay, the account must be reimbursed.

The State ex. rel. *Gabalac v. Firestone Bank*, 346 N.E. 2d 326 (Ohio 1975).

Certified Checks

There are no primary parties on a check as it is normally issued. The drawer is a party secondarily liable, and the drawee and payee are not liable until their signatures are on the item. The check is not an assignment of funds for the benefit of the payee or any subsequent holder,[37] and for this reason the bank can

---

[36] UCC 4–406(4).

[37] UCC 3–409.

not be compelled to pay by a holder. It is, however, liable to customers for wrongful dishonor of checks and other items.[38]

When a bank certifies a check, it becomes a primary party analogous to a maker of a note.[39] The certification or acceptance will be written or stamped on the instrument by an authorized officer of the bank.[40] The bank is not obligated to provide this service,[41] so it will normally charge a fee when certification is requested.

Certification by a *holder* has the effect of discharging the drawer and all indorsers *prior to the holder* who is having the check certified.[42] For example, if D issued a check to P, who indorsed to A and so on to H, a certification by the drawee bank at the request of H would discharge D, P, and A from further liability on the check. The reason for this is that the instrument is now the primary debt and responsibility of the certifying bank. Certification is analogous to cashing the check, and it is easy to see that if the drawee had paid H cash, all parties prior to H would be discharged. Anyone who indorses it following the certification, however, will incur the usual secondary liability.

When a *drawer* has an instrument certified, no one is discharged. Obviously there is no one prior to the drawer to be discharged.

Missing Indorsements and Bank Collection Indorsements

In an effort to speed up the collection process and make it more efficient, depositary banks may supply any necessary indorsement of a customer, unless the item expressly requires the *payee's* indorsement. Generally the bank's written statement on the instrument that it was deposited to the customer's account is sufficient.[43] Also, the drawee/payor bank may charge its customer's account for any item which is properly payable from that account even if the charge creates an overdraft.[44] This is illustrated in the following case.

Facts
The plaintiffs, Barretts, are husband and wife. Mr. Barrett made a check payable to Aquatic Industries on July 19, 1975 for $1,500 drawn on their joint checking account at the drawee defendant bank. Aquatic Industries did not indorse the check when it deposited the check in its account at the Rosewell Bank. The Rosewell Bank, failing to add Aquatic's indorsement as it was authorized to do by UCC 4–205(1), sent the check through banking channels to the defendant bank. Upon receiving the check, the bank debited plaintiffs' account and returned it to them. Plaintiffs contended that the check should not have been paid because it was never indorsed.

Decision
For the drawee bank.

---

[38] UCC 4–402.

[39] UCC 3–413(1).

[40] UCC 3–410(1).

[41] UCC 3–411(2).

[42] UCC 3–411(1). Their contract that the instrument would be honored is performed by the certification.

[43] UCC 4–205(1).

[44] UCC 4–401(1).

Reasoning

The check was properly payable. Since it was properly payable, a bank may charge against its customer's account any item which is otherwise properly payable from that account even though the charge creates an overdraft. UCC 4–401(1). The absence of the payee's indorsement and the failure of the collecting Rosewell Bank to supply the missing indorsement as it was authorized to do did not affect the payor bank's right to pay this check and to debit the plaintiffs' account. In absence of the indorsement of the payee, the instrument was not transferred by negotiation, and any subsequent transferee of the instrument could not acquire the status of a holder in due course. UCC 3–201(1).

First National Bank of Gwinnett v. Gerald Barrett, 233 S.E. 2d. 24 (Ga. 1977).

Intermediary banks and nondepositary payor banks are not in any way given notice or affected by any restrictive indorsement except that of its immediate transferor. For example, if P indorses restrictively in trust for M, "Pay to T for the benefit of M, [signed] P," the depositary bank must exercise due care in receiving this instrument from T, but subsequent banks in the collection channel need not pay any attention to it. They need only obey the instructions contained in the restrictive indorsement *of the bank* which transfers the check to them.[45]

Lost, Destroyed, or Stolen Instruments

If an instrument has been lost, stolen, or destroyed, the owner may still sue on it and recover from any party who is liable. This person, now a plaintiff in a lawsuit, will have to prove his ownership, the facts which prevent his production of the instrument (e.g., if it was destroyed by fire, this would have to be proven), and the terms of the instrument.[46]

Keep in mind that a contract is really more than the paper on which it is written. Even if the paper is destroyed, the contract, with its rights and duties agreed upon by the parties, continues to exist. It is now much harder to prove, but witnesses can be called and the owner's own testimony is admissible.

In order to protect the one who pays from having to pay a second time (assuming that the instrument eventually surfaces in the hands of a legitimate party), the court may require security. This protection against fraud or mistake could be in the form of a bond or insurance policy which the owner would have to post before the court will allow him to collect.

Summary Statement

1. Checks are demand drafts drawn on banks. The drawer is entitled to order the drawee bank to pay money from the checking account because of the contractual relationship that exists between them. The bank is the debtor of its customer, the drawer, to the extent of the checking account balance.

---

[45] UCC 3–206(2)(3)(4), 4–205(2).   [46] UCC 3–804.

2. A bank becomes an agent of its customer in the check clearing process. It will forward checks through bank channels to the drawee-payor for collection. Each bank that participates in the process must take proper action on the check before its midnight deadline—midnight of the next banking day following receipt of an item—or be held accountable for the amount of the check.

3. A holder can not compel a drawee bank to honor a check, but if the drawee wrongfully dishonors, it is liable to the customer for actual damages, direct and consequential, proximately caused by such dishonor. The drawee may honor an item even though it creates an overdraft, and, generally speaking, payment of a check (whether it creates an overdraft or not) is final in favor of an HIDC and those who have in good faith substantially changed their position in reliance on payment. A drawee bank may charge its customer for the original tenor of a materially altered item or for the completed tenor of an item that was issued incomplete.

4. Once a check has been issued, the drawer may (for any reason) direct the bank to stop payment. Oral stop orders are valid for fourteen calendar days; written orders for six months. When the check "bounces" back into the hands of the holder or HIDC, the drawer must be ready to prove a personal or real defense; otherwise a judgment may be entered against him.

5. If the drawee overlooks the stop order and through negligence pays the check anyway, the drawer-customer may recover from the drawee upon proof of the amount of loss caused by the drawee's negligence.

6. A drawee bank is not obligated to honor uncertified checks that have been in circulation more than six months, but it may do so in good faith. Death of a customer does not automatically terminate the drawee's right to pay checks that were drawn previously. Even with knowledge of death and an opportunity to act on it, the drawee may for ten days after date of death pay or certify such checks unless ordered to stop by a person claiming an interest in the account.

7. When the drawee periodically mails its customer a statement of account along with his cancelled checks, the customer has a duty to examine the checks promptly and put the bank on notice of irregularities. If the customer does not act reasonably and promptly in the performance of this duty, and if such negligence or breach of duty causes the bank to suffer a loss, the customer will be responsible for the loss. However, if the drawee bank itself has been negligent, then the customer will *not* be responsible for the loss.

8. There are no primary parties on a check as originally issued, and the check does not operate as an assignment of funds for the payee or anyone else. When a check is certified, the drawee becomes a primary party-acceptor analogous to the maker of a note. All parties *prior* to the one having the check certified are discharged from further liability on the instrument.

9. An intermediary or a nondepositary payor bank is not in any way affected by a restrictive indorsement *except* that of its immediate transferor. Depositary banks are entitled to indorse for deposit on behalf of their customers unless the item expressly requires the payee's signature.

10. The owner of a lost, stolen, or destroyed instrument may still recover on it with proof of ownership, of the facts which prevent its production, and the terms of the instrument. To protect the payor against the possibility of a second payment, the court may require the owner to provide security for the payor's benefit.

The following case is presented as an illustration of how the court interprets legislative intent in the area of banking law.

Rock Island Auction Sales, Inc. v. Empire Packing Co., Inc.
204 N.E.2d 721 (Ill. 1965)

Empire Packing Co., Inc. drew a check on its bank (Illinois National Bank and Trust Company, the drawee-payor) to the order of the plaintiff, Rock Island Auction Sales, Inc., in payment for cattle. The drawee-payor bank, Illinois National, received the check through clearinghouse channels for collection but held it for five days on assurance from Empire that funds would soon be deposited to cover it. Shortly afterward, the check was returned by the drawee-payor marked "Insufficient Funds." A petition in bankruptcy was filed against Empire. The plaintiff, Rock Island, was successful against Illinois National in the District Court, and Illinois National appeals.

Plaintiff argues "that [as] the payor bank [Illinois National] became liable for the amount of the check because it held the check without payment, return or notice of dishonor, beyond the time limit fixed in 4-302. . . ."

The defendant argues that the amount for which it is liable [is determined by] UCC 4-103(5) which provides that the "measure of damages for failure to exercise ordinary care in handling an item is the amount of the item reduced by an amount which could not have been realized by the use of ordinary care." The defendant continues that section 4-302 is invalid and discriminatory "because it imposes a liability upon a payor bank for failing to act prior to its midnight deadline that is more severe than the liability which section 4-103(5) imposes upon a depositary bank or a collecting bank for the same default."

But the legislature may legitimately have concluded that there are differences in function and in circumstances that justify different consequences. Depositary and collecting banks act primarily as conduits. The steps that they take can only indirectly affect the determination of whether or not a check is to be paid, which is the focal point in the collection process. The legislature could have concluded that the failure of such a bank to meet its deadline would most frequently be the result of negligence, and fixed liability accordingly. The role of a payor bank in the collection process, on the other hand, is crucial. It knows whether or not the drawer has funds available to pay the item. The legislature could have considered that the failure of such a bank to meet its deadline is likely to be due to factors other than negligence, and that the relationship between a payor bank and its customer may so influence its conduct as to cause a conscious disregard of its statutory duty. The present case is illustrative. The defendant, in its position as payor bank, deliberately aligned itself with its customer in order to protect that customer's credit and consciously disregarded the duty imposed upon it. The statutory scheme emphasizes the importance of speed in the collection process.

A legislative sanction designed to prevent conscious disregard of deadlines cannot be characterized as arbitrary or unreasonable, nor can it be said to constitute a legislative encroachment on the functions of the judiciary.

Affirmed for plaintiff.

Questions and Case Problems

1. D purchased inventory from P with a $5,000 check. Drawee Bank wrongfully dishonored D's check, and P repossessed the inventory. This caused D much embarrassment and at least $1,000 in good will. In addition, D lost a $2,000 breach-of-contract suit to X for failure to deliver merchandise. If D's inventory had not been repossessed, D could have fulfilled the contract with X. D then sued Drawee Bank. Result?

2. D issued a $100 check on Drawee Bank payable to the order of P. P materially altered the amount (words and figures) to $1,000 and negotiated it to an HIDC. The HIDC forwarded it to Drawee Bank for collection and received $1,000. When these facts were revealed by D's examination of his monthly statement and cancelled checks, he proceeded against Drawee Bank to reinstate his account. Result?

3. Faye Zappacosta, bookkeeper for Arrow Builders, drew checks on defendant-drawee (Royal National Bank) purportedly representing social security and income taxes withheld from the wages of Arrow's employees. For twenty-three months she drew fifty-four such checks. Twenty-three were properly applied and the others were presented individually by Zappacosta and honored by the defendant-drawee (Royal National). This scheme could have been detected by Arrow's chief accountant after the first month's embezzlement if Zappacosta's work had been properly supervised.

   Arrow proceeded against defendant Royal National after these facts came to light. Result? [*Arrow Builders Supply Corp. v. Royal National Bank,* 288 N.Y. Supp. 2d 609 (1968).]

4. D drew a $1,650 check on Drawee Bank payable to the order of P, seller, for a used Harley Davidson bike sold to D. The check was purposely post-dated to give D time to try out his new bike. D was not satisfied with the bike's performance, so he phoned a stop order and later confirmed it in writing. He tried to return the bike to P but P refused to accept it. P deposited D's check and the Drawee Bank paid it despite the stop order. P left town with the money and D seeks reimbursement from Drawee Bank. Result?

5. Granite filed a written stop order with the drawee Hempstead Bank on a check issued to Overseas Equipment Co. Granite then delivered a new check to Overseas. More than a year later the first check was presented to Hempstead and paid. Granite claimed that the drawee bank is liable to it for paying the first check. [*Granite Equipment Leasing Corp. v. Hempstead Bank,* 326 N.Y. Supp. 2d 881 (1971).]

6. D issued a $1,000 check on June 1 payable to the order of P. P negotiated it to A, an HIDC, on June 10, and A deposited it for collection on July 10. The check was returned to A unpaid because the Drawee Bank became insolvent on July 5. The Drawee Bank can pay only a fraction of its customers' deposits. Discuss A's rights against P and D. Would your answer to A's rights against D be the same if the Drawee Bank became insolvent on June 25 (other facts remain unchanged)?

7. X forged the signature of D as drawer on a check and subsequently negotiated it to an HIDC, who collected the instrument from the drawee bank. The drawee returned the check to D at the end of the month along with a statement of his account. D did not examine this material for more than three months. When D finally discovered the forgery, his bank refused to reimburse his account because he did not bring the forgery to its attention within a "reasonable period not exceeding fourteen calendar days." Result?

8. D drew a $500 check on Drawee Bank dated September 8—two days before he was fatally injured in an accident. The Drawee Bank learned of D's death on September 15, and it honored the check on September 22. D's legal heirs insist that Drawee Bank should not have honored the check and that D's account should be credited for $500. Result?

9. D drew a $100 check on Drawee Bank payable to the order of P. P had the check certified at Drawee Bank. Following the certification, P "expertly" materially altered the words and figures to $1,000. Then P negotiated the check to A, an HIDC, who forwarded the instrument for collection and received $1,000. These facts came to light when D discovered that several checks he drew later that month "bounced." D insisted that Drawee Bank reinstate his account. Result?

10. In the case of *Rock Island Auction Sales, Inc. v. Empire Packing Co., Inc.*, 204 N.E. 2d 721 (Ill. 1965),[47] explain what Illinois National should have done both to protect itself and also to accommodate Rock Island Auction Sales.

---

[47] See pp. 584-85.

Deadlines and Discharge

31

After you have read this chapter, you should be able to:

1. Distinguish between presentment for payment and presentment for acceptance.
2. Learn when presentment is necessary.
3. Become familiar with the mechanics of presentment—how it is made, to whom, and the length of time allowed.
4. Recognize the importance of giving notice of dishonor, and find how such notice is to be given.
5. Review the methods of discharging one's liability on an instrument.

Introduction

The duties one asssmes and the rights brought into existence by the creation of a negotiable instrument do not last forever. The same law that provided for the creation of commercial paper also provides for its ending. It was important for you to know how to create a formal contract, and it is equally important to know how to discharge (end) the formal contract.

Once an instrument has been created negotiable in form and issued to a payee under some contractual arrangement, it may be further negotiated to a holder or an HIDC. At maturity, the holder will expect to be paid, so he will take the very practical step of "presenting" it to the maker, acceptor, or, if it is an unacceptable draft, to the drawee.

When a holder of an instrument is finally paid according to its terms by one of these parties, the holder is satisfied and the liability of all parties to the instrument is discharged. If it is not paid—if the instrument is dishonored—then the holder may institute a lawsuit and be faced with an array of real or personal defenses.

Instead of bringing suit immediately and undergoing the expense and anxiety that it entails, the holder may seek other avenues of recovery. After all, he had no part of the potential defendant's dispute with the payee.

At this stage, the holder will think of the secondary or conditional liability of the drawer or indorsers. These secondary parties, or any of them, will be liable on the instrument if the holder takes the preliminary steps of timely presentment for payment and, if the instrument is not paid, notice of dishonor.

This chapter deals with the procedures that must be followed to bind primary and secondary parties, and with the ways in which a party can discharge his liability on an instrument.

Presentment, Dishonor and Notice—In General

Presentment of an instrument *for payment*[1] at the proper time[2] and, under some circumstances, presentment *for acceptance* prior to payment,[3] is the first step a holder must take to preserve the liability of secondary parties—drawers and indorsers. Once *any* presentment has been made (whether presentment for acceptance or for payment, and whether presentment is necessary or optional), the instrument is **dishonored**[4] if the responsible party does not accept or pay within certain time deadlines.[5] Secondary parties engage to be liable only if the instrument is duly presented for acceptance or payment to the drawee, acceptor, or maker. Therefore, it is essential that presentment be made if, on dishonor of the instrument, they are to be held liable by the holder.

presentment
"a demand for acceptance or payment made upon the maker, acceptor, drawee or other payor by or on behalf of the holder"
UCC 3–504(1)

dishonor
the refusal of the drawee to accept the draft, or of the drawee, acceptor, or maker to pay the draft or note

---

[1] UCC 3–501(1)(b).

[2] UCC 3–503.

[3] UCC 3–501(1)(a), 3–503(1)(a).

[4] UCC 3–507(1)(a).

[5] UCC 3–506.

Finally, the *holder* must give notice of dishonor to secondary parties,[6] and this notice must be *sent* prior to midnight of the *third* business day following dishonor or receipt of notice of dishonor.[7] For *banks,* the deadline is midnight of the *next banking day* following dishonor or receipt of notice of dishonor.[8]

Presentment

How Made
Presentment—that is, the demand for payment or acceptance—is made upon the maker, acceptor, or drawee by or on behalf of the holder. It may be made by mail, through a clearinghouse, or personally at the place designated in the instrument. If no place is specified, then the business address or residence is acceptable. Presentment is excused if no one can be located at any of these places to accept or pay the instrument.[9]

Rights of the Party to Whom Presentment Is Made
The maker, acceptor, or drawee (or their authorized agent) may require the following things *without dishonoring* the instrument:

(a) exhibition or physical display of the note or draft;
(b) reasonable proof of identification and, if the presenter is an agent, reasonable proof of his authority;
(c) presentment at the specified place, or, if none is specified, at a place reasonable in the circumstances; and
(d) a signed receipt on the instrument for full or partial payment, and surrender of the instrument if paid in full.[10]

Failure to comply with any of these requirements invalidates the presentment. However, the presenter must be given a reasonable time to comply—e.g., the presenter who is an agent may need some time to produce proof of this authority to act on behalf of the owner.[11]

Time Allowed for Acceptance or Payment
The instrument is not dishonored if *acceptance* is deferred until the close of the next business day following presentment. Even beyond that, the *holder* may allow postponement for an additional business day in a good faith effort to obtain acceptance.[12] As a general rule, *payment* may be deferred while reasonable steps are taken to determine whether the instrument is properly payable, but payment must be made before the close of business *on the day of presentment* to avoid dishonor.[13]

---

[6] UCC 3–501(2).
[7] UCC 3–508(2)(4).
[8] UCC 4–104(h).
[9] UCC 3–504.

[10] UCC 3–505(1).
[11] UCC 3–505(2).
[12] UCC 3–506(1).
[13] UCC 3–506(2).

Time of Presentment

When an instrument contains a *due date,* presentment *for payment* should be made on that date.[14] If payments have been accelerated, presentment for payment is due within a reasonable time after acceleration.[15] Any presentment *for acceptance* must be made on or before the date when payment is due.[16]

Presentment for payment or acceptance of *all other instruments*—i.e., those without due dates—is due within a reasonable time after date or issue or after the secondary party becomes liable.[17] Otherwise the secondary party is discharged.

A reasonable period of time is determined from the nature of the instrument, banking or **trade usage,** and the facts of the particular case. For uncertified checks drawn and payable in the U.S., a reasonable period of time for presentment or for the initiation of the bank collection process is *presumed* to be

(a) 30 days after date or issue (whichever is later) with respect to the *drawer's* liability, and

(b) 7 days after indorsement with respect to indorser's liability.[18]

Effect of Late Presentment

The holder's failure to make a proper and timely presentment,[19] as well as the holder's failure to give proper and timely notice of dishonor,[20] has the effect of discharging *secondary* parties. Indorsers will be fully discharged under these circumstances; drawers *may* be fully or partially discharged.

The *drawer* of a domiciled instrument—one payable at a particular bank—will not automatically receive a full discharge. The discharge is limited to the extent that funds placed on deposit in that bank and intended for payment of a domiciled instrument have "shrunk" because of the bank's insolvency during the delay, i.e., the period of time beyond thirty days. To qualify for this discharge, the drawer must make a written assignment to the holder of all the rights he has against the now insolvent bank.[21]

To illustrate, suppose that the drawee originally held sufficient funds to pay a customer-drawer's $1,000 check, but that the payee or subsequent party held the check for more than thirty days before presenting it or initiating the bank collection process. If the drawee bank becomes insolvent during the delay (the period in excess of thirty days) and only $500 are ultimately available to pay the check, the drawer may discharge his liability by written assignment to the holder of his rights against the bank for $500. In the following case, the drawee bank did not become insolvent, thus the drawer's obligation was not discharged because of the payee's delay in presentment.

---

[14] UCC 3–503(1)(c).

[15] UCC 3–503(1)(d).

[16] UCC 3–503(1)(a)(b).

[17] UCC 3–503(1)(e).

[18] UCC 3–503(2).

[19] UCC 3–503(1)(e), 3–502(1), 3–501(b)(c).

[20] UCC 3–501(2), 3–502(1).

[21] UCC 3–503(1)(b).

Facts

At issue is whether the defendant drawer's obligation to pay dishonored uncertified checks is discharged by failure of the plaintiff payee to demand payment within a reasonable amount of time. The district court ruled that the obligation was not discharged and entered a judgment for the payee. The checks were held by the payee for over thirty days after date of issue. When they were finally presented for payment, they were returned due to a lack of sufficient funds.

Decision

For the payee.

Reasoning

Presentment does not in itself discharge the drawer since the record does not show that the drawee bank became insolvent during the delay, thereby depriving the drawer of funds with which to cover the checks. UCC 3–502(1) states: "Where without excuse any necessary presentment or notice of dishonor is delayed beyond the time when it is due (a) any indorser is discharged; and (b) any drawer or the acceptor of a draft payable at a bank or the maker of a note payable at a bank who, because the drawee or payor bank becomes insolvent during the delay, is deprived of funds maintained with the drawee or payor bank to cover the instrument may discharge his liability by written assignment to the holder of his rights against the drawee or payor bank in respect of such funds, but such drawer, acceptor or maker is not otherwise discharged."

Grist v. Osgood, 521 P.2d 368 (Nev. 1974).

Indorsers of uncertified checks are fully discharged if the instrument is presented or the collection process begun more than seven days after their indorsement. In essence, the payee or holder is being penalized because of the failure to make a timely presentment.

Notice of Dishonor

Notice of dishonor may be given to anyone who may be liable on the instrument by the holder or his bank or agent.[22] To be effective, any notice of dishonor must be given *by a bank* before its one-day midnight deadline (midnight on its next banking day following the banking day on which it receives the item or notice of its dishonor), and *by all other persons* before the three-day midnight deadline (midnight of the third business day after dishonor or notice of dishonor).[23]

Banks have shorter deadlines than their customers.

Failure to give timely notice of dishonor will result in the discharge of secondary parties in the same manner as a failure to make a timely presentment.[24] While memorizing dates and deadlines can be quite a chore, it could be very beneficial to a person in the long-run to remain familiar with this one.

Notice may be given in any reasonable manner, written or oral. It must be sufficient to identify the dishonored instrument. A misdescription which is not misleading will still be effective as a notice.[25]

---

[22] UCC 3–508(1).

[23] UCC 3–508(2), 4–104(h).

[24] UCC 3–501(2), 3–502(1).

[25] UCC 3–508(3).

Notice operates for the benefit of all who have rights against the party notified.[26] For example, if H presents an instrument at maturity and it is dishonored, one notice by H to indorsers A and B is all that is needed. If H recovers from B, B can pursue A without giving further notice to A. If H gives notice to B only, then B has a full three-day period to notify A.

Written notice is given when *sent* although it is never received.[27] It may consist of the instrument itself with the stamped or written statement that acceptance or payment has been refused.[28]

Protest

Protest is a formal method of preserving proof that presentment was made and that the instrument was dishonored.

Protest is required for drafts which, on their face, appear to be drawn or payable outside the states and territories of the United States and the District of Columbia.[29] Such drafts at times are called "international" or "foreign" drafts. On all other drafts, protest is optional. It is a certificate of dishonor made by a U.S. consul, vice consul, notary public, or other authorized person according to the law of the place of dishonor. The protest must identify the instrument, and it may certify that some or all of the parties have been notified.[30]

Delayed, Waived, or Excused Presentment, Protest, or Notice

Delay

Delay in presentment, protest, or notice of dishonor is excused if the party does not know that it is due—e.g., the holder received it after acceleration by a prior party but without notice of the acceleration.[31] Delay is also excused if it is caused by circumstances beyond the party's control and he exercises reasonable diligence after the cause of the delay ceases.[32]

Waiver or Excuse

Presentment, protest, or notice of dishonor is completely excused if

(a) it has been expressly or impliedly waived,
(b) the party has dishonored or countermanded (stopped) payment or otherwise has no reason to expect or right to require that the instrument be accepted or paid, or
(c) presentment, protest, or notice can not be given by the exercise of reasonable diligence.[33]

Presentment alone is excused if the maker, acceptor, or drawee is dead or insolvent. If payment or acceptance is refused for reasons other than the want of a proper presentment—e.g., the holder is told by the maker that he will not

---

[26] UCC 3–508(8).   [29] UCC 3–501(3).   [32] UCC 3–511(1).

[27] UCC 3–508(4).   [30] UCC 3–509.   [33] UCC 3–511(2).

[28] UCC 3–508(3).   [31] UCC 3–511(1).

pay at maturity because the payee defrauded him—then presentment is excused because it would simply be useless.[34]

Waiver of protest is a waiver of presentment and notice of dishonor as well, even though protest is not required. Waiver of presentment, notice, or protest embodied in the instrument itself is binding on all parties. If it is written above the signature of one or more indorsers, it binds those only.[35]

Discharge

A party is **discharged** from liability on an instrument by any act or agreement with the other party that would discharge a simple contract for the payment of money.[36] Payment discharges the instrument, as is illustrated in the following case.

discharge
(in contracts) the termination of a contractual duty to perform a promise

Facts
Bruce Small, minor son of the defendant, Genevieve, purchased an automobile from the plaintiff, George Allen, for $225. He paid $100 down, and a note for the balance was signed by Bruce and Genevieve. Bruce paid the note, and it was marked "Paid in full, George S. Allen" and delivered to Bruce Small, who had the lien on the automobile discharged of record. Later Bruce Small, still a minor, by written notice rescinded his contract with the plaintiff. He assigned his ownership to the plaintiff by transferring the ownership using the form provided on the registration certificate. He then returned the car to the plaintiff's garage and demanded that the plaintiff return the $225, which plaintiff refused to do. Bruce Small successfully sued the plaintiff, who then returned the $225 to him. Plaintiff later sued Genevieve on the note, contending that Genevieve is liable to him on the note to the extent of its face amount. He argued that since Bruce rescinded his contract with the plaintiff, the lien note

was restored to its former status as far as the defendant was concerned, she being an accommodation maker.

Decision
For defendant, Genevieve Small.

Reasoning
There is no question that the note was fully paid according to its terms and tenor, and the court so found. Payment is the final act which extinguishes a negotiable instrument and transmits it into a cancelled voucher. There is no longer a holder of the instrument and no suit may thereafter be maintained.

The findings establish that the defendant signed the note to insure its payment. The full payment was made. The surrender of a note by the holder to the maker, with intent thereby to discharge it, does discharge it. Whatever acts Bruce Small took on his own behalf, as a minor, were between him and the plaintiff and could not affect the rights of the defendant.

George S. Allen d/b/a Allen's Garage v. Genevieve Small, 271 A.2d 840 (Vt. 1970).

---

[34] UCC 3–511(3).

[35] UCC 3–511(5)(6).

[36] UCC 3–601(2).

The following methods of discharge are exclusive insofar as the provisions of UCC Article 3 are concerned, but the Article does not prevent or affect discharge arising from other rules of law, e.g., bankruptcy:

satisfaction
the discharge of an obligation by paying what is due

renunciation
the abandonment of a right by a person

1. payment or **satisfaction** (Section 3–603); or
2. tender of payment (Section 3–604); or
3. cancellation or **renunciation** (Section 3–605); or
4. impairment of right of recourse or of collateral (Section 3–606); or
5. reacquisition of the instrument by a prior party (Section 3–208); or
6. fraudulent and material alteration (Section 3–407); or
7. certification of a check (Section 3–411); or
8. acceptance varying a draft (Section 3–412); or
9. unexcused delay in presentment or notice of dishonor or protest (Section 3–502).[37]

The liability of *all parties* is discharged when one who has no right of action—i.e., no recourse against anyone on the instrument—reacquires it or is himself discharged.[38] For example, a note issued from M to P and negotiated from P to A to H may be reacquired by M prior to maturity or paid by M at maturity. Both reacquisition and payment discharge all parties to the instrument at that time.

If M chooses to reissue the note he purchased before maturity, he will of course be liable to subsequent parties. Intervening parties, P, A, and H, are discharged with respect to M and subsequent holders *not* in due course. If their indorsements are cancelled, they will not be liable even to an HIDC.[39]

Effect of a Discharge
No discharge *provided by Article 3* is effective against a subsequent HIDC unless he has notice of the discharge when he takes the instrument.[40] Discharges provided by *other* rules of law, e.g., bankruptcy, are effective despite lack of notice.

Payment or Satisfaction
In order to receive the benefit of a discharge, payment or satisfaction must be made to a *holder* or his authorized agent. Payment offered in full settlement may be accepted in partial settlement only. Always consult your state law. In the following case, the payee's cashing of a check marked "in full satisfaction" but payable only for a lesser amount did not constitute consent by the payee who wrote on the check to that effect.

Facts
During 1971 the plaintiff, Wesley Scholl, did work for the defendants, Clinton and Virginia Tallman. As of February 18, 1971 plaintiff's books indicated that the Tallmans owed him $2,927.37. The Tallmans made payments during the course of 1971-72, but as of November 4, 1974 they allegedly still owed $2,077.37. Defendants believe plaintiff's figure to be too high; they felt that several hundred dollars in cash payments had not been credited to their account. They then sent a $500 check to Scholl

---

[37] UCC 3–601(1).   [38] UCC 3–601(3).   [39] UCC 3–208.   [40] UCC 3–602.

with the words "Wesley Scholl Settlement in Full for all Labor and Materials to Date" typed on the back of the check. No further payments were made.

A short time later Scholl cashed the check but not until he had scratched out the typing on the back and wrote "Restriction of payment in full refused. $1,826.65 remains due and payable." He then brought this suit to collect payment.

The trial court found in favor of the defendants on **accord and satisfaction.** It was proved that the plaintiff had failed to record two checks, but the cash payments were not proved. The plaintiff appealed.

Decision

Reversed. For the plaintiff, Scholl.

Reasoning

The question before the court is whether there has been an accord and satisfaction of the disputed claim. The offer and consideration are not disputed here; the controversy involves acceptance. South Dakota's version of the UCC addresses the issue: "Part performance of an obligation . . . when expressly accepted by the creditor in writing in satisfaction . . . extinguishes the obligation."

The question is whether indorsement of the check with knowledge of the condition on the face of the check constitutes acceptance in writing under the statute. UCC 1-207 provides: "A party who with explicit reservation of rights performs or promises performance or assents to performance in a manner demanded or offered by the other party does not thereby prejudice the rights reserved." The case was remanded for determination of how much was due to the plaintiff.

Scholl v. Tallman, 247 N.W.2d 490 (S.D. 1976).

accord and satisfaction
a new contract (accord) which discharges a party from a previous contractual obligation; the old contract is discharged (satisfied)

Jus Tertii: The Law of the Third Party

The maker, acceptor, or drawee is discharged even though payment is made with knowledge that some other party has a claim of ownership on the instrument unless, prior to payment, the party with the claim either (1) secures or idemnifies the one seeking a discharge, or (2) gets a court order (injunction) against payment.[41]

To illustrate: suppose that the payee, P, is fraudulently induced to negotiate a note to A; or, if P is a minor, simply assume that he indorses the paper to A in a transaction for goods. In either case, P will have a claim on the instrument. Knowledge of this claim, however, will not affect the maker-M's right to pay A or a subsequent holder at maturity and receive a full discharge. After all, the maker has *no defense of his own* against the payee or the holder. He expects at maturity to be able to pay a holder and receive a discharge, and he does not want to be drawn into a dispute between P and A. Payment and discharge can be prevented only if P, the party with the claim, (1) posts security or **indemnity** for M, or (2) gets an injunction against payment.[42]

indemnity
an absolute obligation to pay for another's loss

---

[41] UCC 3-603(1).   [42] UCC 3-306(d).

Payment at maturity does *not* result in a discharge if it is made in bad faith or with knowledge that the holder acquired by theft or acquired through a thief. However, bearer paper could be stolen and still be negotiated to an HIDC. If this happens, payment to an HIDC who innocently acquired through a thief is a discharge even though this fact is known at the time of payment.[43]

Finally, no discharge results if payment is inconsistent with the terms of a restrictive indorsement.[44] Assume that P indorses a note issued by M as follows: "Pay to A upon completion of contract #61384, [signed] P." If A presents this instrument to M for payment at maturity, M must take reasonable steps to determine that the contract has been completed. If it has not been completed, payment to A will not discharge M from liability to P.

You will recall, however, that intermediary banks and payor banks that are not also depositaries are only affected by the restrictive indorsement *of their transferor*. In the situation described above, these banks would not have to be concerned with P's restrictive indorsement.[45]

Tender of Payment

tender
proffer, make available

Tender or offer of full payment at maturity or at a later time discharges a party only to the extent of all subsequent liability for interest, costs, and attorney's fees.[46] A tender before maturity has no effect unless the terms permit a party who is liable on the instrument to accelerate payment and avoid the running of interest. For example, a note may provide that the maker promises to pay "on or before" the due date.

If the holder refuses tender of payment by a party (M, maker, for example), any party on the instrument who has a right of recourse against M is fully discharged.[47] On an instrument issued by M and indorsed from P to A to H, H's refusal of M's tender completely discharges P and A because H had a chance to get his money and refused to take it.

The primary party on a time instrument makes tender if he is ready and able to pay at every place designated at maturity. Tender of payment of a domiciled note or draft—one payable at a bank—can be made at maturity if funds are available at that bank and instructions have been given to pay.[48]

Cancellation and Renunciation

A holder may discharge the liability of any party on the instrument in any manner apparent on the face of the paper or the indorsements.[49] Since this discharge is in the nature of a gift, no consideration is necessary.

---

[43] UCC 3–603(1)(a).

[44] UCC 3–603(1)(b).

[45] UCC 3–206(2), 4–205(2).

[46] UCC 3–604(1).

[47] UCC 3–604(2).

[48] UCC 3–604(3).

[49] UCC 3–605(1)(a).

The holder who is discharging a party from further liability may do so by intentionally cancelling the instrument or the party's signature.[50] He may renounce his rights either in a signed writing which is delivered to the party being discharged or by surrender of the instrument to that party.[51] Neither cancellation nor renunciation affects the title to the instrument unless it is surrendered.[52]

Impairment of Recourse or of Collateral

recourse
a right to resort to
some one or thing

Assume that M issued P a $1,000 note that was subsequently indorsed to A and, finally, to H. If M dishonored at maturity and A was held secondarily liable to H on the indorsement contract, A could normally expect to seek reimbursement from P. After all, P was the one who got him into this fix to begin with.

collateral
"the personal property
subject to a security
interest"
UCC 9-105(1)(c)

However, what if H released or discharged P? Is A left to seek recovery against M alone? M, remember, already refused to pay once, and he is likely to refuse again. Does it seem fair then for H, acting unilaterally and without A's consent, to defeat A's initial expectation of falling back on P?

No! One's gut reaction is that this is not fair, and the Code reenforces this conclusion.[53] A is fully discharged if H releases P. However, if H released P and *reserved his rights against A* at the time P was discharged, A would remain liable to H but he would be entitled to recourse against P.[54] The basic thought to keep in mind is that A's right to seek reimbursement from prior parties can not be jeopardized or destroyed by the unilateral conduct of H. In the following case the holder's undue extension of time of payment on a note discharged the payee indorser.

Facts

Two promissory notes payable to Beermann "Quality" Fertilizers, defendant, were executed on October 2, 1967 by the maker, David Vavra. Each of the notes provided on the face that "the makers, sureties, and guarantors of this note hereby severally waive presentment for payment, notice of non-payment, protest, and notice of protest, and diligence in bringing suit against any party thereto and consent that time of payment may be extended without notice thereof." The notes were indorsed in blank and transferred before maturity to the plaintiff bank by the payee for their full value. The payee, Beermann Brothers, is a defendant.

The notes were not paid at their maturity on January 2, 1968 and on August 29, 1968 Vavra executed two extension notes to the plaintiff which extended the time of payment of the original notes to December 20, 1968. The extension notes were executed without the knowledge or consent of the defendant except as authorized by the original notes. These extension notes were not paid at maturity, and action was brought on May 2, 1969 against Beermann Brothers and Vavra on the two October 2, 1967 notes. The defendant, Beermann Brothers, appealed from judgment for the plaintiff.

---

[50] UCC 3-605(1)(a). [52] UCC 3-605(2). [54] UCC 3-606(2)(c).

[51] UCC 3-605(1)(b). [53] UCC 3-606(1)(a).

Decision

Reversed, for the defendant.

Reasoning

Under UCC 3-118(f), unless otherwise specified, a consent to extension of a promissory note authorizes a single extension for not longer than the original period of the note. Here, extension was for 113 days, 21 days longer than the period of the original notes. Under UCC 3-606(1)(a), an agreement by the holder to suspend the right to enforce a promissory note against the maker, without the consent of the defendant indorser and without an express reservation of rights against him, discharges the indorser from liability. There being no reservation of rights against the defendant, the extension to Vavra by the plaintiff bank for a period of time longer than the original term authorized in the note discharged the defendant payee.

Citizens State Bank v. Beermann Brothers, 198 N.W. 2d 458 (Neb. 1972).

This principle holds true in situations where H releases collateral security that A was depending on as well. Modify the M to P to A to H hypothetical to the extent that M pledges valuable goods, jewels, stocks, or commodities (or mortgages property) as security for the note. If H releases this security without the consent of A, or of P, they are discharged to the extent of their injury or loss. If $500 worth of security was **pledged** or mortgaged to strengthen the note, A or P would be discharged to that extent if H released or surrendered the security. Once again, the reason for this rule is that H can not unilaterally inflict harm or alter the contract of those parties who precede him.

Reacquisition of the Instrument by a Prior Party

Suppose that D drew a check payable to the order of P. The check was then negotiated by the indorsement of A, B, and C to P. A, B, and C are discharged because, on dishonor, they are liable to P, the holder, who as payee is, in turn, liable to them. In this way, persons who are liable to another, who then becomes liable to them, are spared the problem of circuity of action.

Summary Statement

1. When an instrument is *presented* by a holder to a maker, acceptor, or drawee for *payment* at maturity, or for *acceptance* at or prior to maturity, the instrument is *dishonored* if it is not paid or accepted within the deadline. Presentment for *payment* should be made on the due date or, if the instrument has been accelerated, within a reasonable time after acceleration. Presentment for *acceptance* must be made on or before maturity. *Any other presentment*—i.e., presentment of an instrument without a due date—must be made within a *reasonable time* after date or issue or after a secondary party becomes liable.

pledge
the possessory security interest in bailed goods acquired by the bailee when there is a bailment for the purpose of security

2. A reasonable period of time depends on the type of instrument, trade usage, and the facts of the particular case. For an *uncertified check* drawn and payable in the U.S., a reasonable period of time is presumed to be *thirty days from issue* with respect to the *drawer's* liability and *seven days from indorsement* for a *secondary party's* liability. Failure to make a proper presentment, unless excused, will *fully* discharge *indorsers.* The drawer, acceptor, or maker of an instrument *payable at a bank* may be *fully or partially discharged* if the drawee-payor bank becomes insolvent during the delay depending on the extent of such insolvency.

3. Once an instrument has been dishonored, the *holder* must send notice of dishonor to secondary parties by midnight of the *third* business day following dishonor; *for banks,* the period is trimmed to midnight of the *next banking day.* Notice may be given in any reasonable manner, written or oral, which sufficiently identifies the instrument. It is effective if *sent* within the deadline even though it is never received. Failure to give proper notice, unless excused, will *fully* discharge *indorsers;* the drawer, maker, or acceptor of an instrument payable at a bank may be fully or partially discharged if the drawee-payor bank becomes insolvent during the delay, depending on the extent of such insolvency.

4. Protest, made in the presence of an authorized official, is a formal way of preserving proof of presentment, dishonor, and notice of dishonor. It is required on "international" or "foreign" drafts.

5. A party is discharged from all liability on an instrument by any act or agreement that would discharge a simple contract, e.g., payment to a holder at maturity. If a person reacquires an instrument, *all intervening parties* are discharged from liability to the reacquirer; intervening parties will *not* be liable to subsequent holders, but they will be liable to subsequent HIDCs *unless* their indorsements are cancelled.

6. No discharge under Article 3 is effective against a subsequent HIDC unless he has notice of it at the time he takes the instrument. To be effective, payment or satisfaction must be made to a *holder* or his authorized agent. The discharge is available even though payment is made with knowledge that some party has a claim of ownership on the instrument unless, prior to payment, the party with the claim either (a) secures or indemnifies the one seeking a discharge, or (b) gets an injunction against payment. Payment at maturity will not result in a discharge if it is made with knowledge that the holder acquired by theft or through a thief (unless the holder has the right of an HIDC). Neither will payment at maturity amount to a discharge if it is inconsistent with the terms of a restrictive indorsement.

7. Tender of full payment at or after maturity discharges one from liability for interest, costs, and attorney's fees. If the holder refuses a proper tender, all parties who had a right of recourse against the one making tender are discharged.

8. A *holder* may discharge the liability of any party by intentionally cancelling the instrument or the party's signature. If the holder releases a previous signatory against whom some intervening party has a right of recourse, the release will have the effect of discharging the intervening party as well, *unless* the holder reserves rights against the intervening party. In the event that the holder does reserve such right of recourse against the intervening party, the intervening party retains his original right to seek recovery against the one that the holder discharged. Similarly, if the holder releases collateral that a party on the instrument had access to as security for his original obligation on the instrument, that party will be discharged to the extent of injury or loss caused by such release.

In the following case, note how the court held that, when the holder of a note surrendered the collateral security for the note, a maker of the note was discharged not completely but only to the extent of the value of the collateral surrendered.

Christensen v. McAtee
473 P.2d 659 (Or. 1970)

Denecke, Justice. The plaintiff secured a judgment on a promissory note executed by the defendants, and the defendant, Paul McAtee, appealed. The note was secured by a mortgage executed by the defendant, McAtee Builders, Inc., on real property owned by McAtee Builders, Inc. Paul McAtee's defense was that he was discharged from his obligation because the plaintiff, without Paul McAtee's consent, released the mortgage given by McAtee Builders.

Section 73.6060(1)(b) [Oregon Statutory reference to UCC 3-606] of the Uniform Commercial Code provides:

(1) The holder discharges any party to the instrument to the extent that without such party's consent the holder:

. . . .

(b) Unjustifiably impairs any collateral for the instrument given by or on behalf of the party or any person against whom he has a right of recourse.

The trial court in its written opinion correctly stated:

It was the rule of the negotiable instruments law prior to the adoption of the Uniform Commercial Code, and it is the rule of the Uniform Commercial Code that the so-called suretyship defense, which is the essence of the defense in this case, is not an absolute discharge of the note, but merely operates as a discharge pro tanto according to the value of the lost security. Note the language of ORS [Oregon Statutes] 73.6060, "The holder discharges any party to the instrument to the extent that. . . ."

The trial court found:

The Court finds that the defendant has failed to prove the value of the security released and that hence the Court has no way of measuring the extent of the defendant's loss, if any, even if the Court should find that the defendant is a party who had a right to recourse against the co-defendant.

No direct evidence of value was introduced. Plaintiff urges that generally the value of property mortgaged exceeds the amount of the debt. Assuming this to be true, it does not create such an overwhelming inference that we must conclude error in the trial court's finding of no satisfactory evidence of value of the security released.

Affirmed.

Questions and Case Problems

1. Bermes was required by state law to file his accident claim with the Industrial Commission within one year after *final payment* for his injuries under an insurance policy. The insurance company drew a draft to the order of Bermes which he received on May 3 and which was honored or paid in cash on May 6. He filed his claim with The Industrial Commission on May 4 of the next year. Did he file in time? [*Consolidated Freightways v. The Industrial Commission,* 269 N.E. 2d 291 (Ill. 1971)].

2. The defendant, New House Products, Inc., offered to make part payment at maturity of a promissory note that it had issued to the payee, Commercial Plastics. The offer was rejected. Commercial then instituted this suit for the entire amount of the principal, interest, and attorney's fees. What was the effect of New House's tender? [*New House Products, Inc. v. Commercial Plastics and Supply Corp.,* 233 S.E. 2d 45 (Ga. 1977).]

3. M created a negotiable promissory note payable to the order of P. P indorsed to A, A to B, and B indorsed to H. H released and agreed not to sue P, his nephew. H did not ask for or receive the consent of any other party on the instrument. Finally, H expressly reserved his rights against B in accordance with one of the terms in the body of the note. B claims that H's release of P discharges him (B) because H had knowledge of B's right of recourse against P. Result?

4. Glover and Ferguson, partners, signed a ninety-day $20,000 note to the plaintiff-payee bank, National Bank of Commerce. Before the note was due, Ferguson bought Glover's partnership interest. Glover informed the bank that Ferguson was assuming all partnership obligations. Glover further related that he did not want the note extended nor would he sign a renewal.

    Five months later Ferguson was discharged in bankruptcy, and the bank proceeded against Glover for the balance. Glover alleged that the bank agreed not to sue Ferguson and that this had the effect of discharging him (Glover) from any further liability under UCC 3-606(1)(a). Glover further alleged that the bank was estopped from pursuing him because Ferguson's checking account on several occasions exceeded the overdue and unpaid balance and the bank failed to off-set against it. Result? [*Glover v. National Bank of Commerce of Pine Bluff,* 529 S.W. 2d 333 (Ark. 1975).]

5. M issued a $500 negotiable promissory note to P in return for merchandise. P was then defrauded by A, who induced her to negotiate the note to him in payment for a piece of antique sculpture. When she (P) discovered that the sculpture was junk, she insisted that M should refuse to pay A at maturity of the note. Result?

6. M issued a $1,000 note payable to the order of P. P indorsed "Pay to T in trust for X, [signed] P," and negotiated the instrument to T. T indorsed in blank and discounted the note with Rocky Mountain Co. (Rocky). Rocky Mountain took the instrument without knowledge that T was misappropriating X's funds. However, by the time the instrument matured, X discovered several embezzlements by T (including the money attributable to this note) and sought to prevent payment by M to Rocky. Can M pay Rocky and be discharged from further liability? X argues that UCC 3-603(1)(b) will prevent M from being discharged. Result?

7. M issued a $1,000 negotiable promissory note to P and is quite satisfied with the goods he received in return. P indorsed the instrument specially to A as collateral security for a loan, but, P claims, she never received the loan. A negotiated the note to H, who knew of the dispute between P and A. H, who claims to be an HIDC since the dispute did not involve a defense of the maker, seeks payment from M at maturity. Since M is satisfied with the goods he received from P and has known all along that he would have to pay at the due date, he would prefer to pay H and receive a discharge. Is he entitled to do so despite P's objection?

8. M issued a negotiable instrument to P for $100. P raised the amount to $200 and presented it to M for payment at maturity. M detected the alteration and refused to pay any amount. Is M liable to P for the original $100?

9. M issued a negotiable promissory note payable to the order of P for $800. P negotiated to A, and the instrument was subsequently negotiated to B, to C, then back to A, and finally to H. H did not qualify as an HIDC, however, because he received the instrument as a gift. At maturity, M refused to pay, and H gave timely notice to all indorsers. B and C claim that they have been discharged by A's reacquisition. Result? Would your response be the same if H qualified as an HIDC?

10. In the case of *Christensen v. McAtee*, 473 P. 2d 659 (Or. 1970),[55] explain the reasoning for the law that the surrender of collateral security for a note by the holder of the note does not release a maker completely but, rather, only to the extent of the value of the collateral.

---

[55] See pp. 600–601.

Summary

The purpose of federal governmental regulation of business is fundamentally to protect our freedom to do business by curbing and preventing abuses. The government regulation discussed in chapter 32 is intended to protect free enterprise and fair competition. Administrative agencies, as discussed in chapter 33, have the responsibility to monitor business and establish rules and regulations to carry out the federal laws. In chapter 34 the laws that identify and protect the rights of labor to organize and of management to manage are discussed. Laws to protect the human and physical environment from private and public abuse and unnecessary waste are discussed in chapter 35.

32 Antitrust Law

After you have read this chapter, you should be able to:

1. Define pure monopoly and pure competition.
2. Explain the reason for the Sherman Act of 1890.
3. Explain why group boycotts are illegal.
4. Explain why Congress passed the Clayton Act.
5. Explain exclusive dealing contracts, tying arrangements, stock acquisitions designed to lessen competition, and horizontal versus vertical constraints.
6. Identify the Federal Trade Commission.
7. Understand the Robinson-Patman Act of 1936.
8. Understand the major defenses against the Robinson-Patman Act of 1936.

Introduction

Imagine that you are an entrepreneur in a small midwestern town. Your company sells oil to consumers within a forty-mile radius and has been expanding rapidly since you began it ten years ago. You are finally making a decent living from the business. Suddenly you discover that your competitors are involved in a scheme which will allow them not only to control the industry but to wipe out your firm.

The stockholders of your larger competitors are turning their power to vote in corporate matters over to a select group of people called trustees. These trustees thereby gain enormous power in many firms at once and can control the supply (and so the price) of oil for the entire nation, including the area in which you have traditionally done business. By raising the price of oil in one state and making a great deal of profit, they can lower the price in another area, even to the point of taking a loss for a while, to drive out competition—including your firm. How would you feel?

This scheme is far more than a story. During the late 1800s and early 1900s, such business trusts were common. People like John D. Rockefeller and Cornelius Vanderbilt made their fortunes using schemes just like this one. The public became greatly concerned as business power became more and more concentrated in the hands of a few individuals. They therefore turned to law for help.

Freedom to compete is a healthy concept and goes hand in hand with the principles of freedom and liberty on which the United States was founded. The early governmental policy of laissez faire (governmental noninterference with business) made it possible for such freedoms to be abused as business sought to increase its power. The policy had to be modified by federal statute to check the increasing tide of unreasonable restraint of trade which interfered with free enterprise and fair competition.

Accordingly, the issue became: how to balance free enterprise and fair competition on the one hand with governmental regulation of business on the other hand. The same issue exists today. This chapter analyzes the strains of public and private interests and the government's current reaction to them in controlling monopolies, combinations, and unfair restraints in business.

We shall see in this chapter the purposes of the various major antitrust statutes, how these statutes have worked, the type of business activities restrained, and the impact of the federal courts in interpreting and enforcing these statutes.

The Response of Law to Undue Concentration of Business Power

The United States was created with the intention of providing maximum opportunity for free competition in business. The doctrine of **laissez-faire**—that is, to let business alone—was dominant and worked well, at least until the industrial expansion after the Civil War. Then, with business growing by leaps and bounds, it became necessary to monitor the activities of some firms.

laissez-faire
government's policy of not interfering with business

The amount and type of government regulation of business has always been hotly debated in the world of work, but such regulation does exist. In this chapter we will examine the major federal antitrust laws: the Sherman Antitrust Act of 1890; the Clayton Act of 1914; the Federal Trade Commission Act of 1914; and the Robinson-Patman Act of 1936 amending the Clayton Act. Students should be aware that a number of other laws also regulate business, but they are somewhat less important.

What is it we want to regulate? Anyone who has followed a winning baseball team knows that things tend to get exciting when the competition is a little too close for comfort. When your team is leading by four or five runs the game can become boring, but when the lead is cut to one and the opposition has a tying run on third base with no outs, the situation is entirely different. For many people, the world of business provides the same kind of excitement. Competition forces firms to do their best to stay ahead, and by and large this is a good thing for all of us. Firms come up with new products, increase their sales, and improve current products—all to be the leader of the industry. Once in a while, however, a firm becomes as strong or stronger than its competitors and can drive its rivals completely out of business. If this happens, the leader becomes the *only* one with a particular product and can establish any price it wants, no matter how exorbitant.

The difficulty for the government is to determine when the law should exert control over competition. When there are many firms of equal strength, control may not be needed. When there is but one firm, and that firm is in a position to hurt the public, control is clearly needed. But what about the case in the middle, where a few firms control an industry? And, what about the case of an industry where one firm rather than many would be desirable? For example, it would be useless to have thirty or forty different telephone companies competing in the same city. Think of all the wires the telephone company now puts up. Could you imagine thirty times as many wires? As you can see, finding an answer is not easy. The government has set down some guidelines on when they will exert control and when they will not. Before we can examine those laws, you need to understand two terms: pure monopoly and pure competition.

Pure Monopoly versus Pure Competition

On rare occasions a firm discovers that it has no competitors. For example, most utility companies are unlikely to have competition in a given town. One gas company or one electric company satisfies the needs of the entire community; duplication is simply unnecessary. In a small community, one barber shop may be enough to cut everyone's hair. In these cases, it is either impossible for a competitor to enter the market or merely improbable or unlikely. The more improbable or unlikely competition is, the closer the market is to a **pure monopoly**—a market situation where only one firm is producing a product or providing a service.

pure monopoly
a market in which there is a single firm with no competitors

608   Government Regulation of Business

More often, however, a number of firms compete with each other for business. On occasion, the products are so similar that consumers can not distinguish between the goods of different firms. There may also be so many sellers that the size of the market for each firm is small, and an individual company can not have any meaningful influence over the price of the goods. If both things happen at the same time, we approach **pure competition.**

pure competition
a market in which many firms compete and no one firm has very much power

The market for wheat is an example of nearly pure competition. Many farmers produce wheat, and there is little if any difference between their end products. Furthermore, no individual farmer can influence the price very much because the market is so large. If one farmer tried to get $.10 more per bushel, buyers would merely move on to the next farmer. Thus, we can say that there is pure competition for wheat.

Controlling Monopolies, Combinations, and Unfair Restraints

Federal statutory modification of laissez-faire.

As you can imagine, monopolies in key industries can become enormous and wield tremendous power. Unfortunately, this power is not always used to benefit consumers. The first example in this chapter pointed out how some firms try to drive out competition in the hope of ultimately forming a monopoly. The practice of giving controlling blocks of stock to trustees was the first target of federal regulation and the genesis of today's **antitrust laws.**

antitrust laws
laws that limit monopolies, combinations, and unfair restraints to help prevent the undue concentration of economic power

Sherman Antitrust Act of 1890

It is highly unlikely that any firm will be an absolute monopoly, so the United States government had to develop a law to control situations that were approaching monopolistic competition. The first law to do this was the Sherman Antitrust Act of 1890. The two major sections of this law are:

Section 1: Every contract, combination in the form of trust or otherwise, or conspiracy, in restraint of trade or commerce among the several States, or with foreign nations, is hereby declared to be illegal.

Section 2: Every person who shall monopolize, or attempt to monopolize, or combine or conspire with any other person or persons, to monopolize any part of the trade or commerce among the several States, or with foreign nations, shall be deemed guilty of a felony. . . .[1]

Section 1 makes restraint of trade illegal; section 2 goes on to explain that individuals who engage in such restraint can be prosecuted for their actions.

Boycotts. Part of the Sherman Act has been interpreted by the courts to limit the opportunity for firms to join in not doing business with another company. Although any company can decide with whom it will or will not deal, if many firms get together in a concerted effort to boycott one firm, they are participating in a **group boycott,** which is a violation *per se* (of itself) of the Sherman Act. This is illustrated by the following case.

group boycott
a concerted effort by a number of firms to avoid doing business with a particular individual or firm

---

[1] See Sherman Antitrust Act, 15 U.S.C.A., secs. 1–7.

Facts

Klor's Inc., plaintiff, was a San Francisco retail store, and Broadway-Hale Stores, Inc., defendant, was its principal competitor. The owners of Klor's accused Broadway-Hale of trying to get the manufacturers of household appliances to agree not to sell to Klor's or to discriminate against Klor's by offering them goods at unreasonable prices. Judgment for plaintiff. Defendant appealed.

Decision

Affirmed, for plaintiff.

Reasoning

The plaintiff's contention that this concerted effort on the part of Broadway-Hale, Inc. and others violated the Sherman Act was sustained. Mr. Justice Black wrote: "Group boycotts . . . have long been held to be in the forbidden category. . . . Plainly the allegations of this complaint disclose such a boycott. This is not a case of a single trader refusing to deal with another, nor even of a manufacturer and a dealer agreeing to an exclusive distributorship. Alleged in this complaint is a wide combination consisting of manufacturers, distributors and a retailer. It deprives the manufacturers and distributors of their freedom to sell to Klor's at the same prices . . . made available to Broadway-Hale. . . . It clearly has, by its nature and character, a monopolistic tendency."

Klor's Inc. v. Broadway-Hale Stores, Inc.,
359 U.S. 207 (1959).

Violations of the Sherman Act may be punished by a jail sentence or a fine or both. Over the years, Congress has increased the fine by amending the Act.[2] Today a corporate violator can be required to pay $1 million, and individuals to pay as much as $100,000. The government also has the power to enjoin violators from further action. Finally, individuals whose businesses have been injured by a violation of the Act can sue for treble (triple) the amount of injury sustained, plus related court costs.

The Clayton Act of 1914

The Sherman Act did not succeed in halting all of the abuses that Congress had hoped it would cover. As a result, Congress passed the Clayton Act of 1914. Among the more important parts of the Act are provisions dealing with exclusive-dealing contracts, tying sales, and stock acquisition designed to substantially lessen competition or tending to create a monopoly.

Exclusive-Dealing Contracts. If you were a manufacturer, you might want to get retailers to agree not to sell the products of your competitors. Some retailers might even find the arrangement beneficial. The retailer would get to know your product very well and could depend on you for a constant supply. If enough retailers agreed to such an arrangement, you could effectively wipe out your competition. If your firm were powerful enough to exert some influence on the retailer, you might consider forcing the retailer into such an arrangement. Whatever its effect on the retailer, such an arrangement *might* substantially decrease

---

[2] Amendments to Sherman Act, sec. 2.

competition. The Clayton Act prohibits this kind of activity and labels it an **exclusive-dealing contract.**

Tying Arrangements.   A **tying arrangement** is another technique "to substantially lessen competition" or "tending to create a monopoly." Here is how a tying contract works. Suppose you were the owner of a medium-size manufacturing plant. You decide to purchase 1,000 fountain pens from Ajax Pen Company. Ajax gives you a good deal on the fountain pens, but as part of that deal makes you sign a contract agreeing to purchase only Ajax *ink* for those pens. Clearly, if Ajax has a monopoly on pens and can get its customers to sign such agreements, it soon will have a monopoly on ink as well. Tying contracts are regulated by section 3 of the Clayton Act. They have been declared illegal where the contract will "substantially lessen competition or tend to create a monopoly in any line of commerce."

The law does not require that there be a monopoly in an industry before it will step in to regulate the firms involved. It merely requires that the action substantially lessen competition by foreclosing competitors from substantial volume of the tied market. In the case above, Ajax would be lessening competition by limiting the ability of other ink companies to sell their products. But how large a volume of tied sales is necessary to effectively limit competition? In the landmark case,[3] the court decided that tied sales should amount to at least $500,000 to require regulatory action.

Stock Acquisitions Designed to Lessen Competition.   It was suggested earlier in this chapter that the courts often face difficult questions when a firm becomes large enough to wield a great deal of power. One problem that has been particularly perplexing is whether the sheer size of the firm should dictate governmental control, or whether the firm must actually use that power to restrain trade in some way. The government's answer came in section 7 of the Clayton Act as amended by the Cellar-Kefauver Act of 1950:

No corporation shall acquire, directly or indirectly, the whole or any part of the stock or other share capital and no corporation subject to the jurisdiction of the Federal Trade Commission shall acquire the whole or any part of the assets of one or more corporations engaged in commerce, where in any line of commerce in any section of the country, the effect of such acquisition, of such stocks or assets, or of the use of such stock by the voting or granting of proxies or otherwise, *may* be substantially to lessen competition, or *tend* to create a monopoly. [Emphasis added.]

Notice that such acquisition need not *result* in substantially lessening competition or creating a monopoly in order to be unlawful. All that is required is that it "may" or "tend to" produce the unlawful result.

Corporate acquisition of stock may result in a horizontal or vertical merger, and if it *may* substantially lessen competition or *tend to* create a monopoly, it is unlawful. The example below illustrates the concept of horizontal and vertical mergers. Stop Time, Inc. is a firm that manufactures and sells pocket watches.

---

[3] *International Salt Co., Inc. v. United States,* 332 U.S. 392 (1947).

To manufacture these watches, Stop Time must purchase the raw materials, put them together as pocket watches, and sell the watches to retailers, who sell to the public. Stop Time probably competes with companies such as Timex, Westclox, and Benrus, to name a few. A diagram of Stop Time's competitive situation would probably look like this:

Figure 32.1 Diagrammatic Representation of Stop Time, Inc.'s Competitive Situation

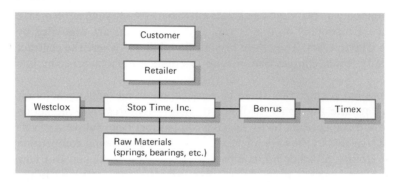

If Stop Time purchased stock in Timex, Benrus, or Westclox, that would be a **horizontal merger**; Stop Time would be combining forces with its competitors. On the other hand, if Stop Time bought a controlling interest in all retailers of pocket watches or in all sources of raw materials, that would be a **vertical merger**.

According to section 7 of the Clayton Act, horizontal mergers were illegal; vertical ones were not. Today, because of complex case law and vast and overlapping administrative rules and regulations, students are advised to see a legal specialist if their problem seems to extend beyond this brief description. Although both types of combinations could cause problems, the Act limited only horizontal mergers. This was an important weakness in the law.

In the following case the court held that the proposed merger of the two firms "may be to substantially lessen competition" and, therefore, would violate the Clayton Act.

horizontal merger
a merger of competing firms

vertical merger
a merger between a firm and one of its major suppliers or customers

Facts
The plaintiff, Brown Shoe Co., Inc., initiated a suit against the United States government in November 1955, when the government tried to stop Brown from merging with G. R. Kinney Co., Inc. through an exchange of stock. By dollar volume, Brown was the third largest seller of shoes in the United States, and Kinney was the eighth largest. Judgment for the United States government. Plaintiff appealed.

Decision
Affirmed, for the United States government.

Reasoning
"[T]he government contended that the effect of the merger of Brown . . . and Kinney . . . 'may be substantially to lessen competition or to tend to create a monopoly' by eliminating actual or potential competition in the production of shoes for the national wholesale market and in the sale of shoes at

retail in the nation." In deciding whether this merger would violate section 7 of the Clayton Act as amended, the court examined both the vertical and horizontal aspects of the contemplated merger. It also examined congressional intent in amending section 7 of the Clayton Act:

"Congress sought to assure the Federal Trade Commission and the courts the power to brake this [merger] force at its outset and before it gathered momentum."

"Congress indicated plainly that a merger had to be functionally viewed, in the context of its particular industry."

"Congress used the words *may be* to substantially lessen competition."

. . . "On the basis of the record before us, we believe that the Government sustained the burden of proof. . . . The judgment is affirmed."

Brown Shoe Co., Inc. v. United States, 370 U.S. 294 (1962).

The Federal Trade Commission Act

The **Federal Trade Commission** was created in 1914 when Congress passed the Federal Trade Commission Act. Congress intended the FTC to monitor two areas: (1) unfair methods of competition, and (2) unfair or deceptive acts or practices in or affecting commerce.

Implications of the Federal Trade Commission Act for Other Laws. Congress gave the FTC power to enforce antitrust laws. Specifically, the FTC monitors the performance of firms to see that they meet the criteria established in both the Sherman Antitrust Act and the Clayton Act. The FTC also monitors other less well known laws. For example, it may move to cancel deceptive trademarks under the Lanham Act of 1946, or monitor the kinds of fiber in wool products under the Wool Products Labeling Act of 1939. The following case came under the Lanham Act and held that there was trademark infringement.

Facts

Plaintiff, Ye Olde Tavern Cheese Products, registered its trademark properly. Commencing at least as early as 1958, plaintiff has been packaging and distributing various snacks, including nuts in individual cellophane bags stapled to large cards. . . . The bags bore the label "Ye Old Tavern."

In 1964 Planters Peanuts, a division of Standard Brands, defendant, placed on sale a product which it identified as "Planters Ye Old Tavern Nuts." [This product was displayed in a way similar to the plaintiff's product.] Three months later the defendant reintroduced the same product as "Planters Tavern Nuts."

This is a suit by the plaintiff for trademark infringement, unfair competition, trademark dilution, and injury to business reputation, taken under the Lanham Act.

Decision

Judgment for the plaintiff.

Reasoning

The court stated that a plaintiff in a trademark infringement suit has an easier burden of proof, in that the prior use of the trademark gives rise to a presumption of exclusive right to it, and renders proof of an actual intent to defraud unnecessary.

Ye Olde Tavern Cheese Products, Inc. v. Planters Peanuts Division of Standard Brands, Inc., 261 F.Supp. 200 (1966), aff'd 394 F.2d 833 (1967).

Federal Trade Commission May Act on Its Own Initiative. If the Federal Trade Commission believed that a firm is using some unfair method of competition, it would probably try to prosecute the firm under an appropriate section of one of the major antitrust laws. However, on many occasions the FTC has moved on its own to stop deceptive acts in commerce, as in the following case.

Facts

The case arose out of Colgate's attempt to prove on television that its shaving cream, Rapid Shave, outshaves them all. Colgate had three one-minute commercials designed to show that Rapid Shave could soften even the toughness of sandpaper. The announcer informed the audience that "to prove Rapid Shave's super-moisturizing power, we put it right from the can onto tough, dry sandpaper. Apply . . . soak . . . off in a stroke." It appeared that sandpaper was being used, but it was really a "simulated sandpaper" made of plexiglass to which sand had been applied. The Federal Trade Commission found that the commercial was a material deceptive device. Colgate appealed.

Decision

Affirmed, for the Federal Trade Commission.

Reasoning

The court had to decide whether it was a deceptive practice under section 5 of the FTC Act to represent falsely that a televised test, experiment, or demonstration provides a viewer with visual proof of a product claim. The court held: "We agree with the Commission that the undisclosed use of plexiglass in the present commercials was a material deceptive practice, independent and separate from the other misrepresentations found. We find unpersuasive Colgate's other objections to this conclusion. They claim that it will be impractical to inform the viewing public that it is not seeing an actual test . . . but we think . . . that the ingenious advertising would well be able . . ., if it so desires, to conform to the Commission's insistence that the public not be misinformed."

Federal Trade Commission v. Colgate-Palmolive Co., 380 U.S. 374 (1965).

If a firm is found to be violating the law, a number of punishments are available, ranging from civil penalties to criminal prosecution. The FTC has generally used a combination of consent decrees and orders. These are similar to settlements with the offending firm and are not nearly as severe as criminal prosecution.

Robinson-Patman Act of 1936

Section 2(a) of the Clayton Act was difficult for both courts and businesses to understand. In an attempt to clear the air, Congress passed the Robinson-Patman Act of 1936, amending section 2(a). This Act was specifically designed to deal with **price discrimination**. Experts today contend that the Robinson-Patman Act has not actually clarified the issue to the satisfaction of all interested parties. It does, however, state that it shall be "unlawful to discriminate in price between

price discrimination
the practice of offering the same product to different competing customers at different prices

Government Regulation of Business

different purchasers of commodities of like grade and quality, where . . . the effect of such discrimination may be (a) to substantially lessen competition, or (b) to tend to create a monopoly in any line of commerce or (c) to injure, destroy, or prevent competition with any person who either grants or knowingly receives the benefit of such discrimination, or with customers of either of them."[4]

The Uses of the Robinson-Patman Act. The Act is used to eliminate a number of unfair practices. One of these is to lower the price of goods in a geographical area to drive out the competition. A second practice is to give discounts on goods to one seller but not to another, where the only reasonable explanation of the discount is an intent to destroy competition or create a monopoly. A third practice is to discriminate against purchasers by charging inordinately high freight costs with the intent to destroy competition. In the following case the FTC held that the firm's charging lower prices for its product in certain geographical areas drove out competition and was violative of the Clayton Act.

Facts

"Dean Milk Co. maintained [ed] its executive offices in Franklin Park, Illinois, and [was] engaged in the processing and sale of fluid milk . . . in a number of states. . . . Its prices in Evansville, Indiana . . . and Lexington, Kentucky, all of which are served by the Louisville processing plant, were lower than prices in Louisville." The FTC had to decide whether the price difference reflected a violation of section 2(a) of the Clayton Act.

Decision

Dean's price difference was such a violation.

Reasoning

The dairy argued that evidence of a "reasonable possibility" of adverse competition effects on competition is not enough to issue an order to cease. The FTC disagreed, "Congress clearly intended to prevent in their incipiency practices which might harm the competitive process and thus explicitly provided that a showing of actual injury was not necessary. [Here] we think the conditions . . . in the market—the low profit margins and the high mortality rate in the smaller dairies—support a conclusion that there is a reasonable possibility that continued sales . . . where they can not realize a reasonable profit . . . will cause the demise of other small dairies.

Respondent [Dean Milk Co.] will be ordered to cease charging lower prices . . ."

In re *Dean Milk Company,* 68 FTC 710 (1965).

Resale Price Fixing. Resale price fixing occurs when the price is fixed at which the purchased product is to be resold by the buyer. When two or more competing suppliers agree to so fix the price, there is *horizontal* price fixing. When the supplier so agrees with his buyer, there is *vertical* price fixing. Both are illegal today.

---

[4] Robinson-Patman Act, (1936) 15 U.S.C., sec. 13.

Defenses Against a Charge Under the Robinson-Patman Act. Not all price differences or discounts are violations *per se* of the Robinson-Patman Act. If a buyer purchases such a large quantity of goods that the manufacturer can save money on production or on purchase of raw materials, a discount may be offered. If a change in conditions makes the goods sell for more (or less), this would not be a violation. If you can demonstrate that you did not attempt to lessen competition, but merely acted in good faith to challenge your competitors, you will be safe. This was the point of the following case, which held that there was no violation of the Robinson-Patman Act.

Facts

Defendant, Standard Oil Co., sold gasoline to four comparatively large "jobbers" (customers) in Detroit at a lower price per gallon than it sold to many comparatively smaller service-station customers in the same area. Defendant appealed from a judgment in favor of the FTC.

Decision

Reversed, for the defendant.

Reasoning

Standard Oil Co. argued that it lowered prices in good faith to retain jobbers as customers—that is, it met the lower prices of competitors to retain customers. The Supreme Court ruled: "It is enough to say that Congress did not seek, by the Robinson-Patman Act, either to abolish competition or so radically to curtail it that a seller would have no substantial right of self-defense against a price raid by a competitor. The heart of our national economic policy long has been faith in the value of competition . . ., which it sought to protect, and monopoly, which it sought to prevent.

Judgment of lower court reversed. . . . We agree [that] the lower price was justified."

Standard Oil Co. v. FTC, 340 U.S. 231 (1951).

Summary Statement

1. With a stated belief in free competition, the United States has grown from an agrarian economy to the world's foremost industrialized nation. Sometimes competition becomes extremely stiff, and weak, ineffective firms are driven out of the market. This may lead to a monopoly. Not all monopolies are evil and not all require governmental regulation. In some circumstances, however, the government may wish to intervene.
2. We examined the major federal antitrust laws: the Sherman Antitrust Act of 1890; the Clayton Act of 1914 with the Cellar-Kefauver Amendment; the Federal Trade Commission Act of 1914; and the Robinson-Patman Act of 1936 amending section 2(a) of the Clayton Act. We noted some defenses against the Robinson-Patman Act, to emphasize that firms sometimes discriminate among their customers for good commercial reasons, with the apparent result of hurting competitors. The government is not trying to eliminate competition, it is trying to regulate abuses.

3. We noted the important role of the Federal Trade Commission in today's antitrust regulations. The commission monitors performance of companies around the criteria of the Sherman and Clayton Acts.
4. We saw that the Robinson-Patman Act is used to eliminate unfair practices such as unfair discounts or discrimination in pricing.
5. Finally, we looked at the various defenses under the Robinson-Patman Act and noted that there were certain violations that could be defended against by showing that they were just good business and not designed to lessen competition.

In the following well known case, the court found a tying arrangement in violation of the Sherman Act.

Siegel v. Chicken Delight, Inc.
448 F.2d 43 (1971), cert. denied 405 U.S. 955 (1972)

Before Madden, Judge of the United States Court of Claims, and Merrill and Hufstedler, Circuit Judges.

Merrill, J. This antitrust suit is a class action in which certain franchisees of Chicken Delight seek treble damages for injuries allegedly resulting from illegal restraints imposed by Chicken Delight's standard form franchise agreements. The restraints in question are Chicken Delight's contractual requirements that franchisees purchase certain essential cooking equipment, dry-mix food items, and trademark bearing packaging exclusively from Chicken Delight as a condition of obtaining a Chicken Delight trademark license. These requirements are asserted to constitute a tying arrangement, unlawful per se under section 1 of the Sherman Act.

II. The Existence of an Unlawful Tying Arrangement

In order to establish that there exists an unlawful tying arrangement plaintiffs must demonstrate: First that the scheme in question involves two distinct items and provides that one (the tying product) may not be obtained unless the other (the tied product) is also purchased. . . . Second, that the tying product possesses sufficient economic power appreciably to restrain competition in the tied product market. . . . Third, that a "not insubstantial" amount of commerce is affected by the arrangement. . . . Chicken Delight concedes that the third requirement has been satisfied. It disputes the existence of the first two. Further it asserts that . . . there is a fourth issue: whether there exists a special justification for the particular tying arrangement in question. . . .

A. Two Products

The District Court ruled that the license to use the Chicken Delight name, trademark, and method of operations was "a tying item in the traditional sense," the tied items being the cookers and fryers, packaging products, and mixes.

The hallmark of a tie-in is that it denies competitors free access to the tied product market, not because the party imposing the arrangement has a superior product in that market, but because of the power or leverage exerted by the tying product.

Sale of a franchise license, with the attendant rights to operate a business in the prescribed manner and to benefit from the goodwill of the tradename, in no way requires the forced sale by the franchisor of some or all of the component articles. . . .

. . . The relevant question is not whether the items are essential to the franchise, but whether it is essential to the franchise that the items be purchased from Chicken Delight. This raises not the issue of whether there is a tie-in but rather the issue of whether the tie-in is justifiable, a subject to be discussed below.

We conclude that the District Court was not in error.

B. Economic Power

Under the per se theory of illegality, plaintiffs are required to establish not only the existence of a tying arrangement but also that the tying product possesses sufficient economic power to appreciably restrain free competition in the tied product markets.

. . . It is not the nature of the public interest that has caused the legal barrier to be erected that is the basis for the presumption, but the fact that such a barrier does exist. Accordingly we see no reason why the presumption that exists in the case of the patent and copyright does not equally apply to the trademark.

C. Justification

Chicken Delight maintains that, even if its contractual arrangements are held to constitute a tying arrangement, it was not an unreasonable restraint under the Sherman Act. Three different bases for justification are urged.

First, Chicken Delight contends that the arrangement was a reasonable device for measuring and collecting revenue.

Second, Chicken Delight advances as justification the fact that when it first entered the fast food field in 1952 it was a new business and was then entitled to the protection afforded by *United States v. Jerrold Electronics Corp.* . . .

The third justification Chicken Delight offers is the "marketing identity" purpose, the franchisor's preservation of the distinctiveness, uniformity and quality of its product.

We conclude that the District Court was not in error in holding as matter of law (and upon the limited jury verdict) that Chicken Delight's contractual requirements constituted a tying arrangement in violation of section 1 of the Sherman Act. . . . [J]udgment is affirmed.

The District Court judgment was reversed and remanded for limited trial on several damage questions.

Questions and Case Problems

1. Soft Top Ice Cream, Inc. sells franchises that allow the purchaser of the franchise to sell several different flavors of soft ice cream. However, Soft Top Ice Cream, Inc. demands that retailers purchase a special machine from them to make the product. They explain that only the combination of their special machine and special mix will produce the product which is sold as "Soft Top Ice Cream." Is this a violation of the Clayton Act? [*Engbrecht v. Dairy Queen Co. of Mexico, Missouri*, 203 F.Supp. 714 (1962).]

2. Ajax Candy, Karmel Kandie, and Sweet Tooth Kandi are members of an association of candy jobbers. They have frequently refused to deal with any manufacturer of candy who will not agree to their scheme of price fixing. They also attempt to get dealers to refuse to deal in the candies of their competitors. Is this unlawful? Explain. [*Boyle v. United States,* 40 F.2d 49 (1930).]

3. Karasel Film, Neat-O-Film, and others join together to limit the use of their films to those theaters who buy all their supplies, such as projectors and popcorn, from them. They also require theaters to pay royalties to them, no matter from whom the projectors were purchased. Is this illegal? [*U.S. v. Motion Picture Patents Co.,* 225 F. 800 (1915).]

4. Big Yellow Co. is regularly engaged in the business of producing, transporting, and importing bananas into the United States. They already have a substantial share of the market. In fact, they are considering increasing their control of the market by purchasing a block of stock in a competitor's business. May they proceed? [*U.S. v. United Fruit Co.* (D.C. La. 1958), para. 6894.]

5. Real Hair Co. has an advertising campaign that states that their hair looks exactly like the "real thing" and will never fall out. Several people decide to use the services of Real Hair. The hair does not look real and falls out immediately. Recourse? [In re *Medi-Hair International, et al.,* 80 FTC 627 (1972).]

6. U Drive Um Auto Company decides to sell some of its cars. In an effort to get customers, it tells them the cars are new. This turns out to be false. Recourse? [In re *Arlington Imports, Inc.,* 77 FTC 1109 (1970).]

7. V. Smokes M Cigarette Company decided to offer certain grocery stores additional packs of cigarettes at no charge when they purchased a certain brand of cigarette. This offer was made only to certain grocers. The cigarette dealers also provided free displays to these customers and not to others. Is this illegal? [In re *P. Lorillard Co.,* 44 FTC 1180 (1948).]

8. Irving Dairies was in a fierce battle with other dairies in the area of Patchogue, New York. Irving was granting discounts in excess of 20 percent (the usual for the market) to certain customers. Is this illegal price discrimination? [*Jones v. Borden Co.,* 430 F.2d 568 (1970).]

9. Aladdin Tire Co. had certain accounts called "commercial accounts." These accounts operated through a number of stores in greater Boston; coincidentally Aladdin owned and operated these stores. Prices of tires were lower at these stores than elsewhere. Illegal? [In re *U.S. Rubber Co., et al.,* 28 FTC 1489 (1939).]

10. In the case of *Siegel v. Chicken Delight, Inc.,* 448 F.2d 43 (1971), cert. denied 405 U.S. 955 (1972),[5] the court said that "the relevant question is not whether the items are essential to the franchise, but whether it is essential to the franchise that the items be purchased from Chicken Delight. This raises not the issue of whether there is a tie-in but rather the issue of whether the tie-in is justifiable." Discuss this statement by the court and explain how a business may so operate as to avoid violation of this part of the Sherman Act.

---

[5] See pp. 617–18.

33 Administrative Law

After you have read this chapter, you should be familiar with all of the following terms:

1. Administrative Procedures Act of 1946.
2. Administrative investigations.
3. Informal settlements.
4. Adjudicative procedures.
5. Judicial review.
6. Substantial evidence test.
7. Administrative reparations.
8. License.

Introduction

Most of us assume that when we purchase a drug prescribed by our family physician, it will be pure and safe when taken as directed. But did you ever wonder who sets the standards against which the drugs are measured? Often we were told in elementary civics courses that legislators make laws and, therefore, the laws establishing drug standards must have been passed by legislators. But is it that easy? Let us stop and consider that statement for a moment.

Let us think of all the drugs currently on the market. Many of them have names that a layman can barely pronounce—and much less can a layman understand their chemical makeup and action. How many of our senators or representatives have degrees in pharmacology? Obviously, very few, if any! Then how do they have the expertise necessary to legislate on the safety of each and every drug? Obviously they do *not* have the expertise—and they do *not* legislate on each drug. Even if the legislature were inclined to begin the impossible task of passing laws about each drug, do you think they would have the time to complete the job and do all the other things legislators are supposed to do? Again, obviously, the answer is no!

So how are the standards established to assure our safety when we take a prescribed medicine? The bulk of the work is assumed by administrative agencies. Some of the major federal administrative agencies that you may have heard about are: the Federal Trade Commission (FTC); the Federal Communications Commission (FCC); the National Labor Relations Board (NLRB); the Federal Reserve Board; the Internal Revenue Service; and the group that regulates the safety of medicine, the Food and Drug Administration (FDA). In this chapter we look at the range and limits of activities of our federal administrative agencies. There are also state administrative agencies concerned with state matters.

Congress provided for the creation of federal administrative agencies because it needed help to implement legislation it enacted. These agencies have the following responsibilities: (1) creating administrative rules and regulations; (2) establishing administrative procedures necessary for administrative action; (3) monitoring and providing for administrative investigation of industries for violations of antitrust laws and for consumer protection; and (4) adjudicating violation of such laws and administrative rules and regulations.

In this chapter we will consider the establishment and growth of federal administrative agencies, and observe how they operate. We will note again the problem of how far government, through its administrative agencies in the fulfillment of their responsibilities, should interfere in our daily business and private life.

Response of the Law

Administrative agencies are so numerous today that just listing them with a brief description of the function of each would take up the rest of this book and a major portion of another. A more manageable task for us is to present an overview of the growth of administrative agencies and provide some idea of how they

Administrative agencies.

operate. We will therefore examine the foundation upon which administrative law has grown from the federal Administrative Procedures Act of 1946, 60 Stat. 237 (1946).

Administrative agencies do far more than set standards. Once standards are set in the form of rules, these rules must be enforced. Note that administrative agencies establish rules, not laws, which are made only by Congress as a legislative body authorized by the U.S. Constitution. Agencies monitor performance. If persons do not meet their standards, the agencies often have the power to levy fines or revoke previously granted privileges. These powers are not unlimited and, on occasion, agency decisions are overturned by courts of law through a process known as "judicial review."

Both the number and the domain of concern of administrative agencies have grown rapidly in the past twenty years. In reading the materials that follow, students should recall the question asked at the beginning of Part 7, Governmental Regulation of Business: How great an involvement do we, as managers of major industries and as private citizens, want the government to have in our lives?

Delegation

The Problem of Time

In the opening of this chapter we suggested that elementary civics texts traditionally told students that legislators make laws. We then went on to say that this was not always the case. Administrative agencies have the power to create rules and regulations also, which all of us must obey. Where does that power come from? Article I, section 1 of the United States Constitution states: "All legislative powers herein granted shall be vested in a Congress of the United States, which shall consist of a Senate and a House of Representatives." Reading on, you simply never come across a section stating that there shall be a Federal Trade Commission.

The power comes from a concept familiar to management students known as "delegation." Suppose you were to start a small business, perhaps a gas station. At first you might be able to handle all of the issues that come up during the day. You can pump gas, change the tires, and fix all of the engines that need fixing. As the business grows, however, you may be faced with growing lines of customers demanding gasoline. As you spend more and more time at the pumps, you get further and further behind on your repairs. You might throw up your hands in disgust and shout, "There aren't enough hours in a day to do all of the things I would like to do." So you might hire an assistant to pump gas—i.e., you delegate the responsibility to someone else, thus freeing you to do the more enjoyable task of fixing broken Mercedes and Jaguars.

Congress did the same thing when it delegated the responsibility for rule-making to administrative agencies. It simply did not have the *time* to create all the rules necessary for the smooth operation of our nation. It may not lack the interest, but it very well may have far too many other things to do.

Source of administrative agency power.

Delegation.

One reason for delegation is lack of time.

The Problem of Expertise

If we go back to our gas station example: suppose the assistant gas pumper works out well, and you go back to the job of fixing engines. Then a customer approaches you with a Classic 19XX Stutz Bearcat. If you have never been trained in making repairs on classic automobiles and if you thought that such repairs might become a significant part of your business, you would consider delegating the responsibility for repairs. Certainly you would want to keep your role as owner and manager of the work of your assistants, but if others have expertise which you lack, you delegate to them the responsibility for getting the job done.

Once again, Congress sought to delegate its responsibility when it discovered that it did not have nearly as much collective specialized knowledge about particular areas as could be marshalled in an administrative agency. This combination of pressures on Congress—too little time and insufficient expertise—led to the creation of the huge number of federal administrative agencies. At first, some people considered this delegation a potential violation of the Constitution. But the power to delegate responsibility downward from Congress to administrative agencies has long been guaranteed. The case which follows is a classic because it is one of the very few instances of a delegation downward from Congress being held *invalid*. It has come to be known as the *Hot Oil* case. Its companion, the *Sick Chicken* case, is printed at the end of this chapter.

Another reason for delegation is lack of expertise.

Facts

In 1933 the United States was in the midst of a great depression. However, in the state of Texas, huge oil reserves were discovered. This led to a vast oversupply of oil in the marketplace. Through the National Industrial Recovery Act, section 9(c), President Roosevelt was authorized to prohibit transportation in interstate commerce of petroleum and the products thereof . . . (48 Stat. 200 (1933)). The Panama Refining Company sued (ultimately to the Supreme Court), claiming that the President's directions to the Secretary of the Interior to promulgate implementatory regulations to enforce section 9(c) were unconstitutional delegations. Was the President's delegation unconstitutional in this case?

Decision

Judgment for Panama Refining Co.

Reasoning

"Thus, in every case in which the question has been raised, the court has recognized that there are limits of delegation which there is no constitutional authority to transcend. We think that section 9(c) goes beyond these limits."

Panama Refining Co. v. Ryan, 293 U.S. 388 (1935).

Administrative Procedures

While agencies vary somewhat in the procedures they use, it is still possible to create a composite picture of what happens when it is necessary for an agency to take action against a business firm for violation of a rule. In the next few

Administrative procedures necessary for administrative action.

pages we shall examine some typical administrative techniques for dispute resolution. The agency we shall examine is the Federal Trade Commission (FTC).

You will recall that in the previous chapter the FTC was identified as the agency responsible for monitoring industries for violation of antitrust laws. In addition to having that responsibility, the FTC is actively involved in consumer protection. For example, the FTC has consistently prosecuted individuals involved in false advertising or those who make deceptive claims, as is illustrated in the following case.

Facts

A manufacturer produced a cream designed for cosmetic use. According to its own claims, the cream "restores natural moisture necessary for a live, healthy skin"; "your face need know no drought years"; and the preparation brings to the user's "skin quickly the clear radiance . . . the petal-like quality and texture of youth." The cream is called "Rejuvenescence Cream." The Federal Trade Commission sued to stop the use of the name "Rejuvenescence Cream." Is the name deceptive in that it would lead people to believe that the cream would actually rejuvenate skin?

Decision

Judgment for the Federal Trade Commission.

Reasoning

Representations merely having the capacity to deceive are unlawful. The Federal Trade Commission had produced an expert who testified that the average woman, conditioned by talk in magazines and over the radio . . . might take rejuvenescence to mean that "this is one of the modern miracles" and is something which would actually cause her youth to be restored.

Charles of the Ritz Distrib. Corp. v. FTC, 143 F.2d 676 (1944).

Administrative investigation.

Investigations

In order to do its job effectively, administrative agencies need to have the power to investigate instances in which they believe rules have been violated. The Federal Trade Commission has that power. Typically, federal agencies have large groups of staff members who spend their time continuously collecting data on the industry or industries being monitored. Therefore, it is likely that instances of deviation from the rules would rapidly come to the attention of the agency staff. If the problem becomes acute, the enforcement arm of the agency can initiate some action.

The Federal Trade Commission, like most other agencies, has the power to compel people to testify before them. To accomplish this task, they may issue what is known as a **subpoena.** Subpoenas are designed to elicit testimony from particular witnesses, but they may be insufficient and unrealistic as a technique for gathering the quantity of information constantly needed for monitoring purposes. Therefore, administrative agencies also have the power to demand the periodic filing of reports. While some businessmen complain about the volume of paperwork, the advantage of these reporting procedures is that a wide range of activities can be carefully monitored at once.

subpoena
an order to appear before a judicial body for the purpose of giving testimony

Informal Settlements

Attempt for informal settlements.

In chapter 2, Organization of the United States Legal System, we mentioned that, when a dispute arises, lawyers rarely try to bring the case to court immediately. Rather, they try to discuss the problem with the adversary in the hope of arriving at some mutually satisfactory settlement. The Federal Trade Commission and most other agencies have mechanisms which facilitate informal enforcement of standards.

Needless to say, the degree to which the agency is willing to settle informally depends upon the nature of the infraction (is it a major offense?) and the number of infractions which that firm had been involved in previously. If an agreement is struck between the parties, the FTC requires that a formal affidavit be filed detailing the nature of the complaint and providing the agency with written assurance that there will be no further violations of the rules.

Adjudicative Proceedings

Adjudicative proceedings.

Certainly not all matters can be settled informally. Therefore, agencies have established adjudicative procedures designed to formally decide cases of alleged violations of administrative rules.

Complaint. An administrative agency issues a complaint. This is a document designed to serve as notice to the business involved that the agency believes that the business has violated a particular standard. The Federal Trade Commission, for example, issues an "adjudicative complaint." (Also known as a Part III complaint since it is issued pursuant to Part III of the FTC's rules.)

Hearings. At first glance, administrative hearings appear to be much like any other courtroom trial. However, closer examination reveals several significant differences. Just as in formal courts, administrative hearings are presided over by a judge. The judges are called "administrative law judges," and they are employees of the agency. They are *not* members of the state or federal judiciary.

At the hearing the administrative law judge allows each side to present evidence. In FTC proceedings, parties may cross-examine witnesses and make motions and objections. In fact, in the case of an indigent (poor person), the FTC can make arrangements to have counsel appointed to represent the indigent. Once all of the evidence has been presented, the judge issues an opinion. As we will see shortly, this opinion may be appealed to a higher authority if deemed necessary.

Evidence. One major difference between formal state and federal courts, on the one hand, and administrative agencies, on the other, is in the kind of evidence which they will find acceptable. Formal court systems tend to be more restrictive about the kinds of evidence they will receive. The formal courts have grown up with a system which is based upon exclusionary rules of evidence. That is, the courts have rather rigorously tended to exclude evidence if it may in any way be undependable. The classic example being the courts' reluctance to accept "**hearsay.**"

hearsay
matter not personally known but heard from others

Administrative hearings are conducted less formally than state or federal court hearings. They also allow evidence of a much broader scope. The federal Administrative Procedures Act defines the scope of acceptable evidence in section 7(c):

Any oral or documentary evidence may be received, but every agency shall as a matter of policy provide for the exclusion of irrelevant immaterial or unduly repetitious evidence and no sanction shall be imposed or rule or order be issued except upon consideration of the whole record or such portions thereof as may be cited by any party and as supported by and in accordance with the reliable, probative and substantial evidence.

This means that evidence which would otherwise be unacceptable may be included as part of an administrative hearing for its probative value, as is illustrated in the following case.

Facts
Powers was an employee of Cities Service Oil Company. As shipping master, Powers interviewed applicants for jobs. Powers often questioned potential employees about their union affiliations and told people that he would not hire members of the National Maritime Union. This is a violation of potential employees' rights under the National Labor Relations Act. Was the NLRA trial examiner wrong in accepting or rejecting testimony concerning Powers' behavior if such testimony is hearsay?

Decision
No. Judgment for the NLRB.

Reasoning
Counsel admits that the evidence is hearsay and, while the Board is entirely free to accept such evidence, we cannot say that it commits reversible error in excluding it.

NLRB v. Cities Service Oil Co., 129 F.2d 933 (1942).

Decision. The administrative judge considers all of the evidence and issues an opinion. This opinion is usually subject to review by the entire administrative agency and they may either accept the opinion or reject it. The opinion may contain a recommendation for a sanction. For example, the Federal Trade Commission judge may decide that a particular business advertising practice should not continue, and he may therefore issue a cease and desist order.

Judicial review of
administrative
adjudications.

Judicial Review

Decisions made by administrative agencies are reviewable. By this we mean that if you, as an aggrieved party, are not satisfied with a decision made by an agency, you may appeal the decision to a court of law. However, courts do not automatically have to hear your case. Indeed, there is a tendency on the part of federal courts to resist review in favor of relying on the administrative agencies' expertise.

The standard which the courts use in deciding whether or not to review an administrative agency's decision is the *substantial evidence* test. This test declares that courts will review issues that involve questions of law. However, questions of fact are reviewed only if the decision violates a test of reasonableness. While this is the dominant view today, there are some *state* statutes which give the courts the right to have a trial *de novo*[1] (new trial). The argument in favor of allowing de novo trials is that this assures that the courts will have an opportunity to provide a somewhat stronger check on arbitrary administrative action. Finally, the Administrative Procedures Act, section 706, provides useful guidance on the scope of review, as is illustrated in the following case.

Facts

Appellant, Charlton, was an investigator for the United States Internal Revenue Service. He was charged with failing to properly care for official documents and to report a proffered bribe. The district court said that it would review only to determine whether there had been substantial compliance with applicable procedures and statutes. Is this the proper test?

Decision

Judgment for Charlton.

Reasoning

Section 706 of the Administrative Procedures Act says in part: "The reviewing court shall—Hold unlawful and set aside agency action found to be (a) arbitrary, capricious, and abuse of discretion . . . (d) without observance of procedure required by law and . . . (e) unsupported by substantial evidence in a case subject to sections 556 and 557 of this title. . . ."

Charlton v. United States, 412 F.2d 390 (1969).

Types of Powers Held by Administrative Agencies

Administrative agencies have several different ways in which to exert control over their respective companies. It is, of course, possible for an administrative agency to simply use the power of moral persuasion to obtain compliance with its rules. However, the chances of this technique working satisfactorily are quite limited. Perhaps the most common technique used is to *fine* rule-breakers. Another form of sanction is to force the regulated party to pay *reparations* to the injured party. Finally, a third technique employed by administrative agencies is the granting, revocation, and withholding of a *license.*

At the state level, one example of a licensing requirement is the license you must earn to drive your car. A driver's license is a privilege granted to you after you have demonstrated a rudimentary understanding of automobile safety and handling. If you violate too many driving laws, your license can be suspended or revoked.

---

[1] See 82 AM. JUR. Workmen's Compensation, sec. 618; and Ohio Rev. Code, Title 41, *Labor and Industry,* sec. 4123.519.

Summary Statement

1. In this chapter we examined the scope of activity of federal administrative agencies. We began by observing that federal administrative agencies are a creation born of necessity. Although the federal Constitution says that legislators make laws, reality dictates that rule-making procedures be delegated to administrative agencies.
2. There are so many administrative agencies that it is impossible to outline all of the different structures which exist. However, we noted that there exists a substantial body of federal laws guiding their action. The most important of these laws is the Administrative Procedures Act.
3. Administrative agencies investigate violations of rules and may take informal action to settle disputes. However, there are more formal alternatives available. Agencies may hold hearings, complete with elaborate procedures (formal or informal), and may issue decisions which the regulated groups must follow.
4. The decisions of administrative agencies may be appealed to courts of law, but courts are reluctant to use their power of *judicial* review.
5. Finally, agencies vary in their strength. Some agencies can fine rule violators; others have the power to license and revoke licenses.

In the following classic case the court held that Congress had unconstitutionally and, therefore, illegally delegated its code-making legislative power to the President in the National Industrial Recovery Act by not *establishing standards* of fair competition and, instead, delegating this power to the President. In short, it was an illegal delegation of legislative power instead of a delegation of authority to *implement standards*, which can be established only by the Congress.

Schechter Poultry Corp. v. United States
295 U.S. 495 (1935)

Mr. Chief Justice Hughes delivered the opinion of the Court. Petitioners . . . were convicted . . . on eighteen counts of an indictment charging violations of what is known as the "Live Poultry Code," and on an additional count for conspiracy to commit such violations. . . . [T]he defendants contended (1) that the Code had been adopted pursuant to an unconstitutional delegation by Congress of legislative power. . . .

The Circuit Court of Appeals sustained the conviction . . . [and] this Court granted writs of certiorari, April 15, 1935. . . .

. . . Schechter Poultry Corporation and Schechter Live Poultry Market are corporations conducting wholesale poultry slaughterhouse markets in Brooklyn, New York City. . . . Defendants ordinarily purchase their live poultry from commission men at the West Washington Market in New York City or at the railroad terminals serving the City, but occasionally they purchase from commission men in Philadelphia. They buy the poultry for slaughter and resale. After the poultry is trucked to their slaughterhouse markets in Brooklyn, it is there sold [to butchers who sell to the public]. . . . Defendants do not sell poultry in interstate commerce.

The "Live Poultry Code" was promulgated under section 3 of the National Industrial Recovery Act. That section—the pertinent provisions of which are set forth in the margin—authorizes the President to approve "codes of fair competition.". . .

The President approved the Code by an executive order in which he found that the application for his approval had been duly made in accordance with the provisions of Title I of the National Industrial Recovery Act, that there had been due notice and hearings, that the Code constituted "a code of fair competition" as contemplated by the Act and complied with its pertinent provisions including clauses (1) and (2) of subsection (a) of section 3 of Title I; and that the Code would tend "to effectuate the policy of Congress as declared in section 1 of Title I. . . ."

Second. The question of the delegation of legislative power. We recently had occasion to review the pertinent decisions and the general principles which govern the determination of this question. . . . The Constitution provides that "All legislative powers herein granted shall be vested in a Congress of the United States, which shall consist of a Senate and House of Representatives." Art. I, section 1. And the Congress is authorized "To make all laws which shall be necessary and proper for carrying into execution" its general powers. Art. I, section 8, par. 18. The Congress is not permitted to abdicate or to transfer to others the essential legislative functions with which it is thus vested. We have repeatedly recognized the necessity of adapting legislation to complex conditions [in our society]. . . . The wide range of administrative authority which has been developed by means of them cannot be allowed to obscure the limitations of the authority to delegate if our constitutional system is to be maintained. . . .

Accordingly, we look . . . to see whether Congress has overstepped these limitations. . . .

Such a sweeping delegation of legislative power finds no support in the decision upon which the Government especially relies. By the Interstate Commerce Act, Congress has itself provided a code of laws regulating the activities of the common carriers subject to the Act, in order to assure the performance of their services upon just and reasonable terms, with adequate facilities and without unjust discrimination. Congress from time to time has elaborated its requirements, as needs have been disclosed. To facilitate the application of the standards prescribed by the Act, Congress has provided an expert body. That administrative agency, in dealing with particular cases, is required to act upon notice and hearing, and its orders must be supported by findings of fact which in turn are sustained by evidence. . . .

. . . [S]ection 3 of the Recovery Act is without precedent. It supplies no standards for any trade, industry or activity. It does not undertake to prescribe rules of conduct to be applied to particular states of fact determined by appropriate administrative procedure. Instead of prescribing rules of conduct, it authorizes the making of codes to prescribe them. For that legislative undertaking, section 3 sets up no standards, aside from the statement of the general aims of rehabilitation, correction and expansion described in section one. In view of the scope of that broad declaration, and of the nature of the few restrictions that are imposed. . . . [w]e think that the code-making authority thus conferred is an unconstitutional delegation of legislative power. . . .

In view of these conclusions, we find it unnecessary to discuss other questions which have been raised as to the validity of certain provisions of the Code under the due process clause of the Fifth Amendment.

On . . . the grounds we have discussed, the attempted delegation of legislative power, and the attempted regulation of intrastate transactions which affect interstate commerce only indirectly, we hold the code provisions here in question to be invalid and that the judgment of conviction must be reversed.

Mr. Justice Cardozo, concurring.

The delegated power of legislation which has found expression in this code is not canalized within banks that keep it from overflowing. It is unconfined and vagrant. . . .

This court has held that delegation may be unlawful though the act to be performed is definite and single, if the necessity, time and occasion of performance have been left in the end to the discretion of the delegate. . . . I pointed out in an opinion that there had been "no grant to the Executive of any roving commission to inquire into evils and then, upon discovering them, do anything he pleases." . . . Choice, though within limits, had been given him "as to the occasion, but none whatever as to the means.". . . Here, in the case before us, is an attempted delegation not confined to any single act nor to any class or group of acts identified or described by reference to a standard. Here in effect is a roving commission to inquire into evils and upon discovery correct them.

Questions and Case Problems

1. A trade association representing a group of community antenna television systems petitions the U.S. Supreme Court for review of a revised fee schedule which set the annual fee at $.30 per subscriber. May Congress delegate its job of lawmaking to others? [*National Cable Television Ass'n., Inc. v. United States*, 415 U.S. 336 (1974).]

2. Must all agencies attempt to resolve disputes informally before moving to a hearing?

3. The FCC decides that it shall prohibit the telephone company from furnishing CATV service in their telephone service area, either directly or through affiliates. In arriving at its decision, is the FCC bound by the rules of evidence, as they might be in federal courts? [*General Telephone Co. of the Southwest v. United States*, 449 F.2d 846 (1971).]

4. The Commission of Food and Drugs issues a regulation requiring that labels and advertisements for prescription drugs which bear proprietary names for the drugs or the ingredients shall carry the corresponding "established name" every time the trade (proprietary) name is used. May the courts review this action? [*Abbott Laboratories v. Gardner*, 387 U.S. 136 (1967).]

5. Describe the purpose of a complaint issued by an administrative agency.

6. Make a list of the ten largest independent administrative agencies in the federal government. Consult your government documents librarian for assistance.

7. The wheat Farmer Jones grows on his farm is entirely consumed at the farm. Since Congress authorized the NLRB (a federal administrative body in the labor field) to cover any enterprise "affecting commerce," may the NLRB regulate employees at the Jones farm? [*Wickard v. Filburn*, 317 U.S. 111 (1942).]

8. Hearst Publications, Inc. refuses to bargain collectively with newsboys who distribute its newspapers. It claims that the newsboys are independent contractors, not employees. Will the NLRB's ruling that they *are* employees be easily overturned by the U.S. Supreme Court? [*NLRB v. Hearst Publications, Inc.*, 322 U.S. 111 (1944).]

9. The Pottsville Broadcasting Company asked the Federal Communications Commission for permission to build a broadcasting station. The Commission denies the application for valid reasons. Will the courts overturn a ruling of the FCC if some minor procedural matters seem to have been poorly handled? [*FCC v. Pottsville Broadcasting Co.*, 309 U.S. 134 (1940).]

10. In the case of *Schechter Poultry Corp. v. United States*, 295 U.S. 495 (1935),[2] Schechter operates a slaughterhouse in New York. Part of the slaughterhouse violates a code of a federal administrative agency. Schechter argues that administrative agencies may not create their own rules and regulations but must look to Congress for guidance. Do you agree?

---

[2] See pp. 628–30.

34 Labor Law

After you have read this chapter, you should be familiar with all of the following terms:

1. Craft union.
2. Industrial union.
3. Knights of Labor.
4. AFL-CIO.
5. Criminal conspiracy.
6. Injunction.
7. Yellow dog contract.
8. Norris-La Guardia Act.
9. Wagner Act.
10. Taft-Hartley Act.
11. Unfair labor practices.
12. Bargaining unit.
13. Boulwarism.
14. Executive Orders 10988 & 11491.
15. Hot Cargo.

Introduction

A small business owned and operated by one person is called a **sole proprietorship.** Obviously, therefore, sole proprietorships tend to be small organizations. Thus, if you were to work for such a firm, there is an excellent chance that you would know the owner personally. If you had a problem concerning your wages, hours, or the conditions of employment, it would be relatively easy to bring your concern to the proper authority. Further, in a small organization, since your labor is a significant part of the whole, management has a great deal of interest in your well-being.

In a **partnership,** the organization may tend to grow. There may be a division of work among the partners such that one partner manages the firm while the other participates largely through investment of capital. As an employee, you may rarely see one of the partners. **Incorporated** firms have the potential of growing to be huge organizations. Examples of organizations in this category abound and include Ford, General Motors, A.T. & T. and General Mills. It is highly unlikely that people working on the assembly line will know anyone in top management. If problems arise concerning wages, hours, or conditions of employment, an employee might raise his concern with a foreman and perhaps with the personnel department, but his voice is just one among the crowd. Unlike the situation in a sole proprietorship, one employee rarely makes up a significant part of the workforce.

The question of how an employee can have his or her voice heard in a large organization has been answered in the United States by labor unions. Labor organizations such as the American Federation of Teachers, the United Auto Workers, and the American Federation of State, County, and Municipal Employees have flourished in the past several decades in response to employees' needs for representation in the workplace.

Not only have these unions pressed employers for better labor contracts, but they have also been instrumental in pressing legislators to pass pieces of legislation which have improved our lives immeasurably.

sole proprietorship
a business owned and operated by one person

partnership
an association of two or more persons to carry on as co-owners a business for profit

corporation
a legal entity created by statute authorizing an association of persons to carry on an enterprise

Response of the Law

Unions were not always welcome additions to the world of work. Indeed, at first they were strenuously resisted by employers. Today unions are generally accepted as part of the work environment, but many employers resist union organizing efforts because they believe unions will drive up wages or take away management prerogatives. We, the authors, do not take any position on the impact of unions in the workplace. Our job is to present, educationally, the labor union as a present-day factor in business, except to note that the issue is certainly unresolved. This chapter presents an overview of the major federal laws which govern labor-management relations.

At first, employers resisted unions by dismissing employees who exhibited pro-union tendencies, and the courts were supportive of employers' actions for many years. Gradually, as we shall see, the courts and the legislators have sought to strike a balance between the unions' right to organize employees and the employers' right to manage the business free from outside interference. Laws such as the Wagner Act, Taft-Hartley, and Landrum-Griffin Acts are frequently referred to by contemporary labor relations specialists as they attempt to discern the best course of action in resolving a labor dispute.

The law has also attempted to provide benefits to employees of the federal government. For example, the following pieces of federal legislation are all part of the domain of Labor Law: (a) Executive Order 10988 and (b) Executive Order 11491, discussed later.

In this chapter we will examine some of these laws in order to understand their impact on employees and management.

A Brief History of Unions

The Origin of Craft Unionism

As we all learned in history courses, the United States was largely an agricultural nation during its early years. Unions were virtually nonexistent then. However, even in colonial America, farmers could not produce all of the items they needed to survive, and gradually craftsmen and their stores began to flourish. These craftsmen hired employees to assist in filling orders, and they often trained these employees in the skilled crafts.

Craftsmen would often join with others to discuss their trade and to socialize. Their primary motive was not to induce an employer to increase their wages or improve their working conditions; rather, their common bond was that they shared a skill. In fact, often the craftsmen were independent employers. These groups represented the beginnings of craft style unions in our country.

As our country continued to grow, the craft unions began to do more than just socialize. In an attempt to maintain high quality workmanship, they began to set standards for entrance into their trade. People interested in joining a particular craft union were given **apprentice** status for a period of time. If they succeeded as an apprentice, they ultimately were given the rank of **journeyman** and were allowed to work on their own.

apprentice
a student learning a particular craft

journeyman
a skilled craftsman

Some historians have made the point that these unions were designed not only to maintain high quality standards, but also to keep out "undesirables." In the early years of our nation, almost any newcomer was viewed suspiciously and as potentially undesirable competition. In fact, these early unions were attempting to limit competition. Apprentice groups were one technique they employed. Another technique designed to limit competition was the creation of a **closed shop**. A closed shop means that an employer may hire only union workers to perform a particular task. Failure to do so would not usually result in some sort of retribution during these early years, but employers risked having lower quality products produced.

closed shop
an employer who, by agreement with a union, will employ only union members

The Origins of Industrial Unions

As our nation developed, it moved from an agrarian economy to an industrial nation and, as corporations began to grow, the workplace became increasingly less personal. Furthermore, technological change began to alter the nature of work. Companies needed fewer and fewer skilled craftsmen. The very work which these craftsmen once did slowly and painstakingly was gradually usurped by a machine and some unskilled laborers working at low wages. Who would organize these people? At first, nobody. Employees had to protect themselves, if they could, from an employer who cared little about his employees' well-being.

The Civil War marked the point in our history when industrialization began to move at a pace unparalleled in the history of any other nation in the world. While our nation produced goods at rates previously unheard of, the employees producing those goods were often locked into poverty by well-to-do employers and were unable to take part in the great society of which they were a part. When they finally realized that they were in an untenable position, they began to organize for collective action.

One of the first unions to gain national recognition was the Knights of Labor. The Knights were led in their quest by the Grand Master Workman Terrance Powderly. Powderly did not succeed for long, however. One of the major difficulties faced by the Knights was that they were organized to accept any person who worked for a living. Thus, craftsmen and unskilled laborers formed mixed assemblies, which often led to internal quarrels. This organizational strategy, plus a disastrous and violent demonstration at Haymarket Square in Chicago, ultimately led to their extinction.

Knights of Labor.

Workingmen did not enjoy being part of violent unions. Just as the Knights of Labor failed, so too did the International Workers of the World (I.W.W., or Wobblies). Although this group also grew to national size, it never established a firm hold on the workers because it was associated with violence and radical behavior. Other early unions grew for a while and then died. Many—such as the socialist labor unions—died because American workmen separated their political life from their "bread and butter" (wage and hour) concerns.

Contemporary Unions

Out of these early unions grew today's powerful union groups. The American Federation of Labor (AFL) grew under the early leadership of Samuel Gompers. Gompers was concerned about representing the skilled craftsmen. The AFL craft locals represent craft autonomy, that is, for each particular skill there is a union group which represents their interests. Gompers, for example, was a member of the cigar-makers. Other craft-oriented unions include the carpenters, the plumbers, and the electricians.

American Federation of Labor.

Industrial unions were formed because people like John L. Lewis, of the coal miners union, believed that the AFL was ineffective in representing the interests of workers who were semi-skilled or unskilled in mass production industries. In the 1930s people were able to join with others in massive organizing campaigns which resulted in large numbers of people joining labor unions. The AFL and the CIO were not always joined in one organization, as they are today. In fact, for many years a bitter rivalry existed between the two groups. At first, the CIO was called the Committee (later Congress) of Industrial Organizations and was a branch of the AFL. Internal disputes and rivalries over organizing strategies

Congress of Industrial Organizations.

led to a split which lasted until 1955, when new leaders of each organization were brought together by a man named Arthur Goldberg. (Mr. Goldberg subsequently was a member of the U.S. Supreme Court and then U.S. Ambassador to the United Nations.)

Today unions within the AFL-CIO and independent unions are rivals for control of a major group of largely unorganized employees. These are white collar workers, professionals, and government employees. As we shall see, the law has had a significant impact upon the growth of unions in our country, and we can expect further growth of unions among government employees to be shaped by social control exerted through law.

Early Attempts to Control Labor Unions

Criminal Conspiracy

Employers have traditionally resisted union organizing attempts. The earliest strategy adopted by employers to quash a union was to accuse the union of having unlawfully combined into a **conspiracy** to control wages. The logic of this argument was that, if wages were driven up, eventually the consuming public would suffer, since prices would rise. Thus, any time a worker joined with others to ask for a wage increase he was risking a court action. During the first half of the nineteenth century this doctrine was quite effective.

conspiracy
a combination of persons for the purpose of committing an unlawful act

Then, in a landmark decision, the courts of the state of Massachusetts decided the following case.

Facts
The defendants were bootmakers who were organized into a union group. They were accused of unlawfully attempting to extort great sums of money from the employer by means of organizing a union. Was the formation of a union a conspiracy?

Decision
No. Judgment for the defendants.

Reasoning
The manifest intent of the association is to induce all those engaged in the same occupation to become members of it. Such a purpose is not unlawful. . . . An association may be formed, the declared object of which is innocent and laudable. If the plaintiff wanted to demonstrate that this union was formed for criminal purpose, it should have brought this forward as part of the evidence.

Commonwealth v. Hunt, 4 Metcalf 111 (Mass. 1842), 44 Mass. Reports.

The conspiracy doctrine, which began with an incident involving shoemakers in Philadelphia in 1806, ended following the *Hunt* case just noted. It was a powerful weapon for its time but finally yielded to the injunction.

injunction
a court order requiring a person to do or not to do something

Injunction

Another early weapon used against employees was the **injunction**. An injunction is an order issued by a court ordering that a person do or not do something. For

Government Regulation of Business

example, if students decided to march and perhaps take violent action against a professor's decision to give an entire class failing grades, it would be possible for the university to obtain a stop order, an injunction. In the case of a labor dispute, if a union embarked on a course of action which seemed likely to injure the employer in any way, the employer would request an injunction. Needless to say, in the late 1800s such an order was relatively easy to obtain, the potential damage to the employer would be minimal, and the injunction would still be issued.

In 1894 the U.S. Supreme Court affirmed the use of injunctions in labor disputes when it heard *In re* Debs (158 U.S. 564 (1895)). Since that time injunctions have been used in labor disputes. However, courts are much more careful about the circumstances under which they issue a stop order.

Associated with the injunction was a tactic used by employers called the **yellow dog contract.** Under these contracts, employees had to promise their employer not to join a union. If they did join, they were automatically fired for violating a condition of employment. Such contracts are illegal because they unfairly hinder union members' ability to organize for collective action. The reason a yellow dog contract is associated with the injunction is that employers would seek an injunction from the courts to stop unions from attempting to organize workers who had previously signed yellow dog agreements. Yellow dog contracts have been declared illegal.

yellow dog contract
an agreement between an employer and employee that the employee will not be, nor continue to be, a member of a union

Sherman Act

In chapter 32, Antitrust Law, we mentioned that the first attempt to regulate monopolistic competition by business was a federal enactment called the Sherman Antitrust Act. This law not only made monopolies illegal, but it also said that combinations or conspiracies to restrain trade were illegal. The sections of the Sherman Act which should provide us with guidance about whether Congress intended unions to be covered by the Act were, in fact, silent on the issue. Thus, the case of the *Danbury Hatters*, which brought the issue to the Supreme Court, was an important decision.

Sherman Act.

Facts
A union group composed of hatmakers in Danbury, Connecticut attempted to organize Loewe and Company. One of its tactics was to initiate a boycott of Loewe hats. This strategy caused the managers of Loewe to bring an action against the union under the Sherman Act. Was the union activity a combination in restraint of trade as contemplated by the Sherman Act?

Decision
Yes. Judgment for Loewe and Company.

Reasoning
The hatters union members violated the Sherman Act by their actions. The boycott of plaintiff's goods was ordered for the purpose of obstructing the flow of commerce. Thus, Loewe and Company would not be able to engage in business as effectively as they might have. This is the kind of action that Congress intended to restrain through antitrust legislation.

Lawlor v. Loewe, 235 U.S. 522 (1915).

Thus, the impact of the *Danbury Hatters* case was to bring unions within the domain of the antitrust statutes. Employers used this decision as a weapon until Congress acted to change the state of affairs in the Clayton Act of 1914. Section 6 of the Clayton Act specifically held that neither labor organizations nor "the members thereof . . . be held or construed to be illegal combinations or conspiracies in restraint of trade, under the antitrust laws."

Unfortunately for labor unions, section 6 of the Clayton Act has suffered at the hands of the courts. In a series of Supreme Court decisions, the justices claimed the power to determine whether the unions were carrying out "legitimate objects." This posture was clearly adhered to in *Bedford Cut Stone Co. v. Journeymen Stone Cutters Association,* 274 U.S. 37 (1927).

Contemporary Federal Labor Legislation

Norris-La Guardia Act.

Norris-La Guardia Act

Until the 1930s labor unions were at the mercy of employers. Early in the '30s, when the United States was in the midst of a severe depression, President Hoover attempted to deal with the extremely high rate of unemployment and low wages by offering workingmen a piece of legislation designed to give employees an advantage in the labor-management relations arena which they had not previously enjoyed. It was the Norris-La Guardia Act of 1932, and it has several noteworthy provisions. First, it declared yellow dog contracts to be illegal. Second, it guaranteed employees the right to organize into unions and to bargain collectively with their employers. This principle remains an important part of our federal labor laws today.

Wagner Act.

Wagner Act

In 1933 the Roosevelt administration was attempting to do what the Hoover administration had failed to do—that is, bring our country out of the depression. One attempt to move in this direction was the National Industrial Recovery Act. The critical section with respect to labor relations was 7(a), which specifically endorsed employees' rights "to bargain collectively through representatives of their own choosing." The Supreme Court held that the NIRA was unconstitutional.

Within two years Congress acted again to protect labor's interests. In 1935 it passed the National Labor Relations Act. The NLRA is usually referred to as the Wagner Act. It remains today as one of the most important pieces of federal labor legislation. The following case illustrates its purpose to safeguard the rights of employees.

Government Regulation of Business

Facts

Jones & Laughlin Steel produced steel in Pennsylvania and sold their goods throughout the United States. One of the elements defined by the Wagner Act as an unfair labor practice is the discharge of employees for union activity. Jones & Laughlin had committed this act and so were charged by the NLRB with an unfair labor practice. Jones & Laughlin fought the NLRB by arguing that the Wagner Act was unconstitutional and that their manufacturing business was not in the "stream of commerce." Is the Wagner Act unconstitutional and is Jones & Laughlin in commerce?

Decision

Judgment for NLRB.

Reasoning

We think it clear that the National Labor Relations Act may be construed to operate within the sphere of constitutional authority. The statute goes no further than to safeguard the rights of employees. Further, Jones & Laughlin clearly fits as in the stream of commerce and so is subject to federal regulations.

NLRB v. Jones & Laughlin Steel Corp., 301 U.S. 1 (1937).

As referred to in the Jones & Laughlin case, the Wagner Act defined some practices which were designed to give employees more rights to organize for labor action. These were called **unfair labor practices** by *employers*. Later the Taft-Hartley Act defined unfair labor practices by a *union*.

There are five unfair labor practices by employers. Employers may *not*:

1. refuse to bargain with employee representatives;
2. discharge an employee just because he has filed a complaint under the Wagner Act;
3. encourage or discourage union membership or discriminate when hiring or retaining employees just because of their union leanings;
4. interfere with employees in any way in their right to determine who shall represent them; and
5. dominate or interfere with any labor organization or contribute to its support in any way.

Needless to say, such a powerful Act would not be effective unless it had some administrative support. Thus, Congress created the National Labor Relations Board to handle disputes as they arose. In addition to the unfair labor practices as enumerated, the NLRB also was charged with the task of setting up union election procedures and defining the appropriate **bargaining unit.**

The bargaining unit is a group of employees appropriately joined together for the purpose of collective bargaining. In an industrial setting, for example, the bargaining unit might be all of the employees within a particular department, or all employees doing essentially the same job. The NLRB enters the scene if there is a dispute concerning whether or not particular employees should be in the unit. Disputes often arise in this regard. For example, employers may argue that particular employees, such as first line foremen, have managerial responsibility, while the union argues that they are members of the unit.

unfair labor practices
tactics by an employer or a union which are legally prohibited as unfair

bargaining unit
a group of employees appropriately joined together for the purpose of collective bargaining

Taft-Hartley

Some labor law experts argue that labor laws and labor sentiment in our country move in pendulum swings. That is, strongly pro-labor laws are passed, then strongly pro-management laws are enacted. Since the Wagner Act was clearly pro-labor, protecting employees' rights to organize, the Taft-Hartley Act would be pro-management. Indeed, it was precisely that. Passed in 1947, it was designed to redress an imbalance which Congress and the American people perceived in the labor area. It is not difficult to imagine why they believed there was a need for a law controlling labor. In the period just prior to passage of Taft-Hartley our nation was embroiled in strikes. Not only was there a nationwide coal strike, but telephone company, steel, oil, textile, and maritime workers also had work stoppages, and many other unions were involved in labor disputes of one kind or another.

State Right-to-Work Provisions. One of the most controversial sections of the Taft-Hartley Act is section 14(b), the "right-to-work" section. This portion of the Act allows states to pass right-to-work laws. These laws allow companies to make contracts which have very weak union security clauses. In effect, they permit people to work in a union plant without joining the union. The merits of right-to-work laws have been argued for a number of years.

Free Speech. Taft-Hartley made several important changes in the state of labor law in the United States. First, it allowed employers to comment more freely on union organizing activities than they had been able to do in the past. Prior to Taft-Hartley, employers had to be extremely careful about what they said to employees about the union. Taft-Hartley directly addresses the subject of free speech in section 8(c), where it says that employers would not commit an unfair labor practice to speak to employees, unless they threaten reprisal or promise some benefit to employees. This is the so-called "free speech" amendment.

Unfair Labor Practices. Another important part of the Taft-Hartley Act is its section on unfair labor practices. This time the unfair practices were aimed at labor rather than at management. There are a number of such unfair labor practices by unions. First, it is an unfair labor practice for the union to try to coerce employees to join unions. In other words, no harsh tactics can be used to get an employee to join. Second, certain kinds of strikes and boycotts are unfair labor practices. Strikes or boycotts designed to make an employer assign work to a particular craft group, strikes or boycotts designed to force an employer to recognize a union without NLRB precertification, and secondary boycotts are all held to be unfair labor practices.

secondary boycott
the bringing of pressure by a union on a neutral party who will then pressure the employer with whom the union has a dispute

Secondary Boycott. A **secondary boycott** is a union attempt to place *concerted pressure* on an otherwise *uninvolved party* in order to get that party to pressure the union's real adversary into capitulating. The following case held that there was insufficient concerted activity present and, therefore, no secondary boycott.

Government Regulation of Business

Facts

The teamsters were picketing several rice mills in Louisiana, one of these being International Rice Co. The union was charged with an unfair labor practice of secondary boycott when the pickets told two employees of Sales & Service House, a customer of the mill, that they were on strike and that the two employees could, and should, not purchase from the mill. International Rice claimed that there was a secondary boycott by the union. Was this a secondary boycott?

Decision

No. Judgment for NLRB.

Reasoning

The most that can be concluded is that the union did encourage two employees of a neutral customer to turn back from an intended trip to the mill. A secondary boycott involves "concerted activity" to a far greater extent than exhibited here.

NLRB v. International Rice Milling Co., 341 U.S. 665 (1951).

Other unfair labor practices defined by this Act include:

1. Union attempts to charge excessive dues.
2. A prohibition against featherbedding. Featherbedding is forcing an employer to keep unneeded employees, such as on jobs which no longer exist. An example is forcing a railroad to continue to hire coal shovelers for the electric locomotive.
3. Union refusal to bargain in good faith.
4. Union attempts to force employers to discriminate against employees who are not interested in the union, in an attempt to influence union membership.

The duty to bargain in *good faith* is now shouldered regularly by both the union and management, as part of the collective bargaining process. An interesting case emerged in 1964 which tested the principle of good faith bargaining. General Electric instituted a policy which has come to be known as *Boulwarism*, named after Mr. Boulware, an executive at General Electric. The case is as follows:

Facts

General Electric negotiated a contract with the International Union of Electrical Workers (I.U.E.). G.E.'s strategy involved making considerable efforts prior to negotiation to determine what was right and fair for the employees. They then presented the package to the union and made it clear that it would not make any changes which it did not consider "correct" merely because of an actual or threatened strike. The NLRB decided that G.E.'s conduct was not bargaining in good faith. G.E. petitioned for review.

Decision

Petition denied.

Reasoning

G.E.'s bargaining technique, its campaign among employees, and its conduct at the bargaining table, all complementing each other, were calculated to disparage the union. This is not bargaining in good faith.

NLRB v. General Electric Company, 418 F.2d 736 (1969).

Because of all the strikes which had occurred in the period immediately preceding the Taft-Hartley Act, Congress decided to build in a provision which would give the government power to act when a vital industry was adversely affected by a labor action. In the event that a dispute in an industry (or in a substantial part thereof) "imperils the nation's health or safety," the President may appoint a Board of Inquiry to report on the dispute. This can result in an order by the court to stop the strike for sixty days and then again for another twenty days, if needed. During the second period, an election is conducted among the workers to see whether they would accept the last offer of the employer. If no progress results, the President then reports to Congress about the state of affairs and makes recommendations which he believes to be appropriate.

Landrum-Griffin Act.

Landrum-Griffin Act

The technical name for the Landrum-Griffin Act is the Labor Management Reporting and Disclosure Act of 1959. The reason for this Act was largely to clean up the internal affairs of unions. In the mid 1950s Senator McClellan began an investigation into the activities of unions and uncovered massive amounts of corruption and violence. The public was sufficiently alarmed to push for strong reform legislation, and in 1959 that is precisely what the public received in the form of the Landrum-Griffin Act.

For our purposes, the most important part of the Landrum-Griffin Act is Title I, which is also known as a "bill of rights" for union members. This is because it assures that all union members will have an opportunity to participate in the internal affairs of their organization in some meaningful way. For example, Landrum-Griffin Title I guarantees members the right to vote in union elections. Titles II–VI contain other provisions to deal with internal union problems, such as the election of officers and the prohibition of certain kinds of people (for example, certain convicted offenders) from holding union office.

Title VII of Landrum-Griffin contains amendments to Taft-Hartley. Perhaps the most important amendment was to make it an unfair labor practice to become involved in a **hot-cargo agreement.** Hot cargo agreements generally were union decisions not to handle items that were produced by or were going to support an anti-union company.

hot cargo agreement
an agreement between an employer and a union that the employer is not to handle or otherwise deal with goods of another employer

Government Employees

The federal government has always been rather slow in managing its own labor-management relations. Although there are examples of some concerted labor activity in the federal government in the 1800s, union-management relations in the public service were virtually dead until President Kennedy enacted Executive Order 10988 in 1961. The thrust of this Order was to have three kinds of union recognition in the federal sector. "Informal recognition" allowed employees to gather together but management did not have to consult the group before acting. "Exclusive recognition" meant that a union represented at least 10 percent of the number of the employees in question. The union was then entitled to bargain a contract for all employees in the unit, and management had to meet with the representatives. "Formal recognition" was an intermediate step which obligated the managers only to speak with the union prior to acting.

President Nixon discarded Executive Order 10988 in 1962 and in 1970 added Executive Order 11491, which was designed to do away with all but the exclusive form of recognition. This change, in addition to other amendments, has marked a period of rapid expansion of interest of federal employees in union groups. Today there are well over 1,000,000 government employees represented by union organizations, such as the American Federation of Government Employees.

However, the range of items and the power of federal government union groups is still rather limited. Indeed, by comparison with private sector employees, government employees are decades behind the times.

The Strike: Public versus Private Sector

Almost all of us take for granted the right of employees to strike for higher wages. In fact, we are often surprised to learn that the courts can sometimes stop groups from striking.

In the *private* sector, the right to strike is so much a part of labor relations that it is rarely interfered with by the courts. The only time the courts will stop a private sector strike is in the event of violence.

In the *public* sector, the right to strike is much more restricted. The courts have repeatedly ruled that strikes in the public sector are illegal. The reason given by the courts is that if government employees strike they threaten the well-being of the entire community. However, there is some debate about this argument, and we may one day see legal public sector strikes.

In both the public and private sectors, management has a limited arsenal of weapons to fight the strike. These weapons include the *lockout* and the *injunction*. By the injunction, the court is ordering a group to "stop" a certain kind of behavior which may cause damage. A lockout is, as its name suggests, a closing of a plant before the union strikes.

Summary Statement

1. The origins of craft unionism and industrial unions are quite different. Industrial unions exist as a response to technological change.
2. Various methods have been used to control labor unions. Early attempts at labeling unions as criminal conspiracies gave way to attempts to use antitrust laws, followed by a regularized pattern of laws.
3. Today's labor laws have their roots in the Norris-La Guardia Act. However, the three major contemporary laws are the Wagner Act, the Taft-Hartley Act, and the Landrum-Griffin Act.
4. Government employees represent an ever-increasing number of potential union members. Special executive orders regulate labor-management relations between government and its employees.

In the following case, the court held that the employer had not bargained in good faith with the union representing its employees. This case was briefly presented previously;[1] however, because of the great importance of the court's language, a large part of the court's opinion is presented here.

NLRB v. General Electric Company
418 F.2d 736 (1969)

Irving R. Kaufman, Circuit Judge. Almost ten years after the events that gave rise to this controversy, we are called upon to determine whether an employer may be guilty of bad faith bargaining, though he reaches an agreement with the union, albeit on the Company's terms. We must also decide if the Company committed three specific violations of the duty to bargain by failing to furnish information requested by the union, by attempting to deal separately with I.U.E. locals, and by presenting a personal accident insurance program on a take-it-or-leave-it basis. . . .

. . . The Board found that G.E.'s bargaining stance and conduct, considered as a whole, were designed to derogate the Union in the eyes of its members and the public at large. This plan had two major facets: first, a take-it-or-leave-it approach ("firm, fair offer") to negotiations in general which emphasized both the powerlessness and uselessness of the Union to its members, and second, a communications program that pictured the Company as the true defendant of the employees' interests. . . .

G.E. argues forcefully that it made so many concessions in the course of negotiations—concessions which, under section 8(d), it was not obliged to make—that its good faith and the absence of a take-it-or-leave-it attitude were conclusively proven, despite any contrary indicia on which the Trial Examiner and the Board rely. The dissent proceeds under the misapprehension that we consider lack of major concessions as evidence of bad faith. Rather, we discuss them only because while the absence of concessions would not prove bad faith, their presence would, as G.E. claims, raise a strong inference of good faith. . . .

The Company's stand, however, would be utterly inexplicable without the background of its publicity program. Only when viewed in that context does it become meaningful. . . . G.E., the Trial Examiner found, chose to rely "entirely" on its communications program to the virtual exclusion of genuine negotiations, which it sought to evade by any means possible. Bypassing the national negotiators in favor of direct settlement dealings with employees and local officials forms another consistent thread in this pattern. The aim, in a word, was to deal with the Union through the employees, rather than with the employees through the Union.

The Company's refusal to withhold publicizing its offer until the Union had had an opportunity to propose suggested modifications is indicative of this attitude. Here two interests diverged. The command of the Boulware approach was clear: employees and the general public must be barraged with communications that emphasized the generosity of the offer, and restated the firmness of G.E.'s

[1] See p. 641.

position. A genuine desire to reach a mutual accommodation might, on the other hand, have called for G.E. to await Union comments before taking a stand from which it would be difficult to retreat. . . .

The most telling effect of G.E.'s marketing campaign was not on the Union, but on G.E. itself. Having told its employees that it had made a "firm, fair offer," that there was "nothing more to come," and that it would not change its position in the face of "threats" or a strike, G.E. had in effect rested all on the expectation that it could institute its offer without significant modification. Properly viewed, then, its communications approach determined its take-it-or-leave-it bargaining. . . .

. . . [T]he Company, having created a view of the bargaining process that admitted of no compromise, was trapped by its own creation. It could no longer seek peace without total victory, for it had by its own words and actions branded any compromise a defeat.

G.E. urges that section 8(c), 29 U.S.C. section 158(c) (1964), prohibits the Board from considering its publicity efforts in passing on the legality of its bargaining conduct. The section reads:

(c) The expressing of any views, argument, or opinion, or the dissemination thereof, whether in written, printed, graphic, or visual form, shall not constitute or be evidence of an unfair labor practice under any of the provisions of this subchapter, if such expression contains no threat of reprisal or force or promise of benefit.

. . . The legislative history, past decisions, and the logic of the statutory framework, however, indicate a contrary conclusion. . . .

While it is clear that the Board is not to control the substantive terms of a collective bargaining contract, nonetheless the parties must do more than meet. . . .

. . . [T]he petition for enforcement of the Board's order is granted.

Questions and Case Problems

1. Distinguish between a craft and an industrial union.

2. Can employers still request an injunction against a union group, even though we live in an age of enlightened human resource management?

3. Define the concept of yellow dog contracts. Why are these illegal today?

4. A corporation donates $10,000 to a union group for an attempt by that union to organize the corporation's competitors. Is this illegal?

5. Faculty members at Kendall College were unionized. All full-time faculty members were organized into a union. Part-time employees were not in the union if they were hired and paid "per course." Can the union force these employees into the bargaining unit? [*Packard Motor Car Co. v. NLRB*, 330 U.S. 485, 491 (1947).] See also *Kendall College v. NLRB*, U.S. Ct. of Appeals 7th Circuit, 97 LRRM 2878 (February 1978).

6. A union group becomes involved in a labor dispute with Mueller-Anderson, Inc., a general contractor of an apartment complex. The union began picketing each of the two entrances to the workplace even though one was reserved for the particular workers involved in the dispute and the other was reserved for

subcontractors. Where there is an attempt to get uninvolved subcontractors to stop doing business with Mueller-Anderson, is there a violation of the law? [*Carpenters Local 470 v. NLRB (Mueller-Anderson, Inc.)*, U.S. Ct. of Appeals 9th Circuit (San Francisco), 97 LRRM 2281 (November 1977).]

7. An employer declares to his employees, members of a union, that he is unable to continue granting wage increases because of "economic incapacity." The union demands to see the financial records that brought the employer to make the statement. Must the records be provided? [*Teleprompter Corp. et al. v. NLRB*, No. 77-1054, U.S. Ct. App. 1st Cir. (Boston) 97 LRRM 2455 (December 1977).]

8. A union group of employees of Allis-Chalmers Mfg. Co. decides to engage in a lawful strike against Allis-Chalmers Mfg. Co. Some employee members of the union decide they do not want to participate in the strike and so they cross the picket line. The union fines them. The employees claim their rights under Landrum-Griffin have been violated. Do they have a case? [*NLRB v. Allis-Chalmers Mfg. Co.*, 388 U.S. 175 (1967).]

9. The following clause appears in a contract: "Employers shall not contract any work covered by this agreement to be done at the site of the construction, alteration . . . of a building structure or other work to any person, firm, or company who does not have an existing labor agreement with the union covering such work." Is this clause legal? [*Henderson v. Operating Engineers*, U.S. District Ct. of Oregon, 97 LRRM 2348 (November 1977).]

10. This question is in connection with the case of *NLRB v. General Electric Company*, 418 F.2d. 736 (1969)[2] For several years General Electric Company adopted a special position in labor relations. The company would enter negotiations with what it considered to be a very generous and fair offer and would not easily be persuaded to move from that position. If the union did not see eye to eye with management, management would try to go around the union officials and appeal directly to the employees. Do you believe that this is, or should be, "bargaining in good faith" as the law demands?

---

[2] See pp. 644–45.

Environmental Law

35

After you have read this chapter, you should be able to:

1. Discuss the major components of the National Environmental Policy Act.
2. Understand the purpose and function of the National Environmental Protection Agency.
3. Trace the development of the Clean Air Act and the Clean Water Act as recently amended.
4. Introduce the main concepts of the Toxic Substances Control Act, the Resource Conservation and Recovery Act, and the federal Environmental Pesticide Control Act.
5. Analyze the Noise Control Act and compare its strategy with that of the air and water Acts.
6. Highlight the provisions of the Endangered Species Act and its recent amendments.
7. Distinguish state from federal land use powers.

Introduction

One student defined the *environment* as "the universe, and all that surrounds it." This droll and provocative description, while accurate, is somewhat broad for our purposes. The focus of our present inquiry is the *ecosphere*—that intricate web of the earth's living things and the thin global skin of air, water, and soil which supports its existence. The *human environment* is still more complex because it consists not merely of our physical surroundings—it encompasses the vast interplay of our emotional, intellectual, and cultural life as well.

A study of environmental law, then, is the study of mankind's efforts to regulate intrusions on the ecosphere, particularly those intrusions that stress the environment beyond its natural capacity to adjust. In the broadest sense, this includes worldwide and peaceful attempts to enhance the human environment as well. The efforts include measures designed

1. to control population growth and minimize pollution;
2. to encourage food production and an equitable distribution of the world's material goods;
3. to regulate the extraction of nonrenewable resources and promote alternative energy technologies; and
4. to bring the economic system into a harmonious relationship with the ecosystem.

As a practical matter, this chapter will be limited to an examination of environmental protective measures within the U.S. and how they interrelate to form a national strategy for maintaining the integrity of the ecosphere.

Federal Regulation—The Environmental Protection Agency

The necessity for federal regulation and the EPA.

The *Environmental Protection Agency* (EPA) was established by a 1970 executive reorganization plan designed to consolidate federal environmental activities into a single agency.[1] The objective was to structure a coordinated response to a broad range of pollutants—air, water, noise, solid wastes, toxic chemicals, pesticides, and radiation. Generally speaking, Congress has conferred upon EPA a twofold task: (a) creating national pollution standards, and (b) enforcement of these standards (normally in conjunction with the states).

The problems are enormous, however. First, within each area, millions of dollars in research are needed to make way for enlightened regulation. Second, environmentally sound solutions often run into opposition from energy and production-minded interests—e.g., emission control limits on automobiles sometimes frustrate fuel economy and production schedules. Finally, progress in one area may provoke difficulties in another area. To illustrate, cleaner air and water require the removal of solid and chemical wastes. Disposal of these wastes creates land-use problems that are not entirely within the jurisdiction of EPA. The cooperative efforts of federal, state, regional, and local governmental agencies are frequently essential to progress toward an environmentally acceptable solution. Such problems are not respecters of political boundaries.

---

[1] Reorganization Plan #3 of 1970, 35 Fed. Reg. 15623, 84 Stat. 2086 (1970).

National Environmental Policy Act

The *National Environmental Policy Act* (NEPA)[2] is the kingpin of U.S. environmental laws. Contrary to popular belief, it does not set a single pollution standard for air, water, noise, radiation, hazardous substances, or solid wastes. Neither does it establish a veto over harmful environmental projects. The *Council on Environmental Quality* (CEQ), which was chartered by NEPA, merely serves as the President's policy advisor. It has issued regulations to all federal agencies on the implementation of NEPA,[3] but it does not have enforcement powers.

NEPA.

CEQ.

On the other hand, NEPA does firmly command a *rigorous decision-making process for all agencies of the federal government*. Federal agencies are required to implement these procedures to the fullest extent possible in order to achieve the environmental standards or goals set forth in section 101:

1. Safe, healthful, productive, and esthetically and culturally pleasing surroundings.
2. Preserve important historic, cultural, and natural aspects of our natural heritage.
3. Achieve a balance between population and resource use.
4. Enhance the quality of renewable resources and promote recycling of depletable resources.

Congress directed that all laws, policies, and regulations of the U.S. be interpreted and administered in accordance with NEPA. Federal agencies were ordered to utilize an interdisciplinary approach to decision making and to give environmental values appropriate consideration along with economic and technical factors.

Environmental Impact Statements

The most dramatic innovation introduced by NEPA is the section 102 requirement for *Environmental Impact Statements* (EIS). *These statements must accompany every proposal for legislation and other major federal actions significantly affecting the quality of the human environment*. CEQ regulations require the following format:

EIS.

1. A statement of the purpose and need for the project.
2. A rigorous comparison of the reasonable alternatives.
3. A succinct description of the environment of the area to be affected by the proposed project.
4. A discussion of the environmental consequences of the proposal and of alternatives (including direct and indirect effects, energy requirements and conservation potential, mitigation measures, depletable resource requirements, impacts on urban quality and historic and cultural resources, and possible conflicts with state or local land-use plans, policies, and controls).
5. A list of the names and qualifications of the people primarily responsible for preparing the EIS and of the agencies to which the EIS was sent.
6. An appendix.

---

[2] 42 U.S.C. secs. 4321–4347, 83 Stat. 852, Pub. L. 91–190 (1970) as amended by Pub. L. 94–52 (1975), and Pub. L. 94–83 (1975).

[3] 40 Code of Federal Regulations, secs. 1500–1508.

Purpose. The genius of this approach is the *early alert* it gives federal agencies. Since Congress has established as a national policy that environmental values be integrated into the decision-making process to assure an overall balance, the EIS is designed to give *advance warning* of harmful environmental consequences. Full disclosure of all the environmental, technological, and economic pros and cons should avoid wasteful expenditures on projects and proposals that have not been well thought out. In short, NEPA simply requires the federal bureaucracy to do what conscientious citizens and taxpayers had every reason to expect in the first place. The CEQ regulations introduced a "scoping process" which requires prompt and full administrative analysis of important issues. The regulations also demand a written record which documents the reasonable alternatives, the steps taken to mitigate environmental harm, and the justification for the agency's decision.

Theory and Practice. That, at least, is the way things are supposed to work. However, as everyone knows, there is frequently a big gap between theory and practice—and that is precisely the case with NEPA.

In the first place, NEPA, like the U.S. Constitution, is not self-executing. It relies upon the integrity of government bureaucracies, the alertness of concerned citizens, and the supervision of federal courts to carry out its mandate.

For example, when a federal agency undertakes a project, it must first determine whether the EIS process has been triggered—i.e., whether there is a *major federal action significantly affecting the quality of the human environment.* If, contrary to your own analysis, the agency decides that an impact statement is not necessary, there is *no one except you* or other concerned citizens to step in and do something about it. The Council on Environmental Quality is not authorized to stop the project; neither is the Environmental Protection Agency. Congress and the President have the power to influence administrative decision, but NEPA does not supply an automatic stop on environmentally harmful projects. People have to make it work.

NEPA and the courts.

NEPA and the Courts

Once an agency has prepared an EIS—and we will assume that it is a fair, adequate, and objective evaluation of the pros and cons—what happens if the agency decides to proceed with a project despite your protest that it is environmentally disastrous? Does NEPA make demands beyond mere procedural compliance? Once the formalities of NEPA are satisfied, can the federal agency proceed with business as usual?

Surprisingly enough, some courts have found NEPA's requirements to be procedural only, but the better-reasoned decisions insist that the procedural aspects of the Act are designed to achieve a substantive national policy of environmental protection. The following case views EISs as a *means* toward the achievement of certain *ends* or *objectives.* If the impact analysis indicates that more harm will result from a project than good—that the costs outweigh the

Government Regulation of Business

benefits—further action on such a project will be regarded by the federal courts as arbitrary and capricious. In such a case the court would have the power to enjoin (stop) the project permanently.

Facts

A citizens group, The Environmental Defense Fund, Inc. sought an injunction against the U.S. Corps of Engineers to prevent completion of a dam on the free-flowing Cossatot River in Arkansas. The U.S. District Court held that an adequate Environmental Impact Statement had been prepared and that the National Environmental Policy Act contained no substantive standards beyond the procedural step of "full disclosure" embodied in the EIS.

Decision

For U.S. Corps of Engineers.

Reasoning

The district court found that NEPA "falls short of creating the type of 'substantive rights' claimed by the plaintiffs," and therefore "plaintiffs are relegated to the procedural requirements of the Act."

We disagree. The language of NEPA, as well as its legislative history, make it clear that the Act is more than an environmental full-disclosure law. NEPA was intended to effect substantive changes in decision making. The Act states that agencies have an obligation "to use all practical means, consistent with other essential considerations of national policy, to improve and coordinate federal plans, functions, programs, and resources to preserve and enhance the environment." To this end, section 101 sets out specific environmental goals to serve as a set of policies to guide agency action affecting the environment.

Section 102(1) directs that the policies, regulations and public laws of the United States be interpreted in accordance with these policies to the fullest extent possible. Section 102(2), of course, sets forth the procedural requirements of the Act. The purpose is to "insure that the policies enunciated in section 101 are implemented." The procedures included in section 102 of NEPA are not ends in themselves. They are intended to be "action forcing."

Environmental Defense Fund, Inc. v. Corps of Engineers of the U.S. Army, 470 F.2d 289 (1972).

The Clean Air Act

Introduction

The Clean Air Act Amendments of 1977 continue the impressive but difficult task which Congress undertook in 1970.[4] Implementation of the Act necessitated separate treatment of emissions from stationary sources (factories, utilities) and from mobile sources (automobiles, trucks). Control of both types was expected to lead to the achievement of ambient (surrounding) air quality standards by certain target dates. Figure 35.1 on the following page summarizes the chief pollutants by source and health effects.

---

[4] 42 U.S.C. secs. 1857–1858a, 84 Stat. 1676, Pub. L. 91–604 (1970), as amended by 42 U.S.C. secs. 7401–7642, 91 Stat. 685, Pub. L. 95–96 (1977).

Figure 35.1 Air Pollutants, by Sources and Health Effects

	Pollutant	Source	Health Effect
1	Sulphur dioxide (SO_2)	Power plants; automotive emissions	Causes and aggravates respiratory ailments
2	Particulates	Power plants; oil and coal combustion; agricultural operations	Injury to lungs; throat and eye irritation
3	Carbon monoxide (CO)	Automotive emissions	Decreases blood oxygen; impairs heart functions; impairs visual perception and alertness
4	Photochemical oxidants (ozone)	Refineries; petrochemical plants; automotive emissions	Aggravates respiratory ailments; causes eye irritation
5	Nitrogen dioxide (NO_2)	Power plants; oil and coal combustion	Combines with hydrocarbons to form photochemical oxidants (ozone)
6	Hydrocarbons	Petroleum products, refineries, automobiles	Combines with nitrogen oxides to form photochemical oxidants (ozone)

Stationary Sources

EPA was authorized by the 1970 Act to formulate *primary standards* to protect *public health* and *secondary standards* to protect *public welfare*—visibility, vegetation, animal life. States were expected first to inventory their air quality and then to subdivide their geographical area into manageable air quality control regions (AQCR). Next, the states were required to hold public hearings and to formulate state implementation plans (SIPs) which described the means and methods of achieving those standards within each AQCR.

Each state was given three years following EPA approval of its SIP to reach the primary standard. A reasonable period of time was allotted for the secondary standard.

Mobile Sources

Congress dealt with emissions from automobiles by requiring that carbon monoxide and hydrocarbons be reduced by 90 percent between 1970–75 and nitrogen dioxides by 90 percent between 1971–76. EPA awarded automakers a two-year delay on these deadlines.

With regard to both stationary and mobile sources, great strides were made toward ambient air quality standards. None of them was achieved on the national level, however. This gave rise to the 1977 Clean Air Act Amendments.

AQCR.

SIP.

Government Regulation of Business

The 1977 Clean Air Act Amendments

Congress extended the basic strategy of the 1970 Act in its 1977 amendments. New state implementation plans (SIPs) were required to be submitted to EPA by January 1, 1979. EPA then had six months to approve, disapprove, or seek state modification of the SIP. Attainment under these new plans is targeted for December 31, 1982. EPA regulations allow states to treat a plant as if it had a bubble over the top—the "bubble" concept—and to reduce high cost controls for a pollutant in exchange for an equal increase in the control of that pollutant in the same plant where abatement is less expensive.

For states that are seriously affected by automobile emissions and will not attain the standards by 1982, revised plans which impose all requirements to meet the standards by 1987 must be submitted. In sum, this means that the 1977 amendments extend the deadline for most pollutants until 1982 and for automobile-related pollutants until 1987.

Figure 35.2   National Ambient Air Quality Standards

National Ambient Air Quality Standards			
Pollutant	Averaging Time	Primary Standard Levels	Secondary Standard Levels
		Micrograms per cubic meter ($\mu g/m^3$) or parts per million (ppm)	
Particulate matter	Annual (geometric mean)	75 $\mu g/m^3$	60 $\mu g/m^3$
	24 hours[b]	260 $\mu g/m^3$	150 $\mu g/m^3$
Sulfur oxides	Annual (arithmetic mean)	80 $\mu g/m^3$ (0.03 ppm)	—
	24 hour[b]	365 $\mu g/m^3$ (0.14 ppm)	
	3 hour[b]	—	1300 $\mu g/m^3$ (0.5 ppm)
Carbon monoxide	8 hour[b]	10 mg/m^3 (9 ppm)	10 mg/m^3 (9 ppm)
	1 hour[b]	40 mg/m^3 (35 ppm)	40 mg/m^3 (35 ppm)
Nitrogen dioxide	Annual (arithmetic mean)	100 $\mu g/m^3$ (0.05 ppm)	100 $\mu g/m^3$ (0.05 ppm)
Ozone	1 hour[b]	235 $\mu g/m^3$ (0.12 ppm)	235 $\mu g/m^3$ (0.12 ppm)
Hydrocarbons (nonmethane)[a]	3 hour (6 to 9 a.m.)	160 $\mu g/m^3$ (0.24 ppm)	160 $\mu g/m^3$ (0.24 ppm)

[a] A nonhealth=related standard used as a guide for ozone control.

[b] Not to be exceeded more than once per year.

Source: U.S. Environmental Protection Agency.

New SIPs begin with an air quality index of each AQCR. Next, the states detailed their approach to *nonattainment* (dirty air) regions and *nondeterioration* (clean air) regions. Nonattainment regions include those AQCRs within the state that were not reaching the ambient air quality standards for one or more pollutants. Nondeterioration areas contain air of higher quality than the law demands. This may sound confusing, but a single AQCR could be classified nonattainment for one pollutant (a dirty air region for SO_2, for example) and nondeterioration for another (a clean air region for CO). It all depends on that region's mix of stationary and mobile sources.

Nonattainment Areas

If a SIP submitted by January 1, 1979 meets EPA's approval within six months, then the air quality control board can begin evaluating permit applicants on July 1, 1979. After that date new or modified major stationary source applicants in nonattainment areas will be issued permits under the following conditions:

1. The net effect is reduced emissions (existing sources are retrofitted so that they will more than offset new or modified sources within the area).
2. The source meets lowest achievable emission rate.
3. All other facilities of the applicant within the state are in compliance.

If EPA rejects the SIP, then, until a new plan meets its approval, there can be no new industrial construction within the state. Additionally, EPA and Department of Transportation funds will be withheld, except funds for safety, mass transit, and air quality improvement projects.

Prevention of Significant Deterioration

In those parts of the country where the air is cleaner than it is required to be under national standards, Congress established three air quality categories. Within these categories emission limitations have been established for particulates and sulfur dioxide. In August, 1980, EPA limitations for hydrocarbons, carbon monoxide, photochemical oxidants, and nitrogen oxides became effective.

In Class I, very little air pollution is tolerated. It includes international parks as well as national parks and wilderness areas in excess of 5,000 or more acres (there are occasions, however, when a plant may receive a limited variance for sulfur dioxide emissions). Class II areas are susceptible to moderate amounts of air quality deterioration. In Class III areas, degradation is permissible to the limits of national primary standards. Except for certain federal lands discussed above, procedures are available to redesignate land from Class II to Class III so that industrial expansion may be accommodated.

Enforcement

Congress placed at the disposal of EPA a variety of criminal and civil enforcement measures. The most innovative contribution of the 1977 amendments is an economic penalty that eliminates any cost advantage of being out of compliance. States can enforce their own air pollution laws if they do not substantially burden interstate commerce and if they have not been preempted by Congress. The following case illustrates this point.

Government Regulation of Business

Facts

New York City enacted an ordinance requiring exhaust emission controls for licensed taxicabs. The plaintiffs, fifteen licensed taxicab companies, sought an injunction prohibiting enforcement of the ordinance and a declaratory judgment that it was null and void.

Decision

For New York City.

Reasoning

There was no actual conflict between the Clean Air Act and the city ordinance. Since the city did not create an automobile emission standard contrary to the federal standard, there is no interference with interstate commerce in the sale of new cars.

Where exercise of the local police power serves the purpose of a federal Act, the preemptive effect of that Act should be narrowly construed. We think the purpose of the federal Act is served by the challenged ordinance. Surely New York City has the power at least to try to clean the very air that people breathe. Plainly, that is the purpose of the ordinance, and it is clearly compatible with the goal of the federal Clean Air Act. Moreover, both the history and text of the Act show that the preemption section was made, not to hamstring localities in their fight against air pollution, but to prevent the burden on interstate commerce which would result if, instead of uniform standards, every state and locality were left free to impose different standards for exhaust emission control devices for the manufacture and sale of new cars.

Allway Taxi, Inc. v. The City of New York, 340 F. Supp. 1120 (S.Q.N.Y. 1972), aff'd per curiam 468 F.2d 624 (1973).

The 1977 Clean Water Act

Background

The 1977 *Clean Water Act* (CWA) amends the 1972 *Federal Water Pollution Control Act* (FWPCA).[5] The announced goals of the 1972 Act were: *no effluent discharges by 1985,* and *water clean enough for swimming and other recreational values by 1983.*

CWA.

FWPCA.

These goals were to be accomplished in stages—first, by establishing quality standards based on water use, such as human consumption, recreation, and industrial purposes; next, by treating effluents that are discharged into waters of the U.S. from *point* sources (e.g., ditches, pipes, defined channels). These effluents are controlled by EPA-specified technology. *Nonpoint,* or undefined, sources are dealt with through a planning process somewhat resembling SIPs under the Clean Air Act.

Industrial discharges were required to install the *best practicable control technology* by July 1, 1977, and the *best available technology economically achievable* by July 1, 1983. Municipalities were subjected to less stringent demands. *Secondary* treatment was required by 1977, and *best practicable* by 1983. For a fee, industrial dischargers can use municipal facilities if the effectiveness of these publicly owned treatment works is not jeopardized.

---

[5] 33 U.S.C. secs. 1251–1376, 86 Stat. 816, Pub. L. 92–500 (1977), as amended by 91 Stat. 1567, 1575, Pub. L. 95–217 (1977).

Both industrial and municipal discharges were required to obtain National Pollutant Discharge Elimination System (NPDES) permits prior to commencing operations. The permit system was designed to bolster the monitoring and enforcement provisions of the Act.

New Developments Under the 1977 CWA

Funding. A *Buy America* provision requires funds to be spent on domestic construction materials. This section of the Act does not apply if EPA finds it to be inconsistent with the public interest, if costs are unreasonable, or if the materials are not available in satisfactory quality and quantity.

Effluent Requirements. The 1977 CWA classifies pollutants as conventional (sanitary waste), toxic (65 designated chemicals), and nonconventional (all other). Regarding conventional pollutants, EPA must publish regulations and set effluent limitations requiring *best conventional technology* (BCT). Industrial compliance is targeted for July 1, 1984.

For toxic chemicals, the July 1, 1984 deadline is applicable as well. However, industry must comply with more stringent effluent limitation requirements—*best available technology economically achievable* (BAT). Nonconventional pollutants must be controlled by BAT not later than July 1, 1984, with the possibility of a variance until July 1, 1987.

Enforcement

The civil and criminal enforcement sections of the Act substantially parallel those of the Clean Air Act. While there is no provision that deprives a firm of the economic advantage of noncompliance, it resembles the Clean Air Act in that states retain some flexibility in enforcing their own statutes. The case which follows illustrates this flexibility.

Facts
The city of Chicago adopted an ordinance providing that the sale of detergents containing any phosphorus constituted a criminal offense. The plaintiff, Proctor & Gamble, sought declaratory and injunctive relief, alleging that the ordinance violated the commerce clause of the U.S. Constitution.

Decision
For the City of Chicago.

Reasoning
The Proctor & Gamble Company could not prove convincingly that the Chicago City Council was wrong in its conclusion that limiting phosphorus in waters under its jurisdiction could someday be the key to clean water. The ordinance will not solve the problem, but it is a significant first step. Since interstate commerce is only slightly affected, and since states (and cities through their state-granted city charters) have Tenth Amendment powers to protect the public health, this ordinance is valid.

The Proctor & Gamble Company v. City of Chicago, 509 F.2d 69 (1975), cert. denied 421 U.S. 978 (1975).

Toxic Substances Control Act

Prior to the 1976 *Toxic Substances Control Act* (TSCA),[6] national policy addressed to the production and sale of toxic chemical substances was one of reaction from crisis to crisis. Toxicity and environmental studies were generally undertaken only after the damage had been done.

The 1976 Act revamped this essentially "wait and see" approach. The TSCA expands, systematizes, and exploits information on production, use, and toxicity to prevent hazardous environmental and human exposure.

Congress charted a course between affirmative clearance of new chemicals by EPA before sale and no premarket notification at all. The federal government can now control and stop the production or use of chemical substances that may present an unreasonable risk of injury to health or the environment. Manufacturers of *new chemicals* and chemicals for *new uses* must notify EPA ninety days prior to beginning production.

Manufacturers may also be required to test selected chemicals or to report production quantities, use, biological properties, and other information necessary for hazard assessment. The following criteria are utilized to pinpoint those substances which must undergo the rigorous testing procedures mandated by the Act:

1. Does substantial exposure to the chemical imply an unreasonable risk to health or the environment?
2. If data for predicting health and environmental effects are inadequate, testing is necessary to develop data.

EPA was authorized to require reports on the name and identity of each chemical, proposed uses, production level, by-products, adverse effects, and number of workers exposed. Trade secrets and financial data required by the Act are confidential, but health and safety information is subject to public disclosure. Records of significant adverse health effects must be kept for thirty years; information regarding environmental damage must be kept for five years.

Resource Conservation and Recovery Act of 1976

Within six months of enactment, the *Resource Conservation and Recovery Act*[7] required EPA to identify areas with common solid waste management problems and appropriate planning units. Not later than eighteen months following enactment, EPA was required to publish guidelines to aid state development of solid waste management plans. Ambient air standards, groundwater quality,

---

[6] 15 U.S.C. secs. 2601–2629, 90 Stat. 2003, Pub. L. 94–469 (1976).

[7] 42 U.S.C. secs. 6901–6987, 90 Stat. 2796, Pub. L. 89–272, as added Pub. L. 94–580 (1976).

waste collection, open dumps, resource recovery, and markets for recovered materials are the chief considerations of these management plans. Before EPA will approve the state plan:

1. state, local, and regional responsibilities must be identified;
2. strategy for coordinating regional planning must be specified;
3. establishment of new open dumps must be prohibited and old ones must be improved or phased out;
4. nonhazardous wastes must be disposed of in sanitary landfills or used for resource recovery.

There are a number of incentives embodied in the plan—economic, technical assistance, and personnel training. While its success is largely contingent upon the states' voluntary acceptance of responsibility, there are certain coercive measures. If a state does not present a plan that meets EPA's approval, or if it does not revise the plan to accommodate EPA's objections, EPA can impose upon the state a plan of its own. The real effectiveness of such an alternative is open to question, however, because EPA simply does not have the resources to enforce it.

Hazardous Wastes

One of the more significant features of the Act directs EPA to identify hazardous wastes that threaten the human environment. Once these wastes have been identified, owners and operators of hazardous waste treatment and storage facilities must apply for EPA permits (or state permits under EPA approved plans). Applications must detail composition, quantity, location, and the method and rate of disposal.

Essentially hazardous wastes are to be tracked from the manufacturing stage through transportation, treatment, storage, and disposal. A *manifest system* designed along a pathways approach is the chief component of this strategy. It is enforced with civil *and* criminal penalties, both with a maximum of $25,000 per day. Imprisonment for not more than one year is also a possibility.

Noise Control Act of 1972

Both the Clean Air Act and the Clean Water Act begin with national quality standards. These standards, you recall, are to be achieved mainly through the application of appropriate technology.

Noise Control Act.

The *Noise Control Act*[8] differs from this approach in that Congress did not establish a national standard of quietness. It focused instead on a technology-based strategy that required EPA to identify the principal sources of noise. Newly manufactured products so identified became subject to noise emission regulations

---

[8] 42 U.S.C. sec. 4901 et seq. (1972).

Government Regulation of Business

set by EPA. These regulations are expected to be tough enough to protect public health, safety, and welfare while taking into consideration:

1. conditions of product use;
2. amount of noise reduction achievable through most modern technology available;
3. cost.

The federal Act preempts state rules and regulations that are different from the required noise-suppressant technology of EPA-designated products. States can address the problem through their zoning authority, however, and may further limit the sound level by restricting the movement and operation of such products.

Products that do not conform to the requirements of the Act can not be imported, nor can they be distributed in interstate commerce. In addition to this, manufacturers are not permitted to remove any noise-suppressant devices, notices, or labels required to be affixed to the product prior to its sale to the ultimate consumer. Any use of a product following the removal (or rendering inoperative) of its muffler system is forbidden as well.

Manufacturers must warrant the noise-emission components of each product against defects in materials and workmanship during useful product life (assuming normal maintenance and operation). EPA can require manufacturers to affix appropriate labels, maintain records, supply information, and conduct tests necessary to ascertain full compliance with the Act.

The principal incentive to encourage compliance is the requirement that federal agencies purchase EPA-designated low-noise-emission products if their cost does not exceed 125 percent of the retail price for a "reasonably substitutable" commodity. Civil and criminal sanctions are available to reinforce this and other provisions of the Act.

Pesticide Regulation

The federal *Insecticide, Fungicide, and Rodenticide Act* of 1947 and the federal *Environmental Pesticide Control Act* of 1972[9] require registration and labeling of agricultural pesticides. The objective is to prevent unreasonable risk to human life and health and to the environment, with the social, environmental, and economic costs and benefits being taken into account.

Statutes for pesticide control.

Pesticides must be classified for "general" or "restricted" use. Those within the latter category may be used only by or under the supervision of state-certified and EPA-approved applicators.

The use of any registered pesticide in a manner contrary to labeling instructions is prohibited. EPA may issue a "stop sale, use and removal" order when a pesticide is found to be in violation of federal statutes. Such pesticides may also be seized.

---

[9] 7 U.S.C. secs. 136–136y, 86 Stat. 975, Pub. L. 92–516 (1972), as amended by 87 Stat. 903, Pub. L. 93–205 (1973), 89 Stat. 754, Pub. L. 94–140 (1975).

Manufacturing plants must be registered with EPA, and they must furnish information on the types and amounts of pesticides produced, distributed, and sold. Federal inspectors with appropriate warrants are entitled to enter and inspect such establishments and take samples.

Criminal sanctions for knowing violations ranging up to $1,000 or thirty days imprisonment (or both) can be imposed on farmers and private applicators. Registered manufacturers, commercial applicators, wholesalers, distributors, and retailers who knowingly violate the law face the possibility of a maximum $25,000 criminal fine or one year imprisonment (or both).

The Endangered Species Act

Endangered Species Act.

Most people never heard of the *Endangered Species Act*[10] until the now-famous Snail Darter was discovered in the waters of the Little Tennessee River. Approximately $102 million had been sunk into the Tellico Dam by this time and there was strong pressure for completion. *TVA v. Hill*,[11] included at the close of this chapter, gives you the U.S. Supreme Court's analysis of the Act, but Congress has since modified it to exclude the Tellico Dam from its coverage.[12]

The Endangered Species Act authorizes the Secretary of Interior, in consultation with representatives from the states, to designate species of fish, wildlife, and plants threatened with extinction and those that might become endangered in the foreseeable future. Federal agencies must avoid jeopardizing endangered species. Fines ranging from $1,000 to $10,000 can be imposed on private citizens who buy, sell, transport in interstate commerce, import, or export in violation of the Act.

Congress created a three-member review panel to examine controversial federal projects. The review is not undertaken, however, until all alternatives to the project have been pursued in good faith. After the review panel has compiled a detailed report on the merits of granting an exemption, the report is considered by a seven-person cabinet-level committee. The committee may then finally exempt a project on the basis of the following criteria:

1. Benefits of the project clearly outweigh benefits of alternative action consistent with conserving the species or its critical habitat.
2. The project is in the public interest.
3. There are no reasonable and prudent alternatives.

If the committee does not grant an exemption, the project can not be continued. In the case of Tellico Dam, the statute remains intact, but the dam was removed from the committee's jurisdiction.

---

[10] 16 U.S.C. secs. 1531–1543, 87 Stat. 884, Pub. L. 93–205 (1973), as amended.

[11] *Tennessee Valley Authority v. Hill*, 437 U.S. 153 (1978).

[12] Pub. L. 96–69 (1979).

Land Use

In the final analysis, all pollution problems come down to decisions regarding land use. If property is zoned for industrial purposes or devoted to highway or automobile-related uses, air pollution is a likely result. With less land available for food production, demands for increased yields per acre require the application of chemical fertilizers, insecticides, and pesticides—and therefore invite their related problems. Land dedicated to airport and other transportation uses will likely raise complaints about excessive noise. Sanitary landfills frequently evoke criticism based on aesthetics, odor, and, perhaps, contamination of groundwater. The following examples document the relationship between pollution and land use. We will include illustrations on the state and federal level.

Zoning

Zoning of real property is discussed in detail in chapter 45, Real Property and Its Ownership.

Zoning ordinances are exercises of local *police powers*—i.e., powers reserved under the Tenth Amendment, designed to protect the public health, morals, and safety. If zoning regulations exceed a certain degree, they amount to a *taking,* and the owner must be paid a reasonable value for the property so condemned. While no clear and unmistakable lines are drawn between regulation and taking, the prohibition of some uses merely amounts to regulation. If all uses are forbidden, or if title to the property is transferred to someone else, then a compensable taking has occurred.[13]

Translated to *environmental* terms, this means that a state or the District of Columbia may *take* private property for the purpose of devoting it to a better balanced and more attractive community.

Miserable and disreputable housing conditions may do more than spread disease and crime and immorality. They may also suffocate the spirit by reducing the people who live there to the status of cattle. They may indeed make living an almost insufferable burden. They may also be an ugly sore, a blight on the community which robs it of charm, which makes it a place from which men turn. The misery of housing may despoil a community as an open sewer may ruin a river.[14]

Private property may be *regulated* without payment of compensation to the owner. For example, the Supreme Court has upheld a zoning ordinance limiting to two the number of unrelated, unmarried persons forming a household. This caused certain landlords the loss of tenants—hence, an economic loss.

---

[13] *South Terminal Corp. v. EPA,* 504 F.2d 646 (1974).

[14] *Berman v. Parker,* 348 U.S. 26, 32–33 (1954).

It is said, however, that if two unmarried people can constitute a "family," there is no reason why three or four may not. But every line drawn by a legislature leaves some out that might well have been included. That exercise of discretion, however, is a legislative, not a judicial, function. . . . A quiet place where yards are wide, people few, and motor vehicles restricted are legitimate guidelines in a land-use project addressed to family needs. This goal is a permissible one. . . . The police power is not confined to elimination of filth, stench, and unhealthy places. It is ample to lay out zones where family values, youth values, and the blessings of quiet seclusion and clean air make the area a sanctuary for people.[15]

Solar Zoning

A special application of zoning regulation—and one that you may fully expect to have an immense social impact in years to come—is solar zoning. In a sense, this means parceling out the sun's rays in a manner that accommodates both public and private interests.

Suppose, for example, that you and your spouse plan to build a home utilizing solar energy for heating and cooling. Typically, this will entail the installation of solar collectors on the roof and the use of a liquid or gaseous medium to transfer the heat for direct use (hot water tank, radiator, heat pump) or indirect use (storage as chemical energy in a battery).

The technology for these systems has been available for years and is relatively simple. Depending on the part of the country you are in (the sunny Southwest versus colder climates) and the size of your house (currently solar collectors occupy roofspace which is the equivalent of 30–60 percent of your floorspace), the system may cost from $1,500 to $9,000. In any event, the investment necessary for solar heating is sufficiently large to make you think twice. At a minimum, you will expect certain assurances that the solar panels will not be shielded from the sunlight by obstructions on neighboring lands. The issue is simply this—are you entitled to the uninterrupted flow of sunlight across adjacent property? Could you expect to win a lawsuit against an offending property owner if he caused obstruction of sunlight that would otherwise fall on your solar collectors? The following case, which arose in Florida a number of years ago, addresses a similar issue.

Facts

The Eden Roc Hotel in Miami Beach objected to a fourteen-story addition by a competitor, the Fontainebleau, because it shaded portions of Eden Roc's pool and beach. Eden Roc based its suit on the doctrine of Ancient Lights, an English common law concept that the uninterrupted use of light through a window for twenty years or more gave the recipient an easement that the adjoining landowner can not terminate.

Decision

For the defendant, Fontainebleau.

---

[15] *Village of Belle Terre v. Boraas,* 416 U.S. 1 (1974).

Reasoning

Even though placement of the Fontainebleau was motivated partly by spite (the high-rise could have been situated in a less troublesome spot), public policy favors the development of real estate. So long as the development is reasonable, does not create a nuisance, or violate any restrictive covenants or zoning ordinances, a property owner is free to build any structure he pleases.

Furthermore, the twenty-year prescriptive easement might deprive a property owner, such as the Fontainebleau, of the right to fully utilize property even though it had no knowledge of a neighbor's intent to gain an easement by adverse possession. An essential ingredient in adverse possession is notice—i.e., open, public, and hostile possession that gives the other party an opportunity to object. The Fontainebleau had no notice that the Eden Roc was pursuing such a course, so it had no reason to file an objection.

Fontainebleau Hotel Corp. v. Forty-Five Twenty-Five, Inc., 114 S. 2d 357 (Fla. 1959).

You can see that the doctrine of Ancient Lights was not effective for Eden Roc's purpose. Historically, it applied to indirect light only—when the remaining natural light on the "window-half" of an affected room became insufficient for normal reading, the doctrine became operable.[16] If the doctrine were reinstated, its emphasis on indirect light should not be insurmountable. After all, indirect light inside the home is generated by direct sunlight outside, and obstacles on neighboring property that diminish one diminish the other. However, the prescriptive period for such an easement—whether it be for one year, twenty years, or thirty years—inflicts a degree of uncertainty that may give many people second thoughts about investing in a solar unit.

Does this mean, then, that there are no legal means to protect and encourage the installation of solar units? No! Courts aligned with the Fontainebleau case could reverse their pro-development stance in view of a critical energy shortage and the environmental virtues of solar units. **Stare decisis** does not freeze the law into an unbreakable mold. However, even a reversal would not eliminate the uncertainty factor—the prescription period—so the doctrine of Ancient Lights does not promise a full solution.

stare decisis
a principle of law that courts will follow case precedent if it is still applicable

With these formidable obstacles to be dealt with, local zoning ordinances offer a more likely solution. For highly developed areas, zoning regulations in the form of building restrictions offer no easy answers. Many structures already existing would be characterized as nonconforming uses, and no controls could be installed until new ones take their place.

Zoning offers greater promise for newly developing rural and suburban areas, however. Restrictive covenants can be useful as well. Height limitations placed on houses and other buildings will assure neighboring property owners of uninterrupted, direct sunlight.

---

[16] An imaginary Grumble Line is drawn through the middle of a room. If there is not enough natural light on the window side of this line for the average person to read without "grumbling," the offending landowner becomes liable for his conduct.

Such restrictions are quite in line with traditional measures to promote open spaces and an aesthetically pleasing community. There are no constitutional or other prohibitions that would frustrate this approach. Of course, it is not an overnight solution. Local governing bodies prodded by thoughtful citizens will need to phase in these controls in anticipation of expanded use. This pattern of development is illustrative of the adaptability and flexibility of our legal system when confronted with a new and exciting challenge.

Federal Land Use—Surface Mining

There is no single comprehensive piece of federal legislation that controls land use. About one-third of the nation's land is federally owned, and it ranges from wilderness areas to multiple-use lands that may be leased for minerals, timber, and grazing. In addition to the federal anti-pollution laws discussed so far, tax laws, federally guaranteed loan programs, and agricultural subsidies influence the use of privately owned land that is within the jurisdiction of state and local zoning authorities.

Surface Mining and Reclamation Act.

The *Surface Mining Control and Reclamation Act* of 1977,[17] based on Congress' commerce power, regulates the use of privately owned land. In line with the Clean Air Act and Clean Water Act, the regulatory functions will be carried out by the states if permanent regulatory programs meeting minimum federal standards are enacted by state legislatures. Otherwise, the program will be administered by the Department of Interior.

As a prerequisite for eligibility to administer its own regulatory program, each state must establish a mechanism for designating certain lands as unsuitable for mining. As for the land that is appropriate for development, mine operators are required to restore topsoil and revegetate after mining, and treat harmful minerals so that groundwater and surface water will not be contaminated.

Prime farmlands can not be mined unless the operator has the technological capacity to restore the area to equivalent or higher levels of yield. Alluvial valley floors can not be mined if the mining would damage farming in the valleys or the quantity or quality of waters that supply the valley floors.

Reclamation plans must be filed by the mine operator as part of the permit application, and a $10,000 performance bond must be posted as well. Where federal coal lies beneath privately owned land, the consent of the owner is necessary before operations can begin. There is no legal maximum that can be demanded by the surface owner for this privilege.

A citizen suit provision allows any person who is or may be adversely affected by some failure to comply with this Act to file suit against the responsible regulatory body. Finally, the Act created an abandoned mine reclamation fund to repair land from previous strip operations, and it established within the Department of Interior the Office of Surface Mining Reclamation and Enforcement to administer the Act's provisions.

---

[17] 30 U.S.C. secs. 1201–1328, 91 Stat. 447, Pub. L. 95–87 (1977).

Summary Statement

1. The National Environmental Policy Act (NEPA) established high goals of environmental protection to be achieved through vigorous decision-making procedures.

2. Environmental Impact Statements (EISs) guide proposals for legislation and other major federal actions that significantly affect the quality of the human environment.

3. NEPA created the Council on Environmental Quality (CEQ) as a policy advisor to the President, and by Executive Order the President organized the Environmental Protection Agency (EPA) to exercise certain important standard setting and enforcement functions.

4. The 1977 Clean Air Act amendments reaffirm EPA's high air quality standards and, if new state implementation plans (SIPs) are approved, give until 1982 to meet these standards. If automobile-related pollutants create the problem, the deadline may be extended until 1987.

5. The 1977 Clean Water Act continues to focus chiefly on *point* sources of pollution. It requires the application of the *best conventional technology* (BCT) for most pollutants and the *best available technology economically achievable* (BAT) for toxic and nonconventional wastes. The National Pollutant Discharge Elimination System requires the installation of this technology before permits are granted to dischargers of conventional, toxic, or nonconventional effluents. Target date for the goal of "water clean enough for swimming and other recreational values" has been moved to 1984 (with a likely extension for nonconventional pollutants through 1987). The goal of no effluent discharges into waters of the U.S. is still maintained for 1985.

6. EPA has been empowered by the 1976 Toxic Substances Control Act to control and stop the manufacture or use of chemicals that may present unreasonable risk of injury to health or the environment. Manufacturers may be required to test chemicals, and their reports to EPA are public information.

7. Solid waste management problems are the subject of the 1976 Resource Conservation and Recovery Act. It embodies economic, technical, and other incentives, but success depends upon full state cooperation. Hazardous wastes are given special treatment by the Act—they are literally tracked by a permit system from manufacture through disposal.

8. The 1972 Noise Control Act authorizes EPA to *identify* newly manufactured products that are principal sources of noise and to *require* the application of noise-suppressant technology. EPA regulations are expected to protect public health, safety, and welfare while taking into consideration product use, noise-reduction technology, and cost.

9. The 1972 Federal Environmental Pesticide Control Act—amending earlier legislation—controls registration, labeling, and application of pesticides. Its objective is to prevent unreasonable risk to human life and health and to the environment, while taking into account the social, environmental, and economic costs and benefits.

10. The Endangered Species Act as amended authorizes the Secretary of Interior to protect certain plants, fish, and wildlife (including their habitat) from extinction. If federal projects jeopardize the life or habitat of endangered species, a seven-person cabinet-level panel must determine the outcome.
11. State and federal governments formulate land-use policies. Whether a state is proceeding on its U.S. Constitution Tenth Amendment reserved powers, or the federal government on its Article I legislative powers, a just compensation must be paid to the private landowner for property that is taken for a public purpose. If the private property is merely *regulated*, for example, through local zoning ordinances or federal strip-mining controls, the landowner is not entitled to compensation.

The following long classic case is reproduced almost in its entirety because of its clear and authoritative analysis of the National Environmental Policy Act, *which makes environmental protection a part of the mandate of every federal agency and department*. Thus, in the following case, the Atomic Energy Commission must concern itself with adverse environmental effects of its actions. Notice how the court determines that it has power to decide this case.

Calvert Cliffs' Coordinating Committee, Inc. v. AEC
449 F.2d 1109 (1971)

J. Skelly Wright, Circuit Judge: These cases are only the beginning of what promises to become a flood of new litigation—litigation seeking judicial assistance in protecting our natural environment. Several recently enacted statutes attest to the commitment of the Government to control, at long last, the destructive engine of material "progress." But it remains to be seen whether the promise of this legislation will become a reality. Therein lies the judicial role. . . .

Petitioners argue that rules recently adopted by the Atomic Energy Commission to govern consideration of environmental matters fail to satisfy the rigor demanded by NEPA. The Commission, on the other hand, contends that the vagueness of the NEPA mandate and delegation leaves much room for discretion and that the rules challenged by petitioners fall well within the broad scope of the Act. We find the policies embodied in NEPA to be a good deal clearer and more demanding than does the Commission. We conclude that the Commission's procedural rules do not comply with the congressional policy. Hence we remand these cases for further rule making. . . .

[Ed. note: Following this case the Atomic Energy Commission (now the Nuclear Regulatory Commission) amended its rules to require its hearing board to conduct an independent review of staff environmental recommendations along with its recommendations on economic and technical factors.]

The relevant portion of NEPA is Title I, consisting of five sections. Section 101 sets forth the Act's basic substantive policy: that the federal government "use all practicable means and measures" to protect environmental values. Congress did not establish environmental protection as an exclusive goal; rather, it desired a reordering of priorities, so that environmental costs and benefits will assume their proper place along with other considerations. In section 101(b), imposing an explicit duty on federal officials, the Act provides that "it is the continuing responsibility of the Federal Government to use all practicable means, consistent with other essential considerations of national policy," to avoid environmental degradation, preserve "historic, cultural, and natural" resources, and promote "the widest range of beneficial uses of the environment without . . . undesirable and unintended consequences."

Thus the general substantive policy of the Act is a flexible one. It leaves room for a responsible exercise of discretion and may not require particular substantive results in particular problematic instances. However, the Act also contains very important "procedural" provisions—provisions which are designed to see that all federal agencies do in fact exercise the substantive discretion given them. These provisions are not highly flexible. Indeed, they establish a strict standard of compliance.

NEPA, first of all, makes environmental protection a part of the mandate of every federal agency and department. [Emphasis added.] The Atomic Energy Commission, for example, had continually asserted, prior to NEPA, that it had no statutory authority to concern itself with the adverse environmental effects of its actions. Now, however, its hands are no longer tied. It is not only permitted, but compelled, to take environmental values into account. Perhaps the greatest importance of NEPA is to require the Atomic Energy Commission and other agencies to consider environmental issues just as they consider other matters within their mandates. This compulsion is most plainly stated in section 102. There, "Congress authorizes and directs that, to the fullest extent possible: (1) the policies, regulations, and public laws of the United States shall be interpreted and administered in accordance with the policies set forth in this Act. . . ." Congress also "authorizes and directs" that "(2) all agencies of the Federal Government shall" follow certain rigorous procedures in considering environmental values. . . . In order to include all possible environmental factors in the decisional equation, agencies must "identify and develop methods and procedures . . . which will insure that presently unquantified environmental amenities and values may be given appropriate consideration in decision making along with economic and technical considerations." "Environmental amenities" will often be in conflict with "economic and technical considerations." To "consider" the former "along with" the latter must involve a balancing process. In some instances environmental costs may outweigh economic and technical benefits, and in other instances they may not. But NEPA mandates a rather finely tuned and "systematic" balancing analysis in each instance.

To ensure that the balancing analysis is carried out and given full effect, section 102(2)(c) requires that responsible officials of all agencies prepare a "detailed statement" covering the impact of particular actions on the environment, the environmental costs which might be avoided, and alternative measures which might alter the cost-benefit equation. The apparent purpose of the "detailed statement" is to aid in the agencies' own decision-making process and to advise other interested agencies and the public of the environmental consequences of planned federal action.

Of course, . . . all of these section 102 duties are qualified by the phrase "to the fullest extent possible." We must stress as forcefully as possible that this language does not provide an escape hatch for footdragging agencies; it does not make NEPA's procedural requirements somehow "discretionary." Congress did not intend the Act to be such a paper tiger. Indeed, the requirement of environmental consideration "to the fullest extent possible" sets a high standard for the agencies, a standard which must be rigorously enforced by the reviewing courts.

Unlike the substantive duties of section 101(b), which require agencies to "use all practical means consistent with other essential considerations," the procedural duties of section 102 must be fulfilled to the "fullest extent possible."
. . .

Thus the section 102 duties are not inherently flexible. They must be complied with to the fullest extent, unless there is a clear conflict of statutory authority. Considerations of administrative difficulty, delay, or economic cost will not suffice to strip the section of its fundamental importance.

We conclude, then, that section 101 of NEPA mandates a particular sort of careful and informed decision-making process and creates judicially enforceable duties. The reviewing courts probably can not reverse a substantive decision on its merits, under section 101, unless it is shown that the actual balance of costs and benefits that was struck was arbitrary or clearly given insufficient weight to environmental values. But if the decision was reached procedurally without individualized consideration and balancing of environmental factors—conducted fully and in good faith—it is the responsibility of the courts to reverse. As one District Court has said of section 102 requirements: "It is hard to imagine a clearer or stronger mandate to the Courts." . . .

The following recent case illustrates the mandatory power of congressional legislation with which the courts *must* comply irrespective of other considerations.

Tennessee Valley Authority v. Hill
437 U.S. 153 (1978)

. . . The Tennessee Valley Authority, a wholly owned public corporation of the United States, began constructing the Tellico Dam and Reservoir Project in 1967, shortly after funds for its development were authorized. Tellico is a multipurpose regional development project designed principally to stimulate shoreline development, generate sufficient electric current to heat 20,000 homes, provide flatwater recreation and flood control, as well as improve economic conditions in "an area characterized by underutilization of human resources and outmigration of young people." Of particular relevance to this case is one aspect of the project, a dam which TVA determined to place on the Little Tennessee, a short distance from where the river's waters meet with the Big Tennessee. When fully operational, the dam would impound water covering some 16,500 acres—much of which represents valuable and productive farmland—thereby, converting the river's shallow, fast-flowing waters into a deep reservoir over thirty miles in length.

The Tellico Dam has never opened, however, despite the fact that construction has been virtually completed and the dam is, essentially, ready for operation. Although Congress has appropriated monies for Tellico every year since 1967, progress was delayed, and ultimately stopped, by a tangle of lawsuits and administrative proceedings. After unsuccessfully urging TVA to consider alternatives to damming the Little Tennessee, local citizens and national conservation groups brought suit in the District Court, claiming that the project did not conform to the requirements of the National Environmental Policy Act of 1969 (NEPA), 42 U.S.C. section 4331 et seq. After finding TVA to be in violation of NEPA, the District Court enjoined the dam's completion pending the filing of an appropriate Environmental Impact Statement.

A few months prior to the District Court's decision dissolving the NEPA injunction, a discovery was made in the waters of the Little Tennessee which would profoundly affect the Tellico Project. Exploring the area around Coytee Springs, which is about seven miles from the mouth of the river, a University of Tennessee ichthyologist, Dr. David A. Etnier, found a previously unknown species of perch, the snail darter, or Percina Imostoma tanasi. This three-inch tannish-colored fish, whose numbers are estimated to be in the range of 10,000 to 15,000, would soon engage the attention of environmentalists, the TVA, the Department of the Interior, the Congress of the United States, and ultimately the federal courts, as a new and additional basis to halt construction of the dam.

The moving force behind the snail darter's sudden fame came some four months after its discovery, when the Congress passed the Endangered Species Act of 1973, 87 Stat. 884, 16 U.S.C. 1531 et seq. 1976 ("Act"). This legislation, among other things, authorizes the Secretary of the Interior to declare species of animal life "endangered" and to identify the "critical habitat" of these creatures.

[Ed. note: The snail darter was then listed by the Department of Interior as an endangered species. Since section 7 of the Act prohibited federal projects from jeopardizing the existence of endangered species, a permanent injunction was issued to prohibit further work on the dam until Congress reexamined the issue.]

Two questions are presented: (a) would TVA be in violation of the Act if it completed and operated the Tellico Dam as planned? (b) if TVA's actions would offend the Act, is an injunction the appropriate remedy for the violation? For the reasons stated hereinafter, we hold that both questions must be answered in the affirmative.

It may seem curious to some that the survival of a relatively small number of three-inch fish among all the countless millions of species extant would require the permanent halting of a virtually completed dam for which Congress has expended more than $100 million. The paradox is not minimized by the fact that Congress continued to appropriate large sums of public money for the project, even after congressional appropriations committees were apprised of its apparent impact upon the survival of the snail darter. We conclude, however, that the explicit provisions of the Endangered Species Act require precisely that result.

One would be hard pressed to find a statutory provision whose terms were any plainer than those in section 7 of the Endangered Species Act. Its very words affirmatively command all federal agencies "to insure that actions authorized, funded, or carried out by them do not jeopardize the continued existence" of an endangered species or "result in the destruction or modification of habitat of such species . . ." 16 U.S.C. section 1536. This language admits of no exception. Nonetheless, petitioner urges, as do the dissenters, that the Act can not reasonably be interpreted as applying to a federal project which was well under way when Congress passed the Endangered Species Act of 1973. To sustain that position, however, we would be forced to ignore the ordinary meaning of plain language. It has not been shown, for example, how TVA can close the gates of the Tellico Dam without "carrying out" an action that has been "authorized" and "funded" by a federal agency. Nor can we understand how such action will "insure" that the snail darter's habitat is not disrupted. Accepting the Secretary's determination, as we must, it is clear that TVA's proposed operation of the dam will have precisely the opposite effect, namely the eradication of an endangered species.

Concededly, this view of the Act will produce results requiring the sacrifice of the anticipated benefits of the project and of many millions of dollars in public funds. But examination of the language, history, and structure of the legislation under review here indicates beyond doubt that Congress intended endangered species to be afforded the highest of priorities.

Questions and Case Problems

1. The National Environmental Policy Act requires Environmental Impact Statements on *major* federal actions *significantly* affecting the quality of the human environment. Did Congress then intend for minor federal actions which had a significant effect to escape the EIS process? [*Minnesota Public Interest Research Group v. Butz,* 498 F.2d 1314 (1974).]

2. Congress designed Environmental Impact Statements to give an "early alert" regarding the environmental consequences of certain federal actions. How is this early alert system implemented?

3. Among the purposes of the Clean Air Act of 1970, Congress established the following:

   To protect and enhance the quality of the Nation's air resources so as to promote the public health and welfare and the productive capacity of its population . . .

   Following EPA approval of State Implementation Plans that allowed industrial expansion in previously undeveloped and underdeveloped regions, the Sierra Club brought suit alleging that this section of the Clean Air Act had been violated. EPA argued that the plans it approved promoted industrial growth and protected against air pollution below the national standards. Result? [*Sierra Club v. Ruckelshaus,* 344 F.Supp. 253 (1972), aff'd 412 U.S. 541 (1973).]

4. Discuss the strategy established by Congress in the 1970 Clean Air Act. What is the relationship between the approach to stationary and mobile sources?

5. Discuss the approach Congress took to clean air areas and dirty air areas under the 1977 Clean Air Act Amendments.

6. The *Buy America* provision of the 1977 Clean Water Act does not direct the purchase of domestic construction materials under all circumstances. What are the criteria that EPA must use to determine whether the purchase of foreign or domestic goods is appropriate?

7. Since the 1972 federal Water Pollution Control Act, the U.S. no longer pins its clean-up efforts exclusively on water quality standards. It requires effluent-control technology as well. What is the difference between these two approaches? Discuss.

8. The Toxic Substances Control Act may require manufacturers to test selected chemicals. What are the *criteria* that are used to determine those substances which must undergo the testing procedures mandated by the Act?

9. Compare the approach Congress took in establishing national uniform clean air standards with its approach in establishing noise standards under the Noise Control Act of 1972.

10. In the case of *Calvert Cliffs' Coordinating Committee, Inc. v. AEC,* 449 F.2d 1109 (1971),[18] the court stated that "NEPA mandates a rather finely tuned and 'systematic' balancing analysis. . . ." How does the Act ensure that this balancing analysis will be carried out?

---

[18] See pp. 666–68.

Business Organizations
A. Partnerships and Special Ventures

36. Creation and Termination of Partnerships
The nature of a partnership; kinds of partnership; how a partnership is created, dissolved and terminated; and how partnership assets are distributed on dissolution.

37. Partnership Management and the Authority of Partners
The express, implied, and apparent authority of partners in the management of a partnership, in the absence of partnership agreement to the contrary.

38. Rights, Duties, and Remedies of Partners Among Themselves
The inter-partner relationship with respect to the rights, duties, and remedies of the partners among themselves, with particular reference to the Uniform Partnership Act.

39. Special Ventures
Other noncorporate forms of business entity distinguished from the general partnership.

Summary

The oldest known form of business organization is the partnership. Although partnerships are easy to create, their structure is complex with consequent exposure to liability. If you ever become a partner, these chapters will help you understand the managerial problems you can expect to encounter. As a partner you will have many legal rights and duties to your copartners as well as to third persons dealing with your firm. These chapters explain the resulting rights and duties.

Chapter 39, Special Ventures, will acquaint you with various types of noncorporate business ventures, such as the limited partnership, joint venture, mining partnership, business trust, unincorporated association, joint-stock company, and the franchise.

36

Creation and Termination
of Partnerships

After you have read this chapter, you should be able to:

1. Define a general partnership.
2. Identify the source of partnership law.
3. List and explain the classifications of partnerships.
4. List and explain the classifications of partners.
5. Explain what is generally found in the Articles of Partnership.
6. Explain who may be partners.
7. Explain what is necessary to create a partnership.
8. Explain and define partnership by estoppel.
9. List and explain the five characteristics of tenancy in partnership.
10. Discuss partnership dissolution.
11. List and explain the four methods of dissolution by acts of the partners.
12. List and explain the four methods of dissolution by operation of law.
13. List and explain the six instances when a partnership can be dissolved by decree of the court.
14. Explain when and why notice of dissolution must be given to partners and to third parties.
15. Discuss the winding up of partnership affairs.
16. Explain the order of distributing partnership assets after dissolution.

Introduction

Partnership is one of the oldest forms of business organization. Hammurabi, a king of Babylon, made reference to the regulation of partnerships in the 20th century B.C. The development of ancient partnership law has its origin with the Italian merchants of the late Middle Ages.

Under the name of La Société en commandite, it has existed in France from the time of the Middle Ages; mention being made of it in the most ancient commercial records, and in the early mercantile regulations of Marseilles and Montpelier. . . . In the statutes of Pisa and Florence, it is recognized so far back as the year 1166. . . . In the Middle Ages it was one of the most frequent combinations of trade, and was the basis of the ancient and widely extended commerce of the opulent maritime cities of Italy.[1]

However, modern partnership law, as it exists in the United States, evolved from the English law. The civil law, the law merchant, the common law, and equity all contributed to a confused state that demanded a statutory body of partnership law. The result in England was the adoption of the *Partnership Act of 1890.* In the United States the *Uniform Partnership Act* (U.P.A.) was approved by the Conference of Commissioners on Uniform States Laws in 1914 and has been adopted by most states.[2]

The purpose of the U.P.A. is to codify the principles of partnership law for **general partnerships,** as distinguished from limited partnerships, which are discussed in chapter 39, Special Ventures. *Unless stated otherwise, reference to "partnership" is to the general partnership.* Unless the Act provides otherwise, the common law rules of contract and agency will govern partnership transactions.[3] The law governing partnerships is essentially the *state* statutory law of the Uniform Partnership Act. The Uniform Partnership Act is reproduced as Appendix B at the back of this book.

> **general partnership**
> a partnership as defined by the U.P.A.

Nature of Partnership

A **partnership** has been defined in U.P.A., section 6, as "an association of two or more persons to carry on as co-owners a business for profit." It is a contractual agreement between competent parties to pool their capital and/or services in a business and to share the profits and losses. The definition for *tax* purposes is considerably broader. The Internal Revenue Code, section 761 (a), defines a partnership as "*a syndicate, group, pool, joint venture, or other unincorporated organization through . . . which any business . . . is carried on, and which is not . . . a corporation or a trust or estate.*"

Our concern will be limited to the legal relationships between the partners and between the partnership and third parties. The Uniform Partnership Act will be cited as the applicable law throughout the text. You may refer to it in Appendix B. Notice how the court in the following case applies the partnership definition to the facts.

> **partnership**
> "an association of two or more persons to carry on as co-owners a business for profit" U.P.A., sec. 6

---

[1] *Ames v. Downing,* 1 Brad. 321, 329 (N.Y. Surr. Ct. 1850).

[2] The U.P.A. has been adopted by all states except Louisiana, Georgia, and Mississippi.

[3] U.P.A., sec. 4.

Facts

Grau brought suit and alleged a partnership with Mitchell in the operation of a business. He sought dissolution of the partnership and distribution of the profits according to their respective rights and interests. The real estate was owned by Mitchell, and there is nothing in the record to establish Grau's interest in the real property and improvements thereon. As to the operation of the business, Mitchell kept the books, maintained the bank account in her name, paid all the bills, and compensated Grau in cash for all the work that he did. No partnership returns were filed with either the federal or state government. Mitchell's remuneration had no relationship with the business' making or losing money. Grau was not able to establish any agreement for a share of the profits, and there was nothing to make him liable for any of the debts. Is there sufficient evidence to support the claim of a partnership?

Decision

No. Judgment for defendant, Mitchell.

Reasoning

A partnership is a contract, express or implied, between two or more competent persons to place their money, effects, labor or skill, or some or all of them into a business and to divide the profits and bear the losses in certain proportions.

There is no agreement, oral or written, express or implied, wherein the parties were joined together to carry on the business for a profit and to share the losses.

Grau v. Mitchell, 397 P.2d 488 (Colo. 1964).

Kinds of Partnership

Partnerships have been divided into several classes regarding their extent of business activity and the nature of their employment. This classification is helpful in determining whether a partner has customary authority as an agent to bind the partnership with third parties, as discussed in chapter 37.

trading partnership
a partnership in the business of buying and selling property

A partnership is a **trading partnership** when it *buys and sells property*. Some trading partnerships—e.g., plumbing contractors or T.V. repair shops—combine the sale of goods with the furnishing of services.

nontrading partnership
a partnership in the business of selling only services

A **nontrading partnership** engages in providing only services, generally on a fee-for-services basis, such as one of lawyers, physicians, and accountants.

This classification shows that the customary authority of a partner in a trading partnership will be substantially broader than in a nontrading partnership. The implied authority of partners in trading and nontrading partnerships is discussed in chapter 37.

Kinds of Partners

A *dormant partner* is one who is not active in the business and is not known to the public as a partner. An example would be a retired accountant still sharing in the firm profits after having sold his practice.

Business Organizations: A. Partnerships and Special Ventures

A *nominal partner* is not a partner but holds himself out as a partner or allows others to hold him out as a partner—as, for example, by permitting his name to appear on firm stationery as a member of the partnership. To illustrate, if a partnership is purchased, it may be helpful to retain the name of the selling partner. He is not a partner and is often referred to as an "ostensible" partner. Because he is held out to be a partner, he may be held liable as such by "estoppel."

A *secret partner* takes an active part in firm management but is not known to the public as a partner.

An *ostensible* or *public partner* holds himself out, or permits himself to be held out, as a partner and actively engages in the partnership business. If he does not actively so engage, he is a *silent* partner.

A *general partner* is an *ordinary* partner in a general partnership or in a limited partnership.

A *limited partner* is a partner in a limited partnership who is not a general partner. He is sometimes called a "special partner."

Creation of the Partnership

A partnership is generally created by the contractual agreement of the parties. If the parties intended to create a partnership, as between each other, there is a partnership. However, when the question concerns the firm's liability to third parties, a partnership may be implied in law by the courts.

Requisites for a partnership.

Form

Unless the state statutory law requires a writing, no particular form is required to create a partnership agreement. If it falls within the statute of frauds,[4] there must be written evidence of the partners' contract. For example, an accounting partnership agreement should be in writing under the statute of frauds, as it will normally exist for a specified time of more than one year. It is always desirable to have a written partnership agreement to avoid a misunderstanding regarding its terms.

Articles of Partnership

The partnership contract is called the *articles of partnership*. The agreement generally includes the date of formation, the names and addresses of the partners and the partnership, its purpose and duration, the capital contribution of each partner, the proportions by which the partners share in the profits and losses, salaries and drawing accounts, the duties and restrictions on managing the firm, the method of accounting and the fiscal year, rights and duties on voluntary termination, disability, retirement, death of a partner, and dissolution procedures.

The agreement.

---

[4] See pp. 161–62 for a discussion of the statute of frauds.

Figure 36.1   General Partnership Agreement (Short Form)

GENERAL PARTNERSHIP AGREEMENT (Short Form)

Agreement, made this _____ day of _____ , 19 _____ , by and between John Doe, of _____ , and Richard Roe, of _____ .

Whereas, Richard Roe has acquired an undivided one-half interest in the real estate and insurance business heretofore owned and conducted by John Doe, with office and place of business located at _____ ;

It is agreed as follows:

1. **Name and Duration.** The parties hereby agree to continue the operation of said business as partners under the name of _____ , the partnership to continue for an indefinite time and until terminated as herein provided or as may be mutually agreed upon.

2. **Capital.** The amount of capital contributed to the partnership by the parties is hereby agreed to be the sum of $ _____ each, and is represented by the following personal property: [*here describe*] .

3. **Reserve Fund.** An additional sum of_____ dollars ($ _____) shall be set up and reserved from the profits of the partnership business, and shall become and be a part of the invested capital, it being agreed that not less than____% of the net earnings shall be so reserved until said amount is accumulated.

4. **Banking.** The funds of the partnership shall be deposited in its name in the_____ Bank of _____ , and all trust funds shall be deposited in such bank in a separate account. All such funds, partnership or trust, shall be subject to withdrawal only by check made in the name of the partnership and signed by either partner.

5. **Duties.** Each partner shall devote all his time and attention to the business of the partnership, and shall not, directly or indirectly, engage in any other business without the consent of the other partner.

6. **Books.** Full and accurate accounts of the transactions of the partnership shall be kept in proper books, and each partner shall cause to be entered therein full and accurate accounts of all his transactions in behalf of the partnership. Such books shall be kept at the place of business of the partnership, and each party shall at all times have access to and may inspect and copy any of them.

7. **Drawings.** Each party shall be entitled to withdraw such amounts and at such times, from the partnership earnings, as shall from time to time be fixed and agreed upon.

8. **Profits and Losses.** At the end of each calendar year, a full and accurate inventory shall be prepared, and the assets, liabilities, and income, both gross and net, shall be ascertained, and the net profits or net losses of the partnership shall be fixed and determined. The net profits or net losses shall be divided equally between the parties, and the account of each shall be credited or debited with his proportionate share thereof.

9. **Limitations.** Neither party shall, without the written consent of the other, make, execute, deliver, indorse or guaranty any commercial paper, nor agree to answer for, or indemnify against, any act, debt, default or miscarriage of any person, partnership, association or corporation, other than that of the parties hereto.

10. **Termination.** The partnership may be terminated by either party upon giving 60 days notice to the other party of his desire to withdraw, in which event an accounting shall be had and a division of the partnership assets made, provided, however, that the party to whom notice is given shall have the right to acquire the whole interest of the partnership at a price not to exceed the book value thereof, on such terms as may be agreed upon, and to continue the partnership business under the same name.

In Witness Whereof, the parties have signed this agreement.

_____   _____

[Signatures]

Source: Reprinted with permission from Edmund O. Belsheim's ''Modern Legal Forms.'' Copyright © 1971 by West Publishing Co.

     Business Organizations: A. Partnerships and Special Ventures

Firm Name

The partnership may select any name it desires provided it complies with state statutory law. It may use a fictitious trade name or the names of the partners. The name can not be *deceptively similar* to an existing business. State statutes usually require the partnership to file a *business certificate* in the city hall where the firm is located, indicating the name and location of the partnership and the names and addresses of the partners. The purpose of this is to allow a party who wants to sue the firm to discover who the partners are who own the business.

Illegality

A partnership agreement must comply with contract law concerning the legality of its operation. If the agreement is illegal under statutory law or court decision for public policy reasons, it is a void agreement. The courts will attempt to separate the legal portion of the partnership agreement from its illegal part and allow the partnership to exist only for its legal purpose.

Unless the parties agree to change the effect of the U.P.A., where allowed, the U.P.A. becomes part of the partnership agreement. For instance, *unless the partnership agreement provides otherwise,* all partners have equal rights in the management and conduct of the partnership business regardless of their capital contribution.[5]

> The U.P.A. becomes part of the agreement unless changed by the partners.

An Association

You recall that section 6 of the U.P.A. defined a partnership "as an association of two or more persons. . . ." An association as partners is not a master/servant or employer/employee relationship. It is a relationship that makes each member a coprincipal and a general agent for the firm in transacting partnership business. Although it does not pay tax itself, a partnership is a unique entity for tax purposes and is required to calculate its income or loss and file an information return. This taxable income or loss is then passed through to the partners,[6] who show it on their individual tax returns.

Two or More Partners.   The "two or more persons" requirement immediately will distinguish the partnership from the sole proprietorship, where one person earns the profits and bears all losses. The "person" under U.P.A., section 2, "includes individuals, partnerships, corporations, and other associations." However, the *person* must have the *capacity to contract.*

Infants or Minors.   Under most state laws, an infant may be a partner with partnership rights. The infant's agreement will be voidable during his minority or a reasonable time thereafter. He can disaffirm and withdraw during that time without incurring liability for breach of contract. He may also disaffirm his individual liability on partnership contracts with third parties, although some states will not allow a minor of an insolvent partnership to withdraw his capital contribution.

---

[5] U.P.A., sec. 18(e).

[6] See Int. Rev. Code of 1954 ch. 1, subch. K (26 U.S.C.A.) for the tax effect of partnership transactions.

Insane Persons.   The state law governing competency of the mentally ill to contract will determine their ability to be partners. Generally, their contracts will be voidable unless they have been adjudicated to be insane, in which case they have no capacity to contract and can not be partners.[7]

Corporations.   Modern corporation laws and the U.P.A., sections 2 and 6, permit corporations to become partners.[8]

Carrying on a Business for Profit

Partners must "carry on as co-owners a business for profit." To illustrate, if X and Z invested in an apartment building and agreed to share the rental income, this in itself will not create a partnership;[9] it is not a business. A business must carry on a number of *continuous commercial transactions* as an enterprise. A fraternity or sorority or other nonprofit organization can not be a partnership.

Co-owners of a Business

U.P.A., section 7(2) lists a number of forms of co-owned property which do not, in themselves, establish a partnership. Joint tenancy, tenancy in common, tenancy by the entirety, joint property or part ownership—even if the co-owners share profits made by use of the property—are not partnerships.

Sharing Profits.   The *sharing of profits* is *prima facie evidence* that a person is a partner in a business. However, under U.P.A., section 7(4), no such inference may be drawn when profits are received in payment: (a) as a debt, by installments or otherwise; (b) as wages of an employee or rent to a landlord; (c) as an annuity to a widow or representative of a deceased partner; (d) as interest on a loan; or (e) as the consideration for the sale of the goodwill of a business. However, in any of these instances, if the recipient of the profits also has the *right to participate in the management of the business,* there is *a co-ownership* and a resulting partnership.

   In order for there to be a partnership, the business enterprise, subject to the partnership agreement, must merge the individual rights and liabilities of each member as well as the control of the partnership property.

   Fixed payment is not evidence of a partnership. The partner must have an interest in the profits granting him the *control* of an owner. For instance, if X, a doctor, is to receive a fixed percentage of the profits from his associate without any control over the medical practice, he is not a partner. As is illustrated in the following case, sharing in the *gross* profits is insufficient to prove that a partnership existed; they must share in the *net* profits.

---

[7] See above pp. 137, 140–41 on capacity to contract.

[8] Model Business Corporation Act sec. 4(p) (published for American Bar Foundation by West Publishing Co., 1971).

[9] U.P.A., sec. 7(3).

Facts

Jenkins, defendant, transported cattle and leased the truck-tractors to pull the trailers from various individuals, including Joe Lewis, under a written lease agreement. The gross income from the operation was divided, with Jenkins receiving 30 percent and Lewis 70 percent. Under the terms of the agreement, Jenkins had exclusive control over the entire operation. Jenkins kept books on the operation and collected all money due for the hauling. After the parties operated under this agreement for about a year, Lewis commenced negotiating with Brodnax White Truck Company, plaintiff, to trade for a new truck. Brodnax required a down payment of approximately $2,500 and advised him that he would have to have a cosigner on the chattel mortgage. Lewis and a representative of Brodnax called on Jenkins to see if he would cosign the chattel mortgage. Subsequently the truck was involved in a collision, and Lewis returned it to Brodnax for repairs, which forms the basis of this suit. When the repairs were completed, Brodnax presented Lewis a bill for $1,304.48. He was unable to pay the account, and Brodnax sued Jenkins upon the theory that Lewis contracted the repairs as his partner. Does the sharing of gross income constitute a partnership?

Decision

No. Judgment for defendant, Jenkins.

Reasoning

The mere participation of two persons in the gross receipts of an enterprise in which their capital, skill, and labor may be combined cannot of itself make them partners. To constitute a partnership, the parties in the business or transaction must be entitled to share in the net profits. It is not sufficient that they participate in the "gross profits."

It is apparent that neither Lewis nor Jenkins contemplated joint ownership of the profits as such. They merely intended to share in the gross receipts and used such division as a guide to determine the compensation due each of them.

Jenkins v. Brodnax White Truck Company, 437 S.W.2d 922 (Tex. 1969).

Partner by Estoppel

A person who is not a member of a partnership may incur partnership *liability* to a third party *as though* he were a partner under the doctrine of *partnership by estoppel*. This occurs when a person who is not a partner by words or conduct *represents* himself, or permits himself to be represented, to anyone as a partner and a third party *relies* on that belief[10] and *extends credit* to the partnership in reasonable reliance on the holding out. The person is really not a partner and does not become a firm member but is a *nominal partner* and can not deny liability. By estoppel, he is liable to third persons as a partner. For example, Jones permits Moran to inform Peters that Jones and Moran are partners when, in fact, they are not partners. Moran tells Peters that Jones is his partner, and Peters, in reliance on Moran's statement, extends credit through Moran to the apparent Jones/Moran partnership. Jones is estopped to assert that he and Moran are not partners, and Jones is liable as a partner to Peters.

Partnership liability of a nonpartner by estoppel.

---

[10] U.P.A., sec. 16(1).

The following case illustrates how an associate in an accounting firm may be held out to the public as being a partner, but between members he is not a partner. *Partnership by estoppel applies only to a third party's claim that a person is a partner.*

Facts

In 1964 Kelley and Galloway were partners in an accounting business. Smith left another firm and came to work for them. For three and one-half years Smith drew $1,000 a month plus $100 a month for travel expenses. At the end of the year he was paid a relatively small additional sum as a bonus out of the profits of the business. Not until Smith left the Kelley-Galloway firm in 1968 did he make any claim that he was entitled to a fixed percentage of the profits. In this lawsuit he asserted he had a twenty percent interest therein.

There was no writing evidencing a partnership agreement. However, during the years Smith worked for the firm he was held out to the public as a partner. In a contract entered into between Kelley, Galloway, Smith and a third party, Smith was designated a partner. Partnership tax returns listed him as such; so did a statement filed with the Kentucky Board of Accountancy. In a suit filed in the circuit court against a third party, he was designated a partner.

On the other hand, there was no agreement that Smith would be a partner or have a right to share in the profits; he made no contribution to the assets of the partnership; he took no part in the management; he had no authority to hire or fire employees or to make purchases for the firm; he did not sign any notes when the firm was borrowing money; and he was not obligated to stand any losses of the firm.

Smith sued the partnership and claimed that he was a partner and was entitled to a twenty percent interest in the profits. Was Smith a partner?

Decision

No. Judgment for the defendant firm.

Reasoning

A partnership is a contractual relationship, and the intention to create it is necessary. As to third parties, a partnership may arise by estoppel, but our question is whether the parties intended to and did create such a relationship as would entitle Smith to share in the profits.

The conduct of the parties over a three-and-one-half-year period confirms the conclusion that, though Smith was held out to the public as a partner, between themselves a partnership relationship was not intended to be and was not created.

Smith v. Kelley, 465 S.W.2d 39 (Ky. 1971).

Partnership Property

Partnership assets and property.

The *assets* of a partnership consist of the *partnership property* and the *contributions of the partners necessary for the payment of the partnership liabilities.* U.P.A., section 8(1) defines partnership property as "all property originally brought into the partnership stock or subsequently acquired by purchase or otherwise, on account of the partnership."

Creditors

Firm Creditors.   The issue of partnership property is important when the firm is insolvent and its creditors are seeking satisfaction of their claims.

Individual Creditors.   The partners of a firm in their individual capacity may incur personal debts. The creditors, in that instance, may reach that partner's interest in the firm by means of a *charging order.*[11] It then becomes necessary to determine what is firm property.

Title to Partnership Property

U.P.A., section 8(3) allows the partnership to hold title to *real property* in the firm name. A majority of states allow the partnership to hold title under a fictitious name.

Transfer of the Partnership Property

Personal Property.   Any partner with express, implied, or apparent authority may transfer **personal property** owned by the firm to another party. For example, X, a partner in a construction firm, may sell a truck owned by the partnership to Z without the actual authority of his copartners if there is **customary authority** in that business to sell equipment.

Real Property.   If title to the **real property** is in the name of the partnership on the deed, the title can be transferred by any partner executing the deed in the partnership name. The partner must have authority or **apparent authority** to make the conveyance. If he does not, the partnership can recover the property.

Title to Partnership Property Held in the Name of an Individual Partner.
An individual partner may have the title to partnership property in his own name. For example, he may have owned property before the partnership was formed and contributed that property to the firm but failed to transfer record title to the partnership. The partner holds the title as a trustee, in constructive trust, for the benefit of his copartners.

Tenancy in Partnership

Each partner has a property interest in firm property and is a co-owner in such property. Title to firm property is held by the partners as a *tenancy in partnership.*[12]

This concurrent ownership has characteristics that distinguish it from a **tenancy in common** and a **joint tenancy.** For example, a joint tenant has full survivorship rights upon the death of a co-tenant; a surviving partner does not.

---

[11] U.P.A., sec. 28.

[12] U.P.A., sec. 25.

personal property
a movable thing, along with interests and rights in the thing

customary authority
implied authority to do those acts that conform to the general custom or usage

real property
land and immovable things attached to land, along with interests and rights in the land

apparent authority
the power of a person (A) to act as though he were an agent, created by another's (P's) manifestation to a third person (T) that A is P's agent

tenancy in common
a form of ownership of property by more than one person without survivorship

joint tenancy
a form of ownership of property by more than one person with the right of survivorship

The characteristics of a tenancy in partnership are as follows:

1. A partner, subject to any agreement between them, has an equal right with his partners to use *specific* partnership property for partnership purposes.
2. A partner's right in *specific* partnership property can not be transferred by him (sold, assigned, or mortgaged) without the consent of all his co-partners.
3. A partner's right in *specific* partnership property is not subject to attachment by his *personal* creditors.
4. On the death of a partner, his right in *specific* partnership property vests in the surviving partners, except when the deceased was the last surviving partner; then his right in such property vests in his legal representative,[13] who holds it in trust for partnership purposes.
5. A partner's right in *specific* partnership property is not subject to any interest of his surviving spouse.

State statutes must be examined to determine what interested parties must do when having any connection with a partnership, as is illustrated in the following case.

Facts
Harold Kerry, a partner, gave an assignment of his interest in the partnership to his wife as security for his indebtedness to her. Ruth never recorded the assignment as required by state law. Kerry was subsequently adjudged bankrupt on his voluntary petition. Ruth Kerry, his wife, filed a petition to require Schneider, trustee of the bankrupt, to abandon the partnership interest. Are the personal creditors of Kerry, represented by the trustee in bankruptcy, entitled to a lien on his partnership interest?

Decision
Yes. Judgment for the defendant, Schneider.

Reasoning
Because the partner's assignment was not recorded, as required by state law, his wife had no enforceable right to her husband's partnership interest. She was, hence, a mere general creditor, and the bankruptcy trustee had a right to the partnership interest free of any pledge to his wife.

Kerry v. Schneider, 239 F.2d 896 (1956).

We have seen what a partnership is and how it comes into existence. The operation of a partnership may be interrupted by any number of events resulting in its *dissolution* or in *termination* of its legal entity as a partnership. These are now to be discussed.

Dissolution, Winding Up, and Termination

Termination of partnership entity after dissolution and winding up.

The termination of the partnership is a process involving the sale of its assets, the payment of its liabilities, ultimate distribution of cash to the partners, and ending with the termination of the partnership entity. Termination is preceded by *dissolution* and *winding up,* which occur in that order.

---

[13] U.P.A., sec. 25(d).

Business Organizations: A. Partnerships and Special Ventures

Dissolution

Dissolution is defined by U.P.A., section 29 as follows:

> The dissolution of a partnership is the change in the relation of the partners caused by any partner ceasing to be associated in the carrying on as distinguished from the winding up of the business.

The "change in the relation of the partners" may be the result of a partner leaving the firm, of disability, of retirement, or of death. The well designed partnership agreement will provide for the continuance of the partnership, giving the remaining partners the right to purchase the leaving partner's interest and a pay-off of his distributive share of the profits.

The legal effect of dissolution is to terminate all authority of any partner to act for the partnership[14] except to wind up the partnership business. After dissolution, the partnership remains obligated to pay its liabilities. For instance, a deceased partner's estate is liable for the deceased partner's share of the partnership debts.

It is important to recognize that the partnership entity is *not* terminated by dissolution. The partnership will continue in accordance with the partnership agreement during the winding up of its affairs.

Causes for Dissolution. Dissolution is effected by the acts of the partners, by operation of law, and by decree of court.

1. By Acts of the Partners.

a. Agreement. The partnership agreement may provide for its dissolution upon a specified period of time or the occurrence of an event.[15] For example, a partnership may have been created for the purpose of buying, developing, and selling a condominium. When the dissolution occurs in accordance with the partnership agreement, there is no liability for any partner.

b. Withdrawal. For any number of reasons, a partner may decide to withdraw from the firm in *violation* of his partnership agreement. Although he has the power to withdraw, he may thereby incur damages for breach of the partnership agreement. Usually the partnership agreement will provide for a partner's withdrawal by giving proper advance notice to his associates. U.P.A., section 31(b), states: "Dissolution is caused by the express will of any partner when no definite term or particular undertaking is specified."

c. Expulsion. A partner may be expelled by his co-partners for cause. The partnership agreement may specify certain reasons for dismissal. A partnership is dissolved by the expulsion of any partner for cause.[16]

2. By Operation of Law.

a. Death. U.P.A., section 31(4) provides for the automatic dissolution of the partnership upon the death of a partner.

---

[14] U.P.A., sec. 33.

[15] U.P.A., sec. 31(1)(a).

[16] U.P.A., sec. 31(1)(d).

b. Bankruptcy. Bankruptcy of any partner or of the partnership will cause the firm to dissolve.[17] The partner or firm in bankruptcy can not *carry on* the partnership business.

3. By Decree of Court. An individual partner may petition the court to obtain its dissolution under certain circumstances. The issue before the court is whether or not the firm can continue to *carry on* partnership business. U.P.A., section 32 provides upon petition that the court *shall* decree a dissolution whenever any of the following occur:

a. Insanity. A partner has been declared a lunatic in any judicial proceeding or is shown to be of unsound mind.

b. Incapacity. A partner becomes in any way incapable of performing his part of the partnership contract. For example, if a partner suffered a physical disability that prevented him from providing services, that fact would allow the court to dissolve the partnership even over the disabled partner's objections.

c. Misconduct. The conduct of a partner which tends to affect prejudicially the carrying on of the business is ground for another partner to petition for a dissolution. For instance, the conduct of a partner who continues to cause a disruption in the working relationship affecting the carrying on of the business is ground for dissolution.

d. Operation Only at a Loss. The statutory definition of a partnership (U.P.A., section 6) is to carry on the business for a profit. When the business of the partnership can be carried on only at a loss, a partner may petition the court for dissolution.

e. Equitable Necessity. U.P.A. provides a "catch all" provision in section 32(f), which allows dissolution "whenever other circumstances render a dissolution equitable." An example is, when a person is fraudulently induced to enter a partnership based on a misrepresentation in its financial statements.

Notice of Dissolution. The legal effect of dissolution is to terminate all authority of any partner to act for the partnership, except so far as may be necessary to wind up the partnership affairs.[18]

Notice to Third Parties. The winding up process may be done by partners who have not wrongfully caused dissolution. They have implied authority to sell the partnership assets and pay off the various firm creditors with the proceeds.

A partner who has wrongfully caused a dissolution (for example, by a withdrawal in violation of the partnership agreement) may have *apparent authority* to engage in the winding up process in dealings with third parties who knew of the partnership but not of the dissolution. In order to eliminate the apparent authority, *notice* must be given to third parties that the partnership has been dissolved. When dissolution is caused by operation of law (e.g., death or bankruptcy), notice to third parties is not required.

---

[17] U.P.A., sec. 31(5). As noted in chapter 52, Bankruptcy Under the Bankruptcy Reform Act of 1978, a partnership is not entitled to a discharge in bankruptcy.

[18] U.P.A., sec. 33.

Business Organizations: A. Partnerships and Special Ventures

In the following case, the partnership creditor had notice of the dissolution of the partnership and, therefore, could not hold the partners liable for new partnership obligations sought to be imposed on the partnership after the dissolution.

Facts

Defendants had been partners doing business under the firm name of Belmont Upholstering Company and as partners they signed a five-year lease. Plaintiff, LaHood, was the lessor. In 1956 Belmont Upholstering Company ceased doing business as a partnership, though they filed no certificate of dissolution, and formed a corporation, the Belmont Furniture Company, Inc. Sometime prior to the lease expiration, LaHood, the landlord, tendered to Teschendorf, a new member of the partnership, a new five-year written lease, at a higher rental, naming the same partnership and partners as lessees. Teschendorf objected to its rent provisions and refused to sign. LaHood thereafter went to defendant Wieladt, a partner of the dissolved partnership, who did sign. The defendant continued for a number of months to deliver to plaintiff checks for the rent. These checks, as had been true for the previous year, no longer named the partnership "Belmont Upholstering Company" as payor, but instead "Belmont Furniture Company," the name of the corporation. This is an action against all the members of the partnership for the due rent. Could the landlord, LaHood, rely upon Wieladt's apparent authority to bind the dissolved partnership?

Decision

No. Judgment for defendants, former partners.

Reasoning

One partner may bind another, but here there was no partnership when the second lease was signed by Wieladt. The lease, by its terms, did not purport to be a partnership lease, but one between LaHood and Wieladt, and the rental payments were not out of Teschendorf's or partnership funds, but were payments by the corporation.

LaHood v. Wieladt, 105 N.W.2d 39 (Mich. 1960).

1. *Actual Notice.* Third parties who have *extended credit* to the partnership (for example, past creditors) must be given actual notice; that is, they must actually receive notice that the firm has been dissolved. This will destroy any apparent or customary authority.

2. *Constructive Notice.* To third parties who knew of the partnership but never had extended credit to the firm, a local newspaper publication is sufficient to eliminate apparent authority. A third party is held to have notice even though he never read the notice.

Notice to Partners. When dissolution is caused by an act of the partner (for instance, a partner who became disabled and could not continue working), he must give notice to the other partners of his intent to withdraw from the firm. If he fails to give notice of his withdrawal, he is liable to his co-partners for his share of any liability created by any partner acting for the partnership as if the partnership had not been dissolved.

Winding Up Partnership Affairs

The winding up of partnership affairs is the orderly liquidation of partnership assets and the distribution of proceeds to partnership creditors and then to the partners themselves. Throughout the winding up process the partners continue to owe a fiduciary duty to each other. They are prevented from taking on new partnership business. The following case illustrates this.

Facts

Groves, a partner, died and Aegerter, his surviving partner, continued to conduct partnership business and wind up the partnership. Aegerter accepted new retainer contracts which were only in prospect at the time of dissolution and during the lifetime of Groves. This is an action by the deceased partner's widow to oust the surviving partner from the control of the partnership for misconduct in the management of the business. Was Aegerter guilty of mismanagement by taking on new contracts?

Decision

No. Judgment for Aegerter.

Reasoning

A surviving partner has no power to bind the estate of a deceased partner by making new contracts. He has no authority to continue the business as distinguished from winding it up. If the surviving partner continues business he does so at his own risk. He must answer for any loss incurred. It does not appear that Aegerter concealed the fees derived from these contracts, or that he was acting in bad faith or that the deceased partner's estate is in any danger of losing the fees.

Groves v. Aegerter, 42 S.W.2d 974 (Mo. 1931).

Right to Wind Up Partnership Affairs. U.P.A., section 37 provides that "unless otherwise agreed the partners who have not wrongfully dissolved the partnership or the legal representative of the last surviving partner, not bankrupt, have the right to wind up the partnership affairs." A court-appointed receiver will wind up the partnership if the dissolution is by court decree. A surviving partner is entitled to reasonable compensation for his services in winding up the partnership affairs.

Upon dissolution, each partner has the right to be paid his interest in the partnership. To prevent a liquidation, partners commonly enter into a "buy and sell" agreement that provides for a method to evaluate and pay the partners' interests.

Distribution of Assets. U.P.A., section 40 establishes the rules for settling accounts between the partners after dissolution as a part of the winding up process. The partners may by their own agreement change the statutory order of payments *among themselves.*

Firm creditors who are not partners have first claim on the partnership assets, followed by (a) a partner's claim for advances made to the firm, (b) a partner's refund of capital contributed to the firm, and (c) distribution of the remaining assets equally as profits.

Business Organizations: A. Partnerships and Special Ventures

Summary Statement

1. A partnership is an association of two or more persons to carry on as co-owners a business for profit. Each element in this definition must be satisfied for there to be a partnership.
2. With the exception of Louisiana, Georgia, and Mississippi, the Uniform Partnership Act is the statutory source of partnership law.
3. Partnerships are classified as trading and nontrading.
4. General partners are classified as dormant, nominal, secret, and general.
5. The Articles of Partnership or Partnership Agreement generally include many items so that there is no uncertainty about the terms of the partners' relationship.
6. Any person competent to contract may be a partner, as well as another partnership or a corporation.
7. A partnership is a contractual relationship, and hence the parties must agree to its creation.
8. A partnership by estoppel occurs when a person by words or conduct represents himself, or permits himself to be represented, as a partner, and the third party in reasonable reliance on that holding out extends credit to the partnership.
9. Partnership property is held as a *tenancy-in-partnership* with the following characteristics:
   a. Any partner may use it for partnership purposes.
   b. A partner may not, without the consent of his co-partners, transfer his interest in it.
   c. Personal creditors of a partner may not attach his right in it.
   d. Upon a partner's death, his right in partnership property vests in the surviving partners.
   e. The surviving spouse of a partner has no interest in the deceased partner's property.
10. Dissolution is the change in the relation of the partners caused by any partner ceasing to be associated in the carrying on of the business. Upon dissolution, no partner is authorized to act for the partnership except to wind up partnership business.
11. Dissolution does not terminate the partnership entity.
12. Dissolution may be caused by the acts of the partners or by operation of law.
13. Actual notice of dissolution must be given to third parties who had extended credit to the partnership, and constructive notice (e.g., newspaper publication) to third parties who knew of the partnership but had never extended credit to the firm.
14. Winding up of a partnership is the liquidation of partnership assets and distribution of proceeds to partnership creditors and then the partners themselves.

15. After dissolution, partnership assets are distributed as follows:
    a. firm creditors who are not partners,
    b. partners' advances,
    c. partners' capital contributions,
    d. remaining assets are distributed as profits.

In the following case, the court must determine if a partnership existed. Notice that the parties must agree to share profits and losses, and that at the trial the burden of proof is on the party seeking to prove a partnership existed.

In re Wells' Will
321 N.Y.Supp.2d 200 (1971)

Gabrielli, Justice. Frank Wells died on March 10, 1969 and was survived by three sons and five daughters. By his will executed on September 13, 1968 he devised and bequeathed his estate to the petitioner, in trust, for the benefit equally of his eight children with the remainder to their issue. The principal assets are three farms valued at $267,300 and livestock and farm equipment valued at $14,950, the last-mentioned not being the subject of any controversy on these appeals. All three farms, recorded in decedent's name, had been worked as a dairy farm, and the livestock and equipment referred to were used on the farm.

The executor-trustee (petitioner) has filed a petition for the judicial settlement of its intermediate account and seeks a determination of the title to the farm and the ownership of the livestock and farm equipment, as well as a declaration that it has general authority to sell the farm. Objections to the account were filed by the three sons (objectants), in which they assert they were partners with decedent in the operation of the farm, and they also claim title thereto, including the livestock and farm equipment thereon. Decedent's daughters (respondents) filed replies controverting these objections.

To set the stage for discussion of the issues, a recitation of the background facts is in order. Decedent purchased the three farms separately, the first acquisition having occurred in 1937. The other two farms were acquired in 1939 and 1944, title being taken in the name of decedent and his wife, who later predeceased him. Thereafter title to all three farms continued in his name. When each son attained the age of fourteen, he quit school and went to work full time on the farm. They have continued to work there since. As each married, he received $50 a month, his maintenance, and the free use of a residence on the farm. Thereafter and for some six years prior to decedent's death, he paid each son a salary of $300 per month plus the free use of a residence. Throughout all this time decedent made all decisions relating to the financial operation and management of the farm, and objectants performed the required labor to operate it. All income realized from the sale of produce and milk sold from the farm was received by and paid to decedent, and all the proceeds from the operation of the farm went into his personal account. Decedent consistently filed individual personal and farm income tax returns which showed deductions for wages paid to the sons. No partnership tax return was ever filed. Additionally, all real estate taxes were paid by decedent and taken by him as an income tax deduction. It also appears that

Business Organizations: A. Partnerships and Special Ventures

the objectants filed individual returns and never, of course, deducted any losses from the farm operation or reported any profits therefrom, reporting as income only the salary paid by decedent. Of further interest, each continued to receive his salary, despite business losses sustained by decedent during certain years. Significantly, decedent recited in paragraph VI of his will that "I presently own certain farm properties which are being operated by [my] sons for me," following which he made certain provisions for the continuance of the operation of the farm.

On the other hand, there is testimony that objectants had purchased farm equipment and livestock with their own funds; that decedent considered the farm operation "a four-way deal"; that the farm was "all theirs (decedent and the three sons) together"; and they were to "work and sell together"; that the farms "were his and theirs together"; that he "bought them [the farms] for the boys"; that "the boys owned the farms"; and that in 1955 decedent has prepared a personal inventory of the farm property in which, after totaling the value, he divided the total thereof by four and made the statement that "each share including my share is $11,230." Accordingly, the Surrogate found that a partnership existed among decedent and objectants and directed that there be an accounting of the assets and profits of the partnership from 1943 until decedent's death and, further, that the objectants be awarded a three-quarter interest in the partnership profits.

Objectants now contend that, having found that a partnership existed, the court was also required to include the farm property as an asset of the partnership, that decedent had title to the farm as trustee for the benefit of the objectants and, hence, that a constructive trust should be imposed upon the farm. On the other hand, petitioner and respondents assert that no partnership existed at all and that legal and equitable title to the farm remained in decedent at all times.

We agree with the Surrogate's refusal to impose a constructive trust for the benefit of objectants.

However, we disagree with the determination that a partnership existed between decedent and objectants and, as a corollary, that there should be an accounting therefor. Naturally, a partnership may result not only from an express agreement, but from circumstantial evidence as well. An indispensable requirement of a partnership is "a mutual promise or undertaking of the parties to share in the profits of the business and submit to the burden of making good the losses." Even if we were to conclude that the decedent and objectants are considered to have placed their money, efforts, and skills in a common business, they have not divided the profits nor borne the losses in any proportion, and objectants have not sustained their burden of showing the existence of a partnership. The evidence clearly establishes (and objectants concede) that missing are the indispensable essentials of a mutual promise to share the profits and an undertaking to assume the burden of making good the losses, without which no contract of partnership can be created under either the Common Law or statutory law of New York.

The decree should be modified by deleting so much therefrom as (1) declares that a partnership existed among decedent and objectants and (2) directs that there be an accounting of the assets and profits thereof, and as so modified, it should be affirmed.

Questions and Case Problems

1. X, Y, and Z owned a restaurant as partners. Z died and under his will left "all my property, both real and personal, to my wife." Z's wife wants to maintain her deceased husband's status as a partner in the restaurant. May she do so?

2. In 1959 plaintiff met Philip Miller. Later, Mr. Miller asked plaintiff to marry him, to move to Jackson, and to help him run the nursery business. Plaintiff gave up her well-paying job to move to Jackson. The business was close to failing at the time of their marriage. By 1974, the time of Mr. Miller's death, the business was prosperous. Plaintiff did not make any capital contribution to the partnership, although she held a management position in the nursery business and did physical labor. She kept all the books and hired and fired employees. In 1960 a business registration certificate was filed for the nursery listing it as a partnership. Annual tax forms listed the business as a sole proprietorship and plaintiff's occupation as a housewife. There never was any formal written partnership agreement. Mrs. Miller, the plaintiff, sued defendant bank, her husband's executor, claiming that she was a partner in the nursery business with her deceased husband. Was there a partnership? [*Miller v. City Bank and Trust Company,* 266 N.W.2d 687 (Mich. 1978).]

3. X owns a building with a restaurant rented to Z. Z is the manager of the restaurant and is authorized by X to make all food purchases in X's name. In addition to rental payments, Z pays X 15 percent of the monthly net profits. Y, a creditor of the restaurant, sued X and Z as partners. Are they partners?

4. Plaintiff, Anderson Hay and Grain Co., Inc., was engaged in the business of selling feed to race track concessions. Plaintiff claims that defendants, Dunn and Welch, were partners in a business known as Ruidoso Downs Feed Concession. A bank account was maintained in the name of Ruidoso Downs Feed Concession, and both Dunn and Welch were authorized to sign checks and make withdrawals from the capital account. For the year 1968 Welch filed a partnership income tax return. Credit was extended by plaintiff to Ruidoso Downs Feed Concession on the strength of Dunn's financial responsibility. Dunn, defendant, claims that the plaintiff knew that Ruidoso Downs Feed Concession was a sole proprietorship operated by Welch and that he and Welch were not partners. Was Dunn a partner by estoppel? [*Anderson Hay and Grain Co., Inc. v. Dunn,* 467 P.2d 5 (N.M. 1970).]

5. Juanita Bailes and Fred Bailes were married in 1953. They began operation of a business, Bailes Best Made Dog Food, as a partnership in 1958, and continued such operation until Fred Bailes died intestate in 1969. Surviving him were Juanita, his wife, and an only son Fred, Jr., by a previous marriage. Plaintiff, Fred, Jr., claims that all the assets of the business should become part of the estate of his father and should be distributed according to the law of descent and distribution. Juanita Bailes, defendant, objects. Is plaintiff entitled to his father's interest in the partnership? [*Bailes v. Bailes,* 549 S.W.2d 69 (Ark. 1977).]

6. X, Y, and Z were doctors who owned their medical building as partners. The building was owned free and clear of any mortgage debt. Z died and his widow sued X and Y for her husband's interest in the medical building. Decide.

7. Plaintiff, a judgment creditor of defendant partner, seeks to impose a lien on defendant's undivided interest in *partnership* real estate. The court held that foreclosing on real estate of a partnership to satisfy the judgment debt of an individual partner was illegal. Plaintiff appealed. You decide. [*Buckman v. Goldblatt,* 314 N.E.2d 188 (Ohio 1974).]

8. Chris and Mike Balafas were brothers who ran a shoe repair business. All their expenses were paid out of a joint fund. There was no formal business agreement. Mike married Mary and Mike's will provided that Chris was to inherit all of his estate except for a $10,000 bequest to Mary. Upon Mike's death, Mary brought this suit to have the shoe repair business declared a partnership and to claim her share of the assets. The court found that the business was a partnership and that Mike intended to leave Chris the business upon his death. Can a partner provide how he is going to dispose of the partnership property upon his death? [*Balafas v. Balafas,* 117 N.W.2d 20 (Minn. 1962).]

9. Plaintiff is the widow of a deceased partner. When plaintiff married, her husband was in a construction and agricultural partnership business with his two brothers. The partnership profits were divided equally. The partnership traded one of the partnership properties for a house into which plaintiff and her husband moved. The property was taken in the name of plaintiff and her husband. The bookkeeper reduced the capital account of plaintiff and her husband by $23,000. At about this time the partnership became inactive, and it remained inactive through the death of plaintiff's husband. Plaintiff brought this action for an accounting and division of properties of the partnership. Defendant, the surviving partner, claims that, since plaintiff's husband's capital account was reduced by $23,000, his widow should receive a reduced share of the profits to reflect the $23,000 trade, rather than the agreed one-half. You decide. [*Mahan v. Mahan,* 489 P.2d 1197 (Ariz. 1971).]

10. In re *Wells' Will,* 321 N.Y.Supp.2d 200 (1971),[19] if you were one of the sons of the decedent, what would you have done while your father was alive so as to be able, after his death, to establish that there was a partnership?

---

[19] See pp. 690–91.

37

Partnership Management and the Authority of Partners

After you have read this chapter, you should be able to:

1. Identify the source of law regarding the management of a partnership.
2. Identify trading and nontrading partnerships.
3. Explain the source of a partner's implied authority.
4. Explain what is meant by the implied authority of a partner, and list and give examples.
5. List and explain the five prohibited transactions under the U.P.A. on a partner's implied authority to bind the firm.
6. Discuss the express authority of a partner.
7. Explain what is meant by a partner's apparent authority.
8. Explain when a majority is required to effect a partnership decision; explain when a unanimous vote is required.

Introduction

Partnerships engage in a broad spectrum of business activities ranging from the small hardware store to the New York Wall Street law offices. The management problems and contractual relationships encountered by each partnership will vary, depending upon the size and nature of the partnership.

This chapter examines the legal procedures established by the Uniform Partnership Act to manage the partnership and engage in contracts with third parties. The law of **agency** as discussed in Part 3, Agency and Employment, will apply.[1]

Actual Authority of the Partners

*Each partner is an **agent** of the partnership for the purpose of carrying on, in the usual way, the partnership business.*[2] Hence, all partners have **actual authority** to bind the firm with third parties unless prohibited by the partnership agreement. The partners also have equal voice in the internal management of the business, unless denied by the agreement.[3] In addition to the actual authority, a partner may have *apparent authority* to bind the firm with third parties as he carries on the partnership business in the usual and customary manner.

Express Authority
Partners have, by virtue of their agreement, **express authority** to act on behalf of the partnership. Thus, a managing partner of a retail department store has *express authority* to purchase inventory on credit and thereby obligate the firm. The partnership agreement will determine the extent of the individual partners' express authority.

Implied Authority
A partner may have **implied authority** to bind the firm with third parties. This may occur even if the partnership agreement or the partners do not give him any authority. The extent of his implied authority will depend upon the scope of the firm's business and its character as a "trading" or "nontrading" partnership.[4] A *trading* partnership is engaged in buying and selling *property*. A *nontrading* partnership is engaged in selling *services*. The following are common examples of a partner's implied authority to contract with third persons on behalf of the partnership.

Contracts to Buy and Sell. The authority of a partner to buy or sell the firm's assets depends upon whether the firm is a trading or nontrading partnership. A

agency
a legal relationship between two persons who agree that one is to act on behalf of the other, subject to the other's control

agent
a person authorized to act on behalf of another and subject to the other's control

actual authority
express and implied authority

express authority
an agent's authority specifically expressed in his principal's manifestation to him

implied authority
an agent's authority which the agent reasonably can understand he has from his principal's manifestation to him, but not expressed therein

---

[1] U.P.A., sec. 4(3), and *Rice v. Jackson,* 171 Pa. 89 (1895).

[2] U.P.A., sec. 9(1).

[3] U.P.A., sec. 18(e).

[4] See p. 676 for classification of partnerships.

partnership engaged in manufacturing, wholesaling, or retailing is a trading partnership. Partnerships of lawyers, accountants, and doctors are nontrading partnerships. In the following case the court characterized the partnership operations as nontrading and found that a partner was not acting within the scope of the business when he sold lumber to the plaintiff.

Facts

Bole, the plaintiff, instituted this suit against Lyle, Peters, and Barton, partners of the Cherokee Box and Handle Company, to recover funds advanced to defendants for the purchase of lumber which was never delivered. Cherokee Box owned and operated a manufacturing business and made packing crates. It sold most of its stock to the U.S. Government. Barton, the managing partner, signed the sales contract on behalf of the partnership. Bole paid Barton for the lumber. The partnership received no part of the proceeds of the check, and the other partners knew nothing of the transaction until plaintiff's claim was made after the dissolution of the partnership. Is each of the partners liable for the claim?

Decision

No. Judgment for defendants.

Reasoning

Each partner is a general agent of the firm but only for the purpose of carrying on the business of the partnership. If the act is within the partnership business according to the ordinary and usual course of conducting it, the partnership is bound regardless of whether the partner, in performing the act, proceeds in good faith or bad faith toward his co-partners. Sales made by a partner in a trading firm are not viewed with the same strictness as in nontrading firms, such as here involved, because in trading firms sales are usually within the scope of the business while in nontrading firms they are exceptional and only incidental to the main business. In this case there was nothing in the firm name to suggest that it was in the business of selling lumber. Plaintiff, Bole, chose to deal with Barton without knowing anything of the nature of the partnership, and the nonparticipating partners were in no way responsible for his loss; recovery should be against Barton alone.

Bole v. Lyle et al., 287 S.W.2d 931 (Tenn. 1956).

To Borrow Money and Execute Commercial Paper. A trading partnership that is buying and selling inventory will have frequent needs to borrow money and execute promissory notes in the firm name. A partner in such a firm has implied authority to do both and to pledge partnership property, provided that it is reasonably necessary to carry on the partnership business. A partner in a nontrading partnership does not have this implied authority unless an emergency requires it or it is customary for that business to borrow money and sign notes. In the following case, the court held that a third person's payment to the partner of a partnership is payment to the partnership, and what the partner does with the money is of no concern to the third person.

Facts

Roe, the plaintiff, was a partner with the defendant, Cooke, in a law firm. As partners, they agreed to divide equally all fees received from their client and co-defendant, Quirk. Quirk paid the fee with a check payable to Cooke, who appropriated it to his own use. Roe claims that since the partnership was noncommercial and nontrading in character, Cooke did not have authority to accept or indorse the check issued by Quirk. Was the check paid to co-partner Cooke binding on both partners?

Decision

Yes. Judgment for defendants.

Reasoning

It would afford the debtor of a law firm virtually no protection in paying a partnership debt to one member of the firm if he was bound to see that the money paid to a single member was properly applied by the partner receiving it.

Roe v. Cooke, 112 N.E.2d 511 (Ill. 1953).

Employment. Partners have implied authority to employ personnel whose services are necessary to carry on the partnership business.

Firm Debts. A partner has implied authority to pay the *partnership's creditors* with partnership funds. However, a partner may not pay his *personal creditors* with firm funds.

Settle and Compromise Claims. A partner has implied authority to settle and compromise a claim of a partnership creditor.

Representations and Admissions. A partner has implied authority to make representations and admissions that may bind the firm, provided that they are made in the ordinary and usual course of firm business. For example, X, a partner, admitted to Z, a firm creditor, that Z's claim was owed. X's admission will bind the firm.[5]

Notice to a Partner. A partner has implied authority to receive notice on any matter relating to partnership affairs, and such notice will bind the partnership, except in the case of fraud.[6] To illustrate, if a landlord gave notice of an increase in the partnership rent to a partner, the notice will bind the firm.

Limitation on Authority

Partners have no implied authority to perform acts that are not customary and usual in the carrying on of the partnership business. The partnership agreement, however, may give a partner express authority to do acts not for the carrying on of usual partnership business. However, certain transactions are prohibited under U.P.A., section 9(3).

A partner may not assign the partnership property for the benefit of creditors. If a partner made such an assignment, it would prevent the firm from

---

[5] U.P.A., sec. 11.

[6] U.P.A., sec. 12.

conducting its usual business. The U.P.A. allows an assignment if authorized by the other partners.[7]

A partner may not dispose of the good will of the business. A partner has no implied authority to sell the partnership good will, because this would cause a discontinuance of firm business. Partnership authorization would be required from *all* the other partners.[8] This is illustrated in the following case.

Facts
This is a suit by two partners of a retail grocery business to dissolve their partnership by acquiring the interest of the third partner, the defendant. The partnership agreement was for an indefinite term, permitting any partner to terminate upon notice and giving the remaining partners the option to purchase the retiring partner's interest. The court ordered all the property of the partnership sold except the partnership name. The plaintiffs claimed that the defendant had no interest in the good will of the business. Did the court have the authority to exclude the partnership name from the sale of the partnership assets?

Decision
Yes. Judgment for the defendant.

Reasoning
The good will of a business is the reasonable expectation of its continued profitable operation. It consists of the name of the firm, its reputation for doing business, its location, the number of its customers, and the former success of the business. One partner has no implied authority to dispose of the good will of a partnership. Hence, the court was right in ordering all of the property of the partnership sold except the partnership name.

Young v. Cooper, 203 S.W.2d 376 (Tenn. 1947).

A partner may not do any act which would make it impossible to carry on the ordinary business of the partnership. For example, an individual partner has no implied authority to sell an office computer that is required to process its monthly billings.[9]

A partner may not confess a judgment. An individual partner has no implied authority to admit that a claim is due, because the partners have the right to defend the claim in court.[10] For example, in a malpractice claim against a medical partnership, an admission of liability by a doctor who treated the patient will not bind the firm.

A partner may not submit a partnership claim to arbitration. A partner can not submit a firm dispute to arbitration without the consent of the other partners unless the firm has ceased doing business.[11] Since arbitration is becoming a common method of resolving disputes[12] and is found in many contracts, third persons dealing with a partnership should insist on unanimous consent in a contract that provides for arbitration.

---

[7] U.P.A., sec. 9(3)(a).   [10] U.P.A., sec. 9(3)(d).

[8] U.P.A., sec. 9(3)(b).   [11] U.P.A., sec. 9(3)(e).

[9] U.P.A., sec. 9(3)(c).   [12] See pp. 23–24 for a discussion of arbitration.

Apparent Authority

Partners have apparent authority to carry on in the usual way the partnership business, and third persons who reasonably rely on such authority can bind the firm.[13] A partner without actual or apparent authority can not bind the firm with third parties. If the third person knows of the lack of authority, he can not bind the firm for the partner's unauthorized acts.

Firm Management

The internal management of the partnership is accomplished by the partners' vote in the decision-making process.

Ordinary Business

At a partnership meeting the *decision of the majority* will govern, provided that it is an *ordinary business* matter and the vote does not contradict an agreement between the parties. Hence, the majority may decide those business affairs that are *normal and customary* in carrying out the firm's business.[14] For example, in a construction firm, the majority may decide to rent construction equipment over the objection of the minority. All of the partners will be bound under the equipment lease.

Extraordinary Business

A *unanimous vote* by the partners is necessary for a business decision that would change the partnership agreement.[15] Thus, changing the location of the firm is a matter all the partners must agree to, unless the partnership agreement provides otherwise.

In the following case the partners incorporated part of the business without the consent of one partner, who brought suit to reach his partnership interest in the corporation.

Facts

Fortugno, plaintiff, a member of a family partnership that was organized to collect and sell manure, brought an action for its dissolution. The partnership, Hudson Manure Company, sold its manure to mushroom growers in southeastern Pennsylvania. In the course of its operation, the partnership found it convenient to put certain of its activities in corporate form in order to limit the liability of the individual partners. Fortugno refused to authorize the corporate division of the partnership and claimed that the enterprises constitute a single integrated partnership, whether or not any phase of the business was conducted in corporate form. He sought to be paid in cash for his partnership interest in both the partnership and the corporation and requested the court to order the sale of the corporate assets. May the partnership property be traced into the corporation?

---

[13] U.P.A., sec. 9(1). [14] U.P.A., sec. 18(h). [15] U.P.A., sec. 18(h).

Decision

Yes. Judgment for Fortugno.

Reasoning

Less than all the partners may not bind the partnership by an act not performed for the purpose of carrying on the usual partnership business, unless authorized by the other partners. Because Fortugno never ratified the act of incorporating part of the partnership, no assets of the partnership may remain in the corporation.

Fortugno v. Hudson Manure Company, 144 A.2d 207 (N.J. 1958).

Summary Statement

1. Partnership management is governed by the Uniform Partnership Act and agency law. The partners by agreement may change the effect of the U.P.A., which states that "all partners have equal rights in the management and operation of the partnership business."
2. The extent of a partner's contribution to the firm does not affect his equal voice in management.
3. The partnership agreement grants to each partner *express authority* to act as an agent on behalf of the partnership.
4. Implied authority of a partner to act on behalf of the firm depends upon whether it is a trading or nontrading firm.
5. The implied authority of a partner depends on the nature of the firm; some common examples of a partner's implied authority are authority to:
   a. buy and sell inventory in a trading partnership;
   b. borrow money and execute commercial paper in a trading partnership;
   c. employ personnel;
   d. pay firm debts with partnership funds;
   e. settle and compromise claims;
   f. make admissions that will bind the firm if made in the ordinary and usual course of firm business;
   g. receive notice on any matter relating to partnership affairs.
6. Unless authorized by *all* the other partners, or unless they have abandoned the business, a partner may not:
   a. assign the partnership property in trust for creditors;
   b. dispose of the partnership's good will;
   c. do any other act which would make it impossible to carry on the ordinary partnership business;
   d. confess a judgment;
   e. submit a partnership claim to arbitration.
7. A majority vote is required to effect *ordinary* business decisions connected with the partnership business.
8. A unanimous vote of the partners is required to change the partnership agreement or any material agreement between the partners.

The following case involves a partner who signed a promissory note on behalf of the partnership without express authorization from his co-partner to do so. Notice how the court refused to apply the doctrine of apparent authority because the lending bank's agent knew that the co-partner did not authorize the loan.

Matanuska Valley Bank v. Arnold
223 F.2d 778 (Alaska 1955)

Orr, Circuit Judge. Appellant, plaintiff in the lower court, sued appellees, defendants in the lower court, to recover payment of three notes purported to have been executed on behalf of a partnership consisting of appellees—Mrs. Irene Arnold and Willard Davis—and signed by Willard Davis.

Davis was engaged in the contracting business in Palmer, a small community in Alaska. He secured a contract from the United States to erect a garage and storage building. Being without sufficient funds to enable him to finance the project, he contacted Mrs. Arnold, whose credit at the bank was good, and induced her to enter into an agreement with him for the purpose of carrying out the contract. Mrs. Arnold was to secure the bond required by the contract and to supply the capital necessary to carry the work until it could be paid for out of the progress payments on the contract. Pursuant to the agreement, Mrs. Arnold executed two notes of $5,000 each in favor of the bank. In the course of time, one of the $5,000 notes was paid from such proceeds and was cancelled and returned to Mrs. Arnold.

Later, Davis, without consulting Mrs. Arnold or in any manner informing her of his intended action, executed a note in favor of the bank in the sum of $5,100, signing the name of the partnership, "Davis Construction Company, by Willard Davis," thereto. This note was accepted as payment of the remaining $5,000 note held by the bank and executed by Mrs. Arnold, and later the note was returned to her. Subsequently, two other notes in suit, each in the sum of $3,000, were executed by Davis, signed "Davis Construction Company, Willard Davis."

Davis seems to have had other business ventures during the period in question and was not careful in segregating the financial transactions of the one from the other, with the result that funds were commingled, and indebtedness incurred in transactions other than the partnership project were paid for out of funds in the partnership account.

The notes in the sums of $5,100, $3,000, and $3,000 were not paid, and the bank sought to hold Mrs. Arnold, apparently the only solvent member of the partnership, liable. She defended on the ground that Davis had no authority, either apparent or real, to bind the partnership by his sole signature.

The sole purpose of the partnership agreement between Mrs. Arnold and Davis was to build the garage and storage building for the United States.

In the instant case we find no evidence of express authority having been given Davis to execute the notes on behalf of the firm, nor can authority be implied.

We now consider whether Davis had apparent authority to bind the firm. Maze, the manager of the bank, was fully conversant with the agreement between Davis and Mrs. Arnold and the circumstances surrounding it. If the knowledge of Maze can be imputed to the bank, there can have been no apparent authority. The bank argues that the knowledge of its agent, Maze, should not be imputed to it for the reason that Maze was acting adversely to the interests of appellant, his principal. This argument is bottomed on a finding of the trial court that a scheme existed on the part of Maze and Davis to defraud Mrs. Arnold and that said scheme involved covertly extending the bank's credit to Davis on behalf of the firm for use on other than firm's business.

But assuming that Maze was acting adversely to appellant, his principal, his knowledge should nevertheless be imputed to appellant under the sole actor doctrine. Maze was the manager of the bank and appears to have been in complete charge of its affairs; he was the sole representative of the bank in all dealings connected with the execution of the notes upon which this suit is brought. The bank is foreclosed from taking the inconsistent position of claiming on the one hand apparent authority based upon dealings with its sole agent, Maze, and on the other hand disclaiming the imputation of Maze's knowledge.

There exists an additional reason why Davis had no authority to bind the firm, at least insofar as the note in the sum of $3,000, executed by Davis on the 17th day of October 1951, is concerned. The trial court found that the money received by Davis from the bank on the firm's notes executed by him was used in the construction of a house for Maze and the Butte Road House.

The judgment denying recovery on the notes sued upon is affirmed.

Questions and Case Problems

1. X, Y, and Z operated a supermarket as partners. Z borrowed $25,000 from S Bank for the purpose of buying food. Z signed as a partner, but X and Y never consented to the loan. Z used the money to pay his personal debts. S Bank demanded payment of the $25,000 from the partners. Decide.

2. Oswald, plaintiff, and Leckey, defendant, signed a partnership agreement to conduct an accounting practice. The partnership was not harmonious and was terminated. Plaintiff seeks an accounting and claims defendant had no authority to write off uncollectible accounts without his consent while winding up the partnership affairs. Defendant claimed he acted in good faith and has the power to compromise claims. You decide. [*Oswald v. Leckey,* 572 P.2d 1316 (Or. 1977).]

3. X, Y, and Z ran a college bookstore as partners. At a partnership meeting they agreed that X and Y would work in the store but Z would be the only partner authorized to order textbooks. A salesman who knew that X was a partner, but did not know that he was without authority to order textbooks, took an order from him for 1,000 books. The partnership refused to accept or pay for the books. Can the textbook company collect?

4. X and Z were partners in a medical practice. Y, a patient of Z, was billed $600 for an operation. Y claimed that the bill was unfair, and Z agreed to compromise by accepting $300 as payment in full. X told Z that he had no authority to accept less than the original bill and told Y that he was going to sue for the additional $300. Y claimed that partner X was bound by the compromise. Decide.

5. C owed X, Y, and Z a fee of $2,000 for accounting services rendered by their partnership. C paid the money to X, who used it to pay off a home improvement loan. Y and Z insisted that C repay the $2,000 fee. Decide.

6. X, Y, and Z owned, as partners, an antique business in Boston. X and Y desired to move the firm to Vermont. At a partnership meeting, Z objected to the move. X and Y claim the majority rule. Are they correct?

7. X and Y operated a construction business as partners. Z, a customer, complained to X that the construction of his apartment building was defective. X found Z to be unreasonable but agreed to submit the dispute to arbitration. Y protested the arbitration procedure and claimed that the partnership is not bound to arbitrate. Is Y correct?

8. X, Y, and Z are partners in an accounting firm. X and Y want to rent additional space on the floor where they always operated the firm. Z feels it is too expensive to do so and votes against it. X and Y sign the lease and rent the new space. Is Z liable as a partner on the lease?

9. Feingold, plaintiff, sued William and Charlotte Davis, husband and wife and owners of Davis Nursing Home as a partnership. Mr. Davis signed a purchase and sale agreement to sell the nursing home to Feingold, including its assets and good will. Mrs. Davis, his co-partner, never signed nor consented to the agreement and refused to convey the property. Feingold sought specific performance of the purchase and sale agreement. Decide. [*Feingold v. Davis,* 282 A.2d 291 (Pa. 1971).]

10. In the case of *Matanuska Valley Bank v. Arnold,* 223 F.2d 778 (Alaska 1955),[16] would the result have been any different if Maze was not in complete charge of the bank's affairs? Would the bank have any liability for the fraud of its agent, Maze, and if so would this have any impact on the bank's claim for payment of the note from Mrs. Arnold? Disregard the facts in the last paragraph of the case for the purpose of your answer.

---

[16] See pp. 701–2.

38

Rights, Duties, and Remedies of Partners Among Themselves

After you have read this chapter, you should be able to:

1. List and explain the eight rights of a partner as an owner of the firm.
2. List and explain the five duties of partners to each other.
3. Explain the remedies of a partner.
4. Analyze and discuss the nature of a partner's liability on firm contracts and torts committed by a partner or an employee of the firm.
5. Explain the liability of an incoming partner entering an existing firm.
6. Explain the nature and extent of a partner's liability.
7. Explain the effect of dissolution of the firm on a partner's existing liability.
8. List and explain the three property rights a partner has in the partnership.

Introduction

Many students will be partners, and will be dealing with partners, in business. They should be carefully aware of the nature of *their* duties and rights, just as they should be aware of those of partners in other firms that are dealing with them. The liability of a partner to his partners and, particularly, to third persons is great.

This chapter explains the rights and duties of the partners among themselves as well as the partnership's liability to third persons who have dealt with the firm. The U.P.A., section 18 establishes the rules that determine the rights and duties of the partners, *unless their partnership agreement provides otherwise.* Also, since partners are general agents of the partnership, the law of agency applies[1] and spells out the common law agent duties of each partner, unless the partnership agreement provides otherwise.

Rights of Partners

Each partner, as a co-owner of the partnership, has, *unless otherwise agreed,* the following statutory rights under U.P.A., section 18.

Share Equally in Profits and Losses

Profits and losses.

Unless otherwise agreed, each partner has the right to share in the profits and surplus equally.[2] This rule is not affected by a disproportionate amount of capital and contributions or the amount of services rendered by a partner. Thus, if A contributes $10,000 and B $5,000 and C services only, they each will equally share the profits unless otherwise agreed. Unless otherwise agreed, losses are shared as profits are shared.

Equal Rights in Management

Participation in management.

Each partner has an equal right in the management of the firm.[3] Thus, a partner who provides only services has the same voice in management as the partner who made a substantial capital contribution.

Payment of Interest

Loans. A partner who makes a loan to the firm shall be paid interest from the date of the loan. An advance by a partner, beyond the amount of capital which the partnership agreement obligated him to contribute, is a loan to the partnership. The lending partner is entitled to interest from the date of advance and to repayment when the loan is due. If partnership funds are insufficient to pay the note on its due date, the co-partners must contribute their share of the amount due.

Receipt of interest.

---

[1] U.P.A., sec. 4(3).

[2] U.P.A., secs. 26 and 18(a).

[3] U.P.A., sec. 18(e).

Capital Contributions. A partner who makes a capital contribution shall receive interest *from the date when repayment should be made.* The contribution used in the business should be returned upon dissolution after partnership debts have been paid. If the contribution is then not returned to the partner, he is, unless otherwise agreed, entitled to interest on the amount due. In the following case, a partner's skill and labor on behalf of the partnership were determined to be a part of his capital contribution to the firm to which he was entitled on dissolution as well as interest thereon when the other partner refused to make payment.

Facts

Plaintiff, Thompson, was a partner with defendant, Beth, in a business organized to erect and operate a resort area. Thompson was a skilled cabinet maker and electrician who invested $400 and contributed 2,000 hours of labor in building the lake resort. Upon dissolution of the partnership, plaintiff made demand for an accounting and payment of his share of the proceeds from the sale of the property. Defendant refused. Thompson claimed he was entitled to compensation for his 2,000 hours of labor as a capital investment and to interest on his share from the date of his sale of the partnership assets.

Decision

Judgment for plaintiff, Thompson.

Reasoning

A partner who has been active in contributing his skill and labor on a day-to-day basis is compensated by a share in the partnership profits. This rule does not apply where the skill and labor of the partner are his contribution to the capital assets of the partnership. Here, Thompson's return of his contribution on liquidation is not remuneration, but a return on capital investment, and he is entitled to interest from the date of sale of the partnership assets.

Thompson v. Beth, 111 N.W.2d 171 (Wis. 1961).

Availability of partnership books.

Partnership Books

The partnership books and records shall be kept at the principal place of business of the partnership. Each partner has the right to inspect and copy the books at any time. However, the partnership agreement may prevent a partner from inspecting the books and using the information for other than partnership purposes. In the following case, the court ordered that, pursuant to the request of one of the partners, there should be a dissolution and an accounting even though the partnership books were poorly kept.

Facts

Plaintiff, Luchs, formed a partnership with defendant, Ormsby, to service government contracts for specialized construction work. Plaintiff brought this action for a dissolution and an accounting. The lower court entered a judgment against the defendant and he appealed. Defendant stated at the trial that he would accept the accountants' report, and that any incompleteness in their report was through negligent bookkeeping of the partnership. Defendant then claimed that the accountants' report was inadequate and demanded a new audit.

Business Organizations: A. Partnerships and Special Ventures

Decision

Judgment for plaintiff, Luchs.

Reasoning

Any incompleteness in the accountants' report was due to the negligent bookkeeping of the partnership, and a better job could not have been done under the circumstances.

Luchs v. Ormsby, 340 P.2d 702 (Cal. 1959).

New Partners

A new partner may be admitted only with the consent of *all* the partners unless the partnership agreement provides otherwise. Recall that a partnership is a contractual relationship, and the admission of a new member is a material change in the agreement. The new incoming partner is liable for partnership obligations before and after his becoming a partner. However, his personal assets can not be reached to satisfy partnership creditors whose claims existed *before* he became a partner.

If a new partner promises his co-partners that he will pay old creditors, the latter will generally be entitled to enforce his promise as third party creditor beneficiaries.[4]

If the incoming partner buys a partnership interest from a retiring partner, the transaction is not within the bulk sales law because the new partner is bound to pay the old partner's debts from partnership property. However, the incoming partner must give public notice of the purchase.[5]

Partnership Assets

Partnership *property* is what the partnership has accumulated. It is a part of the *assets* of the partnership, which consist of (1) the *partnership property* and (2) the *contributions of each of the partners* necessary for payment of all partnership liabilities.

Reimbursement and Indemnity

Provided that a partner is acting reasonably and in good faith, he is entitled to be **reimbursed** for payments made and reasonable personal debts incurred by him in properly carrying on the partnership business. For example, if an accountant paid for office supplies with a personal check, he is entitled to be reimbursed by the firm. He is also entitled to be **indemnified** for damage to his property while used in the partnership business, as is illustrated by the following case.

Admission of new partners.

Partnership assets.

reimbursement
one person's right against another to be repaid money paid on the other's behalf for which the latter was responsible

idemnity
an absolute obligation to pay for another's loss

---

[4] See pp. 178–79 for a discussion of third party beneficiaries.

[5] UCC 6–103(6); see pp. 409–11 for a discussion of the bulk sales law.

Facts

Plaintiff, Smith, is one of the eight partners who owned and operated a coal mine with a fleet of thirty trucks. Smith sued the partnership to recover damages for the value of his personally owned truck which was damaged as the result of the negligence of an employee of the partnership. Is Smith entitled to reimbursement for his loss?

Decision

Yes. Judgment for plaintiff, Smith.

Reasoning

If the negligence of the partnership caused damage to the property of a stranger, the partnership would be liable. There is no reason to deny recovery where the damaged property is that of a partner. The negligence was that of a firm employee acting within the scope of his employment. The partners are jointly and severally liable for the loss.

Smith v. Hensley, 354 S.W.2d 744 (Ky. 1962).

Compensation for services rendered to the partnership.

Compensation

No partner is entitled to extra compensation for his services in carrying on partnership business. It is important for the partnership agreement to provide for salaries to be paid to the partners because sharing the profits is considered adequate compensation, unless the parties otherwise agree. It is not unusual in a professional partnership for one partner to be authorized as a general manager. For example, a law firm may designate a partner who will expend additional time in managing the law practice. Unless the partnership agreement entitles him or her to additional compensation for additional services, there is no extra compensation. The U.P.A. does provide for reasonable compensation for a *surviving* partner's services in winding up the partnership affairs.[6] In the following case, the partners agreed to pay a partner a salary for his services, which the court enforced.

Facts

Plaintiff, Chambers, is a partner with defendant, Sims, both of whom did not draw money from the partnership at regular intervals but instead drew out money as they needed it. The partnership agreement stated that "the partners shall be entitled to compensate themselves for their services as an expense of operation of the business before computation of profits." Plaintiff claimed that the partners orally agreed to pay him a salary of $350 per month and never

did. The lower court found this to be a fact, and that the practice of compensating full-time service had been established. Plaintiff was awarded the reasonable value of his services to the partnership, and defendant appealed. Was the plaintiff entitled to remuneration for his services?

Decision

Yes. Judgment for the plaintiff, Chambers.

---

[6] U.P.A., sec. 18(f).

Reasoning

Generally a partner is not entitled to any remuneration for his services in the absence of any agreement by the partners to that effect. Here the partnership agreement contemplated compensation, and the practice of paying salaries had been established. In such a case it is presumed that payment of reasonable salaries was intended.

Chambers v. Sims, 374 P.2d 841 (Utah 1962).

Accounting

A partner may, under limited circumstances as provided by U.P.A., section 22, require a *formal* accounting during the ordinary operation of the partnership. This right should be distinguished from the informal process of inspecting and copying the books and records. The right to a formal accounting occurs:

1. when he is wrongfully excluded from the partnership business, or
2. when the right to a formal accounting exists under the partnership agreement, or
3. when a partner has acquired secret profits without the consent of the other partners from any transaction connected with the firm, or
4. whenever other circumstances render it just and reasonable.

Remedies of Partners

Contracts

The partnership is liable for the contracts of its partners as agents of the firm.

> Every partner is an agent of the partnership for the purpose of its business. . . . [U.P.A., section 9.]

Hence, contract liability *of the partners* in carrying out partnership business is the responsibility of the firm. As to third persons, the partners are liable *jointly* for partnership *contracts*.

A breach of the partnership agreement subjects the wrongdoer to contract liability. Generally the usual common law remedies for breach of contract are available to partners among themselves.[7] A partner has the remedy of an *accounting* if he sues the partnership.

Tort

All partners are *jointly and severally* liable to third persons *for **torts*** committed in the ordinary course of the partnership business.

tort
a civil (private) noncontractual wrong for which a court will give a remedy

> Where, by any wrongful act or omission of any partner acting in the ordinary course of the business of the partnership . . . loss or injury is caused to any person, not being a partner in the partnership . . . the partnership is liable therefor to the same extent as the partner so acting or omitting to act. [U.P.A., section 13.]

---

[7] See pp. 187–91 for remedies on breach of contract.

To illustrate, if Doctor X is a partner in a medical partnership and negligently treats a patient, the malpractice negligence claim may be brought against Doctor X and the partnership.

Notice in the following case that it is not necessary that the two co-partners participate in the negligent act to be held jointly and severally liable to the injured party.

Facts

Plaintiff, Roux, sued Lawand, as the surviving partner of a partnership, to recover damages for personal injury for a tort committed by a partner acting in the scope of the partnership business. The negligent partner, while cleaning a hat in the back room of a shoe-shining shop, struck a match to light a cigarette and caught the hat afire, then picked it up and threw it toward the sink, where it fell into a pail of flammable fluid which burst into flames. He took the pail of blazing liquid and hurled the contents through a doorway and burned the plaintiff. Is the partnership liable for the torts of its partners?

Decision

Yes. Judgment for the plaintiff, Roux.

Reasoning

Partners are liable jointly and severally for the tortious acts of a co-partner, done in the reasonable scope of the partnership business, whether they personally participate therein or only have knowledge thereof. If a partnership is liable for a tort, each member is individually liable.

Roux v. Lawand, 160 A. 756 (Me. 1932).

Of course, partners are liable to each other and to the partnership for their torts committed on each other and on the partnership.

Duties of Partners

Partnership Agreement

A partnership is created by a contract between the parties. Thus, each partner has a duty to comply with the terms of the partnership agreement. A partner is liable for any loss caused to the firm for violation of his duties.

Duty to inform.

Information

Each partner has the statutory duty to render full information of partnership matters to any partner. A similar duty is owed by agents to their principals. The duty is based on the *fiduciary status* of partners who act on behalf of the partnership. This duty to render information "on demand" extends to the legal representative of a partner.

Reasonable Care

Duty to act carefully.

Each partner is under a common law duty to exercise reasonable care and skill in transacting partnership business. A partner is personally liable to the partnership for any loss proximately caused by his negligence. He is *not* liable for honest mistakes or errors of judgment.

Good Faith

A partner's **fiduciary** status obligates him to act with complete *loyalty* to the firm. This fiduciary duty prohibits a partner from making a *secret profit*. A partner holds all profits in *trust* for the partnership.

fiduciary
a person with a duty to act primarily for the benefit of another

Each partner is under the fiduciary duty not to compete with the firm. This obligates the partner to devote his full time and effort to the partnership. The co-partners may, however, agree to a partner engaging in a competing business.

In the following case, a partner was held liable for secret commissions even though his partner knew he was operating another business.

Facts

Plaintiff, Liggett, sued the defendant, Lester, to dissolve the partnership they operated as a service station. Shortly after the formation of the partnership, Lester, with Liggett's consent, became owner and operator of a bulk plant for the handling of large volumes of petroleum products for wholesale consumers. Lester arranged with the oil company to receive an additional discount as a "jobber," ranging from $.01 to $.015 per gallon. He did not pass this profit on to the partnership. Liggett was not aware of this transaction. When Liggett discovered the secret profit-taking, he closed the station.

Lester claimed that a partner may engage in an enterprise in his own behalf, provided that he act in good faith. He alleged good faith because Liggett knew of the bulk plant operation. Was Lester obligated to account for the secret profits?

Decision

Yes. Judgment for plaintiff, Liggett.

Reasoning

The conduct of Lester in concealing his additional profits constituted a breach of a fiduciary duty one partner owes another. Lester's profits on such purchases amounted to secret commissions wrongfully withheld from his partner. Although Liggett was aware of Lester's bulk plant operation, he was not aware of discounts received. Lester not only failed to offer his partner an opportunity to share in the discount, he also tried to keep him from learning of it. Liggett's consent was not truly obtained.

Liggett v. Lester, 390 P.2d 351 (Or. 1964).

Keep Accounts

Each partner has a fiduciary duty to keep accounts of his partnership business. Usually a managing partner assumes this duty on behalf of the firm.

Summary Statement

1. Unless the partners agree otherwise, each partner as an owner, has the following rights:
   a. to manage the firm (U.P.A., sec. 18(e));
   b. to inspect the books (U.P.A., sec 19);
   c. to share the profits and surplus (U.P.A., sec. 26);
   d. to receive interest on his capital contribution from the date when repayment should be made (U.P.A., sec. 18(d));
   e. to receive interest on loans from the date of the loan (U.P.A., sec. 18(c));
   f. to be indemnified by the partnership for payment made and personal liabilities incurred in carrying on firm business (U.P.A., sec. 18(b));
   g. to be repaid his capital contributions by his co-partners after all liabilities are paid (U.P.A., sec. 18(a));
   h. to receive, upon dissolution, after the payment of all creditors and loans by partners, return of his capital contribution (U.P.A., sec 40(b) III);
   i. to vote on the admission of new partners (U.P.A., sec. 18(g)).
2. Each partner, as an agent and a fiduciary, owes to his co-partners the following duties:
   a. good faith and loyalty;
   b. to act with reasonable care in transacting firm business;
   c. to keep an account and record of his partnership business (U.P.A., sec. 21);
   d. to render information to his co-partners on all important matters affecting the firm;
   e. to obey the partnership agreement;
   f. unless otherwise agreed, to share in the losses in the same ratio as they share in the profits.
3. Each partner is liable jointly with the other partners on partnership *contracts* made in its name and within the scope of another partner's actual or apparent authority.
4. Each partner is liable jointly and severally for the *torts* of other partners and firm employees acting in the ordinary course of the business or with the authority of his co-partners (U.P.A., sec. 13).
5. A partner admitted into an existing partnership is liable for all previously incurred firm obligations, and this liability is satisfied only out of partnership property (U.P.A., sec. 17).
6. Dissolution of the firm does not discharge the liability of the partners unless the firm creditors agree.
7. The partnership assets are the partnership property *and* the contributions of the partners necessary for the payment of all partnership liabilities.

In the following case, a suit was brought by a husband against a medical partnership for the alienation of his wife's affections by one of the physician partners. The U.P.A., section 13, provides for partnership liability where any partner acting in the ordinary course of the business caused loss or injury to any person not being a partner.

Business Organizations: A. Partnerships and Special Ventures

Kelsey-Seybold Clinic v. Maclay

466 S.W.2d 716 (Tex. 1971)

This is a suit for alienation of affections in which the trial court rendered summary judgment for the defendant, Kelsey-Seybold Clinic, a medical partnership. [Plaintiff appealed, and the appellate court reversed and sent the case back for trial. Defendant medical partnership now appeals to this Supreme Court claiming there is no issue of fact and, therefore, summary judgment is proper.] The question to be decided is whether the Clinic established conclusively that it is not liable for the damages alleged to have been caused by the acts of one of the partners.

Plaintiff alleged that Dr. Brewer and the Clinic had treated him, his wife, and their children for several years; that Dr. Brewer, who is a pediatrician and one of the partners in the Clinic, was the doctor to whom his wife had taken their children; that beginning in late 1966, Dr. Brewer conceived and entered into a scheme to alienate the affections of plaintiff's wife, Mrs. Maria Maclay; that he showered his attentions and gifts upon her until April or May, 1967, when her affections were alienated as a direct result of his actions, causing her to separate from plaintiff on or about July 25, 1967.

Plaintiff further alleged that Dr. Brewer's actions designed to alienate Mrs. Maclay's affections occurred while he was acting as a medical doctor for plaintiff's family and in the course and scope of his employment as a partner in the Clinic; that various acts of undue familiarity occurred both on and off the premises of the Clinic; that prior to April, 1967, the Clinic, through Dr. Mavis Kelsey, one of the senior partners, had knowledge of Dr. Brewer's actions; that at the time this knowledge was acquired, the Clinic was providing medical treatment for plaintiff and his entire family; and that the "partnership approved of, consented to, and ratified and condoned such conduct of its partner, Brewer, and refused to come to the aid of your plaintiff or in any way attempt to halt or disapprove the actions of Brewer." Plaintiff prayed for the recovery of damages both actual and exemplary, from Dr. Brewer and the Clinic, jointly and severally.

Where a partner proposes to do, in the name or for the benefit of the partnership, some act that is not in the ordinary course of the business, consent by the other partners may constitute his authority to do the act for the partnership. We also recognize that even a willful or malicious act outside the ordinary scope of the partnership business may be so related to the business that tacit consent of the other partners could fairly be regarded as a grant of authority. In this instance, however, Dr. Brewer was acting solely for his own personal gratification. His conduct could not benefit the Clinic in any way, and no one would have supposed that he was acting for the partnership. It is our opinion that in these circumstances the "consent" that might be inferred from the silence or inaction of the Clinic after learning of his conduct does not render the Clinic vicariously liable for the damages claimed by the plaintiff.

We are also of the opinion that the Clinic owed a duty to the families of its patients to exercise ordinary care to prevent a tortious interference with family relations. It was not required to maintain constant surveillance over personnel on duty or to inquire into and regulate the personal conduct of partners and employees while engaged in their private affairs. But if and when the partnership received information from which it knew or should have known that there might be a need to take action, it was under a duty to use reasonable means at its disposal to prevent any partner or employee from improperly using his position with the Clinic to work a tortious invasion of legally protected family interests.

The rather meager information in the present record does not necessarily indicate that the Clinic was under a duty to act or that it could have done anything to prevent the damage when Dr. Kelsey first learned of the situation. On the other hand, it does not affirmatively and clearly appear that the Clinic could or should have done nothing. Mrs. Maclay's affections may have been alienated from her husband before anyone talked with Dr. Kelsey, but the facts in that respect are not fully developed. There is no proof as to when, where, or under what circumstances the misconduct, if any, on Dr. Brewer's part occurred. Dr. Kelsey testified that he did not believe anything improper occurred at the Clinic, but the proofs do not establish as a matter of law that he was justified in not making further inquiry after his conversations with plaintiff and Mrs. Maclay's uncle. The record does not show whether there is a partnership agreement that might have a bearing on the case, and we have no way of knowing the extent to which the Clinic might have determined which patients were to be seen by Dr. Brewer or controlled his actions while on duty. Dr. Kelsey's testimony suggests that the partners might have been in a position to prevent improper conduct by one of their number on the premises of the Clinic. In our opinion the Clinic has failed to discharge the heavy, and in the case of this character virtually impossible, burden of establishing as a matter of law at the summary judgment stage that it is not liable under any theory fairly presented by the allegations of the petition. [The court held that there was *an issue of fact* as to whether the medical partnership breached its duty to use reasonable means at its disposal to prevent Dr. Brewer from improperly using his position with the Clinic to work a tortious invasion of legally protected family interests, thus precluding summary judgment. The decision of the appellate court was affirmed.]

Questions and Case Problems

1. Stroud and Freeman formed a general partnership to sell groceries under the name of Stroud's Food Center. Plaintiff, National Biscuit Company, sold bread to the partnership. The partners' power and authority were not restricted or limited by the partnership agreement. Stroud advised National Biscuit that he personally would not be responsible for any additional bread sold by National Biscuit to Stroud's Food Center. After this notice to plaintiff, at the request of Freeman, plaintiff sold and delivered bread to Stroud's Food Center. Did Freeman's act bind the partnership and Stroud? [*National Biscuit Co. v. Stroud,* 106 S.E.2d 692 (N.C. 1959).]

2. X and Z operated a collection agency as partners. While attempting to collect a debt for the firm, Y, a firm employee, committed an assault and battery on W. When W sued the firm, C, a new partner, was joined as a party defendant. Is C liable along with the other partners?

3. Plaintiff, Bovy, was a partner with the defendants, Graham, Cohen, and Wampold in a law partnership. The written partnership agreement did not provide for the distribution of fees upon dissolution. The partners entered into a subsequent agreement which specified how fees should be divided upon dissolution. The partnership was dissolved, and Bovy brought this suit to

compel compliance, with the subsequent agreement regarding the division of fees. The defendants claim that, during the negotiations for the new agreement, Bovy had not fully disclosed the number of cases in which he claimed a contingent fee. Was Bovy subject to a fiduciary duty of disclosure to divulge the number of cases and value of their contingent fees during the negotiation of the subsequent partnership agreement? [*Bovy v. Graham, Cohen & Wampold,* 564 P.2d 1175 (Wash. 1977).]

4. Claude Bass, the plaintiff, entered into a one-year oral partnership to operate a farm. Ben Daetwyler, the defendant, agreed to furnish the farm, oats for the animals, and the equipment, provided that Bass did all the work. After all expenses were paid, the profits were to be divided equally. Daetwyler kept all the books and partnership records but did not make an accounting to Bass. He deducted his rent for the farm, equipment used, and oats for the animals from the gross income of the partnership. Bass claimed he had no right to do so. Decide. [*Bass v. Daetwyler,* 305 S.W.2d 339 (Mo. 1957).]

5. Plaintiff, Koenig, and defendant, Huber, were partners engaged in a plumbing and heating business. They signed a partnership agreement which provided that the parties were to employ themselves diligently in the business; that each partner was to contribute equally to the capital of the firm in the form of equipment and machinery; and that all debts and obligations of the partnership would be shared equally and all profits would be distributed equally. Koenig filed suit for the dissolution of the partnership and an accounting. The lower court failed to consider "extra time" spent by Koenig in the partnership business while the defendant, Huber, was operating an oil station. Is a partner entitled to be paid for "extra time" spent in a partnership business? [*Koenig v. Huber,* 210 N.W.2d 825 (S.D. 1973).]

6. Weiss was one of the partners in Pike Associates that was formed to build and operate a shopping center. Weiss put up all his right, title, and interest in the shopping center as security for a personal loan to Weiss made by the defendant. Plaintiff bank also loaned Weiss money some years earlier. Defendant attempted to foreclose on its interest in the shopping center partnership after Weiss was in default on his note to the defendant. Plaintiff seeks to enjoin the foreclosure and to establish that its interest has priority because a partner can not pledge specific partnership property for a personal loan. May a partner pledge as security an interest in the partnership assets? [*Madison National Bank v. Newrath,* 275 A.2d 495 (Md. 1971).]

7. A partnership was formed for the production of a movie. The members were Rose, a film specialist, Young, a producer, and Cominas and Greenberg, who were scriptwriters. Rose contributed his camera, film, for which he would be reimbursed, as well as services and cash. All the other partners contributed services only. The agreement provided for an equal division of profits. When 80 percent of the picture had been made, Greenberg was terminated by the partners. He sued the partners for one-fourth of the net profits of the movie. The lower court found his termination was not justified and awarded him his agreed share of the profits. Defendants appealed and argue that he is only entitled to compensation for his services up to the date of termination. Is Greenberg entitled to share in the profits? [*Greenberg v. Rose,* 342 P.2d 522 (Cal. 1959).]

8. Cook, the plaintiff, brought this action against Vennigerholz, the widow of his deceased partner, for an accounting of amounts due—namely, interest on advances made in payment of taxes. The partnership was formed to buy and develop land. During the term of the partnership from 1940 to 1952, Cook paid all the taxes on the land. Is Cook entitled to a credit for payment of the taxes plus interest? [*Cook v. Vennigerholz*, 269 P.2d 824 (Wash. 1954).]

9. Harris, the president of defendant company, International Realty Ltd., formed a partnership with a group of physicians to purchase an apartment house under construction as a good "tax shelter." Harris stated the purchase price as $1,010,000 but failed to disclose that it could have been purchased for $907,500. Harris also did not disclose to his partners that the defendant, of which he was the president and major stockholder, would receive a $100,000 commission. The doctors, plaintiffs, brought this suit to require Harris to account to the partnership for the commission received by him without their consent. Harris claims that the doctors knew someone was going to make a commission and, therefore, no disclosure was required. You decide. [*Starr v. International Realty Ltd.*, 533 P.2d 165 (Or. 1975).]

10. In light of the case of *Kelsey-Seybold Clinic v. Maclay*, 466 S.W.2d 716 (Tex. 1971),[8] if you were a partner in a partnership, what basic guidelines would you help to establish and observe so that matters of partner impropriety could be so handled as to minimize the risk of partnership liability for such impropriety?

---

[8] See pp. 713–14.

Special Ventures 39

After you have read this chapter, you should be able to:

1. Define a limited partnership.
2. Explain the liability of:
   a. a general partner.
   b. a limited partner.
3. Explain how a limited partnership is formed.
4. Define a joint venture.
5. Define a mining partnership.
6. Explain a business trust.
7. Explain an unincorporated association.
8. Define a joint-stock company.
9. Define and explain a franchise.
10. Explain the relationship of a trademark to a franchise; define a trademark.

Introduction

When you enter business you will find that there are many different kinds of business all operating within some kind of formal or loose business structure. We have just discussed the ordinary partnership, and in chapters 40–44 we will study the corporation. There are still other forms of business organization which are likely to have importance for you, as a participant in one or more of them, or because you have dealings with them. It is therefore important for you to have an opportunity to learn about them, their character, their legal status, and their liability.

Special Venture Organizations

Limited Partnership

limited partnership
a partnership of one or more general partners and one or more limited partners formed in compliance with the Uniform Limited Partnership Act

The **limited partnership** is a noncorporate business organization that protects the capital investor from liability for losses beyond the investment. It is a form of partnership that can be created only in states that have adopted the Uniform Limited Partnership Act (U.L.P.A.). This entitles a limited partner to share profits without sharing losses beyond his investment. The general partners manage the business.

A limited partnership is a partnership formed by two or more persons . . . having as members one or more general partners and one or more limited partners. [U.L.P.A., section 1.]

Notice that each limited partnership must have at least one general partner with unlimited liability.

The U.L.P.A. was revised in 1976 and is now being considered by the various states. Because the revised Act has not been adopted widely yet, this text will deal only with the current adopted 1916 Act. However, a few comments about the new 1976 Act will be made at the end of this section.

Formation. The partners must sign and swear to a limited partnership *certificate* that states the firm name, character, location, names and addresses of general and limited partners and their investment and share of the profits, and other information. The certificate must be filed with the "designated official" (usually in the county clerk's office or the registry of deeds) where the firm is doing business. A limited partnership can be formed only by *complete* or *substantial* compliance in good faith with the statutory requisites.

In the following case a limited partner was held not to be liable as a general partner because of minor defects in the partnership certificate because the creditor seeking recovery was not misled by it.

Facts

Griffith was a limited partner in Midfield Packing. A number of minor errors were made in filing the limited partnership certificate. Rathke, a partnership creditor, brought suit against both Griffith and the general partners. The lower court found that Griffith would be liable as a general partner because of the minor defects in the partnership certificate. Will minor defects in forming a limited partnership subject the limited partner to unlimited liability?

Decision

No. Judgment for Griffith, the limited partner.

Reasoning

The general rule is that minor technical defects will not subject the limited partner to liability unless creditors were misled and suffered financial loss to them.

Rathke v. Griffith, 218 P.2d 757 (Wash. 1950).

A limited partner's *capital* contribution can be only cash or other property, but not services. He may be *employed* by the firm to render services and be paid for his work like anyone else.

Liability of a Limited Partner. The limited partners are not personally liable for firm debts *provided that they do not participate in firm management.* They are non-participating investors. The *general* partners have the duty to manage and control the firm and, therefore, are personally liable for the firm's obligations. If a limited partner does engage in firm management and hence "takes part in the *control* of the business," he will be held *personally* liable for firm debts. What constitutes "taking part in the control of the business" is not clearly defined. U.L.P.A., section 5 generally prohibits the use of a limited partner's surname (last name) as part of the firm name, unless it is the same as that of a general partner or it appeared in the partnership name before he became a limited partner. The limited partner is liable to the partnership for capital contributions to the firm that he agreed in the certificate of partnership that he would make but had not yet made. When creditors have a claim against the firm, a limited partner can not withdraw his capital contribution.

A managing general partner may desire to invest in the limited partnership and thereby become a limited partner. U.L.P.A., section 12(2) provides for this and grants to him all the rights and duties of a general partner.

Rights of a Limited Partner. U.L.P.A., section 10 provides that a limited partner shall have the following rights:

1. to inspect and copy partnership books;
2. to have on demand true and full information of all things affecting the partnership, and a formal account of partnership affairs whenever circumstances render it just and reasonable;
3. to have a dissolution and winding up by decree of court; and
4. to receive a share of the profits or other compensation by way of income, and to the return of his contribution as provided in the partnership certificate, except as otherwise provided in the U.L.P.A., sections 15 and 16.

Figure 39.1 Form of Limited Partnership Certificate

FORM OF LIMITED PARTNERSHIP CERTIFICATE

We, the undersigned, for the purpose of forming a limited partnership pursuant to the Uniform Limited Partnership Act as set forth in Sections _____ of the _____ Code, hereby certify:

1. **Name.** The name of the partnership is _____ .
2. **Character of Business.** The character of the business to be carried on is to engage in the business of _____ .
3. **Place of Business.** The location of the principal place of business of the partnership is _____ .
4. **General Partners.** The name and place of residence of each general partner are:

> _____   _____
> _____   _____

Limited Partners. The name and place of residence of each limited partner are:

> _____   _____
>   _____

5. **Term.** The term for which the parntership is to exist is indefinite [*or* from _____ , 19__, to the close of business on _____ , 19__, and thereafter from year to year] .
6. **Initial Contribution of Each Limited Partner.** The amount of cash and a description of and the agreed value of the other property contributed by each limited partner are:

Name	Cash	Description of Other Property	Agreed Value of Other Property
_____	_____	_____	_____
_____	_____	_____	_____

7. **Additional Contributions of Each Limited Partner.** Each limited partner may (but shall not be obliged to) make such additional contributions to the capital of the partnership as may from time to time be agreed upon by the general partners.
8. **Return of Contribution to Each Limited Partner.** The contribution of each limited partner is to be returned to him as may from time to time be agreed upon by the general partners.
9. **Profit Shares of Each Limited Partner.** The share of the profits or other compensation by way of income which each limited partner shall receive by reason of his contribution is:

> _____   _____ %
> _____   _____ %

10. **Assignment of Limited Partner's Interest.** Each limited partner is given the right to substitute an assignee as contributor in his place, provided that the assignment is approved by all the general partners.
11. **Admission of Additional Limited Partners.** The general partners are given the right to admit additional limited partners, provided that the admissions are approved by all the general partners, but in no event other than upon a cash contribution to the partnership and upon the same terms as herein expressed.
12. **Death, Retirement or Insanity of General Partner.** In the event of the death, retirement or insanity of a general partner, the remaining general partners shall have the right to continue the business of the partnership under the same name by themselves or in conjunction with any other person or persons they may select.
13. **Right of Limited Partner to Receive Property Other Than Cash.** Each limited partner is given the right to demand and receive property other than cash in return for his contribution, and the value of such property shall be that shown on the books of the partnership.

Signed the _____ day of _____ , 19__ .

[Signatures of general and limited partners]

Subscribed and sworn to before me this _____ day of _____ , 19_____ .

> _____
> Notary Public

Source: Reprinted with permission from Edmund O. Belsheim's ''Modern Legal Forms.''
Copyright © 1971 by West Publishing Co.

Liquidation. Upon liquidation, each limited partner has priority over general partners in net assets. After payment to outside partnership creditors and to limited partners who have made loans to the firm, the limited partners receive their share of profits and then their capital contribution. General partners are then paid back their loans, share of profits, and, lastly, their capital contributions.[1]

Use of Limited Partnership. The popularity of the limited partnership today is found in a venture where the investor seeks both limited liability and the right to deduct expenses and losses against their other income.[2] For example, X is a high-income earner who wants to invest in a project with high risk and high earning potential. If the project should fail, X as a limited partner can claim the loss as a deduction against his income.

(Revised) Uniform Limited Partnership Act (1976). Because of its newness, not many states have adopted the revised Act at the present time. However, a few items in the revised Act should be mentioned briefly.

Revised U.L.P.A.

The name of the limited partnership must contain the words "limited partnership" in full. The partnership must maintain a registered agent in the state for service of process on the partnership, at whose office certain partnership records shall be kept. The certificate of limited partnership must be filed in the office of the secretary of state. The capital contribution of a limited partner may be the performance of services, cash, or property.

A limited partner who actively participates in the control of the business is liable only to persons who transact business with the partnership, knowing of such participation in control. The Act also specifies (under section 303b) exactly what does *not* constitute participation in the control of the business, which should be of enormous help to courts in adopting states, namely,

1. being a contractor for, or an agent or employee of, the partnership;
2. consulting with and advising a partner with respect to the business;
3. acting as surety for the partnership;
4. approving or disapproving of an amendment to the partnership agreement; and
5. voting on various matters, such as: dissolution; winding up; the transfer of all or substantially all of the assets, or the incurring of debt, other than in the ordinary course of the business; change in the nature of the business; removal of a general partner.

Joint Venture

A **joint venture,** sometimes referred to as a joint adventure, has many characteristics similar to a partnership but is generally organized for a single transaction. Hence, it does not meet the statutory definition of a partnership under section 6 of the U.P.A., which requires the partners to "carry on" a business. It

joint venture
an association of two or more persons as co-owners to engage in a limited business transaction for a profit

---

[1] U.L.P.A., sec. 23.

[2] Int. Rev. Code of 1954, secs. 701–02 (26 U.S.C.A.).

can be defined as an association of two or more persons as co-owners to form a limited business transaction for a profit. Generally it is a single undertaking for a limited duration. For example, X and Z purchase recreational property for investment purposes. They agree to share the rental income and expenses. When the property is sold, they will share the "profits" or "gains." Both X and Z have other full-time jobs.

In the above example, X as a joint venturer has authority to bind his associate Z or the joint venture within the actual or apparent scope of his authority. Due to the narrow scope of the business, a joint venturer's authority is limited to a greater extent than that of a general partner.

The negligence of one joint associate is imputed to the others in a joint venture. Any associate may be held liable to injured third persons caused by the negligence of another associate.[3]

Because of the close similarity of a joint venture to a partnership, it is commonly held that their rights and duties are governed by the Uniform Partnership Act. Hence, the joint members have the consequent fiduciary duties to account for profits. Similar to a partnership, profits of the joint venture are taxable when earned, whether or not distributed.[4]

Joint-stock company.

Joint-Stock Company

The joint-stock company or association is generally a nonstatutory business organization with many characteristics of a corporation. Its articles of association, which need not be filed with a government office, may provide for centralization of management in a board of trustees, continuity of existence, and transferability of shares.

The popularity of the joint-stock company occurred in the early 19th century when free enterprise was rapidly expanding. Obtaining a corporate charter from the state was a difficult process. The joint-stock company, like a general partnership, required only a private contract for its existence. However, it never attained limited liability, unless a third party business creditor by contract agreed to look only to company assets. It was always liable for tort claims.

Today with the relative ease of forming a corporation, there is no need to seek corporate attributes in another business organization.

Business trust.

Business Trust

The business trust, sometimes called a Massachusetts trust, is similar to a common law trust with the trustees acting as business managers and the beneficiaries as capital investors and holders of transferable shares. The trust is formed by a trust instrument that describes the nature of the business, a description of the trust property, the trustees and their powers, the beneficiaries' interests, and the rights of creditors dealing with the trustees.

---

[3] *Keiswetter v. Rubenstein,* 209 N.W. 154 (Mich. 1926).

[4] Int. Rev. Code of 1954, sec. 761(a) (26 U.S.C.A.).

Business Organizations: A. Partnerships and Special Ventures

Early statutory law in Massachusetts did not allow corporations to deal in real property, and this was the reason for the common use of the name "business trust" and for its popularity. At one time it was not regulated nor subject to corporate taxation, and its members were free from personal liability. Legislation has gradually subjected the business trust to the same federal income taxation as corporations, and has imposed personal liability on the trustees, and also on its beneficiaries only if they have the power to control.

Generally the beneficiaries will be held personally liable for trust obligations if they have power to control the trust management. For example, if they retain powers to instruct the trustees or to alter, amend, or terminate the trust, they are held to be principals and, hence, liable to the trust creditors.

Although the trust instrument will probably state that the trustees and beneficiaries can not be held personally liable for trust debts, it has no effect against creditors who do not assent to it. For instance, if a tenant is injured due to defective stairs in a building owned and managed by a business trust, the trustees are personally liable for the damages resulting from the tort of negligence.

Notice that the court in the following case held that the plaintiff's mere knowledge of the trustee's status is not enough to relieve the trustee of liability as a contracting party. There must be an agreement to that effect to accomplish that result.

Facts

Plaintiff, Larson, entered into a construction contract with the defendant, Sylvester, as trustee of the Winchester Building Trust. Larson knew that Sylvester acted as trustee of the Winchester Building Trust but never agreed with Sylvester that he would not be held personally responsible for the contract. Was mere knowledge that Sylvester was acting as trustee enough to bind Larson to an agreement that Sylvester should not be personally liable?

Decision

No. Judgment for Larson, the plaintiff.

Reasoning

Contracts with regard to the rights and property affected by trusts are the contracts of the trustee. The trustee may avoid personal liability by agreeing with another that the latter will look only to the trust property for compensation for breach of the trust agreement and not to the trustee. The facts that Sylvester was acting as trustee of the Winchester Building Trust and not individually, and that Larson knew it, would not relieve him of liability. There must have been an agreement that the trustee, Sylvester, should not be liable personally in order to confine Larson to recourse against the trust. Mere knowledge that Sylvester was acting as trustee would not be enough to bind Larson to an agreement that Sylvester should not be personally liable.

Larson v. Sylvester, 185 N.E. 44 (Mass. 1933).

Mining Partnership

The development of oil and gas by co-owners who share the profits and losses of the operation in some states creates a distinct form of association called a mining partnership.[5] Some states have enacted statutory law that recognizes the mining partnership.[6]

Differs from Partnership. Unlike a general partnership, a mining partnership is not dissolved by the bankruptcy or death of a partner. A mining partner has limited authority to bind his co-partners although he has implied authority to charge them for necessary business expenses. Each partner is personally liable for such an expense. In the following case, the partners in a mining partnership were held to be jointly and severally liable for tortious conduct.

Facts

Plaintiff, Dunkin, acquired a three-year agricultural lease on 240 acres of land in Oklahoma. Thereafter the defendant, Mikel Drilling Co., a mining partnership, acquired oil and gas leases on a portion of the 240 acres. Plaintiff claimed that the defendant mining partners commenced drilling on his cropland and they cut his fence and left his gates down, causing injury to plaintiff's cattle when drinking oil and salt water that had flowed over and across the surface of plaintiff's land. The court found the defendants jointly and severally liable for the damage caused to the plaintiff's cattle. Are partners of a mining partnership subject to joint and several liability?

Decision

Yes. Judgment for plaintiff, Dunkin.

Reasoning

By virtue of the joint control and management of a mining partnership, every general partner is liable to third persons for all the obligations of the partnership, jointly with his co-partners.

Mikel Drilling Co. v. Dunkin, 318 P.2d 435 (Okla. 1957).

Franchising

Franchising is a composition of marketing, management, finance, and law. The marketing development of the chain store that slowly replaced the individual entrepreneur in the late 1940s initiated the phenomenal growth of franchising. The small-business owner simply could not compete with the purchasing power and advertising of the postwar chain store giants. Franchising outlets for goods and services created a new method of distribution that has affected the lives of everyone.

---

[5] *McAnally v. Cochran,* 46 P.2d 955 (Okla. 1935); mining partnership recognized by judicial decision in California, Colorado, Kansas, Kentucky, Michigan, Montana, Oklahoma, Texas, Utah, West Virginia and Wyoming.

[6] Alabama, California, Idaho, and Montana all require a written document to create a mining partnership.

Definition

Franchising is a business relationship between a *franchisor,* who markets goods or services through a *franchisee,* who has the right to use the franchisor's tradename, and trademark, and methods of operation. In return, the franchisee agrees to sell the services or products under the control of the franchisor.

Franchise.

Why franchise? Any company that has established a sound business may consider the advantages of becoming a franchisor. The franchisor has a controlled outlet enabling it to maintain its reputation and goodwill for its merchandise. The distribution takes place over a large geographic area. The franchisor will sell a franchise for a fee that provides it with a source of capital for further expansion. Other advantages allow the franchisor to have independent operators run the various franchises and purchase merchandise from their designated suppliers.

The court in the following case upheld the right of a franchisor to compel their franchisees to buy only from designated suppliers and sell only approved products.

Facts

Thomas Carvel, president of Carvel Corporation, defendant, went into the ice cream business in 1934. In 1948 the business issued franchises and sold freezers for the operation of soft ice cream stores under the Carvel name. This is an action by franchise operators under franchise agreements with Carvel Corporation claiming that the supplier, H.P. Hood & Sons, and Carvel Corporation violated the antitrust laws by their refusal to deal directly with them. The franchisees allege that they have the right to purchase Carvel Mix ice cream, made pursuant to Carvel's secret formula, other than on the terms Carvel Corporation prescribed in the franchise agreement. Did Carvel Corporation violate the antitrust laws by requiring its franchise operators to deal only with its supplier of ice cream, H.P. Hood & Sons?

Decision

No. Judgment for defendant, Carvel Corporation.

Reasoning

Carvel Corporation had the right to bind the dairy companies to manufacture this secret formula mix solely for its own use or for persons whom it might designate. No outsider, without Carvel Corporation's approval, had the right to require the dairy companies to sell them this special formula mix. The plaintiff did not contend that Carvel Corporation engaged in any common conspiracy with the supplier, H.P. Hood & Sons.

Susser v. Carvel Corporation, 206 F.Supp 636 (1962).

Trademark

Trademark.

A company that desires to franchise should acquire federal registration in the United States Patent Office of its trademark and tradename. The Lanham Act in section 5 defines a trademark as "any word, name, symbol, or device, or any combination thereof adopted and used by manufacturer or merchant to identify his goods and distinguish them from those manufactured by others." Once the trademark is registered, the owner may grant to another (the franchisee) the right to use it in accordance with the franchise contract. Well known trademarks are McDonald, Shell, Holiday Inn, etc.

Exclusivity

The franchise contract includes a provision that designates a geographical area where the franchisee can operate.

The court in the following case found no antitrust violation in an exclusive dealership franchise.

Facts

Hudson, the defendant, urged Schwing, the plaintiff, a Ford dealer in Baltimore, to establish a Hudson agency in the Baltimore area. Schwing agreed to become a master franchise dealer for Hudson upon assurance that Schwing would receive an annual quota of 150 Hudson automobiles. Thereafter Bankert was granted an exclusive dealership franchise with Hudson and opened in Baltimore. Schwing's dealership was not renewed. Plaintiff claims that the purpose of the nonrenewal was to eliminate him from competition with Bankert and thereby create a monopoly in the Baltimore area to the end that higher prices might be obtained from the public. May Hudson grant an exclusive dealership and thereby give a dealer an actual monopoly?

Decision

Yes. Judgment for defendant, Hudson Sales Corporation.

Reasoning

Every *manufacturer* has a natural and complete monopoly on his particular product, especially when sold under his own brand or tradename. A manufacturer may prefer to deal with one person rather than another, and may grant exclusive dealership to sell in a particular territory. An exclusive dealership to sell in a particular area is not invalid. The public was not injured since the automobile market remained in its normal competitive state. Unless the manufacturer dominates the market, he has the right to give a dealer an actual monopoly.

Schwing Motor Company v. Hudson Sales Corporation, 138 F.Supp. 899 (1956).

"Tying Arrangement." Many franchisors recognize the importance of a location. Hence they purchase the buildings and lease the premises to a franchisee. To ensure a standardized image and decor, the layout, design, and equipment are considered part of the trademark image. The items in the "franchise package" must all interrelate as part of the franchise outlet in order to justify its anticompetitive effect; otherwise the franchise arrangement will be held to be illegal.

Service or Product Control

The franchisor has an interest in maintaining the good will of the business that the purchasing public has come to associate with its tradename. Hence a common provision found in a franchising contract obligates the franchisee to purchase *all* its products from the franchisor or its authorized suppliers. Since this is "full-line" forcing—that is, a *full* line of products must be taken by the franchisee in order to obtain *any* of the franchisor's products—such an arrangement is *not* an unlawful tying under the Clayton Antitrust Act.

Termination

If a court finds that the franchisee operates the franchise in violation of an agreed standard, it will allow the franchisor to terminate the contract, as is illustrated by the following case.

Facts

Plaintiff, Seegmiller, claimed that the defendant, Western Men, Inc., wrongfully terminated an employment agency service franchise. Seegmiller agreed to operate the franchise in an office properly identified as Western Men, Inc. in a suitable place in a downtown office building. Seegmiller did not do so, but rather attempted to carry on the business by telephone from her house. Was the defendant justified in terminating the franchise?

Decision

Yes. Judgment for the defendant.

Reasoning

Franchise contracts are almost always drawn up by the franchisor and are presented to the dealer for acceptance and signature rather than for negotiation as to terms. When there is no express provision that it may be cancelled without cause, it is fair to assume that both parties intended that, if services are performed in a satisfactory manner, it will not be cancelled arbitrarily. The requirement of a suitable office was material to the proper performance of the franchise contract, and its noncompliance was proper grounds for termination.

Seegmiller v. Western Men, Inc., 437 P.2d 892 (Utah 1968).

Summary Statement

1. A limited partnership is a partnership formed by two or more persons having as members one or more general partners and one or more limited partners. A limited partner shall not become liable as a general partner unless he takes part in the control of the business.
2. (a) The general partners in a limited partnership are personally liable for partnership debts. (b) The limited partners are liable to the partnership for capital contributions to the firm which they agreed in the certificate of partnership that they would make but had not yet made.
3. A limited partnership must be formed by a signed and sworn certificate, which generally is filed in the county clerk's office or the registry of deeds where the firm business is carried on.
4. A joint venture is an association of two or more persons organized as co-owners to engage in a *limited* business transaction for a profit.
5. A mining partnership is an association of co-owners organized to develop oil and gas production and share the profits and losses. It is not dissolved by the death or bankruptcy of a partner.

6. A business trust is formed by a trust instrument with the trustees acting as business managers and the beneficiaries as capital investors and holders of transferable shares. The beneficiaries will be held personally liable for trust obligations only if they have power to control the trust management.

7. A joint-stock company is a nonstatutory business organization created by contract that provides for centralized management and transferability of shares. It is generally taxable as a corporation with unlimited liability for its members.

8. Franchising is a contractual arrangement whereby one party, the franchisor, consents to another party, the franchisee, using its tradename, trademark, supplied products, equipment, and managerial expertise. The franchisee agrees to sell the services or products under the control and supervision of the franchisor.

The court in the following case examined the issue of when a limited partner becomes liable as a general partner. The Uniform Limited Partnership Act in section 7 provides: "A limited partner shall not become liable as a general partner unless, in addition to the exercise of his rights and powers as a limited partner, he takes part in the control of the business." Note how the court must examine the evidence introduced in order to determine the degree of the limited partner's participation in the control of the business.

Plasteel Products Corp. v. Helman
271 F.2d 354 (1959)

This is an appeal from a judgment of the United States District Court for the District of Massachusetts entered following the allowance of appellees' motions for summary judgment.

Plaintiff, a Pennsylvania corporation, sued appellees, among others, all Massachusetts citizens, as "co-partners doing business as Copley Steel Products Company" for $6,555.29 as unpaid balance for merchandise sold and delivered to Copley. Several of the defendants filed motions for summary judgment on the ground that they were limited partners only, and submitted uncontradicted supporting affidavits.

The question of law involved here is whether Mass. Gen. Laws Ann. c. 109, sec. 7 (Uniform Limited Partnership Act), makes appellees liable as general partners as a result of their execution of the December 1955 agreement. This section reads: "A limited partner shall not become liable as a general partner unless, in addition to exercise of his rights and powers as a limited partner, he takes part in the control of the business."

Plaintiff-appellant contends that appellees took part in the control of the business by the selection of Paul L. Sriberg as general sales manager and by providing for joint control by him and the general partner of financial aspects of the business.

Appellees contend that the absence of tenure provisions for Paul L. Sriberg negates any purpose of appellees to control the partnership; that the disputed provisions of the agreement evince only a desire for Paul L. Sriberg's services and a willingness both to concede some profits to obtain his services and to allow some protection for the Sriberg Trust interest. Appellees also contend that none of the decided cases interpreting and applying section 7 would support a holding of general liability here.

There are very few cases which afford much assistance in the interpretation and application of section 7. The cases applying statutes in force prior to the Uniform Limited Partnership Act cannot be relied on since the uniform Act was drawn to overcome the strict interpretations which were frustrating the purpose of statutory limited partnerships.

The cases that do interpret and apply section 7 contain some elements which aid in reaching a decision here. In *Rathke v. Griffith . . .* the co-partners had drawn bylaws that provided that the affairs of the partnership should be handled by a board of directors and named the defendant, a purported limited partner, as one of the directors. But in view of testimony that the defendant had never functioned as a director, the court refused to hold that this arrangement itself constituted participation in control of the business sufficient to make the defendant generally liable. In the instant case the only conduct relied on to charge appellees as general partners is the signing of the limited partnership agreement. By analogy to the Rathke case, this does not constitute participation such as to impose general liability.

Paul L. Sriberg could have been discharged at any time by the general partner. This would lead to the surrender of the interest of the trust for his children and the end of any necessity for joint signing by Sriberg and the general partner. This factor makes the case somewhat analogous to *Grainger v. Antoyan* . . . in which the defendant was authorized to cosign the checks, but they also could be signed without him. There the court held that, with no other evidence of taking part in control of the business, the defendant was not subject to general liability. The power here to discharge Sriberg and terminate any apparent control clearly distinguishes this case from *Holzman v. DeEscamilla, . . .* in which the purported limited partners were necessary to the issuance of any checks, and, indeed, could issue checks without the general partner's approval. There, general liability was imposed.

In our view of these cases the ground solely relied on by the appellant to charge appellees with general liability is insufficient to constitute taking part in the control of the business.

Questions and Case Problems

1. Kitchell Corporation sued John Hermansen to recover money due to it under a promissory note. The note was signed by "John Hermansen, President of Arizona-Utah Investment Company, a limited partnership." Is John Hermansen individually liable as the general partner of Arizona-Utah Land Investment Company, and may a corporation be a general partner of a limited partnership? [*Kitchell Corp. v. Hermansen,* 446 P.2d 934 (Ariz. 1968).]

2. Rowlett and McRea were co-partners of a limited partnership in the automobile sales and repair business, doing business as McRea Motor Co. The plaintiff, Silvola, is an accountant who sued Rowlett for money due for accounting services rendered to McRea Motor Co., claiming that Rowlett was

a general rather than a limited partner. Rowlett, a limited partner under the partnership agreement, was the foreman of the automobile repair shop but in all business matters acted under the direction and control of McRea. McRea was the general partner and Rowlett the sole limited partner. Rowlett contributed tools and cash when the limited partnership was formed. Did Rowlett become liable as a general partner by providing services to the partnership as foreman to the automobile repair shop? [*Silvola v. Rowlett*, 272 P.2d 287 (Colo. 1954).]

3. Plaintiff, Polikoff, and Levy, the defendant, with others, formed a joint venture known as the State House Inn. The members, over the objection of the plaintiff, caused all of the assets to be transferred to a new corporation, the State House Inn, Inc. Polikoff brought this suit claiming that co-venturers can not arbitrarily dispose of the assets of the venture over the objection of one co-venturer. He asked the court to have the assets disposed of by a judicial sale. You decide. [*Polikoff v. Levy*, 270 N.E.2d 540 (Ill. 1971).]

4. Frigidaire Sales Corporation, plaintiff, entered into a contract with Commercial Investors, a limited partnership. Mannon and Baxter, the defendants, were the limited partners of Commercial and were also officers, directors, and shareholders of Union Properties, Inc., the only general partner of Commercial Investors. Mannon and Baxter controlled Union Properties, and through their control of Union Properties they exercised the day-to-day control and management of Commercial. Commercial breached the contract, and Frigidaire Sales Corporation brought suit against Union Properties and Mannon and Baxter individually. Did Mannon and Baxter incur general liability for Commercial's obligations by reason of their control over the general partner, Union Properties, Inc.? [*Frigidaire Sales Corporation v. Union Properties, Inc.*, 562 P.2d 244 (Wash. 1977).]

5. Fidelity Lease Limited, defendant, is a limited partnership organized to lease restaurant locations. It is composed of 22 limited partners and a corporate general partner, Interlease Corporation. Interlease's officers, directors, and shareholders were Crombie, Kahn, and Sanders, who were also limited partners of Fidelity. Delaney, the plaintiff, is a building contractor who entered into an agreement with the limited partnership, Fidelity, acting by and through its corporate general partner, Interlease, to lease a fast-food restaurant to the partnership. Delaney built the restaurant, but Fidelity failed to take possession or pay rent. Delaney brought suit for damages for breach of the lease agreement, naming as defendants the limited partnership of Fidelity Lease Limited, its corporate general partner, Interlease Corporation, and all of its limited partners individually. Are Crombie, Kahn, and Sanders—the officers, directors, and shareholders of Interlease—personally liable? [*Delaney v. Fidelity Lease Limited*, 526 S.W.2d 543 (Tex. 1975).]

6. North Dade Imported Motors was an authorized dealer in the Miami area, Florida, in 1956. Brundage Motors was distributor for Volkswagon products in Florida. Prior to granting North Dade a franchise for 1960, Brundage: required that North Dade construct new facilities of the type and design requested by Brundage Motors and that a manager of Brundage's choice run the business; specified how many vehicles North Dade had to sell, what parts it had to stock, the type used and the manner of keeping its books, and who could own

its stock. North Dade complied with these requirements. Brundage Motors requested North Dade to change its present and general manager due to a decline in sales. Brundage forced North Dade to sell the business dealership to a person of Brundage's choosing upon the terms and conditions dictated by Brundage. North Dade refused to do so, and Brundage therefore ceased shipping parts and vehicles to North Dade and ceased advertising North Dade as an authorized Volkswagon dealer. North Dade sued Brundage for breach of its franchise agreement. Was Brundage's conduct an unfair trade practice? [*North Dade Imported Motors, Inc. v. Brundage Motors, Inc.,* 221 So.2d 170 (Fla. 1969).]

7. Loomis Land & Cattle Co., plaintiff, brought suit to enjoin the sale of a shopping center under the terms of a note and deed executed by Loomis Land & Cattle Co. and Richard Loomis as guarantor to the defendant, Diversified Mortgage Investors. The right to have the sale enjoined was based upon the ground that Diversified Mortgage was a Massachusetts business trust and not a recognizable entity under the laws of Texas and was, therefore, without standing in court to pursue any of the remedies arising under the sales contract. Defendant argues that it has standing to sue in the Texas courts because a Massachusetts trust is to be treated as an unincorporated joint-stock company. May a state regard a Massachusetts business trust as a joint-stock company? [*Loomis Land & Cattle Company v. Diversified Mortgage Investors,* 533 S.W.2d 420 (Tex. 1976).]

8. Richardson, the plaintiff and co-trustee of a business trust, brought this action to nullify two leases and a purchase and sale agreement executed by two of the three trustees. The Brattle Craigie Trust was created in 1913 by Joseph Clarke and two other individuals under a declaration of trust for the purpose of "purchasing, improving, holding, managing, disposing and otherwise dealing with real estate." In September 1942, by a unanimous vote of all the business trustees, including Richardson, the instrument creating the Brattle Craigie Trust was amended to permit the powers of the business trustees to be exercised by a majority. Richardson, the plaintiff, now contends that the amendment is invalid because it deprives the trustees of their power and duty to control the operation of the business trust. May a business trust be amended to provide for majority control of trust business? [*Richardson v. Clarke,* 364 N.E.2d 804 (Mass. 1977).]

9. The Olympic Limited Partnership owns and manages many buildings. Mrs. Jones is a limited partner employed by the partnership with full responsibility for the management of one of the partnership's large apartment buildings, for which she is paid a substantial salary. Does she thereby participate in the control of the partnership and thus become liable as a general partner? Explain your answer.

10. After reading the case of *Plasteel Products Corp. v. Helman,* 271 F.2d 354 (1959),[7] what specific additional conduct by Mr. Sriberg would cause him to participate in the control of the limited partnership and thereby become liable as a general partner? Explain your answer.

---

[7] See pp. 728–29.

40. Nature and Classes
The background, concept, and need for the corporate form of legal entity, created with permission of the state or federal governments. The various kinds of corporation are examined.

41. Creation and Termination
The statutory requirements for creation and termination of a corporation, as well as the function and liability of promoters.

42. Corporate Powers
The source, nature, and extent of corporate express and implied power or authority without which a corporation could not function. The effect of corporate conduct which exceeds its powers is also considered.

43. Corporate Stock and Shareholders
The meaning of corporate stock owned by shareholders, and the various kinds of shares, rights of shareholders, and transferability of shares.

44. Corporate Management
How a corporation actually operates; the functions of the board of directors and corporate officers who participate in that operation as managers, and their duties, powers, and liability. The managerial function of shareholders is examined also.

Summary

The need for corporations in a government-regulated free-enterprise system is discussed, followed by a brief history of the corporation and descriptions of the various kinds. You will see how a corporation is formed and dissolved. The powers granted to a corporation by the state are reviewed. As you will probably own stock in a corporation, the rights of stockholders are explained as well as the few instances when a shareholder may be held personally liable. Finally, the managerial functions of a corporation's officers and directors are discussed from a legal viewpoint.

40 Nature and Classes

After you have read this chapter, you should be able to:

1. Define a corporation.
2. Explain "limited liability."
3. Identify the source of corporation law.
4. Explain the contribution to corporate law from the following:
   a. Roman law.
   b. Canon law.
   c. Civil law.
   d. Common law.
   e. Overseas trading companies.
   f. Model Business Corporation Act.
5. List and explain the classification of corporations.
6. Explain what is meant by "doing business" in a foreign state.
7. List activities that generally do not constitute transacting business in a foreign state.
8. Explain what is a "resident agent" and what is his purpose.
9. Explain how private corporations are regulated by the government.
10. Explain the constitutional restrictions on government regulation of a corporation.
11. Explain what is meant by disregarding the corporate entity and when the court may do so.
12. List and explain the corporate attributes.
13. Explain what is a Subchapter S corporation.
14. Explain what is meant by "piercing the corporate veil."

Introduction

You are one of five people who wish to engage in business together but who have two main problems: they need capital, the money to get the business started and operating; and they don't want to have the risk of their individual properties being available to pay creditors of the business. They also want to be able to transfer their shares or interests in the business easily to other persons without affecting the continuation of the business. The corporation came into being as a result of these and other needs.

Nature

A **corporation** is a legal entity created by statute authorizing an association of persons to carry on an enterprise. The corporation exists as a *legal person* with many powers. For example, it can own property, real and personal, in its own name; make contracts; incur debts; issue stocks and bonds; and sue and be sued. As a legal person, its owners, the **shareholders** or stockholders, are distinct from the legal entity and can not be sued for corporate liabilities. This is known as *limited liability*—that is, the corporate investor's risk is limited to the loss of his investment. A shareholder can not be held personally liable for corporate debts. For example, if you purchased **shares of stock** for $5,000, corporate creditors could not sue you personally, although your investment may be lost.

A corporation is granted its existence from the state. The formation of a corporation, under modern statutory law, is accomplished by submitting to the secretary of state a document called the *articles of incorporation*. The articles, discussed in a later chapter, identify the name and location of the corporation, the nature of its business, the directors, officers, and authorized capitalization.

Larger business organizations function as corporations because the corporate form affords them the many advantages of *corporate attributes*. They consist of:

1. the ability to raise substantial capital by dividing its ownership into *shares of stock* that may be sold to the general public;
2. the ability to continue in existence upon the death of an owner, called *perpetual succession;*
3. an easy method of *transferring* corporate stock;
4. the *centralization of management* by a board of directors;
5. the *limited liability* of its stock investors;
6. the *legal entity theory* that creates an artificial person liable for its obligations.

Historical Background

Roman Law

The concept of the government creating an "artificial person" with certain characteristics having legal status has an ancient origin. During the early Roman Republic various religious, educational, and governmental groups began to develop. The Roman Empire's rulers, desiring control over these groups, granted them legal authorization only by express approval. This created the origin of a business association requiring governmental authorization.

Canon Law

The law of the Roman Catholic Church affected corporate law by regulating ecclesiastical property ownership. Pope Innocent IV (1243–1254) developed the concept of an "artificial person" that would own church property and permit its use without personal ownership by the clergy, thus creating the principle of a legal entity separate and distinct from its owners.

Civil Law

A codified legal system based on the Roman law also recognizes the corporation as a separate entity. The codification of the civil law in some European countries adopted many characteristics of the Roman law.

Common Law

In England, as early as the 14th century, many ecclesiastical, charitable, and municipal corporations developed. Their most common trait was *perpetual existence,* which became a corporate characteristic.

Overseas Trading Companies

The British government granted powers to explore, trade with, and colonize foreign territory. The British East India Company (1600), the Virginia Company (1609)—which founded the Virginia Colony and brought the Pilgrims to America—and the South Sea Company (1711) are examples of business associations that were the prototypes of the modern business corporation.

The United States enacted corporate laws as early as 1795 in North Carolina. A 20th century demand to incorporate created a need to modernize corporate law, which led to the development of the Model Business Corporation Act (MBCA) first published in 1946. The Act was last revised in 1979. Many states have amended their corporate law statutes in accordance with the MBCA. Today, in most states, filing the articles of incorporation, paying the necessary fee, and getting state approval cause the creation of an "artificial legal person"—the corporation.

Classification of Corporations

The needs of our society are commonly provided for by corporate institutions. For example, educational and health care needs are served by colleges and hospitals that may be *nonprofit corporations*. When the general public is served by the corporation—for example, a municipality—it is a *public corporation*. If substantial business is carried on in interstate commerce, it is a *foreign corporation* in other than its state of origin.

Public, Private, and Quasi-Public Corporations

A *public corporation* is one organized by the state or federal government to administer government affairs. The government may then employ recognized business procedures in such matters as the purchase of property and management of its functions. For example, a city is a *municipal public corporation* granted authority to operate by the state.

Private corporations are created by private parties and may serve a profit or nonprofit purpose but not a governmental function. For instance, the national corporations that constitute our free-enterprise system are private corporations although their stock is sold to the public. They engage in business for a *profit* and to provide a return on the stockholder's investment by way of a *dividend*. Private corporations are now highly regulated by governmental agencies such as the Department of Labor and the Federal Trade Commission.[1] Most of our discussion in these chapters on corporations will be concerned with the private corporation organized for a profit and selling its stock to the public. They are "business corporations" and sometimes referred to as "public" because of their stock ownership.

Quasi-public corporations are known as "public service corporations." They provide services that the general public has an interest in, such as supplying gas and electricity and operating railroads. Because of their public involvement, they are subjected to greater governmental regulation than private corporations.

Domestic and Foreign Corporations

A *domestic corporation* is a corporation formed and created under the laws of the state that granted its corporate charter. In all other states or countries it is a *foreign corporation*. For example, if you were to incorporate in Massachusetts but did extensive business in New York and Florida and all the stockholders reside in Connecticut, you would be a domestic corporation in Massachusetts and a foreign corporation in New York and Florida.

It is not unusual for many large corporations to do business in several states. When a foreign corporation transacts business in a *substantial and continuous manner as opposed to a casual transaction,* it must obtain permission for this intrastate business in the foreign state. For example, if a corporate representative procured purchase orders in Texas that would be accepted by a Massachusetts corporation in Massachusetts, where its permanent corporate office was located, it would not be "doing business" in Texas.

. . . a foreign corporation shall not be considered to be transacting business in this state . . . by reason of carrying on . . . any of the following activities:
1) Holding meetings of its directors or shareholders or carrying on other activities concerning its internal affairs
2) maintaining bank accounts
3) effecting sales through independent contractors
4) transacting business in interstate commerce . . . [MBCA, sec. 106].

---

[1] See chapters 32–34 on government regulation of business.

In the following case the court notes the question of "doing business" must be resolved upon the facts of each particular case.

Facts

Plaintiff, Boney, a resident of South Carolina, brought this action for injury sustained while traveling downstream on the Savannah River. The defendant, Trans-State Dredging Co., a Florida corporation, for over ten months had been performing dredging operations in South Carolina. Boney signaled for permission to pass Trans-State's dredge and was signaled by the defendant to proceed. The dredge shifted its position, causing a cable running from it to rise up and overturn the plaintiff's boat. Pursuant to statute, the Secretary of State of South Carolina was served a substitute summons, and the defendant moved to set aside the service as ineffectual to bring the defendant within the jurisdiction of the court. Was the defendant "doing business" in South Carolina at the time of the accident?

Decision

Yes. Judgment for plaintiff.

Reasoning

No universal formula has been devised for determining what constitutes "doing business" by a foreign corporation within a state so as to subject it to the jurisdiction of the courts of that state. The question must be resolved upon the facts of the particular case. Defendant's operations extended over a continuous period of more than ten months and over an area of one hundred and forty-two miles of the Savannah River, the middle of which is the boundary between South Carolina and Georgia. We are of the opinion that the defendant's operations, although not continuously performed in South Carolina, constituted corporate activity within that state sufficient to satisfy the "doing business" test and, therefore, to render the defendant subject to the jurisdiction of the court.

Boney v. Trans-State Dredging Co., 115 S.E.2d 508 (S.C. 1960).

State corporate statutes require a foreign corporation that intends to do intrastate business to procure a *certificate of authority*. The application generally requires filing the foreign corporation's articles of incorporation with the secretary of state and paying the filing fee. Of most importance is the name and office address of the corporation's registered agent to receive service of process in the event the foreign corporation is sued.

In the following case the court reviewed the corporate activity in the foreign state and, although the corporation appeared to have only *casual transactions*, filing in the foreign state was nevertheless required to comply with the foreign state statute.

Facts

Plaintiff, Sinwellan Corporation, organized under the laws of Maryland, brought this action against the defendant, Farmers Bank of the State of Delaware, alleging that Farmers wrongfully dishonored certain checks drawn on Sinwellan's checking account. Farmers Bank brought a motion to dismiss the complaint on the grounds that Sinwellan is a "foreign corporation" doing business in Delaware and it has not filed the

Business Organizations: B. Corporations

appropriate certificate with the secretary of state and hence has no right to sue in Delaware.

Sinwellan maintained a Delaware bank account in its corporate name, advertised in two Delaware newspapers, stored its financial records in Delaware, executed contracts with Delaware residents in Delaware, sold securities and engaged in credit transactions with Delaware residents, and provided a taxi service in Delaware.

The lower court applied the "doing business" test and found the activities inadequate to require filing and hence denied the defendant's motion to dismiss the complaint.

Decision
Reversed. Judgment for defendant.

Reasoning
The Maryland statute on foreign corporations requires it to file a certificate stating the name and address of its registered agent in Maryland. The primary object of the statute is to secure to the state and its people a way to serve process on a corporation which is organized elsewhere and which comes here to act through officers or agents. Given the scope of intrastate activities in which Sinwellan is engaged, the statute requires that it formalize its presence here through the nomination of a registered agent, the identification of an office, and by otherwise complying with the Maryland statute.

Farmers Bank v. Sinwellan Corporation, 367 A.2d 180 (Del. 1976).

Foreign corporations are subject to the foreign state regulating agencies and corporate state taxation.

Close Corporations

It is a common misconception that the corporate organization with its many advantages is reserved for "big business." Many small companies desire to incorporate and thereby obtain limited liability. In a *close corporation* the stock is generally owned by one individual or his family. Hence, the managerial control of the corporation is in the owners. The closely held stock is not traded publicly, and the business is referred to as a close corporation. It has a separate corporate entity with all the corporate attributes of any corporation. Many state statutes authorize one person to incorporate, own all the stock, and serve as sole director and president.[2]

Subchapter S Corporation

Profits earned by a corporation normally are taxed two times! First the *corporation* is taxed on the profits and then, on distribution of the profits as corporate dividends to shareholders, the *shareholders* must include such dividends as taxable income in their income tax returns.

Under the federal Internal Revenue Code, shareholders of certain closely held *small* business corporations may elect to be *individually* taxed as partners.[3] If the corporation qualifies, the individual shareholders are taxed on their shares of the corporation's income, or can deduct their proportionate share of its losses.

---

[2] See, for example, MASS. GEN. LAWS, ch. 156, A sec. 8 (1963).

[3] Int. Rev. Code of 1958, subch. S, secs. 1371–1377 (26 U.S.C.A.).

The corporation, as an entity, pays no *federal* income tax. (It may have to pay a state corporate income tax.) Hence, the shareholders are relieved of the double-tax burden on corporate income—namely, a corporate tax on the profit when made and also a tax on the dividend when the profits are distributed. The sub-chapter S corporation must have no more than fifteen shareholders of the same class of stock, with many other requirements to qualify under the Internal Revenue Code. Because of the tax advantages, a small closely held corporation should always investigate the feasibility of a subchapter S election.

Professional Corporations

As the result of professional groups attempting to obtain various corporate advantages by way of tax-sheltered qualified pension and profit-sharing plans and other employee fringe benefits, every state has enacted corporate legislation allowing professionals to incorporate their practice. Members of the professions have found themselves annually confronted with a substantial tax liability because of their status as employers or proprietorships or partnerships. By incorporating their practice, they become owner-employees and are thereby eligible to participate in employee fringe benefits such as pension and profit-sharing plans. Contributions to these plans are tax deductible by the professional corporation, and the trust income invested is tax free until distributed to the employees at retirement.

Nonprofit Corporations

A *nonprofit* (eleemosynary) corporation is organized for charitable purposes, examples being colleges and hospitals. Because they are given preferential tax treatment, special statutes govern their formation and operation.[4]

Corporate Regulations

Our economy may be described today as a highly regulated free-enterprise system. If you were to incorporate, state statutory law would grant you various corporate powers. However, as a domestic corporation in the state of formation, your company would be subject to the state tax laws and state regulating agencies. For example, if you were manufacturing raw materials, the state environmental protection agency would regulate the extent of the allowed pollution caused by the company. If you were "doing business" in a foreign state, the company would be subject to the regulating agencies and tax law of that state also. Interstate business would require you to comply with the regulations of the federal agencies, such as the Federal Trade Commission.

Constitutional Restrictions

State and federal administrative agencies are subject to certain constitutional restrictions in regulating a corporation's activities.

---

[4] See the Revenue Act of 1978 (Pub. L. 95–600), sec. 341, and amendments thereunder.

Corporation as a Legal Person

When a corporation comes into existence by filing the necessary documents with the appropriate state office, a legal entity is formed that exists independently of its owners. Today the corporation is highly regulated by various state and federal administrative agencies that have the right to review not only its books and records (e.g., the Internal Revenue Service), but also its operational procedures (e.g., the Department of Labor). As a legal person it has constitutional rights to protect itself from arbitrary governmental intervention. For example, an administrative summons issued by the I.R.S. to review corporate books and records is subject to a court "show cause" hearing.

The United States Constitution allows the corporation the right of the "people" under the Fourth Amendment (to be secure against unreasonable searches and seizures), the Fifth Amendment (right not to be deprived of liberty or property without due process of law), and the Fourteenth Amendment (the right not to be denied the equal protection of the laws). State constitutions commonly have similar restrictions. In the following case a state court held a state statute violative of the state and federal constitutions' equal protection and due process clauses.

Facts

This is a criminal action prosecuted by the State of Michigan against the defendant, John McDonald, a licensed cosmetologist, for cutting the hair of a male without obtaining a barber's license. The Michigan Barber Licensing and Regulation Act permits a licensed barber to cut the hair of "any person" and a licensed cosmetologist to cut the hair of "any female" and not any male person unless he or she first obtained a barber's license. McDonald challenged the statutory distinction between licensed barbers and licensed cosmetologists as violating the equal protection and due process of the state and federal constitution.

Decision

Judgment for McDonald.

Reasoning

The purpose of regulating both barbers and cosmetologists is to ensure qualified practitioners and sanitary facilities. We are unable to perceive any rational or reasonable relationship between these objectives and the restrictions of the haircutting activity of cosmetologists to female persons. There is no showing that different sanitary measures are required to cut men's hair that are not included in the sanitary requirements to cut women's hair. Cosmetologists are qualified to cut hair; they seek only to render the same service for men's hair that they already provide for women's hair. Insofar as the statute prevents cosmetologists from rendering to male patrons the same hair-cutting services they may lawfully provide to female customers, it violates the equal protection and due process clauses of the state and federal constitutions.

People v. McDonald, 240 N.W.2d 268 (Mich. 1976).

Disregard of Corporate Entity

The corporation as a legal entity distinct from its shareholders is the basis for limited liability. If the corporation is sued, the law will generally insulate the shareholders from personal liability, as is illustrated in the following case.

Facts

Plaintiff, Walkovszky, was severely injured in New York City when he was run down by a taxicab owned by the Seon Cab Corporation and negligently operated by Marchese. The defendant, Carlton, is the stockholder of ten corporations, including Seon Cab, each of which has two cabs registered in its name. Although seemingly independent of one another, the corporations are alleged to be "operated as a single entity, unit and enterprise" with regard to financing, supplies, repairs, employees, and garaging. The plaintiff asserts that he is entitled to hold Carlton personally liable as the stockholder for his damages because the multiple corporate structure constitutes an unlawful attempt "to defraud members of the general public" who might be injured by the cabs.

Decision

Judgment for the defendant, Carlton.

Reasoning

The law permits the incorporation of a business for the very purpose of enabling its proprietors to escape personal liability. The courts will disregard the corporate form to "pierce the corporate veil" whenever necessary to prevent fraud or to achieve equity. The corporation form may not be disregarded merely because the assets of the corporation are insufficient to assure the recovery sought.

Walkovszky v. Carlton, 223 N.E.2d 6 (N.Y. 1966).

The courts have the power, under certain circumstances, to treat the corporation and the shareholders as identical parties. In the following case, the court held an individual shareholder who dissolved the corporation personally liable on a corporate debt.

Facts

The plaintiff, Daisy Lee Williams, the personal representative of the deceased Daisy Burrell, brought this suit against Philip F. Cohen, who was the only stockholder, director, and officer of the dissolved Mobile Roofing and Construction Company, Inc. Daisy Burrell obtained a judgment against the Mobile Roofing and Construction Company for damages resulting from a home construction contract. When the corporation went out of business, Williams sued Cohen, the only stockholder, personally on the corporate judgment. The lower court found for Williams and Cohen appealed. Is Cohen personally liable for the corporation's debt?

Decision

Yes. Judgment for the plaintiff, Williams.

Business Organizations: B. Corporations

Reasoning

Under the evidence, this is an appropriate case to treat Mobile Roofing and Construction Company, Inc. as identical with Philip F. Cohen, the owner of all its stock and assets. A corporation is a distinct and separate entity from the individuals who compose it as stockholders or who manage it as directors or officers. In a proper case, when the corporate form is being used to evade personal responsibility, the court can impose liability on the person controlling the corporation. When Cohen dissolved the corporation, there were no assets from which the judgment could be collected. He personally assumed liability for all corporate debts except the Burrell judgment. A corporation dissolved to evade creditors can enjoy no more standing as an entity separate and apart from its sole stockholder than a corporation formed to accomplish such evasion.

Cohen v. Williams, 318 So.2d 279 (Ala. 1975).

The corporation serves as a form of legal entity to answer the needs of business society. It serves small as well as large businesses. However, because it is formed with the permission of society, it is subject to societal constraints and can not do what society condemns. When it attempts to do so, the courts will "pierce the corporate veil" and look behind the corporate legal entity to determine such impropriety.

Subsidiaries

A **subsidiary corporation** has a majority of its outstanding and issued stock owned by a parent corporation. When the parent corporation owns all the stock it is a wholly owned subsidiary. For example, a new line of merchandise may involve such a substantial risk to a corporation that it desires to fragment its liability by forming a subsidiary to sell the new products. Generally, the officers and directors of the parent corporation will also serve in the subsidiary corporation. If the parent corporation exercises control over the wholly owned subsidiary, it will be liable for the contracts and torts of the subsidiary.

subsidiary corporation
a corporation owned
by another corporation

Summary Statement

1. A corporation is a legal entity created by statute authorizing an association of individuals to carry on an enterprise.
2. The corporation as a legal person is a distinct legal entity and hence the corporate stockholders can not be sued for corporate liabilities. This is known as "limited liability." A stockholder's liability is limited to his investment.
3. Corporation law is found in state statutory law. Each state has its own corporation laws, and many have modernized them to comply with the Model Business Corporation Act.
4. Roman law required government approval for a corporation.
5. Canon law developed the concept of an "artificial person" that could own property in its own name.
6. Civil law recognized the corporation as a separate entity.

7. Common law established the perpetual existence of a corporation.
8. Corporations may be classified as:
    a. public,
    b. private,
    c. quasi-public,
    d. domestic, or
    e. foreign.
9. A foreign corporation is one that is "doing business" in a substantial and continuous manner where it was not originally organized.
10. A foreign corporation must maintain a resident agent in the foreign state to receive service of process in the event the corporation is sued.
11. Private corporations are highly regulated by the state and federal governments. As a "legal person," a corporation is entitled to many constitutional rights.
12. The courts may disregard the corporate entity and "pierce the corporate veil" whenever necessary to prevent fraud.
13. A corporation that qualifies under the Internal Revenue Code may elect to be taxed similarly to a partnership. It is referred to as a "subchapter S corporation."
14. Corporations have numerous attributes that make them a very popular form of business, namely,
    a. perpetual succession;
    b. centralization of management;
    c. no shareholder liability for corporate obligations;
    d. they may sell their stock to raise capital;
    e. ease of transferring corporate stock;
    f. the legal entity theory makes them liable for their own obligations.

In the following case, decided by the United States Supreme Court, the issue of localized *intrastate* activity is examined to determine whether a foreign corporation must qualify to do business. Because Article I, section 8 of the U.S. Constitution states that "Congress shall have power . . . to regulate commerce . . . among the several states," the states have no authority to require foreign corporate registration of *interstate* business. Notice how the court distinguishes the facts in this case from prior similar cases with respect to *intrastate activity*.

Allenberg Cotton Co., Inc. v. Pittman
419 U.S. 20 (1974)

Mr. Justice Douglas. This is an appeal from a judgment of the Supreme Court of Mississippi, which held that under the applicable Mississippi statute appellant [Allenberg Cotton Co.] might not recover damages for breach of a contract to deliver cotton because of its failure to qualify to do business in the State. Appellant claims that that Mississippi statute as applied to the facts of the case is repugnant to the Commerce Clause of the Constitution.

   Appellant is a cotton merchant with its principal office in Memphis, Tenn. It had arranged with one Covington, a local cotton buyer in Marks, Miss., "to

Business Organizations: B. Corporations

contract cotton" to be produced the following season by farmers in Quitman County, Miss. The farmer, Pittman [appellee], in the present case, made the initial approach to Covington, seeking a contract for his cotton; in other instances Covington might contact the local farmers. In either event, Covington would obtain all the information necessary for a purchase contract and telephone the information to appellant in Memphis, where a contract would be prepared, signed by an officer of appellant, and forwarded to Covington. The latter would then have the farmer sign the contract. For these services Covington received a commission on each bale of cotton delivered to appellant's account at the local warehouse. When the farmers delivered the cotton, Covington would draw on appellant and pay them the agreed price.

The Supreme Court of Mississippi held that appellant's transactions with Mississippi farmers were wholly *intrastate* in nature, being completed upon delivery of the cotton at the warehouse, and that the fact that appellant might subsequently sell the cotton in *interstate* commerce was irrelevant to the federal question "as the Mississippi transaction had been completed and the cotton then belonged exclusively to Allenberg, to be disposed of as it saw fit, at its sole election and discretion," . . . Under the contract which Covington negotiated with appellee, Pittman, the latter was to plant, cultivate, and harvest a crop of cotton on his land, deliver it to a named company in Marks, Miss., for ginning, and then turn over the ginned cotton to appellant at a local warehouse. The suit brought by appellant alleged a refusal of Pittman to deliver the cotton and asked for injunctive relief and damages. One defense tendered by Pittman was that appellant could not use the courts of Mississippi to enforce its contracts, as it was doing business in the State without the requisite certificate. The Supreme Court of Mississippi sustained that plea, reversing a judgment in favor of appellant, and dismissed the complaint.

Appellant's arrangements with Pittman and the broker, Covington, are representative of a course of dealing with many farmers whose cotton, once sold to appellant, enters a long interstate pipeline. That pipeline ultimately terminates at mills across the country or indeed around the world, after a complex sorting and matching process designed to provide each mill with the particular grade of cotton which the mill is equipped to process.

We deal here with a species of control over an intricate interstate marketing mechanism. The cotton exchange has federal protection under the Commerce Clause. . . . Delivery of the cotton to a warehouse, taken in isolation, is an intrastate transaction. But that delivery is also essential for the completion of the interstate transaction, for sorting and classification in the warehouse are essential before the precise interstate destination of the cotton, whether in this country or abroad, is determined. The determination of the precise market cannot indeed be made until the classification is made. The cotton in this Mississippi sale, . . . though temporarily in a warehouse, was still in the stream of interstate commerce. . . .

The Mississippi Supreme Court, as noted, ruled that appellant was doing business in Mississippi. Appellant, however, has no office in Mississippi, nor does it own or operate a warehouse there. It has no employees soliciting business in Mississippi or otherwise operating there on a regular basis; its contracts are arranged through an independent broker, whose commission is paid either by appellant or by the farmer himself and who has no authority to enter into contracts on behalf of appellant. These facts are in sharp contrast to the situation in Eli

Lilly, where Lilly operated a New Jersey office with eighteen salaried employees whose job was to promote use of Lilly's products. . . . There is no indication that the cotton which makes up appellant's "perpetual inventory" in Mississippi is anything other than what appellant has claimed it to be, namely, cotton which is awaiting necessary sorting and classification as a prerequisite to its shipment in interstate commerce.

In short, appellant's contacts with Mississippi do not exhibit the sort of localization or intrastate character which we have required in situations where a State seeks to require a foreign corporation to qualify to do business. Whether there were local tax incidents of those contacts which could be reached is a different question on which we express no opinion. Whether the course of dealing would subject appellant to suits in Mississippi is likewise a different question on which we express no view. We hold only that Mississippi's refusal to honor and enforce contracts made for interstate or foreign commerce is repugnant to the Commerce Clause.

The judgment is reversed and the cause remanded for proceedings not inconsistent with this opinion.

Questions and Case Problems

1. X owned all the stock in Z Co., Inc., his incorporated gas station. X never had any officers or directors, nor did he ever have a corporate meeting. X mixed his personal funds in the corporate checking account. C, a customer, was injured by a corporate employee and he sued X as an individual for damages. May C hold X personally liable?

2. Home Owner's Aid, Inc., a public service corporation, sued defendant, Union Savings Association, on behalf of their client. Home Owners contended that a corporation is the same as a natural person and has the right to represent itself and its clients through an appointed agent who need not be an attorney. Home Owners further claimed that it has the constitutional right to litigate in this manner under the due process and equal protection of the law. May a corporation maintain a legal action through an officer of the corporation who is not an attorney? [*Union Savings Association v. Home Owners Aid, Inc.*, 262 N.E.2d 558 (Ohio 1970).]

3. Colin sought to evict a tenant under a rent control regulation. Altman, the rent commissioner, denied the request. The building was owned by 130 West 112th Street Corp. and all the stock was owned by Colin. Colin claimed that he desired the apartment for his own personal use. The rent commissioner denied the application on the ground that Colin had no standing (no legal status in the case) because he was not the owner of the building, and the rental regulations do not recognize a corporation as having a necessity to occupy housing. Colin claimed, because he owned all the stock, the court should disregard the corporate entity. May the corporate veil be pierced for the benefit of the corporation or its stockholders? [*Colin v. Altman*, 333 N.Y. Supp.2d 432 (1972).]

4. Emma Galler, plaintiff, brought suit to compel specific performance of a shareholders agreement made between her deceased husband, Benjamin Galler, and Isadore Galler, the defendant. Isadore and Benjamin were brothers

who were the only shareholders in a corporation without creditors. They executed a shareholders agreement to provide for their families in the event of death. The agreement provided that the surviving widow receive salary continuation payments and name a successor to her husband in the event of death. Specific dollar amounts of dividends were mandated by the shareholders agreement. May a shareholders agreement of a close corporation that pertains to director selection and the payment of dividends be enforced? [*Galler v. Galler,* 203 N.E.2d 577 (Ill. 1965).]

5. Edson, the plaintiff, is a licensed physician and surgeon. He was a staff member of Griffin Hospital and was denied the right to use hospital facilities for surgical procedures as a result of a change in the hospital bylaws. Edson sued the hospital and claimed that, since it is a public corporation serving the public, his patients are entitled to the facilities as a matter of law. The hospital is the recipient of state aid, special grants from the surrounding towns, and contributions from the United Fund and Community Chest. Ninety-five percent of its income is derived from charges for services rendered. Edson claimed that the hospital is a public corporation and can not adopt private regulations for use of its facilities. Is the hospital a private or a public corporation? [*Edson v. Griffin Hospital,* 144 A.2d 341 (Conn. 1958).]

6. X, Y, and Z are doctors who decided to incorporate their practice, which was formerly a partnership. E has been their secretary for many years. The doctors would like to offer her stock in the newly formed medical corporation. May they do so?

7. X, Y, and Z are stockholders of a real estate business they operate as a corporation. They have purchased a building for office use and formed a separate corporation to own the building. The real estate office and other tenants will pay rent to the corporation that owns the building. P, a client, brought suit against the real estate corporation for return of his down payment and has attached the building owned by the separate corporation. May the court disregard the corporate entity that owns the building and allow P's attachment?

8. X owned a small department store as a sole proprietor. X had many personal and business creditors. In an attempt to save his business, he incorporated the store and purchased all the stock. X's personal creditors sought to reach the corporate assets to collect their claims. X claimed that the store as a corporation owned assets distinct from his personal assets. Decide.

9. X is a corporation organized "to assist in the planning and organization of a new corporation." Z signed the articles of incorporation of a newly formed business as president of X, Inc. The secretary of state refused to accept a corporation as an incorporator. Could he do so?

10. In the case of *Allenberg Cotton Co., Inc. v. Pittman,* 419 U.S. 20 (1974),[5] the court decided that the appellant corporation was engaged in interstate, and not intrastate, business and, therefore, was not doing business in Mississippi. Discuss how a variation in how the appellant did business would cause it to be doing an intrastate business in Mississippi.

---

[5] See pp. 744–46.

41 Creation and Termination

After you have read this chapter, you should be able to:

1. Define and explain the function of a promoter.
2. Explain why a promoter is a fiduciary.
3. Explain the information required in the articles of incorporation.
4. Define and explain a *de jure* corporation.
5. Define and explain a *de facto* corporation.
6. Define and explain a so-called "corporation by estoppel."
7. Explain involuntary dissolution by the state.
8. Explain when the incorporators may dissolve a corporation.
9. Explain when the shareholders may dissolve a corporation.
10. Distinguish a merger from a consolidation.
11. Explain the legal effect of a merger or a consolidation.

Introduction

After you have decided to join with other persons to form a corporation, where would you look to determine how to form the corporation, and what societal limitations exist to your doing so? You probably will want to retain an attorney to give you this advice. It may come as a surprise to learn that a corporation can be formed only by permission of the state and, therefore, only by compliance with the laws of the state. Also, only the state can terminate corporate existence. You and your associates are called *promoters,* and all of you assume certain duties and liabilities in connection with organizing the corporation and contracts made before the corporation came into existence. We will begin with a discussion of promoters.

Creation

Promoters

If you were to plan the incorporation of a business venture, it would be necessary to consider whether contracts have to be signed *before* the corporation is formed. For example, will it own or lease its place of operation? Who will invest in the business? Or will it have to borrow funds from a bank? Planning the corporation and attending to its organization is the function of a **promoter.**

The promoter is not always associated with the business after it obtains corporate existence. Modern statutes authorize corporate formation upon filing the articles of incorporation and paying the necessary fee. At that point, the corporate officers are capable of signing on behalf of the corporation and, hence, do not require the services of a promoter. If the officers sign in their respective capacities on behalf of the corporation, they are not personally liable. In a later chapter we will discuss the liability of corporate officers. This liability is based on the agency theory that a disclosed principal (the corporation) is liable for authorized contracts made on its behalf by an agent (the corporate officer) with third parties. Hence, once the corporation is formed, a promoter is no longer necessary because the corporation can contract on its own behalf through the corporate officers.

promoter
a person who organizes and brings a corporation into existence

Promoter's Liability. Because the promoter performs various functions *before* formation of the corporation, he is not its agent. Accordingly, he is personally liable on contracts made on behalf of the proposed corporation. For example, as a promoter, you would be personally liable if you signed an office lease on behalf of a nonexisting corporation. If the corporation later occupied the premises, it may also be liable; however, this would not relieve the promoter from his liability to the landlord.

After incorporation, the corporation may become bound *to the terms* of the preincorporation contract, but the courts differ on how this may be accomplished. One theory is *adoption,* whereby the corporation adopts or assumes the obligation of performing the preincorporation contract either by corporate resolution of its board of directors or impliedly by knowingly accepting the benefits of the contract. The promoter is still liable as a party to the contract. A second, and the most used, theory is **novation,**[1] whereby the nonpromoter party to the preincorporation contract agrees to discharge the contract and, by a new contract, take the corporation in place of the promoter. A third theory is *continuing offer,* whereby the preincorporation contract is construed to be a continuing offer to the corporation by the nonpromoter party, and the corporation on its creation can accept it and be bound. A fourth theory, not legally sound, is *ratification,* whereby the corporation seeks to authenticate the making of the contract on its behalf retroactively as of the time the preincorporation contract was made. The ratification theory is not sound because the corporation was not in existence at the time the preincorporation contract was made and, therefore, could not at that time appoint an agent nor authorize the contract to be made.

Although the promoter is not an agent for the proposed corporation, he is under a duty to act for its benefit and hence is a **fiduciary.**[2] In that capacity he owes the corporation he is promoting and its stock subscribers a high degree of care. Upon incorporation, a promoter is obligated to make a full disclosure to the board of directors of any contract signed on its behalf. All transactions made by the promoter on behalf of the corporation must be accounted for. A promoter is personally liable for any secret profit made, and the corporation or the shareholders may sue him for their damages.

Incorporators

State corporate laws require the **incorporator** to sign and file the articles of incorporation with the secretary of state. While some states insist on three incorporators, the modern trend requires only one. Generally the statutes require the incorporators to be natural persons, and often citizens of the state or of the United States. Because incorporation is a contractual undertaking, the incorporators must not be minors, with their limited capacity to contract. The modern statutory trend is to allow a corporation to act as an incorporator.

Articles of Incorporation

State corporate statutes establish the procedures involved in incorporating a business. The **articles of incorporation** is the written application to the state for permission to incorporate. It must be filed with the secretary of state and generally must have the following information.

The Name of the Corporation. The incorporators may not select a name that is *deceptively similar* to another corporation.[3] State statutes generally allow for the reservation of the corporate name (for three or four months) in advance of

novation
a new contract with a new party immediately discharging the old contract

fiduciary
a person with a duty to act primarily for the benefit of another

incorporators
the persons who sign the articles of incorporation

articles of incorporation
the written application to the state for permission to incorporate

---

[1] See p. 180 for a discussion of novation.

[2] See pp. 241–43 for an explanation of the implied duties of a fiduciary.

[3] MODEL BUSINESS CORPORATION ACT sec. 10 (published for American Bar Foundation by West Pub. Co., 1971).

the filing date.[4] This may be a convenient way of assuring the organizing members that the selected name will qualify. The name must contain one of the following words or its abbreviation: "corporation," "company," "incorporated," or "limited."

The Purpose.   There must be a statement of the purpose for which the corporation is organized. As we previously discussed under the classification of corporations, the members may incorporate for a profit, nonprofit, professional, or charitable purpose. State statutes establish the rules to qualify as a special class of corporation. For example, separate laws exist for the incorporation of a professional medical practice because of its stock ownership by the licensed physicians and medical purpose to deliver health services.

Capital Stock Authorization.   The amount and class of shares the corporation shall have authority to issue is stated in the articles of incorporation. This is not the amount of stock the corporation must issue. For example, the corporation may initially issue 5,000 shares of stock although it is authorized 25,000 shares, the remaining 20,000 shares may be issued at a later date. The 5,000 are referred to as *issued and outstanding.*

Any restrictions placed on the transfer of shares of stock are also specified. For instance, closely held corporations commonly provide that a shareholder who desires to sell his stock first notify the directors of the selling price and grant the corporation the option to redeem the shares at the same price. This method assures control of the voting stock by the owner-directors of the small corporation. The transfer of stock is discussed in a later chapter.

Place of Business.   The post office address of the initial principal office of the corporation must be listed. This qualifies it as a *domestic* corporation in that state.

Directors and Officers.   Most states require a listing of the names and addresses of the initial directors and officers of the corporation.

The directors need not be residents of the state of incorporation nor shareholders of the corporation. The directors may be one or more in number, and they may be increased or decreased by amending the articles of incorporation. The initial directors hold office until the organizational stockholders' meeting, when they are ratified or new directors are elected by the stockholders. Each director will hold office generally until the next annual stockholders' meeting or until his successor is elected. A director may resign prior to that time or be terminated by the stockholders for cause. After approval of the articles of incorporation by the state, which is now called the corporate *charter,* the directors named therein hold an organizational meeting for the purpose of adopting the bylaws, electing the corporate officers,[5] and transacting whatever other business comes before the meeting—e.g., approve of any previous contracts entered into by the promoters.

---

[4] Id., sec. 9.   [5] Id., sec. 57.

The officers appointed by the board of directors generally consist of a president, one or more vice presidents, a secretary, and a treasurer. Many states allow the same person to be both secretary and treasurer. The directors and officers are discussed in a later chapter.

Incorporators. The incorporator must sign and file the articles of incorporation under the penalties of **perjury,** stating that the information they contain is correct.

Registered Agent. The name and address of the registered agent is placed in the articles to provide a claimant access to whom and where legal service can be made. The articles of incorporation are a matter of public information in the office of the secretary of state and may be viewed there by anyone. A person desirous of suing the corporation may send legal process to the resident agent or a corporate officer. Many states require a resident agent only when the applicant is a foreign corporation.

Bylaws. The rules and regulations of a corporation for its internal management and operation are its **bylaws.** They implement the charter and must be reasonable and not contrary to law. The shareholders have the right to enact bylaws, in the absence of statute and charter to the contrary. The Model Business Corporation Act gives to the initial directors the power to enact the initial bylaws[6] and also, in most states, the power to amend and repeal them in the absence of statute or charter to the contrary.

Certificate of Incorporation

Upon the filing of the articles of incorporation and payment of the filing fee, a certificate of incorporation is issued by the secretary of state. In most states, following the Model Business Corporation Act, corporate existence then begins.[7] The approved articles of incorporation are now called the **charter.** At this stage, creditors deal with the corporation as a separate entity from its stockholders, and the officers may do business in their respective capacities to avoid personal liability. The first order of business will be an organizational meeting for the stockholders to elect the directors, who will appoint the officers. The directors then adopt the bylaws, open a corporate checking account, and commence the management of the business.

Defective Incorporations

De Jure *Corporation.* Upon issuance of the corporate certificate, the corporate entity is formed. Although minor errors occur in attempting to comply with the statutory requirements for incorporation, a *de jure* (by law) corporation exists. For example, an incorporator may have failed to list a director's address in the articles of incorporation, or the seals required by statute to be next to the signatures of the incorporators may have been omitted. As most states follow typical procedures for the review by government officials of incorporation papers before issuance of the certificate, the chances of a defective filing are remote. If *complete*

---

[6] Id., sec. 27.   [7] Id., sec. 56.

Business Organizations: B. Corporations

or *substantial* compliance with the mandatory requirements of the incorporation statute and the prerequisites for the organization of the corporation have occurred, a valid *de jure* corporation exists.

De Facto *Corporation.* When a *de jure* corporation can not be found, the courts will determine if a defective incorporation is in "sufficient compliance" with the mandatory provisions of the corporation law. If it finds (1) a colorable attempt (i.e., real effort) in good faith (2) to comply with the mandatory provisions of a valid corporate law for its incorporation and (3) business use of the corporation beyond just the organizational meeting, a ***de facto*** (by fact) corporation has been formed. It exists in fact although not by law, and a *de facto* corporate debtor can not avoid liability on the basis of its being defective. Although a *de facto* corporate defendant may not attack its legal existence for the reason stated, the state may do so. The certificate of incorporation is conclusive evidence of corporate existence. Often the phrase "colorable compliance" is used to describe "colorable attempt," and it means that some real effort has been made to comply, but the compliance is less than substantial, although getting close to it.

Corporate status, whether *de jure* or *de facto,* is very important with respect to the liability of the corporate members (shareholders) because, with the corporate status as a shield, the members are not liable for corporate obligations. Without corporate status, they are personally liable for their contractual obligations. This is illustrated in the following case where the court held that there was no colorable attempt to comply with the state corporate statute and, therefore, since there was no *de facto* corporation, the members were personally liable.

> **de facto corporation**
> a corporation which has not complied substantially with the mandatory requirements of a valid state incorporation statute but has made a colorable attempt to do so, in good faith, and has begun to operate as a corporation

Facts

Conway, the plaintiff, entered into a contract with Trend Set Construction Corporation for remodeling work on Conway's home. Samet, the defendant, signed the contract as president of Trend Set Construction Corporation. Conway subsequently learned that Trend Set had never filed a certificate of incorporation. Suit was then brought against Samet personally. Samet defended on the ground that her attorney was supposed to have incorporated the business. The attorney told Samet she was incorporated and gave her a corporate seal. Her attorney had all the necessary information to incorporate and was paid the incorporation fees. Samet claimed she had a *de facto* corporation. Was this a *de facto* corporation?

Decision

No. Judgment for the plaintiff, Conway.

Reasoning

More is required to establish the *de facto* corporation defense than giving instructions to an attorney to incorporate. There must be a colorable attempt to comply with the statute governing incorporations made before the contract. Without any certificate of incorporation having been even prepared or acknowledged, there can be no *de facto* corporation.

Conway v. Samet, 300 N.Y.Supp.2d 243 (1969).

Corporation by Estoppel

The so-called "corporation by estoppel" occurs when business associates hold themselves out as being a corporation to third persons who materially changed their position in reasonable reliance on the misrepresentation. The estoppel prevents such associates from later denying corporate existence, but it does not create a corporation. There is an estoppel to deny corporate status.

Notice how the court in the following case decided that the doctrine of corporation by estoppel is distinct from a *de facto* corporation.

Facts

Bukacek, the plaintiff, and three others were the incorporators of Pell City Farms, Inc., the defendant. Pursuant to an agreement between the incorporators and Pell City Farms, Inc., Bukacek conveyed his 300-acre tract to Pell City Farms, Inc. Bukacek then claimed that Pell City was incapable of taking legal title to the property as a corporation because it had not filed its articles of incorporation. Bukacek executed the deed, transferring his interest in the land to the corporation; he was an incorporator, officer, director, and stockholder of the corporation and participated in the business activities of the corporation relating to the land after the articles of incorporation were filed. May Bukacek have the corporation's title to the land set aside?

Decision

No. Judgment for defendant, Pell City Farms.

Reasoning

The incidence of corporate existence may exist *as between the parties* by virtue of an estoppel. Corporations by estoppel are not based upon the same principles as corporations *de facto*. A *de facto* corporation can not be created by estoppel. The only effect of an estoppel is to prevent the raising of the question of the existence of a corporation.

Bukacek was one of the incorporators who dealt with the corporation as a corporation both before and after the articles of incorporation were filed. Bukacek is estopped to deny the existence of the corporation at the time he voluntarily executed a deed transferring property to the corporation even though the articles of incorporation had not been filed at that time.

Bukacek v. Pell City Farms, Inc., 237 So.2d 851 (Ala. 1970).

Termination

The state creates corporate existence, and only the state can authorize its dissolution. Unlike a sole proprietorship or a partnership, a corporation will not terminate upon the death of an owner. When a stockholder dies, his shares, as personal property, become an asset of his estate. As previously discussed, this continuity of the corporation is called "perpetual succession." Our discussion will focus on methods of terminating a corporation either voluntarily by the incorporators or shareholders, or involuntarily by the state, shareholders, or creditors.

Voluntary Dissolution

A corporation has statutory power to voluntarily terminate, provided that it complies with the state corporate laws. In some instances the incorporators may dissolve the corporation; however, it is usually the shareholders. The directors have no power to dissolve without the stockholders' approval.

By Incorporators. After having filed the articles of incorporation and being granted the corporate charter by the state, the corporation may be unable to issue its stock and, therefore, may decide not to commence business. The incorporators may file *articles of dissolution* stating the following:

1. the corporate name;
2. the issuance date of the certificate of incorporation;
3. that none of its shares was issued;
4. that it has not commenced business;
5. that money paid on stock subscriptions has been returned;
6. that the corporation has no debts; and
7. that a majority of the incorporators elect to dissolve.[8]

Upon approval, the secretary of state will issue a *certificate of dissolution,* and corporate existence will terminate.

By Shareholders. The shareholders may, by following state corporate law, dissolve the corporation for any reason. The board of directors adopts a resolution recommending dissolution that is submitted to a vote at a shareholders' meeting. In most states, at least a majority vote is required. Articles of dissolution are then filed, and the certificate of dissolution will be issued by the secretary of state.

In states that follow the Model Business Corporation Act, a statement of intent to dissolve is filed prior to the articles of dissolution. The corporation must notify and pay the creditors, pay any taxes due, collect the receivables, liquidate the assets, and distribute the remainder of the assets to the shareholders.

Involuntary Dissolution

The court, on a petition brought by the shareholders or the state, may dissolve the corporation.

By Shareholders. The shareholders may bring a petition to dissolve the corporation for gross mismanagement *by the board of directors* (e.g., voting for plant expansion with insufficient funds to finance the venture); on the ground of unfair advantage by the majority over the minority stockholders; or on the grounds of dissension and deadlock.

In the following case, judicial dissolution resulted from the "persistent unfairness" to a minority shareholder of a family corporation. Notice that the burden of proof is on the shareholder seeking dissolution.

---

[8] Id., sec. 82.

Facts

The defendant, C. E. Stumpf & Sons, Inc., was formed to conduct a masonry and general contracting business. It was wholly owned, in equal shares, by Stumpf and his two sons. As the result of a managerial dispute, the plaintiff, Donald Stumpf, one of the sons, ceased to be employed by the corporation. Thereafter he was removed as an officer of the corporation and received no salary, dividends, or other revenue from his investment. The corporation invested all its profits in rental properties. Stumpf brought this suit under the state corporate statute which allows for involuntary dissolution where "those in control of the corporation have knowingly countenanced abuse of authority or persistent unfairness toward any shareholder . . ."

Decision

Judgment for the plaintiff, Donald Stumpf.

Reasoning

A corporation may be involuntarily dissolved by the shareholders when it is reasonably necessary to protect their interests and rights. Involuntary dissolution is not an automatic remedy but rather a matter for the court's discretion. The shareholders must persuade the court that fairness requires drastic relief. Here Stumpf had no managerial voice in the business and received no salary or revenue from his investment. Such corporate conduct constituted unfair conduct and is grounds for involuntary dissolution.

Stumpf v. C. E. Stumpf & Sons, Inc., 120 Cal. Rptr. 671 (1975).

By State. The state, acting through the attorney general's office, may cause an involuntary dissolution for a corporation's failure to pay state taxes, for not filing annual reports, for fraudulently filing articles of incorporation, for the failure of a foreign corporation to appoint a resident agent, or for abuse of its corporate authority.

Bankruptcy

A corporation may voluntarily elect to file for bankruptcy, or its creditors may commence involuntary bankruptcy proceedings by petitioning the bankruptcy court. The corporate assets will then be liquidated and applied to creditors' claims. Once bankruptcy proceedings have commenced, a board of directors' resolution to dissolve adopted by a majority of the shareholders will effect a dissolution.[9]

Mergers and Consolidations

merger
the absorption of one corporation by another corporation

Merger

In a **merger,** one corporation is absorbed by another corporation, which continues to exist as the surviving corporation while the other terminates. State corporate

---

[9] See chapter 52, Bankruptcy Under the Bankruptcy Reform Act of 1978. A corporation is not entitled to a discharge in bankruptcy.

statutes have specific procedures that must be followed. Generally each board of directors involved approves a plan of merger that includes:

1. the names of the merging corporations and the name of the corporation into which they propose to merge, called the *surviving corporation;*
2. the terms and conditions of the proposed merger;
3. the manner of converting the shares of each corporation into the shares of the surviving corporation or into cash or other property;
4. a statement of any changes in the articles of incorporation of the surviving corporation;
5. approval by shareholders' vote at shareholders' meetings of each of the corporations involved;
6. upon the shareholders' approval, submission of the plan to the secretary of state's office as the articles of merger;
7. if the documents are in order, issuance of a certificate of merger by the secretary of state.[10]

In the following case, a shareholder contested a sale of the corporation on the grounds that it was, in fact, a merger and that the merger statute, which required a two-thirds shareholders' vote, was not followed.

Facts

Applestein, the plaintiff, a shareholder of United, the defendant corporation, sought to enjoin a proposed sale of 40 percent of the corporation's stock to Epstein, the sole shareholder of Interstate corporation, in exchange for all of Interstate's stock. Interstate would then cease to exist, and United would then take over all its assets and liabilities. Applestein argued that this was a merger rather than a sale and hence, required a vote of approval of two-thirds of the stockholders. United claimed that it had the right to purchase stock without shareholders' approval.

Decision

Judgment for plaintiff, Applestein.

Reasoning

A merger of two corporations contemplates that one will be absorbed by the other and go out of existence but the absorbing company will remain. As a consequence of the legislative power to legalize mergers, the state can prescribe the terms and conditions for a valid merger. This is more than a simple purchase by United of the assets of Interstate. In substance, the transaction is a merger. Accordingly, the shareholders of United were entitled to be notified of their statutory rights of dissent. The failure of the corporate officers of United to take these steps to obtain stockholder approval of the agreement by the statutory two-thirds vote at a proper stockholders' meeting would render the proposed corporate action invalid.

Applestein v. United Board and Carton Corp., 159 A.2d 146 (N.J. 1960).

---

[10] Id., secs. 71, 73, 74.

Consolidation

In a **consolidation,** two or more corporations combine together, forming a *new* corporation. In a merger, the corporations combine together, resulting in a *surviving corporation* rather than a *new* corporation that is formed under a *plan of consolidation.* Thus, X, Y, and Z corporations *merge* into Z, the surviving corporation; X, Y, and Z *consolidate* forming a new corporation, C corporation.

However, the legal effects of both a merger and consolidation are similar. The following, as found in the Model Business Corporation Act, section 76, are illustrative:

1. The existence of all corporations shall cease, except the surviving or new corporation.
2. The surviving merged or new consolidated corporation shall have all the rights and duties of a corporation organized under the law.
3. The surviving or new corporation shall possess all property, real and personal, and all debts belonging to each of the corporations so merged or consolidated.
4. The rights of creditors of any such corporations shall not be impaired by a merger or consolidation.
5. The articles of incorporation in a surviving corporation (merger) shall be deemed to be amended to the extent that changes in its articles of incorporation are stated in the plan of merger.
6. The articles of incorporation of a new corporation (consolidation) shall comply with the statements set forth in the articles of consolidation.

Some Reasons for Consolidation or Merger. A corporation may wish to merge with another to acquire a related or unrelated line of merchandise in order to diversify and reduce some of its economic risks; or it may wish to invest accumulated income rather than pay a dividend or tax as it is. If the effect is to lessen interstate competition, it may violate a federal antitrust law. For example, a large computer corporation may acquire a smaller one for all of the above reasons. There are always significant tax consequences to any merger or consolidation.

Summary Statement

1. Promoters plan the corporation and attend to its organization. In doing so, they frequently sign preincorporation contracts. Unless the formed corporation adopts the contract, a promoter is personally liable to third parties thereon.
2. A promoter is a fiduciary because he is under a duty to act for the benefit of the corporation. He is liable to the corporation for any secret profits made while acting as a promoter.
3. The articles of incorporation must be filed and approved by the secretary of state's office. The corporate name, purpose, capital stock authorization, place of business, names and addresses of directors and officers, fiscal year, and resident agent are listed in the articles of incorporation that are signed by the incorporators.

4. A defectively formed corporation may be given legal status in certain circumstances.

5. A *de jure* (by right) corporation exists by complete or substantial compliance with the statutory requirements for incorporation.

6. A *de facto* (in fact) corporation exists when there was a good faith colorable attempt to organize under a state corporation law and there is business use of the defectively formed corporation.

7. A corporation by estoppel does not create a corporation but prevents the denial of corporate existence by associates who held themselves out as being a corporation to third parties who materially changed their position in reasonable reliance on the misrepresentation.

8. The state, acting through the attorney general's office, may dissolve a corporation that fails to act legally.

9. Shareholders may voluntarily dissolve the corporation by voting to adopt the board of directors' resolution to dissolve, or the corporation may be involuntarily dissolved with court approval.

10. A merger is the absorption of one corporation by another corporation, which continues to exist while the other terminates.

11. A consolidation is the combination of two or more corporations forming a new corporation.

12. The legal effect of a merger or consolidation is the termination of all corporations except the surviving corporation (merger) or new corporation (consolidation); the surviving or new corporation has all the rights and duties of a corporation, and the rights of creditors are not impaired.

In the following case, the court found the promoter was not liable for a preincorporation debt because the creditor agreed to look solely to the corporation.

Sherwood & Roberts-Oregon, Inc. v. Alexander
525 P.2d 135 (Or. 1974)

Deneke, J. The defendants are real estate developers. They held title to some land either as individuals or in an unincorporated joint venture known as Iron Mountain Investment Company. Defendants planned to develop this land. The plaintiff is in the business of lending money and securing loans from other sources for plaintiff's customers. Defendants sought financing through plaintiff, who suggested securing a commitment for a long-term loan—that is, an offer by a lender to make defendants a loan, the offer to continue for an agreed period of time.

Under existing financial conditions, the interest on the loan would be at least twelve percent. Twelve percent is a usurious rate to charge individuals; therefore, plaintiff informed defendants that any loan would have to be made to a corporation. Corporations are not subject to the same usury laws as individuals.

When the plaintiff was preparing the [promissory] note which was to be the good faith deposit, plaintiff asked defendant Alexander what corporation would borrow the money and execute the good faith deposit note. Alexander did not have any corporation but told plaintiff the corporation's name would be "Iron

Mountain Investment Co., Inc." The note was so prepared and signed by Alexander for the corporation. Plaintiff knew that at this time there was no corporate entity.

Plaintiff secured a commitment; however, it was not acceptable to defendants. . . . Because the commitment was rejected, plaintiff brought this action on the good faith deposit note. Defendants never attempted to form a corporation. Judgment was for the defendants, and the plaintiff appeals.

Since all parties were fully informed of the purely prospective existence of the corporation, the note is best termed a preincorporation contract. Parties in the position of the defendants are termed "promoters." . . .

The common law rule governing these preincorporation contracts is stated: "It is settled by the authorities that a promoter, though he may assume to act on behalf of the projected corporation and not for himself, will be personally liable on the contract unless the other party agreed to look to some other person or fund for payment. . . ."

The next step is to determine if there was any evidence that the plaintiff agreed to accept the obligation of a to-be-formed corporation solely and not to look for payment from the defendants as individuals. The trial court made a finding of fact:

"Defendants did not at any time assume to act as a corporation but simply agreed to subsequently organize a corporation. Plaintiff made no attempt verbally or in writing to hold defendants individually as co-signers or as guarantors." This finding probably was intended to be to the effect that the plaintiff was not looking to the individuals for payment of the note.

We find there was evidence that plaintiff looked solely to the to-be-formed corporation for payment of the note. Unlike the creditor in the usual case, the plaintiff in this case is the party that insisted that the contract show a corporation as the obligor and would not do business otherwise, although plaintiff knew when the note was executed that no corporation existed. Plaintiff's officer who handled the transaction testified that plaintiff would look to the defendant individuals as well as to the corporation for payment of the principal note and mortgage, had it been consummated. He testified the defendants and their wives would have been required to execute these documents in their individual capacity. The commitment tendered to defendants had blanks for defendants and their wives to sign, individually, indicating their acceptance. That the note, prepared by plaintiff, was not prepared for the signature of either defendant as an individual, whereas all the other documents were so prepared, is also some evidence that plaintiff did not intend to have the defendants, as individuals, obligated on the note.

Further evidence is the testimony of plaintiff's officer that when the note was signed, he did not intend to proceed further in securing a commitment until defendants provided him with their articles of incorporation. The trial court could infer from this testimony that the plaintiff was not going to look to the individual defendants to repay it for the expense of finding a commitment; rather the plaintiff desired to conduct all parts of this transaction with a corporate entity. This desire on plaintiff's part is reasonable as plaintiff's officer was concerned that, if the corporation was considered a sham to avoid the usury statute, plaintiff would be subject to the penalties of the usury statute.

Judgment is affirmed.

Questions and Case Problems

1. Radom, the plaintiff, and Neidorff were the sole shareholders in a corporation in the music publication business. Upon Neidorff's death, his wife, Anna, succeeded to his shares. Due to the mutual mistrust of Anna and Radom, they were unable to agree upon a board of directors and the declaration of dividends. The deadlock continued over a three-year period while the corporation continued to prosper. To resolve the dispute, Radom petitioned the court for dissolution. Will the court dissolve a close corporation where the stockholders can not agree to the election of directors and the declaration of dividends? [In re *Radom & Neidorff, Inc.,* 119 N.E.2d 563 (N.Y. 1954).]

2. Neal was an incorporator for Main Street Electric Company, Inc. He filed the articles of incorporation with the secretary of state in Texas. The articles were refused because there already existed a Main Street Electronic Company, Inc. in Texas. May the secretary of state refuse an application on these grounds?

3. Chartrand agreed with O'Malia to purchase stock for $80,000 in a new corporation to be formed named Barney's Club, Inc., the defendant. Each was to receive 25.5 percent of the issued stock. When the corporation was formed, it refused to issue the shares to Chartrand in the agreed amount. Chartrand brought suit to compel an equal division of the shares and claimed that Barney's Club knew of the agreement and accepted its benefit since O'Malia was its president and director. Barney's Club, Inc. claimed it never adopted the agreement. Was Barney's Club, Inc. liable under the preincorporation agreement made between Chartrand and O'Malia? [*Chartrand v. Barney's Club, Inc.,* 380 F.2d 97 (1967).]

4. Boss, the defendant, was the promoter of a new corporation. He contracted with Stanley J. How & Associates, Inc., the plaintiff, wherein How agreed to provide architectural services for the new corporation. Boss signed as agent for the new corporation, which was never formed. How provided plans and was never paid for its services. How sued Boss, who defended by claiming that How agreed to look solely to the new corporation for payment. Is Boss, as promoter, liable on the contract entered into in behalf of a new corporation to be formed although How agreed to be paid by the corporation to be formed? [*Stanley J. How & Associates, Inc. v. Boss,* 222 F.Supp. 936 (1963).]

5. Levin, an incorporator, filed the articles of incorporation and named the corporation "Levin's, Limited." The secretary of state's office refused to accept the articles because "limited" would not indicate to the public that the business is a corporation, and hence the name is improper. Decide.

6. X, Y, and Z, as incorporators, formed W Corporation. Z neglected to sign the articles of incorporation, and the secretary of state's office certified the articles. X, Y, and Z believed that they were a corporation and commenced business. B, an officer of the corporation, contracted in the name of the corporation with T. When T discovered that the articles were not properly filed, he sued X, Y, and Z as individuals for his damages. Decide.

Creation and Termination   761

7. Colorado Indoor Trap Shoot, Inc., the plaintiff, sued Tucker, doing business as Consolidated Sales Company. Plaintiff was to purchase from defendant the necessary equipment to open and operate one of the indoor trap shoot establishments in Colorado. Plaintiff was to pay the defendant $2,100,000 for the exclusive rights to sell, lease, and distribute all such indoor trap shoot equipment in the State of Colorado for a maximum period of five years. Defendant claims that the contract was entered into on behalf of its company which was to be formed by him as a promoter, and this was known to the plaintiff. Is Tucker, as a promoter, personally liable on the preincorporation contract? [*Tucker d/b/a Consolidated Sales Co. v. Colorado Indoor Trap Shoot, Inc.,* 471 P.2d 912 (Okla. 1970).]

8. The plaintiff, Stephens Wholesale Bldg. Supply Co., sold merchandise to the defendant, Norman R. Harris, individually, and doing business as Bessemer Building and Improvement Company. Prior to the filing of incorporation papers by defendant, Harris, on April 2, 1969, a corporate checking account was opened, a lease for corporate office space and a bid on a construction job were made in the name of the corporation. Harris opened his business relationship with Stephens in an individual capacity, although he subsequently operated as a corporation. Was Harris personally liable under contract with Stephens before he incorporated? [*Harris v. Stephens Wholesale Bldg. Supply Co., Inc.,* 309 So.2d 115 (Ala. 1975).]

9. Johnston, plaintiff, owns 50 percent of the stock in defendant, Livingston Nursing Home, Inc., and Mr. and Mrs. Vick own the remaining 50 percent. All three parties serve as the corporation's directors and officers. Johnston complained that the business affairs of the corporation have been grossly mismanaged under the control of his sister, Lessie Vick, and her husband, Henry Vick. He further complained of neglect of the patients and poor quality of the food. Johnston contends that the officers of Livingston Nursing Home have come to an impasse and, due to dissension and bickering among the stockholders, that it is impossible to carry on the corporation and its business affairs. Johnston requested the equity court to appoint a receiver, dissolve the corporation, and sell the assets for payment of debts and distribution of the excess among the stockholders. There is no contention that the corporation is insolvent. May the court dissolve the corporation? [*Johnston v. Livingston Nursing Home, Inc.,* 211 S.2d 151 (Ala. 1968).]

10. In the case of *Sherwood & Roberts-Oregon, Inc. v. Alexander,* 525 P.2d 135 (Or. 1974),[11] the court held that the defendants were liable on the contract as promoters for a corporation to be formed. If the corporation had been formed later and you were one of the promoters, discuss what could be done to terminate the liability of the promoters.

---

[11] See pp. 759–60.

Corporate Powers

42

After you have read this chapter, you should be able to:

1. Explain the function of the "purpose clause" in the articles of incorporation.
2. Explain the source of the corporation's *express powers*.
3. Discuss the *implied powers* of a corporation.
4. List and explain the corporate statutory powers.
5. Explain the function of corporate bylaws.
6. Explain the doctrine of *ultra vires*.
7. Explain the remedies for *ultra vires* acts.

Introduction

While the corporation may exist as a legal entity by permission of the state, it can not function without authority or power. The state is the source of all corporate power and determines what a corporation may and may not do. Accordingly, it is necessary to consider the nature and extent of corporate powers.

Nature of Corporate Powers

In the planning stages of the corporation it is necessary to determine the purpose of its formation. This is described in the *purpose clause* of the articles of incorporation. Once authorized by the state to function as a corporation, it has the consequent **express powers** as stated in the articles of incorporation and the corporate statutes to carry out its business purpose. For instance, as an "artificial person" the corporation may, in its own name, own property, sell stock, borrow money, and hire employees. If the incorporators anticipate a new line of business, the purpose clause should be broadly descriptive of its express powers so as to avoid a later necessary amendment of the articles of incorporation, requiring stockholders' approval.

Many states, following the Model Business Corporation Act, allow a purpose clause authorizing the corporation to engage in any lawful business transaction. For example, a typical purpose clause for a restaurant business may state that the purpose is "to engage in the restaurant business and any legal business transactions related thereto." The powers that are reasonably necessary to carry out the express powers are called **implied powers.** Corporate officers have no authority to bind a corporation without express, implied, or statutory power. This is illustrated in the following case.

corporate express powers
those powers specifically stated in the corporation's articles of incorporation and in the corporation statutes

corporate implied powers
those powers reasonably necessary to carry out the express powers

Facts
Plaintiff, Brinson, was a shareholder of defendant corporation, Mill Supply Co. He sued to prevent it from paying a guaranty contract. A. F. Peterson was the president and secretary of defendant corporation, who signed, in the corporate name, a contract of guaranty of a promissory note signed by Alfred Peterson in his individual capacity. Brinson claimed that the president had no authority to have the corporation guarantee payment of Peterson's personal note.

Decision
Judgment for plaintiff, Brinson.

Reasoning
For a contract executed by a corporate officer to be binding on the corporation, it must appear that (1) it was incidental to the business of the corporation; or (2) it was expressly authorized; and (3) it was properly executed. The powers granted to the corporation under the articles of incorporation do not expressly or impliedly authorize it to issue accommodation paper or to guarantee the obligations of a third party. To permit the payment of the claim would clearly result in an invasion of the assets of the defendant corporation.

Brinson v. Mill Supply Co., 14 S.E.2d 505 (N.C. 1941).

Corporate Statutory Powers

The state where the corporation is organized gives it various statutory powers. These powers are the reasons why the corporation is the most desirable way of operating a business. Section 4 of the Model Business Corporation Act lists the following powers that are representative of state corporate laws.

Perpetual Succession. "Each corporation shall have power: (a) to have perpetual succession by its corporate name unless a limited period of duration is stated in its articles of incorporation."

You will recall that a partnership is dissolved by a change in the relationship among the partner-owners. This will not occur in a corporation as the death of a shareholder causes the stock to pass to the representative for his estate. For example, the death of a shareholder or a change in management will not affect its perpetual existence. The stability provided by this attribute makes it the only proper business form for the larger corporations with many shareholders.

To Sue and Be Sued in Its Corporate Name. "(b) to sue and be sued, complain and defend, in its corporate name."

Sole proprietors and partners are sued and sue in their own names. The corporation as a distinct and independent legal person sues in *its* own name. This is a significant advantage because the owners and managers are not personally liable for corporate debts.

To Have a Corporate Seal. "(c) to have a corporate seal. . . ."

This right is consistent with the *legal person* aspect of the corporation. The seal is commonly used on important documents to evidence corporate authorization of the transaction. For example, banks generally require a corporate seal when a corporate checking account is opened, and the certificate of stock normally has the corporate seal on it.

To Acquire Property. "(d) to purchase, take, receive, lease or otherwise acquire, . . . real or personal property."

A corporation may purchase property in its own name either as an investment or for its own use. The property then becomes a corporate asset, subject to the rights of creditors. For example, a corporate restaurant, that does not pay its debts and owns its own kitchen equipment, may have the equipment attached and liquidated by its creditors and the proceeds used to satisfy their claims.

To Dispose of Its Property. "(e) to sell, convey, mortgage, pledge, lease, . . . or otherwise dispose of . . . its property."

We will see in a later chapter that the decision to sell corporate property generally requires board authorization because of its effect on the stockholders' investment. Once authorized, it is the corporation, as a legal person, who sells the property, and not the board of directors or corporate officers.

To Financially Assist Its Employees. "(f) to lend money and use its credit to assist its employees."

Prudent investment of corporate profit is an obligation of the board of directors. The directors may use corporate funds for employee benefits. For example, employee credit unions and profit and pension plans commonly give employees the right to borrow corporate money at a favorable interest rate.

To Buy and Sell Stocks and Bonds in Other Corporations, etc. "(g) to purchase . . . or sell . . . shares or other interests in, or obligations of other . . . corporations, associations, partnerships . . . or obligations of the United States, a state or municipality."

This power clearly identifies the investment potential of the corporation beyond its own business purpose. A corporation may own, in its own name, stock or bonds in another business or government.

To Make Contracts and Incur Debts. "(h) to make contracts and incur liabilities, borrow money, . . . issue its notes, bonds or other obligations by mortgage . . . of all or any of its property, franchises and income."

This corporate power to engage in debt financing is commonly used to meet cash flow demands. The ability to raise money by the issuance of bonds and notes is an essential statutory power.

The following case illustrates how a court will extend the power to contract beyond the corporation's immediate expressed purpose, provided that the contract is executed and not contrary to public policy.

Facts

Plaintiff, Miller, sued the defendant, Temple Lumber Company, for breach of a contract to construct a dwelling house for plaintiff. Temple Lumber was to furnish all labor and materials in the construction of a house for Miller and was to do the construction according to a set of plans and specifications. Temple Lumber's corporate charter set out the purpose of the corporation as that of "manufacturing lumber and the purchase and sale of material used in such business and doing all things necessary and incident to such lumber business." Temple Lumber claimed it was not liable on the contract since construction of a building was not an act within its "purpose" clause and, therefore, was beyond the powers of the corporation.

Decision

Judgment for plaintiff, Miller.

Reasoning

An act of a corporation is *ultra vires* when it is beyond the scope either of the express or implied power of the charter. If the act is not one prohibited by law or public policy, and it enures to the direct benefit of the corporation, and is executed, it is not, strictly speaking, *ultra vires.* Acts which are not enumerated in the purpose clause of the charter of a corporation but are not prohibited and are appropriate, convenient, and suitable in carrying out the purposes for which the charter was expressly granted are the "implied powers and authority" of a corporation.

Temple Lumber Co. v. Miller, 169 S.W.2d 256 (Tex. 1943).

To Lend and Invest. "(i) to lend money for its corporate purposes, invest. . . ."

To Engage in Intrastate and Interstate Business Activities. "(j) to conduct its business . . . and have offices within or without this State."

Many corporations carry on business activities, not only in its state of formation, but in many others. Our economy could not function without this power.

To Have Officers and Agents. "(k) to elect or appoint officers and agents of the corporation, and define their duties and fix their compensation."

In a later chapter we will explain the management of the corporation. Although the corporation is a legal person, it has no means of operating the daily affairs of its business except through its officers.

To Make and Alter Bylaws. "(l) to make and alter bylaws, not inconsistent with its articles of incorporation or with the laws of this State for the administration and regulation of the affairs of the corporation."

Bylaws determine the policy of the corporation and establish the authority of the officers, directors and stockholders. They can grant extraordinary powers to the board of directors allowing them to make decisions that ordinarily would require stockholders' approval. The initial bylaws are usually adopted by the board of directors who have the power to alter or amend unless the articles of incorporation reserve that to the stockholders.[1]

To Make Charitable Contributions. "(m) to make donations for the public welfare or for charitable, scientific or educational purposes."

This power allows the corporation to make tax deductible charitable contributions. Our society, with its numerous nonprofit organizations (e.g., colleges and hospitals) relies upon substantial corporate contributions for their funding.

To Transact Lawful Business. "(n) to transact any lawful business which the board of directors shall find will be in aid of governmental policy."

The board of directors, as the principal governing body of the corporation, will be discussed in a later chapter. The directors are generally elected by the stockholders and their number is fixed by the bylaws.

To Establish Incentive Plans. "(o) to . . . establish pension plans . . . and other incentive plans for any or all of its directors, officers and employees."

Essential to the well-being of our labor force is planning for retirement. The Employee Retirement Income Security Act[2] governs the procedure and tax advantages of the pension area. Many small business associations have elected to incorporate to obtain these benefits.

To Be a Member of Another Enterprise. "(p) to be a promoter, partner, or manager of any partnership, joint venture, trust or other enterprise."

---

[1] Model Business Corporation Act (published for American Bar Foundation by West Pub. Co., 1971).

[2] 29 U.S.C., ch. 18.

This power may be exercised to give a corporate general partner of a limited partnership unlimited liability.[3]

To Have All Implied Powers to Effect Its Purposes.   "(q) to have . . . all powers necessary to effect its purposes. . . ."

Unauthorized Corporate Acts

Ultra Vires Acts

ultra vires
beyond the powers

A corporation may perform only those acts that are authorized by its express, implied, or statutory powers. These powers are derived from the state of incorporation as established in corporate statutory law, the articles of incorporation, and its reasonably implied powers. If it should engage in an unauthorized act, it is ***ultra vires***—that is, beyond the powers of the corporation. For example, if the board of directors of a computer corporation were to authorize the expenditure of funds to purchase conservation land in order to protect the wild life, although this may be socially desirable, it would be beyond the authority of a computer corporation and *ultra vires.*

Illegal Acts Distinguished from Ultra Vires.   Corporate action in excess of *corporate* authority is *ultra vires,* but it is not *illegal* unless it is contrary to statute or public policy as declared by the courts. For example, in the above illustration, while the board action was in excess of *corporate authority,* such action was not illegal as contrary to *public law.* However, if the board had *bribed* a Congressman to vote in Congress to make the land available to the corporation, this would be contrary to federal statute and public policy, be illegal, and be a crime.

Legal Effect of Ultra Vires Acts.   At common law, *ultra vires* business transactions were void because they were performed without legal authorization. Under modern statutory law, the defense of *ultra vires* is abolished in a suit for breach of contract by or against a corporation.

No act of a corporation and no conveyance or transfer of real or personal property to or by a corporation shall be invalid by reason of the fact that the corporation was without capacity or power to do such act. . . . [Model Business Corporation Act, section 7.]

The following case illustrates this when the defendant's corporate president acted beyond his authority.

Facts
Southeastern Beverage & Ice Equipment Company, Inc., the plaintiff, brought suit against the Free For All Missionary Baptist Church, Inc., the defendant, for rent due under a lease for liquor dispensing equipment. The lease was signed by the president and secretary of the defendant corporation. The church contends that the lease was *ultra vires* and unauthorized.

Decision
Judgment for plaintiff.

---

[3] See pp. 718–21 for a discussion of the limited partnership.

Reasoning

Incapacity or lack of power on the part of the church corporation does not make the lease invalid, and the defense of *ultra vires* is not available. The State Business Corporation Code abolished the doctrine of *ultra vires* as a means of avoiding a transaction which the corporation later claims is beyond its capacity or power. The corporation is not relieved of liability to any third persons for acts of its officers by reason of any limitation upon the power of the officers not known to such third persons. There is no evidence that Southeastern Beverage as lessor knew of any limitation upon the power of the Baptist Church president.

Free For All Missionary Baptist Church, Inc. v. Southeastern Beverage & Ice Equipment Company, Inc., 218 S.E.2d 169 (Ga. 1975).

Many courts will allow *ultra vires* as a defense where the contract is executory—that is, not yet performed. If the corporation or the other party have received full performance of the contract, they can not avoid liability by the defense of *ultra vires*. This occurred in the following case.

Facts

Plaintiff, Total Automation, was a corporation with a checking account in the defendant bank, Illinois National Bank. The bank operated a travel department that was owed money by Total Automation. The bank deducted the amount owed to the travel department from Total's checking account. Plaintiff claims that the bank had no right to setoff because the operation of a travel agency by a national bank is an *ultra vires* act.

Decision

Judgment for defendant, Illinois National Bank & Trust Co.

Reasoning

The defense of *ultra vires* is not favored by the courts where it is raised by a private party seeking to avoid payment for a benefit received. Total Automation is not aggrieved as a private person by having to pay for services it used, nor can it be heard to say it is aggrieved as a member of the public by a departure from sound policy relating to banking, since it voluntarily entered into the *ultra vires* transaction and reaped its benefits.

Total Automation, Inc. v. Illinois National Bank & Trust Co. of Rockford, 351 N.E.2d 879 (Ill. 1976).

Remedies for Ultra Vires Acts. The corporation may protect itself in the following ways from *ultra vires* activity engaged in by the officers or directors:

1. By an injunction obtained by a shareholder against the corporation to restrain and enjoin the further commission of *ultra vires* acts.
2. The corporation either directly or acting through a receiver, trustee, or other legal representative, or through shareholders in a representative suit, may sue the corporate officers or directors.
3. The attorney general of the state of incorporation may bring a proceeding to dissolve the corporation or to enjoin it from the further transaction of unauthorized business.[4]

---

[4] Model Business Corporation Act, sec. 7.

Summary Statement

1. The "purpose clause" of the articles of incorporation give it express and implied powers to engage in the stated purpose.
2. The *express powers* of a corporation are found in the articles of incorporation and the corporate statutory law.
3. The *implied powers* grant to the corporation authority to perform those reasonably incidental acts in carrying on corporate business.
4. The corporate statutory powers give to a corporation the implied authority:
   a. of perpetual succession,
   b. to have a corporate name,
   c. to sue and be sued in its corporate name,
   d. to have a corporate seal,
   e. to acquire and dispose of its property,
   f. to financially assist its employees,
   g. to buy and sell stocks and bonds in other corporations, etc.,
   h. to make contracts and incur debts,
   i. to lend and invest,
   j. to engage in intrastate and interstate business activity,
   k. to have officers and agents,
   l. to make and alter bylaws,
   m. to make charitable contributions,
   n. to transact lawful business,
   o. to establish incentive plans,
   p. to be a member of another enterprise,
   q. to elect a board of directors,
   r. to have all implied powers to effect its purposes.
5. The bylaws regulate the internal affairs of the corporation. They establish the authority of the directors, officers, and shareholders as well as procedures for calling meetings.
6. Acts of the corporation outside the scope of the corporate authority are *ultra vires*. Executed corporate contracts are valid, and the creditor can not use the defense of *ultra vires;* if executory, either party may use the *ultra vires* defense.
7. If officers or directors propose an *ultra vires* act, the shareholders may enjoin the act, the shareholders in a representative suit may sue the officers or directors personally, or the attorney general may bring a proceeding to dissolve the corporation.

Notice how the court in the following case examines the nature of the contract signed by the corporate president and found it to be "unusual and extraordinary," thus requiring express authority to execute.

Goldenberg v. Bartell Broadcasting Corporation

262 N.Y.Supp.2d 274 (1965)

Wilfred A. Waltemade, Justice. In the case on trial, the plaintiff sets forth two causes of action, both of which seek recovery of damages for an alleged breach of a written contract of employment. The first cause of action is against the defendant Bartell Broadcasting Corporation, an entity incorporated under the laws of the State of Delaware. It is alleged in substance that on or about March 16, 1961, the plaintiff and the defendant Bartell Broadcasting Corporation entered into a written contract wherein the plaintiff was engaged as an assistant to Gerald A. Bartell, the president of the defendant Bartell Broadcasting Corporation. The plaintiff's primary duties were to engage in corporate development in the field of pay television. The contract, which was for a period of three years, provided for (1) payment to the plaintiff of $1,933 per month; and (2) for the delivery to plaintiff of 12,000 shares of "Free Registered" stock of defendant Bartell Broadcasting Corporation, which stock was payable in three installments of 4,000 shares each in the months of January 1962, 1963, and 1964; and (3) the payment of plaintiff's traveling and living expenses in connection with the services to the employer; and (4) that the defendant Bartell Broadcasting Corporation would provide the plaintiff with a private office and proper office facilities; and (5) that the agreement would be binding on any successor corporation or any corporation with which defendant Bartell Broadcasting would merge.

This written contract was signed by the plaintiff and by Gerald A. Bartell in his capacity as the president of Bartell Broadcasting Corporation. It is further claimed that on or about May 1961, this contract was amended to increase plaintiff's monthly compensation from $1,933 to $2,400. It is further contended that the plaintiff was not paid his monthly compensation commencing with the month of November 1961; that the defendant Bartell Broadcasting Corporation failed to deliver 4,000 shares of stock allegedly due in January 1962; and that in July 1962, the defendant Bartell Broadcasting Corporation denied the validity of plaintiff's employment contract. . . .

The court will now turn its consideration to the first cause of action set forth in the complaint.

A corporation can only act through its directors, officers, and employees. They are the conduit by and through which the corporation is given being and from which its power to act and reason springs. Therefore in every action in which a person sues a corporation on a contract executed on behalf of the corporation by one of its officers, one of the issues to be determined is whether the officer had the express, implied, or apparent authority to execute the contract in question.

The authority of an officer to act on behalf of a corporation may be express, implied, or apparent. There has been no proof offered in this case indicating that Gerald A. Bartell, as president of the defendant Bartell Broadcasting Corporation, had express authority to enter into the agreement, dated March 16, 1961, which is the subject of the first cause of action.

Did Gerald A. Bartell then have either implied or apparent authority to execute the contract?

Implied authority is a species of actual authority, which gives an officer the power to do the necessary acts within the scope of his usual duties. Generally the president of a corporation has the implied authority to hire and fire corporate employees and to fix their compensation. However, the president of a corporation does not have the implied power to execute "unusual or extraordinary" contracts of employment. . . .

The agreement of March 16, 1961 not only provides for the payment of a substantial monthly compensation, but also requires the delivery of 12,000 shares of "free registered" stock of the defendant Bartell Broadcasting Corporation. While the payment of the monthly compensation would not make the contract of March 16, 1961 "unusual or extraordinary," the Court is of the opinion that the inclusion in the contract of the provision requiring the delivery to plaintiff of 12,000 shares of "free registered" stock does bring the agreement within the category of being an "unusual and extraordinary" contract.

With the varied and broad business experience acquired by the plaintiff in his wide business association as evidenced by his career resumé furnished to the defendants . . . and by plaintiff's own testimony, it can be truly said that he not only was presumed to have knowledge of the statutory provisions of the law pertaining to corporations, but that he apparently also had actual knowledge of such laws. It is reasonable to infer that the plaintiff was aware, or at the least had reason to be aware, that the authority for the issuance of corporate stock rests solely within the powers of the Board of Directors of the corporation, and that in the absence of express authority, the president of a corporation does not have the implied or apparent authority to enter into an employment contract which provides for the issuance of corporate stock as compensation.

The Court concludes, after a careful analysis of the evidence and the application of the law reviewed herein that the plaintiff has not made out a prima facie case of express, implied, or apparent authority of the president of the defendant Bartell Broadcasting Corporation to execute the contract of employment.

Accordingly, the motion by the defendants to dismiss the complaint is granted.

Questions and Case Problems

1. The "purpose clause" of Z Corporation stated that it was organized to operate a sporting goods store. The directors authorized the corporate purchase of an apartment. S, a shareholder of Z Corporation, brought an action against the corporation, claiming that it was about to perform an *ultra vires* act. The directors claim they have the statutory power "to purchase real property wherever situated." Is the shareholder correct?

2. X Co., Inc. was a life insurance agency. X Co. purchased a car wash and began its operation. X Co. had ten shareholders who knew of the car wash purchase and did not object although X Co. never amended its articles of incorporation. X Co. purchased various shop products from S on open account and owed it $5,000. When sued by S, X Co. defended on the ground that, as a life insurance agency, the entire car wash business was *ultra vires,* and hence it is not liable under any contract with S. Decide.

3. Smith, the president of XYZ Co., Inc., was very friendly with Jones, the deceased vice-president. Without approval of the board of directors, Smith

paid $1,000 per month to Mrs. Jones as a corporate benefit. When the shareholders discovered this, they sued Smith for the corporate loss. Smith claimed that he had express power to make charitable contributions. Decide.

4. Legal Aid Services, Inc., plaintiff, brought an action against American Legal Aid, Inc., defendant, to enjoin it from using the term "Legal Aid" in defendant's business transactions on the grounds that it was deceptively similar to plaintiff's name. Legal Aid Services, Inc., plaintiff, was organized in 1966 as a Wyoming nonprofit corporation for the purpose of rendering free legal services to persons of low income. The Natrona County Bar Association and members contribute through the plaintiff approximately 700 hours annually in free legal service to the poor. Plaintiff corporation was funded by a federal grant through the Office of Economic Opportunity. American Legal Aid, Inc., defendant, was incorporated in 1970. It sold memberships to the general public for reimbursement of attorney's fees incurred in specified areas according to a schedule. There was considerable evidence that many people were confused about the two corporations. Defendant claims that it has the express statutory power to have its own corporate name. Decide. [*American Legal Aid, Inc. v. Legal Aid Services, Inc.,* 503 P.2d 1201 (Wyo. 1972).]

5. XYZ Co., Inc. applied to a local bank for a corporate loan of $50,000. The bank requested security for the loan, and XYZ's board of directors transferred its stock to be held as collateral by the bank. A group of minority shareholders sought to enjoin the issuance of the stock on the grounds that the corporation is not authorized to pledge its security to acquire a loan. Decide.

6. Marsili and other shareholders, plaintiffs, brought a derivative action against Pacific Gas & Electric Company, defendant, and allege that a contribution to Citizens for San Francisco was *ultra vires* because neither defendant's articles of incorporation nor the state law permits a corporation to make political donations. The Citizens group was an association organized to defeat a local ballot proposition that would prohibit the construction of buildings exceeding seventy-two feet unless approved in advance by the voters. Did the board of directors have authority to make the contribution? [*Marsili v. Pacific Gas & Electric Company,* 124 Cal.Rptr. 313 (1975).]

7. Thermal Supply of Harlingen, Inc., plaintiff, brought this action against defendant, Rio Refrigeration Company, for merchandise furnished to Coastal Refrigeration that defendant purchased. Rio Refrigeration bought all the business of Coastal, including its trucks, inventory, supplies and tools, office equipment, and accounts receivable. Rio assumed payment of all of Coastal's accounts payable, including the unpaid account that is the basis of this action. Defendant claims that the contract with Coastal to assume its debts was *ultra vires* because a corporation has no right to act as surety or guarantor for the debts of another. Was the contract *ultra vires?* [*Rio Refrigeration Company v. Thermal Supply of Harlingen, Inc.,* 368 S.W.2d 128 (Tex. 1963).]

8. National Organization for Women, Essex County Chapter, plaintiff, brought this action against Little League Baseball, Inc. to admit girls aged eight to twelve to participate in local Little League baseball teams. Plaintiff claims that Congressional Charter of Little League Baseball, Inc. with a purpose clause "to promote, develop, supervise and voluntarily assist in all lawful ways to interest boys who will participate in Little League baseball" violates the New Jersey statutory policy of sex discrimination in places of public accommodation. Decide. [*National Organization for Women, Essex County Chapter v. Little League Baseball, Inc.*, 318 A.2d 33 (N.J. 1974).]

9. Alfalfa Electric Co-op, Inc., plaintiff, brought this action against First National Bank & Trust Co. of Oklahoma City, defendant, to determine if a loan granted by the bank to plaintiff was unlawful. Alfalfa claims that its board of directors had no authority to encumber a portion of its assets by pledging them as collateral for loans to a nonprofit development corporation created by the plaintiff. Alfalfa seeks a declaratory judgment to determine whether the loan was *ultra vires* and, if so, it requests return of the encumbered assets from defendant, First National Bank. Is pledging corporate assets as collateral for a corporate loan within the powers of the corporation? [*Alfalfa Electric Co-op, Inc. v. First National Bank & Trust Co. of Oklahoma City*, 525 P.2d 644 (Okla. 1974).]

10. In the case of *Goldenberg v. Bartell Broadcasting Corporation*, 262 N.Y. Supp.2d 274 (1965),[5] the court held that the corporation had acted *ultra vires*. Discuss the court's holding and explain how the court reached this conclusion.

---

[5] See pp. 771–72.

Business Organizations: B. Corporations

Corporate Stock and Shareholders

43

After you have read this chapter, you should be able to:

1. Define a share of stock.
2. List and explain the rights of a shareholder.
3. Distinguish the two basic kinds of stock.
4. Explain cumulative voting by shareholders.
5. Explain voting by proxy.
6. Define and explain a voting trust.
7. Define a dividend and explain a "surplus" for its payment.
8. Distinguish a "certificated security" from an "uncertificated security" and explain the transferring of each.
9. Explain the procedures for restricting the transfer of stock.
10. Explain a shareholders' derivative suit.
11. Give examples when a shareholder may be held personally liable to corporate creditors.
12. Explain the function of the state and federal regulation of stock issuance.
13. Define a wasting asset corporation.
14. Explain the purpose and function of the Foreign Corrupt Practices Act.

Introduction

We have learned that the corporation is a legal entity separate and distinct from its shareholders. As a result, shareholders are not liable for obligations of the corporation; the obligations are not obligations of the shareholders. The corporate stock is owned by the shareholders and, therefore, it becomes important to discuss what is meant by corporate stock and to understand the rights of the shareholders.

Corporate Stock

Nature

share of stock (stock)
a unit of interest in a corporation

When you purchase shares of stock in a corporation, a stock certificate is generally issued as evidence of your fractional ownership in the business.[1] **"Shares mean the units into which the proprietary interests in a corporation are divided"** (Model Bus. Corp. Act, sec. 2 (d) (1971)). As an owner you would have numerous

Figure 43.1a   Example of Certificate of Stock (Front)

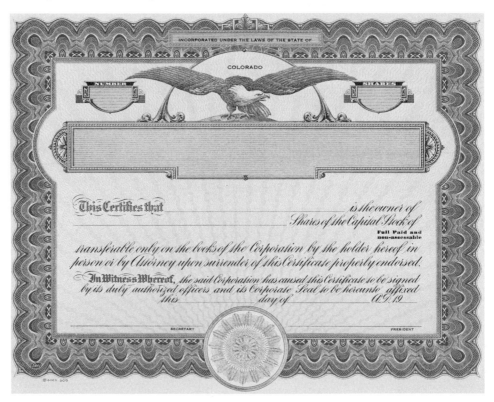

---

[1] Revised Article 8 of the Uniform Commercial Code (1977) has been extended to cover a registered security interest not represented by a written instrument called an "uncertificated security." See p. 787 for further discussion.

rights, depending on the kind of stock purchased. Generally a **shareholder** (stock-holder) has: (1) the right to share in the profits of the corporation by way of a dividend distribution; (2) the right to share in the surplus upon dissolution; (3) the right to vote at stockholders' meetings; and (4) the right to transfer his stock. However, because the corporation owns the assets in its own name, as a shareholder you do not have any interest in *specific* corporate property. A corporation's ability to raise substantial capital by dividing its ownership into shares of stock that may be sold to the general public is part of the foundation of our free-enterprise system.

Classes of Stock

The articles of incorporation require the incorporators to state the initial capitalization of the corporation—that is, the number of shares and kind of stock the corporation will have the authority to issue. A selection of the kinds of stock

Figure 43.1b   Example of Certificate of Stock (Back)

will depend upon the nature of the business. The capitalization may subsequently be changed by amending the articles of incorporation with the stockholders' approval.

Common Stock. The two basic kinds of stock are *common* and *preferred.* Common stock has the ordinary rights of participation in a corporation, such as the right to vote at shareholders' meetings, share in the dividends, and share in the distribution of corporate assets on dissolution.

Par value stock is stock with a certain minimum dollar price when issued—e.g., $1 par value means that each share is to be sold by the corporation at not less than $1 as determined by the board of directors, payable by the purchaser to the corporation. *No-par value* stock is stock issued for any price as determined by the board of directors, in the absence of charter provision to the contrary.

Preferred Stock. A holder of **preferred stock** is given preferential rights over a holder of common stock. These rights make the stock more attractive to an investor. Generally they give preference in the payment of **dividends** and in the distribution of assets upon dissolution. Although they do not have a *promise* of receiving a dividend, they will be paid before the holders of common stock. The articles of incorporation generally deny holders of preferred stock the right to vote.

Cumulative preferred stock entitles the holder to a certain dividend distribution each year, which, if not paid, accumulates over the years until funds become available. When a dividend is declared, it can not be paid until all back accumulations are paid first. *Noncumulative preferred stock* does not have such an accumulation, but it does have priority over dividends declared on common stock. *Participating preferred stock* entitles the holder to participate with the holders of common stock in any dividend distribution remaining after dividends are first paid on the preferred stock. *Non-participating preferred stock* is not entitled to participate in the surplus that is distributed to the holders of common stock. Even preferred shareholders have no right to demand a dividend when the directors honestly decide not to declare one.

Rights of Shareholders

A shareholder has a contractual relationship with the corporation whereby it agrees to give the shareholder certain rights for the consideration (selling price) of the stock.

The consideration for the issuance of shares may be paid, in whole or in part, in money, cash, or in other property, or in labor or services actually performed for the corporation. [Model Bus. Corp. Act, sec. 19 (1971).]

The following case illustrates the requirement that the price must be paid before issuance of corporate shares.

Business Organizations: B. Corporations

Facts

Plaintiffs, Manhart and others, filed this suit individually and as major stockholders against defendants United Steel Industries, Inc., Hurt, and Griffitts, alleging that the corporation had issued Hurt 5,000 shares of its stock in consideration of Hurt agreeing to perform CPA and bookkeeping services for the corporation for one year in the future, and had issued Griffitts 4,000 shares of its stock in consideration for the promised conveyance of a five-acre tract of land to the corporation, which land was never conveyed. The lower court entered judgment declaring the stock issued to Hurt and Griffitts void. Defendants appealed.

Decision

Judgment for plaintiffs.

Reasoning

Article 12, section 6, Texas Constitution, Vernon's Ann. St. provides: "No corporation shall issue stock . . . except for money paid, labor done, or property actually received." The 5,000 shares were issued to Hurt before the CPA services were rendered and hence were illegally issued and void. The 4,000 shares issued to Griffitts were issued for a promise to convey land in the future and were also illegally issued and void. The board of directors does not have authority to issue shares contrary to state statutory law for services to be performed in the future (as in the case of Hurt) or for property not received (as in the case of Griffitts).

United Steel Industries, Inc. v. Manhart 405 S.W.2d 231 (Tex. 1966).

As evidence of the contractual relationship, the shareholder may receive a stock certificate (certificated security) duly executed by the corporate officers, generally the president and secretary.

The shares of a corporation shall be represented by certificates signed by the president . . . and the secretary. Each certificate representing shares shall state upon the face thereof:
(a) that the corporation is organized under the laws of this state,
(b) the name of the person to whom issued,
(c) the number and class of shares, and the designation of the series,
(d) the par value of each share or a statement that the shares are without par value.
No certificate shall be issued for any share until such share is fully paid. [Model Bus. Corp. Act, sec. 23 (1971).]

As an owner of the stock, the shareholder may generally sell it at any price, transfer his title to another as a gift, or pledge it as security for a loan.

Stockholders usually have the following rights: (1) the right to vote at shareholders' meetings; (2) the right to receive a dividend; (3) the right to inspect the corporate books; (4) pre-emptive rights; (5) the right to transfer the stock; (6) the right to sue the corporation or third parties for improper action; and (7) the right to share in the profits upon dissolution.

Right to Vote

Shareholders have the right to vote for the directors and on other appropriate matters at their annual meeting or at any duly called special stockholders' meeting. The right to vote may be denied to any class of stock in the articles of incorporation, in which event a stockholder has *nonvoting shares*. Changes in the articles of incorporation require stockholders' approval and the amended articles to be filed at the office of the secretary of state.[2] For example, a corporate name change or recapitalization generally requires approval by a majority of the stockholders. Treasury shares—i.e., its own shares reacquired by the corporation—do not have any voting rights. The corporation may reacquire its shares in various ways, such as by buying them.

Who May Vote.　The corporation maintains a stock transfer book that records the shareholders who are entitled to receive notice of all meetings. Generally only those recorded shareholders may vote.[3]

A shareholder may desire to **pledge** the stock to obtain a loan. In that event he maintains the right to vote unless the shares are transferred to the pledgee.[4] For example, if a bank required you to pledge your I.B.M. stock as security for a $5,000 loan, you would maintain voting rights during the term of the loan. If you defaulted and transferred the shares to the bank, it would have voting rights.

Nonvoting shareholders may have the statutory right to vote as a class upon certain amendments to the articles of incorporation. Examples of such amendments are: (1) an increase or decrease of the aggregate number of authorized shares of the nonvoting stock; (2) an increase or decrease in the par value of the nonvoting stock; (3) an increase in the number of authorized shares having superior rights to the nonvoting stock; or (4) a cancellation of accrued dividends of the nonvoting stock that have not been declared.[5]

Number of Votes.　Under the common law a shareholder was entitled to only one vote regardless of the number of shares he owned. Today by statute a stockholder may vote as many shares of voting stock as he owns.

State statutes generally provide for **cumulative voting** by shareholders in the election of directors. The articles of incorporation will grant this right that entitles a shareholder to as many votes as he has shares of voting stock multiplied by the number of directors to be elected. Your vote = number of shares you own x number of directors to be elected. For example, if the corporate board consisted of 10 directors and you had 100 shares of voting stock, you may have 1,000 votes that may be cast for any one director or in any other manner. The minority

pledge
the possessory security interest in bailed goods acquired by the bailee when there is a bailment for the purpose of security

bailment
a delivery of goods by a bailor to a bailee which are to be returned to the bailor or as he directs, in accordance with the bailment agreement

cumulative voting
a method of voting whereby a shareholder has as many votes as he has shares of voting stock multiplied by the number of directors to be elected

---

[2] See MODEL BUS. CORP. ACT, sec. 59 (1971) for procedures to amend articles of incorporation.

[3] UCC 8–207(1).

[4] UCC 8–207.

[5] MODEL BUS. CORP. ACT, sec. 60 (1971).

shareholders are thereby given an indirect voice in the management of the corporation that could otherwise be denied to them by 51 percent of the voting shareholders.

Voting by Proxy.   Many shareholders of large corporations do not desire to personally attend the annual shareholders' meeting and other special meetings but wish to exercise their voting right. The shareholder may, by written **proxy**, authorize another to vote for him.

Minority shareholders of large corporations occasionally engage in a proxy fight in an attempt to vote as a block for a particular issue or to elect directors. Proxy solicitation is now regulated by the Securities and Exchange Commission, which requires that sufficient information be provided shareholders regarding the nature of the proxy fight.[6] In the following case, such information was not provided, resulting in illegality.

proxy
a shareholder's written authorization to another person to vote his shares at a corporate meeting; also the person with such authority

Facts
The plaintiff, Securities and Exchange Commission, sued defendant, Lockheed Aircraft Corp., seeking a permanent injunction against Lockheed for violation of security laws. During the period from 1968 to at least September 1975, Lockheed made secret payments of at least $25 million (at times in cash) to foreign government officials to aid Lockheed in procuring and maintaining contracts with foreign government customers. This information was not disclosed in proxy statements sent to its shareholders. Is a corporation required to disclose illegal activity in proxy solicitations?

Decision
Yes. Judgment for plaintiff, Securities and Exchange Commission.

Reasoning
Use of the mails to submit proxies to shareholders that fail to disclose illegal activity is false and misleading and a violation of section 14(a) of the Securities Exchange Act.

Securities and Exchange Commission v. Lockheed Aircraft Corp., C.C.H. Fed. Sec. L.Rep. Sec. 95, 509 (D.D.C. 1976).

Voting Trust.   The shareholders may agree to pool their voting stock in an attempt to control the management of the corporation. A **voting trust** is a trust created by an agreement between the shareholders to transfer legal title to their voting stock to a party serving as a trustee who is authorized by the trust to vote the stock as a unit. The trustee is a **fiduciary** with implied duties owed to the stockholders to protect their interest and with limited powers to act in accordance with the voting trust agreement. In the following case, the voting trust was upheld as legal in concept and duration.

voting trust
a trust created by an agreement between the shareholders to transfer legal title to their voting stock to a party (trustee) who is authorized to vote the stock as a unit

fiduciary
a person with a duty to act primarily for the benefit of another

---

[6] Securities Exchange Act of 1934, sec. 14(a).

Facts

Plaintiff, Nathan Weil, was a director of Self Service Sales Corporation along with Edward Beresth, Gershon Weil, and Raymond Harrison. As holders of the majority stock, they entered into a stockholders' voting trust that provided "as long as each remained a stockholder of Self Service Sales Corporation, he would vote for the election of the other parties to the board of directors." At a later date the other directors voted to adopt new bylaws not consistent with the agreement. Nathan Weil objected and brought this suit to enforce the voting agreement. The defendants claim that the voting trust violated public policy and was unenforceable.

Decision

Judgment for plaintiff, Nathan Weil.

Reasoning

A voting agreement is not invalid under the common law. Although stockholders can not by contract alter their statutory powers, they can agree to limit their exercise of these powers. The defendants' claim of invalidity is based on an alleged lack of a limit as to the duration of the agreement, which they claim is contrary to the public policy of Connecticut. The voting agreement here is not unlimited in duration. The obligation of each stockholder to vote for the other signatories as directors expressly exists only "so long as he is a stockholder of Self Service Sales Corporation." Thus, even if there were a public policy forbidding voting agreements of unlimited duration, it can not be said that the policy has been violated.

Weil v. Beresth, 220 A.2d 456 (Conn. 1966).

Dividends

If you were to invest in a corporation as a stockholder, you would expect a return on your investment by way of a dividend and an increase in the market value of the stock. A dividend is a portion of the corporate net profits or *surplus* set aside for distribution to the shareholders. It is within the discretion of the directors to declare a dividend, but it is not to be declared when the corporation is insolvent. *Until a dividend is declared by the board of directors, the stockholders have no right to receive one.* If the directors refuse to declare a dividend and have clearly abused their discretion by continuously voting against a "declaration," a court may require the payment of a dividend. This is illustrated by the following well known case.

Facts

Plaintiffs, shareholders in the Ford Motor Company, defendant, brought an action to compel the company's board of directors to declare a special dividend. The company had made substantial profits over the years, and a regular quarterly dividend of five percent per month on its capital stock had been paid since 1911, with additional special dividends of from $1 million to $10 million per year from 1911 to 1915. In 1916 the board of directors decided to continue the regular five percent per month dividend but no longer to make any additional special dividends. At that time the company's surplus was $112 million, its yearly profits $60 million, its liabilities including capital stock less than $20 million, and its cash on hand $54 million. The company had planned improvements costing $24 million. Judgment was for the plaintiffs, and the company appealed.

Decision

Affirmed in part for plaintiffs and reversed in part for defendant.

Reasoning

Mr. Ford's testimony creates the impression that he thinks the Ford Motor Company has made too much money, has had too large profits, and that, although large profits might still be earned, a sharing of them with the public by reducing the price of the output of the company ought to be undertaken.

A business corporation is organized and carried on primarily for the benefit of its stockholders. The powers of the directors are to be exercised in the choice of means to attain that end and do not extend to a change in the end itself, to the reduction of profits or to the nondistribution of profits among stockholders in order to devote them to other purposes. It is not within the lawful powers of a board of directors to shape and conduct the affairs of a corporation for the merely incidental benefit of shareholders and for the primary purpose of benefiting others. There was a large daily, weekly, monthly receipt of cash. The output was practically continuous and was continuously, and within a few days, turned into cash. Moreover, the contemplated expenditures were not to be immediately made. It would appear that, accepting and approving the plan of the directors, it was their duty to distribute on or near the 1st of August 1916 a very large sum of money to stockholders.

Dodge v. Ford Motor Co., 170 N.W. 668 (Mich. 1919).

However, the courts are hesitant to substitute their judgment for the dividend policy of the directors who were elected by the shareholders to use their discretion in managing the corporation. This is illustrated by the following case.

Facts

Gay, the plaintiff, was a minority shareholder in defendant corporation, Gay's Super Markets, Inc. He brought this suit against the corporation and its directors, alleging that their refusal to declare a dividend was not done in good faith. The defendant claimed that, although it had $125,000 in cash, the directors felt that due to the expansion commitments of the company, the funds could not be considered available for dividends. Is this an abuse of the directors' discretion?

Decision

No. Judgment for defendant, Gay's Super Markets, Inc.

Reasoning

To justify judicial intervention it must be shown that the decision not to declare a dividend amounted to fraud, bad faith, or an abuse of discretion on the part of the corporate officials authorized to make the determination. If there are plausible business decisions supportive of the board of directors' judgment not to declare a dividend, a court will not interfere. It is not our function to referee every corporate squabble or disagreement.

Gay v. Gay's Super Markets, Inc., 343 A.2d 577 (Me. 1975).

Fund for Declaration of Dividends. A dividend is declared when the board of directors votes to approve a resolution on a dividend and announces its distribution. There must be a "surplus" for the payment—that is, an amount of assets that exceeds the liabilities and the issued and outstanding shares.

The shareholders entitled to the dividend then become *general creditors* of the corporation and may enforce the debt if the corporation should become insolvent prior to distributing the dividends. Once the dividend has been declared, announced, and set aside, the fund is held in trust for the benefit of the shareholders. Corporate creditors can not reach the assets in this fund. If the stock is transferred to a new owner after the dividend is declared but before the announced record date for payment, the transferee is generally entitled to receive the dividend.

As an exception to the rules discussed regarding the need for a surplus before the directors can declare a dividend, a *wasting assets corporation* may pay dividends out of current net profits. For instance, an off-coast oil drilling venture is a wasting asset corporation because it is organized to exhaust or use up the assets (oil) of the corporation, in contrast to an industrial corporation organized to manufacture computers on a continuing basis.

Effective Date of Dividend Distribution. As the owner of stock, you generally have the right to sell it at any time. If the directors declare a dividend, the question arises as to whom it should be paid if the holder transferred the stock *after* the declaration date. For example, the board may declare a dividend today *(declaration date)* to be effective in one month *(effective date)* and payable to the stockholders of record in two months *(payment date)*. The vote to declare a dividend is irrevocable and the registered holder on the effective date will be sent the dividend on the payment date. If the corporation is not aware that a transfer took place and paid the *registered holder* who sold the stock to a transferee, the corporation is protected and the transferee must sue the transferor for the money received, *not the corporation.*[7]

Right to Inspect Corporate Books

As a stockholder in a corporation, you are an owner of a fractional interest. In that capacity you are entitled to exercise certain ownership rights over the stock, such as selling, pledging, or giving it to another, as well as the right to inspect the property held by the corporation. Other owners have the same rights and hence their property interests must also be protected. The common law, therefore, granted to a shareholder the right to inspect the corporate books and records at reasonable times for a proper purpose. It is the "proper purpose" aspect of this right that frequently causes a problem. Review of the books as a "fishing expedition" is not permitted. For example, may a public interest group, such as the environmentalists, purchase a block of stock (100 shares) in a corporation and demand the right to review the minute book of the board of directors and shareholders? Generally no, because a shareholder does not demonstrate a

---

[7] UCC 8–207.

"proper purpose" by disapproving of a corporate activity such as a manufacturing company causing a high rate of pollution. The federal Environmental Protection Agency has authority to regulate air standards; it would be the proper party to investigate the alleged illegal act.[8]

If the corporation improperly refuses an inspection of the records, the shareholder may seek court action. In the following case, the court refused to require a corporation to permit inspection by a shareholder for an improper purpose.

Facts
Plaintiff, Pillsbury, bought several shares of Honeywell stock during the Vietnam War to give himself a voice in Honeywell's affairs so that he could persuade the company to cease munitions productions. He made formal demands that Honeywell permit him access to its shareholder ledger and all corporate records dealing with weapons manufacture. Honeywell rejected the demands and argued that a "proper purpose" for inspection must be one that involves an economic concern.

Decision
Judgment for defendant, Honeywell.

Reasoning
The right to inspect is based on the shareholder's economic concern. The shareholder must have a proper purpose to examine the corporate books. Pillsbury would have the right to inspect the records only if he were concerned with the long- or short-term effect of Honeywell's production of munitions. Pillsbury was not here interested even in Honeywell's long-term well-being or in the enhancement of the value of his shares. His sole purpose was to persuade the company to adopt his social and political concerns regardless of any economic benefit to himself or Honeywell.

State ex rel. *Pillsbury v. Honeywell, Inc.,* 191 N.W.2d 406 (Minn. 1971).

Most states have statutory laws regulating the inspection right. Some give the shareholder the absolute right while others go beyond the "proper purpose" limitation of the common law. The Model Business Corporation Act grants the right only to holders of record "at least six months immediately preceding his demand . . . and who own at least five percent of all the outstanding shares of the corporation, upon written demand stating the purpose thereof." This type of a statute will preclude most public interest groups from challenging what they believe to be improper corporate activity through an investigation of the books and records.

A shareholder may authorize an attorney or other agent to inspect the books on his behalf.

Financial Statements
An inspection of the corporate books may include the minutes of the directors' and stockholders' meetings, the stock transfer books, and the books of account. Due to their personal nature, we have seen most states require a "proper purpose"

---

[8] See pp. 621–27 for a discussion of administrative regulations.

to inspect. There is generally no such limitation to the shareholders' right to receive financial statements showing the corporation's assets, liabilities, and operations.

Pre-emptive Rights

You will recall that the incorporators established the original *authorized* capitalization in the articles of incorporation filed with the secretary of state. The corporation then had the right to issue shares up to the authorized amount. If the corporation desires to exceed that initial authorization, it must amend the articles by the directors voting a resolution and having it approved by a majority of the voting shareholders. When the amended articles of incorporation are filed and approved by the state, new stock may be issued. A **pre-emptive right** is the right of the voting stockholders of record to purchase the new stock in proportion to their old stock interest before the new stock may be offered to the public. Hence, a shareholder may maintain his relative voting power and dividend interest.

Most states prohibit the pre-emptive right for an issuance of treasury stock or for an issuance to employees as a part of a stock purchase plan.

The modern trend of corporate law generally follows the Model Business Corporation Act and limits or abolishes the pre-emptive right.

The following case shows how the common law viewed the nature of stock ownership to include pre-emptive rights.

pre-emptive right
a shareholder's right to subscribe to a newly authorized issue of stock proportionate to his holdings in the corporation

Facts
The plaintiff, Stokes, a shareholder in defendant corporation, Continental Trust Co. of the City of New York, brought suit to compel the defendant to issue to him at par such a proportion of an increase made in its capital stock as the number of shares held by him before such increase bore to the number of all the shares originally issued. Defendant was a banking corporation organized in 1890 with a capital stock of $500,000 consisting of 5,000 shares of the par value of $100 each. Plaintiff was one of the original shareholders of the corporation. The directors of defendant met and authorized a special stockholders' meeting for the purpose of voting on the increase of stock. The stockholders voted to increase the stock and the plaintiff demanded from

defendant the right to subscribe for his proportionate increase of the new stock and offered to pay immediately for the same.

Decision
Judgment for plaintiff.

Reasoning
The question presented for decision is whether, according to the facts found, the plaintiff had a legal right to subscribe for and take the same number of shares of the new stock that he held of the old. What is the nature of the right acquired by a stockholder through the ownership of shares of stock? While he does not own and can not dispose of any specific property of the corporation, yet he and his associates own the corporation itself, its charter, franchises, and all rights conferred

thereby, including the right to increase stock. He has an inherent right to his proportionate share of any dividend declared, of any surplus arising upon dissolution, and he can prevent waste or misappropriation of the property of the corporation by those in control. Finally, he has the right to vote for directors and upon all propositions subject by law to the control of the stockholders, and this is his supreme right and main protection. Stockholders have no direct voice in transacting the corporate business, but through their right to vote they can select those whom the law invests with the power of management and control. The power to manage its affairs resides in the directors, who are its agents, but the power to elect directors resides in the stockholders. The power of the individual stockholder to vote in proportion to the number of his stocks is vital and can not be cut off or curtailed by the action of all the other stockholders even with the cooperation of the directors and officers.

Stokes v. Continental Trust Co. of the City of New York, 78 N.E. 1090 (N.Y. 1906).

Transfer of Shares

The rights and duties of corporations and stockholders to transfer stock is governed by Article 8 of the Uniform Commercial Code. Article 8 was revised in 1977 to include a security investment not represented by a written certificate defined as an "uncertificated security."[9] The issuance of an "uncertificated security" is *registered* upon the security transfer book maintained by the corporation. An *initial transaction statement* is then sent to the shareholder. The official Comment to the Uniform Commercial Code, section 8–101 states: "This Article does not purport to determine whether a particular issue of securities should be represented by certificates, in whole or in part. That determination is left to the parties involved, subject to federal and state law."

Transfer of Uncertificated Securities. An uncertificated security is transferred by the transferor (seller) instructing the corporation to issue a *transaction statement* to the new owner (or pledgee) and register the transaction on its transfer ledger. *Within two business days after the registration of a transferred uncertificated security,* the corporation must send the new registered owner (or registered pledgee) and the transferor a *transaction statement.* The transaction statement serves as registration notice to the new owner and a reduction of interest notice to the transferor-seller.

A *periodic statement* must be sent at least annually to the registered owners describing the issuance of which the uncertificated security is a part.[10]

Transfer of Certificated Securities. To effect a proper transfer of a certificated security (stock certificate), the transferor-seller must deliver the certificate and if necessary indorse it over to the purchaser. If the transfer is of a temporary nature (e.g., a pledge of the stock as security for a bank loan), the owner may make the assignment on a separate instrument which requires delivery of both the separate document pledging the stock and the stock certificate.[11]

---

[9] UCC 8–102(b).   [10] UCC 8–408.   [11] UCC 8–309.

"Bona Fide Purchaser." Article 8 of the Uniform Commercial Code deals with "investment securities" that include stock and bonds. These securities may be transferred to a **bona fide purchaser** who may acquire greater rights than the transferor-holder.[12]

A bona fide purchaser is a purchaser for value in good faith and without notice of any adverse claims . . . [UCC 8–302].

This is a change from the common law of assignments that limited the transferee's rights in the stock to those of the transferor. Article 8 allows the "bona fide purchaser" to defeat a claim by the owner of the stock that could be asserted against the transferor; for example, if the stock was acquired by fraud, deceit, or without consideration by the transferor from the owner.

Example 1: A fraudulently induced O, the owner of a stock certificate for 100 shares of X corporation, to indorse and deliver the certificate to A. O can avoid the transaction and reacquire the certificate. However, if A then sells and delivers the certificate to B, a bona fide purchaser, B acquires the title to the certificate and the shares represented thereby.

Example 2: T steals O's certificate of stock and sells and delivers it to Z, an innocent purchaser for value. Since O never indorsed the certificate, nobody can later become a **holder.** Therefore, no later person can become a bona fide purchaser. However, if O had indorsed it (signed his name) making it a bearer certificate, and then T had stolen it and sold and delivered it to Z, Z would be a holder and become a bona fide purchaser with title to the certificate and the shares represented thereby.

Statute of Frauds. If you orally contracted to *sell* your stock, it would be unenforceable regardless of the selling price under UCC 8–319, a special statute of frauds provision. Under the Code, if the contract *for sale* of securities is in writing, it is enforceable. If it is oral, it is unenforceable unless proved in one of four ways. Reference should be made to section 8–319 of the Code.

In the following case, there was no contract for sale but, rather, an agency contract, and therefore the contract did not come under any statute of frauds and was enforceable even though oral.

Facts

The plaintiff, Reinhart, was a stockholder who hired the defendant, Rauscher Pierce Securities Corp., to sell his stock. He instructed the defendant to sell when its value decreased by more than ten percent of the cost to Reinhart. The defendant failed to sell, and Reinhart sued for damages. The defense was that there was no liability for an oral contract to sell stock. From a decision in favor of the defendant, the plaintiff appealed.

---

[12] Although a security is a negotiable instrument, its transfer is not governed by Article 3 on Commercial Paper but rather by Article 8 of the Uniform Commercial Code.

Decision
Judgment for Reinhart, the plaintiff.

Reasoning
UCC section 8–319 does not apply here because this is not a "sale of securities" but rather an agency relationship. Reinhart never said he wanted Rauscher Pierce Securities Corp. to hold his stock for a year or more. He could terminate the agency within a year. Hence, the statute of frauds does not apply.

Reinhart v. Rauscher Pierce Securities Corp., 490 P.2d 240 (N.M. 1971).

Restrictions on Transfer.   The incorporators of a closely held corporation may decide to issue its stock to select shareholders. For instance, a family business may desire to keep control of its ownership and management. The articles of incorporation and the bylaws may state a restriction allowing the corporation or its shareholders the right to purchase the stock before it is offered to outsiders. The selling price may be established in accordance with a stated formula stated in the text of the restriction or it may be the current market price. Restrictions on stock are generally valid if they are conspicuous and reasonable. Because a purchaser is generally not aware of restrictions in the articles of incorporation or bylaws, the stock certificate must conspicuously note the restriction, unless the buyer has actual knowledge of it, in order for it to be effective.

In order to be conspicuously noted, the Code requires it to be written so that a reasonable person ought to have noticed it, as a printing or heading in capitals or in larger or contrasting type or color.[13] The stock certificate need not state the terms of the restriction, but the purchaser must have the right to read the full text that generally appears in the articles of incorporation or the bylaws.

If the security is uncertificated, the *initial transaction statement* sent to the registered owner must note the restriction.[14]

Shareholders' Remedies
As a stockholder, you own a fractional portion of the corporation with contractual rights. If the directors act wrongfully and deprive the stockholders of their rights, they may sue for breach of contract. For example, the stockholder may sue the directors for not being permitted to exercise any of his rights previously discussed, such as his right to a dividend when one should have been declared, to vote at meetings, to inspect the corporate books for a proper purpose, or to exercise his pre-emptive right. In any of these instances, more than one stockholder will be *individually* injured and any one, on behalf of the others, may bring a *derivative* suit against the corporation. This is illustrated in the following case upholding a derivative action.

---

[13] UCC 1–201(10).

[14] UCC 8–204(b).

Facts

The plaintiff, Rosa Taormina, as the widow and executrix of the estate of Calogero Taormina, sued Taormina Corporation and the officers and directors of the corporation as individual defendants. The Taormina Corporation carried on the business of canning goods. Calogero Taormina owned 498 shares of stock, and the individual defendants owned the remaining shares. The directors and officers formed a partnership under the name of Taormina Company and caused the assets and goodwill of the corporation to be transferred to the partnership. The same canning business developed by the corporation was thereafter conducted by the partnership. The plaintiff claimed that the defendants unjustly profited themselves at the expense of the corporation and asked the court that they account for all profits made by the partnership. The defendants contend that the injury was to Calogero Taormina individually and that the only remedy is a direct suit against the corporation to recover a share of the profits obtained from the business conducted by the partnership.

Decision

Judgment for the plaintiff, Rosa Taormina.

Reasoning

The relief to be obtained in a derivative action is relief to the corporation in which all stockholders, whether guilty or innocent of the wrongs complained of, shall share indirectly. If the argument of the defendant was accepted, it would mean that no derivative action could be maintained by a stockholder to redress corporate wrongs if those wrongs had resulted in loss to the value of the stockholdings.

Taormina v. Taormina Corp., 78 A.2d 473 (Del. 1951).

Shareholders' Liability

Shareholders are not liable for *corporate* contracts or tort claims because the corporation, as a legal entity, is separate and distinct from its owners, the shareholders. However, shareholders contract with the corporation in the purchase of stock and are obligated to pay *to the corporation* the full consideration of the shares.

Corporate creditors who can not satisfy their claims from corporate assets may bring a "bill in equity" against a stockholder who failed to pay his subscription price. In this way the price becomes available through the corporation to the corporate creditors.

Watered Stock

watered stock
corporate stock reduced in value by the issuance of par value shares for less than their par value

You recall that the consideration for stock issuance of shares may be paid in property or services actually performed for the corporation. If such property or services are overvalued and worth less than the par value of the share, the share is diluted; hence the name "**watered stock**." Par value stock may also be issued for less than par value for (1) insufficient cash; (2) payment of a stock dividend

Business Organizations: B. Corporations

without transferring the surplus to the capital account;[15] (3) a stock bonus; or (4) a gratuitous issue. In such events, both the corporation and the stockholders are liable in tort for deceiving the corporate creditors who relied upon the misrepresented outstanding par value capital stock as having been paid for in an amount of at least its par value.

Securities Regulations

Blue-Sky Laws

The *intrastate* issuance of securities is regulated in many states by *blue-sky laws* (so called because stock was praised to the blue sky). If securities are sold to the public, the state may establish procedures to assure public protection from a fraudulent issuance. A stockholder may rescind a stock sale made in violation of a "blue-sky" law. The issuing corporation is generally required to register and have its security approved by the state security commission prior to public sale.

Federal Securities Act of 1933

If you purchased a security offered to the public on an *interstate* basis, the Federal Securities Act of 1933 requires the corporation to file a *registration statement* and a prospectus with the Securities and Exchange Commission describing the offering if it exceeds $2,000,000. If less, the corporation must file *notification* and the *offering circular* with the SEC. Fraudulent statements that are mailed interstate to stockholders are a violation of the Securities Exchange Act.[16] This is illustrated by the following case where fraud was not alleged in the complaint.

Facts

Stewart, the plaintiff and a potential purchaser of securities, brought suit against Bennett, the defendant, an officer and director of Viatron Corporation, underwriters of the security offering, and Viatron's accounting firm, alleging misstatements and omissions in the registration statement filed by Viatron with the Securities and Exchange Commission. Defendants claim that the plaintiff did not allege and prove fraud and hence they are not liable under the Securities Act.

Decision

Judgment for defendants.

Reasoning

A security purchaser must prove fraud under the Securities Act to obtain relief. The Act imposes civil liability for untrue or misleading information that appears in a registration statement. The stockholder must prove reasonable reliance on the misrepresentation relating to the purchase and the use of the mails or other instrument of interstate commerce. The complaint fails to allege fraud and hence does not state a claim under the Securities Act.

Stewart v. Bennett, 359 F. Supp. 878 (Mass. 1973).

---

[15] See p. 784 on Fund for Declaration of Dividends.

[16] Securities Exchange Act of 1934, 15 U.S.C. sec. 78(b) and Rule 10b–5, 17 C.F.R. sec. 240 10b–5.

Foreign Corrupt Practices Act of 1977

Investigations by the Securities and Exchange Commission disclosed corrupt foreign payments by over 300 U.S. corporations involving hundreds of millions of dollars. Congress responded to these corporate abuses by enacting the Foreign Corrupt Practices Act of 1977. The Act amends section 13 (b) of the Securities Exchange Act of 1934 to require reporting corporations to comply with certain *accounting standards.* In addition, the Act makes it unlawful for such reporting corporations *or any domestic concern (i.e., any business association) not subject to the Securities Exchange Act* to engage in *corrupt practices* with foreign officials.

Accounting Standards

The accounting standards provision applies only to reporting corporations subject to SEC jurisdiction. It requires them to *keep books, records, and accounts which, in reasonable detail, accurately and fairly reflect the transactions and dispositions of corporate assets.* Foreign bribery is often paid from off-the-books slush funds that are made illegal by the Act. Corporations subject to the SEC are also required *to devise and maintain a system of internal accounting controls* sufficient to provide reasonable assurance that transactions are executed in accordance with management's specific authorization and are recorded as necessary to permit preparation of financial statements in conformity with generally accepted accounting principles or other applicable criteria and to maintain accountability for its assets. Access to assets is permitted only in accordance with management authorization and the recorded accountability for assets is compared with existing assets at reasonable intervals. The Act requires appropriate action to be taken with respect to any differences.[17]

Foreign Corrupt Practices

This portion of the Act applies to reporting corporations subject to the SEC, their officers, directors, employees, agents (of the corporation), or stockholders and to any individuals of a domestic concern (any business association) who make use of the mails or any means of interstate commerce to corruptly pay any official of a foreign government or a foreign political party for the purpose of influencing any decision in order to obtain or retain business.

Penalties for Violation

A corporation may be fined up to $1,000,000 for violation and an individual may be fined up to $10,000 and imprisoned for a term of up to five years or both.

---

[17] 15 U.S.C. sec. 78q–1(b).

Summary Statement

1. Stockholders have a contractual relationship with the corporation with consequent rights.
2. Generally a stockholder has the following rights:
   a. to vote for the election of the directors and the other appropriate matters at a meeting of the stockholders;
   b. to receive a declared dividend;
   c. to inspect corporate books for a proper purpose;
   d. to transfer the stock subject to any restrictions;
   e. to sue the corporation for improper action when authorized by corporate state law;
   f. to purchase new stock in proportion to his old stock held before the new stock is offered to the public (pre-emptive right); and
   g. to share in the profits upon dissolution of the corporation.
3. Common stock is the ordinary voting stock of the corporation.
4. Preferred stock has preference over other kinds of stock with respect to dividends and, generally, a priority on distribution of the profits upon dissolution. Preferred stock may be:
   a. cumulative,
   b. non-cumulative,
   c. participating,
   d. non-participating.
5. Cumulative voting entitles a stockholder to as many votes as he has shares of voting stock multiplied by the number of directors to be elected.
6. Proxy vote is written authorization given to another to vote on behalf of a shareholder. The SEC regulates proxy solicitation.
7. A voting trust is a stockholders' agreement whereby title to their stock is transferred to a trustee who votes the stock as a unit.
8. A dividend is a portion of the corporate net profits set aside for distribution to the shareholders. It is declared by the directors.
9. An "uncertificated security" is not represented by a stock certificate. The shareholder receives a transaction statement from the corporation as evidence of his registered interest.
10. Stock transfer may be restricted if the terms are conspicuous and reasonable.
11. A stockholder may sue the directors if wrongfully deprived of his rights.
12. Stockholders may be held personally liable to corporate creditors if they fail to pay the full consideration of the purchased shares or for the purchase of "watered stock."
13. State and federal governments have extensive regulations on stock offered to the public.

The following case illustrates how the court construes the term "security" to include an investment of money in an enterprise with the expectation of profits. Notice how the court finds an investment contract even though the investor contributed some effort to obtain a return on his investment.

Securities and Exchange Commission v. Glenn W. Turner Enterprises, Inc.

474 F.2d 476 (1973), cert. denied, 414 U.S. 821 (1973)

Duniway, J. This is an appeal from an order granting the Securities and Exchange Commission a preliminary injunction. The injunction prohibits offering and selling by appellants [defendants in the lower court] of certain of their "Adventures" and "Plans," and also any withdrawal by appellants of funds from the assets of the corporate defendants other than in the regular course of business. Dare to Be Great, Inc. (Dare), a Florida corporation, is a wholly owned subsidiary of Glenn W. Turner Enterprises, Inc. The individual defendants are, or were, officers, directors, or employees of the defendant corporation.

The trial court's findings, which are fully supported by the record, demonstrate that defendants' scheme is a gigantic and successful fraud. *The question presented is whether the "Adventures" or "Plans" enjoined are "securities" within the meaning of the federal securities laws.*

The definitions of security that are found in each Act are almost identical. Both definitions include the terms "investment contract," "certificate of interest or participation in any profit-sharing agreement," and any "instrument commonly known as a 'security'." The district court held that the plans in question fell into all three categories of securities. Because we find them to be investment contracts, we need not decide whether the other definitions are applicable as well.

The 1933 and 1934 Acts are remedial legislation, among the central purposes of which is full and fair disclosure relative to the issuance of securities. . . . It is a familiar canon of legislative construction that remedial legislation should be construed broadly. . . . The Acts were designed to protect the American public from speculative or fraudulent schemes of promoters. For that reason Congress defined the term "security" broadly, and the Supreme Court has in turn construed the definition liberally. . . . And in the recent case of *Tcherepnin v. Knight*, the Court stated, "[I]n searching for the meaning and scope of the word 'security' in the Act, form should be disregarded for substance and the emphasis should be on economic reality." . . .

In *SEC v. W.J. Howey Co.*, the Supreme Court set out its by now familiar definition of an investment contract: "The test is whether the scheme involves an investment of money in a common enterprise with profits to come solely from the efforts of others." . . .

For purposes of the present case, the sticking point in the Howey definition is the word "solely," a qualification which of course exactly fitted the circumstances in Howey. All the other elements of the Howey test have been met here. There is an investment of money, a common enterprise, and the expectation of profits to come from the efforts of others. Here, however, the investor, or purchaser, must himself exert some efforts if he is to realize a return on his initial cash outlay. He must find prospects and persuade them to attend Dare Adventure Meetings, and at least some of them must then purchase a plan if he is to realize that return. Thus it can be said that the returns or profits are not coming "solely" from the efforts of others.

Strict interpretation of the requirement that profits to be earned must come "solely" from the efforts of others has been subject to criticism. . . . Adherence to such an interpretation could result in a mechanical, unduly restrictive view of what is and what is not an investment contract. It would be easy to evade by adding a requirement that the buyer contribute a modicum of effort. Thus the fact that the investors here were required to exert some efforts if a return were to be achieved should not automatically preclude a finding that the Plan or Adventure is an investment contract. To do so would not serve the purpose of the legislation. Rather we adopt a more realistic test, whether the efforts made by those other than the investor are the undeniably significant ones, those essential managerial efforts which affect the failure or success of the enterprise.

In this case, Dare's source of income is from selling the Adventures and the Plan. The purchaser is sold the idea that he will get a fixed part of the proceeds of the sales. In essence, to get that share, he invests three things: his money, his efforts to find prospects and bring them to the meetings, and whatever it costs him to create an illusion of his own affluence. He invests them in Dare's get-rich-quick scheme. What he buys is a share in the proceeds of the selling efforts of Dare. Those efforts are the sine qua non of the scheme; those efforts are what keeps it going; those efforts are what produces the money which is to make him rich. In essence, it is the right to share in the proceeds of those efforts that he buys. In our view, the scheme is no less an investment contract merely because he contributes some effort as well as money to get into it.

Our holding in this case represents no major attempt to redefine the essential nature of a security. Nor does our holding represent any real departure from the Supreme Court's definition of an investment contract as set out in Howey. We hold only that the requirement that profits come "solely" from the efforts of others would, in circumstances such as these, lead to unrealistic results if applied dogmatically, and that a more flexible approach is appropriate.

Affirmed.

Questions and Case Problems

1. Blackhawk Holding Corp., the defendant, when organized issued Class A common stock and Class B common stock. Owners of Class B stock were not entitled to dividends or to participate in the distribution of assets but did have the right to vote. Class B stock represented 28 percent of the total stock issuance. Stroh, a Class B stockholder and plaintiff, claimed that Class B stock was not valid because there was no economic interest in the corporation associated with its ownership. Is stock that only confers a right to vote valid? [*Stroh v. Blackhawk Holding Corp.*, 272 N.E. 2d 1 (Ill. 1971).]

2. X Corporation had 50,000 shares of issued and outstanding Class A voting common stock. The board of directors voted to submit to the shareholders a plan to increase the aggregate number of authorized shares of the nonvoting stock. The Class A shareholders voted in favor of the increase. Class B shareholders were not permitted to vote, and they claim that the increase was not validly approved. Decide.

3. XYZ Corp.'s board of directors never declared a dividend in its fifteen years of business. The company always earned a profit, but the directors believed a large cash account was much safer than declaring dividends. The shareholders sued the company to force a dividend. Decide.

4. American Independent Oil was a close corporation organized by the plaintiff, Abercrombie, the defendant, Davies, and nine oil companies. Davies and five of the oil companies agreed to transfer their stock to a trustee in order that the shares may be voted as a block. Abercrombie brought suit to have the agreement set aside because the voting trust did not comply with statutory requirements. May a private voting agreement be valid if it violates a statute on voting trusts? [*Abercrombie v. Davies,* 130 A.2d 338 (Del. 1957).]

5. Goldman, plaintiff, owned one-half of one percent of the stock in defendant corporation, Trans-United Industries, Inc. Goldman contends that the affairs of Trans-United were not being properly managed. The complaint states that Goldman desires to ascertain the names of stockholders and the extent of their holdings. Trans-United alleged that the true purpose in seeking examination of all the corporate books is to gain control of the corporation. May Goldman inspect the stockholders list of Trans-United? May he inspect the corporate books and records? [*Goldman v. Trans-United Industries, Inc.,* 171 A.2d 788 (Pa. 1961).]

6. Issner, plaintiff and shareholder in National Distillers Corporation, brought a derivative suit against defendant, Panhandle Eastern Pipe Line and National Helium Corporation and their respective boards of directors. Panhandle and Distillers formed a jointly owned subsidiary, National Helium, to extract helium from natural gas products by Panhandle. Each company owned 50 percent of the stock of National Helium. Issner alleged that the board of directors of Panhandle conceived of a plan and imposed it upon National Helium with primary regard to Panhandle's own interest while disregarding the interest of National Helium. May a shareholder maintain a derivative action and challenge a board of directors' decision without alleging that it was wrongfully motivated? [*Issner v. Aldrich,* 254 F.Supp. 696 (Del. 1966).]

7. Wilkes, the plaintiff, and three individual defendants organized a corporation to run a nursing home. Each party was an equal shareholder and director. They all received $100 per week for services rendered to the nursing home. The business was successful for fifteen years, when the plaintiff and another shareholder had a misunderstanding. The relationship degenerated to the point where in January of 1967 plaintiff gave notice to sell his shares for their appraised value. At the board of directors' meeting in February 1967, plaintiff's salary was cancelled and at the annual stockholders' meeting in March he was not re-elected as a director or officer. Plaintiff sued the corporation and the individual defendants for damages for lost salary and for breach of the fiduciary duties owed to minority shareholders. Decide. [*Wilkes v. Springside Nursing Home, Inc.,* 353 N.E.2d 657 (Mass. 1976).]

8. Skoglund and Ackerly, plaintiffs, brought an action against Ormand Industries, Inc. to inspect their books. Ormand Industries is engaged in the outdoor advertising business in California. Skoglund had bought and sold several

communication corporations engaged in the outdoor advertising business. Ackerly is the president of Ackerly Communications Inc., a closely held Seattle outdoor advertising company in which Skoglund is a major shareholder. Skoglund and Ackerly are substantial shareholders of Ormand. They believed that Ormand was being mismanaged and requested an inspection of the corporate books and a list of the shareholders. Ormand refused because the plaintiffs failed to show a proper purpose, and because they are in a competitive position with Ormand because of their outdoor advertising interests in the Seattle area. Decide. [*Skoglund v. Ormand Industries, Inc.,* 372 A.2d 204 (Del. 1976).]

9. XYZ Co., Inc. was a domestic corporation in New York. The corporation proposed to sell $750,000 worth of no-par common stock to the general public within the State of New York. The board of directors claimed that this stock offering is exempt from SEC registration and prospectus requirements. Decide.

10. In the case of *Securities and Exchange Commission v. Glenn W. Turner Enterprises, Inc.,* 474 F.2d 476 (1973), cert. denied, 414 U.S. 821 (1973),[18] the court briefly quotes a sentence from the case *SEC v. W.J. Howey Co.* Discuss the court's holding in the Turner Enterprises case and explain how that case can be distinguished from the quoted sentence in the Howey case.

---

[18] See pp. 794–95.

44

Corporate Management

After you have read this chapter, you should be able to:

1. Explain the managerial function of a shareholder.
2. Explain when stockholders' approval is necessary for corporate management.
3. Define a quorum.
4. Explain the managerial role of the directors.
5. Explain how board action may be taken without a formal meeting.
6. Explain the significance of a director being a fiduciary.
7. Give an illustration of a director's breach of a fiduciary duty.
8. Explain how directors are elected and removed.
9. Explain what is meant by the indemnification of a corporate officer or director.
10. Explain the managerial role of the corporate officers.
11. Explain when a corporate officer may be held personally liable.

Introduction

Society today, more than ever before, depends upon efficient management of its corporate institutions. You may serve as an employee for a corporation and depend upon it for your livelihood, well-being, and a dignified retirement. To administer these needs, corporate policy must be clearly defined and implemented. State corporate laws, the articles of incorporation, and the corporate bylaws grant authority to the stockholders, the board of directors, and the corporate officers to effectively manage the corporation. Our discussion will focus on the managerial functions of each group and their respective roles therein.

Shareholders

Shareholders are given their authority from state corporate law, the articles of incorporation, and the bylaws. In the last chapter we discussed the rights of a shareholder as a fractional owner of the corporation and his concern with making a profit from the investment. This was generally accomplished by a dividend and an increase in the market value of the stock. The principal managerial function of the shareholder is to elect the board of directors at a legal shareholders' meeting. Hence, they are not directly involved with policy decisions, which are reserved to the board of directors. A voting majority of shareholders dissatisfied with corporate policy may elect a new board of directors.

Authority.

Limited managerial functions.

Managerial decisions that would substantially change the nature of the corporation require approval by the voting stockholders: for example, changes in the articles of incorporation such as the corporate name, changes in its authorized stock, changes in corporate purpose, or a merger or a consolidation.

Shareholders' Meetings

The shareholders may vote and act legally only at a duly called and properly held regular or special stockholders' meeting.

Voting at shareholders' meeting.

Time. The time of the annual stockholders' meeting is fixed in the articles of incorporation and the bylaws. Most state statutes require a regular annual meeting.[1] Notice to the stockholders of the annual meeting is often not required but is usually given. However, *advance written notice* of a *special* meeting is required. The notice must indicate the time, place, date, and purpose of the meeting.

The bylaws generally allow a majority of the stockholders the right to call a special meeting of the stockholders.

A closely held corporation may find it burdensome to give written notice of the meeting to its few shareholders. Most statutes allow a written *waiver of notice* signed by the shareholders either before or after the meeting.

In the following case, the court held that attendance at a stockholders' meeting will not waive proper notice.

---

[1] See, for example, MASS. GEN. LAWS ANN. ch. 156, sec. 28.

Facts

Darvin, the plaintiff, brought this action to set aside actions taken at the stockholders' meeting of defendant, Belmont Industries, Inc. Darvin and four other stockholders owned all of the shares in Belmont Industries, Inc. They were also directors and officers of the corporation. A dispute over corporate management arose between Darvin and the other directors, who no longer wanted Darvin in the corporation. Accordingly, a special meeting of the stockholders and directors was scheduled for September 12, 1969. Darvin received notice of the meeting on September 11. At the meeting Darvin was eliminated as a director and officer. The bylaws of the corporation provided that shareholders shall receive notice "at least ten days prior to any meeting." Darvin claims that the actions taken at the meeting are ineffective because he was given notice only one day in advance. Was Darvin's attendance at the meeting together with the nonvoting of his shares sufficient participation to waive the notice requirement?

Decision

No. Judgment for plaintiff, Darvin.

Reasoning

The purpose of the time-notice requirement is to provide a shareholder with sufficient opportunity to study contemplated action at the shareholders' meeting and the legality thereof. Although the notice given to Darvin was sufficient to obtain his physical presence at the meeting, it was not sufficient to allow him time to ascertain what action was to be taken at the special meeting. Darvin's mere attendance at the meeting coupled with the nonvoting of his shares was not sufficient participation to waive the notice requirement.

[*Darvin v. Belmont Industries, Inc.*, 199 N.W. 2d 542 (Mich. 1972).]

Quorum. A legal stockholders' meeting requires a quorum to transact business. A **quorum** is a specified number of shareholders required to be present or a specified number of shares required to be represented before the shareholders' meeting can begin. State statutes, the articles of incorporation, and the bylaws determine the specific number that generally is a percentage of the voting stockholders or shares represented. A shareholders' meeting that opens with a quorum may generally continue to transact corporate business after a sufficient number of shareholders leave the meeting and break the quorum. This provides for a continuation of the meeting over the objection of dissident stockholders who have left.

quorum
the number of persons necessary to be present or shares necessary to be represented at a meeting in order to transact business

Shareholders' Action without a Meeting. Small closely held corporations may wish to transact business that requires shareholders' approval but decide not to call a special meeting. Most corporate statutes allow this if the shareholders sign their consent to the action taken without a meeting.

Directors

Corporate management.

The directors elected by the shareholders manage the business and establish corporate policy. In that capacity they do not carry on the day-to-day business. The authority of the board to manage the corporation is derived from state statutes, the articles of incorporation, and the bylaws.

Powers of Directors

The board of directors acts on behalf of the corporation. While acting within the scope of their authority they have the power to bind the corporation. The board delegates the administration of corporate policy to the officers authorizing them to carry out the day-to-day business. The board votes on policy and functions only as a body; individual members have no authority to act without board consent.

Number of Directors

Most state corporate statutes require at least three board members. The articles of incorporation or the bylaws will fix the exact number. To accommodate the closely held corporation and the professional corporations, many states allow as few as one director.

Qualifications

Generally any person may be a director, including a nonresident, minor, or nonshareholder. Corporate statutes, the articles of incorporation, or the bylaws may place restrictions on eligibility. It is not unusual for the bylaws to impose stock ownership requirements on the directors. Larger corporations encourage "outside directors" to serve as board members.

Directors' Meetings

The directors may vote on corporate matters only at a legally held board meeting. The bylaws may provide for regular board meetings to be held with or without notice. Special meetings require notice to the directors unless it is impracticable to do so. If proper notice was not sent and a director should attend a meeting, he may be deemed to have waived the notice requirement. Board action may be taken without a meeting when all the directors sign a *consent statement* that recites the action taken. This is especially convenient in a closely held corporation where the directors and stockholders are the same parties. Bylaws may require the meetings to be held at a particular place, but most states allow meetings within or without the state of incorporation.

Board acts only through board meetings.

Liability of Directors

Directors may be held personally liable to the corporation or to the shareholders in the management of the corporation if they violate a duty owed to either of them causing a financial loss. This duty is based upon the director being a *fiduciary* that manages the company on behalf of the corporation and the shareholders.

Directors as fiduciaries.

Directors are not liable for honest errors of judgment if they acted in good faith and with due diligence. For example, if the board of directors in exercising its discretion votes to adopt a new line of merchandise that results in a financial loss, it can not be held personally liable. They have a common law duty to exercise the standard of care of an ordinary prudent director in a similar business, and are held liable for their negligent acts.[2]

---

[2] *Atherton v. Anderson,* 99 F.2d 883 (1938) and *Murphy v. Hanlon,* 79 N.E.2d 292 (Mass. 1948).

State corporate statutes commonly provide duties that establish a director's liability with respect to an illegal declaration of dividends, purchase of treasury stock, or the illegal distribution of assets during corporate liquidation.

Director's Breach of Fiduciary Duties

A director, as a fiduciary, must account to the corporation for *secret profits* received in violation of his *duty of loyalty* as well as *secret profits* made by using inside information acquired at a board of directors' meeting. A director will be protected from suit for breach of a fiduciary duty if he makes a *full disclosure* of any financial interest he may have in the contract to the board of directors or to the voting shareholders, who approve. The corporation or the shareholders may sue the director for breach of a fiduciary duty and compel the director to pay any secret profits to the corporation. In the following case the corporation sued its former director for breach of his fiduciary duty to disclose material facts to the corporation.

Facts

Plaintiff, Aero Drapery of Ky., Inc., brought suit against Engdahl, the defendant, an officer and treasurer of Aero. While employed by Aero, the defendant entered into a contract with several of Aero's key employees to leave and form a new corporation in direct competition with it. Engdahl and the other employees then quit and began competing with Aero, who alleged breach of fiduciary duties against Engdahl.

Decision

Judgment for plaintiff, Aero Drapery of Ky., Inc.

Reasoning

Engdahl as a director and officer was a fiduciary of Aero. Whenever a fiduciary possesses information and the withholding of that information will damage the corporation, it is his duty to fully disclose these facts to the corporation. Engdahl should have terminated his duties as director and treasurer when he first began preparation to directly compete with Aero.

Aero Drapery of Ky., Inc. v. Engdahl, 507 S.W.2d 166 (Ky. 1974).

Removal of Directors

The stockholders may call a meeting to remove a director or the board of directors. State statutory law generally provides specific grounds for a director to be removed "for cause." Generally a majority of the shareholders may remove a director "without cause."

Corporate Officers

Function of corporate officers.

State corporate statutes require corporations to have officers, elected and removed by a board of directors. These officers carry out on a day-to-day basis the policy established by the board. The officers as well as the term of office and the duties of the officers are stated in the bylaws. They usually consist of a president, secretary, and treasurer and as many vice-presidents as required in the bylaws.

Business Organizations: B. Corporations

Powers of Officers

The powers of a corporate officer are determined by the law of agency because they are agents of the corporation. The board of directors, the articles of incorporation, and the bylaws delegate authority to the officers. An officer must not misuse his powers so as to breach his duty of loyalty to the corporation, as is illustrated in the following case.

Agency law applicable.

Facts

Plaintiff, Wilshire Oil Company of Texas, sued Riffe, the defendant and its former corporate officer, to recover profits made by Riffe by participating in competitive enterprises, and to recover compensation paid during the period he was involved in the competitive corporation. Riffe claims he is entitled to compensation because his services were properly performed.

Decision

Judgment for plaintiff, Wilshire Oil Company of Texas.

Reasoning

When a corporate officer engages in conduct which constitutes a breach of his duty of loyalty, or if it is a willful breach of his contract of employment, he is not entitled to compensation for services during such period of time although part of his services may have been properly performed. In the Restatement (Second) of Agency, sec. 469, the above doctrine is set forth:

An agent who without the acquiescence of his principal, acts . . . in competition with the principal . . . is not entitled to compensation. . . .

Wilshire Oil Company of Texas v. Riffe, 406 F.2d 1061 (1969).

Liability of Officers

The officers are acting on behalf of the corporation and, therefore, are *fiduciaries*. Similar to directors, the officers have a duty to exercise that degree of care that an ordinary prudent officer would exercise under the circumstances.

Fiduciaries with duty of care.

In the following case, a corporate president is held personally liable for breach of his fiduciary duty of loyalty when he supplied a competitor with a list of the corporation's employees and their salaries.

Facts

Plaintiff, Bancroft-Whitney Co., brought this action against Glen, its past corporate president. Glen signed a contract with Bender Co. to become president of its division. Without resigning or giving notice to the plaintiff, he offered employees of Bancroft a job at more favorable terms. Was Glen liable to the plaintiff for breach of his fiduciary duty?

Decision

Yes. Judgment for plaintiff.

Reasoning

Corporate officers and directors are not permitted to use their position of trust and confidence to further their private interests. The mere fact that the officer makes preparations to compete before he resigns his office is not sufficient to constitute a breach of duty. It is the nature of his preparation which is significant. A corporate officer breaches his fiduciary duties when, with the purpose of facilitating the recruiting of the corporation's employees by a competitor, he supplies the competitor with a selective list of the corporation's employees, together with the salary the competitor should offer in order to be successful in recruitment.

Bancroft-Whitney Co. v. Glen, 411 P.2d 921 (Cal. 1966).

Indemnification of Officers, Directors, Employees, and Agents

Corporate officers or directors may believe that they are acting in good faith but still may be sued by shareholders or other aggrieved parties. The cost of defending the lawsuit and the risk of being found liable may discourage competent individuals from accepting such an office. Under the common law, the expenses involved in defending a director or officer in a suit were borne by them. Today many state statutes, following the Model Business Corporation Act, authorize the corporation to indemnify a corporate officer, director, or agent. Insurance companies will write indemnification policies to cover this loss. The articles of incorporation and bylaws should state the terms of indemnification, such as under the Model Business Corporation Act, section 5:

Indemnification.

A corporation shall have power to indemnify any person who is a party . . . to any . . . suit or proceeding, whether civil, criminal, administrative or investigative . . . by reason of the fact that he is or was a director, officer, employee, or agent of the corporation . . . against expenses (including attorney fees), judgments, fines, and amounts paid in settlement . . . incurred by him in connection with such suit . . . if he acted in good faith and in a manner he reasonably believed to be not opposed to the best interests of the corporation, and, [if] a criminal action, had no reasonable cause to believe his conduct was unlawful.

Although corporate debts and taxes are generally the obligation of the corporation, some state statutes impose personal liability on the officers and directors for corporate debts, wages, taxes, and crimes.

Summary Statement

1. Shareholders indirectly manage the corporation by voting to elect the board of directors at the shareholders' meeting.
2. Managerial decisions that substantially change the nature of the corporation require approval by the shareholders.
3. A quorum is a specified number of shareholders required to be present or shares represented before the shareholders' meeting can begin.
4. Directors manage the business affairs and establish corporate policy.
5. Board action may be taken without a meeting when all directors sign a *consent statement* that recites the action taken.
6. A director is a fiduciary because he manages the company on behalf of the stockholders. Directors are not liable for honest errors of judgment if they act in good faith.
7. A director, as a fiduciary, is liable for secret profits received in violation of his duty of loyalty.
8. The stockholders elect and may remove the directors.
9. A corporation may *indemnify* a director or officer for any loss incurred in connection with a suit, provided that they acted in good faith.

Business Organizations: B. Corporations

10. Corporate officers are elected by the directors to carry out the day-to-day business of the corporation.
11. Officers act on behalf of the corporation and are fiduciaries. They can be held liable for breach of a fiduciary duty of loyalty.

In the following case the court examined the power of a managing director to determine if he could initiate a lawsuit on behalf of the corporation without board approval or authority under the bylaws.

Covington Housing Development Corp. v. City of Covington
381 F.Supp. 427 (1974), aff'd, 513 F.2d 630, cert. denied, 423 U.S. 869 (1975)

Swinford, J. The complaint in this civil rights action commenced by the Covington Housing Development Corporation and its executive director, alleges that on October 5, 1972 the corporation contracted with the City of Covington for the development of residential areas under the Demonstration Cities and Metropolitan Development Act, 42 U.S.C. sec. 3301 et seq. Because the executive director of the Authority (Thompson) was a negro, city officials deliberately misrepresented certain facts to the Department of Housing and Urban Development in a successful attempt to halt further funding to the project. The corporation alternately seeks damages or reinstatement of the development. . . .

. . . The record is now before the court on the defendants' motion for summary judgment on the ground that Thompson lacks the capacity to sue in the name of the Covington Housing Development Corporation. It is contrarily asserted that the plaintiff's power to initiate this action is derived from his managerial position as reflected in governing statutes and corporate records; that several directors informally agreed to the commencement of this action; and that the corporation has ratified Thompson's action. An examination of the cited standards compels dismissal of the complaint.

The plaintiff's assertion of an inherent authority to institute this action in the name of the entity reveals a fallacious interpretation of both the corporate records and the legal principles outlining the extent of a manager's authority. Kentucky law vests control over corporate affairs in a board of directors, "except as may be otherwise provided in the articles of incorporation." K.R.S. 271A.175. The Board may in turn delegate a portion of its decision-making authority to responsible corporate officers: "All officers and agents of the corporation, as between themselves and the corporation, shall have such authority and perform such duties in the management of the corporation as may be provided in the bylaws, or as may be determined by resolution of the board of directors not inconsistent with the bylaws." K.R.S. 271A.250(2). The Articles of the Covington Housing Development Corporation direct the board of directors to "appoint such officers and agents as the affairs of the corporation may require and to define their duties. . . ." The responsibilities of the executive director are thus enunciated in the corporation's bylaws. . . .

While the executive director is not expressly denied the authority to institute legal proceedings, the court is cited to no article, bylaw, or resolution vesting such responsibility in the plaintiff. The depositions and interrogatories of other participants in the operation reveal that the executive director was at no time vested with the authority to commence litigation; indeed, the corporate minutes strongly suggest that Thompson was not even a company official at the time this action was initiated. While a managing director enjoys a broad range of commercial responsibility, the court is unaware of any decision construing in such inherent control the right to commence litigation of this magnitude. Rather, it is well settled that a manager's authority is limited to the conduct of ordinary business affairs. . . .

The plaintiff's reliance upon any informally granted authority to commence this litigation ignores the "well settled doctrine that a corporation can act only through its directors at an official meeting regularly held, and that its acts can be proven only by the records of such meeting." . . . [A] business will not be bound by agreements secured among isolated directors. . . . The claimed ratification of Thompson's decision to sue is similarly unsupported by any suggestion of express or implicit approval of the plaintiff's action. . . .

For defendant.

Questions and Case Problems

1. Mount, the defendant, and other shareholders held a majority of the shares in Seagrave Corp., the plaintiff. Mount and seven others were members of the board of directors. As a board member, Mount sent out a proxy statement outlining a merger of Fyr-Fyter Co. with Seagrave wherein Mount proposed to sell 35,000 shares of Seagrave stock at $5 per share over the market price. Mount stated in the proxy statement that he was selling 23,400 of his shares in Seagrave to Wetzel regardless of the number of shares other stockholders desired to sell. The minority shareholders brought this suit against Mount, claiming that as a director he had breached his fiduciary duty of loyalty. Decide. [*Seagrave Corp. v. Mount,* 212 F.2d 389 (1954).]

2. Barr, the plaintiff and shareholder of Talcott, brought a derivative shareholders' suit against Wackman and other directors of Talcott. Because of the self-dealing and breach of fiduciary duties of Talcott's directors, First Capital, a subsidiary of Gulf and Western had been able to obtain board approval of an unfair stock offer. Wackman claims that the derivative action can not be maintained since no demand was made on the board to rescind the offer. Must demand be first made on the directors before the stockholders bring a derivative suit? [*Barr v. Wackman,* 329 N.E.2d 180 (N.Y. 1975).]

3. Smith, a director of XYZ Corporation, attended a corporate board meeting when a dividend was declared. Due to an inadequate surplus, this was an illegal dividend. Smith did not vote against the dividend. The next day Smith decided he should vote against the declaration of the dividend and sent a registered letter to the secretary. Creditors of XYZ Corporation sued the directors, including Smith, for declaring an illegal dividend. Is Smith liable?

4. Jones, the president of XYZ Co., with the directors' approval, franchised a successful business throughout the east coast. As a result of this new franchising venture, the corporation overextended and became insolvent. A shareholders' suit was brought against Jones, alleging a breach of his fiduciary duty as the chief executive officer to transact business in a reasonable manner. Decide.

5. Segal and Martinez were two physicians who formed plaintiff corporation, Patient Care Services, to provide comprehensive health services to a

hospital. Both physicians were directors, officers, and stockholders of Patient Care Services. The hospital that engaged its services did not renew the contract. A new medical corporation formed, owned, and managed by Segal was awarded the new contract. Segal informed Martinez of his intent to negotiate with the hospital on behalf of his corporation. Was Segal liable for breach of his fiduciary duty of loyalty? [*Patient Care Services, S.C. v. Segal*, 337 N.E.2d 471 (Ill. 1975).]

6. Jones, the president of XYZ Corporation, developed a competing corporation during his office as president. The directors knew of this but never attempted to stop Jones. XYZ Corp. became insolvent because of this competition. The shareholders brought suit against Jones and the directors for breach of their fiduciary duty of loyalty. The directors claim that they are not liable because they did not participate in the competing company. Decide.

7. Gimbel, plaintiff and shareholder of Signal Companies, Inc., defendant, sued to enjoin the sale of its stock in a subsidiary corporation. Gimbel represents a minority group of shareholders who object to a proposed sale of all the capital stock of Signal Oil, a wholly owned subsidiary of defendant corporation. A special meeting of the defendant's board of directors was called without notice of its purpose. Three of the four outside directors were unaware of the proposed sale prior to the meeting. A handwritten outline of the transaction was handed to the directors and an oral presentation was made supporting it. The tax consequences of the sale were discussed. The general financial status of Signal Oil Co., including its sales, income, cash flow, balance sheet, projected expenditures, and risks were also reviewed. Gimbel attacked the proposed sale on the grounds that the directors recklessly authorized the sale without informed reasonable deliberations. Judgment for whom? [*Gimbel v. Signal Companies, Inc.*, 316 A.2d 599 (Del. 1974).]

8. Devine, defendant, was a director of Continental Growth Fund, a mutual fund and co-defendant, in an action by the Securities and Exchange Commission, plaintiff, claiming that Devine breached his fiduciary duty in failing to discover the misappropriation of the mutual fund's assets by another director. Devine sought indemnification from the Fund for reasonable costs and expenses incurred in connection with his defense to Securities and Exchange Commission. The articles of incorporation provided for indemnification except in cases involving gross negligence or reckless disregard of duties. The Securities and Exchange Commission objected to indemnification because it would be contrary to the purpose of the Investment Company Act of 1940 to protect the investors from negligence. Decide. [*Securities and Exchange Commission v. Continental Growth Fund*, CCH Fed. Sec. L.Reptr., para. 91, 437 (S.D.N.Y. 1964).]

9. Dr. Smith, a physician, would like to incorporate his solo practice. He wants to be the only officer, director, and 100 percent shareholder. May he do so?

10. Examine the case of *Covington Housing Development Corp. v. City of Covington*, 381 F.Supp. 427 (1974), aff'd, 513 F.2d 630, cert. denied, 423 U.S. 869 (1975),[3] and explain how Thompson could obtain the power to sue in the name of Covington Housing Development Corporation.

---

[3] See pp. 805–6.

Part **9**

Real Property

Summary

The following three chapters discuss the law of real property. This law developed earlier than almost any other body of law discussed in this text. As a result, it sometimes reflects its age and also the fact that it developed in a primarily agricultural society. As you read through the chapters, see if you can spot aspects of the law which reflect these ancient and rural characteristics.

Another feature of real property law is that it is enormously complex. Even so, there are a very large number of transactions handled each day in every area. The great complexity causes transfer costs to be fairly high. Thus, real estate brokers typically charge four to ten percent of the sale price for helping transactions conclude smoothly. As you read through the chapters, try to think of workable ways to simplify real property transactions.

Finally, when reading the chapters think about strategies and tactics you could adopt as a prospective seller, buyer, landlord, or tenant. If you master the material in these chapters, and devise common-sense strategies, you can often dramatically improve your legal position in real estate transactions.

In summary, then, you should attempt to spot the old agricultural aspects of the law, look for ways to simplify it, and devise sensible strategies for handling these transactions which you will encounter many times in your life.

45

Real Property and Its Ownership

After you have read this chapter, you should be able to:

1. Identify the physical parts of real property and distinguish them from personal property.
2. Understand the legal relationship between persons who co-own real estate.
3. Identify the powers over realty possessed by owners.
4. Identify the rights which the government may take from the owner.
5. Identify the rights which the owner may give to another without actually transferring ownership.

Introduction

Problems frequently arise where the law must decide what is and what is not real property. For example, if a student leases certain "real property," has he also leased the stove and refrigerator on the premises? And if someone sells or wills "real property," exactly what passes by the sale or will?

Once we know what real property is, then we can examine the ways that more than one person can own the same realty. Of course, that introduces problems concerning the relationships among the owners. For example, if a husband and wife own realty together, should either be allowed to sell his or her interest without the spouse's consent?

Exactly what powers should the law give to owners? Should they be allowed to cause ownership to stay forever in their family? And can an owner sell some of his ownership rights and keep others for himself?

How much power should be given to the government to restrict an owner's use of his property? If the government does restrict the use, should the owner be compensated for any loss in property value?

As you read through this material on real property and its ownership, ask yourself whether the rules of law seem fair and just for *all* the parties. If you disagree with the law, can you propose an alternative that will work better?

Physical Characteristics of Real Property

The basic physical element of realty is land. The buyer of real property usually purchases the *surface rights* or the right to occupy the surface of a piece of land.

Surface rights.

In addition, the earth beneath the surface is part of the realty. The right to dig or mine that earth is called a *mineral right*. One person may own the surface rights while another owns the mineral rights. The mineral rights extend to the center of the earth.

Mineral rights.

The air space above the surface of the land is also part of the realty. Ownership of that space is called the *right to air space*. The ownership power, except for the right to exclude aircraft overflight,[1] extends to the upper atmosphere. Therefore, if the branch of a neighbor's tree grows into your air space, you have the right to force its removal.

Right to air space.

Further, water on the surface or under the ground is part of the realty. Control of the water by a landowner is called a *water right*. Because water is mobile—i.e., it flows across and under land—the owner's control of water is not as absolute as is his control of surface rights, mineral rights, and air space. Thus, an owner could not divert the path of a river, changing its course through other property downstream.

Water rights.

The *right to lateral and subjacent support* means that the physical support for the land surface can not be removed by a neighbor or the owner of the mineral right.[2] Thus, one could not excavate along the property line, thereby causing the neighbor's soil to slide into the trench.

Right to lateral and subjacent support.

---

[1] See *United States v. Causby,* 328 U.S. 256 (1946).

[2] *Empire Star Mines Co., Limited v. Butler,* 145 P.2d 49 (Cal. 1944).

The ability to distinguish between real and personal property is critical to understanding real estate transactions. This is so because different bodies of law govern transfers of real and personal property. In general, **real property** is land and immovable things attached to the land. In contrast, **personal property** is a movable thing. Sometimes real and personal property are very closely connected, as are a stove and a house. Then we categorize things with the tests discussed in chapter 19, Personal Property.[3] They are the tests of *intention, attachment,* and *annexation.* Thus, the intention of the person attaching something to a structure may determine whether the thing is real or personal. In some cases the permanency of the attachment determines whether it is real or personal. In other instances the importance of the thing to the functioning of the structure may cause it to be classified as real property.

Thus, crops are sometimes part of the realty and sometimes personal property. When a crop is frequently harvested, as is corn, then it is treated as personal property even while in the ground because it is not *permanently* attached to the land. On the other hand, if the crops are infrequently harvested, such as Christmas trees, they are a part of the realty until severed from the ground. Avocado trees, grape vines, and rose bushes would be real property. Avocados, grapes, and roses raised by a florist would be personal property.

Structures or buildings are part of the real property if they are *permanently* attached to the land. Thus, office buildings and college classrooms are part of the realty. However, a house trailer sitting on its wheels is usually considered personal property. Mobile homes on *rented* foundations are not *permanently* attached to the land and are also personalty. A small garden shed resting on top of the ground would be personalty. If the wheels of the house trailer were removed and it were set on a permanent foundation, it would be realty. If the garden shed were bolted to a cement pad, it would be realty.

Personal property like stoves and dishwashers become a part of the realty if they are permanently attached. In most cases a free-standing stove is personalty, but a built-in stove is realty. Personal property which becomes realty by permanent attachment is called a **fixture.**

The fixtures attached by business tenants are called **trade fixtures.** Unlike other fixtures, trade fixtures are treated as *personalty* because they are usually not intended to be permanent. Thus, if a baker permanently attached ovens to a *rented* bakery shop, they would still be treated as personalty because the landlord and tenant probably *intended* that they should be removed at the end of the lease period.

Co-ownership

When real estate is owned by one person alone, he is said to own the realty in *severalty.* Co-ownership exists when realty is owned by more than one person. Thus, two persons may buy together a condominium and become co-owners of the property.

---

[3] See pp. 298 et seq.

There are several types of co-ownership. The major types of co-ownership are tenancy in common, joint tenancy, tenancy by entirety, and community property. These names are labels defining four or five characteristics of the relationships among co-owners. The characteristics generally involved are the potential number of co-owners, the possible percentage of ownership, co-owners' rights to sell their portions of ownership, and the distribution of a co-owner's interest in the realty on death. In general, the use of such words as "tenancy in common" in a deed or a lease is sufficient to bind the co-owners to all of the characteristics of that form of co-ownership.

All methods of co-ownership have a common characteristic: it is that co-owners all have equal rights to occupy all the property. Thus, one co-owner may not exclude any other co-owner from any portion of their co-owned property.

In **tenancy in common** the interest of the co-owner passes on his death to his **heirs** or devisees (the persons named in the decedent's will to receive real property). Any number may co-own as tenants in common. They may have unequal percentage ownerships. For example, one may own 99 percent while the other co-owner owns 1 percent. Each of these co-owners may sell his or her interest without the other's consent unless there is a contract provision to the contrary.

In **joint tenancy** on the death of a co-owner, his or her interest is evenly divided among the remaining joint tenants. This is called the **right of survivorship.** Any number may own as joint tenants, but each must have an equal interest. Thus, if there are four joint tenants, each must own 25 percent. Each joint tenancy owner may sell his or her interest without the consent of the other co-owners, unless there is a contract provision to the contrary.

Tenancy by entirety is a form of co-ownership only for married couples. This method of co-ownership has all the characteristics of joint tenancy—including survivorship—except that a party may *not* sell his or her interest without the consent of the spouse. Further, a divorce or separation transforms tenancy by entirety into tenancy in common.

Some states recognize **community property** as a substitute for tenancy by entirety. Again, this method of co-ownership is only for married couples. In these states, property acquired during marriage is generally presumed to be community property. However, property owned by one spouse before marriage or received during the marriage by gift or inheritance is presumed to be that person's separate property. As such, it is not community property.

Survivorship is treated differently in different community property states. Some provide that, on death, half the community property goes to the surviving spouse while the other half can pass to devisees. If the decedent's one half is *not* willed away, it also goes to the surviving spouse. Other states treat survivorship in the same way as in tenancy by entirety. Often both spouses must consent to any conveyance of community real property.

tenancy in common
a form of ownership of property by more than one person without survivorship

heirs
persons who, by statute, are entitled to property not disposed of by a decedent's will

joint tenancy
a form of ownership of property by more than one person with the right of survivorship

right of survivorship
a relationship among co-owners where death of one owner causes his interest to be transferred to the remaining owners

tenancy by entirety
a form of co-ownership between husband and wife with the right of survivorship

community property
a form of ownership by husband and wife of property acquired by their efforts during their marriage

Figure 45.1 Characteristics of Co-ownership

Type of Co-ownership	Legal Characteristics				
	Only available to married couples	Interest willable, or passes to co-owner on death	*All* interest passes to co-owner on death	Ownership interests must be equal	Consent required from co-owner for sale of interest
Tenants in common					
Joint tenants			✓	✓	
Tenants by entirety	✓		✓	✓	✓
Community property	✓	✓		✓	✓

Nature of Ownership

estate
a bundle of ownership rights in, or powers over, realty

Ownership of realty is usually acquired by purchase, gift, or inheritance. But everyone does not receive the same powers of ownership. The powers of ownership are defined by the **estate** in land which the new owner receives. Each estate is composed of a certain bundle of ownership rights. The words used in the deed, will, lease, or other instrument transferring ownership determine which estate the new owner receives.

One parcel of land usually supports only a single estate. For example, most owner-occupied homes involve just one estate. Occasionally, however, two or more estates exist in the same parcel. Thus, both the landlord and his tenant own estates in the rented apartment. The tenant's ownership rights include the right to occupy the property. The landlord's ownership rights include the powers to collect the rent and regain possession at the end of the lease.

When more than one estate exists in a single parcel, these owners do not co-own, for example, as in tenancy in common. Rather, each owns a separate estate with separate powers of ownership. Co-owners own together a single estate. The following paragraphs discuss the powers of ownership of the major estates in land.

fee simple absolute
the greatest bundle of ownership rights in and powers over realty

Fee simple absolute is the estate with *all* the ownership rights. The owner of this estate exercises all the power allowed by law. If this estate is present, there can be no other estate in the same land. Most buyers of homes and farms and commercial property purchase the fee simple absolute estate.

conditional estate
an estate where ownership is dependent upon some act or event

Conditional estates make the ownership conditional on some act or event. For example, ownership may exist only "so long as no alcoholic beverages are served on the premises." If scotch were served, ownership would shift from the owner of the conditional estate to the one who conditionally sold the property.

Whenever there is a conditional estate there must also be another corresponding estate. This second estate is made up of the ownership power retained by the seller of the property. The retained power permits the seller to receive back all the owership rights held by the owner of the conditional estate if the condition is violated. This owner would then have a fee simple absolute because he would be the owner of the only estate in the property.

A **life estate** is ownership only for the length of a life. This owner exercises all the ownership powers except the right to permanently dispose of the property. The length of the ownership period is generally measured by the life of the holder of the life estate. For example, a husband might convey "to my wife Julia, for life." Occasionally the period is measured by the life of someone else. When the life estate lasts for the life of one other than the owner, it is called a *life estate pur autre vie*. For example, a father may will a home to a nurse for the life of his mentally ill son.

Nonfreehold estates, called tenancies, involve ownership for a limited period of time. *Tenants* own nonfreehold estates. The length of ownership is specified in a lease, or indicated by the payment period, or is only for so long as the landlord desires. These estates are discussed in detail in chapter 47, Renting Realty.

Future interests are estates that usually give possession of the realty when a life or a conditional estate terminates. If the right of possession returns to the one who originally granted the life or conditional estate, the future interest is usually called a *reversion*. If the right of possession goes to another person, it is sometimes called a *remainder*. Thus, if a hunting guide were to convey his mountain cabin "to my brother Albonzo for life, and then to his son Fredrico," the son would, on his father's death, receive a remainder. If the guide conveyed simply "to my brother Albonzo for life," the law would probably conclude that the guide intended to regain ownership on Albonzo's death. The guide would receive a reverter.

Future interests are also classified as *vested* or *contingent*. *Vested* interests arise when there is *certainty* that the estate will become *possessory*—that is, the grantee *will* acquire the possessory estate. For example, if a deed conveyed property from "grandfather to son for life and then to grandson, Mark, and his heirs," the future interest of Mark is *vested*. It is certain that he or his heirs will possess the estate. However, if the conveyance were from "grandfather to son for life and then to grandson provided that he shall then be unmarried," this grandson's future interest is *contingent*. It will not vest if the grandson is married when the son dies. One *can not be certain* that the grandson or his heirs will ever possess the estate.

The distinction between vested and contingent future interests is especially important because the *rule against perpetuities* makes void contingent future interests which do not vest within 21 years plus the length of a life *in being at the time of the conveyance*. This rule is intended to ensure that property is not burdened for long periods of time when the identity of the ultimate owner is uncertain. To illustrate, suppose a successful business woman were to convey her

life estate
an estate that lasts only for the length of a particular person's life

Future interests.

Rule against perpetuities.

estate "to my daughter, Alberta, for life, and then to my firstborn granddaughter on her 25th birthday, provided she is then a registered democrat, and if not. . . ." The conveyance is contingent on the granddaughter's political affiliation. And at least 25 years would be required for her interest to vest. This violates the requirement that the interest vest within "21 years plus the length of a life in being." The time in this illustration is not measured by a "life in being" since no granddaughter has yet been born. The 21 years would be measured by the *granddaughter's* life. Thus the attempted conveyance to the granddaughter violates the rule.

Others' Rights in the Owner's Land

Licenses

When someone owns a possessory estate in land, whether in severalty or as a co-owner, they control all the ownership rights associated with that particular estate. Frequently the owner will give some right in his land to another. For example, a theatre owner may grant someone the right to sit through one showing of a film. This kind of temporary, oral right to come upon the land of another is called a **license.** Stores grant implied licenses to their customers to enter the store to shop for goods. Dinner guests are on the host's property by right of a license.

Generally oral licenses are *revocable.* Thus, the theatre patron or the dinner guest would become *trespassers* if they failed to leave immediately when asked. The theatre patron may be entitled to a refund of his money, but he can not legally sit through the show when asked to leave. In many places trespass is a criminal offense and the police will assist in removing the trespasser. Usually an oral license is revoked when the one who granted it sells the land.

Easements

Easements are usually *irrevocable* rights to some limited use of another's land. In contrast with licenses, easements are generally given for substantial periods of time, like five or ten or fifty years. To comply with the statute of frauds, they should be in writing. Easements may be granted which allow another to drive across the owner's land, bury a sewer pipe, hang power lines over the land, or make any other use which does not constitute exclusive possession. Easements may be *appurtenant* or *in gross.*

Easements Appurtenant.   When easements are given to neighboring landowners and the easement *benefits* the neighbor's land, then it is called an *easement appurtenant.* Appurtenant means attached to the land. Thus an easement to drive farm equipment across another's land in order to farm an otherwise inaccessible parcel would be an easement appurtenant.

The land of the one who grants the appurtenant easement is called the **servient tenement.** That land is in a sense the servant of the benefited land. The servient tenement is burdened with the easement. The land benefited is named the **dominant tenement.**

license
a temporary, revocable right to some use of another's land

easement
a right to the limited use of another's land which can not be revoked by the latter owner

servient tenement
property in which someone has an easement appurtenant

dominant tenement
property which is benefited by an easement appurtenant in nearby land

Figure 45.2   Easement Appurtenant for the Benefit of Property A

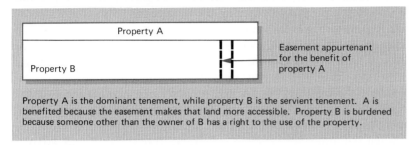

Property A is the dominant tenement, while property B is the servient tenement. A is benefited because the easement makes that land more accessible. Property B is burdened because someone other than the owner of B has a right to the use of the property.

Easements for access roads or water ditches are easements appurtenant. These easements are transferred with the dominant tenement. However, the servient tenement is bound after its transfer only if the buyer of the servient tenement had notice of the easement prior to the purchase.

Easements in Gross.   Easements which do not benefit neighboring land, like easements for access given to a nonneighbor or for telegraph lines and poles are called *easements in gross*. Easements in gross pass when the burdened property is sold. However, the person benefited generally can not transfer his rights.

Zoning Ordinances

The owner's use of his realty can also be restricted by zoning ordinances. An **ordinance** is a municipal law or legislation. Zoning ordinances may be adopted by cities or counties to regulate the location of residential, business, and industrial districts. The purpose of zoning is to ensure fair use and orderly development of land within the community.

The legal power to enact zoning ordinances comes from the Constitution of the United States, which recognizes the **police power** of the separate states. Generally the states can not use police power except to promote the health, safety, morals, and general welfare of the community. State legislatures usually pass statutes which permit the cities and counties to enact the zoning ordinances.

The zoning power is very broad. Courts generally support the right of cities and counties to enforce community zoning goals at the expense of individual land owners. Thus, an ordinance may change the zoning from one land use to another. For example, a commercial area could be rezoned residential. If the zoning reduces the value of the owner's land, he bears the loss and could not recover for his financial injury from the local government.

On the other hand, zoning can not be used unreasonably to eliminate an *existing use*. Thus, a zoning ordinance restricting use of an area to residential could not be used to eliminate an already existing cemetery.[4] The cemetery in

Zoning ordinances.

ordinance
municipal legislation

police power
the power of a state or federal government to legislate reasonably for the general public welfare

---

[4] See *Lockard v. City of Los Angeles*, 202 P.2d 38 (Cal. 1949).

a residential zone is called a *non-conforming use*. If the city wished to eliminate the cemetery, it must go through **condemnation** procedures, which permit the city to take title to the property by paying the owners the reasonable value of the property. Recently, however, some states have begun to allow reasonable zoning ordinances which eliminate existing uses. Thus, an ordinance requiring the elimination of billboard signs within five years would be enforceable in some states.

Spot zoning is the treatment of a single property in a manner inconsistent with the treatment of similar properties in the area. It is usually prohibited.[5] Further, zoning will not be enforceable if it exceeds the police power of the state. This occurs when the ordinance is clearly arbitrary, unreasonable, and without substantial relation to the public health, safety, morals, and general welfare, as is illustrated in the following case.

Facts
Plaintiff, Sherman, resided in Del Fanta, California. The city enacted a zoning ordinance prohibiting the use of engines in excess of five horsepower within the residential district. Sherman sued the city.

Decision
The ordinance is not enforceable.

Reasoning
Engine horsepower bears no reasonable relation to the health, safety, morals, or general welfare of Del Fanta residents.

Del Fanta v. Sherman, 290 P. 1087 (Cal. 1955).

A *variance* may be granted by a city or county to allow a land owner to make some use of his land which is inconsistent with the general zoning ordinance. Usually the owner must appear before the variance board and establish hardship and lack of injury to others. For example, a particular zoning ordinance may prohibit fences taller than five feet. A property owner might obtain a variance allowing a six-foot fence by showing that all his neighbors consent and by arguing that the taller fence is needed to keep four fierce large dogs in the yard.

Building codes specify the construction techniques and standards that must be used in the city or county.

Restrictive Covenants

Even when there are no zoning restrictions, the owner may still be prohibited from certain uses. This occurs when a former owner created a restrictive **covenant** or when the nature of the neighborhood creates an *equitable servitude*. A restrictive covenant is a promise usually made by the buyer to the seller. It is often written in the deed or contract for sale or other recordable document. Usually the promise limits the use of the land in some way. For example, the buyer may contract with the seller, promising not to graze sheep on the land. This buyer is almost always bound by the restrictive covenant.

---

[5] *Smith v. County of Washington*, 406 P.2d 545 (Or. 1965).

If the buyer who gave the covenant resells, the new owner is bound only if the covenant is the kind that **runs with the land.** Restrictive covenants run with the land when they meet all four of the following legal tests:

1. The original parties must have *intended* the covenant to run.
2. It must touch and concern the land. This means that the covenant must affect the use of the property or affect the title to the property.
3. The buyer must have had notice of the covenants at the time he purchased. Notice exists when the buyer is told about the restrictive covenant or when a copy of the restrictive covenant is recorded.
4. There must be a chain of ownership connections between the original promisee and the current owner. This is called *privity of estate.*

If one of the tests is not passed, then the restrictive covenant does not bind subsequent purchasers. For example, if the buyer promises not to serve alcoholic beverages on the property, then this restrictive covenant binds the buyer but not subsequent purchasers. This would be so because this particular promise does not touch and concern the land.

Note that sellers can extract the same promise from buyers by a restrictive covenant, or by transferring a conditional estate, or by private contract. If the restrictive covenant is broken, the owner may be required to pay damages or may be enjoined from future breaches. In contrast, if the condition of conveyance is violated, the violator loses his ownership.

Equitable servitudes may arise even when there is no written covenant. The general building plan or scheme of development in the area may give notice to a purchaser that his use of the property must conform with the general use. When this occurs, the purchaser is said to be bound by an equitable servitude.

Owner's Tort Duties

Owner's tort duties.

A person who possesses land may owe certain tort duties to other persons who come on the land. The extent of the duties depends upon whether the persons who come on the land are trespassers, licensees, or invitees.

Trespasser. A *trespasser* is a person who is on the land without any right to be there. Thus, when a neighbor walks upon your land without your consent, he is a trespasser. Generally, a trespasser takes the property as he finds it. The owner or possessor does not have any duty to the trespasser to keep his land in a reasonably safe condition. However, the owner or possessor can not intentionally cause harm to the trespasser. Further, if the owner or possessor knows that the trespasser is on the land, or that persons constantly trespass on the land, then various tort duties are imposed upon the possessor with respect to the condition of the land. An **attractive nuisance** attracts children to trespass and broadens the landowner's responsibility.

Licensee. A *licensee* is a person whom the possessor of land has permitted to be on that land. A social guest is an example. A licensee takes the premises for what they appear to be, and therefore the possessor has the duty to disclose to the licensee nonobvious dangers on the land known to the possessor and which the licensee would not likely discover.

Invitee. An *invitee* is a person who is either a *public* invitee—that is, a member of the public invited to enter or remain on the land by its possessor for a public purpose—or a *business visitor*—one who is invited by the possessor of land to enter or remain on the land for the purpose of doing business with the possessor. An example of a public invitee occurs when the possessor of land invites people to come on the land for a public meeting. An example of a business visitor occurs when a retail store invites prospective customers to enter the store and consider making purchases. Thus, a social guest is not an invitee because neither of the two purposes (public or business) is present. The possessor of land has the duty to keep the premises in a reasonably safe condition and to warn invitees of dangers on the land of which the possessor should, on reasonable examination, be aware and which are not reasonably discoverable by the invitee.

Summary Statement

1. The physical elements of real property include surface rights, air rights, mineral rights, and water rights.
2. Personal property becomes realty when that is what is intended, or when it is permanently attached to the realty, or when it is adapted to the realty. It is then a fixture. Trade fixtures, however, are usually personal property. Crops are classified as real or personal property according to their permanence in the ground.
3. Co-ownership can take the form of tenancy in common, joint tenancy, tenancy by entirety, or community property. All but tenancy in common have some right of survivorship.
4. The rights and powers of ownership are determined by the estate in land received by the purchaser. Fee simple absolute is the most common and greatest estate. Other major estates are conditional estates, life estates, non-freehold estates, and future interests.
5. A license is an oral, temporary right to come upon the land of another. Easements are rights to some use of another's land which can not be revoked by the land owner. Easements may be appurtenant or in gross.
6. Zoning is an exercise of police power. Spot zoning, attempts to eliminate current uses, and arbitrary and unreasonable zoning are generally unenforceable.
7. Only those restrictive covenants which run with the land bind later purchasers.
8. Land owners owe tort duties to trespassers, greater duties to licensees and invitees.

The following case confronts the problems associated with covenants which run with the land. The case is intended to illustrate the way a court will scrutinize the words creating the covenant. The reader is asked to think about whether or not prior owners should be allowed to control current use of realty.

Parrish v. Richards
336 P.2d 122 (Utah 1959)

This is an action to enjoin maintenance of a tennis court and fence allegedly built in violation of a real property restrictive covenant.

The parties are contiguous owners of real property. . . . Defendants' residence is located between those of plaintiffs, Parrish and Peterson. Prior to the acquisition by any of the parties of any of the tracts of land here involved, there had been placed upon and against such lands certain restrictive covenants recorded in the office of the County Recorder of Salt Lake County, Utah. The covenant here involved reads as follows:

Use of Land: Each lot is hereby designated as a residential lot, and none of said lots shall be improved, used or occupied for other than private residence purposes, and no flat or apartment house . . . shall be erected thereon, *and no structure shall be erected* . . . other than a one-, two-, or three-car garage, and one single family residence, not to exceed one story in height. . . . [Emphasis added.]

Prior to August 1, 1955 defendants leveled their land on the south side and laid down a concrete apron in the southwest corner measuring 78 feet by 36 feet for a tennis court. Around and upon such concrete defendants placed a six-foot wire fence. Defendants testified that they do not intend to put up any overhead lights or floodlights whatsoever over the tennis court.

Plaintiffs brought suit alleging that the described construction of the tennis court is a "structure" erected and placed upon the property in violation of the above-mentioned restrictive covenant. Plaintiffs also alleged that the construction interfered with their view; that there had been no waiver of the covenant on their part; that the value of their property had diminished as a result of the construction; and they prayed for an injunction permanently enjoining the defendants from proceeding with the construction.

The trial court followed the correct doctrine that in the construction of uncertain or ambiguous restrictions, the courts will resolve all doubts in favor of the free and unrestricted use of property and that it will "have recourse to every aid, rule, or canon of construction to ascertain the intention of the parties." In applying that doctrine to the situation, the court concluded that the fence surrounding said tennis court does not violate the covenant. Garages and other similar buildings which are of solid construction are of a different character entirely. Structures of that kind, which are solid, obstruct the view for the neighborhood and crowd the area with buildings, which would reduce the beauty of it. It seems quite plain that the covenant was intended to prevent the blocking of the view and the crowding of the buildings which would reduce the beauty and utility and therefore depreciate the value of the property within the subdivision. But the objections which validly may be made against solid constructions do not exist in regard to a flat concrete slab for a tennis court. Nor does the wire fence around it obstruct the view. Based upon the foregoing, it is our opinion that the trial court was correct in its conclusion that the tennis court and fence are not the type of structure prohibited by the covenant.

Affirmed, for defendants.

Questions and Case Problems

1. Frensley deeded a one-acre tract of land to the Assembly of God Church. The deed recited that the church was to own such land "so long as said premises shall be held, kept and used . . . for a place of divine worship. . . ."

   Later, oil and gas were discovered under the surface and production was initiated. The church was maintained on the premises at all times.

   Frensley's heirs asserted that the above clause limited the transfer to surface rights and that the mineral rights had been retained by Frensley. Accordingly, his heirs leased the mineral rights which they claim they received under Frensley's will to Skelly Oil Company.

   Further, the heirs assert that, even if the mineral rights were conveyed, then the church received only a conditional estate and that production of gas and oil violated the condition. Therefore, the heirs are now owners in fee simple absolute.

   The church through its trustee, White, files suit to determine the ownership rights of the church and heirs. Who prevails and on what theories? [*Frensley v. White,* 254 P.2d 982 (Okla. 1953).]

2. Wicks, a farmer, entered into an oral contract for the sale of four acres of uncut barley to Candle, a grocer, for $450. The parties agreed that the crop was to be severed three weeks after the agreement was made. Because the market price for barley rose nearly 60 percent, Wicks barred Candle from cutting the crop. Candle sues, and Wicks defends by citing that part of the statute of frauds which requires that a contract for the sale of an interest in land must be in writing. Who prevails?

3. In 1939 Cyrus M. Beachy conveyed real property to a trust for the benefit of his grandchildren, ages eleven and fifteen. Beachy required that the property pass from the trust to the children "when the youngest . . . shall have attained the age of forty (40) or would have attained such age had he survived."

   If either grandchild died before the property passed, his interest was to go to his children, if any, and to his heirs at law if no children were born.

   In 1945 Beachy died. His will left all his property to the grandchildren. The grandchildren claim that the conveyance to the trust violates the rule against perpetuities and is therefore void. If void, the property was part of the estate that passed through the will. Thus, the grandchildren would have immediate possession. Must the grandchildren wait the remaining 23 years before receiving the property? [*McEwen v. Enoch,* 204 P.2d 736 (Kan. 1949).]

4. Phil Porkey, a gourmet butcher, rented space from Larry Lessor for his butcher shop. The parties executed a three-year lease. Phil installed heavy refrigerated display counters which were attached to the floor with bolts, connected to a water pipe, and wired directly into the building's electrical system. Larry becomes insolvent and his creditors sue to attach the valuable counters. Phil objects, claiming that the counters are his personal property. Who prevails, Phil or Larry's creditors?

5. Clarence sold to Delbert a parcel of land on which there was a home, barn, unharvested crop, and housetrailer. Delbert protested when Clarence removed the trailer and Delbert sues to recover it. Will he prevail?

6. Mr. Thomas and Mr. Sturgeon were elderly gentlemen with heart ailments living in a home owned by them in joint tenancy in Fresno, California. On September 2nd, 1947, at about 9:00 P.M., a neighbor heard Mr. Sturgeon yell asking the neighbor to call a doctor. After calling, the neighbor went over and saw Mr. Thomas lying on the ground. The neighbor thought Mr. Thomas' body was cold and felt for a pulse but none was present. At that same time he heard a thud in the house. On investigation he found Mr. Sturgeon lying with his head on the piano pedals. Artificial respiration was administered. Within thirty minutes Mr. Sturgeon stopped breathing.

   Shortly thereafter, the fire chief arrived and observed that Mr. Thomas' body was discolored and cool while Mr. Sturgeon's body was still warm and had good color.

   At the trial between the heirs of Mr. Thomas and Mr. Sturgeon, evidence was introduced that an autopsy could not establish who had died first.

   Further, a physician testified that body temperature as felt at the scene would not be a good indication of who died first.

   California has a provision in its Probate Code which states:

   Where there is no sufficient evidence that two joint tenants have died otherwise than simultaneously the property so held shall be distributed one-half as if one had survived and one-half as if the other had survived.

   The trial court found that Thomas died first and his heirs appealed the case. What decision by the appellate court? [*Thomas v. Anderson*, 215 P.2d 478 (Cal. 1950).]

7. Purcey gave a written easement to his neighbor Pistol allowing Pistol to run a water ditch across Purcey's property to irrigate Pistol's land. Purcey sells his property to Rifle, who fills in the ditch because "it's dangerous for my kids." Pistol sues. Who prevails?

8. Holmes was engaged in the business of raising and processing chickens. In 1963 he bought property in Clackamas County, Oregon on which he planned to erect a chicken-processing plant. To prepare for construction he spent $33,000 to install a well system, plant special grass, and run soil tests to determine where drain fields for the plant's sewage should be located. In 1967 Clackamas County enacted an ordinance zoning the property Rural Agricultural-Single Family Residential. The zoning prohibited further construction of the chicken-processing plant. Holmes continued work and the county sued. The trial court enjoined defendant from further construction and he appealed. What result? [*Clackamas County v. Holmes*, 508 P.2d 190 (Or. 1973).]

9. The Davis family rented an apartment in a complex controlled by McDougall. The laundry room in the complex contained a Maytag washing machine with tub, agitator, and roller type wringer. The roller wringer was designed to release automatically when misused. However, the release mechanism was defective. Jodi Davis, age 3½, climbed up on a stool, started the washer and inserted her hand in the roller wringer, causing permanent injuries to her fingers, hand, and wrist. Her parents sued on her behalf, alleging that the landlord maintained an attractive nuisance. The trial court granted McDougall's motion for summary judgment and ruled that the washing machine was not an attractive nuisance. Jodi's parents appealed. What result? [*Davis v. McDougall,* 480 P.2d 907 (Ida. 1971).]

10. In the case of *Parrish v. Richards,* 336 P.2d 122 (Utah 1959),[6] is there anything which suggests the kind of attitude this court has toward restrictive covenants? Explain.

---

[6] See p. 821.

Transferring Ownership of Realty

46

After you have read this chapter, you should be able to:

1. Describe in detail the process of transferring ownership with deeds.
2. Describe the major methods of *financing* ownership and indicate the advantages and disadvantages of each method.
3. Identify the consequence of recording a document associated with realty.
4. Describe the steps involved in the typical sales transaction.
5. Identify methods for transferring ownership other than by a sale.

Introduction

Ownership of realty is most frequently transferred as a part of a *sales transaction.* Basically, the seller transfers ownership, through the *deeding process,* in return for the buyer's payment of the purchase price. Since most buyers do not have enough cash to pay the full price, they usually borrow most of the money from a lender such as a bank. The lender usually protects its interest by requiring the buyer to execute an *instrument of finance,* such as a mortgage or a trust deed. These instruments generally allow the lender to collect the loan by selling the realty if payments are not made as promised.

Ownership is often transferred without being part of a sales transaction. Further, the deeding process is not always needed to effectuate a transfer. For example, a city may *condemn* realty. In this process it forces a transfer of ownership without the consent of the private party.

This chapter examines ownership transfers by scrutinizing the deeding process and by evaluating the instruments of finance. Once these basic processes are developed, one can then examine the whole of the sales process. The nonsale transfers of ownership, such as condemnation, are discussed separately.

As you read through this material, ask yourself whether the average college graduate who has successfully completed a course in business law can competently handle his own purchase or sale. How about the college graduate without a background in business law? Or the person who did not graduate from high school? If you conclude that the average consumer needs professional help, then think about the kind of background such a professional person ought to have.

The Deeding Process

Historical Development

livery of seisin
an ancient ceremony
used to transfer
ownership of land

The law of deeds has its roots in the ancient rite of **livery of seisin.** That ceremony served as the forerunner of the modern deeding process at a time when very few persons could write. This method of transferring ownership required that the buyer and seller gather a group of local residents on the property to be sold. All the persons would march around the boundaries of the property and then assemble at its center. There the seller would dig up a chunk of sod and offer it to the buyer with the local residents as witnesses. While offering the sod, the seller would recite the terms of the transaction. Ownership was transferred when the buyer accepted the chunk of sod from the hands of the seller. While the modern deeding process has replaced the old rite of *livery of seisin,* it is easier to understand the modern process when it is compared with the old ceremony.

Overview of the Modern Deeding Process

deed
a formal document
used to transfer title to
real estate

Today paper replaces the chunk of sod. Usually a **deed** is a single piece of paper. (See figure 46.1.) Like the sod, a new deed is created each time there is a sale. Like the ancient ceremony of *livery of seisin,* it is the whole deeding process which transfers ownership. All the parts of the modern process must be completed

Figure 46.1 Warranty Deed

WARRANTY DEED
(Joint Tenancy Form)

_____and_____ husband and
wife grantors of_____ , County of_____ ,
State of Utah, hereby convey and WARRANT to
_____ and_____ husband and wife
as joint tenants and not as tenants in common, with full rights of survivorship,
Grantees of_____ for the sum of
_____ (   )
the following described tract of land in_____County,
State of Utah

WITNESS, the hand of said grantors, this_____ day of_____
A.D.   19 ____

    Signed in the presence of

_____   _____

_____   _____

_____   _____

_____   _____

STATE OF UTAH   RECORDING DATA
                              ss.   Entry No.   Fee $

County of _____   Recorded   Indexed
                                         Platted   Abstracted
    On the_____ day of_____   Compared   Delivered

personally appeared before me the
signer of the within instrument,
who duly acknowledged to me that
he executed the same.

_____
        Notary Public

Commission expires:
Residing in_____

before ownership is transferred. These elements of the modern deeding process are *execution, delivery,* and *acceptance.*

Execution refers to the format, language, and signing of the document. Many states have enacted statutes which specify a form for short, simple deeds. These are called statutory deeds. While all deeds are essentially similar, there are slight variations from state to state. For example, while some states require

notarize
verification by a proper
public official of the
authenticity of a
signature

that deeds be notarized to be valid, most states do not. **Notarizing** involves marking signed documents in a way which indicates that an official of the state has determined that the signatures are valid.

By itself, execution of a valid deed does not transfer ownership. Delivery and acceptance are also required to complete the deeding process. **Delivery,** like transferring the chunk of sod, merely involves transferring possession of a properly executed deed with the *intention* of shifting ownership. Delivery can be made to either the buyer or his agent. Thus, if a mother executed a deed in favor of a daughter but the deed was left in the mother's safe-deposit box until her death, the deed would not transfer ownership because it was not delivered. Further, if a deed were delivered just as security for a debt, ownership would not be transferred because there was no *intent* to shift ownership.

Acceptance merely means that the buyer indicates his willingness to assume ownership. Retaining the deed after delivery usually constitutes acceptance.

delivery
(in realty) the voluntary
transfer of a deed with
the intent thereby to
transfer ownership of
the realty

The deed's contents.

The Deed Document

All deeds contain about the same information (see figure 46.1). The major sections of deeds include:

1. the names of the grantor(s), (sellers);
2. the words of conveyance;
3. names of the grantee(s), (purchasers);
4. the consideration statement;
5. the property description;
6. the habendum;
7. the signatures and certifications.

Each section communicates important information about the nature of the parties or the property or the transaction. Since the deed is the heart of most real estate transactions, it must be scrutinized carefully by both the buyer and the seller if they are to protect their interests.

Grantor(s) Name(s).   The person giving up ownership is the grantor. The person receiving the deed is the grantee. The name(s) of those executing the deed as grantor(s) appears first. These persons must be owners of the estate conveyed in order for that interest to pass.

Words of Conveyance.   The words of conveyance generally determine which promises or warranties the grantor makes to the grantee. When the words "warrant and convey" or "grant and convey" are used, this indicates that the grantor promises or warrants:

encumbrance
a person's right in
another person's
property

1. that the grantor owns the estate transferred and will pay the grantee for his injury if it turns out that he doesn't receive the estate described in the deed;
2. that there are no liens, leases, easements, mortgages, or **encumbrances** which bind the grantee other than those disclosed in the deed.

Deeds of this type are generally called **warranty deeds** or *grant deeds*. They are the kind most frequently used.

The other major type of deed is called the **quitclaim deed.** The words of conveyance for it often include the word "quitclaim." This deed merely transfers the grantor's ownership, if any. No promises or warranties are implied in the deed. Thus, if a teacher gave a student a warranty deed to the school building in exchange for $10,000, the student could sue and recover the money if it turned out that the teacher did not own the building. If, however, a quitclaim deed were given, the student could not recover the money.

Quitclaim deeds are often used to remove "clouds on title." For example, if a divorced man sold property and then died and the buyer feared that the man's ex-wife might have a **dower** claim, the buyer could ask the ex-wife to execute a quitclaim deed. She might sign—perhaps in return for $25—but her lawyer would surely advise her not to execute a warranty deed because she is not certain that she owns any interest in the property.

In the absence of other indications, the law generally presumes that the grantor and grantee intended the conveyance of the fee simple absolute estate. Conditional and life estates can usually be identified by examining the words of conveyance. For example, the words "warrant and convey so long as no sheep are grazed on the land" would transfer a conditional estate. The words "quitclaim for life" would convey only a life estate.

Grantee(s) Name(s). Aside from identifying the grantees, this section indicates the form of co-ownership, if it exists, and each co-owner's percentage of ownership. In community property states, a statement that the grantees are husband and wife would create a presumption that community property is the form of co-ownership with each co-owning fifty percent. Tenancy by entirety would be presumed from the husband and wife designation in some, but not all, states which recognize that form of co-ownership.

Where no relationship is stated and the grantees are not married, the law in almost all states presumes that the parties co-own as tenants in common with equal percentage ownerships. Of course, when the ownership percentages are stated, they will govern. Thus, one could convey to "Oliver Wendell Holmes as to ninety-nine percent (99 percent) and John Marshall as to one percent (1 percent)," and Marshall would own one percent, not fifty.

Generally joint tenancy must be specifically identified. Some states demand extremely clear and emphatic language to create joint tenancy. Many lawyers use phrases like A to B and C "as joint tenants, with full rights of survivorship, and not as tenants in common."

Consideration. Generally most deeds recite a fictitious amount like "ten dollars" as the stated consideration. This protects the privacy of the parties because then the actual consideration for the sale does not become a part of the public record when the deed is recorded. In many cases consideration is not required for effective deeding.

---

warranty deed
a deed conveying title and giving warranties to the grantee

quitclaim deed
a document used in transferring the grantor's interest in realty, if any, without any warranties

dower
(at common law but generally abolished by statute today) a widow's life estate in a portion of the land of her deceased husband

Description of the Property. This section of the deed describes the physical boundaries of the parcel being conveyed. Frequently deeds must contain a legal description of the property to satisfy the execution requirement for deeding. Legal descriptions include subdivision lot descriptions, and meets and bounds descriptions. Street addresses and farm names do not qualify as legal descriptions. Thus, in some states a deed describing property as "1600 Pennsylvania Avenue" would not be recordable even though the city, county, and state were identified.

The Habendum. That portion of the deed immediately below the property description is called the **habendum**. It is in this section of the deed that the grantor defines the estate being conveyed and indicates the encumbrances which will affect the grantee's estate. Recall that in the words of conveyance of the warranty deed the grantor promises that there are no encumbrances except those listed on the deed. If an encumbrance, such as an easement or mortgage, exists but is not excepted (recited) in the habendum of a warranty deed, the grantor would be liable for any financial loss suffered by an innocent grantee because of the encumbrance. It is not necessary to recite encumbrances on a quitclaim deed because that deed does not warrant anything.

Signature and Notarizing. Generally only the grantor(s) signs the deed. Grantees usually need not sign although some grantors may require it as proof of acceptance. In some states the grantor's signature must be witnessed and the deed notarized.

Instruments of Finance

Most buyers of realty do not have enough cash to pay the full purchase price. So buyers usually borrow part of the price. Lenders want to be very certain they will be repaid. So they almost always require that the borrower give the lender the legal right to force the sale of the property if loan payments are not made as promised. The lender then can use the money from the forced sale to pay off the loan. The three major instruments of finance used to protect lenders are the "mortgage," the "trust deed," and the "land sale contract." Realty can also be transferred with the seller's existing financing.

Mortgages

Mortgages are the most common instrument for financing the acquisition of realty. (See figures 46.2 and 46.3.) Generally the buyer will give a **mortgage** to a lender such as a bank or savings and loan association. The mortgage gives the lender the legal right to file suit in court to *foreclose* (cut off) the buyer's ownership rights in the property in the event loan payments are not made as promised. After the suit is initiated and the judge hears the evidence, he issues a decree of **foreclosure**. After the decree is issued, the lender can cause a *sheriff's sale,* where the property is auctioned off to the highest bidder. The money received from the sheriff's sale is used to repay the debt owed the lender. If the

habendum
that portion of a deed which defines the estate in land being conveyed and indicates the encumbrances

mortgage
the nonpossessory security interest in realty; also the instrument which gives lenders the power to sell the mortgaged realty, to repay the debt, when the borrower defaults on the payments

foreclosure
the cutting off of the owner's interest in realty by sale pursuant to court decree

Figure 46.2   Minnesota Short Form Mortgage

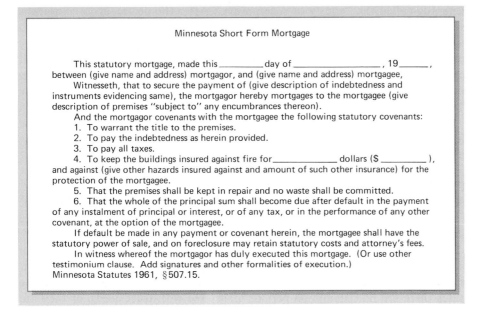

Minnesota Short Form Mortgage

This statutory mortgage, made this _____ day of _____ , 19 _____ , between (give name and address) mortgagor, and (give name and address) mortgagee,

Witnesseth, that to secure the payment of (give description of indebtedness and instruments evidencing same), the mortgagor hereby mortgages to the mortgagee (give description of premises "subject to" any encumbrances thereon).

And the mortgagor covenants with the mortgagee the following statutory covenants:
1. To warrant the title to the premises.
2. To pay the indebtedness as herein provided.
3. To pay all taxes.
4. To keep the buildings insured against fire for _____ dollars ($ _____), and against (give other hazards insured against and amount of such other insurance) for the protection of the mortgagee.
5. That the premises shall be kept in repair and no waste shall be committed.
6. That the whole of the principal sum shall become due after default in the payment of any instalment of principal or interest, or of any tax, or in the performance of any other covenant, at the option of the mortgagee.

If default be made in any payment or covenant herein, the mortgagee shall have the statutory power of sale, and on foreclosure may retain statutory costs and attorney's fees.

In witness whereof the mortgagor has duly executed this mortgage. (Or use other testimonium clause. Add signatures and other formalities of execution.)
Minnesota Statutes 1961, §507.15.

Figure 46.3   Mortgage "Closing"

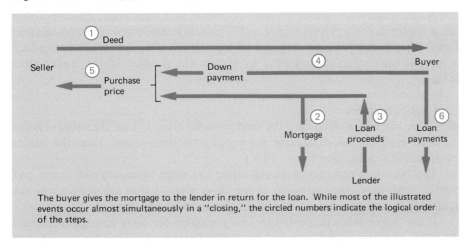

The buyer gives the mortgage to the lender in return for the loan. While most of the illustrated events occur almost simultaneously in a "closing," the circled numbers indicate the logical order of the steps.

money received exceeds the debt, the surplus goes to the mortgagor (the borrower). If the money is not sufficient to pay the debt, the lender can usually obtain a deficiency judgment against the borrower for the balance due.

Mortgagors are protected in most states with rights of **redemption.** Prior to the decree of foreclosure, the mortgagor can sometimes stop the foreclosure

redemption
the reclaiming of a foreclosed ownership interest in realty

Transferring Ownership of Realty   831

process by simply paying all past-due installments along with those expenses incurred by the lender because of the default. This ability to stop foreclosure is generally called the "equity of redemption." After the decree of foreclosure is issued, the mortgagor is still protected in a majority of states by a redemption period—usually six months to a year—during which he can regain the property by paying off the *whole* amount of the mortgage along with the lender's default expenses. This is generally called the right of "statutory redemption." Mortgages sometimes contain clauses which waive rights of redemption. Generally these clauses can not be enforced.

The process of mortgage foreclosure is usually very time consuming. The delays associated with the suit, sheriff's sale, and possible redemption can often delay the sale for one or two years.

Trust Deeds

trust deed
a deed of land to a trustee in trust as security for performance of an obligation with power to sell the land on default; basically, a real property mortgage

With this method of financing the buyer first obtains the deed from the seller. The buyer then gives a **trust deed** to a **trustee.** (See figure 46.4.) The trustee holds the trust deed on behalf of the lender. The trust deed contains language which allows the trustee to sell the property if the buyer defaults on the loan payments. Note that a court order is not required to cause the sale, and that it is a private sale conducted by the trustee rather than by the sheriff. In some states there are no redemption periods associated with trust deeds, or they are very short. For these reasons, sale after default often occurs more rapidly under a trust deed than under a mortgage. Therefore, lenders frequently prefer trust deeds to mortgages.

trustee
(in realty) the one who holds the trust deed for the benefit of the lender

A mortgage with "power of sale" is similar to a trust deed. No foreclosure suit is required, and a private sale occurs. This sale is conducted by the mortgagee. Some states do not permit mortgages with powers of sale, and those states which do permit them carefully regulate by statute the conduct of the lender after default.

Land sale contracts.

Land Sale Contracts

With this method of financing the lender—who often is also the seller—keeps the deed until all the contracted payments have been made. Then the lender must deliver a deed. (See figure 46.5.)

The land sale contract gives the buyer the right to occupy the realty and treat it as his own. The law refers to the buyer under a land sale contract as the *equitable owner* even though he has not yet received the deed.

If the buyer defaults, the lender in some states can have him removed from the property in about the same way a landlord evicts a tenant who has not paid the rent. While this involves a lawsuit, it is sometimes concluded much more rapidly than either a mortgage foreclosure or a sale by trustee. In these states the lender can sometimes treat the installment payments as though they were rental charges so that the defaulting buyer loses everything.

Real Property

Figure 46.4 Trust Deed "Closing"

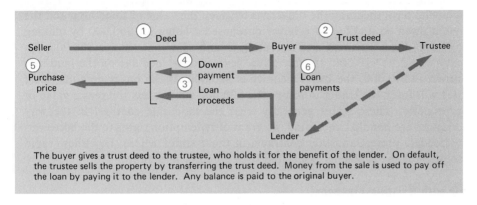

The buyer gives a trust deed to the trustee, who holds it for the benefit of the lender. On default, the trustee sells the property by transferring the trust deed. Money from the sale is used to pay off the loan by paying it to the lender. Any balance is paid to the original buyer.

Figure 46.5 Performance of a Land Sale Contract

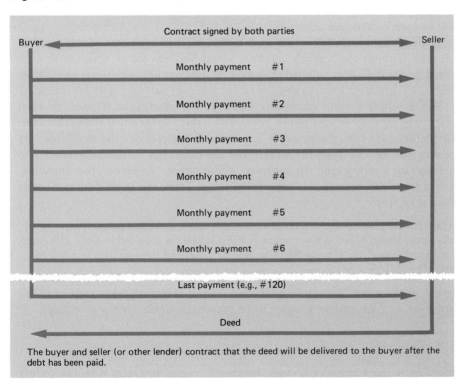

The buyer and seller (or other lender) contract that the deed will be delivered to the buyer after the debt has been paid.

Most other states force the lender in the land sale contract to return to the defaulting buyer his equity in the property. The word "equity" as used here is a financial term meaning the difference between the value of something and the amount owed on it. Thus, if a buyer purchased a home for $60,000 by making a $10,000 down payment and executing a land sale contract for $50,000, his equity would be $10,000. If after a few years the balance due on the land sale contract is $40,000, the buyer's equity is $20,000. If the buyer defaults, most states will force the lender to return the $20,000 equity, less the rental value of the property. These states generally treat the land sale contract in the way mortgages are handled, including the grant of redemption rights to the borrower.

Lenders prefer land sale contracts in those states where they allow rapid resolution of the problems associated with a debtor in default.

Sale with existing financing.

Sale with Existing Financing

Another method of financing involves the sale of the property with the existing financing intact. Thus, the seller may deed mortgaged property to the buyer. This mortgage should then be recited in the habendum of the deed as an encumbrance. The property can be transferred when encumbered by a mortgage, trust deed, or even a land sale contract.

Some lenders include clauses in their financial instruments which prohibit such sales without the lender's consent. About half the states which have confronted the issue have concluded that such restrictions are sometimes unenforceable.

While sellers remain personally liable to the mortgagee (lender) in such sales, the buyer may or may not be personally liable. Generally if the deed recites in the habendum that the property is conveyed "subject to" the mortgage, the property may be foreclosed on default, but the buyer has no personal liability to the foreclosing mortgagee. In contrast, if the buyer "assumes" the financing, then he as well as the seller is personally liable. Thus, the habendum portion of a deed may state:

Grantee hereby assumes the mortgage against the above described property in favor of Wells Fargo Bank, N.A., in the amount of $283,219.00, as recorded in Book 218, page 21 of the records of the County Recorder for the County of Cache, State of Utah on January 1, 1901.

The use of the word "assumes" instead of stating "Grantee takes *subject to* the mortgage . . ." causes the grantee to be personally liable for the mortgage.

Recording of realty documents.

priority
the order in which claims against realty are satisfied

Recording

Recording is the process of filing a document related to realty with the county clerk or commissioner of deeds. Deeds, mortgages, land sale contracts, easements, and liens are among the many documents usually recorded. In general, the purpose of recording is to give *notice* to the world and to influence **priority** with respect to any other claims against the realty.

Priority

Priority determines the order in which claims against the realty are satisfied. Thus, if there are two mortgages recorded against a property and foreclosure occurs, the mortgage first recorded will be paid completely before any funds are applied to the second. Similarly, if an owner gives two deeds for the same realty to different persons, in most states the grantee who first records his deed will become the final owner even if he had received the second deed, i.e., second in time. Generally this second grantee (who first records his deed) must not have known of the first conveyance, and must have paid for the deed, in order for him to receive first priority.

Notice

Every buyer of realty is assumed by law to have *notice* of all claims and encumbrances recorded against the property. This is so even though the buyer did not know of the claim and did not examine the public record. This is called "constructive notice." Thus, if an easement for a right of way is recorded against a property which is later bought for development into a housing tract, the developer is bound by the easement. He is bound even though he was not actually aware of the easement and even though it makes his development impossible. (Note that if the seller gave a warranty deed which did not indicate the easement, then the seller would be liable to the developer.)

Also, if a claim against property, like a mortgage, is *not* recorded and the property is sold, the buyer takes the property free of the claim. However, the buyer must not have had actual knowledge of the claim and he must have paid value for the property. If he knew of the claim or received the property as a gift, generally he is bound by the unrecorded claim.

The Sale Process

Overview

Deeding and financing are at the heart of most realty transactions. Once one understands these processes, they can be integrated into the typical sale process. By examining the total sale process, one can gain a perspective on the way many legally intense business transactions are structured. Such a perspective can also illustrate the way several bodies of law can merge in a single transaction.

The typical process for selling a single-family residence involves a sequence of steps by the seller, the real estate broker, and the buyer. Each step involves contract law or agency law or real property law. Some steps involve the application of all three bodies of law. Figure 46.6 depicts the structure of the typical residential transaction. The remaining paragraphs of this section provide an overview of the major steps involved in transferring ownership in the context of a *sale*.

Figure 46.6 The Legal Environment of Real Estate Sales

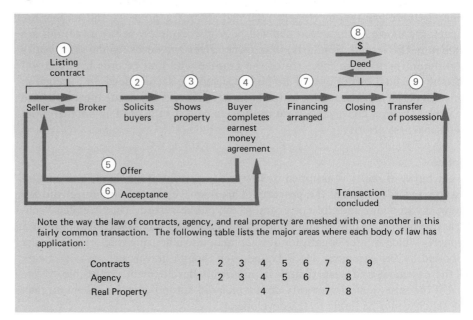

Note the way the law of contracts, agency, and real property are meshed with one another in this fairly common transaction. The following table lists the major areas where each body of law has application:

Contracts	1	2	3	4	5	6	7	8	9
Agency	1	2	3	4	5	6		8	
Real Property				4			7	8	

Listing. Usually the owner of realty, such as a house, will sign a **listing** contract with a real estate broker. This contract makes the broker the **special** or **professional agent** of the seller. Usually the broker can collect the negotiated commission once he has produced a ready, willing, and able buyer who offers to purchase the property under the same terms as those indicated in the listing contract. Brokers can not agree among themselves to fix commission rates. Commission rates must be determined through negotiation between the seller and the broker.

Sales Efforts and the Earnest Money Agreement. The broker then must use reasonable efforts in finding prospective buyers. The prospective buyers are escorted around the property by the broker. He generally explains the terms under which the seller might be willing to sell. Then the broker persuades the prospect to make what is sometimes called an "earnest money offer." While the broker aids the buyer by filling in the blank spaces on this standard form, he is still the agent and fiduciary of the seller and represents the seller's best interests. The earnest money offer proposes a contract which generally specifies the following:

1. the buyer's name(s);
2. the amount of the earnest money (the amount of money given the seller which he may keep if the buyer breaches the contract);
3. the estate transferred and a description of the property;
4. the sale price and method of financing (e.g., land sale contract);
5. the date of closing (when the final financing is to be concluded; for example, the date when the deed and money will be exchanged in a cash sale);

6. the date of possession (when the buyer can move into the property);
7. the date of proration (when the buyer assumes liability for property taxes, insurance obligations, utilities, etc.);
8. the buyer's form of co-ownership if any;
9. the party who shall pay for the abstract of title or title insurance policy.

Arranging Financing. Frequently the buyer will make his offer conditioned upon, or subject to, obtaining appropriate financing or obtaining an appraisal of the realty for a certain amount. The broker will usually assist the buyer in arranging the financing or appraisal.

Closing. After financing has been arranged, the closing can take place. The closing is the meeting where the remainder of the purchase price is usually paid and arrangements are made for the proration of property taxes, insurance, and utilities. The deed can be delivered to the buyer at this time if the earnest money contract so provides.

Transfer of Possession. Physical possession is transferred on the date specified in the earnest money agreement.

Escrow

Frequently the closing or settlement process is fairly complex and involves large amounts of money. The parties may then direct that the transaction be closed in **escrow.** This means that the buyer and seller execute a detailed contract with an escrow officer—someone other than the buyer or seller—which directs the officer as to the exact procedures to be used in closing. When an escrow is not used, the broker, lender, attorney, or title insurance company may close the transaction by relying on the earnest money agreement and the oral instructions of the buyer and seller.

escrow
the conditional delivery of property to a person who is to deal with it on the occurrence of specified conditions

When land sale contracts are used, the buyer will often require that the seller execute a deed and deliver it into escrow. The escrow officer then accepts the deed for the buyer and, following the instructions in the escrow contract, the officer will turn the deed over to the buyer after all the payments have been made.

Title Insurance

While warranties of title protect buyers of realty, the value of a warranty depends upon the financial strength of the seller. Thus, if a seller conveys fee simple absolute by warranty deed then loses all his money gambling in Atlantic City, the buyer has no effective remedy if he discovers that the seller owned only a life estate.

A search of the chain of title would have revealed the problem, but most buyers do not know how to check the county recorder's records. Sometimes an attorney will be retained to prepare an *abstract of title*. That document summarizes the history of transactions associated with the property. And if the buyer is injured by an undisclosed defect in the title, he may be able to collect in a suit against the attorney for negligence.

Title insurance often can be purchased as a substitute for an abstract of title. The policy contracts to pay the buyer for injuries arising from undisclosed defects of title up to the face amount of the policy. Generally such policies are limited to defects which could be identified from an examination of the recorded documents in the chain of title. Since most states have laws regulating the financial structure of title insurance companies, the injured buyer with title insurance can recover from a financially stable company.

RESPA

The Federal Real Estate Settlement Procedures Act of 1974 (RESPA) along with later amendments and regulations[1] is intended to educate consumers, reduce the costs associated with transferring ownership of realty, and eliminate abusive practices like kickbacks.

RESPA covers all transactions where the sale is financed by a *federally* related mortgage loan on residential structures other than large apartment buildings. In such transactions the *lender* must provide the buyer with a copy of an information booklet and an opportunity to obtain estimates of settlement costs in advance of the closing. Further, the party *conducting the closing* or settlement must use a Uniform Settlement Statement. That federal document is intended to clearly identify settlement costs incurred by the buyer and seller.

Finally, the Act prohibits kickbacks and unearned fees. For example, brokers, lenders, sellers, or buyers can not receive compensation for referring a buyer or seller to a particular bank, attorney, title insurance company, or fire insurance company. Such action can be *criminal* conduct. However, brokers *can* operate cooperative brokerage arrangements and multiple listing services.

Lenders have a limited exemption from this provision. They can require the seller to pay a prepayment penalty on the old mortgage if the new loan is not made with the same lender. Thus, sellers will often ask buyers to borrow from the old lender. That tactic increases the lender's volume of business.

Sellers may not specify a particular title company to be used by the buyer even though there is no kickback. Lenders, however, may specify a title company since one title policy is usually written for them in the amount of their loan.

Further, the Act requires that lenders who collect from the borrower advance payments (sometimes called "impounds") for expenses like property taxes and insurance can only collect a reasonable amount.

Nonsale Transfers of Ownership

Other Deed-Related Transfers

While the deeding process is generally associated with transactions involving the *sale* of realty, deeding is also involved with transfers of ownership through gifts and wills.

---

[1] *HUD Regulations,* subtitle B, part 3500 et seq.

Ownership of realty is also transferred when one dies without a will. Decedents dying without a will are said to have died "intestate." In these cases the laws of descent and distribution will determine who among the surviving relatives will become the new owner or owners. Thus, in many states if a man dies intestate without children, all of the property goes to his surviving wife. If there are no heirs of the person who dies intestate, then his property "escheats" to the state. This means the state becomes the owner.

Dedication

Dedication.

If a developer wants to give land to a local government—perhaps for use as public streets—then he can dedicate it. However, ownership is not transferred until the government *accepts* the transfer.

Condemnation

Condemnation.

When a government wants private property for a public use, it may exercise its power of **eminent domain** and take title through condemnation if it pays the owner the reasonable value of the property.

eminent domain
government power to appropriate private land for public use on payment of just compensation without the owner's consent

Adverse Possession

If one who thinks he owns property acts as the owner for a substantial period of time, the law will acknowledge his asserted ownership as true under the doctrine of **adverse possession.** The time period varies dramatically from state to state, but it usually is five to fifteen years. In addition to the time period requirement, the following tests must also be met:

1. open, notorious, exclusive use of the property by the claimant;
2. *continuous* use for the prescribed period; and
3. color of title.

Color of title means that the occupant came upon the property with some basis for believing he was the owner. In addition to the above requirements, some states require that the claimant have paid the property taxes during the period of use.

adverse possession
a method of acquiring title to land by actual, exclusive, and continuous possession of land under color of title adverse or hostile to the true owner in an open and notorious manner for a statutory period of time

Prescription

The method for acquiring ownership by **prescription** is analogous to adverse possession. However, prescription applies to those "uses" which are associated with easements. Accordingly, property taxes need not be paid. In some cases where a claimant would not qualify as an adverse possessor for failure to pay taxes, he may prevail in a claim for prescription. For example, a person who reasonably believed that he was the owner of a pasture and grazed cattle there for thirty years, but whose property tax assessment did not include the pasture, might not qualify for adverse possession, but he probably could win the prescription right to continue grazing cattle because of his previous use of the pasture.

prescription
(in real property) a method of obtaining the right to use of another's land as an easement by open and continuous possession and use of the land under a claim of right to such use for a statutory period of time

Accretion

When a boundary line is defined by a creek, river, stream, or shoreline, then the very gradual change in the location of the water will shift the location of the boundary. This method of acquiring ownership of the additional land caused by such gradual change is called **accretion.** When the shift is rapid and radical, the physical process is called *avulsion.* Avulsion does not change the boundary.

accretion
a method of obtaining title to another's land caused by gradual changes in the natural boundaries of such land

Summary Statement

1. The deeding process is the most common method used to transfer ownership of realty. It requires execution of the deed document, delivery, and acceptance.
2. Warranty deeds warrant (assure) transfer of the indicated estate free of all encumbrances except those stated in the deed. Quitclaim deeds transfer only the grantor's interest, if any. The grantor does not warrant that he has an interest to transfer or that all encumbrances have been disclosed in the deed.
3. The language used in deeds determines the estate transferred, the form of co-ownership, the physical boundaries of the estate, and the limitations on the ownership of the grantee, such as restrictive covenants and mortgages.
4. Financing the purchase of realty usually involves either a mortgage, trust deed, land sale contract, or a sale with existing financing.
5. Generally the debtor in default can be removed from the property most rapidly under a land sale contract, less rapidly under a trust deed, and most slowly under a mortgage.
6. Recording influences the priority among competing claims and gives notice of the recorded document to the whole world.
7. Escrows are contracts which direct a person to perform specific acts in connection with property, such as recording a deed. They are often used in closing a real estate sale.
8. Title insurance and abstracts of title allow a buyer to collect from someone other than the grantor when the buyer is injured by a defect of title not disclosed in the insurance policy nor in the abstract.
9. RESPA requires distribution of a pamphlet and use of the Uniform Settlement Statement, prohibits most referral kickbacks, and limits amounts collected for lender's prepayment accounts for insurance and taxes.
10. Ownership can be transferred without using the deeding process. This can occur through condemnation, adverse possession, prescription, and accretion.

The following case is presented to illustrate the complex nature of problems encountered in real property transactions. Can you perceive the role of contract, agency, and real property law in the transaction leading to the lawsuit?

Bailey v. Kuida
213 P.2d 895 (Ariz. 1950)

Joseph and Eva Bailey brought this action against Walter and Christine Kuida to rescind a contract of sale of real estate.

The sale was negotiated through J. W. Carter, a real estate broker, as agent for defendants. Carter represented to plaintiffs before an agreement was signed that, in his opinion, the property could be used for construction of an apartment house thereon.

Defendants had no knowledge of any representation made by their agent, J. W. Carter, to plaintiffs concerning the property until about one year . . . [after the transaction was concluded].

At the time the agreement of sale was executed there was then on record in the office of the County Recorder, Maricopa County, restrictions to the uses to which said . . . [land] . . . could be put which prohibited its use for apartment house property, and restricted the use of said property in other respects.

Plaintiffs never saw the warranty deed which contained restrictions against the use of the property for apartment house purposes until approximately a year after plaintiffs had entered into said agreement. Plaintiffs had no actual notice of the restrictions on the property.

Plaintiffs sued defendants on two causes of action for rescission. The first cause of action was based upon the claim that defendants agreed to convey the property free and clear of all encumbrances, restrictions, reservations, conditions, and limitations, and further agreed to deliver to the escrow agent a warranty deed conveying a fee simple title to plaintiffs.

The second cause of action was based on fraud, for the misrepresentation that the property could be used to construct an apartment house thereon. The lower court rendered judgment in favor of defendants, and from this judgment the plaintiffs appeal.

. . . This court has ruled that when a purchaser of real estate discovers that he has been defrauded, he has two courses open to him. He may either ratify the transaction so far as the owner is concerned and make the payments, notwithstanding the false representations, reserving the right to sue the agent in damages for such fraud and deception, or he may go to the owner and, stating the fraud, offer to rescind. If the owner, after due notice of the fraud and offer of rescission, insists upon holding the purchaser to the transaction, he will then be deemed to have ratified the alleged representations of the agent, and the purchaser may pursue as against such owner any remedy which he would have had, had the false representations been made by the owner in person. If, on the other hand, the owner accepts the rescission and returns the money paid, the parties are in status quo ante contractus [before making the contract] and justice as between them is satisfied. . . .

Defendants, having accepted the benefits of the transaction based upon the misrepresentation made by their agent Carter that the property was available for the construction of an apartment house thereon, and having refused to rescind when so advised by plaintiffs, are bound by Carter's misrepresentations.

The term "warranty deed" has a definite legal meaning. " 'Warranty deed' purports to convey fee title to property free and clear of all encumbrances." . . . Section 71-408, A.C.A. 1939, provides:

From the use of the word "grant" or "convey" in any conveyance by which an estate of inheritance or fee simple is to be passed, the following covenants, and none other, on the part of the grantor for himself and his heirs to the grantee, his heirs and assigns, are implied, unless restrained by express terms contained in such conveyances: That previous to the time of the execution of such conveyance the grantor has not conveyed the same estate or any right, title or interest therein, to any person other than the grantee; that such estate is at the time of the execution of such conveyance free from encumbrances. . . .

Defendants in this case by contract agreed to sell and convey the property to plaintiffs, to deliver to the escrow agent a warranty deed, and did not make any reference whatsoever in the contract to restrictions. Regardless of what restrictions may have been of record in the County Recorder's office in Maricopa County pertaining to this particular piece of property, *the contract between the parties must govern the obligations and rights of each of the parties.* [Emphasis added.]

Defendants deposited a deed entitled "Warranty Deed" with the escrow agent which contained the restrictions hereinbefore referred to, instead of the warranty deed contracted for by the parties with no encumbrances thereon. This constituted a breach of the contract of sale, and plaintiffs had the right to refuse further payments on the purchase price and to recover the amount paid thereon, for it is apparent from the evidence that defendants could not perform.

Plaintiffs complain that the lower court erred in its conclusion of law that where defendants contracted to deliver to plaintiffs a fee simple title, plaintiffs were charged with constructive notice of the public records and of the private records of the escrow agent, and by reason of such notice were entitled only to a fee simple minus the encumbrances and restrictions shown by those public and private records. Section 71-426, A.C.A. 1939, provides as follows:

The record of any grant, deed or instrument of writing authorized or required to be recorded, which has been duly acknowledged and recorded in the proper county, shall be taken and held as notice to all persons of the existence of such grant, deed or instrument. . . .

Public records are of course notice to any person of the existence and contents of their properly recorded instruments.

The trial court did not err in holding that plaintiffs had constructive notice of the encumbrances of record in connection with this property, with the County Recorder of Maricopa County, but did err as to the legal conclusion reached by reason of such notice. However, it is of no moment whether or not the plaintiffs did have notice. The defendants had notice as well, but in the face of such knowledge defendants saw fit to enter into a contract with plaintiffs agreeing to deliver to them a warranty deed, without any mention whatsoever [in the contract] of encumbrances.

. . . But the purpose of the recording acts is to protect the persons who claim rights under the recorded instruments. It has never been held that an encumbrance was excepted from an agreement to convey good title merely because the encumbrance was of record at the time the agreement was made. . . .

Plaintiffs had the right to rely on the written agreements whereby defendants agreed to convey the property by warranty deed, and it is immaterial under the facts in this case whether or not plaintiffs had constructive notice of the restriction.

Judgment is reversed, with directions to the trial court to enter judgment in favor of plaintiffs in accordance with the prayer of the complaint.

Questions and Case Problems

1. Arthur Glander received a deed to a small farm from his parents. A month after receiving that deed, Arthur executed a quitclaim deed for the property to his brother and his sister, Gladys. The deed was in proper form, signed and notarized. The deed was given to Arthur's father for him to hold. The father was to give the deed to the brother and sister if Arthur died. Gladys moved to New York. Thirteen years later, while visiting the father's home and rummaging through his papers, Gladys found the deed. She promptly recorded it. Arthur now sues, asking the court to determine who is the true owner in a quiet title action. Who prevails, Arthur or Gladys? [*Glander v. Glander*, 239 P.2d 254 (Ida. 1951).]

2. Sly Hick orally promised his girlfriend, Sally Showgirl, that he would give her his farm in return for her continued affection. So Sally conferred great affection on Sly. Then one night Sly died of a heart attack. Sally believes that she owns the farm. Sly's relatives assert that she owns nothing. Who is right?

3. In 1919 Nix and Nix Company purchased land for a substantial sum of money from Tooele County in Utah. Title was transferred with a quitclaim deed. The Nixes paid property taxes to the county for the property for twenty years. Then they discovered that an honest mutual mistake had been made because the county never owned any interest in the land. Nix and Nix Company now sue Tooele County to recover the purchase price. Who prevails? [*Nix v. Tooele County*, 118 P.2d 376 (Utah 1941).]

4. The Kendricks owned property in Snohomish County, Washington. In 1961 they sold two houses and lots for $18,500 with a down payment of $1,100 and monthly payments of $120 under a land sale contract. The land sale contract was recorded. The buyers were Millard C. Davis and his wife. They mortgaged this interest under the land sale contract to a Finance Company to secure a loan of $1,000. In 1965 the buyers defaulted on the land sale contract. The Kendricks (the sellers) recorded and sent a Notice of Declaration of Forfeiture and Cancellation of Contract to the Davises. The Kendricks filed a **lis pendens,** which gives notice that a suit is pending, and initiated a suit to quiet title. The Finance Company became a party to the suit and offered to pay off the balance of the land sale contract in return for acquiring ownership. The Kendricks, sellers, want clear title to the property free of the mortgage. Who prevails, the Kendricks or the Finance Company? [*Kendrick v. Davis*, 452 P.2d 222 (Wash. 1969).]

   lis pendens
   a suit is pending

5. Erasmus Wiley occupied an old house in a commercial area for about twenty years. On his sixtieth birthday he executed a warranty deed to his neighbor, Buster Blue, in return for $200,000 in cash. Erasmus retained the right to occupy the property for an additional three months. Buster did not record his

deed. After two months Erasmus executed a quitclaim deed for $150,000 in favor of Jerry Green, a politician. Jerry had no knowledge of the prior deed, and he immediately recorded his quitclaim deed. Erasmus now resides in a Brazilian resort and is incommunicado. What are the rights of the parties?

6. Winnie Selsor, a full-blood Creek Indian, owned 160 acres of unimproved, unfenced, poorly wooded mountainous land. When she failed to pay the property taxes, the county sold the property to L. P. Kelley. Later Winnie deeded the property to Eddie Cox. Kelley asked Herman Johnson to take care of the land. Johnson ran 35 to 40 head of cattle on the property and came upon the land about 50 times a year to check on the cattle and the land. Cox claims that the tax deed is void. Kelley asserts title through adverse possession. Cox counters that, while other requirements may have been met, Kelley did not possess the land. Who prevails? [*Cox v. Kelley*, 295 P.2d 1061 (Okla. 1956).]

7. Able leased a room in a home owned by widow Wilma. The parties executed a written lease for two years so Able would complete graduate school. Six months later Wilma sold the house to Professor Pickey. When Pickey discovered Able, he told him to leave because Pickey intends to use the room to display his rodent collection. Able claims he has the right to rent the room for another 1½ years. The lease was not recorded, and Pickey could not tell when he inspected the property that the one room had been rented out. Who prevails?

8. Frank Willett and George Miller owned lands on opposite shores of the Camarron River. From 1913 until 1930 the Camarron River moved about a half mile into Miller's property. Over 200 acres of Miller's former property are now on Willett's side of the river. The change was caused by several floods, each lasting about five days, which shifted the river's location as much as 300 feet. Willett and Miller now claim ownership of the property between the old location of the river and the new location. Who prevails? [*Willett v. Miller*, 55 P.2d 90 (Okla. 1936).]

9. Monte Bucks, the holder of a bachelor's degree in Business Administration, bought a large apartment house by putting $2,000 down and taking the property "subject to" an existing mortgage of about $750,000. He installed a former go-go dancer as the manager in the hope that she would lure many of her friends into renting apartments in his building. The plan worked, and occupancy approached 100 percent. However, rental receipts declined dramatically because the tenants spent all their money on things other than rent. In addition, maintenance expenses rose significantly because the new tenants treated the property harshly. Monte could not make the mortgage payments. The lender foreclosed on the mortgage and recovered $600,000 on the sale of the distressed apartment building. The lender now sues Monte for the other $150,000. Who prevails?

10. In the case of *Bailey v. Kuida*, 213 P.2d 895 (Ariz. 1950),[2] was the real estate salesman adequately prepared to perform the job for which he was paid? Explain.

---

[2] See pp. 841–43.

Renting Realty

47

After you have read this chapter, you should be able to:

1. Describe the kinds of rental relationships which landlords and tenants may establish.
2. Describe the promises implied in most leases.
3. Describe the covenants and conditions which should be included in a residential lease.
4. Describe the tenant's powers to transfer their rights in leased property.
5. Describe the rights and obligations of landlords and tenants on termination of a lease.

Historical Development

By the early 1700s the common law of England had developed a sophisticated body of case law clearly defining the landlord-tenant relationship. That case law was transplanted to each of our states as they adopted the common law of England for their state law. After the initial adoption, and with the passage of time, the uniform body of law was transformed significantly by the statutory and case law of each state. Today landlord-tenant law varies dramatically from state to state. While a Uniform Landlord Tenant Act was drafted in 1972, it has as yet been adopted in only a few states.

Basic Nature of the Landlord-Tenant Relationship

freehold estates
fee simple absolute, conditional and life estates

demise
(in realty) to lease or rent

leasehold estate
the estate in realty owned by tenants

lease
a form of contract giving one person, the tenant, the exclusive right to occupy for a period the property of another, the landlord

The landlord-tenant relationship arises when the owner of a **freehold estate** (e.g., fee simple absolute, a conditional estate, or a life estate) transfers to another the right to temporarily possess the realty. Generally the right of possession is given in exchange for the payment of *rent*. The temporary transfer of the right of possession is referred to as **demising** or *leasing* the property. Since the transfer of possession is temporary, the owner of the freehold will eventually regain possession. This power to regain possession is called the *right of reversion*. The owner of the freehold is called the *landlord* or *lessor,* and the party receiving the temporary right of possession is called the *tenant* or *lessee.* After transfer, the tenant is said to own a **leasehold estate.** (See figure 47.1.)

When a written document evidences the relationship between the parties, the document is usually called the **lease** or *rental agreement.* Most leases constitute a blending of the law of *conveyancing* (i.e., transferring ownership of realty) and the law of contracts. The conveyancing aspect of the transaction is concerned with transferring a leasehold estate to the tenant. The contract aspects

Figure 47.1   Creation and Termination of a One Year Leasehold Estate

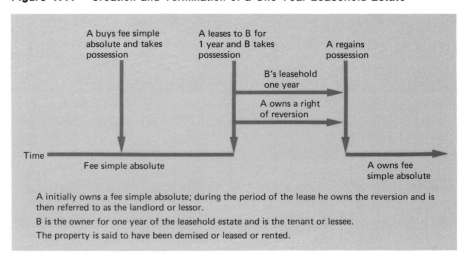

A initially owns a fee simple absolute; during the period of the lease he owns the reversion and is then referred to as the landlord or lessor.

B is the owner for one year of the leasehold estate and is the tenant or lessee.

The property is said to have been demised or leased or rented.

relate to the agreements between the parties on such issues as payment of the rent, who shall repair the realty, the amount of security or cleaning deposits and the conditions under which they can be returned, and limitation on uses of the property.

The law treats the tenants as owners of *nonfreehold* estates. These estates do not occupy the same status in the law as freehold estates. The owners of freehold estates are said to be *seised* of the property. Owners of estates are seised when they acquire possession of a freehold with a deed. Tenants are not seised, though they do possess the realty. Because of this, the landlord retains some obligations of ownership, like the duty to pay the property taxes. Further, the tenant's estate will be treated as personalty. Thus, if a tenant dies, his leasehold interest may pass via his will to those who receive the decedent's *personalty*.

Because leases are part contracts, the law assumes that the parties negotiate the terms of the lease at arm's length with each party protecting his own self-interest. Accordingly, there is no standard lease document. Most printed lease documents have been prepared by the attorneys for landlords. If tenants arc too shy to negotiate changes in the printed forms, they may be severely injured.

Creation of the Rental Relationship

Oral Leases

A lease may be created in a variety of ways. It can be created orally, and is then called a **parol lease**; or it can be created without words—by implication from the acts of the parties. While oral leases are often enforceable, every state requires that certain leases be placed in writing. Generally it is the statute of frauds[1] for each state which determines which leases must be written.

parol lease
a lease not reduced to writing

Statute of Frauds

The states vary dramatically in defining when a lease falls *within* the **statute of frauds.** Most states require leases to be in writing only when they exceed a term specified by statute, usually one or three years. While most states do not treat leases as the sale of an "interest in land," a few do. In these states all leases must be written. In general, the consequence of failing to comply with the statute is that the lease is treated as terminable at the will of the lessor or lessee, either without notice or with minimal notice.

statute of frauds
a statute requiring that certain kinds of contract be proved only by a proper writing

Generally the statute of frauds requires that the writing be signed by the defendant and that it contain all the essential terms of the lease, so that a court need not hear oral testimony to determine the rights of the parties. Even when a lease is within the statute of frauds and not in writing, the lease may still be enforced in an equity action if the plaintiff can establish that *part performance* has cured the defective creation. Generally part performance occurs when there has been transfer of possession, payment of rent, and substantial improvement of the property by the lessee.

---

[1] See chapter 11, Contractual Form—Requirement of a Writing for Enforceability, Statute of Frauds.

Leasehold Estates

If a landlord-tenant relationship comes into being, the law will classify it as an estate at sufferance, an estate at will, a periodic estate, or an estate for years. The distinctions among the types of estates are important because the estates are terminated differently.

Estate at sufferance.

Estate at Sufferance. This estate arises when one rightfully takes possession of property as a lessee but then remains in possession *after* termination of the lease. A few states allow landlords to use self-help eviction if no force is used. But most states require notice of termination of an estate at sufferance and permit eviction only by a police officer after a lawsuit.

Estate at will.

Estate at Will. When someone takes possession of the realty with the landlord's consent, but *without* entering into an oral or written lease, he or she owns an *estate at will.* This usually occurs when the parties agree that the prospective tenant can move in and that the lease will be negotiated later.

This landlord-tenant relationship can be terminated at any time by either party. Some states protect the lessee by requiring notice before dispossession.

Periodic estate.

Periodic Estate. This relationship arises when the parties agree on the terms and conditions of the lease but *do not specify its term or length.* For example, the parties may agree that the rent is "five dollars per day payable monthly in advance." There is a clear implication in this language that the lease is intended to run for longer than one month, yet the lease specifies no ending date. The law allows this tenant a *periodic estate.* In general, this estate continues for the *length of the payment period* and is automatically renewed unless one party gives adequate notice of termination. Usually the notice of termination must equal the length of the payment period. Thus, where rent is paid every two months, most states would require a two-month notice to terminate.

The main characteristic of periodic leases is their flexibility. Since both the landlord and tenant can terminate, in most instances with a thirty-day notice, the terms of the lease are open to easy revision. For example, a landlord who wants to raise the rent 30 percent can submit a new lease to the tenant. For all practical purposes, the tenant must accept it or be forced to leave within about thirty days. On the other hand, the student who rented a periodic estate in the worst apartment in town on the first day of classes can easily move out in the middle of the term when more attractive accommodations become available.

Estate for years.

Estate for Years. This estate arises when the parties *agree on the beginning date and ending date for the lease.* The term "estate for years" is misleading because it can be for any length of time, such as one week, or two months, or 340 days, or five years. Because the parties know the date when the lease ends, no notice is required to terminate. Further, neither the landlord nor the tenant may terminate the lease without cause before the agreed termination date. Thus, if a student executed a nine-month lease and moves out after three months, he or she may be liable for six months' rent! That liability arises only when the landlord has used reasonable efforts to rerent but has not found a new tenant.

Figure 47.2 Methods of Terminating Leasehold Estates

Estate	Self–Help Dispossession	Notice Required to Terminate	Termination on Death of Party or Transfer
Sufferance	Y*	N*	Y
Will	N	N*	Y
Periodic	N	Y	N
Years	N	N	N

*In some but not all states.

If a new tenant rerents after a vacancy of three months, the original tenant will be liable for the amount of rent for the three months' vacancy. (See figure 47.2.)

Holdover Tenants. Frequently tenants remain in possession after termination of the estate. When this occurs, the landlord generally has a choice of several remedies.

The holdover tenant can be **evicted**—that is, forceably removed from the property by the sheriff. Further, the tenant is liable for reasonable rent for the holdover period. In some states the landlord can collect double or triple rent for the holdover period.

If the tenant holds over, the landlord may elect to compel the tenant to remain. This is an alternative to eviction. In general, the tenant will thereby become liable for rent for a period equal to the length of the original term. Thus, if Harvey Hardsnoz rented an apartment to Suzie Pillow for one year to terminate on January 1, and Suzie held over until January 3, Hardsnoz could in some states treat her as his tenant for the remainder of the year. If, however, Suzie had a month-to-month tenancy and held over, she would be liable for only one month's rent.

eviction
the dispossession of a tenant from the leased premises

Covenants and Conditions in Leases

When parties enter into a lease agreement, there are generally numerous promises flowing from both the landlord and the tenant. For example, the lessor may promise to deliver possession on a certain date, while the lessee may promise to pay $150 as a cleaning deposit before the end of the first month of occupancy. Promises in leases can be classified as covenants or conditions. Breach of a **condition** automatically gives the other party the legal right not to perform his obligations. In contrast, breach of a *covenant* does not eliminate the obligation of the injured party to perform. It merely gives the injured party the right to sue for damages caused by the breach of the covenant. Leases which have been well drafted by a landlord's lawyer will make all the tenant's promises conditions.

condition
an uncertain event on the occurrence of which a contractual obligation is made contingent or dependent

Covenants and conditions in a lease are different kinds of promise.

Thus, if the lease contains a condition prohibiting any pet of any kind in the residence, and the tenant kept a caged hamster, the landlord could evict him. If, on the other hand, the lease did not make the tenant's promise a condition, the landlord could only sue for the damages resulting from keeping the hamster, if any can be proved. Some states have enacted statutes which cause all the tenant's promises to be treated as conditions.

In general, the law assumes that the lessor and lessee will negotiate all the covenants and conditions needed to establish a workable relationship. In many cases, however, the parties agree only on the very basic terms of the transaction, such as the rental amount and the length of the lease. In these situations the law will recognize the existence of *implied* covenants and conditions.

Implied Covenants and Conditions

In general, these implied promises favor landlords rather than tenants. Thus, most wise tenants will insist on executing a detailed written lease.

Duty to Repair.   The majority of states place the duty to repair the rented property on the *tenant*. This duty stems from the common law obligation imposed on all who temporarily occupy realty not to allow the property to *waste* (deteriorate).[2] However, if the landlord's conduct *causes* the defect, he may be obligated to repair. Further, if this landlord-caused defect makes the property unfit for the intended use, and the landlord refuses to repair, the tenant may treat the situation as a **constructive eviction** by moving out and paying no further rent. For example, if the landlord failed to repair the heating system in a large apartment complex during the middle of a very cold winter, the tenants could move out and not be liable for rent even though six months of the lease period were remaining.

Tort Duties.   In general, the lessee assumes liability for tortious injuries to himself and to others which occur on the leased property. An exception to this rule exists when the defective condition is known to the landlord but not disclosed to the tenant, and the tenant would not be able to identify the problem after a reasonable inspection. Further, the landlord is also liable for injuries occurring on portions of the property, such as hallways, which he *controls*. In general, the landlord controls the *common areas*. These are areas used by all the tenants. Thus, if a tenant's guest is injured because of a defective diving board in the pool area of an apartment complex, the landlord is likely to be liable.

Quiet Enjoyment.   The landlord impliedly promises that the tenant will not be dispossessed by someone with title superior to the landlord's.

Fixtures.   Generally under *residential* leases the personal property permanently affixed to leased realty becomes real property and therefore remains at the end

---

[2] The following states *do* require the *landlord* to keep the premises in good repair: California, Connecticut, Georgia, Indiana, Iowa, Kentucky, Louisiana, Massachusetts, Utah, Montana, New Jersey, New York, North Dakota, Oklahoma, Pennsylvania, South Dakota, and Wisconsin. But even in these states the tenant's duty to prevent *waste* generally still exists.

Real Property

of the lease as the landlord's property. Similarly, alterations and improvements of the realty accrue to the landlord, and the tenant is not entitled to compensation for their value. When the lease is for *commercial* property, the law presumes that the fixture may be removed by the tenant. However, the tenant must remove the fixture during the term of the lease. He may not be able to remove it after the termination.

Emblements. An emblement is what is sown and produced on the land. A corn crop can be an emblement. When *farm* property is leased and cultivated by the tenant, the law implies a right to harvest those crops. In some states the crop may be harvested by the tenant even after the lease expires.

Taxes, Insurance, and Utilities. The law implies, in the absence of a contrary agreement between the parties, that the landlord will pay the property taxes. However, neither party is obligated to insure the property. The tenant generally must pay for utilities such as garbage, electricity, gas, and water.

Use of the Property. In the absence of a contrary agreement, the lessee may make any use of the property which is legal. Thus, a tenant can not be evicted for having pets, giving parties, installing a hot plate, or even playing loud country-rock music unless the lease so states.

Prohibition Against Discrimination Statute. The federal Fair Housing Act of 1968 and its amendments makes unlawful discrimination on the basis of race, color, religion, sex, or national origin in the *rental* or advertising of realty.

Express Covenants and Conditions
Nearly all the *implied* promises discussed above can be negated by an *express* agreement between the lessor and the lessee. However, **exculpatory clauses,** which attempt to limit the lessor's *tort* liability, have been nullified by a few states. Of course, no agreement can give the lessor the right to discriminate on the basis of race, color, religion, sex, or national origin.

Duty to Repair. Most tenants will want an affirmative promise in writing from the landlord, phrased as a condition, whereby the duty to repair rests with the lessor.

Cleaning Deposits. Most tenants should require a written promise stating that the cleaning deposit will be refunded if the premises are returned in the same condition as when leased, less normal wear and tear. The promise should also state that the landlord may only retain amounts actually paid others for cleaning prior to the rerenting of the premises.

Most cleaning deposit disputes arise because tenants do not plan their legal affairs intelligently. If they generate evidence of the condition of the premises before they move in and after they move out, their chances of recovering the full cleaning deposit are very high. For example, the lessee can walk through the property before and after occupancy with a respected mature person who would be a good witness in a small claims court. Then, if the issue is litigated, the

emblements
what is sown and produced on the land

Taxes, insurance, utilities.

Use of the property.

Discrimination.

Express covenants and conditions.

exculpatory clause
a clause which relieves one from liability

Repair.

Cleaning deposits.

tenant is likely to prevail even when the landlord lies. Note that, without the witness, it is the tenant's word against that of the landlord, and the tenant has the burden of proof. Therefore, the landlord is likely to win.

Security Deposits.   Frequently lessors will require that tenants pay substantial rent in advance as security in the event that the leases are broken. For example, the lessee may be required to pay the first and last month's rent in advance.

Liquidated Damages.   Many tenants want to limit their risk under leases so they include **liquidated damages** clauses which limit the liability for rent. For example, a freshman student executing a nine-month lease on an apartment near campus might want to be able to terminate the lease if he flunks out, and pay only two months' additional rent, rather than risk greater liability.

Transfer of the Lessee's Interest

In the absence of a contrary agreement between the lessor and the lessee, the lessee generally has the legal power to transfer his right of possession to another. If this power exists, the lessor has no control over the tenant's choice of a new occupant. Further, the new occupant is also allowed to transfer his possessory interest to another. Therefore, landlords who want to carefully scrutinize tenants frequently include a clause in their leases prohibiting such transfers. These clauses are valid and enforceable. In addition, a few states have enacted statutes which prohibit such transfers without the lessor's consent.

While landlords dislike the lessee's power to transfer his interest, it can be very valuable to the tenant. When a tenant decides to vacate, he can reduce his financial risk if he can rerent the property to another. If a higher rent is obtained, the tenant can retain the surplus and thereby reap significant profits!

Such transfers can be either **assignments** or *sublettings*. The rights of the parties vary significantly, depending upon which method of transfer is used. They are so distinct that the courts will often permit an assignment when the lease document prohibits just subletting. The reverse is also true.

Assignment

In order for a tenant to assign his interest in realty, he must transfer his interest for *all* the time remaining on his lease. When this occurs, the original tenant is called the "**assignor**" and the new tenant is called the "assignee." (See figure 47.3.)

If all the remaining term of the lease has been transferred so that assignment has occurred, then one can determine the rights and liabilities of the parties (lessor, lessee, and assignee) by analyzing the concepts of **privity of contract** and **privity of estate.** In general, privity of contract means that parties are linked by legal rights and duties stemming from a contract between them. Similarly, privity of estate means that persons are legally connected by rights and duties flowing from ownership or possession of the same realty. For example, if Mrs. Seller deeds property to Mrs. Buyer, they are said to be in privity of estate. If Mrs.

Figure 47.3 Timing of Lease Assignment Events

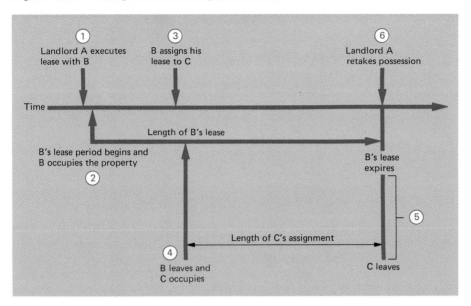

Seller recorded restrictive covenants during her ownership, they would bind Mrs. Buyer because of privity of estate.

In the landlord-tenant area, one can define the rights of the parties before and after assignments by referring to the following rules about privity:

1. Privity of *contract* always exists (before and after assignment) between the original lessor and the original lessee until the expiration of the lease.
2. Privity of *estate* exists only between the landlord and the tenant in possession (usually the most recent assignee).

These rules help us to define the relationships among the parties because certain rights and duties flow via privity of estate and certain others flow via privity of contract. Generally privity of contract is a conduit for *all* the obligations contained in a *lease*. Thus, a landlord can enforce all the lease provisions against those in privity of contract. However, most assignees are not in privity of contract and, therefore, the lessor may not be able to assert some provisions of the lease against them. But an assignee *will* become bound via privity of contract if he assumes the lease in addition to taking an assignment of it. **Assumption** occurs when an assignee agrees with the assignor to be bound by the terms in the original lease.

The tenant in possession is in privity of estate with the landlord. Privity of estate is a conduit for only those terms of the lease which *run with the land*. Terms and conditions of leases run with the land when they touch and concern the land. Thus, a covenant in a lease whereby the tenant promises to graze cattle on the land but not farm it would bind assignees in privity of estate with the

assumption of a lease an agreement by an assignee with the assignor to become bound by all the terms and conditions in the lease executed by the assignor

Figure 47.4   Lease Assignment Relationships

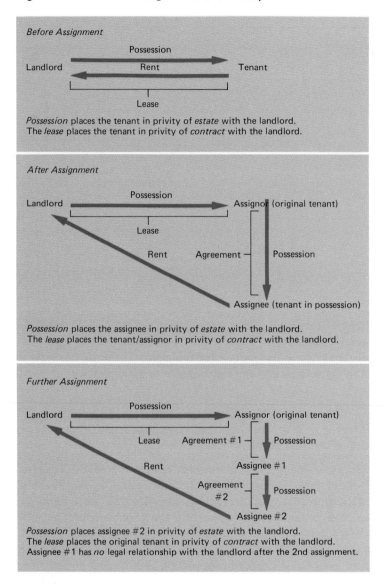

Before Assignment

Landlord — Possession → Rent ← Tenant

Lease

Possession places the tenant in privity of *estate* with the landlord.
The *lease* places the tenant in privity of *contract* with the landlord.

After Assignment

Landlord — Possession → Assignor (original tenant)

Lease

Rent   Agreement — Possession

Assignee (tenant in possession)

Possession places the assignee in privity of *estate* with the landlord.
The *lease* places the tenant/assignor in privity of *contract* with the landlord.

Further Assignment

Landlord — Possession → Assignor (original tenant)

Lease   Agreement #1 — Possession

Rent   Assignee #1

Agreement #2 — Possession

Assignee #2

Possession places assignee #2 in privity of *estate* with the landlord.
The *lease* places the original tenant in privity of *contract* with the landlord.
Assignee #1 has *no* legal relationship with the landlord after the 2nd assignment.

personal covenant
a promise in a lease
which does not touch
and concern the realty

landlord. In contrast, a covenant by the tenant promising not to drink alcohol on the premises does *not* touch and concern the land. It is called a **personal covenant.** The landlord can enforce this covenant against the original lessee (who is in privity of contract) but not against an assignee who is only in privity of estate. Covenants to pay rent, make repairs, extend the lease, or permit the tenant to option the realty are illustrations of covenants which generally touch and concern the land and, therefore, run with it to assignees.

Real Property

Figure 47.5 Timing of Subletting Events

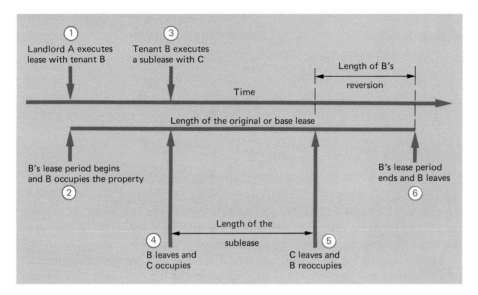

The relationship between the original tenant and his assignee is governed by the assignment contract. Since the original tenant is liable for the personal covenants contained in the lease, he should extract from the assignee promises that no personal covenants will be breached. Otherwise the assignee may breach the covenant without liability, and the original tenant will be liable to the landlord for the breach!

Note that, when an assignee assigns his interest, he is neither in privity of contract nor privity of estate with the landlord. His only liability stems from the assignment agreement he made with his assignor. (See figure 47.4.)

Subletting

Subletting occurs when the tenant transfers the right to exclusive possession to another for a period *shorter* than the remaining term of his lease. The original tenant thereby retains a reversionary interest. Therefore, at the end of the subletting period, the sublessor (the original tenant) regains possession for the remainder of his lease period. (See figure 47.5.) Subletting creates a set of relationships among the parties which differ in important ways from those associated with assignments. In general, a sublessor is neither in privity of contract nor privity of estate with the original lessor.

It is the presence of the tenant's reversion which distinguishes assigning and subletting. The tenant's reversion may be for any period of time. If the owner in fee simple leases to a tenant for five years, and that tenant immediately transfers to another the right to exclusive possession for four years and 364 days, thereby retaining a reversion for one day, the tenant has sublet rather than assigned. Subletting does not affect the legal relationship between the original landlord

sublet
a transfer by the lessee of a *part* of the remaining term of his lease

Figure 47.6   Relationships in Lease Subletting

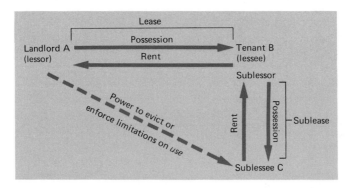

and tenant. The landlord usually continues to collect the rent from his original tenant. The landlord may sue this tenant for breach of any term of the lease, even when the breach is caused by the sublessee.

Subletting establishes a landlord-tenant relationship between the sublessor and the sublessee. The sublessor is entitled to collect the rent, and the sublessee is entitled to the undisturbed use of the premises.

Subletting may be disadvantageous to the sublessee. His legal relationship with the *original lessor* is minimal and to some extent one-sided. Thus, the sublessee can not prevail in a suit against the original lessor to enforce provisions of the original lease. On the other hand, the sublessee *is* bound by the provisions of the original lease which limit the *use* of the property. Thus, if the original lease prohibits use of the property for anything except farming, the lessor would win a suit against a lessee attempting to operate a gas station on the property. Further, while the sublessee is legally bound to pay rent to the sublessor and is *not* liable to the original lessor for the rent, he may be evicted if the original lessor is not paid. But eviction is the extent of the original lessor's remedy against the sublessee. If the original lessor is entitled to collect damages for past or future unpaid rent, he must collect from his original tenant. (See figure 47.6.)

Transfer of the Lessor's Interest

Landlords also have the legal power to transfer their interests in rented property. In general, the new owner takes the property subject to the rights of the tenants. Thus, a tenant can assert the same rights against the new owner that he could have asserted against the old owner. For example, a new owner of a student dormitory can not raise rents if the student tenants leased with fixed rents for the remainder of the academic year with an estate for years.

The new owner is bound by the old leases because, in most cases, he has knowledge of the leases from the presence of the tenants on the property. If the tenants are not on the property and the buyer is not aware of the lease when he becomes the new owner, he usually takes free of the lease.

Tenants who do not visibly occupy the realty can protect themselves by *recording* their leases. This gives **constructive notice** to all the world of the lessee's interest. Thus, if a college freshman visited the college community in mid-August and found an apartment which was a great bargain close to campus, he could execute a lease at that time, with possession to begin when school started. To protect himself from a buyer who might want to raise the rent, the student can *record* his lease. This establishes and protects his ownership priority.

Recording the lease.

constructive notice
knowledge of a fact presumed or imputed by law

Termination of Leases

Leases can be terminated in a variety of ways by both the landlord and the tenant. But there must be some legal basis for termination or the lease continues to be effective. Thus, if a landlord discovered that a tenant occupying under an estate for years kept a dog in the apartment and he served the tenant with an impressive looking notarized legal document titled *Notice to Vacate or Be Evicted,* the tenant could continue occupying the property with the dog unless the lease prohibited pets. This landlord has no basis for terminating the relationship. The following paragraphs discuss the legal basis for termination of the rental relationship.

Expiration of the Lease

Estates for years have well-defined ending dates. Periodic estates do not. The arrival of the ending date of the estate for years terminates the rental relationship without notice. If appropriate advance notice is given before the end of a periodic estate, the rental relationship will be terminated. The tenancy at will and tenancy at sufferance are terminated by the sale of the property or death of the landlord. No advance notice of termination is usually required.

Expiration of the lease.

Surrender and Acceptance

If a lessee wants to terminate the lease before expiration of the term, the lessee can accomplish this by *surrendering* the lease to the landlord. However, to terminate the tenant's obligations, the landlord must *accept* the surrender. Surrender and acceptance are acts of the parties which clearly indicate that they both intend the obligations under the lease to be terminated. Thus, if a tenant leased an apartment for five years and, after two and one-half years was transferred by his employer to a new city, he could approach the landlord and state that he wants to back out of the lease. If the landlord assents and takes possession of the apartment, the tenant's obligations may be terminated.

Surrender of a lease and the landlord's acceptance of the surrender.

Constructive Eviction

If, after execution of the lease, the landlord causes the leased premises to become unfit for their intended use by the tenant—as, for example, by refusing to provide heat to an apartment—the tenant's obligations may be terminated if he moves out because of the unfit condition.

Constructive eviction.

Breach of Condition

If either party breaches a condition contained in the lease, that relieves the other party of his obligations under the lease. Thus, if a tenant violates a condition prohibiting green plants on the premises, the landlord can deprive the tenant of possession through eviction. Conversely, a tenant can move out and not be liable for further rent if the landlord breaches an express condition promising to keep the premises in good repair.

Eviction

Generally self-help eviction is available in only a few states. Landlords must almost always sue to evict. The proceedings are frequently called actions for *unlawful detainer*. As in all court actions, the defendant (in this situation the tenant) is given advance notice of the lawsuit. Courts try to handle this action speedily so that tenants can be dispossessed as rapidly as possible. If the landlord is, in fact, entitled to evict the tenant and the tenant fails to leave voluntarily, the *sheriff* will physically remove the tenant and his property from the premises.

In order to win the eviction proceedings the landlord must prove that the lease has been terminated.

Summary Statement

1. Real property law is very old and reflects the agrarian society in which it developed.
2. The basic nature of the rental relationship involves a temporary transfer of possession in return for the payment of rent.
3. Oral leases are generally enforceable only if they are for a short period.
4. The rental relationships recognized by law are estates at will, estates at sufferance, periodic estates, and estates for years.
5. There are express and implied covenants and conditions in leases.
6. If one party breaches a covenant, the injured party must still perform his or her duties under the lease. If, however, a condition is breached, the injured party need not perform.
7. An assignment is the transfer of all the remaining term of a lease. A sub-letting is the transfer of just a part of the remaining term.
8. Buyers of realty generally are bound by the leases executed by the seller.
9. A holdover tenant may be liable for all the rent for an additional lease period.
10. A lease may be terminated by expiration of the term, surrender and acceptance, constructive eviction, and breach of condition.

The following case is presented to illustrate the legal concepts of constructive eviction, implied covenants, and the nature of the landlord's duty to repair.

Cherberg v. Peoples National Bank of Washington

564 P.2d 1137 (Wash. 1977)

Utter, Associate Justice. James Cherberg and his wife brought a claim based in part upon the tort of intentional interference with business expectancies arising from the willful refusal of the Joshua Green Corporation, as their landlord, to perform duties owed them under a commercial lease. A jury verdict for $42,000 was entered in favor of the Cherbergs. . . .

In 1967 the petitioners, James and Arlene Cherberg, leased a portion of the Lewis Building on Fifth Avenue in downtown Seattle and invested some $80,000 in the establishment and operation of a restaurant business at that location. The respondent, Joshua Green Corporation, acquired the Lewis Building in February of 1972, subject to the lease of the petitioners. In April of 1972, Peoples National Bank of Washington, the owner of the property abutting the Lewis Building on the south, commenced demolition of the existing buildings on its property for the purpose of constructing a high-rise office tower. The demolition work resulted in the exposure of the south wall of the Lewis Building. It was found to be structurally unsafe and in need of substantial repairs to satisfy requirements of the City of Seattle Building Department. The demised premises here at issue were located within the Lewis Building but did not abut the south wall.

The lease between the parties required the lessee to make necessary repairs to maintain the demised premises, excepting the outside walls and other structural components of the building, and reserved to the lessor the use of the roof and outside walls of the building. The lease does not contain an express covenant concerning the responsibility to maintain the structural components of the building.

Upon learning of the problems with the south wall, the lessor contacted the Cherbergs directly and through its attorneys, indicating that the Green Corporation would probably elect not to repair the wall and that the City might order the building closed. The Cherbergs responded that the lessor was obligated under the lease to make repairs and that they would suffer substantial damage should their tenancy be disrupted.

Thereafter, the lessor terminated the lease and informed the Cherbergs of its intention to post the building as unsafe. The Cherbergs closed their business for approximately one week. An independent consultant then informed the Cherbergs that repair of the wall was, in fact, feasible. Petitioners reopened their business when the Green Corporation failed to actually post the building and at that time reiterated their demands to the lessor. The bank, not wishing to be delayed further in its construction plans, eventually repaired the wall at its own expense (estimated at $30,000 to $50,000).

This action was brought against the bank and the Green Corporation, alleging breach of the lessor's duty to repair, negligent demolition by the bank, and that the defendants had engaged in a conspiracy to destroy petitioners' business. Undisputed evidence was presented demonstrating that there were close ties between Joshua Green, III, the Green Corporation, and Peoples National Bank of Washington. The evidence disclosed that the Green Corporation viewed the Lewis Building as an adequately profitable investment under the circumstances existing at the time of purchase, but that it was the Corporation's desire to regain control of the premises as soon as possible in order to demolish the existing structure on the property and erect a new building which they felt might be more profitable.

Demolition of the Lewis Building during the course of the new construction would have been of substantial economic benefit both to the Green Corporation and to the bank. In early 1972 both the bank and the Green Corporation had requested the same agent to engage in efforts to negotiate a sale of petitioners' leasehold in order that the Green Corporation might regain control of the premises.

The trial court, at the conclusion of testimony, dismissed the bank from the suit and also dismissed the negligence and conspiracy claims. Respondent's other motions pertinent to this appeal were denied. The jury was instructed that respondent was liable for damages caused by the failure to repair the outside wall. It further instructed the jury with regard to the elements of the tort of intentional interference with business expectations and that, if the jury concluded that the defendant's actions were willful, damages for mental suffering, inconvenience, and discomfort would be compensable. The jury made a special finding of willful action and returned a verdict of $42,000. The only evidence of economic loss due to the temporary closure and attendant disruption of business was in the amount of $3,100.

The Court of Appeals held that the lessor did have a duty to make repairs to the wall on the basis of a mandate so to do from competent government authority. However, it reversed and remanded, holding that the Green Corporation was entitled to a directed verdict on the claim of interference with business expectations and the assessment of damages for inconvenience, discomfort, and mental distress.

The first issue is the rights and duties of the parties with regard to the unsafe condition of the south wall of the building. We agree with the holding of the Court of Appeals that an implied duty on the part of the lessor exists to make those repairs mandated by competent government authority where, as here, the appropriate authority determines that, in the interest of the public welfare, a defective condition of a building must be remedied. We also agree that the evidence presented established that the refusal of the respondent to take action to fulfill this duty, within a reasonable time after notification from the City, breached an implied covenant of quiet enjoyment and resulted in an actionable constructive eviction. . . .

In addition, however, even absent a mandate from government authority, the lessor was under a duty to make the repairs here in question. The general rule is that a landlord has no duty to make repairs to the demised premises absent an express covenant requiring such action. . . . While it is true that this lease did not contain an express covenant abrogating this common law rule, the area requiring repair was not a part of the demised premises but was an area of the building over which the landlord had expressly retained control.

A landlord has a duty to maintain, control, and preserve retained portions of the premises subject to a leasehold in a manner rendering the demised premises adequate for the tenant's use and safe for occupany by both the tenant and his invitees. . . . Failure to fulfill this duty results in liability on the part of the lessor for injury caused thereby, . . . and failure to fulfill this duty, by omission to repair, can in a proper case constitute an actionable constructive eviction. . . .

The willful refusal to adequately maintain retained portions of a building so as to allow the tenant to enjoy the beneficial use of the demised portion of the building is a breach of an implied duty owed by the landlord to the tenant under Washington law. On these facts, this breach of duty was sufficient to constitute an actionable constructive eviction and provides a basis for the conclusion that the landlord was liable for any damages stemming from that breach, . . . independent of any directive to repair issued by the City of Seattle. . . .

The decision of the Court of Appeals is reversed and the judgment in favor of the petitioners reinstated. It is so ordered.

Questions and Case Problems

1. Sally Studious arrived in town one month before the start of school. She entered into an oral agreement to rent an attractive apartment at a bargain price. She agreed to take possession within thirty days. Before Sally moved in, Snidely Whiplash bought the complex and raised the rents 50 percent. Snidely knew of Sally's lease when he purchased, but he now refuses to deliver possession unless she agrees to the higher rent. Sally sues. Who prevails?

2. Industrial Investment Company leased certain property located in the State of Hawaii. It then subleased to Frank Hayashi. Frank then assigned his leasehold interest to Obed Hanuna. Obed assigned the leasehold estate to Mrs. Park. But Mrs. Park did not pay the rent as agreed. Since Industrial Investment Company is not receiving rental income, it sues Frank Hayashi. Must Frank pay? [*Broida v. Hayashi,* 464 P.2d 285 (Hawaii 1970).]

3. Sniffle Student, president of the campus leapfrog club, moved into an apartment two months before school started because the monthly rental was so low. He didn't sign a lease and there was no agreement with the landlord on how long Sniffle would occupy the property. At the beginning of the school term the landlord discovered that Sniffle was raising frogs in the apartment. The landlord gave Sniffle a sixty-day notice to vacate. Sniffle refuses to move, stating that the landlord didn't indicate his bias against frogs at the beginning of the lease. The landlord sues. Who prevails?

4. Fidel rented property from De Baca. The lease agreement contained a covenant against assignments. Fidel sublet a portion of the property for a period shorter than the unexpired term of the lease. De Baca sues to evict Fidel. Who prevails?

5. Dr. Eldredge leased a 45-acre farm located in Gem County, Idaho to Joseph W. Jensen and Rhea Bell Jensen for five years. After the first year, the Jensens defaulted in their rental payments but remained in possession. At the beginning of the fourth year, Dr. Eldredge sold the property to third parties. The Jensens elected to treat the sale as constructive eviction and abandoned the premises. Dr. Eldredge sued for unpaid rent of $1,200. The Jensens defended, claiming damages of $5,000 for early termination of the lease. Who prevails? [*Eldredge v. Jensen,* 404 P.2d 624 (Ida. 1965).]

6. Betty Reiman, a fourteen-year-old girl, went to the apartment of Mrs. Green, who had been ill, to assist in preparations for Mrs. Green's return from the hospital. Betty helped with the washing and drying of Mrs. Green's linen. The linen was dried by hanging it on a clothes line located on the roof of the apartment building. A skylight was also on the roof near the door giving tenants access to the clothes line area. Betty's cousin, Leah, helped her collect the clothes off the line, stacking them in Betty's arms. After stripping the line, Leah went ahead to open the door for Betty. When Leah pulled the door part way open, Betty stepped back to allow it to swing completely open. In so doing, her heel struck an object, causing her to fall backward through the skylight to the floor below. She now sues for the injuries sustained. The owner of the building, Moore, denies responsibility for the injuries. Who prevails? [*Reiman v. Moore*, 108 P.2d 452 (Cal. 1940).]

7. Rich executed a lease on an apartment owned by Scrudge. The lease stated that Rich's possession was conditioned upon fulfilling all of the tenant's promises made in the lease. One clause prohibited any alterations and required Rich to obtain Scrudge's consent before applying wallpaper or repainting the walls. Rich substantially upgraded the apartment by repainting but did not obtain Scrudge's consent. Scrudge now sues, seeking eviction. Rich defends, claiming that Scrudge has not been injured. Who prevails?

8. Peterson leased property from Platt for a ten-year period. Peterson operated an Arctic Circle Drive Inn on the property. When Peterson fell two months behind in the rent, Platt waited until the property was vacant, took possession of the premises, changed the locks, and denied entry to Peterson and his employees. As a consequence, certain tasty goods perished. Peterson sued Platt, claiming that Platt took possession illegally and, therefore, Platt should be liable for Peterson's injuries. Who prevails? [*Peterson v. Platt*, 400 P.2d 507 (Utah 1965).]

9. Sid Scholar leased an apartment near the women's dorms for a nine-month period. The lease agreement did not indicate who was to be responsible for repairs. When the toilet broke, Sid asked the landlord to repair it. He refused. Sid moved out five months before the end of the lease. The landlord sues Sid for the cost of repairing the toilet and for five months' rent. Who prevails?

10. In the case of *Cherberg v. Peoples National Bank of Washington*, 564 P.2d 1137 (Wash. 1977),[3] describe what motivated the landlord to refuse to make the repairs.

---

[3] See pp. 859–60.

Part **10** Secured Transactions,
Insurance, and Bankruptcy

Summary

In this Part we will examine four legal topics that are important to most individuals and businesses—secured transactions involving personal property, suretyship, insurance, and bankruptcy. A secured transaction is one in which an interest in personal property, such as a car, is given as collateral for a loan. Insurance involves the shifting of risks from one party, the insured, to another party, the insurer. Insurance has become so important that it has an impact on virtually every personal or business transaction, from birth (which is covered by health insurance) to death (which is covered by "life" insurance). We also examine the law relating to bankruptcy. While we hope that bankruptcy law will not affect you individually, the law is extremely important to businesses forced to write off many thousands of dollars worth of debts discharged in bankruptcy.

48

Creation of Security Interests in Personal Property

After you have read this chapter, you should be able to:

1. Describe a secured transaction.
2. List the three major types of collateral.
3. Define after-acquired property and future advances.
4. Describe the floating lien.
5. List two methods used to *create* a security interest.
6. Describe the four methods used to *perfect* a security interest.

Introduction

As consumers increase their use of credit in making purchases, the law of secured transactions becomes especially important. In most consumer transactions the creditor will want something more than the mere promise of the consumer to repay the debt. Many creditors will require the consumer to give the creditor a security interest in property which the consumer owns. Some creditors will require, additionally, the promise of another person, a surety, to pay the debt on the consumer's default. In this chapter and the next we will discuss these two credit transactions: the personal property secured transaction and suretyship.

Although secured transactions are important for the consumer, they are especially important for the person in business. This is because the businessman will often enter into a secured transaction as a debtor in acquiring goods and will enter into a second secured transaction as a creditor in selling goods to a consumer.

The law of secured transactions is at times technical and complicated. However, it is important to keep in mind as you read these chapters that this material is especially important to the person who is not an attorney because, in most cases, the person entering into a secured transaction does not retain an attorney but, instead, acts as his own attorney. While this practice is not recommended, it is often necessary because secured transactions are so common that it would usually be impractical and expensive to retain an attorney.

Definitions

After graduating from college, Rufus decided to buy a new car. The average price of new cars was $7,000; however, Rufus had only $2,000 in his savings account. Consequently, Rufus went to First Bank and borrowed $5,000, giving the bank a note in that amount. At this point Rufus becomes a *debtor* and First Bank is a *creditor*.

If the bank required nothing more than the note from Rufus, the law of secured transactions would be unnecessary. However, creditors like the bank usually do want something else: they want the right to repossess Rufus' property if Rufus fails to make his agreed payments or if he goes into bankruptcy. In this case the bank would want such an interest, called a **security interest,** in Rufus' car. A creditor with a security interest is called a **secured party,** and the whole transaction would now be described as a **secured transaction.**

In many cases the creditor extends credit in order that the debtor may purchase the property which is then used as **collateral** for the loan. This is called a *purchase money security interest*. In Rufus' case, he has given the bank a purchase money security interest in the car because he used the loan to purchase the car. If he had borrowed money to buy the car but had given the bank a security interest in only his speedboat, the security would *not* be a *purchase money security interest*.

security
a creditor's interest in specific property, or in the obligation of a third person, as assurance for the performance of the debtor's obligation

security interest
an interest in personal property or fixtures which secures payment or performance of an obligation

secured party
a creditor with a security interest

secured transaction
a transaction used to create a security interest

collateral
the personal property subject to a security interest

Source of Law

The law of secured transactions is found in Article 9 of the Uniform Commercial Code. Because the UCC has been adopted in all states but Louisiana, the law of secured transactions is generally uniform throughout the United States.

The UCC provides that Article 9 applies "to any transaction (regardless of its form) which is intended to create a security interest in personal property or fixtures. . . ." (Section 9–102(1)(a).) This statement has two major consequences. First, if the creditor asks for real estate as security instead of personal property, the transaction is not a secured transaction but, instead, is a *mortgage*. Mortgage law is derived from real estate cases and statutes and has been discussed in Part 9, Real Property.

The second consequence is that, regardless of what a transaction is called by the debtor and the creditor, it is a secured transaction if the parties intend to create a security interest in personal property or fixtures. In the following case the court held that a lease with an option to buy was, in substance, a secured transaction.

Facts
Franklin National Bank leased three dump trucks and other equipment to Noyes Paving Company. Under the terms of the leases, Noyes was given the option to purchase the leased goods at the end of the term for $1. The bank did not comply with the law of secured transactions. Noyes also gave a security interest in its "Construction Equipment Motor Vehicles" to James Talcott, Inc. Noyes later defaulted in his payments to the bank and to Talcott, and both parties claimed the trucks and equipment.

Decision
Talcott wins.

Reasoning
The policy of the UCC is to look to the substance of the agreement rather than the form. The bank's lease, in substance, was really a secured transaction, and the bank should have treated it as such, which it did not do.

James Talcott, Inc. v. Franklin National Bank of Minneapolis, 194 N.W.2d 775 (Minn. 1972).

Types of Collateral

The personal property which is subject to a security interest is called *collateral*. The types of personal property which may be used as security are either *tangible* (e.g., goods) or *intangible* (e.g., accounts receivable) and may be broken down into three major categories: tangible goods, intangibles, and paper. These categories will become important later when we discuss methods of "perfecting" a security interest and priorities among several secured parties.

Tangible Goods
Goods are generally defined as tangible things which are movable when the security interest is created or which are fixtures. Specifically, there are four types of goods.

Consumer Goods. *Consumer goods* are goods which are used or bought for use primarily for personal, family, or household purposes. (UCC 9–109(1).) If Rufus purchased his car primarily for a personal or family purpose, the car would be considered a consumer good.

Consumer goods.

Equipment. Goods which are used or bought for use primarily in business (including farming or a profession) are classified as *equipment* (UCC9–109(2)). If Rufus was a travelling salesman and used the car primarily for travelling to customers, the car would be equipment.

Equipment.

Inventory. Goods which are held for sale or lease are considered to be *inventory.* If Waldo were a car dealer and bought his car for purposes of resale, the car would be inventory.

Inventory.

Farm Products. Crops, livestock, and supplies used or produced in farming operations which are in the possession of a debtor engaged in farming fall under the heading of *farm products.*

Farm products.

Intangibles

Two types of intangibles, one specific and one general, can be used as security. The specific type of intangible is the **account.** Accounts include the *account receivable,* a right to payment for goods which have been sold or for services which have been rendered. Accounts also include a right to payment under a contract even where the right has not yet been earned by performance.

account
a right to payment under a contract

The other type of intangible is **general intangibles** which includes all personal property other than the property which we specifically list in this section. For example, good will, copyrights, patents, and trademarks would be considered general intangibles because they do not fall within the other categories.

general intangibles
a catchall category covering a variety of personal property

Paper

In many cases a right is evidenced by a piece of paper, and the paper may be used as a security. The UCC specifically provides that a security interest may be created in the following three types of paper.

Chattel Paper. Chattel paper is defined as a writing or writings which evidence both a monetary obligation and a security interest in or lease of specific goods. (UCC 9–105(1)(b).) Suppose, for example, that Rufus, instead of financing his car at the bank, had financed the purchase at the dealership under the type of security arrangement called a **conditional sale,** whereby the seller reserves title to the car until the buyer completes making payments. Under this arrangement Rufus would sign both a note and a contract, and these writings together are chattel paper.

conditional sale
a sale in which the seller reserves title until the buyer completes payments

In many cases the dealership can not wait three or four years for Rufus to pay because the dealership needs cash to purchase more automobiles. Consequently, the dealer might go to a bank, borrow money, and give the bank a security interest in the chattel paper. The bank would then have a security interest in the dealership's security interest and, if the dealer defaulted in his payments to the bank, the bank would then begin receiving payments from Rufus.

Creation of Security Interests in Personal Property

instrument
a writing which
evidences a right to
payment of money,
including negotiable
instruments and
certificated securities

Instruments. An **instrument** is any writing, apart from a security agreement or lease, which evidences a right to payment of money. One common type of instrument is the *negotiable instrument* (covered in Part 6, Commercial Paper), which includes drafts, checks, and notes. Another instrument is the *certificated security,* which is a share or other interest in property or in an enterprise of the issuer which is represented by an instrument in bearer or registered form and which is commonly dealt in on securities exchanges or commonly recognized as a medium for investment. (UCC 8–102(1)(a).)

Documents of Title. A document of title is a document which entitles the person in possession of it to hold and dispose of the document or the goods it covers as he sees fit. Common examples are the *bill of lading,* a document issued by a carrier which evidences receipt of goods, and a *warehouse receipt,* a receipt issued by a person in the business of storing goods.

Proceeds and After-Acquired Property

In addition to the categories of goods, the security interest might also cover proceeds and after-acquired property. **Proceeds** cover whatever the debtor receives upon selling, exchanging, or otherwise disposing of the collateral. Although there are a number of specific rules governing proceeds, the general rule is that a security interest in collateral also covers identifiable proceeds when the debtor disposes of the collateral. For utmost protection, however, a secured party should file a financing statement, described below, which specifically covers proceeds.

proceeds
what the debtor
receives when he
disposes of collateral

After-acquired property refers to property acquired after the debtor and creditor have entered into a security agreement. UCC 9–204 specifically provides that the security agreement may cover after-acquired collateral. The section also provides that the security agreement may include future loans made by the secured party. The combination of these two provisions allows a secured party to create a **floating lien** to cover present and future advances and acquisitions with the agreement.

**after-acquired
property**
property acquired after
the security agreement
is made

floating lien
a security device
which covers after-
acquired property and
future advances

The floating lien is especially useful when the collateral is inventory. Suppose, for example, that Alpha Appliance Store borrows cash from First Bank and gives to the bank a security interest in present and future inventory. The security agreement also covers future advances by the bank and proceeds. One day Alpha sells a new stove to a customer in exchange for cash and an old stove is taken as a trade-in. Alpha then borrows money from the bank and purchases another new stove from a manufacturer. There is no need for the bank to create a new security interest because, under the floating lien concept, the original agreement covers the old stove (proceeds), the new stove (after-acquired property), and the new loan (future advances).

Creation of Security Interests

In order to acquire rights in the debtor's property, the creditor must create a valid security interest. However, in order to create rights that are superior to those of other creditors and to ensure that he is paid first when the property is sold, the creditor must *perfect* the security interest. At first we will discuss *creation* of the security interest, and then we will discuss *perfection* of the security interest.

Form

Two methods are used to create a security interest. First, the creditor and debtor might enter into a **security agreement**, an agreement which must under the Code: (1) be in writing, (2) be signed by the debtor, and (3) contain a description of the collateral.

security agreement
an agreement which creates or provides for a security interest (UCC 9-105(1)(I))

The following excerpt from a security agreement has been taken from a Massachusetts case:

[The debtor does] hereby grant, sell, assign, transfer and deliver to Grantee the following goods, chattels, and automobiles, namely: The business located at and numbered 574 Washington Street, Canton, Mass. together with all its goodwill, fixtures, equipment and merchandise. The fixtures specifically consist of the following: *All contents of luncheonette including equipment such as: booths and tables; stand and counter; tables; chairs; booths; steam tables; salad unit; potato peeler, a U.S. Slicer; range; case; fryer; compressor; bobtail; milk dispenser; silex; 100 Class air conditioner; signs; pastry case; mixer; dishes; silverware; tables; hot fudge; Haven Ex.; 2-door stationwagon 1957 Ford A57R107215* together with all property and articles now and which may hereafter be, used or mixed with, added or attached to, and/or substituted for, any of the foregoing described property.

The most common legal question regarding such agreements involves the question of whether the description of the collateral is sufficient, as is illustrated in the following case.

Facts
On November 18, 1960 Firestone made a loan to Kozy Kitchen, and Kozy Kitchen signed the security agreement quoted above, giving Firestone a security interest, which Firestone perfected the same day. On November 19, 1960 National Cash Register (NCR) delivered a cash register to Kozy Kitchen under a conditional sales contract, and a month later NCR perfected its security interest. Firestone later took possession of the cash register and sold it. NCR claims that it should receive proceeds from the sale because Firestone's security agreement does not mention the cash register.

Decision
Firestone wins.

Reasoning
Firestone's security agreement was broad enough to cover the cash register. At the end of the agreement there is reference to after-acquired property, which would include the cash register.

National Cash Register Company v. Firestone & Co., Inc., 191 N.E.2d 471 (Mass. 1963).

pledge
a possessory security
interest in bailed
goods acquired by the
bailee when there is a
bailment for the
purpose of security

The other method used to create a security interest is the **pledge**, whereby the secured party actually takes *possession* of the collateral. In most cases the pledge is not used, because the debtor wants to keep possession of the property for his own use and enjoyment. However, the pledge is the preferred method of creating a security interest when paper is used as collateral. In the following case a security agreement was not signed by the debtor and, since the lender did not have possession of any collateral, he did not have a security interest in anything.

Facts

Rutkin lent money to Burdette Electric, Inc. Burdette assigned to Rutkin an account receivable owed by B. J. Builders, Inc. as security for the loan. However, a security agreement was never signed by Burdette. Rutkin now claims that it is entitled to the account.

Decision

Rutkin loses.

Reasoning

A security interest is created by either a written agreement or by taking possession of the collateral. As an intangible, an account receivable can not be possessed, and there was no written agreement.

M. Rutkin Electric Supply Co., Inc. v. Burdette Electric, Inc., 237 A.2d 500 (N.Y. 1967).

Requirements

Regardless of whether the security agreement or pledge is used, the UCC imposes three requirements which must be met if the security interest is to *attach* to the collateral—that is, if it is to be enforceable by the creditor. *First,* the debtor and creditor must agree that it will attach. This requirement would automatically be met if a security agreement was used. *Second,* the creditor must give value. **Value,** generally, means *any consideration* sufficient under contract law. Under the UCC, value is also specifically defined to include a creditor's *binding commitment to extend credit* and a creditor's taking security for *a pre-existing claim.* *Third,* the debtor must have rights in the collateral although, as we discussed above, the security interest may attach to after-acquired property.

value
any consideration
sufficient to support a
contract, or a
commitment to extend
credit, or a past debt

Perfection of Security Interests

When the three requirements for attachment have been met, the secured party may enforce his interest against the debtor. But often another party besides the debtor may claim an interest in the collateral. Suppose, for example, that Heidi purchased a refrigerator under a conditional sales contract from Bill's Appliance Store and that Bill's security interest attached to the refrigerator. Heidi used the refrigerator in her grocery store, thus making the refrigerator *equipment.* In each of the following three cases a third party might claim an interest in the collateral. (1) Heidi might sell the refrigerator to a friend who had no knowledge of Bill's security interest. (2) Another creditor might make a loan to Heidi and perfect a security interest in the refrigerator. (3) Heidi might go into bankruptcy and the trustee in bankruptcy would claim that the value of the refrigerator should be divided evenly among all her creditors.

In each of the three cases Bill's interest would be subordinate to that of the third party, even though the interest would be enforceable against Heidi alone. In order for Bill to gain rights superior to such third parties, he must give **constructive notice** (notice by law) to them that he has a security interest. This is called **perfection of a security interest.** Four common methods are used to perfect security interests.

constructive notice
knowledge of a fact presumed or imputed by law

perfection of a security interest
when the creditor complies with Article 9 of the Code's requirements for perfection

Financing Statement

The *most common method* used commercially to perfect security interests *is to file* a short document called a **financing statement** either locally in a county office, such as the registrar's office, or centrally with the secretary of state. The place of filing depends on the type of collateral and on the law in each particular state. For instance, in some states if an automobile is used as collateral, the financing statement should be filed locally unless the automobile is considered to be inventory, in which case there must be a central filing. Regardless of the place of filing, the financing statement is effective for *five years* from the date of filing, and it lapses after that time unless a *continuation statement* is filed before the lapse.

financing statement
a document which is filed by the secured party to give public notice of the security interest in personal property.

The formal requirements for the financing statement are simple. The statement must: (1) list the names and addresses of the debtor and of the secured party, (2) be signed by the debtor, and (3) contain a statement describing or indicating the types of the collateral. The following example of a financing statement is taken from a Pennsylvania case:

15110 of 1955
Financing Statement

This financing statement is presented to a filing officer for filing pursuant to the Uniform Commercial Code.

1. Debtor (or assignor)—Fort Pitt Packaging Co., Inc., 5615 Butler Street, Pittsburgh 1, Pa.

2. Secured Party (or assignee)—Provident Trust Co., 900 East Ohio St., Pittsburgh 1, Pa.

3. Maturity date of obligation _____

4. The financing statement covers the following types of property: All present and future accounts receivable submitted.

For Pitt Packaging Co., Inc.
Leo A. Levy, Treas.
Provident Trust Company
A. W. Charlton
Executive Vice Pres.

In most cases where the validity of the financing statement is at issue, the major legal question relates to the third requirement: Does the financing statement adequately describe the collateral? This was the question in the following case.

Facts

Provident Trust Co. filed the above financing statement locally in Allegheny County on August 18, 1955 and centrally with the Secretary of the Commonwealth on August 19, 1955. In March, 1957 Fort Pitt assigned to Provident Trust Co., which was acting as an agent for another company, its accounts under a contract with the U.S. Government. Fort Pitt was later placed in receivership, and the receiver claimed that the financing statement did not specifically describe the U.S. Government account.

Decision

Provident Trust Co. wins.

Reasoning

Under section 9–110 of the UCC, "Any description is sufficient whether or not it is specific if it reasonably identifies the thing described." The UCC also allows the security agreement to cover after-acquired property.

Industrial Packaging Products Co. v. Fort Pitt Packaging International Inc., 161 A.2d 19 (Pa. 1960).

Secured parties often, through ignorance of the law or laziness, attempt to use a security agreement as a financing statement or the financing statement as a security agreement. Two different documents should be used because the requirements differ. For instance, a security agreement can not be used as a financing statement because the financing statement contains the additional requirement that the addresses of the parties be indicated. And the financing statement does not meet the requirements for a security agreement, as illustrated by the following case.

Facts

On February 21, 1962 American Card Company executed a note for $12,373 payable to Hillman. The company and Hillman both signed a financing statement which was properly filed. However, a written security agreement was never signed. Hillman now claims that the financing statement may serve as the security agreement.

Decision

Hillman loses.

Reasoning

While it is possible for one document to serve as both the financing statement and the security agreement, the separate requirements for each must be met by the document. The financing statement in question did not contain the required agreement by the debtor that Hillman be granted a security interest.

American Card Co. v. H.M.H. Co., 196 A.2d 150 (R.I. 1963).

Going back to our original example of Bill's sale of a refrigerator to Heidi, if Bill had filed a financing statement covering Heidi's refrigerator, Bill would be giving constructive notice to the world of his security interest in the refrigerator. It is important to note the practical implication of this rule: when you purchase property from someone outside the normal course of business, you should first check to determine whether the property is subject to a security interest. If there is a perfected security interest, the secured party of the seller

Secured Transactions, Insurance, and Bankruptcy

may repossess the property from you, an innocent buyer. However, the secured party will be protected only when the financing statement is filed and indexed properly. In the following case the financing statement was filed under the wrong name.

Pledge

A *second method of perfection* is the *pledge,* whereby the secured party takes *possession* of the goods. The pledge gives clear notice to the world of the security interest by virtue of the secured party's possession.

The pledge obviously can not be used when one of the three types of collateral, namely intangibles, is used as security because by their very nature there is nothing to physically possess. On the other hand, the pledge in most cases must be used when the collateral is *paper* because of long-standing commercial practices. For instance, the UCC provides that, with few exceptions, a security interest in instruments can be perfected only by the secured party taking possession. A security interest in the other two types of paper—namely, chattel paper and negotiable documents—may be perfected by filing, but to be absolutely safe, the creditor should still take possession because certain purchasers are given priority over the secured party who has perfected by filing.

In a pledge the secured party takes *possession* of the collateral.

Automatic Perfection

In cases where a person purchases *consumer* goods and gives a creditor a *purchase money security interest* in those goods, the secured party's security interest will be perfected *automatically.* However, it is still a safe practice for the secured party to perfect the security interest by filing a financing statement because, if the statement is not filed, a buyer from the consumer takes the goods free of the security interest if: (1) he buys without knowledge of the interest; (2) he pays value; and (3) he buys for his personal use. For example, in the situation where Bill sold the refrigerator to Heidi, Bill's security interest would be automatically perfected if, instead of equipment, the refrigerator was a consumer good bought for Heidi's personal use. Since there is perfection, Bill's security interest would prevail over other *creditors* and the *trustee in bankruptcy*. But if Heidi sells the refrigerator to a friend who has no notice of Bill's security interest and who buys for his own personal, family, or household purposes, the friend will take the refrigerator free and clear of the security interest. In the following case the purchase money security interest in consumer goods was not defeated by the debtor's gift of the collateral since the donee did not give value.

Facts
Rike-Kumber sold a diamond ring to Nicolosi on July 7, 1964. Nicolosi signed a purchase money security agreement, but a financing statement was not filed. Nicolosi gave the ring to his fiancee and later declared bankruptcy. Now Rike-Kumber claims the ring.

Decision
Rike-Kumber is entitled to the ring.

Reasoning
Rike-Kumber's security interest was automatically perfected. The fiancee did not give value.

In re *Nicolosi*, 4 UCC Rptr. 111 (Ohio, 1966).

Certificate of Title Laws

In most states there are certificate of title laws which cover automobiles and may also cover other vehicles such as trailers, mobile homes, boats, and farm tractors. If goods are subject to such laws, filing a financing statement is not effective to perfect a security interest; instead, the security interest is perfected by notation on the certificate of title.

Multi-County and Multi-State Transactions

In our mobile society it is common for debtors to move from one county to another or from one state to another, taking with them the property that is subject to a perfected security interest. When such a move takes place, does the security interest continue to be perfected? When the move is *from one county to another in the same state,* the states follow two different approaches. In some states if the financing statement was originally filed properly, it continues to be effective after the debtor moves. In other states the secured party must file a copy of the financing statement within four months in the new county; otherwise the security interest becomes unperfected.

When the move is *from one state to another state,* there are two general UCC rules which apply, although these rules are subject to a number of exceptions. First, under section 1–105, the parties may agree that the laws of a particular state or nation are to govern their rights and duties if the transaction bears a reasonable relation to such state or nation. Second, there is a provision governing perfection to the effect that perfection is governed by the law of the state where the collateral is located when the *last* event occurs which is necessary to perfect the interest. This event will usually be filing the financing statement. If the security interest in the collateral is perfected under the law of that state and then the collateral is moved to another state, it will remain perfected if, *within four months,* the secured party perfects the interest in the *new* state. The UCC also has detailed rules governing goods covered by a certificate of title, mobile goods *normally* used in more than one jurisdiction (e.g., commercial harvesting machinery), accounts, general intangibles, chattel paper, and minerals.

Summary Statement

1. A secured transaction is one in which a debtor gives to a creditor an interest in property owned by the debtor.
2. There are three major classifications of collateral: (a) tangible goods, (b) intangibles, and (c) paper.
3. The Uniform Commercial Code specifically provides that the security agreement may cover after-acquired property and future advances. This allows a secured party to create a floating lien with one security agreement.
4. A security interest may be created by (a) security agreement or (b) pledge.
5. The most common methods used to perfect a security interest are the pledge and filing a financing statement.

In the following case the court discusses the general policy of the UCC regarding description of collateral in a security agreement.

In re Amex-Protein Development Corporation
504 F.2d 1056 (1974)

Plant Reclamation claimed a security interest in personal property held by Amex-Protein, which was in bankruptcy. Plant Reclamation claimed that the security interest was created by a promissory note which included the following language: "This note is secured by a Security Interest in subject personal property as per invoices." The invoices referred to in the note were submitted by Plant Reclamation when it sold equipment to Amex-Protein. Plant Reclamation also filed a financing statement listing the equipment.

The appellate court adopted the opinion of the District Judge:

I. Did the Promissory Note "Create or Provide for" a Security Interest?

This issue turns on whether there has been compliance with the following pertinent sections of the California Commercial Code [Cal.Com.C] which govern the creation and enforcement of a security interest:

Section 9105 (1)(h):

"Security agreement" means an agreement which creates or provides for a security interest;

Section 120 (37):

"Security interest" means an interest in personal property or fixtures which secures payment or performance of an obligation. . . .

Section 9203:

(1) Subject to the provisions of Section 4208 on the security interest of a collecting bank and Section 9113 on a security interest arising under the division on sales, a security interest is not enforceable against the debtor or third parties unless

(a) The collateral is in the possession of the secured party; or

(b) The debtor has signed a security agreement which contains a description of the collateral. . . .

No magic words or precise form are necessary to create or provide for a security interest so long as the minimum formal requirements of the Code are met. . . . This liberal approach is mandated by an expressed purpose of the secured transaction provisions of the Code:

"The aim of this Article is to provide a simple and unified structure within which the immense variety of present-day secured financing transactions can go forward with less cost and with greater certainty. . . .

The Article's flexibility and simplified formalities should make it possible for new forms of secured financing, as they develop, to fit comfortably under its provisions. . . ." Comment to UCC and Cal.Com.C. section 9101.

Accordingly, the promissory note herein qualifies as a security agreement which by its terms "creates or provides for" a security interest.

II. Adequacy of Description of the Collateral

The trustee urges a second ground for sustaining the Order of the Referee complained of here, namely the inadequacy of the description of the collateral in the promissory note and hence the failure to comply with Cal.Com.C. section 9203 (1)(b), *supra.* Cal.Com.C. section 9110 provides:

For the purposes of this division any description of personal property or real estate is sufficient whether or not it is specific if it reasonably identifies what is described. Personal Property may be referred to by general kind or class if the property can be reasonably identified as falling within such kind or class or if it can be so identified when acquired by the debtor. . . .

Although the promissory note does not describe the collateral within the four corners of the document, such description is provided (1) through incorporation by reference of the subject invoices, as well as (2) through reference to the more specific description of the collateral contained in the financing statement.

The use of such extrinsic aids is clearly permissible to identify the collateral:

Under the Uniform Commercial Code there is no reason why parol evidence may not be admitted in aid of the description of the collateral, even where the collateral has been reasonably and sufficiently identified in the security agreement. In many instances, a description in a security agreement may be in general terms; parol evidence should therefore be admissible to explain or supplement the general description, or to resolve ambiguities. [Footnotes omitted.] 44 Cal.Jr.2d Rev. Secured Transactions section 107 at 386.

The doctrine of incorporation by reference is likewise available in this area:

There is nothing in the Uniform Commercial Code to prevent reference in the security agreement to another writing for particular terms and conditions of the transaction. There is also nothing in the Uniform Commercial Code to prevent reference in the Security Agreement to another writing for a description of the collateral, so long as the reference in the security agreement is sufficient to identify reasonably what it described. In other words, it will at times be expedient to give a general description of the collateral in the security agreement and refer to a list or other writing for more exact description. In addition, the security agreement could itself consist of separate parts, one a general description of the obligation secured and the rights and duties of the parties, and the other a description of the collateral, both such writings being signed by the debtor and stated to comprise a single security agreement or referring to each other. [Footnotes omitted.] Id. section 109 at 387-388. . . .

It is manifest that the reference to the invoices in the subject promissory note, coupled with the existence of a financing statement containing a more specific description, satisfies the requirements of Cal.Com.C. sections 9203 (1)(b) and 9110.

The judgment is affirmed.

Questions and Case Problems

1. The comptroller of Fibre Glass Boat Corporation sent the following letter to a creditor, Teleflex: "Pursuant to our telephone conversation, please find a duly executed copy of a financing statement received from your company, wherein the Fibre Glass Boat Corporation agrees to guarantee all inventory used in the production of boats, limited in the amount of fifteen thousand dollars, in order to cover all merchandise that may be purchased from your company." Teleflex later claimed that this letter created a security interest. Is Teleflex correct? [In re *Fibre Glass Boat Corporation*, 324 F.Supp. 1054 (1971).]

2. Alpha purchased a pair of skis from his roommate Beta. Alpha agreed to make monthly payments on the skis over a period of six months and entered into an oral agreement with Beta that, in the event of a default on any payment, Beta could repossess the skis. Alpha later defaulted. May Beta legally repossess under their security agreement? Why?

3. Willard signed a security agreement giving Popular Finance Company (PFC) a security interest in "1 2-pc. living room suite, wine; 1 5-pc. chrome dinette set, yellow; 1 3-pc. panel bedroom suite, lime oak, matt. & spgs." The agreement provided that this property was to be kept at Willard's residence and the address was stated in the agreement. When Willard later declared bankruptcy, it was claimed that the security interest was invalid because the description of the property was insufficient. Is the description sufficient? [In re *Drane*, 202 F.Supp. 221 (1962).]

4. Elmer borrowed money from Friendly Finance (FF) and gave FF a security interest in all of his lawn equipment. FF filed a financing statement covering the equipment. Later Elmer sold his lawn mower to his next door neighbor, Rufus, who bought the mower in good faith, paid value, and was unaware of FF's security interest. If Elmer defaults in his loan payments, may FF repossess the mower from Rufus? Why?

5. Marby's, a clothing store, borrowed $25,000 from a bank and signed a security agreement covering the store's equipment. The store also signed a financing statement that covered equipment, inventory, and accounts receivable, and the bank filed the statement. Does the bank have a perfected security interest in Marby's equipment, inventory, and accounts receivable? [*Mitchell v. Shepherd Mall State Bank*, 458 F.2d 700 (1972).]

6. A creditor took a security interest in the crops of a farmer. The security agreement included the kind of crops, the names of the farms where the crops were grown, and legal descriptions of the farms. A financing statement was filed that covered the farmer's crops "which are now growing or are hereafter planted, grown, and produced on land owned or leased by debtor in Cherokee County, Kansas." Later the farmer sold the crops to a third party, who claimed that the financing statement was insufficient to perfect a security interest in the crops and, therefore, the creditor had no lien on the crops. Is the third party correct? [*Chanute Production Credit Ass'n. v. Wier Grain & Supply, Inc.*, 499 P.2d 517 (Kan. 1972).]

7. Excel Stores, Inc., a Connecticut corporation engaged in the business of selling toys and other merchandise, purchased six cash registers on credit from National Cash Register Company (NCR). NCR took a security interest in the cash registers. However, in signing the security agreement, the treasurer of Excel Stores inadvertently used the name "Excel Department Stores," and this name was also used on the financing statement. Does NCR have a perfected security interest? [In re *Excel Stores, Inc.*, 341 F.2d 961 (1965).]

8. A bank agreed to lend money to a company, and the company signed a security agreement covering all existing and future accounts receivable. The bank filed a financing statement which described the collateral as "Accounts Receivable." The company later went into receivership, and the receiver claimed that the security interest was unperfected as to accounts receivable which arose after the date of the financing statement because the financing statement did not mention *future* accounts receivable. Is the receiver correct? [*South County Sand & Gravel Co. v. Bituminous Pavers Co.*, 256 A.2d 514 (R.I. 1969).]

9. Clyde purchased a stereo system from Loud Sounds (LS) on credit. Clyde signed a security agreement, but a financing statement was not filed. Later Clyde sold his speakers to a friend, Jake, who knew of the security interest but wanted them for his personal use. Clyde sold the rest of the system to a store, Used Stereos (US), which was unaware of the security interest. When Clyde defaulted on his payments to LS, LS attempted to repossess the collateral from Jake and US. Should the repossession be allowed? Why?

10. In the case of In re *Amex-Protein Development Corporation*, 504 F.2d 1056 (1974),[1] the court concluded that a promissory note could be used to create a security interest. What Code policy is served by this liberal approach?

---

[1] See pp. 877–78.

Enforcement of Personal Property Security Interests; and Suretyship

49

After you have read this chapter, you should be able to:

1. Determine which of two secured parties has priority when both have perfected by filing a financing statement.
2. Discuss the rights of a secured party against a mortgagee who claims a fixture.
3. List the procedure which a secured party will follow after the debtor's default.
4. Define the three parties involved in a suretyship arrangement.
5. Discuss the three options available to a surety after paying the creditor.
6. Explain the types of defenses which are available to a surety.

Introduction to
Enforcement of Personal Property Security Interests

In chapter 48 we examined three basic questions relating to the law of secured transactions: (1) What type of collateral may be used as security? (2) How is a security interest created? (3) How is a security interest perfected? However, even when a creditor meets all the requirements for creating and perfecting a security interest, it is possible that other creditors will have better rights to repossess the collateral when the debtor defaults. We will begin this chapter with a discussion of the rules which determine which creditor has priority upon the debtor's default. These rules are litigated frequently and are very important because a creditor can lose thousands of dollars in collateral if a court determines that he does not have priority. Once a determination is made as to which creditor has priority, there is one key security question left to consider: What right does the creditor with priority have to repossess and to sell the collateral?

After concluding our examination of the law of secured transactions, we will look at another type of security arrangement, suretyship. This arrangement—under which the creditor obtains the promise of another person, a surety, to repay the obligor's debt (or to perform some other obligation of the obligor)—requires an understanding of the law of suretyship.

The problem of priorities.

Priorities

George owned a $1,000 stereo. In need of cash, he borrowed $2,000 from Andy and gave Andy a security interest in the stereo. Later, having spent the $2,000, George borrowed another $2,000 from Bob and gave Bob a security interest in the same stereo. If George defaults on both of his loan payments, who has the right to repossess the stereo, Andy or Bob? As noted in chapter 48, a secured party with a perfected security interest has priority over unperfected security interests. Thus, if Bob had perfected his security interest and Andy did not perfect, Bob would in most cases be entitled to the stereo. Many cases, however, can not be resolved this easily, and the decision will depend on additional factors. Eight common fact situations which raise priority questions will be discussed below.

Creditors Perfect by Filing

If both creditors have perfected their security interests by filing a financing statement, *the first secured party to file has priority*. This rule illustrates the importance of filing the financing statement as soon as possible, even before the loan is made. For example, on June 1 Andy promised to lend George $2,000, took a security interest in the stereo, and filed a financing statement. On July 1 Bob loaned Andy $2,000, took a security interest in the stereo, and filed a financing statement. On August 1 Andy made his promised loan. Who has priority? The answer under the above rule is that Andy has priority because he filed his financing statement first, even though he did not lend the money until after Bob's loan. Before extending credit on July 1, Bob should have checked the public records and, if he had done so, would have discovered that the stereo was already subject to a security interest.

Creditors Perfect Using Different Methods

If each creditor uses a different method of perfection, the creditor who has either filed a financing statement or perfected first has priority. Let us suppose that on June 1 Andy loaned $2,000 to George and took a security interest in George's stereo. On July 1 Bob loaned $2,000, took a security interest in the stereo, and perfected by taking possession—that is, by pledge. On August 1 Andy filed a financing statement covering the stereo. Bob would have priority because his interest was *perfected* first, even though his security interest was not the first to attach. Andy's security interest had *attached* on June 1, but his *perfection* did not occur until August 1.

Neither Creditor Perfected

If neither Andy nor Bob had perfected his security interest, the secured party who first created a security interest will prevail. This rule will be rarely used because as soon as a secured party realizes that other security interests exist, he will immediately attempt to perfect his security interest, thus making the case subject to the above rules.

Fixtures

A **fixture** is property which, although at one time personal property, has been attached to real estate in such a way that it is legally considered to be part of the real estate, although it still may be used as collateral in a secured transaction. Because it is legally part of the real estate, a new type of creditor now enters the picture: a creditor with a mortgage covering the real estate. To illustrate, we might assume that our debtor, George, lives in a house that he has mortgaged to First Bank. If he builds his stereo system into a wall in such a way that it is considered to be a fixture, the stereo, as part of the real estate, becomes subject to the mortgage of First Bank. If the mortgage is foreclosed, First Bank can claim not only the house and land but also the stereo.

fixture
a chattel which has become permanently attached to realty and thus becomes part of the realty; it still can be used as collateral for a security interest

The situation becomes complicated when George gives a creditor, *Second Bank,* a security interest in the stereo to secure another loan. If George defaults on both loans, who has priority: the creditor with a mortgage or the secured party? Although the rules governing this situation are very complex and subject to exception, it may be generally stated that to gain priority over a creditor with a recorded mortgage, the secured party must have a *purchase money security interest,* and the security interest must be perfected by a fixture filing *before* the goods become fixtures or *within ten days after* they become fixtures. A **fixture filing** is a filing of the financing statement in the office where mortgages are recorded.

fixture filing
filing a financing statement in the office where mortgages are recorded

Noninventory Financing

Noninventory financing is especially important to a person in business and to creditors which lend to businesses. To illustrate a typical situation, we might assume that George runs a business—a restaurant—and that he borrows $2,000 from First Bank, giving First Bank a perfected security interest in all of the *equipment* which he now owns or may acquire later. As discussed in chapter 48, after-acquired property may be included in a security agreement. George then buys a stereo on credit from a local store, Loud Sounds, and gives Loud Sounds a security interest in the stereo. George uses the stereo to play music to customers. If George defaults on his payments to First Bank and to Loud Sounds, who has priority with regard to the stereo? In most cases, First Bank, with its prior, perfected security interest, prevails. However, there is a major exception which protects secured parties with a *purchase money security interest* such as that of Loud Sounds. If there is a purchase money security interest, the purchase money creditor has priority if it *perfects within ten days after the debtor receives the collateral*. In many cases an issue is raised concerning the meaning of possession, as is illustrated in the following case.

Facts

National Acceptance Company loaned $692,000 to Ultra Precision and took a perfected security interest in Ultra's present and after-acquired equipment on March 7, 1967. In June, 1968 Ultra ordered a machine from Wolf subject to the condition that Ultra obtain satisfactory financing. The machine was delivered August 7, 1968, satisfactory financing was obtained and a security agreement was executed on October 23, 1968, and the security interest was perfected on October 30, 1968. Now a question has arisen: Which secured party has priority?

Decision

Wolf's interest has priority.

Reasoning

Wolf's interest was perfected within ten days after Ultra received possession of the machine. Possession means more than physical delivery; in this case, possession occurred when Ultra became obligated to pay for the machine—that is, when the security agreement was signed after satisfactory financing was obtained.

In re *Ultra Precision Industries, Inc.,* 503 F.2d 414 (1974).

Inventory Financing

One might think initially that inventory financing should be treated in the same manner as equipment financing; that is, the secured party with an interest in after-acquired property should have priority over all other creditors except for the purchase money security interest. However, in practice, inventory financing differs from equipment financing in that inventory is bought and sold more frequently than equipment and, to finance the continuing purchase of new inventory, lenders often will automatically make periodic loans to a business. Loans made under this arrangement are secured by a security agreement covering both future advances and after-acquired inventory, as noted in our discussion of the floating lien in chapter 48. A secured party with such a perfected security interest will have priority over later security interests, except a secured party who has (1) a purchase money security interest in inventory; (2) given notice before the debtor receives possession that he intends to acquire a security interest; and (3) perfected before the debtor receives possession. Since the earlier secured party now has notice, he will not make the usual periodic advance, knowing that the loan is not required since the purchase has been financed under the purchase money arrangement.

To illustrate, George now operates a stereo store and has given First Bank a perfected security interest covering all present and future inventory. George later purchased a truckload of RCA stereos on credit, giving RCA a security interest in the stereos. In order to gain priority over the earlier perfected interest of First Bank, RCA must do two things *before delivering* the stereos: (1) give notice to First Bank of its intention to acquire a security interest, and (2) perfect its security interest.

Buyers in Ordinary Course of Business

If a customer, Alex, visited George's stereo store, he might be unaware that the RCA stereos in the store are subject to the security interests of both First Bank and RCA. Does this mean that, if Alex buys a stereo, it might be repossessed by one of the creditors if George defaults on his payments? Such a result would have a detrimental effect on commerce, and the UCC specifically provides that a buyer in the ordinary course of business, such as Alex, buys free and clear of security interests created by the seller. This protection extends even to a case where the security interest is perfected or the buyer knows of the interest. The buyer in ordinary course of business prevailed in the following case.

Facts

Homish was an automobile dealer who gave a security interest in all of his vehicles to Sterling Acceptance Company. Homish then sold a new Dodge automobile to Grimes, who paid the sale price in full. Homish never delivered the certificate of title, however, and because of Homish's financial difficulties, Sterling now wants to repossess the automobile from Grimes.

Decision

Sterling loses.

Reasoning

Grimes purchased the automobile in the ordinary course of business from a dealer. Therefore, he purchases free and clear of all security interests, even when those interests are perfected and he knows of them.

Sterling Acceptance Co. v. Grimes, 168 A.2d 600 (Pa. 1961).

bailment
a delivery of goods by a bailor to a bailee which are to be returned to the bailor or as he directs in accordance with the bailment agreement

bailee
the person to whom goods are bailed

bailee's lien
the bailee's legal right to retain possession of the bailed goods as security for the obligation owing to the bailee, usually payment for the bailee's services and for materials supplied to the bailed goods

Bailee's Liens

In many cases the interest of a secured party will conflict with that of a **bailee** who has repaired or improved the collateral and who claims a **bailee's lien** in order to secure payment for his services and for materials supplied to the collateral. In such cases, a bailee *in possession* of the collateral and with a valid bailee's lien under the relevant state law takes priority over a perfected security interest, as is illustrated in the following case.

Facts

A debtor borrowed money from the Gulf Coast State Bank in order to purchase a car, and the bank took a perfected security interest in the car. Later the car was damaged in an automobile accident and taken to an auto repair shop. After the car was repaired, the debtor did not pay the repair bill, and the repair shop claimed a bailee's lien on the car. The bank claimed that its perfected security interest had priority.

Decision

The repair shop wins.

Reasoning

A bailee with a lien upon goods in his possession has priority unless the state lien law expressly provides otherwise. The Texas lien law did not change the UCC rule.

Gulf Coast State Bank v. Nelms, 525 S.W.2d 866 (Tex. 1975).

Rights of Secured Party on Default

When a debtor defaults in his payments, the secured party with priority will normally take two courses of action. He will (1) repossess the collateral and (2) either retain or sell the collateral.

Repossession

Dolly obtained financing from First Bank to purchase a new car and gave the bank a security interest in the car. Dolly parked the car every night in her driveway, which was her private property. One morning she discovered that the car was gone and, after calling the police, learned that the bank had repossessed the car during the night because she had missed two payments. Are such repossessions legal?

The answer is to be found in UCC 9–503 which provides: "Unless otherwise agreed a secured party has on default the right to take possession of the collateral . . . without judicial process if this can be done without breach of the peace." As interpreted by the courts, this allows a secured party to trespass secretly onto the debtor's property in the middle of the night in order to remove the collateral so long as there is no breach of the peace.

A **breach of the peace,** as defined by most courts, results from an act of violence or an act which is likely to produce violence. Using this definition, secured parties have been allowed to remove a car from a private driveway and an airplane from an open hangar. No breach of the peace occurred in the following case.

breach of peace
an act of violence or an act likely to produce violence

Facts

The Bank of Babylon entered into a security agreement covering property owned by Elwood Auto Parts. The agreement gave the bank the right to enter the debtor's premises and take away the property with or without legal process. After Elwood's default, the bank entered the premises, using a key obtained from a locksmith, and removed the property. A question later arose as to whether the bank's actions constituted a breach of the peace.

Secured Transactions, Insurance, and Bankruptcy

Decision

This was not a breach of the peace.

Reasoning

Even though the bank might have committed a "breaking" into the premises, the bank did not commit an act of violence and did nothing to disturb the peace and quiet of the community. Also, in this situation the use of the key was not likely to result in violence.

Cherno v. Bank of Babylon, 282 N.Y. Supp.2d 114 (1967).

In addition to self-help repossession, a secured party might also commence an action to obtain a court order that the debtor turn over collateral. Because court proceedings involve state action, the due process clause of the federal Constitution requires that the debtor be given notice of the court hearing and an opportunity to present his defense before the property is seized. In a few states, courts have decided that even self-help repossession involves state action, and these courts require a court hearing before the collateral is seized.

After Repossession

A secured party who has possession of the collateral through self-help or a court order has two options. First, the secured party may sell the collateral at a public or private sale. The sale must be commercially reasonable with regard to the method, manner, terms, place, and time of sale. Furthermore, although subject to specific exceptions, such as a sale of perishable goods, the secured party must give reasonable notification of the sale to the debtor and to other secured parties who have sent written notice (to the repossessing secured party) claiming an interest in the collateral. If the sale of the collateral results in a surplus after secured parties have been paid, the debtor is entitled to the surplus. But if the proceeds are not sufficient to cover the secured debt, the debtor is liable for any deficiency.

The other option is for the secured party to keep the collateral in full satisfaction of the debt. This option will be used most frequently by a secured party when the collateral is worth more than the unpaid debt. In order to protect the debtor and prevent unfair enrichment of the secured party, the UCC provides that in most cases the secured party must send written notice to the debtor, and to other secured parties claiming an interest in the collateral, proposing to keep the collateral in satisfaction of the debt. If the debtor or another secured party objects within 21 days after the notice was sent, the repossessing secured party must sell the collateral. If no objection is raised, the secured party may keep the collateral in satisfaction of the debt.

Compulsory resale.

The UCC provides special protection for the debtor where the collateral is *consumer goods* and the debtor has paid *sixty percent* of the loan or of the price. In such cases, the creditor must obtain from the debtor a written, signed statement under which the debtor allows the creditor to retain the collateral. A creditor without this statement must sell or dispose of the collateral within ninety days after taking possession.

Introduction to Suretyship

On the day when he reached the age of eighteen and legally became an adult, Junior decided to purchase a used car from Dealer. Junior selected a car and signed a conditional sales contract whereby he was to make monthly payments to Dealer for two years. But Dealer decided that he wanted more than Junior's promise to repay the debt; he wanted some type of security to protect him in the event of Junior's default.

There are two common types of security arrangements used in business. One type is the secured transaction discussed above where the debtor gives the creditor a security interest in certain collateral. The other security arrangement, which may be used separately or in conjunction with the secured transaction, is **suretyship.** Under this arrangement another person—for example, Junior's Father—would also sign Junior's note and promise to pay the debt.

Definitions

suretyship
a legal relationship in which one person (surety) and another person (principal, the debtor) are obligated to perform the same obligation to a third person (creditor) who is entitled to only one performance, and as between the surety and the principal the latter is to perform the obligation and is ultimately liable therefor

principal
the debtor in a suretyship arrangement

surety
a person who promises the creditor to pay the principal's debt or to perform his obligation

surety bond
a promise by a professional surety to pay if the principal defaults or commits a wrongful act

guarantor
a type of surety

In security arrangements using a surety, there are typically three parties. The **principal** or *principal debtor* is the debtor, in our case Junior. The principal is indebted to the *creditor,* Dealer. The **surety** (Father in the above example) is a third party who agrees to become liable on the debt of the principal (Junior).

A very common business arrangement is the **surety bond** under which a professional surety promises to make payment if a principal defaults or commits a wrongful act. In many cases surety bonds are required by contract. For example, a person building a new office building might require the contractor to furnish a construction bond to cover a possible failure of the contractor to complete the contract or to pay his subcontractors. Other bonds are required by statute. These include bonds required of public officials, bonds required of fiduciaries such as the executor of an estate, and bail bonds.

In some states a distinction is made between two categories of surety: one is the *strict surety* and the other the **guarantor.** The strict surety is a *co-debtor* with the principal. For example, a son wants to buy an automobile on credit, but the seller will not sell to the son without the father as surety. Accordingly, the father and son sign the contract and promissory note for *their* purchase, on credit, of an automobile for the son, with the agreement between *them* that the son is to pay for the automobile. As to the creditor seller, the father and son are the co-debtor purchasers; as between the father and son, the son is the principal and the father is the strict surety. However, if the automobile had been sold to the son as the purchaser and the father agreed with the *seller* to be responsible for the son's payment and liable on his default, the father would be a guarantor, liable only on the son's default.

Secured Transactions, Insurance, and Bankruptcy

A guarantor is liable only in accordance with the terms of his suretyship contract. There are various types of guaranty differing only in their contract terms, two of which will be considered here.

The *absolute guaranty* is a contract that the guarantor will perform only on the principal's *default*. A common example is the "guaranty of payment," such as X's statement to Z, "Extend credit to A, and if he does not pay, I will." At the maturity date, if A does not pay, Z can recover from X.

The *conditional guaranty* states a condition which must occur before the surety is liable to the creditor. A commonly used example is the "guaranty of collection," when the guarantor must pay only if the debt is *uncollectible*—that is, the creditor can not collect it from the principal. It is uncollectible when the creditor has sued the principal, the resulting judgment can not be paid, and the surety is notified of this within a reasonable time.

Statute of Frauds

The distinction between a strict surety and a guarantor is important under the statute of frauds. The contract of a strict surety is not within that portion of the statute of frauds which provides that a promise to answer for the debt, default, or miscarriage (e.g., an employee's embezzlement of a firm's cash) *of another* is unenforceable without a proper writing. Since the strict surety is a co-debtor with the principal, he is a co-principal, and he does not condition his liability on the default of the other principal. He is liable on the obligation together with the other principal.

In contrast, the guarantor promises to pay or perform the principal's obligation *only on the principal's nonperformance* and, therefore, a contract of guaranty is within the statute and unenforceable without a proper writing. The writing may be the signed contract itself, or a note or memorandum of an oral contract signed by the party to be charged with performance (the guarantor) or by his lawfully authorized agent.

The Suretyship Contract

A suretyship contract is created in the same manner as other contracts and must meet basic contractual requirements in addition to the statute of frauds, such as offer and acceptance, consideration, and legality. For example, we have learned under the law of contracts that, when an offer is made for a *unilateral* contract, unless otherwise agreed, the law requires the offeree to notify the offeror of his performance. His failure to do so discharges the offeror, provided that the offeror would not learn of such performance within a reasonable time in the ordinary course of affairs. This is the law of suretyship also, as illustrated in the following case.

Facts

Milo Black sent the following letter to the Electric Storage Battery Company: "In regard to credit rating for Gerald Black, I will guarantee payment of material purchased." Gerald made purchases from August 29, 1960 to December 29, 1961. Electric Storage did not acknowledge Milo's letter but, finally, in 1962 wrote him demanding payment for the purchases. Milo refused to pay.

Decision

Milo is not liable.

Reasoning

Electric Storage never notified Milo that it had accepted his offer.

Electric Storage Battery Co. v. Black, 134 N.W.2d 481 (Wis. 1965).

Surety's Defenses

Complete defenses of the surety against the creditor.

Complete Defenses

Both the principal and the surety may have defenses against the creditor when he seeks to enforce their contracts with him. There are the usual contract defenses (discussed in Part 2, Contracts) such as fraud, duress, coercion, and undue influence, which the principal and surety may assert against the creditor in their respective contracts. If Father is a *strict surety* with the principal Junior on a note signed by them for the purchase of a car from Dealer but Dealer never delivered the car, neither would be liable on the note because of failure of consideration—Dealer's failure to render the agreed consideration, namely, delivery of the car. If Father were a *guarantor,* he could also assert Junior principal's defenses in a suit against him by Dealer.

It must be emphasized that all of the principal's defenses which are not personal to him are also available to the surety (guarantor). For example, assume that Dealer fraudulently induced Junior to buy the car. On Junior's default by his nonpayment, Father surety (guarantor) can assert the fraud if he is sued by Dealer.

There are a few contract defenses, however, which are personal to the principal and can not be raised by the surety. These include the principal's discharge in bankruptcy, the principal's power of avoidance resulting from his infancy or insanity, and the running of the statute of limitations on the principal's obligation. The last is illustrated in the following case.

Facts

Yockey purchased oil well supplies on credit from Bomud Company under an oral agreement. The agreement was guaranteed in writing by Osborn. Yockey later defaulted but was not liable because the statute of limitations is very short for oral agreements. Bomud then sued Osborn, the statute of limitations not having run on the written agreement. Osborn claims that since the principal is not liable, he should not be liable either.

Decision
Bomud wins.

Reasoning
Osborn, as a guarantor, made a separate agreement to perform Yockey's contract. The fact that Bomud can not collect from Yockey is of no consequence with regard to this separate agreement.

Bomud Company v. Yockey Oil Company and Osborn, 299 P.2d 72 (Kan. 1956).

There are special defenses which are unique to the suretyship arrangements. When the creditor and the principal agree to a modification of their contract without the consent of the surety, if the modification agreement is binding on them (e.g., there is consideration), and it would increase the possibility of the surety's risk, the surety is discharged from his suretyship obligation. However, all modifications will not result in discharge, as is shown by the following case involving a *paid* surety.

Facts
Bayer, a general contractor, hired Deschenes, a subcontractor, to do excavation work beginning on November 24, 1958. The work was to be completed by March 1, 1959. Aetna Insurance Company furnished a performance bond for Deschenes in the amount of $91,000. Deschenes started the work late and never completed the project. Aetna, however, claims that it is not liable as a surety because Bayer gave extension of the time for performance to Deschenes.

Decision
Aetna loses.

Reasoning
A compensated surety such as Aetna is discharged only when it is harmed by the contract modification. Aetna could prove no harm.

Bayer & Mingolla Construction Co. v. Deschenes, 205 N.E.2d 208 (Mass. 1965).

The surety will also be discharged in cases where the creditor does not perform the suretyship contract—for example, by failing to mail copies of the principal's bills to the surety. Furthermore, the surety will be discharged when the principal's debt is paid or when a proper tender of payment is rejected by the creditor.

Partial Defenses
We have considered the surety's defenses which *completely discharge* the surety. However, there are some defenses which only partially discharge the surety. A few are considered here.

Partial defenses.

Surrender or Impairment of Property Security. When the creditor has property as security as well as a surety and he surrenders the property to the principal or wrongfully impairs its value, the surety is discharged only to the extent of the value of the surrendered property or of its impairment.

Release of a Co-Surety.   There may be more than one surety on the same obligation of the principal. They are called *co-sureties*. When the creditor releases one of various co-sureties without the consent of the others, thereby causing them to lose their contributive shares from the released co-surety in the event the principal defaults, the other co-sureties are discharged to the extent of the loss of such contributive shares. For example, P owes C $900 and X, Y, and Z are equal co-sureties as guarantors on the debt. C releases Z without the consent of X and Y and without reserving his rights against Z.[1] P defaults and has no assets, and X, Y, and Z individually are solvent with sufficient assets to pay the debt. C can collect only $600 from X and Y because, by his release of Z, he prevented X and Y from recovering Z's contributive share on the $900 debt.

Guaranty of Collection.   When there is a guaranty of collection, if the creditor *delays* in his collection from the principal or *delays* in his notice of uncollectibility to the surety so as to cause loss to the surety in his effort to be reimbursed by the principal, the surety is discharged to the extent of such loss.

Surety's Rights

Surety's rights against the principal.

In cases where the surety has no defense or only a partial defense and must pay the creditor on the principal's default, there are three options available to the surety to cover the loss. First, the surety is entitled to **reimbursement** from the principal. For instance, if Father paid Dealer, Junior would be liable to Father for those payments.

reimbursement
(in suretyship) the surety's right to recover from the principal

Second, the surety is entitled to be subrogated to the rights of the creditor. With a **subrogation,** the surety steps into the shoes of the creditor and takes over all his rights to collect the debt. We might assume, for example, that Junior had given Dealer a security interest in his car. If Junior defaulted and Father paid off Dealer, Father would succeed to Dealer's rights, in this case the right to collect the debt and to repossess the collateral.

subrogation
(in suretyship) the surety succeeds to the creditor's rights against the principal

Finally, in cases where there are several sureties for the same debt, the liability of the sureties is joint and several; that is, a creditor may collect from all sureties jointly or may decide to sue and collect from only one of the sureties. If the creditor collects from less than all of the sureties, those who pay are entitled to **contribution** from the other sureties and, unless the surety contract provides otherwise, the loss will be shared equally by the sureties.

Surety's rights against his co-sureties.

contribution
(in suretyship) the right of sureties who have paid the creditor to collect part of the payment from other sureties

Summary Statement

Enforcement of Personal Property Security Interests
1. When two or more creditors claim an interest in the same collateral and all creditors have perfected by filing a financing statement, the first creditor to file has priority.

---

[1] If C had *reserved his rights against Z*, the courts would construe C's reservation of his rights against Z as meaning that C is *promising not to sue Z* rather than *discharging* Z from his obligation to C.

2. A secured party will prevail over a mortgagee who claims a fixture if the secured party has a purchase money security interest and has perfected by a fixture filing within ten days after the goods become fixtures.

3. A perfected security interest in *equipment* is subject to the priority of a purchase money security interest which has been perfected within ten days after the debtor receives the collateral.

4. A perfected security interest in *after-acquired inventory* has priority over later security interests, except as against a secured party with a purchase money security interest in inventory who, before the debtor obtains possession, gives notice of his intention to acquire a security interest and perfects the security interest.

5. Buyers in the ordinary course of business take property free from a previously perfected security interest in the property created by the seller.

6. Generally a bailee's lien has priority over a previously perfected security interest in the bailed goods.

7. After a debtor defaults, a secured party will (a) repossess the collateral through self-help or court order and (b) sell the collateral or, subject to certain limitations, keep the collateral in full payment of the debt.

Suretyship

8. Three parties are involved in a suretyship relationship: (a) a principal, who is the debtor; (b) a creditor; and (c) a surety who promises the creditor to pay the debt either as a co-debtor with the principal or as a guarantor on the principal's default.

9. A strict surety is a co-debtor with the principal on his contract with the creditor and his contract is not within the statute of frauds. A guarantor's contract is within the statute.

10. A guaranty of collection is enforceable only when the debt is uncollectible.

11. All of the principal's defenses which are not personal to him may be asserted by the surety against the creditor on the principal's default.

12. Defenses personal to the principal are (a) the principal's discharge in bankruptcy, (b) the principal's power of avoidance resulting from his infancy or insanity, and (c) the running of the statute of limitations on the principal's obligation.

13. Binding modification of the principal's contract by the principal and the creditor without the surety's consent, which increases the possibility of the surety's risk, discharges the surety.

14. The surety has partial defenses and he is partially discharged by the creditor's (a) surrendering or impairing property security held by him, (b) releasing a co-surety without a reservation of rights, and (c) delaying collection on a guaranty of collection.

15. A surety who has paid the creditor is entitled to (a) reimbursement from the principal, (b) subrogation to the creditor's rights, and (c) contribution from other co-sureties.

In the following case, the court considers the constitutionality of self-help repossession under the Uniform Commercial Code.

Frost v. Mohawk National Bank
74 Misc.2d 912 (N.Y. 1973)

Edward S. Conway, Justice: This is a motion by the plaintiff for a preliminary injunction and temporary restraining order enjoining the defendants during the pendency of the action from continuing to deprive plaintiff of the use and benefit of a certain 1971 Fiat automobile and for an order directing defendants to return it to the plaintiff.

Plaintiff purchased a certain 1971 Fiat automobile from Hickey Ford Sales on July 7, 1971. The purchase was financed by defendant Mohawk National Bank under a retail installment contract which called for 36 monthly installments of $55.45 each, commencing August 20, 1971 and ending on July 20, 1974.

After the plaintiff had failed to make the payments due for April and May under the installment contract, the defendant Mohawk National Bank repossessed the automobile through its agent, defendant Edward F. Dunleavy, by removing it from its parking place on First Street in Troy.

There is no longer any question but that where repossession is obtained through judicial process under the replevin statutes, a person must be afforded notice and an opportunity to be heard prior to any taking, except in extraordinary circumstances. . . .

In the opinion of this Court, the rationale of the Sniadach and Fuentes cases is that in the exercise of "due process" by the state, notice and an opportunity to be heard must be given where the object of the action is the taking of property in which the possessor has a significant property interest, except in extraordinary circumstances.

The Court has examined the retail installment contract in the instant case and finds that there is a clause which allows the seller, in the event of a default, the right without notice or demand, to enter upon any premises where the vehicle may be found and take possession of and remove the vehicle without process of law.

Section 9-503 of the Uniform Commercial Code provides in part:

Unless otherwise agreed a secured party has on default the right to take possession of the collateral. In taking possession a secured party may proceed without judicial process if this can be done without breach of the peace or may proceed by action. . . .

Many text writers on the Uniform Commercial Code have expressed opinions that "self-help" under section 9-503 of the Code may very well be struck down under the rationale of *Sniadach v. Family Finance Corp.,* . . . and *Fuentes v. Shevin.* . . . However, they all make a distinction between "self-help" and replevin prior to a hearing even though both involve a "taking" of the debtor's property before any judicial determination of the validity of the taking. Most of them make a distinction when self-help repossession is authorized by a private contract and the consumer has contracted for the security interest.

It is the opinion of this Court that an agreement entered into in compliance with section 9-503 of the Uniform Commercial Code must be held to be legal, especially where the debtor has expressly authorized the "self-help" provisions of the contract. Such an agreement can not be held to be unconscionable when such terms are expressly authorized by statute. To stretch the rationale of the Sniadach case and later cases following it to include a prohibition of "self-help" under a security agreement would require this Court to go beyond the point permitted by good reason under the circumstances of this case.

The motion of the plaintiff is therefore denied, and the order of this Court to show cause, dated June 6, 1973, is vacated.

Questions and Case Problems

Enforcement of Personal Property Security Interests

1. Burrows purchased livestock from Bailey on an installment sale arrangement. Burrows later borrowed $80,000 from Walker Bank, which took a perfected security interest in the livestock Burrows was purchasing. Bailey then filed a financing statement covering the livestock being sold to Burrows. Does the bank have a security interest that is prior to Bailey's interest? [*Walker Bank and Trust Co. v. Burrows*, 507 P.2d 384 (Utah 1973).]

2. Central Bank had a perfected security interest in "equipment now owned or hereafter acquired" by Galleon. Lewyn sold a machine to Galleon on credit, keeping title to the machine until Galleon made payment. The machine was delivered to Galleon and Lewyn did not file a financing statement. Who has priority to the machine—Lewyn or Central Bank? Why? [*Galleon Industries, Inc. v. Lewyn Machinery Co., Inc.*, 279 So.2d 137 (Ala. 1973).]

3. Clyde works for First Bank as a lending officer. Clyde is considering a loan to Disco Duds Clothing Store (DD) to enable the store to purchase a new stock of inventory, in which the bank will take a security interest. However, Clyde learns that Second Bank already has a perfected security interest in Disco's present and future inventory. Can Clyde and First Bank gain priority over Second Bank's interest? If so, how?

4. National Shawmut Bank had a perfected security interest in a car owned by Wever. Wever sold the car to Hanson-Rock, an automobile dealer, who resold the car to Jones. Now National Shawmut wants to repossess Jones' car. May it? [*National Shawmut Bank of Boston v. Jones*, 236 A.2d 484 (N.H. 1967).]

5. Corbin Deposit Bank had a perfected security interest in Foreman's car. Foreman took his car to King, who was in the business of repairing cars, for repair work. Foreman did not pay King for the repair work, and King claimed a lien on the car, which was still in his possession. Foreman also failed to pay his debt to the bank. The car was sold. Who is entitled to the proceeds? [*Corbin Deposit Bank v. King*, 384 S.W.2d 302 (Ky. 1964).]

6. Henry borrowed money from a bank, purchased a new pickup truck, and gave the bank a perfected security interest in the truck. Later Henry defaulted on his payments and the bank repossessed his truck by towing it from a parking lot while Henry was at work. The bank then sold the car at an auction without notifying Henry. Henry claims that the repossession and sale were illegal. Is he correct? Why?

7. In the case of *Frost v. Mohawk National Bank,* 74 Misc.2d 912 (N.Y. 1973),[2] a clause in the retail installment contract allowed the seller, after default, to enter the buyer's premises and to remove the vehicle without giving prior notice. Under this clause, could a seller go to court and, without notice to the buyer, obtain a court order directing a local sheriff to repossess the car? Explain.

Suretyship

8. Watkins Company signed a contract with Baker, who was to sell Watkins Company products. Sanders also signed the contract, as a surety. When Watkins Company later sued Sanders on his guaranty, Sanders claimed that his signature was obtained by fraud. He claimed that Baker had told him the contract was only a recommendation and Sanders, who did not have his glasses handy, signed it without reading the document. Does Baker's fraud relieve Sanders of liability? Why? [*J.R. Watkins Co. v. Lankford,* 256 S.W.2d 788 (Mo. 1953).]

9. Cardwell guaranteed purchases by McPeters from Failing. The guaranty provided that Failing would promptly mail copies of all invoices to Cardwell. Failing waited seven months after one purchase before mailing the invoice. If McPeters fails to pay the invoice, is Cardwell liable? [*George E. Failing Co. v. Cardwell Investment Co.,* 376 P.2d 892 (Kan. 1962).]

10. In 1933, Keyes signed a note promising to pay a debt to Laney. Dyer was a surety on the note. When Keyes failed to pay the note, Dyer paid Laney in 1946 and sued Keyes for reimbursement in 1948. Keyes defended by claiming that Dyer could not bring suit on the 1933 note in 1948 because the statute of limitations requires lawsuits to be brought within three years after the cause of action arises. Is Keyes correct? [*Keyes v. Dyer,* 243 P.2d 710 (Okla. 1952).]

---

[2] See pp. 894–95.

General Principles of Insurance Law

After you have read this chapter, you should be able to:

1. List the major types of insurance.
2. Define insurance.
3. Describe the regulation of insurance transactions.
4. Explain what is meant by an insurable interest and indicate when the insurable interest must exist.
5. Explain why warranties, representation, and concealment are important and how they are used as defenses by insurance companies.

Introduction

A knowledge of insurance is extremely important to every individual on both a personal and a business level. Like death and taxes, insurance is certain to affect you at some time during your lifetime, and if you own an automobile, a house, or a business, or wish to provide financial security for your family, insurance represents a key element in personal, business, and estate planning.

In this chapter we will examine the general principles of the law relating to insurance contracts. In chapter 51 we will examine closely the three most common types of insurance: (1) life insurance, (2) homeowner's insurance, and (3) automobile insurance.

To illustrate both the importance and the various types of insurance, we might assume that a recent college graduate, Fred, is married, has a child, and has recently purchased a small clothing store. There are many different kinds of insurance that Fred should consider in his personal and business transactions.

Types of insurance.

Types of Insurance

Homeowner's Insurance

Fred should purchase a homeowner's policy that will provide coverage for losses due to damage or destruction of his home. As discussed in chapter 51, the policy should also protect Fred in the event he is sued by someone whom he accidentally injures or who is injured while on Fred's property.

Life Insurance

Fred should create an estate plan that includes a will and life insurance, and possibly also a trust and lifetime gifts. The types and form of life insurance policies will be discussed in chapter 51.

Health Insurance

Health care costs are rising faster than the costs of most products and services. In some communities the charge for spending one night in the hospital runs into hundreds of dollars, not including medical treatment and other services. Consequently, it is extremely important that Fred obtain insurance covering hospital expenses, medical and surgical fees, and other services such as X rays, radiological treatment, and laboratory tests. It is common for individuals to supplement their health insurance with a major medical insurance policy that provides coverage for extended illness, which might cost more than the coverage provided by the primary insurance policy.

Disability Insurance

If Fred should become ill, his health insurance will pay for his hospital and medical treatment, but a source of income will be needed to support his family until his recovery. A disability insurance policy can be purchased that will provide a monthly income for Fred until he recovers.

Annuity

In planning for his eventual retirement, Fred might decide to purchase an **annuity** policy. An annuity is a type of insurance policy that will pay Fred a designated amount periodically, the payments to begin at a date set in the policy. Fred might choose to purchase a fixed dollar annuity that pays a set amount—e.g., $10,000 per year. Alternatively, he might choose a variable annuity where the annuity premiums are invested in stocks or bonds and the benefit rises or falls, depending on the current value of the portfolio.

Automobile Insurance

Fred will need either regular or no-fault automobile insurance for his car. Both types of insurance will be discussed in chapter 51.

Title Insurance

When Fred purchased his home, it is likely that he purchased **title insurance,** which protects Fred in the event that the person who sold him the house did not have clear title to the property. For instance, there might be a deed on record with a hidden defect, such as a voidable deed signed by a minor. Title insurance will protect Fred for as long as he owns the property. With title insurance, only one premium is paid—at the closing—although if the owner mortgages the house, the bank usually will require him to purchase a second policy to protect the bank's interest.

Social Insurance

Today approximately ninety percent of workers are covered by social security, even when they are self-employed, and almost all of our country's population over 65 years of age is covered by Medicare, which is provided by the federal government. During their working years, employees covered by social security make contributions that are automatically deducted from wages; the employer matches the amount of the deduction and forwards the total to the Internal Revenue Service. A worker who is self-employed will pay the social security contribution when he files an annual income tax return. The social security contributions are used (1) to pay workers a retirement income when they retire at age 62 or later, (2) to pay disability income to workers who are unable to work because of a disability, and (3) to pay the survivors of a deceased worker.

Medicare provides hospital and medical insurance for persons 65 or older and for disabled persons who have been receiving social security benefits for at least two years. Everyone 65 or older who is entitled to receive social security payments automatically receives hospital insurance. Medical insurance, to cover doctor's fees and other services, is available for a modest monthly premium.

Workers' Compensation Insurance

Workers' (sometimes called "workmen's") compensation laws protect workers who are injured on the job. In almost every state these laws provide that employers, such as Fred in his role as the owner of a clothing store, must pay for all accidental injuries occurring on the job. For instance, if one of Fred's employees carelessly leaves a coat hanger on the floor and later injures himself when he trips on the hanger, Fred is liable for damages resulting from the injury. Most employers purchase a workers' compensation insurance policy from a private company or purchase coverage through a state workers' compensation fund. A few employers use self-insurance; that is, they pay injured workers from company assets.

Business Insurance

In addition to workers' compensation insurance, there are several types of insurance that Fred will need for his business. As he did for his home, Fred should purchase fire and liability insurance for his business as well as automobile insurance if automobiles are used in the business. Fred might purchase **business interruption insurance,** which will reimburse him for lost revenues in the event he has to close his business temporarily because of property damage. If Fred ships his clothing in the ordinary course of business, he will want to purchase **inland marine insurance** to cover against loss while the goods are in transit. *Crime insurance* can be purchased to protect Fred from dishonesty of his employees or theft by outsiders. A number of the personal insurance coverages discussed above can be purchased by the employer as a fringe benefit for the employees, including group life, medical disability, and retirement insurance. Finally, if Fred is considered the key person in his business, the business should purchase key employee life insurance coverage to cover financial losses suffered by the company when Fred dies.

Excess Liability Insurance

Damage awards to injured persons have increased greatly in recent years, and liability coverage under standard homeowner's automobile and business policies is often inadequate. For instance, homeowner's insurance usually provides liability coverage for $50,000; if Fred injures someone—for example, by accidentally hitting him in the eye with a golf ball—the damages could easily run over $100,000. Consequently, it is wise to purchase an excess liability policy, sometimes called an "umbrella" policy, which will provide liability coverage for at least $1 million.

Self-Insurance

When insurance coverage becomes too expensive, many businesses and organizations use some type of self-insurance mechanism. Some companies simply "go bare"; they purchase no insurance and use company assets to pay losses. Some companies self-insure for most losses but purchase supplementary catastrophic loss insurance. Other companies or organizations group together to form insurance "pools" and thus spread their losses among the group. Finally, many companies in recent years have formed subsidiaries, called "captive" insurance companies, and then purchase coverage from the captives, thus avoiding brokerage commissions and other costs.

business interruption insurance
insurance that covers lost revenues when a business is closed as the result of property damage

inland marine insurance
insurance that covers goods that are being shipped

Secured Transactions, Insurance, and Bankruptcy

Definition of Insurance

Before we proceed further, it will be useful to define insurance. There are two different types of insurance definitions. *First,* most courts have adopted a very general definition: **insurance** is a contract, usually called an insurance policy, where one party (called the **insurer** or underwriter) agrees to pay another party (the **insured**) for losses affecting the insured's interests (the insurable interest). The consideration which the insurer receives for paying such losses is called the *premium.*

Second, state insurance commissioners are guided by specific statutory definitions of insurance which they use in deciding whether a particular activity is subject to insurance regulation. For example, section 22 of the California Insurance Code defines insurance as a "contract whereby one undertakes to indemnify another against loss, damage, or liability arising from a contingent or unknown event." Certain companies in California offered home buyers a "homeowner's protection plan" that required the companies to repair plumbing, electrical, and heating systems that become defective within one year after the home was purchased. The California Attorney General, in an opinion dated May 3, 1978, advised those companies that, under the statutory definition of insurance, the companies were engaged in the insurance business and were thus subject to insurance regulation. In the following case the court held that a plan for prepaid legal services was not insurance.

insurance
a contract where the insurer agrees to pay the insured for losses affecting the insured's interests

insurer
the person who assumes another's risk (in the insurance contract)

insured
the person whose risk has been assumed by another (in the insurance contract)

Facts
The New York County Lawyer's Association and a Teamsters Union local created two experimental plans for prepaid legal services. The New York statutes define insurance as an agreement whereby one party (the insurer) is obligated to pay another party (the insured) upon the happening of a fortuitous event. A fortuitous event is an occurrence which is beyond the control of either party. Do the prepaid legal services plans constitute insurance?

Decision
Prepaid legal services plans do not constitute insurance.

Reasoning
Many of the events covered by the legal services plan are not fortuitous. These services include legal assistance in estate planning, divorce, and the purchase of real estate.

Feinstein v. Attorney General of the State of New York, 326 N.E.2d 288 (N.Y. 1975).

Organization of Insurers

Insurer organization.

Many insurance companies, especially those that write fire and casualty insurance, are organized as typical business corporations. That is, they authorize, issue, and sell stock to shareholders, who own the business and receive dividends. However, two other methods of organization are also commonly used by insurance companies.

First, a substantial amount of insurance at the international level is underwritten by Lloyd's of London. Lloyd's is not a company but, instead, is a society with thousands of members who join together to form syndicates, each of which specializes in a certain type of insurance. A person who purchases insurance from Lloyd's is really purchasing insurance from one or more of these individual syndicates. In an effort to make American insurers more competitive with Lloyd's, the state of New York enacted legislation in 1978 that provides for the creation of the New York Insurance Exchange, which is modeled after Lloyd's.

mutual company
a company owned by
the insureds

Second, many American insurers—especially those that underwrite life insurance—are mutual companies. A **mutual company** is one that is owned by the insureds, with the result that the insureds are purchasing insurance at cost since there are no shareholders to be paid. A few mutual companies sell assessable policies, which means that the policyholders must pay an amount in addition to the premium if the company suffers losses. For example, after a Colorado insurance company failed in 1975, the policyholders, many of whom were unaware that their policies were assessable, were charged an average of $500 to cover the company's losses.

In addition to the type of organization, insurance companies can be classified by the type of insurance they sell. At one time an insurance company could sell only one type of insurance—fire, life, or casualty. Today, however, all states allow multiple-line underwriting under which a nonlife insurer can sell all types of insurance except for life insurance. Most states today have gone one step further and allow all-line companies to sell all types of insurance.

Government regulation.

Insurance Regulation

Unlike most contracts, the contract of insurance is closely regulated by the government. Insurance regulations govern the financial condition of insurers, policy premiums, policy forms, and the licensing of insurers and their agents. The overriding legal question with regard to insurance regulation has been whether the individual states or the federal government should be primarily responsible for regulating insurance. The question arises because the commerce clause of the United States Constitution, Article 1, Section 8, provides that Congress has the power to regulate *interstate* commerce. But in the 1868 case of *Paul v. Virginia,*[1] the Supreme Court of the United States ruled that issuing an insurance policy is not an act of commerce and, therefore, the states have the right to regulate insurance contracts. This case was followed until 1944, when the Supreme Court ruled in *United States v. South-Eastern Underwriters Association*[2] that an insurance company that conducts business across state lines is engaged in interstate commerce and subject to regulation by Congress. However, Congress reacted to this decision by enacting the McCarran-Ferguson Act,

---

[1] 8 Wall. 168 (1868).

[2] 322 U.S. 533 (1944).

which became effective in 1945. This Act declared that state regulation of insurance should continue unless a federal law is specifically directed toward the insurance industry. The Act also provided that federal antitrust Acts would not apply to the insurance industry if states established their own regulations. Most states have developed their own regulations and, consequently, today insurance is regulated chiefly by the states.

However, state regulation of insurance is still a live issue today because Congress periodically considers the question of whether the federal government could regulate the insurance industry better than state governments. Furthermore, even with our present system of regulation, questions of federal versus state regulation are frequently raised in the courts, as is illustrated in the following case.

Facts
An insurance agent handled the insurance for Sports Car Club of America (SCCA), which required its members across the country to purchase SCCA-approved coverage. After several years SCCA hired another agency to handle its insurance plan. The original agent filed suit, claiming that SCCA's plan violated federal antitrust statutes. The trial court dismissed the complaint because the state where the agent resided, Missouri, had a statute regulating the business of insurance. The agent appealed the dismissal.

Decision
The trial court decision is reversed and the case remanded.

Reasoning
The agent's complaint alleged a nationwide conspiracy. Consequently, the trial court should have determined whether the other states involved also regulate insurance, thereby exempting the defendant's activity from federal law.

Seasongood v. K & K Insurance Agency, 548 F.2d 729 (1977).

Insurable Interest

One of the key distinctions between an insurance contract and other types of contract is the requirement that the insured have some type of interest, called an **insurable interest,** in the risk covered by the insurance contract. There are three reasons why the law requires the insured to have an insurable interest. *First,* insurance is usually considered to be a contract of indemnity; that is, the purpose of insurance is to provide compensation for losses suffered by the insured. Without the requirement of insurable interest, a person could insure property he does not own and thus be overindemnified for a loss.

Second, the insurable interest requirement is designed to prevent gambling contracts, which are void in most states. For example, if Jack insures something in which he has an interest (as when he purchases collision insurance on his own car), he is not gambling but, instead, is merely shifting an existing risk to the insurer in exchange for his payment of premiums. However, if Jack purchased

insurable interest
an interest the insured has in the risk covered by the insurance contract

collision insurance on Sam's car, a car in which he had no interest, the insurance "contract" would be a wager; Jack would be betting the company that Sam's car will be damaged in a collision.

Third, an insurable interest is required because of the moral risks that would be created by allowing a person to insure a risk in which he has no interest. For instance, if we allow Jack to insure Sam's life or car when Jack has no interest in either, Jack will be tempted to destroy the car or even to murder Sam in order to collect on the policies.

Insurable interest in *life.*

Although these reasons underlie insurable interest theory, in practice the theory is applied differently for life and property insurance. *With life insurance,* insurable interest means that the insured has a reasonable expectation of *economic benefit* or a *legal interest* in the life being insured. To illustrate, if Clyde took in a young orphan with the intention of caring for and supporting him, the orphan would have an insurable interest in Clyde's life based on the reasonable expectation of economic benefit provided by Clyde, even though the orphan was not legally adopted. If Clyde legally adopted the orphan, the orphan would have an even better case because of his legal relationship to Clyde under which Clyde is required to provide support. Thus, the orphan could take out a policy of life insurance on Clyde's life.

With life insurance, the insurable interest must *exist when the policy is purchased,* but it is not required that there be an interest at the time of the loss. Once an insurable interest is established, the insured may purchase any amount of life insurance on the insured which the insurer is willing to sell. In the following case the insurable interest in life existed when the policy was purchased but not at the time of death.

Facts

Jack was employed by Pioneer Foundry for nine years. During Jack's employment, the company had an insurable interest in Jack's life, and it purchased a $50,000 policy on his life, the company being named as beneficiary on the policy. When Jack later left the company, the company continued to pay the premiums on the policy until Jack's death. Is the company, which had no insurable interest at the time of Jack's death, entitled to recover $50,000 on the policy?

Decision

The company is entitled to recover the proceeds.

Reasoning

If the insurable interest requirement is met when the policy is issued, the policy proceeds must be paid even if there is no insurable interest at death. The company is not limited in its recovery to the amount of its financial loss, which in this case was nothing.

Secor v. Pioneer Foundry Co., Inc., 173 N.W.2d 780 (Mich. 1970).

Insurable interest in *property.*

There are two views as to what constitutes an insurable interest in *property.* In some states the insured must actually have some type of *legal interest* in the insured property. For instance, Jack obviously has an insurable interest in his own car if he is the legal owner of the car. In other states an insurable interest

Secured Transactions, Insurance, and Bankruptcy

exists if a person expects to *suffer an economic loss* if the property is destroyed. Under this theory, if Jack owned a pizza shop and often borrowed his friend Sam's car to make deliveries, Jack would have an insurable interest in Sam's car because Jack would suffer an economic loss if Sam's car were destroyed (a loss of sales because he would be unable to make deliveries).

In the following case, the court applied the legal interest test.

Facts
A turnpike company contributed one-third of the cost of a public bridge used by persons traveling on the turnpike. The company then purchased fire insurance on the bridge. When the bridge was later destroyed by fire, the company suffered a loss of tolls and attempted to collect on its insurance policy.

Decision
The company may not collect on the policy.

Reasoning
The company does not have an insurable interest. In this state (Pennsylvania), the interest of the insured must arise from a legal title. The company's contribution when the bridge was built does not give it such an interest because the contribution was voluntary.

Farmers Mutual Ins. Co. v. New Holland Turnpike Road Co., 15 A. 563 (Pa. 1888).

Unlike life insurance, with property insurance the insurable interest must *exist at the time of loss,* and the insured may recover *only up to the value of his interest* at the time of loss. For instance, if Jack purchased automobile insurance on his car but later sold the car, his insurable interest would cease at the time of sale. He could recover nothing if the car were destroyed after the sale.

Insurance Company Defenses

Insurers' defense against payment.

It is a common belief that insurance companies often refuse to make payment on their policies because of fine print provisions in the policies—or, stated another way, "the large print giveth and the fine print taketh away!" While this is, of course, an exaggeration, there are indeed many cases where a company has a legitimate defense in its refusal to pay. Most of these defenses fall within one of three categories.

Warranties

warranty
(in insurance) a statement of fact or a promise made by the insured which is part of the insurance contract and which must be true if the insurer is to be liable on the contract

A **warranty** is a statement of fact or a promise made by the insured which is part of the insurance contract and which must be true if the insurer is to be liable on the contract. Under the common law, the insurance company would be justified in rescinding the policy if the warranty was untrue. For example, if Jack purchased insurance on his frame house and warranted in the policy that the house was brown when it actually was pink, under the common law rule he could not recover for fire losses because his statement was untrue. This harsh rule has been changed in most states by statutes which provide that, unless the contract provides otherwise, statements of fact or promises made by the insured are interpreted to be representations.

Representations

A **representation** is a statement of fact made by the insured during negotiations with the insurer before the policy is issued. It is not a part of the insurance contract and normally is made in the application for insurance. For instance, when Jack applied for fire insurance, he might have stated that his house was brown, but the statement might not be incorporated into the policy. If Jack's representation is not true—i.e., if the house is pink—may the company avoid liability on the policy? In the absence of fraud, the general rule is that the company may not *avoid* liability unless the representation was *material* to its decision whether to issue the policy. In other words, the question is whether the company would have issued the policy even if the representation had not been made. The color of Jack's house would not be material and, therefore, Jack's misrepresentation would be no defense. However, if Jack had represented that the house was made of stone when in fact it was a frame house, the company could *avoid* liability because of the misrepresentation of a material fact. The following case illustrates this.

Facts

In applying for automobile insurance, Johnny stated in his application that he had no arrests for offenses other than traffic violations, that he had not been fined or convicted for a moving violation, and that he did not use alcoholic beverages. In fact, Johnny had a number of convictions for traffic violations, forgery, and drunkenness. The company issued the policy, and Johnny's car was later involved in an accident. Johnny was not driving the car at the time of the accident. May the company cancel the policy and avoid liability because of Johnny's false statement?

Decision

The company is not liable.

Reasoning

Johnny's misrepresentations were material to the risk. Consequently the policy was void.

Countryside Casualty Co. v. Orr, 523 F.2d 870 (1975).

Concealment

Concealment occurs when the insured intentionally fails to disclose a *material fact* to the insurer. Generally the insured must disclose material facts and may not recover on the policy if such facts were concealed with the intention of defrauding the company. In the following case, the information not disclosed by the insured was material to the insurer's decision to insure.

Secured Transactions, Insurance, and Bankruptcy

Facts

A husband was listed as the beneficiary in a $25,000 life insurance policy on his wife. When the policy was originally issued, the wife failed to disclose the *name* of her psychiatrist and, shortly after applying for the insurance, she was hospitalized for severe depression. The wife died two years after the policy was issued, and the husband's right to collect on the policy was questioned by the company, which sought to rescind the policy.

Decision

The husband may not collect on the policy.

Reasoning

The court decided that the *name* of the psychiatrist was *material* to the company's decision whether to issue the policy, especially since the psychiatrist treated the wife for depression and alcoholism.

Massachusetts Mutual Life Insurance Company v. Tate, 369 N.E.2d 767 (N.Y. 1977).

Summary Statement

1. There are several types of insurance that directly affect the average person. Among the most important types are life insurance, homeowner's insurance, and automobile insurance.
2. Insurance is generally defined as a contract where one party agrees to pay another party for specified losses.
3. Under the federal McCarran-Ferguson Act, the regulation of the insurance business is primarily a matter for individual states.
4. An insured person must have an insurable interest in the risk covered by the contract to acquire insurance.
5. For life insurance, the insured must have an insurable interest in the insured life at the time the contract is formed; while for property insurance, the insured must have an insurable interest in the property at the time of property loss.
6. In most cases an insurance company can not raise a warranty or representation as a defense unless the statement was material to its decision whether to issue the policy.

The following case illustrates the application of the legal rules regarding misrepresentation by an applicant for insurance.

Vaughn v. American National Insurance Company
543 P.2d 1404 (Okla. 1975)

Lavender, Justice: Action brought by beneficiary on life insurance policy providing coverage of $5,000 as to ordinary life and an additional coverage of $5,000 for accidental death. The insured, Marvin Edward Vaughn, was the son of the beneficiary, Wanda Mae Vaughn. She was the plaintiff. April 4, 1972, the insured died from an automobile accident. It was an accidental death. American National Insurance Company (insurer) refused coverage on its life policy based on misrepresentations found in the application. By cross-petition, insurer sought cancellation of its policy. Trial court rendered judgment for insurer on its cross-petition to rescind. Court of Appeals reversed the judgment of rescission.

The application for insurance was taken from Marvin Vaughn October 19, 1971. American's agent filled in the application from information and answers to the questions given to the agent by Marvin Vaughn. Vaughn then signed the application. Material to this action are the following questions and answers. . . .

15. State name and address of family physician, specialist or clinic for principal proposed insured:
Name: Dr. D.R.
Address: 1217 N. Shartel, Oklahoma City
Date last seen: May 1968
Reason: Pencillin shot—flu . . .

19. Has any proposed insured . . .

(f) Ever been under observation or treatment in any hospital, sanitarium, clinic, or rest home?

	Yes	No
	( )	(X)

. . .

(j) Consulted or been treated or examined by any physician or practitioner for any cause not previously mentioned in this application?

	Yes	No
	( )	(X)

. . .

As a part of the application, a medical authorization (to receive any and all information about the applicant with reference to health and medical history and as to any hospitalization, advice, diagnosis, treatment, disease or ailment) was given by the applicant to the insurance company.

In an investigation by the insurer upon the filing of a claim under the policy by the beneficiary after her son's death, it was determined:

The family physician, Dr. R., hospitalized deceased in Deaconess Hospital for "post natural gas inhalation" complications on June 6, 1967. That physician consulted with Dr. W., a psychiatrist. Deceased was transferred to the psychiatric ward at Baptist Hospital, where he was treated for depression until discharged by Dr. W. on June 24, 1967.

Because of these established facts, both the trial court and the Court of Appeals found the answers to questions 19(f) and (j) were false.

The Court of Appeals holds the insurer should be charged with knowledge of applicant's mental and emotional problems for it (1) knew the applicant had a family physician, (2) knew that physician's identity, and (3) had authority from the applicant to secure his medical information. That court excused the false answers because applicant had freely given his family physician's name in the application. The false answers are excused because the applicant was not familiar with the underwriting requirement of the defendant. He did not know what to reveal and what to conceal.

The rationale for the Court of Appeals' holding is based on "actual notice" as defined in *Creek Land & Improvement Co. v. Davis*. . . .

The words "actual notice" do not always mean in law what in metaphysical strictness they import. They more often mean knowledge of facts and circumstances sufficiently pertinent in character to enable reasonably cautious and prudent persons to investigate and ascertain as to the ultimate facts.

We do not agree the knowledge gained in the answers to the questions contained in the application was "knowledge of facts and circumstances sufficiently pertinent in character for reasonably cautious and prudent persons to investigate and ascertain as to the ultimate facts." Applicant's answer to question 15 revealed the applicant had a family physician in 1968 and who he was. That revealed fact was tempered with the circumstance or reason for the last visit of May, 1968, "penicillin shot—flu." By answers to questions 19(f) and (j), the application gave knowledge of (1) no observation or treatment in any hospital, sanitarium, or clinic and (2) no consultation, treatment, or examination by any physician for any cause other than a penicillin shot for flu. Those revealed facts were false. The insurer was not alerted by the revealed information in the application so as to investigate and ascertain the ultimate fact that the applicant had a history of an emotional problem. The insurer was lulled into complacency by false answers. The agent had no "actual knowledge" to be imputed over to the insurer as "imputed knowledge" as applied by the Court of Appeals.

Under 36 O.S. 1971, section 3609 misrepresentations, omissions, concealment of facts, and incorrect statements in the application for insurance prevent recovery under the policy if (1) fraudulent; or (2) material to the acceptance of the risk; or (3) the insurer in good faith would not have issued the policy, or in as large an amount, if the true facts had been made known as required by the application.

In *Massachusetts Mutual Life Ins. Co. v. Allen* . . . this court said:

A "misrepresentation" in negotiations for a life insurance policy under 36 O.S. 1961, section 3609, is a statement as a fact of something which is untrue, and which the insured knows or should know is untrue . . . and which has a tendency to mislead, where such misrepresentation is material to the risk.

The false information given by the applicant in the application of his not being hospitalized and of no consultation or treatment by a physician, except for flu, concealed from the insurer true facts. These true facts, if revealed, would have given the insurer knowledge requiring a prudent insurer to investigate and would have led to the discovery of applicant's prior emotional problems.

We hold that false information was a misrepresentation. That misrepresentation was material to the acceptance of the risk on the life of the applicant. The insurer is entitled to a judgment of rescission.

Decision of the Court of Appeals vacated and judgment of the trial court affirmed.

Questions and Case Problems

1. A home appliance service company sold plans to homeowners who were planning to sell their homes. Under the plans the company performed a check on the appliances in the home and agreed to repair the appliances during a one-year period if the home buyer experienced problems with them. Is this plan a contract of insurance? [Opinion No. 78-20 of the New Mexico Attorney General, October 4, 1978.]

2. In question 1, would the plan be considered a contract of insurance if it was offered as a guaranty by the appliance manufacturers? Would the plan be insurance if the service company obligated itself to inspect and repair the appliances on a regular basis? Why?

3. Nancy purchased a life insurance policy from Friendly Mutual Insurance Company. Nancy now is trying to discover who owns the company so that, if the company fails, she will know where to look in order to recover the cash value of her policy. Who owns Nancy's company? Are the owners liable? Why?

4. Mary purchased an insurance policy on the life of her husband, Steve, in the amount of $600,000. Mary and Steve were later divorced, but Mary continued to pay premiums on the insurance policy. Later, when Steve died, the company refused to pay Mary on the grounds that (1) she had no insurable interest in Steve's life because of the divorce or (2) if she did have an insurable interest, its value was only $300,000 as determined by the size of Steve's alimony payments and his life expectancy. Is the company correct on either of these grounds? Why?

5. One week before he reached the age of majority, a minor made a down payment on an automobile and was given a receipt by the car dealer. He immediately applied for car registration, and his father applied for insurance as the owner of the car. Before the policy was issued to the father, the son reached the age of majority. After the policy was issued, the car was involved in an accident and the company denied coverage on the grounds that the insured—the father—had no insurable interest. Is the company correct? [*DiGerolamo v. Liberty Mutual Insurance Company*, 355 So.2d 622 (La. 1978).]

6. An automobile that had been stolen in Ohio was sold to an innocent purchaser in Alabama. The purchaser bought an automobile insurance policy on the car, including fire and theft coverage. The car was later stolen from the purchaser and was destroyed by fire. The insurance company claimed that the purchaser was not entitled to collect on the policy because he had no insurable interest in the car. Is the company correct? Why? [Ex parte *Granite State Insurance Company v. Lowe*, 362 So.2d 240 (Ala. 1978).]

7. A mortgage company obtained a mortgage on real estate and purchased fire insurance on the property. The company immediately assigned the mortgage to the Federal National Mortgage Association (FNMA) and promised FNMA to maintain insurance on the property. When the property was later destroyed by fire, the insurance company refused to pay for the loss, claiming that the mortgage company had no insurable interest. Is the insurer correct? [*Capital Mortgage Corporation v. Michigan Basic Property Insurance Assoc.*, 261 N.W. 2d 5 (Mich. 1977).]

8. A woman who was covered by a health insurance policy fell from a horse and suffered serious skull and brain injuries. As a result, the woman had to undergo surgery and therapy, which were paid for by the insurer. The insurer later sent the woman a life insurance application, which was completed and returned to the insurer. On the application it was stated that the woman had received head injuries but had recovered. The insurer issued the policy and shortly thereafter the woman died after undergoing another skull operation. The company claimed that it was not liable on the policy because of the misrepresentation. The beneficiary claimed that the company was liable

because it knew of the woman's condition, having made payments under the health insurance policy. Who is correct? [*Murray v. Montgomery Ward Life Insurance Company,* 563 P.2d 20 (Colo. 1977).]

9. Arthur, in completing an insurance application, answered "no" to the following question: "Have you ever had or been told by a physician or other practitioner that you had . . . heart trouble?" In fact, Arthur had been told—and had been treated for a heart condition. When Arthur died, the company refused to pay the insurance proceeds to Arthur's widow. May the widow recover the proceeds? Why? [*Weeser v. Provident Mutual Life Ins. Co.,* 322 So.2d 230 (La. 1975).]

10. In the case of *Vaughn v. American National Insurance Company,* 543 P.2d 1404 (Okla. 1975),[3] would the decision have been different if the court had concluded that the applicant's answers in the application were warranties rather than representations? Why?

---

[3] Scc pp. 907–8.

51

Life, Fire, and Automobile Insurance Law

After you have read this chapter, you should be able to:

1. Describe the three most common types of life insurance and explain their coverages.
2. Discuss the legal effect of a conditional receipt.
3. Define the term "incontestability" as it is used in an insurance contract.
4. List the types of homeowner's insurance policy forms and explain their coverages.
5. Compare traditional and no-fault automobile insurance.

Introduction

In chapter 50 we examined the general principles of insurance law, including the different types of insurance, the definition of insurance, the methods of organization used by insurers, insurance regulation, the concept of insurable interest, and various defenses used by insurers. In this chapter we will focus on the three most important types of insurance for the average person: (1) life insurance, (2) homeowner's insurance, and (3) automobile insurance.

Life Insurance

Types of Life Insurance

There are three general types of life insurance policies. **Term insurance** is insurance sold for a specified time period. If the person dies within the time period, the company will pay the face value of the policy. If the insured does not die within the term, the insurance terminates and the company usually has the right to keep all premiums—i.e., there is no cash value. Term policies are "level term" when the policy value remains the same throughout the life of the policy, and they are "decreasing term" when the face value decreases as the policy termination date approaches. Term policies may also be convertible to whole life insurance or may include a right to renew the policy without proof of insurability. Term life insurance is especially popular with young married couples because it is the cheapest type of insurance and can provide insurance for a term long enough to cover the family in the event the breadwinner dies before the mortgage on the family home is paid off or before the children graduate from college or otherwise get started in life.

term insurance
insurance sold for a specified time period, with no cash value

Whole life insurance (sometimes called straight life, ordinary life, or permanent life insurance) provides coverage throughout the life of the insured. Whole life insurance includes cash values which build up through the years. The policyholder is entitled to borrow money from the company up to the cash value or to turn in the policy to the insurance company for cash.

whole life insurance
insurance for the entire life of the insured, with cash values that increase through the years

Endowment insurance is insurance that pays the policyholder a lump sum of money at a date specified in the policy. If the insured person dies before that date, the money is paid to the beneficiary at death. This type of policy is popular with persons who will need a large sum of money at a future date—e.g., for college expenses or retirement.

endowment insurance
insurance that pays the policyholder a lump sum at a specified date

An insurance policy might be a combination of some of the above three types of insurance. For instance, in recent years companies have developed "adjustable life" insurance that combines term and whole life insurance. With adjustable life, the amount of coverage and the premiums can be raised or lowered to meet changes in insurance needs resulting from births, deaths, marriages, and other events. For example, if a policyholder becomes a father, he might want to increase his term coverage but shorten the length of the term to reduce expenses. Or if the policyholder receives a substantial raise, he might want to convert his term policy to whole life which, although more expensive, can be cashed in at a later date.

Settlement Options

When the insured party dies, the beneficiary might decide to receive a lump sum payment. However, most policies give the beneficiary at least three optional methods of settling with the company. First, the lump sum might be left on deposit, with the company to pay a specified annual interest rate. Second, the beneficiary might elect to receive periodic income from the proceeds for a specified number of years. Third, the beneficiary may elect to receive a lifetime annuity—equal monthly payments for life, with a certain number of payments guaranteed in the event the insured dies in the early years of the annuity.

Conditional Receipts

There is often a time gap between the application for life insurance and the approval of the application by the insurer. This is because life insurance represents a long-term, potentially costly commitment on the part of the insurer, and the insurer will normally require the applicant to undergo a medical examination before approving the policy. However, most applicants want coverage during this time gap in the event that something should happen after the application date. And it is to the company's advantage to provide coverage during the gap as a means of preventing the applicant from changing his mind. The **conditional receipt** has been developed to meet these needs.

conditional receipt
a receipt that provides an applicant for life insurance with temporary coverage until the application is approved by the company

Although conditional receipts vary in form, the most common type of receipt provides that coverage is effective on the date of application unless the company determines that the applicant was not an acceptable or insurable risk according to company rules and standards on that date. If, under company rules and standards, the applicant is considered insurable, there is coverage even when the applicant dies before company approval of the policy, as is illustrated by the following case.

Facts
On March 14, 1974 a man applied for a $125,000 life insurance policy. He paid the first month's premium and was given a conditional receipt stating that he was covered immediately if the company was satisfied that he was insurable on that date. The next day he was examined by a physician who recommended the man as a first class risk. On March 19, before the application reached the home office, the man was killed in an automobile accident. The company refused coverage.

Decision
The company was wrong in refusing coverage.

Reasoning
The court concluded, on the basis of expert testimony, that the man was an insurable risk on March 14. Consequently there was coverage under the conditional receipt.

Vernon v. Provident Life & Accident Ins. Co., 222 S.E.2d 501 (S.C. 1976).

Incontestability

Let us assume that Clyde purchased a life insurance policy naming his wife as beneficiary. Clyde died after the policy had been in effect for nine years. After his death the company refused coverage, claiming that Clyde had lied about his health on the application. The company's refusal obviously puts the beneficiary in a difficult position; it will be hard to prove what Clyde's health was nine years ago, and the person best able to testify, Clyde, is dead. To avoid undue burden on beneficiaries, state law usually requires insurance companies to include an **incontestability clause** in life insurance policies. This clause provides that the company may not contest the coverage, except for non-payment of premiums, after the policy has been in effect for a stated time period, usually one or two years.

incontestability clause
a clause in a life insurance policy providing that the company may not contest coverage after the policy has been in effect for a stated time period

Suicide

Life insurance policies usually contain a clause stating that if the insured commits suicide within a certain period (e.g., two years) from the date the policy was issued, the company is not liable. Such clauses are upheld by the courts, which have decided that the public policy of enforcing the contract and providing for the beneficiary outweighs the public policy of discouraging suicide. Furthermore, when death occurs within the two-year period, there is a presumption that the death was not a suicide. In the following case it was held that suicide did not occur because the death was not intentional.

Facts

A twenty-year-old Marine served in a fighter squadron as a radar technician. He was familiar with .45 calibre automatic pistols and had given instructions on their use. The Marine was a happy-go-lucky, cheerful person who sometimes tried to "shake up" his friends by placing a .45 to his head and pulling the trigger. One day when the Marine was apparently in good spirits, he suddenly put a pistol to his head, said "Here's to it" to a friend, and pulled the trigger. The gun fired, killing the Marine. The insurance company that insured him claimed this was a suicide.

Decision

The death is not a suicide.

Reasoning

The company must prove that the death was intentional. The burden of proof was not met here.

Angelus v. Government Personnel Life Ins. Co., 321 P.2d 545 (Wash. 1958).

Beneficiaries

The **beneficiary** in an insurance policy is the person designated to receive the death benefit after the person dies. Most policies provide for the designation of second beneficiaries, who will take the death benefit if the first beneficiary is not alive when the insured dies.

beneficiary
the person designated in a life insurance policy to receive the death benefit

Although, as a general rule, contract rights of a third party beneficiary can not be altered, the insurance contract is an exception to this rule. In most policies the contract stipulates that the policy owner can change the beneficiary by following a procedure set forth in the policy. The change of beneficiary is usually not effective unless the company records the change at its home office.

As a general rule under common law, a person will not be allowed to benefit from his own wrongful act. As applied to the insurance contract, this rule means that a beneficiary who murders the insured can not recover on the insurance policy. In the following case the court discussed profiting from one's wrong as precluding recovery on a life insurance policy.

Facts

Ruby was the beneficiary of her husband's insurance policy. Ruby allegedly killed her husband and pleaded guilty to manslaughter. However, she later withdrew her plea and was acquitted by a jury when she was tried for second degree murder. Ruby claims that because of the acquittal she is entitled to collect on the policy.

Decision

Ruby's acquittal does not automatically entitle her to the proceeds.

Reasoning

The beneficiary can not profit from her own wrongful act. In determining whether Ruby intentionally killed her husband, the criminal trial is irrelevant because it involves a different standard of proof (beyond a reasonable doubt) from that used in a civil trial (preponderance of the evidence).

Carter v. Carter, 88 So.2d 153 (Fla. 1956).

Homeowner's Insurance

The purchase of a house represents the largest investment ever made by most individuals. Consequently, it is extremely important that this investment is protected with the proper insurance coverage. Most homeowner's policies today represent a package of property and liability coverages.

Policy Forms

Four types of policy forms are commonly used today. The *Basic Form* provides protection for eleven types of perils, including fire, windstorm, hail, explosion, and vandalism. The *Broad Form* policy, probably the most popular policy, adds coverage for five additional perils: (1) the weight of ice and snow, (2) the collapse of a building, (3) accidents from steam or water systems, (4) accidents from electrical equipment, and (5) falling objects such as trees. The *Comprehensive Form* is "all-risk" coverage; that is, all perils are covered with very few exceptions, such as earthquake, tidal waves, war, and nuclear radiation. Finally, a *Special Form* provides Comprehensive Form coverage on the real estate and Broad Form coverage on personal property.

Property Coverage

Three types of property are covered by a homeowner's policy. First, of course, the *dwelling* itself is protected from loss by the above perils. Second, *appurtenant structures* such as a garage or storage sheds are normally covered for an amount equal to ten percent of the coverage on the dwelling. Third, *personal property* such as furniture, clothing, and jewelry is normally covered up to an amount equal to fifty percent of the coverage on the dwelling.

In addition to these property coverages, the standard policy will provide an **additional living expense** in an amount up to twenty percent of the coverage on the dwelling. This is used to cover living expenses incurred by a homeowner who is forced to leave his home while repairs are being made.

Liability Coverage

The standard homeowner's policy includes comprehensive **personal liability coverage.** Most individuals are protected under their automobile insurance policies if they injure someone while driving a car. However, many accidents are not caused by the use of an automobile. For example, if Sam is playing golf and hits another player with a ball, or if a visitor slips on the carpet in Sam's house, Sam might be liable for substantial damages. The personal liability coverage protects the homeowner in the event such claims are made.

As additional protection, the standard homeowner's policy will pay reasonable medical expenses to persons injured in the house or as a result of the insured's activities away from the house. For example, if Charley slipped on the sidewalk when visiting Sam's house, the policy would pay Charley's medical expenses up to a certain amount, even though Sam was not legally responsible for the accident.

Exclusions

The standard homeowner's policy contains certain express exclusions from both property and liability coverage. Examples of exclusions from *property coverage* are losses resulting from volcanic eruptions, earthquakes, landslides, floods, and water that backs up through sewers. Exclusions from *liability coverage* include losses covered by workers' compensation laws; liability resulting from the use of aircraft, motor vehicles, and watercraft; and liability resulting from business pursuits.

In addition to the express exclusions from coverage, certain exceptions from coverage will be implied by the courts. A "friendly fire" exception occurred in the following case.

Facts

A woman wrapped her star sapphire ring in a handkerchief and placed it on her dresser with some Kleenex tissue. Her maid later inadvertently threw the Kleenex and the handkerchief into a wastebasket. Another servant then emptied the wastebasket into a trash burner and burned the trash. The ring, which was later discovered in the trash burner, was damaged to the extent of $900. The woman claimed that her homeowner's policy covered the loss because personal property was insured "against all direct loss or damage by fire."

additional living expense
a homeowner's insurance policy provision that covers living expenses incurred by a homeowner forced to leave the home while repairs are being made

personal liability coverage
a homeowner's insurance policy provision covering liability for accidents on or away from the insured property

Decision

This loss is not covered.

Reasoning

There is an implied exception in homeowner's policies for "friendly fires." Friendly fires are those lighted and contained in a usual place for fire such as a fireplace, an incinerator, or a trash burner.

Youse v. Employers Fire Ins. Co., Boston, Mass., 238 P.2d 472 (Kan. 1951).

Replacement Cost or Coinsurance

Many homeowner's policies contain a provision that may trap an unsuspecting homeowner and result in a loss of thousands of dollars in coverage. This is a provision that requires a homeowner to carry insurance equal to a certain percentage (usually eighty percent) of the full replacement cost of the house. If the owner meets the eighty percent requirement, he is covered for the full cost of the replacement up to the amount of coverage. If the coverage is less than eighty percent, then the homeowner receives the larger of: (1) the actual cash value of the part of the building damaged, or (2) the proportion of the replacement cost which the amount of insurance coverage bears to the required eighty percent of the full replacement cost.

To illustrate, we might assume that Betty purchases for $50,000 an old Victorian home which would cost $75,000 to replace. In order to save premiums, Betty purchased only $30,000 in coverage. If the roof of the house, which had an actual cash value of $500 but which would cost $2,000 to replace, is destroyed by fire, how much can Betty collect? Betty obviously has coverage less than eighty percent of the full replacement cost ($75,000) of the house. Therefore, she can only recover the larger of (1) the actual cash value of the roof ($500), or (2) the proportion of the replacement cost ($2,000) that the insurance ($30,000) bears to eighty percent of the full replacement cost ($60,000). Thus, Betty would recover only $1,000, figured as follows: $\frac{30,000}{60,000} \times 2,000 = \$1,000$.

She would have to pay the other $1,000 required to replace the roof out of her own pocket—i.e., she would become a "co-insurer" for part of the loss.

Automobile Insurance

According to the Insurance Information Institute, during every ten minutes in the year 1975, there were 473 automobile accidents in the United States, which injured 95 persons and killed one person. There are two basic automobile insurance mechanisms in our country to cover injuries and property damage resulting from such accidents: traditional automobile insurance, and no-fault automobile insurance.

Traditional Automobile Insurance

Traditional automobile insurance is a package of four basic types of coverages. *First,* and probably most important, the policy provides **liability insurance** which covers you for damages you might have to pay if you injure someone or damage

Types of automobile insurance.

automobile liability insurance
insurance that covers a driver who injures someone, or damages someone's property, in an automobile accident

someone's property in an automobile accident. The liability coverage insures not only the named insured and residents of his household, but also other persons using the automobile with the permission of the named insured. This coverage for "permittees" often raises complex legal issues, as is illustrated in the following case.

Facts

Hartford issued an automobile insurance policy to Zylka. The policy provided liability coverage for any person using the car with Zylka's permission. Zylka gave permission to her son Michael to use the car when he returned home from college for summer vacation. She told Michael not to let anyone else use the car. Michael let his friend Douglas use the car to pick up a date. Douglas was involved in an automobile accident and several persons sued him. Douglas claimed he was covered by the Hartford policy.

Decision

Douglas is covered.

Reasoning

Although courts are not in agreement, this court adopted an "initial permission" rule. Under this rule, if a person (here Michael) has permission to use an automobile, there is coverage even though he deviates from the scope of the permission or allows another person to use the car.

Odolecki v. Hartford Acc. & Indem. Co., 264 A.2d 38 (N.J. 1970).

The *second* basic coverage is for *medical payments,* including all reasonable expenses for medical, surgical, and hospital services incurred within one year from the date of the accident. Covered persons include the named insured, relatives, and guests riding in the automobile.

The *third* basic coverage provides insurance for *physical damage to the automobile.* Most automobile owners purchase two types of property insurance. **Collision insurance** pays for damage to the insured automobile when it is involved in a collision. **Comprehensive insurance** covers damage to the insured automobile resulting from causes other than collision, such as falling objects, fire, theft, explosion, earthquake, windstorm, hail, flood, or riot. Both collision and comprehensive insurance are often sold with a deductible—e.g., $100. This means that if there is physical damage to the automobile, the owner pays the first $100 and the company pays losses above that amount.

The *fourth and last type* of basic coverage is *uninsured motorist* coverage. It is possible that the insured owner of an automobile, member of his family, or guests in the automobile might be injured in an accident caused by a person who does not have liability insurance as required by law or who is a "hit and run" driver. In such cases **uninsured motorists coverage** pays all sums which the insured is entitled to recover for bodily injury caused by the accident. A "hit and run" accident is defined as one in which there is physical contact between the automobiles at the time of the accident and the identity of the other driver can not be determined. In the following case, no such physical contact occurred.

collision insurance
insurance covering damage to the insured automobile resulting from a collision

comprehensive insurance
insurance covering damage to the insured automobile resulting from causes other than collision

uninsured motorist coverage
insurance that pays all sums that the insured is entitled to recover when he is injured by an uninsured or a "hit and run" driver

An unidentified car stopped suddenly at an intersection. This caused the following car to stop abruptly and a motorcycle to run into the following car. The motorcyclist claimed that he was entitled to recover under the uninsured motorist coverage in his insurance policy.

Decision

The motorcyclist is not covered.

Reasoning

This was not a hit and run accident, and consequently the motorist can not recover. There was no physical contact between the motorcycle and the unidentified first vehicle.

Hensley v. Government Employees Insurance Company, 340 So.2d 603 (La. 1976).

No-Fault Automobile Insurance

No-fault automobile insurance has been enacted in one form or another in approximately half of the states and now covers over half the population of the United States. Since the first no-fault statute was enacted in Massachusetts, effective January 1, 1971, appellate courts in a number of states have approved the no-fault concept and have declared it to be constitutional.

The basic no-fault concept is simple, although the details may vary, depending on the state. No-fault, in essence, gives the victim of an automobile accident the right to be paid by his own insurance policy for *personal injury,* no matter who caused the loss (personal injury protection). But no-fault laws also take away the right to sue the person who caused the accident. The net result is that to recover under no-fault you no longer must prove that another person is "at fault."

To illustrate no-fault, we might assume that twins, Jack and Jill, are involved in similar automobile accidents. In both cases the cars driven by Jack and Jill are rear-ended by careless drivers and their cars, worth $2,000, are totally destroyed. Both Jack and Jill suffer broken right legs and their out-of-pocket losses total $4,000 for medical care and $3,000 in lost wages. The only difference is that Jack is injured in Detroit and, as a Michigan resident, is covered by the most liberal no-fault law in the United States. Jill, an Ohio resident, is injured a few miles south of Detroit in Toledo and is not covered by no-fault.

Advantages of no-fault insurance.

Under the Michigan no-fault system, the victim of an automobile accident is entitled to recover from his own insurance company all charges for medical and hospital care and lost wages for up to three years. In addition to this *required* coverage, a driver has the option, also available in states without no-fault, of purchasing collision coverage for his car. In our case, Jack would immediately collect from his company $4,000 for medical care, $3,000 for lost wages and, if he had purchased enough optional collision coverage, $2,000 for the car.

Disadvantages of no-fault insurance.

But in no-fault states like Michigan, a victim can not sue the person who caused the accident unless the damages are greater than the benefits provided under the law (or unless the victim dies, his bodily functions are seriously impaired, or he is seriously disfigured). Thus, in our case, Jack can not sue the other driver and will receive no compensation for his pain and suffering. Also,

Secured Transactions, Insurance, and Bankruptcy

if he has no collision coverage, he will recover nothing from the other driver for the damage to his car.

Jill, living in a state without no-fault, could recover the value of her car and at least part of the cost of medical care from her own insurance company if she had elected to include these coverages. But even if she had no insurance coverage, she could sue the other driver and might recover not only her out-of-pocket losses, but also a substantial amount for pain and suffering. According to one study, the amount paid in the average settlement is 2.4 times the amount of actual loss, or in this case $21,600.

Advantages of the "fault" system of insurance.

Consequently, if neither Jack nor Jill had purchased collision coverage, Jack would be limited to a total of $7,000 under no-fault, which he can collect only from his own company, while Jill might recover $21,600 from the person who caused the accident.

However, is Jill really in a better position than Jack? Under the *fault* system, in order to recover from the other driver, Jill must prove that the other driver is at fault. If we assume that this can be proven, in many states Jill will still recover nothing if the other driver proves that Jill's own carelessness contributed in even a small way to the accident. Regardless of the final outcome, Jill will have to wait more than five years in some metropolitan areas for her case to come to trial, and in the meantime must pay her own bills. And, if Jill wins the case, it is possible that as much as fifty percent of her recovery will be used for attorney's fees and related costs. It is considerations such as these that have caused Congress and the states without no-fault to continue the debate as to whether no-fault systems should be adopted.

Disadvantages of the "fault" system of insurance.

New Trends

In this chapter and in chapter 50, we have examined the general principles of insurance law and the three types of insurance most important to the average person. As these chapters illustrate, the insurance contract is not only unique but is also often complicated—in fact, often too complicated for the average person to understand. However, two trends have developed in recent years to protect insureds from companies who might try to insert "fine print" clauses in insurance contracts in order to avoid liability.

First, state insurance commissioners in several states have adopted regulations requiring certain types of policies to be readable. For example, the purpose of the Pennsylvania regulation, section 64.1, "is an auto insurance policy that is understandable to a person of average intelligence and education." To carry out this purpose, the regulations require the use of a certain size type, short sentences, and simple words.

Second, courts in several states have developed the doctrine of reasonable expectations to protect the insurance consumer. Under this rule, a person who has reasonable expectations that he is covered by an insurance policy will, in fact, be covered—even though he did not read the policy and the fine print of the policy denies coverage. This is illustrated in the following case.

Facts

Richard applied for a $25,000 life insurance policy from Prudential, paid the first quarterly premium, and was given a conditional receipt. Richard did not appear for a required physical examination and died seven weeks after applying for the insurance. Prudential denied recovery on the grounds that the conditional receipt covered Richard only if he was an insurable risk, and he could not be considered insurable without a physical examination.

Decision

Richard is covered.

Reasoning

Although Prudential is correct under normal principles of contract law, the insurance contract (including the conditional receipt) is unique. Here Richard is covered because he had reason to believe that he was insured.

Prudential Insurance Company of America v. Lamme, 425 P.2d 346 (Nev. 1967).

Summary Statement

1. The three most common types of life insurance are term insurance, whole life insurance, and endowment insurance.
2. A conditional receipt is used to provide insurance coverage between the date of application and the date the company approves the policy, provided that the applicant was insurable on the application date.
3. The incontestability clause in life insurance policies prevents the company from contesting coverage after the policy has been in effect for a specified time, normally one or two years.
4. There are four common types of homeowner's insurance. The most popular type is the Broad Form, which provides coverage for sixteen specific perils.
5. Traditional automobile insurance is a package of four coverages: liability, medical payments, property, and uninsured motorist.
6. With automobile no-fault insurance, a person injured in an automobile accident is compensated by his own insurance company and, in most cases, can not sue the person who caused the accident.

The following case illustrates the problems faced by a person who is injured by an uninsured motorist—even when there is uninsured motorist coverage.

Taft v. Sweeney
373 A.2d 712 (N.J. 1977)

Per Curiam. At issue in this appeal is the availability of Uninsured Motorists coverage (UM) issued to plaintiff as a source of compensation for injuries he received in an automobile accident where the total proceeds of the liability policy insuring the culpable defendant to the statutory minimum has been tendered to and accepted by plaintiff. Plaintiff contends that since the value of the injuries received in the accident exceeds the amount of liability coverage available, defendant must be regarded as uninsured to the extent of such excess and he is therefore entitled to tap his UM coverage for the excess. The trial judge granted the motion for summary judgment interposed by Safeco Insurance Company, the carrier which provided the UM coverage. This appeal ensued. We affirm.

The facts of the underlying accident and the available insurance policies are not complex. On September 29, 1974 an automobile driven by plaintiff collided with defendant Sweeney's automobile. There seems little doubt but that the collision was caused by the negligence of Sweeney, who was charged with operating his vehicle while under the influence of alcohol and subsequently pleaded guilty to the charge. At the time of the accident Sweeney was insured by defendant Transamerica Insurance Company through a liability policy which limited coverage to $15,000 per person and $30,000 maximum for each accident, the minimum amounts required by N.J.S.A. 39:6B-1. . . .

Fundamental to the issue raised in this appeal is the meaning to be attributed to the word "uninsured" in N.J.S.A. 17:28-1.1 which sets forth the requirement for uninsured motorists coverage. It reads as follows:

> No automobile liability policy . . . of insurance . . . shall be issued in this State . . . unless it includes coverage, in limits for bodily injury or death as follows:
> a. an amount or limit of $15,000, exclusive of interest and costs, on account of injury to, or death of, one person, in any one accident . . .
> . . . for payment of all or part of the sums which the insured . . . shall be legally entitled to recover as damages from the operator or owner of an *uninsured* automobile, or hit and run automobile. . . . [Emphasis added.]

The coverage afforded by the policy in question is consistent with the foregoing statutory requirements. Hence, it is clear that that coverage afforded is triggered by the insured's accident with an "uninsured" automobile.

This essential element of uninsured motorists coverage is not tainted by ambiguity. Such coverage becomes available only when the insured is injured by an uninsured motor vehicle or a hit and run automobile. Neither is involved in this case.

Defendant Sweeney was insured to the statutory minimum. Nothing in N.J.S.A. 17:28-1.1 suggests that UM coverage is to be made available as excess insurance whenever a liability policy, meeting the statutory minimum limits of coverage, proves an inadequate source of compensation to the injured insured. The essential requirement for such coverage is lack of insurance, not inadequate insurance.

Neither of the two cases cited by plaintiff supports his contentions. *Motor Club of America Ins. Co. v. Phillips* . . . held that a person injured by an uninsured motorist is entitled to UM coverage under more than one policy affording him such coverage. Basic to that holding, however, is the fact that the insured was injured by an uninsured motorist. In this case plaintiff's injuries were caused by an insured motorist. *Gorton v. Reliance Ins. Co.* . . . held that each of several injured plaintiffs could recover under his own uninsured motorists coverage the difference between the amounts received under the defendant tortfeasor's liability policy and the existing statutory limit for bodily injury or death. In this case, however, plaintiff has received the full statutory limit from Sweeney's liability carrier. *Gorton* has no application to this case.

The statutory scheme is clear. The Legislature intended . . . to guarantee to each person injured by an automobile in this State an available source of reparation for the injuries received up to the statutory minimum. . . . That goal has been achieved in this case.

Affirmed.

Questions and Case Problems

1. Tom and Mary, a young married couple, have just purchased their first home after obtaining a twenty-year mortgage from First Bank. Tom and Mary both work and need their incomes to make the mortgage payments. However, they are afraid that if one of them should die, the other would be unable to make the payments. What type of insurance protection would you recommend for Tom and Mary? Why?

2. An attorney represented an engineering company for a fee of $300 a month and was provided coverage under the company's group life insurance plan. Although the engineering company did not withhold taxes for the attorney and she was not listed on the payroll, the company did send a letter to the insurer listing her as an employee. However, the attorney did not meet the definition of employee within the policy because she was not employed on a full-time basis. The attorney died after the policy had been in effect for two years, and the insurer refused to pay the beneficiary. Must the insurer pay? Why? [*Bonitz v. Travelers Insurance Company,* 372 N.E.2d 254 (Mass. 1978).]

3. A life insurance company issued a policy on Edward's life. One day Edward's wife, Angela, discovered Edward dead in their bedroom. Edward had been shot in the temple, but there was no evidence that he had held the murder weapon. Angela was charged with murder but acquitted. The insurance company claimed that Angela was not entitled to the proceeds because this was a suicide within two years of the date of the policy. Is the company correct? [*Lincoln Income Life Ins. Co. v. Parker,* 224 S.E.2d 781 (Ga. 1976).]

4. An insured owned a life insurance policy which named certain beneficiaries. The insured executed a will in which he provided that persons other than the named beneficiaries were to receive the insurance proceeds. He died the day after signing the will. Who should receive the proceeds—the beneficiaries named in the will or the beneficiaries named in the policy? [*Pena v. Salinas,* 536 S.W.2d 671 (Tex. 1976).]

5. A homeowner (with homeowner's liability insurance coverage) worked at a research center. One of his duties at the center was to take care of a wolf named Sophie and, in order to fulfill this duty, he kept Sophie at his home. One day while at the home Sophie bit a child. The insurance company claimed that the homeowner had no liability coverage for the bite. Is the company correct? Why? [*North River Insurance Company v. Poos,* 553 S.W.2d 500 (Mo. 1977).]

6. Mac recently purchased a home for $50,000. His homeowner's insurance policy contains a standard eighty percent replacement cost clause. Mac has purchased $40,000 worth of coverage because he thinks that if he does not have at least eighty percent of the home's value covered he can recover only eighty percent of any losses. Is Mac correct? Why?

7. A truck driver, in making a delivery of goods, learned that the goods could not be unloaded for a couple of days. He unhitched the trailer and on the following day picked up several strangers and began to visit a number of local bars. After he had around nine beers, the driver drove the truck into a utility pole,

which caught fire and damaged a school. The company that insured the owner of the truck claimed that there was no coverage. Is the company correct? [*Louisville Gas and Electric Company v. Employer's Mutual Liability Insurance Co.*, 548 S.W.2d 843 (Ky. 1977).]

8. William owned a 1977 Plymouth. He allowed his son Robert to use the car but instructed Robert not to let anyone else drive the car. One night Robert used the car to drive two friends to a particular destination. When they were ready to leave, Robert's friends went to the car, found the keys, and decided to drive the car to where Robert was standing. Robert did not give them permission to drive the car. On the way to Robert, the car was involved in a collision. Does William's insurance provide coverage? [*Western States Mutual Insurance Company v. Verucchi*, 363 N.E.2d 826 (Ill. 1977).]

9. Suzanne was driving her car west on a highway when an approaching car crossed the center line and forced her off the highway. She crashed into several trees and another automobile. The approaching car, which did not strike her car, did not stop and was not identified. Suzanne now claims that her own insurer must pay the damages, which she claimed were $27,500, under her uninsured motorists coverage. Is she correct? Why? [*Jett v. Doe*, 551 S.W.2d 221 (Ky. 1977).]

10. In the case of *Taft v. Sweeney*, 373 A.2d 712 (N.J. 1977),[1] assume that four passengers riding with Taft were seriously injured in the accident along with Taft. Would Taft and the passengers be entitled to collect under Taft's uninsured motorists coverage? Why?

---

[1] See pp. 922–23.

52

Bankruptcy Under the Bankruptcy Reform Act of 1978

After you have read this chapter, you should be able to:

1. Discuss the source of bankruptcy law.
2. Describe the bankruptcy court system.
3. Distinguish between voluntary and involuntary bankruptcy.
4. Describe the property in the debtor's estate.
5. Discuss the distribution of the estate after liquidation.
6. Suggest two alternatives to bankruptcy.

Introduction

In recent years the use of credit to finance the purchase of property and services has become extremely popular with both consumers and businesses. The popularity of credit purchases, however, has resulted in an unfortunate and unexpected consequence for many borrowers—a trip to bankruptcy court. There are approximately 200,000 bankruptcy filings each year in the United States, with business bankruptcies accounting for around fifteen percent of the total.

In this chapter we will examine what happens when an individual files for bankruptcy and the effect of the bankruptcy on the debtor and his creditors. We will also examine two alternative courses of action available under the bankruptcy law: wage earner plans for individuals with regular income, and reorganization plans for businesses.

Source of Bankruptcy Law

The United States Constitution, Article 1, Section 8, provides that "the Congress shall have power . . . to establish . . . uniform laws on the subject of Bankruptcies throughout the United States." This means that bankruptcy is a *federal* matter and that the states do not have the power to enact bankruptcy laws.

Congress has used its power to enact bankruptcy Acts five times—in 1800, 1841, 1867, 1898, and 1978. The current one, the *Bankruptcy Reform Act of 1978* (effective on October 1, 1979) repealed the 1898 Act and made a number of changes in bankruptcy law. These reforms include: (1) a new court and trustee system; (2) a change in the list of property that is exempt from liquidation; (3) a clarification of the law governing the debtor's reaffirmation of discharged debts; (4) simplification of the method for commencing a bankruptcy case; (5) changes in the law allowing trustees to avoid certain property transfers made by the debtor; and (6) a consolidation of the chapters in the prior law covering business reorganization.

The Bankruptcy Reform Act of 1978 will, unless otherwise indicated, be the source for the following discussion of bankruptcy law. This Act is so new that few cases have been decided interpreting its provisions. Consequently, case summaries have been omitted from the text although ten hypothetical cases have been included at the end of the chapter. Many attorneys refer to the new Act as the "Bankruptcy Code" in order to distinguish it from the old 1898 Act.

Administrative Framework

Under the 1978 Act, a new bankruptcy court system is established and phased in between the years 1979 and 1984. The federal district courts have exclusive jurisdiction over bankruptcy cases, but this jurisdiction is delegated to a bankruptcy court that is created as an adjunct for each district.

Bankruptcy judges for the new courts are appointed by the President with the advice and consent of the Senate. The judges serve fourteen-year terms and

Federal jurisdiction over bankruptcy law.

Bankruptcy Reform Act of 1978—the law governing bankruptcy effective October 1, 1979.

are paid an annual salary of $50,000. The bankruptcy court is given exclusive jurisdiction over the debtor's property, can handle all proceedings related to bankruptcy cases, and has all powers of any court of law or equity, except that the bankruptcy judge may not enjoin (restrain) other courts and is limited in its use of criminal contempt as a punishment. Appeals from bankruptcy court decisions go initially to the federal district court, although the parties involved may agree to take the appeal directly to the federal circuit court of appeals.

While the new bankruptcy judges are given broad judicial powers, the judges are not allowed to administer the debtor's estate. For example, the 1978 Act provides in section 341 that the bankruptcy judge may not preside at—and can not even attend—the first meeting of creditors to plan for the administration of the debtor's estate because the judge might learn something at the meeting that would bias his later judicial decisions. Consequently, the administration of the estate is handled by a separate officer, the **trustee** in bankruptcy.

Trustees are initially appointed by the bankruptcy judge from a panel of private trustees. However, at the first meeting of creditors, a new trustee may be elected if the election is requested by creditors holding at least twenty percent of the unsecured claims. The trustee generally serves as the representative of the bankrupt's estate and handles a wide range of administrative duties, such as collecting and selling the debtor's property, investigating the financial affairs of the debtor, and making a final report and accounting to the court.

Bankruptcy Procedure

To illustrate the procedure followed in a typical bankruptcy case, let us assume that Micawber, a young college graduate, has made a number of purchases on credit and suddenly discovers that he has $10,000 in debts and only $2,000 worth of assets. Micawber is unable to make the installment payments on his debts as they become due and he is afraid that his wages will be subject to **garnishment.** He is now considering filing for bankruptcy.

Commencement of the Case

A bankruptcy case is commenced with the filing of a petition by a *debtor,* which is called a **voluntary case,** or by the debtor's creditors, which is called an **involuntary case.** The term "debtor" includes persons, corporations, or partnerships that reside, or have a domicile, a place of business, or property in the United States.

In a *voluntary case,* the debtor may be any person except a railroad, bank, insurance company, savings and loan association, or building and loan association. Insolvency of the debtor is not required. The petition may be filed by husband and wife jointly. The voluntary filing of a petition automatically acts as an *order for relief* under the bankruptcy law—that is, an order adjudicating bankruptcy of the debtor.

In an *involuntary case,* the debtor may be any person except the above five types of organization excluded in a voluntary case and except a farmer or a charitable corporation. If the debtor has twelve or more creditors, the petition

trustee
(in bankruptcy) the officer responsible for administering the debtor's estate

garnishment
a statutory proceeding begun by a judgment creditor to reach the intangible assets of the judgment debtor— e.g., the debtor's right to his salary

voluntary case
a bankruptcy case in which the petition is filed by the debtor

involuntary case
a bankruptcy case in which the petition is filed by the creditor

may be filed by three or more creditors whose *unsecured* claims total at least $5,000. If there are fewer than twelve creditors, the petition may be filed by one or more of such creditors whose total claims amount to at least $5,000. The debtor, Micawber in our case, may choose not to contest the petition, in which case the court will order the relief requested in the petition. If the debtor does contest the petition, the court will order relief only if, after a trial, it is determined that the debtor is not paying his debts as they become due or that a custodian was appointed or took possession of the debtor's property within 120 days before the filing of the petition. If the court dismisses the petition, it may award the debtor costs, attorney's fees, and damages, including, in some cases, **punitive damages.**

The filing of the petition acts as a **stay** of (1) judicial, administrative, or other proceedings against the debtor; (2) the enforcement of a judgment against the debtor; and (3) the creation or enforcement of any lien against the debtor's estate. Thus, Micawber's creditors could not start a suit or enforce their judgments by garnishment or otherwise after a petition is filed. There are, however, certain actions that are excluded from the operation of the stay, including criminal proceedings, the collection of alimony or support, and an action of the Department of Housing and Urban Development to foreclose a mortgage insured under the National Housing Act. Also, under section 361 of the 1978 Act, certain measures, such as requiring cash payments to creditors, may be taken to provide adequate protection for creditors harmed by the stay.

Creditors' Claims

Within a reasonable time after the order for relief, there will be a meeting of the creditors. The debtor, here Micawber, is required to appear at this meeting and to testify under oath if any creditor wants to question him. As previously noted, the judge is not allowed to attend this meeting and the creditors in certain cases may elect a trustee to replace the one appointed by the court. The creditors may also elect a **creditors' committee** that may consult with, and make recommendations to, the trustee and submit questions to the court regarding administration of the case.

Each creditor may file a **proof of claim,** which is automatically allowed unless an objection is raised by a party affected by the bankruptcy. If there is an objection, the court will allow the claim unless it determines that the claim falls within a specified list of claims that are not allowed, such as claims that are unenforceable against the debtor, claims for unmatured interest, and unmatured alimony and support that is not discharged by the bankruptcy.

If a **claim** is **contingent** or unliquidated, the court may estimate the value of the claim to determine the amount of the allowance. And when a creditor has a claim secured by a security interest or other lien on the debtor's property, the allowance is treated as a secured claim to the extent of the value of the property and an unsecured claim to the extent that the claim exceeds the property value. For example, C has a $10,000 claim against D and has D's office furniture worth $6,000 as security. C's unsecured claim is for $4,000.

punitive damages
the money judicially awarded in excess of compensatory damages to punish for malicious, wanton, or intentional wrongful conduct

stay
a halt

creditors' committee
(in bankruptcy) a committee elected by the creditors to advise the trustee in bankruptcy

proof of claim
the claim filed by a creditor in a bankruptcy case

contingent claim
a claim not certain of occurring, depending on a possible future event

The Estate

The trustee is responsible for collecting the property of the debtor's **estate,** reducing the property to money, and closing the estate in a manner that serves the best interests of the parties. The estate generally includes all legal or equitable interests which the debtor has in property as of the date the case was commenced. There are, however, three ways in which additional property might be added to the estate even though the debtor had no interest in the property on commencement of the case.

First, the estate includes property acquired by the debtor within 180 days after the petition was filed (1) by inheritance, bequest, or devise; (2) as a beneficiary on a life insurance policy; or (3) as the result of a property settlement agreement with a spouse for a divorce.

Second, the trustee has the right, called a *voidable preference,* to avoid certain transfers of property by the debtor, called preferences, and thus bring the property back into the estate. A **preference** is a transfer of property to a creditor for a debt owed before the transfer was made. The transfer must have been made while the debtor was **insolvent** (defined as a financial condition where the debts are greater than the assets, exclusive of fraudulent transfers and property exempted under the Code) and within ninety days before the petition was filed; however, there are special rules governing transfer to insiders such as a relative of an individual debtor or a director of a corporation. It also must be shown that the transfer enabled the creditor to receive preferential treatment. Additionally, the trustee may avoid fraudulent transfers made by the debtor within a year before the petition was filed and also transfers voidable under state law.

There are several important exceptions to the rules allowing the trustee to avoid preferences. For example, the trustee may not avoid a transfer: (1) that was a contemporaneous exchange for new value given to the debtor; (2) that was in payment of a debt incurred in the ordinary course of business so long as the transfer was made within 45 days after the debt was incurred; (3) of a purchase money security interest that secured new value which is perfected within ten days after the security interest attaches; (4) to a creditor to the extent that, after the transfer, the creditor gave new value not secured by an unavoidable security interest; and (5) of a perfected security interest in inventory or receivables or the proceeds of either, although there are limitations for transfers made ninety days before the filing of the petition.

The *third* possibility for adding property to the estate is for the trustee to use his rights as a **lien creditor** to avoid certain transfers by the debtor. The trustee's rights include the power of: (1) a creditor who has a judicial lien; (2) a creditor who has obtained a writ of execution that was returned unsatisfied; and (3) a bona fide purchaser of real property from the debtor. To illustrate the trustee's rights, we might assume that our debtor, Micawber, gave an unperfected security interest in his boat to a creditor, Heep. Because Heep's interest in the boat is not perfected, a lien creditor would have priority with regard to the boat.

estate
(in bankruptcy) the debtor's legal or equitable interest in property on the date the case commences

preference
(in bankruptcy) a debtor's transfer of his property made when insolvent and within ninety days before a petition in bankruptcy was filed which gives a creditor preferential treatment

insolvency
(in bankruptcy) when the debtor's assets are less than his liabilities

lien creditor
a creditor with a judicial lien or a writ of execution

Secured Transactions, Insurance, and Bankruptcy

Thus, the trustee, with the powers of a lien creditor, can avoid Heep's interest in the boat. Heep's only recourse is to file a claim as an unsecured creditor and share Micawber's assets with other unsecured creditors.

Although the trustee may make additions to the estate by avoiding preferences and by exercising his rights as a lien creditor, certain property is exempt and will not be included in the estate. A debtor may choose to use the **exemptions** listed in the federal bankruptcy statute or, *alternatively,* may elect the exemptions available under state law, although the states have the right to require the debtor to use the state exemptions. Property exempt *under the federal law* includes: (1) the debtor's residence up to a maximum interest of $7,500; (2) *one* motor vehicle up to $1,200 in value; (3) household furnishings, wearing apparel, appliances, books, animals, crops, or musical instruments held for personal, family, or household use up to a maximum $200 value for *each* item; (4) up to $500 in jewelry; (5) implements, professional books, tools of the debtor's trade up to $750 in value; (6) an unmatured life insurance contract owned by the debtor other than credit life insurance; (7) prescribed health aids; (8) various state and federal benefits including social security, unemployment compensation, local public assistance, veterans', and disability benefits; (9) private benefits including the debtor's right to alimony and support payments, pension, profit-sharing and other plans, to the extent reasonably necessary for the support of the debtor; and (10) the debtor's right to receive certain payments such as an award under a law compensating victims of a crime, a payment under a life insurance policy on a person of whom the debtor was a dependent, and a payment of up to $7,500 on account of personal injury. The debtor is also entitled to exempt any other property up to a value of $400, plus any unused amount under (1) above. Thus, under this last provision, a debtor who is not a homeowner may exempt $7,900 in any property.

The state exemption laws are not uniform and, if the debtor elects the state exemptions, his rights will vary considerably, depending on the state of his residence. Additionally, many of the state laws were drafted many years ago and the exemptions are not as useful today as they once were. For instance, the Michigan law exempts, among other property, 10 sheep, 2 cows, 5 swine, 100 hens, 5 roosters, and enough hay and grain to feed the animals and poultry for six months!

exemption
(in bankruptcy) a debtor's property that is not liquidated and not distributed to creditors in bankruptcy

Distribution of the Estate

After the trustee has collected and liquidated the debtor's property, the property will be distributed according to the following **priorities:** (1) administrative expenses and specified fees and charges; (2) unsecured claims, in an involuntary case, arising in the ordinary course of business after the case was commenced but before the order for relief or the appointment of trustees; (3) unsecured claims up to $2,000 for wages, salaries, or commissions earned by an individual within ninety days before the filing of the petition or the cessation of the debtor's business; (4) unsecured claims for contributions to employee benefit plans arising from services rendered within 180 days before the petition was filed or the debtor

priorities
claims that are paid first after the estate has been liquidated

ceased doing business, but only to the extent of $2,000 per employee less amounts paid for wage claims and to other employee benefit plans; (5) unsecured claims up to $900 owed to individuals who have deposited money for the purchase of consumer goods or services which were not delivered or provided; and (6) unsecured tax claims of governmental units. Any property remaining after priority claims and expenses have been paid will be distributed on a pro rata basis to unsecured creditors who have filed a proof of claim.

Discharge

After the estate has been liquidated and distributed, the court will order a **discharge.** However, a discharge will not be allowed if the case falls within one of seven main categories. *First,* discharges are allowed only to *individuals,* not to corporations or partnerships (in order to avoid what a U.S. House of Representatives report referred to as "trafficking in corporate shells and bankrupt partnerships"). However, corporations and partnerships may utilize chapter 11 of the new Act on business reorganization or they may liquidate under state law. *Second,* a discharge is not allowed if the debtor has transferred, destroyed, or concealed property within one year before, or any time after, the petition was filed with the intent to hinder, delay, or defraud creditors. *Third,* a debtor who has concealed, destroyed, falsified, or failed to preserve recorded information relating to the debtor's financial condition or business transactions will not be granted a discharge unless the act was justified. *Fourth,* a debtor who fraudulently makes a false oath, presents a false claim, gives or receives property for acting or failing to act, or withholds recorded information from officials is not entitled to a discharge. *Fifth,* a discharge is not allowed when the debtor has failed to explain satisfactorily a loss or deficiency of assets. *Sixth,* a debtor who refuses to obey a lawful order of the court will not be discharged. *Finally,* a discharge is not allowed if the debtor has been granted a discharge in an earlier bankruptcy case commenced within six years before the petition in the current case was filed.

If these exceptions do not apply and the *discharge* is granted, it serves to release the debtor from debts that arose before the date of the order for relief. The discharge also voids judgments relating to such debts and operates as an injunction against the collection of the debts.

However, even after a discharge, certain types of debts must still be paid by the debtor. These include: (1) certain taxes—e.g., taxes for which the debtor failed to file a return or filed a fraudulent return; (2) debts incurred in obtaining property or services by false pretenses or false financial statements reasonably relied on by creditors; (3) debts owed to creditors whose names were not given to the court by the debtor; (4) debts resulting from breach of fiduciary duty, larceny, or embezzlement; (5) debts owed for alimony or support; (6) debts resulting from a willful and malicious injury caused by the debtor; and (7) certain debts owed to a governmental unit. Included in this last category are educational loans owed to a governmental unit or nonprofit institution of higher education.

Secured Transactions, Insurance, and Bankruptcy

In addition to these nondischargeable debts, it is possible for a debtor to become liable for a debt that was discharged in bankruptcy by reaffirming (reassuming) the debt after the bankruptcy proceedings. However, reaffirmation is subject to abuse by certain creditors who might pressure the debtor into making a promise to reaffirm and, under the 1978 Act, Congress has made it more difficult for creditors to obtain such promises. For example, in cases where an individual wants to reaffirm a debt, the bankruptcy court must inform the debtor at a hearing that the reaffirmation is not required under law and of the legal effect of the reaffirmation. If the debt is a consumer debt, the court must also determine that the reaffirmation does not impose undue hardship on the debtor and is in the debtor's best interest.

Plans for Individuals with Regular Income

As an alternative to the straight bankruptcy procedure described above, which leads to liquidation and distribution of the debtor's estate, it is possible for a debtor to propose a plan for the payment of debts under chapter 13 of the Bankruptcy Reform Act. A **chapter 13** case, commonly called a "wage earner's plan," is commenced by the filing of a *voluntary petition,* which operates as an automatic stay of proceedings in the same manner as a straight bankruptcy petition.

chapter 13 plan
a plan for the payment of debts proposed by an individual as an alternative to a straight bankruptcy

The debtor then proposes a plan which provides for the submission of future income to the control of the trustee and provides for payments to creditors, including full payment of the claims entitled to priority discussed above. Chapter 13 contains a number of provisions that may be included in the plan, including the modification of the claims of secured creditors. The plan may not provide for payments over a period exceeding three years unless the court feels that there is cause to extend the plan an additional two years.

After the debtor has filed the plan, the court will schedule a **confirmation hearing,** at which time creditors may object to the plan. The court will then decide whether or not to confirm the plan after considering various requirements set forth in section 1325 of the Act, including adequate protection of secured creditors. If the plan is confirmed and the debtor makes all payments promised under the plan, he will be discharged of the debts provided for by the plan, although there are certain exceptions such as alimony and support payments.

confirmation hearing
the hearing at which a chapter 13 plan is considered by the court

Business Reorganization

As an *alternative to bankruptcy,* a business may choose to reorganize under **chapter 11** of the 1978 Act. A chapter 11 proceeding may be commenced by the filing of a voluntary *or* involuntary petition. Once a petition is filed, only the debtor may file a plan for 120 days after the order for relief unless a trustee has been appointed, in which case any party in interest may file a plan. The court may order the appointment of a trustee for cause (including fraud, dishonesty, incompetence, or gross mismanagement) or if the appointment is in the interest of creditors, security holders, or other interests of the estate.

chapter 11 plan
a plan for the reorganization of a business

In addition to the possible appointment of a trustee, the court is also required to appoint a creditors' committee as soon as possible after the order for relief. The creditors' committee consults with the debtor or trustee concerning administration of the estate, investigates all matters relevant to the formulation of a plan, participates in the formulation of a plan, and performs other services as representative of other creditors.

The contents of the plan are set forth in section 1123 of the Act. This section requires that the plan: (1) designate classes of claims; (2) specify which claims or interests are not impaired by the plan; (3) specify the treatment given claims or interests that are impaired by the plan; (4) provide the same treatment for claims within a particular class; and (5) provide adequate means for executing the plan.

After the plan is formulated, it will be transmitted, along with a written disclosure statement approved by the court, to holders of claims, who may accept or reject the plan. The court will then schedule a hearing and will confirm the plan if it complies with chapter 11. If the plan is fair and equitable, it may be confirmed even though all classes of claims have not accepted the plan; once confirmed, it binds all interested parties.

Summary Statement

1. Under the U.S. Constitution, bankruptcy is a federal matter; states do not have the power to enact bankruptcy laws.
2. The federal district courts have jurisdiction over bankruptcy cases, but this jurisdiction is delegated to a bankruptcy court that is created as an adjunct for each district.
3. A voluntary bankruptcy is one filed by the debtor, while involuntary petitions are filed by creditors. The court will order relief under an involuntary petition if it determines that the debtor is not paying his debts as they become due.
4. The debtor's estate includes all legal or equitable interests which the debtor has in property as of the date the case was commenced.
5. After liquidation, the estate will be distributed first to creditors with priority and then to unsecured creditors.
6. As an alternative to bankruptcy, an individual might file a plan under chapter 13, and a business might file a reorganization plan under chapter 11.

In the following case, the court discusses the question of whether a private college can refuse to issue copies of a student's transcript after the student's college loans have been discharged in bankruptcy. It should be noted that this case was decided in 1977, before the new law became effective, and the issue has not been litigated under the new Act.

Girardier v. Webster College

563 F.2d 1267 (1977)

Urbom, Chief District Judge. The issue here is whether a college may refuse to release transcripts of credits to former students for the sole reason that those students have not repaid to the college their National Defense Education Act loans and have obtained discharges in bankruptcy of those loans.

The plaintiff, Robert Girardier, took out a National Defense Student Loan with the defendant, Webster College, under subchapter 11 of the National Defense Education Act, 20 U.S.C. sections 421–429. He received his bachelor's degree in May 1972. Thereafter, the plaintiff defaulted on the loan and filed bankruptcy papers, listing the college as an unsecured creditor in the sum of $1,500. He was subsequently discharged in bankruptcy from the payment of the loan. At a later time he applied to the defendant for a transcript of his undergraduate credits, tendering the $2 fee therefor. The defendant refused, for the sole reason that the plaintiff owed the defendant $1,500 from the plaintiff's discharged student loan, citing a provision in the college handbook: "No transcript is released until all accounts are paid." Counsel for the defendant admits that, if the plaintiff were to pay the obligation in full, the college would furnish the requested transcript. The plaintiff alleges that a transcript is necessary for him to receive his master's degree, to which he is otherwise entitled, from the University of Missouri-St. Louis.

The plaintiff Luzkow is in an almost identical posture. Sometime after receiving her bachelor's degree from Webster College in May 1973, she too defaulted on her National Defense Student Loan. She filed bankruptcy, listing the college as an unsecured creditor in the amount of $1,900, and was subsequently discharged. She then sought copies of her college transcript, and the defendant similarly refused her request. She alleges that she needs a transcript as a necessary part of her applications to graduate school.

Although the complaints were filed separately, they have been dealt with by the parties and the district court as if consolidated. The Girardier complaint seeks damages only, while the Luzkow complaint asks for declaratory, injunctive, and monetary relief. . . .

Prior to 1970 there was sound authority for inflicting various hardships on bankrupts following their discharge, based solely on the fact of bankruptcy. Indeed, the Supreme Court of the United States had twice sanctioned such hardships in the area of motorists' financial responsibility laws. . . .

Along with the provisions giving the bankruptcy court greater powers to determine the effect of discharge, Congress in 1970 passed 11 U.S.C. section 32(f)(2), which states:

An order of discharge shall . . .
(2) enjoin all creditors whose debts are discharged from thereafter instituting or continuing any action or employing any process to collect such debts as personal liabilities of the bankrupt.

The plaintiffs urge that the language "employing any process" extends to cover the action of the defendant. They argue that the absence of the adjective "legal" before the word "process" implies a Congressional intent to include informal means of debt collection within the proscription of the statute.

We find no Congressional intent that the language be so broad. . . . In *Wood v. Fiedler* . . . this court said:

The 1970 amendments were enacted to prevent creditors from instituting state court actions in the hope that the bankrupt would ignore the proceedings based on a misplaced reliance on the discharge or due to a lack of funds to defend.

That the 1970 amendments did not serve to prohibit nonlegal, informal means of inducing the debtor to make payment on or revive the discharged obligation is apparent from the legislative history. Just before passage of the bill, Professor Lawrence King's memorandum for the National Bankruptcy Conference was read into the record as the "Explanatory Memorandum to Accompany S. 4247" (the 1970 amendments), 116 Cong.Rec. 34818-34820 (October 5, 1970):

This proposed legislation also does not affect in any way a bankrupt's obligation upon a discharged debt which is subsequently revived by a new promise. In the absence of any statutory directive, the case law has permitted enforcement of such new promise made after the commencement of the bankruptcy proceeding. . . .

In providing a uniform system of bankruptcy, Congress has made fundamental policy of the Act the providing of a means for (1) the effective rehabilitation of the bankrupt and (2) the equitable distribution of the bankrupt's assets among his creditors. . . .

It is true that the first purpose has been variously stated as giving the debtor a new opportunity in life and a clear field for future effort, unhampered by the pressure and discouragement of preexisting debt. . . . *Lines v. Frederick*. . . .

The court in *Lines* said:

The various provisions of the bankruptcy Act were adopted in the light of that view and are to be construed when reasonably possible in harmony with it so as to effectuate the general purpose and policy of the Act.

But that does not necessarily mean that every conceivable mechanism for furthering this goal has been written into the Act so as to become law. Historically, the Congress has rested on the discharge provisions of the Act to effectuate this goal; as of 1970, the Congress has further implemented this goal by the injunctive provisions of 11 U.S.C. section 32(f)(2). The Supreme Court of the United States has extended this protection by striking down state laws which create "a powerful weapon for collection of a debt [that has] been released by [operation of] federal law." But this is as far as the Congress or the courts have gone. The plaintiffs urge that they are entitled to be treated in a nondiscriminatory manner by reason of their bankruptcy, unless the disparity in treatment is rationally supported. This may be a proper legislative end for the Congress to consider, but it is not the present law. . . .

The Bankruptcy Act, as now written, does not prohibit a private college's refusing to furnish transcripts to persons who have received a discharge in bankruptcy of their college loans. . . .

The judgment of the district court is vacated and the action is remanded to that court with directions to dismiss the complaints for failure to state a claim on which relief may be granted.

Questions

1. Sam, a young college graduate, recently discovered that his debts substantially exceed his assets. Sam is now considering filing for bankruptcy. However, because Sam has fewer than twelve creditors and because his total debts are less than $5,000, he feels that he can not use the federal bankruptcy court and must use the state bankruptcy court instead. Should Sam commence a state bankruptcy proceeding? Why?

2. In question 1 above, is Sam insolvent under the bankruptcy definition? If he is not insolvent, may creditors file an involuntary petition?

3. Rollo, while driving his automobile one Sunday afternoon, was involved in an automobile accident in which Harry, a passenger in another automobile, was killed. Harry's family brought suit against Rollo, claiming that the accident was caused by his negligence. The local authorities also charged Rollo under the state criminal law with negligent homicide. After these two actions were commenced, Rollo filed a voluntary petition in bankruptcy. Rollo claimed that the petition operated as a stay of both proceedings. Is he correct? Why?

4. In question 3 above, what effect would a discharge in bankruptcy have on the claim for damages by Harry's family? Would the result be different if the family proved that Rollo intentionally and maliciously caused the accident? Why?

5. Clara had two elderly aunts, Millie and Tillie. Under Millie's will, Clara was to receive all of Millie's property. Tillie named Clara as the beneficiary in her life insurance policy. Clara was deeply in debt and decided to file for bankruptcy in order to discharge her debts and avoid using the inheritance and insurance money to pay her creditors. A petition was filed on January 15. Aunt Tillie died the following May 15 and Aunt Millie died the following November 15. Are the inheritance and the insurance proceeds included in Clara's estate and thus available to creditors? Why?

6. Kermit filed a voluntary bankruptcy petition. Sixty days before filing the petition, Kermit had given a security interest in his boat to First Bank, at which time First Bank made a $1,000 loan to Kermit. At the time of this transaction, Kermit was not insolvent. The trustee now wants to avoid the security interest. First Bank claims that the trustee can not avoid the interest because (1) Kermit was not insolvent and (2) the bank gave new value to Kermit. Who wins? Why?

7. Sara decided to file a voluntary bankruptcy petition. At the time of the filing, Sara had two debts outstanding: a $5,000 unsecured loan owed to First Bank, and a $5,000 unsecured loan owed to her college, Ivory Towers. Sara's assets are: (1) an automobile worth $1,000; (2) an oboe worth $200; (3) a sofa, chair, bookcase, and bed—each worth $200; (4) an ankle bracelet worth $500; and (5) a wide-screen color television set with matching stereo components worth $6,000. How much will each creditor receive in the bankruptcy proceedings if Sara elects the exemptions available under federal law? Why?

8. In question 7 above, what will be the effect of a discharge in bankruptcy? Why?

9. Clarence was granted a discharge in bankruptcy in a case commenced August 1, 1980. On August 1, 1985 Clarence transfers a valuable piece of real estate to his brother for a nominal consideration in an attempt to defraud his creditors. On the same day he destroys all his financial records. On August 20, 1986 Clarence files a bankruptcy petition. Should the court grant a discharge? Why?

10. Corporation X is in financial difficulty but wants to avoid a straight bankruptcy. The corporation is now considering filing a petition for a chapter 13 wage earner's plan under which the corporation would turn its future income over to a trustee, who would make payments to creditors over a three-year period. What problem might the corporation encounter with this plan? Can you suggest a solution?

Appendix A
An Explanation of the Civil Trial Process

Introduction

The judicial system with its use of courts deals with the interpretation, validity, declaration, and application of law to the factual situations confronting the court. In this process law is made, indicating what is legal now and, therefore, as case precedent what applies for the future. The court acts only on matters brought before it by parties who want judicial action. It has only the jurisdiction and powers given to it by federal or state statute.

Some cases involve the Constitution, administrative rules and regulations, while other cases involve the common law and equity in the absence of constitutional or legislative guidance. The decisions of the courts are law, providing guidance to society as to what may or may not be legally done. It is therefore important to understand the meaning of these decisions by reading and analyzing them. All too often members of the public have no concept of how their judicial system works through the courts. An explanation here of the civil trial process will be helpful.

The opinions of the courts in deciding cases are often contained in reports of those cases, which are available in libraries in court buildings, law schools, and other public places. Reference to a court opinion is called a *case citation*. For example, *Vigil v. Lamm,* 190 Colo. 180, 544 P.2d 631 (1976) refers to a Colorado case report found in volume 190 of the Colorado Reports at page 180, which may also be found in the regional Pacific Reporter in volume 544 second series at page 631. The date of the case is 1976. The report may be of a case or, more importantly, of its appellate review by the next higher court or by the highest court in the judicial system.

One of the most important ways law is made is by the published opinions of appellate courts. Most of the abbreviated court decisions in this text are edited versions of appellate court opinions. To understand how the parties to a legal dispute get to an appellate court to have their case heard, we offer here a brief overview of the civil trial process. The process described may vary slightly from state to state, but the definitions of the terms used are widely accepted.

The Trial of a Civil Case[1]

plaintiff
the party who initiates a civil suit by filing a complaint in the proper court

complaint
the first pleading in a civil action

summons
a writ or process served on the defendant in a civil action notifying him of the action and summoning him to appear and plead

defendant
the party against whom a civil suit (or criminal action) is brought

counterclaim
a claim asserted by the defendant against the plaintiff's claim in a civil action

A civil suit is initiated by the **plaintiff,** who files several documents in a trial court of general jurisdiction (usually a county court located in the county government building). The document of greatest importance is called the **complaint,** which is filed by the plaintiff. The complaint must contain the following information:

1. the names of the parties to the case, the plaintiff(s) and defendant(s);
2. a statement sufficient to show that the court has jurisdiction to hear the matter; and
3. a short and plain statement of the facts, indicating:
   a. the existence of a legal duty and
   b. the breach of this duty and
   c. a claim for relief in the form of a request for a given amount of money damages and/or a claim for equitable relief, such as a request for an injunction or an order for specific performance of a contract.

The complaint is filed together with a **summons,** which directs the server of the papers (usually a county sheriff if the case is filed in a county court, or a federal marshall if filed in a federal court) to the last known address of the **defendant.** Usually a copy of the complaint is included for the purpose of this *service.* When the server of the papers locates the defendant(s) or, in some states, when the server locates the permanent residence of the defending party(ies), the papers are left with someone of suitable age and discretion residing therein. The server then files a sworn statement with the court, often called a *return,* in which the server swears that the defendant(s) was (were) served.

The defendant may file a document with the court responding to the complaint, called an *answer,* within a given time period, usually twenty to thirty days. A copy of the answer is given to the plaintiff. The answer may admit all, part, or none of the facts as alleged in the complaint, and may admit or deny any or all of the legal consequences. In addition, the answer may include a claim for relief against the plaintiff, called a **counterclaim,** if the grounds exist.

The general rule defining those persons who may be plaintiffs or defendants is that they must have a direct interest in the subject matter of the suit; that is, these persons must be directly affected by the outcome. This rule has been expanded somewhat recently by permitting *class action* suits.

Class action suits were first widely used on the federal level, but gradually states have been adopting procedures which provide for this type of litigation. The class action procedural rules provide that one or more members of a class may sue or be sued as representatives of a class of persons if: (1) the class is so numerous that joinder of all members of the class is not practicable; (2) there are questions of law or fact that are common to all members of the class; (3) the claims or defenses of the parties representing the class are typical of the claims or defenses of the class; (4) the representatives of the class will fairly protect the

---

[1] Some of this material is from A. Wolfe and F. Neffzinger, *Legal Perspectives of American Business Associations* (Columbus, Ohio: Grid Pub. Co., 1977).

interests of the class; and (5) all the members of the class must be identifiable (within reason). In addition to these prerequisites, the court must find that the class action is superior to other available methods for the fair and efficient adjudication of the controversy.

If a party is properly served with the complaint and fails to file an answer within the time period provided by law, then the plaintiff may ask the court to enter a *default* judgment. If such is entered, the court is making a judgment that the plaintiff is entitled to the relief claimed in the complaint.

As stated earlier, a defendant may *answer,* or the defendant may challenge the plaintiff's case by **motion** before the issue is formally tried. There are several motions the parties may use to challenge the legal arguments of the other party asserted through the **pleadings** filed with the court. The first such opportunity to present such a motion is presented by the defendant, who may make a motion to the court to dismiss the complaint for failure to state a claim upon which relief may be granted. In this case the motion is made by filing a document labeled "Motion" with the court.

> **motion**
> a procedural device asking the court to take some action

> **pleadings**
> the formal documents filed with a court that usually include the complaint, answer, and motions regarding them

The filing of the "Motion to Dismiss for Failure to State a Claim" by the defendant requires the judge to rule on whether or not the plaintiff has stated the existence and breach of a legal duty. The judge must consider the complaint and the facts stated therein and resolve every inference created by the facts in favor of the plaintiff. When this is done, the court will grant or deny the motion to dismiss.

Discovery

If the defendant files an answer, then the litigation moves into a phase of the process generally called the *discovery* stage. Generally the objectives of this *pre-trial* procedure are to: (1) simplify the issues; (2) obtain admissions of fact to avoid unnecessary arguments and avoid surprise; (3) limit the number of expert witnesses; and (4) cover any other matters which would expedite the trial.

The following legal devices permit an adverse party to discover almost all information relevant to the trial of a civil suit. The best known discovery device is the **deposition.** A deposition is a sworn statement of any person, including a party to the action (the plaintiff or defendant) or any witness, which is made in response to questions from the attorneys for the opposing sides. The deposition is used to discover physical evidence, to discover what a witness will say at trial, or to discover any other matter relevant to the subject of the case. A deposition is taken under oath or affirmation, usually in front of attorneys for both parties, and is transcribed by a court reporter. The final copy is signed as a true statement by the one being deposed and is filed with the court. This signed statement may be used at the trial if the witness is unavailable, or it may be used at the trial to challenge the oral testimony of the deposing witness if such testimony varies from that in the deposition.

> **deposition**
> a written statement made by a person under oath or affirmation in a judicial proceeding where there is opportunity for cross-examination before trial

If the party or witness can not be interviewed in person, then a series of written questions may be sent and must be answered under oath. These written questions are called **interrogatories.**

> **interrogatory**
> a written question

In addition to depositions and interrogatories, a party may ask the court to order another party, if good cause is shown, to produce documents and other items of evidence for inspection, copying, or photographing. The subject of this order may be books, papers, accounts, letters, photographs, objects or tangible things, or other items which constitute evidence relating to the subject of the suit. If the mental or physical condition of the party is in controversy, the court may order the party to submit to a physical or mental examination by a physician if good cause is shown. This latter method of discovery is used in many cases where personal injury is the subject of the case.

Courts in the various states adopted many of these discovery procedures in the 1960s so they are viewed as relatively new. This adoption has resulted in many more cases being settled out of court because the procedures allow a party to discover almost all of the relevant evidence of the opposing party. The only evidence which is not obtainable by an opposing party are those materials which are **privileged.** Generally such materials include an attorney's work product (thoughts and research on a case) and communications between the client and his attorney or the patient and his doctor.

If the parties decide to *settle* the case out of court, the attorneys ask the permission of the judge to dismiss the case. If this dismissal is done *with prejudice,* it means that a party will be barred from filing the suit again. If the pretrial procedures do not result in settlement, then the parties usually ask the judge to rule on another series of motions challenging the legal assertions of the adverse parties. After the pleadings are all filed, either party may make a motion to dismiss the claims of an adverse party and enter judgment for the moving party by asking for a *judgment on the pleadings* or **summary judgment.** Some procedural systems make a distinction between these two motions but, in essence, they are the same. Like the initial motion to dismiss described above, these motions require the judge to consider the arguments made in all of the pleadings, resolve every reasonable inference against the moving party, and make a finding as to whether or not the arguments made and facts asserted warrant submission of the case to the jury in a trial on the facts. Generally, if the judge finds that the legal arguments and facts presented could lead to but one reasonable conclusion, and that is in favor of the moving party, then the motion must be granted. If there are issues of fact present which would lead reasonable minds to differ, then the motion should be overruled.

A matter may be tried before a **jury** or a judge alone. If a party in a civil suit desires a jury trial, it must be demanded, usually during the initial pleading phase. In federal courts, the U.S. Constitution guarantees a trial by jury in all civil actions at common law where the value of the controversy exceeds twenty dollars. The U.S. Constitution does not guarantee the right of a trial by jury in civil cases in state courts. However, the constitutions of the states usually provide that there is such a right in cases similar to those where the common law gave such a right at the time the constitution was adopted. Practically speaking, this means that almost all matters involving judgments of fact and requests for money damages may be tried before a jury. Usually negligence cases, and other personal

privileged communication
a communication between certain persons which, because of their relationship, is inadmissible in evidence without a waiver of the privilege

summary judgment
a judgment rendered on a motion by a party in a civil action that, solely on the basis of the pleadings, judgment should be rendered without the necessity of a trial on the facts

jury
a group of people selected to decide the facts in a trial

injury cases, are tried before a jury. On the other hand, cases involving the equity powers of the court or those involving very complex issues such as antitrust suits or breaches of industrial contracts and other cases where evaluation of the evidence requires rigorous analysis and expertise are usually tried before the judge alone. In very exceptional cases, the judge may appoint a *master* or *referee* to hear some of the evidence and make findings of fact.

The process of questioning prospective jurors to determine which of them will be permitted to sit on the jury is called **voire dire.** This phrase is French in origin and means "to speak the truth." The voire dire procedure allows the court and parties to reject a prospective juror if, after questioning, it is revealed that the person is barred by *statute* to serve in that case (e.g., wife of the plaintiff) or might be prejudiced or unable to render an impartial judgment. Usually each party is given three challenges to use for *any* reason—called *peremptory challenges;* additional challenges can be made for sufficient cause (statutory cause)—called *challenge for cause.*

voire dire
the examination before trial of a prospective juror or witness in which he or she is to answer the questions truthfully

Trial

At the trial, the plaintiff, through the attorney representing the plaintiff's interests, presents its side of the **evidence.** After each witness is sworn and "directly" examined by the plaintiff's attorney, the defendant's attorney may "cross-examine" the witness on matters brought out on direct examination. It must be emphasized at this point that, since most of the cases which proceed to trial do involve disputes of fact, the process by which the facts are "found" is the process of *direct examination* of a witness by the attorney who initially uses the witness followed by *cross-examination* by the attorney for the other side. The jury or the judge, by watching the witnesses respond to the questions asked, must determine whether they are telling the truth or accurately recalling an event. The answers which are given by the witness are considered by the fact-finder (jury or judge) together with the witness's demeanor (facial expressions and hand movements).

evidence
a fact from which an inference may be drawn of another fact

Following the plaintiff's version of the facts in the case, the defendant presents the evidence relevant to its side.

During the trial itself, a party may challenge the entire case of an adverse party by moving for a **directed verdict.** Either party may move this, and it requires the judge to rule on whether or not there are still issues of fact present which warrant the continuation of the trial. If reasonable minds could differ about the interpretation or existence of certain crucial facts, or the inferences to be drawn from the facts, then the court will overrule the motion and the trial will proceed.

directed verdict
a jury verdict as directed by the judge

At the close of the defendant's case, both sides make summary arguments emphasizing the aspects of the testimony and other evidence they believe most pertinent to their arguments. Before the jury retires to make its finding of fact, the judge instructs the jury on the appropriate rules of law which the jurors are to apply to the facts as determined by them. Below is an example of the type of "instruction" the judge may give to the jury in a negligence case:

Negligence is lack of ordinary care. It is a failure to exercise that degree of care which a reasonably prudent person would have exercised under the same circumstances. It may arise from doing an act which a reasonably prudent person would not have done under the same circumstances, or, on the other hand, from failing to do an act which a reasonably prudent person would have done under the circumstances.[2]

In applying this statement of the law, each juror must decide by using his or her own life experience as a guide whether or not the defendant acted as a "reasonably prudent person" would have, given the circumstances.

The judge gives the jury instructions on each matter of law argued in the case. After the instructions, the jury retires to the jury room, where it applies all the rules stated by the judge to the facts as presented to them at the trial by the parties, witnesses, attorneys, and other evidence and reaches a verdict both as to liability (was the defendant legally at fault for a breach of a rule?) and **damages** (if the defendant was liable, what is the appropriate amount of damages that will compensate the plaintiff for the breach of the rule?)

A motion for *judgment notwithstanding the verdict* may be made by an aggrieved party against whom the verdict has been announced after the trial of the issues. This motion requires the judge to rule on whether or not the jury could reasonably have reached the verdict it did, given the evidence and the court's instructions. This motion is granted only when the judge believes that the jury reached a verdict by ignoring the instructions, or where, after hearing and seeing all of the evidence, the jury could not logically have reached the verdict it did. This motion, like the one for summary judgment or the one for a directed verdict, essentially challenges the legal sufficiency of a party's case. It must not be confused with a motion for a new trial, which may be made after a verdict is reached but is granted only where substantial errors in the trial process occurred.

The Appellate Process

If either of the parties believes that there was an error during the trial and that this error caused an unfavorable verdict, the party may appeal. The error must be one in the process of introducing evidence or in the statement of the law or in the application of the rule to the facts. *Parties usually can not appeal the finding of a fact.* For example, if the jury finds that, as a matter of fact, the defendant did *sign* an agreement in question on a given date, then this may not be appealed. However, a party may appeal the issue of whether or not signing the agreement did legally *bind* the party. This latter conclusion is one which is a mixture of fact-finding and law application and is appropriate for appeal. The

damages
the money judicially awarded for another's wrongful conduct

---

[2] 1 New York Pattern Jury Instructions—Civil, Committee on Pattern Jury Instructions, Assoc. of Supreme Court Justices, vol. 1, 2d ed. (Rochester: The Lawyers Co-operative Pub. Co., 1974), p. 126.

reasons for this are that a party should get only one chance to introduce the evidence the party deems appropriate. Therefore, the trial courts are set up to take evidence; all the procedures at this level are adopted to ensure the fairness of the evidence-producing process. The right to cross-examination, the right to demand and examine other evidence, and the right to object to the introduction of irrelevant or excessively prejudicial evidence all exist at the trial level.

Appellate courts are not equipped to hear testimony or inspect evidence. Appellate courts are composed of three or more judges who hear the arguments of the appealing parties as to why the statements of the rules in the trial court were erroneous or why the process of rule application was erroneous.

An appeal may be initiated by either party. The one appealing is called the **appellant** or, in some courts, the *petitioner*. The one answering the appeal is the **appellee** or the *respondent*. At the trial stage, the case is given a name or "style" (in legal language); almost always this is done by putting the name of the plaintiff first, followed by the name of the defendant. However, on appeal, some courts, but not all, put the name of the appellant first when reporting the case. So if the defendant appeals, his name goes first in the official report. You should be cautioned that the appellate case's style does not reveal who is the plaintiff or defendant in the original trial of the matter. This may be determined only by reading the appellate opinion.

appellant
a party who appeals a case decision against him

appellee
a party against whom an appeal is taken

The appellant must file with the appellate court at least two documents. One is the transcribed version of what occurred in the trial. During the trial a court reporter took down all of the testimony, all objections and motions, and other relevant happenings in a special form of shorthand. This shorthand version of the trial is not transcribed into prose unless it is requested and paid for by one of the parties. Together with this transcript, the appellant files a legal brief which contains his legal arguments. The appellate court considers the trial transcript, the written legal arguments (briefs) of both parties, and in many cases allows attorneys for the parties to appear before it to orally answer questions asked by the appellate court and, in general, to argue the merits of the issues advanced. For the reasons stated above, the appellate court does not consider additional evidence, can not call new or recall the old witnesses, or, generally, view the evidence again. The *facts* as found by the trial court must be taken as given.

The appellate court then takes the matter under consideration, does considerable legal research on the matter, votes, and writes its opinion. If some of the judges do not agree with the majority of the court, they may write dissenting opinions stating their reasons. This appellate opinion is usually published and is available to all persons.

If either party is still of the belief that a *substantial* error in the statement of the rule or in the application of the rule to the facts was made by either the trial or intermediate appellate court, the party may appeal the case to the next higher level, the supreme court of the state or federal system, which is usually the highest level. Again, the party appealing this time is called the appellant or petitioner and the answering party is the appellee or respondent. The name of the appellant is usually placed first. The same general practice is followed in filing the appeals papers and hearing the arguments, except that additional arguments are made either supporting or attacking the decision of the first appellate court.

An appellate court (either intermediate or supreme court) may do one of three things with the case before it. It may *affirm* the holding of the court immediately below it and state its reasons for affirming the holding. If it affirms the decision, the same party who won the case in the court below wins again.

The appellate court may *reverse* the decision being appealed and enter its own judgment, giving the reasons. The third option is to order all or part of the case *tried again* using the interpretation of the law as stated by the appellate court. In this case, if the parties so desire, the case will be tried again. The same trial judge may preside again, but a new jury will be chosen.

This concludes our presentation of material on the trial and appeal of a civil case. The terms defined above and the processes outlined are crucial to our understanding of how to study law because the published opinions of appellate judges are the best source available to indicate how the law is applied. For this reason we have used in this book excerpts of mostly appellate cases to illustrate the application of important legal principles discussed in this book. We have made an attempt to edit the irrelevant portions out of these opinions and have attempted to leave in enough information so that you may discern the complete outlines of how the dispute developed and how the legal rules were applied to solve the dispute.

Kinds of Material in This Book

In this text we have presented three different kinds of material. First, there is textual material which presents a statement of the general rules of law applicable to most of the important areas of business activity. These rules are both legislative and judicial in origin.

However, presenting the written rules is only a starting point. A second type of information illustrates how some of the important rules are applied by those in charge of rule application, either the state or federal governments or private individuals. This rule application is illustrated by presenting both short and long excerpts from appellate case opinions. These case opinions demonstrate how the abstract statements presented by the written rules of law are applied to reality. The cases literally breathe life into the rules and are absolutely necessary to an understanding of how the law "works." Therefore, you are encouraged to read them carefully and to make notes on them as described below.

Third, we have presented at the end of the chapters review questions and case problems and also one or two long, important cases. Some of these review case problems are actual cases; others, created by us, should not be viewed as portraying an actual occurrence.

Briefing Appellate Cases

Some of the appellate cases excerpted in the text, especially the longer ones at the end of the chapters, are very complex and will require some effort on your part to fully understand them. We suggest that you keep notes on these cases. These notes are called "briefs" by students of the law. The briefs usually have the following components:

1. A statement of the "facts" of the case as found by the trial court and restated by the appellate court.
2. A statement of the "legal" arguments advanced by both the plaintiff and the defendant.
3. A precise statement of the legal issue or legal problem facing the court; this usually involves an application of a legal principle (rule) or principles (rules) to the facts.
4. A summary of the court's reasoning used to reach its conclusion; this is best accomplished by stating in your own words which facts the court finds are "legally operative" and then summarizing how the legal principle or rule applies to these facts.

Appendix B
Uniform Partnership Act (1914)

Part I   Preliminary Provisions

Section 1.   Name of Act

This act may be cited as Uniform Partnership Act.

Section 2.   Definition of Terms

In this act, "Court" includes every court and judge having jurisdiction in the case.

"Business" includes every trade, occupation, or profession.

"Person" includes individuals, partnerships, corporations, and other associations.

"Bankrupt" includes bankrupt under the Federal Bankruptcy Act or insolvent under any state insolvent act.

"Conveyance" includes every assignment, lease, mortgage, or encumbrance.

"Real property" includes land and any interest or estate in land.

Section 3.   Interpretation of Knowledge and Notice

(1) A person has "knowledge" of a fact within the meaning of this act not only when he has actual knowledge thereof, but also when he has knowledge of such other facts as in the circumstances shows bad faith.

(2) A person has "notice" of a fact within the meaning of this act when the person who claims the benefit of the notice:

    (a) States the fact to such person, or

    (b) Delivers through the mail, or by other means of communication, a written statement of the fact to such person or to a proper person at his place of business or residence.

Section 4.   Rules of Construction

(1) The rule that statutes in derogation of the common law are to be strictly construed shall have no application to this act.

(2) The law of estoppel shall apply under this act.

(3) The law of agency shall apply under this act.

(4) This act shall be so interpreted and construed as to effect its general purpose to make uniform the law of those states which enact it.

(5) This act shall not be construed so as to impair the obligations of any contract existing when the act goes into effect, nor to affect any action or proceedings begun or right accrued before this act takes effect.

Section 5.   Rules for Cases Not Provided for in This Act

In any case not provided for in this act the rules of law and equity, including the law merchant, shall govern.

Part II   Nature of Partnership

Section 6.   Partnership Defined

(1) A partnership is an association of two or more persons to carry on as co-owners a business for profit.

(2) But any association formed under any other statute of this state, or any statute adopted by authority, other than the authority of this state, is not a partnership under this act, unless such association would have been a partnership in this state prior to the adoption of this act; but this act shall apply to limited partnerships except in so far as the statutes relating to such partnerships are inconsistent herewith.

Section 7. Rules for Determining the Existence of a Partnership

In determining whether a partnership exists, these rules shall apply:

(1) Except as provided by section 16 persons who are not partners as to each other are not partners as to third persons.

(2) Joint tenancy, tenancy in common, tenancy by the entireties, joint property, common property, or part ownership does not of itself establish a partnership, whether such co-owners do or do not share any profits made by the use of the property.

(3) The sharing of gross returns does not of itself establish a partnership, whether or not the persons sharing them have a joint or common right or interest in any property from which the returns are derived.

(4) The receipt by a person of a share of the profits of a business is prima facie evidence that he is a partner in the business, but no such inference shall be drawn if such profits were received in payment:

  (a) As a debt by installments or otherwise,

  (b) As wages of an employee or rent to a landlord,

  (c) As an annuity to a widow or representative of a deceased partner,

  (d) As interest on a loan, though the amount of payment vary with the profits of the business,

  (e) As the consideration for the sale of a good-will of a business or other property by installments or otherwise.

Section 8. Partnership Property

(1) All property originally brought into the partnership stock or subsequently acquired by purchase or otherwise, on account of the partnership, is partnership property.

(2) Unless the contrary intention appears, property acquired with partnership funds is partnership property.

(3) Any estate in real property may be acquired in the partnership name. Title so acquired can be conveyed only in the partnership name.

(4) A conveyance to a partnership in the partnership name, though without words of inheritance, passes the entire estate of the grantor unless a contrary intent appears.

Part III   Relations of Partners to Persons Dealing with the Partnership

Section 9. Partner Agent of Partnership as to Partnership Business

(1) Every partner is an agent of the partnership for the purpose of its business, and the act of every partner, including the execution in the partnership name of any instrument, for apparently carrying on in the usual way the business of the partnership of which he is a member binds the partnership, unless the partner so acting has in fact no authority to act for the partnership in the particular matter, and the person with whom he is dealing has knowledge of the fact that he has no such authority.

(2) An act of a partner which is not apparently for the carrying on of the business of the partnership in the usual way does not bind the partnership unless authorized by the other partners.

(3) Unless authorized by the other partners or unless they have abandoned the business, one or more but less than all the partners have no authority to:

  (a) Assign the partnership property in trust for creditors or on the assignee's promise to pay the debts of the partnership,

  (b) Dispose of the good-will of the business,

  (c) Do any other act which would make it impossible to carry on the ordinary business of a partnership,

  (d) Confess a judgment,

  (e) Submit a partnership claim or liability to arbitration or reference.

(4) No act of a partner in contravention of a restriction on authority shall bind the partnership to persons having knowledge of the restriction.

Section 10. Conveyance of Real Property of the Partnership

(1) Where title to real property is in the partnership name, any partner may convey title to such property by a conveyance executed in the partnership name; but the partnership may recover such property unless the partner's act binds the partnership under the provisions of paragraph (1) of section 9, or unless such property has

been conveyed by the grantee or a person claiming through such grantee to a holder for value without knowledge that the partner, in making the conveyance, has exceeded his authority.

(2) Where title to real property is in the name of the partnership, a conveyance executed by a partner, in his own name, passes the equitable interest of the partnership, provided the act is one within the authority of the partner under the provisions of paragraph (1) of section 9.

(3) Where title to real property is in the name of one or more but not all the partners, and the record does not disclose the right of the partnership, the partners in whose name the title stands may convey title to such property, but the partnership may recover such property if the partners' act does not bind the partnership under the provisions of paragraph (1) of section 9, unless the purchaser or his assignee, is a holder for value, without knowledge.

(4) Where the title to real property is in the name of one or more or all the partners, or in a third person in trust for the partnership, a conveyance executed by a partner in the partnership name, or in his own name, passes the equitable interest of the partnership, provided the act is one within the authority of the partner under the provisions of paragraph (1) of section 9.

(5) Where the title to real property is in the names of all the partners a conveyance executed by all the partners passes all their rights in such property.

Section 11. Partnership Bound by Admission of Partner

An admission or representation made by any partner concerning partnership affairs within the scope of his authority as conferred by this act is evidence against the partnership.

Section 12. Partnership Charged with Knowledge of or Notice to Partner

Notice to any partner of any matter relating to partnership affairs, and the knowledge of the partner acting in the particular matter, acquired while a partner or then present to his mind, and the knowledge of any other partner who reasonably could and should have communicated it to the acting partner, operate as notice to

or knowledge of the partnership, except in the case of a fraud on the partnership committed by or with the consent of that partner.

Section 13. Partnership Bound by Partner's Wrongful Act

Where, by any wrongful act or omission of any partner acting in the ordinary course of the business of the partnership or with the authority of his co-partners, loss or injury is caused to any person, not being a partner in the partnership, or any penalty is incurred, the partnership is liable therefor to the same extent as the partner so acting or omitting to act.

Section 14. Partnership Bound by Partner's Breach of Trust

The partnership is bound to make good the loss:

(a) Where one partner acting within the scope of his apparent authority receives money or property of a third person and misapplies it; and

(b) Where the partnership in the course of its business receives money or property of a third person and the money or property so received is misapplied by any partner while it is in the custody of the partnership.

Section 15. Nature of Partner's Liability

All partners are liable

(a) Jointly and severally for everything chargeable to the partnership under sections 13 and 14.

(b) Jointly for all other debts and obligations of the partnership; but any partner may enter into a separate obligation to perform a partnership contract.

Section 16. Partner by Estoppel

(1) When a person, by words spoken or written or by conduct, represents himself, or consents to another representing him to any one, as a partner in an existing partnership or with one or more persons not actual partners, he is liable to any such person to whom such representation has been made, who has, on the faith of such

representation, given credit to the actual or apparent partnership, and if he has made such representation or consented to its being made in a public manner he is liable to such person, whether the representation has or has not been made or communicated to such person so giving credit by or with the knowledge of the apparent partner making the representation or consenting to its being made.

> (a) When a partnership liability results, he is liable as though he were an actual member of the partnership.
>
> (b) When no partnership liability results, he is liable jointly with the other persons, if any, so consenting to the contract or representation as to incur liability, otherwise separately.

(2) When a person has been thus represented to be a partner in an existing partnership, or with one or more persons not actual partners, he is an agent of the persons consenting to such representation to bind them to the same extent and in the same manner as though he were a partner in fact, with respect to persons who rely upon the representation. Where all the members of the existing partnership consent to the representation, a partnership act or obligation results; but in all other cases it is the joint act or obligation of the person acting and the persons consenting to the representation.

Section 17. Liability of Incoming Partner

A person admitted as a partner into an existing partnership is liable for all the obligations of the partnership arising before his admission as though he had been a partner when such obligations were incurred, except that this liability shall be satisfied only out of partnership property.

Part IV   Relations of Partners to One Another

Section 18. Rules Determining Rights and Duties of Partners

The rights and duties of the partners in relation to the partnership shall be determined, subject to any agreement between them, by the following rules:

> (a) Each partner shall be repaid his contributions, whether by way of capital or advances to the partnership property and share equally in the profits and surplus remaining after all liabilities, including those to partners, are satisfied; and must contribute towards the losses, whether of capital or otherwise, sustained by the partnership according to his share in the profits.
>
> (b) The partnership must indemnify every partner in respect of payments made and personal liabilities reasonably incurred by him in the ordinary and proper conduct of its business, or for the preservation of its business or property.
>
> (c) A partner, who in aid of the partnership makes any payment or advance beyond the amount of capital which he agreed to contribute, shall be paid interest from the date of the payment or advance.
>
> (d) A partner shall receive interest on the capital contributed by him only from the date when repayment should be made.
>
> (e) All partners have equal rights in the management and conduct of the partnership business.
>
> (f) No partner is entitled to remuneration for acting in the partnership business, except that a surviving partner is entitled to reasonable compensation for his services in winding up the partnership affairs.
>
> (g) No person can become a member of a partnership without the consent of all the partners.
>
> (h) Any difference arising as to ordinary matters connected with the partnership business may be decided by a majority of the partners; but no act in contravention of any agreement between the partners may be done rightfully without the consent of all the partners.

Section 19. Partnership Books

The partnership books shall be kept, subject to any agreement between the partners, at the principal place of business of the partnership, and every partner shall at all times have access to and may inspect and copy any of them.

Section 20. Duty of Partners to Render Information

Partners shall render on demand true and full information of all things affecting the partnership to any partner or the legal representative of any deceased partner or partner under legal disability.

Section 21. Partner Accountable as a Fiduciary

(1) Every partner must account to the partnership for any benefit, and hold as trustee for it any profits derived by him without the consent of the other partners from any transaction connected with the formation, conduct, or liquidation of the partnership or from any use by him of its property.

(2) This section applies also to the representatives of a deceased partner engaged in the liquidation of the affairs of the partnership as the personal representatives of the last surviving partner.

Section 22. Right to an Account

Any partner shall have the right to a formal account as to partnership affairs:

> (a) If he is wrongfully excluded from the partnership business or possession of its property by his co-partners,
>
> (b) If the right exists under the terms of any agreement,
>
> (c) As provided by section 21,
>
> (d) Whenever other circumstances render it just and reasonable.

Section 23. Continuation of Partnership Beyond Fixed Term

(1) When a partnership for a fixed term or particular undertaking is continued after the termination of such term or particular undertaking without any express agreement, the rights and duties of the partners remain the same as they were at such termination, so far as is consistent with a partnership at will.

(2) A continuation of the business by the partners or such of them as habitually acted therein during the term, without any settlement or liquidation of the partnership affairs, is prima facie evidence of a continuation of the partnership.

Part V   Property Rights of a Partner

Section 24. Extent of Property Rights of a Partner

The property rights of a partner are (1) his rights in specific partnership property, (2) his interest in the partnership, and (3) his right to participate in the management.

Section 25. Nature of a Partner's Right in Specific Partnership Property

(1) A partner is co-owner with his partners of specific partnership property holding as a tenant in partnership.

(2) The incidents of this tenancy are such that:

> (a) A partner, subject to the provisions of this act and to any agreement between the partners, has an equal right with his partners to possess specific partnership property for partnership purposes; but he has no right to possess such property for any other purpose without the consent of his partners.
>
> (b) A partner's right in specific partnership property is not assignable except in connection with the assignment of rights of all the partners in the same property.
>
> (c) A partner's right in specific partnership property is not subject to attachment or execution, except on a claim against the partnership. When partnership property is attached for a partnership debt the partners, or any of them, or the representatives of a deceased partner, cannot claim any right under the homestead or exemption laws.
>
> (d) On the death of a partner his right in specific partnership property vests in the surviving partner or partners, except where the deceased was the last surviving partner, when his right in such property vests in his legal representative. Such surviving partner or partners, or the legal representative of the last surviving partner, has no right to possess the partnership property for any but a partnership purpose.
>
> (e) A partner's right in specific partnership property is not subject to dower, curtesy, or allowances to widows, heirs, or next of kin.

Section 26. Nature of Partner's Interest in the Partnership

A partner's interest in the partnership is his share of the profits and surplus, and the same is personal property.

Section 27. Assignment of Partner's Interest

(1) A conveyance by a partner of his interest in the partnership does not of itself dissolve the partnership, nor, as against the other partners in the absence of agreement, entitle the assignee, during the continuance of the partnership, to interfere in the management or administration of the partnership business or affairs, or to require any information or account of partnership transactions, or to inspect the partnership books; but it merely entitles the assignee to receive in accordance with his contract the profits to which the assigning partner would otherwise be entitled.

(2) In case of a dissolution of the partnership, the assignee is entitled to receive his assignor's interest and may require an account from the date only of the last account agreed to by all the partners.

Section 28. Partner's Interest Subject to Charging Order

(1) On due application to a competent court by any judgment creditor of a partner, the court which entered the judgment, order, or decree, or any other court, may charge the interest of the debtor partner with payment of the unsatisfied amount of such judgment debt with interest thereon; and may then or later appoint a receiver of his share of the profits, and of any other money due or to fall due to him in respect of the partnership, and make all other orders, directions, accounts and inquiries which the debtor partner might have made, or which the circumstances of the case may require.

(2) The interest charged may be redeemed at any time before foreclosure, or in case of a sale being directed by the court may be purchased without thereby causing a dissolution:

(a) With separate property, by any one or more of the partners, or

(b) With partnership property, by any one or more of the partners with the consent of all the partners whose interests are not so charged or sold.

(3) Nothing in this act shall be held to deprive a partner of his right, if any, under the exemption laws, as regards his interest in the partnership.

Part VI Dissolution and Winding Up

Section 29. Dissolution Defined

The dissolution of a partnership is the change in the relation of the partners caused by any partner ceasing to be associated in the carrying on as distinguished from the winding up of the business.

Section 30. Partnership not Terminated by Dissolution

On dissolution the partnership is not terminated, but continues until the winding up of partnership affairs is completed.

Section 31. Causes of Dissolution

Dissolution is caused:

(1) Without violation of the agreement between the partners,

(a) By the termination of the definite term or particular undertaking specified in the agreement,

(b) By the express will of any partner when no definite term or particular undertaking is specified,

(c) By the express will of all the partners who have not assigned their interests or suffered them to be charged for their separate debts, either before or after the termination of any specified term or particular undertaking,

(d) By the expulsion of any partner from the business bona fide in accordance with such a power conferred by the agreement between the partners;

(2) In contravention of the agreement between the partners, where the circumstances do not permit a dissolution under any other provision of this section, by the express will of any partner at any time;

(3) By any event which makes it unlawful for the business of the partnership to be carried on or for the members to carry it on in partnership;

(4) By the death of any partner;

(5) By the bankruptcy of any partner or the partnership;

(6) By decree of court under section 32.

Section 32. Dissolution by Decree of Court

(1) On application by or for a partner the court shall decree a dissolution whenever:

    (a) A partner has been declared a lunatic in any judicial proceeding or is shown to be of unsound mind,

    (b) A partner becomes in any other way incapable of performing his part of the partnership contract,

    (c) A partner has been guilty of such conduct as tends to affect prejudicially the carrying on of the business,

    (d) A partner wilfully or persistently commits a breach of the partnership agreement, or otherwise so conducts himself in matters relating to the partnership business that it is not reasonably practicable to carry on the business in partnership with him,

    (e) The business of the partnership can only be carried on at a loss,

    (f) Other circumstances render a dissolution equitable.

(2) On the application of the purchaser of a partner's interest under sections 28 or 29:

    (a) After the termination of the specified term or particular undertaking,

    (b) At any time if the partnership was a partnership at will when the interest was assigned or when the charging order was issued.

Section 33. General Effect of Dissolution on Authority of Partner

Except so far as may be necessary to wind up partnership affairs or to complete transactions begun but not then finished, dissolution terminates all authority of any partner to act for the partnership,

(1) With respect to the partners,

    (a) When the dissolution is not by the act, bankruptcy or death of a partner; or

    (b) When the dissolution is by such act, bankruptcy or death of a partner, in cases where section 34 so requires.

(2) With respect to persons not partners, as declared in section 35.

Section 34. Right of Partner to Contribution from Co-partners after Dissolution

Where the dissolution is caused by the act, death or bankruptcy of a partner, each partner is liable to his co-partners for his share of any liability created by any partner acting for the partnership as if the partnership had not been dissolved unless

    (a) The dissolution being by act of any partner, the partner acting for the partnership had knowledge of the dissolution, or

    (b) The dissolution being by the death or bankruptcy of a partner, the partner acting for the partnership had knowledge or notice of the death or bankruptcy.

Section 35. Power of Partner to Bind Partnership to Third Persons after Dissolution

(1) After dissolution a partner can bind the partnership except as provided in Paragraph (3).

    (a) By any act appropriate for winding up partnership affairs or completing transactions unfinished at dissolution;

    (b) By any transaction which would bind the partnership if dissolution had not taken place, provided the other party to the transaction

        (I) Had extended credit to the partnership prior to dissolution and had no knowledge or notice of the dissolution; or

        (II) Though he had not so extended credit, had nevertheless known of the partnership prior to dissolution, and, having no knowledge or notice of dissolution, the fact of dissolution had not been advertised in a newspaper of general circulation in the place (or in each place if more than one) at which the partnership business was regularly carried on.

(2) The liability of a partner under Paragraph (1b) shall be satisfied out of partnership assets alone when such partner had been prior to dissolution

(a) Unknown as a partner to the person with whom the contract is made; and

(b) So far unknown and inactive in partnership affairs that the business reputation of the partnership could not be said to have been in any degree due to his connection with it.

(3) The partnership is in no case bound by any act of a partner after dissolution

(a) Where the partnership is dissolved because it is unlawful to carry on the business, unless the act is appropriate for winding up partnership affairs; or

(b) Where the partner has become bankrupt; or

(c) Where the partner has no authority to wind up partnership affairs; except by a transaction with one who

(I) Had extended credit to the partnership prior to dissolution and had no knowledge or notice of his want of authority; or

(II) Had not extended credit to the partnership prior to dissolution, and, having no knowledge or notice of his want of authority, the fact of his want of authority has not been advertised in the manner provided for advertising the fact of dissolution in Paragraph (1b II).

(4) Nothing in this section shall affect the liability under Section 16 of any person who after dissolution represents himself or consents to another representing him as a partner in a partnership engaged in carrying on business.

Section 36.   Effect of Dissolution on Partner's Existing Liability

(1) The dissolution of the partnership does not of itself discharge the existing liability of any partner.

(2) A partner is discharged from any existing liability upon dissolution of the partnership by an agreement to that effect between himself, the partnership creditor and the person or partnership continuing the business; and such agreement may be inferred from the course of dealing between the creditor having knowledge of the dissolution and the person or partnership continuing the business.

(3) Where a person agrees to assume the existing obligations of a dissolved partnership, the partners whose obligations have been assumed shall be discharged from any liability to any creditor of the partnership who, knowing of the agreement, consents to a material alteration in the nature or time of payment of such obligations.

(4) The individual property of a deceased partner shall be liable for all obligations of the partnership incurred while he was a partner but subject to the prior payment of his separate debts.

Section 37.   Right to Wind Up

Unless otherwise agreed the partners who have not wrongfully dissolved the partnership or the legal representative of the last surviving partner, not bankrupt, has the right to wind up the partnership affairs; provided, however, that any partner, his legal representative or his assignee, upon cause shown, may obtain winding up by the court.

Section 38.   Rights of Partners to Application of Partnership Property

(1) When dissolution is caused in any way, except in contravention of the partnership agreement, each partner, as against his co-partners and all persons claiming through them in respect of their interests in the partnership, unless otherwise agreed, may have the partnership property applied to discharge its liabilities, and the surplus applied to pay in cash the net amount owing to the respective partners. But if dissolution is caused by expulsion of a partner, bona fide under the partnership agreement and if the expelled partner is discharged from all partnership liabilities, either by payment or agreement under section 36(2), he shall receive in cash only the net amount due him from the partnership.

(2) When dissolution is caused in contravention of the partnership agreement the rights of the partners shall be as follows:

(a) Each partner who has not caused dissolution wrongfully shall have,

  (I) All the rights specified in paragraph (1) of this section, and

  (II) The right, as against each partner who has caused the dissolution wrongfully, to damages for breach of the agreement.

(b) The partners who have not caused the dissolution wrongfully, if they all desire to continue the business in the same name, either by themselves or jointly with others, may do so, during the agreed term for the partnership and for that purpose may possess the partnership property, provided they secure the payment by bond approved by the court, or pay to any partner who has caused the dissolution wrongfully, the value of his interest in the partnership at the dissolution, less any damages recoverable under clause (2a II) of this section, and in like manner indemnify him against all present or future partnership liabilities.

(c) A partner who has caused the dissolution wrongfully shall have:

  (I) If the business is not continued under the provisions of paragraph (2b) all the rights of a partner under paragraph (1), subject to clause (2a II), of this section,

  (II) If the business is continued under paragraph (2b) of this section the right as against his co-partners and all claiming through them in respect of their interests in the partnership, to have the value of his interest in the partnership, less any damages caused to his co-partners by the dissolution, ascertained and paid to him in cash, or the payment secured by bond approved by the court, and to be released from all existing liabilities of the partnership; but in ascertaining the value of the partner's interest the value of the good-will of the business shall not be considered.

Section 39. Rights Where Partnership is Dissolved for Fraud or Misrepresentation

Where a partnership contract is rescinded on the ground of the fraud or misrepresentation of one of the parties thereto, the party entitled to rescind is, without prejudice to any other right, entitled,

(a) To a lien on, or a right of retention of, the surplus of the partnership property after satisfying the partnership liabilities to third persons for any sum of money paid by him for the purchase of an interest in the partnership and for any capital or advances contributed by him; and

(b) To stand, after all liabilities to third persons have been satisfied, in the place of the creditors of the partnership for any payments made by him in respect of the partnership liabilities; and

(c) To be indemnified by the person guilty of the fraud or making the representation against all debts and liabilities of the partnership.

Section 40. Rules for Distribution

In settling accounts between the partners after dissolution, the following rules shall be observed, subject to any agreement to the contrary:

(a) The assets of the partnership are:

  (I) The partnership property,

  (II) The contributions of the partners necessary for the payment of all the liabilities specified in clause (b) of this paragraph.

(b) The liabilities of the partnership shall rank in order of payment, as follows:

  (I) Those owing to creditors other than partners,

  (II) Those owing to partners other than for capital and profits,

  (III) Those owing to partners in respect of capital,

  (IV) Those owing to partners in respect of profits.

(c) The assets shall be applied in the order of their declaration in clause (a) of this paragraph to the satisfaction of the liabilities.

(d) The partners shall contribute, as provided by section 18 (a) the amount necessary to satisfy the liabilities; but if any, but not all, of the partners are insolvent, or, not being subject to process, refuse to contribute, the other partners shall contribute their share of the liabilities, and, in the relative proportions in which they share the profits, the additional amount necessary to pay the liabilities.

(e) An assignee for the benefit of creditors or any person appointed by the court shall have the right to enforce the contributions specified in clause (d) of this paragraph.

(f) Any partner or his legal representative shall have the right to enforce the contributions specified in clause (d) of this paragraph, to the extent of the amount which he has paid in excess of his share of the liability.

(g) The individual property of a deceased partner shall be liable for the contributions specified in clause (d) of this paragraph.

(h) When partnership property and the individual properties of the partners are in possession of a court for distribution, partnership creditors shall have priority on partnership property and separate creditors on individual property, saving the rights of lien or secured creditors as heretofore.

(i) Where a partner has become bankrupt or his estate is insolvent the claims against his separate property shall rank in the following order:

(I) Those owing to separate creditors,

(II) Those owing to partnership creditors,

(III) Those owing to partners by way of contribution.

Section 41. Liability of Persons Continuing the Business in Certain Cases

(1) When any new partner is admitted into an existing partnership, or when any partner retires and assigns (or the representative of the deceased partner assigns) his rights in partnership property to two or more of the partners, or to one or more of the partners and one or more third persons, if the business is continued without liquidation of the partnership affairs, creditors of the first or dissolved partnership are also creditors of the partnership so continuing the business.

(2) When all but one partner retire and assign (or the representative of a deceased partner assigns) their rights in partnership property to the remaining partner, who continues the business without liquidation of partnership affairs, either alone or with others, creditors of the dissolved partnership are also creditors of the person or partnership so continuing the business.

(3) When any partner retires or dies and the business of the dissolved partnership is continued as set forth in paragraphs (1) and (2) of this section, with the consent of the retired partners or the representative of the deceased partner, but without any assignment of his right in partnership property, rights of creditors of the dissolved partnership and of the creditors of the person or partnership continuing the business shall be as if such assignment had been made.

(4) When all the partners or their representatives assign their rights in partnership property to one or more third persons who promise to pay the debts and who continue the business of the dissolved partnership, creditors of the dissolved partnership are also creditors of the person or partnership continuing the business.

(5) When any partner wrongfully causes a dissolution and the remaining partners continue the business under the provisions of section 38(2b), either alone or with others, and without liquidation of the partnership affairs, creditors of the dissolved partnership are also creditors of the person or partnership continuing the business.

(6) When a partner is expelled and the remaining partners continue the business either alone or with others, without liquidation of the partnership affairs, creditors of the dissolved partnership are also creditors of the person or partnership continuing the business.

(7) The liability of a third person becoming a partner in the partnership continuing the business, under this section, to the creditors of the dissolved partnership shall be satisfied out of partnership property only.

(8) When the business of a partnership after dissolution is continued under any conditions set forth in this section

the creditors of the dissolved partnership, as against the separate creditors of the retiring or deceased partner or the representative of the deceased partner, have a prior right to any claim of the retired partner or the representative of the deceased partner against the person or partnership continuing the business, on account of the retired or deceased partner's interest in the dissolved partnership or on account of any consideration promised for such interest or for his right in partnership property.

(9) Nothing in this section shall be held to modify any right of creditors to set aside any assignment on the ground of fraud.

(10) The use by the person or partnership continuing the business of the partnership name, or the name of a deceased partner as part thereof, shall not of itself make the individual property of the deceased partner liable for any debts contracted by such person or partnership.

Section 42. Rights of Retiring or Estate of Deceased Partner When the Business is Continued

When any partner retires or dies, and the business is continued under any of the conditions set forth in section 41(1, 2, 3, 5, 6), or section 38(2b) without any settlement of accounts as between him or his estate and the person or partnership continuing the business, unless otherwise agreed, he or his legal representative as against such persons or partnership may have the value of his interest at the date of dissolution ascertained, and shall receive as an ordinary creditor an amount equal to the value of his interest in the dissolved partnership with interest, or, at his option or at the option of his legal representative, in lieu of interest, the profits attributable to the use of his right in the property of the dissolved partnership; provided that the creditors of the dissolved partnership as against the separate creditors, or the representative of the retired or deceased partner, shall have priority on any claim arising under this section, as provided by section 41(8) of this act.

Section 43. Accrual of Actions

The right to an account of his interest shall accrue to any partner, or his legal representative, as against the winding up partners or the surviving partners or the person or partnership continuing the business, at the date of dissolution, in the absence of any agreement to the contrary.

Part VII Miscellaneous Provisions

Section 44. When Act Takes Effect

This act shall take effect on the . . . . day of . . . . one thousand nine hundred and . . . .

Section 45. Legislation Repealed

All acts or parts of acts inconsistent with this act are hereby repealed.

Appendix C
Uniform Commercial Code (1978 Text)

Title

An Act

To be known as the Uniform Commercial Code, Relating to Certain Commercial Transactions in or regarding Personal Property and Contracts and other Documents concerning them, including Sales, Commercial Paper, Bank Deposits and Collections, Letters of Credit, Bulk Transfers, Warehouse Receipts, Bills of Lading, other Documents of Title, Investment Securities, and Secured Transactions, including certain Sales of Accounts, Chattel Paper, and Contract Rights; Providing for Public Notice to Third Parties in Certain Circumstances; Regulating Procedure, Evidence and Damages in Certain Court Actions Involving such Transactions, Contracts or Documents; to Make Uniform the Law with Respect Thereto; and Repealing Inconsistent Legislation.

Article 1   General Provisions

Part 1   Short Title, Construction, Application and Subject Matter of the Act

Section 1—101.   Short Title

This Act shall be known and may be cited as Uniform Commercial Code.

Section 1—102.   Purposes; Rules of Construction; Variation by Agreement

(1) This Act shall be liberally construed and applied to promote its underlying purposes and policies.

(2) Underlying purposes and policies of this Act are

  (a) to simplify, clarify and modernize the law governing commercial transactions;

  (b) to permit the continued expansion of commercial practices through custom, usage and agreement of the parties;

  (c) to make uniform the law among the various jurisdictions.

(3) The effect of provisions of this Act may be varied by agreement, except as otherwise provided in this Act and except that the obligations of good faith, diligence, reasonableness and care prescribed by this Act may not be disclaimed by agreement but the parties may by agreement determine the standards by which the performance of such obligations is to be measured if such standards are not manifestly unreasonable.

(4) The presence in certain provisions of this Act of the word "unless otherwise agreed" or words of similar import does not imply that the effect of other provisions may not be varied by agreement under subsection (3).

(5) In this Act unless the context otherwise requires

  (a) words in the singular number include the plural, and in the plural include the singular;

  (b) words of the masculine gender include the feminine and the neuter, and when the sense so indicates words of the neuter gender may refer to any gender.

Section 1—103.   Supplementary General Principles of Law Applicable

Unless displaced by the particular provisions of this Act, the principles of law and equity, including the law merchant and the law relative to capacity to contract, principal and agent, estoppel, fraud, misrepresentation, duress, coercion, mistake, bankruptcy, or other validating or invalidating cause shall supplement its provisions.

Section 1—104.   Construction Against Implicit Repeal

This Act being a general act intended as a unified coverage of its subject matter, no part of it shall be deemed to be impliedly repealed by subsequent legislation if such construction can reasonably be avoided.

Section 1—105.   Territorial Application of the Act; Parties' Power to Choose Applicable Law

(1) Except as provided hereafter in this section, when a transaction bears a reasonable relation to this state and also to another state or nation the parties may agree that the law either of this state or of such other state or nation shall govern their rights and duties. Failing such agreement this Act applies to transactions bearing an appropriate relation to this state.

(2) Where one of the following provisions of this Act specifies the applicable law, that provision governs and a contrary agreement is effective only to the extent permitted by the law (including the conflict of laws rules) so specified:

> Rights of creditors against sold goods. Section 2—402.

> Applicability of the Article on Bank Deposits and Collections. Section 4—102.

> Bulk transfers subject to the Article on Bulk Transfers. Section 6—102.

> Applicability of the Article on Investment Securities. Section 8—106.

> Perfection provisions of the Article on Secured Transactions. Section 9—103.

Section 1—106.   Remedies to Be Liberally Administered

(1) The remedies provided by this Act shall be liberally administered to the end that the aggrieved party may be put in as good a position as if the other party had fully performed but neither consequential or special nor penal damages may be had except as specifically provided in this Act or by other rule of law.

(2) Any right or obligation declared by this Act is enforceable by action unless the provision declaring it specifies a different and limited effect.

Section 1—107.   Waiver or Renunciation of Claim or Right After Breach

Any claim or right arising out of an alleged breach can be discharged in whole or in part without consideration by a written waiver or renunciation signed and delivered by the aggrieved party.

Section 1—108.   Severability

If any provision or clause of this Act or application thereof to any person or circumstances is held invalid, such invalidity shall not affect other provisions or applications of the Act which can be given effect without the invalid provision or application, and to this end the provisions of this Act are declared to be severable.

Section 1—109.   Section Captions

Section captions are parts of this Act.

Part 2   General Definitions and Principles of Interpretation

Section 1—201.   General Definitions

Subject to additional definitions contained in the subsequent Articles of this Act which are applicable to specific Articles or Parts thereof, and unless the context otherwise requires, in this Act:

(1) "Action" in the sense of a judicial proceeding includes recoupment, counterclaim, set-off, suit in equity and any other proceedings in which rights are determined.

(2) "Aggrieved party" means a party entitled to resort to a remedy.

(3) "Agreement" means the bargain of the parties in fact as found in their language or by implication from other circumstances including course of dealing or usage of trade or course of performance as provided in this Act (Sections 1—205 and 2—208). Whether an agreement has legal consequences is determined by the provisions of this Act, if applicable; otherwise by the law of contracts (Section 1—103). (Compare "Contract".)

(4) "Bank" means any person engaged in the business of banking.

(5) "Bearer" means the person in possession of an instrument, document of title, or certificated security payable to bearer or indorsed in blank.

(6) "Bill of lading" means a document evidencing the receipt of goods for shipment issued by a person engaged in the business of transporting or forwarding goods, and includes an airbill. "Airbill" means a document serving for air transportation as a bill of lading does for marine or rail transportation, and includes an air consignment note or air waybill.

(7) "Branch" includes a separately incorporated foreign branch of a bank.

(8) "Burden of establishing" a fact means the burden of persuading the triers of fact that the existence of the fact is more probable than its non-existence.

(9) "Buyer in ordinary course of business" means a person who in good faith and without knowledge that the sale to him is in violation of the ownership rights or security interest of a third party in the goods buys in ordinary course from a person in the business of selling goods of that kind but does not include a pawnbroker. All persons who sell minerals or the like (including oil and gas) at wellhead or minehead shall be deemed to be persons in the business of selling goods of that kind. "Buying" may be for cash or by exchange of other property or on secured or unsecured credit and includes receiving goods or documents of title under a pre-existing contract for sale but does not include a transfer in bulk or as security for or in total or partial satisfaction of a money debt.

(10) "Conspicuous": A term or clause is conspicuous when it is so written that a reasonable person against whom it is to operate ought to have noticed it. A printed heading in capitals (as: NON-NEGOTIABLE BILL OF LADING) is conspicuous. Language in the body of a form is "conspicuous" if it is in larger or other contrasting type or color. But in a telegram any stated term is "conspicuous." Whether a term or clause is "conspicuous" or not is for decision by the court.

(11) "Contract" means the total legal obligation which results from the parties' agreement as affected by this Act and any other applicable rules of law. (Compare "Agreement.")

(12) "Creditor" includes a general creditor, a secured creditor, a lien creditor and any representative of creditors, including an assignee for the benefit of creditors, a trustee in bankruptcy, a receiver in equity and an executor or administrator of an insolvent debtor's or assignor's estate.

(13) "Defendant" includes a person in the position of defendant in a cross-action or counterclaim.

(14) "Delivery" with respect to instruments, documents of title, chattel paper, or certificated securities means voluntary transfer of possession.

(15) "Document of title" includes bill of lading, dock warrant, dock receipt, warehouse receipt or order for the delivery of goods, and also any other document which in the regular course of business or financing is treated as adequately evidencing that the person in possession of it is entitled to receive, hold and dispose of the document and the goods it covers. To be a document of title a document must purport to be issued by or addressed to a bailee and purport to cover goods in the bailee's possession which are either identified or are fungible portions of an identified mass.

(16) "Fault" means wrongful act, omission or breach.

(17) "Fungible" with respect to goods or securities means goods or securities of which any unit is, by nature or usage of trade, the equivalent of any other like unit. Goods which are not fungible shall be deemed fungible for the purposes of this Act to the extent that under a particular agreement or document unlike units are treated as equivalents.

(18) "Genuine" means free of forgery or counterfeiting.

(19) "Good faith" means honesty in fact in the conduct or transaction concerned.

(20) "Holder" means a person who is in possession of a document of title or an instrument or a certificated investment security drawn, issued, or indorsed to him or his order or to bearer or in blank.

(21) To "honor" is to pay or to accept and pay, or where a credit so engages to purchase or discount a draft complying with the terms of the credit.

(22) "Insolvency proceedings" includes any assignment for the benefit of creditors or other proceedings intended to liquidate or rehabilitate the estate of the person involved.

(23) A person is "insolvent" who either has ceased to pay his debts in the ordinary course of business or cannot pay his debts as they become due or is insolvent within the meaning of the federal bankruptcy law.

(24) "Money" means a medium of exchange authorized or adopted by a domestic or foreign government as a part of its currency.

(25) A person has "notice" of a fact when

(a) he has actual knowledge of it; or

(b) he has received a notice or notification of it; or

(c) from all the facts and circumstances known to him at the time in question he has reason to know that it exists.

A person "knows" or has "knowledge" of a fact when he has actual knowledge of it. "Discover" or "learn" or a word or phrase of similar import refers to knowledge rather than to reason to know. The time and circumstances under which a notice or notification may cease to be effective are not determined by this Act.

(26) A person "notifies" or "gives" a notice or notification to another by taking such steps as may be reasonably required to inform the other in ordinary course whether or not such other actually comes to know of it. A person "receives" a notice or notification when

(a) it comes to his attention; or

(b) it is duly delivered at the place of business through which the contract was made or at any other place held out by him as the place for receipt of such communications.

(27) Notice, knowledge or a notice or notification received by an organization is effective for a particular transaction from the time when it is brought to the attention of the individual conducting that transaction, and in any event from the time when it would have been brought to his attention if the organization had exercised due diligence. An organization exercises due diligence if it maintains reasonable routines for communicating significant information to the person conducting the transaction and there is reasonable compliance with the routines. Due diligence does not require an individual acting for the organization to communicate information unless such communication is part of his regular duties or unless he has reason to know of the transaction and that the transaction would be materially affected by the information.

(28) "Organization" includes a corporation, government or governmental subdivision or agency, business trust, estate, trust, partnership or association, two or more persons having a joint or common interest, or any other legal or commercial entity.

(29) "Party," as distinct from "third party," means a person who has engaged in a transaction or made an agreement within this Act.

(30) "Person" includes an individual or an organization (See Section 1—102).

(31) "Presumption" or "presumed" means that the trier of fact must find the existence of the fact presumed unless and until evidence is introduced which would support a finding of its non-existence.

(32) "Purchase" includes taking by sale, discount, negotiation, mortgage, pledge, lien, issue or re-issue, gift or any other voluntary transaction creating an interest in property.

(33) "Purchaser" means a person who takes by purchase.

(34) "Remedy" means any remedial right to which an aggrieved party is entitled with or without resort to a tribunal.

(35) "Representative" includes an agent, an officer of a corporation or association, and a trustee, executor or administrator of an estate, or any other person empowered to act for another.

(36) "Rights" includes remedies.

(37) "Security interest" means an interest in personal property or fixtures which secures payment or performance of an obligation. The retention or reservation of title by a seller of goods notwithstanding shipment or delivery to the buyer (Section 2—401) is limited in effect to a reservation of a "security interest." The term also includes any interest of a buyer of accounts or chattel paper which is subject to Article 9. The special property interest of a buyer of goods on identification of such goods to a contract for sale under Section 2—401 is not a "security interest," but a buyer may also acquire a "security interest" by complying with Article 9. Unless a lease or consignment is intended as security, reservation of title thereunder is not a "security interest" but a consignment is in any event subject to the provisions on consignment sales (Section 2—326). Whether a lease is intended as security is to be determined by the facts of each case; however, (a) the inclusion of an option to purchase does not of itself make the lease one intended for security, and (b) an agreement that upon compliance with the terms of the lease the lessee shall become or has the option to become the owner of the property for no additional consideration or for a nominal consideration does make the lease one intended for security.

(38) "Send" in connection with any writing or notice means to deposit in the mail or deliver for transmission by any other usual means of communication with postage or cost of transmission provided for and properly addressed and in the case of an instrument to an address specified thereon or otherwise agreed, or if there be none to any address reasonable under the circumstances. The receipt of any writing or notice within the time at which it would have arrived if properly sent has the effect of a proper sending.

(39) "Signed" includes any symbol executed or adopted by a party with present intention to authenticate a writing.

(40) "Surety" includes guarantor.

(41) "Telegram" includes a message transmitted by radio, teletype, cable, any mechanical method of transmission, or the like.

(42) "Term" means that portion of an agreement which relates to a particular matter.

(43) "Unauthorized" signature or indorsement means one made without actual, implied or apparent authority and includes a forgery.

(44) "Value." Except as otherwise provided with respect to negotiable instruments and bank collections (Sections 3—303, 4—208 and 4—209) a person gives "value" for rights if he acquires them

    (a) in return for a binding commitment to extend credit or for the extension of immediately available credit whether or not drawn upon and whether or not a chargeback is provided for in the event of difficulties in collection; or

    (b) as security for or in total or partial satisfaction of a pre-existing claim; or

    (c) by accepting delivery pursuant to a pre-existing contract for purchase; or

    (d) generally, in return for any consideration sufficient to support a simple contract.

(45) "Warehouse receipt" means a receipt issued by a person engaged in the business of storing goods for hire.

(46) "Written" or "writing" includes printing, typewriting or any other intentional reduction to tangible form.

Section 1—202. Prima Facie Evidence by Third Party Documents

A document in due form purporting to be a bill of lading, policy or certificate of insurance, official weigher's or inspector's certificate, consular invoice, or any other document authorized or required by the contract to be issued by a third party shall be prima facie evidence of its own authenticity and genuineness and of the facts stated in the document by the third party.

Section 1—203. Obligation of Good Faith

Every contract or duty within this Act imposes an obligation of good faith in its performance or enforcement.

Section 1—204. Time; Reasonable Time; "Seasonably"

(1) Whenever this Act requires any action to be taken within a reasonable time, any time which is not manifestly unreasonable may be fixed by agreement.

(2) What is a reasonable time for taking any action depends on the nature, purpose and circumstances of such action.

(3) An action is taken "seasonably" when it is taken at or within the time agreed or if no time is agreed at or within a reasonable time.

Section 1—205. Course of Dealing and Usage of Trade

(1) A course of dealing is a sequence of previous conduct between the parties to a particular transaction which is fairly to be regarded as establishing a common basis of understanding for interpreting their expressions and other conduct.

(2) A usage of trade is any practice or method of dealing having such regularity of observance in a place, vocation or trade as to justify an expectation that it will be observed with respect to the transaction in question. The existence and scope of such a usage are to be proved as facts. If it is established that such a usage is embodied in a written trade code or similar writing the interpretation of the writing is for the court.

(3) A course of dealing between parties and any usage of trade in the vocation or trade in which they are engaged or of which they are or should be aware give particular meaning to and supplement or qualify terms of an agreement.

(4) The express terms of an agreement and an applicable course of dealing or usage of trade shall be construed wherever reasonable as consistent with each other; but when such construction is unreasonable express terms control both course of dealing and usage of trade and course of dealing controls usage of trade.

(5) An applicable usage of trade in the place where any part of performance is to occur shall be used in interpreting the agreement as to that part of the performance.

(6) Evidence of a relevant usage of trade offered by one party is not admissible unless and until he has given the other party such notice as the court finds sufficient to prevent unfair surprise to the latter.

Section 1—206. Statute of Frauds for Kinds of Personal Property Not Otherwise Covered

(1) Except in the cases described in subsection (2) of this section a contract for the sale of personal property is not enforceable by way of action or defense beyond five thousand dollars in amount or value of remedy unless there is some writing which indicates that a contract for sale has been made between the parties at a defined or stated price, reasonably identifies the subject matter, and is signed by the party against whom enforcement is sought or by his authorized agent.

(2) Subsection (1) of this section does not apply to contracts for the sale of goods (Section 2—201) nor of securities (Section 8—319) nor to security agreements (Section 9—203).

Section 1—207. Performance or Acceptance Under Reservation of Rights

A party who with explicit reservation of rights performs or promises performance or assents to performance in a manner demanded or offered by the other party does not thereby prejudice the rights reserved. Such words as "without prejudice," "under protest" or the like are sufficient.

Section 1—208. Option to Accelerate at Will

A term providing that one party or his successor in interest may accelerate payment or performance or require collateral or additional collateral "at will" or "when he deems himself insecure" or in words of similar import shall be construed to mean that he shall have power to do so only if he in good faith believes that the prospect of payment or performance is impaired. The burden of establishing lack of good faith is on the party against whom the power has been exercised.

Section 1—209. Subordinated Obligations

An obligation may be issued as subordinated to payment of another obligation of the person obligated, or a creditor may subordinate his right to payment of an obligation by agreement with either the person obligated or another creditor of the person obligated. Such a subordination does not create a security interest as against either the common debtor or a subordinated creditor. This section shall be construed as declaring the law as it existed prior to the enactment of this section and not as modifying it.

Note: *This new section is proposed as an optional provision to make it clear that a subordination agreement does not create a security interest unless so intended.*

Article 2 Sales

Part 1 Short Title, General Construction and Subject Matter

Section 2—101. Short Title

This Article shall be known and may be cited as Uniform Commercial Code—Sales.

Section 2—102. Scope; Certain Security and Other Transactions Excluded From This Article

Unless the context otherwise requires, this Article applies to transactions in goods; it does not apply to any transaction which although in the form of an unconditional contract to sell or present sale is intended to operate only as a security transaction nor does this Article impair or repeal any statute regulating sales to consumers, farmers or other specified classes of buyers.

Section 2—103. Definitions and Index of Definitions

(1) In this Article unless the context otherwise requires

    (a) "Buyer" means a person who buys or contracts to buy goods.

    (b) "Good faith" in the case of a merchant means honesty in fact and the observance of reasonable commercial standards of fair dealing in the trade.

(c) "Receipt" of goods means taking physical possession of them.

(d) "Seller" means a person who sells or contracts to sell goods.

(2) Other definitions applying to this Article or to specified Parts thereof, and the sections in which they appear are:

"Acceptance." Section 2—606.
"Banker's credit." Section 2—325.
"Between merchants." Section 2—104.
"Cancellation." Section 2—106(4).
"Commercial unit." Section 2—105.
"Confirmed credit." Section 2—325.
"Conforming to contract." Section 2—106.
"Contract for sale." Section 2—106.
"Cover." Section 2—712.
"Entrusting." Section 2—403.
"Financing agency." Section 2—104.
"Future goods." Section 2—105.
"Goods." Section 2—105.
"Identification." Section 2—501.
"Installment contract." Section 2—612.
"Letter of Credit." Section 2—325.
"Lot." Section 2—105.
"Merchant." Section 2—104.
"Overseas." Section 2—323.
"Person in position of seller." Section 2—707.
"Present sale." Section 2—106.
"Sale." Section 2—106.
"Sale on approval." Section 2—326.
"Sale or return." Section 2—326.
"Termination." Section 2—106.

(3) The following definitions in other Articles apply to this Article:

"Check." Section 3—104.
"Consignee." Section 7—102.
"Consignor." Section 7—102.
"Consumer goods." Section 9—109.
"Dishonor." Section 3—507.
"Draft." Section 3—104.

(4) In addition Article 1 contains general definitions and principles of construction and interpretation applicable throughout this Article.

Section 2—104. Definitions: "Merchant"; "Between Merchants"; "Financing Agency"

(1) "Merchant" means a person who deals in goods of the kind or otherwise by his occupation holds himself out as having knowledge or skill peculiar to the practices or goods involved in the transaction or to whom such knowledge or skill may be attributed by his employment of an agent or broker or other intermediary who by his occupation holds himself out as having such knowledge or skill.

(2) "Financing agency" means a bank, finance company or other person who in the ordinary course of business makes advances against goods or documents of title or who by arrangement with either the seller or the buyer intervenes in ordinary course to make or collect payment due or claimed under the contract for sale, as by purchasing or paying the seller's draft or making advances against it or by merely taking it for collection whether or not documents of title accompany the draft. "Financing agency" includes also a bank or other person who similarly intervenes between persons who are in the position of seller and buyer in respect to the goods (Section 2—707).

(3) "Between merchants" means in any transaction with respect to which both parties are chargeable with the knowledge or skill of merchants.

Section 2—105. Definitions: Transferability; "Goods"; "Future" Goods; "Lot"; "Commercial Unit"

(1) "Goods" means all things (including specially manufactured goods) which are movable at the time of identification to the contract for sale other than the money in which the price is to be paid, investment securities (Article 8) and things in action. "Goods" also includes the unborn young of animals and growing crops and other identified things attached to realty as described in the section on goods to be severed from realty (Section 2—107).

(2) Goods must be both existing and identified before any interest in them can pass. Goods which are not both existing and identified are "future" goods. A purported present sale of future goods or of any interest therein operates as a contract to sell.

(3) There may be a sale of a part interest in existing identified goods.

(4) An undivided share in an identified bulk of fungible goods is sufficiently identified to be sold although the quantity of the bulk is not determined. Any agreed proportion of such a bulk or any quantity thereof agreed upon by number, weight or other measure may to the extent of the seller's interest in the bulk be sold to the buyer who then becomes an owner in common.

(5) "Lot" means a parcel or a single article which is the subject matter of a separate sale or delivery, whether or not it is sufficient to perform the contract.

(6) "Commercial unit" means such a unit of goods as by commercial usage is a single whole for purposes of sale and division of which materially impairs its character or value on the market or in use. A commercial unit may be a single article (as a machine) or a set of articles (as a suite of furniture or an assortment of sizes) or a quantity (as a bale, gross, or carload) or any other unit treated in use or in the relevant market as a single whole.

Section 2—106. Definitions: "Contract"; "Agreement"; "Contract for Sale"; "Sale"; "Present Sale"; "Conforming" to Contract; "Termination"; "Cancellation"

(1) In this Article unless the context otherwise requires "contract" and "agreement" are limited to those relating to the present or future sale of goods. "Contract for sale" includes both a present sale of goods and a contract to sell goods at a future time. A "sale" consists in the passing of title from the seller to the buyer for a price (Section 2—401). A "present sale" means a sale which is accomplished by the making of the contract.

(2) Goods or conduct including any part of a performance are "conforming" or conform to the contract when they are in accordance with the obligations under the contract.

(3) "Termination" occurs when either party pursuant to a power created by agreement or law puts an end to the contract otherwise than for its breach. On "termination" all obligations which are still executory on both sides are discharged but any right based on prior breach or performance survives.

(4) "Cancellation" occurs when either party puts an end to the contract for breach by the other and its effect is the same as that of "termination" except that the cancelling party also retains any remedy for breach of the whole contract or any unperformed balance.

Section 2—107. Goods to Be Severed From Realty: Recording

(1) A contract for the sale of minerals or the like (including oil and gas) or a structure or its materials to be removed from realty is a contract for the sale of goods within this Article if they are to be severed by the seller but until severance a purported present sale thereof which is not effective as a transfer of an interest in land is effective only as a contract to sell.

(2) A contract for the sale apart from the land of growing crops or other things attached to realty and capable of severance without material harm thereto but not described in subsection (1) or of timber to be cut is a contract for the sale of goods within this Article whether the subject matter is to be severed by the buyer or by the seller even though it forms part of the realty at the time of contracting, and the parties can by identification effect a present sale before severance.

(3) The provisions of this section are subject to any third party rights provided by the law relating to realty records, and the contract for sale may be executed and recorded as a document transferring an interest in land and shall then constitute notice to third parties of the buyer's rights under the contract for sale.

Part 2 Form, Formation and Readjustment of Contract

Section 2—201. Formal Requirements; Statute of Frauds

(1) Except as otherwise provided in this section a contract for the sale of goods for the price of $500 or more is not enforceable by way of action or defense unless there is some writing sufficient to indicate that a contract for sale has been made between the parties and signed by the party against whom enforcement is sought or by his authorized agent or broker. A writing is not insufficient because it omits or incorrectly states a term agreed upon but the contract is not enforceable under this paragraph beyond the quantity of goods shown in such writing.

(2) Between merchants if within a reasonable time a writing in confirmation of the contract and sufficient against the sender is received and the party receiving it has reason to know its contents, it satisfies the requirements of subsection (1) against such party unless written

notice of objection to its contents is given within 10 days after it is received.

(3) A contract which does not satisfy the requirements of subsection (1) but which is valid in other respects is enforceable

    (a) if the goods are to be specially manufactured for the buyer and are not suitable for sale to others in the ordinary course of the seller's business and the seller, before notice of repudiation is received and under circumstances which reasonably indicate that the goods are for the buyer, has made either a substantial beginning of their manufacture or commitments for their procurement; or

    (b) if the party against whom enforcement is sought admits in his pleading, testimony or otherwise in court that a contract for sale was made, but the contract is not enforceable under this provision beyond the quantity of goods admitted; or

    (c) with respect to goods for which payment has been made and accepted or which have been received and accepted (Sec. 2—606).

Section 2—202. Final Written Expression: Parol or Extrinsic Evidence

Terms with respect to which the confirmatory memoranda of the parties agree or which are otherwise set forth in a writing intended by the parties as a final expression of their agreement with respect to such terms as are included therein may not be contradicted by evidence of any prior agreement or of a contemporaneous oral agreement but may be explained or supplemented

    (a) by course of dealing or usage of trade (Section 1—205) or by course of performance (Section 2—208); and

    (b) by evidence of consistent additional terms unless the court finds the writing to have been intended also as a complete and exclusive statement of the terms of the agreement.

Section 2—203. Seals Inoperative

The affixing of a seal to a writing evidencing a contract for sale or an offer to buy or sell goods does not constitute the writing a sealed instrument and the law with respect to sealed instruments does not apply to such a contract or offer.

Section 2—204. Formation in General

(1) A contract for sale of goods may be made in any manner sufficient to show agreement, including conduct by both parties which recognizes the existence of such a contract.

(2) An agreement sufficient to constitute a contract for sale may be found even though the moment of its making is undetermined.

(3) Even though one or more terms are left open a contract for sale does not fail for indefiniteness if the parties have intended to make a contract and there is a reasonably certain basis for giving an appropriate remedy.

Section 2—205. Firm Offers

An offer by a merchant to buy or sell goods in a signed writing which by its terms give assurance that it will be held open is not revocable, for lack of consideration, during the time stated or if no time is stated for a reasonable time, but in no event may such period of irrevocability exceed three months; but any such term of assurance on a form supplied by the offeree must be separately signed by the offeror.

Section 2—206. Offer and Acceptance in Formation of Contract

(1) Unless otherwise unambiguously indicated by the language or circumstances

    (a) an offer to make a contract shall be construed as inviting acceptance in any manner and by any medium reasonable in the circumstances;

    (b) an order or other offer to buy goods for prompt or current shipment shall be construed as inviting acceptance either by a prompt promise to ship or by the prompt or current shipment of conforming or non-conforming goods, but such a shipment of non-conforming goods does not constitute an acceptance if the seller seasonably notifies the buyer that the shipment is offered only as an accommodation to the buyer.

(2) Where the beginning of a requested performance is a reasonable mode of acceptance an offeror who is not notified of acceptance within a reasonable time may treat the offer as having lapsed before acceptance.

Section 2—207. Additional Terms in Acceptance or Confirmation

(1) A definite and seasonable expression of acceptance or a written confirmation which is sent within a reasonable time operates as an acceptance even though it states terms additional to or different from those offered or agreed upon, unless acceptance is expressly made conditional on assent to the additional or different terms.

(2) The additional terms are to be construed as proposals for addition to the contract. Between merchants such terms become part of the contract unless:

    (a) the offer expressly limits acceptance to the terms of the offer;

    (b) they materially alter it; or

    (c) notification of objection to them has already been given or is given within a reasonable time after notice of them is received.

(3) Conduct by both parties which recognizes the existence of a contract is sufficient to establish a contract for sale although the writings of the parties do not otherwise establish a contract. In such case the terms of the particular contract consist of those terms on which the writings of the parties agree, together with any supplementary terms incorporated under any other provisions of this Act.

Section 2—208. Course of Performance or Practical Construction

(1) Where the contract for sale involves repeated occasions for performance by either party with knowledge of the nature of the performance and opportunity for objection to it by the other, any course of performance accepted or acquiesced in without objection shall be relevant to determine the meaning of the agreement.

(2) The express terms of the agreement and any such course of performance, as well as any course of dealing and usage of trade, shall be construed whenever reasonable as consistent with each other; but when such construction is unreasonable, express terms shall control course of performance and course of performance shall control both course of dealing and usage of trade (Section 1—205).

(3) Subject to the provisions of the next section on modification and waiver, such course of performance shall be relevant to show a waiver or modification of any term inconsistent with such course of performance.

Section 2—209. Modification, Rescission and Waiver

(1) An agreement modifying a contract within this Article needs no consideration to be binding.

(2) A signed agreement which excludes modification or rescission except by a signed writing cannot be otherwise modified or rescinded, but except as between merchants such a requirement on a form supplied by the merchant must be separately signed by the other party.

(3) The requirements of the statute of frauds section of this Article (Section 2—201) must be satisfied if the contract as modified is within its provisions.

(4) Although an attempt at modification or rescission does not satisfy the requirements of subsection (2) or (3) it can operate as a waiver.

(5) A party who has made a waiver affecting an executory portion of the contract may retract the waiver by reasonable notification received by the other party that strict performance will be required of any term waived, unless the retraction would be unjust in view of a material change of position in reliance on the waiver.

Section 2—210. Delegation of Performance; Assignment of Rights

(1) A party may perform his duty through a delegate unless otherwise agreed or unless the other party has a substantial interest in having his original promisor perform or control the acts required by the contract. No delegation of performance relieves the party delegating of any duty to perform or any liability for breach.

(2) Unless otherwise agreed all rights of either seller or buyer can be assigned except where the assignment would materially change the duty of the other party, or increase materially the burden or risk imposed on him by his contract, or impair materially his chance of obtaining return performance. A right to damages for breach of the whole contract or a right arising out of the assignor's due performance of his entire obligation can be assigned despite agreement otherwise.

(3) Unless the circumstances indicate the contrary a prohibition of assignment of "the contract" is to be construed as barring only the delegation to the assignee of the assignor's performance.

(4) An assignment of "the contract" or of "all my rights under the contract" or an assignment in similar general terms is an assignment of rights and unless the language or the circumstances (as in an assignment for security) indicate the contrary, it is a delegation of performance of the duties of the assignor and its acceptance by the assignee constitutes a promise by him to perform those duties. This promise is enforceable by either the assignor or the other party to the original contract.

(5) The other party may treat any assignment which delegates performance as creating reasonable grounds for insecurity and may without prejudice to his rights against the assignor demand assurances from the assignee (Section 2—609).

Part 3 General Obligation and Construction of Contract

Section 2—301. General Obligations of Parties

The obligation of the seller is to transfer and deliver and that of the buyer is to accept and pay in accordance with the contract.

Section 2—302. Unconscionable Contract or Clause

(1) If the court as a matter of law finds the contract or any clause of the contract to have been unconscionable at the time it was made the court may refuse to enforce the contract, or it may enforce the remainder of the contract without the unconscionable clause, or it may so limit the application of any unconscionable clause as to avoid any unconscionable result.

(2) When it is claimed or appears to the court that the contract or any clause thereof may be unconscionable the parties shall be afforded a reasonable opportunity to present evidence as to its commercial setting, purpose and effect to aid the court in making the determination.

Section 2—303. Allocation or Division of Risks

Where this Article allocates a risk or a burden as between the parties "unless otherwise agreed," the agreement may not only shift the allocation but may also divide the risk or burden.

Section 2—304. Price Payable in Money, Goods, Realty, or Otherwise

(1) The price can be made payable in money or otherwise. If it is payable in whole or in part in goods each party is a seller of the goods which he is to transfer.

(2) Even though all or part of the price is payable in an interest in realty the transfer of the goods and the seller's obligations with reference to them are subject to this Article, but not the transfer of the interest in realty or the transferor's obligations in connection therewith.

Section 2—305. Open Price Term

(1) The parties if they so intend can conclude a contract for sale even though the price is not settled. In such a case the price is a reasonable price at the time for delivery if

(a) nothing is said as to price; or

(b) the price is left to be agreed by the parties and they fail to agree; or

(c) the price is to be fixed in terms of some agreed market or other standard as set or recorded by a third person or agency and it is not so set or recorded.

(2) A price to be fixed by the seller or by the buyer means a price for him to fix in good faith.

(3) When a price left to be fixed otherwise than by agreement of the parties fails to be fixed through fault of one party the other may at his option treat the contract as cancelled or himself fix a reasonable price.

(4) Where, however, the parties intend not to be bound unless the price be fixed or agreed and it is not fixed or agreed there is no contract. In such a case the buyer must return any goods already received or if unable so to do must pay their reasonable value at the time of delivery and the seller must return any portion of the price paid on account.

Section 2—306. Output, Requirements and Exclusive Dealings

(1) A term which measures the quantity by the output of the seller or the requirements of the buyer means such actual output or requirements as may occur in good faith, except that no quantity unreasonably disproportionate to any stated estimate or in the absence of a

stated estimate to any normal or otherwise comparable prior output or requirements may be tendered or demanded.

(2) A lawful agreement by either the seller or the buyer for exclusive dealing in the kind of goods concerned imposes unless otherwise agreed an obligation by the seller to use best efforts to supply the goods and by the buyer to use best efforts to promote their sale.

Section 2—307.   Delivery in Single Lot or Several Lots

Unless otherwise agreed all goods called for by a contract for sale must be tendered in a single delivery and payment is due only on such tender but where the circumstances give either party the right to make or demand delivery in lots the price if it can be apportioned may be demanded for each lot.

Section 2—308.   Absence of Specified Place for Delivery

Unless otherwise agreed

(a) the place for delivery of goods is the seller's place of business or if he has none his residence; but

(b) in a contract for sale of identified goods which to the knowledge of the parties at the time of contracting are in some other place, that place is the place for their delivery; and

(c) documents of title may be delivered through customary banking channels.

Section 2—309.   Absence of Specific Time Provisions; Notice of Termination

(1) The time for shipment or delivery or any other action under a contract if not provided in this Article or agreed upon shall be a reasonable time.

(2) Where the contract provides for successive performances but is indefinite in duration it is valid for a reasonable time but unless otherwise agreed may be terminated at any time by either party.

(3) Termination of a contract by one party except on the happening of an agreed event requires that reasonable notification be received by the other party and an agreement dispensing with notification is invalid if its operation would be unconscionable.

Section 2—310.   Open Time for Payment or Running of Credit; Authority to Ship Under Reservation

Unless otherwise agreed

(a) payment is due at the time and place at which the buyer is to receive the goods even though the place of shipment is the place of delivery; and

(b) if the seller is authorized to send the goods he may ship them under reservation, and may tender the documents of title, but the buyer may inspect the goods after their arrival before payment is due unless such inspection is inconsistent with the terms of the contract (Section 2—513); and

(c) if delivery is authorized and made by way of documents of title otherwise than by subsection (b) then payment is due at the time and place at which the buyer is to receive the documents regardless of where the goods are to be received; and

(d) where the seller is required or authorized to ship the goods on credit the credit period runs from the time of shipment but post-dating the invoice or delaying its dispatch will correspondingly delay the starting of the credit period.

Section 2—311.   Options and Cooperation Respecting Performance

(1) An agreement for sale which is otherwise sufficiently definite (subsection (3) of Section 2—204) to be a contract is not made invalid by the fact that it leaves particulars of performance to be specified by one of the parties. Any such specification must be made in good faith and within limits set by commercial reasonableness.

(2) Unless otherwise agreed specifications relating to assortment of the goods are at the buyer's option and except as otherwise provided in subsections (1) (c) and (3) of Section 2—319 specifications or arrangements relating to shipment are at the seller's option.

(3) Where such specification would materially affect the other party's performance but is not seasonably made or where one party's cooperation is necessary to

the agreed performance of the other but is not seasonably forthcoming, the other party in addition to all other remedies

> (a) is excused for any resulting delay in his own performance; and
>
> (b) may also either proceed to perform in any reasonable manner or after the time for a material part of his own performance treat the failure to specify or to cooperate as a breach by failure to deliver or accept the goods.

Section 2—312. Warranty of Title and Against Infringement; Buyer's Obligation Against Infringement

(1) Subject to subsection (2) there is in a contract for sale a warranty by the seller that

> (a) the title conveyed shall be good, and its transfer rightful; and
>
> (b) the goods shall be delivered free from any security interest or other lien or encumbrance of which the buyer at the time of contracting has no knowledge.

(2) A warranty under subsection (1) will be excluded or modified only by specific language or by circumstances which give the buyer reason to know that the person selling does not claim title in himself or that he is purporting to sell only such right or title as he or a third person may have.

(3) Unless otherwise agreed a seller who is a merchant regularly dealing in goods of the kind warrants that the goods shall be delivered free of the rightful claim of any third person by way of infringement or the like but a buyer who furnishes specifications to the seller must hold the seller harmless against any such claim which arises out of compliance with the specifications.

Section 2—313. Express Warranties by Affirmation, Promise, Description, Sample

(1) Express warranties by the seller are created as follows:

> (a) Any affirmation of fact or promise made by the seller to the buyer which relates to the goods and becomes part of the basis of the bargain creates an express warranty that the goods shall conform to the affirmation or promise:

> (b) Any description of the goods which is made part of the basis of the bargain creates an express warranty that the goods shall conform to the description.
>
> (c) Any sample or model which is made part of the basis of the bargain creates an express warranty that the whole of the goods shall conform to the sample or model.

(2) It is not necessary to the creation of an express warranty that the seller use formal words such as "warrant" or "guarantee" or that he have a specific intention to make a warranty, but an affirmation merely of the value of the goods or a statement purporting to be merely the seller's opinion or commendation of the goods does not create a warranty.

Section 2—314. Implied Warranty: Merchantability; Usage of Trade

(1) Unless excluded or modified (Section 2—316), a warranty that the goods shall be merchantable is implied in a contract for their sale if the seller is a merchant with respect to goods of that kind. Under this section the serving for value of food or drink to be consumed either on the premises or elsewhere is a sale.

(2) Goods to be merchantable must be at least such as

> (a) pass without objection in the trade under the contract description; and
>
> (b) in the case of fungible goods, are of fair average quality within the description; and
>
> (c) are fit for the ordinary purposes for which such goods are used; and
>
> (d) run, within the variations permitted by the agreement, of even kind, quality and quantity within each unit and among all units involved; and
>
> (e) are adequately contained, packaged, and labeled as the agreement may require; and
>
> (f) conform to the promises or affirmations of fact made on the container or label if any.

(3) Unless excluded or modified (Section 2—316) other implied warranties may arise from course of dealing or usage of trade.

Section 2—315. Implied Warranty: Fitness for Particular Purpose

Where the seller at the time of contracting has reason to know any particular purpose for which the goods are required and that the buyer is relying on the seller's skill or judgment to select or furnish suitable goods, there is unless excluded or modified under the next section an implied warranty that the goods shall be fit for such purpose.

Section 2—316. Exclusion or Modification of Warranties

(1) Words or conduct relevant to the creation of an express warranty and words or conduct tending to negate or limit warranty shall be construed wherever reasonable as consistent with each other; but subject to the provisions of this Article on parol or extrinsic evidence (Section 2—202) negation or limitation is inoperative to the extent that such construction is unreasonable.

(2) Subject to subsection (3), to exclude or modify the implied warranty or merchantability or any part of it the language must mention merchantability and in case of a writing must be conspicuous, and to exclude or modify any implied warranty of fitness the exclusion must be by a writing and conspicuous. Language to exclude all implied warranties of fitness is sufficient if it states, for example, that "There are no warranties which extend beyond the description on the face hereof."

(3) Notwithstanding subsection (2)

  (a) unless the circumstances indicate otherwise, all implied warranties are excluded by expressions like "as is," "with all faults" or other languages which in common understanding calls the buyer's attention to the exclusion of warranties and makes plain that there is no implied warranty; and

  (b) when the buyer before entering into the contract has examined the goods or the sample or model as fully as he desired or has refused to examine the goods there is no implied warranty with regard to defects which an examination ought in the circumstances to have revealed to him; and

  (c) an implied warranty can also be excluded or modified by course of dealing or course of performance or usage of trade.

(4) Remedies for breach of warranty can be limited in accordance with the provisions of this Article on liquidation or limitation of damages and on contractual modification of remedy (Sections 2—718 and 2—719).

Section 2—317. Cumulation and Conflict of Warranties Express or Implied

Warranties whether express or implied shall be construed as consistent with each other and as cumulative, but if such construction is unreasonable the intention of the parties shall determine which warranty is dominant. In ascertaining that intention the following rules apply:

  (a) Exact or technical specifications displace an inconsistent sample or model or general language of description.

  (b) A sample from an existing bulk displaces inconsistent general language of description.

  (c) Express warranties displace inconsistent implied warranties other than an implied warranty of fitness for a particular purpose.

Section 2—318. Third Party Beneficiaries of Warranties Express or Implied

Note: *If this Act is introduced in the Congress of the United States this section should be omitted. (States to select one alternative.)*

Alternative A

A seller's warranty whether express or implied extends to any natural person who is in the family or household of his buyer or who is a guest in his home if it is reasonable to expect that such person may use, consume or be affected by the goods and who is injured in person by breach of the warranty. A seller may not exclude or limit the operation of this section.

Alternative B

A seller's warranty whether express or implied extends to any natural person who may reasonably be expected to use, consume or be affected by the goods and who is injured in person by breach of the warranty. A seller may not exclude or limit the operation of this section.

Alternative C

A seller's warranty whether express or implied extends to any person who may reasonably be expected to use, consume or be affected by the goods and who is injured by breach of the warranty. A seller may not exclude or limit the operation of this section with respect to injury to the person of an individual to whom the warranty extends.

Section 2—319. F.O.B. and F.A.S. Terms

(1) Unless otherwise agreed the term F.O.B. (which means "free on board") at a named place, even though used only in connection with the stated price, is a delivery term under which

   (a) when the term is F.O.B. the place of shipment, the seller must at that place ship the goods in the manner provided in this Article (Section 2—504) and bear the expense and risk of putting them into the possession of the carrier; or

   (b) when the term is F.O.B. the place of destination, the seller must at his own expense and risk transport the goods to that place and there tender delivery of them in the manner provided in this Article (Section 2—503);

   (c) when under either (a) or (b) the term is also F.O.B. vessel, car or other vehicle, the seller must in addition at his own expense and risk load the goods on board. If the term is F.O.B. vessel the buyer must name the vessel and in an appropriate case the seller must comply with the provisions of this Article on the form of bill of lading (Section 2—323).

(2) Unless otherwise agreed the term F.A.S. vessel (which means "free alongside") at a named port, even though used only in connection with the stated price, is a delivery term under which the seller must

   (a) at his own expense and risk deliver the goods alongside the vessel in the manner usual in that port or on a dock designated and provided by the buyer; and

   (b) obtain and tender a receipt for the goods in exchange for which the carrier is under a duty to issue a bill of lading.

(3) Unless otherwise agreed in any case falling within subsection (1) (a) or (c) or subsection (2) the buyer must seasonably give any needed instructions for making delivery, including when the term is F.A.S. or F.O.B. the loading berth of the vessel and in an appropriate case its name and sailing date. The seller may treat the failure of needed instructions as a failure of cooperation under this Article (Section 2—311). He may also at his option move the goods in any reasonable manner preparatory to delivery or shipment.

(4) Under the term F.O.B. vessel or F.A.S. unless otherwise agreed the buyer must make payment against tender of the required documents and the seller may not tender nor the buyer demand delivery of the goods in substitution for the documents.

Section 2—320. C.I.F. and C. & F. Terms

(1) The term C.I.F. means that the price includes in a lump sum the cost of the goods and the insurance and freight to the named destination. The term C. & F. or C.F. means that the price so includes cost and freight to the named destination.

(2) Unless otherwise agreed and even though used only in connection with the stated price and destination, the term C.I.F. destination or its equivalent requires the seller at his own expense and risk to

   (a) put the goods into the possession of a carrier at the port for shipment and obtain a negotiable bill or bills of lading covering the entire transportation to the named destination; and

   (b) load the goods and obtain a receipt from the carrier (which may be contained in the bill of lading) showing that the freight has been paid or provided for; and

   (c) obtain a policy or certificate of insurance, including any war risk insurance, of a kind and on terms then current at the port of shipment in the usual amount, in the currency of the contract, shown to cover the same goods covered by the bill of lading and providing for payment of loss to the order of the buyer or for the account of whom it may concern; but the seller may add to the price the amount of the premium for any such war risk insurance; and

(d) prepare an invoice of the goods and procure any other documents required to effect shipment or to comply with the contract; and

(e) forward and tender with commercial promptness all the documents in due form and with any indorsement necessary to perfect the buyer's rights.

(3) Unless otherwise agreed the term C. & F. or its equivalent has the same effect and imposes upon the seller the same obligations and risks as a C.I.F. term except the obligation as to insurance.

(4) Under the term C.I.F. or C. & F. unless otherwise agreed the buyer must make payment against tender of the required documents and the seller may not tender nor the buyer demand delivery of the goods in substitution for the documents.

Section 2—321. C.I.F. or C. & F.: "Net Landed Weights"; "Payment on Arrival"; Warranty of Condition on Arrival

Under a contract containing a term C.I.F. or C. & F.

(1) Where the price is based on or is to be adjusted according to "net landed weights," "delivered weights," "out turn" quantity or quality or the like, unless otherwise agreed the seller must reasonably estimate the price. The payment due on tender of the documents called for by the contract is the amount so estimated, but after final adjustment of the price a settlement must be made with commercial promptness.

(2) An agreement described in subsection (1) or any warranty of quality or condition of the goods on arrival places upon the seller the risk of ordinary deterioration, shrinkage and the like in transportation but has no effect on the place or time of identification to the contract for sale or delivery or on the passing of the risk of loss.

(3) Unless otherwise agreed where the contract provides for payment on or after arrival of the goods the seller must before payment allow such preliminary inspection as is feasible; but if the goods are lost delivery of the documents and payment are due when the goods should have arrived.

Section 2—322. Delivery "Ex-Ship"

(1) Unless otherwise agreed a term for delivery of goods "ex-ship" (which means from the carrying vessel) or in equivalent language is not restricted to a particular ship and requires delivery from a ship which has reached a place at the named port of destination where goods of the kind are usually discharged.

(2) Under such a term unless otherwise agreed

(a) the seller must discharge all liens arising out of the carriage and furnish the buyer with a direction which puts the carrier under a duty to deliver the goods; and

(b) the risk of loss does not pass to the buyer until the goods leave the ship's tackle or are otherwise properly unloaded.

Section 2—323. Form of Bill of Lading Required in Overseas Shipment; "Overseas"

(1) Where the contract contemplates overseas shipment and contains a term C.I.F. or C. & F. or F.O.B. vessel, the seller unless otherwise agreed must obtain a negotiable bill of lading stating that the goods have been loaded on board or, in the case of a term C.I.F. or C. & F., received for shipment.

(2) Where in a case within subsection (1) a bill of lading has been issued in a set of parts, unless otherwise agreed if the documents are not to be sent from abroad the buyer may demand tender of the full set; otherwise only one part of the bill of lading need be tendered. Even if the agreement expressly requires a full set

(a) due tender of a single part is acceptable within the provisions of this Article on cure of improper delivery (subsection (1) of Section 2—508); and

(b) even though the full set is demanded, if the documents are sent from abroad the person tendering an incomplete set may nevertheless require payment upon furnishing an indemnity which the buyer in good faith deems adequate.

(3) A shipment by water or by air or a contract contemplating such shipment is "overseas" insofar as by usage of trade or agreement it is subject to the commercial, financing or shipping practices characteristic of international deep water commerce.

Section 2—324.   "No Arrival, No Sale" Term

Under a term "no arrival, no sale" or terms of like meaning, unless otherwise agreed,

    (a) the seller must properly ship conforming goods and if they arrive by any means he must tender them on arrival but he assumes no obligation that the goods will arrive unless he has caused the non-arrival; and

    (b) where without fault of the seller the goods are in part lost or have so deteriorated as no longer to conform to the contract or arrive after the contract time, the buyer may proceed as if there had been casualty to identified goods (Section 2—613).

Section 2—325.   "Letter of Credit" Term; "Confirmed Credit"

(1) Failure of the buyer seasonably to furnish an agreed letter of credit is a breach of the contract for sale.

(2) The delivery to seller of a proper letter of credit suspends the buyer's obligation to pay. If the letter of credit is dishonored, the seller may on seasonable notification to the buyer require payment directly from him.

(3) Unless otherwise agreed the term "letter of credit" or "banker's credit" in a contract for sale means an irrevocable credit issued by a financing agency of good repute and, where the shipment is overseas, of good international repute. The term "confirmed credit" means that the credit must also carry the direct obligation of such an agency which does business in the seller's financial market.

Section 2—326.   Sale on Approval and Sale or Return; Consignment Sales and Rights of Creditors

(1) Unless otherwise agreed, if delivered goods may be returned by the buyer even though they conform to the contract, the transaction is

    (a) a "sale on approval" if the goods are delivered primarily for use, and

    (b) a "sale or return" if the goods are delivered primarily for resale.

(2) Except as provided in subsection (3), goods held on approval are not subject to the claims of the buyer's creditors until acceptance; goods held on sale or return are subject to such claims while in the buyer's possession.

(3) Where goods are delivered to a person for sale and such person maintains a place of business at which he deals in goods of the kind involved, under a name other than the name of the person making delivery, then with respect to claims of creditors of the person conducting the business the goods are deemed to be on sale or return. The provisions of this subsection are applicable even though an agreement purports to reserve title to the person making delivery until payment or resale or uses such words as "on consignment" or "on memorandum." However, this subsection is not applicable if the person making delivery

    (a) complies with an applicable law providing for a consignor's interest or the like to be evidenced by a sign, or

    (b) establishes that the person conducting the business is generally known by his creditors to be substantially engaged in selling the goods of others, or

    (c) complies with the filing provisions of the Article on Secured Transactions (Article 9).

(4) Any "or return" term of a contract for sale is to be treated as a separate contract for sale within the statute of frauds section of this Article (Section 2—201) and as contradicting the sale aspect of the contract within the provisions of this Article on parol or extrinsic evidence (Section 2—202).

Section 2—327.   Special Incidents of Sale on Approval and Sale or Return

(1) Under a sale on approval unless otherwise agreed

    (a) although the goods are identified to the contract the risk of loss and the title do not pass to the buyer until acceptance; and

    (b) use of the goods consistent with the purpose of trial is not acceptance but failure seasonably to notify the seller of election to return the goods is acceptance, and if the goods conform to the contract acceptance of any part is acceptance of the whole; and

    (c) after due notification of election to return, the return is at the seller's risk and expense but a merchant buyer must follow any reasonable instructions.

(2) Under a sale or return unless otherwise agreed

    (a) the option to return extends to the whole or any commercial unit of the goods while in substantially their original condition, but must be exercised seasonably; and

    (b) the return is at the buyer's risk and expense.

Section 2—328. Sale by Auction

(1) In a sale by auction if goods are put up in lots each lot is the subject of a separate sale.

(2) A sale by auction is complete when the auctioneer so announces by the fall of the hammer or in other customary manner. Where a bid is made while the hammer is falling in acceptance of a prior bid the auctioneer may in his discretion reopen the bidding or declare the goods sold under the bid on which the hammer was falling.

(3) Such a sale is with reserve unless the goods are in explicit terms put up without reserve. In an auction with reserve the auctioneer may withdraw the goods at any time until he announces completion of the sale. In an auction without reserve, after the auctioneer calls for bids on an article or lot, that article or lot cannot be withdrawn unless no bid is made within a reasonable time. In either case a bidder may retract his bid until the auctioneer's announcement of completion of the sale, but a bidder's retraction does not revive any previous bid.

(4) If the auctioneer knowingly receives a bid on the seller's behalf or the seller makes or procures such a bid, and notice has not been given that liberty for such bidding is reserved, the buyer may at his option avoid the sale or take the goods at the price of the last good faith bid prior to the completion of the sale. This subsection shall not apply to any bid at a forced sale.

Part 4 Title, Creditors and Good Faith Purchasers

Section 2—401. Passing of Title; Reservation for Security; Limited Application of This Section

Each provision of this Article with regard to the rights, obligations and remedies of the seller, the buyer, purchasers or other third parties applies irrespective of title to the goods except where the provision refers to such title. Insofar as situations are not covered by the other provisions of this Article and matters concerning title become material the following rules apply:

(1) Title to goods cannot pass under a contract for sale prior to their identification to the contract (Section 2—501), and unless otherwise explicitly agreed the buyer acquires by their identification a special property as limited by this Act. Any retention or reservation by the seller of the title (property) in goods shipped or delivered to the buyer is limited in effect to a reservation of a security interest. Subject to these provisions and to the provisions of the Article on Secured Transactions (Article 9), title to goods passes from the seller to the buyer in any manner and on any conditions explicitly agreed on by the parties.

(2) Unless otherwise explicitly agreed title passes to the buyer at the time and place at which the seller completes his performance with reference to the physical delivery of the goods, despite any reservation of a security interest and even though a document of title is to be delivered at a different time or place; and in particular and despite any reservation of a security interest by the bill of lading

    (a) if the contract requires or authorizes the seller to send the goods to the buyer but does not require him to deliver them at destination, title passes to the buyer at the time and place of shipment; but

    (b) if the contract requires delivery at destination, title passes on tender there.

(3) Unless otherwise explicitly agreed where delivery is to be made without moving the goods,

    (a) if the seller is to deliver a document of title, passes at the time when and the place where he delivers such documents; or

    (b) if the goods are at the time of contracting already identified and no documents are to be delivered, title passes at the time and place of contracting.

(4) A rejection or other refusal by the buyer to receive or retain the goods, whether or not justified, or a justified revocation of acceptance revests title to the goods in the seller. Such revesting occurs by operation of law and is not a "sale."

Section 2—402. Rights of Seller's Creditors Against Sold Goods

(1) Except as provided in subsections (2) and (3), rights of unsecured creditors of the seller with respect to goods which have been identified to a contract for sale are subject to the buyer's rights to recover the goods under this Article (Sections 2—502 and 2—716).

(2) A creditor of the seller may treat a sale or an identification of goods to a contract for sale as void if as against him a retention of possession by the seller is fraudulent under any rule of law of the state where the goods are situated, except that retention of possession in good faith and current course of trade by a merchant-seller for a commercially reasonable time after a sale or identification is not fraudulent.

(3) Nothing in this Article shall be deemed to impair the rights of creditors of the seller

    (a) under the provisions of the Article on Secured Transactions (Article 9); or

    (b) where identification to the contract or delivery is made not in current course of trade but in satisfaction of or as security for a pre-existing claim for money, security or the like and is made under circumstances which under any rule of law of the state where the goods are situated would apart from this Article constitute the transaction a fraudulent transfer or voidable preference.

Section 2—403. Power to Transfer; Good Faith Purchase of Goods; "Entrusting"

(1) A purchaser of goods acquires all title which his transferor had or had power to transfer except that a purchaser of a limited interest acquires rights only to the extent of the interest purchased. A person with voidable title has power to transfer a good title to a good faith purchaser for value. When goods have been delivered under a transaction of purchase the purchaser has such power even though

    (a) the transferor was deceived as to the identity of the purchaser, or

    (b) the delivery was in exchange for a check which is later dishonored, or

    (c) it was agreed that the transaction was to be a "cash sale," or

    (d) the delivery was procured through fraud punishable as larcenous under the criminal law.

(2) Any entrusting of possession of goods to a merchant who deals in goods of that kind gives him power to transfer all rights of the entruster to a buyer in ordinary course of business.

(3) "Entrusting" includes any delivery and any acquiescence in retention of possession regardless of any condition expressed between the parties to the delivery or acquiescence and regardless of whether the procurement of the entrusting or the possessor's disposition of the goods have been such as to be larcenous under the criminal law.

(4) The rights of other purchasers of goods and of lien creditors are governed by the Articles on Secured Transactions (Article 9), Bulk Transfers (Article 6) and Documents of Title (Article 7).

Part 5 Performance

Section 2—501. Insurable Interest in Goods; Manner of Identification of Goods

(1) The buyer obtains a special property and an insurable interest in goods by identification of existing goods as goods to which the contract refers even though the goods so identified are nonconforming and he has an option to return or reject them. Such identification can be made at any time and in any manner explicitly agreed to by the parties. In the absence of explicit agreement identification occurs.

    (a) when the contract is made if it is for the sale of goods already existing and identified;

    (b) if the contract is for the sale of future goods other than those described in paragraph (c), when goods are shipped, marked or otherwise designated by the seller as goods to which the contract refers;

    (c) when the crops are planted or otherwise become growing crops or the young are conceived if the contract is for the sale of unborn young to be born within twelve months after contracting or for the sale of crops to be harvested within twelve months or the next normal harvest season after contracting whichever is longer.

(2) The seller retains an insurable interest in goods so long as title to or any security interest in the goods remains in him and where the identification is by the seller alone he may until default or insolvency or notification to the buyer that the identification is final substitute other goods for those identified.

(3) Nothing in this section impairs any insurable interest recognized under any other statute or rule of law.

Section 2—502. Buyer's Right to Goods on Seller's Insolvency

(1) Subject to subsection (2) and even though the goods have not been shipped a buyer who has paid a part or all of the price of goods in which he has a special property under the provisions of the immediately preceding section may on making and keeping good a tender of any unpaid portion of their price recover them from the seller if the seller becomes insolvent within ten days after receipt of the first installment on their price.

(2) If the identification creating his special property has been made by the buyer he acquires the right to recover the goods only if they conform to the contract for sale.

Section 2—503. Manner of Seller's Tender of Delivery

(1) Tender of delivery requires that the seller put and hold conforming goods at the buyer's disposition and give the buyer any notification reasonably necessary to enable him to take delivery. The manner, time and place for tender are determined by the agreement and this Article, and in particular

    (a) tender must be at a reasonable hour, and if it is of goods they must be kept available for the period reasonably necessary to enable the buyer to take possession; but

    (b) unless otherwise agreed the buyer must furnish facilities reasonably suited to the receipt of the goods.

(2) Where the case is within the next section respecting shipment tender requires that the seller comply with its provisions.

(3) Where the seller is required to deliver at a particular destination tender requires that he comply with subsection (1) and also in any appropriate case tender documents as described in subsections (4) and (5) of this section.

(4) Where goods are in the possession of a bailee and are to be delivered without being moved

    (a) tender requires that the seller either tender a negotiable document of title covering such goods or procure acknowledgment by the bailee of the buyer's right to possession of the goods; but

    (b) tender to the buyer of a non-negotiable document of title or of a written direction to the bailee to deliver is sufficient tender unless the buyer seasonably objects, and receipt by the bailee of notification of the buyer's rights fixes those rights as against the bailee and all third persons; but risk of loss of the goods and of any failure by the bailee to honor the non-negotiable document of title or to obey the direction remains on the seller until the buyer has had a reasonable time to present the document or direction, and a refusal by the bailee to honor the document or to obey the direction defeats the tender.

(5) Where the contract requires the seller to deliver documents

    (a) he must tender all such documents in correct form, except as provided in this Article with respect to bills of lading in a set (subsection (2) of Section 2—323); and

    (b) tender through customary banking channels is sufficient and dishonor of a draft accompanying the documents constitutes non-acceptance or rejection.

Section 2—504. Shipment by Seller

Where the seller is required or authorized to send the goods to the buyer and the contract does not require him to deliver them at a particular destination, then unless otherwise agreed he must

    (a) put the goods in the possession of such a carrier and make such a contract for their transportation as may be reasonable having regard to the nature of the goods and other circumstances of the case; and

(b) obtain and promptly deliver or tender in due form any document necessary to enable the buyer to obtain possession of the goods or otherwise required by the agreement or by usage of trade; and

(c) promptly notify the buyer of the shipment.

Failure to notify the buyer under paragraph (c) or to make a proper contract under paragraph (a) is a ground for rejection only if material delay or loss ensues.

Section 2—505. Seller's Shipment Under Reservation

(1) Where the seller has identified goods to the contract by or before shipment:

(a) his procurement of a negotiable bill of lading to his own order or otherwise reserves in him a security interest in the goods. His procurement of the bill to the order of a financing agency or of the buyer indicates in addition only the seller's expectation of transferring that interest to the person named.

(b) a non-negotiable bill of lading to himself or his nominee reserves possession of the goods as security but except in a case of conditional delivery (subsection (2) of Section 2—507) a non-negotiable bill of lading naming the buyer as consignee reserves no security interest even though the seller retains possession of the bill of lading.

(2) When shipment by the seller with reservation of a security interest is in violation of the contract for sale it constitutes an improper contract for transportation within the preceding section but impairs neither the rights given to the buyer by shipment and identification of the goods to the contract nor the seller's powers as a holder of a negotiable document.

Section 2—506. Rights of Financing Agency

(1) A financing agency by paying or purchasing for value a draft which relates to a shipment of goods acquires to the extent of the payment or purchase and in addition to its own rights under the draft and any document of title securing it any rights of the shipper in the goods including the right to stop delivery and the shipper's right to have the draft honored by the buyer.

(2) The right to reimbursement of a financing agency which has in good faith honored or purchased the draft under commitment to or authority from the buyer is not impaired by subsequent discovery of defects with reference to any relevant document which was apparently regular on its face.

Section 2—507. Effect of Seller's Tender; Delivery on Condition

(1) Tender of delivery is a condition to the buyer's duty to accept the goods and, unless otherwise agreed, to his duty to pay for them. Tender entitles the seller to acceptance of the goods and to payment according to the contract.

(2) Where payment is due and demanded on the delivery to the buyer of goods or documents of title, his right as against the seller to retain or dispose of them is conditional upon his making the payment due.

Section 2—508. Cure by Seller of Improper Tender or Delivery; Replacement

(1) Where any tender or delivery by the seller is rejected because non-conforming and the time for performance has not yet expired, the seller may seasonally notify the buyer of his intention to cure and may then within the contract time make a conforming delivery.

(2) Where the buyer rejects a non-conforming tender which the seller had reasonable grounds to believe would be acceptable with or without money allowance the seller may if he seasonably notifies the buyer have a further reasonable time to substitute a conforming tender.

Section 2—509. Risk of Loss in the Absence of Breach

(1) Where the contract requires or authorizes the seller to ship the goods by carrier

(a) if it does not require him to deliver them at a particular destination, the risk of loss passes to the buyer when the goods are duly delivered to the carrier even though the shipment is under reservation (Section 2—505); but

(b) if it does require him to deliver them at a particular destination and the goods are there duly tendered while in the possession of the carrier, the risk of loss passes to the buyer when the goods are there duly so tendered as to enable the buyer to take delivery.

(2) Where the goods are held by a bailee to be delivered without being moved, the risk of loss passes to the buyer

(a) on his receipt of a negotiable document of title covering the goods; or

(b) on acknowledgment by the bailee of the buyer's right to possession of the goods; or

(c) after his receipt of a non-negotiable document of title or other written direction to deliver, as provided in subsection (4) (b) of Section 2—503.

(3) In any case not within subsection (1) or (2), the risk of loss passes to the buyer on his receipt of the goods if the seller is a merchant; otherwise the risk passes to the buyer on tender of delivery.

(4) The provisions of this section are subject to contrary agreement of the parties and to the provisions of this Article on sale on approval (Section 2—327) and on effect of breach on risk of loss (Section 2—510).

Section 2—510. Effect of Breach on Risk of Loss

(1) Where a tender or delivery of goods so fails to conform to the contract as to give a right of rejection the risk of their loss remains on the seller until cure or acceptance.

(2) Where the buyer rightfully revokes acceptance he may to the extent of any deficiency in his effective insurance coverage treat the risk of loss as having rested on the seller from the beginning.

(3) Where the buyer as to conforming goods already identified to the contract for sale repudiates or is otherwise in breach before risk of their loss has passed to him, the seller may to the extent of any deficiency in his effective insurance coverage treat the risk of loss as resting on the buyer for a commercially reasonable time.

Section 2—511. Tender of Payment by Buyer; Payment by Check

(1) Unless otherwise agreed tender of payment is a condition to the seller's duty to tender and complete any delivery.

(2) Tender of payment is sufficient when made by any means or in any manner current in the ordinary course of business unless the seller demands payment in legal tender and gives any extension of time reasonably necessary to procure it.

(3) Subject to the provisions of this Act on the effect of an instrument on an obligation (Section 3—802), payment by check is conditional and is defeated as between the parties by dishonor of the check on due presentment.

Section 2—512. Payment by Buyer Before Inspection

(1) Where the contract requires payment before inspection non-conformity of the goods does not excuse the buyer from so making payment unless

(a) the non-conformity appears without inspection; or

(b) despite tender of the required documents the circumstances would justify injunction against honor under the provisions of this Act (Section 5—114).

(2) Payment pursuant to subsection (1) does not constitute an acceptance of goods or impair the buyer's right to inspect or any of his remedies.

Section 2—513. Buyer's Right to Inspection of Goods

(1) Unless otherwise agreed and subject to subsection (3), where goods are tendered or delivered or identified to the contract for sale, the buyer has a right before payment or acceptance to inspect them at any reasonable place and time and in any reasonable manner. When the seller is required or authorized to send the goods to the buyer, the inspection may be after their arrival.

(2) Expenses of inspection must be borne by the buyer but may be recovered from the seller if the goods do not conform and are rejected.

(3) Unless otherwise agreed and subject to the provisions of this Article on C.I.F. contracts (subsection (3) of Section 2—321), the buyer is not entitled to inspect the goods before payment of the price when the contract provides

(a) for delivery "C.O.D." or on other like terms; or

(b) for payment against documents of title, except where such payment is due only after the goods are to become available for inspection.

(4) A place or method of inspection fixed by the parties is presumed to be exclusive but unless otherwise expressly agreed it does not postpone identification or shift the place for delivery or for passing the risk of loss. If compliance becomes impossible, inspection shall be as provided in this section unless the place or method fixed was clearly intended as an indispensable condition failure of which avoids the contract.

Section 2—514.   When Documents Deliverable on Acceptance; When on Payment

Unless otherwise agreed documents against which a draft is drawn are to be delivered to the drawee on acceptance of the draft if it is payable more than three days after presentment; otherwise, only on payment.

Section 2—515.   Preserving Evidence of Goods in Dispute

In furtherance of the adjustment of any claim or dispute

(a) either party on reasonable notification to the other and for the purpose of ascertaining the facts and preserving evidence has the right to inspect, test and sample the goods including such of them as may be in the possession or control of the other; and

(b) the parties may agree to a third party inspection or survey to determine the conformity or condition of the goods and may agree that the findings shall be binding upon them in any subsequent litigation or adjustment.

Part 6   Breach, Repudiation and Excuse

Section 2—601.   Buyer's Rights on Improper Delivery

Subject to the provisions of this Article on breach in installment contracts (Section 2—612) and unless otherwise agreed under the sections on contractual limitations of remedy (Sections 2—718 and 2—719), if the goods or the tender of delivery fail in any respect to conform to the contract, the buyer may

(a) reject the whole; or

(b) accept the whole; or

(c) accept any commercial unit or units and reject the rest.

Section 2—602.   Manner and Effect of Rightful Rejection

(1) Rejection of goods must be within a reasonable time after their delivery or tender. It is ineffective unless the buyer seasonably notifies the seller.

(2) Subject to the provisions of the two following sections on rejected goods (Sections 2—603 and 2—604),

(a) after rejection any exercise of ownership by the buyer with respect to any commercial unit is wrongful as against the seller; and

(b) if the buyer has before rejection taken physical possession of goods in which he does not have a security interest under the provisions of this Article (subsection (3) of Section 2—711), he is under a duty after rejection to hold them with reasonable care at the seller's disposition for a time sufficient to permit the seller to remove them; but

(c) the buyer has no further obligations with regard to goods rightfully rejected.

(3) The seller's rights with respect to goods wrongfully rejected are governed by the provisions of this Article on Seller's remedies in general (Section 2—703).

Section 2—603.   Merchant Buyer's Duties as to Rightfully Rejected Goods

(1) Subject to any security interest in the buyer (subsection (3) of Section 2—711), when the seller has no

agent or place of business at the market of rejection a merchant buyer is under a duty after rejection of goods in his possession or control to follow any reasonable instructions received from the seller with respect to the goods and in the absence of such instructions to make reasonable efforts to sell them for the seller's account if they are perishable or threaten to decline in value speedily. Instructions are not reasonable if on demand indemnity for expenses is not forthcoming.

(2) When the buyer sells goods under subsection (1), he is entitled to reimbursement from the seller or out of the proceeds for reasonable expenses of caring for and selling them, and if the expenses include no selling commission then to such commission as is usual in the trade or if there is none to a reasonable sum not exceeding ten per cent on the gross proceeds.

(3) In complying with this section the buyer is held only to good faith and good faith conduct hereunder is neither acceptance nor conversion nor the basis of an action for damages.

Section 2—604. Buyer's Options as to Salvage of Rightfully Rejected Goods

Subject to the provisions of the immediately preceding section on perishables if the seller gives no instructions within a reasonable time after notification of rejection the buyer may store the rejected goods for the seller's account or reship them to him or resell them for the seller's account with reimbursement as provided in the preceding section. Such action is not acceptance or conversion.

Section 2—605. Waiver of Buyer's Objections by Failure to Particularize

(1) The buyer's failure to state in connection with rejection a particular defect which is ascertainable by reasonable inspection precludes him from relying on the unstated defect to justify rejection or to establish breach

(a) where the seller could have cured it if stated seasonably; or

(b) between merchants when the seller has after rejection made a request in writing for a full and final written statement of all defects on which the buyer proposes to rely.

(2) Payment against documents made without reservation of rights precludes recovery of the payment for defects apparent on the face of the documents.

Section 2—606. What Constitutes Acceptance of Goods

(1) Acceptance of goods occurs when the buyer

(a) after a reasonable opportunity to inspect the goods signifies to the seller that the goods are conforming or that he will take or retain them in spite of their non-conformity; or

(b) fails to make an effective rejection (subsection (1) of Section 2—602), but such acceptance does not occur until the buyer has had a reasonable opportunity to inspect them; or

(c) does any act inconsistent with the seller's ownership; but if such act is wrongful as against the seller it is an acceptance only if ratified by him.

(2) Acceptance of a part of any commercial unit is acceptance of that entire unit.

Section 2—607. Effect of Acceptance; Notice of Breach; Burden of Establishing Breach After Acceptance; Notice of Claim or Litigation to Person Answerable Over

(1) The buyer must pay at the contract rate for any goods accepted.

(2) Acceptance of goods by the buyer precludes rejection of the goods accepted and if made with knowledge of a non-conformity cannot be revoked because of it unless the acceptance was on the reasonable assumption that the non-conformity would be seasonably cured but acceptance does not of itself impair any other remedy provided by this Article for non-conformity.

(3) Where a tender has been accepted

(a) the buyer must within a reasonable time after he discovers or should have discovered any breach notify the seller of breach or be barred from any remedy; and

(b) if the claim is one for infringement or the like (subsection (3) of Section 2—312) and the buyer is sued as a result of such a breach he must so notify the seller within a reasonable time after he receives notice of the litigation or be barred from any remedy over for liability established by the litigation.

(4) The burden is on the buyer to establish any breach with respect to the goods accepted.

(5) Where the buyer is sued for breach of a warranty or other obligation for which his seller is answerable over

   (a) he may give his seller written notice of the litigation. If the notice states that the seller may come in and defend and that if the seller does not do so he will be bound in any action against him by his buyer by any determination of fact common to the two litigations, then unless the seller after seasonable receipt of the notice does come in and defend he is so bound.

   (b) if the claim is one for infringement or the like (subsection (3) of Section 2—312) the original seller may demand in writing that his buyer turn over to him control of the litigation including settlement or else be barred from any remedy over and if he also agrees to bear all expense and to satisfy any adverse judgment, then unless the buyer after seasonable receipt of the demand does turn over control the buyer is so barred.

(6) The provisions of subsections (3), (4) and (5) apply to any obligation of a buyer to hold the seller harmless against infringement or the like (subsection (3) of Section 2—312).

Section 2—608.   Revocation of Acceptance in Whole or in Part

(1) The buyer may revoke his acceptance of a lot or commercial unit whose non-conformity substantially impairs its value to him if he has accepted it

   (a) on the reasonable assumption that its non-conformity would be cured and it has not been seasonably cured; or

   (b) without discovery of such non-conformity if his acceptance was reasonably induced either by the difficulty of discovery before acceptance or by the seller's assurances.

(2) Revocation of acceptance must occur within a reasonable time after the buyer discovers or should have discovered the ground for it and before any substantial change in condition of the goods which is not caused by their own defects. It is not effective until the buyer notifies the seller of it

(3) A buyer who so revokes has the same rights and duties with regard to the goods involved as if he had rejected them.

Section 2—609.   Right to Adequate Assurance of Performance

(1) A contract for sale imposes an obligation on each party that the other's expectation of receiving due performance will not be impaired. When reasonable grounds for insecurity arise with respect to the performance of either party the other may in writing demand adequate assurance of due performance and until he receives such assurance may if commercially reasonable suspend any performance for which he has not already received the agreed return.

(2) Between merchants the reasonableness of grounds for insecurity and the adequacy of any assurance offered shall be determined according to commercial standards.

(3) Acceptance of any improper delivery or payment does not prejudice the aggrieved party's right to demand adequate assurance of future performance.

(4) After receipt of a justified demand failure to provide within a reasonable time not exceeding thirty days such assurance of due performance as is adequate under the circumstances of the particular case is a repudiation of the contract.

Section 2—610.   Anticipatory Repudiation

When either party repudiates the contract with respect to a performance not yet due the loss of which will substantially impair the value of the contract to the other, the aggrieved party may

   (a) for a commercially reasonable time await performance by the repudiating party; or

   (b) resort to any remedy for breach (Section 2—703 or Section 2—711), even though he has notified the repudiating party that he would await the latter's performance and has urged retraction; and

(c) in either case suspend his own performance or proceed in accordance with the provisions of this Article on the seller's right to identify goods to the contract notwithstanding breach or to salvage unfinished goods (Section 2—704).

Section 2—611.   Retraction of Anticipatory Repudiation

(1) Until the repudiating party's next performance is due he can retract his repudiation unless the aggrieved party has since the repudiation cancelled or materially changed his position or otherwise indicated that he considers the repudiation final.

(2) Retraction may be by any method which clearly indicates to the aggrieved party that the repudiating party intends to perform, but must include any assurance justifiably demanded under the provisions of this Article (Section 2—609).

(3) Retraction reinstates the repudiating party's rights under the contract with due excuse and allowance to the aggrieved party for any delay occasioned by the repudiation.

Section 2—612.   "Installment Contract"; Breach

(1) An "installment contract" is one which requires or authorizes the delivery of goods in separate lots to be separately accepted, even though the contract contains a clause "each delivery is a separate contract" or its equivalent.

(2) The buyer may reject any installment which is nonconforming if the non-conformity substantially impairs the value of that installment and cannot be cured or if the non-conformity is a defect in the required documents; but if the non-conformity does not fall within subsection (3) and the seller gives adequate assurance of its cure the buyer must accept that installment.

(3) Whenever non-conformity or default with respect to one or more installments substantially impairs the value of the whole contract there is a breach of the whole. But the aggrieved party reinstates the contract if he accepts a non-conforming installment without seasonably notifying of cancellation or if he brings an action with respect only to past installments or demands performance as to future installments.

Section 2—613.   Casualty to Identified Goods

Where the contract requires for its performance goods identified when the contract is made, and the goods suffer casualty without fault of either party before the risk of loss passes to the buyer, or in a proper case under a "no arrival, no sale" term (Section 2—324) then

(a) if the loss is total the contract is avoided; and

(b) if the loss is partial or the goods have so deteriorated as no longer to conform to the contract the buyer may nevertheless demand inspection and at his option either treat the contract as avoided or accept the goods with due allowance from the contract price for the deterioration or the deficiency in quantity but without further right against the seller.

Section 2—614.   Substituted Performance

(1) Where without fault of either party the agreed berthing, loading, or unloading facilities fail or an agreed type of carrier becomes unavailable or the agreed manner of delivery otherwise becomes commercially impracticable but a commercially reasonable substitute is available, such substitute performance must be tendered and accepted.

(2) If the agreed means or manner of payment fails because of domestic or foreign governmental regulation, the seller may withhold or stop delivery unless the buyer provides a means or manner of payment which is commercially a substantial equivalent. If delivery has already been taken, payment by the means or in the manner provided by the regulation discharges the buyer's obligation unless the regulation is discriminatory, oppressive or predatory.

Section 2—615.   Excuse by Failure of Presupposed Conditions

Except so far as a seller may have assumed a greater obligation and subject to the preceding section on substituted performance:

(a) Delay in delivery or non-delivery in whole or in part by a seller who complies with paragraphs (b) and (c) is not a breach of his duty under a contract for sale if performance as agreed has been made impracticable by the occurrence of a contingency the non-occurrence of which was a basic assumption on which the contract was made or by compliance in good faith with any applicable foreign or domestic governmental regulation or order whether or not it later proves to be invalid.

(b) Where the causes mentioned in paragraph (a) affect only a part of the seller's capacity to perform, he must allocate production and deliveries among his customers but may at his option include regular customers not then under contract as well as his own requirements for further manufacture. He may so allocate in any manner which is fair and reasonable.

(c) The seller must notify the buyer seasonably that there will be delay or non-delivery and, when allocation is required under paragraph (b), of the estimated quota thus made available for the buyer.

Section 2—216.   Procedure on Notice Claiming Excuse

(1) Where the buyer receives notification of a material or indefinite delay or an allocation justified under the preceding section he may by written notification to the seller as to any delivery concerned, and where the prospective deficiency substantially impairs the value of the whole contract under the provisions of this Article relating to breach of installment contracts (Section 2—612), then also as to the whole,

(a) terminate and thereby discharge any unexecuted portion of the contract; or

(b) modify the contract by agreeing to take his available quota in substitution.

(2) If after receipt of such notification from the seller the buyer fails so to modify the contract within a reasonable time not exceeding thirty days the contract lapses with respect to any deliveries affected.

(3) The provisions of this section may not be negated by agreement except in so far as the seller has assumed a greater obligation under the preceding section.

Part 7   Remedies

Section 2—701.   Remedies for Breach of Collateral Contracts Not Impaired

Remedies for breach of any obligation or promise collateral or ancillary to a contract for sale are not impaired by the provisions of this Article.

Section 2—702.   Seller's Remedies on Discovery of Buyer's Insolvency

(1) Where the seller discovers the buyer to be insolvent he may refuse delivery except for cash including payment for all goods theretofore delivered under the contract, and stop delivery under this Article (Section 2—705).

(2) Where the seller discovers that the buyer has received goods on credit while insolvent he may reclaim the goods upon demand made within ten days after the receipt, but if misrepresentation of solvency has been made to the particular seller in writing within three months before delivery the ten day limitation does not apply. Except as provided in this subsection the seller may not base a right to reclaim goods on the buyer's fraudulent or innocent misrepresentation of solvency or of intent to pay.

(3) The seller's right to reclaim under subsection (2) is subject to the rights of a buyer in ordinary course or other good faith purchaser under this Article (Section 2—403). Successful reclamation of goods excludes all other remedies with respect to them.

Section 2—703.   Seller's Remedies in General

Where the buyer wrongfully rejects or revokes acceptance of goods or fails to make a payment due on or before delivery or repudiates with respect to a part or the whole, then with respect to any goods directly affected and, if the breach is of the whole contract (Section 2—612), then also with respect to the whole undelivered balance, the aggrieved seller may

(a) withhold delivery of such goods;

(b) stop delivery by any bailee as hereafter provided (Section 2—705);

(c) proceed under the next section respecting goods still unidentified to the contract;

(d) resell and recover damages as hereafter provided (Section 2—706);

(e) recover damages for non-acceptance (Section 2—708) or in a proper case the price (Section 2—709);

(f) cancel.

Section 2—704. Seller's Right to Identify Goods to the Contract Notwithstanding Breach or to Salvage Unfinished Goods

(1) An aggrieved seller under the preceding section may

(a) identify to the contract conforming goods not already identified if at the time he learned of the breach they are in his possession or control;

(b) treat as the subject of resale goods which have demonstrably been intended for the particular contract even though those goods are unfinished.

(2) Where the goods are unfinished an aggrieved seller may in the exercise of reasonable commercial judgment for the purposes of avoiding loss and of effective realization either complete the manufacture and wholly identify the goods to the contract or cease manufacture and resell for scrap or salvage value or proceed in any other reasonable manner.

Section 2—705. Seller's Stoppage of Delivery in Transit or Otherwise

(1) The seller may stop delivery of goods in the possession of a carrier or other bailee when he discovers the buyer to be insolvent (Section 2—702) and may stop delivery of carload, truckload, planeload or larger shipments of express or freight when the buyer repudiates or fails to make a payment due before delivery or if for any other reason the seller has a right to withhold or reclaim the goods.

(2) As against such buyer the seller may stop delivery until

(a) receipt of the goods by the buyer; or

(b) acknowledgment to the buyer by any bailee of the goods except a carrier that the bailee holds the goods for the buyer; or

(c) such acknowledgment to the buyer by a carrier by reshipment or as warehouseman; or

(d) negotiation to the buyer of any negotiable document of title covering the goods.

(3) (a) To stop delivery the seller must so notify as to enable the bailee by reasonable diligence to prevent delivery of the goods.

(b) After such notification the bailee must hold and deliver the goods according to the directions of the seller but the seller is liable to the bailee for any ensuing charges or damages.

(c) If a negotiable document of title has been issued for goods the bailee is not obliged to obey a notification to stop until surrender of the document.

(d) A carrier who has issued a non-negotiable bill of lading is not obliged to obey a notification to stop received from a person other than the consignor.

Section 2—706. Seller's Resale Including Contract for Resale

(1) Under the conditions stated in Section 2—703 on seller's remedies, the seller may resell the goods concerned or the undelivered balance thereof. Where the resale is made in good faith and in a commercially reasonable manner the seller may recover the difference between the resale price and the contract price together with any incidental damages allowed under the provisions of this Article (Section 2—710), but less expenses saved in consequence of the buyer's breach.

(2) Except as otherwise provided in subsection (3) or unless otherwise agreed resale may be at public or private sale including sale by way of one or more contracts to sell or of identification to an existing contract of the seller. Sale may be as a unit or in parcels and at any time and place and on any terms but every aspect of the sale including the method, manner, time, place and terms must be commercially reasonable. The resale must be reasonably identified as referring to the broken contract, but it is not necessary that the goods be in existence or that any or all of them have been identified to the contract before the breach.

(3) Where the resale is at private sale the seller must give the buyer reasonable notification of his intention to resell.

(4) Where the resale is at public sale

   (a) only identified goods can be sold except where there is a recognized market for a public sale of futures in goods of the kind; and

   (b) it must be made at a usual place or market for public sale if one is reasonably available and except in the case of goods which are perishable or threaten to decline in value speedily the seller must give the buyer reasonable notice of the time and place of the resale; and

   (c) if the goods are not to be within the view of those attending the sale the notification of sale must state the place where the goods are located and provide for their reasonable inspection by prospective bidders; and

   (d) the seller may buy.

(5) A purchaser who buys in good faith at a resale takes the goods free of any rights of the original buyer even though the seller fails to comply with one or more of the requirements of this section.

(6) The seller is not accountable to the buyer for any profit made on any resale. A person in the position of a seller (Section 2—707) or a buyer who has rightfully rejected or justifiably revoked acceptance must account for any excess over the amount of his security interest, as hereinafter defined (subsection (3) of Section 2—711).

Section 2—707.   "Person in the Position of a Seller"

(1) A "person in the position of a seller" includes as against a principal an agent who has paid or become responsible for the price of goods on behalf of his principal or anyone who otherwise holds a security interest or other right in goods similar to that of a seller.

(2) A person in the position of a seller may as provided in this Article withhold or stop delivery (Section 2—705) and resell (Section 2—706) and recover incidental damages (Section 2—710).

Section 2—708.   Seller's Damages for Non-acceptance or Repudiation

(1) Subject to subsection (2) and to the provisions of this Article with respect to proof of market price (Section 2—723), the measure of damages for non-acceptance or repudiation by the buyer is the difference between the market price at the time and place for tender and the unpaid contract price together with any incidental damages provided in this Article (Section 2—710), but less expenses saved in consequence of the buyer's breach.

(2) If the measure of damages provided in subsection (1) is inadequate to put the seller in as good a position as performance would have done then the measure of damages is the profit (including reasonable overhead) which the seller would have made from full performance by the buyer, together with any incidental damages provided in this Article (Section 2—710), due allowance for costs reasonably incurred and due credit for payments or proceeds of resale.

Section 2—709.   Action for the Price

(1) When the buyer fails to pay the price as it becomes due the seller may recover, together with any incidental damages under the next section, the price

   (a) of goods accepted or of conforming goods lost or damaged within a commercially reasonable time after risk of their loss has passed to the buyer; and

   (b) of goods identified to the contract if the seller is unable after reasonable effort to resell them at a reasonable price or the circumstances reasonably indicate that such effort will be unavailing.

(2) Where the seller sues for the price he must hold for the buyer any goods which have been identified to the contract and are still in his control except that if resale becomes possible he may resell them at any time prior to the collection of the judgment. The net proceeds of any such resale must be credited to the buyer and payment of the judgment entitles him to any goods not resold.

(3) After the buyer has wrongfully rejected or revoked acceptance of the goods or has failed to make a payment due or has repudiated (Section 2—610), a seller who is held not entitled to the price under this section shall nevertheless be awarded damages for non-acceptance under the preceding section.

Section 2—710. Seller's Incidental Damages

Incidental damages to an aggrieved seller include any commercially reasonable charges, expenses or commissions incurred in stopping delivery, in the transportation, care and custody of goods after the buyer's breach, in connection with return or resale of the goods or otherwise resulting from the breach.

Section 2—711. Buyer's Remedies in General; Buyer's Security Interest in Rejected Goods

(1) Where the seller fails to make delivery or repudiates or the buyer rightfully rejects or justifiably revokes acceptance then with respect to any goods involved, and with respect to the whole if the breach goes to the whole contract (Section 2—612), the buyer may cancel and whether or not he has done so may in addition to recovering so much of the price as has been paid

> (a) "cover" and have damages under the next section as to all the goods affected whether or not they have been identified to the contract; or
>
> (b) recover damages for non-delivery as provided in this Article (Section 2—713).

(2) Where the seller fails to deliver or repudiates the buyer may also

> (a) if the goods have been identified recover them as provided in this Article (Section 2—502); or
>
> (b) in a proper case obtain specific performance or replevy the goods as provided in this Article (Section 2—716).

(3) On rightful rejection or justifiable revocation of acceptance a buyer has a security interest in goods in his possession or control for any payments made on their price and any expenses reasonably incurred in their inspection, receipt, transportation, care and custody and may hold such goods and resell them in like manner as an aggrieved seller (Section 2—706).

Section 2—712. "Cover"; Buyer's Procurement of Substitute Goods

(1) After a breach within the preceding section the buyer may "cover" by making in good faith and without unreasonable delay any reasonable purchase of or contract to purchase goods in substitution for those due from the seller.

(2) The buyer may recover from the seller as damages the difference between the cost of cover and the contract price together with any incidental or consequential damages as hereinafter defined (Section 2—715), but less expenses saved in consequence of the seller's breach.

(3) Failure of the buyer to effect cover within this section does not bar him from any other remedy.

Section 2—713. Buyer's Damages for Non-Delivery or Repudiation

(1) Subject to the provisions of this Article with respect to proof of market price (Section 2—723), the measure of damages for non-delivery or repudiation by the seller is the difference between the market price at the time when the buyer learned of the breach and the contract price together with any incidental and consequential damages provided in this Article (Section 2—715), but less expenses saved in consequence of the seller's breach.

(2) Market price is to be determined as of the place for tender or, in cases of rejection after arrival or revocation of acceptance, as of the place of arrival.

Section 2—714. Buyer's Damages for Breach in Regard to Accepted Goods

(1) Where the buyer has accepted goods and given notification (subsection (3) of Section 2—607) he may recover as damages for any non-conformity of tender the loss resulting in the ordinary course of events from the seller's breach as determined in any manner which is reasonable.

(2) The measure of damages for breach of warranty is the difference at the time and place of acceptance between the value of the goods accepted and the value they would have had if they had been as warranted, unless special circumstances show proximate damages of a different amount.

(3) In a proper case any incidental and consequential damages under the next section may also be recovered.

Section 2—715. Buyer's Incidental and Consequential Damages

(1) Incidental damages resulting from the seller's breach include expenses reasonably incurred in inspection, receipt, transportation and care and custody of goods rightfully rejected, any commercially reasonable

charges, expenses or commissions in connection with effecting cover and any other reasonable expense incident to the delay or other breach.

(2) Consequential damages resulting from the seller's breach include

(a) any loss resulting from general or particular requirements and needs of which the seller at the time of contracting had reason to know and which could not reasonably be prevented by cover or otherwise; and

(b) injury to person or property proximately resulting from any breach of warranty.

Section 2—716. Buyer's Right to Specific Performance or Replevin

(1) Specific performance may be decreed where the goods are unique or in other proper circumstances.

(2) The decree for specific performance may include such terms and conditions as to payment of the price, damages, or other relief as the court may deem just.

(3) The buyer has a right of replevin for goods identified to the contract if after reasonable effort he is unable to effect cover for such goods or the circumstances reasonably indicate that such effort will be unavailing or if the goods have been shipped under reservation and satisfaction of the security interest in them has been made or tendered.

Section 2—717. Deduction of Damages From the Price

The buyer on notifying the seller of his intention to do so may deduct all or any part of the damages resulting from any breach of the contract from any part of the price still due under the same contract.

Section 2—718. Liquidation or Limitation of Damages; Deposits

(1) Damages for breach by either party may be liquidated in the agreement but only at an amount which is reasonable in the light of the anticipated or actual harm caused by the breach, the difficulties of proof of loss, and the inconvenience or nonfeasibility of otherwise obtaining an adequate remedy. A term fixing unreasonably large liquidated damages is void as a penalty.

(2) Where the seller justifiably withholds delivery of goods because of the buyer's breach, the buyer is entitled to restitution of any amount by which the sum of his payments exceeds

(a) the amount to which the seller is entitled by virtue of terms liquidating the seller's damages in accordance with subsection (1), or

(b) in the absence of such terms, twenty per cent of the value of the total performance for which the buyer is obligated under the contract or $500, whichever is smaller.

(3) The buyer's right to restitution under subsection (2) is subject to offset to the extent that the seller establishes

(a) a right to recover damages under the provisions of this Article other than subsection (1), and

(b) the amount or value of any benefits received by the buyer directly or indirectly by reason of the contract.

(4) Where a seller has received payment in goods their reasonable value or the proceeds of their resale shall be treated as payments for the purposes of subsection (2); but if the seller has notice of the buyer's breach before reselling goods received in part performance, his resale is subject to the conditions laid down in this Article on resale by an aggrieved seller (Section 2—706).

Section 2—719. Contractual Modification or Limitation of Remedy

(1) Subject to the provisions of subsections (2) and (3) of this section and of the preceding section on liquidation and limitation of damages,

(a) the agreement may provide for remedies in addition to or in substitution for those provided in this Article and may limit or alter the measure of damages recoverable under this Article, as by limiting the buyer's remedies to return of the goods and repayment of the price or to repair and replacement of non-conforming goods or parts; and

(b) resort to a remedy as provided is optional unless the remedy is expressly agreed to be exclusive, in which case it is the sole remedy.

(2) Where circumstances cause an exclusive or limited remedy to fail of its essential purpose, remedy may be had as provided in this Act.

(3) Consequential damages may be limited or excluded unless the limitation or exclusion is unconscionable. Limitation of consequential damages for injury to the person in the case of consumer goods is prima facie unconscionable but limitation of damages where the loss is commercial is not.

Section 2—720. Effect of "Cancellation" or "Rescission" on Claims for Antecedent Breach

Unless the contrary intention clearly appears, expressions of "cancellation" or "rescission" of the contract or the like shall not be construed as a renunciation or discharge of any claim in damages for an antecedent breach.

Section 2—721. Remedies for Fraud

Remedies for material misrepresentation or fraud include all remedies available under this Article for non-fraudulent breach. Neither rescission or a claim for rescission of the contract for sale nor rejection or return of the goods shall bar or be deemed inconsistent with a claim for damages or other remedy.

Section 2—722. Who Can Sue Third Parties for Injury to Goods

Where a third party so deals with goods which have been identified to a contract for sale as to cause actionable injury to a party to that contract

    (a) a right of action against the third party is in either party to the contract for sale who has title to or a security interest or a special property or an insurable interest in the goods; and if the goods have been destroyed or converted a right of action is also in the party who either bore the risk of loss under the contract for sale or has since the injury assumed that risk as against the other;

    (b) if at the time of the injury the party plaintiff did not bear the risk of loss as against the other party to the contract for sale and there is no arrangement between them for disposition of the recovery, his suit or settlement is, subject to his own interest, as a fiduciary for the other party to the contract;

    (c) either party may with the consent of the other sue for the benefit of whom it may concern.

Section 2—723. Proof of Market Price: Time and Place

(1) If an action based on anticipatory repudiation comes to trial before the time for performance with respect to some or all of the goods, any damages based on market price (Section 2—708 or Section 2—713) shall be determined according to the price of such goods prevailing at the time when the aggrieved party learned of the repudiation.

(2) If evidence of a price prevailing at the times or places described in this Article is not readily available the price prevailing within any reasonable time before or after the time described or at any other place which in commercial judgment or under usage of trade would serve as a reasonable substitute for the one described may be used, making any proper allowance for the cost of transporting the goods to or from such other place.

(3) Evidence of a relevant price prevailing at a time or place other than the one described in this Article offered by one party is not admissible unless and until he has given the other party such notice as the court finds sufficient to prevent unfair surprise.

Section 2—724. Admissibility of Market Quotations

Whenever the prevailing price or value of any goods regularly bought and sold in any established commodity market is in issue, reports in official publications or trade journals or in newspapers or periodicals of general circulation published as the reports of such market shall be admissible in evidence. The circumstances of the preparation of such a report may be shown to affect its weight but not its admissibility.

Section 2—725. Statute of Limitations in Contracts for Sale

(1) An action for breach of any contract for sale must be commenced within four years after the cause of action has accrued. By the original agreement the parties may reduce the period of limitation to not less than one year but may not extend it.

(2) A cause of action accrues when the breach occurs, regardless of the aggrieved party's lack of knowledge of the breach. A breach of warranty occurs when tender

of delivery is made, except that where a warranty explicitly extends to future performance of the goods and discovery of the breach must await the time of such performance the cause of action accrues when the breach is or should have been discovered.

(3) Where an action commenced within the time limited by subsection (1) is so terminated as to leave available a remedy by another action for the same breach such other action may be commenced after the expiration of the time limited and within six months after the termination of the first action unless the termination resulted from voluntary discontinuance or from dismissal for failure or neglect to prosecute.

(4) This section does not alter the law on tolling of the statute of limitations nor does it apply to causes of action which have accrued before this Act becomes effective.

Article 3   Commercial Paper

Part 1   Short Title, Form and Interpretation

Section 3—101.   Short Title

This Article shall be known and may be cited as Uniform Commercial Code—Commercial Paper.

Section 3—102.   Definitions and Index of Definitions

(1) In this Article unless the context otherwise requires

    (a) "Issue" means the first delivery of an instrument to a holder or a remitter.

    (b) An "order" is a direction to pay and must be more than an authorization or request. It must identify the person to pay with reasonable certainty. It may be addressed to one or more such persons jointly or in the alternative but not in succession.

    (c) A "promise" is an undertaking to pay and must be more than an acknowledgment of an obligation.

    (d) "Secondary party" means a drawer or endorser.

    (e) "Instrument" means a negotiable instrument.

(2) Other definitions applying to this Article and the sections in which they appear are:

    "Acceptance." Section 3—410.
    "Accommodation party." Section 3—415.
    "Alteration." Section 3—407.
    "Certificate of deposit." Section 3—104.
    "Certification." Section 3—411.
    "Check." Section 3—104.
    "Definite time." Section 3—109.
    "Dishonor." Section 3—507.
    "Draft." Section 3—104.
    "Holder in due course." Section 3—302.
    "Negotiation." Section 3—202.
    "Note." Section 3—104.
    "Notice of dishonor." Section 3—508.
    "On demand." Section 3—108.
    "Presentment." Section 3—504.
    "Protest." Section 3—509.
    "Restrictive Indorsement." Section 3—205.
    "Signature." Section 3—401.

(3) The following definitions in other Articles apply to this Article:

    "Account." Section 4—104.
    "Banking Day." Section 4—104.
    "Clearing house." Section 4—104.
    "Collecting bank." Section 4—105.
    "Customer." Section 4—104.
    "Depositary Bank." Section 4—105.
    "Documentary Draft." Section 4—104.
    "Intermediary Bank." Section 4—105.
    "Item." Section 4—104.
    "Midnight deadline." Section 4—104.
    "Payor bank." Section 4—105.

(4) In addition Article 1 contains general definitions and principles of construction and interpretation applicable throughout this Article.

Section 3—103.   Limitations on Scope of Article

(1) This Article does not apply to money, documents of title or investment securities.

(2) The provisions of this Article are subject to the provisions of the Article on Bank Deposits and Collections (Article 4) and Secured Transactions (Article 9).

Section 3—104.   Form of Negotiable Instruments; "Draft"; "Check"; "Certificate of Deposit"; "Note"

(1) Any writing to be a negotiable instrument within this Article must

    (a) be signed by the maker or drawer; and

    (b) contain an unconditional promise or order to pay a sum certain in money and no other promise, order, obligation or power given by the maker or drawer except as authorized by this Article; and

    (c) be payable on demand or at a definite time; and

    (d) be payable to order or to bearer.

(2) A writing which complies with the requirements of this section is

    (a) a "draft" ("bill of exchange") if it is an order;

    (b) a "check" if it is a draft drawn on a bank and payable on demand;

    (c) a "certificate of deposit" if it is an acknowledgment by a bank of receipt of money with an engagement to repay it;

    (d) a "note" if it is a promise other than a certificate of deposit.

(3) As used in other Articles of this Act, and as the context may require, the terms "draft," "check," "certificate of deposit" and "note" may refer to instruments which are not negotiable within this Article as well as to instruments which are so negotiable.

Section 3—105.   When Promise or Order Unconditional

(1) A promise or order otherwise unconditional is not made conditional by the fact that the instrument

    (a) is subject to implied or constructive conditions; or

    (b) states its consideration, whether performed or promised, or the transaction which gave rise to the instrument, or that the promise or order is made or the instrument matures in accordance with or "as per" such transaction; or

    (c) refers to or states that it arises out of a separate agreement or refers to a separate agreement for rights as to prepayment or acceleration; or

    (d) states that it is drawn under a letter of credit; or

    (e) states that it is secured, whether by mortgage, reservation of title or otherwise; or

    (f) indicates a particular account to be debited or any other fund or source from which reimbursement is expected; or

    (g) is limited to payment out of a particular fund or the proceeds of a particular source, if the instrument is issued by a government or governmental agency or unit; or

    (h) is limited to payment out of the entire assets of a partnership, unincorporated association, trust or estate by or on behalf of which the instrument is issued.

(2) A promise or order is not unconditional if the instrument

    (a) states that it is subject to or governed by any other agreement; or

    (b) states that it is to be paid only out of a particular fund or source except as provided in this section. As amended 1962.

Section 3—106.   Sum Certain

(1) The sum payable is a sum certain even though it is to be paid

    (a) with stated interest or by stated installments; or

    (b) with stated different rates of interest before and after default or a specified date; or

    (c) with a stated discount or addition if paid before or after the date fixed for payment; or

    (d) with exchange or less exchange, whether at a fixed rate or at the current rate; or

    (e) with costs of collection or an attorney's fee or both upon default.

(2) Nothing in this section shall validate any term which is otherwise illegal.

Section 3—107. Money

(1) An instrument is payable in money if the medium of exchange in which it is payable is money at the time the instrument is made. An instrument payable in "currency" or "current funds" is payable in money.

(2) A promise or order to pay a sum stated in a foreign currency is for a sum certain in money and, unless a different medium of payment is specified in the instrument, may be satisfied by payment of that number of dollars which the stated foreign currency will purchase at the buying sight rate for that currency on the day on which the instrument is payable or, if payable on demand, on the day of demand. If such an instrument specifies a foreign currency as the medium of payment the instrument is payable in that currency.

Section 3—108. Payable on Demand

Instruments payable on demand include those payable at sight or on presentation and those in which no time for payment is stated.

Section 3—109. Definite Time

(1) An instrument is payable at a definite time if by its terms it is payable

    (a) on or before a stated date or at a fixed period after a stated date; or

    (b) at a fixed period after sight; or

    (c) at a definite time subject to any acceleration; or

    (d) at a definite time subject to extension at the option of the holder, or to extension to a further definite time at the option of the maker or acceptor or automatically upon or after a specified act or event.

(2) An instrument which by its terms is otherwise payable only upon an act or event uncertain as to time of occurrence is not payable at a definite time even though the act or event has occurred.

Section 3—110. Payable to Order

(1) An instrument is payable to order when by its terms it is payable to the order or assigns of any person therein specified with reasonable certainty, or to him or his order, or when it is conspicuously designated on its face as "exchange" or the like and names a payee. It may be payable to the order of

    (a) the maker or drawer; or

    (b) the drawee; or

    (c) a payee who is not maker, drawer or drawee; or

    (d) two or more payees together or in the alternative; or

    (e) an estate, trust or fund, in which case it is payable to the order of the representative of such estate, trust or fund or his successors; or

    (f) an office, or an officer by his title as such in which case it is payable to the principal but the incumbent of the office or his successors may act as if he or they were the holder; or

    (g) a partnership or unincorporated association, in which case it is payable to the partnership or association and may be indorsed or transferred by any person thereto authorized.

(2) An instrument not payable to order is not made so payable by such words as "payable upon return of this instrument properly indorsed."

(3) An instrument made payable both to order and to bearer is payable to order unless the bearer words are handwritten or typewritten.

Section 3—111. Payable to Bearer

An instrument is payable to bearer when by its terms it is payable to

    (a) bearer or the order of bearer; or

    (b) a specified person or bearer; or

    (c) "cash" or the order of "cash," or any other indication which does not purport to designate a specific payee.

Section 3—112. Terms and Omissions Not Affecting Negotiability

(1) The negotiability of an instrument is not affected by

    (a) the omission of a statement of any consideration or of the place where the instrument is drawn or payable; or

(b) a statement that collateral has been given to secure obligations either on the instrument or otherwise of an obligor on the instrument or that in case of default on those obligations the holder may realize on or dispose of the collateral; or

(c) a promise or power to maintain or protect collateral or to give additional collateral; or

(d) a term authorizing a confession of judgment on the instrument if it is not paid when due; or

(e) a term purporting to waive the benefit of any law intended for the advantage or protection of any obligor; or

(f) a term in a draft providing that the payee by indorsing or cashing it acknowledges full satisfaction of an obligation of the drawer; or

(g) A statement in a draft drawn in a set of parts (Section 3—801) to the effect that the order is effective only if no other part has been honored.

(2) Nothing in this section shall validate any term which is otherwise illegal.

Section 3—113.   Seal

An instrument otherwise negotiable is within this Article even though it is under a seal.

Section 3—114.   Date, Antedating, Postdating

(1) The negotiability of an instrument is not affected by the fact that it is undated, antedated or postdated.

(2) Where an instrument is antedated or postdated the time when it is payable is determined by the stated date if the instrument is payable on demand or at a fixed period after date.

(3) Where the instrument or any signature thereon is dated, the date is presumed to be correct.

Section 3—115.   Incomplete Instruments

(1) When a paper whose contents at the time of signing show that it is intended to become an instrument is signed while still incomplete in any necessary respect it cannot be enforced until completed, but when it is completed in accordance with authority given it is effective as completed.

(2) If the completion is unauthorized the rules as to material alteration apply (Section 3—407), even though the paper was not delivered by the maker or drawer; but the burden of establishing that any completion is unauthorized is on the party so asserting.

Section 3—116.   Instruments Payable to Two or More Persons

An instrument payable to the order of two or more persons

(a) if in the alternative is payable to any one of them and may be negotiated, discharged or enforced by any of them who has possession of it;

(b) if not in the alternative is payable to all of them and may be negotiated, discharged or enforced only by all of them.

Section 3—117.   Instruments Payable With Words of Description

An instrument made payable to a named person with the addition of words describing him

(a) as agent or officer of a specified person is payable to his principal but the agent or officer may act as if he were the holder;

(b) as any other fiduciary for a specified person or purpose is payable to the payee and may be negotiated, discharged or enforced by him;

(c) in any other manner is payable to the payee unconditionally and the additional words are without effect on subsequent parties.

Section 3—118.   Ambiguous Terms and Rules of Construction

The following rules apply to every instrument:

(a) Where there is doubt whether the instrument is a draft or a note the holder may treat it as either. A draft drawn on the drawer is effective as a note.

(b) Handwritten terms control typewritten and printed terms, and typewritten control printed.

(c) Words control figures except that if the words are ambiguous figures control.

(d) Unless otherwise specified a provision for interest means interest at the judgment rate at the place of payment from the date of the instrument, or if it is undated from the date of issue.

(e) Unless the instrument otherwise specifies two or more persons who sign as maker, acceptor or drawer or indorser and as a part of the same transaction are jointly and severally liable even though the instrument contains such words as "I promise to pay."

(f) Unless otherwise specified consent to extension authorizes a single extension for not longer than the original period. A consent to extension, expressed in the instrument, is binding on secondary parties and accommodation makers. A holder may not exercise his option to extend an instrument over the objection of a maker or acceptor or other party who in accordance with Section 3—604 tenders full payment when the instrument is due.

Section 3—119.   Other Writings Affecting Instrument

(1) As between the obligor and his immediate obligee or any transferee the terms of an instrument may be modified or affected by any other written agreement executed as a part of the same transaction, except that a holder in due course is not affected by any limitation of his rights arising out of the separate written agreement if he had no notice of the limitation when he took the instrument.

(2) A separate agreement does not affect the negotiability of an instrument.

Section 3—120.   Instruments "Payable Through" Bank

An instrument which states that it is "payable through" a bank or the like designates that bank as a collecting bank to make presentment but does not of itself authorize the bank to pay the instrument.

Section 3—121.   Instruments Payable at Bank

Note: *If this Act is introduced in the Congress of the United States this section should be omitted. (States to select either alternative)*

Alternative A—

A note or acceptance which states that it is payable at a bank is the equivalent of a draft drawn on the bank payable when it falls due out of any funds of the maker or acceptor in current account or otherwise available for such payment.

Alternative B—

A note or acceptance which states that it is payable at a bank is not of itself an order or authorization to the bank to pay it.

Section 3—122.   Accrual of Cause of Action

(1) A cause of action against a maker or an acceptor accrues

    (a) in the case of a time instrument on the day after maturity;

    (b) in the case of a demand instrument upon its date or, if no date is stated, on the date of issue.

(2) A cause of action against the obligor of a demand or time certificate of deposit accrues upon demand, but demand on a time certificate may not be made until on or after the date of maturity.

(3) A cause of action against a drawer of a draft or an indorser of any instrument accrues upon demand following dishonor of the instrument. Notice of dishonor is a demand.

(4) Unless an instrument provides otherwise, interest runs at the rate provided by law for a judgment

    (a) in the case of a maker, acceptor or other primary obligor of a demand instrument, from the date of demand;

    (b) in all other cases from the date of accrual of the cause of action.

Part 2   Transfer and Negotiation

Section 3—201.   Transfer: Right to Indorsement

(1) Transfer of an instrument vests in the transferee such rights as the transferor has therein, except that a transferee who has himself been a party to any fraud or illegality affecting the instrument or who as a prior holder had notice of a defense or claim against it cannot

improve his position by taking from a later holder in due course.

(2) A transfer of a security interest in an instrument vests the foregoing rights in the transferee to the extent of the interest transferred.

(3) Unless otherwise agreed any transfer for value of an instrument not then payable to bearer gives the transferee the specifically enforceable right to have the unqualified indorsement of the transferor. Negotiation takes effect only when the indorsement is made and until that time there is no presumption that the transferee is the owner.

Section 3—202.   Negotiation

(1) Negotiation is the transfer of an instrument in such form that the transferee becomes a holder. If the instrument is payable to order it is negotiated by delivery with any necessary indorsement; if payable to bearer it is negotiated by delivery.

(2) An indorsement must be written by or on behalf of the holder and on the instrument or on a paper so firmly affixed thereto as to become a part thereof.

(3) An indorsement is effective for negotiation only when it conveys the entire instrument or any unpaid residue. If it purports to be of less it operates only as a partial assignment.

(4) Words of assignment, condition, waiver, guaranty, limitation or disclaimer of liability and the like accompanying an indorsement do not affect its character as an indorsement.

Section 3—203.   Wrong or Misspelled Name

Where an instrument is made payable to a person under a misspelled name or one other than his own he may indorse in that name or his own or both; but signature in both names may be required by a person paying or giving value for the instrument.

Section 3—204.   Special Indorsement; Blank Indorsement

(1) A special indorsement specifies the person to whom or to whose order it makes the instrument payable. Any instrument specially indorsed becomes payable to the order of the special indorsee and may be further negotiated only by his indorsement.

(2) An indorsement in blank specifies no particular indorsee and may consist of a mere signature. An instrument payable to order and indorsed in blank becomes payable to bearer and may be negotiated by delivery alone until specially indorsed.

(3) The holder may convert a blank indorsement into a special indorsement by writing over the signature of the indorser in blank any contract consistent with the character of the indorsement.

Section 3—205.   Restrictive Indorsements

An indorsement is restrictive which either

  (a) is conditional; or

  (b) purports to prohibit further transfer of the instrument; or

  (c) includes the words "for collection," "for deposit," "pay any bank," or like terms signifying a purpose of deposit or collection; or

  (d) otherwise states that it is for the benefit or use of the indorser or of another person.

Section 3—206.   Effect of Restrictive Indorsement

(1) No restrictive indorsement prevents further transfer or negotiation of the instrument.

(2) An intermediary bank, or a payor bank which is not the depositary bank, is neither given notice nor otherwise affected by a restrictive indorsement of any person except the bank's immediate transferor or the person presenting for payment.

(3) Except for an intermediary bank, any transferee under an indorsement which is conditional or includes the words "for collection," "for deposit," "pay any bank," or like terms (subparagraphs (a) and (c) of Section 3—205) must pay or apply any value given by him for or on the security of the instrument consistently with the indorsement and to the extent that he does so he becomes a holder for value. In addition such transferee is a holder in due course if he otherwise complies with the requirements of Section 3—302 on what constitutes a holder in due course.

(4) The first taker under an indorsement for the benefit of the indorser or another person (subparagraph (d) of Section 3—205) must pay or apply any value given by him for or on the security of the instrument consistently with the indorsement and to the extent that he does so

he becomes a holder for value. In addition such taker is a holder in due course if he otherwise complies with the requirements of Section 3—302 on what constitutes a holder in due course. A later holder for value is neither given notice nor otherwise affected by such restrictive indorsement unless he has knowledge that a fiduciary or other person has negotiated the instrument in any transaction for his own benefit or otherwise in breach of duty (subsection (2) of Section 3—304).

Section 3—207. Negotiation Effective Although It May Be Rescinded

(1) Negotiation is effective to transfer the instrument although the negotiation is

(a) made by an infant, a corporation exceeding its powers, or any other person without capacity; or

(b) obtained by fraud, duress or mistake of any kind; or

(c) part of an illegal transaction; or

(d) made in breach of duty.

(2) Except as against a subsequent holder in due course such negotiation is in an appropriate case subject to rescission, the declaration of a constructive trust or any other remedy permitted by law.

Section 3—208. Reacquisition

Where an instrument is returned to or reacquired by a prior party he may cancel any indorsement which is not necessary to his title and reissue or further negotiate the instrument, but any intervening party is discharged as against the reacquiring party and subsequent holders not in due course and if his indorsement has been cancelled is discharged as against subsequent holders in due course as well.

Part 3 Rights of a Holder

Section 3—301. Rights of a Holder

The holder of an instrument whether or not he is the owner may transfer or negotiate it and, except as otherwise provided in Section 3—603 on payment or satisfaction, discharge it or enforce payment in his own name.

Section 3—302. Holder in Due Course

(1) A holder in due course is a holder who takes the instrument

(a) for value, and

(b) in good faith; and

(c) without notice that it is overdue or has been dishonored or of any defense against or claim to it on the part of any person.

(2) A payee may be a holder in due course.

(3) A holder does not become a holder in due course of an instrument:

(a) by purchase of it at judicial sale or by taking it under legal process; or

(b) by acquiring it in taking over an estate; or

(c) by purchasing it as part of a bulk transaction not in regular course of business of the transferor.

(4) A purchaser of a limited interest can be a holder in due course only to the extent of the interest purchased.

Section 3—303. Taking for Value

A holder takes the instrument for value

(a) to the extent that the agreed consideration has been performed or that he acquires a security interest in or a lien on the instrument otherwise than by legal process; or

(b) when he takes the instrument in payment of or as security for an antecedent claim against any person whether or not the claim is due; or

(c) when he gives a negotiable instrument for it or makes an irrevocable commitment to a third person.

Section 3—304. Notice to Purchaser

(1) The purchaser has notice of a claim or defense if

(a) the instrument is so incomplete, bears such visible evidence of forgery or alteration, or is otherwise so irregular as to call into question its validity, terms or ownership or to create an ambiguity as to the party to pay; or

(b) the purchaser has notice that the obligation of any party is voidable in whole or in part, or that all parties have been discharged.

(2) The purchaser has notice of a claim against the instrument when he has knowledge that a fiduciary has negotiated the instrument in payment of or as security for his own debt or in any transaction for his own benefit or otherwise in breach of duty.

(3) The purchaser has notice that an instrument is overdue if he has reason to know

(a) that any part of the principal amount is overdue or that there is an uncured default in payment of another instrument of the same series; or

(b) that acceleration of the instrument has been made; or

(c) that he is taking a demand instrument after demand has been made or more than a reasonable length of time after its issue. A reasonable time for a check drawn and payable within the states and territories of the United States and the District of Columbia is presumed to be thirty days.

(4) Knowledge of the following facts does not of itself give the purchaser notice of a defense or claim

(a) that the instrument is antedated or postdated;

(b) that it was issued or negotiated in return for an executory promise or accompanied by a separate agreement, unless the purchaser has notice that a defense or claim has arisen from the terms thereof;

(c) that any party has signed for accommodation;

(d) that an incomplete instrument has been completed, unless the purchaser has notice of any improper completion;

(e) that any person negotiating the instrument is or was a fiduciary;

(f) that there has been default in payment of interest on the instrument or in payment of any other instrument, except one of the same series.

(5) The filing or recording of a document does not of itself constitute notice within the provisions of this Article to a person who would otherwise be a holder in due course.

(6) To be effective notice must be received at such time and in such manner as to give a reasonable opportunity to act on it.

Section 3—305. Rights of a Holder in Due Course

To the extent that a holder is a holder in due course he takes the instrument free from

(1) all claims to it on the part of any person; and

(2) all defenses of any party to the instrument with whom the holder has not dealt except

(a) infancy, to the extent that it is a defense to a simple contract; and

(b) such other incapacity, or duress, or illegality of the transaction, as renders the obligation of the party a nullity; and

(c) such misrepresentation as has induced the party to sign the instrument with neither knowledge nor reasonable opportunity to obtain knowledge of its character or its essential terms; and

(d) discharge in insolvency proceedings; and

(e) any other discharge of which the holder has notice when he takes the instrument.

Section 3—306. Rights of One Not Holder in Due Course

Unless he has the rights of a holder in due course any person takes the instrument subject to

(a) all valid claims to it on the part of any person; and

(b) all defenses of any party which would be available in an action on a simple contract; and

(c) the defenses of want or failure of consideration, non-performance of any condition precedent, non-delivery, or delivery for a special purpose (Section 3—408); and

(d) the defense that he or a person through whom he holds the instrument acquired it by theft, or that payment or satisfaction to such holder would be inconsistent with the terms of a restrictive indorsement. The claim of any third person to the instrument is not otherwise available as a defense to any party liable thereon unless the third person himself defends the action for such party.

Section 3—307.   Burden of Establishing Signatures, Defenses and Due Course

(1) Unless specifically denied in the pleadings each signature on an instrument is admitted. When the effectiveness of a signature is put in issue

(a) the burden of establishing it is on the party claiming under the signature; but

(b) the signature is presumed to be genuine or authorized except where the action is to enforce the obligation of a purported signer who has died or become incompetent before proof is required.

(2) When signatures are admitted or established, production of the instrument entitles a holder to recover on it unless the defendant establishes a defense.

(3) After it is shown that a defense exists a person claiming the rights of a holder in due course has the burden of establishing that he or some person under whom he claims is in all respects a holder in due course.

Part 4   Liability of Parties

Section 3—401.   Signature

(1) No person is liable on an instrument unless his signature appears thereon.

(2) A signature is made by use of any name, including any trade or assumed name, upon an instrument, or by any word or mark used in lieu of a written signature.

Section 3—402.   Signature in Ambiguous Capacity

Unless the instrument clearly indicates that a signature is made in some other capacity it is an indorsement.

Section 3—403.   Signature by Authorized Representative

(1) A signature may be made by an agent or other representative, and his authority to make it may be established as in other cases of representation. No particular form of appointment is necessary to establish such authority.

(2) An authorized representative who signs his own name to an instrument

(a) is personally obligated if the instrument neither names the person represented nor shows that the representative signed in a representative capacity;

(b) except as otherwise established between the immediate parties, is personally obligated if the instrument names the person represented but does not show that the representative signed in a representative capacity, or if the instrument does not name the person represented but does show that the representative signed in a representative capacity.

(3) Except as otherwise established the name of an organization preceded or followed by the name and office of an authorized individual is a signature made in a representative capacity.

Section 3—404.   Unauthorized Signatures

(1) Any unauthorized signature is wholly inoperative as that of the person whose name is signed unless he ratifies it or is precluded from denying it; but it operates as the signature of the unauthorized signer in favor of any person who in good faith pays the instrument or takes it for value.

(2) Any unauthorized signature may be ratified for all purposes of this Article. Such ratification does not of itself affect any rights of the person ratifying against the actual signer.

Section 3—405.   Impostors; Signature in Name of Payee

(1) An indorsement by any person in the name of a named payee is effective if

(a) an impostor by use of the mails or otherwise has induced the maker or drawer to issue the instrument to him or his confederate in the name of the payee; or

(b) a person signing as or on behalf of a maker or drawer intends the payee to have no interest in the instrument; or

(c) an agent or employee of the maker or drawer has supplied him with the name of the payee intending the latter to have no such interest.

(2) Nothing in this section shall affect the criminal or civil liability of the person so indorsing.

Section 3—406. Negligence Contributing to Alteration or Unauthorized Signature

Any person who by his negligence substantially contributes to a material alteration of the instrument or to the making of an unauthorized signature is precluded from asserting the alteration or lack of authority against a holder in due course or against a drawee or other payor who pays the instrument in good faith and in accordance with the reasonable commercial standards of the drawee's or payor's business.

Section 3—407. Alteration

(1) Any alteration of an instrument is material which changes the contract of any party thereto in any respect, including any such change in

(a) the number or relations of the parties; or

(b) an incomplete instrument, by completing it otherwise than as authorized; or

(c) the writing as signed, by adding to it or by removing any part of it.

(2) As against any person other than a subsequent holder in due course.

(a) alteration by the holder which is both fraudulent and material discharges any party whose contract is thereby changed unless that party assents or is precluded from asserting the defense;

(b) no other alteration discharges any party and the instrument may be enforced according to its original tenor, or as to incomplete instruments according to the authority given.

(3) A subsequent holder in due course may in all cases enforce the instrument according to its original tenor, and when an incomplete instrument has been completed, he may enforce it as completed.

Section 3—408. Consideration

Want or failure of consideration is a defense as against any person not having the rights of a holder in due course (Section 3—305), except that no consideration is necessary for an instrument or obligation thereon given in payment of or as security for an antecedent obligation of any kind. Nothing in this section shall be taken to displace any statute outside this Act under which a promise is enforceable notwithstanding lack or failure of consideration. Partial failure of consideration is a defense pro tanto whether or not the failure is in an ascertained or liquidated amount.

Section 3—409. Draft Not an Assignment

(1) A check or other draft does not of itself operate as an assignment of any funds in the hands of the drawee available for its payment, and the drawee is not liable on the instrument until he accepts it.

(2) Nothing in this section shall affect any liability in contract, tort or otherwise arising from any letter of credit or other obligation or representation which is not an acceptance.

Section 3—410. Definition and Operation of Acceptance

(1) Acceptance is the drawee's signed engagement to honor the draft as presented. It must be written on the draft, and may consist of his signature alone. It becomes operative when completed by delivery or notification.

(2) A draft may be accepted although it has not been signed by the drawer or is otherwise incomplete or is overdue or has been dishonored.

(3) Where the draft is payable at a fixed period after sight and the acceptor fails to date his acceptance the holder may complete it by supplying a date in good faith.

Section 3—411. Certification of a Check

(1) Certification of a check is acceptance. Where a holder procures certification the drawer and all prior indorsers are discharged.

(2) Unless otherwise agreed a bank has no obligation to certify a check.

(3) A bank may certify a check before returning it for lack of proper indorsement. If it does so the drawer is discharged.

Section 3—412. Acceptance Varying Draft

(1) Where the drawee's proffered acceptance in any manner varies the draft as presented the holder may refuse the acceptance and treat the draft as dishonored in which case the drawee is entitled to have his acceptance cancelled.

(2) The terms of the draft are not varied by an acceptance to pay at any particular bank or place in the United States, unless the acceptance states that the draft is to be paid only at such bank or place.

(3) Where the holder assents to an acceptance varying the terms of the draft each drawer and indorser who does not affirmatively assent is discharged.

Section 3—413. Contract of Maker, Drawer and Acceptor

(1) The maker or acceptor engages that he will pay the instrument according to its tenor at the time of his engagement or as completed pursuant to Section 3—115 on incomplete instruments.

(2) The drawer engages that upon dishonor of the draft and any necessary notice of dishonor or protest he will pay the amount of the draft to the holder or to any indorser who takes it up. The drawer may disclaim this liability by drawing without recourse.

(3) By making, drawing or accepting the party admits as against all subsequent parties including the drawee the existence of the payee and his then capacity to indorse.

Section 3—414. Contract of Indorser; Order of Liability

(1) Unless the indorsement otherwise specifies (as by such words as "without recourse") every indorser engages that upon dishonor and any necessary notice of dishonor and protest he will pay the instrument according to its tenor at the time of his indorsement to the holder or to any subsequent indorser who takes it up, even though the indorser who takes it up was not obligated to do so.

(2) Unless they otherwise agree indorsers are liable to one another in the order in which they indorse, which is presumed to be the order in which their signatures appear on the instrument.

Section 3—415. Contract of Accommodation Party

(1) An accommodation party is one who signs the instrument in any capacity for the purpose of lending his name to another party to it.

(2) When the instrument has been taken for value before it is due the accommodation party is liable in the capacity in which he has signed even though the taker knows of the accommodation.

(3) As against a holder in due course and without notice of the accommodation oral proof of the accommodation is not admissible to give the accommodation party the benefit of discharges dependent on his character as such. In other cases the accommodation character may be shown by oral proof.

(4) An indorsement which shows that it is not in the chain of title is notice of its accommodation character.

(5) An accommodation party is not liable to the party accommodated, and if he pays the instrument has a right of recourse on the instrument against such party.

Section 3—416. Contract of Guarantor

(1) "Payment guaranteed" or equivalent words added to a signature mean that the signer engages that if the instrument is not paid when due he will pay it according to its tenor without resort by the holder to any other party.

(2) "Collection guaranteed" or equivalent words added to a signature mean that the signer engages that if the instrument is not paid when due he will pay it according to its tenor, but only after the holder has reduced his claim against the maker or acceptor to judgment and execution has been returned unsatisfied, or after the maker or acceptor has become insolvent or it is otherwise apparent that it is useless to proceed against him.

(3) Words of guaranty which do not otherwise specify guarantee payment.

(4) No words of guaranty added to the signature of a sole maker or acceptor affect his liability on the instrument. Such words added to the signature of one of two or more makers or acceptors create a presumption that the signature is for the accommodation of the others.

(5) When words of guaranty are used presentment, notice of dishonor and protest are not necessary to charge the user.

(6) Any guaranty written on the instrument is enforcible notwithstanding any statute of frauds.

Section 3—417. Warranties on Presentment and Transfer

(1) Any person who obtains payment or acceptance and any prior transferor warrants to a person who in good faith pays or accepts that

    (a) he has a good title to the instrument or is authorized to obtain payment or acceptance on behalf of one who has a good title; and

    (b) he has no knowledge that the signature of the maker or drawer is unauthorized, except that this warranty is not given by a holder in due course acting in good faith

        (i) to a maker with respect to the maker's own signature; or

        (ii) to a drawer with respect to the drawer's own signature, whether or not the drawer is also the drawee; or

        (iii) to an acceptor of a draft if the holder in due course took the draft after the acceptance or obtained the acceptance without knowledge that the drawer's signature was unauthorized; and

    (c) the instrument has not been materially altered, except that this warranty is not given by a holder in due course acting in good faith

        (i) to the maker of a note; or

        (ii) to the drawer of a draft whether or not the drawer is also the drawee; or

        (iii) to the acceptor of a draft with respect to an alteration made prior to the acceptance if the holder in due course took the draft after the acceptance, even though the acceptance provided "payable as originally drawn" or equivalent terms; or

        (iv) to the acceptor of a draft with respect to an alteration made after the acceptance.

(2) Any person who transfers an instrument and receives consideration warrants to his transferee and if the transfer is by indorsement to any subsequent holder who takes the instrument in good faith that

    (a) he has a good title to the instrument or is authorized to obtain payment or acceptance on behalf of one who has a good title and the transfer is otherwise rightful; and

    (b) all signatures are genuine or authorized; and

    (c) the instrument has not been materially altered; and

    (d) no defense of any party is good against him; and

    (e) he has no knowledge of any insolvency proceeding instituted with respect to the maker or acceptor or the drawer of an unaccepted instrument.

(3) By transferring "without recourse" the transferor limits the obligation stated in subsection (2) (d) to a warranty that he has no knowledge of such a defense.

(4) A selling agent or broker who does not disclose the fact that he is acting only as such gives the warranties provided in this section, but if he makes such disclosure warrants only his good faith and authority.

Section 3—418. Finality of Payment or Acceptance

Except for recovery of bank payments as provided in the Article on Bank Deposits and Collections (Article 4) and except for liability for breach of warranty on presentment under the preceding section, payment or acceptance of any instrument is final in favor of a holder in due course, or a person who has in good faith changed his position in reliance on the payment.

Section 3—419. Conversion of Instrument; Innocent Representative

(1) An instrument is converted when

    (a) a drawee to whom it is delivered for acceptance refuses to return it on demand; or

    (b) any person to whom it is delivered for payment refuses on demand either to pay or to return it; or

    (c) it is paid on a forged indorsement.

(2) In an action against a drawee under subsection (1) the measure of the drawee's liability is the face amount of the instrument. In any other action under subsection (1) the measure of liability is presumed to be the face amount of the instrument.

(3) Subject to the provisions of this Act concerning restrictive indorsements a representative, including a depositary or collecting bank, who has in good faith and in accordance with the reasonable commercial standards applicable to the business of such representative dealt with an instrument or its proceeds on behalf of one who was not the true owner is not liable in conversion or otherwise to the true owner beyond the amount of any proceeds remaining in his hands.

(4) An intermediary bank or payor bank which is not a depositary bank is not liable in conversion solely by reason of the fact that proceeds of an item indorsed restrictively (Sections 3—205 and 3—206) are not paid or applied consistently with the restrictive indorsement of an indorser other than its immediate transferor.

Part 5 Presentment, Notice of Dishonor and Protest

Section 3—501. When Presentment, Notice of Dishonor, and Protest Necessary or Permissible

(1) Unless excused (Section 3—511) presentment is necessary to charge secondary parties as follows:

(a) presentment for acceptance is necessary to charge the drawer and indorsers of a draft where the draft so provides, or is payable elsewhere than at the residence or place of business of the drawee, or its date of payment depends upon such presentment. The holder may at his option present for acceptance any other draft payable at a stated date;

(b) presentment for payment is necessary to charge any indorser;

(c) in the case of any drawer, the acceptor of a draft payable at a bank or the maker of a note payable at a bank, presentment for payment is necessary, but failure to make presentment discharges such drawer, acceptor or maker only as stated in Section 3—502(1) (b).

(2) Unless excused (Section 3—511)

(a) notice of any dishonor is necessary to charge any indorser:

(b) in the case of any drawer, the acceptor of a draft payable at a bank or the maker of a note payable at a bank, notice of any dishonor is necessary, but failure to give such notice discharges such drawer, acceptor or maker only as stated in Section 3—502(1) (b)

(3) Unless excused (Section 3—511) protest of any dishonor is necessary to charge the drawer and indorsers of any draft which on its face appears to be drawn or payable outside of the states, territories, dependencies and possessions of the United States, the District of Columbia and the Commonwealth of Puerto Rico. The holder may at his option make protest of any dishonor of any other instrument and in the case of a foreign draft may on insolvency of the acceptor before maturity make protest for better security.

(4) Notwithstanding any provision of this section, neither presentment nor notice of dishonor nor protest is necessary to charge an indorser who has indorsed an instrument after maturity.

Section 3—502. Unexcused Delay; Discharge

(1) Where without excuse any necessary presentment or notice of dishonor is delayed beyond the time when it is due

(a) any indorser is discharged; and

(b) any drawer or the acceptor of a draft payable at a bank or the maker of a note payable at a bank who because the drawee or payor bank becomes insolvent during the delay is deprived of funds maintained with the drawee or payor bank to cover the instrument may discharge his liability by written assignment to the holder of his rights against the drawee or payor bank in respect of such funds, but such drawer, acceptor or maker is not otherwise discharged.

(2) Where without excuse a necessary protest is delayed beyond the time when it is due any drawer or indorser is discharged.

Section 3—503. Time of Presentment

(1) Unless a different time is expressed in the instrument the time for any presentment is determined as follows:

(a) where an instrument is payable at or a fixed period after a stated date any presentment for acceptance must be made on or before the date it is payable;

(b) where an instrument is payable after sight it must either be presented for acceptance or negotiated within a reasonable time after date or issue whichever is later;

(c) where an instrument shows the date on which it is payable presentment for payment is due on that date;

(d) where an instrument is accelerated presentment for payment is due within a reasonable time after the acceleration;

(e) with respect to the liability of any secondary party presentment for acceptance or payment of any other instrument is due within a reasonable time after such party becomes liable thereon.

(2) A reasonable time for presentment is determined by the nature of the instrument, any usage of banking or trade and the facts of the particular case. In the case of an uncertified check which is drawn and payable within the United States and which is not a draft drawn by a bank the following are presumed to be reasonable periods within which to present for payment or to initiate bank collection:

(a) with respect to the liability of the drawer, thirty days after date or issue whichever is later; and

(b) with respect to the liability of an indorser, seven days after his indorsement.

(3) Where any presentment is due on a day which is not a full business day for either the person making presentment or the party to pay or accept, presentment is due on the next following day which is a full business day for both parties.

(4) Presentment to be sufficient must be made at a reasonable hour, and if at a bank during its banking day.

Section 3—504. How Presentment Made

(1) Presentment is a demand for acceptance or payment made upon the maker, acceptor, drawee or other payor by or on behalf of the holder.

(2) Presentment may be made

(a) by mail, in which event the time of presentment is determined by the time of receipt of the mail; or

(b) through a clearing house; or

(c) at the place of acceptance or payment specified in the instrument or if there be none at the place of business or residence of the party to accept or pay. If neither the party to accept or pay nor anyone authorized to act for him is present or accessible at such place presentment is excused.

(3) It may be made

(a) to any one of two or more makers, acceptors, drawees or other payors; or

(b) to any person who has authority to make or refuse the acceptance or payment.

(4) A draft accepted or a note made payable at a bank in the United States must be presented at such bank.

(5) In the cases described in Section 4—210 presentment may be made in the manner and with the result stated in that section.

Section 3—505. Rights of Party to Whom Presentment Is Made

(1) The party to whom presentment is made may without dishonor require

(a) exhibition of the instrument; and

(b) reasonable identification of the person making presentment and evidence of his authority to make it if made for another; and

(c) that the instrument be produced for acceptance or payment at a place specified in it, or if there be none at any place reasonable in the circumstances; and

(d) a signed receipt on the instrument for any partial or full payment and its surrender upon full payment.

(2) Failure to comply with any such requirement invalidates the presentment but the person presenting has a reasonable time in which to comply and the time for acceptance or payment runs from the time of compliance.

Section 3—506. Time Allowed for Acceptance or Payment

(1) Acceptance may be deferred without dishonor until the close of the next business day following presentment. The holder may also in a good faith effort to obtain acceptance and without either dishonor of the instrument or discharge of secondary parties allow postponement of acceptance for an additional business day.

(2) Except as a longer time is allowed in the case of documentary drafts drawn under a letter of credit, and unless an earlier time is agreed to by the party to pay, payment of an instrument may be deferred without dishonor pending reasonable examination to determine whether it is properly payable, but payment must be made in any event before the close of business on the day of presentment.

Section 3—507. Dishonor; Holder's Right of Recourse; Term Allowing Re-Presentment

(1) An instrument is dishonored when

    (a) a necessary or optional presentment is duly made and due acceptance or payment is refused or cannot be obtained within the prescribed time or in case of bank collections the instrument is seasonably returned by the midnight deadline (Section 4—301); or

    (b) presentment is excused and the instrument is not duly accepted or paid.

(2) Subject to any necessary notice of dishonor and protest, the holder has upon dishonor an immediate right of recourse against the drawers and indorsers.

(3) Return of an instrument for lack of proper indorsement is not dishonor.

(4) A term in a draft or an indorsement thereof allowing a stated time for re-presentment in the event of any dishonor of the draft by nonacceptance if a time draft or by nonpayment if a sight draft gives the holder as against any secondary party bound by the term an option to waive the dishonor without affecting the liability of the secondary party and he may present again up to the end of the stated time.

Section 3—508. Notice of Dishonor

(1) Notice of dishonor may be given to any person who may be liable on the instrument by or on behalf of the holder or any party who has himself received notice, or any other party who can be compelled to pay the instrument. In addition an agent or bank in whose hands the instrument is dishonored may give notice to his principal or customer or to another agent or bank from which the instrument was received.

(2) Any necessary notice must be given by a bank before its midnight deadline and by any other person before midnight of the third business day after dishonor or receipt of notice of dishonor.

(3) Notice may be given in any reasonable manner. It may be oral or written and in any terms which identify the instrument and state that it has been dishonored. A misdescription which does not mislead the party notified does not vitiate the notice. Sending the instrument bearing a stamp, ticket or writing stating that acceptance or payment has been refused or sending a notice of debit with respect to the instrument is sufficient.

(4) Written notice is given when sent although it is not received.

(5) Notice to one partner is notice to each although the firm has been dissolved.

(6) When any party is in insolvency proceedings instituted after the issue of the instrument notice may be given either to the party or to the representative of his estate.

(7) When any party is dead or incompetent notice may be sent to his last known address or given to his personal representative.

(8) Notice operates for the benefit of all parties who have rights on the instrument against the party notified.

Section 3—509. Protest; Noting for Protest

(1) A protest is a certificate of dishonor made under the hand and seal of a United States consul or vice consul or a notary public or other person authorized to certify dishonor by the law of the place where dishonor occurs. It may be made upon information satisfactory to such person.

(2) The protest must identify the instrument and certify either that due presentment has been made or the reason why it is excused and that the instrument has been dishonored by nonacceptance or nonpayment.

(3) The protest may also certify that notice of dishonor has been given to all parties or to specified parties.

(4) Subject to subsection (5) any necessary protest is due by the time that notice of dishonor is due.

(5) If, before protest is due, an instrument has been noted for protest by the officer to make protest, the protest may be made at any time thereafter as of the date of the noting.

Section 3—510. Evidence of Dishonor and Notice of Dishonor

The following are admissible as evidence and create a presumption of dishonor and of any notice of dishonor therein shown:

(a) a document regular in form as provided in the preceding section which purports to be a protest;

(b) the purported stamp or writing of the drawee, payor bank or presenting bank on the instrument or accompanying it stating that acceptance or payment has been refused for reasons consistent with dishonor;

(c) any book or record of the drawee, payor bank, or any collecting bank kept in the usual course of business which shows dishonor, even though there is no evidence of who made the entry.

Section 3—511. Waived or Excused Presentment, Protest or Notice of Dishonor or Delay Therein

(1) Delay in presentment, protest or notice of dishonor is excused when the party is without notice that it is due or when the delay is caused by circumstances beyond his control and he exercises reasonable diligence after the cause of the delay ceases to operate.

(2) Presentment or notice or protest as the case may be is entirely excused when

(a) the party to be charged has waived it expressly or by implication either before or after it is due; or

(b) such party has himself dishonored the instrument or has countermanded payment or otherwise has no reason to expect or right to require that the instrument be accepted or paid; or

(c) by reasonable diligence the presentment or protest cannot be made or the notice given.

(3) Presentment is also entirely excused when

(a) the maker, acceptor, or drawee of any instrument except a documentary draft is dead or in insolvency proceedings instituted after the issue of the instrument; or

(b) acceptance or payment is refused but not for want of proper presentment.

(4) Where a draft has been dishonored by nonacceptance a later presentment for payment and any notice of dishonor and protest for nonpayment are excused unless in the meantime the instrument has been accepted.

(5) A waiver of protest is also a waiver of presentment and of notice of dishonor even though protest is not required.

(6) Where a waiver of presentment or notice or protest is embodied in the instrument itself it is binding upon all parties; but where it is written above the signature of an indorser it binds him only.

Part 6 Discharge

Section 3—601. Discharge of Parties

(1) The extent of the discharge of any party from liability on an instrument is governed by the sections on

(a) payment or satisfaction (Section 3—603); or

(b) tender of payment (Section 3—604); or

(c) cancellation or renunciation (Section 3—605); or

(d) impairment of right of recourse or of collateral (Section 3—606); or

(e) reacquisition of the instrument by a prior party (Section 3—208); or

(f) fraudulent and material alteration (Section 3—407); or

(g) certification of a check (Section 3—411); or

(h) acceptance varying a draft (Section 3—412); or

(i) unexcused delay in presentment or notice of dishonor or protest (Section 3—502).

(2) Any party is also discharged from his liability on an instrument to another party by any other act or agreement with such party which would discharge his simple contract for the payment of money.

(3) The liability of all parties is discharged when any party who has himself no right of action or recourse on the instrument

(a) reacquires the instrument in his own right; or

(b) is discharged under any provision of this Article, except as otherwise provided with respect to discharge for impairment of recourse or of collateral (Section 3—606).

Section 3—602. Effect of Discharge Against Holder in Due Course

No discharge of any party provided by this Article is effective against a subsequent holder in due course unless he has notice thereof when he takes the instrument.

Section 3—603. Payment or Satisfaction

(1) The liability of any party is discharged to the extent of his payment or satisfaction to the holder even though it is made with knowledge of a claim of another person to the instrument unless prior to such payment or satisfaction the person making the claim either supplies indemnity deemed adequate by the party seeking the discharge or enjoins payment or satisfaction by order of a court of competent jurisdiction in an action in which the adverse claimant and the holder are parties. This subsection does not, however, result in the discharge of the liability

(a) of a party who in bad faith pays or satisfies a holder who acquired the instrument by theft or who (unless having the rights of a holder in due course) holds through one who so acquired it; or

(b) of a party (other than an intermediary bank or a payor bank which is not a depositary bank) who pays or satisfies the holder of an instrument which has been restrictively indorsed in a manner not consistent with the terms of such restrictive indorsement.

(2) Payment or satisfaction may be made with the consent of the holder by any person including a stranger to the instrument. Surrender of the instrument to such a person gives him the rights of a transferee (Section 3—201).

Section 3—604. Tender of Payment

(1) Any party making tender of full payment to a holder when or after it is due is discharged to the extent of all subsequent liability for interest, costs and attorney's fees.

(2) The holder's refusal of such tender wholly discharges any party who has a right of recourse against the party making the tender.

(3) Where the maker or acceptor of an instrument payable otherwise than on demand is able and ready to pay at every place of payment specified in the instrument when it is due, it is equivalent to tender.

Section 3—605. Cancellation and Renunciation

(1) The holder of an instrument may even without consideration discharge any party

(a) in any manner apparent on the face of the instrument or the indorsement, as by intentionally cancelling the instrument or the party's signature by destruction or mutilation, or by striking out the party's signature; or

(b) by renouncing his rights by a writing signed and delivered or by surrender of the instrument to the party to be discharged.

(2) Neither cancellation nor renunciation without surrender of the instrument affects the title thereto.

Section 3—606. Impairment of Recourse or of Collateral

(1) The holder discharges any party to the instrument to the extent that without such party's consent the holder

(a) without express reservation of rights releases or agrees not to sue any person against whom the party has to the knowledge of the holder a right of recourse or agrees to suspend the right to enforce against such person the instrument or collateral or otherwise discharges such person, except that failure or delay in effecting any required presentment, protest or notice of dishonor with respect to any such person does not discharge any party as to whom presentment, protest or notice of dishonor is effective or unnecessary; or

(b) unjustifiably impairs any collateral for the instrument given by or on behalf of the party or any person against whom he has a right of recourse.

(2) By express reservation of rights against a party with a right of recourse the holder preserves

(a) all his rights against such party as of the time when the instrument was originally due; and

(b) the right of the party to pay the instrument as of that time; and

(c) all rights of such party to recourse against others.

Part 7   Advice of International Sight Draft

Section 3—701.   Letter of Advice of International Sight Draft

(1) A "letter of advice" is a drawer's communication to the drawee that a described draft has been drawn.

(2) Unless otherwise agreed when a bank receives from another bank a letter of advice of an international sight draft the drawee bank may immediately debit the drawer's account and stop the running of interest pro tanto. Such a debit and any resulting credit to any account covering outstanding drafts leaves in the drawer full power to stop payment or otherwise dispose of the amount and creates no trust or interest in favor of the holder.

(3) Unless otherwise agreed and except where a draft is drawn under a credit issued by the drawee, the drawee of an international sight draft owes the drawer no duty to pay an unadvised draft but if it does so and the draft is genuine, may appropriately debit the drawer's account.

Part 8   Miscellaneous

Section 3—801.   Drafts in a Set

(1) Where a draft is drawn in a set of parts, each of which is numbered and expressed to be an order only if no other part has been honored, the whole of the parts constitutes one draft but a taker of any part may become a holder in due course of the draft.

(2) Any person who negotiates, indorses or accepts a single part of a draft drawn in a set thereby becomes liable to any holder in due course of that part as if it were the whole set, but as between different holders in due course to whom different parts have been negotiated the holder whose title first accrues has all rights to the draft and its proceeds.

(3) As against the drawee the first presented part of a draft drawn in a set is the part entitled to payment, or if a time draft to acceptance and payment. Acceptance of any subsequently presented part renders the drawee liable thereon under subsection (2). With respect both to a holder and to the drawer payment of a subsequently presented part of a draft payable at sight has the same effect as payment of a check notwithstanding an effective stop order (Section 4—407).

(4) Except as otherwise provided in this section, where any part of a draft in a set is discharged by payment or otherwise the whole draft is discharged.

Section 3—802.   Effect of Instrument on Obligation for Which It Is Given

(1) Unless otherwise agreed where an instrument is taken for an underlying obligation

(a) the obligation is pro tanto discharged if a bank is drawer, maker or acceptor of the instrument and there is no recourse on the instrument against the underlying obligor; and

(b) in any other case the obligation is suspended pro tanto until the instrument is due or if it is payable on demand until its presentment. If the instrument is dishonored action may be maintained on either the instrument or the obligation; discharge of the underlying obligor on the instrument also discharges him on the obligation.

(2) The taking in good faith of a check which is not postdated does not of itself so extend the time on the original obligation as to discharge a surety.

Section 3—803. Notice to Third Party

Where a defendant is sued for breach of an obligation for which a third person is answerable over under this Article he may give the third person written notice of the litigation, and the person notified may then give similar notice to any other person who is answerable over to him under this Article. If the notice states that the person notified may come in and defend and that if the person notified does not do so he will in any action against him by the person giving the notice be bound by any determination of fact common to the two litigations, then unless after seasonable receipt of the notice the person notified does come in and defend he is so bound.

Section 3—804. Lost, Destroyed or Stolen Instruments

The owner of an instrument which is lost, whether by destruction, theft or otherwise, may maintain an action in his own name and recover from any party liable thereon upon due proof of his ownership, the facts which prevent his production of the instrument and its terms. The court may require security indemnifying the defendant against loss by reason of further claims on the instrument.

Section 3—805. Instruments Not Payable to Order or to Bearer

This Article applies to any instrument whose terms do not preclude transfer and which is otherwise negotiable within this Article but which is not payable to order or to bearer, except that there can be no holder in due course of such an instrument.

Article 4   Bank Deposits and Collections

Part 1   General Provisions and Definitions

Section 4—101. Short Title

This Article shall be known and may be cited as Uniform Commercial Code—Bank Deposits and Collections.

Section 4—102. Applicability

(1) To the extent that items within this Article are also within the scope of Articles 3 and 8, they are subject to the provisions of those Articles. In the event of conflict the provisions of this Article govern those of Article 3 but the provisions of Article 8 govern those of this Article.

(2) The liability of a bank for action or non-action with respect to any item handled by it for purposes of presentment, payment or collection is governed by the law of the place where the bank is located. In the case of action or non-action by or at a branch or separate office of a bank, its liability is governed by the law of the place where the branch or separate office is located.

Section 4—103. Variation by Agreement; Measure of Damages; Certain Action Constituting Ordinary Care

(1) The effect of the provisions of this Article may be varied by agreement except that no agreement can disclaim a bank's responsibility for its own lack of good faith or failure to exercise ordinary care or can limit the measure of damages for such lack or failure; but the parties may by agreement determine the standards by which such responsibility is to be measured if such standards are not manifestly unreasonable.

(2) Federal Reserve regulations and operating letters, clearing house rules, and the like, have the effect of agreements under subsection (1), whether or not specifically assented to by all parties interested in items handled.

(3) Action or non-action approved by this Article or pursuant to Federal Reserve regulations or operating letters constitutes the exercise of ordinary care and, in the absence of special instructions, action or non-action consistent with clearing house rules and the like or with a general banking usage not disapproved by this Article, prima facie constitutes the exercise of ordinary care.

(4) The specification or approval of certain procedures by this Article does not constitute disapproval of other procedures which may be reasonable under the circumstances.

(5) The measure of damages for failure to exercise ordinary care in handling an item is the amount of the item reduced by an amount which could not have been realized by the use of ordinary care, and where there is bad faith it includes other damages, if any, suffered by the party as a proximate consequence.

Section 4—104. Definitions and Index of Definitions

(1) In this Article unless the context otherwise requires

  (a) "Account" means any account with a bank and includes a checking, time, interest or savings account;

  (b) "Afternoon" means the period of a day between noon and midnight;

  (c) "Banking day" means that part of any day on which a bank is open to the public for carrying on substantially all of its banking functions;

  (d) "Clearing house" means any association of banks or other payors regularly clearing items;

  (e) "Customer" means any person having an account with a bank or for whom a bank has agreed to collect items and includes a bank carrying an account with another bank;

  (f) "Documentary draft" means any negotiable or non-negotiable draft with accompanying documents, securities or other papers to be delivered against honor of the draft;

  (g) "Item" means any instrument for the payment of money even though it is not negotiable but does not include money;

  (h) "Midnight deadline" with respect to a bank is midnight on its next banking day following the banking day on which it receives the relevant item or notice or from which the time for taking action commences to run, whichever is later;

  (i) "Properly payable" includes the availability of funds for payment at the time of decision to pay or dishonor;

  (j) "Settle" means to pay in cash, by clearing house settlement, in a charge or credit or by remittance, or otherwise as instructed. A settlement may be either provisional or final;

  (k) "Suspends payments" with respect to a bank means that it has been closed by order of the supervisory authorities, that a public officer has been appointed to take it over or that it ceases or refuses to make payments in the ordinary course of business.

(2) Other definitions applying to this Article and the sections in which they appear are:

  "Collecting bank." Section 4—105.
  "Depositary bank." Section 4—105.
  "Intermediary bank." Section 4—105.
  "Payor bank." Section 4—105.
  "Presenting bank." Section 4—105.
  "Remitting bank." Section 4—105.

(3) The following definitions in other Articles apply to this Article:

  "Acceptance." Section 3—410.
  "Certificate of deposit." Section 3—104.
  "Certification." Section 3—411.
  "Check." Section 3—104.
  "Draft." Section 3—104.
  "Holder in due course." Section 3—302.
  "Notice of dishonor." Section 3—508.
  "Presentment." Section 3—504.
  "Protest." Section 3—509.
  "Secondary party." Section 3—102.

(4) In addition Article 1 contains general definitions and principles of construction and interpretation applicable throughout this Article.

Section 4—105. "Depositary Bank"; "Intermediary Bank"; "Collecting Bank"; "Payor Bank"; "Presenting Bank"; "Remitting Bank"

In this Article unless the context otherwise requires:

  (a) "Depositary bank" means the first bank to which an item is transferred for collection even though it is also the payor bank;

  (b) "Payor bank" means a bank by which an item is payable as drawn or accepted;

  (c) "Intermediary bank" means any bank to which an item is transferred in course of collection except the depositary or payor bank;

  (d) "Collecting bank" means any bank handling the item for collection except the payor bank;

  (e) "Presenting bank" means any bank presenting an item except a payor bank;

  (f) "Remitting bank" means any payor or intermediary bank remitting for an item.

Section 4—106. Separate Office of a Bank

A branch or separate office of a bank [maintaining its own deposit ledgers] is a separate bank for the purpose of computing the time within which and determining the place at or to which action may be taken or notices or orders shall be given under this Article and under Article 3.

Note: *The brackets are to make it optional with the several states whether to require a branch to maintain its own deposit ledgers in order to be considered to be a separate bank for certain purposes under Article 4. In some states "maintaining its own deposit ledgers" is a satisfactory test. In others branch banking practices are such that this test would not be suitable.*

Section 4—107. Time of Receipt of Items

(1) For the purpose of allowing time to process items, prove balances and make the necessary entries on its books to determine its position for the day, a bank may fix an afternoon hour of 2 P.M. or later as a cut-off hour for the handling of money and items and the making of entries on its books.

(2) Any item or deposit of money received on any day after a cut-off hour so fixed or after the close of the banking day may be treated as being received at the opening of the next banking day.

Section 4—108. Delays

(1) Unless otherwise instructed, a collecting bank in a good faith effort to secure payment may, in the case of specific items and with or without the approval of any person involved, waive, modify or extend time limits imposed or permitted by this Act for a period not in excess of an additional banking day without discharge of secondary parties and without liability to its transferor or any prior party.

(2) Delay by a collecting bank or payor bank beyond time limits prescribed or permitted by this Act or by instructions is excused if caused by interruption of communication facilities, suspension of payments by another bank, war, emergency conditions or other circumstances beyond the control of the bank provided it exercises such diligence as the circumstances require.

Section 4—109. Process of Posting

The "process of posting" means the usual procedure followed by a payor bank in determining to pay an item and in recording the payment including one or more of the following or other steps as determined by the bank:

    (a) verification of any signature;

    (b) ascertaining that sufficient funds are available;

    (c) affixing a "paid" or other stamp;

    (d) entering a charge or entry to a customer's account;

    (e) correcting or reversing an entry or erroneous action with respect to the item.

Part 2 Collection of Items: Depositary and Collecting Banks

Section 4—201. Presumption and Duration of Agency Status of Collecting Banks and Provisional Status of Credits; Applicability of Article; Item Indorsed "Pay Any Bank"

(1) Unless a contrary intent clearly appears and prior to the time that a settlement given by a collecting bank for an item is or becomes final (subsection (3) of Section 4—211 and Sections 4—212 and 4—213) the bank is an agent or sub-agent of the owner of the item and any settlement given for the item is provisional. This provision applies regardless of the form of indorsement or lack of indorsement and even though credit given for the item is subject to immediate withdrawal as of right or is in fact withdrawn; but the continuance of ownership of an item by its owner and any rights of the owner to proceeds of the item are subject to rights of a collecting bank such as those resulting from outstanding advances on the item and valid rights of set-off. When an item is handled by banks for purposes of presentment, payment and collection, the relevant provisions of this Article apply even though action of parties clearly establishes that a particular bank has purchased the item and is the owner of it.

(2) After an item has been indorsed with the words "pay any bank" or the like, only a bank may acquire the rights of a holder

    (a) until the item has been returned to the customer initiating collection; or

    (b) until the item has been specially indorsed by a bank to a person who is not a bank.

Section 4—202. Responsibility for Collection; When Action Seasonable

(1) A collecting bank must use ordinary care in

    (a) presenting an item or sending it for present-ment; and

    (b) sending notice of dishonor or non-payment or returning an item other than a documentary draft to the bank's transferor [or directly to the depositary bank under subsection (2) of Section 4—212] (*see note to Section 4—212*) after learning that the item has not been paid or accepted, as the case may be; and

    (c) settling for an item when the bank receives final settlement; and

    (d) making or providing for any necessary pro-test; and

    (e) notifying its transferor of any loss or delay in transit within a reasonable time after discov-ery thereof.

(2) A collecting bank taking proper action before its midnight deadline following receipt of an item, notice or payment acts seasonably; taking proper action within a reasonably longer time may be seasonable but the bank has the burden of so establishing.

(3) Subject to subsection (1) (a), a bank is not liable for the insolvency, neglect, misconduct, mistake or de-fault of another bank or person or for loss or destruction of an item in transit or in the possession of others.

Section 4—203. Effect of Instructions

Subject to the provisions of Article 3 concerning con-version of instruments (Section 3—419) and the provi-sions of both Article 3 and this Article concerning restrictive indorsements only a collecting bank's trans-feror can give instructions which affect the bank or con-stitute notice to it and a collecting bank is not liable to prior parties for any action taken pursuant to such in-structions or in accordance with any agreement with its transferor.

Section 4—204. Methods of Sending and Presenting; Sending Direct to Payor Bank

(1) A collecting bank must send items by reasonably prompt method taking into consideration any relevant instructions, the nature of the item, the number of such

items on hand, and the cost of collection involved and the method generally used by it or others to present such items.

(2) A collecting bank may send

    (a) any item direct to the payor bank;

    (b) any item to any non-bank payor if authorized by its transferor; and

    (c) any item other than documentary drafts to any non-bank payor, if authorized by Federal Reserve regulation or operating letter, clear-ing house rule or the like.

(3) Presentment may be made by a presenting bank at a place where the payor bank has requested that pre-sentment be made.

Section 4—205. Supplying Missing Indorsement; No Notice from Prior Indorsement

(1) A depositary bank which has taken an item for col-lection may supply any indorsement of the customer which is necessary to title unless the item contains the words "payee's indorsement required" or the like. In the absence of such a requirement a statement placed on the item by the depositary bank to the effect that the item was deposited by a customer or credited to his account is effective as the customer's indorsement.

(2) An intermediary bank, or payor bank which is not a depositary bank, is neither given notice nor otherwise affected by a restrictive indorsement of any person ex-cept the bank's immediate transferor.

Section 4—206. Transfer Between Banks

Any agreed method which identifies the transferor bank is sufficient for the item's further transfer to another bank.

Section 4—207. Warranties of Customer and Collecting Bank on Transfer or Presentment of Items; Time for Claims

(1) Each customer or collecting bank who obtains pay-ment or acceptance of an item and each prior customer and collecting bank warrants to the payor bank or other payor who in good faith pays or accepts the item that

    (a) he has a good title to the item or is authorized to obtain payment or acceptance on behalf of one who has a good title; and

(b) he has no knowledge that the signature of the maker or drawer is unauthorized, except that this warranty is not given by any customer or collecting bank that is a holder in due course and acts in good faith

    (i) to a maker with respect to the maker's own signature; or

    (ii) to a drawer with respect to the drawer's own signature, whether or not the drawer is also the drawee; or

    (iii) to an acceptor of an item if the holder in due course took the item after the acceptance or obtained the acceptance without knowledge that the drawer's signature was unauthorized; and

(c) the item has not been materially altered, except that this warranty is not given by any customer or collecting bank that is a holder in due course and acts in good faith

    (i) to the maker of a note; or

    (ii) to the drawer of a draft whether or not the drawer is also the drawee; or

    (iii) to the acceptor of an item with respect to an alteration made prior to the acceptance if the holder in due course took the item after the acceptance, even though the acceptance provided "payable as originally drawn" or equivalent terms; or

    (iv) to the acceptor of an item with respect to an alteration made after the acceptance.

(2) Each customer and collecting bank who transfers an item and receives a settlement or other consideration for it warrants to his transferee and to any subsequent collecting bank who takes the item in good faith that

(a) he has a good title to the item or is authorized to obtain payment or acceptance on behalf of one who has a good title and the transfer is otherwise rightful; and

(b) all signatures are genuine or authorized; and

(c) the item has not been materially altered; and

(d) no defense of any party is good against him; and

(e) he has no knowledge of any insolvency proceeding instituted with respect to the maker or acceptor or the drawer of an unaccepted item.

In addition each customer and collecting bank so transferring an item and receiving a settlement or other consideration engages that upon dishonor and any necessary notice of dishonor and protest he will take up the item.

(3) The warranties and the engagement to honor set forth in the two preceding subsections arise notwithstanding the absence of indorsement or words of guaranty or warranty in the transfer or presentment and a collecting bank remains liable for their breach despite remittance to its transferor. Damages for breach of such warranties or engagement to honor shall not exceed the consideration received by the customer or collecting bank responsible plus finance charges and expenses related to the item, if any.

(4) Unless a claim for breach of warranty under this section is made within a reasonable time after the person claiming learns of the breach, the person liable is discharged to the extent of any loss caused by the delay in making claim.

Section 4—208. Security Interest of Collecting Bank in Items, Accompanying Documents and Proceeds

(1) A bank has a security interest in an item and any accompanying documents or the proceeds of either

(a) in case of an item deposited in an account to the extent to which credit given for the item has been withdrawn or applied;

(b) in case of an item for which it has given credit available for withdrawal as of right, to the extent of the credit given whether or not the credit is drawn upon and whether or not there is a right of charge-back; or

(c) if it makes an advance on or against the item.

(2) When credit which has been given for several items received at one time or pursuant to a single agreement is withdrawn or applied in part the security interest remains upon all the items, any accompanying documents or the proceeds of either. For the purpose of this section, credits first given are first withdrawn.

(3) Receipt by a collecting bank of a final settlement for an item is a realization on its security interest in the item, accompanying documents and proceeds. To the extent and so long as the bank does not receive final settlement for the item or give up possession of the item or accompanying documents for purposes other than collection, the security interest continues and is subject to the provisions of Article 9 except that

    (a) no security agreement is necessary to make the security interest enforceable (subsection (1) (a) of Section 9—203); and

    (b) no filing is required to perfect the security interest; and

    (c) the security interest has priority over conflicting perfected security interests in the item, accompanying documents or proceeds.

Section 4—209. When Bank Gives Value for Purposes of Holder in Due Course

For purposes of determining its status as a holder in due course, the bank has given value to the extent that it has a security interest in an item provided that the bank otherwise complies with the requirements of Section 3—302 on what constitutes a holder in due course.

Section 4—210. Presentment by Notice of Item Not Payable by, Through or at a Bank; Liability of Secondary Parties

(1) Unless otherwise instructed, a collecting bank may present an item not payable by, through or at a bank by sending to the party to accept or pay a written notice that the bank holds the item for acceptance or payment. The notice must be sent in time to be received on or before the day when presentment is due and the bank must meet any requirement of the party to accept or pay under Section 3—505 by the close of the bank's next banking day after it knows of the requirement.

(2) Where presentment is made by notice and neither honor nor request for compliance with a requirement under Section 3—505 is received by the close of business on the day after maturity or in the case of demand items by the close of business on the third banking day after notice was sent, the presenting bank may treat the item as dishonored and charge any secondary party by sending him notice of the facts.

Section 4—211. Media of Remittance; Provisional and Final Settlement in Remittance Cases

(1) A collecting bank may take in settlement of an item

    (a) a check of the remitting bank or of another bank on any bank except the remitting bank; or

    (b) a cashier's check or similar primary obligation of a remitting bank which is a member of or clears through a member of the same clearing house or group as the collecting bank; or

    (c) appropriate authority to charge an account of the remitting bank or of another bank with the collecting bank; or

    (d) if the item is drawn upon or payable by a person other than a bank, a cashier's check, certified check or other bank check or obligation.

(2) If before its midnight deadline the collecting bank properly dishonors a remittance check or authorization to charge on itself or presents or forwards for collection a remittance instrument of or on another bank which is of a kind approved by subsection (1) or has not been authorized by it, the collecting bank is not liable to prior parties in the event of the dishonor of such check, instrument or authorization.

(3) A settlement for an item by means of a remittance instrument or authorization to charge is or becomes a final settlement as to both the person making and the person receiving the settlement

    (a) if the remittance instrument or authorization to charge is of a kind approved by subsection (1) or has not been authorized by the person receiving the settlement and in either case the person receiving the settlement acts seasonably before its midnight deadline in presenting, forwarding for collection or paying the instrument or authorization,—at the time the remittance instrument or authorization is finally paid by the payor by which it is payable;

    (b) if the person receiving the settlement has authorized remittance by a non-bank check or obligation or by a cashier's check or similar primary obligation of or a check upon the payor or other remitting bank which is not of a kind approved by subsection (1) (b),—at the time of the receipt of such remittance check or obligation; or

(c) if in a case not covered by sub-paragraphs (a) or (b) the person receiving the settlement fails to seasonably present, forward for collection, pay or return a remittance instrument or authorization to it to charge before its midnight deadline,—at such midnight deadline.

Section 4—212.   Right of Charge-Back or Refund

(1) If a collecting bank has made provisional settlement with its customer for an item and itself fails by reason of dishonor, suspension of payments by a bank or otherwise to receive a settlement for the item which is or becomes final, the bank may revoke the settlement given by it, charge back the amount of any credit given for the item to its customers' account or obtain refund from its customer whether or not it is able to return the items if by its midnight deadline or within a longer reasonable time after it learns the facts it returns the item or sends notification of the facts. These rights to revoke, charge-back and obtain refund terminate if and when a settlement for the item received by the bank is or becomes final (subsection (3) of Section 4—211 and subsections (2) and (3) of Section 4—213).

[(2) Within the time and manner prescribed by this section and Section 4—301, an intermediary or payor bank, as the case may be, may return an unpaid item directly to the depositary bank and may send for collection a draft on the depositary bank and obtain reimbursement. In such case, if the depositary bank has received provisional settlement for the item, it must reimburse the bank drawing the draft and any provisional credits for the item between banks shall become and remain final.]

Note: *Direct returns is recognized as an innovation that is not yet established bank practice, and therefore, Paragraph 2 has been bracketed. Some lawyers have doubts whether it should be included in legislation or left to development by agreement.*

(3) A depositary bank which is also the payor may charge-back the amount of an item to its customer's account or obtain refund in accordance with the section governing return of an item received by a payor bank for credit on its books (Section 4—301).

(4) The right to charge-back is not affected by

(a) prior use of the credit given for the item; or

(b) failure by any bank to exercise ordinary care with respect to the item but any bank so failing remains liable.

(5) A failure to charge-back or claim refund does not affect other rights of the bank against the customer or any other party.

(6) If credit is given in dollars as the equivalent of the value of an item payable in a foreign currency the dollar amount of any charge-back or refund shall be calculated on the basis of the buying sight rate for the foreign currency prevailing on the day when the person entitled to the charge-back or refund learns that it will not receive payment in ordinary course.

Section 4—213.   Final Payment of Item by Payor Bank; When Provisional Debits and Credits Become Final; When Certain Credits Become Available for Withdrawal

(1) An item is finally paid by a payor bank when the bank has done any of the following, whichever happens first:

(a) paid the item in cash; or

(b) settled for the item without reserving a right to revoke the settlement and without having such right under statute, clearing house rule or agreement; or

(c) completed the process of posting the item to the indicated account of the drawer, maker or other person to be charged therewith; or

(d) made a provisional settlement for the item and failed to revoke the settlement in the time and manner permitted by statute, clearing house rule or agreement.

Upon a final payment under subparagraphs (b), (c) or (d) the payor bank shall be accountable for the amount of the item.

(2) If provisional settlement for an item between the presenting and payor banks is made through a clearing house or by debits or credits in an account between them, then to the extent that provisional debits or credits for the item are entered in accounts between the presenting

and payor banks or between the presenting and successive prior collecting banks seriatim, they become final upon final payment of the item by the payor bank.

(3) If a collecting bank receives a settlement for an item which is or becomes final (subsection (3) of Section 4—211, subsection (2) of Section 4—213) the bank is accountable to its customer for the amount of the item and any provisional credit given for the item in an account with its customer becomes final.

(4) Subject to any right of the bank to apply the credit to an obligation of the customer, credit given by a bank for an item in an account with its customer becomes available for withdrawal as of right

   (a) in any case where the bank has received a provisional settlement for the item,—when such settlement becomes final and the bank has had a reasonable time to learn that the settlement is final;

   (b) in any case where the bank is both a depositary bank and a payor bank and the item is finally paid,—at the opening of the bank's second banking day following receipt of the item.

(5) A deposit of money in a bank is final when made but, subject to any right of the bank to apply the deposit to an obligation of the customer, the deposit becomes available for withdrawal as of right at the opening of the bank's next banking day following receipt of the deposit.

Section 4—214.   Insolvency and Preference

(1) Any item in or coming into the possession of a payor or collecting bank which suspends payment and which item is not finally paid shall be returned by the receiver, trustee or agent in charge of the closed bank to the presenting bank or the closed bank's customer.

(2) If a payor bank finally pays an item and suspends payments without making a settlement for the item with its customer or the presenting bank which settlement is or becomes final, the owner of the item has a preferred claim against the payor bank.

(3) If a payor bank gives or a collecting bank gives or receives a provisional settlement for an item and thereafter suspends payments, the suspension does not prevent or interfere with the settlement becoming final if

such finality occurs automatically upon the lapse of certain time or the happening of certain events (subsection (3) of Section 4—211, subsections (1) (d), (2) and (3) of Section 4—213).

(4) If a collecting bank receives from subsequent parties settlement for an item which settlement is or becomes final and suspends payments without making a settlement for the item with its customer which is or becomes final, the owner of the item has a preferred claim against such collecting bank.

Part 3   Collection of Items; Payor Banks

Section 4—301.   Deferred Posting; Recovery of Payment by Return of Items; Time of Dishonor

(1) Where an authorized settlement for a demand item (other than a documentary draft) received by a payor bank otherwise than for immediate payment over the counter has been made before midnight of the banking day of receipt the payor bank may revoke the settlement and recover any payment if before it has made final payment (subsection (1) of Section 4—213) and before its midnight deadline it

   (a) returns the item; or

   (b) sends written notice of dishonor or nonpayment if the item is held for protest or is otherwise unavailable for return.

(2) If a demand item is received by a payor bank for credit on its books it may return such item or send notice of dishonor and may revoke any credit given or recover the amount thereof withdrawn by its customer, if it acts within the time limit and in the manner specified in the preceding subsection.

(3) Unless previous notice of dishonor has been sent an item is dishonored at the time when for purposes of dishonor it is returned or notice sent in accordance with this section.

(4) An item is returned:

   (a) as to an item received through a clearing house, when it is delivered to the presenting or last collecting bank or to the clearing house or is sent or delivered in accordance with its rules; or

(b) in all other cases, when it is sent or delivered to the bank's customer or transferor or pursuant to his instructions.

Section 4—302. Payor Bank's Responsibility for Late Return of Item

In the absence of a valid defense such as breach of a presentment warranty (subsection (1) of Section 4—207), settlement effected or the like, if an item is presented on and received by a payor bank the bank is accountable for the amount of

(a) a demand item other than a documentary draft whether properly payable or not if the bank, in any case where it is not also the depositary bank, retains the item beyond midnight of the banking day of receipt without settling for it or, regardless of whether it is also the depositary bank, does not pay or return the item or send notice of dishonor until after its midnight deadline; or

(b) any other properly payable item unless within the time allowed for acceptance or payment of that item the bank either accepts or pays the item or returns it and accompanying documents.

Section 4—303. When Items Subject to Notice, Stop-Order, Legal Process or Setoff; Order in Which Items May Be Charged or Certified

(1) Any knowledge, notice or stop-order received by, legal process served upon or setoff exercised by a payor bank, whether or not effective under other rules of law to terminate, suspend or modify the bank's right or duty to pay an item or to charge its customer's account for the item, comes too late to so terminate, suspend or modify such right or duty if the knowledge, notice, stop-order or legal process is received or served and a reasonable time for the bank to act thereon expires or the setoff is exercised after the bank has done any of the following:

(a) accepted or certified the item;

(b) paid the item in cash;

(c) settled for the item without reserving a right to revoke the settlement and without having such right under statute, clearing house rule or agreement;

(d) completed the process of posting the item to the indicated account of the drawer, maker or other person to be charged therewith or otherwise has evidenced by examination of such indicated account and by action its decision to pay the item; or

(e) become accountable for the amount of the item under subsection (1) (d) of Section 4—213 and Section 4—302 dealing with the payor bank's responsibility for late return of items.

(2) Subject to the provisions of subsection (1) items may be accepted, paid, certified or charged to the indicated account of its customer in any order convenient to the bank.

Part 4 Relationship Between Payor Bank and Its Customer

Section 4—401. When Bank May Charge Customer's Account

(1) As against its customer, a bank may charge against his account any item which is otherwise properly payable from that account even though the charge creates an overdraft.

(2) A bank which in good faith makes payment to a holder may charge the indicated account of its customer according to

(a) the original tenor of his altered item; or

(b) the tenor of his completed item, even though the bank knows the item has been completed unless the bank has notice that the completion was improper.

Section 4—402. Bank's Liability to Customer for Wrongful Dishonor

A payor bank is liable to its customer for damages proximately caused by the wrongful dishonor of an item. When the dishonor occurs through mistake liability is limited to actual damages proved. If so proximately caused and proved damages may include damages for an arrest or prosecution of the customer or other consequential damages. Whether any consequential damages are proximately caused by the wrongful dishonor is a question of fact to be determined in each case.

Section 4—403. Customer's Right to Stop Payment; Burden of Proof of Loss

(1) A customer may by order to his bank stop payment of any item payable for his account but the order must be received at such time and in such manner as to afford the bank a reasonable opportunity to act on it prior to any action by the bank with respect to the item described in Section 4—303.

(2) An oral order is binding upon the bank only for fourteen calendar days unless confirmed in writing within that period. A written order is effective for only six months unless renewed in writing.

(3) The burden of establishing the fact and amount of loss resulting from the payment of an item contrary to a binding stop payment order is on the customer.

Section 4—404. Bank Not Obligated to Pay Check More Than Six Months Old

A bank is under no obligation to a customer having a checking account to pay a check, other than a certified check, which is presented more than six months after its date, but it may charge its customer's account for a payment made thereafter in good faith.

Section 4—405. Death or Incompetence of Customer

(1) A payor or collecting bank's authority to accept, pay or collect an item or to account for proceeds of its collection if otherwise effective is not rendered ineffective by incompetence of a customer of either bank existing at the time the item is issued or its collection is undertaken if the bank does not know of an adjudication of incompetence. Neither death nor incompetence of a customer revokes such authority to accept, pay, collect or account until the bank knows of the fact of death or of an adjudication of incompetence and has reasonable opportunity to act on it.

(2) Even with knowledge a bank may for 10 days after the date of death pay or certify checks drawn on or prior to that date unless ordered to stop payment by a person claiming an interest in the account.

Section 4—406. Customer's Duty to Discover and Report Unauthorized Signature or Alteration

(1) When a bank sends to its customer a statement of account accompanied by items paid in good faith in support of the debit entries or holds the statement and items pursuant to a request or instructions of its customer or otherwise in a reasonable manner makes the statement and items available to the customer, the customer must exercise reasonable care and promptness to examine the statement and items to discover his unauthorized signature or any alteration on an item and must notify the bank promptly after discovery thereof.

(2) If the bank establishes that the customer failed with respect to an item to comply with the duties imposed on the customer by subsection (1) the customer is precluded from asserting against the bank

> (a) his unauthorized signature or any alteration on the item if the bank also establishes that it suffered a loss by reason of such failure; and

> (b) an unauthorized signature or alteration by the same wrongdoer on any other item paid in good faith by the bank after the first item and statement was available to the customer for a reasonable period not exceeding fourteen calendar days and before the bank receives notification from the customer of any such unauthorized signature or alteration.

(3) The preclusion under subsection (2) does not apply if the customer establishes lack of ordinary care on the part of the bank in paying the item(s).

(4) Without regard to care or lack of care of either the customer or the bank a customer who does not within one year from the time the statement and items are made available to the customer (subsection (1)) discover and report his unauthorized signature or any alteration on the face or back of the item or does not within 3 years from that time discover and report any unauthorized indorsement is precluded from asserting against the bank such unauthorized signature or indorsement or such alteration.

(5) If under this section a payor bank has a valid defense against a claim of a customer upon or resulting from payment of an item and waives or fails upon request to assert the defense the bank may not assert against any collecting bank or other prior party presenting or transferring the item a claim based upon the unauthorized signature or alteration giving rise to the customer's claim.

Section 4—407. Payor Bank's Right to Subrogation on Improper Payment

If a payor bank has paid an item over the stop payment order of the drawer or maker or otherwise under circumstances giving a basis for objection by the drawer or maker, to prevent unjust enrichment and only to the extent necessary to prevent loss to the bank by reason of its payment of the item, the payor bank shall be subrogated to the rights

   (a) of any holder in due course on the item against the drawer or maker; and

   (b) of the payee or any other holder of the item against the drawer or maker either on the item or under the transaction out of which the item arose; and

   (c) of the drawer or maker against the payee or any other holder of the item with respect to the transaction out of which the item arose.

Part 5 Collection of Documentary Drafts

Section 4—501. Handling of Documentary Drafts; Duty to Send for Presentment and to Notify Customer of Dishonor

A bank which takes a documentary draft for collection must present or send the draft and accompanying documents for presentment and upon learning that the draft has not been paid or accepted in due course must seasonably notify its customer of such fact even though it may have discounted or bought the draft or extended credit available for withdrawal as of right.

Section 4—502. Presentment of "On Arrival" Drafts

When a draft or the relevant instructions require presentment "on arrival," "when goods arrive" or the like, the collecting bank need not present until in its judgment a reasonable time for arrival of the goods has expired. Refusal to pay or accept because the goods have not arrived is not dishonor; the bank must notify its transferor of such refusal but need not present the draft again until it is instructed to do so or learns of the arrival of the goods.

Section 4—503. Responsibility of Presenting Bank for Documents and Goods; Report of Reasons for Dishonor; Referee in Case of Need

Unless otherwise instructed and except as provided in Article 5 a bank presenting a documentary draft

   (a) must deliver the documents to the drawee on acceptance of the draft if it is payable more than three days after presentment; otherwise, only on payment; and

   (b) upon dishonor, either in the case of presentment for acceptance or presentment for payment, may seek and follow instructions from any referee in case of need designated in the draft or if the presenting bank does not choose to utilize his services it must use diligence and good faith to ascertain the reason for dishonor, must notify its transferor of the dishonor and of the results of its effort to ascertain the reasons therefor and must request instructions.

But the presenting bank is under no obligation with respect to goods represented by the documents except to follow any reasonable instructions seasonably received; it has a right to reimbursement for any expense incurred in following instructions and to prepayment of or indemnity for such expenses.

Section 4—504. Privilege of Presenting Bank to Deal With Goods; Security Interest for Expenses

(1) A presenting bank which, following the dishonor of a documentary draft, has seasonably requested instructions but does not receive them within a reasonable time may store, sell, or otherwise deal with the goods in any reasonable manner.

(2) For its reasonable expenses incurred by action under subsection (1) the presenting bank has a lien upon the goods or their proceeds, which may be foreclosed in the same manner as an unpaid seller's lien.

Article 5 Letters of Credit

Section 5—101. Short Title

This Article shall be known and may be cited as Uniform Commercial Code—Letters of Credit.

Section 5—102. Scope

(1) This Article applies

    (a) to a credit issued by a bank if the credit requires a documentary draft or a documentary demand for payment; and

    (b) to a credit issued by a person other than a bank if the credit requires that the draft or demand for payment be accompanied by a document of title; and

    (c) to a credit issued by a bank or other person if the credit is not within subparagraphs (a) or (b) but conspicuously states that it is a letter of credit or is conspicuously so entitled.

(2) Unless the engagement meets the requirements of subsection (1), this Article does not apply to engagements to make advances or to honor drafts or demands for payment, to authorities to pay or purchase, to guarantees or to general agreements.

(3) This Article deals with some but not all of the rules and concepts of letters of credit as such rules or concepts have developed prior to this act or may hereafter develop. The fact that this Article states a rule does not by itself require, imply or negate application of the same or a converse rule to a situation not provided for or to a person not specified by this Article.

Section 5—103. Definitions

(1) In this Article unless the context otherwise requires

    (a) "Credit" or "letter of credit" means an engagement by a bank or other person made at the request of a customer and of a kind within the scope of this Article (Section 5—102) that the issuer will honor drafts or other demands for payment upon compliance with the conditions specified in the credit. A credit may be either revocable or irrevocable. The engagement may be either an agreement to honor or a statement that the bank or other person is authorized to honor.

    (b) A "documentary draft" or a "documentary demand for payment" is one honor of which is conditioned upon the presentation of a document or documents. "Document" means any

paper including document of title, security, invoice, certificate, notice of default and the like.

    (c) An "issuer" is a bank or other person issuing a credit.

    (d) A "beneficiary" of a credit is a person who is entitled under its terms to draw or demand payment.

    (e) An "advising bank" is a bank which gives notification of the issuance of a credit by another bank.

    (f) A "confirming bank" is a bank which engages either that it will itself honor a credit already issued by another bank or that such a credit will be honored by the issuer or a third bank.

    (g) A "customer" is a buyer of other person who causes an issuer to issue a credit. The term also includes a bank which procures issuance or confirmation on behalf of that bank's customer.

(2) Other definitions applying to this Article and the sections in which they appear are:

    "Notation of Credit." Section 5—108.
    "Presenter." Section 5—112(3).

(3) Definitions in other Articles applying to this Article and the sections in which they appear are:

    "Accept" or "Acceptance." Section 3—410.
    "Contract for sale." Section 2—106.
    "Draft." Section 3—104.
    "Holder in due course." Section 3—302.
    "Midnight deadline." Section 4—104.
    "Security." Section 8—102.

(4) In addition, Article 1 contains general definitions and principles of construction and interpretation applicable throughout this Article.

Section 5—104. Formal Requirements; Signing

(1) Except as otherwise required in subsection (1) (c) of Section 5—102 on scope, no particular form of phrasing is required for a credit. A credit must be in writing and signed by the issuer and a confirmation must be in writing and signed by the confirming bank. A modification of the terms of a credit or confirmation must be signed by the issuer or confirming bank.

(2) A telegram may be a sufficient signed writing if it identifies its sender by an authorized authentication. The authentication may be in code and the authorized naming of the issuer in an advice of credit is a sufficient signing.

Section 5—105. Consideration

No consideration is necessary to establish a credit or to enlarge or otherwise modify its terms.

Section 5—106. Time and Effect of Establishment of Credit

(1) Unless otherwise agreed a credit is established

   (a) as regards the customer as soon as a letter of credit is sent to him or the letter of credit or an authorized written advice of its issuance is sent to the beneficiary; and

   (b) as regards the beneficiary when he receives a letter of credit or an authorized written advice of its issuance.

(2) Unless otherwise agreed once an irrevocable credit is established as regards the customer it can be modified or revoked only with the consent of the customer and once it is established as regards the beneficiary it can be modified or revoked only with his consent.

(3) Unless otherwise agreed after a revocable credit is established it may be modified or revoked by the issuer without notice to or consent from the customer or beneficiary.

(4) Notwithstanding any modification or revocation of a revocable credit any person authorized to honor or negotiate under the terms of the original credit is entitled to reimbursement for or honor of any draft or demand for payment duly honored or negotiated before receipt of notice of the modification or revocation and the issuer in turn is entitled to reimbursement from its customer.

Section 5—107. Advice of Credit; Confirmation; Error in Statement of Terms

(1) Unless otherwise specified an advising bank by advising a credit issued by another bank does not assume any obligation to honor drafts drawn or demands for payment made under the credit but it does assume obligation for the accuracy of its own statement.

(2) A confirming bank by confirming a credit becomes directly obligated on the credit to the extent of its confirmation as though it were its issuer and acquires the rights of an issuer.

(3) Even though an advising bank incorrectly advises the terms of a credit it has been authorized to advise the credit is established as against the issuer to the extent of its original terms.

(4) Unless otherwise specified the customer bears as against the issuer all risks of transmission and reasonable translation or interpretation of any message relating to a credit.

Section 5—108. "Notation Credit"; Exhaustion of Credit

(1) A credit which specifies that any person purchasing or paying drafts drawn or demands for payment made under it must note the amount of the draft or demand on the letter or advice of credit is a "notation credit."

(2) Under a notation credit

   (a) a person paying the beneficiary or purchasing a draft or demand for payment from him acquires a right to honor only if the appropriate notation is made and by transferring or forwarding for honor the documents under the credit such a person warrants to the issuer that the notation has been made; and

   (b) unless the credit or a signed statement that an appropriate notation has been made accompanies the draft or demand for payment the issuer may delay honor until evidence of notation has been procured which is statisfactory to it but its obligation and that of its customer continue for a reasonable time not exceeding thirty days to obtain such evidence.

(3) If the credit is not a notation credit

   (a) the issuer may honor complying drafts or demands for payment presented to it in the order in which they are presented and is discharged pro tanto by honor of any such draft or demand;

(b) as between competing good faith purchasers of complying drafts or demands the person first purchasing has priority over a subsequent purchaser even though the later purchased draft or demand has been first honored.

Section 5—109.   Issuer's Obligation to Its Customer

(1) An issuer's obligation to its customer includes good faith and observance of any general banking usage but unless otherwise agreed does not include liability or responsibility

(a) for performance of the underlying contract for sale or other transaction between the customer and the beneficiary; or

(b) for any act or omission of any person other than itself or its own branch or for loss or destruction of a draft, demand or document in transit or in the possession of others; or

(c) based on knowledge or lack of knowledge of any usage of any particular trade.

(2) An issuer must examine documents with care so as to ascertain that on their face they appear to comply with the terms of the credit but unless otherwise agreed assumes no liability of responsibility for the genuineness, falsification or effect of any document which appears on such examination to be regular on its face.

(3) A non-bank issuer is not bound by any banking usage of which it has no knowledge.

Section 5—110.   Availability of Credit in Portions; Presenter's Reservation of Lien or Claim

(1) Unless otherwise specified a credit may be used in portions in the discretion of the beneficiary.

(2) Unless otherwise specified a person by presenting a documentary draft or demand for payment under a credit relinquishes upon its honor all claims to the documents and a person by transferring such draft or demand or causing such presentment authorizes such relinquishment. An explicit reservation of claim makes the draft or demand non-complying.

Section 5—111.   Warranties on Transfer and Presentment

(1) Unless otherwise agreed the beneficiary by transferring or presenting a documentary draft or demand for payment warrants to all interested parties that the necessary conditions of the credit have been complied with. This is in addition to any warranties arising under Articles 3, 4, 7 and 8.

(2) Unless otherwise agreed a negotiating, advising, confirming, collecting or issuing bank presenting or transferring a draft or demand for payment under a credit warrants only the matters warranted by a collecting bank under Article 4 and any such bank transferring a document warrants only the matters warranted by an intermediary under Articles 7 and 8.

Section 5—112.   Time Allowed for Honor or Rejection; Withholding Honor or Rejection by Consent; "Presenter"

(1) A bank to which a documentary draft or demand for payment is presented under a credit may without dishonor of the draft, demand or credit

(a) defer honor until the close of the third banking day following receipt of the documents; and

(b) further defer honor if the presenter has expressly or impliedly consented thereto.

Failure to honor within the time here specified constitutes dishonor of the draft or demand and of the credit [except as otherwise provided in subsection (4) of Section 5—114 on conditional payment].

Note: *The bracketed language in the last sentence of subsection (1) should be included only if the optional provisions of Section 5—114(4) and (5) are included.*

(2) Upon dishonor the bank may unless otherwise instructed fulfill its duty to return the draft or demand and the documents by holding them at the disposal of the presenter and sending him an advice to that effect.

(3) "Presenter" means any person presenting a draft or demand for payment for honor under a credit even though that person is a confirming bank or other correspondent which is acting under an issuer's authorization.

Section 5—113. Indemnities

(1) A bank seeking to obtain (whether for itself or another) honor, negotiation or reimbursement under a credit may give an indemnity to induce such honor, negotiation or reimbursement.

(2) An indemnity agreement inducing honor, negotiation or reimbursement

    (a) unless otherwise explicitly agreed applies to defects in the documents but not in the goods; and

    (b) unless a longer time is explicitly agreed expires at the end of ten business days following receipt of the documents by the ultimate customer unless notice of objection is sent before such expiration date. The ultimate customer may send notice of objection to the person from whom he received the documents and any bank receiving such notice is under a duty to send notice to its transferor before its midnight deadline.

Section 5—114. Issuer's Duty and Privilege to Honor; Right to Reimbursement

(1) An issuer must honor a draft or demand for payment which complies with the terms of the relevant credit regardless of whether the goods or documents conform to the underlying contract for sale or other contract between the customer and the beneficiary. The issuer is not excused from honor of such a draft or demand by reason of an additional general term that all documents must be satisfactory to the issuer, but an issuer may require that specified documents must be satisfactory to it.

(2) Unless otherwise agreed when documents appear on their face to comply with the terms of a credit but a required document does not in fact conform to the warranties made on negotiation or transfer of a document of title (Section 7—507) or of a certificated security (Section 8—306) or is forged or fraudulent or there is fraud in the transaction:

    (a) the issuer must honor the draft or demand for payment if honor is demanded by a negotiating bank or other holder of the draft or demand which has taken the draft or demand under the credit and under circumstances which would make it a holder in due course

(Section 3—302) and in an appropriate case would make it a person to whom a document of title has been duly negotiated (Section 7—502) or a bona fide purchaser of a certificated security (Section 8—302); and

    (b) in all other cases as against its customer, an issuer acting in good faith may honor the draft or demand for payment despite notification from the customer of fraud, forgery or other defect not apparent on the face of the documents but a court of appropriate jurisdiction may enjoin such honor.

(3) Unless otherwise agreed an issuer which has duly honored a draft or demand for payment is entitled to immediate reimbursement of any payment made under the credit and to be put in effectively available funds not later than the day before maturity of any acceptance made under the credit.

[(4) When a credit provides for payment by the issuer on receipt of notice that the required documents are in the possession of a correspondent or other agent of the issuer

    (a) any payment made on receipt of such notice is conditional; and

    (b) the issuer may reject documents which do not comply with the credit if it does so within three banking days following its receipt of the documents; and

    (c) in the event of such rejection, the issuer is entitled by charge back or otherwise to return of the payment made.]

[(5) In the case covered by subsection (4) failure to reject documents within the time specified in sub-paragraph (b) constitutes acceptance of the documents and makes the payment final in favor of the beneficiary.]

Note: *Subsections (4) and (5) are bracketed as optional. If they are included the bracketed language in the last sentence of Section 5—112(1) should also be included.*

Section 5—115. Remedy for Improper Dishonor or Anticipatory Repudiation

(1) When an issuer wrongfully dishonors a draft or demand for payment presented under a credit the person entitled to honor has with respect to any documents the

rights of a person in the position of a seller (Section 2—707) and may recover from the issuer the face amount of the draft or demand together with incidental damages under Section 2—710 on seller's incidental damages and interest but less any amount realized by resale or other use or disposition of the subject matter of the transaction. In the event no resale or other utilization is made the documents, goods or other subject matter involved in the transaction must be turned over to the issuer on payment of judgment.

(2) When an issuer wrongfully cancels or otherwise repudiates a credit before presentment of a draft or demand for payment drawn under it the beneficiary has the rights of a seller after anticipatory repudiation by the buyer under Section 2—610 if he learns of the repudiation in time reasonably to avoid procurement of the required documents. Otherwise the beneficiary has an immediate right of action for wrongful dishonor.

Section 5—116.   Transfer and Assignment

(1) The right to draw under a credit can be transferred or assigned only when the credit is expressly designated as transferable or assignable.

(2) Even though the credit specifically states that it is nontransferable or nonassignable the beneficiary may before performance of the conditions of the credit assign his right to proceeds. Such an assignment is an assignment of an account under Article 9 on Secured Transactions and is governed by that Article except that

(a) the assignment is ineffective until the letter of credit or advice of credit is delivered to the assignee which delivery constitutes perfection of the security interest under Article 9; and

(b) the issuer may honor drafts or demands for payment drawn under the credit until it receives a notification of the assignment signed by the beneficiary which reasonably identifies the credit involved in the assignment and contains a request to pay the assignee; and

(c) after what reasonably appears to be such a notification has been received the issuer may without dishonor refuse to accept or pay even to a person otherwise entitled to honor until the letter of credit or advice of credit is exhibited to the issuer.

(3) Except where the beneficiary has effectively assigned his right to draw or his right to proceeds, nothing in this section limits his right to transfer or negotiate drafts or demands drawn under the credit.

Section 5—117.   Insolvency of Bank Holding Funds for Documentary Credit

(1) Where an issuer or an advising or confirming bank or a bank which has for a customer procured issuance of a credit by another bank becomes insolvent before final payment under the credit and the credit is one to which this Article is made applicable by paragraphs (a) or (b) of Section 5—102(1) on scope, the receipt or allocation of funds or collateral to secure or meet obligations under the credit shall have the following results:

(a) to the extent of any funds or collateral turned over after or before the insolvency as indemnity against or specifically for the purpose of payment of drafts or demands for payment drawn under the designated credit, the drafts or demands are entitled to payment in preference over depositors or other general creditors of the issuer or bank; and

(b) on expiration of the credit or surrender of the beneficiary's rights under it unused any person who has given such funds or collateral is similarly entitled to return thereof; and

(c) a charge to a general or current account with a bank if specifically consented to for the purpose of indemnity against or payment of drafts or demands for payment drawn under the designated credit falls under the same rules as if the funds had been drawn out in cash and then turned over with specific instructions.

(2) After honor or reimbursement under this section the customer or other person for whose account the insolvent bank has acted is entitled to receive the documents involved.

Article 6   Bulk Transfers

Section 6—101.   Short Title

This Article shall be known and may be cited as Uniform Commercial Code—Bulk Transfers.

Section 6—102. "Bulk Transfers"; Transfers of Equipment; Enterprises Subject to This Article; Bulk Transfers Subject to This Article

(1) A "bulk transfer" is any transfer in bulk and not in the ordinary course of the transferor's business of a major part of the materials, supplies, merchandise or other inventory (Section 9—109) of an enterprise subject to this Article.

(2) A transfer of a substantial part of the equipment (Section 9—109) of such an enterprise is a bulk transfer if it is made in connection with a bulk transfer of inventory, but not otherwise.

(3) The enterprises subject to this Article are all those whose principal business is the sale of merchandise from stock, including those who manufacture what they sell.

(4) Except as limited by the following section all bulk transfers of goods located within this state are subject to this Article.

Section 6—103. Transfers Excepted From This Article

The following transfers are not subject to this Article:

(1) Those made to give security for the performance of an obligation;

(2) General assignments for the benefit of all the creditors of the transferor, and subsequent transfers by the assignee thereunder;

(3) Transfers in settlement or realization of a lien or other security interests;

(4) Sales by executors, administrators, receivers, trustees in bankruptcy, or any public officer under judicial process;

(5) Sales made in the course of judicial or administrative proceedings for the dissolution or reorganization of a corporation and of which notice is sent to the creditors of the corporation pursuant to order of the court or administrative agency;

(6) Transfers to a person maintaining a known place of business in this State who becomes bound to pay the debts of the transferor in full and gives public notice of that fact, and who is solvent after becoming so bound;

(7) A transfer to a new business enterprise organized to take over and continue the business, if public notice of the transaction is given and the new enterprise assumes the debts of the transferor and he receives nothing from the transaction except an interest in the new enterprise junior to the claims of creditors;

(8) Transfers of property which is exempt from execution.

Public notice under subsection (6) or subsection (7) may be given by publishing once a week for two consecutive weeks in a newspaper of general circulation where the transferor had its principal place of business in this state an advertisement including the names and addresses of the transferor and transferee and the effective date of the transfer.

Section 6—104. Schedule of Property, List of Creditors

(1) Except as provided with respect to auction sales (Section 6—108), a bulk transfer subject to this Article is ineffective against any creditor of the transferor unless:

    (a) The transferee requires the transferor to furnish a list of his existing creditors prepared as stated in this section; and

    (b) The parties prepare a schedule of the property transferred sufficient to identify it; and

    (c) The transferee preserves the list and schedule for six months next following the transfer and permits inspection of either or both and copying therefrom at all reasonable hours by any creditor of the transferor, or files the list and schedule in (a public office to be here identified).

(2) The list of creditors must be signed and sworn to or affirmed by the transferor or his agent. It must contain the names and business addresses of all creditors of the transferor, with the amounts when known, and also the names of all persons who are known to the transferor to assert claims against him even though such claims are disputed. If the transferor is the obligor of an outstanding issue of bonds, debentures or the like as to which there is an indenture trustee, the list of creditors need include only the name and address of the indenture trustee and the aggregate outstanding principal amount of the issue.

(3) Responsibility for the completeness and accuracy of the list of creditors rests on the transferor, and the transfer is not rendered ineffective by errors or omissions therein unless the transferee is shown to have had knowledge.

Section 6—105.   Notice to Creditors

In addition to the requirements of the preceding section, any bulk transfer subject to this Article except one made by auction sale (Section 6—108) is ineffective against any creditor of the transferor unless at least ten days before he takes possession of the goods or pays for them, whichever happens first, the transferee gives notice of the transfer in the manner and to the persons hereafter provided (Section 6—107).

[Section 6—106.   Application of the Proceeds

In addition to the requirements of the two preceding sections:

(1) Upon every bulk transfer subject to this Article for which new consideration becomes payable except those made by sale at auction it is the duty of the transferee to assure that such consideration is applied so far as necessary to pay those debts of the transferor which are either shown on the list furnished by the transferor (Section 6—104) or filed in writing in the place stated in the notice (Section 6—107) within thirty days after the mailing of such notice. This duty of the transferee runs to all the holders of such debts, and may be enforced by any of them for the benefit of all.

(2) If any of said debts are in dispute the necessary sum may be withheld from distribution until the dispute is settled or adjudicated.

(3) If the consideration payable is not enough to pay all of the said debts in full distribution shall be made pro rata.]

Note: *This section is bracketed to indicate division of opinion as to whether or not it is a wise provision, and to suggest that this is a point on which State enactments may differ without serious damage to the principle of uniformity.*

In any State where this section is omitted, the following parts of sections, also bracketed in the text, should also be omitted, namely:

> Section 6—107(2) (e).
> 6—108(3) (c).
> 6—109(2).

In any State where this section is enacted, these other provisions should be also.

[(4) The transferee may within ten days after he takes possession of the goods pay the consideration into the (specify court) in the county where the transferor had its principal place of business in this state and thereafter may discharge his duty under this section by giving notice by registered or certified mail to all the persons to whom the duty runs that the consideration has been paid into that court and that they should file their claims there. On motion of any interested party, the court may order the distribution of the consideration to the persons entitled to it.]

Note: *Optional subsection (4) is recommended for those states which do not have a general statute providing for payment of money into court.*

Section 6—107.   The Notice

(1) The notice to creditors (Section 6—105) shall state:

(a) that a bulk transfer is about to be made; and

(b) the names and business addresses of the transferor and transferee, and all other business names and addresses used by the transferor within three years last past so far as known to the transferee; and

(c) whether or not all the debts of the transferor are to be paid in full as they fall due as a result of the transaction, and if so, the address to which creditors should send their bills.

(2) If the debts of the transferor are not to be paid in full as they fall due or if the transferee is in doubt on that point then the notice shall state further:

(a) the location and general description of the property to be transferred and the estimated total of the transferor's debts;

(b) the address where the schedule of property and list of creditors (Section 6—104) may be inspected;

(c) whether the transfer is to pay existing debts and if so the amount of such debts and to whom owing;

(d) whether the transfer is for new consideration and if so the amount of such consideration and the time and place of payment; [and]

[(e) if for new consideration the time and place where creditors of the transferor are to file their claims.]

(3) The notice in any case shall be delivered personally or sent by registered or certified mail to all the persons shown on the list of creditors furnished by the transferor (Section 6—104) and to all other persons who are known to the transferee to hold or assert claims against the transferor.

Note: *The words in brackets are optional. See Note under § 6—106.*

Section 6—108.   Auction Sales; "Auctioneer"

(1) A bulk transfer is subject to this Article even though it is by sale at auction, but only in the manner and with the results stated in this section.

(2) The transferor shall furnish a list of his creditors and assist in the preparation of a schedule of the property to be sold, both prepared as before stated (Section 6—104).

(3) The person or persons other than the transferor who direct, control or are responsible for the auction are collectively called the "auctioneer." The auctioneer shall:

  (a) receive and retain the list of creditors and prepare and retain the schedule of property for the period stated in this Article (Section 6—104);

  (b) give notice of the auction personally or by registered or certified mail at least ten days before it occurs to all persons shown on the list of creditors and to all other persons who are known to him to hold or assert claims against the transferor; [and]

  [(c) assure that the net proceeds of the auction are applied as provided in this Article (Section 6—106).]

(4) Failure of the auctioneer to perform any of these duties does not affect the validity of the sale or the title of the purchasers, but if the auctioneer knows that the auction constitutes a bulk transfer such failure renders the auctioneer liable to the creditors of the transferor as a class for the sums owing to them from the transferor up to but not exceeding the net proceeds of the auction. If the auctioneer consists of several persons their liability is joint and several.

Note: *The words in brackets are optional. See Note under § 6—106.*

Section 6—109.   What Creditors Protected; [Credit for Payment to Particular Creditors]

(1) The creditors of the transferor mentioned in this Article are those holding claims based on transactions or events occurring before the bulk transfer, but creditors who become such after notice to creditors is given (Sections 6—105 and 6—107) are not entitled to notice.

[(2) Against the aggregate obligation imposed by the provisions of this Article concerning the application of the proceeds (Section 6—106 and subsection (3) (c) of 6—108) the transferee or auctioneer is entitled to credit for sums paid to particular creditors of the transferor, not exceeding the sums believed in good faith at the time of the payment to be properly payable to such creditors.]

Note: *The words in brackets are optional. See Note under § 6—106.*

Section 6—110.   Subsequent Transfers

When the title of a transferee to property is subject to a defect by reason of his non-compliance with the requirements of this Article, then:

(1) A purchaser of any of such property from such transferee who pays no value or who takes with notice of such non-compliance takes subject to such defect, but

(2) A purchaser for value in good faith and without such notice takes free of such defect.

Section 6—111.   Limitation of Actions and Levies

No action under this Article shall be brought nor levy made more than six months after the date on which the transferee took possession of the goods unless the transfer has been concealed. If the transfer has been concealed, actions may be brought or levies made within six months after its discovery.

Note to Article 6: *Section 6—106 is bracketed to indicate division of opinion as to whether or not it is a wise provision, and to suggest that this is a point on which State enactments may differ without serious damage to the principle of uniformity.*

Article 7   Warehouse Receipts, Bills of Lading and Other Documents of Title

Part 1   General

Section 7—101.   Short Title

This Article shall be known and may be cited as Uniform Commercial Code—Documents of Title.

Section 7—102.   Definitions and Index of Definitions

(1) In this Article, unless the context otherwise requires:

    (a) "Bailee" means the person who by a warehouse receipt, bill of lading or other document of title acknowledges possession of goods and contracts to deliver them.

    (b) "Consignee" means the person named in a bill to whom or to whose order the bill promises delivery.

    (c) "Consignor" means the person named in a bill as the person from whom the goods have been received for shipment.

    (d) "Delivery order" means a written order to deliver goods directed to a warehouseman, carrier or other person who in the ordinary course of business issues warehouse receipts or bills of lading.

    (e) "Document" means document of title as defined in the general definitions in Article 1 (Section 1—201).

    (f) "Goods" means all things which are treated as movable for the purposes of a contract of storage or transportation.

    (g) "Issuer" means a bailee who issues a document except that in relation to an unaccepted delivery order it means the person who orders the possessor of goods to deliver. Issuer includes any person for whom an agent or employee purports to act in issuing a document if the agent or employee has real or apparent authority to issue documents, notwithstanding that the issuer received no goods or that the goods were misdescribed or that in any other respect the agent or employee violated his instructions.

    (h) "Warehouseman" is a person engaged in the business of storing goods for hire.

(2) Other definitions applying to this Article or to specified Parts thereof, and the sections in which they appear are:

    "Duly negotiate." Section 7—501.
    "Person entitled under the document." Section 7—403(4).

(3) Definitions in other Articles applying to this Article and the sections in which they appear are:

    "Contract for sale." Section 2—106.
    "Overseas." Section 2—323.
    "Receipt" of goods. Section 2—103.

(4) In addition Article 1 contains general definitions and principles of construction and interpretation applicable throughout this Article.

Section 7—103.   Relation of Article to Treaty, Statute, Tariff, Classification or Regulation

To the extent that any treaty or statute of the United States, regulatory statute of this State or tariff, classification or regulation filed or issued pursuant thereto is applicable, the provisions of this Article are subject thereto.

Section 7—104.   Negotiable and Non-Negotiable Warehouse Receipt, Bill of Lading or Other Document of Title

(1) A warehouse receipt, bill of lading or other document of title is negotiable

    (a) if by its terms the goods are to be delivered to bearer or to the order of a named person; or

(b) where recognized in overseas trade, if it runs to a named person or assigns.

(2) Any other document is non-negotiable. A bill of lading in which it is stated that the goods are consigned to a named person is not made negotiable by a provision that the goods are to be delivered only against a written order signed by the same or another named person.

Section 7—105. Construction Against Negative Implication

The omission from either Part 2 or Part 3 of this Article of a provision corresponding to a provision made in the other Part does not imply that a corresponding rule of law is not applicable.

Part 2 Warehouse Receipts: Special Provisions

Section 7—201. Who May Issue a Warehouse Receipt; Storage Under Government Bond

(1) A warehouse receipt may be issued by any warehouseman.

(2) Where goods including distilled spirits and agricultural commodities are stored under a statute requiring a bond against withdrawal or a license for the issuance of receipts in the nature of warehouse receipts, a receipt issued for the goods has like effect as a warehouse receipt even though issued by a person who is the owner of the goods and is not a warehouseman.

Section 7—202. Form of Warehouse Receipt; Essential Terms; Optional Terms

(1) A warehouse receipt need not be in any particular form.

(2) Unless a warehouse receipt embodies within its written or printed terms each of the following, the warehouseman is liable for damages caused by the omission to a person injured thereby:

(a) the location of the warehouse where the goods are stored;

(b) the date of issue of the receipt;

(c) the consecutive number of the receipt;

(d) a statement whether the goods received will be delivered to the bearer, to a specified person, or to a specified person or his order;

(e) the rate of storage and handling charges, except that where goods are stored under a field warehousing arrangement a statement of that fact is sufficient on a non-negotiable receipt;

(f) a description of the goods or of the packages containing them;

(g) the signature of the warehouseman, which may be made by his authorized agent;

(h) if the receipt is issued for goods of which the warehouseman is owner, either solely or jointly or in common with others, the fact of such ownership; and

(i) a statement of the amount of advances made and of liabilities incurred for which the warehouseman claims a lien or security interest (Section 7—209). If the precise amount of such advances made or of such liabilities incurred is, at the time of the issue of the receipt, unknown to the warehouseman or to his agent who issues it, a statement of the fact that advances have been made or liabilities incurred and the purpose thereof is sufficient.

(3) A warehouseman may insert in his receipt any other terms which are not contrary to the provisions of this Act and do not impair his obligation of delivery (Section 7—403) or his duty of care (Section 7—204). Any contrary provisions shall be ineffective.

Section 7—203. Liability for Non-Receipt or Misdescription

A party to or purchaser for value in good faith of a document of title other than a bill of lading relying in either case upon the description therein of the goods may recover from the issuer damages caused by the non-receipt or misdescription of the goods, except to the extent that the document conspicuously indicates that the issuer does not know whether any part or all of the goods in fact were received or conform to the description, as where the description is in terms of marks or labels or kind, quantity or condition, or the receipt or description is qualified by "contents, condition and quality unknown," "said to contain" or the like, if such indication be true, or the party or purchaser otherwise has notice.

Section 7—204. Duty of Care; Contractual Limitation of Warehouseman's Liability

(1) A warehouseman is liable for damages for loss of or injury to the goods caused by his failure to exercise such care in regard to them as a reasonably careful man would exercise under like circumstances but unless otherwise agreed he is not liable for damages which could not have been avoided by the exercise of such care.

(2) Damages may be limited by a term in the warehouse receipt or storage agreement limiting the amount of liability in case of loss or damage, and setting forth a specific liability per article or item, or value per unit of weight, beyond which the warehouseman shall not be liable; provided, however, that such liability may on written request of the bailor at the time of signing such storage agreement or within a reasonable time after receipt of the warehouse receipt be increased on part or all of the goods thereunder, in which event increased rates may be charged based on such increased valuation, but that no such increase shall be permitted contrary to a lawful limitation of liability contained in the warehouseman's tariff, if any. No such limitation is effective with respect to the warehouseman's liability for conversion to his own use.

(3) Reasonable provisions as to the time and manner of presenting claims and instituting actions based on the bailment may be included in the warehouse receipt or tariff.

(4) This section does not impair or repeal . . .

Note: *Insert in subsection (4) a reference to any statute which imposes a higher responsibility upon the warehouseman or invalidates contractual limitations which would be permissible under this Article.*

Section 7—205. Title Under Warehouse Receipt Defeated in Certain Cases

A buyer in the ordinary course of business of fungible goods sold and delivered by a warehouseman who is also in the business of buying and selling such goods takes free of any claim under a warehouse receipt even though it has been duly negotiated.

Section 7—206. Termination of Storage at Warehouseman's Option

(1) A warehouseman may on notifying the person on whose account the goods are held and any other person known to claim an interest in the goods require payment of any charges and removal of the goods from the warehouse at the termination of the period of storage fixed by the document, or, if no period is fixed, within a stated period not less than thirty days after the notification. If the goods are not removed before the date specified in the notification, the warehouseman may sell them in accordance with the provisions of the section on enforcement of a warehouseman's lien (Section 7—210).

(2) If a warehouseman in good faith believes that the goods are about to deteriorate or decline in value to less than the amount of his lien within the time prescribed in subsection (1) for notification, advertisement and sale, the warehouseman may specify in the notification any reasonable shorter time for removal of the goods and in case the goods are not removed, may sell them at public sale held not less than one week after a single advertisement or posting.

(3) If as a result of a quality or condition of the goods of which the warehouseman had no notice at the time of deposit the goods are a hazard to other property or to the warehouse or to persons, the warehouseman may sell the goods at public or private sale without advertisement on reasonable notification to all persons known to claim an interest in the goods. If the warehouseman after a reasonable effort is unable to sell the goods he may dispose of them in any lawful manner and shall incur no liability by reason of such disposition.

(4) The warehouseman must deliver the goods to any person entitled to them under this Article upon due demand made at any time prior to sale or other disposition under this section.

(5) The warehouseman may satisfy his lien from the proceeds of any sale or disposition under this section but must hold the balance for delivery on the demand of any person to whom he would have been bound to deliver the goods.

Section 7—207. Goods Must Be Kept Separate; Fungible Goods

(1) Unless the warehouse receipt otherwise provides, a warehouseman must keep separate the goods covered by each receipt so as to permit at all times identification and delivery of those goods except that different lots of fungible goods may be commingled.

(2) Fungible goods so commingled are owned in common by the persons entitled thereto and the warehouseman is severally liable to each owner for that owner's share. Where because of overissue a mass of fungible goods is insufficient to meet all the receipts which the warehouseman has issued against it, the persons entitled include all holders to whom overissued receipts have been duly negotiated.

Section 7—208. Altered Warehouse Receipts

Where a blank in a negotiable warehouse receipt has been filled in without authority, a purchaser for value and without notice of the want of authority may treat the insertion as authorized. Any other unauthorized alteration leaves any receipt enforceable against the issuer according to its original tenor.

Section 7—209. Lien of Warehouseman

(1) A warehouseman has a lien against the bailor on the goods covered by a warehouse receipt or on the proceeds thereof in his possession for charges for storage or transportation (including demurrage and terminal charges), insurance, labor, or charges present or future in relation to the goods, and for expenses necessary for preservation of the goods or reasonably incurred in their sale pursuant to law. If the person on whose account the goods are held is liable for like charges or expenses in relation to other goods whenever deposited and it is stated in the receipt that a lien is claimed for charges and expenses in relation to other goods, the warehouseman also has a lien against him for such charges and expenses whether or not the other goods have been delivered by the warehouseman. But against a person to whom a negotiable warehouse receipt is duly negotiated a warehouseman's lien is limited to charges in an amount or at a rate specified on the receipt or if no charges are so specified then to a reasonable charge for storage of the goods covered by the receipt subsequent to the date of the receipt.

(2) The warehouseman may also reserve a security interest against the bailor for a maximum amount specified on the receipt for charges other than those specified in subsection (1), such as for money advanced and interest. Such a security interest is governed by the Article on Secured Transactions (Article 9).

(3) (a) A warehouseman's lien for charges and expenses under subsection (1) or a security interest under subsection (2) is also effective against any person who so entrusted the bailor with possession of the goods that a pledge of them by him to a good faith purchaser for value would have been valid but is not effective against a person as to whom the document confers no right in the goods covered by it under Section 7—503.

(b) A warehouseman's lien on household goods for charges and expenses in relation to the goods under subsection (1) is also effective against all persons if the depositor was the legal possessor of the goods at the time of deposit. "Household goods" means furniture, furnishings, and personal effects used by the depositor in a dwelling.

(4) A warehouseman loses his lien on any goods which he voluntarily delivers or which he unjustifiably refuses to deliver.

Section 7—210. Enforcement of Warehouseman's Lien

(1) Except as provided in subsection (2), a warehouseman's lien may be enforced by public or private sale of the goods in block or in parcels, at any time or place and on any terms which are commercially reasonable, after notifying all persons known to claim an interest in the goods. Such notification must include a statement of the amount due, the nature of the proposed sale and the time and place of any public sale. The fact that a better price could have been obtained by a sale at a different time or in a different method from that selected by the warehouseman is not of itself sufficient to establish that the sale was not made in a commercially reasonable manner. If the warehouseman either sells the goods in the usual manner in any recognized market therefor, or if he sells at the price current in such market at the time of his sale, or if he has otherwise sold in conformity with commercially reasonable practices among dealers in the

type of goods sold, he has sold in a commercially reasonable manner. A sale of more goods than apparently necessary to be offered to insure satisfaction of the obligation is not commercially reasonable except in cases covered by the preceding sentence.

(2) A warehouseman's lien on goods other than goods stored by a merchant in the course of his business may be enforced only as follows:

(a) All persons known to claim an interest in the goods must be notified.

(b) The notification must be delivered in person or sent by registered or certified letter to the last known address of any person to be notified.

(c) The notification must include an itemized statement of the claim, a description of the goods subject to the lien, a demand for payment within a specified time not less than ten days after receipt of the notification, and a conspicuous statement that unless the claim is paid within that time the goods will be advertised for sale and sold by auction at a specified time and place.

(d) The sale must conform to the terms of the notification.

(e) The sale must be held at the nearest suitable place to that where the goods are held or stored.

(f) After the expiration of the time given in the notification, an advertisement of the sale must be published once a week for two weeks consecutively in a newspaper of general circulation where the sale is to be held. The advertisement must include a description of the goods, the name of the person on whose account they are being held, and the time and place of the sale. The sale must take place at least fifteen days after the first publication. If there is no newspaper of general circulation where the sale is to be held, the advertisement must be posted at least ten days before the sale in not less than six conspicuous places in the neighborhood of the proposed sale.

(3) Before any sale pursuant to this section any person claiming a right in the goods may pay the amount necessary to satisfy the lien and the reasonable expenses incurred under this section. In that event the goods must not be sold, but must be retained by the warehouseman subject to the terms of the receipt and this Article.

(4) The warehouseman may buy at any public sale pursuant to this section.

(5) A purchaser in good faith of goods sold to enforce a warehouseman's lien takes the goods free of any rights of persons against whom the lien was valid, despite non-compliance by the warehouseman with the requirements of this section.

(6) The warehouseman may satisfy his lien from the proceeds of any sale pursuant to this section but must hold the balance, if any, for delivery on demand to any person to whom he would have been bound to deliver the goods.

(7) The rights provided by this section shall be in addition to all other rights allowed by law to a creditor against his debtor.

(8) Where a lien is on goods stored by a merchant in the course of his business the lien may be enforced in accordance with either subsection (1) or (2).

(9) The warehouseman is liable for damages caused by failure to comply with the requirements for sale under this section and in case of willful violation is liable for conversion.

Part 3 Bills of Lading: Special Provisions

Section 7—301.   Liability for Non-Receipt or Misdescription; "Said to Contain"; "Shipper's Load and Count"; Improper Handling

(1) A consignee of a non-negotiable bill who has given value in good faith or a holder to whom a negotiable bill has been duly negotiated relying in either case upon the description therein of the goods, or upon the date therein shown, may recover from the issuer damages caused by the misdating of the bill or the non-receipt or misdescription of the goods, except to the extent that the document indicates that the issuer does not know whether any part or all of the goods in fact were received or conform to the description, as where the description is

in terms of marks or labels or kind, quantity, or condition or the receipt or description is qualified by "contents or condition of contents of packages unknown," "said to contain," "shipper's weight, load and count" or the like, if such indication be true.

(2) When goods are loaded by an issuer who is a common carrier, the issuer must count the packages of goods if package freight and ascertain the kind and quantity if bulk freight. In such cases "shipper's weight, load and count" or other words indicating that the description was made by the shipper are ineffective except as to freight concealed by packages.

(3) When bulk freight is loaded by a shipper who makes available to the issuer adequate facilities for weighing such freight, an issuer who is a common carrier must ascertain the kind and quantity within a reasonable time after receiving the written request of the shipper to do so. In such cases "shipper's weight" or other words of like purport are ineffective.

(4) The issuer may by inserting in the bill the words "shipper's weight, load and count" or other words of like purport indicate that the goods were loaded by the shipper; and if such statement be true the issuer shall not be liable for damages caused by the improper loading. But their omission does not imply liability for such damages.

(5) The shipper shall be deemed to have guaranteed to the issuer the accuracy at the time of shipment of the description, marks, labels, number, kind, quantity, condition and weight, as furnished by him; and the shipper shall indemnify the issuer against damage caused by inaccuracies in such particulars. The right of the issuer to such indemnity shall in no way limit his responsibility and liability under the contract of carriage to any person other than the shipper.

Section 7—302. Through Bills of Lading and Similar Documents

(1) The issuer of a through bill of lading or other document embodying an undertaking to be performed in part by persons acting as its agents or by connecting carriers is liable to anyone entitled to recover on the document for any breach by such other persons or by a connecting carrier of its obligation under the document but to the extent that the bill covers an undertaking to be performed overseas or in territory not contiguous to the continental United States or an undertaking including matters other than transportation this liability may be varied by agreement of the parties.

(2) Where goods covered by a through bill of lading or other document embodying an undertaking to be performed in part by persons other than the issuer are received by any such person, he is subject with respect to his own performance while the goods are in his possession to the obligation of the issuer. His obligation is discharged by delivery of the goods to another such person pursuant to the document, and does not include liability for breach by any other such persons or by the issuer.

(3) The issuer of such through bill of lading or other document shall be entitled to recover from the connecting carrier or such other person in possession of the goods when the breach of the obligation under the document occurred, the amount it may be required to pay to anyone entitled to recover on the document therefor, as may be evidenced by any receipt, judgment, or transcript thereof, and the amount of any expense reasonably incurred by it in defending any action brought by anyone entitled to recover on the document therefor.

Section 7—303. Diversion; Reconsignment; Change of Instructions

(1) Unless the bill of lading otherwise provides, the carrier may deliver the goods to a person or destination other than that stated in the bill or may otherwise dispose of the goods on instructions from

    (a) the holder of a negotiable bill; or

    (b) the consignor on a non-negotiable bill notwithstanding contrary instructions from the consignee; or

    (c) the consignee on a non-negotiable bill in the absence of contrary instructions from the consignor, if the goods have arrived at the billed destination or if the consignee is in possession of the bill; or

    (d) the consignee on a non-negotiable bill if he is entitled as against the consignor to dispose of them.

(2) Unless such instructions are noted on a negotiable bill of lading, a person to whom the bill is duly negotiated can hold the bailee according to the original terms.

Section 7—304. Bills of Lading in a Set

(1) Except where customary in overseas transportation, a bill of lading must not be issued in a set of parts. The issuer is liable for damages caused by violation of this subsection.

(2) Where a bill of lading is lawfully drawn in a set of parts, each of which is numbered and expressed to be valid only if the goods have not been delivered against any other part, the whole of the parts constitute one bill.

(3) Where a bill of lading is lawfully issued in a set of parts and different parts are negotiated to different persons, the title of the holder to whom the first due negotiation is made prevails as to both the document and the goods even though any later holder may have received the goods from the carrier in good faith and discharged the carrier's obligation by surrender of his part.

(4) Any person who negotiates or transfers a single part of a bill of lading drawn in a set is liable to holders of that part as if it were the whole set.

(5) The bailee is obliged to deliver in accordance with Part 4 of this Article against the first presented part of a bill of lading lawfully drawn in a set. Such delivery discharges the bailee's obligation on the whole bill.

Section 7—305. Destination Bills

(1) Instead of issuing a bill of lading to the consignor at the place of shipment a carrier may at the request of the consignor procure the bill to be issued at destination or at any other place designated in the request.

(2) Upon request of anyone entitled as against the carrier to control the goods while in transit and on surrender of any outstanding bill of lading or other receipt covering such goods, the issuer may procure a substitute bill to be issued at any place designated in the request.

Section 7—306. Altered Bills of Lading

An unauthorized alteration or filling in of a blank in a bill of lading leaves the bill enforceable according to its original tenor.

Section 7—307. Lien of Carrier

(1) A carrier has a lien on the goods covered by a bill of lading for charges subsequent to the date of its receipt of the goods for storage or transporation (including demurrage and terminal charges) and for expenses necessary for preservation of the goods incident to their transportation or reasonably incurred in their sale pursuant to law. But against a purchaser for value of a negotiable bill of lading a carrier's lien is limited to charges stated in the bill or the applicable tariffs, or if no charges are stated then to a reasonable charge.

(2) A lien for charges and expenses under subsection (1) on goods which the carrier was required by law to receive for transportation is effective against the consignor or any person entitled to the goods unless the carrier had notice that the consignor lacked authority to subject the goods to such charges and expenses. Any other lien under subsection (1) is effective against the consignor and any person who permitted the bailor to have control or possession of the goods unless the carrier had notice that the bailor lacked such authority.

(3) A carrier loses his lien on any goods which he voluntarily delivers or which he unjustifiably refuses to deliver.

Section 7—308. Enforcement of Carrier's Lien

(1) A carrier's lien may be enforced by public or private sale of the goods, in block or in parcels, at any time or place and on any terms which are commercially reasonable, after notifying all persons known to claim an interest in the goods. Such notification must include a statement of the amount due, the nature of the proposed sale and the time and place of any public sale. The fact that a better price could have been obtained by a sale at a different time or in a different method from that selected by the carrier is not of itself sufficient to establish that the sale was not made in a commercially reasonable manner. If the carrier either sells the goods in the usual manner in any recognized market therefor or if he sells at the price current in such market at the time of his sale or if he has otherwise sold in conformity with commercially reasonable practices among dealers in the type of goods sold he has sold in a commercially reasonable manner. A sale of more goods than apparently necessary to be offered to ensure satisfaction of the obligation is not commercially reasonable except in cases covered by the preceding sentence.

(2) Before any sale pursuant to this section any person claiming a right in the goods may pay the amount necessary to satisfy the lien and the reasonable expenses incurred under this section. In that event the goods must

not be sold, but must be retained by the carrier subject to the terms of the bill and this Article.

(3) The carrier may buy at any public sale pursuant to this section.

(4) A purchaser in good faith of goods sold to enforce a carrier's lien takes the goods free of any rights of persons against whom the lien was valid, despite noncompliance by the carrier with the requirements of this section.

(5) The carrier may satisfy his lien from the proceeds of any sale pursuant to this section but must hold the balance, if any, for delivery on demand to any person to whom he would have been bound to deliver the goods.

(6) The rights provided by this section shall be in addition to all other rights allowed by law to a creditor against his debtor.

(7) A carrier's lien may be enforced in accordance with either subsection (1) or the procedure set forth in subsection (2) of Section 7—210.

(8) The carrier is liable for damages caused by failure to comply with the requirements for sale under this section and in case of willful violation is liable for conversion.

Section 7—309. Duty of Care; Contractual Limitation of Carrier's Liability

(1) A carrier who issues a bill of lading whether negotiable or non-negotiable must exercise the degree of care in relation to the goods which a reasonably careful man would exercise under like circumstances. This subsection does not repeal or change any law or rule of law which imposes liability upon a common carrier for damages not caused by its negligence.

(2) Damages may be limited by a provision that the carrier's liability shall not exceed a value stated in the document if the carrier's rates are dependent upon value and the consignor by the carrier's tariff is afforded an opportunity to declare a higher value or a value as lawfully provided in the tariff, or where no tariff is filed he is otherwise advised of such opportunity; but no such limitation is effective with respect to the carrier's liability for conversion to its own use.

(3) Reasonable provisions as to the time and manner of presenting claims and instituting actions based on the shipment may be included in a bill of lading or tariff.

Part 4   Warehouse Receipts and Bills of Lading: General Obligations

Section 7—401.   Irregularities in Issue of Receipt or Bill or Conduct of Issuer

The obligations imposed by this Article on an issuer apply to a document of title regardless of the fact that

    (a) the document may not comply with the requirements of this Article or of any other law or regulation regarding its issue, form or content; or

    (b) the issuer may have violated laws regulating the conduct of his business; or

    (c) the goods covered by the document were owned by the bailee at the time the document was issued; or

    (d) the person issuing the document does not come within the definition of warehouseman if it purports to be a warehouse receipt.

Section 7—402.   Duplicate Receipt or Bill; Overissue

Neither a duplicate nor any other document of title purporting to cover goods already represented by an outstanding document of the same issuer confers any right in the goods, except as provided in the case of bills in a set, overissue of documents for fungible goods and substitutes for lost, stolen or destroyed documents. But the issuer is liable for damages caused by his overissue or failure to identify a duplicate document as such by conspicuous notation on its face.

Section 7—403.   Obligation of Warehouseman or Carrier to Deliver; Excuse

(1) The bailee must deliver the goods to a person entitled under the document who complies with subsections (2) and (3), unless and to the extent that the bailee establishes any of the following:

    (a) delivery of the goods to a person whose receipt was rightful as against the claimant;

    (b) damage to or delay, loss or destruction of the goods for which the bailee is not liable [, but the burden of establishing negligence in such cases is on the person entitled under the document];

(c) previous sale or other disposition of the goods in lawful enforcement of a lien or on warehouseman's lawful termination of storage;

(d) the exercise by a seller of his right to stop delivery pursuant to the provisions of the Article on Sales (Section 2—705);

(e) a diversion, reconsignment or other disposition pursuant to the provisions of this Article (Section 7—303) or tariff regulating such right;

(f) release, satisfaction or any other fact affording a personal defense against the claimant;

(g) any other lawful excuse.

(2) A person claiming goods covered by a document of title must satisfy the bailee's lien where the bailee so requests or where the bailee is prohibted by law from delivering the goods until the charges are paid.

(3) Unless the person claiming is one against whom the document confers no right under Sec. 7—503(1), he must surrender for cancellation or notation of partial deliveries any outstanding negotiable document covering the goods, and the bailee must cancel the document or conspicuously note the partial delivery thereon or be liable to any person to whom the document is duly negotiated.

(4) "Person entitled under the document" means holder in the case of a negotiable document, or the person to whom delivery is to be made by the terms of or pursuant to written instructions under a non-negotiable document.

Section 7—404. No Liability for Good Faith Delivery Pursuant to Receipt or Bill

A bailee who in good faith including observance of reasonable commercial standards has received goods and delivered or otherwise disposed of them according to the terms of the document of title or pursuant to this Article is not liable therefor. This rule applies even though the person from whom he received the goods had no authority to procure the document or to dispose of the goods and even though the person to whom he delivered the goods had no authority to receive them.

Part 5 Warehouse Receipts and Bills of Lading: Negotiation and Transfer

Section 7—501. Form of Negotiation and Requirements of "Due Negotiation"

(1) A negotiable document of title running to the order of a named person is negotiated by his indorsement and delivery. After his indorsement in blank or to bearer any person can negotiate it by delivery alone.

(2) (a) A negotiable document of title is also negotiated by delivery alone when by its original terms it runs to bearer.

   (b) When a document running to the order of a named person is delivered to him the effect is the same as if the document had been negotiated.

(3) Negotiation of a negotiable document of title after it has been indorsed to a specified person requires indorsement by the special indorsee as well as delivery.

(4) A negotiable document of title is "duly negotiated" when it is negotiated in the manner stated in this section to a holder who purchases it in good faith without notice of any defense against or claim to it on the part of any person and for value, unless it is established that the negotiation is not in the regular course of business or fiancancing or involves receiving the document in settlement or payment of a money obligation.

(5) Indorsement of a non-negotiable document neither makes it negotiable nor adds to the transferee's rights.

(6) The naming in a negotiable bill of a person to be notified of the arrival of the goods does not limit the negotiability of the bill nor constitute notice to a purchaser thereof of any interest of such person in the goods.

Section 7—502. Rights Acquired by Due Negotiation

(1) Subject to the following section and to the provisions of Section 7—205 on fungible goods, a holder to whom a negotiable document of title has been duly negotiated acquires thereby:

(a) title to the document;

(b) title to the goods;

(c) all rights accruing under the law of agency

or estoppel, including rights to goods delivered to the bailee after the document was issued; and

(d) the direct obligation of the issuer to hold or deliver the goods according to the terms of the document free of any defense or claim by him except those arising under the terms of the document or under this Article. In the case of a delivery order the bailee's obligation accrues only upon acceptance and the obligation acquired by the holder is that the issuer and any indorser will procure the acceptance of the bailee.

(2) Subject to the following section, title and rights so acquired are not defeated by any stoppage of the goods represented by the document or by surrender of such goods by the bailee, and are not impaired even though the negotiation or any prior negotiation constituted a breach of duty or even though any person has been deprived of possession of the document by misrepresentation, fraud, accident, mistake, duress, loss, theft or conversion, or even though a previous sale or other transfer of the goods or document has been made to a third person.

Section 7—503.   Document of Title to Goods Defeated in Certain Cases

(1) A document of title confers no right in goods against a person who before issuance of the document had a legal interest or a perfected security interest in them and who neither

(a) delivered or entrusted them or any document of title covering them to the bailor or his nominee with actual or apparent authority to ship, store or sell or with power to obtain delivery under this Article (Section 7—403) or with power of disposition under this Act (Sections 2—403 and 9—307) or other statute or rule of law; nor

(b) acquiesced in the procurement by the bailor or his nominee of any document of title.

(2) Title to goods based upon an unaccepted delivery order is subject to the rights of anyone to whom a negotiable warehouse receipt or bill of lading covering the goods has been duly negotiated. Such a title may be defeated under the next section to the same extent as the rights of the issuer or a transferee from the issuer.

(3) Title to goods based upon a bill of lading issued to a freight forwarder is subject to the rights of anyone to whom a bill issued by the freight forwarder is duly negotiated; but delivery by the carrier in accordance with Part 4 of this Article pursuant to its own bill of lading discharges the carrier's obligation to deliver.

Section 7—504.   Rights Acquired in the Absence of Due Negotiation; Effect of Diversion; Seller's Stoppage of Delivery

(1) A transferee of a document, whether negotiable or non-negotiable, to whom the document has been delivered but not duly negotiated, acquires the title and rights which his transferor had or had actual authority to convey.

(2) In the case of a non-negotiable document, until but not after the bailee receives notification of the transfer, the rights of the transferee may be defeated

(a) by those creditors of the transferor who could treat the sale as void under Section 2—402; or

(b) by a buyer from the transferor in ordinary course of business if the bailee has delivered the goods to the buyer or received notification of his rights; or

(c) as against the bailee by good faith dealings of the bailee with the transferor.

(3) A diversion or other change of shipping instructions by the consignor in a non-negotiable bill of lading which causes the bailee not to deliver to the consignee defeats the consignee's title to the goods if they have been delivered to a buyer in ordinary course of business and in any event defeats the consignee's rights against the bailee.

(4) Delivery pursuant to a non-negotiable document may be stopped by a seller under Section 2—705, and subject to the requirement of due notification there provided. A bailee honoring the seller's instructions is entitled to be indemnified by the seller against any resulting loss or expense.

Section 7—505.   Indorser Not a Guarantor for Other Parties

The indorsement of a document of title issued by a bailee does not make the indorser liable for any default by the bailee or by previous indorsers.

Section 7—506. Delivery Without Indorsement: Right to Compel Indorsement

The transferee of a negotiable document of title has a specifically enforceable right to have his transferor supply any necessary indorsement but the transfer becomes a negotiation only as of the time the indorsement is supplied.

Section 7—507. Warranties on Negotiation or Transfer of Receipt or Bill

Where a person negotiates or transfers a document of title for value otherwise than as a mere intermediary under the next following section, then unless otherwise agreed he warrants to his immediate purchaser only in addition to any warranty made in selling the goods

(a) that the document is genuine; and

(b) that he has no knowledge of any fact which would impair its validity or worth; and

(c) that his negotiation or transfer is rightful and fully effective with respect to the title to the document and the goods it represents.

Section 7—508. Warranties of Collecting Bank as to Documents

A collecting bank or other intermediary known to be entrusted with documents on behalf of another or with collection of a draft or other claim against delivery of documents warrants by such delivery of the documents only its own good faith and authority. This rule applies even though the intermediary has purchased or made advances against the claim or draft to be collected.

Part 6 Warehouse Receipts and Bills of Lading: Miscellaneous Provisions

Section 7—601. Lost and Missing Documents

(1) If a document has been lost, stolen or destroyed, a court may order delivery of the goods or issuance of a substitute document and the bailee may without liability to any person comply with such order. If the document was negotiable the claimant must post security approved by the court to indemnify any person who may suffer loss as a result of non-surrender of the document. If the document was not negotiable, such security may be required at the discretion of the court. The court may also in its discretion order payment of the bailee's reasonable costs and counsel fees.

(2) A bailee who without court order delivers goods to a person claiming under a missing negotiable document is liable to any person injured thereby, and if the delivery is not in good faith becomes liable for conversion. Delivery in good faith is not conversion if made in accordance with a filed classification or tariff or, where no classification or tariff is filed, if the claimant posts security with the bailee in an amount at least double the value of the goods at the time of posting to indemnify any person injured by the delivery who files a notice of claim within one year after the delivery.

Section 7—602. Attachment of Goods Covered by a Negotiable Document

Except where the document was originally issued upon delivery of the goods by a person who had no power to dispose of them, no lien attaches by virtue of any judicial process to goods in the possession of a bailee for which a negotiable document of title is outstanding unless the document be first surrendered to the bailee or its negotiation enjoined, and the bailee shall not be compelled to deliver the goods pursuant to process until the document is surrendered to him or impounded by the court. One who purchases the document for value without notice of the process or injunction takes free of the lien imposed by judicial process.

Section 7—603. Conflicting Claims; Interpleader

If more than one person claims title or possession of the goods, the bailee is excused from delivery until he has had a reasonable time to ascertain the validity of the adverse claims or to bring an action to compel all claimants to interplead and may compel such interpleader, either in defending an action for non-delivery of the goods, or by original action, whichever is appropriate.

Article 8 Investment Securities

Part 1 Short Title and General Matters

Section 8—101. Short Title

This Article shall be known and may be cited as Uniform Commercial Code—Investment Securities.

Section 8—102. Definitions and Index of Definitions

(1) In this Article, unless the context otherwise requires:

   (a) A "certificated security" is a share, participation, or other interest in property of or an enterprise of the issuer or an obligation of the issuer which is

   (i) represented by an instrument issued in bearer or registered form;

   (ii) of a type commonly dealt in on securities exchanges or markets or commonly recognized in any area in which it is issued or dealt in as a medium for investment; and

   (iii) either one of a class or series or by its terms divisible into a class or series of shares, participations, interests, or obligations.

   (b) An "uncertificated security" is a share, participation, or other interest in property or an enterprise of the issuer or an obligation of the issuer which is

   (i) not represented by an instrument and the transfer of which is registered upon books maintained for that purpose by or on behalf of the issuer;

   (ii) of a type commonly dealt in on securities exchanges or markets; and

   (iii) either one of a class or series or by its terms divisible into a class or series of shares, participations, interests, or obligations.

   (c) A "security" is either a certificated or an uncertificated security. If a security is certificated, the terms "security" and "certificated security" may mean either the intangible interest, the instrument representing that interest, or both, as the context requires. A writing that is a certificated security is governed by this Article and not by Article 3, even though it also meets the requirements of that Article. This Article does not apply to money. If a certificated security has been retained by or surrendered to the issuer or its transfer agent for reasons other than registration of transfer, other temporary purpose, payment, exchange, or acquisition by the issuer, that security shall be treated as an uncertificated security for purposes of this Article.

   (d) A certificated security is in "registered form" if

   (i) it specifies a person entitled to the security or the rights it represents; and

   (ii) its transfer may be registered upon books maintained for that purpose by or on behalf of the issuer, or the security so states.

   (e) A certificated security is in "bearer form" if it runs to bearer according to its terms and not by reason of any indorsement.

(2) A "subsequent purchaser" is a person who takes other than by original issue.

(3) A "clearing corporation" is a corporation registered as a "clearing agency" under the federal securities laws or a corporation:

   (a) at least 90 percent of whose capital stock is held by or for one or more organizations, none of which, other than a national securities exchange or association, holds in excess of 20 percent of the capital stock of the corporation, and each of which is

   (i) subject to supervision or regulation pursuant to the provisions of federal or state banking laws or state insurance laws,

   (ii) a broker or dealer or investment company registered under the federal securities laws, or

(iii) a national securities exchange or association registered under the federal securities laws; and

(b) any remaining capital stock of which is held by individuals who have purchased it at or prior to the time of their taking office as directors of the corporation and who have purchased only so much of the capital stock as is necessary to permit them to qualify as directors.

(4) A "custodian bank" is a bank or trust company that is supervised and examined by state or federal authority having supervision over banks and is acting as custodian for a clearing corporation.

(5) Other definitions applying to this Article or to specified Parts thereof and the sections in which they appear are:

"Adverse claim." Section 8—302.
"Bona fide purchaser." Section 8—302.
"Broker." Section 8—303.
"Debtor." Section 9—105.
"Financial intermediary." Section 8—313.
"Guarantee of the signature." Section 8—402.
"Initial transaction statement." Section 8—408.
"Instruction." Section 8—308.
"Intermediary bank." Section 4—105.
"Issuer." Section 8—201.
"Overissue." Section 8—104.
"Secured Party." Section 9—105.
"Security Agreement." Section 9—105.

(6) In addition, Article 1 contains general definitions and principles of construction and interpretation applicable throughout this Article.

Section 8—103.   Issuer's Lien

A lien upon a security in favor of an issuer thereof is valid against a purchaser only if:

(a) the security is certificated and the right of the issuer to the lien is noted conspicuously thereon; or

(b) the security is uncertificated and a notation of the right of the issuer to the lien is contained in the initial transaction statement sent to the purchaser or, if his interest is transferred to him other than by registration

of transfer, pledge, or release, the initial transaction statement sent to the registered owner or the registered pledgee.

Section 8—104.   Effect of Overissue; "Overissue"

(1) The provisions of this Article which validate a security or compel its issue or reissue do not apply to the extent that validation, issue, or reissue would result in overissue; but if:

(a) an identical security which does not constitute an overissue is reasonably available for purchase, the person entitled to issue or validation may compel the issuer to purchase the security for him and either to deliver a certificated security or to register the transfer of an uncertificated security to him, against surrender of any certificated security he holds; or

(b) a security is not so available for purchase, the person entitled to issue or validation may recover from the issuer the price he or the last purchaser for value paid for it with interest from the date of his demand.

(2) "Overissue" means the issue of securities in excess of the amount the issuer has corporate power to issue.

Section 8—105.   Certificated Securities Negotiable; Statements and Instructions Not Negotiable; Presumptions

(1) Certificated securities governed by this Article are negotiable instruments.

(2) Statements (Section 8—408), notices, or the like, sent by the issuer of uncertificated securities and instructions (Section 8—308) are neither negotiable instruments nor certificated securities.

(3) In any action on a security:

(a) unless specifically denied in the pleadings, each signature on a certificated security, in a necessary indorsement, on an initial transaction statement, or on an instruction, is admitted;

(b) if the effectiveness of a signature is put in issue, the burden of establishing it is on the party claiming under the signature, but the signature is presumed to be genuine or authorized;

(c) if signatures on a certificated security are admitted or established, production of the security entitles a holder to recover on it unless the defendant establishes a defense or a defect going to the validity of the security;

(d) if signatures on an initial transaction statement are admitted or established, the facts stated in the statement are presumed to be true as of the time of its issuance; and

(e) after it is shown that a defense or defect exists, the plaintiff has the burden of establishing that he or some person under whom he claims is a person against whom the defense or defect is ineffective (Section 8—202).

Section 8—106. Applicability

The law (including the conflict of laws rules) of the jurisdiction of organization of the issuer governs the validity of a security, the effectiveness of registration by the issuer, and the rights and duties of the issuer with respect to:

(a) registration of transfer of a certificated security;

(b) registration of transfer, pledge, or release of an uncertificated security; and

(c) sending of statements of uncertificated securities.

Section 8—107. Securities Transferable; Action for Price

(1) Unless otherwise agreed and subject to any applicable law or regulation respecting short sales, a person obligated to transfer securities may transfer any certificated security of the specified issue in bearer form or registered in the name of the transferee, or indorsed to him or in blank, or he may transfer an equivalent uncertificated security to the transferee or a person designated by the transferee.

(2) If the buyer fails to pay the price as it comes due under a contract of sale, the seller may recover the price of:

(a) certificated securities accepted by the buyer;

(b) uncertificated securities that have been transferred to the buyer or a person designated by the buyer; and

(c) other securities if efforts at their resale would be unduly burdensome or if there is no readily available market for their resale.

Section 8—108. Registration of Pledge and Release of Uncertificated Securities

A security interest in an uncertificated security may be evidenced by the registration of pledge to the secured party or a person designated by him. There can be no more than one registered pledge of an uncertificated security at any time. The registered owner of an uncertificated security is the person in whose name the security is registered, even if the security is subject to a registered pledge. The rights of a registered pledgee of an uncertificated security under this Article are terminated by the registration of release.

Part 2 Issue—Issuer

Section 8—201. "Issuer"

(1) With respect to obligations on or defenses to a security, "issuer" includes a person who:

(a) places or authorizes the placing of his name on a certificated security (otherwise than as authenticating trustee, registrar, transfer agent, or the like) to evidence that it represents a share, participation, or other interest in his property or in an enterprise, or to evidence his duty to perform an obligation represented by the certificated security;

(b) creates shares, participations, or other interests in his property or in an enterprise or undertakes obligations, which shares, participations, interests, or obligations are uncertificated securities;

(c) directly or indirectly creates fractional interests in his rights or property, which fractional interests are represented by certificated securities; or

(d) becomes responsibile for or in place of any other person described as an issuer in this section.

(2) With respect to obligations on or defenses to a security, a guarantor is an issuer to the extent of his guaranty, whether or not his obligation is noted on a certificated security or on statements of uncertificated securities sent pursuant to Section 8—408.

(3) With respect to registration of transfer, pledge, or release (Part 4 of this Article), "issuer" means a person on whose behalf transfer books are maintained.

Section 8—202. Issuer's Responsibility and Defenses; Notice of Defect or Defense

(1) Even against a purchaser for value and without notice, the terms of a security include:

  (a) if the security is certificated, those stated on the security;

  (b) if the security is uncertificated, those contained in the initial transaction statement sent to such purchaser, or, if his interest is transferred to him other than by registration of transfer, pledge, or release, the initial transaction statement sent to the registered owner or registered pledgee; and

  (c) those made part of the security by reference, on the certificated security or in the initial transaction statement, to another instrument, indenture, or document or to a constitution, statute, ordinance, rule, regulation, order or the like, to the extent that the terms referred to do not conflict with the terms stated on the certificated security or contained in the statement. A reference under this paragraph does not of itself charge a purchaser for value with notice of a defect going to the validity of the security, even though the certificated security or statement expressly states that a person accepting it admits notice.

(2) A certificated security in the hands of a purchaser for value or an uncertificated security as to which an initial transaction statement has been sent to a purchaser for value, other than a security issued by a government or governmental agency or unit, even though issued with a defect going to its validity, is valid with respect to the purchaser if he is without notice of the particular defect unless the defect involves a violation of constitutional provisions, in which case the security is valid with respect to a subsequent purchaser for value

and without notice of the defect. This subsection applies to an issuer that is a government or governmental agency or unit only if either there has been substantial compliance with the legal requirements governing the issue or the issuer has received a substantial consideration for the issue as a whole or for the particular security and a stated purpose of the issue is one for which the issuer has power to borrow money or issue the security.

(3) Except as provided in the case of certain unauthorized signatures (Section 8—205), lack of genuineness of a certificated security or an initial transaction statement is a complete defense, even against a purchaser for value and without notice.

(4) All other defenses of the issuer of a certificated or uncertificated security, including nondelivery and conditional delivery of a certificated security, are ineffective against a purchaser for value who has taken without notice of the particular defense.

(5) Nothing in this section shall be construed to affect the right of a party to a "when, as and if issued" or a "when distributed" contract to cancel the contract in the event of a material change in the character of the security that is the subject of the contract or in the plan or arrangement pursuant to which the security is to be issued or distributed.

Section 8—203. Staleness as Notice of Defects or Defenses

(1) After an act or event creating a right to immediate performance of the principal obligation represented by a certificated security or that sets a date on or after which the security is to be presented or surrendered for redemption or exchange, a purchaser is charged with notice of any defect in its issue or defense of the issuer if:

  (a) the act or event is one requiring the payment of money, the delivery of certificated securities, the registration of transfer of uncertificated securities, or any of these on presentation or surrender of the certificated security, the funds or securities are available on the date set for payment or exchange, and he takes the security more than one year after that date; and

(b) the act or event is not covered by paragraph (a) and he takes the security more than 2 years after the date set for surrender or presentation or the date on which performance became due.

(2) A call that has been revoked is not within subsection (1).

Section 8—204. Effect of Issuer's Restrictions on Transfer

A restriction on transfer of a security imposed by the issuer, even if otherwise lawful, is ineffective against any person without actual knowledge of it unless:

(a) the security is certificated and the restriction is noted conspicuously thereon; or

(b) the security is uncertificated and a notation of the restriction is contained in the initial transaction statement sent to the person or, if his interest is transferred to him other than by registration of transfer, pledge, or release, the initial transaction statement sent to the registered owner or the registered pledgee.

Section 8—205. Effect of Unauthorized Signature on Certificated Security or Initial Transaction Statement

An unauthorized signature placed on a certificated security prior to or in the course of issue or placed on an initial transaction statement is ineffective, but the signature is effective in favor of a purchaser for value of the certificated security or a purchaser for value of an uncertificated security to whom the initial transaction statement has been sent, if the purchaser is without notice of the lack of authority and the signing has been done by:

(a) an authenticating trustee, registrar, transfer agent, or other person entrusted by the issuer with the signing of the security, of similar securities, or of initial transaction statements or the immediate preparation for signing of any of them; or

(b) an employee of the issuer, or of any of the foregoing, entrusted with responsible handling of the security or initial transaction statement.

Section 8—206. Completion or Alteration of Certificated Security or Initial Transaction Statement

(1) If a certificated security contains the signatures necessary to its issue or transfer but is incomplete in any other respect:

(a) any person may complete it by filling in the blanks as authorized; and

(b) even though the blanks are incorrectly filled in, the security as completed is enforceable by a purchaser who took it for value and without notice of the incorrectness.

(2) A complete certificated security that has been improperly altered, even though fraudulently, remains enforceable, but only according to its original terms.

(3) If an initial transaction statement contains the signatures necessary to its validity, but is incomplete in any other respect:

(a) any person may complete it by filling in the blanks as authorized; and

(b) even though the blanks are incorrectly filled in, the statement as completed is effective in favor of the person to whom it is sent if he purchased the security referred to therein for value and without notice of the incorrectness.

(4) A complete initial transaction statement that has been improperly altered, even though fraudulently, is effective in favor of a purchaser to whom it has been sent, but only according to its original terms.

Section 8—207. Rights and Duties of Issuer With Respect to Registered Owners and Registered Pledgees

(1) Prior to due presentment for registration of transfer of a certificated security in registered form, the issuer or indenture trustee may treat the registered owner as the person exclusively entitled to vote, to receive notifications, and otherwise to exercise all rights and powers of an owner.

(2) Subject to the provisions of subsections (3), (4), and (6), the issuer or indenture trustee may treat the registered owner of an uncertificated security as the person exclusively entitled to vote, to receive notifications, and otherwise to exercise all the rights and powers of an owner.

(3) The registered owner of an uncertificated security that is subject to a registered pledge is not entitled to registration of transfer prior to the due presentment to the issuer of a release instruction. The exercise of conversion rights with respect to a convertible uncertificated security is a transfer within the meaning of this section.

(4) Upon due presentment of a transfer instruction from the registered pledgee of an uncertificated security, the issuer shall:

    (a) register the transfer of the security to the new owner free of pledge, if the instruction specifies a new owner (who may be the registered pledgee) and does not specify a pledgee;

    (b) register the transfer of the security to the new owner subject to the interest of the existing pledgee, if the instruction specifies a new owner and the existing pledgee; or

    (c) register the release of the security from the existing pledge and register the pledge of the security to the other pledgee, if the instruction specifies the existing owner and another pledgee.

(5) Continuity of perfection of a security interest is not broken by registration of transfer under subsection (4)(b) or by registration of release and pledge under subsection (4)(c), if the security interest is assigned.

(6) If an uncertificated security is subject to a registered pledge:

    (a) any uncertificated securities issued in exchange for or distributed with respect to the pledged security shall be registered subject to the pledge;

    (b) any certificated securities issued in exchange for or distributed with respect to the pledged security shall be delivered to the registered pledgee; and

    (c) any money paid in exchange for or in redemption of part or all of the security shall be paid to the registered pledgee.

(7) Nothing in this Article shall be construed to affect the liability of the registered owner of a security for calls, assessments, or the like.

Section 8—208.   Effect of Signature of Authenticating Trustee, Registrar, or Transfer Agent

(1) A person placing his signature upon a certificated security or an initial transaction statement as authenticating trustee, registrar, transfer agent, or the like, warrants to a purchaser for value of the certificated security or a purchaser for value of an uncertificated security to whom the initial transaction statement has been sent, if the purchaser is without notice of the particular defect, that:

    (a) the certificated security or initial transaction statement is genuine;

    (b) his own participation in the issue or registration of the transfer, pledge, or release of the security is within his capacity and within the scope of the authority received by him from the issuer; and

    (c) he has reasonable grounds to believe the security is in the form and within the amount the issuer is authorized to issue.

(2) Unless otherwise agreed, a person by so placing his signature does not assume responsibility for the validity of the security in other respects.

Part 3   Transfer

Section 8—301.   Rights Acquired by Purchaser

(1) Upon transfer of a security to a purchaser (Section 8—313), the purchaser acquires the rights in the security which his transferor had or had actual authority to convey unless the purchaser's rights are limited by Section 8—302(4).

(2) A transferee of a limited interest acquires rights only to the extent of the interest transferred. The creation or release of a security interest in a security is the transfer of a limited interest in that security.

Section 8—302.   "Bona Fide Purchaser"; "Adverse Claim"; Title Acquired by Bona Fide Purchaser

(1) A "bona fide purchaser" is a purchaser for value in good faith and without notice of any adverse claim:

    (a) who takes delivery of a certificated security in bearer form or in registered form, issued or indorsed to him or in blank;

(b) to whom the transfer, pledge, or release of an uncertificated security is registered on the books of the issuer; or

(c) to whom a security is transferred under the provisions of paragraph (c), (d)(i), or (g) of Section 8—313(1).

(2) "Adverse claim" includes a claim that a transfer was or would be wrongful or that a particular adverse person is the owner of or has an interest in the security.

(3) A bona fide purchaser in addition to acquiring the rights of a purchaser (Section 8—301) also acquires his interest in the security free of any adverse claim.

(4) Notwithstanding Section 8—301(1), the transferee of a particular certificated security who has been a party to any fraud or illegality affecting the security, or who as a prior holder of that certificated security had notice of an adverse claim, cannot improve his position by taking from a bona fide purchaser.

Section 8—303. "Broker"

"Broker" means a person engaged for all or part of his time in the business of buying and selling securities, who in the transaction concerned acts for, buys a security from, or sells a security to, a customer. Nothing in this Article determines the capacity in which a person acts for purposes of any other statute or rule to which the person is subject.

Section 8—304. Notice to Purchaser of Adverse Claims

(1) A purchaser (including a broker for the seller or buyer, but excluding an intermediary bank) of a certificated security is charged with notice of adverse claims if:

(a) the security, whether in bearer or registered form, has been indorsed "for collection" or "for surrender" or for some other purpose not involving transfer; or

(b) the security is in bearer form and has on it an unambiguous statement that it is the property of a person other than the transferor. The mere writing of a name on a security is not such a statement.

(2) A purchaser (including a broker for the seller or buyer, but excluding an intermediary bank) to whom the transfer, pledge, or release of an uncertificated security is registered is charged with notice of adverse claims as to which the issuer has a duty under Section 8—403(4) at the time of registration and which are noted in the initial transaction statement sent to the purchaser or, if his interest is transferred to him other than by registration of transfer, pledge, or release, the initial transaction statement sent to the registered owner or the registered pledgee.

(3) The fact that the purchaser (including a broker for the seller or buyer) of a certificated or uncertificated security has notice that the security is held for a third person or is registered in the name of or indorsed by a fiduciary does not create a duty of inquiry into the rightfulness of the transfer or constitute constructive notice of adverse claims. However, if the purchaser (excluding an intermediary bank) has knowledge that the proceeds are being used or that the transaction is for the individual benefit of the fiduciary or otherwise in breach of duty, the purchaser is charged with notice of adverse claims.

Section 8—305. Staleness as Notice of Adverse Claims

An act or event that creates a right to immediate performance of the principal obligation represented by a certificated security or sets a date on or after which a certificated security is to be presented or surrendered for redemption or exchange does not itself constitute any notice of adverse claims except in the case of a transfer:

(a) after one year from any date set for presentment or surrender for redemption or exchange; or

(b) after 6 months from any date set for payment of money against presentation or surrender of the security if funds are available for payment on that date.

Section 8—306. Warranties on Presentment and Transfer of Certificated Securities; Warranties of Originators of Instructions

(1) A person who presents a certificated security for registration of transfer or for payment or exchange warrants to the issuer that he is entitled to the registration,

payment, or exchange. But, a purchaser for value and without notice of adverse claims who receives a new, reissued, or re-registered certificated security on registration of transfer or receives an initial transaction statement confirming the registration of transfer of an equivalent uncertificated security to him warrants only that he has no knowledge of any unauthorized signature (Section 8—311) in a necessary indorsement.

(2) A person by transferring a certificated security to a purchaser for value warrants only that:

    (a) his transfer is effective and rightful;

    (b) the security is genuine and has not been materially altered; and

    (c) he knows of no fact which might impair the validity of the security.

(3) If a certificated security is delivered by an intermediary known to be entrusted with delivery of the security on behalf of another or with collection of a draft or other claim against delivery, the intermediary by delivery warrants only his own good faith and authority, even though he has purchased or made advances against the claim to be collected against the delivery.

(4) A pledgee or other holder for security who redelivers a certificated security received, or after payment and on order of the debtor delivers that security to a third person, makes only the warranties of an intermediary under subsection (3).

(5) A person who originates an instruction warrants to the issuer that:

    (a) he is an appropriate person to originate the instruction; and

    (b) at the time the instruction is presented to the issuer he will be entitled to the registration of transfer, pledge, or release.

(6) A person who originates an instruction warrants to any person specially guaranteeing his signature (subsection 8—312(3)) that:

    (a) he is an appropriate person to originate the instruction; and

    (b) at the time the instruction is presented to the issuer

        (i) he will be entitled to the registration of transfer, pledge, or release; and

        (ii) the transfer, pledge, or release requested in the instruction will be registered by the issuer free from all liens, security interests, restrictions, and claims other than those specified in the instruction.

(7) A person who originates an instruction warrants to a purchaser for value and to any person guaranteeing the instruction (Section 8—312(6)) that:

    (a) he is an appropriate person to originate the instruction;

    (b) the uncertificated security referred to therein is valid; and

    (c) at the time the instruction is presented to the issuer

        (i) the transferor will be entitled to the registration of transfer, pledge, or release;

        (ii) the transfer, pledge, or release requested in the instruction will be registered by the issuer free from all liens, security interests, restrictions, and claims other than those specified in the instruction; and

        (iii) the requested transfer, pledge, or release will be rightful.

(8) If a secured party is the registered pledgee or the registered owner of an uncertificated security, a person who originates an instruction of release or transfer to the debtor or, after payment and on order of the debtor, a transfer instruction to a third person, warrants to the debtor or the third person only that he is an appropriate person to originate the instruction and, at the time the instruction is presented to the issuer, the transferor will be entitled to the registration of release or transfer. If a transfer instruction to a third person who is a purchaser for value is originated on order of the debtor, the debtor makes to the purchaser the warranties of paragraphs (b), (c)(ii) and (c)(iii) of subsection (7).

(9) A person who transfers an uncertificated security to a purchaser for value and does not originate an instruction in connection with the transfer warrants only that:

    (a) his transfer is effective and rightful; and

    (b) the uncertificated security is valid.

(10) A broker gives to his customer and to the issuer and a purchaser the applicable warranties provided in this section and has the rights and privileges of a purchaser under this section. The warranties of and in favor of the broker, acting as an agent are in addition to applicable warranties given by and in favor of his customer.

Section 8—307. Effect of Delivery Without Indorsement; Right to Compel Indorsement

If a certificated security in registered form has been delivered to a purchaser without a necessary indorsement he may become a bona fide purchaser only as of the time the indorsement is supplied; but against the transferor, the transfer is complete upon delivery and the purchaser has a specifically enforceable right to have any necessary indorsement supplied.

Section 8—308. Indorsements; Instructions

(1) An indorsement of a certificated security in registered form is made when an appropriate person signs on it or on a separate document an assignment or transfer of the security or a power to assign or transfer it or his signature is written without more upon the back of the security.

(2) An indorsement may be in blank or special. An indorsement in blank includes an indorsement to bearer. A special indorsement specifies to whom the security is to be transferred, or who has power to transfer it. A holder may convert a blank indorsement into a special indorsement.

(3) An indorsement purporting to be only of part of a certificated security representing units intended by the issuer to be separately transferable is effective to the extent of the indorsement.

(4) An "instruction" is an order to the issuer of an uncertificated security requesting that the transfer, pledge, or release from pledge of the uncertificated security specified therein be registered.

(5) An instruction originated by an appropriate person is:

    (a) a writing signed by an appropriate person; or

    (b) a communication to the issuer in any form agreed upon in a writing signed by the issuer and an appropriate person.

If an instruction has been originated by an appropriate person but is incomplete in any other respect, any person may complete it as authorized and the issuer may rely on it as completed even though it has been completed incorrectly.

(6) "An appropriate person" in subsection (1) means the person specified by the certificated security or by special indorsement to be entitled to the security.

(7) "An appropriate person" in subsection (5) means:

    (a) for an instruction to transfer or pledge an uncertificated security which is then not subject to a registered pledge, the registered owner; or

    (b) for an instruction to transfer or release an uncertificated security which is then subject to a registered pledge, the registered pledgee.

(8) In addition to the persons designated in subsections (6) and (7), "an appropriate person" in subsections (1) and (5) includes:

    (a) if the person designated is described as a fiduciary but is no longer serving in the described capacity, either that person or his successor;

    (b) if the persons designated are described as more than one person as fiduciaries and one or more are no longer serving in the described capacity, the remaining fiduciary or fiduciaries, whether or not a successor has been appointed or qualified;

    (c) if the person designated is an individual and is without capacity to act by virtue of death, incompetence, infancy, or otherwise, his executor, administrator, guardian, or like fiduciary;

    (d) if the persons designated are described as more than one person as tenants by the entirety or with right of survivorship and by reason of death all cannot sign, the survivor or survivors;

    (e) a person having power to sign under applicable law or controlling instrument; and

    (f) to the extent that the person designated or any of the foregoing persons may act through an agent, his authorized agent.

(9) Unless otherwise agreed, the indorser of a certificated security by his indorsement or the originator of an instruction by his origination assumes no obligation that the security will be honored by the issuer but only the obligations provided in Section 8—306.

(10) Whether the person signing is appropriate is determined as of the date of signing and an indorsement made by or an instruction originated by him does not become unauthorized for the purposes of this Article by virtue of any subsequent change of circumstances.

(11) Failure of a fiduciary to comply with a controlling instrument or with the law of the state having jurisdiction of the fiduciary relationship, including any law requiring the fiduciary to obtain court approval of the transfer, pledge, or release, does not render his indorsement or an instruction originated by him unauthorized for the purposes of this Article.

Section 8—309. Effect of Indorsement Without Delivery

An indorsement of a certificated security, whether special or in blank, does not constitute a transfer until delivery of the certificated security on which it appears or, if the indorsement is on a separate document, until delivery of both the document and the certificated security.

Section 8—310. Indorsement of Certificated Security in Bearer Form

An indorsement of a certificated security in bearer form may give notice of adverse claims (Section 8—304) but does not otherwise affect any right to registration the holder possesses.

Section 8—311. Effect of Unauthorized Indorsement or Instruction

Unless the owner or pledgee has ratified an unauthorized indorsement or instruction or is otherwise precluded from asserting its ineffectiveness:

(a) he may assert its ineffectiveness against the issuer or any purchaser, other than a purchaser for value and without notice of adverse claims, who has in good faith received a new, reissued, or re-registered certificated security

on registration of transfer or received an initial transaction statement confirming the registration of transfer, pledge, or release of an equivalent uncertificated security to him; and

(b) an issuer who registers the transfer of a certificated security upon the unauthorized indorsement or who registers the transfer, pledge, or release of an uncertificated security upon the unauthorized instruction is subject to liability for improper registration (Section 8—404).

Section 8—312. Effect of Guaranteeing Signature, Indorsement or Instruction

(1) Any person guaranteeing a signature of an indorser of a certificated security warrants that at the time of signing:

(a) the signature was genuine;

(b) the signer was an appropriate person to indorse (Section 8—308); and

(c) the signer had legal capacity to sign.

(2) Any person guaranteeing a signature of the originator of an instruction warrants that at the time of signing:

(a) the signature was genuine;

(b) the signer was an appropriate person to originate the instruction (Section 8—308) if the person specified in the instruction as the registered owner or registered pledgee of the uncertificated security was, in fact, the registered owner or registered pledgee of the security, as to which fact the signature guarantor makes no warranty;

(c) the signer had legal capacity to sign; and

(d) the taxpayer identification number, if any, appearing on the instruction as that of the registered owner or registered pledgee was the taxpayer identification number of the signer or of the owner or pledgee for whom the signer was acting.

(3) Any person specially guaranteeing the signature of the originator of an instruction makes not only the warranties of a signature guarantor (subsection (2)) but also warrants that at the time the instruction is presented to the issuer:

(a) the person specified in the instruction as the registered owner or registered pledgee of the uncertificated security will be the registered owner or registered pledgee; and

(b) the transfer, pledge, or release of the uncertificated security requested in the instruction will be registered by the issuer free from all liens, security interests, restrictions, and claims other than those specified in the instruction.

(4) The guarantor under subsections (1) and (2) or the special guarantor under subsection (3) does not otherwise warrant the rightfulness of the particular transfer, pledge, or release.

(5) Any person guaranteeing an indorsement of a certificated security makes not only the warranties of a signature guarantor under subsection (1) but also warrants the rightfulness of the particular transfer in all respects.

(6) Any person guaranteeing an instruction requesting the transfer, pledge, or release of an uncertificated security makes not only the warranties of a special signature guarantor under subsection (3) but also warrants the rightfulness of the particular transfer, pledge, or release in all respects.

(7) No issuer may require a special guarantee of signature (subsection (3)), a guarantee of indorsement (subsection (5)), or a guarantee of instruction (subsection (6)) as a condition to registration of transfer, pledge, or release.

(8) The foregoing warranties are made to any person taking or dealing with the security in reliance on the guarantee, and the guarantor is liable to the person for any loss resulting from breach of the warranties.

Section 8—313. When Transfer to Purchaser Occurs; Financial Intermediary as Bona Fide Purchaser; "Financial Intermediary"

(1) Transfer of a security or a limited interest (including a security interest) therein to a purchaser occurs only:

(a) at the time he or a person designated by him acquires possession of a certificated security;

(b) at the time the transfer, pledge, or release of an uncertificated security is registered to him or a person designated by him;

(c) at the time his financial intermediary acquires possession of a certificated security specially indorsed to or issued in the name of the purchaser;

(d) at the time a financial intermediary, not a clearing corporation, sends him confirmation of the purchase and also by book entry or otherwise identifies as belonging to the purchaser

  (i) a specific certificated security in the financial intermediary's possession;

  (ii) a quantity of securities that constitute or are part of a fungible bulk of certificated securities in the financial intermediary's possession or of uncertificated securities registered in the name of the financial intermediary; or

  (iii) a quantity of securities that constitute or are part of a fungible bulk of securities shown on the account of the financial intermediary on the books of another financial intermediary;

(e) with respect to an identified certificated security to be delivered while still in the possession of a third person, not a financial intermediary, at the time that person acknowledges that he holds for the purchaser;

(f) with respect to a specific uncertificated security the pledge or transfer of which has been registered to a third person, not a financial intermediary, at the time that person acknowledges that he holds for the purchaser;

(g) at the time appropriate entries to the account of the purchaser or a person designated by him on the books of a clearing corporation are made under Section 8—320;

(h) with respect to the transfer of a security interest where the debtor has signed a security agreement containing a description of the security, at the time a written notification, which, in the case of the creation of the security interest, is signed by the debtor (which may be a copy of the security agreement) or which, in the case of the release or assignment of the security interest created pursuant to this paragraph, is signed by the secured party, is received by

    (i) a financial intermediary on whose books the interest of the transferor in the security appears;

    (ii) a third person, not a financial intermediary, in possession of the security, if it is certificated;

    (iii) a third person, not a financial intermediary, who is the registered owner of the security, if it is uncertificated and not subject to a registered pledge; or

    (iv) a third person, not a financial intermediary, who is the registered pledgee of the security, if it is uncertificated and subject to a registered pledge;

(i) with respect to the transfer of a security interest where the transferor has signed a security agreement containing a description of the security, at the time new value is given by the secured party; or

(j) with respect to the transfer of a security interest where the secured party is a financial intermediary and the security has already been transferred to the financial intermediary under paragraphs (a), (b), (c), (d), or (g), at the time the transferor has signed a security agreement containing a description of the security and value is given by the secured party.

(2) The purchaser is the owner of a security held for him by a financial intermediary, but cannot be a bona fide purchaser of a security so held except in the circumstances specified in paragraphs (c), (d)(i), and (g) of subsection (1). If a security so held is part of a fungible bulk, as in the circumstances specified in paragraphs (d)(ii) and (d)(iii) of subsection (1), the purchaser is the owner of a proportionate property interest in the fungible bulk.

(3) Notice of an adverse claim received by the financial intermediary or by the purchaser after the financial intermediary takes delivery of a certificated security as a holder for value or after the transfer, pledge, or release of an uncertificated security has been registered free of the claim to a financial intermediary who has given value is not effective either as to the financial intermediary or as to the purchaser. However, as between the financial intermediary and the purchaser the purchaser may demand transfer of an equivalent security as to which no notice of adverse claim has been received.

(4) A "financial intermediary" is a bank, broker, clearing corporation, or other person (or the nominee of any of them) which in the ordinary course of its business maintains security accounts for its customers and is acting in that capacity. A financial intermediary may have a security interest in securities held in account for its customer.

Section 8—314. Duty to Transfer, When Completed

(1) Unless otherwise agreed, if a sale of a security is made on an exchange or otherwise through brokers:

    (a) the selling customer fulfills his duty to transfer at the time he:

        (i) places a certificated security in the possession of the selling broker or a person designated by the broker;

        (ii) causes an uncertificated security to be registered in the name of the selling broker or a person designated by the broker;

        (iii) if requested, causes an acknowledgment to be made to the selling broker that a certificated or uncertificated security is held for the broker; or

        (iv) places in the possession of the selling broker or of a person designated by the broker a transfer instruction for an uncertificated security, providing the issuer does not refuse to register the requested transfer if the instruction is presented to the issuer for registration within 30 days thereafter; and

    (b) the selling broker, including a correspondent broker acting for a selling customer, fulfills his duty to transfer at the time he:

        (i) places a certificated security in the possession of the buying broker or a person designated by the buying broker;

(ii) causes an uncertificated security to be registered in the name of the buying broker or a person designated by the buying broker;

(iii) places in the possession of the buying broker or of a person designated by the buying broker a transfer instruction for an uncertificated security, providing the issuer does not refuse to register the requested transfer if the instruction is presented to the issuer for registration within 30 days thereafter; or

(iv) effects clearance of the sale in accordance with the rules of the exchange on which the transaction took place.

(2) Except as provided in this section or unless otherwise agreed, a transferor's duty to transfer a security under a contract of purchase is not fulfilled until he:

(a) places a certificated security in form to be negotiated by the purchaser in the possession of the purchaser or of a person designated by the purchaser;

(b) causes an uncertificated security to be registered in the name of the purchaser or a person designated by the purchaser; or

(c) if the purchaser requests, causes an acknowledgment to be made to the purchaser that a certificated or uncertificated security is held for the purchaser.

(3) Unless made on an exchange, a sale to a broker purchasing for his own account is within subsection (2) and not within subsection (1).

Section 8—315. Action Against Transferee Based Upon Wrongful Transfer

(1) Any person against whom the transfer of a security is wrongful for any reason, including his incapacity, as against anyone except a bona fide purchaser, may:

(a) reclaim possession of the certificated security wrongfully transferred;

(b) obtain possession of any new certificated security representing all or part of the same rights;

(c) compel the origination of an instruction to transfer to him or a person designated by him an uncertificated security constituting all or part of the same rights; or

(d) have damages.

(2) If the transfer is wrongful because of an unauthorized indorsement of a certificated security, the owner may also reclaim or obtain possession of the security or a new certificated security, even from a bona fide purchaser, if the ineffectiveness of the purported indorsement can be asserted against him under the provisions of this Article on unauthorized indorsements (Section 8—311).

(3) The right to obtain or reclaim possession of a certificated security or to compel the origination of a transfer instruction may be specifically enforced and the transfer of a certificated or uncertificated security enjoined and a certificated security impounded pending the litigation.

Section 8—316. Purchaser's Right to Requisites for Registration of Transfer, Pledge, or Release on Books

Unless otherwise agreed, the transferor of a certificated security or the transferor, pledgor, or pledgee of an uncertificated security on due demand must supply his purchaser with any proof of his authority to transfer, pledge, or release or with any other requisite necessary to obtain registration of the transfer, pledge, or release of the security; but if the transfer, pledge, or release is not for value, a transferor, pledgor, or pledgee need not do so unless the purchaser furnishes the necessary expenses. Failure within a reasonable time to comply with a demand made gives the purchaser the right to reject or rescind the transfer, pledge, or release.

Section 8—317. Creditors' Rights

(1) Subject to the exceptions in subsections (3) and (4), no attachment or levy upon a certificated security or any share or other interest represented thereby which is outstanding is valid until the security is actually seized by the officer making the attachment or levy, but a certificated security which has been surrendered to the issuer may be reached by a creditor by legal process at the issuer's chief executive office in the United States.

(2) An uncertificated security registered in the name of the debtor may not be reached by a creditor except by legal process at the issuer's chief executive office in the United States.

(3) The interest of a debtor in a certificated security that is in the possession of a secured party not a financial intermediary or in an uncertificated security registered in the name of a secured party not a financial intermediary (or in the name of a nominee of the secured party) may be reached by a creditor by legal process upon the secured party.

(4) The interest of a debtor in a certificated security that is in the possession of or registered in the name of a financial intermediary or in an uncertificated security registered in the name of a financial intermediary may be reached by a creditor by legal process upon the financial intermediary on whose books the interest of the debtor appears.

(5) Unless otherwise provided by law, a creditor's lien upon the interest of a debtor in a security obtained pursuant to subsection (3) or (4) is not a restraint on the transfer of the security, free of the lien, to a third party for new value; but in the event of a transfer, the lien applies to the proceeds of the transfer in the hands of the secured party or financial intermediary, subject to any claims having priority.

(6) A creditor whose debtor is the owner of a security is entitled to aid from courts of appropriate jurisdiction, by injunction or otherwise, in reaching the security or in satisfying the claim by means allowed at law or in equity in regard to property that cannot readily be reached by ordinary legal process.

Section 8—318. No Conversion by Good Faith Conduct

An agent or bailee who in good faith (including observance of reasonable commercial standards if he is in the business of buying, selling, or otherwise dealing with securities) has received certificated securities and sold, pledged, or delivered them or has sold or caused the transfer or pledge of uncertificated securities over which he had control according to the instructions of his principal, is not liable for conversion or for participation in breach of fiduciary duty although the principal had no right so to deal with the securities.

Section 8—319. Statute of Frauds

A contract for the sale of securities is not enforceable by way of action or defense unless:

(a) there is some writing signed by the party against whom enforcement is sought or by his authorized agent or broker, sufficient to indicate that a contract has been made for sale of a stated quantity of described securities at a defined or stated price;

(b) delivery of a certificated security or transfer instruction has been accepted, or transfer of an uncertificated security has been registered and the transferee has failed to send written objection to the issuer within 10 days after receipt of the initial transaction statement confirming the registration, or payment has been made, but the contract is enforceable under this provision only to the extent of the delivery, registration, or payment;

(c) within a reasonable time a writing in confirmation of the sale or purchase and sufficient against the sender under paragraph (a) has been received by the party against whom enforcement is sought and he has failed to send written objection to its contents within 10 days after its receipt; or

(d) the party against whom enforcement is sought admits in his pleading, testimony, or otherwise in court that a contract was made for the sale of a stated quantity of described securities at a defined or stated price.

Section 8—320. Transfer or Pledge Within Central Depository System

(1) In addition to other methods, a transfer, pledge, or release of a security or any interest therein may be effected by the making of appropriate entries on the books of a clearing corporation reducing the account of the transferor, pledgor, or pledgee and increasing the account of the transferee, pledgee, or pledgor by the amount of the obligation or the number of shares or rights transferred, pledged, or released, if the security is shown on the account of a transferor, pledgor, or pledgee on the books of the clearing corporation; is subject to the control of the clearing corporation; and

(a) if certificated,

    (i) is in the custody of the clearing corporation, another clearing corporation, a custodian bank, or a nominee of any of them; and

    (ii) is in bearer form or indorsed in blank by an appropriate person or registered in the name of the clearing corporation, a custodian bank, or a nominee of any of them; or

(b) if uncertificated, is registered in the name of the clearing corporation, another clearing corporation, a custodian bank, or a nominee of any of them.

(2) Under this section entries may be made with respect to like securities or interests therein as a part of a fungible bulk and may refer merely to a quantity of a particular security without reference to the name of the registered owner, certificate or bond number, or the like, and, in appropriate cases, may be on a net basis taking into account other transfers, pledges, or releases of the same security.

(3) A transfer under this section is effective (Section 8—313) and the purchaser acquires the rights of the transferor (Section 8—301). A pledge or release under this section is the transfer of a limited interest. If a pledge or the creation of a security interest is intended, the security interest is perfected at the time when both value is given by the pledgee and the appropriate entries are made (Section 8—321). A transferee or pledgee under this section may be a bona fide purchaser (Section 8—302).

(4) A transfer or pledge under this section is not a registration of transfer under Part 4.

(5) That entries made on the books of the clearing corporation as provided in subsection (1) are not appropriate does not affect the validity or effect of the entries or the liabilities or obligations of the clearing corporation to any person adversely affected thereby.

Section 8—321. Enforceability, Attachment, Perfection and Termination of Security Interests

(1) A security interest in a security is enforceable and can attach only if it is transferred to the secured party or a person designated by him pursuant to a provision of Section 8—313(1).

(2) A security interest so transferred pursuant to agreement by a transferor who has rights in the security to a transferee who has given value is a perfected security interest, but a security interest that has been transferred solely under paragraph (i) of Section 8—313(1) becomes unperfected after 21 days unless, within that time, the requirements for transfer under any other provision of Section 8—313(1) are satisfied.

(3) A security interest in a security is subject to the provisions of Article 9, but:

(a) no filing is required to perfect the security interest; and

(b) no written security agreement signed by the debtor is necessary to make the security interest enforceable, except as provided in paragraph (h), (i), or (j) of Section 8—313(1). The secured party has the rights and duties provided under Section 9—207, to the extent they are applicable, whether or not the security is certificated, and, if certificated, whether or not it is in his possession.

(4) Unless otherwise agreed, a security interest in a security is terminated by transfer to the debtor or a person designated by him pursuant to a provision of Section 8—313(1). If a security is thus transferred, the security interest, if not terminated, becomes unperfected unless the security is certificated and is delivered to the debtor for the purpose of ultimate sale or exchange or presentation, collection, renewal, or registration of transfer. In that case, the security interest becomes unperfected after 21 days unless, within that time, the security (or securities for which it has been exchanged) is transferred to the secured party or a person designated by him pursuant to a provision of Section 8—313(1).

Part 4 Registration

Section 8—401. Duty of Issuer to Register Transfer, Pledge, or Release

(1) If a certificated security in registered form is presented to the issuer with a request to register transfer or an instruction is presented to the issuer with a request

to register transfer, pledge, or release, the issuer shall register the transfer, pledge, or release as requested if:

    (a) the security is indorsed or the instruction was originated by the appropriate person or persons (Section 8—308);

    (b) reasonable assurance is given that those indorsements or instructions are genuine and effective (Section 8—402);

    (c) the issuer has no duty as to adverse claims or has discharged the duty (Section 8—403);

    (d) any applicable law relating to the collection of taxes has been complied with; and

    (e) the transfer, pledge, or release is in fact rightful or is to a bona fide purchaser.

(2) If an issuer is under a duty to register a transfer, pledge, or release of a security, the issuer is also liable to the person presenting a certificated security or an instruction for registration or his principal for loss resulting from any unreasonable delay in registration or from failure or refusal to register the transfer, pledge, or release.

Section 8—402. Assurance that Indorsements and Instructions Are Effective

(1) The issuer may require the following assurance that each necessary indorsement of a certificated security or each instruction (Section 8—308) is genuine and effective:

    (a) in all cases, a guarantee of the signature (Section 8—312(1) or (2)) of the person indorsing a certificated security or originating an instruction including, in the case of an instruction, a warranty of the taxpayer identification number or, in the absence thereof, other reasonable assurance of identity;

    (b) if the indorsement is made or the instruction is originated by an agent, appropriate assurance of authority to sign;

    (c) if the indorsement is made or the instruction is originated by a fiduciary, appropriate evidence of appointment or incumbency;

    (d) if there is more than one fiduciary, reasonable assurance that all who are required to sign have done so; and

    (e) if the indorsement is made or the instruction is originated by a person not covered by any of the foregoing, assurance appropriate to the case corresponding as nearly as may be to the foregoing.

(2) A "guarantee of the signature" in subsection (1) means a guarantee signed by or on behalf of a person reasonably believed by the issuer to be responsible. The issuer may adopt standards with respect to responsibility if they are not manifestly unreasonable.

(3) "Appropriate evidence of appointment or incumbency" in subsection (1) means:

    (a) in the case of a fiduciary appointed or qualified by a court, a certificate issued by or under the direction or supervision of that court or an officer thereof and dated within 60 days before the date of presentation for transfer, pledge, or release; or

    (b) in any other case, a copy of a document showing the appointment or a certificate issued by or on behalf of a person reasonably believed by the issuer to be responsible or, in the absence of that document or certificate, other evidence reasonably deemed by the issuer to be appropriate. The issuer may adopt standards with respect to the evidence if they are not manifestly unreasonable. The issuer is not charged with notice of the contents of any document obtained pursuant to this paragraph (b) except to the extent that the contents relate directly to the appointment or incumbency.

(4) The issuer may elect to require reasonable assurance beyond that specified in this section, but if it does so and, for a purpose other than that specified in subsection (3)(b), both requires and obtains a copy of a will, trust, indenture, articles of co-partnership, by-laws, or other controlling instrument, it is charged with notice of all matters contained therein affecting the transfer, pledge, or release.

Section 8—403. Issuer's Duty as to Adverse Claims

(1) An issuer to whom a certificated security is presented for registration shall inquire into adverse claims if:

    (a) a written notification of an adverse claim is received at a time and in a manner affording the issuer a reasonable opportunity to act on it prior to the issuance of a new, reissued, or re-registered certificated security, and the notification identifies the claimant, the registered owner, and the issue of which the security is a part, and provides an address for communications directed to the claimant; or

(b) the issuer is charged with notice of an adverse claim from a controlling instrument it has elected to require under Section 8—402(4).

(2) The issuer may discharge any duty of inquiry by any reasonable means, including notifying an adverse claimant by registered or certified mail at the address furnished by him or, if there be no such address, at his residence or regular place of business that the certificated security has been presented for registration of transfer by a named person, and that the transfer will be registered unless within 30 days from the date of mailing the notification, either:

(a) an appropriate restraining order, injunction, or other process issues from a court of competent jurisdiction; or

(b) there is filed with the issuer an idemnity bond, sufficient in the issuer's judgment to protect the issuer and any transfer agent, registrar, or other agent of the issuer involved from any loss it or they may suffer by complying with the adverse claim.

(3) Unless an issuer is charged with notice of an adverse claim from a controlling instrument which it has elected to require under Section 8—402(4) or receives notification of an adverse claim under subsection (1), if a certificated security presented for registration is indorsed by the appropriate person or persons the issuer is under no duty to inquire into adverse claims. In particular:

(a) an issuer registering a certificated security in the name of a person who is a fiduciary or who is described as a fiduciary is not bound to inquire into the existence, extent, or correct description of the fiduciary relationship; and thereafter the issuer may assume without inquiry that the newly registered owner continues to be the fiduciary until the issuer receives written notice that the fiduciary is no longer acting as such with respect to the particular security;

(b) an issuer registering transfer on an indorsement by a fiduciary is not bound to inquire whether the transfer is made in compliance with a controlling instrument or with the law of the state having jurisdiction of the fiduciary relationship, including any law requiring the fiduciary to obtain court approval of the transfer; and

(c) the issuer is not charged with notice of the contents of any court record or file or other recorded or unrecorded document even though the document is in its possession and even though the transfer is made on the indorsement of a fiduciary to the fiduciary himself or to his nominee.

(4) An issuer is under no duty as to adverse claims with respect to an uncertificated security except:

(a) claims embodied in a restraining order, injunction, or other legal process served upon the issuer if the process was served at a time and in a manner affording the issuer a reasonable opportunity to act on it in accordance with the requirements of subsection (5);

(b) claims of which the issuer has received a written notification from the registered owner or the registered pledgee if the notification was received at a time and in a manner affording the issuer a reasonable opportunity to act on it in accordance with the requirements of subsection (5);

(c) claims (including restrictions on transfer not imposed by the issuer) to which the registration of transfer to the present registered owner was subject and were so noted in the initial transaction statement sent to him; and

(d) claims as to which an issuer is charged with notice from a controlling instrument it has elected to require under Section 8—402(4).

(5) If the issuer of an uncertificated security is under a duty as to an adverse claim, he discharges that duty by:

(a) including a notation of the claim in any statements sent with respect to the security under Sections 8—408 (3), (6), and (7); and

(b) refusing to register the transfer or pledge of the security unless the nature of the claim does not preclude transfer or pledge subject thereto.

(6) If the transfer or pledge of the security is registered subject to an adverse claim, a notation of the claim must be included in the initial transaction statement and all subsequent statements sent to the transferee and pledgee under Section 8—408.

(7) Notwithstanding subsections (4) and (5), if an uncertificated security was subject to a registered pledge at the time the issuer first came under a duty as to a particular adverse claim, the issuer has no duty as to that claim if transfer of the security is requested by the registered pledgee or an appropriate person acting for the registered pledgee unless:

(a) the claim was embodied in legal process which expressly provides otherwise;

(b) the claim was asserted in a written notification from the registered pledgee;

(c) the claim was one as to which the issuer was charged with notice from a controlling instrument it required under Section 8—402(4) in connection with the pledgee's request for transfer; or

(d) the transfer requested is to the registered owner.

Section 8—404. Liability and Non-Liability for Registration

(1) Except as provided in any law relating to the collection of taxes, the issuer is not liable to the owner, pledgee, or any other person suffering loss as a result of the registration of a transfer, pledge, or release of a security if:

(a) there were on or with a certificated security the necessary indorsements or the issuer had received an instruction originated by an appropriate person (Section 8—308); and

(b) the issuer had no duty as to adverse claims or has discharged the duty (Section 8—403).

(2) If an issuer has registered a transfer of a certificated security to a person not entitled to it, the issuer on demand shall deliver a like security to the true owner unless:

(a) the registration was pursuant to subsection (1);

(b) the owner is precluded from asserting any claim for registering the transfer under Section 8—405(1); or

(c) the delivery would result in overissue, in which case the issuer's liability is governed by Section 8—104.

(3) If an issuer has improperly registered a transfer, pledge, or release of an uncertificated security, the issuer on demand from the injured party shall restore the records as to the injured party to the condition that would have obtained if the improper registration had not been made unless:

(a) the registration was pursuant to subsection (1); or

(b) the registration would result in overissue, in which case the issuer's liability is governed by Section 8—104.

Section 8—405. Lost, Destroyed, and Stolen Certificated Securities

(1) If a certificated security has been lost, apparently destroyed, or wrongfully taken, and the owner fails to notify the issuer of that fact within a reasonable time after he has notice of it and the issuer registers a transfer of the security before receiving notification, the owner is precluded from asserting against the issuer any claim for registering the transfer under Section 8—404 or any claim to a new security under this section.

(2) If the owner of a certificated security claims that the security has been lost, destroyed, or wrongfully taken, the issuer shall issue a new certificated security or, at the option of the issuer, an equivalent uncertificated security in place of the original security if the owner:

(a) so requests before the issuer has notice that the security has been acquired by a bona fide purchaser;

(b) files with the issuer a sufficient indemnity bond; and

(c) satisfies any other reasonable requirements imposed by the issuer.

(3) If, after the issue of a new certificated or uncertificated security, a bona fide purchaser of the original certificated security presents it for registration of transfer, the issuer shall register the transfer unless registration would result in overissue, in which event the issuer's liability is governed by Section 8—104. In addition to any rights on the indemnity bond, the issuer may recover the new certificated security from the person to whom it was issued or any person taking under him except a bona fide purchaser or may cancel the uncertificated security unless a bona fide purchaser or any person taking under a bona fide purchaser is then the registered owner or registered pledgee thereof.

Section 8—406. Duty of Authenticating Trustee, Transfer Agent, or Registrar

(1) If a person acts as authenticating trustee, transfer agent, registrar, or other agent for an issuer in the registration of transfers of its certificated securities or in the registration of transfers, pledges, and releases of its uncertificated securities, in the issue of new securities, or in the cancellation of surrendered securities:

> (a) he is under a duty to the issuer to exercise good faith and due diligence in performing his functions; and

> (b) with regard to the particular functions he performs, he has the same obligation to the holder or owner of a certificated security or to the owner or pledgee of an uncertificated security and has the same rights and privileges as the issuer has in regard to those functions.

(2) Notice to an authenticating trustee, transfer agent, registrar or other agent is notice to the issuer with respect to the functions performed by the agent.

Section 8—407. Exchangeability of Securities

(1) No issuer is subject to the requirements of this section unless it regularly maintains a system for issuing the class of securities involved under which both certificated and uncertificated securities are regularly issued to the category of owners, which includes the person in whose name the new security is to be registered.

(2) Upon surrender of a certificated security with all necessary indorsements and presentation of a written request by the person surrendering the security, the issuer, if he has no duty as to adverse claims or has discharged the duty (Section 8—403), shall issue to the person or a person designated by him an equivalent uncertificated security subject to all liens, restrictions, and claims that were noted on the certificated security.

(3) Upon receipt of a transfer instruction originated by an appropriate person who so requests, the issuer of an uncertificated security shall cancel the uncertificated security and issue an equivalent certificated security on which must be noted conspicuously any liens and restrictions of the issuer and any adverse claims (as to which the issuer has a duty under Section 8—403(4)) to which the uncertificated security was subject. The certificated security shall be registered in the name of and delivered to:

> (a) the registered owner, if the uncertificated security was not subject to a registered pledge; or

> (b) the registered pledgee, if the uncertificated security was subject to a registered pledge.

Section 8—408. Statements of Uncertificated Securities

(1) Within 2 business days after the transfer of an uncertificated security has been registered, the issuer shall send to the new registered owner and, if the security has been transferred subject to a registered pledge, to the registered pledgee a written statement containing:

> (a) a description of the issue of which the uncertificated security is a part;

> (b) the number of shares or units transferred;

> (c) the name and address and any taxpayer identification number of the new registered owner and, if the security has been transferred subject to a registered pledge, the name and address and any taxpayer identification number of the registered pledgee;

> (d) a notation of any liens and restrictions of the issuer and any adverse claims (as to which the issuer has a duty under Section 8—403(4)) to which the uncertificated security

is or may be subject at the time of registration or a statement that there are none of those liens, restrictions, or adverse claims; and

(e) the date the transfer was registered.

(2) Within 2 business days after the pledge of an uncertificated security has been registered, the issuer shall send to the registered owner and the registered pledgee a written statement containing:

(a) a description of the issue of which the uncertificated security is a part;

(b) the number of shares or units pledged;

(c) the name and address and any taxpayer identification number of the registered owner and the registered pledgee;

(d) a notation of any liens and restrictions of the issuer and any adverse claims (as to which the issuer has a duty under Section 8—403(4)) to which the uncertificated security is or may be subject at the time of registration or a statement that there are none of those liens, restrictions, or adverse claims; and

(e) the date the pledge was registered.

(3) Within 2 business days after the release from pledge of an uncertificated security has been registered, the issuer shall send to the registered owner and the pledgee whose interest was released a written statement containing:

(a) a description of the issue of which the uncertificated security is a part;

(b) the number of shares or units released from pledge;

(c) the name and address and any taxpayer identification number of the registered owner and the pledgee whose interest was released;

(d) a notation of any liens and restrictions of the issuer and any adverse claims (as to which the issuer has a duty under Section 8—403(4)) to which the uncertificated security is or may be subject at the time of registration

or a statement that there are none of those liens, restrictions, or adverse claims; and

(e) the date the release was registered.

(4) An "initial transaction statement" is the statement sent to:

(a) the new registered owner and, if applicable, to the registered pledgee pursuant to subsection (1);

(b) the registered pledgee pursuant to subsection (2); or

(c) the registered owner pursuant to subsection (3).

Each initial transaction statement shall be signed by or on behalf of the issuer and must be identified as "Initial Transaction Statement."

(5) Within 2 business days after the transfer of an uncertificated security has been registered, the issuer shall send to the former registered owner and the former registered pledgee, if any, a written statement containing:

(a) a description of the issue of which the uncertificated security is a part;

(b) the number of shares or units transferred;

(c) the name and address and any taxpayer identification number of the former registered owner and of any former registered pledgee; and

(d) the date the transfer was registered.

(6) At periodic intervals no less frequent than annually and at any time upon the reasonable written request of the registered owner, the issuer shall send to the registered owner of each uncertificated security a dated written statement containing:

(a) a description of the issue of which the uncertificated security is a part;

(b) the name and address and any taxpayer identification number of the registered owner;

(c) the number of shares or units of the uncertificated security registered in the name of the registered owner on the date of the statement;

(d) the name and address and any taxpayer identification number of any registered pledgee and the number of shares of units subject to the pledge; and

(e) a notation of any liens and restrictions of the issuer and any adverse claims (as to which the issuer has a duty under Section 8—403(4)) to which the uncertificated security is or may be subject or a statement that there are none of those liens, restrictions, or adverse claims.

(7) At periodic intervals no less frequent than annually and at any time upon the reasonable written request of the registered pledgee, the issuer shall send to the registered pledgee of each uncertificated security a dated written statement containing:

(a) a description of the issue of which the uncertificated security is a part;

(b) the name and address and any taxpayer identification number of the registered owner;

(c) the name and address and any taxpayer identification number of the registered pledgee;

(d) the number of shares or units subject to the pledge; and

(e) a notation of any liens and restrictions of the issuer and any adverse claims (as to which the issuer has a duty under Section 8—403(4)) to which the uncertificated security is or may be subject or a statement that there are none of those liens, restrictions, or adverse claims.

(8) If the issuer sends the statements described in subsections (6) and (7) at periodic intervals no less frequent than quarterly, the issuer is not obliged to send additional statements upon request unless the owner or pledgee requesting them pays to the issuer the reasonable cost of furnishing them.

(9) Each statement sent pursuant to this section must bear a conspicuous legend reading substantially as follows: "This statement is merely a record of the rights of the addressee as of the time of its issuance. Delivery of this statement, of itself, confers no rights on the recipient. This statement is neither a negotiable instrument nor a security."

Article 9   Secured Transactions; Sales of Accounts and Chattel Paper

Part 1   Short Title, Applicability and Definitions

Section 9—101.   Short Title

This Article shall be known and may be cited as Uniform Commercial Code—Secured Transactions.

Section 9—102.   Policy and Subject Matter of Article

(1) Except as otherwise provided in Section 9—104 on excluded transactions, this Article applies

(a) to any transaction (regardless of its form) which is intended to create a security interest in personal property or fixtures including goods, documents, instruments, general intangibles, chattel paper or accounts; and also

(b) to any sale of accounts or chattel paper.

(2) This Article applies to security interests created by contract including pledge, assignment, chattel mortgage, chattel trust, trust deed, factor's lien, equipment trust, conditional sale, trust receipt, other lien or title retention contract and lease or consignment intended as security. This Article does not apply to statutory liens except as provided in Section 9—310.

(3) The application of this Article to a security interest in a secured obligation is not affected by the fact that the obligation is itself secured by a transaction or interest to which this Article does not apply.

Note: *The adoption of this Article should be accompanied by the repeal of existing statutes dealing with conditional sales, trust receipts, factor's liens where the factor is given a nonpossessory lien, chattel mortgages, crop mortgages, mortgages on railroad equipment, assignment of accounts and generally statutes regulating security interests in personal property.*

Where the state has a retail installment selling act or small loan act, that legislation should be carefully examined to determine what changes in those acts are needed to conform them to this Article. This Article primarily sets out rules defining rights of a secured party against persons dealing with the debtor; it does not prescribe regulations and controls which may be necessary to curb abuses arising in the small loan business or in the financing of consumer purchases on credit.

Accordingly there is no intention to repeal existing regulatory acts in those fields by enactment or re-enactment of Article 9. See Section 9—203(4) and the Note thereto.

Section 9—103. Perfection of Security Interest in Multiple State Transactions

(1) Documents, instruments and ordinary goods.

    (a) This subsection applies to documents and instruments and to goods other than those covered by a certificate of title described in subsection (2), mobile goods described in subsection (3), and minerals described in subsection (5).

    (b) Except as otherwise provided in this subsection, perfection and the effect of perfection or non-perfection of a security interest in collateral are governed by the law of the jurisdiction where the collateral is when the last event occurs on which is based the assertion that the security interest is perfected or unperfected.

    (c) If the parties to a transaction creating a purchase money security interest in goods in one jurisdiction understand at the time that the security interest attaches that the goods will be kept in another jurisdiction, then the law of the other jurisdiction governs the perfection and the effect of perfection or non-perfection of the security interest from the time it attaches until thirty days after the debtor receives possession of the goods and thereafter if the goods are taken to the other jurisdiction before the end of the thirty-day period.

    (d) When collateral is brought into and kept in this state while subject to a security interest perfected under the law of the jurisdiction from which the collateral was removed, the security interest remains perfected, but if action is required by Part 3 of this Article to perfect the security interest,

        (i) if the action is not taken before the expiration of the period of perfection in the other jurisdiction or the end of four months after the collateral is brought into this state, whichever period first expires, the security interest becomes unperfected at the end of that period and is thereafter deemed to have been unperfected as against a person who became a purchaser after removal;

        (ii) if the action is taken before the expiration of the period specified in subparagraph (i), the security interest continues perfected thereafter;

        (iii) for the purpose of priority over a buyer of consumer goods (subsection (2) of Section 9—307), the period of the effectiveness of a filing in the jurisdiction from which the collateral is removed is governed by the rules with respect to perfection in subparagraphs (i) and (ii).

(2) Certificate of title.

    (a) This subsection applies to goods covered by a certificate of title issued under a statute of this state or of another jurisdiction under the law of which indication of a security interest on the certificate is required as a condition of perfection.

    (b) Except as otherwise provided in this subsection, perfection and the effect of perfection or non-perfection of the security interest are governed by the law (including the conflict of laws rules) of the jurisdiction issuing the certificate until four months after the goods are removed from that jurisdiction and thereafter until the goods are registered in another jurisdiction, but in any event not beyond surrender of the certificate. After the expiration of that period, the goods are not covered by the certificate of title within the meaning of this section.

    (c) Except with respect to the rights of a buyer described in the next paragraph, a security interest, perfected in another jurisdiction otherwise than by notation on a certificate of title, in goods brought into this state and thereafter covered by a certificate of title issued by this state is subject to the rules stated in paragraph (d) of subsection (1).

(d) If goods are brought into this state while a security interest therein is perfected in any manner under the law of the jurisdiction from which the goods are removed and a certificate of title is issued by this state and the certificate does not show that the goods are subject to the security interest or that they may be subject to security interests not shown on the certificate, the security interest is subordinate to the rights of a buyer of the goods who is not in the business of selling goods of that kind to the extent that he gives value and receives delivery of the goods after issuance of the certificate and without knowledge of the security interest.

(3) Accounts, general intangibles and mobile goods.

(a) This subsection applies to accounts (other than an account described in subsection (5) on minerals) and general intangibles (other than uncertificated securities) and to goods which are mobile and which are of a type normally used in more than one jurisdiction, such as motor vehicles, trailers, rolling stock, airplanes, shipping containers, road building and construction machinery and commercial harvesting machinery and the like, if the goods are equipment or are inventory leased or held for lease by the debtor to others, and are not covered by a certificate of title described in subsection (2).

(b) The law (including the conflict of laws rules) of the jurisdiction in which the debtor is located governs the perfection and the effect of perfection or non-perfection of the security interest.

(c) If, however, the debtor is located in a jurisdiction which is not a part of the United States, and which does not provide for perfection of the security interest by filing or recording in that jurisdiction, the law of the jurisdiction in the United States in which the debtor has its major executive office governs the perfection and the effect of perfection or non-perfection of the security interest through filing. In the alternative, if the debtor is located in a jurisdiction which is not a part of the United States or Canada and the collateral is accounts or general intangibles for money due or to become due, the security interest may be perfected by notification to the account debtor. As used in this paragraph, "United States" includes its territories and possessions and the Commonwealth of Puerto Rico.

(d) A debtor shall be deemed located at his place of business if he has one, at his chief executive office if he has more than one place of business, otherwise at his residence. If, however, the debtor is a foreign air carrier under the Federal Aviation Act of 1958, as amended, it shall be deemed located at the designated office of the agent upon whom service of process may be made on behalf of the foreign air carrier.

(e) A security interest perfected under the law of the jurisdiction of the location of the debtor is perfected until the expiration of four months after a change of the debtor's location to another jurisdiction, or until perfection would have ceased by the law of the first jurisdiction, whichever period first expires. Unless perfected in the new jurisdiction before the end of that period, it becomes unperfected thereafter and is deemed to have been unperfected as against a person who became a purchaser after the change.

(4) Chattel paper. The rules stated for goods in subsection (1) apply to a possessory security interest in chattel paper. The rules stated for accounts in subsection (3) apply to a non-possessory security interest in chattel paper, but the security interest may not be perfected by notification to the account debtor.

(5) Minerals. Perfection and the effect of perfection or non-perfection of a security interest which is created by a debtor who has an interest in minerals or the like (including oil and gas) before extraction and which attaches thereto as extracted, or which attaches to an account resulting from the sale thereof at the wellhead or minehead are governed by the law (including the conflict of laws rules) of the jurisdiction wherein the wellhead or minehead is located.

(6) Uncertificated securities. The law (including the conflict of laws rules) of the jurisdiction of organization of the issuer governs the perfection and the effect of perfection or non-perfection of a security interest in uncertificated securities.

Section 9—104. Transactions Excluded From Article

This Article does not apply

    (a) to a security interest subject to any statute of the United States, to the extent that such statute governs the rights of parties to and third parties affected by transactions in particular types of property; or

    (b) to a landlord's lien; or

    (c) to a lien given by statute or other rule of law for services or materials except as provided in Section 9—310 on priority of such liens; or

    (d) to a transfer of a claim for wages, salary or other compensation of an employee; or

    (e) to a transfer by a government or governmental subdivision or agency; or

    (f) to a sale of accounts or chattel paper as part of a sale of the business out of which they arose, or an assignment of accounts or chattel paper which is for the purpose of collection only, or a transfer of a right to payment under a contract to an assignee who is also to do the performance under the contract or a transfer of a single account to an assignee in whole or partial satisfaction of a preexisting indebtedness; or

    (g) to a transfer of an interest in or claim in or under any policy of insurance, except as provided with respect to proceeds (Section 9—306) and priorities in proceeds (Section 9—312); or

    (h) to a right represented by a judgment (other than a judgment taken on a right to payment which was collateral); or

    (i) to any right of set-off; or

    (j) except to the extent that provision is made for fixtures in Section 9—313, to the creation or transfer of an interest in or lien on real estate, including a lease or rents thereunder; or

    (k) to a transfer in whole or in part of any claim arising out of tort; or

    (l) to a transfer of an interest in any deposit account (subsection (1) of Section 9—105), except as provided with respect to proceeds (Section 9—306) and priorities in proceeds (Section 9—312).

Section 9—105. Definitions and Index of Definitions

(1) In this Article unless the context otherwise requires:

    (a) "Account debtor" means the person who is obligated on an account, chattel paper or general intangible;

    (b) "Chattel paper" means a writing or writings which evidence both a monetary obligation and a security interest in or a lease of specific goods, but a charter or other contract involving the use or hire of a vessel is not chattel paper. When a transaction is evidenced both by such a security agreement or a lease and by an instrument or a series of instruments, the group of writings taken together constitutes chattel paper;

    (c) "Collateral" means the property subject to a security interest, and includes accounts and chattel paper which have been sold;

    (d) "Debtor" means the person who owes payment or other performance of the obligation secured, whether or not he owns or has rights in the collateral, and includes the seller of accounts or chattel paper. Where the debtor and the owner of the collateral are not the same person, the term "debtor" means the owner of the collateral in any provision of the Article dealing with the collateral, the obligor in any provision dealing with the obligation, and may include both where the context so requires;

    (e) "Deposit account" means a demand, time, savings, passbook or like account maintained with a bank, savings and loan association, credit union or like organization, other than an account evidenced by a certificate of deposit;

    (f) "Document" means document of title as defined in the general definitions of Article 1

(Section 1—201), and a receipt of the kind described in subsection (2) of Section 7—201;

(g) "Encumbrance" includes real estate mortgages and other liens on real estate and all other rights in real estate that are not ownership interests;

(h) "Goods" includes all things which are movable at the time the security interest attaches or which are fixtures (Section 9—313), but does not include money, documents, instruments, accounts, chattel paper, general intangibles, or minerals or the like (including oil and gas) before extraction. "Goods" also includes standing timber which is to be cut and removed under a conveyance or contract for sale, the unborn young of animals, and growing crops;

(i) "Instrument" means a negotiable instrument (defined in Section 3—104), or a certificated security (defined in Section 8—102) or any other writing which evidences a right to the payment of money and is not itself a security agreement or lease and is of a type which is in ordinary course of business transferred by delivery with any necessary indorsement or assignment;

(j) "Mortgage" means a consensual interest created by a real estate mortgage, a trust deed on real estate, or the like;

(k) An advance is made "pursuant to commitment" if the secured party has bound himself to make it, whether or not a subsequent event of default or other event not within his control has relieved or may relieve him from his obligation;

(l) "Security agreement" means an agreement which creates or provides for a security interest;

(m) "Secured party" means a lender, seller or other person in whose favor there is a security interest, including a person to whom accounts or chattel paper have been sold. When the holders of obligations issued under an indenture of trust, equipment trust agreement or the like are represented by a trustee or other person, the representative is the secured party;

(n) "Transmitting utility" means any person primarily engaged in the railroad, street railway or trolley bus business, the electric or electronics communications transmission business, the transmission of goods by pipeline, or the transmission or the production and transmission of electricity, steam, gas or water, or the provision of sewer service.

(2) Other definitions applying to this Article and the sections in which they appear are:

"Account." Section 9—106.
"Attach." Section 9—203.
"Construction mortgage." Section 9—313 (1).
"Consumer goods." Section 9—109 (1).
"Equipment." Section 9—109 (2).
"Farm products." Section 9—109 (3).
"Fixture." Section 9—313 (1).
"Fixture filing." Section 9—313 (1).
"General intangibles." Section 9—106.
"Inventory." Section 9—109 (4).
"Lien creditor." Section 9—301 (3).
"Proceeds." Section 9—306 (1).
"Purchase money security interest." Section 9—107.
"United States." Section 9—103.

(3) The following definitions in other Articles apply to this Article:

"Check." Section 3—104.
"Contract for sale." Section 2—106.
"Holder in due course." Section 3—302.
"Note." Section 3—104.
"Sale." Section 2—106.

(4) In addition Article 1 contains general definitions and principles of construction and interpretation applicable throughout this Article.

Section 9—106. Definitions: "Account"; "General Intangibles"

"Account" means any right to payment for goods sold or leased or for services rendered which is not evidenced by an instrument or chattel paper, whether or not it has been earned by performance. "General intangibles" means any personal property (including things in action) other than goods, accounts, chattel paper, documents, instruments, and money. All rights to payment earned or unearned under a charter or other contract involving the use or hire of a vessel and all rights incident to the chart or contract are accounts.

Section 9—107. Definitions: "Purchase Money Security Interest"

A security interest is a "purchase money security interest" to the extent that it is

   (a) taken or retained by the seller of the collateral to secure all or part of its price; or

   (b) taken by a person who by making advances or incurring an obligation gives value to enable the debtor to acquire rights in or the use of collateral if such value is in fact so used.

Section 9—108. When After-Acquired Collateral Not Security for Antecedent Debt

Where a secured party makes an advance, incurs an obligation, releases a perfected security interest, or otherwise gives new value which is to be secured in whole or in part by after-acquired property his security interest in the after-acquired collateral shall be deemed to be taken for new value and not as security for an antecedent debt if the debtor acquires his rights in such collateral either in the ordinary course of his business or under a contract of purchase made pursuant to the security agreement within a reasonable time after new value is given.

Section 9—109. Classification of Goods; "Consumer Goods"; "Equipment"; "Farm Products"; "Inventory"

Goods are

(1) "consumer goods" if they are used or bought for use primarily for personal, family or household purposes;

(2) "equipment" if they are used or bought for use primarily in business (including farming or a profession) or by a debtor who is a non-profit organization or a governmental subdivision or agency or if the goods are not included in the definitions of inventory, farm products or consumer goods;

(3) "farm products" if they are crops or livestock or supplies used or produced in farming operations or if they are products of crops or livestock in their unmanufactured states (such as ginned cotton, wool-clip, maple syrup, milk and eggs), and if they are in the possession of a debtor engaged in raising, fattening, grazing or

other farming operations. If goods are farm products they are neither equipment nor inventory;

(4) "inventory" if they are held by a person who holds them for sale or lease or to be furnished under contracts of service or if he has so furnished them, or if they are raw materials, work in process or materials used or consumed in a business. Inventory of a person is not to be classified as his equipment.

Section 9—110. Sufficiency of Description

For the purposes of this Article any description of personal property or real estate is sufficient whether or not it is specific if it reasonably identifies what is described.

Section 9—111. Applicability of Bulk Transfer Laws

The creation of a security interest is not a bulk transfer under Article 6 (see Section 6—103).

Section 9—112. Where Collateral Is Not Owned by Debtor

Unless otherwise agreed, when a secured party knows that collateral is owned by a person who is not the debtor, the owner of the collateral is entitled to receive from the secured party any surplus under Section 9—502(2) or under Section 9—504(1), and is not liable for the debt or for any deficiency after resale, and he has the same right as the debtor

   (a) to receive statements under Section 9—208;

   (b) to receive notice of and to object to a secured party's proposal to retain the collateral in satisfaction of the indebtedness under Section 9—505;

   (c) to redeem the collateral under Section 9—506;

   (d) to obtain injunctive or other relief under Section 9—507(1); and

   (e) to recover losses caused to him under Section 9—208(2).

Section 9—113. Security Interests Arising Under Article on Sales

A security interest arising solely under the Article on Sales (Article 2) is subject to the provisions of this Article except that to the extent that and so long as the debtor does not have or does not lawfully obtain possession of the goods

> (a) no security agreement is necessary to make the security interest enforceable; and
>
> (b) no filing is required to perfect the security interest; and
>
> (c) the rights of the secured party on default by the debtor are governed by the Article on Sales (Article 2).

Section 9—114. Consignment

(1) A person who delivers goods under a consignment which is not a security interest and who would be required to file under this Article by paragraph (3) (c) of Section 2—326 has priority over a secured party who is or becomes a creditor of the consignee and who would have a perfected security interest in the goods if they were the property of the consignee, and also has priority with respect to identifiable cash proceeds received on or before delivery of the goods to a buyer, if

> (a) the consignor complies with the filing provision of the Article on Sales with respect to consignments (paragraph (3) (c) of Section 2—326) before the consignee receives possession of the goods; and
>
> (b) the consignor gives notification in writing to the holder of the security interest if the holder has filed a financing statement covering the same types of goods before the date of the filing made by the consignor; and
>
> (c) the holder of the security interest receives the notification within five years before the consignee receives possession of the goods; and
>
> (d) the notification states that the consignor expects to deliver goods on consignment to the consignee, describing the goods by item or type.

(2) In the case of a consignment which is not a security interest and in which the requirements of the preceding subsection have not been met, a person who delivers goods to another is subordinate to a person who would have a perfected security interest in the goods if they were the property of the debtor.

Part 2   Validity of Security Agreement and Rights of Parties Thereto

Section 9—201.   General Validity of Security Agreement

Except as otherwise provided by this Act a security agreement is effective according to its terms between the parties, against purchasers of the collateral and against creditors. Nothing in this Article validates any charge or practice illegal under any statute or regulation thereunder governing usury, small loans, retail installment sales, or the like, or extends the application of any such statute or regulation to any transaction not otherwise subject thereto.

Section 9—202.   Title to Collateral Immaterial

Each provision of this Article with regard to rights, obligations and remedies applies whether title to collateral is in the secured party or in the debtor.

Section 9—203.   Attachment and Enforceability of Security Interest; Proceeds; Formal Requisites

(1) Subject to the provisions of Section 4—208 on the security interest of a collecting bank, Section 8—321 on security interests in securities and Section 9—113 on a security interest arising under the Article on Sales, a security interest is not enforceable against the debtor or third parties with respect to the collateral and does not attach unless:

> (a) the collateral is in the possession of the secured party pursuant to agreement, or the debtor has signed a security agreement which contains a description of the collateral and in addition, when the security interest covers crops growing or to be grown or timber to be cut, a description of the land concerned;
>
> (b) value has been given; and
>
> (c) the debtor has rights in the collateral.

(2) A security interest attaches when it becomes enforceable against the debtor with respect to the collateral. Attachment occurs as soon as all of the events specified in subsection (1) have taken place unless explicit agreement postpones the time of attaching.

(3) Unless otherwise agreed a security agreement gives the secured party the rights to proceeds provided by Section 9—306.

(4) A transaction, although subject to this Article, is also subject to . . . . *, and in the case of conflict between the provisions of this Article and any such statute, the provisions of such statute control. Failure to comply with any applicable statute has only the effect which is specified therein.

*Note: At * in subsection (4) insert reference to any local statute regulating small loans, retail installment sales and the like.*

The foregoing subsection (4) is designed to make it clear that certain transactions, although subject to this Article, must also comply with other applicable legislation.

This Article is designed to regulate all the "security" aspects of transactions within its scope. There is, however, much regulatory legislation, particularly in the consumer field, which supplements this Article and should not be repealed by its enactment. Examples are small loan acts, retail installment selling acts and the like. Such acts may provide for licensing and rate regulation and may prescribe particular forms of contract. Such provisions should remain in force despite the enactment of this Article. On the other hand if a retail installment selling act contains provisions on filing, rights on default, etc., such provisions should be repealed as inconsistent with this Article except that inconsistent provisions as to deficiencies, penalties, etc., in the Uniform Consumer Credit Code and other recent related legislation should remain because those statutes were drafted after the substantial enactment of the Article and with the intention of modifying certain provisions of this Article as to consumer credit.

Section 9—204. After-Acquired Property; Future Advances

(1) Except as provided in subsection (2), a security agreement may provide that any or all obligations covered by the security agreement are to be secured by after-acquired collateral.

(2) No security interest attaches under an after-acquired property clause to consumer goods other than accessions (Section 9—314) when given as additional security unless the debtor acquires rights in them within ten days after the secured party gives value.

(3) Obligations covered by a security agreement may include future advances or other value whether or not the advances or value are given pursuant to commitment (subsection (1) of Section 9—105).

Section 9—205. Use or Disposition of Collateral Without Accounting Permissible

A security interest is not invalid or fraudulent against creditors by reason of liberty in the debtor to use, commingle or dispose of all or part of the collateral (including returned or repossessed goods) or to collect or compromise accounts or chattel paper, or to accept the return of goods or make repossessions, or to use, commingle or dispose of proceeds, or by reason of the failure of the secured party to require the debtor to account for proceeds or replace collateral. This section does not relax the requirements of possession where perfection of a security interest depends upon possession of the collateral by the secured party or by a bailee.

Section 9—206. Agreement Not to Assert Defenses Against Assignee; Modification of Sales Warranties Where Security Agreement Exists

(1) Subject to any statute or decision which establishes a different rule for buyers or lessees of consumer goods, an agreement by a buyer or lessee that he will not assert against an assignee any claim or defense which he may have against the seller or lessor is enforceable by an assignee who takes his assignment for value, in good faith and without notice of a claim or defense, except as to defenses of a type which may be asserted against a holder in due course of a negotiable instrument under the Article on Commercial Paper (Article 3). A buyer who as part of one transaction signs both a negotiable instrument and a security agreement makes such an agreement.

(2) When a seller retains a purchase money security interest in goods the Article on Sales (Article 2) governs the sale and any disclaimer, limitation or modification of the seller's warranties.

Section 9—207. Rights and Duties When Collateral is in Secured Party's Possession

(1) A secured party must use reasonable care in the custody and preservation of collateral in his possession. In the case of an instrument or chattel paper reasonable care includes taking necessary steps to preserve rights against prior parties unless otherwise agreed.

(2) Unless otherwise agreed, when collateral is in the secured party's possession

(a) reasonable expenses (including the cost of any insurance and payment of taxes or other charges) incurred in the custody, preservation, use or operation of the collateral are chargeable to the debtor and are secured by the collateral;

(b) the risk of accidental loss or damage is on the debtor to the extent of any deficiency in any effective insurance coverage;

(c) the secured party may hold as additional security any increase or profits (except money) received from the collateral, but money so received, unless remitted to the debtor, shall be applied in reduction of the secured obligation;

(d) the secured party must keep the collateral identifiable but fungible collateral may be commingled;

(e) the secured party may repledge the collateral upon terms which do not impair the debtor's right to redeem it.

(3) A secured party is liable for any loss caused by his failure to meet any obligation imposed by the preceding subsections but does not lose his security interest.

(4) A secured party may use or operate the collateral for the purpose of preserving the collateral or its value or pursuant to the order of a court of appropriate jurisdiction or, except in the case of consumer goods, in the manner and to the extent provided in the security agreement.

Section 9—208.   Request for Statement of Account or List of Collateral

(1) A debtor may sign a statement indicating what he believes to be the aggregate amount of unpaid indebtedness as of a specified date and may send it to the secured party with a request that the statement be approved or corrected and returned to the debtor. When the security agreement or any other record kept by the secured party identifies the collateral a debtor may similarly request the secured party to approve or correct a list of the collateral.

(2) The secured party must comply with such a request within two weeks after receipt by sending a written correction or approval. If the secured party claims a security interest in all of a particular type of collateral owned by the debtor he may indicate that fact in his reply and need not approve or correct an itemized list of such collateral. If the secured party without reasonable excuse fails to comply he is liable for any loss caused to the debtor thereby; and if the debtor has properly included in his request a good faith statement of the obligation or a list of the collateral or both the secured party may claim a security interest only as shown in the statement against persons misled by his failure to comply. If he no longer has an interest in the obligation or collateral at the time the request is received he must disclose the name and address of any successor in interest known to him and he is liable for any loss caused to the debtor as a result of failure to disclose. A successor in interest is not subject to this section until a request is received by him.

(3) A debtor is entitled to such a statement once every six months without charge. The secured party may require payment of a charge not exceeding $10 for each additional statement furnished.

Part 3   Rights of Third Parties; Perfected and Unperfected Security Interests; Rules of Priority

Section 9—301.   Persons Who Take Priority Over Unperfected Security Interests; Rights of "Lien Creditor"

(1) Except as otherwise provided in subsection (2), an unperfected security interest is subordinate to the rights of

(a) persons entitled to priority under Section 9—312;

(b) a person who becomes a lien creditor before the security interest is perfected;

(c) in the case of goods, instruments, documents, and chattel paper, a person who is not a secured party and who is a transferee in bulk or other buyer not in ordinary course of business or is a buyer of farm products in ordinary course of business, to the extent that he gives value and receives delivery of the collateral without knowledge of the security interest and before it is perfected;

(d) in the case of accounts and general intangibles, a person who is not a secured party and who is a transferee to the extent that he gives value without knowledge of the security interest and before it is perfected.

(2) If the secured party files with respect to a purchase money security interest before or within ten days after the debtor receives possession of the collateral, he takes priority over the rights of a transferee in bulk or of a lien creditor which arise between the time the security interest attaches and the time of filing.

(3) A "lien creditor" means a creditor who has acquired a lien on the property involved by attachment, levy or the like and includes an assignee for benefit of creditors from the time of assignment, and a trustee in bankruptcy from the date of the filing of the petition or a receiver in equity from the time of appointment.

(4) A person who becomes a lien creditor while a security interest is perfected takes subject to the security interest only to the extent that it secures advances made before he becomes a lien creditor or within 45 days thereafter or made without knowledge of the lien or pursuant to a commitment entered into without knowledge of the lien.

Section 9—302. When Filing Is Required to Perfect Security Interest; Security Interests to Which Filing Provisions of This Article Do Not Apply

(1) A financing statement must be filed to perfect all security interests except the following:

(a) a security interest in collateral in possession of the secured party under Section 9—305;

(b) a security interest temporarily perfected in instruments or documents without delivery under Section 9—304 or in proceeds for a 10 day period under Section 9—306;

(c) a security interest created by an assignment of a beneficial interest in a trust or a decedent's estate;

(d) a purchase money security interest in consumer goods; but filing is required for a motor vehicle required to be registered; and fixture filing is required for priority over conflicting interests in fixtures to the extent provided in Section 9—313;

(e) an assignment of accounts which does not alone or in conjunction with other assignments to the same assignee transfer a significant part of the outstanding accounts of the assignor;

(f) a security interest of a collecting bank (Section 4—208) or in securities (Section 8—321) or arising under the Article on Sales (see Section 9—113) or covered in subsection (3) of this section;

(g) an assignment for the benefit of all the creditors of the tansferor, and subsequent transfers by the assignee thereunder.

(2) If a secured party assigns a perfected security interest, no filing under this Article is required in order to continue the perfected status of the security interest against creditors of and transferees from the original debtor.

(3) The filing of a financing statement otherwise required by this Article is not necessary or effective to perfect a security interest in property subject to

(a) a statute or treaty of the United States which provides for a national or international registration or a national or international certificate of title or which specifies a place of filing different from that specified in this Article for filing of the security interest; or

(b) the following statutes of this state; [list any certificate of title statute covering automobiles, trailers, mobile homes, boats, farm tractors, or the like, and any central filing statute*.]; but during any period in which collateral is inventory held for sale by a person who is in the business of selling goods of that kind, the filing provisions of this Article (Part 4) apply to a security interest in that collateral created by him as debtor; or

(c) a certificate of title statute of another jurisdiction under the law of which indication of a security interest on the certificate is required as a condition of perfection (subsection (2) of Section 9—103).

(4) Compliance with a statute or treaty described in subsection (3) is equivalent to the filing of a financing statement under this Article, and a security interest in

property subject to the statute or treaty can be perfected only by compliance therewith except as provided in Section 9—103 on multiple state transactions. Duration and renewal of perfection of a security interest perfected by compliance with the statute or treaty are governed by the provisions of the statute or treaty; in other respects the security interest is subject to this Article.

*Note: *It is recommended that the provisions of certificate of title acts for perfection of security interests by notation on the certificates should be amended to exclude coverage of inventory held for sale.*

Section 9—303. When Security Interest Is Perfected; Continuity of Perfection

(1) A security interest is perfected when it has attached and when all of the applicable steps required for perfection have been taken. Such steps are specified in Sections 9—302, 9—304, 9—305 and 9—306. If such steps are taken before the security interest attaches, it is perfected at the time when it attaches.

(2) If a security interest is originally perfected in any way permitted under this Article and is subsequently perfected in some other way under this Article, without an intermediate period when it was unperfected, the security interest shall be deemed to be perfected continuously for the purposes of this Article.

Section 9—304. Perfection of Security Interest in Instruments, Documents, and Goods Covered by Documents; Perfection by Permissive Filing; Temporary Perfection Without Filing or Transfer of Possession

(1) A security interest in chattel paper or negotiable documents may be perfected by filing. A security interest in money or instruments (other than certificated securities or instruments which constitute part of chattel paper) can be perfected only by the secured party's taking possession, except as provided in subsections (4) and (5) of this section and subsections (2) and (3) of Section 9—306 on proceeds.

(2) During the period that goods are in the possession of the issuer of a negotiable document therefor, a security interest in the goods is perfected by perfecting a security interest in the document, and any security interest in the goods otherwise perfected during such period is subject thereto.

(3) A security interest in goods in the possession of a bailee other than one who has issued a negotiable document therefor is perfected by issuance of a document in the name of the secured party or by the bailee's receipt of notification of the secured party's interest or by filing as to the goods.

(4) A security interest in instruments (other than certificated securities) or negotiable documents is perfected without filing or the taking of possession for a period of 21 days from the time it attaches to the extent that it arises for new value given under a written security agreement.

(5) A security interest remains perfected for a period of 21 days without filing where a secured party having a perfected security interest in an instrument (other than a certificated security), a negotiable document or goods in possession of a bailee other than one who has issued a negotiable document therefor

  (a) makes available to the debtor the goods or documents representing the goods for the purpose of ultimate sale or exchange or for the purpose of loading, unloading, storing, shipping, transshipping, manufacturing, processing or otherwise dealing with them in a manner preliminary to their sale or exchange, but priority between conflicting security interests in the goods is subject to subsection (3) of Section 9—312; or

  (b) delivers the instrument to the debtor for the purpose of ultimate sale or exchange or of presentation, collection, renewal or registration of transfer.

(6) After the 21 day period in subsections (4) and (5) perfection depends upon compliance with applicable provisions of this Article.

Section 9—305. When Possession by Secured Party Perfects Security Interest Without Filing

A security interest in letters of credit and advices of credit (subsection (2) (a) of Section 5—116), goods, instruments (other than certificated securities), money, negotiable documents, or chattel paper may be perfected by the secured party's taking possession of the collateral. If such collateral other than goods covered by a negotiable document is held by a bailee, the secured party is deemed to have possession from the time the bailee receives notification of the secured party's interest. A security interest is perfected by possession from the time possession is taken without a relation back and continues only so long as possession is retained, unless otherwise specified in this Article. The security interest may be otherwise perfected as provided in this Article before or after the period of possession by the secured party.

Section 9—306. "Proceeds"; Secured Party's Rights on Disposition of Collateral

(1) "Proceeds" includes whatever is received upon the sale, exchange, collection or other disposition of collateral or proceeds. Insurance payable by reason of loss or damage to the collateral is proceeds, except to the extent that it is payable to a person other than a party to the security agreement. Money, checks, deposit accounts, and the like are "cash proceeds." All other proceeds are "non-cash proceeds."

(2) Except where this Article otherwise provides, a security interest continues in collateral notwithstanding sale, exchange or other disposition thereof unless the disposition was authorized by the secured party in the security agreement or otherwise, and also continues in any identifiable proceeds including collections received by the debtor.

(3) The security interest in proceeds is a continuously perfected security interest if the interest in the original collateral was perfected but it ceases to be a perfected security interest and becomes unperfected ten days after receipt of the proceeds by the debtor unless

    (a) a filed financing statement covers the original collateral and the proceeds are collateral in which a security interest may be perfected by filing in the office or offices where the financing statement has been filed and, if the proceeds are acquired with cash proceeds, the description of collateral in the financing statement indicates the types of property constituting the proceeds; or

    (b) a filed financing statement covers the original collateral and the proceeds are identifiable cash proceeds; or

    (c) the security interest in the proceeds is perfected before the expiration of the ten day period.

Except as provided in this section, a security interest in proceeds can be perfected only by the methods or under the circumstances permitted in this Article for original collateral of the same type.

(4) In the event of insolvency proceedings instituted by or against a debtor, a secured party with a perfected security interest in proceeds has a perfected security interest only in the following proceeds:

    (a) in identifiable non-cash proceeds and in separate deposit accounts containing only proceeds;

    (b) in identifiable cash proceeds in the form of money which is neither commingled with other money nor deposited in a deposit account prior to the insolvency proceedings;

    (c) in identifiable cash proceeds in the form of checks and the like which are not deposited in a deposit account prior to the insolvency proceedings; and

    (d) in all cash and deposit accounts of the debtor in which proceeds have been commingled with other funds, but the perfected security interest under this paragraph (d) is

        (i) subject to any right to set-off; and

        (ii) limited to an amount not greater than the amount of any cash proceeds received by the debtor within ten days before the institution of the insolvency proceedings less the sum of (I) the payments to the secured party on account of cash proceeds received by the debtor during such period and (II) the cash proceeds received by the debtor during such period to which the secured party is entitled under paragraphs (a) through (c) of this subsection (4).

(5) If a sale of goods results in an account or chattel paper which is transferred by the seller to a secured party, and if the goods are returned to or are repossessed by the seller or the secured party, the following rules determine priorities:

    (a) If the goods were collateral at the time of sale, for an indebtedness of the seller which is still unpaid, the original security interest attaches again to the goods and continues as a perfected security interest if it was perfected at the time when the goods were sold. If the security interest was originally perfected by a filing which is still effective, nothing further is required to continue the perfected status; in any other case, the secured party must take possession of the returned or repossessed goods or must file.

(b) An unpaid transferee of the chattel paper has a security interest in the goods against the transferor. Such security interest is prior to a security interest asserted under paragraph (a) to the extent that the transferee of the chattel paper was entitled to priority under Section 9—308.

(c) An unpaid transferee of the account has a security interest in the goods against the transferor. Such security interest is subordinate to a security interest asserted under paragraph (a).

(d) A security interest of an unpaid transferee asserted under paragraph (b) or (c) must be perfected for protection against creditors of the transferor and purchasers of the returned or repossessed goods.

Section 9—307.   Protection of Buyers of Goods

(1) A buyer in ordinary course of business (subsection (9) of Section 1—201) other than a person buying farm products from a person engaged in farming operations takes free of a security interest created by his seller even though the security interest is perfected and even though the buyer knows of its existence.

(2) In the case of consumer goods, a buyer takes free of a security interest even though perfected if he buys without knowledge of the security interest, for value and for his own personal, family or household purposes unless prior to the purchase the secured party has filed a financing statement covering such goods.

(3) A buyer other than a buyer in ordinary course of business (subsection (1) of this section) takes free of a security interest to the extent that it secures future advances made after the secured party acquires knowledge of the purchase, or more than 45 days after the purchase, whichever first occurs, unless made pursuant to a commitment entered into without knowledge of the purchase and before the expiration of the 45 day period.

Section 9—308.   Purchase of Chattel Paper and Instruments

A purchaser of chattel paper or an instrument who gives new value and takes possession of it in the ordinary course of his business has priority over a security interest in the chattel paper or instrument

(a) which is perfected under Section 9—304 (permissive filing and temporary perfection) or under Section 9—306 (perfection as to proceeds) if he acts without knowledge that the specific paper or instrument is subject to a security interest; or

(b) which is claimed merely as proceeds of inventory subject to a security interest (Section 9—306) even though he knows that the specific paper or instrument is subject to the security interest.

Section 9—309.   Protection of Purchasers of Instruments, Documents and Securities

Nothing in this Article limits the rights of a holder in due course of a negotiable instrument (Section 3—302) or a holder to whom a negotiable document of title has been duly negotiated (Section 7—501) or a bona fide purchaser of a security (Section 8—302) and the holders or purchasers take priority over an earlier security interest even though perfected. Filing under this Article does not constitute notice of the security interest to such holders or purchasers.

Section 9—310.   Priority of Certain Liens Arising by Operation of Law

When a person in the ordinary course of his business furnishes services or materials with respect to goods subject to a security interest, a lien upon goods in the possession of such person given by statute or rule of law for such materials or services takes priority over a perfected security interest unless the lien is statutory and the statute expressly provides otherwise.

Section 9—311.   Alienability of Debtor's Rights: Judicial Process

The debtor's rights in collateral may be voluntarily or involuntarily transferred (by way of sale, creation of a security interest, attachment, levy, garnishment or other judicial process) notwithstanding a provision in the security agreement prohibiting any transfer or making the transfer constitute a default.

Section 9—312. Priorities Among Conflicting Security Interests in the Same Collateral

(1) The rules of priority stated in other sections of this Part and in the following sections shall govern when applicable: Section 4—208 with respect to the security interests of collecting banks in items being collected, accompanying documents and proceeds; Section 9—103 on security interests related to other jurisdictions; Section 9—114 on consignments.

(2) A perfected security interest in crops for new value given to enable the debtor to produce the crops during the production season and given not more than three months before the crops become growing crops by planting or otherwise takes priority over an earlier perfected security interest to the extent that such earlier interest secures obligations due more than six months before the crops become growing crops by planting or otherwise, even though the person giving new value had knowledge of the earlier security interest.

(3) A perfected purchase money security interest in inventory has priority over a conflicting security interest in the same inventory and also has priority in identifiable cash proceeds received on or before the delivery of the inventory to a buyer if

(a) the purchase money security interest is perfected at the time the debtor receives possession of the inventory; and

(b) the purchase money secured party gives notification in writing to the holder of the conflicting security interest if the holder had filed a financing statement covering the same types of inventory (i) before the date of the filing made by the purchase money secured party, or (ii) before the beginning of the 21 day period where the purchase money security interest is temporarily perfected without filing or possession (subsection (5) of Section 9—304); and

(c) the holder of the conflicting security interest receives the notification within five years before the debtor receives possession of the inventory; and

(d) the notification states that the person giving the notice has or expects to acquire a purchase money security interest in inventory of the debtor, describing such inventory by item or type.

(4) A purchase money security interest in collateral other than inventory has priority over a conflicting security interest in the same collateral or its proceeds if the purchase money security interest is perfected at the time the debtor receives possession of the collateral or within ten days thereafter.

(5) In all cases not governed by other rules stated in this section (including cases of purchase money security interests which do not qualify for the special priorities set forth in subsections (3) and (4) of this section), priority between conflicting security interests in the same collateral shall be determined according to the following rules:

(a) Conflicting security interests rank according to priority in time of filing or perfection. Priority dates from the time a filing is first made covering the collateral or the time the security interest is first perfected, whichever is earlier, provided that there is no period thereafter when there is neither filing nor perfection.

(b) So long as conflicting security interests are unperfected, the first to attach has priority.

(6) For the purposes of subsection (5) a date of filing or perfection as to collateral is also a date of filing or perfection as to proceeds.

(7) If future advances are made while a security interest is perfected by filing, the taking of possession, or under Section 8—321 on securities, the security interest has the same priority for the purposes of subsection (5) with respect to the future advances as it does with respect to the first advance. If a commitment is made before or while the security interest is so perfected, the security interest has the same priority with respect to advances made pursuant thereto. In other cases a perfected security interest has priority from the date the advance is made.

Section 9—313. Priority of Security Interests in Fixtures

(1) In this section and in the provisions of Part 4 of this Article referring to fixture filing, unless the context otherwise requires

(a) goods are "fixtures" when they become so related to particular real estate that an interest in them arises under real estate law

(b) a "fixture filing" is the filing in the office where a mortgage on the real estate would be filed or recorded of a financing statement covering goods which are or are to become fixtures and conforming to the requirements of subsection (5) of Section 9—402

(c) a mortgage is a "construction mortgage" to the extent that it secures an obligation incurred for the construction of an improvement on land including the acquisition cost of the land, if the recorded writing so indicates.

(2) A security interest under this Article may be created in goods which are fixtures or may continue in goods which become fixtures, but no security interest exists under this Article in ordinary building materials incorporated into an improvement on land.

(3) This Article does not prevent creation of an encumbrance upon fixtures pursuant to real estate law.

(4) A perfected security interest in fixtures has priority over the conflicting interest of an encumbrancer or owner of the real estate where

(a) the security interest is a purchase money security interest, the interest of the encumbrancer or owner arises before the goods become fixtures, the security interest is perfected by a fixture filing before the goods become fixtures or within ten days thereafter, and the debtor has an interest of record in the real estate or is in possession of the real estate; or

(b) the security interest is perfected by a fixture filing before the interest of the encumbrancer or owner is of record, the security interest has priority over any conflicting interest of a predecessor in title of the encumbrancer or owner, and the debtor has an interest of record in the real estate or is in possession of the real estate; or

(c) the fixtures are readily removable factory or office machines or readily removable replacements of domestic appliances which are consumer goods, and before the goods become fixtures the security interest is perfected by any method permitted by this Article; or

(d) the conflicting interest is a lien on the real estate obtained by legal or equitable proceedings after the security interest was perfected by any method permitted by this Article.

(5) A security interest in fixtures, whether or not perfected, has priority over the conflicting interest of an encumbrancer or owner of the real estate where

(a) the encumbrancer or owner has consented in writing to the security interest or has disclaimed an interest in the goods as fixtures; or

(b) the debtor has a right to remove the goods as against the encumbrancer or owner. If the debtor's right terminates, the priority of the security interest continues for a reasonable time.

(6) Notwithstanding paragraph (a) of subsection (4) but otherwise subject to subsections (4) and (5), a security interest in fixtures is subordinate to a construction mortgage recorded before the goods become fixtures if the goods become fixtures before the completion of the construction. To the extent that it is given to refinance a construction mortgage, a mortgage has this priority to the same extent as the construction mortgage.

(7) In cases not within the preceding subsections, a security interest in fixtures is subordinate to the conflicting interest of an encumbrancer or owner of the related real estate who is not the debtor.

(8) When the secured party has priority over all owners and encumbrancers of the real estate, he may, on default, subject to the provisions of Part 5, remove his collateral from the real estate but he must reimburse any encumbrancer or owner of the real estate who is not the debtor and who has not otherwise agreed for the cost of repair of any physical injury, but not for any diminution in value of the real estate caused by the absence of the goods removed or by any necessity of replacing them. A person entitled to reimbursement may refuse permission to remove until the secured party gives adequate security for the performance of this obligation.

Section 9—314. Accessions

(1) A security interest in goods which attaches before they are installed in or affixed to other goods takes priority as to the goods installed or affixed (called in this section "accessions") over the claims of all persons to

the whole except as stated in subsection (3) and subject to Section 9—315(1).

(2) A security interest which attaches to goods after they become part of a whole is valid against all persons subsequently acquiring interests in the whole except as stated in subsection (3) but is invalid against any person with an interest in the whole at the time the security interest attaches to the goods who has not in writing consented to the security interest or disclaimed an interest in the goods as part of the whole.

(3) The security interests described in subsections (1) and (2) do not take priority over

   (a) a subsequent purchaser for value of any interest in the whole; or

   (b) a creditor with a lien on the whole subsequently obtained by judicial proceedings; or

   (c) a creditor with a prior perfected security interest in the whole to the extent that he makes subsequent advances

if the subsequent purchase is made, the lien by judicial proceedings obtained or the subsequent advance under the prior perfected security interest is made or contracted for without knowledge of the security interest and before it is perfected. A purchaser of the whole at a foreclosure sale other than the holder of a perfected security interest purchasing at his own foreclosure sale is a subsequent purchaser within this section.

(4) When under subsections (1) or (2) and (3) a secured party has an interest in accessions which has priority over the claims of all persons who have interests in the whole, he may on default subject to the provisions of Part 5 remove his collateral from the whole but he must reimburse any encumbrancer or owner of the whole who is not the debtor and who has not otherwise agreed for the cost of repair of any physical injury but not for any diminution in value of the whole caused by the absence of the goods removed or by any necessity for replacing them. A person entitled to reimbursement may refuse permission to remove until the secured party gives adequate security for the performance of this obligation.

Section 9—315. Priority When Goods Are Commingled or Processed

(1) If a security interest in goods was perfected and subsequently the goods or a part thereof have become

part of a product or mass, the security interest continues in the product or mass if

   (a) the goods are so manufactured, processed, assembled or commingled that their identity is lost in the product or mass; or

   (b) a financing statement covering the original goods also covers the product into which the goods have been manufactured, processed or assembled.

In a case to which paragraph (b) applies, no separate security interest in that part of the original goods which have been manufactured, processed or assembled into the product may be claimed under Section 9—314.

(2) When under subsection (1) more than one security interest attaches to the product or mass, they rank equally according to the ratio that the cost of the goods to which each interest originally attached bears to the cost of the total product or mass.

Section 9—316. Priority Subject to Subordination

Nothing in this Article prevents subordination by agreement by any person entitled to priority.

Section 9—317. Secured Party Not Obligated on Contract of Debtor

The mere existence of a security interest or authority given to the debtor to dispose of or use collateral does not impose contract or tort liability upon the secured party for the debtor's acts or omissions.

Section 9—318. Defenses Against Assignee; Modification of Contract After Notification of Assignment; Term Prohibiting Assignment Ineffective; Identification and Proof of Assignment

(1) Unless an account debtor has made an enforceable agreement not to assert defenses or claims arising out of a sale as provided in Section 9—206 the rights of an assignee are subject to

   (a) all the terms of the contract between the account debtor and assignor and any defense or claim arising therefrom; and

   (b) any other defense or claim of the account debtor against the assignor which accrues before the account debtor receives notification of the assignment.

(2) So far as the right to payment or a part thereof under an assigned contract has not been fully earned by performance, and notwithstanding notification of the assignment, any modification of or substitution for the contract made in good faith and in accordance with reasonable commercial standards is effective against an assignee unless the account debtor has otherwise agreed but the assignee acquires corresponding rights under the modified or substituted contract. The assignment may provide that such modification or substitution is a breach by the assignor.

(3) The account debtor is authorized to pay the assignor until the account debtor receives notification that the amount due or to become due has been assigned and that payment is to be made to the assignee. A notification which does not reasonably identify the rights assigned is ineffective. If requested by the account debtor, the assignee must seasonably furnish reasonable proof that the assignment has been made and unless he does so the account debtor may pay the assignor.

(4) A term in any contract between an account debtor and an assignor is ineffective if it prohibits assignment of an account or prohibits creation of a security interest in a general intangible for money due or to become due or requires the account debtor's consent to such assignment or security interest.

Part 4   Filing

Section 9—401.   Place of Filing; Erroneous Filing; Removal of Collateral

First Alternative Subsection (1)

(1) The proper place to file in order to perfect a security interest is as follows:

  (a) when the collateral is timber to be cut or is minerals or the like (including oil and gas) or accounts subject to subsection (5) of Section 9—103, or when the financing statement is filed as a fixture filing (Section 9—313) and the collateral is goods which are or are to become fixtures, then in the office where a mortgage on the real estate would be filed or recorded;

  (b) in all other cases, in the office of the [Secretary of State].

Second Alternative Subsection (1)

(1) The proper place to file in order to perfect a security interest is as follows:

  (a) when the collateral is equipment used in farming operations, or farm products, or accounts or general intangibles arising from or relating to the sale of farm products by a farmer, or consumer goods, then in the office of the . . . . in the county of the debtor's residence or if the debtor is not a resident of this state then in the office of the . . . . in the county where the goods are kept, and in addition when the collateral is crops growing or to be grown in the office of the . . . . in the county where the land is located;

  (b) when the collateral is timber to be cut or is minerals or the like (including oil and gas) or accounts subject to subsection (5) of Section 9—103, or when the financing statement is filed as a fixture filing (Section 9—313) and the collateral is goods which are or are to become fixtures, then in the office where a mortgage on the real estate would be filed or recorded;

  (c) in all other cases, in the office of the [Secretary of State].

Third Alternative Subsection (1)

(1) The proper place to file in order to perfect a security interest is as follows:

  (a) when the collateral is equipment used in farming operations, or farm products, or accounts or general intangibles arising from or relating to the sale of farm products by a farmer, or consumer goods, then in the office of the . . . . . . in the county of the debtor's residence or if the debtor is not a resident of this state then in the office of the . . . . in the county where the goods are kept, and in addition when the collateral is crops growing or to be grown in the office of the . . . . . . in the county where the land is located;

(b) when the collateral is timber to be cut or is minerals or the like (including oil and gas) or accounts subject to subsection (5) of Section 9—103, or when the financing statement is filed as a fixture filing (Section 9—313) and the collateral is goods which are or are to become fixtures, then in the office where a mortgage on the real estate would be filed or recorded;

(c) in all other cases, in the office of the [Secretary of State] and in addition, if the debtor has a place of business in only one county of this state, also in the office of . . . . . . of such county, or, if the debtor has no place of business in this state, but resides in the state, also in the office of . . . . . of the county in which he resides.

Note: *One of the three alternatives should be selected as subsection (1).*

(2) A filing which is made in good faith in an improper place or not in all of the places required by this section is nevertheless effective with regard to any collateral as to which the filing complied with the requirements of this Article and is also effective with regard to collateral covered by the financing statement against any person who has knowledge of the contents of such financing statement.

(3) A filing which is made in the proper place in this state continues effective even though the debtor's residence or place of business or the location of the collateral or its use, whichever controlled the original filing, is thereafter changed.

Alternative Subsection (3)

[(3) A filing which is made in the proper county continues effective for four months after a change to another county of the debtor's residence or place of business or the location of the collateral, whichever controlled the original filing. It becomes ineffective thereafter unless a copy of the financing statement signed by the secured party is filed in the new county within said period. The security interest may also be perfected in the new county after the expiration of the four-month period; in such case perfection dates from the time of perfection in the new county. A change in the use of the collateral does not impair the effectiveness of the original filing.]

(4) The rules stated in Section 9—103 determine whether filing is necessary in this state.

(5) Notwithstanding the preceding subsections, and subject to subsection (3) of Section 9—302, the proper place to file in order to perfect a security interest in collateral, including fixtures, of a transmitting utility is the office of the [Secretary of State]. This filing constitutes a fixture filing (Section 9—313) as to the collateral described therein which is or is to become fixtures.

(6) For the purposes of this section, the residence of an organization is its place of business if it has one or its chief executive office if it has more than one place of business.

Note: *Subsection (6) should be used only if the state chooses the Second or Third Alternative Subsection (1).*

Section 9—402. Formal Requisites of Financing Statement; Amendments; Mortgage as Financing Statement

(1) A financing statement is sufficient if it gives the names of the debtor and the secured party, is signed by the debtor, gives an address of the secured party from which information concerning the security interest may be obtained, gives a mailing address of the debtor and contains a statement indicating the types, or describing the items, of collateral. A financing statement may be filed before a security agreement is made or a security interest otherwise attaches. When the financing statement covers crops growing or to be grown, the statement must also contain a description of the real estate concerned. When the financing statement covers timber to be cut or covers minerals or the like (including oil and gas) or accounts subject to subsection (5) of Section 9—103, or when the financing statement is filed as a fixture filing (Section 9—313) and the collateral is goods which are or are to become fixtures, the statement must also comply with subsection (5). A copy of the security agreement is sufficient as a financing statement if it contains the above information and is signed by the debtor. A carbon, photographic or other reproduction of a security agreement or a financing statement is sufficient as a financing statement if the security agreement so provides or if the original has been filed in this state.

(2) A financing statement which otherwise complies with subsection (1) is sufficient when it is signed by the secured party instead of the debtor if it is filed to perfect a security interest in

(a) collateral already subject to a security interest in another jurisdiction when it is brought into this state, or when the debtor's location is changed to this state. Such a financing statement must state that the collateral was brought into this state or that the debtor's location was changed to this state under such circumstances; or

(b) proceeds under Section 9—306 if the security interest in the original collateral was perfected. Such a financing statement must describe the original collateral; or

(c) collateral as to which the filing has lapsed; or

(d) collateral acquired after a change of name, identity or corporate structure of the debtor (subsection (7)).

(3) A form substantially as follows is sufficient to comply with subsection (1):

Name of debtor (or assignor) . . . .
Address . . . .
Name of secured party (or assignee) . . . .
Address . . . .

    1. This financing statement covers the following types (or items) of property:

       (Describe) . . . .

    2. (If collateral is crops) The above described crops are growing or are to be grown on:

       (Describe Real Estate) . . . .

    3. (If applicable) The above goods are to become fixtures on*

       (Describe Real Estate) . . . .
       . . . . and this financing statement is to be filed [for record] in the real estate records. (If the debtor does not have an interest of record) The name of a record owner is . . . .

    4. (If products of collateral are claimed) Products of the collateral are also covered.

       (use whichever is applicable)

    . . . .
    Signature of Debtor (or Assignor)

    . . . .
    Signature of Secured Party (or Assignee)

(4) A financing statement may be amended by filing a writing signed by both the debtor and the secured party. An amendment does not extend the period of effectiveness of a financing statement. If any amendment adds collateral, it is effective as to the added collateral only from the filing date of the amendment. In this Article, unless the context otherwise requires, the term "financing statement" means the original financing statement and any amendments.

(5) A financing statement covering timber to be cut or covering minerals or the like (including oil and gas) or accounts subject to subsection (5) of Section 9—103, or a financing statement filed as a fixture filing (Section 9—313) where the debtor is not a transmitting utility, must show that it covers this type of collateral, must recite that it is to be filed [for record] in the real estate records, and the financing statement must contain a description of the real estate [sufficient if it were contained in a mortgage of the real estate to give constructive notice of the mortgage under the law of this state]. If the debtor does not have an interest of record in the real estate, the financing statement must show the name of a record owner.

(6) A mortgage is effective as a financing statement filed as a fixture filing from the date of its recording if

    (a) the goods are described in the mortgage by item or type; and

    (b) the goods are or are to become fixtures related to the real estate described in the mortgage; and

    (c) the mortgage complies with the requirements for a financing statement in this section other than a recital that it is to be filed in the real estate records; and

    (d) the mortgage is duly recorded.

No fee with reference to the financing statement is required other than the regular recording and satisfaction fees with respect to the mortgage.

(7) A financing statement sufficiently shows the name of the debtor if it gives the individual, partnership or corporate name of the debtor, whether or not it adds other trade names or names of partners. Where the debtor so changes his name or in the case of an organization its name, identity or corporate structure that a filed financing statement becomes seriously misleading, the filing is not effective to perfect a security interest

in collateral acquired by the debtor more than four months after the change, unless a new appropriate financing statement is filed before the expiration of that time. A filed financing statement remains effective with respect to collateral transferred by the debtor even though the secured party knows of or consents to the transfer.

(8) A financing statement substantially complying with the requirements of this section is effective even though it contains minor errors which are not seriously misleading.

Note: *Language in brackets is optional.*

Note: *Where the state has any special recording system for real estate other than the usual grantor-grantee index (as, for instance, a tract system or a title registration or Torrens system) local adaptations of subsection (5) and Section 9—403(7) may be necessary. See Mass. Gen. Laws Chapter 106, Section 9—409.*

*Where appropriate substitute either "The above timber is standing on . . . ." or "The above minerals or the like (including oil and gas) or accounts will be financed at the wellhead or minehead of the well or mine located on . . . ."

Section 9—403. What Constitutes Filing; Duration of Filing; Effect of Lapsed Filing; Duties of Filing Officer

(1) Presentation for filing of a financing statement and tender of the filing fee or acceptance of the statement by the filing officer constitutes filing under this Article.

(2) Except as provided in subsection (6) a filed financing statement is effective for a period of five years from the date of filing. The effectiveness of a filed financing statement lapses on the expiration of the five year period unless a continuation statement is filed prior to the lapse. If a security interest perfected by filing exists at the time insolvency proceedings are commenced by or against the debtor, the security interest remains perfected until termination of the insolvency proceedings and thereafter for a period of sixty days or until expiration of the five year period, whichever occurs later. Upon lapse the security interest becomes unperfected, unless it is perfected without filing. If the security interest becomes unperfected upon lapse, it is deemed to have been unperfected as against a person who became a purchaser or lien creditor before lapse.

(3) A continuation statement may be filed by the secured party within six months prior to the expiration of the five year period specified in subsection (2). Any such continuation statement must be signed by the secured party, identify the original statement by file number and state that the original statement is still effective. A continuation statement signed by a person other than the secured party of record must be accompanied by a separate written statement of assignment signed by the secured party of record and complying with subsection (2) of Section 9—405, including payment of the required fee. Upon timely filing of the continuation statement, the effectiveness of the original statement is continued for five years after the last date to which the filing was effective whereupon it lapses in the same manner as provided in subsection (2) unless another continuation statement is filed prior to such lapse. Succeeding continuation statements may be filed in the same manner to continue the effectiveness of the original statement. Unless a statute on disposition of public records provides otherwise, the filing officer may remove a lapsed statement from the files and destroy it immediately if he has retained a microfilm or other photographic record, or in other cases after one year after the lapse. The filing officer shall so arrange matters by physical annexation of financing statements to continuation statements or other related filings, or by other means, that if he physically destroys the financing statements of a period more than five years past, those which have been continued by a continuation statement or which are still effective under subsection (6) shall be retained.

(4) Except as provided in subsection (7) a filing officer shall mark each statement with a file number and with the date and hour of filing and shall hold the statement or a microfilm or other photographic copy thereof for public inspection. In addition the filing officer shall index the statement according to the name of the debtor and shall note in the index the file number and the address of the debtor given in the statement.

(5) The uniform fee for filing and indexing and for stamping a copy furnished by the secured party to show the date and place of filing for an original financing statement or for a continuation statement shall be $. . . . . if the statement is in the standard form prescribed by the [Secretary of State] and otherwise shall be $. . . . ., plus in each case, if the financing statement is subject to subsection (5) of Section 9—402, $. . . . . . The uniform fee for each name more than one required to be indexed shall be $. . . . . The secured party may at his option show a trade name for any person and an extra uniform

indexing fee of $. . . . . shall be paid with respect thereto.

(6) If the debtor is a transmitting utility (subsection (5) of Section 9—401) and a filed financing statement so states, it is effective until a termination statement is filed. A real estate mortgage which is effective as a fixture filing under subsection (6) of Section 9—402 remains effective as a fixture filing until the mortgage is released or satisfied of record or its effectiveness otherwise terminates as to the real estate.

(7) When a financing statement covers timber to be cut or covers minerals or the like (including oil and gas) or accounts subject to subsection (5) of Section 9—103, or is filed as a fixture filing, [it shall be filed for record and] the filing officer shall index it under the names of the debtor and any owner of record shown on the financing statement in the same fashion as if they were the mortgagors in a mortgage of the real estate described, and, to the extent that the law of this state provides for indexing of mortgages under the name of the mortgagee, under the name of the secured party as if he were the mortgagee thereunder, or where indexing is by description in the same fashion as if the financing statement were a mortgage of the real estate described.

Note: *In states in which writings will not appear in the real estate records and indices unless actually recorded the bracketed language in subsection (7) should be used.*

Section 9—404. Termination Statement

(1) If a financing statement covering consumer goods is filed on or after . . . ., then within one month or within ten days following written demand by the debtor after there is no outstanding secured obligation and no commitment to make advances, incur obligations or otherwise give value, the secured party must file with each filing officer with whom the financing statement was filed, a termination statement to the effect that he no longer claims a security interest under the financing statement, which shall be identified by file number. In other cases whenever there is no outstanding secured obligation and no commitment to make advances, incur obligations or otherwise give value, the secured party must on written demand by the debtor send the debtor, for each filing officer with whom the financing statement was filed, a termination statement to the effect that he no longer claims a security interest under the financing statement, which shall be identified by file number. A termination statement signed by a person other than the secured party of record must be accompanied by a separate written statement of assignment signed by the secured party of record complying with subsection (2) of Section 9—405, including payment of the required fee. If the affected secured party fails to file such a termination statement as required by this subsection, or to send such a termination statement within ten days after proper demand therefor, he shall be liable to the debtor for one hundred dollars, and in addition for any loss caused to the debtor by such failure.

(2) On presentation to the filing officer of such a termination statement he must note it in the index. If he has received the termination statement in duplicate, he shall return one copy of the termination statement to the secured party stamped to show the time of receipt thereof. If the filing officer has a microfilm or other photographic record of the financing statement, and of any related continuation statement, statement of assignment and statement of release, he may remove the originals from the files at any time after receipt of the termination statement, or if he has no such record, he may remove them from the files at any time after one year after receipt of the termination statement.

(3) If the termination statement is in the standard form prescribed by the [Secretary of State], the uniform fee for filing and indexing the termination statement shall be $. . . . . ., and otherwise shall be $. . . . . ., plus in each case an additional fee of $. . . . . for each name more than one against which the termination statement is required to be indexed.

Note: *The date to be inserted should be the effective date of the revised Article 9.*

Section 9—405. Assignment of Security Interest; Duties of Filing Officer; Fees

(1) A financing statement may disclose an assignment of a security interest in the collateral described in the financing statement by indication in the financing statement of the name and address of the assignee or by an assignment itself or a copy thereof on the face or back of the statement. On presentation to the filing officer of such a financing statement the filing officer shall mark the same as provided in Section 9—403(4). The uniform fee for filing, indexing and furnishing filing data for a financing statement so indicating an assignment shall be $. . . . . if the statement is in the standard form prescribed by the [Secretary of State] and otherwise shall

be $. . . . ., plus in each case an additional fee of $. . . . . for each name more than one against which the financing statement is required to be indexed.

(2) A secured party may assign of record all or part of his rights under a financing statement by the filing in the place where the original financing statement was filed of a separate written statement of assignment signed by the secured party of record and setting forth the name of the secured party of record and the debtor, the file number and the date of filing of the financing statement and the name and address of the assignee and containing a description of the collateral assigned. A copy of the assignment is sufficient as a separate statement if it complies with the preceding sentence. On presentation to the filing officer of such a separate statement, the filing officer shall mark such separate statement with the date and hour of the filing. He shall note the assignment on the index of the financing statement, or in the case of a fixture filing, or a filing covering timber to be cut, or covering minerals or the like (including oil and gas) or accounts subject to subsection (5) of Section 9—103, he shall index the assignment under the name of the assignor as grantor and, to the extent that the law of this state provides for indexing the assignment of a mortgage under the name of the assignee, he shall index the assignment of the financing statement under the name of the assignee. The uniform fee for filing, indexing and furnishing filing data about such a separate statement of assignment shall be $. . . . . if the statement is in the standard form prescribed by the [Secretary of State] and otherwise shall be $. . . . ., plus in each case an additional fee of $. . . . . for each name more than one against which the statement of assignment is required to be indexed. Notwithstanding the provisions of this subsection, an assignment of record of a security interest in a fixture contained in a mortgage effective as a fixture filing (subsection (6) of Section 9—402) may be made only by an assignment of the mortgage in the manner provided by the law of this state other than this Act.

(3) After the disclosure or filing of an assignment under this section, the assignee is the secured party of record.

Section 9—406. Release of Collateral; Duties of Filing Officer; Fees

A secured party of record may by his signed statement release all or a part of any collateral described in a filed financing statement. The statement of release is sufficient if it contains a description of the collateral being released, the name and address of the debtor, the name and address of the secured party, and the file number of the financing statement. A statement of release signed by a person other than the secured party of record must be accompanied by a separate written statement of assignment signed by the secured party of record and complying with subsection (2) of Section 9—405, including payment of the required fee. Upon presentation of such a statement of release to the filing officer he shall mark the statement with the hour and date of filing and shall note the same upon the margin of the index of the filing of the financing statement. The uniform fee for filing and noting such a statement of release shall be $. . . . . if the statement is in the standard form prescribed by the [Secretary of State] and otherwise shall be $. . . . ., plus in each case an additional fee of $. . . . . for each name more than one against which the statement of release is required to be indexed.

[Section 9—407. Information From Filing Officer]

[(1) If the person filing any financing statement, termination statement, statement of assignment, or statement of release, furnishes the filing officer a copy thereof, the filing officer shall upon request note upon the copy the file number and date and hour of the filing of the original and deliver or send the copy to such person.]

[(2) Upon request of any person, the filing officer shall issue his certificate showing whether there is on file on the date and hour stated therein, any presently effective financing statement naming a particular debtor and any statement of assignment thereof and if there is, giving the date and hour of filing of each such statement and the names and addresses of each secured party therein. The uniform fee for such a certificate shall be $. . . . . if the request for the certificate is in the standard form prescribed by the [Secretary of State] and otherwise shall be $. . . . . Upon request the filing officer shall furnish a copy of any filed financing statement or statement of assignment for a uniform fee of $. . . . . per page.]

Note: *This section is proposed as an optional provision to require filing officers to furnish certificates. Local law and practices should be consulted with regard to the advisability of adoption.*

Section 9—408. Financing Statements Covering Consigned or Leased Goods

A consignor or lessor of goods may file a financing statement using the terms "consignor," "consignee," "lessor," "lessee" or the like instead of the terms specified in Section 9—402. The provisions of this Part shall apply as appropriate to such a financing statement but its filing shall not of itself be a factor in determining whether or not the consignment or lease is intended as security (Section 1—201(37)). However, if it is determined for other reasons that the consignment or lease is so intended, a security interest of the consignor or lessor which attaches to the consigned or leased goods is perfected by such filing.

Part 5 Default

Section 9—501. Default; Procedure When Security Agreement Covers Both Real and Personal Property

(1) When a debtor is in default under a security agreement, a secured party has the rights and remedies provided in this Part and except as limited by subsection (3) those provided in the security agreement. He may reduce his claim to judgment, foreclose or otherwise enforce the security interest by any available judicial procedure. If the collateral is documents the secured party may proceed either as to the documents or as to the goods covered thereby. A secured party in possession has the rights, remedies and duties provided in Section 9—207. The rights and remedies referred to in this subsection are cumulative.

(2) After default, the debtor has the rights and remedies provided in this Part, those provided in the security agreement and those provided in Section 9—207.

(3) To the extent that they give rights to the debtor and impose duties on the secured party, the rules stated in the subsections referred to below may not be waived or varied except as provided with respect to compulsory disposition of collateral (subsection (3) of Section 9—504 and Section 9—505) and with respect to redemption of collateral (Section 9—506) but the parties may by agreement determine the standards by which the fulfillment of these rights and duties is to be measured if such standards are not manifestly unreasonable:

> (a) subsection (2) of Section 9—502 and subsection (2) of Section 9—504 insofar as they

require accounting for surplus proceeds of collateral;

> (b) subsection (3) of Section 9—504 and subsection (1) of Section 9—505 which deal with disposition of collateral;

> (c) subsection (2) of Section 9—505 which deals with acceptance of collateral as discharge of obligation;

> (d) Section 9—506 which deals with redemption of collateral; and

> (e) subsection (1) of Section 9—507 which deals with the secured party's liability for failure to comply with this Part.

(4) If the security agreement covers both real and personal property, the secured party may proceed under this Part as to the personal property or he may proceed as to both the real and the personal property in accordance with his rights and remedies in respect of the real property in which case the provisions of this Part do not apply.

(5) When a secured party has reduced his claim to judgment the lien of any levy which may be made upon his collateral by virtue of any execution based upon the judgment shall relate back to the date of the perfection of the security interest in such collateral. A judicial sale, pursuant to such execution, is a foreclosure of the security interest by judicial procedure within the meaning of this section, and the secured party may purchase at the sale and thereafter hold the collateral free of any other requirements of this Article.

Section 9—502. Collection Rights of Secured Party

(1) When so agreed and in any event on default the secured party is entitled to notify an account debtor or the obligor on an instrument to make payment to him whether or not the assignor was theretofore making collections on the collateral, and also to take control of any proceeds to which he is entitled under Section 9—306.

(2) A secured party who by agreement is entitled to charge back uncollected collateral or otherwise to full or limited recourse against the debtor and who undertakes to collect from the account debtors or obligors must proceed in a commercially reasonable manner and may deduct his reasonable expenses of realization from the collections. If the security agreement secures an indebtedness, the secured party must account to the debtor

for any surplus, and unless otherwise agreed, the debtor is liable for any deficiency. But, if the underlying transaction was a sale of accounts or chattel paper, the debtor is entitled to any surplus or is liable for any deficiency only if the security agreement so provides.

Section 9—503. Secured Party's Right to Take Possession After Default

Unless otherwise agreed a secured party has on default the right to take possession of the collateral. In taking possession a secured party may proceed without judicial process if this can be done without breach of the peace or may proceed by action. If the security agreement so provides the secured party may require the debtor to assemble the collateral and make it available to the secured party at a place to be designated by the secured party which is reasonably convenient to both parties. Without removal a secured party may render equipment unusable, and may dispose of collateral on the debtor's premises under Section 9—504.

Section 9—504. Secured Party's Right to Dispose of Collateral After Default; Effect of Disposition

(1) A secured party after default may sell, lease or otherwise dispose of any or all of the collateral in its then condition or following any commercially reasonable preparation or processing. Any sale of goods is subject to the Article on Sales (Article 2). The proceeds of disposition shall be applied in the order following to

(a) the reasonable expenses of retaking, holding, preparing for sale or lease, selling, leasing and the like and, to the extent provided for in the agreement and not prohibited by law, the reasonable attorneys' fees and legal expenses incurred by the secured party;

(b) the satisfaction of indebtedness secured by the security interest under which the disposition is made;

(c) the satisfaction of indebtedness secured by any subordinate security interest in the collateral if written notification of demand therefor is received before distribution of the proceeds is completed. If requested by the secured party, the holder of a subordinate security interest must seasonably furnish reasonable proof of his interest, and unless he does so, the secured party need not comply with his demand.

(2) If the security interest secures an indebtedness, the secured party must account to the debtor for any surplus, and, unless otherwise agreed, the debtor is liable for any deficiency. But if the underlying transaction was a sale of accounts or chattel paper, the debtor is entitled to any surplus or is liable for any deficiency only if the security agreement so provides.

(3) Disposition of the collateral may be by public or private proceedings and may be made by way of one or more contracts. Sale or other disposition may be as a unit or in parcels and at any time and place and on any terms but every aspect of the disposition including the method, manner, time, place and terms must be commercially reasonable. Unless collateral is perishable or threatens to decline speedily in value or is of a type customarily sold on a recognized market, reasonable notification of the time and place of any public sale or reasonable notification of the time after which any private sale or other intended disposition is to be made shall be sent by the secured party to the debtor, if he has not signed after default a statement renouncing or modifying his right to notification of sale. In the case of consumer goods no other notification need be sent. In other cases notification shall be sent to any other secured party from whom the secured party has received (before sending his notification to the debtor or before the debtor's renunciation of his rights) written notice of a claim of an interest in the collateral. The secured party may buy at any public sale and if the collateral is of a type customarily sold in a recognized market or is of a type which is the subject of widely distributed standard price quotations he may buy at private sale.

(4) When collateral is disposed of by a secured party after default, the disposition transfers to a purchaser for value all of the debtor's rights therein, discharges the security interest under which it is made and any security interest or lien subordinate thereto. The purchaser takes free of all such rights and interests even though the secured party fails to comply with the requirements of this Part or of any judicial proceedings

(a) in the case of a public sale, if the purchaser has no knowledge of any defects in the sale and if he does not buy in collusion with the secured party, other bidders or the person conducting the sale; or

(b) in any other case, if the purchaser acts in good faith.

(5) A person who is liable to a secured party under a guaranty, indorsement, repurchase agreement or the like and who receives a transfer of collateral from the secured party or is subrogated to his rights has thereafter the rights and duties of the secured party. Such a transfer of collateral is not a sale or disposition of the collateral under this Article.

Section 9—505. Compulsory Disposition of Collateral; Acceptance of the Collateral as Discharge of Obligation

(1) If the debtor has paid sixty per cent of the cash price in the case of a purchase money security interest in consumer goods or sixty per cent of the loan in the case of another security interest in consumer goods, and has not signed after default a statement renouncing or modifying his rights under this Part a secured party who has taken possession of collateral must dispose of it under Section 9—504 and if he fails to do so within ninety days after he takes possession the debtor at his option may recover in conversion or under Section 9—507(1) on secured party's liability.

(2) In any other case involving consumer goods or any other collateral a secured party in possession may, after default, propose to retain the collateral in satisfaction of the obligation. Written notice of such proposal shall be sent to the debtor if he has not signed after default a statement renouncing or modifying his rights under this subsection. In the case of consumer goods no other notice need be given. In other cases notice shall be sent to any other secured party from whom the secured party has received (before sending his notice to the debtor or before the debtor's renunciation of his rights) written notice of a claim of an interest in the collateral. If the secured party receives objection in writing from a person entitled to receive notification within twenty-one days after the notice was sent, the secured party must dispose of the collateral under Section 9—504. In the absence of such written objection the secured party may retain the collateral in satisfaction of the debtor's obligation.

Section 9—506. Debtor's Right to Redeem Collateral

At any time before the secured party has disposed of collateral or entered into a contract for its disposition under Section 9—504 or before the obligation has been discharged under Section 9—505(2) the debtor or any other secured party may unless otherwise agreed in writing after default redeem the collateral by tendering fulfillment of all obligations secured by the collateral as well as the expenses reasonably incurred by the secured party in retaking, holding and preparing the collateral for disposition, in arranging for the sale, and to the extent provided in the agreement and not prohibited by law, his reasonable attorneys' fees and legal expenses.

Section 9—507. Secured Party's Liability for Failure to Comply With This Part

(1) If it is established that the secured party is not proceeding in accordance with the provisions of this Part disposition may be ordered or restrained on appropriate terms and conditions. If the disposition has occurred the debtor or any person entitled to notification or whose security interest has been made known to the secured party prior to the disposition has a right to recover from the secured party any loss caused by a failure to comply with the provisions of this Part. If the collateral is consumer goods, the debtor has a right to recover in any event an amount not less than the credit service charge plus ten per cent of the principal amount of the debt or the time price differential plus 10 per cent of the cash price.

(2) The fact that a better price could have been obtained by a sale at a different time or in a different method from that selected by the secured party is not of itself sufficient to establish that the sale was not made in a commercially reasonable manner. If the secured party either sells the collateral in the usual manner in any recognized market therefor or if he sells at the price current in such market at the time of his sale or if he has otherwise sold in conformity with reasonable commercial practices among dealers in the type of property sold he has sold in a commercially reasonable manner. The principles stated in the two preceding sentences with respect to sales also apply as may be appropriate to other types of disposition. A disposition which has been approved in any judicial proceeding or by any bona fide creditors' committee or representative of creditors shall conclusively be deemed to be commercially reasonable, but this sentence does not indicate that any such approval must be obtained in any case nor does it indicate that any disposition not so approved is not commercially reasonable.

[Articles 10 and 11 are omitted as unnecessary.]

Glossary of Legal Terms and Definitions

a

ab initio   from the beginning

abandoned property   discarded goods in which the owner has voluntarily relinquished all interest

abstract of title   a record of the history of the title to land as found in official records

abuse of civil legal process   to make excessive and improper use of the right to sue in an attempt to exhaust someone into submission

acceptance   the offeree's expressed assent to the offer in reliance on and in compliance with the offer

acceptor   the drawee on a draft who has assented in writing on the draft to pay it

accession   the increase in property by what it produces or by the addition of other property to it

accommodation party   a person who signs commercial paper as an accommodation to another person whose signature is on the instrument for the purpose of assisting the latter to obtain credit

accord   a new contract which provides that, on its performance, a previous contract as well as the new contract are discharged

accord and satisfaction   a new contract (accord) which discharges a party from a previous contractual obligation; the old contract is discharged (satisfied)

account   a right to payment under a contract

account stated   an account which has been settled and the matured items and balance expressly or impliedly agreed to by the parties

accretion   a method of obtaining title to another's land caused by gradual changes in the natural boundaries of such land

acknowledgement   the formal written declaration, admission, or confirmation made to a proper public official (usually a notary public) that he executed a particular legal instrument

act of God   an unexpected force of nature

action   a judicial proceeding concerning legal interests

actual authority   express and implied authority

ad litem   during the action

adjudicate   to determine by judicial authority

administrative law   rules and regulations created by an administrative agency, thereby becoming law

administrator (administratrix)   a court-appointed man (woman) not named in a will who administers the estate of a decedent

adverse possession   a method of acquiring title to land by actual, exclusive, and continuous possession of land under color of title adverse or hostile to the true owner in an open and notorious manner for a statutory period of time

affidavit   the formal written statement of a person voluntarily confirmed by oath or affirmation before a public official with authority to administer oaths or affirmations (usually a notary public)

after-acquired property   (in security) property acquired after the security agreement is made

agency   a legal relationship between two persons who agree that one is to act on behalf of the other, subject to the other's control

agent   a person authorized to act on behalf of another and subject to the other's control

agreement   a manifestation of mutual assent between parties by offer and acceptance

air space, right to   ownership of the air space above the surface of land

annuity   an insurance policy that pays the insured a designated amount periodically, beginning at a date set in the policy

anticipatory breach   a party's material breach of contract made by his repudiation before his performance is due

anticipatory repudiation   a party's manifestation of an intent not to perform his contractual obligation, made before his performance is due; *see* **repudiation**

antitrust laws   laws that limit monopolies, combinations, and unfair restraints to help prevent the undue concentration of economic power

apparent authority   the power of a person (A) to act as though he were an agent, created by another's (P's) manifestation to a third person (T) that A is P's agent

appellant   a party who appeals a case decision against him

appellee   a party against whom an appeal is taken

apprentice   a student learning a particular craft

arbitration   a method for deciding disputes outside of court by persons called arbitrators, appointed by the disputing parties

arson   the willful and malicious burning of the dwelling house of another (at common law); today, by statute, arson includes one's own insured house and the buildings of another

articles of incorporation   the written application to the state for permission to incorporate

artisan's lien   a person's possessory lien on goods owned by another and improved at the owner's request

assault   an unprivileged act intentionally causing another to apprehend a harmful or offensive bodily contact

assignee   the person to whom a contract right is transferred

assignment   the transfer of a contract right; (in realty) a transfer by the lessee of *all* the remaining term of his lease

assignor   the transferor of a contract right; (in realty) one who transfers *all* the remaining term of his lease

assumption of risk   voluntarily assuming a known risk of harm

attachment   the seizure of tangible property by a proper public officer (usually a sheriff) pursuant to a writ of attachment pending an action

attempt   (in criminal law) a preparatory crime

attractive nuisance   a dangerous and attractive condition of realty which may lure children into trespassing

auction   a public sale of property by public outcry to the highest bidder

auctioneer   a person licensed by law to sell property of another at a public sale

authority   an agent's power to act for his principal in accordance with the principal's manifestation of consent to the agent; *see* **actual authority, apparent authority, customary authority, express authority, implied authority, incidental authority**

avoid   to void, annul

b

bailee   the person to whom goods are bailed

bailment   a delivery of goods by a bailor to a bailee which are to be returned to the bailor or as he directs in accordance with the bailment agreement

bailor   the person who bails goods

bankruptcy   a federal procedure whereby a debtor's nonexempt assets are gathered together and used to discharge the debtor from most of his debts

bargaining unit   a group of employees appropriately joined together for the purpose of collective bargaining

battery   an act intentionally causing harmful or offensive bodily contact with another

bearer   the person in possession of an instrument, document of title, or certificated security payable or deliverable to bearer or indorsed in blank (a signature without additional words)

beneficiary   a person who is to receive a benefit; (in insurance) the person designated in a life insurance policy to receive the death benefit

bilateral contract   a contract in which the consideration is mutual promises

bill of lading   a document issued to the shipper by a carrier of goods

bill of sale   a formal document used to transfer personal property

binder   an insurance company's memorandum of an oral contract of insurance pending the issuance of a formal policy

blank indorsement   an indorsement which does not specify any particular indorsee; *see* **indorsement**

blue-sky laws   state laws regulating the sale and transfer of securities

bona fide   in good faith

bona fide purchaser   a purchaser for value in good faith and without notice of any adverse claim or defense with respect to what is being purchased; (in corporations) a purchaser for value in good faith and without notice of any adverse claim, and who is either a holder of a certificated security or registered on the corporate books as the owner

boycott   the act of a combination of persons to cause business harm to another by refraining from doing business with that other and inducing others to do likewise; *see* **group boycott**

breach of contract   wrongful nonperformance of a contractual promise

breach of the peace   an act of violence or an act likely to produce violence

broker   a person authorized to represent another and negotiate for him with others

bulk transfer   "any transfer in bulk and not in the ordinary course of the transferor's business of a major part of the materials, supplies, merchandise or other inventory of an enterprise subject to Article 6" UCC 6–102(1)

burglary   the breaking and entering in the night, of the home of another, with the intent to commit a felony therein

buyer in ordinary course of business   "a person who, in good faith and without knowledge that the sale to him is in violation of the ownership rights or security interest of a third party in the goods, buys in ordinary course from a person in the business of selling goods of that kind but does not include a pawnbroker" UCC 1–201(9)

bylaws   (in corporations) rules and regulations of a corporation for its internal management and operation

c

C. & F.   cost plus freight

C.I.F.   cost, insurance, freight

C.O.D.   collect on delivery

cancellation   the nullification of a contractual obligation

capital   corporate net assets

capital stock   *see* **stated capital**

case law   *see* **stare decisis**

cashier's check   a check drawn by a bank on itself and payable to the order of a payee

caveat emptor   let the buyer beware

caveat venditor   let the seller beware

certificate of deposit   a written "acknowledgement by a bank of receipt of money with an engagement to repay it," and which is in compliance with the UCC as being a negotiable instrument UCC 3–104(2)(c).

certiorari, writ of   an appellate court's certification to an inferior court that a case will be reviewed by the appellate court

charter   articles of incorporation approved by the state

chattel   a tangible, movable thing

check   a negotiable "draft drawn on a bank payable on demand" UCC 3–104(2)(b)

chose in action   intangible personal property, such as an account receivable

closed container rule   a bailee is not responsible for the contents of a closed container unless he knows or should know the contents

closed shop an employer who, by agreement with a union, will employ only union members

code a comprehensive, systematic collection of statutes in a particular legal area

collateral the personal "property subject to a security interest . . . " UCC 9–105(1)(c)

collecting bank "any bank handling the item for collection except the payor bank" UCC 4–105(d)

commercial frustration an excuse offered by a party to a contract justifying nonperformance of an obligation, usually because performance has been made impossible in fact

commercial unit "such a unit of goods as by commercial usage is a single whole for purposes of sale and division of which materially impairs its character or value on the market or in use" UCC 2–105(6)

common carrier a carrier which offers its services to the general public for a fee

common law principles of non-statutory law reflecting the customs and usages of society and found in judicial decisions

common stock corporate stock with the ordinary rights of participation in a corporation; *see* **share of stock**

community property a form of ownership by husband and wife of property acquired by their efforts during their marriage

compensatory damages the money judicially awarded to compensate for damage caused by another's wrongful conduct; *see* **damages**

complaint the first pleading in a civil action

composition (outside of bankruptcy) an agreement among some or all of the creditors with their insolvent or financially embarrassed debtor, each to take something less than what is owed to him and, on the debtor's performance, the debtor is discharged fully

compromise an agreement resolving a dispute outside of court reached through concessions offered by the aggrieved parties

condemnation forcing a property owner to transfer property to a government in exchange for just compensation

condition an uncertain event on the occurrence of which a contractual obligation is made contingent or dependent; *see* **condition concurrent, condition precedent,** and **condition subsequent**

condition concurrent a condition which must occur at the same time as another condition; *see* **condition**

condition precedent a condition which must occur or not occur before a dependent promise becomes performable; *see* **condition**

condition subsequent a condition, on the occurrence or nonoccurrence of which, after a promise becomes performable, excuses the duty of performance; *see* **condition**

conditional estate an estate where ownership is dependent upon some act or event

conditional receipt a receipt that provides an applicant for life insurance with temporary coverage until the application is approved by the company

conditional sale a sale in which the seller reserves title until the buyer completes payments; now called a secured transaction under Article 9 of the Uniform Commercial Code

confession of judgment a party's consent to jurisdiction and judgment of a court without a trial in a civil case

confirmation an assuring expression of understanding

confusion the mixing of chattels of like kind of different persons so that the chattels of one person can not be distinguished from the chattels of the other persons

consent a person's approval of something, made with full capacity, freely, and without fraud or mistake; (in torts) such approval permitting what would otherwise be an intentional tort

consequential (or special damages) the money judicially awarded for loss which the breaching party reasonably could foresee would be a consequence of his breach; *see* **damages**

consideration   the legal price bargained for a promise and inducing a party to enter into a contract

consignee   one to whom goods are shipped

consignment   the shipment of goods from one person to another

consignor   one who ships goods to another

consolidation   (in corporations) the combination of two or more corporations forming a new corporation

conspiracy   a combination of persons for the purpose of committing an unlawful act

constructive eviction   a tenant's moving out of leased premises because the landlord caused the premises to become unfit for their intended use by the tenant

constructive notice   knowledge of a fact presumed or imputed by law

consumer   a person who buys goods for use primarily for personal, family, or household purposes

consumer goods   goods which "are used or bought for use primarily for personal, family, or household purposes" UCC 9–109(1)

contingent claim   (in insurance) a claim not certain of occurring, depending on a possible future event

contract   a promise which the law recognizes as creating a legal obligation of performance; *see* **executed contract, executory contract, express contract, formal contract, implied contract,** and **simple contract**

contract to sell   a contract to transfer title to goods in the future

contribution   (in suretyship) the right of sureties who have paid the creditor to collect part of the payment from other sureties

contributory negligence   plaintiff's conduct which falls below the standard to which he should conform for his own protection and which is a legally contributing cause with the defendant's negligence causing the plaintiff's harm; *see* **negligence**

conversion   the tort of intentional interference with another's right to possession, control, and dominion of a chattel

conveyance   the transfer of an interest in land

copyright   a governmental grant of protection of original works in a tangible medium of expression

corporate express powers   those powers specifically stated in the corporation's articles of incorporation and in the corporation statutes

corporate implied powers   those powers reasonably necessary to carry out the express powers

corporation   a legal entity created by statute authorizing an association of persons to carry on an enterprise

cost-plus contract   a contract in which the price is the cost of production or performance (whatever it turns out to be) plus an agreed upon profit

costs   (in litigation) allowable recoverable expense by a party in a legal proceeding

counterclaim   a claim asserted by the defendant against the plaintiff's claim in a civil action

counteroffer   an offer which rejects a previous offer

course of dealing   "a sequence of previous conduct between the parties to a particular transaction which is fairly to be regarded as establishing a common basis of understanding for interpreting their expressions and other conduct" UCC 1–205(1)

court   a judicial tribunal

covenant   a promise as a part of a contract

covenant running with the land   the promise of an owner of land which binds future owners of the same land

cover   to seek a substitute performance of a contract

creditor   one to whom money is owed

creditors' committee   (in bankruptcy) a committee elected by the creditors to advise the trustee in bankruptcy

crime   an act, committed or omitted, in violation of a public law governing it; *see* **felony** and **misdemeanor**

cross-examination   a party's initial examination of a witness other than his own in a trial

cumulative voting   a method of voting whereby a shareholder has as many votes as he has shares of voting stock multiplied by the number of directors to be elected

cure   a seller's correction of his failure to deliver conforming goods under a contract for sale before the due date has expired

custom   *see* **usage of trade**

customary authority   implied authority to do those acts that conform to the general custom or usage; *see* **authority**

d

d/b/a/   doing business as

damage   loss or harm

damages   the money judicially awarded for another's wrongful conduct; *see* **compensatory damages, consequential (or special) damages, incidental damages, liquidated damages, nominal damages,** and **punitive (or exemplary) damages**

de facto **corporation**   a corporation which has not complied substantially with the mandatory requirements of a valid state incorporation statute but has made a colorable attempt to do so, in good faith, and has begun to operate as a corporation

de jure **corporation**   a corporation which has completely or substantially complied with the mandatory requirements of a valid state incorporation statute

debtor   one who owes money to another

decedent   one who is dead

deceit   the tort of knowingly misrepresenting a material fact, intending to mislead another person by inducing him to rely on the misrepresentation and to act in a particular business transaction, causing financial damage to him

deed   a formal document used to transfer title to real estate

defamation   a person's unprivileged, wrongful publication to a second person of a false and defamatory statement concerning a third person, harmful to the third person's reputation

default   a failure to perform a legal duty

defendant   the party against whom a civil suit (or criminal action) is brought

delegation   the transfer of one's duty to another, the transferor still being responsible for the duty

delivery   a voluntary transfer of possession

demise   (in realty) to lease or rent

demurrer   a pleading which states that a preceding pleading does not state a cause of action

dependent promise   a promise the performance of which is dependent upon the occurrence of a condition

deposit rule   an acceptance is effective when sent, though never received, if an authorized medium is used timely by the offeree

depositary bank   "the first bank to which an item is transferred for collection even though it is also the payor bank" UCC 4–105(a)

deposition   a written statement made by a person under oath or affirmation in a judicial proceeding where there is opportunity for cross-examination before trial

detriment   doing, or forbearing from doing, something by a party who had no previous obligation so to do or refrain from doing

directed verdict   a jury verdict as directed by the judge

disaffirm   to nullify one's previous consent

discharge   (in contracts) termination of a contractual duty to perform a promise; (under the UCC) cancellation and termination; (in bankruptcy) a court order releasing the individual debtor from his debts after the estate has been liquidated and distributed

disclaimer   denial of an obligation or a claim

disclosed principal   a person known, or who reasonably should be known, by a third party to be a principal for an agent

dishonor   the refusal of the drawee to accept the draft, or of the drawee, acceptor, or maker to pay the draft or note

dividend   a portion of corporate net profits or surplus set aside for distribution to the shareholders

divisible contract   a contract which provides that performance of less than all the obligations on one side will become due by performance of less than all the obligations on the other side

document of title a document evidencing that the person possessing it "is entitled to receive, hold and dispose of the document and the goods it covers" UCC 1–201(15)

documentary draft "any negotiable or non-negotiable draft with accompanying documents, securities or other papers to be delivered against honor of the draft" UCC 4–104(f)

dominant tenement property which is benefited by an easement appurtenant in nearby land

donee the recipient of a gift

donor the person who makes a gift

dower (at common law but generally abolished by statute today) a widow's life estate in a portion of the land of her deceased husband

dowry traditionally, property that the wife brings to the marriage

draft a negotiable instrument containing an unconditional order e.g., "pay"

drawee the person on whom a draft is drawn and ordered to pay

drawer the person who initially draws or creates and signs a draft

due negotiation delivery of a document of title to a holder who purchases it for value, in good faith, and without notice of any claim or defense to the document

duress wrongful inducement to do that which a reasonable person would have been unable to resist

duty a legal obligation not to interfere with another person's interest

e

easement a right to the limited use of another's land which can not be revoked by the latter owner

eleemosynary charitable, benevolent

emancipated minor a minor whose parents have given up their rights to take care of the minor and to have custody of and to claim the minor's earnings

embezzlement depriving someone of his property through breach of a trust relationship

emblements what is sown and produced on the land

eminent domain government power to appropriate private land for public use on payment of just compensation without the owner's consent

encumbrance a person's right in another person's property

enforceable contract a contract which can be proved and enforced by the courts

enjoining an order from a court to desist from doing

equipment goods which "are used or bought for use primarily in business (including farming or a profession) . . ." UCC 9–109(2)

equity principles of justice and fairness which developed when the relief at common law was inadequate

escheat the transfer of property to the state when a person dies without heirs

escrow the conditional delivery of property to a person who is to deal with it on the occurrence of specified conditions

estate a bundle of ownership rights in, or powers over, realty; (in bankruptcy) the debtor's legal or equitable interest in property on the date the case commences

estoppel a principle of law that when one person "holds out" (represents) a material fact to another person, who changes his position materially to his prejudice in reasonable reliance on the holding out, the first person is "estopped" (prohibited) to deny what he asserted previously

et al. abbreviation of a latin phrase meaning "and another" or "and others"

eviction the dispossession of a tenant from the leased premises

evidence a fact from which an inference can be drawn of another fact

exclusive dealing contract an agreement between a seller or lessor and a purchaser or lessee that the latter shall not use or deal in products of a competing seller or lessor

exculpatory clause a clause which relieves one from liability

executed contract   a contract which has been performed by all the parties to it; *see* **contract**

executor (executrix)   a man (woman) who is named in and administers a will

executory contract   a contract which has not been performed by all the parties to it; *see* **contract**

exemplary damages   *see* **punitive damages**

exemption   (in bankruptcy) a debtor's property that is not liquidated and not distributed to creditors in bankruptcy

express authority   an agent's authority specifically expressed in his principal's manifestation to him; *see* **authority**

express contract   a contract in which the promise or promises are expressly made; *see* **contract**

express warranty   a warranty expressed by a party; *see* **warranty**

f

F.A.S.   free alongside

F.O.B.   free on board

factor   a person in business for himself with authority to buy goods, or to sell goods in his possession, in his own name for another

false imprisonment   (false arrest) an unprivileged act intentionally restraining the movement of another who is aware of such restraint

farm products   "crops or livestock or supplies used or produced in farming operations . . . in the possession of a debtor engaged in . . . farming operations" UCC 9–109(3)

featherbedding   make-work arrangements for employees when there is no work for them to perform or their services are not required

Federal District Court   the *trial* level court of the federal legal system

Federal Trade Commission   a government body that monitors unfair competition and commercial practices

fee simple absolute   the greatest bundle of ownership rights in, and powers over, realty

felony   a serious crime for which, usually, the punishment can be more than one year in prison; *see* **crime**

fiduciary   a person with a duty to act primarily for the benefit of another

financing statement   a document which is filed by the secured party to give public notice of the security interest in personal property

firm offer   (UCC) a merchant's signed irrevocable offer to buy or sell goods, giving assurance that it will be kept open; consideration is not required, and its maximum time is three months

fixture   a chattel which has become permanently attached to realty and thus becomes part of the realty; it still can be used as collateral for a security interest

fixture filing   filing a financing statement in the office where mortgages are recorded

floating lien   a security device which covers after-acquired property and future advances

foreclosure   the cutting off of an owner's interest in realty by sale pursuant to court decree

forfeiture   to lose a legal right as a penalty

forgery   (crime) the unauthorized act of imitating or altering a writing with the intent to defraud and impose liability

formal contract   a contract which must be in a certain form; *see* **contract**

franchise   a business relationship between a franchisor, who markets goods or services through a franchisee, who has the right to use the franchisor's trade name, trademark, and methods of operation

fraud   (in contracts) a misrepresentation of fact, known to be false, made to induce another person to make or to refrain from making a contract, and relied on by the other person

freehold   "an interest in land for a period of time the termination of which can not be measured or computed exactly in terms of years, months, and days, and which is not terminable at the will of the transferor" Restatement of Property, sec. 8

fungible goods   every unit of goods is the equivalent of any other like unit, either actually or by contract

future goods   "goods which are not both existing and identified" to the contract UCC 2–105(2)

g

garnishee   the person against whom a writ of garnishment is issued

garnishment   a statutory proceeding begun by a judgment creditor to reach the intangible assets of the judgment debtor by writ of garnishment

general agent   (universal agent) an agent authorized to conduct a series of transactions involving a continuity of service

general intangibles   a catch-all category covering a variety of personal property

general lien   a lien on property other than the property on which services were rendered; *see* **lien**

general partnership   *see* **partnership**

genuineness of assent   reality of consent to an offer or acceptance

gift   a voluntary transfer of a chattel by someone who is not to receive anything in return

gift causa mortis   a conditional, revocable gift by someone facing imminent death from a present illness or impending peril

good faith   "honesty in fact in the conduct or transaction concerned" UCC 1–201(19)

goods   tangible, movable things

group boycott   a concerted effort by a number of firms to avoid doing business with a particular individual or firm; *see* **boycott**

guarantee   (noun) the person to whom a guaranty is made; (verb) to make a guaranty

guarantor   a type of surety

guaranty   a type of suretyship

guardian   a person legally entrusted with the custody and/or the property of another

guardian ad litem   guardian for the legal action, appointed by a court

h

habendum   that portion of a deed which defines the estate in land being conveyed and indicates the encumbrances

harm   *see* **damage**

hearsay   matter not personally known but heard from others

heirs   persons who, by statute, are entitled to property not disposed of by a decedent's will

holder   "a person who is in possession of a document of title or an instrument or a certificated investment security drawn, issued, or indorsed to him or his order or to bearer or in blank" UCC 1–201(20)

holder in due course   the holder of a negotiable instrument who takes it for value, in good faith, and without notice that the instrument is overdue or has been dishonored or of any defense against, or claim to, the instrument by any person

horizontal merger   a merger of competing firms

hot cargo agreement   an agreement between an employer and a union that the employer is not to handle or otherwise deal with goods of another employer

i

illegal   contrary to law

immunity   exemption from liability

implied authority   an agent's authority which the agent reasonably can understand he has from his principal's manifestation to him, but not expressed therein; *see* **authority**

implied contract   a contract in which the promise or promises are implied from conduct; *see* **contract**

implied warranty   a warranty imposed by law; *see* **warranty**

impossibility   performance can not factually be done

incidental authority   implied authority to do what is incidental in carrying out the express authority; *see* **authority**

incidental damages the money judicially awarded for expenses reasonably incurred by the non-breaching party on the other party's breach; *see* **damages**

incontestability clause a clause in a life insurance policy providing that the company may not contest coverage after the policy has been in effect for a stated time period

incorporators the persons who sign the articles of incorporation

indemnity an absolute obligation to pay for another's loss

independent contractor a person who contracts independently for himself to render a result, and who is not acting on behalf of another nor subject to another's control

independent promise a promise the performance of which is not dependent upon the occurrence of a condition

indorsee the person named by an indorser on an instrument to whom it is to be paid

indorsement the indorser's signature on an instrument (or on a paper attached to it); *see* **blank indorsement, qualified indorsement, restrictive indorsement, special indorsement**

indorser the person who signs on an instrument (or on a paper attached to it) other than as a maker, drawer, or acceptor

injunction a court order requiring a person to do or not to do something

injury the wrongful invasion of another person's interest

innkeeper operator of an establishment engaged in making lodging accommodations available to transients

insolvency (in contracts) when the debtor is unable to pay his debts as they mature; (in bankruptcy) when the debtor's assets are less than his liabilities; (UCC) when the debtor "either has ceased to pay his debts in the ordinary course of business, or cannot pay his debts as they become due, or is insolvent within the meaning of the federal bankruptcy law" UCC 1–201(23)

installment contract "one which requires or authorizes the delivery of goods in separate lots to be separately accepted" UCC 2–612(1)

instrument a writing which evidences a right to payment of money, including negotiable instruments and certificated securities

insurable interest an interest the insured has in the risk covered by the insurance contract

insurance a contract where the insurer agrees to pay the insured for losses affecting the insured's interests

insured the person whose risk has been assumed by another

insurer the person who assumes another's risk

interest a person's desire which has been legally recognized as dominant over a similar desire of another person

interlocutory order an intermediate court order pending a final decision

intermediary bank "any bank to which an item is transferred in course of collection except the depositary or payor bank" UCC 4–105(c)

interpleader an equitable remedy of a person who has some thing but does not claim any interest in it, requesting the court to decide who, as between two or more claimants, is entitled to the thing

interrogatory a written question

intestate a decedent without a will

inventory goods which are held for sale or lease

j

joint liability (in contracts) occurs when parties together obligate themselves to perform the same promise

joint tenancy a form of ownership of property by more than one person with the right of survivorship

joint venture an association of two or more persons as co-owners to engage in a limited business transaction for a profit

journeyman a skilled craftsman

judge the government officer who presides over a court

judgment the final decision of a case by a court

jurisdiction the power of a court to hear and decide a case involving a person or subject matter properly brought before the court

jury a group of people selected to decide the facts in a trial

l

laissez-faire government's policy of not interfering with business

land a tangible, immovable thing

larceny the taking and carrying away of the personal property of another without the right to do so

lateral support the physical support for the land surface

law norms established by the official leaders of society; also those desires recognized and secured by society

law-government continuum a method of showing the numerous ways of constructing legal systems

law merchant a body of law which developed by the customs and usages of merchants and which later became part of the common law

lawyer a person who is licensed to practise law by advising and representing clients in legal matters

lease a form of contract giving one person, the tenant, the exclusive right to occupy for a period the property of another, the landlord

leasehold estate the estate in realty owned by tenants

legal in compliance with the law

letter of credit "an engagement by a bank or other person made at the request of a customer and of a kind within the scope of UCC 5–102 that the issuer will honor drafts or other demands for payment upon compliance with the conditions specified in the" letter of credit UCC 5–103(1)(a)

libel a defamatory publication in written or other permanent form

license a temporary, revocable right to some use of another's land

lien a legal right in another's property as security for the performance of an obligation; *see* **general lien, possessory lien,** and **specific lien**

lien creditor a creditor with a judicial lien or a writ of execution

life estate an estate that lasts only for the length of a particular person's life

limited partnership a partnership of one or more general partners and one or more limited partners formed in compliance with the Uniform Limited Partnership Act; *see* **partnership**

liquidated claim a claim for an amount which is either certain, or ascertainable by mathematical calculation, or by operation of law

liquidated damages the money judicially awarded in the amount as agreed to by the parties as reasonable compensation for damage which may be caused by the wrongful conduct of one of the parties in the future; *see* **damages**

lis pendens a suit is pending

listing an agency contract between a broker and a seller of realty

livery of seisin an ancient ceremony used to transfer ownership of land

locus in quo the place in which

lost property goods in a place where they were not put by the owner who does not know where they are

m

majority (in contracts) the legal age at which a minor becomes an adult; also, in voting, one more than half

maker the person who initially makes and signs a promissory note

marshaling of assets an equitable doctrine that, when there are two classes of creditors, one class having recourse to more than one asset while the other class has recourse to only some but not all of those assets, creditors of the first class are to resort first to those assets not available to other creditors and then to the other assets available to the other creditors

master a principal who has the right to control, or controls, the physical conduct of his servant agent

material alteration "any alteration of an instrument is material which changes the contract of any party thereto in any respect" UCC 3–407(1)

mechanic's lien a statutory lien on real property given to a person who, pursuant to contract, has rendered labor, services, or materials for the improvement of the property and who has not been paid

mediation the process of using a third party to bring disputants closer to resolution of their differences

medium an agency, instrument, means, or channel

mens rea the mental element required for a crime

merchant "a person who deals in goods of the kind or otherwise by his occupation holds himself out as having knowledge or skill peculiar to the practices or goods involved in the transaction or to whom such knowledge or skill may be attributed by his employment of an agent or broker or other intermediary who by his occupation holds himself out as having such knowledge or skill" UCC 2–104(1)

merger (in corporations) the absorption of one corporation by another corporation

mineral right right to dig or mine the earth

minor a person who is under the age of full legal capacity

misdemeanor a crime for which the punishment is less than one year in prison; *see* **crime**

misfeasance misdoing

mislaid property goods which the owner has voluntarily laid down and forgotten where they were laid

misrepresentation a representation of what is not true

mistake believing a fact to exist when it does not exist, or believing a fact not to exist when it does exist

mortgage the nonpossessory security interest in realty; also the instrument which gives lenders the power to sell the mortgaged realty, to repay the debt, when the borrower defaults on the payments

mortgagee the person to whom another's realty has been mortgaged

mortgagor the person who has mortgaged his realty

motion a procedural device asking the court to take some action

n

natural law an ideal or cosmic law

negative sanction punishment for deviating from the norm of a group; *see* **sanction**

negligence (conduct) failure to use the degree of care demanded by the circumstances; (tort) negligence proximately causing injury to another person's interest; *see* **contributory negligence**

negotiable document a document of title which states that the goods covered by the document are to be delivered to bearer or to the order of someone

negotiable instrument a writing signed by the maker or drawer containing an unconditional promise or order to pay a sum certain in money payable on demand or at a definite time to order or to bearer

negotiable promissory note a written unconditional promise to pay a sum certain in money, payable on demand or at a definite time, payable to order or to bearer, and signed by the maker

negotiate to deliver a negotiable instrument, or document, or a certificated security to a holder

negotiation the delivery of negotiable paper to a person who thereby becomes a holder

no arrival, no sale a term used by a seller when it or another is shipping goods and does not want to be liable if the goods do not arrive at their destination

nominal damages the money judicially awarded when no damage has occurred from another's wrongful conduct; *see* **damages**

nonfeasance not doing

nonperformance no performance

nonsuit termination of a lawsuit without a finding on the merits of the case

nontrading partnership a partnership in the business of selling only services; *see* **partnership**

no-par stock corporate stock which is issued without any stated nominal price; *see* **share of stock**

norm a group's standard of behavior

notarize verification by a proper public official of the authenticity of a signature

notary public a public officer with the authority to administer oaths and affirmations and to attest and certify documents

novation a new contract with a new party immediately discharging the old contract

nuisance a tort concerned with a person's conduct which is a wrongful interference with the interest of other persons in their private and public use and enjoyment of land

null/nullity of no legal effect

o

obligee the person to whom a legal obligation is owed

obligor the person who owes a legal obligation

offer a promise made in exchange for another's act, forbearance, or return promise

offeree the promisee to whom an offer is made

offeror the promisor making an offer

option the irrevocable offer in an option contract

ordinance municipal legislation

p

par value stock corporate stock which is issued for a stated certain minimum nominal price; *see* **share of stock**

paralegal an individual trained to assist lawyers in their practice

parol oral

parol evidence oral testimony

parol evidence rule a rule of law which provides that, when there is a written contract, it can not be contradicted (added to or varied) by any prior or contemporaneous oral agreement, or by a prior written agreement

parol lease a lease not reduced to writing

partial performance incomplete performance which is insufficient to accomplish, or which defeats, the main purpose of a contract

partition a division of property between joint owners

partnership (general partnerships) "an association of two or more persons to carry on as co-owners a business for profit" U.P.A. sec. 6; *see* **limited partnership, nontrading partnership,** and **trading partnership**

patent a governmental grant of protection of an invention

payee the person to whose order the instrument is originally written

payor bank "a bank by which an item is payable as drawn or accepted" UCC 4–105(b)

per curiam by the court

per se in and of itself

perfection of a security interest when the creditor complies with Article 9 of the Uniform Commercial Code's requirements for perfection

performance the fulfillment of a contractual obligation

perjury knowingly falsely swearing under oath, or affirming, in a judicial or quasi-judicial proceeding

perpetuities, rule against *see* **rule against perpetuities**

personal covenant a promise in a lease which does not touch and concern the realty

personal or limited defense (in negotiable instruments) a defense which is not to *contractual* liability on the instrument but, rather, is to *avoid* liability on the instrument; any defense which is not a real defense

personal property (personalty) a movable thing, along with interests and rights in the thing

plaintiff the party who initiates a civil suit by filing a complaint in the proper court

pleadings the formal documents filed with a court that usually include the complaint, answer, and motions regarding them

pledge the possessory security interest in bailed goods acquired by the bailee when there is a bailment for the purpose of security

police power the power of a state or federal government to legislate reasonably for the general public welfare

positive sanction reward for an action approved by a group; *see* **sanction**

possessory lien a lien which includes the right to possession of the property which is subject to the lien

power of attorney written authority by a principal to an agent

pre-emptive right a shareholder's right to subscribe to a newly authorized issue of stock proportionate to his holdings in the corporation

preference (in bankruptcy) a debtor's transfer of his property made when insolvent and within ninety days before a petition in bankruptcy was filed which gives a creditor preferential treatment

preferred stock corporate stock with a preference over the common stock; *see* **share of stock**

prescription (in real property) a method of obtaining the right to use of another's land as an easement by open and continuous possession and use of the land under a claim of right to such use for a statutory period of time

present sale a contract causing the immediate transfer of the title to goods for a price at the time the contract is made

presenting bank "any bank presenting an item except a payor bank" UCC 4–105(e)

presentment "a demand for acceptance or payment made upon the maker, acceptor, drawee or other payor by or on behalf of the holder" UCC 3–504(1)

price discrimination the practice of offering the same product to different competing customers at different prices

prima facie at first sight

primary parties parties (maker and acceptor) on a negotiable instrument who are absolutely liable for its payment according to the terms at the time they sign

principal (in agency) a person who has authorized an agent to act on his behalf and subject to his control; (in money) the capital sum of a money debt; (in suretyship) the debtor in a suretyship arrangement

priorities (in bankruptcy) claims that are paid first after the estate has been liquidated

private carrier a carrier which does not offer its services to the general public

privilege that which exempts a person from liability for his conduct which, but for the privilege, would subject him to liability for such conduct

privileged communication a communication between certain parties which, because of their relationship, is inadmissible in evidence without a waiver of the privilege

privity a mutuality of relationship between persons or between persons and a particular transaction

privity of contract two parties have rights or duties relating to each other which were created by a contract

privity of estate two parties have rights or duties relating to each other and flowing from ownership or possession of the same realty

probate court a court which has jurisdiction over the estate of a deceased person

professional agent a professional, independent contractor employed as a special agent

promise an assurance or undertaking that something shall or shall not happen

promisee the person to whom a promise is made

promisor the person who makes a promise

promissory estoppel a principle of preventing injustice by enforcing a gratuitous promise as a contract, without consideration and agreement, the promisor reasonably expecting that his promise would be justifiably relied upon substantially by the promisee

promissory note *see* **negotiable promissory note**

promoter a person who organizes and brings a corporation into existence

proof of claim (in bankruptcy) the claim filed by a creditor in a bankruptcy case

property   a thing; also an interest or right in a thing

proscribe   to prohibit

protest   (in negotiable instruments) a formal certificate, issued by a properly authorized person, certifying that a foreign or international draft was duly presented for acceptance or payment and that it was dishonored

proximate cause   the cause of an injury without which the injury would not have occurred

proxy   a shareholder's written authorization to another person to vote his shares at a corporate meeting; also the person with such authority

public policy   the concept of law under which the freedom to act is limited for the good of the community

punitive (or exemplary) damages   the money judicially awarded in excess of compensatory damages to punish for malicious, wanton, or intentional wrongful conduct; *see* **damages**

pure competition   a market in which many firms compete and no one firm has very much power

pure monopoly   a market in which there is a single firm with no competitors

q

qualified indorsement   an indorsement which disclaims or qualifies the liability of the indorser on the instrument; *see* **indorsement**

quality test   (in contracts) the promise must cause the offeree reasonably to believe that the promise was intended to be an offer

quantity test   (in contracts) the promise must have certainty of terms in what it promises and what it asks for

quasi   as if

quasi contract   as if a contract; a contract implied in law

question of fact   a dispute over what happened

question of law   a dispute over the legal effect of what happened

quitclaim deed   a document used in transferring the grantor's interest in realty, if any, without any warranties

quorum   the number of persons necessary to be present, or shares necessary to be represented, at a meeting in order to transact business

r

ratification   (in contracts) a person's waiver of his power of avoidance; (in agency) a person's manifested consent to be bound by another's previously unauthorized act made in his name and not binding on him

real or universal defense   (in negotiable instruments) a defense to contractual liability on an instrument

real property (realty)   land and immovable things attached to land, along with interests and rights in the land; also a freehold interest in land

receiver   a person appointed by a court to receive, preserve, and manage property which is involved in litigation

recognizance   an obligation acknowledged by a person in a court to do something (e.g., to appear in court at a later time), i.e., personal bond

redemption   the reclaiming of a foreclosed ownership interest in realty

reformation   an action to correct a writing so as to reflect correctly the intentions of the parties which mistakenly were not properly expressed in the writing

reimbursement   one person's right against another to be repaid money paid on the other's behalf for which the latter was responsible; (in suretyship) the surety's right to recover from the principal

rejection   (in contracts) the offeree's expression refusing the offer; (in sales) the buyer's refusal to accept goods provided by the seller under a contract for sale

remainder   that remaining part of an estate in land which, on the termination of a preceding estate, passes to someone other than the grantor

remainderman   a person who was not a grantor of an estate in land but who will acquire the remainder of an estate after a preceding estate has terminated

remedy the means by which a right is enforced or protected

renunciation the abandonment of a right by a person

replevin a common law form of action to regain possession of specific chattels

representation (in insurance) a statement of fact made by the insured which is not a part of the insurance contract but, during negotiation, is made to induce formation of the contract

repudiation a party's manifestation of an intent not to perform his obligation; *see* **anticipatory repudiation**

res ipsa loquitur the thing speaks for itself

res judicata the thing has been adjudicated; the principle of law that, once a matter has been litigated and finally adjudicated, it should not be the subject of litigation again between the same parties

rescind cancel

rescission cancellation

respondeat superior let the master (superior) be responsible for the torts of his servant committed while acting within the scope of his employment

restitution a legal remedy restoring one to his original position prior to the particular transaction

restrictive indorsement an indorsement which determines the type of interest in the instrument being transferred; *see* **indorsement**

reversion a future interest which will, or may, be returned to the grantor. In contrast, a remainder goes to one other than the grantor.

revocation (in contracts) the offeror's recalling of the offeree's power to accept as contained in the offer

right a legal claim by the owner of an interest that others shall not interfere with his interest

right of survivorship a relationship among co-owners where death of one owner causes his interest to be transferred to the remaining owners

riparian relating to the bank or shore of a river or stream

robbery the felonious taking of money or goods of value from the person of another or in his presence, against his will, by force or fear

rule against perpetuities the beneficiary of a trust must be identifiable at the time the trust is created or, in most states, within a period for the life of a person or persons in existence at the time the trust is created and 21 years after the death of such person or persons

s

sale the transfer "of title from seller to purchaser for a price" UCC 2–106(1)

sanction a group's technique for controlling its members; *see* **negative sanction** and **positive sanction**

satisfaction the discharge of an obligation by paying what is due

seal a symbol attached to a writing attesting that it is a legal document

secondary boycott the bringing of pressure by a union on a neutral party who will then pressure the employer with whom the union has a dispute

secondary parties (in negotiable instruments) parties on a negotiable instrument who are liable on the instrument only if certain conditions occur

secured party a creditor with a security interest

secured transaction a transaction used to create a security interest

security a creditor's interest in specific property, or in the obligation of a third person, as assurance for the performance of the debtor's obligation

security agreement an agreement which creates or provides for a security interest

security interest "an interest in personal property or fixtures which secures payment or performance of an obligation" UCC 1–201(37)

servant an agent whose physical conduct his master (principal) has the right to control or controls

service usually labor rendered by one person for another

servient tenement property in which someone has an easement appurtenant

several liability (in contracts) occurs when the same performance is separately promised by each party

shareholder (stockholder) the owner of a unit of interest in a corporation

share of stock (stock) a unit of interest in a corporation; *see* **common stock, no-par stock, par value stock, preferred stock,** and **treasury stock**

shipper-carrier a legal relationship between the shipper and the common carrier when goods have been delivered to the carrier for immediate shipment

shop right an employer's free, nonexclusive, irrevocable, nonassignable license to use the invention or discovery of an employee who has used his employment time or the employer's facilities in connection with such invention or discovery

signed "includes any symbol executed or adopted by a party with the present intention to authenticate a writing" UCC 1–201 (39)

simple contract a contract which need not be in any particular form; *see* **contract**

slander a defamatory publication by spoken words, gestures, or other nonpermanent form

social engineering using the law to bring about social change

sole proprietorship a business owned and operated by one person

special agent "an agent authorized to conduct a single transaction or a series of transactions not involving continuity of service" Restatement (Second) of Agency, sec. 3

special damages *see* **consequential damages**

special indorsement an indorsement which specifies a particular indorsee; *see* **indorsement**

specific lien a lien on the specific property on which services were rendered; *see* **lien**

specific performance the exact performance of a contract by a party as ordered by a court

standard an established measure

stare decisis a principle of law that courts will follow case precedent if it is still applicable

stated capital (capital stock) generally, the money received by a corporation from the issuance of its shares exclusive of what has been allocated to capital surplus

statute law created by a legislative body and approved by the executive

statute of frauds a statute requiring that certain kinds of contract be proved only by a proper writing

statute of limitations a statute limiting the time in which a claim may be asserted in court; expiration bars enforcement of the claim

statutory law bills passed by the legislature and signed into law by the president or governor

stay (noun) a halt

stock *see* **share of stock**

straight bill a non-negotiable bill of lading

strict liability absolute liability irrespective of the absence of negligence or fault

strict surety a co-debtor with the principal for the same obligation owing to the creditor

subagent the person appointed by an agent and as to whom the appointing agent is a principal

sublet a transfer by the lessee of a *part* of the remaining term of his lease

subpoena an order to appear before a judicial body for the purpose of giving testimony

subrogation the substitution of one person for another with reference to a claim or right; (in suretyship) the surety succeeds to the creditor's rights against the principal

subsidiary corporation a corporation owned by another corporation

substantial performance incomplete performance which is sufficient to accomplish, and does not defeat, the main purpose of a contract

substantive law that part of the law which creates, defines, and regulates rights

summary judgment a judgment rendered on a motion by a party in a civil action that, solely on the basis of the pleadings, judgment should be rendered without the necessity of a trial on the facts

summons   a writ or process served on the defendant in a civil action notifying him of the action and summoning him to appear and plead

surety   a person who promises the creditor to pay the principal's debt or to perform his obligation

surety bond   a promise by a professional surety to pay if the principal defaults or commits a wrongful act

suretyship   a legal relationship in which one person (surety) and another person (principal, the debtor) are obligated to perform the same obligation to a third person (creditor) who is entitled to only one performance, and as between the surety and the principal the latter is to perform the obligation and is ultimately liable therefor

surface right   the right to occupy the surface of a piece of land

survivorship, right of   a relationship among co-owners where death of one owner causes his interest to be transferred to the remaining owners

t

tenancy   a form of ownership in realty

tenancy by entirety   a form of co-ownership between husband and wife with the right of survivorship

tenancy in common   a form of ownership of property by more than one person without survivorship

tenant   *see* **lease**

tender   (verb) proffer, make available

tenor   what is stated as meant

title insurance   insurance that covers the title to real estate

tort   a civil (private) noncontractual wrong for which a court will give a remedy

tortfeasor   a person who has committed a tort

trade fixture   a chattel attached to leased realty by a business tenant

trademark   any word, name, symbol, or device, or any combination thereof, adopted and used by manufacturer or merchant to identify his goods and distinguish them from those manufactured by others

trading partnership   a partnership in the business of buying and selling property; *see* **partnership**

transfer   (noun) a delivery of some thing

transferee   one to whom another has transferred some thing

transferor   one who has transferred some thing to another

treason   a felony specifically defined by the U. S. Constitution

treasure trove   buried treasure

treasury stock   corporate stock reacquired by the issuing corporation; *see* **share of stock**

trespass   (verb) to wrongfully interfere with another's possession of land or chattels

trust   a legal device whereby legal title to property is held by one person (a trustee) for the benefit of a beneficiary

trust deed   a deed of land to a trustee in trust as security for performance of an obligation with power to sell the land on default; basically, a real property mortgage

trustee   a person who has title to property in trust for the benefit of someone; (in bankruptcy) the officer responsible for administering the debtor's estate; (in realty) the one who holds the trust deed for the benefit of the lender

tying arrangement   an agreement between a seller or lessor and a purchaser or lessee that a sale or lease of a product to the latter is contingent upon the latter's purchase or lease of another product of the seller or lessor

u

ultra vires   beyond the powers

unconscionable   offends the conscience, immoderate, too one-sided

unconscionable contract   a contract in which one of the parties is in too unequal or one-sided a bargaining position

undisclosed principal   a person not known, or who is not reasonably known, to be a principal for an agent by a third party

undue influence   unfair persuasion by one who, because of his relationship with another, dominates the other

unenforceable contract   a contract which the courts will not enforce

unfair labor practices   tactics by an employer or a union which are legally prohibited as unfair

Uniform Commercial Code   a body of statutory law governing commercial transactions concerning personal property (movable things)

unilateral contract   a contract in which the consideration for a promise is an act or a forbearance

union shop   a shop or place of employment where the employer may hire non-union employees but after a short period of time, usually thirty days, the new employees must become members of the union or be discharged

universal agent   *see* **general agent**

unjust enrichment   a legal doctrine that prevents persons from profiting or enriching themselves inequitably at the expense of others

usage of trade   "any practice or method of dealing having such regularity of observance in a place, vocation or trade as to justify an expectation that it will be observed with respect to the transaction in question" UCC 1–205(2); used synonymously with "custom"

usury   charging a rate of interest on a loan higher than that permitted by statute

v

value   (UCC) any consideration sufficient to support a contract, a commitment to extend credit, or a past debt

verdict   a jury's finding of fact

vertical merger   a merger between a firm and one of its major suppliers or customers

void   of no legal effect

voidable contract   a contract which can be avoided by one or more of the parties

voire dire   the examination before trial of a prospective juror or witness in which he or she is to answer questions truthfully

voting trust   a trust created by an agreement between the shareholders to transfer legal title to their voting stock to a party (trustee) who is authorized to vote the stock as a unit

w

warehouse receipt   a document issued to the bailor by a warehouseman

warehouseman   a person in the business of storing goods for a fee

warranty   an express or implied assurance that certain facts exist; (in insurance) a statement of fact or a promise made by the insured which is part of the insurance contract and which must be true if the insurer is to be liable on the contract; (in sale of goods) generally, a promise made by a seller or manufacturer of goods, or a promise implied in a sales transaction by law, that the goods sold are of a certain quality or will perform in a certain manner; *see* **express warranty** and **implied warranty**

warranty deed   a deed conveying title and giving warranties to the grantee

water right   a right to control of the water on the surface or under the ground

watered stock   corporate stock reduced in value by the issuance of par value shares for less than their par value

will   a formal document which governs the transfer of property at death

writ   a court order

writ of execution   a court order authorizing a sheriff to seize tangible property to satisfy a court judgment

writ of garnishment   *see* **garnishment**

wrong   the illegal invasion of another person's interest

y

yellow dog contract   an agreement between an employer and employee that the employee will not be, nor continue to be, a member of a union

Table of Cases

Index

t

Tenancy. *See* Real property
Tender, 395, 596
Third party beneficiary contracts, 178–79, 181–82
Tort, 42, 53, 149, 252, 470, 709
Toxic Substances Act, 655–56
Trade acceptance, 497
Trade fixture, 812
Trade usage, 590
Trademark, 67
Traveller's check, 498–99
Treasure trove, 324
Trespass, 149, 819
Trial. *See* Civil trial process
Trust, 137, 310
Truth-In-Lending Act, 480
Truth-In-Packaging Act, 479
Tying arrangements
  Clayton Act, 610, 611
  defined, 611
  in franchising, 726

u

Ultra vires, 146, 768–69
Unconscionable, 77, 351
Undue influence, 114–15
Unemployment insurance, 286–87
Unfair labor practices, 639–41
Uniform Consumer Credit Code, 481
Unions. *See* Labor law
Unliquidated debt, 127
Usage of trade, 163, 377
Usury, 150, 480, 560

v

Value
  contract law, 123
  UCC, 388
Verdict, 35

w

Wage-hour law, 282
Warehouse receipt, 334, 336
Warehouseman, 333
Warranty, 253, 322, 422, 456–64, 905
Watered stock, 790–91
Workmen's compensation, 65, 284
Wrong, 53

y

Yellow dog contract, 637, 638